THE WORLD ECONOMY
TRADE AND FINANCE

Fourth Edition

Beth V. Yarbrough
Robert M. Yarbrough
both of Amherst College

The Dryden Press
Harcourt Brace College Publishers

Fort Worth Philadelphia San Diego New York Orlando Austin San Antonio
Toronto Montreal London Sydney Tokyo

Acquisitions Editor	Emily Barrosse
Developmental Editor	Stacey Sims
Project Editor	Michele Tomiak
Production Manager	Jessica Iven Wyatt
Art Director	Jeanette Barber
Picture and Rights Editor	Annette Coolidge
Electronic Publishing Coordinator	Kathi Embry
Product Manager	R. Paul Stewart
Copy Editor	Leon Unruh
Proofreader	Tad Gaither
Text Type	10/12 Sabon

Address for Editorial Correspondence
The Dryden Press, 301 Commerce Street, Suite 3700, Fort Worth, TX 76102

Address for Orders
The Dryden Press, 6277 Sea Harbor Drive, Orlando, FL 32887
1-800-782-4479, or 1-800-433-0001 (in Florida)

ISBN: 0-03-017764-2

Library of Congress Catalog Card Number: 96-85126

Printed in the United States of America
7 8 9 0 1 2 3 4 5 039 9 8 7 6 5 4 3 2

The Dryden Press
Harcourt Brace College Publishers

To Beth's parents

THE DRYDEN PRESS SERIES IN ECONOMICS

Baldani, Bradfield, and Turner
Mathematical Economics

Baumol and Blinder
Economics: Principles and Policy
Seventh Edition (Also available in micro and
macro paperbacks)

Baumol, Panzar, and Willig
*Contestable Markets and the Theory of Industry
Structure*
Revised Edition

Berch
*The Endless Day: The Political Economy of
Women and Work*

Breit and Elzinga
*The Antitrust Casebook: Milestones in
Economic Regulation*
Third Edition

Brue
The Evolution of Economic Thought
Fifth Edition

Demmert
Economics: Understanding the Market Process

Dolan and Lindsey
Economics
Seventh Edition (Also available in micro and
macro paperbacks)

Edgmand, Moomaw, and Olson
Economics and Contemporary Issues
Third Edition

Gardner
Comparative Economic Systems
Second Edition

Glahe
Microeconomics: Theory and Application
Second Edition

Green
Macroeconomics: Analysis and Applications

Gwartney and Stroup
Economics: Private and Public Choice
Eighth Edition (Also available in micro and
macro paperbacks)

Gwartney and Stroup
*Introduction to Economics: The Wealth and
Poverty of Nations*

Heilbroner and Singer
*The Economic Transformation of America:
1600 to the Present*
Second Edition

Hirschey and Pappas
Fundamentals of Managerial Economics
Fifth Edition

Hirschey and Pappas
Managerial Economics
Eighth Edition

Hyman
*Public Finance: A Contemporary Application of
Theory to Policy*
Fifth Edition

Kahn
*The Economic Approach to Environmental and
Natural Resources*

Kaserman and Mayo
*Government and Business: The Economics of
Antitrust and Regulation*

Kaufman
The Economics of Labor Markets
Fourth Edition

Kennett and Lieberman
*The Road to Capitalism: The Economic
Transformation of Eastern Europe and the
Former Soviet Union*

Kreinin
International Economics: A Policy Approach
Seventh Edition

Lott and Ray
Applied Econometrics with Data Sets

Marlow
Public Finance: Theory and Practice

Nicholson
Intermediate Microeconomics and Its Application
Seventh Edition

Nicholson
Microeconomic Theory: Basic Principles and Extensions
Sixth Edition

Puth
American Economic History
Third Edition

Ragan and Thomas
Principles of Economics
Second Edition (Also available in micro and macro paperbacks)

Ramanathan
Introductory Econometrics with Applications
Third Edition

Rukstad
Corporate Decision Making in the World Economy: Company Case Studies

Rukstad
Macroeconomic Decision Making in the World Economy: Text and Cases
Third Edition

Samuelson and Marks
Managerial Economics
Second Edition

Scarth
Macroeconomics: An Introduction to Advanced Methods
Third Edition

Stockman
Introduction to Economics
(Also available in micro and macro paperbacks)

Thomas
Economics: Principles and Applications
(Also available in micro and macro paperbacks)

Walton and Rockoff
History of the American Economy
Seventh Edition

Welch and Welch
Economics: Theory and Practice
Fifth Edition

Yarbrough and Yarbrough
The World Economy: Trade and Finance
Fourth Edition

PREFACE

The success of earlier editions of *The World Economy: Trade and Finance* owes much to developments outside the classroom. Specific episodes come and go, but the hectic pace of world events continues to make students, economists, policy makers, and citizens increasingly aware of international economic issues. After ten years' work to complete the Uruguay Round of GATT negotiations, more than 100 countries are overhauling their trade policies, bringing them into line with new rules and with the newly created World Trade Organization. The world's two largest free-trade areas—the European Union and the North American Free-Trade Agreement (NAFTA)—provide models for the rest of the world but also struggle with periodic crises, from Mexico's dramatic peso devaluation to Britain's "mad cow" disease. Debates over the relationship between international trade and wages dominate domestic political discussion in the United States. The Maastricht Treaty's deadlines for a European monetary union, with its common *Euro* currency, come and go. The formerly centrally planned economies of Eastern Europe and the former Soviet Union continue to struggle to integrate themselves into the world economy. Even the names on the world stage change. National "divorces" in the Soviet Union, Czechoslovakia, and Yugoslavia produce new names on the list of sovereign states, while national "marriages" between East and West Germany and between China and Hong Kong remove old ones.

Philosophy and Pedagogy

The pace, scale, and scope of such events underscore a widespread perception of international economics' increased importance for understanding events in the world. Luckily, a few simple tools of economic analysis can provide a great deal of insight into the ever-changing world economy. The goal of this fourth edition of *The World Economy* remains unchanged from that of the first three: To present these tools of international economic analysis clearly, consistently, and comprehensively and to establish the theoretical principles basic to the analysis of international economic problems.

Integrated Theory and Applications

By *combining* up-to-date theory with current events and policy debates, this book emphasizes learning how to *use* international economics as a tool for understanding. By the end of the quarter or semester, students will be able to analyze problems independently, not simply those that happen to dominate the headlines at the time of the book's writing. On the other hand, *The World Economy* has never glorified theory for its own sake. The rule we endeavor to follow remains: Any theory worth presenting is worth teaching students to *use*.

The World Economy is self-contained in that it defines all necessary concepts; it does not rely on students' memory of other economics courses. Numerous tables tie abstract concepts to their measurable counterparts. *We believe that an international economics course should familiarize students with the empirical reality of the world economy as well as with abstract models of it.* This belief is reflected in more frequent use of real-world data than is typical in other books. In addition, we refer frequently to common errors or misinterpretations in the popular press. Learning how to read the newspaper or listen to the evening news with a keen eye and ear is at least as important as learning how to read the scholarly literature.

The integration of clear, concise theory with up-to-date examples and cases sets this book apart from its competitors. One example of this integration is a strong focus on the distributional consequences of policy throughout both the international trade and open-economy macroeconomics sections of the book. These consequences represent the crux of international economic policy controversies, but most textbooks shortchange them with a flurry of tangency conditions. We make extensive use of examples from diverse areas of the world economy—the rapidly developing Pacific Rim, the economies in transition from central planning, Africa, and the Middle East. We highlight the relevance of international economic theory for understanding front-page microeconomic issues such as trends in trade and wages, arguments for trade-based industrial policies, agricultural policy reform, U.S. most-favored-nation status for China, and intellectual property protection and piracy. And, we maintain the lively, up-to-date focus throughout Part Two by examining macroeconomic issues such as Russia's efforts to make the ruble convertible, the United States' external debt, the macroeconomics of German unification, the 1994 Mexican peso crisis, the U.S. government budget deficit and the dollar, the European Union's 1992–1993 currency crises, the Kobe earthquake and the yen, and Chinese macroeconomic reforms.

Careful, Clear Pedagogy

Major sections within each chapter of *The World Economy* are numbered for easy reference. At crucial points in an argument, we ask students "Why?" These queries encourage *active* reading, stopping the reader from moving passively through the argument without confronting its underlying logic; comments from our students indicate that the queries achieve their goal.[1] *The World Economy*'s generous number of graphs, as well as their lively two-color format, make the arguments easy to follow. All graphs are fully integrated into the text and accompanied by self-contained legends. We encourage students to practice active translation between graphs and legends *(Can you cover the graph and draw your own, given the legend? Can you cover the legend and write your own explanation of the graph?)*. Again, the emphasis is on learning to *use* the graphs as tools for understanding, not on memorization or rote manipulation.

Each chapter contains several cases, a summary, a "Looking Ahead" section that links the chapter to the next one, a list of key terms (boldfaced in the text), review questions and problems (including new ones in every chapter of the fourth edition), and a list of supplementary readings. The cases provide examples of the economic concepts and models developed in the chapter as well as extensive empirical information about the countries that the world economy comprises. The end-of-chapter "Questions and Problems for Review" highlight the major concepts from the chapter and relate those concepts to current policy debates; many end-of-chapter questions from earlier editions now appear in the *Study Guide* (a new version of which accompanies this new edition). Unlike the bibliographies in many textbooks,

---

[1] Several students have reported making a game of the queries by trying to read each chapter without being "caught" unprepared to answer a query.

the readings suggested in *The World Economy* include short, up-to-date articles as well as classic treatises and survey articles. We note each reading as appropriate for introductory, intermediate, or advanced students.

Changes from the Third Edition

Although our basic goals, philosophy, and pedagogy remain unchanged, this fourth edition does incorporate many improvements. We have thoroughly updated and revised the book, including the text of each chapter as well as figures, tables, and cases.

Updated Theory and Applications

Current events with new or substantially expanded coverage in this new edition include the growing international trade involving China, voluntary import expansions such as the U.S.–Japan semiconductor pacts, regional trade agreements, the Uruguay Round, the "end"of the developing-country debt crisis, reform and transition in Eastern Europe and the former Soviet Union, growing international capital mobility, macroeconomic interdependence, trends in real exchange rates, and developments in the European Monetary System. In terms of theory, this edition contains new or expanded treatment of wages in the Ricardian and Neoclassical trade models, intra-industry trade, economies of scale, tariffs and quotas with monopoly, interregional trade, intertemporal trade, reform and transition from central planning, the real exchange rate, the current account, external balance, sterilization, reserve-currency countries, long-run equilibrium, long-run exchange rates, supply shocks, and the debate over fixed versus flexible exchange rates.

New Cases

Existing cases have been expanded, and many new cases added, to reflect current events and issues. Just a few of the many new cases include those about the Heckscher-Ohlin theorem and U.S.–China trade, U.S. luxury-car tariffs, contaminated blood, the oilseed dispute, intertemporal trade, growth and reform in transition, U.S. foreign exchange intervention, the real exchange rate and the current account, the dollarization of Cuba, floating the pound, nontraded goods and the real exchange rate, exchange rate target zones, and the markets for Chinese yuan.

Improved Organization

As in the first three editions, *The World Economy* is organized in two parts. Part One (Chapters Two through Eleven) covers international microeconomics and Part Two (Chapters Twelve through Twenty-One), international macroeconomics. The body of each chapter contains basic theoretical development, examples, and cases. Extensions and other optional materials (for example, the derivation of a world production possibilities frontier, Edgeworth boxes, offer curves, and derivation of the aggregate demand curve) are covered in appendixes that instructors can assign or omit at their discretion.

Along with the areas of new coverage already mentioned, we have rearranged existing material to increase flexibility. Several changes improve the organization of Part One. The section on trade adjustment assistance now appears in Chapter Four, "Trade, Distribution, and Welfare." Material on the history of international trade policy and on economic integration, previously in Chapter Eleven, now appears in a redesigned Chapter Nine, "The Political Economy of Trade Policy and Borders." The chapter on "Economic Growth and Factor Mobility" (Chapter Nine in earlier editions) becomes Chapter Ten. And a new Chapter Eleven now closes Part One with an examination of trade-related issues in developing and transitional economies.

In Part Two, we moved material on offshore currency markets and asset approaches to the exchange rate up to Chapter Twelve. Chapter Fourteen, on the market for goods and services, now develops the IS curve, previously in Chapter Fifteen; this section can still be omitted in courses that skip the IS-LM-BOP model. A new Chapter Eighteen presents models related to long-run macroeconomic equilibrium: money neutrality, purchasing power parity, the monetary approach to the exchange rate, and the real exchange rate. Chapter Nineteen contains the aggregate demand-aggregate supply model (from Chapter Eighteen of earlier editions), along with new material on real exchange rate adjustment and on supply shocks. Chapter Twenty contains expanded discussions of "Alternative International Monetary Regimes." Finally, an all-new Chapter Twenty-One closes the book with a systematic treatment of macroeconomic issues related to development and transition, parallel to the role of the new Chapter Eleven in Part One.

Intended Audience

By presenting the fundamentals of international economics clearly but rigorously, *The World Economy* becomes adaptable for a variety of courses. Our correspondence with users of earlier editions indicates that they use the book successfully in many ways. Students with only a one-semester introductory economics course as background have no trouble mastering the material; in fact, we use the book extensively in classes at that level. All appendixes can be omitted without loss of continuity, and any supplementary reading can be chosen from articles denoted as appropriate for beginning students. For students who have completed courses in intermediate micro and macro, the appendixes can be added along with a wider range of supplementary reading. The flexibility of the book serves beginning graduate students with no specific background in international economics and provides a stepping stone to more advanced texts and the professional literature. The book also appeals to students of political science, international relations, and international business by providing insight into economics' unique perspective on international issues.

Alternate Course Outlines

For full-year courses, the entire book can be covered along with a sizable sample of readings. The micro-macro ordering reflects our own teaching preferences but is easily reversible. In a one-semester course emphasizing microeconomic aspects of the world economy, we use Chapters One through Eleven, but any combination of Chapters Five, Nine, Ten, and Eleven could be omitted to permit more extensive use of supplementary readings. In a one-semester course emphasizing macroeconomics, we cover Chapters Twelve through Twenty-One, but it is possible to omit any combination of Sixteen, Seventeen, Eighteen, Twenty, and Twenty-One. By limiting outside readings, a one-semester course easily can cover the essentials of both the micro and macro perspectives. We have taught such a course by concentrating on Chapters Two through Four, Six through Eight, Twelve through Fifteen, and Nineteen. No doubt other permutations are possible.

Supplement Packages by the Authors

Study Guide

The World Economy has its own *Study Guide,* new for the fourth edition and available from The Dryden Press through your local or college bookstore. We wrote the *Guide* ourselves, carefully coordinating it with the text and using the same careful pedagogy. The *Study Guide* contains

- Additional "Problems and Questions for Review" with answers.
- Answers to italicized queries in the chapters.
- Matching exercises for key terms in each chapter.
- List of key points for each chapter.
- Hints for writing a successful term paper on the world economy.
- List of source materials for international data.

Instructor's Manual

The *Instructor's Manual,* also written ourselves, contains

- Suggested test questions for each chapter.
- Answers to the italicized queries in the book.
- Answers to the end-of-chapter "Problems and Questions for Review."
- Chapter-by-chapter key points.
- Information on alternate course structures.

The Dryden Press may provide complimentary instructional aids and supplements or supplement packages to those adopters qualified under our adoption policy. Please contact your sales representative for more information. If as an adopter or potential user you receive supplements you do not need, please return them to your sales representative or send them to

Attn: Returns Department
Troy Warehouse
465 South Lincoln Drive
Troy, MO 63379

Acknowledgments

As always, we are grateful to the entire staff of The Dryden Press, especially Emily Barrosse, Daryl Fox, Stacey Sims, Michele Tomiak, Jeanette Barber, Jessica Wyatt, Kathi Embry, Mike Beaupré, and Annette Coolidge for transforming an occasionally unruly manuscript into a beautiful book. Leon Unruh's careful copyediting helped.

On this fourth edition, our thanks go to an especially careful group of reviewers: George Borts, Brown University; Byron Gangnes, University of Hawaii–Manoa; David Hammes, University of Hawaii–Hilo; Michael Kim, Penn State University; Nolin Masih, Saint Cloud University; Robert Moore, Georgia State University; Sam Skogstad, Georgia State University; Robert Stern, University of Michigan; and Sandra Williamson, University of Pittsburgh. We are grateful to all, and we appreciate the comments we did not use as much as those we did. The kind words and constructive criticisms of *The World Economy* users continue to be invaluable.

The suggestions of several "generations" of students in the international economics courses at Amherst College play a key role in improving the book. Jeanne Reinle provides essential encouragement, reminders, and good humor, as well as a patient sounding board when we fall behind schedule and become cranky. Over the past 14 years, Amherst College deans Dick Fink, Ron Rosbottom, Ralph Beals, and Lisa Raskin, as well as presidents Peter Pouncey and Tom Gerety, have generously supported and encouraged our work on *The World Economy* and on many other research projects.

Beth V. Yarbrough
Robert M. Yarbrough
Amherst, Massachusetts
1996

CONTENTS

Chapter Three
Comparative Advantage II: Factor Endowments and the
Neoclassical Model   71

Chapter Four
Trade, Distribution, and Welfare   109

Chapter Twenty
Alternative International Monetary Regimes   823

Chapter Twenty-One
Macroeconomics of Development and Transition   875

CHAPTER ONE

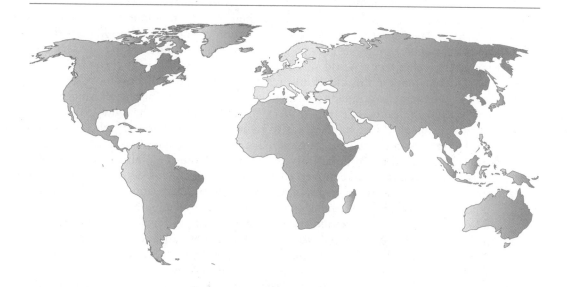

Introduction to the World Economy

1.1 Introduction

Much has happened in the international economic sphere since we wrote the opening chapter of the third edition of *The World Economy*. On the trade side, more than a hundred countries completed a historic (and marathon!) set of international negotiations to reach the Uruguay Round agreement to lower trade barriers and launch the new World Trade Organization. On a smaller scale, the United States, Canada, and Mexico created the North American Free-Trade Agreement. The biggest developing-country debtors, Argentina, Brazil, and Mexico, reached agreements with their major creditors, leading many analysts to declare the "end" of the debt crisis that dominated headlines and threatened world financial institutions during the 1980s. Economies in transition from central planning, including Eastern Europe, the former Soviet Union, and China, integrated themselves—albeit to differing degrees and at different speeds—into the world economy. Many developing countries, after decades of self-imposed isolation from world markets, embarked on programs of economic liberalization that included trade reforms, macroeconomic stabilization, and structural reforms to reduce the role of government and increase the role of markets in their economies. At the same time, in developed countries such as the United States, domestic political debates raged over the domestic consequences of trade, particularly the expanding trade with low-wage developing countries.

On the macroeconomic front, international financial markets continued their dramatic growth as governments reduced their regulation of international financial activity and new information and communication technologies allowed market participants to move funds around the globe more quickly and cheaply. The U.S. dollar, after reaching post-World War II highs in its value relative to the Japanese yen and German mark in the mid-1980s, reached postwar lows against those same currencies. Germany continued to struggle with the macroeconomic aftermath of its costly 1990 unification of East and West. On a broader scale, the (now 15) members of the European Union made plans to issue a common currency, the *Euro,* and implement common macroeconomic policies, but currency crises and domestic recessions forced Britain and Italy to withdraw from the plans. Developed and developing countries alike moved to give their central banks more independence from political pressures in hopes of achieving better macroeconomic performance, especially lower inflation. And Mexico, until 1994 an often-cited model of successful macroeconomic stabilization and economic reform, suffered a significant setback in late 1994 that spilled over to other Latin American developing economies. Among the United States and its major trading partners, the debate continued over the economic effects of the U.S. government budget deficit.

So the world economy has been a lively place.[1] As a result, the complex economic and political ties that bind countries into the world economy are receiving closer scrutiny than ever before. The news is full of discussions of **international interdependence,** and the fact that no nation is an economic island never has been more obvious. Citizens of many countries feel increasingly affected by external events over which they, and sometimes even their national policy makers, exert little control. Most of the major economic stories that occupy newspaper headlines are stories about international interdependence, its ramifications, and policy makers' and citizens' attempts to come to terms with it.

1.2   Why Study International Economics?

All this makes studying international economics more important than ever before, whether you are (or hope to be) a national policy maker, a business owner planning corporate strategy, or simply an informed citizen and voter. *The World Economy: Trade and Finance* provides a basic tool kit. It presents simple models to explain how the world economy works, empirical evidence to evaluate the models' predictions, dozens of case studies and applications from economic history and current events around the globe, plus lots of useful information about the world economy and the countries that comprise it. When you finish the book, you should feel confident weighing politicians' statements about international economic policy, evaluating the key international influences on a firm or industry, and analyzing the linkages between the economic policies followed by your home country and those followed by the rest of the world.

---

[1]In the chapters that follow, we shall examine all the events mentioned in the preceding two paragraphs, plus many more.

Table 1.1 □ Degree Subjects of Top Macroeconomic Policy Makers, 1993

Country	Finance Minister (Fiscal Policy)	Central Bank Governor (Monetary Policy)
Britain	Law	Economics
Canada	None	Philosophy, Politics, and Economics
France	Economics	Law/Literature
Germany	Law and Politics	Economics
Italy	Economics	Economics
Japan	Law	Law
United States	Law	Economics
Argentina	Economics	Economics
Brazil	Sociology	Economics
Chile	Economics	Economics
Mexico	Economics	Economics
China	None	Mechanical Engineering
Indonesia	Economics	Economics
South Korea	Public Administration	Economics
Taiwan	Economics	Economics
Thailand	Economics	Economics
Czech Republic	Economics	Economics
Poland	Economics	Economics
Russia	Economics	Economics

Source: *The Economist*, August 14, 1993, p. 63; data from country embassies and central banks.

It is also worth remembering that many of the individuals formulating the policies we will report and analyze (often critically) in this book have at least some training in economics. Table 1.1 reports the undergraduate training of recent finance ministers (typically in charge of fiscal policy, or government expenditure and taxation) and central bank governors (typically in charge of controlling the money stock) for a sample of developed- and developing-country governments.

1.3 What Do We Mean by International Interdependence?

The term *international interdependence* entered the front-page vocabulary during the 1970s when the industrialized countries, along with oil-importing developing nations, helplessly endured two rounds of sudden and dramatic oil price increases by the Organization of Petroleum Exporting Countries (OPEC). In the early 1980s, countries' roles reversed as OPEC watched the price of oil tumble in response to a policy-induced recession in the industrialized countries. The fall in oil prices was welcome news in most industrial and oil-importing developing countries, but the decline also heightened the debt problem of several developing-country oil exporters, most notably Mexico. The 1980s debt crisis among developing countries, in turn, generated financial uncertainty and a loss of export markets for the developed world and threatened the solvency of several major U.S. commercial banks.

By the mid-1980s, key industries such as steel and automobiles, once dominated by a handful of U.S. firms, spanned the globe. Many U.S. industries struggled against increasingly potent foreign competition, and one by one those industries sought protection in the form of barriers against imports. Because industries are themselves interdependent, one industry's import barriers (which raised prices) made it more difficult for other industries to remain competitive. For example, when the U.S. steel industry won protection, U.S. automobile manufacturers had to pay higher prices for steel and became more vulnerable to competition from foreign car producers. As U.S. auto producers lost their dominance in their home market, they pressured policy makers for their own protection from foreign competition.

Policy makers responded to the auto industry's demands in 1981 with voluntary export restraints on Japanese automobiles. The restraints, which limited Japanese firms' ability to export cars produced in Japan to the United States, prompted an international relocation of much of the world's auto production. Japanese firms such as Honda and Toyota now produce cars *in* the United States and export them to Europe, to South Korea, and even back to Japan. In fact, it no longer makes much sense to talk about "American" cars or "Japanese" cars. Auto-industry analysts now speak of "captive imports" (vehicles such as the Geo, made by a foreign-based company but sold through domestic dealerships) and "transplants" (for example, the Ford-Mazda Probe, built domestically by a foreign-based company). Even though cars no longer can be easily defined by their "nationality," firms recognize that as long as domestic interests dominate the policy-making process, it is to the firms' advantage to appear "domestic." So, a new type of advertising emphasizes firms' links to the domestic economy. Figure 1.1 illustrates this phenomenon. The figure reproduces a recent *Wall Street Journal* advertisement from Toyota in which the firm highlights its many U.S.-based parts suppliers.[2]

A product's "nationality" becomes even more difficult to determine once we recognize that firms assemble their products from components manufactured around the world. Ford, for example, assembles its Escort in Germany from parts produced in 15 countries, from Austria to Canada to Japan.[3] Such production linkages represent one type of economic interdependence, a type that is increasingly prevalent in the world economy. Occasionally, the result is embarrassment for policy makers intent on giving preference to domestic products.[4] For example, a small town in New York, determined to "Buy American," bought a $55,000 John Deere excavator in

---

[2]In 1995, a long-simmering trade dispute between the United States and Japan over trade in auto parts erupted into a near trade war; Case Two in Chapter Six provides details.

[3]Peter Dicken, *Global Shift* (London: Harper & Row, 1986), p. 304.

[4]Chapters Seven and Eight cover the effects of such policies.

Figure 1.1 □ Firms Advertise Their Domestic Economic Linkages

BUYING quality PARTS is not a FOREIGN idea to us.

OVER THE last five years, Toyota in America has purchased more than $20 billion in parts and materials from 510 U.S. suppliers. Today, more than half the Toyota vehicles sold in America are built at our plants in Kentucky and California. Local investment that contributes to America's place in the global economy - it all makes good sense, in any language.

Toyota Avalon. Built in Georgetown, Kentucky.

INVESTING IN THE THINGS WE ALL CARE ABOUT. **TOYOTA**

Some parts that go into our American-built vehicles are purchased overseas. For more information about Toyota in America visit our web site at http://www.toyota.com/antenna/usa.html or write Toyota Motor Corporate Services, 9 West 57th Street, Suite 4900-S9, New York, NY 10019

Source: *The Wall Street Journal*, January 17, 1996, A13.

preference over a comparable $40,000 Komatsu one. Town decision makers then discovered that Komatsu built its machine in Illinois and that Deere built its in Japan.[5]

The debates over international interdependence that heated up in the 1970s and 1980s have not cooled, but some of the details have changed. For example, one of the most important trends of recent years is developing countries' expanding involvement with the world economy. After decades of attempting to isolate themselves from world markets, many developing countries now open their borders and pursue policies designed to integrate themselves into international economic activity. This trend produces new patterns of international interdependence that bring new debates to the fore. What are the implications for developed countries of growing trade with developing economies? Is the "common sense" conclusion—that trade with countries where wages are far below those in the United States must lower wages for unskilled American workers—correct? In other words, as the title of one recent article put it, "Are Your Wages Set in Beijing?"[6] Most economists agree, based on mounting empirical evidence, that trade with low-wage countries has *not* lowered U.S. wages significantly; but the debate continues.[7]

International interdependence and the debates it engenders are not limited to trade in goods and services. In fact, interdependence in financial markets, where firms and governments borrow, lend, and finance investment projects, has grown even more dramatically than that in markets for goods such as oil, steel, and automobiles. Until the mid-1960s, government control of financial flows across national borders, combined with the limitations of transportation and communication technologies, kept national financial markets largely separate. Now, with decreased government regulation and improved technologies, financial activity clusters in international centers such as London, New York, Tokyo, Singapore, Hong Kong, Zurich, Frankfurt, and Paris. The result is a 24-hour market in which a push of a computer button can shift funds from one country or currency to another. Growing numbers of firms based in one country list themselves on foreign stock exchanges to facilitate global finance of their investment projects. Estimates indicate that approximately one in every seven stock (or equity) transactions involves a foreign party.[8] U.S.-based firms now raise funds for investment by issuing bonds denominated not just in dollars but also in Japanese yen, French and Swiss francs, German marks, British pounds, and other currencies and sell those bonds around the world. Figure 1.2 illustrates the recent growth in cross-border security transactions for the large industrial economies.[9]

Firms are not the only parties that have internationalized their patterns of finance. Many governments now sell a substantial share of their bonds—sometimes denominated in the domestic currency and sometimes in foreign ones—to

[5]*The Economist*, February 1, 1992, p. 26.
[6]Richard B. Freeman, *Journal of Economic Perspectives*, 1995, pp. 15–32.
[7]We return to this issue in Chapters Four and Eight.
[8]International Monetary Fund, *World Economic Outlook*, May 1995, p. 80.
[9]Note that the data in the figure report transactions as a percent of gross domestic product (GDP), which itself has grown dramatically since 1980. GDP measures the total market value of all final goods and services produced in a given period within a country's borders.

Figure 1.2 □ **Cross-Border Securities Transactions, 1980, 1992 (Percent of GDP)**

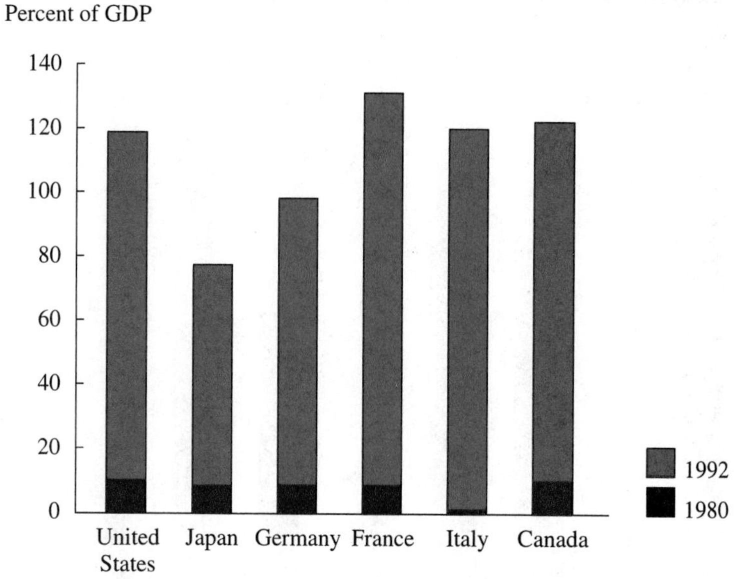

Percent of GDP

Source: International Monetary Fund, *World Economic Outlook*, May 1995, p. 80.

foreign buyers. Such a pattern has long been true for Britain and the United States, the two dominant economies of the twentieth century, and the pattern has now spread to other industrial economies, as documented in Figure 1.3. Despite rapid growth in virtually all international financial markets, the most dramatic growth of all has occurred in the markets for currencies themselves. In 1994, turnover in world foreign exchange markets, where national currencies are traded, reached well over $1 trillion *per day,* an increase of more than 25-fold just since 1980.[10]

All these international financial markets provide opportunities for **international investment,** which plays a vital role in the world economy. From a lender's perspective, the markets allow individuals, firms, and governments with funds to lend to find the most productive investment projects to fund, regardless of the projects' location. From a borrower's perspective, international financial markets allow individuals, firms, and governments with promising investment projects to seek out lenders willing to fund the projects on attractive terms, regardless of the lenders' nationality or place of residence.

[10]International Monetary Fund, *World Economic Outlook*, May 1995, p. 80.

Figure 1.3 □ **Government Bonds Held by Foreign Investors, 1979, 1992 (Percent of Outstanding Amount)**

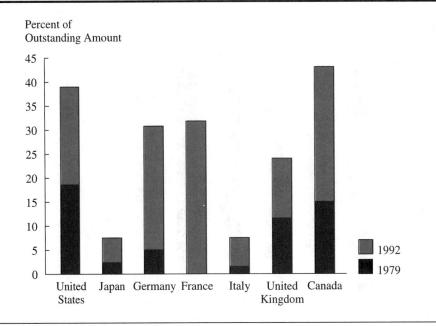

Source: International Monetary Fund, *World Economic Outlook,* May 1995, p. 81.

The growth of international flows of goods and services, financial assets such as stocks, bonds, and currencies, and information reflects declines in the costs of international transportation and communication. Sea cargo, air transport, and telephone calls all have become dramatically cheaper (see Figure 1.4), and these trends encourage international economic activity. However, government policies toward international economic activity also exert an important influence. Since World War II, more and more governments have become convinced of the importance of open international markets for goods, services, and investment and have reduced their restrictions on international transactions.

1.3.1 Policy Implications of International Interdependence

The increase in international economic activity, in turn, has far-flung implications for the world political economy. Policy makers in issue areas once considered domestic—such as antitrust policy, regulation, and taxation—now must reckon with those policies' international ramifications. Trade disputes between the United States and Japan often hinge on the two countries' different approaches to antitrust policy. In 1995, for example, American-based Kodak accused Japanese-based Fuji of engaging in anti-competitive practices to monopolize Japan's photographic-supplies market

Figure 1.4 □ **Transport and Communication Costs, 1930–1990 (Index: 1930 = 100)**

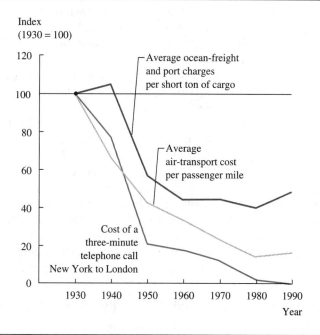

Source: *The Economist,* July 20, 1991; data from Institute for International Economics.

and also accused the Japanese government of complicity in Fuji's activities. In negotiations over the North American Free-Trade Agreement (NAFTA), member countries' different environmental policies posed a major barrier to cooperation. U.S. and Canadian environmental interests feared that firms would take advantage of Mexico's lower environmental standards and enforcement by moving to Mexico and exporting goods produced under the laxer standards to the U.S. and Canadian markets. With increased international mobility, countries that try to tax their citizens at rates above those in other nations risk the loss of some of their most productive citizens. Britain experienced such a loss during the early 1980s when movie stars, rock stars, and celebrity athletes fled England for countries with lower tax rates. In each of these cases, a policy that at first glance appears to have solely domestic effects turns out to be linked to international questions as well. Effective economic policy making requires that these international linkages be taken into account.

The implications of interdependence for macroeconomic policy making—that is, for fiscal, monetary, and exchange rate policy—are at least as dramatic as those for microeconomic policy. In Europe, Germany's tight monetary policy to prevent inflation has angered other members of the European Union and threatened the group's plans to introduce a common currency for Europe. Japan has resisted U.S. lobbying to increase its level of government spending in the economy. As the yen price of a

U.S. dollar fell from ¥360 to ¥80 between 1973 and 1995, Japanese policy makers blamed U.S. macroeconomic policy, especially the government budget deficit, and U.S. policy makers pointed fingers at "unfair" Japanese trade policies toward U.S. goods. Brazil and Argentina suffered "hangovers" or "tequila effects" after Mexico experienced serious macroeconomic instability in late 1994 and early 1995.

International interdependence carries political implications as well as economic ones. As communication and transportation technologies improve, authoritarian governments that attempt to limit their citizens' access to growing world markets face an increasingly difficult task. During the student rebellion of June 1989, fax messages from Chinese citizens living abroad kept Chinese residents informed of events in their own country. Differentials in living standards and personal freedom between East and West exerted pressure, eventually metamorphic, on control-oriented Eastern European and Soviet governments in 1989–1991. Cuba, one of the few remaining authoritarian socialist economies, spends scarce resources to block signals from U.S. television satellites from reaching the island. Nor are developed economies such as the United States immune from the political ramifications of interdependence. Many American workers and politicians blame international trade for declining wages among the lowest skilled workers, even though the bulk of empirical evidence points to other culprits. And some Americans bitterly resented the U.S. financial support package for Mexico during that country's 1994 currency crisis.

1.3.2   Symptoms of International Interdependence

Beyond citing a potentially endless list of examples, it is difficult to define, much less quantify, the idea of interdependence. We can examine two measures as symptoms. The first is simply the trend in the extent of trade, or the volume of goods and services exchanged across national boundaries. Figure 1.5 establishes that merchandise trade has expanded rapidly over the past half-century. Comparing the growth in merchandise *trade* volume with growth in world merchandise *production* in panel (a), we find that trade not only grew but also expanded more than twice as fast as production. Panel (b) reveals that the rate of growth of trade outpaced that of production in all but five years between 1950 and 1993. These trends indicate an increasingly vital role of international trade in allocating the world's resources. Because economics is the study of the allocation of scarce resources among alternative uses, the importance of international issues in the study of economics also has increased.

As we shall see in Chapters Two and Three, international trade improves individuals' well-being by increasing the quantity of goods and services available to consume. Nevertheless, the interdependence of which trade is a symptom often is viewed as a mixed blessing. For U.S. consumers, trade makes available sugar from Brazil, silk from China, and champagne from France. Trade also provides wheat for residents of the former Soviet republics in years of bad harvests and export markets for American farmers. However, U.S. sugar producers, textile manufacturers, and wine growers demand protection from competition by foreign rivals; and U.S. consumers sometimes blame high food prices on the former Soviet Union's failure to undertake agricultural reform.

Figure 1.5 □ **World Merchandise Trade and Output, 1950–1993**

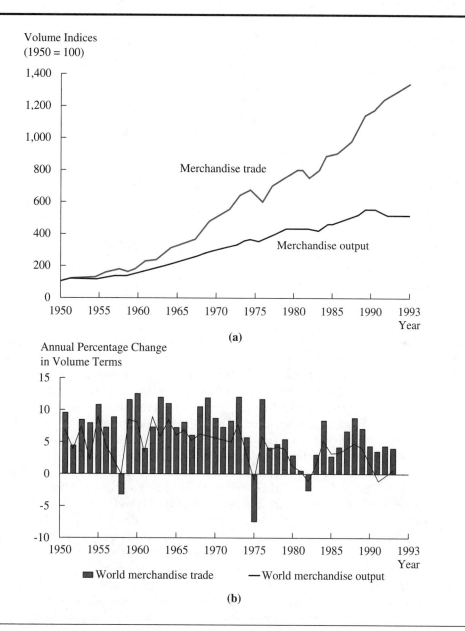

Source: GATT, *International Trade: Trends and Statistics*, 1994.

Table 1.2 ▫ **Merchandise Exports and Imports as Shares of Gross Domestic Product, 1993**

Country	Merchandise Exports/GDP	Merchandise Imports/GDP
Singapore	1.34	1.55
Ireland	.67	.50
Belgium	.53	.59
Côte d'Ivoire	.36	.21
Canada	.30	.28
Indonesia	.23	.19
United Kingdom	.22	.25
China	.22	.24
Russia	.13	.10
India	.10	.10
Tajikistan	.10	.15
Japan	.09	.06
Panama	.08	.33
United States	.07	.10

Source: World Bank, *World Development Report 1995.*

Despite dramatic increases in trade worldwide, countries continue to differ significantly in the extent to which they engage in trade. Table 1.2 presents some examples; it measures a country's involvement in trade by merchandise exports and imports as shares of its total output or gross domestic product (GDP). The 1993 export shares range from a low of 7 percent for the United States to a high of 134 percent for Singapore, a tiny country that specializes in assembly for export. Import percentages range from Japan's 6 percent to Singapore's 155 percent, again reflecting that country's specialization in assembly and reexport tasks.

Other things being equal, large countries such as the United States tend to engage in less trade, as a share of their production, than do smaller countries. The main reason is easy to see: The size and diversity of the United States mean that domestic markets satisfy many needs. On the import side, residents of Rhode Island get corn from Iowa, oil from Texas, and lettuce from California; they go to the beach in Florida, mountain climbing in Colorado, and whale watching in Alaska. They execute financial deals in New York and enjoy movies produced in Hollywood. On the export side, U.S. firms enjoy access to a huge domestic market; many do not export, but this is changing. Although still modest by world standards, as indicated in Table 1.2, U.S. involvement in international trade has increased steadily in recent years. Figure 1.6, which reports the dollar value of U.S. merchandise imports and exports throughout the postwar era, documents this trend.

Countries not only engage in trade to differing extents, but their trade tends to cluster with certain trading partners. This is not surprising because transportation costs, while now low by historical standards, still play a role in determining

Figure 1.6 □ **U.S. Merchandise Imports and Exports, 1946–1993 ($ Billions)**

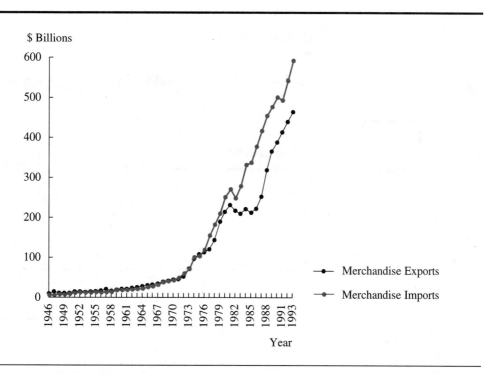

Source: *Economic Report of the President 1995.*

trade patterns.[11] Figure 1.7 highlights this clustering by dividing trade flows into four major groups or blocs of countries, North America, Western Europe, Asia, and the rest of the world. Recently, policy makers have expressed concern over the risk that trade patterns will evolve more in the direction of trade blocs—with open intra-bloc trade but high barriers to trade with countries outside the bloc. This concern underlies some economists' criticisms of the European Union and the NAFTA.[12]

As a symptom of international interdependence, the magnitude and pattern of trade primarily reflect interdependence among producers and consumers in specific markets. International trade in automobiles makes auto consumers and producers worldwide interdependent, and the same is true in thousands of other markets. But economic interdependence goes much deeper. Synchronized changes

---

[11]Chapter Five presents several hypotheses about which groups of countries engage in large amounts of trade with each other.

[12]Chapter Nine covers arguments for and against such trade blocs.

Figure 1.7 □ **Regional Flows of Merchandise Trade, 1992 ($ Billions)**

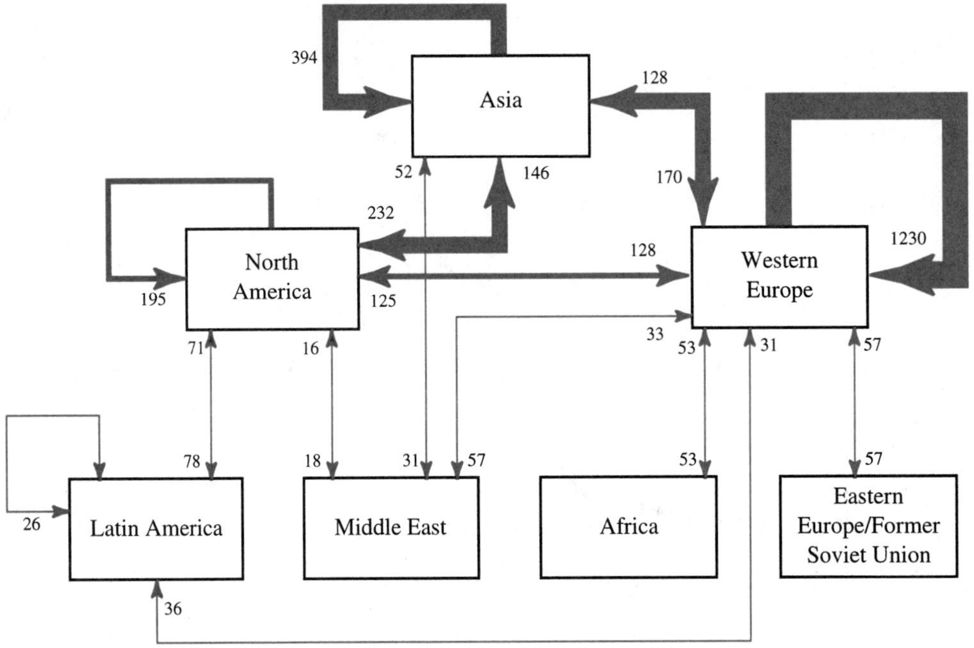

Source: Bernard Hoekman and Michael Kostecki, *The Political Economy of the World Trading System: From GATT to WTO* (Oxford: Oxford University Press, 1995), p. 9; data from GATT.

in macroeconomic activity across countries represent a second important symptom of interdependence. Figure 1.8 illustrates the recent paths of industrial production in a set of major industrialized economies. Notice that the countries exhibit a striking tendency toward simultaneous booms and recessions. This historical evidence suggests that it may be difficult for one economy to expand when its trading partners' economies are growing slowly or shrinking.

Like interdependence within specific markets, this more general macroeconomic interdependence often is viewed as a mixed blessing. Europeans bitterly resented the spillover effects of U.S. anti-inflation policies during the early 1980s, but they appreciated the effects of the strong U.S. recovery after 1983. More recently, the size of the U.S. government budget deficit and the U.S. recession that opened the 1990s raised concerns in the rest of the world over the international implications of economic events and policies in America. Across the Atlantic, Britain and Italy have withdrawn, at least temporarily, from European Union plans for a common currency because of their unwillingness to endure the spillover effects of German macroeconomic policy. In general, macroeconomic spillover effects create the potential for

Figure 1.8 □ **Industrial Production in the Major Industrialized Economies, 1969–1993 (Index: 1987 = 100)**

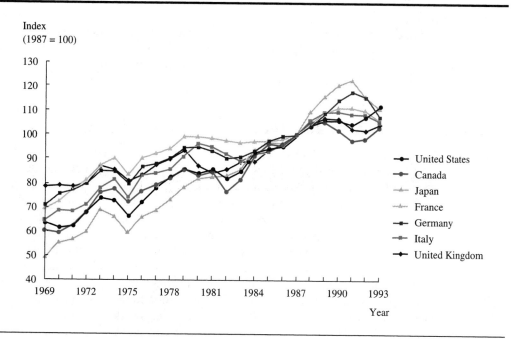

Index
(1987 = 100)

United States
Canada
Japan
France
Germany
Italy
United Kingdom

Year

Source: *Economic Report of the President 1995.*

conflict whenever one country perceives a need to pursue contractionary policies (for example, to fight inflation) while its trading partners want to expand (perhaps to counter unacceptably high unemployment).

Despite the clarity of the pattern observable in Figure 1.8, a cautionary note is in order. Data such as those reported in Figure 1.8 require careful interpretation. After all, each country's experience may have been totally independent of all others'. In other words, it is possible that mere coincidence produced the pattern apparent in Figure 1.8. This general caution must be taken seriously. Historical evidence is very useful in suggesting patterns in economic behavior, but it has little ability to explain the "whys" behind them. Because of the inability of empirical evidence alone to explain observed patterns, we need *theories* of economic behavior to answer questions such as, What are the nature and consequences of the economic ties among the countries of the world economy? Or, how should policy makers respond to particular cases of international economic interdependence?

This book addresses these fundamental questions from the perspective of economics. Within the sphere of countries' international relationships, political and economic elements are difficult, if not impossible, to separate. However, the basic concepts of economic theory can be surprisingly helpful in untangling the maze of issues that constitutes the world economy. Because millions of firms produce hundreds of thousands of commodities in more than 150 countries, we need a systematic framework for analysis—and this is what economic theory can provide. Thus, it is this book's perspective more than its subject matter that marks it as a text in international *economics*. The subjects covered (such as international trade, the transition from central planning, multinational enterprises, relations between developed and developing countries, inflation, debt, and unemployment) are also of direct interest to political scientists, as well as to specialists in international relations, international business, and public policy.

1.4   The Economic Significance of Political Boundaries

International economics traditionally has been the subject of special books and courses, separate from the rest of economics. At the same time, the interaction between international economics and the remainder of economic theory has been rich and, like international trade itself, beneficial to both parties. Economists working specifically on international problems developed many of the analytical techniques now used in all areas of the discipline. Similarly, many recent advances in international economics have built on developments in other areas of economics.

Why does the separate study of international questions persist? The main reason is that the **economic significance of political boundaries** persists. Most people would agree that life in a small New England college town differs radically from life in Los Angeles. From an economist's point of view, however, residents of the two places share a great deal. All use U.S. dollars as a currency or means of payment. All live under a common set of federal laws and a common political and economic system, and many share a common language. All share in the fortunes of the U.S. economy, benefiting from the country's resource endowment and being affected by U.S. policy decisions. Because of all these shared features, most economic transactions between the New Englander and the Californian face a smaller set of barriers than do economic transactions between a U.S. resident and a resident of a foreign country. The Californian can relocate in New England if he or she desires, and the New Englander is free to migrate to California. If the pattern of interest rates makes deposits in California banks or bonds issued by California firms or government agencies attractive, the New Englander can choose to buy those assets, and vice versa for the Californian buying assets in New England.

National boundaries are economically relevant not only in determining the legal, language, and currency barriers to transactions but in determining economic policy. In other words, the nature of the policy-making process also tends to make international economics a separate field of study. Despite the growing internationalization of many markets, economic policy making remains largely a matter of national sovereignty. In fact, many national governments respond to the perception of increased international interdependence by guarding their sovereign policy-making powers even more jealously. As a result, the policy process typically favors the interests of domestic residents over the interests of the world as a whole. This tendency is easy to understand given the realities of policy making. Decisions on policies either universally beneficial or universally harmful are easy—but such easy decisions are rare. The more typical policy decision involves evaluating a policy that benefits some individuals and harms others. In such a situation, we should not be surprised that the consideration given to the policy's effects on domestic residents usually outweighs that given to those on individuals abroad.

At the same time, it is important to realize that the major popular misconception about international trade policy is that policy choices pit the interests of one country against those of the other (for example, that the United States must not let Japan "win" by capturing a larger share of world markets).[13] In fact, trade-policy choices rarely take this form. Instead, trade policy primarily affects the distribution of income *within* each country. If the United States blocks imports of Japanese steel, the main result is not to help the United States at Japan's expense; rather, the main effect is to help American steel producers at the expense of American steel consumers, such as the U.S. automobile industry and American car buyers. Because economists think that individuals act in their own self-interest, evaluating the effects of various international trade policies on different interest groups will be one of our major tasks. By understanding a policy's effects on different groups within the economy, we can understand the observed pattern of political support for and opposition to the policy.

1.5 Studying International Economics

Economists traditionally divide the subject matter of international economics into two parts. The first, called the **theory of international trade,** extends *micro*economic analysis to international questions. Here we consider decisions concerning the quantities of various goods produced, consumed, and traded by different countries. We shall see that the goods and services available for consumers to enjoy are at a maximum when each country specializes in producing those goods that it can produce relatively efficiently. Trade then allows each country's residents to import a variety of other goods to consume. These production and consumption decisions collectively determine the relative prices of both goods and factors of production such as labor, capital, and land. These prices, in turn, determine the distribution of income among individuals in the economy.

Like microeconomics, trade theory traditionally ignores monetary issues by expressing all costs and prices in terms of other goods rather than a monetary unit such as dollars. In other words, goods exchange directly for other goods (one bushel of corn for two bushels of wheat, or four computers for one car). By examining trade's effect on the relative prices of different goods and factors of production, trade theory highlights the distributional impact of trade. Because unrestricted international trade can change relative prices, it also can alter the distribution of income among various groups within each country. An understanding of this interrelationship between

---

[13]The U.S. practice of blaming Japan for U.S. economic problems, known as "Japan bashing," has become so pervasive that a Japanese software company introduced a home-computer game by that name. In the game, players can negotiate over several U.S.–Japan trade disputes including auto quotas, whaling, and drift-net fishing.

trade and income distribution is essential to making sense of the political pressures for **protectionist policies,** which restrict international trade to "protect" domestic producers from foreign competition.

The second major branch of international economics, called *international finance, balance-of-payments theory,* or **open-economy macroeconomics,** applies *macro*economic analysis to aggregate international problems. Major concerns here include the level of employment and output in each economy as well as changes in the price level, balance of payments, and **exchange rates** or relative prices of different national currencies. The most basic issue addressed by open-economy macroeconomics is the interaction of international goals and influences with domestic ones in determining a country's macroeconomic performance and policy. Can a country that engages in international transactions (called an **open economy**) pursue the same macroeconomic policies as a country that engages in no international transactions (a **closed economy**) and achieve the same results? The answer is *no;* so, understanding the implications of openness turns out to be essential to effective macroeconomic policy making.

As in microeconomic analysis of international trade policy, we shall discover that macroeconomic policies have distributional consequences. Policy choices typically stated in terms of domestic interests versus foreign ones actually involve differences in the interests of various groups *within* each economy. For example, journalists, commentators, and politicians often speak of any currency depreciation (that is, a rise in the exchange rate or the domestic currency price of a unit of foreign currency) as an economic problem in need of a remedy. Indeed, sound economic policy making does require that any country experiencing a chronic currency depreciation consider adjusting its macroeconomic policies. We also must recognize, however, that depreciations *help* some groups within the domestic economy, especially import-competing and export industries. Those same currency depreciations also *hurt* other domestic groups, particularly importers and consumers of imported goods.

International trade and open-economy macroeconomics are the subjects of Parts One and Two of this book, respectively. In each part, we begin by building a simple model and then elaborate on it and apply it to many historical and current events in the world economy. The models are just tools to describe the way the world economy works. They may seem overly simple and "unrealistic." However, that's the whole point of building models. After all, a road map would be of little practical use if it illustrated every bump, ant hill, grain of sand, pothole, and roadside sign. We need models like good road maps: as simple as possible while still capturing the key features necessary to understand the world economy. Once you master the basic models in Parts One and Two, you can use them to analyze not only the applications considered in the text but the constantly changing international economic news.

Economists call models that describe in a simplified way how the world economy works *positive models.* For the most part, we shall employ **positive analysis** in this book, using models to understand how the world economy is structured and how it functions. This approach focuses primarily on explanation and prediction. The goal is to understand the world economy well enough to be able to say, "If event X happens, event Y will follow." For example, after reading Chapter Four we might predict that, given the opportunity to choose between unrestricted trade and protectionism, farmers in Japan would tend to choose protectionism. This prediction *does not* depend on whether we, as economists or citizens, believe protectionism is desirable; the prediction follows directly from our model of how the world economy works. We can then look at Japanese farmers' political behavior and see if they do in fact support protectionist policies. (To jump ahead a bit, the answer is *yes*.)

Another type of analysis is **normative** and *does* depend on our judgments about what is and is not desirable. For example, if we think trade is desirable because it maximizes the quantity of goods and services available to consumers, we might conclude that Japanese policy makers should pursue open trade policies in the agricultural sector even though Japanese farmers oppose them. Normative analyses always rely on our values to determine what types of international economic goals and policies we think should be pursued.

From our discussion of the differences between positive and normative economic analysis, we can see that disagreements over international policy issues can come from at least two sources. First, there may be disagreement about the way the world works. One individual may think that "If event X happens, event Y will follow," while another may think that "If event X happens, event Z will follow." For example, one person might argue that opening international trade (X) will reduce economic growth (Y) because imported goods will replace domestic production, while someone else claims that opening trade (X) will increase economic growth (Z) by moving resources into their most productive uses. Analysts usually can resolve such disagreements by conducting further empirical research to determine whether Y or Z will follow X.

Disagreements based on normative judgments typically prove more difficult to resolve. Two policy makers may agree that "If we pursue policy X, result Y will follow." But if the two disagree about whether Y is desirable, they will disagree about whether they should pursue policy X. For example, most economists acknowledge that policies of unrestricted international trade would result in the decline of several U.S. industries, including nonspecialty steel, some types of automobiles, footwear, and many types of textiles and apparel, because those U.S. industries are relatively inefficient compared with their foreign counterparts. Whether one supports policies of unrestricted trade thus depends in part on one's evaluation of the tradeoffs among trade's efficiency benefits, the short-run costs of resource reallocation associated with the decline of certain industries, the costs to consumers of protecting inefficient industries, and the increased interdependence that comes from relying on foreign suppliers.

Throughout this book, both positive and normative issues arise. Although the distinction is not always clear, it is important to keep in mind the conceptual difference between the two. Debates over the desirability of various international economic policies can be useful only when it is clear where the disagreement originates—in our views of the way the world works or in our views of how we would like the world to be.

1.6   Overview of the Book

Like international economics, this book is organized into two major sections. Part One applies *micro*economic analysis to international economic relations. Part Two makes up the open-economy *macro*economic portion of the book. In this section, we highlight some of the major questions addressed in each part.

1.6.1 International Microeconomics

Debates over international economic policy are far from new. As we see in Chapter Two, controversy over trade policy played a major role in the eighteenth-century origin of economics as a discipline. In fact, many of the debates of the 1700s persist in the 1990s. The early chapters of the book demonstrate that unrestricted international trade enlarges the quantity of available goods and services for all participating countries. In other words, even though Chinese wages fall far short of U.S. wages, the popular view that China gains *at America's expense* by selling toys and textiles in the United States is mistaken; and we explain why. In the process, we discover the first of two bases for mutually beneficial international trade: the vitally important, but often misunderstood, concept of comparative advantage. We use the basic building blocks of this argument (presented in Chapters Two and Three) throughout Part One; thus, the time spent mastering them will be well rewarded.

If international trade holds so much potential for improving world welfare, why has free trade been the exception historically rather than the rule? More specifically, why would a major firm such as LTV Corporation not only oppose free trade but also spend the money to take out a full-page advertisement in *USA Today* to plead for support in restricting trade (see Figure 1.9)? Chapter Four introduces the answer: because trade policy alters the distribution of income in a systematic and predictable way. Understanding these distributional effects allows us to understand the patterns of support for and opposition to international trade. For example, U.S. farmers historically have supported unrestricted international trade, while Japanese farmers have supported a complex array of restrictions on Japanese agricultural imports. This reflects the fact that most sectors of U.S. agriculture are highly efficient and, therefore, have little reason to worry about foreign competition in their domestic markets. U.S. farmers support unrestricted international trade because it provides access to export markets for their products. Most Japanese agriculture, on the other hand, is highly inefficient relative to that of other countries, resulting in very high prices for Japanese-grown products.[14] Without trade barriers, Japanese farmers would lose their domestic market to more efficient foreign rivals.

Some specific aspects of international trade are difficult to understand based solely on the basic trade model developed in Chapters Two through Four. For example, does it make sense for Germany to export cars to Japan at the same time that Japan exports cars to Germany (a phenomenon called *intra-industry trade*)? Why do developed countries tend to trade largely with each other rather than with the developing countries? Why does production of many goods, such as televisions, VCRs, and semiconductor chips, move from country to country as the product "ages" from fresh innovation to old standby? Can protection ever help a country "create" comparative advantage? Chapter Five examines these issues and, in the process, uncovers the second basis for mutually beneficial international trade: economies of scale, or some firms' ability to achieve lower average production costs as either their own output or the output of their industry rises. Chapter Five also presents the empirical

---

[14]American visitors to Japan often report trouble enjoying a melon they know cost the yen equivalent of $90!

Figure 1.9 □ "The Steel Imperative"

THE STEEL IMPERATIVE

Good intentions have gone sour.
America is hastening its own dependence
on foreign steel
for everything from our tanks to our toasters.
The time to act is now.

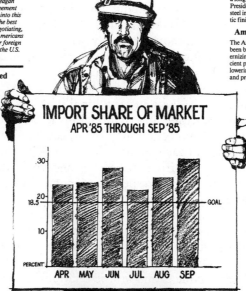

Just over a year ago, President Reagan and the Congress reached an agreement to restrict the flow of unfair steel into this country. But after 14 months of the best of intentions and a lot of hard negotiating, we are worse off than we were. Americans can no longer sit idly by while our foreign trading partners wreak havoc on the U.S. Steel market.

The plan hasn't worked

Last year, instead of enacting quota legislation, Congress went along with the President's plan to negotiate voluntary restraint agreements to try to hold steel imports to 18.5 percent (with 1.7 million tons of semi-finished added, totaling about 20.2% of the domestic market). But today, steel imports—most from state-supported mills—have reached an astounding 30.7 percent.

Everyone is shipping his product into the only open market in the world. Eighteen countries which don't even have steel mills—countries like Belize, Swaziland, Mali, Bhutan, and Fiji—have started exporting steel into the U.S.

The simple fact is, the President's plan has failed and Congress has both the mandate and the opportunity to do something about it.

A new plan "with teeth"

The Steel Import Stabilization Act of 1984 declared that "if the national policy for the steel industry does not produce satisfactory results within a reasonable period of time, the Congress will consider taking such legislative actions concerning steel and iron ore products as may be necessary or appropriate to stabilize conditions in the domestic market for such products."

Rep. Jim Chapman (D-Tex.) has proposed action that enforces that mandate. HR 3459 supports the President's 1984 objectives. It provides that steel imports from any country not party to a bilateral agreement under the President's national policy for steel, shall not exceed 70 percent of the amount of steel imported from such country during the base period of October 1, 1983, to October 1, 1984. This,

we believe, is eminently fair and would go a long way toward helping achieve the President's original goal of limiting all steel imports to 18.5 percent of the domestic finished steel market.

American steel second to none

The American Steel Industry has never been busier building new facilities, modernizing others, painfully closing less efficient plants, streamlining the workplace, lowering costs, developing new products and processes, investing to the very limits of our abilities. And today the industry is vastly different from what it was a few short years ago.

The facts are that in the last two years we have added more high-yield continuous casters than any nation in Europe. More than Japan. Probably more than any other country in the world. And we've done it with our own resources, not with taxpayers' money.

The fact, often overlooked, is that the American Steel Industry is the most productive in the world. Our 5.42 man-hours per net ton produced represents the highest steel productivity among the major industrialized countries of the world. Yes, we're even more productive than Japan, Germany, France and Britain.

Make your voice heard

While HR 3459 won't entirely stem the tide of foreign steel, it is at least a beginning. America would finally be standing up and saying to the rest of the world that we believe in truly *fair* trading and we're going to do something about it.

We urge Congress to get behind HR 3459. We urge our friends in local communities, in state governments, our customers and our employees to let your representatives in Washington know that you are no longer willing to sit idly by while a vital American industry is seriously threatened by unfair trade.

We at LTV and our fellow workers in the American Steel Industry are fighting back. We urge you to join the fight.

LTV The LTV Corporation

Source: *USA Today,* December 3, 1985, 9A.

evidence on how well various economic models of international trade explain observed trade patterns.

Tariffs, the simplest form of protectionist policy, are the focus of Chapter Six, and Chapter Seven examines the more subtle nontariff policies of the "new protectionism," such as voluntary export restraints, anti-dumping policies, voluntary import expansions, and export subsidies. Although governments still use many tariffs, the 1970s and 1980s witnessed a proliferation of nontariff barriers to trade. These barriers raise serious questions for the world trading system and tend to be considerably more complex in their effects than simple tariffs.

Despite rigorous demonstration of potential gains from trade, many arguments for protectionist policies persist, some of them the same basic arguments put forward in the eighteenth century. Should we refuse to buy products produced by foreign workers who earn the equivalent of $1.00 per day? Is free trade inconsistent with national security, making a country vulnerable to a shutoff of vital materials? Does trade prevent an environmentally conscious country from implementing its preferred environmental standards? What about government involvement in trade policies designed to aid "strategic" industries in high-technology sectors of the economy? Chapter Eight analyzes the most commonly heard arguments and evaluates alternative, nonprotectionist policies for dealing with most of the issues raised.

Chapter Nine argues that a fundamental and understandable tension exists between narrowly nationalistic interests, represented by concerns over national sovereignty, and more broadly international interests, represented by international cooperation and trade. International institutions, including trade groups such as the European Union and the NAFTA, can be viewed as responses to this tension. Policy makers in each country must deal with the dilemma of a tradeoff between achieving the gains from cooperation and trade and maintaining sovereign control over all aspects of their respective economies. Occasionally, a government even chooses different trade policies for different parts of the country. China, for example, as an early part of its transition to a more market-oriented economy, allowed relatively unrestricted international trade and investment in "special economic zones" in its southern coastal provinces near Hong Kong and Taiwan, while it maintained more government controls over trade and investment in the rest of the country. Chapter Nine examines the relationship between national boundaries and trade policy. We explore cases in which trade policy making occurs at a level higher than the individual country (for example, the European Union and the NAFTA) as well as cases in which it occurs at lower levels (for example, China's special economic zones).

Some of the most hotly debated areas of international economic policy concern cross-border resource movements. Multinational enterprises have long been controversial, often accused of abandoning their home countries and exploiting their hosts; nevertheless, multinationals have grown rapidly throughout the last half-century. Immigration is also a potent political issue in many parts of the world, including the United States and Western Europe. Some in the United States see uncontrolled immigration, particularly from Mexico and the rest of Central America, as an economic and political threat. Others argue that the strength of the American economy derived from a generation of immigrants and that a growing work force of new immigrants ensures the continued strength of the economy. Similar arguments over immigration policy rage in Europe as postwar barriers between East and West fall. Again, understanding the effects of resource mobility on the distribution of income turns out to be essential to understanding the debate (the subject, along with technological progress, of Chapter Ten).

Some scholars who acknowledge the benefits of free trade for developed countries have argued that such benefits do not apply to developing countries. The role of international trade in the complicated process of economic development has been a subject of debate for decades, although most economists now agree that the record is clear: Open international trade provides benefits regardless of the stage of development. Debates continue, however, between developed and developing economies on many issues related to international trade and participation in the world economy. The first half of Chapter Eleven evaluates these debates. For example, does trade with the developed nations condemn the developing ones to a future of exploitation, producing primary products at ever-falling prices? Is there a connection between the trade policies chosen by developed and developing countries and the latters' debt problem? Do developed economies' trade policies help or hinder developing country efforts to integrate themselves into the world economy? Why can't developed and developing economies agree on environmental issues—or on a system of international protection for intellectual property such as movies, books, and computer software?

A new type of developing economies emerged in the early 1990s: those in transition from central planning. The transitional economies differ in some important respects from traditional developing countries; after all, many of the centrally planned economies were highly (even overly) industrialized. Despite these differences, the two groups exhibit many common problems, challenges, and needs for reform. In the second half of Chapter Eleven, we examine the legacy of central planning, the reform tasks that lie ahead, and the prospects for the transitional economies.

1.6.2 International Macroeconomics

Perhaps the most prominent international macroeconomic issue of the mid-1980s was the rapid appreciation of the U.S. dollar against most other currencies. The "strength" of the dollar received blame for the plight of bankrupt American farmers, the developing-country debt crisis, and the U.S. trade deficit, among other things. Ironically, one of the most prominent economic issues of the late 1970s was the rapid depreciation or "weakness" of the dollar. In the 1990s, dollar depreciation is in the news again. What exactly does it mean when the number of dollars required to buy a yen rises? What can cause such a change? What does this mean for the U.S. economy and for the economies of U.S. trading partners? Chapter Twelve opens Part Two with a study of the mechanics of foreign exchange markets and exchange rate determination.

Probably no concept in international macroeconomics is more bewildering to the person on the street than the balance of payments. The evening news announces surpluses and deficits in the balance of payments, but the figures reported rarely refer to the true balance of payments. Chapter Thirteen examines a country's balance of payments, which is simply a double-entry accounting system that records transactions between the country and its trading partners.

Conventional wisdom holds that a deficit in a country's **current account** (the difference between the value of the country's exports of goods and services and its imports of goods and services) leads to sluggish macroeconomic performance.[15] However, during the 1980s, the United States had both a rapidly growing current-account deficit and a robust recovery from the recession that opened the decade, and in the early 1990s, a U.S. recession coincided with shrinkage of the current-account deficit. Does U.S. experience imply that the conventional wisdom is wrong? Chapter Fourteen resolves these apparent puzzles in the context of a simple open-economy version of a Keynesian model for determining the gross domestic product.

Many linkages join the macroeconomies of the world. U.S. residents purchase British goods and services, buy British assets (bonds or shares of stock issued by British firms), and may hold bank deposits denominated in British pounds sterling. All these transactions affect gross domestic product, interest rates, and exchange rates in both the United States and Britain as well as different macroeconomic policies' abilities to achieve policy makers' desired results. Chapters Fifteen, Sixteen, and Seventeen examine these linkages and their implications for the conduct of macroeconomic policy. Questions we address include: Why does the European Union's Exchange Rate Mechanism carry different implications for Germany than for the other EU members? How did Mexico go from model of reform to currency crisis in 1994? How does a country's chosen mix of fiscal, monetary, and exchange rate policy affect its trading partners?

The models in Chapters Fourteen through Seventeen focus on macroeconomic policies' *short-run* effects. Policy makers often (some would say *too* often) choose policies primarily for their short-run effect. However, we must keep in mind, as must policy makers, that macroeconomic policies also carry *long-run* consequences that may differ sharply from their short-run effects. Chapter Eighteen summarizes what economists know about long-run macroeconomic equilibrium, especially long-run exchange rates. Among other topics in Chapter Eighteen, we explore the effects of interest rates, earthquakes, and nontraded goods on the exchange rate.

A major development in the world economy during the late 1960s and 1970s was the emergence of inflation as a serious problem in the industrialized countries. This forced macroeconomists to reconsider their views of the ways economies function, because the most widely used models had been developed during years when inflation was insignificant. The spread of inflation was a decidedly international issue, because many countries claimed that the United States had generated inflation through its unwise monetary and fiscal policies and, aided by the structure of the then-existing international monetary system, spread the problem to

---

[15]We shall see in Chapter Thirteen that the current account includes several subaccounts; the ones mentioned here are the largest and most important.

other countries.[16] Chapter Nineteen documents the recent history of inflation in the world economy and alters our earlier analysis of macroeconomic policies to account for it. Most importantly, we discover in Chapter Nineteen that many macroeconomic policies that may alter a country's real output in the short run affect primarily the price level in the long run.

For international transactions such as trade and financial activity to proceed smoothly, a well-defined system (called an **international monetary regime**) for handling such tasks as exchanging one currency for another must exist. The major categories of international monetary regimes include a gold standard, a fixed exchange rate regime, a flexible exchange rate regime, and a managed-floating regime. Each has its advantages and disadvantages, and the choice is the subject of periodic debate. Chapter Twenty outlines U.S. experience under the various monetary systems, along with some of the criteria that go into the choice of regime. Since the inflationary experience of the 1970s, a small group of proponents of a return to a gold standard (abandoned for a second time around 1930) have been vocal, and we analyze the strengths and weaknesses of their arguments. Several members of the world economy currently face important decisions about their international monetary regime; for example, the European Union is taking steps toward a common currency for at least some of its 15 member countries.

Chapter Eleven investigated trade-related issues facing developing and transitional economies. In Chapter Twenty-One, we turn our attention to the macroeconomic issues facing these two groups of countries. Can their past policies explain their poor historical macroeconomic performance? What are the key elements of reform required to improve performance? Should these countries try to ensure macroeconomic stabilization before they embark on fundamental structural reform of their economies (the so-called gradualism approach, often associated with China), or is sudden across-the-board reform more likely to succeed (the "big-bang" approach, associated with Poland)? How does a country with no history of market-oriented institutions, such as central banks and foreign exchange markets, go about establishing them? Chapter Twenty-One tackles these questions, first for traditional developing economies, and then for transitional ones.

Throughout the book, we present data on many aspects of the world economy, ranging from international patterns in labor productivity and wages, the largest semiconductor producers, the arms trade, U.S. intervention in foreign exchange markets, the economic effects of German unification, and the emerging foreign exchange markets for Russian rubles and Chinese yuan.

A rich variety of sources of additional information about the world economy exists. In the *Study Guide* written to accompany this book, we suggest useful leads if you want to pursue a particular topic in more detail. If you do not yet have a copy of the *Study Guide,* check with your instructor or your bookstore to order one. Along with data sources on the world economy, the *Guide* contains study aids and questions with answers for each chapter in the text, helpful hints for writing economics papers, and much more.

---

[16]The effect of the U.S. economy on the rest of the world became enshrined in the saying "When the United States sneezes because of a cold, the rest of the world catches pneumonia."

Key Terms

international interdependence	exchange rates
international investment	open economy
economic significance of political boundaries	closed economy
	positive analysis
theory of international trade	normative analysis
protectionist policies	current account
open-economy macroeconomics	international monetary regime

Problems and Questions for Review

1. For each of the types of cost illustrated in Figure 1.4 (air transport, sea transport, telephone costs), explain why a decline in the cost might lead to an increase in international trade.

2. Look at the data in Table 1.2. Why might some countries choose to engage more in international trade than other countries?

3. Name some examples of the economic significance of political boundaries.

4. Figure 1.9 provides an example of a firm buying an advertisement in a national publication to lobby support for its position on an international trade issue. Suppose that you represent Acme Thingamajigs, a major producer of thingamajigs. What kinds of trade policies for the thingamajig market might you support, and why? What would you consider in deciding whether buying an advertisement to lobby for your position would be worthwhile?

5. Name three recent events in international microeconomics that you hope to understand better after mastering Chapters Two through Eleven.

6. Name three recent events in international macroeconomics that you hope to understand better after mastering Chapters Twelve through Twenty-One.

7. Suppose you had been a tourist in Moscow on October 11, 1994, when the ruble price of a U.S. dollar suddenly rose by over 20 percent. How might the ruble depreciation have affected you? Suppose, instead, you had been a Russian firm that used inputs imported from Germany. How might the ruble depreciation have affected you?

References and Selected Readings

Bhagwati, Jagdish. *Protectionism.* Cambridge, Mass.: MIT Press, 1988.
A lively treatment of the history and status of protectionism; for all students.

Destler, I. M. *American Trade Politics.* Washington, D.C.: Institute for International Economics, 1995.
Excellent treatment of the historical evolution of U.S. trade policy-making institutions; for all students.

Economic Report of the President, 1995. Washington, D.C.: U.S. Government Printing Office, 1995.
Accessible discussion of the state of the U.S. economy, plus a convenient set of economic data. Chapter Six covers international issues.

Frieden, Jeffry, and David A. Lake, eds. *International Political Economy: Perspectives on Global Power and Wealth.* New York: St. Martin's Press, 1991.

An introductory collection of readings highlighting different perspectives among political scientists and economists on the major questions of international political economy.

Friedman, Milton. "The Methodology of Positive Economics." In *Essays in Positive Economics*. Chicago: University of Chicago Press, 1953.
The classic (and controversial) article that introduced the positive/normative distinction into economics; accessible to introductory students.

General Agreement on Tariffs and Trade. *International Trade: Trends and Statistics*. Geneva: GATT, annual.
Comprehensive collection of trade statistics by region, country, and industry.

Hetzel, Robert L. "The Free Trade Debate: The Illusion of Security versus Growth." Federal Reserve Bank of Richmond *Quarterly Review* 80 (Spring 1994): 39–58.
Introduction to a key element of the debate over free trade and protectionism.

International Monetary Fund. *World Economic Outlook*. Washington, D.C.: International Monetary Fund, annual.
Useful survey of current international macroeconomic issues; also includes data appendices.

James, Harold. *International Monetary Cooperation Since Bretton Woods*. Washington, D.C.: International Monetary Fund, 1996.
A historian's comprehensive official IMF account of the history of international monetary relations since the Second World War; for all students.

King, Philip. *International Economics and International Economic Policy: A Reader*. New York: McGraw Hill, 1995.
An excellent reader for all students. Well organized to follow along with The World Economy.

Krugman, Paul. "Growing World Trade: Causes and Consequences." *Brookings Papers on Economic Activity* 1 (1995): 327–377.
Survey of recent trends in world trade; for intermediate students.

Obstfeld, Maurice. "International Currency Experience: New Lessons and Lessons Relearned." *Brookings Papers on Economic Activity* 1 (1995): 119–219.
Survey of current issues in international macroeconomics; for intermediate and advanced students.

Spero, Joan Edelman, and Jeffrey A. Hart. *The Politics of International Economic Relations*. New York: St. Martin's Press, 1996.
A highly readable treatment of the intersection between international economics and international politics.

U.S. International Trade Commission. *The Year in Trade: Operation of the Trade Agreements Program*. Washington, D.C.: U.S. Government Printing Office, annual.
Excellent overview of current trade issues, negotiations, and disputes.

World Bank. *Global Economic Prospects and the Developing Countries*. Washington, D.C.: World Bank, annual.
Survey of current economic conditions' implications for the developing economies; includes data appendices.

World Bank. *World Development Report*. New York: Oxford University Press, annual.
Useful survey of international issues focused on developing economies. Each year's annual studies a different issue; 1995's covers "Workers in an Integrating World." Includes data appendices.

Yarbrough, Beth V., and Robert M. Yarbrough. "The 'Globalization' of Trade: What's Changed and Why?" In *Studies in Globalization and Development*, edited by S. Gupta and N. K. Choudry. Norwell, Mass.: Kluwer Academic Publishers, forthcoming 1996.
Recent trends in international trade; for all students.

PART ONE

International Microeconomics

CHAPTER TWO

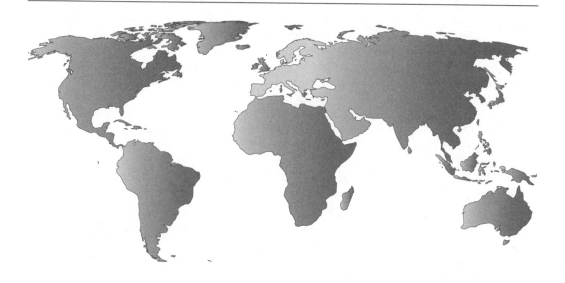

Comparative Advantage I:
Labor Productivity and the Ricardian Model

2.1 Introduction

Nations engage in international trade because they benefit from doing so.[1] The gains from trade arise because trade allows countries to specialize their production in a way that allocates all resources to their most productive uses. Trade plays an essential role in achieving this allocation because it frees each country's residents from having to consume goods in the same combination in which the domestic economy can produce them. If the United States specialized its production but did not engage in international trade, U.S. residents would have large quantities of wheat and soybeans, airplanes, computers and other high-technology equipment, but no coffee or bananas and few shoes or textiles. Japanese residents, on the other hand, would

---

[1]For convenience, we speak of "nations" or "countries" engaging in international trade and making production and consumption decisions. In reality—at least in market-oriented economies—individual firms and consumers, not countries or their governments, make production and consumption decisions and engage in international trade. In nonmarket economies, government enterprises conduct a large percentage of internaional trade as well as control production patterns. Chapter Eight examines government involvement in trade for market economies and Chapter Eleven for nonmarket economies.

find themselves well stocked with automobiles and consumer electronics but without gasoline to run the automobiles and confined to a diet consisting largely of fish.

We can easily see the benefits from productive specialization and trade at the individual level. Most individuals choose to specialize in producing one good (for example, the teaching of economics) and then trade or exchange some of that good for other goods to consume (such as food, clothing, and housing). Any individual who attempted to achieve self-sufficiency by producing everything he or she consumed would face a very difficult task and certainly be constrained to a lower standard of living. Suppose you tried to generate your own electricity and build your own automobile along with growing your own food and building your own house. Providing yourself with these "necessities" would require so much time and effort that there would be little left to produce the "luxuries," such as mountain bikes and CD players, to which you are accustomed. The same holds true for countries that choose to forgo the opportunities provided by productive specialization and trade. The fact that political boundaries divide the world into nation-states does not alter trade's potential for expanding output by efficiently allocating the world's scarce resources to their most productive uses. But policy makers and political economists did not completely understand this simple point until around 1817, and some still forget or ignore it today, as witnessed by the following excerpt:

> The recent trade policy of the United States has encouraged the wage-cutting foreign trade that has been draining away the nation's industries and jobs and created an enormous trade deficit. Given this starting point, the economic state of the nation can be radically improved simply by adopting realistic policies that limit imports so as to bring the nation's foreign trade into balance.[2]

The fact that workers earn lower wages in many other countries than in the United States does *not* mean that trade between those countries and the United States is not mutually beneficial. The imposition of restrictions on trade between low-wage countries and the United States would harm, not help, both parties, as we shall see in the next several chapters.[3]

This chapter demonstrates the existence of gains from trade within the simplest possible context; later chapters extend the analysis to fit reality more closely. The fundamental ideas presented in this chapter—simple though they are—represent not only the heart of international trade theory but also perhaps the most enduring contribution of economics to the goal of improving the welfare of citizens of the world economy.

2.2 Early Trade Theory: The Mercantilists

During the seventeenth and eighteenth centuries, the doctrine of **mercantilism** represented the dominant attitude toward international trade. The period was one of

---

[2]John M. Culbertson, "'Free Trade' Is Impoverishing the West," *The New York Times*, July 28, 1985, F-3.

[3]Chapters Four and Eight explore the proposition that high-wage countries harm themselves by engaging in trade with low-wage countries.

nation building and consolidation of power by newly formed states. Because gold and silver circulated as money, the quantity of these precious metals held by any country symbolized that nation's wealth and power. National leaders wanted to accumulate as much gold and silver as possible. Their efforts to accomplish this involved producing and exporting (selling abroad) as many goods as possible while keeping imports (purchases from abroad) to a minimum. When a nation's exports proved insufficient to pay for its imports, flows of precious metals settled the account balance. Any country that could export more than it imported could enjoy an inflow of gold and silver. The policy prescription based on this mercantilist view was to encourage exports and restrict imports. Mercantilists viewed trade primarily as a way to accumulate gold.

Further, mercantilists assumed trade was a **zero-sum game**—that it could not be **mutually beneficial** to all parties. (Poker is an example of a zero-sum game: Whatever one player wins, the other players lose.) Mercantilists assumed that fixed amounts of goods and of gold existed in the world and that trade merely determined their distribution among the various nations.[4]

2.3   The Decline of Mercantilism

Near the end of the eighteenth century, the doctrine of mercantilism came under attack by leaders of the emerging science of political economy. In 1752, David Hume pointed out two weaknesses in the mercantilists' logic.

First, it is not the quantity of gold and silver a nation holds that matters; rather, it is the quantity of goods and services that the gold and silver can buy. Individuals get satisfaction not by accumulating precious metals but by consuming the goods those metals can buy. The mercantilists wanted to export as many goods and import as few as possible. This implied that other nations would accumulate all the world's output of goods while the mercantilist nation accumulated all the gold. *(Would you want to live in a country that successfully pursued mercantilist policies?)*

The second problem raised by Hume concerns the long-run viability of mercantilist policies. Suppose a country ran a trade surplus (that is, the value of the country's exports exceeded the value of its imports) and obtained the implied inflow of gold. Because gold formed the basis for nations' money supplies during the mercantilist period, the gold inflow would raise both the money supply and prices.[5] As the prices of the nation's goods rose relative to the prices of other nations' goods, the price increase would make the nation's exports less attractive to foreign buyers and imports more attractive to domestic residents. Thus, the price effects of the gold

---

[4]Chapters Nine and Twenty discuss additional aspects of mercantilism. The debate over the causes and consequences of mercantilism can be found in references by Smith, Heckscher, Viner, Ekelund and Tollison, and Irwin in the references at the end of the chapter.

[5]The relationship between a nation's money stock and its price level will be a central issue in Part Two. For now it suffices to recall that, other things being equal, a change in the money stock causes the price level to move in the same direction.

inflow would automatically eliminate the initial surplus. We shall see more about David Hume and his **specie-flow mechanism,** as this automatic adjustment scenario is called, in Part Two.

A second political economist to question mercantilist policies was Adam Smith, writing in 1776. Smith focused on the mercantilists' assumption that trade constituted a zero-sum game. By assuming each country could produce some commodities using less labor than its trading partners, Smith showed that *all* parties to international trade could benefit. How could this be possible? According to Smith, trade improved the allocation of labor, ensuring that each good would be produced in the country in which the good's production required the least labor. The result would be a larger total quantity of goods produced in the world. With more goods available for distribution among the nations, each could be made better off. In this sense, trade would be like a hypothetical poker game in which every player could win simultaneously!

In 1817, David Ricardo showed that even Smith's optimistic view failed to capture all the potential benefits from trade. Ricardo's work provided the basis for our modern understanding of the importance of unrestricted international trade. We are now ready to examine a modern version of Adam Smith's and David Ricardo's revolutionary views of trade. First we discuss some simplifying assumptions of our analysis. We could relax most of these, at the expense of additional complexity, without altering the fundamental results.

2.4 Some Simplifying Assumptions

First, we assume **perfect competition** prevails in both output and factor markets. Each buyer and seller is small enough relative to the market to take the market-determined price as given. Each commodity is homogeneous (that is, all units of each good are identical), and buyers and sellers have good information about market conditions. Entry and exit are easy in each market. The assumption of perfect competition is important, because it implies that the price of each good will equal the good's **marginal cost** of production, or the change in total cost due to production of one additional unit of output.[6]

Second, we assume each country has a fixed endowment of resources available, and these resources are fully employed and homogeneous. The problem each country faces involves allocating the fixed quantity of resources among production of the various goods residents want to consume.[7]

Third, we assume technology does not change. Different countries may use different technologies, but all firms within each country employ a common production method for each good.[8]

Fourth, we assume transportation costs are zero.[9] This implies that consumers will be indifferent between the domestically produced and imported versions of a good

---

[6]Chapters Five and Eight relax this assumption.

[7]For the implications of factor growth or mobility, see Chapter Ten.

[8]Theories of trade that focus on technology can be found in Chapters Five, Eight, and Ten.

[9]Chapter Five contains a discussion of transportation costs.

when the domestic prices of each are the same. Other barriers to trade also are ignored.[10]

Fifth, we assume factors of production (or inputs) such as labor and capital are completely mobile among industries within each country and completely immobile among countries.[11] This assumption obviously is too strong to represent an accurate description of the world, and we shall relax the assumption in Chapter Ten. However, resources that are much more mobile within than among countries capture an essential element of the economic significance of political boundaries. Perfect mobility of resources among industries implies that the price of each factor must be equal in all industries within each country; otherwise, resources would move from low-paying to high-paying industries. Because factors are immobile among countries, the price of each factor generally will differ across countries without trade.

Finally, we assume a world consisting of two countries, each using a single input to produce two commodities. For simplicity, we shall refer to the countries as A and B, the single input as L (for *labor*), and the two goods as X and Y.

2.5   The Ricardian World without Trade

The answer to the question "Does international trade benefit its participants?" requires that we compare a world without international trade to one with trade and show that a larger quantity of goods is available in the latter. We call the case of self-sufficiency, or no trade, **autarky.** In autarky each nation must produce whatever its residents want to consume, for there is no other way to obtain goods for consumption. In other words, the decision made by a country in autarky is simultaneously a production decision *and* a consumption decision. To make this decision, the country must use two pieces of information. First, it must consider the production trade-offs between goods X and Y that are possible given the available resources and technology. Second, it must consider its citizens' subjective tradeoffs between consumption of goods X and Y.

2.5.1   Production in Autarky

We can characterize the various combinations of goods X and Y that countries A and B can produce by developing a production possibilities frontier (or transformation curve) for each country. The **production possibilities frontier** represents all the alternate combinations of goods X and Y a country could produce given its fixed resource endowment. To sketch country A's production possibilities frontier, we must know A's resource endowment—the quantity of labor available in A for use in production—and the technology used to transform labor inputs into output in the form of goods X and Y. We denote country *A*'s *labor* endowment as L^A. Two **input**

---

[10]Chapters Six and Seven concentrate on trade restrictions and their effects.

[11]The specific-factors model in Chapter Four captures the effects of an input that cannot move across industries.

coefficients, a_{LX} and a_{LY}, summarize the production technology. The input coefficients tell us how many units of labor are required to produce one unit of each of the two outputs. In country A, production of one unit of good X requires a_{LX} units of *labor*, and production of one unit of good Y requires a_{LY} units of *labor*.

It helps to have a memory aid for the meaning of the input coefficients. The first letter always refers to the *country*, the first subscript to the *input*, and the second subscript to the *output* produced. For example, a_{LX} might be the number of units of *labor* required to produce a Xerox machine in America, while b_{LY} could denote the number of units of *labor* needed to produce a yo-yo in Britain. The best way to become comfortable with the input coefficients is to practice reading them in terms of what they mean rather than the letters themselves. The statement $a_{LX} = 2$ reads "the number of units of labor required to produce 1 unit of good X in country A is 2." With a little patience and practice, the input coefficients will become familiar and convenient ways to represent the productive technology available in different countries.

Note the relationship between country A's input coefficients, or technology, and the country's labor productivity. The more productive country A's labor is in producing good X, the fewer units of labor will be required to produce 1 unit of X, so the lower a_{LX} will be. Similarly, high labor productivity in the Y industry translates into a low value of a_{LY}. Because Ricardo's model contained only one input (labor), a country's technology simply reflects the country's labor productivity in the two industries.

If country A chooses to use all its labor in production of good X, it can produce L^A/a_{LX} units of X (and zero units of Y). Consider country A with 100 units of labor ($L^A = 100$) where 2 units of labor are required to produce 1 unit of good X ($a_{LX} = 2$) and 5 units of labor are required to produce 1 unit of good Y ($a_{LY} = 5$). If country A chooses to use all the available labor producing good X, it can produce 50 units ($L^A/a_{LX} = 100/2 = 50$). If it chooses instead to use all its labor producing Y, it can produce 20 units of good Y and zero units of X. *(Why?)*

Country A also can produce a variety of alternate combinations containing some of *both* goods. For every unit of X forgone, A can produce a_{LX}/a_{LY} (or 2/5 in our numerical example) additional units of good Y. By producing 1 less unit of X, 2 units of labor (a_{LX}) are released—enough labor to produce 2/5 units of Y, since 5 units of labor (a_{LY}) are required to produce 1 unit of Y. All the possible production choices can be represented graphically as country A's production possibilities frontier, illustrated in Figure 2.1, where ΔY denotes "change in Y" and similarly for ΔX.

The negative slope of the production possibilities frontier reflects the fact that labor is scarce. This means the only way to produce more of one good is to produce less of the other. The rate at which one good can be transformed into the other is a_{LX}/a_{LY}, which defines the (absolute value of the) slope of the production possibilities frontier.[12] In economic terminology, the slope gives the **opportunity cost** of good X, or the number of units of good Y forgone to produce an additional unit of good X. This is called the **marginal**

---

[12]The production possibilities frontier is defined by the requirement that all labor be employed. This can be expressed as $L^A = a_{LX} \cdot X + a_{LY} \cdot Y$; in words, the total quantity of labor must equal the quantity employed in producing good X plus the quantity employed in producing good Y. Along a given production possibilities frontier, the total quantity of labor available, L^A, is held constant. For the full-

Figure 2.1 □ **Country A's Production Possibilities Frontier**

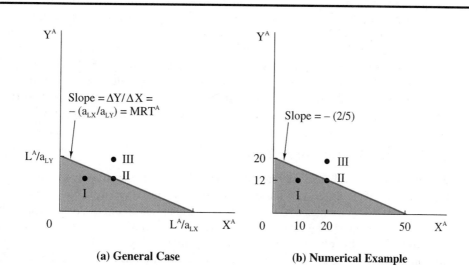

Slope $= \Delta Y / \Delta X = -(a_{LX}/a_{LY}) = MRT^A$

Slope $= -(2/5)$

(a) General Case   **(b) Numerical Example**

Country A can use its labor endowment (L^A, or 100) to produce L^A/a_{LX} (100/2 = 50) units of good X, L^A/a_{LY} (100/5 = 20) units of good Y, or any intermediate combination. The slope of the frontier $(-[a_{LX}/a_{LY}]$, or $-2/5)$ gives the opportunity cost of good X, or the rate at which good X can be "transformed" into good Y.

rate of transformation (MRT), because it is the rate at which good X can be "transformed" into good Y by transferring labor out of the X industry and into the Y industry.

In autarky, residents of country A can choose to produce any combination of goods X and Y that lies on the production possibilities frontier. It also is possible to produce at points inside the frontier, such as point I in Figure 2.1. In the numerical example, country A could produce 10 units of X and 12 units of Y using a total of $2 \cdot 10 + 5 \cdot 12 = 80$ units of labor. However, the country would not choose to locate at an interior point such as I, because it could produce more by moving to a point such as II, on the frontier. At each interior point, either some resources are not being used at all or some are not being used to their full productive potential. Points that lie outside the production possibilities frontier, such as III, are desirable but unattainable due to the constraint imposed by the fixed quantity of labor available. For example, country A could not produce 20 units of good X along with 20 units of good Y because such a combination would require 140 units of labor ($2 \cdot 20 + 5 \cdot 20 = 140$), and only 100 units are available.

---

employment condition to continue to hold when output levels of goods X and Y are varied, it must be true that $\Delta L^A = a_{LX} \cdot \Delta X + a_{LY} \cdot \Delta Y = 0$, where Δ is a shorthand notation for "change in." Rearranging this expression, it must be true that $\Delta Y / \Delta X = -(a_{LX}/a_{LY})$ gives the slope of the production possibilities frontier.

The **Ricardian model** implies the production possibilities frontier is a straight line. The slope of the production possibilities frontier represents the opportunity cost of good X (given by a_{LX}/a_{LY}), which is independent of the particular output combination being produced. For this reason, the Ricardian model sometimes is referred to as a **constant-cost model**. In autarky, the shaded triangle formed in Figure 2.1 by the two axes and the production possibilities frontier represents both the **production opportunity set** (the set of all possible combinations of X and Y the country could produce) and the **consumption opportunity set** (the set of all possible combinations of X and Y its residents could consume). The two sets must coincide in autarky, because domestic production is the only source of goods for consumption.

2.5.2   Consumption in Autarky

The production possibilities frontier tells only half the autarky story by revealing which combinations of goods X and Y it is *possible to produce* given the available labor and technology. To determine which of the many possible points *will be chosen*, we must introduce the tastes, or preferences, of the country's residents. We assume that the level of satisfaction or **utility** enjoyed by residents depends on the quantities of goods X and Y available for consumption and that the production/consumption decision is made in such a way as to maximize utility. A graphical technique called an **indifference curve** shows all the different combinations of goods X and Y that result in a given level of utility.

Indifference curves have four basic properties. First, all indifference curves are downward sloping. Figure 2.2 shows why this must be true. Initially, the country is located at point 1, consuming X_1 units of good X and Y_1 units of good Y. Which other points would produce the same level of satisfaction as point 1? Surely not the points in area III, since they contain less of each good. Points in area II also must be ruled out, because they contain more of each good and therefore would be preferred to point 1. We are left with areas I and IV. Area I points contain less good X than does point 1 but also contain more good Y. Area IV points contain less good Y than does point 1 but also contain more good X. Areas I and IV represent the possibility of *substituting* more of one good for less of the other with no change in overall utility. The fact that residents must be compensated for the loss of one good by more of the other good to maintain the same level of utility implies that indifference curves must be downward sloping.

A second requirement is that indifference curves be convex, or bowed in toward the origin of the graph. The slope of an indifference curve represents the rate at which residents are willing to trade off consumption of the two goods; this rate is called the **marginal rate of substitution (MRS)**. Convexity of the indifference curve implies that this rate of tradeoff changes with movements along the curve. As more X and less Y are consumed (moving down an indifference curve), good Y becomes more highly valued relative to good X; in other words, the amount of additional X required to compensate for further reducing consumption of Y increases.

Suppose, for example, that good X represented food and good Y represented clothing. At a point high and to the left on an indifference curve, a large amount of clothing and very little food would be available. In such a situation, individuals probably would willingly trade a substantial amount of clothing to obtain a small amount of

Figure 2.2 □ **Indifference Curves Are Downward Sloping**

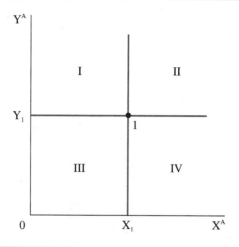

Residents would not be indifferent between point 1 and any point in areas II or III. Points in area II are preferred to point 1 because they contain more of each good. Points in area III are inferior to point 1 because they contain less of each good. All points that result in a level of utility equal to that attained at point 1 must lie in area I or IV.

additional food. The marginal rate of substitution between food and clothing would be high, and the indifference curve steep. At a point low and to the right on the same indifference curve, a large amount of food and very little clothing would be available. Individuals then would willingly give up very little clothing to obtain additional food. The marginal rate of substitution between food and clothing would be low, and the indifference curve relatively flat. Therefore, as we move down and to the right along an indifference curve, it becomes flatter as good X becomes less highly valued relative to good Y. The result is a convex indifference curve.

A third characteristic of indifference curves is that they never intersect. Each point, representing a single combination of goods X and Y, lies on one—and only one—indifference curve. Any consumption bundle consisting of given quantities of the two goods produces a unique level of utility, although we shall discuss some potential problems surrounding this requirement shortly.

Finally, higher indifference curves represent higher levels of utility and therefore are preferred to lower indifference curves. This simply reflects the preference for more goods over fewer goods. The indifference curves in Figure 2.3 satisfy the four requirements discussed.

Economists originally developed indifference curves to represent the tastes of an individual. Here we are using **community indifference curves** to represent the tastes of residents of a country as a group. This obviously is a much more complicated problem than dealing with the tastes of an individual. We shall use community indifference curves exactly as if they were individual indifference curves. However, we should be aware

Figure 2.3 □ Indifference Curves

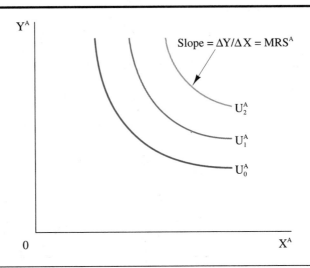

Each curve shows all combinations of goods X and Y that produce a given level of utility. Each indifference curve is downward sloping and convex. Indifference curves do not intersect, and higher curves are preferred to lower ones.

that this sidesteps some potential problems that arise from the issue of **income distribution.** For example, suppose a country has X_0 units of good X and Y_0 units of good Y. How does the country's utility compare if (1) one individual owns all the X_0 and Y_0 and all other residents have nothing or (2) the X_0 and Y_0 are divided evenly among all individuals? Without making interpersonal comparisons of utility, it is impossible to say. We cannot assume that case 2 implies higher utility just because more persons gained than lost in moving there from case 1. There is no "objective" way to compare a loss of utility by one individual with a gain in utility by another. We shall ignore these issues temporarily and return to them in Chapter Four, where we discuss the effects of trade and trade restrictions on the distribution of income within a country. For now we should point out that increased availability of goods always raises **potential utility;** whether or not actual utility increases depends on the distribution of income. Whenever a larger quantity of goods becomes available for distribution, it is possible to make every individual better off. Of course, this outcome rarely occurs automatically; for this reason, other policies designed to alter the distribution of income often accompany trade policies.

2.5.3 Equilibrium in Autarky

In autarky, the country makes its production and consumption decision by maximizing utility subject to the constraint imposed by the production possibilities frontier. Figure 2.4 illustrates this by combining Figures 2.1 and 2.3. Point A* puts residents on indifference curve U_1^A, representing the highest level of satisfaction

Figure 2.4 ▫ **Country A's Autarky Equilibrium**

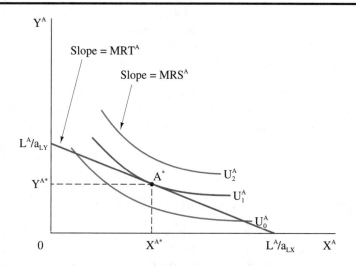

Country A makes its production and consumption decision to maximize utility subject to the constraint imposed by the availability of resources and technology. This decision is represented graphically by the point of tangency between the (highest attainable) indifference curve and the production possibilities frontier at point A^*. At that point—and only at that point—the rate at which it is possible to transform good X into good Y (MRT^A) equals the rate at which residents of A are willing to trade off goods X and Y in consumption (MRS^A).

attainable given the country's resource endowment (L^A) and available technology (a_{LX} and a_{LY}). Point A^* is the country's **autarky equilibrium.** Given that the country does not trade with other countries, point A^* represents the allocation of resources between industries X and Y that produces the highest level of utility for domestic residents. Points along lower indifference curves (illustrated by U_0^A) are less preferred than A^*. Points along higher indifference curves (such as U_2^A) are unattainable because of the resource and technology constraint.

At the autarky equilibrium, the marginal rate of transformation (the rate at which the country is *able* to transform good X into good Y along the production possibilities frontier) equals the marginal rate of substitution (the rate at which residents *willingly* give up some of one good to get more of the other good along an indifference curve). The common slope of the production possibilities frontier and the indifference curve also represents the opportunity cost of good X expressed in terms of good Y. Because all markets are perfectly competitive, the relative price of each good equals its opportunity cost. Therefore, the (absolute value of the) slope of the production possibilities frontier also can be identified with the relative price of good X, or $(P_X/P_Y)^A$, denoting the rate at which units of good X and good Y exchange in the domestic market. This relative price is called the **autarky relative price** of good X in country A. In the numerical example (with $L^A = 100$, $a_{LX} = 2$, and $a_{LY} = 5$), the relative price of good X in country A equals 2/5 units of good Y because production of an additional unit of good X requires that Y production be reduced by 2/5 units.

We can also calculate the wage rate that will prevail in country A in autarky. We shall use three pieces of information. First, labor comprises the only input; so the marginal costs of producing goods X and Y must equal $a_{LX} \cdot w^A$ and $a_{LY} \cdot w^A$, respectively, where w^A denotes the *wage* rate per unit of labor. Second, because all markets exhibit perfect competition, the price of each good must equal its marginal cost. Therefore, $P_X^A = a_{LX} \cdot w^A$ and $P_Y^A = a_{LY} \cdot w^A$. Third, the wage rate must be equal in the two industries. Otherwise, workers would all choose to work in the high-wage industry and production of the other good would fall to zero. We know consumers want to consume *both* goods, so wages must be equal to induce some workers to employment in each industry. Combining these three facts, we arrive at the conclusion that all workers in autarky in country A must earn a wage equal to $w^A = P_X^A/a_{LX} = P_Y^A/a_{LY}$.

2.6   The Ricardian Model with Trade

We have seen that in autarky the production opportunity set and consumption opportunity set a country faces are identical. International trade relaxes this restriction on consumption opportunities; residents can consume combinations of the two goods that could not possibly be produced domestically. To understand the source of this result, we need to introduce country B, a potential trading partner for country A.

Country B's autarky situation resembles country A's. The consumption possibilities of country B are limited to B's production possibilities, defined by the resource endowment (L^B) and the available technology (b_{LX} and b_{LY}). The two input coefficients again define the number of units of *labor* required to produce a unit of good X in country B (b_{LX}) and the number of units of *labor* required to produce a unit of good Y in country B (b_{LY}). Of course, there is no reason to believe that countries A and B will have identical quantities of labor available or use the same technology. If the technologies differ, the production possibilities frontiers of the two countries generally will have different slopes. In fact, these differences form the basis for mutually beneficial trade. We shall see later that if two countries' production possibilities frontiers had the same slope, trade between the two would be pointless. *(Explain why different relative labor productivity in the two industries across countries generates different slopes of the two countries' production possibilities frontiers.)*

Country B's preferences for goods X and Y can be represented by a set of indifference curves. These must satisfy the four restrictions discussed earlier (see section 2.5.2), but there is no reason to expect the preferences of residents of country B to be identical to those of country A's residents.

Combining the production possibilities frontier and the set of indifference curves for country B, Figure 2.5 shows B's autarky equilibrium at B*. As for country A, the slope of B's production possibilities frontier gives the marginal rate of transformation between goods X and Y (MRT^B), or the opportunity cost of good X; and the slope of B's indifference curve represents the marginal rate of substitution (MRS^B), or the rate at which residents of B willingly trade off consumption of the two goods. In autarky equilibrium, these two slopes are equal; country B makes its

Figure 2.5 □ **Country B's Autarky Equilibrium**

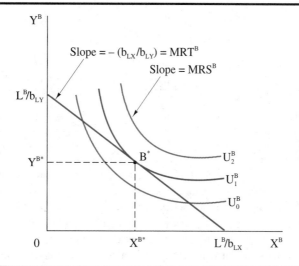

In autarky, country B produces and consumes at B*, the point of tangency between its production possibilities frontier and the (highest attainable) indifference curve, U$_1^B$.

production/consumption decision to maximize utility subject to the production constraint. The (absolute value of the) slope of country B's production possibilities frontier also gives the autarky relative price of good X in B, or $(P_X/P_Y)^B$. Workers in country B in autarky earn a wage rate of $w^B = P_X^B/b_{LX} = P_Y^B/b_{LY}$ per unit of labor, regardless of whether they work in the X or the Y industry. *(Why?)*

To demonstrate the potential of international trade for improving the welfare of residents of countries A and B, it is first necessary to show that the allocation of resources implied by the two autarky equilibria, A* and B*, does *not* maximize total world output. More precisely, by moving away from A* and B*, more of one of the two goods can be produced *without* decreasing production of the other. In other words, we must show that it is possible to produce more output by having countries A and B produce combinations of X and Y different from those represented by A* and B*. Adam Smith first demonstrated this fundamental result using the concept of absolute advantage.

2.6.1 Adam Smith and the Principle of Absolute Advantage

Country A has an **absolute advantage** in production of good X if $a_{LX} < b_{LX}$, that is, if it takes fewer units of labor to produce a unit of good X in country A than in B. Adam Smith asserted that international trade between two countries would be *mutually* beneficial whenever one country had an absolute advantage in production of one good and the other country had an absolute advantage in production of the other good. For example, if $a_{LX} < b_{LX}$ and $a_{LY} > b_{LY}$, country A has an absolute

Table 2.1 □ The Productive Technologies of Countries A and B

The technologies, summarized by the input coefficients for each country, relate the number of units of labor required to produce one unit of each of the outputs.

	General Case		Numerical Example	
	Country A	Country B	Country A	Country B
Labor units needed to produce one X	a_{LX}	b_{LX}	2	3
Labor units needed to produce one Y	a_{LY}	b_{LY}	5	4

advantage in production of good X and country B an absolute advantage in production of good Y; fewer units of labor are required to produce a unit of good X in country A than in B, and fewer units of labor are required to produce a unit of good Y in B than in A. According to the theory of absolute advantage, it would benefit each country to specialize in producing the good in which it had an absolute advantage and to import the good in which it had an **absolute disadvantage.**

To illustrate how specialization and trade along the lines of absolute advantage can increase world output and utility, we summarize the input coefficients of countries A and B in Table 2.1 in both general terms and a specific numerical example. Starting from the autarky positions, A^* and B^*, let country A produce one less unit of good Y (the good in which A has an absolute *dis*advantage); this frees up a_{LY} (or 5) units of labor. Let country B replace the lost output by producing one more unit of Y; this requires b_{LY} (or 4) units of labor. Total world production of good Y is unchanged. But a_{LY} units of labor have been freed up in A, while only b_{LY} additional units of labor are required in B. Since $a_{LY} > b_{LY}$, this implies $5 - 4 = 1$ unit of labor available for production of *additional* X or Y. The greater the extent of B's absolute advantage in production of Y, the more labor available for additional production. *(Why?)* The reader can use a similar exercise to show that switching a unit of X production from country B to country A produces a similar gain. These gains from specializing according to absolute advantage are possible because such specialization involves producing each good in the country in which it can be produced with less labor. By producing each unit of output using the minimum quantity of labor, the world's scarce labor ($L^W = L^A + L^B$) can produce a larger total of goods X and Y.[13]

Adam Smith's discussion represented a giant step forward in understanding the nature and potential of international trade. Its main contribution was the idea that trade is *not* a zero-sum game. International trade policy between the

---

[13]With two goods, the phrase "a larger total of goods X and Y" is defined inadequately, because it is possible to produce more of one good *by producing less of the other*. We use the phrase to convey the notion that it is not possible to produce more of one good *without* reducing production of the other. Moving from a position of autarky to one of productive specialization does allow more of one good to be produced without reducing production of the other good. Once countries are completely specialized, further such gains become impossible.

United States and Japan or the European Union is not like a giant poker game in which one party wins at the expense of the other. However, according to Smith, mutually beneficial trade required each country to have an absolute advantage in one of the goods. This requirement rules out many potential trading relationships in which one of the two countries has an absolute advantage in *both* goods (for example, if $a_{LX} = 2$, $a_{LY} = 5$, $b_{LX} = 8$, $b_{LY} = 10$). But David Ricardo soon demonstrated that even Smith's optimistic view of trade was not optimistic enough.[14]

2.6.2   David Ricardo and the Principle of Comparative Advantage

Perhaps the greatest of David Ricardo's many contributions to economics was the demonstration that mutually beneficial trade is possible even if one of the potential trading partners has an absolute advantage in production of *both* goods. Failure to understand this simple but important point leads to one of the most common fallacies in modern discussions of international trade and trade policy: the claim that developing economies with low labor productivity relative to the rest of the world should isolate themselves from international trade.

Ricardo used the concept of **comparative advantage.** Country A has a comparative advantage in production of good X if $(a_{LX}/a_{LY}) < (b_{LX}/b_{LY})$. The idea of comparative advantage is a simple extension of the concept of opportunity cost. Country A has a comparative advantage in production of good X if, to produce an additional unit of good X in A, it is necessary to forgo fewer units *of good Y* than would be necessary to produce the additional unit of good X in country B.[15] This is equivalent to saying that the opportunity cost of good X in country A (measured in units of good Y) is lower than in B. Table 2.2 reports the opportunity cost of each good in each country in both general form and a numerical example. In country A, $a_{LX} = 2$ units of labor are required to produce a unit of good X and $a_{LY} = 5$ units of labor to produce a unit of good Y. Therefore, production of an additional unit of X means forgoing 2/5 units of Y; in other words, the opportunity cost of producing good X in country A is 2/5 units of Y. Similarly, production of an additional unit of Y in country A is possible only if X production is reduced by 5/2. *(Why?)* In country B, $b_{LX} = 8$ units of labor are required to produce one unit of good X and $b_{LY} = 10$ to produce one Y. This implies that the opportunity cost of producing X in country B is 8/10 units of Y, and the opportunity cost of producing Y in B is 10/8 units of X. In the numerical example, country A has an absolute advantage in *both* goods. *(Why?)* Nonetheless, we shall demonstrate that trade according to comparative advantage can be *mutually beneficial.*

---

[14]Historians of economic thought disagree about whether Adam Smith intended his discussion also to cover cases of comparative advantage. Regardless of one's view on this debate, Smith's achievement in explaining to others the potential benefits of international trade was monumental.

[15]To see that (a_{LX}/a_{LY}) is measured in units of good Y per unit of good X, note that a_{LX} is measured in units of labor per unit of X (or labor/X) while a_{LY} is measured in units of labor per unit of Y (or labor/Y). Therefore, a_{LX}/a_{LY} is in units of Y per unit of X (or Y/X).

Table 2.2 □ Opportunity Costs of Producing Goods X and Y in Countries A and B

The opportunity cost of producing each good in each country equals the number of units of labor required to produce a unit of the good divided by the number of units of labor required to produce a unit of the other good. For example, to produce an additional unit of good X in country B requires $b_{LX} = 8$ units of labor. To obtain the 8 units of labor, Y production in B would have to be cut by 8/10 units, since each unit of Y produced uses $b_{LY} = 10$ units of labor. Therefore, the opportunity cost of the additional unit of X is 8/10 units of Y.

	General Case		Numerical Example	
	Country A	Country B	Country A	Country B
Good X	a_{LX}/a_{LY}	b_{LX}/b_{LY}	(2/5)Y	(8/10)Y
Good Y	a_{LY}/a_{LX}	b_{LY}/b_{LX}	(5/2)X	(10/8)X

Note that one country *cannot* have a comparative advantage in production of both goods. *(Why?)*[16] Note too that tastes are irrelevant in determining comparative advantage under constant costs because the slopes of the production possibilities frontiers are constants. Tastes do affect the particular point at which a country will choose to produce in autarky, but the comparison of opportunity costs in the two countries (the determinant of comparative advantage) is the same regardless of tastes.

The principle of comparative advantage states that it will be beneficial for a country to specialize in production of the good in which it has a comparative advantage and to trade for the good in which it has a comparative disadvantage. Such specialization and trade make both countries potentially better off by expanding their consumption opportunity sets. In other words, specialization and trade allow a country's *consumption* opportunity set to expand beyond its *production* opportunity set. Residents can choose to consume combinations of goods that would be impossible to produce domestically.

In autarky, the domestic production possibilities frontier defines the production and consumption opportunity sets, and its slope defines both the opportunity costs and the relative prices for goods X and Y. We can now demonstrate that specialization and trade along the lines of comparative advantage can increase the total world quantities of the two goods available for consumption and therefore expand the consumption opportunity sets beyond the production opportunity sets.[17]

In Table 2.2, country A has a comparative advantage in good X and country B a comparative advantage in good Y. *(Why?)* Suppose that beginning at its autarky equilibrium, A*, country A produces one additional unit of good X. Its production of good Y must fall by a_{LX}/a_{LY} (or 2/5 in the numerical example), the opportunity cost of good X in A. Now suppose that from its autarky equilibrium, B*, country B produces one less unit of good X. Its production of good Y rises by b_{LX}/b_{LY} (or 8/10), the opportunity cost

---

[16]By definition, country A has a comparative advantage in production of good X if $(a_{LX}/a_{LY}) < (b_{LX}/b_{LY})$ or in good Y if $(a_{LY}/a_{LX}) < (b_{LY}/b_{LX})$. These two statements cannot both be true. *(Use the numerical example from Table 2.1 to see why. If one example is not convincing, make up others by using different numerical values for the input coefficients.)*

[17]The appendix to this chapter presents an alternate way to demonstrate this effect of trade, based on the idea of a world production possibilities frontier.

of good X in B. Because $(a_{LX}/a_{LY}) < (b_{LX}/b_{LY})$ by the definition of comparative advantage in our example, the same fixed quantity of total labor has been used to produce the same quantity of good X and a *larger* quantity of good Y than were being produced in autarky. In fact, the increased production of good Y is equal to the difference in opportunity costs $[(b_{LX}/b_{LY}) - (a_{LX}/a_{LY})]$, or $(8/10 - 2/5 = 4/10)$; therefore, the greater the degree of comparative advantage, the greater the gains from specialization.

The same switching technique (that is, switching production of each good from the comparative disadvantage country to the comparative advantage country) can be repeated until each country is completely specialized in the good in which it has a comparative advantage.[18] This is true in the constant-cost model because, as countries specialize according to comparative advantage, changes in production do not alter the pattern of costs or comparative advantage.

At points A_p and B_p in Figure 2.6, the total quantity of goods X and Y produced in the world is maximized given the available resources and technology; additional units of either good can be produced *only* by decreasing production of the other.

Figure 2.6 □ **Productive Specialization according to Comparative Advantage**

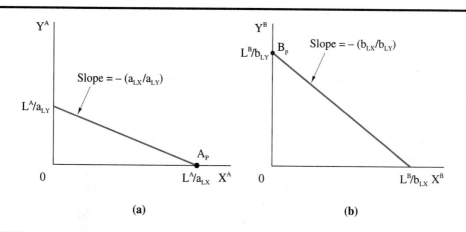

Because the opportunity cost of producing good X is lower in country A than in country B, total output of X can be increased without reducing production of good Y by switching X production from B to A. Once A is completely specialized in producing X (at point A_p), further increases in X production require reductions in Y production. Because country B has a comparative advantage in production of good Y, total output of Y is increased without reducing production of X when B specializes completely in Y (at point B_p).

[18]Each country will specialize completely so long as tastes for the two goods and the countries' sizes do not differ too much. If tastes are strongly biased toward one good (say, everyone likes to consume lots of X but only a little of Y), both countries may continue to produce some X, but the country with a comparative advantage in X will specialize completely. If the countries are very different in size, the small country may not be able to satisfy the large country's demand for the good in which the small country has a comparative advantage. In this case, the small country will specialize completely while the large country will produce some of both goods.

If the countries can produce more by specializing, why did they not choose to specialize in autarky? The reason is that, in autarky, residents of each country must consume goods in the same proportion in which they are produced domestically. If country A specialized completely in production of good X in autarky, its residents would be forced to consume L^A/a_{LX} units of X and none of good Y. However, consumers generally want to diversify their consumption, consuming some of a number of different goods. This characteristic of tastes effectively rules out production specialization without trade. With trade, a country can specialize its production and then trade some of its domestically produced good (produced at relatively low opportunity cost) for some of the good produced in the other country (which could be produced domestically only at a relatively high opportunity cost).

2.6.3   International Equilibrium with Trade

Once both countries have opened trade and specialized production according to comparative advantage, at what relative price ratio will trade occur? How many units of its export good (X) will country A have to give up to obtain a unit of its import good (Y)? And how many units of its export good (Y) will country B have to give up to get a unit of its import good (X)? First, we can see that the equilibrium price ratio at which trade occurs (written as $[P_X/P_Y]^{tt}$ and called the **terms of trade**) must lie between the two autarky price ratios, or $(P_X/P_Y)^A < (P_X/P_Y)^{tt} < (P_X/P_Y)^B$. To see why, consider that each country now has two alternate methods for turning good X into good Y or vice versa. The first is through domestic production (at a rate defined by the domestic opportunity cost that equals the autarky price ratio). The second is through international trade (at a rate defined by the international price ratio or terms of trade). As a result of this choice, a country would never trade voluntarily at international terms of trade less favorable than the country's autarky price ratio.

For example, from the point of productive specialization, A_p in panel (a) of Figure 2.6, country A can transform good X into good Y through domestic production at a rate of $a_{LX}/a_{LY} = (P_X/P_Y)^A$ units of Y obtained per unit of X forgone. In order for country A to choose instead to continue to specialize in production of good X and trade some of it to country B in exchange for some good Y, the trade with B must give A at least $a_{LX}/a_{LY} = (P_X/P_Y)^A$ units of Y imports for each unit of X exported. Graphically, beginning at point A_p country A will find it beneficial to trade with country B only if trade occurs at a relative price represented by the slope of a line from point A_p that is *steeper* than A's production possibilities frontier. Residents of A will purchase Y from B if they can do so at a price below the autarky price of Y, or $(P_Y/P_X)^A$. (Note that a low autarky relative price of X is equivalent to a high autarky relative price of Y.) Panel (a) of Figure 2.7 illustrates this restriction imposed by country A on the international terms of trade.

Country B faces a similar choice of technique for obtaining good X. From the point of productive specialization, B_p in panel (b) of Figure 2.6, country B can obtain good X through domestic production by forgoing good Y at a rate of $b_{LX}/b_{LY} = (P_X/P_Y)^B$ per unit of X produced. If country B can obtain X at a more favorable rate

Figure 2.7 □ **Restrictions on International Terms of Trade**

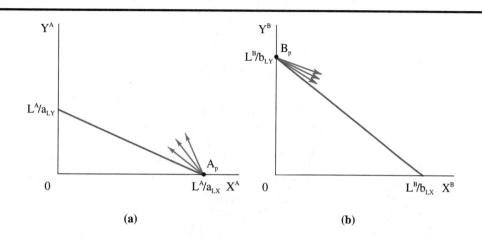

For country A to trade voluntarily with country B, the international terms of trade must be more favor-able to A than are the production possibilities or domestic opportunity costs. For any international terms of trade represented as a line from point A_p that is *steeper* than the production possibilities frontier, country A can obtain more units of good Y for each unit of good X forgone through international trade than through domestic production. Because B can get one unit of X through domestic production by for-going b_{LX}/b_{LY} units of Y, B will trade voluntarily only if it can obtain a unit of X for fewer than b_{LX}/b_{LY} units of Y. Therefore, all the terms of trade at which country B would willingly trade can be represented by lines from point B_p that are *flatter* than B's production possibilities frontier.

through international trade, it will choose to specialize in production of Y and trade with A to get X for consumption. Residents of B will be willing to purchase X from country A at any price below the autarky price, $(P_X/P_Y)^B$. Examples of international terms of trade at which B would choose to trade are illustrated in panel (b) of Figure 2.7 by lines from point B_p that are *flatter* than B's production possibilities frontier.

The international terms of trade must satisfy one additional condition beyond those in Figure 2.7: The equilibrium price ratio also must be the **market-clear-ing price** for the two goods. The quantity of good X that country A wants to *export* at the terms of trade must equal the quantity of good X that country B wants to *import* at the same terms of trade. Simultaneously, the quantity of good Y that country B wants to export at the terms of trade must just equal the quan-tity of good Y that country A wants to import. To incorporate this requirement into our graphical framework, we must go beyond Figure 2.7 to see how each country decides how much of goods X and Y to consume under unrestricted trade.

Each country chooses its consumption point in such a way as to maximize util-ity. We saw the consumption decision under autarky in Figures 2.4 and 2.5. With trade, however, the consumption opportunity set no longer is constrained to equal the production opportunity set. Once country A specializes in producing

Figure 2.8 □ Country A's Free Trade Equilibrium

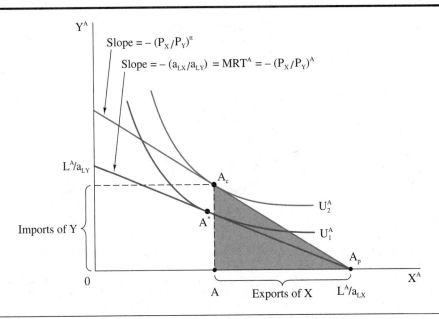

Country A produces at A_p and consumes at A_c, the point of tangency of the indifference curve with the equilibrium terms-of-trade line. At the equilibrium terms of trade, country A's exports of good X just equal country B's imports, and A's imports of good Y just equal B's exports. Country A's trade triangle is AA_cA_p.

good X and opens up trade with country B, residents of A can choose to consume any combination of X and Y that lies on the terms-of-trade line through the production point, A_p. From panel (a) of Figure 2.7, we see that this is clearly an improvement over autarky for country A residents. As a result of specialization and trade, they are able to consume larger quantities of both X and Y than they could under autarky; the consumption opportunity set has expanded. From panel (b) of Figure 2.7, we see that residents of country B enjoy a similar expansion of the consumption opportunity set due to specialization and trade. Each country takes advantage of the new opportunities by locating at the point of tangency of the highest possible indifference curve and the terms-of-trade line.

Figures 2.8 and 2.9 show the results for the two countries. The shaded triangles in the figures, known as **trade triangles,** summarize each country's imports and exports as well as the terms of trade. For country A, the base of triangle AA_cA_p, line AA_p, represents exports of good X and the height, line AA_c, gives the imports of Y. The slope of line A_cA_p measures the equilibrium terms of trade. Triangle BB_pB_c in Figure 2.9 summarizes the analogous information for country B. (*What relationship must hold between the lengths of AA_p and BB_c? AA_c and BB_p? The slopes of A_cA_p and B_pB_c? Why?*)

Figure 2.9 □ **Country B's Free Trade Equilibrium**

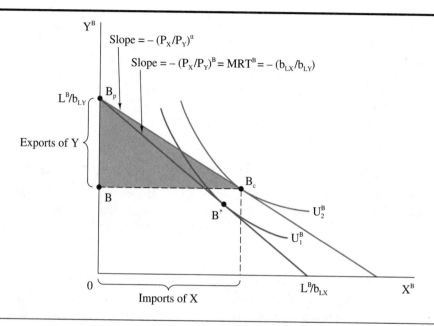

Country B *produces* at point B_p and *consumes* at point B_c, exporting good Y and importing good X. This free trade equilibrium produces a higher level of utility than was attainable under autarky. Country B's trade triangle is BB_pB_c.

Notice that country B partakes of the gains from trade by specializing according to comparative advantage *even though* B suffers an absolute disadvantage in both goods or, equivalently, even though country B labor is less productive than country A's in producing both goods. Often-heard claims that countries with low labor productivity need to isolate themselves from trade with more productive economies represent a fallacy based on a failure to understand comparative advantage. Unfortunately, choosing policies based on this fallacy has proven costly to many developing economies over the last half century.

We can also conclude that wages rise in both countries with the opening of trade. Simply put, this happens because trade allows each country's labor to specialize in producing the good in which it is relatively more productive. Recall that, in autarky, $w^A = P^A_X/a_{LX} = P^A_Y/a_{LY}$ and $w^B = P^B_X/b_{LX} = P^B_Y/b_{LY}$, because workers in each country must produce some of both goods. With trade, country A no longer needs to produce good Y, in which country A labor is *relatively* unproductive; and country B no longer has to produce any good X, in which country B labor is relatively unproductive. Therefore, with trade, the conditions defining equilibrium wages in the two countries simplify to $w^{A*} = P^A_X/a_{LX}$ and $w^{B*} = P^B_Y/b_{LY}$. Figures 2.8 and 2.9 show that P^A_X and P^B_Y have risen with trade. Because each country no longer produces its import good, the declines in those prices that accompany the opening of trade exert no negative effect on wages.

We have demonstrated that trade can be mutually beneficial as long as the countries possess a comparative advantage in production. This does *not* mean the gains from trade necessarily will be shared equally by the trading partners. Specifying the precise division of the gains from trade between the two countries would require additional information. Figure 2.7 clearly shows that trade expands each country's consumption opportunity set by allowing the country to trade at terms that differ from the autarky price ratio. The implication is that a country will capture a larger share of the gains from trade when the equilibrium terms of trade differ significantly from the country's autarky price ratio (or are very close to the trading partner's autarky price ratio).[19]

2.7   The Gains from Trade: Exchange and Specialization

Thus far, we have discussed the gains from trade rather abstractly, implying that all the gains come from specialization according to comparative advantage. In this section, we focus more explicitly on the gains from trade and distinguish two sources.

2.7.1   Gains from Exchange

One portion of the gains from trade, called the **gains from exchange**, comes from allowing unrestricted exchange of goods between countries *without* altering the autarky production patterns. In autarky, the relative prices of the two goods differ between countries, as shown in Figures 2.8 and 2.9. Because the relative price in each country just equals the marginal rate of substitution, the rates at which consumers in the two countries are willing to trade off consumption of the two goods also differ in autarky. In country B, consumers are willing to give up as many as $(P_X/P_Y)^B$ units of good Y for an additional unit of good X; in country A, consumers are willing to give up a unit of good X for as few as $(P_X/P_Y)^A$ units of good Y. By the definition of comparative advantage in our example, $(P_X/P_Y)^A <$ $(P_X/P_Y)^B$. Therefore, an exchange of good X for good Y between countries A and B could be mutually beneficial: Country A values the Y it can get from B more highly than the X it must give up; likewise, country B values the X it can get from A more highly than the Y it must forgo. Figure 2.10 illustrates these gains from exchange for country A.

Each country continues to *produce* at its autarky point; but, rather than consuming the goods produced domestically, residents of A then exchange with residents of B. Firms in country A will be willing to export good X at any relative price higher than the autarky price in A, $(P_X/P_Y)^A$; consumers in country B will

---

[19]The importance of this statement lies in its implications for the division of the gains from trade. Define a small country as one whose participation in a market is small relative to the overall size of the market, so that the country's decisions do not affect the world price in the market. A large country, in contrast, does affect the world price through its production and consumption decisions. In trade between a large country and a small country, the small country captures the gains because the international terms of trade will be the same as the large country's autarky price.

Figure 2.10 □ **Gains from Exchange**

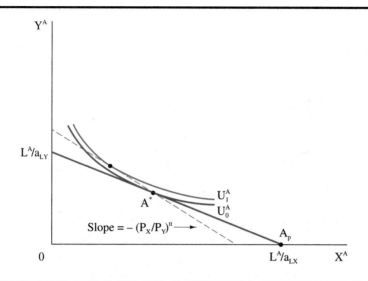

Even if country A continued to produce at its autarky point, A*, exchange with country B at the mutually agreed-on terms of trade would allow A to reach a higher level of utility than would be possible in autarky.

be willing to import good X at any relative price lower than the autarky price in B, $(P_X/P_Y)^B$. *(Why?)* For both countries to trade voluntarily, the international terms of trade must fall between these limits—$(P_X/P_Y)^A < (P_X/P_Y)^{tt} < (P_X/P_Y)^B$. At any terms of trade within this range, the two countries will find exchange mutually beneficial. The precise equilibrium price ratio at which exchange will occur also requires that the markets for the two goods clear. The quantity of good X that country A is willing to export in exchange for a quantity of good Y from country B must match the quantity of X that B is willing to import in exchange for its exports of Y. Through this exchange, each country attains a higher level of utility than in autarky.

In Figure 2.10, the move from U_0^A to U_1^A represents the gains from exchange for country A. *(Test your understanding by drawing the corresponding diagram for country B.)* These gains come from reallocating the same quantities of goods X and Y produced in autarky between the two countries based on their residents' tastes for each good.

2.7.2   Gains from Specialization

The gains from exchange illustrated in Figure 2.10 obviously do not comprise all of country A's gains from trade. The remainder come from production

Figure 2.11 □ Gains from Trade

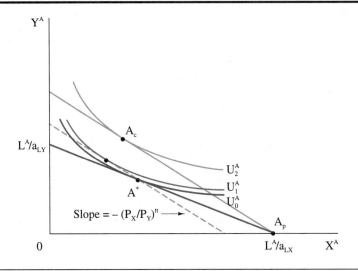

Unrestricted trade allows country A to move from utility level U_0^A in autarky to level U_2^A. The move to U_1^A represents the gains from exchange and the move from U_1^A to U_2^A the gains from specialization.

specialization according to comparative advantage and are called the **gains from specialization.** With the possibility of trade, countries no longer choose to produce the same combination of goods they did in autarky. Each country adjusts its production along the production possibilities frontier, producing more of the good in which it has a comparative advantage and less of the good in which it has a comparative disadvantage.

Figure 2.11 reproduces country A's unrestricted trade equilibria from Figure 2.8, but also illustrates how the total gains from trade (the move from U_0^A to U_2^A) can be broken down into the gains from exchange (U_0^A to U_1^A) and the gains from specialization (U_1^A to U_2^A).

2.8 Demand and Supply under Constant Costs

The autarky and international trade results developed within the production possibilities frontier/indifference curve framework in this chapter also can be presented using demand and supply curves. The demand/supply framework is useful because it allows us to see more directly the determination of the equilibrium terms of trade; it also will prove convenient for analyzing the effects of trade restrictions in Chapters Six and Seven.

2.8.1   Demand and Supply in Autarky

In autarky, the market for each good in each country is isolated from the market for the same good in the other country; therefore, there are four markets (one for each of the two goods in each of the two countries) represented by the four panels of Figure 2.12. In each of the four markets, the interaction of domestic demand and domestic supply determines the good's autarky relative price.

A downward-sloping demand curve for each good represents the tastes of each country's residents. The quantity demanded of each good depends negatively on the good's autarky price, other things being equal.

The opportunity costs of producing the goods determine the shape of the supply curves. The opportunity cost of producing each good in each country is constant out to the maximum amount of the good the country can produce. This gives the supply curves a 90-degree angle: horizontal then suddenly vertical. The level of output at which the supply curve of good X becomes vertical in panel (a) corresponds to the point at which country A's production possibilities frontier intersects the X axis; a similar relationship holds for A's production of good Y in panel (b).

In competitive markets, the price of each good just equals its opportunity cost. The equilibria in the four separate markets represent the same situation as autarky points A^* and B^* in Figures 2.4 and 2.5. Country A, where the autarky relative price is $(P_X/P_Y)^A$, produces X^{A^*} units of X and Y^{A^*} units of Y. Country B, with an autarky relative price of $(P_X/P_Y)^B$, produces X^{B^*} units of X and Y^{B^*} of Y.

Comparison of the two countries' markets for good X in panels (a) and (c) of Figure 2.12 reveals that country A has a comparative advantage in production of good X. Similarly, country B has a comparative advantage in production of good Y, as shown by comparing panels (b) and (d). *(Why?)*

2.8.2   Demand and Supply with Trade

The opening of trade allows countries A and B to participate in a common international market for each good. The two separate markets for good X in panels (a) and (c) of Figure 2.12 combine to become the international market for good X in panel (a) of Figure 2.13. Similarly, panels (b) and (d) from Figure 2.12 form the basis for panel (b) of Figure 2.13.

Panel (a) of Figure 2.12 demonstrates that country A is willing to export good X at any price greater than $(P_X/P_Y)^A$. The horizontal distance between the domestic demand and supply curves measures the supply of exports offered at each price. The Exports$_X^A$ line in panel (a) of Figure 2.13 depicts this supply of exports of good X by country A. Note that Figure 2.13's horizontal axis measures the quantity of good X *traded*, not the quantity produced or consumed as in earlier diagrams. Panel (c) of Figure 2.12 shows that country B's residents demand to import good X from A at any price below $(P_X/P_Y)^B$ in quantities given by the horizontal distance between the domestic demand and supply curves. This demand for imports of good X by country B becomes the Imports$_X^B$ line in panel (a) of Figure 2.13.

Combining the export-supply and import-demand curves yields the unrestricted trade equilibrium in the international market for good X. The international market is in equilibrium when the quantity of the good that one country (A in the case of

Figure 2.12 ▫ **Domestic Markets for Goods X and Y in Autarky under Constant Costs**

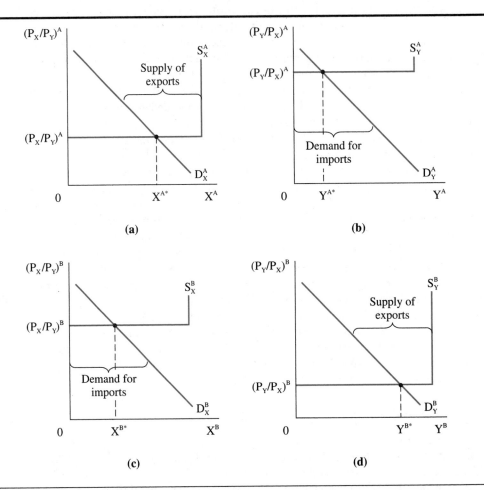

(a)   **(b)**

(c)   **(d)**

In autarky, the relative prices of goods are determined by equality of quantity demanded domestically and quantity supplied domestically. Domestic demand for each good depends negatively on the good's relative price. A country can produce each good at a constant opportunity cost up to the point where the country's entire labor endowment is employed producing the one good; at that point, it becomes impossible to produce any more of the good, so the domestic supply curve becomes vertical. At relative prices at which domestic quantity demanded exceeds quantity supplied of a good, the domestic shortage results in a demand for imports, as illustrated in panels (b) and (c). At relative prices at which domestic quantity supplied exceeds quantity demanded of a good, the domestic surplus results in a supply of exports, as illustrated in panels (a) and (d).

good X) wants to export at the international terms of trade equals the quantity that the other country (here, B) wants to import at the same terms. The equilibrium price of good X is $(P_X/P_Y)^{tt}$, and country A exports X^{tt} to country B. *(We argued in the production possibilities frontier/indifference curve framework that the international terms of trade would lie between the two autarky price ratios. How does the demand and supply framework in Figure 2.13 reflect this restriction?)*

Figure 2.13 ▫ **International Markets for Goods X and Y under Constant Costs**

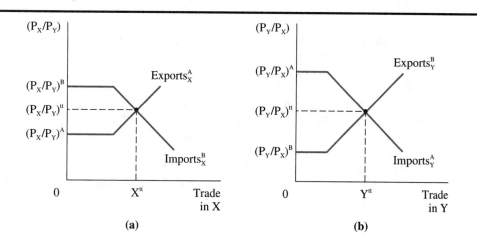

Each country is willing to import its good of comparative disadvantage at prices below its autarky price. At each price, the quantity demanded of imports equals the difference between quantity demanded and quantity produced domestically. Each also is willing to export its good of comparative advantage at prices above its autarky price. At each price, the quantity supplied of exports equals the difference between quantity supplied and quantity demanded domestically. The equilibrium international terms of trade lie between the two autarky prices. At the equilibrium terms of trade, the quantity one country wants to import matches the quantity the other country wants to export.

The same procedure is used to derive the international market for good Y (panel (b) of Figure 2.13) from panels (b) and (d) of Figure 2.12. The demand for imports of good Y by country A comes from panel (b) of Figure 2.12, and the supply of exports of good Y by country B comes from panel (d). *(What determines the vertical intercepts of Imports$_Y^A$ and Exports$_Y^B$?)* The international equilibrium price of good Y is $(P_Y/P_X)^{tt}$, and country B exports Y^{tt} to country A. These results correspond to the information summarized in the trade triangles in Figures 2.8 and 2.9.

In the remainder of the book, we shall use both the demand/supply and production possibilities/indifference curve frameworks. Although the two methods of analysis convey the same information, each is more convenient for answering certain questions. As each issue arises, we shall address it with the more appropriate method. Translating back and forth between the two methods also provides practice in working with the basic ideas of international trade theory.[20]

This completes our development of the basic Ricardian model and the demonstration of the gains from productive specialization and trade. We now turn to three

---

[20]Appendix B to Chapter Three covers a third graphical technique, called the *offer curve* or *reciprocal demand curve*. All information conveyed by offer-curve analysis can be obtained using either the production possibilities frontier/indifference curve or the demand/supply technique.

cases. The first reports the results of several attempts to empirically test the major implications of the Ricardian theory of trade. Can differences in technology or labor productivity among countries actually explain the trade patterns observed in the world economy? Case One suggests that the answer is *yes:* Countries *do* tend to export goods in which their labor is relatively productive and to import those in which their labor is relatively unproductive. Case Two examines a rather subtle assumption of the Ricardian model: that workers or citizens do not mind productive specialization. Provided that production of the two goods pays the same wage (which will be the case so long as labor is mobile among industries in each country), workers are assumed to be indifferent between the productive specialization that occurs under unrestricted trade and the diversified production that occurs in autarky. Case Two explores the issues that arise when we relax that assumption. Case Three reports labor productivity in several industries for the United States, Germany, and Japan, as well as how labor productivity has changed during the postwar period.

Case One
Can the Ricardian Model Explain Trade?

The first and best-known effort to empirically test the major implication of the Ricardian model was made by G. D. A. MacDougall in 1951.[21] MacDougall used data from 1937 on U.S. and U.K. exports in 25 industries. Recall that the Ricardian model implies each country tends to export those goods in which it has a comparative advantage. Its comparative advantage is in those goods in which its labor is highly productive compared to the trading partner's labor.[22] MacDougall combined these two aspects of the Ricardian model to formulate the following testable proposition: Other things being equal, the higher the output per worker in the United States relative to the United Kingdom in a given industry, the higher the share of the world market captured by the United States. Figure 2.14 reports this relationship, and its data clearly support the major implication of the Ricardian model: High relative labor productivity in a given industry accompanies a high market share. Later studies by Balassa and Stern confirm MacDougall's findings using data for different time periods.[23]

---

[21]G. D. A. MacDougall, "British and American Exports: A Study Suggested by the Theory of Comparative Costs," *Economic Journal* 61 (December 1951), 697–724.

[22]Highly productive labor in an industry is equivalent to a low input coefficient. The input coefficient (for example, a_{LX}) measures how many units of labor are needed to produce one unit of output, while labor productivity (or, $1/a_{LX}$) asks how many units of output a unit of labor can produce.

[23]Bela Balassa, "An Empirical Demonstration of Classical Comparative Cost Theory," *Review of Economics and Statistics* (August 1963), 231–238, and Robert M. Stern, "British and American Productivity and Comparative Costs in International Trade," *Oxford Economic Papers* (October 1962), 275–296.

Figure 2.14 ▫ **Relative Labor Productivity and Export Performance**

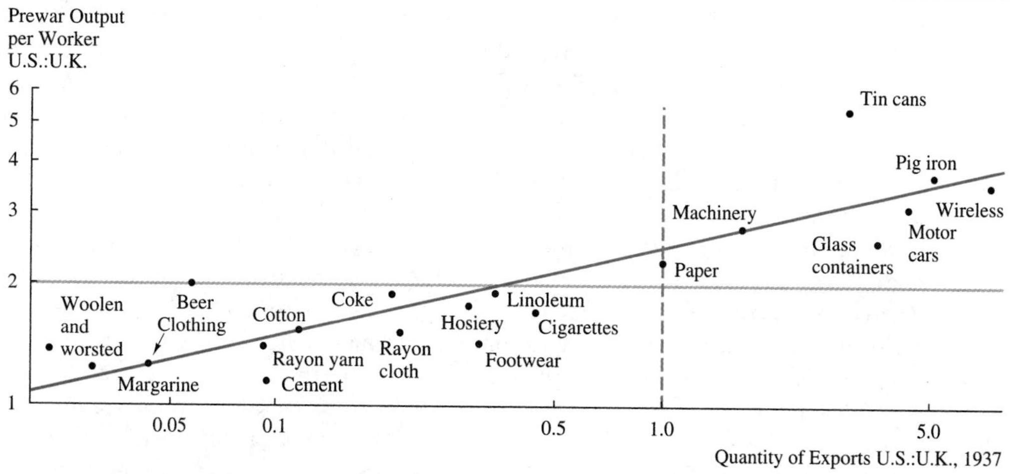

The empirical results clearly support the Ricardian idea that a country tends to export goods in which its labor is relatively productive.

Source: G. D. A. MacDougall, "British and American Exports: A Study Suggested by the Theory of Comparative Costs," *Economic Journal* 61 (December 1951), 697–724.

Notice how Figure 2.14 confirms the importance of *comparative* as opposed to absolute advantage. U.S. labor productivity exceeded U.K. labor productivity in all 25 industries MacDougall examined. On average, U.S. productivity was approximately twice U.K productivity, as illustrated by the pale horizontal line in Figure 2.14. If absolute advantage determined trade patterns, the United Kingdom would not have exported in any of the industries. But, because comparative advantage determines trade patterns, the United Kingdom did export—in those industries in which U.K. labor productivity was closer to that of the United States (for example, woolens, beer, and clothing). The United States exported more in those industries where U.S. labor productivity most significantly exceeded that of the United Kingdom (for example, pig iron and tin cans).

Simply reporting the results of the MacDougall, Balassa, and Stern studies, however, does not really do justice to the power of the findings or to the Ricardian model. Ricardo originally intended the model as a simple framework for highlighting the principle of comparative advantage rather than as a full explanation for observed trade patterns in the world economy. Both the theoretical model and the empirical tests ignore many relevant issues, such as the presence of nonlabor inputs, tariffs, transportation costs, economies of scale, and product differentiation. Considering these omissions, it is surprising that the relationship between labor productivity and export performance still emerges so clearly.

Because several of the crucial variables are difficult, if not impossible, to observe, further complications for empirical testing of the model occur. The theoretical version of the model implies that relative labor productivity (represented by the pattern of input coefficients) determines opportunity costs, which in turn determine autarky price ratios, which in turn determine trade patterns. In the real world, autarky prices typically are unobservable because trade is occurring; thus, empirical tests must seek a direct relationship between labor productivity and trade patterns, bypassing the unobservable autarky prices.[24] That this problem in implementing the model empirically cannot disguise the comparative advantage/export relationship is a tribute to the power of Ricardo's insight.

Since Ricardo wrote in the nineteenth century, economists have come to appreciate many explanations for existing trade patterns. However, in recent years, Ricardo's insights, particularly the importance of cross-country differences in technology and labor productivity, once again have come to the forefront. Two major issues in the world economy in the late twentieth century—the need to integrate developing countries and the formerly centrally planned countries into the world economy—help explain the new appreciation of Ricardo's insights. When a country isolates its economy from the rest of the world, as many developing and centrally planned nations did for decades, and then reemerges and tries to integrate itself into the world economy, the years of isolation leave a legacy of backward technology and low labor productivity. Policy makers must evaluate the implications of this legacy and design policies for confronting it. Almost two centuries after his original contribution, David Ricardo continues to lend a powerful helping hand in this task.

Case Two
The High Price of Self-Sufficiency

Unlike most cases in the book, this case presents a hypothetical example of a trading relationship between two countries. It is constructed with two goals in mind: (1) to provide another numerical example of the Ricardian model of comparative advantage and (2) to highlight some subtle assumptions of the model that have important implications for international trade policy.

We assume that Japan and America have established a trading relationship in steel and wheat. In Japan, 5 units of *l*abor are required to produce a ton of *s*teel ($j_{LS} = 5$) and 15 units of *l*abor are required to produce a ton of *w*heat ($j_{LW} = 15$). In America, 10 units of *l*abor are required to produce a ton of *s*teel ($a_{LS} = 10$) and 5 units of *l*abor are required to produce a ton of *w*heat ($a_{LW} = 5$). Japan has an endowment of 500

---

[24]Occasionally, rare historical circumstances do reveal autarky prices, for example, the case of the opening of Japan to trade during the nineteenth century.

Table 2.3 □ Input Coefficients for Production of Steel and Wheat in Japan and America

	Japan	America
Units of labor per ton of steel	$j_{LS} = 5$	$a_{LS} = 10$
Units of labor per ton of wheat	$j_{LW} = 15$	$a_{LW} = 5$

Table 2.4 □ Opportunity Costs of Producing Steel and Wheat in Japan and America

	Japan	America
Opportunity cost per ton of steel	1/3 tons of wheat	2 tons of wheat
Opportunity cost per ton of wheat	3 tons of steel	1/2 tons of steel

units of labor to allocate between steel and wheat production, and America has 600 units. Table 2.3 summarizes this information.

We can translate the information in Table 2.3 directly into the opportunity cost of producing each good in each country. The opportunity cost of producing 1 ton of steel in Japan is 1/3 tons of wheat, because production of an additional ton of steel requires 5 units of labor that could be used to produce 1/3 tons of wheat. The opportunity cost of 1 ton of wheat in Japan is 3 tons of steel. *(Why?)* Similarly, the opportunity cost of producing 1 ton of steel in America is 2 tons of wheat, because an additional ton of steel requires 10 units of labor, enough to produce 2 tons of wheat. The opportunity cost of producing 1 ton of wheat is 1/2 tons of steel. Table 2.4 summarizes the pattern of opportunity costs.

The Ricardian model of comparative advantage suggests that Japan should specialize in steel and America in wheat to maximize total output. If the two countries choose to specialize according to comparative advantage, total production will be as described in Table 2.5. The result in Table 2.5 is economically efficient: The world's scarce resources (1,100 units of labor) produce the maximum quantity of goods, in the sense that it is impossible to produce more of one good without producing less of the other.

But what if residents of Japan and America reject the goal of economic efficiency? Perhaps workers in each country value the ability to choose in which of the two

Table 2.5 □ Production of Steel and Wheat with Complete Specialization according to Comparative Advantage

	Japan	America	Total
Output of steel	100 (= 500/5)	0	100
Output of wheat	0	120 (= 600/5)	120

Table 2.6 □ **Production Pattern with Incomplete Specialization**

	Japan	America	Total
Output of steel	80 (= 400/5)	12 (= 120/10)	92
Output of wheat	6 2/3 (= 100/15)	96 (= 480/5)	102 2/3

industries to work. Residents of Japan might not want the urban culture associated with large-scale steel production, while residents of America may not want a largely rural environment. Perhaps the Japanese worry about being dependent on America for their food supply, and Americans about dependence on Japan for a vital material such as steel. These concerns might cause the two countries to choose not to specialize completely in their goods of comparative advantage. For example, each might choose to keep a specified share of its labor employed in its comparative-disadvantage industry. What would be the costs of such a decision?

Suppose that each country decides as a matter of policy to keep 20 percent of its labor force employed in the comparative-*disadvantage* industry. In Japan, 400 workers will produce steel and 100 wheat; in America, 480 workers will produce wheat and 120 steel. Table 2.6 gives the new production pattern.

A comparison of Tables 2.5 and 2.6 shows the true opportunity cost of the countries' decisions not to specialize according to comparative advantage. The total quantity of steel available has dropped by 8 units (from 100 to 92), and the total quantity of wheat has dropped by 17 1/3 units (from 120 to 102 2/3). The two countries have provided diversity in their economies and reduced their dependence on each other, but only at the cost of reduced output of both goods. In later chapters, we shall pursue questions concerning the desirability of policies with effects similar to those illustrated in Table 2.6.

In fact, the United States has restricted imports of steel, not only from Japan but also from many other countries, for the last 30 years. Japan, on the other hand, controls the quantity of imports of many agricultural products, including rice, fruit, and beef. We shall examine U.S. import restrictions on steel and Japanese import restrictions on agricultural products in Chapter Seven.

Case Three
Patterns in Labor Productivity

We shall see in Chapters Three and Five that differences in relative labor productivity form only one of several possible bases of comparative advantage and that, in turn, comparative advantage is only one of several possible foundations for mutually beneficial international trade. Nonetheless, we can explore at this point whether significant across-country differences in relative labor productivity exist. Table 2.7 reports recent estimates of value added per hour worked for several major manufacturing

Table 2.7 ▫ **Value Added per Hour Worked in Major Manufacturing Branches, 1950–1990 (U.S. = 100)**

Germany/U.S.: $(1/g_{LX})/(1/a_{LX}) = (a_{LX}/g_{LX})$	1950	1965	1973	1979	1990
Food, beverages, tobacco	53.1	76.9	68.4	74.1	75.8
Textiles, apparel, leather	44.0	78.1	81.0	85.9	88.2
Chemicals, allied products	32.4	64.3	90.5	106.0	76.7
Basic, fabricated metals	30.9	53.6	67.2	90.1	98.8
Machinery, equipment	43.7	77.1	90.0	110.7	87.6
Other manufacturing	34.2	56.6	68.8	80.1	79.3
Japan/U.S.: $(1/j_{LX})/(1/a_{LX}) = (a_{LX}/j_{LX})$					
Food, beverages, tobacco	26.7	25.8	39.5	39.8	37.0
Textiles, apparel, leather	24.7	37.5	53.2	54.9	48.0
Chemicals, allied products	13.0	32.1	60.4	78.0	83.8
Basic, fabricated metals	12.5	23.1	61.4	84.3	95.6
Machinery, equipment	8.0	23.5	50.6	79.6	114.4
Other manufacturing	9.7	20.0	34.0	39.8	54.9

Source: Bart Van Ark and Dirk Pilat, "Productivity Levels in Germany, Japan, and the United States: Differences and Causes," *Brookings Papers on Economic Activity: Microeconomics* 2 (1993), p. 17.

sectors in Germany and Japan relative to the United States. Value added is a measure of output, so value added per hour worked corresponds to the inverse of our input coefficients; because a_{LX} reports the number of units of labor required to produce one unit of X, its inverse, $1/a_{LX}$, measures output per unit of labor.

The top half of Table 2.7 compares labor productivity in Germany and the United States in each of six manufacturing sectors. Each number in the table reports value added per hour of labor in Germany ($1/g_{LX}$ in terms of our input coefficients) divided by value added per hour worked in the United States ($1/a_{LX}$), or (a_{LX}/g_{LX}). To determine the countries' comparative advantage across two sectors, X and Y, we need to compare (a_{LX}/a_{LY}) and (g_{LX}/g_{LY}). When the former exceeds the latter, Germany has a comparative advantage in good X and the United States in good Y; and when the latter exceeds the former, the United States has a comparative advantage in good X and Germany in good Y. The condition (a_{LX}/a_{LY}) > (g_{LX}/g_{LY}) is algebraically equivalent to (a_{LX}/g_{LX}) > (a_{LY}/g_{LY}). So, within each column in the top half of Table 2.7, industries with the highest numbers (that is, sectors with the highest values of [a_{LX}/g_{LX}]) correspond to industries of German comparative advantage relative to the United States, and industries with the lowest numbers (that is, sectors with the lowest values of [a_{LX}/g_{LX}]) correspond to industries of U.S. comparative advantage relative to Germany.

The data suggest that German labor productivity overall has improved relative to that of the United States, but still lags behind. After solid gains during most of the postwar period, German productivity lost ground relative to that of the United States in several sectors between 1979 and 1990. Note also that the pattern of comparative advantage has shifted. During the early postwar years, German comparative advantage relative to the United States was in food, beverages, and tobacco, along with textiles, apparel, and leather, while the United States exhibited an advantage in chemicals and metals. By 1990, metals showed the strongest German comparative advantage. *(Based on the data in the table, what patterns of imports and exports would you expect between Germany and the United States based on comparative advantage? If trade were based on absolute advantage, what would you predict about U.S.-German trade based on the table? Which fits better with what you know about trade?)*

The bottom half of Table 2.7 performs the same exercise for Japan and the United States. Japan's productivity catch-up during the postwar years is even more impressive than Germany's. In 1950, Japan showed a comparative advantage relative to the United States in food and textiles, and a comparative disadvantage in machinery and other manufacturing. By 1990, Japanese comparative advantage had shifted to metals and to machinery, where Japanese productivity surpassed that of the United States. *(Based on the data in the table, what patterns of imports and exports would you expect between Japan and the United States based on comparative advantage? If trade were based on absolute advantage, what would you predict about U.S.-Japan trade based on the table? Which fits better with what you know about trade?)*

Summary

Early trade policies reflected the doctrine of mercantilism, which set a goal of accumulation of gold and silver. At least in the short run, encouraging exports and restricting imports facilitated such accumulation. Mercantilists viewed trade as a zero-sum game that distributed the available gold among countries; whatever one country gained came at the expense of another.

Adam Smith and David Ricardo challenged the zero-sum view of trade. Following the insights of Smith and Ricardo, this chapter demonstrated how the possibility of trading internationally allows a country to separate its production decision from its consumption decision. Gains from trade arise when a country specializes its production according to comparative advantage—based on differences in technology or labor productivity—and then trades with other countries to obtain its preferred set of goods for consumption. The gains in efficiency allow trade to be *mutually* beneficial.

Looking Ahead

The complete specialization of production predicted by the Ricardian model almost never occurs. The two-country, two-good model drastically simplifies the many-country, many-good world economy. In a more realistic setting, most countries produce more than one good, and most goods are produced in more than one country. There are at least two reasons. First, even in a two-country, two-good world, complete specialization would occur only if there were no restrictions on trade, no transportation costs, and no product differentiation, and if each country were large enough to satisfy world demand for its good of comparative advantage. Second, and probably more important, the complete-specialization result follows directly from the assumption of constant costs; we have assumed that comparative advantage never shifts from one country to another—regardless of the degree of productive specialization. Economists believe that constant opportunity cost is the exception rather than the rule. For most production technologies, we expect the opportunity cost of producing a good to rise with the level of production. In Chapter Three, we expand our model of trade to include increasing costs. We shall also see a second major source of comparative advantage: variations in countries' factor endowments. In the process, we shall discover why trade policy has proven so enduringly controversial.

Key Terms

mercantilism
zero-sum game
mutually beneficial trade
specie-flow mechanism
perfect competition
marginal cost
autarky
production possibilities frontier
input coefficient
opportunity cost
marginal rate of transformation
  (MRT)
Ricardian model
constant-cost model
production opportunity set
consumption opportunity set
utility

indifference curve
marginal rate of substitution (MRS)
community indifference curves
income distribution
potential utility
autarky equilibrium
autarky relative price
absolute advantage
absolute disadvantage
comparative advantage
terms of trade
market-clearing price
trade triangles
gains from exchange
gains from specialization

Problems and Questions for Review

1. Let country A's endowment of labor equal 200 and country B's endowment of labor equal 200. The number of units of labor required to produce one unit of good X in country A equals 5, and the number of units of labor required to produce one unit of good Y in country A equals 4. The number of units of labor required to produce one unit of good X in B equals 4, and the number of units of labor required to produce one unit of good Y in B equals 8.
   (a) Draw the production possibilities frontier for each country. Be sure to label carefully.
   (b) Which country has an absolute advantage in which good(s)? Why? What would a theory of absolute advantage imply about the direction of trade? Why?
   (c) If free trade according to absolute advantage were allowed, what degree of productive specialization would occur? Why? How much of each good would be produced?
   (d) Answer the questions in parts (b) and (c) for the principle of comparative advantage rather than absolute advantage.
   (e) How do your answers in (b) and (c) differ from those in (d)? Why?

2. Consider a world consisting of two countries, Continentia and Islandia. Each country has 500 units of labor, the only input. In Continentia, it takes 5 units of labor to produce a computer and 10 units of labor to produce a unit of textiles. In Islandia, it takes 10 units of labor to produce a computer and 5 units of labor to produce a unit of textiles.

   (a) Sketch each country's production possibilities frontier. Label the vertical and horizontal intercepts and the slopes.

   (b) What is the opportunity cost of producing a computer in Continentia? Why? What is the opportunity cost of producing a unit of textiles in Continentia? Why? What is the opportunity cost of producing a computer in Islandia? Why? What is the opportunity cost of producing a unit of textiles in Islandia? Why?

   (c) In autarky, what would be the relative price of computers in Continentia? In Islandia? Why?

   (d) Which country has a comparative advantage in producing which good? Why?

   (e) If Continentia and Islandia specialize according to comparative advantage, how many computers and how many units of textiles will Continentia produce? Islandia? Why?

   (f) After several years of trade, Continentia and Islandia pass new laws stating that half of each country's labor force must be used in each industry. In other words, half of Continentia's labor must produce computers and half must produce textiles. The same is true in Islandia. Under the new laws, how many computers and how many units of textiles will Continentia produce? Islandia? Why?

   (g) How big is the economic cost of the laws that restrict specialization and trade between Continentia and Islandia?

3. Dismalia is a country with an unproductive labor force. It requires more units of labor to produce a unit of any good in Dismalia than in other countries. Dismalia's leaders have decided that the country cannot gain from international trade because the country's labor is so unproductive. According to the theory of international trade, are they correct or incorrect? Explain.

4. How are a country's opportunity costs and the shape of its production possibilities frontier related? How is this chapter's constant-cost assumption reflected in the production possibilities frontiers' shape? How are opportunity costs and the shape of the production possibilities frontier related to autarky relative prices?

5. In autarky, how do a country's residents decide what combination of goods to consume? What limits or constrains their choices? How does this change if we allow international trade?

6. Suppose labor cannot move between industries in either country in the short run. Therefore, each country must continue to produce at its autarky production point. Might it still be worthwhile to allow international trade? Why? How is your answer related to the gains from exchange and the gains from specialization?

7. The table reports the units of labor required to produce 1 unit of good X and of good Y in country A and in country B for three hypothetical cases.

	Case I		Case II		Case III	
	Country A	*Country B*	*Country A*	*Country B*	*Country A*	*Country B*
Good X	1	3	1	2	1	2
Good Y	2	4	2	4	2	1

(a) For each case, in which good(s) does each country have an absolute advantage?

(b) For each case, in which good(s) does each country have a comparative advantage?

(c) In which case(s) would trade be mutually beneficial? Why?

8. Comment on the following statement. "The Ricardian model of trade assumes each country's fixed endowment of labor is fully employed both in autarky and under unrestricted trade. The model also assumes that technology (labor productivity) does not change. Therefore, the world economy cannot produce more output with trade than in autarky."

References and Selected Readings

Chipman, John S. "A Survey of the Theory of International Trade, Part 1: The Classical Theory." *Econometrica* 33 (July 1965): 477–519.
A seminal survey article on international trade, this is of interest primarily to advanced students, although some sections dealing with the historical development of trade theory are appropriate for all students.

Deardorff, Alan V. "Testing Trade Theories and Predicting Trade Flows." In *Handbook of International Economics,* Vol. 1, edited by Ronald W. Jones and Peter B. Kenen, 467–518. Amsterdam: North-Holland, 1984.
A survey of the literature on testing trade theories; appropriate for advanced students.

Dornbusch, Rudiger, Stanley Fischer, and Paul Samuelson. "Comparative Advantage, Trade, and Payments in a Ricardian Model with a Continuum of Goods." *American Economic Review* 67 (December 1977): 823–839.
A modern version of the Ricardian model, with many goods. For intermediate and advanced students.

Ekelund, Robert B., Jr., and Robert D. Tollison. *Mercantilism as a Rent-Seeking Society: Economic Regulation in Historical Perspective.* College Station, TX: Texas A & M Press, 1981.
A modern reinterpretation of mercantilism emphasizing rent seeking; for all students.

Gray, H. Peter. "Non-Competitive Imports and Gains from Trade." *International Trade Journal* 1 (Winter 1986): 107–128.
Incorporates trade in goods that cannot be produced domestically; for intermediate-level students.

Heckscher, Eli F. *Mercantilism.* London: George Allen and Unwin, 1934.
Along with Viner (see below), one of the two classic treatises on mercantilism; for all students.

Hume, David. "Of the Balance of Trade." In *Essays, Moral, Political, and Literary.* London, 1752.
Hume's classic critique of mercantilism.

Irwin, Douglas A. "Strategic Trade Policy and Mercantilist Trade Rivalries." *American Economic Review Papers and Proceedings* 82 (May 1992): 138–143.
Argues that mercantilist trade policies by the seventeenth-century Dutch East India Company provide an example of strategic trade policy (discussed in Chapter Eight).

Jones, Ronald W., and J. Peter Neary. "The Positive Theory of International Trade." In *Handbook of International Economics,* Vol. 1, edited by Ronald W. Jones and Peter B. Kenen, 1–62. Amsterdam: North-Holland, 1984.
A more advanced presentation of many of the concepts treated in this chapter.

Krugman, Paul. "Recent Developments in the Positive Theory of Trade." In *Handbook of International Economics,* Vol. 3, edited by G. M. Grossman and Kenneth Rogoff. Amsterdam: North-Holland, 1995.
Advanced up-to-date survey of recent developments in trade theory.

Krugman, Paul. "What Do Undergrads Need to Know About Trade?" *American Economic Review Papers and Proceedings* 83 (May 1993): 23–26.
An entertaining tour of the many fallacies in supposedly enlightened discussions of international trade policy. Essential reading for all students.

Leamer, Edward, and John Levinsohn. "International Trade Theory: The Evidence." In *Handbook of International Economics,* Vol. 3, edited by G. M. Grossman and Kenneth Rogoff. Amsterdam: North-Holland, 1995.
Advanced up-to-date survey of empirical evidence on international trade theories.

MacDougall, G. D. A. "British and American Exports: A Study Suggested by the Theory of Comparative Costs." *Economic Journal* 61 (December 1951): 697–724, and 62 (September 1952): 487–521.
The first and best-known tests of the Ricardian model; early parts of the article are appropriate for all students, later sections for intermediate or advanced students.

Ricardo, David. *The Principles of Political Economy and Taxation.* Baltimore: Penguin, 1971 (Originally published 1817).
Chapter 7 contains the original, classic version of comparative advantage; appropriate for all students..

Smith, Adam. *An Inquiry into the Nature and Causes of the Wealth of Nations.* New York: Random House, 1937 (Originally published 1776).
The book often credited with founding economics as a discipline. The whole book is accessible to students at all levels; Books I and IV contain the specialization argument.

Van Ark, Bart, and Dirk Pilat. "Productivity Levels in Germany, Japan, and the United States: Differences and Causes." *Brookings Papers on Economic Activity: Microeconomics* 1993 (2):1–70.
Empirical study of across-country productivity differences; intermediate and advanced.

Viner, Jacob. *Studies in the Theory of International Trade.* Clifton, N.J.: Augustus M. Kelley, 1965 (Originally published 1937).
Along with Heckscher (see above), one of the two classic treatises on mercantilism; for all students.

Chapter Two Appendix

The World Production Possibilities Frontier

We can see the gains from trade by constructing a world production possibilities frontier illustrating all the combinations of goods X and Y that can be produced using the world's labor according to the pattern of comparative advantage. The technique for constructing the frontier is similar to that used in section 2.5.1. If all the world's labor ($L^W = L^A + L^B$) were devoted to producing good X, $[(L^A/a_{LX}) + (L^B/b_{LX})]$ units could be produced; this marks the intersection of the world production possibilities frontier and the horizontal axis at point 1 in Figure 2A.1. Similarly,

Figure 2A.1 □ World Production Possibilities Frontier

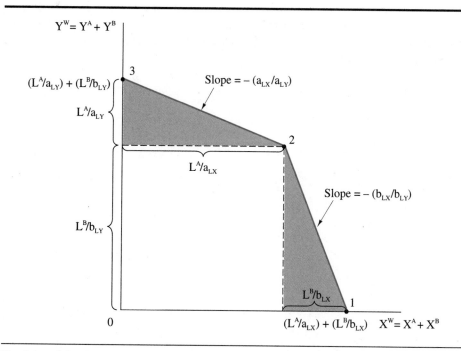

The slopes of the two segments of the world production possibilities frontier represent opportunity costs in the two countries. Moving from point 1 toward point 3, good Y is produced first by country B (from 1 to 2) and then by country A (from 2 to 3). Moving from point 3 toward point 1, good X is produced first by country A (at opportunity cost a_{LX}/a_{LY}) and then by country B (at opportunity cost b_{LX}/b_{LY}).

devoting all labor to producing good Y would permit $[(L^A/a_{LY}) + (L^B/b_{LY})]$ units to be produced, representing the intersection of the world production possibilities frontier with the vertical axis at point 3 in the figure.

Even though costs of production are constant within each country, giving each *country's* production possibilities frontier its straight-line shape, the *world* production possibilities frontier is *not* a straight line. This is true because the opportunity cost of each good differs between the two countries. We assume for the remainder of this appendix that country A has a comparative advantage in good X and B in good Y. Any X produced should be produced first in country A, and any Y produced should come first from country B. *(Why?)* In Figure 2A.1, moving upward and to the left from point 1, where only good X is produced, country B begins to produce good Y; the opportunity cost is b_{LY}/b_{LX}. At point 2, country B can produce no more good Y *(why?)*, so if we continue to move further upward and to the left, the additional good Y must be produced in country A, where the opportunity cost is $(a_{LY}/a_{LX}) > (b_{LY}/b_{LX})$. Similarly, moving downward to the right from point 3, where only good Y is being produced, country A begins to produce good X at an opportunity cost of a_{LX}/a_{LY} per unit. At point 2, country A is completely specialized and can produce no more X. Therefore, any additional X must be produced in country B at an opportunity cost of (b_{LX}/b_{LY}). Note that the two shaded triangles in the figure correspond to the production possibilities frontiers of the two countries, A on the upper left and B on the lower right. *(Suppose the two countries specialize according to their comparative disadvantage rather than their comparative advantage. Construct the world production possibilities frontier under this assumption. How does it compare with the frontier in Figure 2A.1? Why?)*

CHAPTER THREE

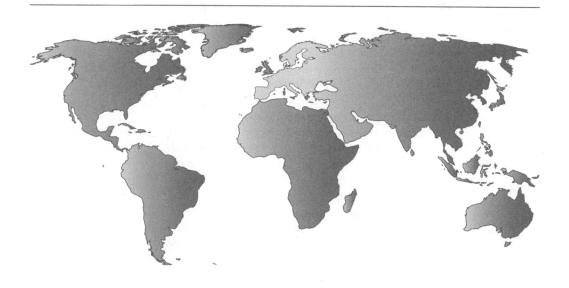

Comparative Advantage II:
Factor Endowments and the Neoclassical Model

3.1 Introduction

Chapter Two's simple model of production, consumption, and trade is useful in showing how and why international trade based on cross-country differences in technology or labor productivity can be mutually beneficial. Case One in that chapter showed that repeated empirical tests have supported the major implication of the Ricardian model—the positive relationship between countries' relative labor productivity and relative market share in various industries. However, as noted in Chapter Two, another implication of the constant-cost model—complete productive specialization—fails to match what we observe in the world economy.[1]

Based on detailed studies of many industries, economists think the opportunity costs of production increase with the level of output rather than remain constant for most goods. This phenomenon of increasing costs forms the focus of this chapter.

---

[1]As mentioned in Chapter Two, differences in country size can result in partial specialization by one of the two countries even with constant costs.

We shall see that incorporating increasing costs into the basic trade model can explain the observed partial rather than complete specialization. In addition, the possibility of increasing costs will allow us to explore sources of comparative advantage beyond the differences in relative labor productivity emphasized by Ricardo. Comparative advantage merely reflects differences in opportunity costs between two countries. But why should opportunity costs differ? Within the context of the Ricardian model, the only possible explanation is differences in the productive technologies, captured by the input coefficients that reflect labor productivity. If relative labor productivity were the same in the two countries, the opportunity costs and autarky relative prices would also be the same, and there would be no potential gains from trade. Thus, although the Ricardian model powerfully demonstrates the gains from trade, we want to look for possible additional explanations of *why* opportunity costs differ.

The increasing-cost model also has a second advantage: the ability to explain why international trade policy is so persistently controversial. Strong feelings on both sides of the issue always accompany trade policy decisions; some groups strongly advocate unrestricted trade, while others support a variety of restrictions.

3.2   The Neoclassical World without Trade

In this chapter, we continue to use the simplifying assumptions introduced in Chapter Two (see section 2.4). Again our goal is to compare the availability of goods in autarky with that under unrestricted trade. In autarky, each country must make a decision concerning the allocation of its available resources between production of two goods. This decision decides not only the country's production but also its consumption.

3.2.1   Production in Autarky

To grasp the idea of increasing costs, we need a new element in the model, that is, a second factor of production. Chapter Two's constant-cost model contained only one factor of production, which we called labor; and each unit of labor was a perfect substitute for any other unit of labor. Here, in the **Neoclassical** or **increasing-cost model,** there are two factors of production—labor (L) and capital (K)—and they are not equally effective in producing the two outputs, X and Y. The word *capital,* when used in trade theory, refers to durable inputs such as machines, buildings, iron mines, and tools.

How can we represent the production technology when there are two inputs? A few products may require the two inputs in **fixed proportions.** In such cases, the technology resembles a recipe that calls for ingredients in certain predetermined proportions. A cake recipe that specifies two cups of flour and one cup of milk will not produce a cake if you reverse the proportions of flour and milk. However, most production processes offer a fairly wide range of opportunities for substituting one input or factor of production for another. For example, automobiles can be built using a large amount of capital equipment, such as mechanized assembly lines and robots, and very little labor. Automobiles also can be built almost entirely by hand, using a large quantity of labor and very little capital in the form of simple tools. The textile industry provides another example. Japan produces textiles using sophisticated, computerized equipment and relatively little labor.

Figure 3.1 □ **Isoquant Map for an X Firm in Country A**

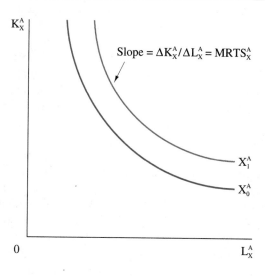

Each isoquant shows all the combinations of labor and capital that can produce a given level of output of good X in country A. Each isoquant is downward sloping, reflecting substitutability of inputs, and convex. Higher isoquants represent higher levels of output (for example, $X_1^A > X_0^A$).

At the same time, many developing countries continue to use large quantities of labor along with simple hand looms to make textiles.

Production Functions and Isoquants

For each industry, the recipe specifying the maximum output that can be produced with given quantities of inputs is called the **production function**. We denote the production functions for the X and Y industries in country A by $X^A = f_X^A(L_X^A, K_X^A)$ and $Y^A = f_Y^A(L_Y^A, K_Y^A)$. Plugging the quantities of resources used in each industry into the right-hand side of the production functions, we can determine the output of each industry. For example, if f_X^A is defined as $X^A = 2L_X^A K_X^A$, employment of 3 units of labor and 2 units of capital will produce $X^A = 2 \cdot 3 \cdot 2 = 12$ units of output. Producers can generate a given quantity of output using a variety of combinations of labor and capital, because the inputs are substitutes for each other. The 12 units of good X produced using 3 units of labor and 2 of capital could also be produced using, for example, 6 units of labor and 1 of capital (because $X^A = 2 \cdot 6 \cdot 1 = 12$) or 2 units of labor and 3 of capital (because $X^A = 2 \cdot 2 \cdot 3 = 12$). The graphical technique for representing these substitution possibilities is called an **isoquant** (or *same-quantity*) map. Each isoquant shows all the different combinations of quantities of labor and capital with which it is technically possible to produce a given amount of output. Figure 3.1 presents an isoquant map for production of good X in country A.

Each isoquant is downward sloping and convex, and higher isoquants correspond to higher levels of output. Isoquants are downward sloping because using less of one input implies that the firm must use more of the other input to maintain the same level of output (that is, to stay on the same isoquant). In other words, the negative slope of an isoquant represents the fact that the two inputs are substitutes for each other—using less of one requires using more of the other. The slope of an isoquant represents the rate at which producers can substitute one input for the other; this rate is called the **marginal rate of technical substitution (MRTS)**. The convexity of the isoquant implies that this rate changes along the curve. As more labor and less capital are used (moving down and to the right along an isoquant), it becomes more difficult to substitute additional labor for capital. The amount of additional labor required to compensate for a given reduction in capital increases.

Given all the possible combinations of labor and capital for producing a given level of good X in country A, we must specify how X-producing firms choose a particular production process. Each firm produces its output at minimum cost. Because profits equal total revenue minus total cost, any firm that did not use the cost-minimizing production process would needlessly forgo profits. Assuming there are only two inputs, an X-producing firm's total costs equal the wage rate paid to labor in A (w^A) times the quantity of labor employed (L_X^A) plus the rental rate for capital (r^A) times the quantity of capital employed (K_X^A). The wage rate and the rental rate for capital are called **factor prices** or **factor rewards**.[2] Total costs can be represented as $C = w^A L_X^A + r^A K_X^A$. For example, if the wage rate in country A equals \$10 per unit of labor and the rental rate for capital is \$15 per unit, the total cost for a firm employing 3 units of labor and 2 of capital would be $C = \$10 \cdot 3 + \$15 \cdot 2 = \$60$.

By using the expression for total cost, we can draw a line representing all the combinations of L and K a firm could hire for a given level of costs as in Figure 3.2. If the firm hired only capital, how many units of capital could it hire? The answer is given by the amount of total cost (C) divided by the rental rate (for example, \$60/\$15 = 4); this forms the vertical intercept of an isocost line (or *same-cost line*). Similarly, if the firm hired only labor, the maximum number of units it could hire for a total cost of C would be C/w^A, or \$60/\$10 = 6. *(Why?)* Connecting these two points yields the **isocost line,** which gives all the possible combinations of labor and capital the firm could hire for a total cost of C given factor prices of w^A and r^A. The slope of the isocost line is $-(w^A/r^A)$, or $-(2/3)$. *(Why?)*[3] The isocost line for a lower level of total cost (such as \$45) would lie parallel to the one drawn for C = \$60 in Figure 3.2, but shifted in toward the origin.

---

[2]Inputs referred to as "capital" are durable in the sense that they provide productive services for more than one period. For example, a machine may last many years even though a firm must purchase it only once. The cost of using such a machine for one period is not its purchase price but only a portion of that price. The true cost of using the machine for one period often is referred to as the *rental rate,* because it corresponds to the cost of renting the machine for one period rather than purchasing it. In our notation, r refers to this rental rate. Of course, the same holds true for labor, since the wage rate represents the cost of renting a unit of labor for a specified period, not the price of buying a worker!

[3]The slope of a line is defined as the rise, or vertical change over the length of the line, divided by the run, or horizontal change over the length of the line. Between the vertical and horizontal intercepts of the isocost line, the vertical change, or change in capital purchased, is $-(C/r^A)$ and the horizontal change, or change in labor purchased, is (C/w^A). Therefore, the slope is $-(C/r^A)/(C/w^A) = -(w^A/r^A)$. With a wage rate of \$10 and a rental rate of \$15, the slope of the isocost would be $-(2/3)$. Hiring an additional unit of labor would require the firm to hire 2/3 units less capital to keep total cost unchanged.

Figure 3.2 □ **Isocost Line for an X Firm in Country A**

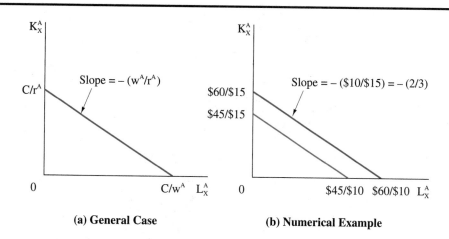

(a) General Case   **(b) Numerical Example**

An isocost line shows all combinations of labor and capital a firm could hire with a given total cost of C. The slope of each isocost equals the (negative) ratio of the input prices. Higher isocost lines correspond to higher levels of total costs.

Combining Figures 3.1 and 3.2 illustrates the firm's choice of production process. The firm produces its output at minimum total cost by choosing the point on the isoquant that lies on the lowest possible isocost line. This occurs at the point of tangency between the isoquant and the isocost line, as illustrated in Figure 3.3. The firm produces output level X_0^A using L_X^{A*} units of labor and K_X^{A*} units of capital at a total cost of $C^* = w^A L_X^{A*} + r^A K_X^{A*}$. At the chosen point, the relative factor prices (given by the absolute slope of the isocost line) just equal the rate at which the firm can substitute the two inputs while maintaining a constant level of output (as measured by the marginal rate of technical substitution along the isoquant). In other words, at this point the rate at which the two inputs can be substituted while keeping total *cost* constant exactly equals the rate at which they can be substituted while keeping *output* constant.

The Capital-Labor Ratio

The ratio of capital to labor the firm chooses is K_X^{A*}/L_X^{A*} and is called the **capital-labor ratio**. The slope of a ray through the origin and the chosen production point gives the capital-labor ratio as shown in Figure 3.3.[4] We can relate the capital-labor

---

[4]At any point along the ray, the vertical distance from the origin measures the amount of capital used while the horizontal distance from the origin measures the quantity of labor. Using the rise/run formula for the slope of a line, the slope of a ray from the origin is K_X^A/L_X^A.

Figure 3.3 □ Firm's Choice of Process for Producing X in Country A

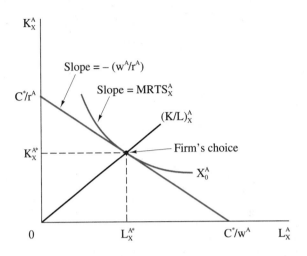

The firm produces its output at the minimum possible total cost. The point of tangency of an isoquant with an isocost line represents this decision. The firm uses L_X^{A*} units of labor and K_X^{A*} units of capital to produce X_0^A units of output. The slope of the straight line from the origin through the production point equals the capital-labor ratio.

ratio quite easily to the idea of input coefficients as used in Chapter Two.[5] Dividing both K_X^{A*} and L_X^{A*} by the number of units of X being produced gives the number of units of capital and labor used to produce each unit of good X. This corresponds to the definition of the input coefficients from Chapter Two, except that now there are two coefficients for the X industry in country A, $a_{KX} = K_X^{A*}/X_0^A$ and $a_{LX} = L_X^{A*}/X_0^A$. The first coefficient represents the number of units of capital used in producing a unit of good X in country A, and the second the number of units of labor used in producing a unit of X in A. Note that $K_X^{A*}/L_X^{A*} = a_{KX}/a_{LX}$. The major difference between these coefficients and the ones in Chapter Two is that these are not constants but depend on the relative prices of the two factors of production. The input coefficients have become.economic choices. In the constant-cost model, a firm in country A had only one way to produce a unit of good X: use a_{LX} units of labor. Now the

---

[5]We shall restrict our attention to production processes in which the firm would choose the same capital-labor ratio regardless of the level of output as long as factor prices remained the same. Production functions that satisfy this condition are called *homothetic*. In economic terms, the marginal rate of technical substitution depends only on the capital-labor ratio, not on the total quantities of the two inputs used or on the level of output. Graphically, this implies that the tangencies of all isoquants with the corresponding isocost lines lie along a straight line from the origin as long as factor prices do not change. We also assume that constant returns to scale characterize production. This means that changing the usage of both inputs by a certain proportion changes output by that same proportion; we shall relax this assumption in Chapter Five.

Figure 3.4 □ **Capital-Labor Ratios in Different Industries**

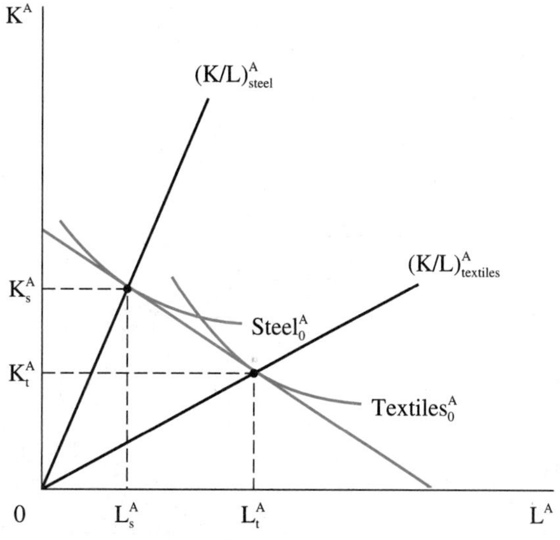

Although industries face the same relative factor prices, they generally choose different capital-labor ratios. This tendency for various industries to utilize factors in different proportions carries important implications for the theory of international trade.

firm can choose from among all the combinations of labor and capital along an iso-quant, and the particular combination chosen depends on the relative prices of the two inputs. For example, a fall in the wage rate relative to the rental rate would cause the firm to use more labor and less capital to produce any given output—that is, the capital-labor ratio would fall. *(How can this be demonstrated graphically in Figure 3.3?)*

Firms that produce good Y in country A go through the same type of decision process as X-producing firms. Each firm chooses its production process to minimize costs, and the choice can be summarized by the ratio of the input coefficients, a_{KY}/a_{LY}. The important point is that the ratios of input coefficients generally will *differ* for the two industries even if the two industries face the *same* relative factor prices, as they will due to mobility of factors within the country. For example, in Figure 3.4 steel-producing firms choose a production technique that uses a large quantity of capital relative to labor, and textile firms choose one using more labor relative to capital, even though both face the same prices for labor and capital.

If $(a_{KX}/a_{LX}) > (a_{KY}/a_{LY})$, good X is said to be the **capital-intensive good.** Note that what matters is the amount of capital used relative to the amount of labor, not just the amount of capital. Perhaps good Y requires more of both labor and capital than does good X (for example, $a_{LX} = 2$, $a_{KX} = 4$, $a_{LY} = 3$, and $a_{KY} = 5$). Nevertheless, if

Figure 3.5 □ **Production Possibilities Frontier with Increasing Costs**

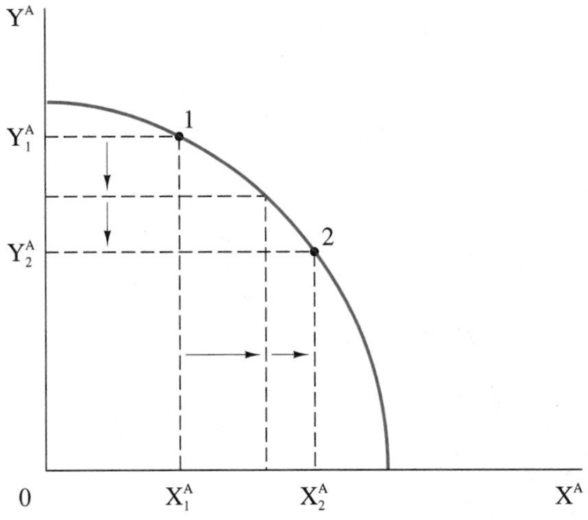

With two factors of production unequally suited for production of the two outputs, the production possibilities frontier bows out from the origin. Reduced production of good Y releases resources in the "wrong" proportion for the X industry. Adjustment becomes increasingly difficult as more and more X is produced, causing X's opportunity cost to rise.

good X requires *relatively* more capital (4/2 > 5/3), good X is capital intensive. As long as there are only two goods and two factors of production, the statement that good X is capital intensive is equivalent to the statement that good Y is **labor intensive.** *(Why?)*[6] In Figure 3.4, steel is the capital-intensive industry and textiles the labor-intensive industry.

The production technologies summarized by the four input coefficients provide one of the two pieces of information necessary to sketch country A's production possibilities frontier. The other required information is A's endowment of labor and capital. We assume that country A has L^A units of labor and K^A units of capital. The fact that the two outputs will be produced using the two factors in different proportions (or different *intensities*) implies that the production possibilities frontier is no longer a straight line as in the constant-cost model; rather, it is concave, or bowed out from the origin. Suppose good X is capital intensive, good Y is labor intensive, and country A is currently at point 1 in Figure 3.5, producing a large amount of Y and a small amount of X. As the country changes its production along the frontier from point 1 toward point 2, the reduced production of good Y (the labor-intensive good) releases relatively large

---

[6]The inequality that defines good X as capital intensive directly implies that $(a_{LY}/a_{KY}) > (a_{LX}/a_{KX})$, the definition of labor intensity of good Y.

amounts of labor and small amounts of capital. These released resources are in the "wrong" proportion for the X industry, which is capital intensive. The further the country moves toward point 2, the greater the adjustment that industry X must make in its production process to absorb the resources released by the shrinking Y industry. This increasingly difficult adjustment implies that successive reductions in Y production lead to smaller and smaller increases in the output of good X. This phenomenon is represented graphically by the concavity of the production possibilities frontier.

The (absolute value of the) slope of the production possibilities frontier at each point along the curve represents the opportunity cost of good X in terms of forgone good Y. *(Why?)* As country A produces more and more X along with less and less Y, the opportunity cost of X rises. Similarly, the opportunity cost of producing Y (1/absolute slope of the production possibilities frontier) increases as A produces more and more Y along with less and less X. The marginal rate of transformation (MRT^A) no longer is constant as in the constant-cost model of Chapter Two; it now depends on the particular combination of X and Y produced. Opportunity costs rise with production because the two factors of production are not perfect substitutes for each other; they are not equally well suited to producing both goods. Efficient production of goods X and Y requires that the two inputs be used with differing intensities in the two industries.

3.2.2 Equilibrium in Autarky

The indifference-curve technique used in Chapter Two to represent tastes and preferences for the two goods also applies under conditions of increasing costs. The production possibilities frontier defines the production opportunity set. In autarky, the country's consumption possibilities are limited to these same combinations of X and Y. Residents of the country will choose the point within the opportunity set that lies on the highest attainable indifference curve, thereby maximizing utility subject to the constraint imposed by resource availability and technology. Figure 3.6 illustrates this result.

Country A reaches the highest attainable level of utility at A^*, the tangency of indifference curve U_0^A with the production possibilities frontier. The autarky equilibrium involves the production and consumption of X^{A^*} units of good X and Y^{A^*} units of good Y. At the equilibrium, the opportunity cost of X in terms of Y is given by the (absolute) slope of the production possibilities frontier at point A^*. Because all markets are assumed to be perfectly competitive, the relative price of good X must equal its opportunity cost; thus, the relative price of X in autarky is given by the (absolute) slope of a line tangent to the production possibilities frontier at A^*. Therefore, in autarky equilibrium $MRT^A = MRS^A = -(P_X/P_Y)^A$. These conditions ensure that country A produces so as to achieve the highest possible level of satisfaction given the available resources and technology. The rate at which it is possible to transform good X into good Y in country A (along the production possibilities frontier) just equals the rate at which residents of A willingly trade off consumption of the two goods (along the indifference curve). However, by introducing country B as a potential trading partner for country A, we can demonstrate that trade allows A to achieve an outcome superior to A^*, the best that is possible in autarky.

Figure 3.6 ▫ Autarky Equilibrium with Increasing Costs

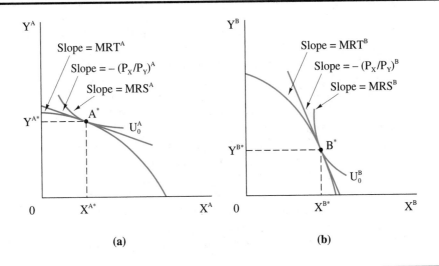

Country A chooses to locate at the tangency of the highest attainable indifference curve and the production possibilities frontier. The absolute slope of the production possibilities frontier at A^* gives the opportunity cost and the relative price of good X. In autarky, country B produces and consumes at B^*, thereby achieving the highest level of utility attainable given the constraint imposed by the availability of resources and technology.

Country B possesses L^B units of labor and K^B units of capital that can be allocated between production of goods X and Y. Firms in each industry in country B choose among all the possible production techniques and select the combination of labor and capital that minimizes the cost of production. The chosen production processes can be summarized by the input coefficients (b_{LX} and b_{KX} for the X industry and b_{LY} and b_{KY} for the Y industry), which, like the coefficients in country A, are not constants but choices that depend on the relative prices of the two factors of production in country B. The factor endowment and the production technology in B combine to determine the production possibilities frontier. In Figure 3.6, country B's autarky equilibrium lies at B^*, where the production possibilities frontier is tangent to the highest attainable indifference curve. The (absolute) slope of the production possibilities frontier at B^* gives the opportunity cost of producing good X in country B. The (absolute) slope of the indifference curve at B^* gives the MRS^B, or the rate at which residents of country B willingly trade off consumption of the two goods. Because all markets are perfectly competitive, the relative price of each good must equal its opportunity cost; thus, the (absolute) slope of a line tangent to the production possibilities frontier at B^* measures the relative price of good X in autarky in country B.

3.3   The Neoclassical Model with Trade

In autarky, the production opportunity set for each country coincides with its consumption opportunity set. Opening up the possibility of trade between countries A and B creates an opportunity for residents of each country to consume combinations of the two goods that lie *outside* the respective production possibilities frontiers. Once again, the key to increased consumption with trade is found in the difference between the autarky prices of goods X and Y in the two countries.

3.3.1 Productive Specialization

In the Neoclassical model, country A is defined as having a **comparative advantage** in production of good X if the relative price of X in A, $(P_X/P_Y)^A$, is lower than that in B, $(P_X/P_Y)^B$. Because all markets are perfectly competitive, this condition also implies that the opportunity cost of good X is lower in A than in B. Graphically, country A has a comparative advantage in good X if the slope of the relative price line in Figure 3.6 representing A's autarky equilibrium is flatter than that representing B's.

Just as in the constant-cost model of Chapter Two, comparative advantage is a natural extension of the concept of opportunity cost. However, in the increasing-cost model, comparative advantage traditionally is defined by comparing autarky relative *prices* (which reflect opportunity costs) rather than by directly comparing opportunity *costs*. The reason for this is that, under increasing costs, opportunity costs change along the production possibilities frontier. By using autarky relative prices, we specify at what points along the two production possibilities frontiers to compare the opportunity costs. This observation points out an important difference between the constant- and increasing-cost models. In both models, determining the direction of comparative advantage involves comparing the slopes of the production possibilities frontiers. Under constant costs, the slope of each frontier is a constant; thus, the determination of comparative advantage does not depend on the country's particular location along the frontier. This implies that tastes play no role in the constant-cost model in determining comparative advantage *(why?)*; advantage is determined on the "supply" side of the model by technology rather than on the "demand" side by tastes. Under increasing costs, the determination of comparative advantage requires that we specify the exact points on the production possibilities frontiers at which to compare the opportunity costs, because costs change along the frontiers. As we shall see later, this fact allows tastes a role in determining comparative advantage.

In Figure 3.6, country A has a comparative advantage in production of good X. *(Why?)* This implies that country B has a comparative advantage in production of good Y. *(Why?)* Suppose each country begins to produce more of the good in which it has a comparative advantage and less of the good in which it has a comparative disadvantage. Each additional unit of good X produced in country A requires forgoing fewer units of good Y than when that unit of X was produced in country B. Similarly, each additional unit of good Y produced in country B requires forgoing fewer units of good X than when that unit of Y was produced in country A. Therefore, specialization according to comparative advantage allows total output to expand; more of one good can be produced *without* producing less of the other good.

In the constant-cost model of Chapter Two, this process of specialization continued until each country produced *only* its good of comparative advantage. Will the complete-specialization result continue to hold under increasing costs? The answer is

Figure 3.7 □ **Productive Specialization with Increasing Costs**

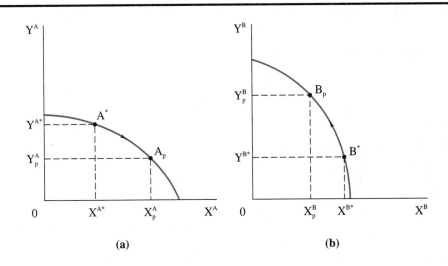

(a)   (b)

From the autarky equilibrium, A^*, country A specializes in its good of comparative advantage, X. As country A produces more X and less Y, the opportunity cost or relative price of good X rises while that of good Y falls. From the autarky equilibrium at B^*, country B increases production of good Y until the opportunity costs of the two goods equalize with those in country A. Specialization continues to point A_p, where the slope of the production possibilities frontier equals the slope of country B's at B_p.

"probably not." Figure 3.7 illustrates. As each country begins to specialize by moving along its production possibilities frontier in the direction of the good of its comparative advantage, the opportunity cost of producing that good rises and the cost of producing the good of comparative disadvantage falls. As the cost of producing good X rises in country A and falls in country B, eventually costs in the two countries are equalized. Similarly, as the cost of producing good Y rises in country B and falls in country A, costs in the two countries eventually converge. When the cost of producing each good becomes equal in the two countries, the advantage to *further* productive specialization disappears. The optimal degree of productive specialization occurs at points A_p and B_p (the p subscripts denote *production*), where the slopes of the two production possibilities frontiers are equal. Country A produces X_p^A and Y_p^A, and country B produces X_p^B and Y_p^B. Notice that if the two countries' autarky prices (and therefore opportunity costs) were equal, there would be no comparative advantage and no reason to specialize.

The condition illustrated in Figure 3.7 ensures that production is allocated efficiently between the two countries or according to comparative advantage. However, this condition alone is not sufficient to determine exactly which combinations of goods X and Y the two countries will produce. After all, there are many pairs of points at which the slopes of the two production possibilities frontiers are equal; points A_p and B_p in the figure comprise only one possible pair of points that satisfies the equal-slope

Figure 3.8 □ Trade Equilibrium with Increasing Costs

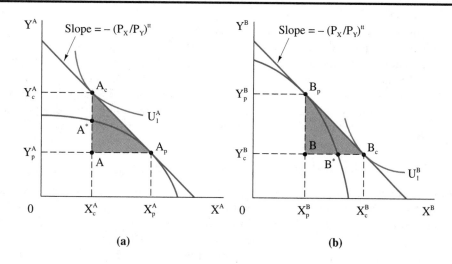

(a)   **(b)**

Country A specializes production in its comparative advantage good, X, until the opportunity cost of X equalizes in the two countries. Trade occurs along the terms-of-trade line until country A reaches its highest attainable indifference curve at point A_c. The trade triangle is AA_cA_p. Country B specializes in producing good Y until the cost of Y equalizes in the two countries at B_p. Trade occurs along the international terms-of-trade line until country B reaches its highest attainable indifference curve at B_c. The trade triangle for B is BB_pB_c.

requirement. At which of these pairs of points will production actually occur? To answer this question, we must reintroduce the role of tastes in the model.

3.3.2   International Equilibrium with Trade

Once productive specialization has occurred so that the two goods' opportunity costs are equalized between the two countries, the goods' relative prices also will be equal in A and B. *(Why?)* Of all the possible sets of relative prices, at which one will trade actually occur? The market-clearing or equilibrium terms of trade will be the one at which the quantity of good X that country A wants to export just equals the quantity of X that country B wants to import, and the quantity of Y that B wants to export equals the quantity that A wants to import. This is the international version of the definition of the **equilibrium price** of any good: the price at which quantity demanded equals quantity supplied. In panel (a) of Figure 3.8, country A can trade along the common relative price line representing the international terms of trade to the point of tangency with the highest attainable indifference curve. This occurs at point A_c, which is A's optimal consumption point under unrestricted trade (the c subscript denotes *consumption*). Country A produces at A_p, exports $(X_p^A - X_c^A)$ units of good X to country B, and imports $(Y_c^A - Y_p^A)$ units of Y from country B.

Panel (b) of Figure 3.8 represents country B's equilibrium. Residents of B can trade with those of A along the terms-of-trade line. The utility-maximizing consumption choice is B_c. Country B imports $(X_c^B - X_p^B)$ from country A in exchange for exporting $(Y_p^B - Y_c^B)$ to A.

Unrestricted trade expands each country's consumption opportunity set by allowing residents to trade at the international terms of trade, obtaining consumption combinations that lie outside the production possibilities frontiers and therefore could not be produced domestically. It would be impossible for country A to produce X_c^A units of good X and Y_c^A units of good Y, and country B could not produce X_c^B and Y_c^B. Trade also equalizes the opportunity cost of each good in both countries by increasing production of each good in the low-cost country and decreasing production in the high-cost country.

3.3.3   Autarky and Trade: The Two Koreas[7]

No country in the modern world exists in complete autarky. Some, however, come much closer than others. Since Korea split into the Republic of (South) Korea and the Democratic Peoples' Republic of (North) Korea during the Korean War of the 1950s, the North's philosophy has been one of *juche,* or self-sufficient industrialization. The government of the North, one of the world's last centrally planned Communist regimes, strictly controls foreign trade, along with other contact with the outside world. The South, on the other hand, has pursued outward- or trade-oriented policies despite frequent disputes with the United States over an alleged lack of openness of South Korean markets for U.S. goods. The difference in results is remarkable, as summarized in Table 3.1.[8] The South's per capita gross domestic product exceeds that of the North by a factor of nine, and the South's recent 8 percent economic growth rate dwarfs the North's negative growth of almost 4 percent.

Of course, North Korea's attempts at self-sufficiency are not the only cause of its economic problems. Estimates place North Korea's army at 1.2 million persons; and military expenditures absorb up to 20 percent of the economy's output. Until recently, the small amount of trade in which the country engaged took the form of oil imports from the Soviet Union to fuel huge state-owned industrial plants and exports of low-quality goods to Eastern Europe.[9] The demise of the Soviet Union means North Korea's factories now run far below capacity because it lacks the foreign currency to buy oil at world prices on the open

---

[7]This section draws on Damon Darlin, "North Korea, Fierce But Broke, Invites Western Investment," *The Wall Street Journal,* May 12, 1992, A1; "North Korea's Economy Staggers Along," *The Wall Street Journal,* May 26, 1992, A12; "Free-Trade Zone May Appear in Far East," *The Wall Street Journal,* June 10, 1992; John J. Fialka, "Korea Face-Off Grows Tense as the Economy of North Deteriorates," *The Wall Street Journal,* September 3, 1993, A1; Steve Glain, "South Korea, Under Corporate Pressure, Ma Drop Its Ban on Trade With North," *The Wall Street Journal,* September 12, 1994; "A Survey of South Korea," *The Economist,* June 3, 1995; and "Against the Odds," *The Economist,* June 8, 1995, 33.

[8]North Korea does not publish economic data; South Korea publishes statistical estimates about the North.

[9]This trade pattern also characterizes most economies in transition, that is, those in the process of changing from central planning to a market-oriented economy; see section 11.9.

Table 3.1 □ **Comparison of North and South Korea, 1993**

Indicator	North Korea	South Korea
Territory (1,000 square meters)	122.1	99.3
Population (million persons)	23.0	44.5
GNP ($100 million)	198	3,769
Per-capita GNP ($)	859	8,470
Economic growth (percent)	–4	8

Source: *The Economist,* June 3, 1995, pp. 5, 7.

market. The decline of central planning in Eastern Europe eliminated the markets for North Korea's few exports, whose low quality makes them noncompetitive in world markets. This combination of events reduced North Korea's trade by 25 percent between 1990 and 1991.[10] These problems have led to rumors of idle fuelless factories, power outages, and occasional hunger. North Korea's only ruler, Kim Il Sung, in power since 1948, died in 1994 and was replaced by his son, Kim Jong Il.

The country has responded to its growing economic problems by opening a crack in the door to the outside world. The government now encourages foreign firms to take advantage of North Korea's low wages by investing in a special economic zone, Rajin-Sonbong, modeled on China's coastal economic zones.[11] But the government still isolates that area from the rest of the country to prevent the spread of political ideas, and investors have been wary. Talks have been underway for years on several major projects involving North Korea. The first is the reunification of the two Koreas, with the obvious hope that the economic strength of the South could revitalize the North. The costs, however, could be enormous; one estimate places the cost to bring the North's economy up to par with the South's at $1.2 trillion. A second project is a possible free-trade zone among North Korea, China, and Russia, along with perhaps Mongolia and South Korea, at the mouth of the Tumen River. Such a zone, with more openness to international trade, would allow North Korea to capture at least a portion of the potential gains from trade. Several South Korean firms have plans for textile and apparel factories, tourist resorts, railroads, and steel mills in North Korea. In May 1995, a South Korean firm won government approval for the first joint venture with a firm from the North since the Korean War. Recently, plans have been stymied by stalemates between North Korea and the United States over the former's nuclear policy. Regardless of the timetables or fates of particular projects, one thing is certain. If North Korea hopes to experience economic growth similar to that in the South, open international trade based on comparative advantage will constitute a vital component of the necessary policy changes.

---

[10]"North Korea's Foreign Trade," *The Wall Street Journal,* June 16, 1992.

[11]Section 9.5.2 examines the role of special economic zones in China's transition.

3.4   More Sources of Comparative Advantage

Under increasing costs, a country has comparative advantage in production of goods whose relative prices are lower there than in the other country. To locate the sources of comparative advantage, it is necessary to examine the determinants of relative prices. As illustrated in Figure 3.6, the interaction of supply (resource availability and technology as summarized in the production possibilities frontier) and demand (tastes as summarized by the indifference curves) determines relative prices in each country. Differences in relative prices can originate from differences in resource availability, technology, tastes, or some combination thereof. Here we restrict our attention to the possible effects of differences in resource endowments and tastes in determining comparative advantage by assuming that the two countries have access to the same technology. We examined the role of technology or labor productivity differences in Chapter Two.

3.4.1   The Role of Factor Endowments

The importance of differences between countries' endowments of various factors of production in determining patterns of opportunity costs was asserted by two Swedish economists, Eli Heckscher and Bertil Ohlin, in the early twentieth century. To demonstrate the role of factor endowments, Heckscher and Ohlin used several simplifying assumptions. In addition to the basic assumptions we used throughout the first two chapters (see section 2.4), they assumed that tastes and technology did not differ between countries, that countries differed in factor abundance, and that goods differed in factor intensity.

Factor Abundance

First, we must define what Heckscher and Ohlin meant by the assumption that countries differ in **factor abundance**. Abundance can be defined in either of two ways. The first definition is based on relative factor quantities. By this definition, country A is **capital abundant** if $(K^A/L^A) > (K^B/L^B)$—that is, if A has more capital per unit of labor than does country B. Note that A could actually have *less* capital than B yet still be the capital-abundant country (for example, if $K^A = 50$, $L^A = 50$, $K^B = 100$, and $L^B = 150$ so that $K^A/L^A = 1$ and $K^B/L^B = 2/3$). What matters is a comparison of capital *per unit of labor,* or the *ratio* of capital to labor, in the two countries. Given two factors and two countries, if country A is capital abundant, country B must be **labor abundant**. *(Why?)* The quantity-based definition of factor abundance obviously depends only on the supply of the factors in each country; the demand for factors plays no role. Table 3.2 highlights the significant differences among countries' factor endowments.[12] *(Which country is the most capital abundant? The least capital abundant?)*

---

[12]The tables from which the data in Table 3.2 come list land separately from capital; if land were included in the capital measure, the capital/labor rankings would be different. Chapter Five explores the implications of a more detailed classification of inputs.

Table 3.2 □ **Factor Endowments**

Country	Capital (Billion 1966 $)	Labor (1,000 Persons)	Capital/Labor (Billion 1966 $ Per 1,000 Persons)
Argentina	24,018	8,496	2.83
Australia	35,053	4,727	7.42
Austria	15,653	3,363	4.65
Bene-Lux	22,563	3,764	5.99
Brazil	30,476	26,463	1.15
Canada	76,537	7,232	10.58
Denmark	13,018	2,230	5.84
Finland	13,929	2,176	6.40
France	146,052	21,233	6.88
Germany	181,079	26,576	6.81
Greece	7,223	4,314	1.67
Hong Kong	2,087	1,525	1.37
Ireland	3,370	1,109	3.04
Italy	90,436	19,998	4.52
Japan	165,976	49,419	3.36
Korea	3,025	9,440	0.32
Mexico	21,639	12,844	1.68
Netherlands	29,941	4,699	6.37
Norway	12,883	1,464	8.80
Philippines	6,597	12,470	0.53
Portugal	3,757	3,381	1.11
Spain	34,792	11,849	2.94
Sweden	31,555	3,450	9.15
Switzerland	23,315	2,843	8.20
United Kingdom	110,717	25,396	4.36
United States	785,933	76,595	10.26
Yugoslavia	14,023	8,837	1.59

Source: Harry P. Bowen, et al., "Multicountry, Multifactor Tests of the Factor Abundance Theory," *American Economic Review*, December 1987, pp. 806–807.

A second possible definition of factor abundance is based on factor *prices* rather than on *quantities*. According to the price-based definition, country A is capital abundant if in autarky $(r^A/w^A) < (r^B/w^B)$ or $(w^A/r^A) > (w^B/r^B)$, that is, if the relative rental rate for capital in country A is lower than in B. The price-based definition considers the role of demand for the two factors as well as their supplies, because the price of each factor represents the interaction of both demand and supply. For our purposes, either definition of factor abundance will suffice; however, because the Heckscher-Ohlin model traditionally is associated with the quantity-based definition, we shall use that one.

The Heckscher-Ohlin Theorem

Heckscher and Ohlin combined the notion of factor *abundance* with the idea that different goods involve different factor *intensities* to infer that a country will have a comparative advantage in the good whose production involves intensive use of the factor that the country possesses in abundance.[13] Further, under unrestricted trade, the country will export the good in which it has a comparative advantage and import the good whose production involves intensive use of the factor that the country possesses in relative scarcity. We assume that if good X is the capital-intensive good in country A (that is, if $[a_{KX}/a_{LX}]$ > $[a_{KY}/a_{LY}]$), it also will be capital intensive in country B ($[b_{KX}/b_{LX}] > [b_{KY}/b_{LY}]$).[14]

As an example, assume country A is labor abundant ($[L^A/K^A] > [L^B/K^B]$) and good X is labor intensive ($[a_{KX}/a_{LX}] < [a_{KY}/a_{LY}]$ and $[b_{KX}/b_{LX}] < [b_{KY}/b_{LY}]$). These two conditions imply that A has a resource endowment relatively well suited to production of good X and B has a resource endowment relatively well suited to production of Y. For example, the United States has a resource endowment well suited to the production of wheat; it is farmland abundant, and wheat is a farmland-intensive good. Hong Kong has a resource endowment well suited to the production of clothing; Hong Kong is labor abundant, and clothing production is a labor-intensive industry. The production possibilities frontier of each country reflects a bias toward the good of comparative advantage, as shown in the two panels of Figure 3.9.

If tastes were identical in the two countries, as Heckscher and Ohlin assumed, the autarky price of wheat would be lower in the United States and that of clothing lower in Hong Kong.[15] Each country then would be the low-cost producer of the good that used its abundant factor intensively. Under unrestricted trade, each country would specialize in and export the good that used the abundant factor intensively because of the good's low autarky price. This result is known as the **Heckscher-Ohlin theorem.** *(Using Table 3.2 and the Heckscher-Ohlin theorem, name a country you would expect to export capital-intensive goods. Name a country you would expect to export labor-intensive goods. What do you know about the trade of the counties you named? Does it fit your predictions?)*

A theory of trade based *solely* on production bias due to factor endowments is somewhat artificial. Under conditions of increasing costs, tastes and productive possibilities interact to determine comparative advantage. What ultimately matters is the comparison of autarky price ratios in the two countries. This is distinct from the constant-cost case, in which comparative advantage is determined on the supply side (by the production possibilities frontier) with demand conditions (tastes) determining primarily the volume of trade.

---

[13]Do not make the mistake of confusing factor abundance and factor intensity. Abundance refers to *countries' endowments* of factors of production. Intensity refers to *industries' usage* of factors of production. For example, the Philippines is (compared with the United States) labor abundant, and the textile industry is (compared with the aircraft industry) labor intensive.

[14]The case in which a good is capital intensive in one country but labor intensive in the other is known as a *factor-intensity reversal.*

[15]The assumption of identical tastes in the two countries does *not* imply that residents of each will consume the two goods in equal quantities or in equal proportions. Identical tastes are defined as identical sets of indifference curves. Imagine a set of indifference curves drawn on a piece of transparent plastic and placed over two graphs containing each country's production possibilities frontier. Even though the indifference curves are identical, the actual consumption point chosen in each graph would differ because of the differences between production possibilities.

Figure 3.9 □ **Production Bias due to Differences in Factor Abundance**

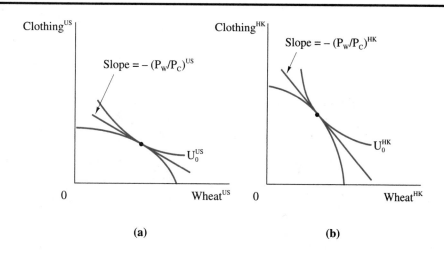

(a)   (b)

Each country's production possibilities frontier exhibits a bias toward the axis representing the good whose production involves intensive use of that country's abundant factor of production. This production bias creates a tendency for each country to have a comparative advantage in the good that uses the abundant factor intensively.

3.4.2   The Role of Tastes

Although the Heckscher-Ohlin model assumes that the production bias resulting from differences in factor endowments forms the basis for trade, there are other possibilities.[16] For example, two countries could have identical production possibilities frontiers (that is, identical factor endowments and technology) but very different tastes. The taste differences would produce different autarky price ratios, as shown in Figure 3.10, and a basis for mutually beneficial trade.

In Figure 3.10, residents of country A have tastes biased toward consumption of good Y, and residents of country B have tastes biased toward consumption of good X. With identical production possibilities, the strong demand for Y in A and for X in B result in different relative prices in each country. This **taste bias** gives country A a comparative advantage in production of good X. Under unrestricted trade, A would specialize in X and B in Y even though the production possibilities are identical. When the identical-taste assumption of Heckscher-Ohlin is relaxed and both factor endowments and tastes are allowed to differ simultaneously, the taste bias can reinforce, partially offset, or totally offset the production bias. Unlike in the constant-cost case, tastes play a significant role in determining the direction of comparative advantage. Case Three presents an example in which differences in consumers' tastes for poultry parts provide a basis for trade.

---

[16]Chapter Two covered technology as a source of comparative advantage. In Chapter Five, we shall add economies of scale as a basis for mutually beneficial trade not based on comparative advantage.

Figure 3.10 ▫ **Taste Bias**

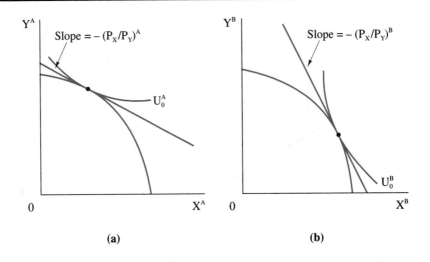

(a)   (b)

If tastes differ between countries A and B, the autarky price ratios will differ even if the production possibilities are identical, and a basis for mutually beneficial trade will exist.

In this chapter, we have seen the effects of introducing increasing costs on the basic trade model. Under increasing costs, trade still is mutually beneficial but productive specialization is incomplete. The reality of incomplete productive specialization perhaps is illustrated best by looking at the actual U.S. trade picture. Case One documents the broad categories of goods that the United States imports and exports. Cases Two and Three examine specific instances of the roles of factor endowment and tastes in determining patterns of productive specialization and trade. Cases Four and Five report on two new and rapidly growing trading relationships, both involving China.

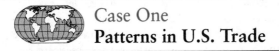

Case One
Patterns in U.S. Trade

Each month the U.S. Department of Commerce publishes figures on the value of U.S. merchandise exports and imports in a number of goods categories. In addition, government statistics record the distribution of U.S. trade among trading partners. Here we summarize the trade of the United States in 1994 in terms of types of goods and destinations and sources of exports and imports.

Figure 3.11 □ U.S. Merchandise Exports by Destination, 1994

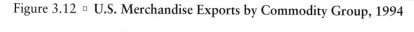

Source: U.S. Department of Commerce, *Survey of Current Business.*

Figures 3.11 and 3.12 depict U.S. exports by destination and commodity group, respectively. In 1994, of a total of $503 billion of merchandise exports, 24 percent went to Western Europe, 23 percent to Canada, and 10 percent to Japan plus 21 percent to the rest of Asia. Eastern Europe and Africa accounted for only 1 percent and less than 1 percent respectively. Overall, the data suggest that the United States exports largely to other developed countries.

This phenomenon has several possible explanations. First, the higher incomes of residents of developed countries mean a greater demand for goods, including

Figure 3.12 □ U.S. Merchandise Exports by Commodity Group, 1994

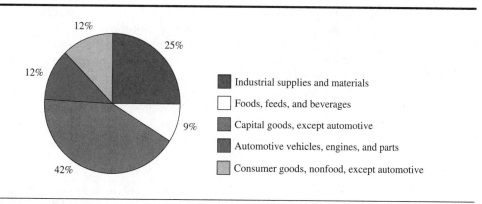

Source: U.S. Department of Commerce, *Survey of Current Business.*

imports. Second, the developed countries have, as a whole, pursued more open, trade-oriented policies than have developing countries (more on this in Chapter Eleven). Third, some analysts have suggested that developed countries tend to trade heavily with one another because they share a taste for types of goods that developing countries do not. Fourth, we shall see in Chapter Five that economies of scale, in addition to comparative advantage, provide a potential basis for mutually beneficial trade, especially among developed economies.

Figure 3.12 reports the shares of total U.S. merchandise exports accounted for by various broad commodity groups. The front-runner is capital goods (excluding automotive products), which comprise 42 percent of total merchandise exports. Other major export categories include industrial supplies and materials (25 percent); automotive vehicles, engines, and parts (12 percent); consumer goods, excluding food and automobiles (12 percent); and foods, feeds, and beverages (9 percent).

Figures 3.13 and 3.14 present corresponding information for U.S. imports, which totaled $669 billion in 1994. The major trading partners as defined by imports are the same as for exports. Partners are mainly developed economies and include the two geographical neighbors and NAFTA partners, Canada and Mexico.

U.S. imports are divided approximately equally among capital goods, industrial supplies and materials, consumer goods, and automotive vehicles, engines, and parts.

Case Two
Factor Endowments and Agriculture in the Middle East[17]

Until the early 1980s, Saudi Arabia imported most of the wheat it consumed, producing only 187,000 metric tons in 1981. Less than a decade later, the country produced over 3 million metric tons per year, over two-thirds of which was sold in export markets. Saudi Arabia produces exportable surpluses of eggs and dairy products as well. The desert blooms with giant green circles, up to 200 acres in size.

While agriculture produces only about 1 percent of the country's gross domestic product (a measure of total output), it employs about 25 percent of the native work force. Because of extensive irrigation and other measures necessary to grow wheat in a largely desert country, Saudi Arabia's domestically produced wheat costs about $1,000 a ton when wheat could be imported for about $80 per ton. Experts have estimated the total cost to the Saudi budget at $1 billion, when the same quantity of wheat could have been imported for $120 million. In addition to these costs, experts believe agriculture consumes over 80 percent of the water used in the country, most

[17]This case draws on Barbara Rosewicz, "Saudi Arabia Battles a Glut, but It Isn't the One You Think," *The Wall Street Journal*, April 2, 1986; Dennis D. Miller, "States Do Good, Arab Economies Done Ill," *The Wall Street Journal*, September 3, 1987; and "Arab Agriculture: Just Add Water," *The Economist*, July 15, 1989.

Figure 3.13 ▫ U.S. Merchandise Imports by Source, 1994

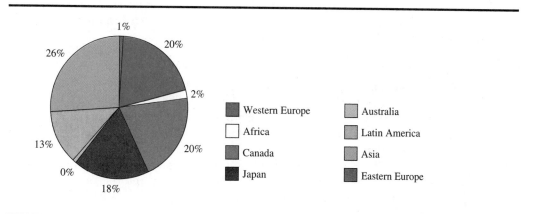

Source: U.S. Department of Commerce, *Survey of Current Business*.

Figure 3.14 ▫ U.S. Merchandise Imports by Commodity Group, 1994

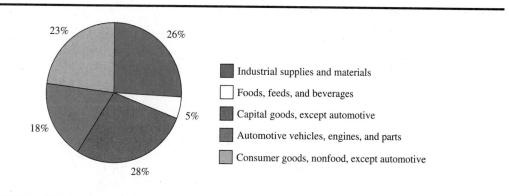

Source: U.S. Department of Commerce, *Survey of Current Business*.

of which (as much as 90 percent by some estimates) comes from aquifers not naturally replenished. Some experts predict exhaustion of the aquifers in as little as 20 years.

How does a country accomplish a pattern of production so counter to its resource-based comparative advantage? The Saudi government encouraged wheat production by guaranteeing farmers artificially high prices, free land, and low-interest loans for machinery, fertilizer, and seed. Farmers responded with a surge of wheat production. Soon the government had to build storage silos to store the surplus grain that could not be sold at the high prices. Grain has been given away as aid to poor countries, and much is sold on international markets, with the Saudi government making up the difference between the high prices paid to Saudi farmers and the lower market prices brought by the grain. *(Draw a production possibilities frontier for Saudi Arabia based on your knowledge of the country's factor endowment. Let the goods on the two axes be wheat and oil.)*

The Saudis are not alone in their support of farming in the desert. Libya is building the "Great Man-Made River" to carry water for irrigation of 500,000 acres of cereal crops and grazing for 2 million sheep and 200,000 cattle. Costs are estimated at $25 billion, making the "river" one of the most expensive engineering projects in the world. But, like in Saudi Arabia, the aquifers feeding the artificial river are nonrenewable, accumulated over thousands if not millions of years. Once those aquifers are exhausted, the Great Man-Made River will be just a pipeline under the Sahara. These agricultural projects reduce the countries' dependence on foreign suppliers of food, but only at enormous costs to both the economy and the environment. In Chapter Eight, we shall consider the arguments for and against such policies.

Case Three
Trade in Chicken Feet?
It's All a Matter of Taste[18]

For years, U.S. poultry producers tossed tons of "unusable" chicken and turkey parts into the garbage. In the state of Virginia alone, approximately 600 tons of chicken feet were disposed of annually. But no longer. The former governor of Virginia, Gerald Baliles, tells of discovering the potential market:

> When I was in China a couple of years ago, I was struck by how often I encountered chicken feet in the soups, foods, and markets. When I got back, I told my people that Virginia has a fairly large poultry industry in the Shenandoah Valley. I said, "Call them up and find out what they do with chicken feet." I got the strangest stares. I found out that the chickens' feet are chopped off on the assembly lines and discarded. I told them, "I think I've found them a new market." Today, we ship 40 tons a month of chicken feet to the Far East.[19]

Tastes for poultry parts differ substantially across countries. Based on these differences in tastes, most parts viewed as unusable by U.S. consumers now are sold abroad, where consumers often consider them delicacies. Chicken feet go to Hong Kong, where cooks use them in soup. Legs and necks are popular in Taiwan. And

---

[18]This case is based on James McGregor, "Now, if We Could Only Get Them to Start Accepting Candied Yams," *The Wall Street Journal*, November 21, 1988; and "China Clucks Over U.S. Chicken Export Decline," *The San Francisco Chronicle*, December 19, 1989.

[19]"Chicken Feet, Chocolate Provide Recipe for Trade," *USA TODAY*, July 27, 1989.

turkey testicles—believed by many male Taiwanese to boost potency—sell in Taiwan for the equivalent of about $3.50 a pair. *(Assume Taiwan and the United States have identical production possibilities frontiers. Illustrate how the difference in tastes for poultry parts could lead to mutually beneficial trade.)* U.S. chicken exports to Japan, on the other hand, are declining. The Japanese increasingly prefer chicken thighs, also popular in the United States, and are turning to Chinese and Brazilian suppliers.

Case Four
China-South Korea Trade: New and Growing[20]

Until a few years ago, (Communist) China and (staunchly anti-Communist) South Korea conducted no direct international trade, despite their geographical proximity. Now things have changed. The two countries have started to exploit the differences in their factor endowments through trade. Labor-abundant China, with a 1992 labor force of 699 million and a relatively small endowment of capital, exports to Korea such labor-intensive products as cotton gloves, fire bricks, umbrellas, and chopsticks. In exchange, South Korea provides more capital-intensive goods, including steel, plastics, paper, and electronics, especially appliances.

As both economies have integrated themselves into the world economy through trade, both have enjoyed unusually high rates of per capita income growth. Throughout the 1980s, when both developing and industrial countries suffered low rates of growth by historical standards, China's and South Korea's per capita incomes each grew by approximately 8 percent per year. China's exports expanded by 12 percent annually, and its imports by over 9 percent. South Korea's exports and imports grew by 12 and 11 percent, respectively. By 1992, China's per capita income had grown to $470 per year, and South Korea's to $6,790; and both were major exporters to industrialized countries as well as to each other. Most experts agree that China's growth prospects are excellent—if it stays on the path of increasing economic openness and trade.

Case Five
Heckscher-Ohlin and U.S.–China Trade

The Heckscher-Ohlin theorem predicts a country will specialize in and export goods that use the country's abundant factor intensively, while importing goods intensive

[20]See Damon Darlin, "New Trade Relationship With China Is Changing South Korea's Economy," *The Wall Street Journal,* November 17, 1992, A15. Statistics in the case come from the World Bank's *World Development Report 1994* (Oxford: Oxford University Press), 1994.

Table 3.3 □ **Composition of U.S.–China Trade, 1990**

Skill Group (Industry Examples)	Percent of Chinese Exports to U.S.	Percent of U.S. Exports to China
1 (Periodicals, office and computing machines)	4.8	7.7
2 (Aircraft and parts, industrial inorganic chemicals)	2.6	48.8
3 (Engines and turbines, fats and oils)	3.9	21.3
4 (Concrete, nonelectric plumbing and heating)	11.5	4.3
5 (Watches, clocks, toys, sporting goods)	18.9	6.3
6 (Wood buildings, blast furnaces, basic steel)	8.2	1.3
7 (Ship building and repair, furniture and fixtures)	4.1	2.8
8 (Cigarettes, motor vehicles, iron and steel foundries)	5.2	1.8
9 (Weaving, wool, leather tanning and finishing)	17.2	0.4
10 (Children's outerwear, nonrubber footwear)	23.5	5.2

Source: Jeffrey D. Sachs and Howard J. Shatz, "Trade and Jobs in U.S. Manufacturing," *Brookings Papers on Economic Activity* 1 (1994), pp. 18, 53.

in the country's scarce factor. As we have seen, the United States possesses human capital in abundance, and unskilled labor is the United States' scarce factor. China, on the other hand, possesses unskilled labor in great abundance. Therefore, the Heckscher-Ohlin theorem predicts that the United States would export to China products whose production involves intensive use of skilled labor (embodying the country's human capital) and that China would export to the United States products intensive in unskilled labor.

Table 3.3 reports data from a recent study that allow us to test informally the Heckscher-Ohlin prediction. The study's authors divided a sample of 131 industries into ten groups (or deciles) according to their skill intensity. Group 1 includes the most skill-intensive industries, and group 10 the least skill intensive. Table 3.3 reports sample industries for each group, along with the group's share of Chinese exports to the United States and of U.S. exports to China.

The pattern of U.S.-China trade in 1990 fits closely the Heckscher-Ohlin-based predictions. U.S. exports to China are concentrated in the high-skill sectors; deciles 1–3 account for 78 percent of U.S. exports. Chinese exports to the United States fall into the lower skill categories; groups 9 and 10, the least skilled, comprise over 40 percent of the total. Chinese exports in groups 4 and 5 include mostly assembly tasks in the radio, television, and toy industries.

Summary

When goods are produced using two inputs that are not perfect substitutes for each other, the opportunity cost of producing each good rises as more of the good is produced. A country has a comparative advantage in production of a good when the opportunity cost of that good is lower there than in the trading partner. When trade is possible, each country will specialize in and export the good in which it has a comparative advantage. We have now encountered two major bases for comparative advantage and mutually beneficial trade: (1) differences in technology or labor productivity, as in Chapter Two's Ricardian model, and (2) differences in factor endowments, emphasized in this chapter's Heckscher-Ohlin theorem.

Looking Ahead

Chapters Two and Three demonstrated the potential of international trade based on comparative advantage in increasing the welfare of the residents of participating countries. Nevertheless, decisions on trade policy always generate controversy, leading us to suspect that the case for trade must be more complicated than we have seen so far. In Chapter Four, we introduce an effect of trade we have ignored up to now: its effect on the distribution of income *within* each country.

Key Terms

Neoclassical (increasing-cost) model
fixed proportions
production function
isoquant
marginal rate of technical
   substitution (MRTS)
factor prices (factor rewards)
isocost line
capital-labor ratio

capital-intensive good
labor-intensive good
comparative advantage
equilibrium price
factor abundance
capital abundance
labor abundance
Heckscher-Ohlin theorem
taste bias

Problems and Questions for Review

1. Assume tastes and technology are identical in Hong Kong and Japan. Assume Hong Kong is labor abundant and Japan is capital abundant. Assume production of clothing is labor intensive and production of automobiles is capital intensive.
   (a) Sketch the production possibilities frontiers for Hong Kong and Japan. Explain briefly why you drew them as you did.
   (b) In autarky, which country has a comparative advantage in production of which good? Show how you know, or why you don't know.
   (c) What does the Heckscher-Ohlin theorem predict would happen if trade were opened between Hong Kong and Japan?
   (d) Show and label the autarky and unrestricted-trade equilibria, production and consumption points, imports and exports, autarky price ratios, and terms of trade.

2. Under increasing costs, will two countries find it beneficial to trade if they have:
   (a) Identical production possibilities and different tastes?
   (b) Identical tastes and different production possibilities?

(c) Identical tastes and identical production possibilities?

Explain and illustrate.

3. How does a concave, or bowed-out, production possibilities frontier reflect increasing costs?

4. In Table 3.2, what are the most capital-abundant countries? The most labor-abundant countries?

5. A firm's production function is X = 5LK. Name three input combinations that would allow the firm to produce 100 units of output. In each case, what is the firm's capital-labor ratio? If the wage rate is $10 per unit and the rental rate on capital is $20 per unit, what are the firm's costs for each of the three input combinations?

6. What determines the capital-labor ratio for each good in each country? Why might both industries use a higher capital-labor ratio in one country than in another? Can you think of circumstances in which each industry would exhibit the same capital-labor ratio in both countries? Explain.

7. Why do the autarky relative prices in the two countries form limits or bounds on the international terms of trade? Explain.

References and Selected Readings

Corden, W. M. "The Normative Theory of International Trade." In *Handbook of International Economics,* Vol. 1, edited by Ronald W. Jones and Peter B. Kenen, 63–130. Amsterdam: North-Holland, 1984.
Advanced treatment of many of the issues covered in this chapter.

Deardorff, Alan V. "Testing Trade Theories and Predicting Trade Flows." In *Handbook of International Economics,* Vol. 1, edited by Ronald W. Jones and Peter B. Kenen, 467–518. Amsterdam: North-Holland, 1984.
Advanced treatment of many of the issues that arise in empirically testing trade theories such as those covered in this chapter.

Ethier, Wilfred J. "Higher Dimensional Issues in Trade Theory." In *Handbook of International Economics,* Vol. 1, edited by Ronald W. Jones and Peter B. Kenen, 131–184. Amsterdam: North-Holland, 1984.
Advanced treatment of the models in this chapter extended to more than two goods, factors of production, and countries.

Heckscher, Eli. "The Effect of Foreign Trade on the Distribution of Income." *Ekonomisk Tidskrift* 21 (1919). Reprinted in American Economic Association, *Readings in the Theory of International Trade.* Philadelphia: Blakiston, 1949, Chap. 13.
The original statement of the Heckscher-Ohlin results.

Humphrey, Thomas M. "The Trade Theorist's Sacred Diagram: Its Origin and Early Development." Federal Reserve Bank of Richmond *Economic Quarterly* 74 (January-February 1988): 3–15.
The history of development of the production possibilities frontier/indifference curve diagram; intermediate.

Humphrey, Thomas M. "When Geometry Emerged: Some Neglected Early Contributions to Offer-Curve Analysis." Federal Reserve Bank of Richmond *Economic Quarterly* 81 (Spring 1995): 39–74.
History of the development of offer-curve analysis and its application to international trade.

Jones, Ronald W. "The Structure of Simple General Equilibrium Models." *Journal of Political Economy* 73 (December 1965): 557–572.
For advanced students, the classic mathematical presentation of the basic trade model.

Jones, Ronald W., and J. Peter Neary. "The Positive Theory of International Trade." In *Handbook of International Economics,* Vol. 1, edited by Ronald W. Jones and Peter B. Kenen, 1–62. Amsterdam: North-Holland, 1984.
Advanced treatment of much of the material contained in this chapter.

Leamer, Edward, and John Levinsohn. "International Trade Theory: The Evidence." In *Handbook of International Economics,* Vol. 3, edited by G. M. Grossman and Kenneth Rogoff. Amsterdam: North-Holland, 1995.
Advanced up-to-date survey of empirical evidence on international trade theories.

Ohlin, Bertil. *Interregional and International Trade.* Cambridge, Mass.: Harvard University Press, 1933.
Ohlin's elaboration of Heckscher's earlier work on the factor-proportions model.

Samuelson, Paul A. "The Gains from International Trade." *Canadian Journal of Economics and Political Science* 9 (1939): 195–205.
Early, readable demonstration of how international trade improves potential welfare.

Samuelson, Paul A. "The Gains from International Trade Once Again." *Economic Journal* 72 (1962): 820–829.
Update of the above paper.

Saxonhouse, Gary R. "What Does Japanese Trade Structure Tell Us About Trade Policy?" *Journal of Economic Perspectives* 7 (Summer 1993): 21–43.
Surveys empirical tests of how Japan's factor endowment affects the country's trade patterns; accessible to all students.

Chapter Three Appendix A

The Edgeworth Box

One of the inconveniences of attempting to understand the world economy as opposed to a single domestic economy is the need to keep track of so many things at once. Even with our simplifying assumption of only two countries and two industries, the analysis usually requires using at least two graphs simultaneously, such as those in Figure 3.6, representing events in country A and country B. Some tasks would be made easier if we could combine information about the two countries in a single graph. One convenient tool for accomplishing this is called an *Edgeworth box* (named after, but apparently not invented by, economist and mathematician Francis Edgeworth). Simply put, an Edgeworth box combines two two-axis diagrams (such as those for our two countries or for two industries within a single country) into a single, box-shaped diagram.

We begin by developing an Edgeworth box that combines information about two industries within a single country (the X and Y industries in country A), where each industry uses two inputs, labor (L) and capital (K). Each industry is characterized by a set of isoquants as illustrated in Figure 3A.1. The lengths of the axes in

Figure 3A.1 □ **Isoquant Maps for X and Y in Country A**

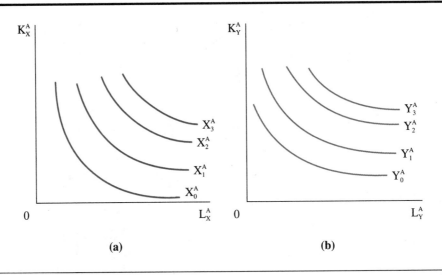

(a)   (b)

The country's resource endowment defines the length of each axis. L^A determines the lengths of the horizontal axes, and K^A the lengths of the vertical axes.

Figure 3A.2 □ Edgeworth Box for X and Y Production in Country A

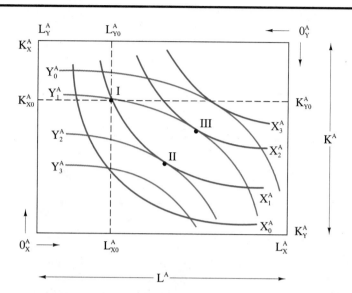

Each point in the box describes an allocation of the total available labor and capital between the X and Y industries. Industry X values are read from left to right and bottom to top from the 0_X^A origin. Industry Y values are read from right to left and top to bottom from the 0_Y^A origin.

Figure 3A.1 are defined by the quantity of labor and capital available in A; it is impossible to use more than L^A units of labor or more than K^A units of capital.

To form an Edgeworth box, we take the Y-industry diagram and rotate it 180 degrees so that the origin lies in its upper right-hand rather than lower left-hand corner. Next, we move the X-industry and Y-industry diagrams toward each other until the two just touch to form a box as in Figure 3A.2.

The horizontal dimension of the box measures the total quantity of labor available in A to be allocated between the X and Y industries. The vertical dimension captures the same information about the capital input. Each point in the box, then, represents an allocation of labor and capital between X production and Y production. For example, point I implies that L_{X0}^A units of labor are being used in the X industry and L_{Y0}^A units (read from right to left from the Y origin) in the Y industry. Similarly, point I involves allocating K_{X0}^A units of capital to the X industry and K_{Y0}^A to the Y industry.

Each point in or on the Edgeworth box represents a point inside or on country A's production possibilities frontier. The points lying *on* the production possibilities frontier can be distinguished by the fact that they are tangencies between the X-industry and Y-industry isoquants. This must be true because at any point in Figure 3A.2 that is not such a tangency, it is possible for country A to produce more of one good without producing less of the other. For example, from point I (a nontangency point), A can produce more good Y without reducing production of X by moving to point II (a tangency point) *or* produce

Figure 3A.3 □ **Country A's Production Possibilities Frontier**

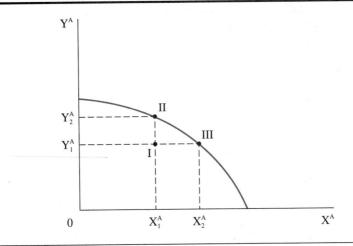

Points I, II, and III correspond to the matching points from Figure 3A.2. All points *on* the production possibilities frontier correspond to points of tangency between an X isoquant and a Y isoquant in the Edgeworth box. All points *inside* the production possibilities frontier correspond to nontangency points in the Edgeworth box, that is, to points from which it is possible to increase production of one good without decreasing production of the other.

more X without reducing production of Y by moving to point III (another tangency point). Points II and III, therefore, lie on country A's production possibilities frontier, while point I is an interior point as illustrated in Figure 3A.3.

We can also use the Edgeworth-box technique to consider the gains from specialization and exchange. Let $X^W = X^A + X^B$ represent the total world quantity of good X produced and $Y^W = Y^A + Y^B$ represent the total world quantity of good Y produced. These two quantities then can form the dimensions of a second type of Edgeworth box. By allowing more of one good to be produced without producing less of the other, productive specialization according to comparative advantage can increase the size of the box. Using the production possibilities frontiers from Chapter Three, Figure 3A.4 illustrates the increase in the size of the box due to productive specialization. Under autarky, $X^W = X^{A^*} + X^{B^*}$ and $Y^W = Y^{A^*} + Y^{B^*}$ from Figure 3.6, while with specialization according to comparative advantage, $X^W = X^A_p + X^B_p > X^{A^*} + X^{B^*}$ and $Y^W = Y^A_p + Y^B_p > Y^{A^*} + Y^{B^*}$ from Figure 3.8.

Once productive specialization has increased the quantity of goods available, residents of A exchange with residents of B according to their tastes for the two goods. In Figure 3A.5, tastes are represented by a set of community indifference curves for each country. Beginning at point p (for *production*), trade occurs along a line (whose slope measures the international terms of trade) to a point of tangency between two indifference curves, one for each country. From such a point (denoted c for *consumption*), it is impossible to move residents of one country onto a higher indifference curve without moving residents of the other onto a lower curve.

Figure 3A.4 □ **Edgeworth Box Showing Total World Production of Goods X and Y**

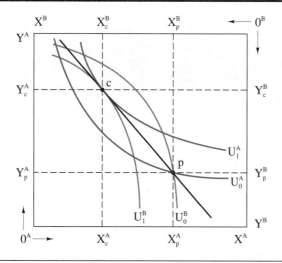

Production at the autarky production points (A* and B* from Figure 3.6) define the dimensions of the box in panel (a). The larger dimensions of the box in panel (b) reflect increased production brought about by productive specialization according to comparative advantage (as illustrated in Figure 3.8).

Figure 3A.5 □ **Edgeworth Box Depiction of Exchange between Countries A and B**

Beginning from the point of productive specialization (p), residents of both countries can make themselves better off through exchange. Trade occurs at the international terms of trade to consumption point c, where it becomes impossible to improve the welfare of residents of one country without reducing the welfare of residents of the other.

Chapter Three Appendix B

Offer Curves

Recall from section 3.3.2 that the equilibrium terms of trade between countries A and B must satisfy two conditions: (1) the terms of trade must lie between the two autarky price ratios, or $(P_X/P_Y)^A < (P_X/P_Y)^{tt} < (P_X/P_Y)^B$ if country A has a comparative advantage in production of X, and (2) the amount of a good one country wants to export at the terms of trade must equal the amount of the good the other country wants to import (that is, the markets must clear). Finding the equilibrium terms of trade in a production possibilities frontier/indifference curve graph like the one in Figure 3.8 is a matter of artistic trial and error. An alternate graphical technique, known as *offer curves* or *reciprocal demand curves,* has two advantages: Offer curves clearly show the equilibrium terms of trade, while allowing information about countries A and B to be presented in a single graph.

The term *offer curve* refers to the curve's illustration of the "offer" one country would make for trade with another at any given terms of trade—that is, country A's offer curve answers the question "At each relative price of goods X and Y, what quantities would A want to export and import?" Country B's offer curve presents the same information about the trade offers B would be willing to make. The other designation, *reciprocal demand curve,* refers to the curve's emphasis on the relationship between exports and imports; a country exports to receive imports in return, or reciprocally. For each relative price or terms of trade, an offer curve shows how much of its export good a country is willing to give up in exchange for a given amount of its import good. Therefore, an offer curve combines the information in an import demand curve *and* an export supply curve, or in an indifference curve map *and* a production possibilities frontier.

Offer curves are drawn in a two-dimensional space with the amount of good X traded measured on the horizontal axis and the amount of good Y traded measured on the vertical axis. Note that this differs slightly from most of the graphs we have used so far, which measure the *total* quantities of the two goods on the axes rather than the internationally *traded* quantities.

Figure 3B.1 illustrates the offer curves for countries A and B. The slope of any ray from the origin measures one possible relative price of good X or one possible value for the terms of trade. This is true because the slope of the ray is given by the line's rise (ΔY) divided by the run (ΔX), or how much good Y must be given up to obtain an additional unit of good X through exchange. Steeper rays represent relatively high prices for good X (and relatively low prices for good Y), while flatter rays represent relatively low prices for X (or relatively high prices for Y).

Figure 3B.1 ▫ **Offer Curves for Countries A and B**

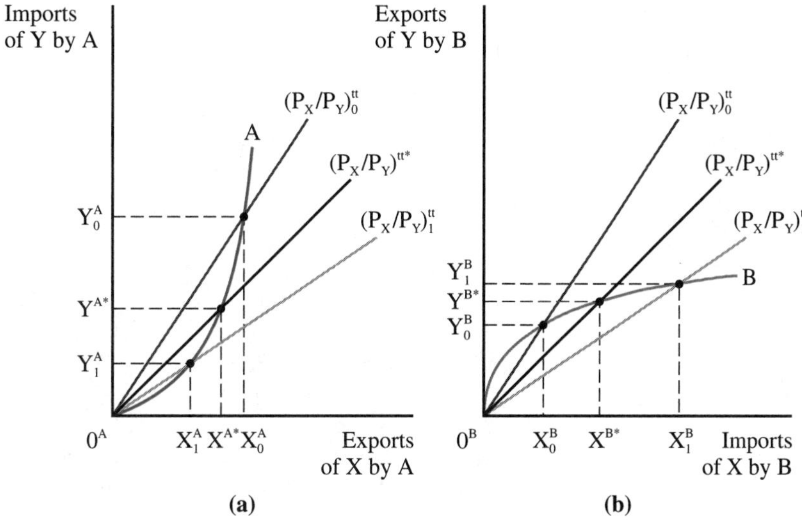

Each country's offer curve illustrates the quantities of the two goods it would want to export and import at different terms of trade, represented by the slopes of rays from the origin.

In panel (a) of Figure 3B.1, A's offer curve reflects A's willingness to export larger quantities of good X as the relative price of X rises. The rising relative price of X means that A is able to obtain more imported Y for each unit of exported X, making exporting more attractive. The curve also reveals A's willingness to import larger quantities of good Y as the relative price of Y falls. The falling price of Y (rising price of X) means Y is less costly in terms of the amount of X that must be exported in exchange. Each point on the curve gives A's desired exports and imports for the terms of trade given by a ray from the origin through that point.

Panel (b) of Figure 3B.1 depicts country B's offer curve. Given the assumption that B has a comparative advantage in good Y, B exports Y and imports X. A steep terms-of-trade line, then, implies country B's imports of X are expensive in terms of exported Y. As a result, the volume of trade in which B wants to engage is relatively small. Along a flatter terms-of-trade line, the price of B's export good is higher relative to the price of its import good, and B chooses to engage in a larger volume of trade.

The convenience of the offer-curve technique for finding the equilibrium terms of trade now is evident. Equilibrium occurs at the terms of trade for which A's desired exports of X just equal B's desired imports of X, and B's desired exports of Y just equal A's desired imports of Y. Obviously, the intersection of the two offer curves meets this condition; thus, $(P_X/P_Y)^{tt^*}$ represents the equilibrium at which the markets for goods X and Y clear.

Figure 3B.2 □ Equilibrium Terms of Trade

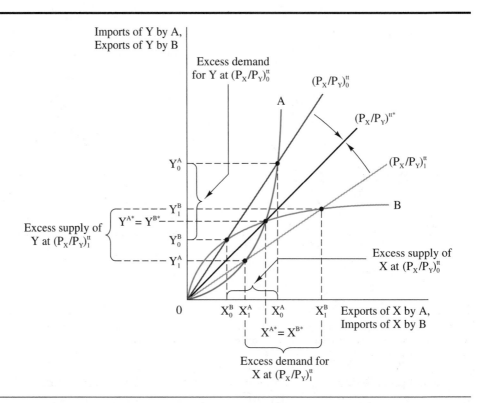

At the equilibrium terms of trade, $(P_X/P_Y)^{tt*}$, the quantity of good X country A wants to export equals the quantity country B wants to import, and the quantity of good Y country B wants to export equals the quantity A wants to import. At any other terms of trade, there is excess supply of one good and excess demand for the other.

Figure 3B.2 illustrates the adjustment that brings the terms of trade to equilibrium. If the relative price of good X is too high for market clearing, such as $(P_X/P_Y)^{tt}_0$, A will want to export more X than B will want to import while B will be willing to export less Y than A will want to import. The excess supply of good X and the excess demand for good Y will cause P_X/P_Y to fall toward equilibrium. On the other hand, if the relative price of good X is too low, such as $(P_X/P_Y)^{tt}_1$, B will want to import more X than A wants to export and A will want to import less Y than B wants to export. The excess demand for good X and the excess supply of good Y will cause P_X/P_Y to rise.

Finally, we note the graphical relationship between the offer-curve diagram and the production possibilities frontier/indifference curve diagram in Figure 3.8. Each point on an offer curve can be thought of as defining a trade triangle. Recall that the base and height of a trade triangle represent imports and exports of the two goods and that the slope of the third side of the triangle measures the terms of trade. Figure 3B.3 uses offer curves to depict the same trade triangles as in Figure 3.8.

Figure 3B.3 □ **Offer Curves and Trade Triangles**

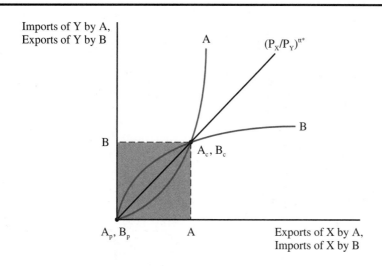

The origin of the offer-curve diagram corresponds to the two countries' production points, A_p and B_p. The intersection of the two offer curves corresponds to the consumption points, A_c and B_c. The slope of the line connecting the origin and the intersection represents the equilibrium terms of trade. The shaded rectangle combines the two countries' trade triangles from Figure 3.8.

CHAPTER FOUR

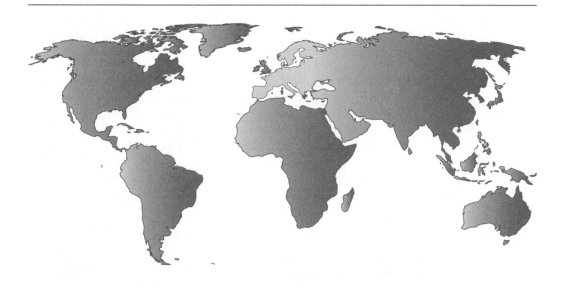

Trade, Distribution, and Welfare

4.1 Introduction

We now come to the heart of the theory of international trade. From the viewpoint of economic *theory,* we shall examine one of the areas in which international trade theory has made major contributions to other aspects of economics: general-equilibrium analysis. From the viewpoint of economic *policy,* we shall explore the primary reason for the controversy that surrounds the issue of free trade versus protection.

4.2 Partial- and General-Equilibrium Analysis

General-equilibrium analysis takes into account the interrelationships among various markets in the economy. **Partial-equilibrium analysis,** on the other hand, focuses on events in one or two markets and assumes that other markets remain unaffected. International economists pioneered the widespread use of general-equilibrium analysis, because the issues that arise in an international context often require looking at many markets at once, for example, both foreign and domestic markets or both input and output markets. A typical problem might involve analyzing the effect of unrestricted steel trade on U.S. employment in the automotive industry. Answering such a question requires general-equilibrium techniques.

However, the general- or partial-equilibrium character of any analysis is a matter of degree, since the two techniques lie on a continuum. At the extreme partial-equilibrium end of the spectrum would be an analysis of the effect of a Florida freeze on orange prices that ignored the impact on all other fruit markets and the effects of changes in growers' incomes. At the extreme general-equilibrium end of the spectrum would be a model of the world economy that included every good, every input, and every country and in which "everything depended on everything else." Of course, no such model exists, because it would prove intractable and, therefore, useless. Choosing a point between the extremes of partial- and general-equilibrium analysis is an art—and learning this art is part of becoming an economist. One of the most important skills for any economist to develop is the ability to pick tools and techniques appropriate for the problem at hand. Although partial-equilibrium techniques are important in all areas of economics, including international trade, a true understanding of many international issues requires mastery of some simple techniques of general-equilibrium analysis. In fact, we already have used such techniques to analyze events in the X and Y industries in countries A and B.

In Chapters Two and Three, we saw that the mechanism by which unrestricted trade produces a more efficient outcome than does autarky involves the reallocation of production such that relative output prices (which reflect opportunity costs) equalize in the two countries. This ensures production of each good in the country where its production requires forgoing less in terms of other goods; this is the essence of efficient production. So far, we have treated this change in relative output prices as the end of the story. However, if we move our analysis along the spectrum of techniques toward a more general-equilibrium theory, we must consider that changes in relative output prices will generate changes in other variables, particularly in the rewards or wages paid to the various factors of production. In other words, the relative price changes that occur when trade opens alter the distribution of income within each country. Any policy that alters the distribution of income will generate controversy, because individuals whose positions improve will support the policy and those harmed will oppose it.

4.3 Output Prices and Factor Prices: The Stolper-Samuelson Theorem

The changes in relative output prices that accompany the opening of trade follow from changes in the two goods' production levels in each country. Capturing the gains from trade requires productive specialization according to comparative advantage. Because production of each good involves using the two inputs in different proportions, changing the *output* combination alters relative demands for the two *inputs*.[1] This change in relative input demands causes changes in relative input prices and in the distribution of income. If production shifts from steel (a capital-intensive good) to textiles (a labor-intensive good), the demand for capital will fall and the demand for labor will rise. The pattern of factor rewards within the economy will reflect these shifts in demand; the price of capital will fall, and the wage rate will rise.

---

[1]For a review, see section 3.2.1, especially Figure 3.4.

Figure 4.1 □ **Effect of Opening Trade on Demand for Inputs in a Labor-Abundant Country**

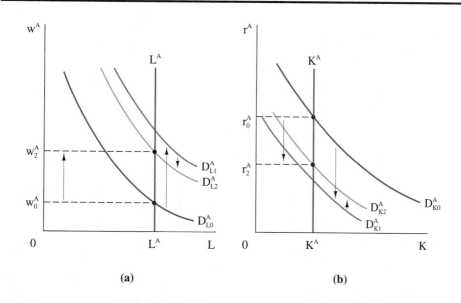

(a)   (b)

As production of the labor-intensive good increases, opening trade generates a net increase in demand for labor. The net effect on demand for capital is negative, because production of the capital-intensive good falls. With fixed factor endowments, the reward paid to the abundant factor rises and that paid to the scarce factor falls. The wage-rental ratio under unrestricted trade exceeds the ratio under autarky.

Under the assumptions of the Heckscher-Ohlin model, opening trade increases production of the good that uses the country's abundant factor intensively, which increases demand for that factor. Similarly, production of the good that uses the scarce factor intensively falls with the opening of trade, reducing demand for that factor. Remember that each country's endowment of each factor is fixed; thus, a vertical line represents the supply of each factor. Increased demand for the abundant factor bids up its price, and decreased demand for the scarce factor bids down its price.

As an example, assume country A is labor abundant and good X is the labor-intensive good. According to the Heckscher-Ohlin theorem, under unrestricted trade country A will specialize in producing good X. Because production of good X involves intensive use of labor, the demand for labor in A will rise. Of course, country A will, at the same time, decrease its production of good Y. *(Why?)* The falling production of Y will release some labor previously used in the Y industry; but because production of Y is capital intensive, the amount of labor released will be relatively small.

Panel (a) of Figure 4.1 shows these effects of trade on labor demand in country A. In autarky, D^A_{L0} gives the demand for labor. Once trade begins, increased production of good X increases demand to D^A_{L1}, and decreased production of good Y decreases demand to D^A_{L2}. The vertical supply curve, L^A, shows the country's fixed endowment of labor; so, trade raises the equilibrium wage or reward paid to labor from w_0^A to w_2^A.

The effects occurring simultaneously in the capital market in country A appear in panel (b) of Figure 4.1. In autarky, the production pattern results in a demand for capital given by D_{K0}^A and an equilibrium rental rate of r_0^A. When trade opens, country A reduces production of good Y, the capital-intensive good, causing demand to shift down to D_{K1}^A. Production of good X increases; but because X is labor intensive, this involves only a small increase in the demand for capital, to D_{K2}^A. The new equilibrium rental rate is r_2^A. Because the wage rate has risen and the rental rate has fallen, the new equilibrium wage-rental ratio, w_2^A/r_2^A, exceeds the ratio that prevailed in autarky, w_0^A/r_0^A. The output price changes that occur when trade restrictions are removed have redistributed income toward owners of labor, the abundant factor, and away from owners of capital, the scarce factor. These changes in relative factor prices must accompany any change in relative output prices.

In fact, we can make an even stronger statement about the relationship between output prices and factor prices: Each factor price changes in the same direction but *more than proportionally* with the price of the output that uses that factor intensively. For example, if the price of the labor-intensive good rises by 10 percent, the wage rate rises by more than 10 percent.[2] If the price of the capital-intensive good remains unchanged when the price of the labor-intensive good rises by 10 percent, the price of capital must fall. To see why, recall that under perfect competition the price of a good must equal the good's marginal cost, or the change in total cost from producing an additional unit. With two inputs, this requirement can be expressed as $P_X = a_{LX} \cdot w + a_{KX} \cdot r = MC_X$ for good X and $P_Y = a_{LY} \cdot w + a_{KY} \cdot r = MC_Y$ for good Y, because the cost of one unit of output equals the number of additional units of labor used times the wage rate plus the number of additional units of capital used times the rental rate. In other words, the price of a good can be written as a weighted sum of the input prices, where the weights are the input coefficients. The expression for P_Y reveals that if P_Y does not change when w rises (due to a rise in P_X), r must fall.[3]

This **magnification effect**—the fact that changes in output prices have a magnified effect on factor prices—carries important implications for evaluating the effects of international trade policy. Suppose labor-abundant country A opens trade. The price of good X rises while the price of good Y falls, and the wage rate rises while the rental rate falls. *(Why?)* Now suppose you are a worker in country A. You now earn a higher wage, but you also must pay a higher price for any good X you consume. Are you better off; that is, has the purchasing power of

---

[2]Similarly, if the price of the labor-intensive good falls by 10 percent, the wage rate falls by more than 10 percent.

[3]The result is easy to see if we make the simplifying assumption that the input coefficients do not change. Then we can take percentage rates of change of both sides of the price-equals-marginal-cost expressions, which gives $(a_{LX}/MC_X) \cdot \hat{w} + (a_{KX}/MC_X) \cdot \hat{r} = \hat{P}_X$ and $(a_{LY}/MC_Y) \cdot \hat{w} + (a_{KY}/MC_Y) \cdot \hat{r} = \hat{P}_Y$, where "hats" denote percentage rates of change in a variable. If $\hat{w} > \hat{P}_X > \hat{P}_Y = 0$, then $\hat{r}$ must be negative; the marginal cost of Y, which must equal P_Y, can remain unchanged when the wage rate rises only if the price of capital falls. This result continues to hold without the simplifying assumption of unchanging input coefficients; for demonstrations using more sophisticated techniques, see the Jones or Jones and Neary reference listed at the end of this chapter.

your wages risen? The magnification-effect analysis allows you to answer *yes* (even if you spend all your income on the now more expensive good X), because wages have risen proportionally more than the price of good X.

On the other hand, suppose you are a capital owner in country A. The rental rate earned on your capital has fallen, but so has the price you must pay for any good Y you consume. Are you better off or worse off in terms of your purchasing power? The magnification effect implies you are worse off (even if you spend all your income on the now cheaper good Y), because the rental rate earned on your capital has fallen proportionally more than the price of good Y.

In discussing the link between changes in output prices and changes in factor prices, we have loosely stated one of the basic theorems of international trade theory. This is called the **Stolper-Samuelson theorem** after Wolfgang Stolper and Paul Samuelson, who co-authored the 1941 paper that first demonstrated it. In its most general form the theorem states that, under the assumptions of our model, a change in the price of a *good* changes, in the same direction and more than proportionally, the price of the *factor* used intensively in the good's production. When the assumptions of the Heckscher-Ohlin model (which imply that a country has a comparative advantage in the good that uses the abundant factor intensively) are added, the Stolper-Samuelson theorem means that opening trade will increase the reward to the abundant factor and lower the reward to the scarce factor. This follows because trade raises production of the good of comparative advantage, increasing the good's opportunity cost and relative price. The Heckscher-Ohlin model defines comparative advantage in terms of intensive use of the abundant factor. Trade raises the price of the good that uses the abundant factor intensively, thereby raising the abundant factor's price.

The Stolper-Samuelson theorem clarifies one reason for the controversial nature of trade policy. Opening trade leads to output price changes that alter factor rewards, creating incentives for owners of the abundant input to support unrestricted trade and for owners of the scarce input to resist moves toward unrestricted trade. It is important to remember that the country as a whole is made potentially better off by trade; that is, owners of the abundant factor gain enough from open trade to allow them to compensate the losers and still be better off. However, such compensation, although theoretically possible, rarely occurs. Therefore, the Stolper-Samuelson theorem clearly pinpoints the existence of at least one constituency for protectionist policies or restrictions on trade. Later, when we discuss various types of protectionist measures and their effects, we also shall examine some policies that aim to eliminate this natural constituency for protection by redistributing the gains from trade.

The Stolper-Samuelson theorem highlights the relationship between *output prices* and *factor prices* within a single country. The next result to emerge from the basic trade model deals with the relationship between relative factor prices in the two countries.

4.4 Trade and Factor Prices: The Factor Price Equalization Theorem

It is easy to see that trade tends to equalize across countries the price of each good traded. But what about *factor* prices in various countries? If factors of production moved freely across national borders, we would expect factor prices to equalize across countries. Labor would flow from countries with low wages to those with high wages, thereby raising wages in the low-wage countries and lowering wages in the high-wage ones. Similarly, capital would flow from countries where it received a low reward to those where it received a high reward. But recall that we have assumed factors of production are *not* mobile among countries.[4] In Chapter One, we argued that restricted mobility of factors among countries constitutes one aspect of the economic significance of political boundaries.[5] While factors are not completely immobile, it is true that factors are much less mobile among countries than within. Some barriers, such as language or cultural barriers, are "natural," and policy makers impose others, including immigration restrictions and capital controls. Factor immobility implies that there is no obvious mechanism by which unrestricted trade in *outputs* can equalize *factor* prices across countries.

When trade begins, a country increases its output of the good in which it possesses a comparative advantage. According to Heckscher and Ohlin, production of this good involves intensive use of the country's abundant factor. Thus, moving from autarky to unrestricted trade raises the price of the abundant factor (which was relatively low in autarky due to the factor's abundance); similarly, such a move lowers the price of the scarce factor (which was high without trade due to scarcity). The same adjustment process occurs in the second country, but with the roles of the two factors reversed. *(Could the same factor be abundant in both countries? Why or why not?)* Trade raises the price of a factor in the country where the factor is abundant and lowers its price in the country where it is scarce. Thus, even when factors are immobile between the two countries, unrestricted trade in goods tends to equalize the relative price of each factor across countries. This is the idea behind the **factor price equalization theorem,** which Paul Samuelson first demonstrated in 1948.

There are a number of formal proofs of the factor price equalization theorem, some of them quite complex and sophisticated. For our purposes, we simply need to understand the basic logic and role of the theorem. The preceding discussion focused on the economy-wide adjustment that results in equalization of factor prices. We also can view the process of factor price equalization from the viewpoint of a firm's adjustment to trade.

As the world economy moves from autarky to unrestricted trade in outputs, each country increases production of the good that uses its abundant factor intensively. Suppose for a moment that production of each good in each country continued to involve use of capital and labor in the same proportions as in autarky. The different output combination produced under trade then would imply more total use of the abundant factor and less total use of the scarce factor in each country. But total usage of each factor in each country (adding the usages by the two industries, X and Y) always must equal the fixed endowment of the input. In other words, it must be true, both in autarky and with trade, that

[4]We shall relax this assumption in Chapter Ten.

[5]The degree of factor mobility is an important distinction between interregional and international trade, as discussed in section 9.5.1.

Figure 4.2 □ **Adjustment of Production Technology Required by the Opening of Trade**

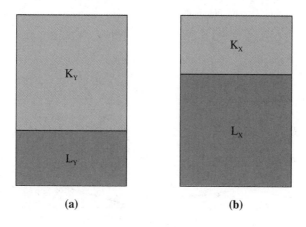

Reduced production of good Y releases inputs in the combination represented in panel (a). To increase production of good X using the same production techniques used in autarky would require inputs in the combination represented in panel (b). The result would be an excess supply of capital and excess demand for labor. Firms in both industries adjust by becoming more capital intensive.

$$L^A = L_X^A + L_Y^A,$$

$$K^A = K_X^A + K_Y^A,$$

$$L^B = L_X^B + L_Y^B,$$

$$K^B = K_X^B + K_Y^B.$$

[4.1]

Therefore, a country cannot produce a *different* combination of the two outputs while continuing to use the *same* production techniques (that is, capital-labor ratios) as before.[6]

Consider the case in which labor-abundant country A opens trade and wants to specialize in producing labor-intensive good X. To increase production of X, country A must decrease production of good Y. This releases a package of inputs composed of capital and labor in the proportion being used in the Y industry. The box in panel (a) of Figure 4.2 illustrates this package of inputs; it includes a relatively large amount of capital and a small amount of labor, because Y is the capital-intensive good. Panel (b) of Figure 4.2 shows the resources needed to produce an additional unit of good X using current production techniques; it includes a relatively large quantity of labor and a small amount of capital. This scenario implies that opening

----

[6]This result can be demonstrated by algebraic manipulation of Equation 4.1; see the Jones reference at the end of this chapter.

Figure 4.3 □ Changes in Capital-Labor Ratios Required to Change Output Mix

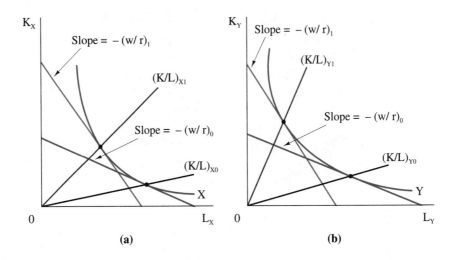

To increase production of the labor-intensive good (X), firms in both industries must increase their capital-labor ratios. The rise in the wage-rental ratio from $(w/r)_0$ to $(w/r)_1$ brings about this adjustment.

trade causes an excess supply of capital as firms in the Y industry release more capital than X firms want to hire. There also is an excess demand for labor as Y firms release less labor than X firms want to hire.

Something must happen to cause the firms to adjust their production techniques. What occurs is a change in the relative prices of the two factors. Capital becomes relatively cheaper, causing Y firms to release less of it and X firms to hire more of it. Labor becomes relatively more expensive, causing Y firms to release more of it and X firms to hire less.

The isoquant diagram of Figure 4.3 illustrates the changes in firms' cost-minimizing production techniques. Recall that firms in each industry choose their capital-labor ratios by equating the marginal rate of technical substitution (given by the slope of the isoquant) to the ratio of the factor prices (given by the slope of the isocost line).[7] A rise in w/r from $(w/r)_0$ to $(w/r)_1$ can be represented as a clockwise rotation of the isocost line, or an increase in (the absolute value of) its slope. Firms respond by using a *higher* capital-labor ratio, $(K/L)_{X1}$ rather than $(K/L)_{X0}$. This adjustment occurs in both industries.

Why would the labor-abundant country need to use a higher capital-labor ratio in production of both goods? When the country engages in trade, it specializes its

---

[7]For a review, see section 3.2.1.

production according to comparative advantage. This means specializing in production of the good that uses the abundant factor intensively—but the country has available only a fixed quantity of that factor. To produce more of the good that uses the abundant factor intensively, production of each unit of both goods must use less of that factor than before so there will be enough of it to go around. The factor price changes predicted by the factor price equalization theorem provide the firm an incentive to undertake the necessary changes in production techniques.

4.4.1 An Alternate View of Factor Price Equalization

Economists initially found the factor price equalization theorem a very surprising result—that is, that trade in outputs could equalize factor prices even when factors were completely immobile among countries. Robert Mundell provided an intuitive and insightful explanation. According to Mundell, trade in outputs serves as a substitute for trade in factors of production. For example, when a labor-abundant country exports a unit of a labor-intensive good, it indirectly exports labor to a labor-scarce country. Similarly, when a labor-abundant country imports a capital-intensive good, it indirectly imports capital from a capital-abundant country. Mundell went even further by "turning the model on its head" and showing that if factors of production were freely traded and outputs immobile among countries, rather than vice versa, trade still would equalize output prices. Unrestricted trade in either output or input markets can serve as a substitute for trade in the other markets.

4.4.2 The Nonobservability of Factor Price Equalization

We never observe full factor price equalization; it is important to understand why.[8] Figure 4.4 reports one measure of hourly wages for eleven countries. Wages differ by a factor of 21; that is, those in the highest-wage country (Germany) are 21 times as high as those in the lowest-wage country (Poland). A reasonable question about the factor price equalization theorem would be: Why are factor prices, as observed in the real world, not equalized? There are several reasons why full factor price equalization never has been observed.

First, we must note that much of the apparent inequality of income and wealth across countries comes from uneven ownership of human and nonhuman capital. The Neoclassical model assumes all labor is homogeneous. However, labor actually differs substantially across countries in terms of skill, training, education, nutrition, and a variety of other attributes. Wage differences reflect these variations; we would not expect a nuclear physicist with 20 years' experience in Germany to earn the same wage as an unskilled laborer entering the work force for the first time in Poland. Also, most individuals in developed countries earn part of their incomes from ownership of capital in addition to what they earn by selling their labor services.

Second, we have assumed each good is produced using the same production technology in all countries. When a new and better technology is developed for production of a good, it does tend to spread and replace older, less effective technologies; but

---

[8]The Leamer and Levinsohn and the Rassekh and Thompson articles in the chapter references survey the empirical literature on factor price equalization.

Figure 4.4 □ **Hourly Pay in Manufacturing (1990 U.S. = 100)**

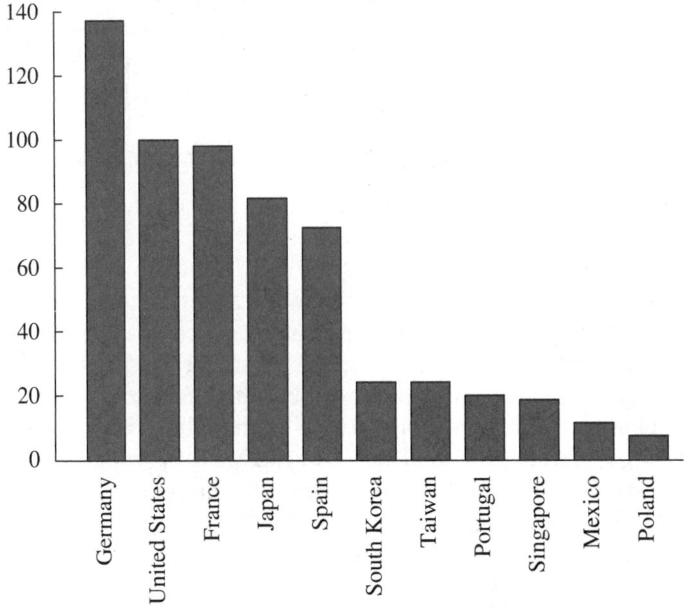

Source: *The Economist*, September 21, 1991, p. 28; data from Olivier Blanchard, Rudiger Dornbusch, et al., *Reform in Eastern Europe*.

the process can be slow, particularly between developed and developing countries. When two countries produce a good using different technologies, the rewards paid to the factors of production will not equalize across countries, even in the presence of trade, although the rewards will tend to move closer together than without trade.

Both differences in ownership of human capital and differences in technology cause factor productivity to vary across countries. Under such circumstances, we would not expect actual factor prices to equalize, but rather factor prices *corrected for productivity differences* to equalize. For example, we would expect countries with labor productivity higher than that of the United States to exhibit wages higher than those in the United States and vice versa. Figure 4.5 presents one test of this relationship. The horizontal axis in panel (a) measures labor productivity relative to that in the United States, and the vertical axis measures the wage rate compared to that in the United States. The data points for 30 countries, representing a wide sample of developed and developing countries cluster around a 45-degree line, just as we would expect. Panel (b) presents the corresponding information for capital.

Figure 4.5 □ **Relative Factor Productivity and Factor Prices**

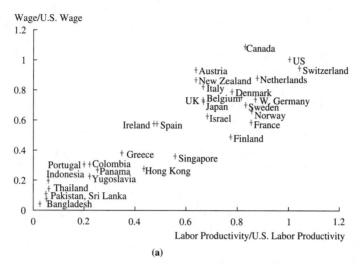

(a)

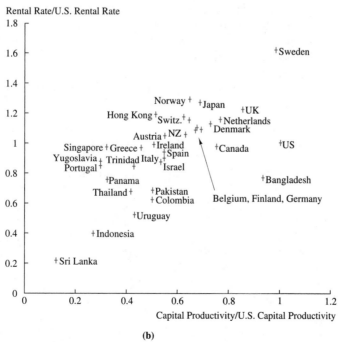

(b)

Relative factor price differences across countries match relative productivity differences.

Source: Data from Daniel Trefler, "International Factor Price Differences: Leontief Was Right!" *Journal of Political Economy* 101 (1993), p. 972.

Third, remember that factor price equalization follows from output price equalization. But, complete output price equalization sometimes does not occur, for reasons including transportation costs, policy barriers to trade, and the existence of goods (for example, haircuts or health care) that rarely are traded.

Despite these problems, the factor price equalization theorem is useful in understanding the effects of trade liberalization. From a theoretical point of view, the theorem highlights the general-equilibrium character of the model and the importance of a rigorous formulation to derive all the implications from a model of the world economy. From a policy point of view, the theorem points out that trade in outputs and trade in inputs are substitutes in terms of their effects on the world economy. Consider the case of an extremely labor-abundant country. In autarky, wages would tend to be very low. Policy makers might be tempted to prescribe policies such as forced emigration to reduce the quantity of labor and raise wages; but the costs of mobility for some factors of production, especially labor, are very high in both economic and psychological terms. The factor price equalization theorem suggests an important policy alternative: Allow free trade in outputs, specialize in labor-intensive production, and export labor indirectly in the form of labor-intensive goods.

Countries including Ireland, the Philippines, India, Jamaica, and Singapore have begun using new technologies to do just that. With new international computer and telecommunication networks, labor-abundant countries such as those mentioned can perform labor-intensive data-processing tasks for foreign firms. Entering data into computers for new databases, creating telephone directories, maintaining computer files for magazine subscriptions, processing computer records for large health-insurance companies, and large-scale telephone operations are just a few of the jobs, not all of which are low-skill occupations. For example, if you call the technical-support line at Quarterdeck Office Systems, Inc., a Santa Monica, California computer software company, the technician answering your questions may be in Dublin, Ireland.[9]

4.5   Short-Run Immobility and Trade: Specific Factors[10]

The Stolper-Samuelson and factor price equalization theorems summarize the effects of opening trade on relative factor prices under the assumption that factors are completely mobile among industries within a country and completely immobile among countries. In the short run, however, the mobility of factors among industries may be imperfect. When factors cannot move easily and quickly among industries, the short-run effects of opening trade differ from the long-run effects captured by the Stolper-Samuelson and factor price equalization theorems.

---

[9]For more examples, see Lawrence MacDonald, "Software Concerns Thrive in Philippines," *The Wall Street Journal,* May 10, 1991; and Bernard Wysocki, "American Firms Send Office Work Abroad to Us Cheaper Labor," *The Wall Street Journal,* August 14, 1991, A1.

[10]Paul Samuelson, "Ohlin Was Right," *Swedish Journal of Economics* 73 (1971), 365–384; and Ronald W. Jones, "A Three-Factor Model in Theory, Trade, and History," in *Trade, Balance of Payments, and Growth,* eds., Jagdish Bhagwati, et al., (Amsterdam: North-Holland, 1971), 3–21, developed the specific-factors model. The historical development of and increased recent interest in the model is discussed in the Jones and Neary reading cited at the end of the chapter.

Table 4.1 □ **Composition of Selected Countries' Capital Stocks**

	Percentage of Net Capital Stock				
Item	United States (1978)	Germany (1977)	Mexico (1978)	India (1975)	Hungary (1977)
Land	23	25	19	35	27
Housing	23	24	25	18	13
Other structures	24	27	25	16	24
Machinery and equipment	12	11	17	12	12
Inventories	9	5	8	9	13
Consumer durables	9	8	5	7	9
Livestock	0	0	2	3	1

Source: World Bank, *World Development Report* 1989, p. 97; data from R. W. Goldsmith, *Comparative National Balance Sheets: A Study of Twenty Countries, 1688–1978* (Chicago: University of Chicago Press, 1985).

4.5.1 Reasons for Short-Run Factor Immobility

Mobility of factors among industries may be less than perfect for several reasons. In the case of physical capital such as machines and factories, the causes of limited mobility are clear. A machine designed to manufacture shoes cannot suddenly accommodate the manufacture of computers. At any moment, a significant share of a country's capital stock takes the form of specialized equipment—equipment suited only for the specific purpose for which it was designed.

How, then, does the nature of the capital stock change over time to reflect the rising and falling fortunes of various industries? As machines, buildings, and other types of physical capital wear out from use and age, firms set aside funds to replace the equipment when the time comes. These funds are called **depreciation allowances** and comprise a form of saving by firms. Just as an individual might save to have funds to buy a new car when the old one wears out, a firm saves to accumulate funds for replacement of worn-out capital equipment. Although a particular piece of capital equipment often cannot become suited for use in a different production process, depreciation funds can be used to buy a different type of capital. In other words, as the economy's capital equipment wears out and is replaced, firms can change the character of the capital stock in response to changes in relative demands for and supplies of various goods. If the relative price of shoes falls, some of the machines used in shoe production will not be replaced when they wear out. On the other hand, if the relative price of computers rises, firms will not only replace machines worn out in computer production but will invest in additional computer-producing equipment as well.

Calculating the value and composition of a country's capital stock is very difficult and complex; however, economists have attempted estimates. Table 4.1 reports the percentages of several countries' capital stocks composed of various capital categories.

The above arguments for the capital stock also apply, with appropriate modifications, to the country's workforce. Individuals learn certain skills suited for use in specific occupations. Some general skills, of course, apply in a wide range of industries; oral and written communication skills, good interpersonal skills, and desirable work habits such as punctuality prove useful in almost any job. Other skills are more specific. A welder cannot become a mathematics professor overnight in response to a decline in the construction industry and a boom in education. Similarly, a mathematics professor cannot suddenly become a welder in response to the opposite trend. A given individual can learn new skills, but the process takes time. As older workers retire and new ones enter the labor force, the skill distribution across the labor force slowly changes in favor of growing industries and away from shrinking ones. This captures the labor-force version of the depreciation of the capital stock.

In the long run, the process of depreciation, retraining, and replacement allows both capital and labor to flow from declining to rising industries. Such mobility may be limited in the short run. The more specialized the capital equipment and skills and the slower the rate of depreciation in a given industry, the more slowly that industry will adjust to change.

4.5.2 Effects of Short-Run Factor Immobility

Suppose country A produces *s*hoes (s) and *c*omputers (c) using labor and capital. Labor is perfectly mobile between the shoe and computer industries, but capital is industry specific. Shoe capital (SK) cannot produce computers, and computer capital (CK) cannot produce shoes. As a result, the wage paid to labor will be equal in the two industries, but the rental rates paid to the two types of capital may differ. *(Why?)*

Figure 4.6 illustrates equilibrium in country A's factor markets. In panel (a), the length of the horizontal axis $(0_s 0_c)$ measures the total quantity of labor available in country A, or L^A. The two vertical axes measure the wage paid to labor in the two industries (w_s on the left axis and w_c on the right). We measure labor used in the shoe industry from left to right from the shoe origin (0_s), and labor used in the computer industry from right to left from the computer origin (0_c). Any point along the horizontal axis represents an allocation of the available labor between the two industries.

The curves VMP_{s0}^L and VMP_{c0}^L represent the *v*alue of the *m*arginal *p*roduct of labor in the two industries, respectively. The value of the marginal product of labor equals the increase in revenue to a firm that hires an additional unit of labor, or marginal product of labor (the number of units of additional output produced when one additional unit of labor is employed) multiplied by the price of the good produced, $VMP^L \equiv MP^L \cdot P$. As the quantity of labor employed in an industry rises, the marginal productivity of labor falls and with it the value of the marginal product of labor; therefore, the VMP curves slope downward when viewed from their respective axes.[11] Because the labor market is assumed to be perfectly competitive,

---

[11]The marginal product of labor falls as the firm uses more and more labor because the marginal product of a factor is defined as the change in output resulting from a one-unit change in use of that factor *with the quantities of all other factors held constant*. As more and more labor is combined with a fixed amount of capital, additional workers become less and less productive *(think of a simple example)*; hence, the marginal product of labor declines.

Figure 4.6 □ **Effect on Factor Markets of an Increase in an Output Price with a Specific Factor**

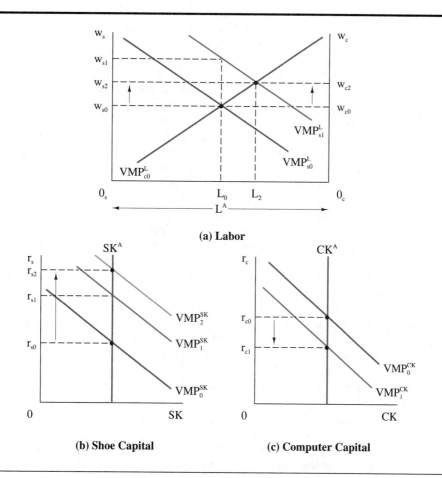

(a) Labor

(b) Shoe Capital

(c) Computer Capital

An increase in the price of shoes raises the wage rate in both industries, but by less than the rise in the price of shoes. The return to capital specific to the shoe industry rises more than proportionally with the price of shoes, and the return to capital specific to the computer industry falls.

labor earns a wage in each industry equal to the value of the productivity of the marginal unit of labor in that industry. In the figure, 0_sL_0 workers work in the shoe industry and 0_cL_0 workers in the computer industry, equalizing wages at $w_{s0} = w_{c0}$. *(Explain why mobility of labor between industries ensures this division of labor between the industries. What would happen if $w_s > w_c$ or vice versa?)*

Panels (b) and (c) of Figure 4.6 illustrate equilibrium in the markets for shoe capital and for computer capital. Country A's endowments of the two inputs are fixed at SK^A and CK^A, respectively, so the supply curve of each is just a vertical line. The demand for each type of capital reflects the value of its marginal product, or the additional revenue to a firm hiring an additional unit of the capital. Because the marginal product of each type of capital falls as more is used, the VMP curves slope downward. Each type of capital earns the rental rate at which the quantity available equals the quantity firms want to hire; so the equilibrium rental rates are r_{s0} and r_{c0}.

What happens if the price of shoes (P_s) rises? The value of the marginal product of labor in the shoe industry rises proportionally with P_s, since $VMP_s^L \equiv MP_s^L \cdot P_s$. The VMP_s^L curve in panel (a) shifts upward. At the initial allocation of labor between the two industries (L_0), $w_{s1} > w_{c0}$, causing workers to move from the computer industry to the shoe industry until wages again equalize at $w_{s2} = w_{c2}$, with L_2 representing the new allocation of labor between industries.

Notice that wages rise *less* than proportionally with the price of shoes (reflected in Figure 4.6 by the fact that $w_{s2} < w_{s1}$); the magnification effect does *not* apply to the mobile factor when one of the factors is immobile between industries. The rise in the price of shoes exerts an ambiguous effect on workers' purchasing power. Wages rise, but by less than the price of shoes. If a worker spent most of his or her income on shoes, the worker's purchasing power would fall; but a worker who spent most of his or her income on computers (whose price is unchanged) would enjoy an increase in purchasing power.

Even though capital cannot move between industries, the change in the price of shoes still affects capital markets. The marginal product of any factor of production depends positively on the quantity of other factors with which the factor works. As labor moves into the shoe industry, shoe capital has more labor to work with and the marginal product of shoe capital rises, shifting the $VMP^{SK} \equiv MP^{SK} \cdot P_s$ line up to VMP_1^{SK}. The exodus of labor from the computer industry, on the other hand, reduces the marginal product of computer capital and shifts $VMP^{CK} \equiv MP^{CK} \cdot P_c$ down to VMP_1^{CK}. The rise in the price of shoes also causes a proportional shift up in $VMP^{SK} \equiv MP^{SK} \cdot P_s$ to VMP_2^{SK}. The net result is that the rental rate earned by shoe capital rises more than proportionally with the price of shoes, while the rental rate earned by computer capital falls. The rise in the price of shoes improves the purchasing power of owners of shoe capital, even if they spend most of their incomes on now more expensive shoes, and reduces the purchasing power of owners of computer capital, even if they spend most of their incomes on computers, whose price has not changed. Therefore, the magnification effect *does* hold for the immobile factor. Table 4.2 summarizes these results.

4.5.3 Trade with an Industry-Specific Factor

Short-run immobility of factors among industries implies that the short-run effects of opening trade on the distribution of income differ from the predictions of the Stolper-Samuelson theorem. To highlight the importance of the degree of mobility in determining the effects on income, we shall continue to consider the case in which labor is highly mobile among industries but capital is immobile in the short run. Suppose a country with a comparative disadvantage in labor-intensive shoe production and a comparative advantage in capital-intensive computer production opens trade. Shoe production falls and computer production rises as the country specializes its production according to comparative advantage.

If both labor and capital were perfectly mobile between the two industries, newly unemployed workers from the shoe industry would flow into the computer industry, and the

---

Table 4.2 □ Effect of a Rise in the Price of Shoes on Factor Prices When Capital Is Immobile

---

The wage rate rises in both industries, but by less than the price of shoes. The effect on workers' purchasing power depends on the shares of shoes and computers in workers' consumption. The return to shoe capital rises more than the price of shoes, so owners of shoe capital enjoy an increase in buying power regardless of their pattern of consumption. The return to computer capital falls, so owners of computer capital suffer a loss of purchasing power regardless of their pattern of consumption.

Effect on	
w_s	+
Purchasing power of w_s	?[a]
w_c	+
Purchasing power of w_c	?[a]
r_s	+
Purchasing power of r_s	+[b]
r_c	−
Purchasing power of r_c	−[b]

[a]No magnification effect.
[b]Magnification effect.

---

computer industry would buy unused capital from the shoe industry. Given our assumption of mobile labor and immobile capital, workers do flow from the shoe to the computer industry, but the machines used in producing shoes are useless in making computers.

What happens to wages and to the rates of return earned by capital? First, note that the price of shoes falls and the price of computers rises as the production pattern shifts. The price of shoes falls as more efficiently produced imports replace relatively inefficient domestic production. The price of computers rises with the level of production, a reflection of increasing costs. The net effect on wages depends on the magnitudes of the rise in P_c and the fall in P_s. *(How could you illustrate this in Figure 4.6? What would happen to VMP_s^L and VMP_c^L?)* Regardless of whether wages rise or fall, the effect on workers' purchasing power depends on the combination of goods they consume. If a worker spends a large share of income on shoes (whose price has fallen) and a small share on computers (whose price has risen), he or she definitely will enjoy an increase in purchasing power, or ability to buy goods. Another worker will be worse off if he or she buys no shoes but does buy a new computer, because the price of computers rises by a greater proportion than do wages. *(Why?)*[12]

---

[12]An increase in the price of a good causes wages to rise less than proportionally with the good's price in the presence of immobile capital, as demonstrated in section 4.5.2. Here the addition of a decline in the price of the second good causes wages to rise even less. If the decline in the price of shoes more than offsets the rise in the price of computers, wages may fall; but the effect on labor's purchasing power will remain ambiguous.

Table 4.3 □ **Short- and Long-Run Effects of Opening Trade on Factor Prices and Purchasing Power**

The country has a comparative advantage in production of computers. In the short run, capital employed in the computer industry and workers who buy more shoes than computers gain from the opening of trade. In the long run, owners of capital, the factor used intensively in computer production, gain from the opening of trade.

	Effect of Trade in	
	Short Run	Long Run
w_s	?	−
Purchasing power of w_s	?[a]	−[b]
w_c	?	−
Purchasing power of w_c	?[a]	−[b]
r_s	−	+
Purchasing power of r_s	−[b]	+[b]
r_c	+	+
Purchasing power of r_c	+[b]	+[b]

[a]No magnification effect.
[b]Magnification effect.

    The effect on the return to capital is clearer. Owners of capital designed to produce shoes are definitely worse off, since the rate of return to shoe-specific capital falls, and by more than the price of shoes. Owners of capital designed to produce computers definitely are better off, because the return to computer-specific capital rises, and by more than the price of computers. In the short run, therefore, the factor owner's consumption pattern and the industry that employs the factor determine the effect on the factor's reward. Only in the long run, when all factors can move among industries, does a factor's relative scarcity or abundance determine the impact of opening trade.
    Table 4.3 illustrates the distinction between short-run and long-run effects on factor prices in terms of the shoe-computer example. In the short run, the returns to capital employed in the expanding computer industry rise. This creates an incentive for investment in capital designed for production of computers. The other side of the adjustment process is a fall in the returns to capital specifically employed in the shoe industry, creating incentives not to replace that capital as it wears out. Again wages may rise or fall, but the effect on workers' purchasing power will depend on whether workers buy primarily (now cheaper) shoes or (now more expensive) computers.
    In the long run, both workers and capital can move between industries. Wages fall throughout the economy, because the expanding computer industry is less labor intensive than the contracting shoe industry. The return to all capital in the economy rises as the economy specializes in production of the capital-intensive good, computers. These long-run results coincide with the predictions of the Stolper-Samuelson theorem.

The existence of factors specific to single industries creates a short-run rigidity, or limitation on the economy's ability to reallocate production among industries quickly and at low cost. The more industry-specific the factors of production, the more costly will be any adjustment to relative price changes in terms of temporary unemployment or underutilization of capital. These short-term costs of adjustment cause a number of policy problems as individuals attempt to insulate themselves from the effects of unfavorable price changes.

Whenever relative prices change and some industries decline, pressure for protection builds from resources tied to those industries. However, interference with relative price changes and the resulting factor price changes can be dangerous to the health of the economy as a whole. As we argued in the shoe-computer example, the temporary fall in the rewards to capital in the shoe industry and the rise in the rewards to capital in the computer industry create the incentives needed for the economy to adjust to trade by specializing according to comparative advantage. Trade, in turn, can improve potential welfare by increasing the total quantity of goods and services available for consumption.

4.6 General-Equilibrium Empirical Models

At the beginning of this chapter, we mentioned the importance of choosing the appropriate technique along the partial- to general-equilibrium continuum when building a theoretical model of international trade. The same issue arises in empirical work aimed at measuring the effects of trade policies. Until recently, virtually all empirical work used partial-equilibrium techniques. Improvements in computer technology are changing that. Many international economists now use **computable general-equilibrium (CGE) models.** Although the models themselves are complex, the logic underlying their use is quite straightforward.

There are four basic steps in building and using a CGE model to study trade policy. The first step involves gathering as much consistent data as possible on world production, consumption, imports, exports, prices, and so forth. The results from the model can be no better than the quality of the data, so this first step is time-consuming and important. In the second step, the model builder uses trade theory (for example, the material covered here in Chapters Two through Four) to construct the model's structure in the form of a set of equations. Third, the economist must set the values of the equations' parameters. This process, called *calibrating the model,* happens in one of two ways. For some parameters, such as elasticities of demand, existing economic literature usually provides estimates that can be used. For parameters with no existing estimates, one chooses values that allow the model to reproduce the actual outcome for a given year. For example, we might know how much steel the United States produced in our base year, but not know the elasticity of supply for steel. In such a case, we would choose a value for the supply elasticity that, when plugged into the model with all the other parameter estimates, would predict the actual base-year level of production. Finally, once the model is calibrated, we can change the value of any variable in the model and observe the effects of the change on all the other variables.

CGE models represent a major advance in economists' ability to study the actual empirical effects of international trade policy.[13] Unfortunately, data limitations still present a big hurdle. International comparability of data is notoriously lacking; and some analysts claim that the calibration process in CGE models introduces too much guesswork to produce reliable estimates.

4.7   Trade and Welfare: Gainers, Losers, and Compensation

The Stolper-Samuelson theorem and the specific-factors model can explain why various groups in the economy may feel quite differently about unrestricted trade. Under the assumptions of the Heckscher-Ohlin theorem, a country indirectly "exports" its abundant factor through trade, thereby increasing demand for that factor and raising its price. Likewise, the country indirectly "imports" its scarce factor, decreasing demand and lowering the factor's relative price. In the short run, when some factors are industry specific, the rewards to factors employed specifically in the comparative-advantage industry rise and the rewards to factors employed specifically in the comparative-disadvantage industry fall. But, in Chapter Three we demonstrated that opening trade increases the total quantity of goods available and makes it possible for everyone to gain. In order for everyone to gain—despite the change in relative factor rewards implied by the Stolper-Samuelson theorem and the specific-factors model—a portion of the gains enjoyed by some would have to be used to compensate others for their losses. If this were done, every person, and therefore society as a whole, could be made better off by trade. In general, however, no automatic mechanism to make this compensatory redistribution exists.

These questions of income distribution and the differential impacts of trade on various groups within a country did not arise in the Ricardian or constant-cost model of Chapter Two. The reason is that the Ricardian model contained only one input, which we called *labor*. In each country, opening trade raised the relative price of the output that the country's labor produced relatively efficiently. Wages rose, and everyone was made better off. In reality, however, things are not so simple.[14] Policy makers usually must deal with hard questions involving evaluation of policies that make some groups better off and others worse off.

4.7.1   Potential and Actual Utility

In Chapters Two and Three, we carefully demonstrated that unrestricted international trade increases the quantity of goods that the world's endowment of scarce resources can produce. With more goods available for consumption, we can see a potential increase in world welfare or utility. Figure 4.7 illustrates this potential increase.[15]

---

[13]The Deardorff and Stern reference at the end of the chapter provides one example.

[14]The result from the Ricardian model carries over to the case of two inputs only if both industries use those inputs in the same proportions. (*Why would the adjustment of production techniques illustrated in Figure 4.3 be unnecessary in this special case?*)

[15]For a review of the basics of indifference curves and some hints at the distributional problems involved in using community indifference curves, see section 2.5.2. The distributional issues central to the analysis of community indifference curves do not arise in the case of individual indifference curves because all goods belong to the individual whose indifference map is being analyzed.

Figure 4.7 □ **Increase in Potential Welfare from Trade**

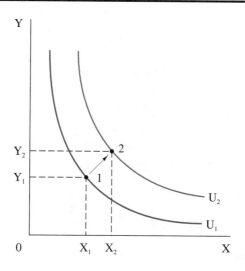

Trade allows production of larger quantities of goods, making a higher indifference curve attainable.

Why must we speak of a *potential* increase in world welfare or utility? We cannot say that a move from point 1 (representing autarky) to point 2 (representing unrestricted trade) in Figure 4.7 increases *actual* utility. After all, we know nothing about the distribution of the goods at either point. At point 1, society produces X_1 units of good X and Y_1 units of good Y. One individual may own all the X and all the Y while everyone else has nothing, or the X and Y may be evenly distributed among all individuals. The same holds true at point 2: There are X_2 units of X and Y_2 units of Y available, but we do not know how these goods are distributed. That point 2 lies on a higher indifference curve than point 1 merely implies that moving from 1 to 2 has the *potential* to make every individual better off (for example, if the additional goods were distributed among all individuals).

4.7.2 Comparing Utility: The Pareto Criterion

Suppose that in moving from point 1 to point 2 in Figure 4.7, the additional goods ($[X_2 - X_1]$ units of X and $[Y_2 - Y_1]$ units of Y) were distributed such that every person ended up with more of each good. In such a case, we could say that the move from point 1 to 2 increased actual world welfare or utility according to one possible criterion for judging the effects of a change on welfare. The **Pareto criterion** (named after economist Vilfredo Pareto) says that any change that makes at least one person better off *without* making any individual worse off produces an increase in welfare. The example in which increased production was distributed among all residents clearly satisfies this requirement.

The Pareto criterion is a useful concept for assessing the welfare effects of various economic policies. Unfortunately, it sidesteps the really tough policy questions. In Chapter One, we suggested that policy makers rarely are lucky enough to evaluate policies that either benefit everyone or harm everyone. Decisions on such policies are relatively easy; both common sense and the Pareto criterion recommend pursuing the former class of policies and avoiding the latter class. Far more common are policy questions that involve benefits to some individuals and costs to others. In these cases, neither common sense nor the Pareto criterion provides much assistance.

4.7.3 Comparing Utility: The Compensation Criterion

Clearly the Pareto criterion cannot answer some questions that arise in evaluating the effect on world welfare of opening international trade. The changes in relative factor prices predicted by the Stolper-Samuelson and factor price equalization theorems and by the specific-factors model imply that opening trade will harm some groups. In the short run, these groups include owners of any specific inputs employed in production of the country's comparative-disadvantage good. In the long run, the losers include owners of the factor that the country uses intensively in producing the comparative-disadvantage good.

Several economists have suggested ways to evaluate the welfare effects of policies that benefit some individuals and harm others, thereby circumventing the inherent boundaries of the issues the Pareto criterion can address. The specific proposals vary; however, a simple idea underlies each. The key question is whether the gainers from a policy gain enough to allow them to compensate the losers for their losses and still enjoy a net gain.

The opening of international trade satisfies the **compensation criterion** for a welfare improvement. Because the world economy can produce more goods with trade, gainers can, in principle, compensate losers and still be better off. The remaining problems arise because such compensation, though possible, rarely occurs.

4.7.4 Adjustment Costs, Compensation, and Trade Adjustment Assistance

Specialization and trade according to comparative advantage are dynamic processes. Countries gain and lose comparative advantage as demand and supply conditions in various markets change. Efficiency requires that industries relocate and adapt to these changes, but such adjustment imposes costs. Resources employed in a shrinking industry may suffer losses due to temporary unemployment, relocation, or retraining. The more specifically resources are designed for certain industries, the larger the dislocation costs are likely to be, because specialized resources, by definition, are ill suited for movement among industries. There can be little doubt that these costs and the associated redistributions of income are an important cause of protectionist policies. Industries have every incentive to lobby for protection to avoid the adjustment costs associated with changing patterns of comparative advantage.

Adjustment costs create three distinct but related policy problems. The first concerns equity in dealing with individuals adversely affected by trade. We have seen that unrestricted international trade maximizes world welfare. We also have seen that certain groups within the economy are harmed by trade. (For a review, see sections 4.3, 4.4, and 4.5) The extent to which society should compensate groups injured by trade represents an important policy question. The second issue concerns how to prevent individuals harmed by trade from successfully lobbying for protectionist policies that reduce total world welfare. The third question is how government can promote the adjustments necessary to realize the full potential gains from international trade.

Most countries have government-administered programs to aid individuals who have lost jobs because of changing patterns of comparative advantage. These programs have the triple purpose of more equitably distributing the adjustment costs incurred to capture the gains from trade, placating the most potent constituency for protectionism, and encouraging and facilitating the necessary adjustments.

The U.S. government administers the **Trade Adjustment Assistance (TAA)** program. The Trade Expansion Act of 1962 contained the first provision for a program aimed specifically at workers displaced for trade-related reasons (in particular, by increased imports resulting from GATT tariff reductions). The act provided for assistance in the forms of extended unemployment benefits and retraining and relocation funds for workers in industries that could prove liberalization of international trade as the cause of their displacement. Requirements for such proof were quite stringent, and no workers qualified for assistance during the first several years of the program (until 1969). Gradually, Congress eased the requirements, and more workers became eligible for benefits.

The Trade Act of 1974 mandated that imports need only "contribute importantly" to displacement rather than be the direct cause. More important, the 1974 act changed the nature of the link between trade and displacement. Congress had designed the 1962 act with the idea that workers injured *by a government policy* (that is, internationally negotiated reductions in tariffs) should receive compensation. The 1974 act altered the purpose of the program to include compensation of workers injured by increases in imports *regardless of the cause* of those increases. The number of workers receiving assistance grew slowly through the 1970s before exploding in 1980, when automobile workers qualified. During fiscal year 1980, expenditures for the TAA program exceeded the program budget by a factor of 4. Budget authorization for TAA expired briefly in 1985 but then was reinstated retroactively. Congress tightened eligibility requirements by requiring that increased imports be no less important than any other cause in a job loss rather than simply an important cause. Table 4.4 reports cash payments to workers under the TAA program.

The primary source of controversy surrounding the TAA program is the fact that its three goals, at least to some extent, conflict. The goal of compensating workers displaced because of international trade interferes with the goal of facilitating the adjustments required by trade according to comparative advantage. Many economists feel the program's heavy emphasis on extended unemployment benefits and weak focus on retraining and relocation assistance actually hamper adjustment. Over the years 1975 through 1987, about $4,400 million went to Trade Readjustment Allowances, or extended unemployment benefits, while only $228 million were spent on retraining, job search, and relocation. The unemployment benefits encourage workers to remain unemployed and await recall to their old jobs rather than seek employment in growing industries.[16] The Omnibus Trade

---

[16]For an accessible discussion of the weaknesses of the Trade Adjustment Assistance program and proposals for reform, see Robert Z. Lawrence and Robert E. Litan, "Living with the Trade Deficit: Adjustment Strategies to Preserve Free Trade," *The Brookings Review* (Fall 1985), 3–13.

Table 4.4 □ **Trade Readjustment Allowance Expenditures**

	Total Outlays ($ Millions)
1976	79
1977	148
1978	257
1979	256
1980	1,622
1981	1,440
1982	103
1983	37
1984	35
1985	43
1986	116
1987	198
1988	186
1989	125
1990	92
1991	116
1992	43
1993	50

Source: U.S. Department of Labor.

and Competitiveness Act of 1988 added the requirement that workers must participate in job training programs in order to be eligible for TAA payments.

4.7.5 Who Is Society?

An alternate way to view distributional issues in evaluating the effects of trade involves considering what we mean by society's welfare or utility. Presumably the welfare of society as a whole is some combination of the welfare of the individuals within it.

The key questions then become: What type of combination, and which individuals? Should the welfare of individuals be added together (implying everyone counts equally), or should the individual welfare terms be weighted (so some individuals count more than others)? Should every individual count? These are questions that economists obviously cannot answer; however, the questions impact policy making in international economics as well as other areas.

The repeal of the Corn Laws in nineteenth-century Britain, the subject of Case One, provides the most famous example of a change in "who counts" causing a change in international trade policy.

Case One
Political Change and the Repeal of the Corn Laws

The political system of nineteenth-century Britain still reserved the bulk of political power for the landed gentry. Parliament consisted of appointees of the large landowners. As a result of the work of the Classical economists (particularly Adam Smith and David Ricardo), Britain drastically reduced or removed tariffs on many goods during the first half of the nineteenth century.[17] The glaring exception was the so-called Corn Laws, which prohibited grain imports at prices below those of British-produced grain. Britain effected this prohibition with a variable tariff on imported grain. The British government periodically adjusted the tariff to ensure that the total price of imported grain to British consumers, including the tariff, exceeded the price of British grain.

Within the framework of the Heckscher-Ohlin model, it is hardly surprising that Britain, a small island nation, lacked a comparative advantage in grain production. The owners of the land on which British grain was grown gained most from the continuation of the Corn Laws. Because these same landowners held the reins of government, the Corn Laws did not disappear as quickly as had many other trade restrictions. However, political change in the Reform Bill of 1832 laid the groundwork for eventual repeal of the laws.[18] The 1832 reforms extended the representation of government to middle-class men who were not landowners; this included large numbers from the capitalist or industrialist class emerging after the Industrial Revolution.

Agriculture in Britain was land intensive, while the developing industries were capital intensive. The specific-factors model suggests free trade in grain would have harmed the landed aristocracy and helped the owners of capital. The newly enfranchised middle class needed an urban workforce to man the factories; and the obvious source of this workforce was the labor that would be released from agriculture if the Corn Laws were repealed.[19] Because of this growing demand for labor in industry and because most agricultural workers spent almost all their incomes on food grain (made artificially expensive by the Corn Laws), workers sided with the middle class and against the aristocracy in favoring the repeal of the laws. *(Why, according to the specific-factors model, might the consumption pattern of workers determine which side they would take in the Corn Law debate?)* In 1846, 14 years after the reform bill

---

[17]An enduring debate among economic historians concerns the Classical economists' impact on Britain's moves toward free trade. For a discussion, see William D. Grampp, "Britain and Free Trade: In Whose Interest?" *Public Choice* 55 (1987), 245–256.

[18]Recent work suggests that another consideration in the repeal was landowners' diversification into industry, giving them as much stake in industry's progress as in the fate of agriculture; see the Schonhardt-Bailey paper in the chapter references.

[19]Research shows that "man" the factories is the correct terminology. Skilled male factory workers used their new political power not only to overturn the Corn Laws but to outlaw factory work by women, teenagers, and children to eliminate competition for jobs. See Gary M. Anderson and Robert D. Tollison, "A Rent-Seeking Explanation of the British Factory Acts," in *Neoclassical Political Economy: The Analysis of Rent-Seeking and DUP Activities,* ed., David C. Colander (Cambridge, Mass.: Ballinger, 1984), 187–201.

whose political realignments had made repeal possible, Parliament repealed the Corn Laws. Although political groups such as the Anti-Corn Law League had crusaded for repeal for years, the Irish potato famine of 1845 provided the final spur to action by requiring imports to make up for a portion of the resulting shortfall in food.

The basic distributional questions raised by trade remain a source of controversy today just as during the debate over repeal of the Corn Laws. Case Two, which analyzes U.S. and Canadian views of Canadian energy exports to the United States, provides one current example of the differing perspectives on free trade.

Case Two
Canadian Energy Policy and U.S. Imports[20]

Canada is the largest energy exporter to the United States. Its exports, including natural gas and electricity, petroleum and petroleum products, and uranium, totaled $11 billion in 1993. This fact, along with recent rapid growth in Canadian-U.S. energy trade, has generated controversy on both sides of the border. Canadian energy producers are relieved that an easing of Canadian export restrictions has allowed increased exports to the United States. Canadian consumer groups express concern that foreign sales could mean higher energy prices, particularly if power companies build costly new plants based on shaky forecasts of the future U.S. market. A related irritation for Canadian consumers came in late 1990 when Canada's National Energy Board ruled that all customers of TransCanada Pipelines must share the cost of a major new gas pipeline to serve the U.S. northeast; Canadians felt the company's U.S. customers should bear the full cost. Other groups worry that Canadians are selling their energy resources now rather than conserving them for future sale at higher prices. Ironically, just such a view caused the Canadian government to restrict petroleum exports during the 1970s, when oil prices reached their peak in real terms. The oil Canada now exports at relatively low prices could, without the export restrictions, have been sold in the mid-1970s at much higher prices.

On the U.S. side of the border, consumer groups enjoy lower energy prices resulting from imports from Canada. U.S. residents, as well as government officials, worry less about dependence on Canada than about reliance on OPEC exporters. American energy producers find themselves divided on the issue. Major U.S. oil and gas companies own large parts of Canadian energy reserves, so those firms don't worry about the imports. Small U.S. energy producers, on the other hand, claim that Canadian exports disrupt markets and depress already low prices. These producers press for protection from exports and take advantage of existing restrictions that require any surplus power from U.S. generators to be purchased ahead of imports. Producers in

---

[20]See Alan Bayless, "Canadian Natural Gas Exports to U.S. Soared 33% in '87; Further Gains Seen," *The Wall Street Journal*, February 24, 1988; and U.S. International Trade Commission, *Operation of the Trade Agreements Program*, 39th Report, 1987 (Washington, D.C.: U.S.G.P.O., 1988).

U.S. manufacturing industries with heavy energy input requirements side with U.S. consumers in welcoming the increasing Canadian exports, since they result in lower energy prices.

Economic relations between Canada and the United States are friendly, especially following the free-trade agreement that took effect in 1989 and evolved into the 1994 North American Free Trade Agreement (NAFTA). That agreement prohibits restrictions on energy imports or exports by either country except for reasons of national security or temporary short-supply conditions. But energy policy seems likely to remain a source of controversy. Canadian energy producers, U.S. consumers, and U.S. producers of energy-intensive goods favor unrestricted trade in energy products between the United States and Canada. U.S. energy producers, Canadian consumers, and Canadian producers of energy-intensive products have incentives to lobby for restrictions on Canadian energy exports to the United States.

Case Three
Trade and Wages in Asia

The Neoclassical model, although a very simplified view of the world economy, highlights some fallacies common in many discussions of international trade policy. One of the model's most important lessons is the fact that factor prices and the pattern of trade are determined *jointly*. Each affects and is affected by the other. Failure to recognize this two-way interaction can result in both nonsensical arguments and poor predictions.

For example, so-called experts on trade often argue that an economy's openness to imports from lower wage countries will result in massive employment shifts to those countries. Recall Ross Perot's famous 1994 prediction of a "giant sucking sound" that would move thousands of jobs from the United States to Mexico under NAFTA. Such an argument has many problems (not the least of which is that the prediction didn't come true!), but a key one is its failure to recognize that wages rise in the low-wage country as production of labor-intensive goods starts to move there in response to the initially low wages. Thailand, South Korea, Singapore, and Taiwan all have experienced such wage increases in recent years as they removed trade barriers and integrated themselves into the world economy, specializing at first in relatively low-skill labor-intensive goods.[21]

As wages begin to rise, several adjustments occur. First, firms have less incentive, other things being equal, to move their labor-intensive production to the country; so the increase in demand for labor moderates. Fewer textile producers are moving to Thailand, and fewer sports-shoe producers to South Korea, in the 1990s than in the 1980s; instead, production moves to countries where wages remain low,

---

[21]See, for example, "How Cheap Can You Get?" *The Economist,* August 21, 1993, 29–30; and Steve Glain, "Korea Is Overthrown as Sneaker Champ," *The Wall Street Journal,* October 7, 1993, A4.

especially Indonesia, China, and Vietnam. Second, firms in the countries where wages have risen shift into new, less unskilled labor-intensive lines of production. For example, South Korean shoe producers have moved from sneakers into hiking boots and in-line skates, products that lower wage countries such as China still lack the skill to produce reliably.

Case Four
Trade and Wages in the United States

Recently, policy makers and economists have turned their attention to the possible relationship among three trends in the U.S. economy during the 1980s. First, the U.S. merchandise trade deficit (that is, the excess of the total value of imported goods over the total value of exported goods) grew rapidly. Second, the upward trend in average U.S. real wages, exhibited throughout the postwar period, stalled. And third, the wage differential between skilled, well-educated U.S. workers and unskilled, poorly educated U.S. workers expanded dramatically. Two obvious questions arise: Did international trade, reflected in the trade deficit, cause the growth in U.S. real wages to stop? And did international trade cause the real incomes of low-skilled and poorly educated workers to fall?

Attempts at empirical tests to answer these questions face many obstacles. One is the fact that so many things change simultaneously in the world economy that attempts to identify causality always runs the risk of misattributing the cause.[22] A second hurdle follows from the discussion in Case Three. Changes in trade patterns may affect wages, but changes in wages also affect trade patterns; and most empirical tests fail to use statistical techniques that can handle the two-way relationship.

Most economists tentatively agree that the trends in wages in the United States during the 1980s stem primarily from changes in technology rather than from international trade.[23] In particular, the increased importance of knowledge-intensive skills such as the use of personal computers has increased demand for workers who possess those skills and decreased demand for less educated workers who lack them. The result has been rapidly rising real wages for skilled, educated workers and falling real wages for unskilled, poorly educated workers, a trend captured in Figure 4.8. These trends have caused economists, policy makers, and the public to focus on the U.S. education system and issues related to educational reform.

Regardless of the outcome of the debate on educational reform, protection does *not* represent a fruitful approach for combating the decline in real wages of low-skill workers. Even if increased openness to international trade were the cause of that decline, and much of the current evidence suggests otherwise, protection would

---

[22]The Bhagwati and Kosters book cited in the chapter references contains detailed discussion of this problem.

[23]See, for example, John Bound and George Johnson, "Changes in the Structure of Wages During the 1980s: An Evaluation of Alternative Explanations," *American Economic Review* 92 (1992), 371–392.

Figure 4.8 □ **Indexed Weekly Wages of White Males, 1940-1990 (1940 = 100)**

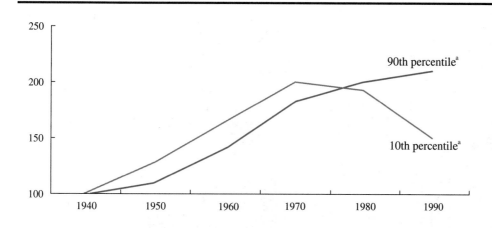

[a]Percentiles refer to percentiles of the wage distribution where workers in the 99th percentile have the highest earnings.

Source: Elaine Buckberg and Alun Thomas, "Wage Dispersion and Job Growth in the United States," *Finance and Development* (June 1995), p. 17; data from C. Huhn, "Wage Inequality and Industrial Change," National Bureau of Economic Research Working Paper No. 4684, March 1994.

impose costs on the economy that would far exceed any benefits to low-skill workers. This does not mean that these workers must bear all the costs of opening trade. We know that unrestricted international trade allows the economy to produce a larger total quantity of goods and services. We also know that some groups gain and others lose when a country opens trade. But the gains from trade guarantee that winners from trade can compensate losers, allowing all to share in the gains.

Summary

This chapter explicitly introduced the concept of general-equilibrium analysis to emphasize some of the many interrelated changes within an economy that result from opening international trade. Figure 4.9 illustrates the key relationships among the various markets.

The basic information the trade model views as exogenous includes tastes, technology, and factor endowments. These three ingredients form the basis for the demand for outputs and the demand for and supply of factors of production. Factor prices, determined by supply and demand, in turn influence incomes, which feed back through the demand for outputs. Factor prices are linked to output prices (which depend on factor endowments according to the Heckscher-Ohlin theorem) through the Stolper-Samuelson theorem and to factor prices in the other country through the factor price equalization theorem. Finally, relative output prices in the two countries determine the pattern of comparative advantage and productive specialization. The equilibrium terms of trade resulting from this process determine the size and allocation of the gains from trade.

Figure 4.9 □ **General-Equilibrium Linkages in the International Trade Model**

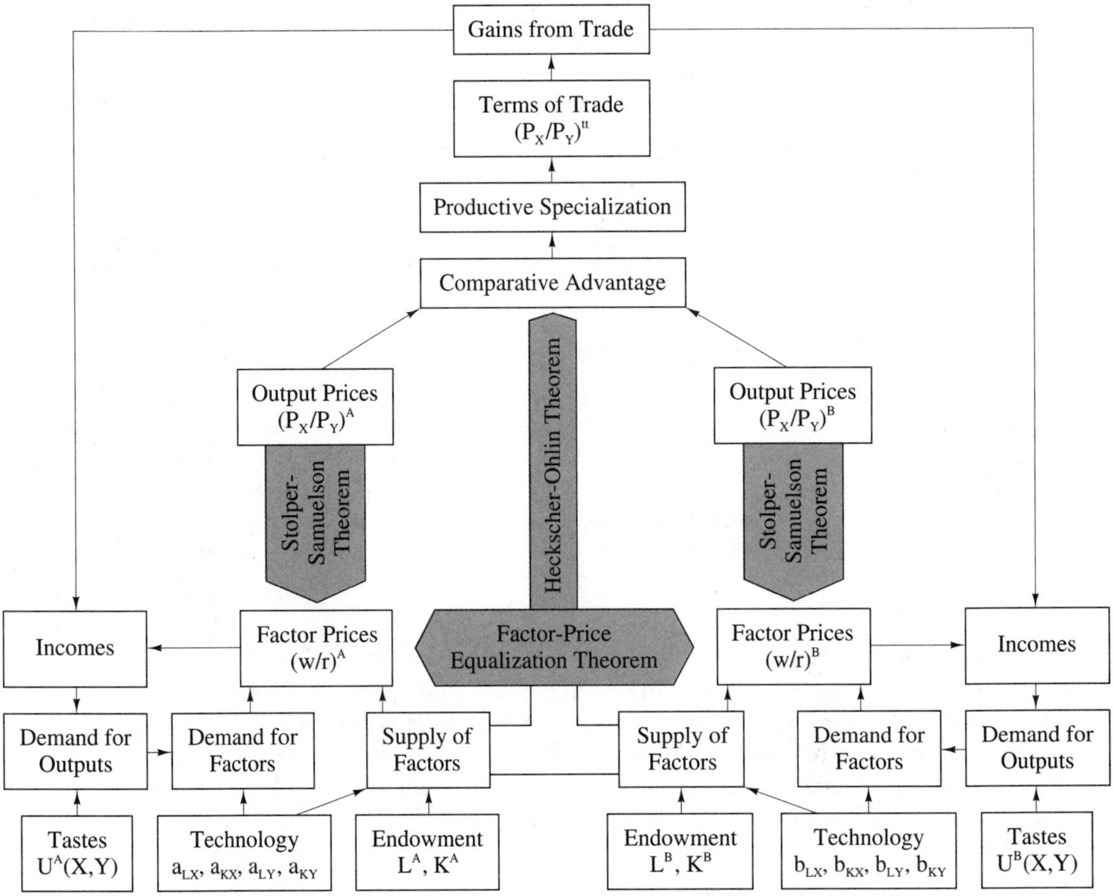

General-equilibrium analysis incorporates the interrelationships among various markets in the world economy. The Heckscher-Ohlin, Stolper-Samuelson, and factor price equalization theorems create linkages between markets in the two countries with trade in outputs.

The Stolper-Samuelson theorem states that opening trade raises the reward of the factor used intensively in producing the good in which the country has a comparative advantage. The factor price equalization theorem states that opening trade in goods equalizes factor prices across countries even when factors are completely immobile internationally. These results highlight the reasons why the impact of international trade varies among different groups within the economy. Owners of resources used intensively in the comparative-advantage industry gain from the output price and factor price changes caused by trade. Owners of resources used intensively in the comparative-disadvantage industry, on the other hand, lose. Nonetheless, the results from Chapters Two and Three still hold: Unrestricted international trade, by increasing the total quantities of goods an economy can produce, increases potential world welfare.

The changes in the distribution of income caused by trade show why changes in potential welfare and changes in actual welfare need not necessarily coincide. To predict changes in actual welfare, we must use some criterion for weighing the gains enjoyed by some groups against the losses suffered by others. By changing the relative weights attached to the gains and losses of various individuals and groups, political change in a country can result in significant changes in that country's trade policies, as the repeal of the Corn Laws in nineteenth-century Britain illustrates.

Looking Ahead

In this chapter, we explored the wide-ranging effects of opening international trade, particularly those on relative factor prices and the distribution of income. In Chapter Five, we shall examine attempts to test the Heckscher-Ohlin explanation of trade patterns and outline some of the resulting refinements and modifications of the theory. Then we shall turn to trade based on economies of scale rather than comparative advantage.

Key Terms

general-equilibrium analysis
partial-equilibrium analysis
magnification effect
Stolper-Samuelson theorem
factor price equalization theorem
depreciation allowance

computable general-equilibrium
  (CGE) models
Pareto criterion
compensation criterion
Trade Adjustment Assistance (TAA)

Problems and Questions for Review

1. Define the following terms:
   (a) Factor abundance.
   (b) Factor intensity.
   (c) Stolper-Samuelson theorem.
   (d) Factor price equalization theorem.
   (e) Pareto welfare criterion.
   (f) Compensation welfare criterion.
   (g) Capital-labor ratio.
   (h) Value marginal product of labor.

2. Assume labor and land are the only two inputs. Farmia is a labor-abundant country that grows coffee and wheat. Coffee production is labor intensive, and wheat production is land intensive. Labor can work in either the coffee or the wheat industry and can move easily back and forth between the two. But, land

is specialized; land on the plains is suited to produce wheat and land in the mountains to produce coffee. "Wheat land" is useless in producing coffee, and "coffee land" is useless in producing wheat. If Farmia opens trade with a country with identical tastes, what will happen in the short run to

(a) Farmia's production of wheat and coffee? What information or theorem did you use as the basis for your answer?

(b) Prices of wheat and coffee in Farmia? How do you know?

(c) Wages in Farmia? How do you know?

(d) The price of wheat land in Farmia? How do you know?

(e) The price of coffee land in Farmia? How do you know?

(f) The welfare or purchasing power of workers, owners of wheat land, and owners of coffee land in Farmia? How do you know?

3. This question continues question 1 from Chapter Three.

(a) If both factors of production are mobile between industries, how would the following groups feel about opening trade: capital owners in Hong Kong, labor in Hong Kong, capital owners in Japan, and labor in Japan?

(b) Now assume that labor is perfectly mobile between industries, but that capital is immobile between industries, that is, some capital is suitable to produce automobiles, but not suitable for producing clothing and vice versa. How would the following groups feel about opening trade: owners of auto-producing capital in Hong Kong, owners of clothing-producing capital in Hong Kong, owners of auto-producing capital in Japan, owners of clothing-producing capital in Japan, labor in Hong Kong, and labor in Japan?

4. Compared with most other countries, the United States is endowed with relatively little unskilled labor. For many years, the unskilled workers in the labor-intensive U.S. textile and apparel industries have been among the most vocal supporters of protectionist policies that limit imports into the United States. Is this what international trade theory would predict? Why, or why not?

5. In debates over international trade policy, it often is the case that workers and capital owners in a given industry take the same side (for example, U.S. auto producers and the United Auto Workers union, or U.S. steel producers and the United Steelworkers union). However, the Stolper-Samuelson theorem predicts that owners of capital and labor would be affected quite differently by trade. How can international trade theory explain the observation?

6. "The Ricardian and Neoclassical models carry different implications about support for and opposition to unrestricted international trade." Explain.

7. Briefly explain why the magnification effect plays an important role in predicting whether various groups in the economy will support or oppose international trade.

8. The labor-abundant countries of Asia have experienced rapidly rising wages since those economies liberalized their international trade policies. Does this observation match the predictions of international trade theory? Explain.

References and Selected Readings

Aho, C. Michael, and Thomas O. Bayard. "Costs and Benefits of Trade Adjustment Assistance." In *The Structure and Evolution of Recent U.S. Trade Policy,* edited by Robert E. Baldwin and Anne O. Krueger, 153–193. Chicago: University of Chicago Press, 1984.
A survey of U.S. experience with Trade Adjustment Assistance and proposals for reform; for all students.

Bernard, Andrew B., and J. Bradford Jensen. "Exporters, Jobs, and Wages in U.S. Manufacturing: 1976-1987." *Brookings Papers on Economic Activity: Microeconomics* (1995): 67–121.
Empirical examination of trade's effects on employment and wages; intermediate and advanced.

Bhagwati, Jagdish, and Marvin H. Kosters, eds. *Trade and Wages.* Washington, D.C.: American Enterprise Institute, 1994.
Accessible overview of theory and empirical evidence on the relationship between changes in international trade and wages.

Burtless, Gary. "International Trade and the Rise in Earnings Inequality." *Journal of Economic Literature* 33 (June 1995): 800–816.
Review of several books on the trade-wage relationship; intermediate level.

"Colloquium on U.S. Wage Trends in the 1980s." Federal Reserve Bank of New York *Economic Policy Review* 1 (January 1995).
Excellent collection of short articles summarizing the latest research on wage trends; for all students.

Deardorff, Alan V., and Robert M. Stern. *Computational Analysis of Global Trading Arrangements.* Ann Arbor, Mich.: University of Michigan Press, 1991.
Recent applications of one of the most famous computable general equilibrium models, known as the Michigan Model. For advanced students.

Deardorff, Alan V., and Robert M. Stern, eds. *The Stolper-Samuelson Theorem: A Golden Jubilee.* Ann Arbor, Mich.: University of Michigan Press, 1994.
Collection of papers celebrating the fiftieth anniversary of the Stolper-Samuelson theorem. The papers vary in level of difficulty.

Ethier, Wilfred J. "Higher Dimensional Issues in Trade Theory." In *Handbook of International Economics,* Vol. 1, edited by Ronald W. Jones and Peter B. Kenen, 131–184. Amsterdam: North-Holland, 1984.
Advanced presentation of many concepts presented in this chapter, relaxing the assumptions of only two factors, two goods, and two countries.

Feenstra, Robert C. "Estimating the Effects of Trade Policy." In *Handbook of International Economics,* Vol. 3., edited by G. M. Grossman and Kenneth Rogoff, 1553–1596. Amsterdam: North-Holland, 1995.
Advanced, up-to-date survey of the empirical literature on the economic effects of various trade policies.

Fieleke, Norman S. "Is Global Competition Making the Poor Even Poorer?" Federal Reserve Bank of Boston *New England Economic Review* (November/December 1994): 3–16.
Introductory overview of the literature on the effect of trade on wages.

Freeman, Richard B. "Are Your Wages Set in Beijing?" *Journal of Economic Perspectives* 9 (Summer 1995): 15–32.
Overview of the relationship between trade and changes in U.S. wages; for all students.

Grossman, Gene M. "Partially Mobile Capital: A General Approach to Two-Sector Trade Theory." *Journal of International Economics* 15 (1983): 1–17.
For intermediate and advanced students; a model that includes the standard and specific-factor models as special cases.

Helpman, Elhanan, and Paul R. Krugman. *Market Structure and Foreign Trade.* Cambridge, Mass.: MIT Press, 1985.
More advanced presentation of many ideas presented in this chapter.

Helpman, Elhanan, and Paul R. Krugman. *Trade Policy and Market Structure.* Cambridge, Mass.: MIT Press, 1989.
More advanced presentation of many ideas discussed in this chapter.

Jones, Ronald W. "The Structure of Simple General Equilibrium Models." *Journal of Political Economy* 73 (December 1965): 557–572.
The classic algebraic demonstration of the magnification effect and related ideas.

Jones, Ronald W., and J. Peter Neary. "The Positive Theory of International Trade." In *Handbook of International Economics,* Vol. 1, edited by Ronald W. Jones and Peter B. Kenen, 1–62. Amsterdam: North-Holland, 1984.
More advanced presentation of many ideas presented in this chapter, including their historical development.

Lawrence, Robert Z., and Matthew J. Slaughter. "International Trade and American Wages in the 1980s: Giant Sucking Sound or Small Hiccup?" *Brookings Papers on Economic Activity: Microeconomics* 2 (1993): 161–226.
Empirical examination of trade's effects on wages; intermediate.

Leamer, Edward, and John Levinsohn. "International Trade Theory: The Evidence." In *Handbook of International Economics,* Vol. 3, edited by G. M. Grossman and Kenneth Rogoff, 1339–1394. Amsterdam: North-Holland, 1995.
Advanced up-to-date survey of empirical evidence on international trade theories.

Mundell, Robert A. "International Trade and Factor Mobility." *American Economic Review* 47 (June 1957): 321–335.
Presents the argument that trade in goods and mobility of factors are substitutes. Although the basic argument is highly readable, the graphical proofs may be difficult for students to follow.

Rassekh, F., and H. Thompson. "Factor Price Equalization: Theory and Evidence." *Journal of International Economic Integration* 8 (1993): 1–32.
Useful survey of the literature on factor price equalization.

Richardson, J. David. "Income Inequality and Trade: How to Think, What to Conclude." *Journal of Economic Perspectives* 9 (Summer 1995): 33–55.
Analysis of the relationship between trade and income inequality; for all students.

Rodrik, Dani. "Political Economy of Trade Policy." In *Handbook of International Economics,* Vol. 3, edited by G. M. Grossman and Kenneth Rogoff, 1457–1494. Amsterdam: North-Holland, 1995.
Advanced, up-to-date survey of the literature on distributional aspects of trade policy and their implications for the policy process.

Sachs, Jeffrey D., and Howard J. Shatz. "Trade and Jobs in U.S. Manufacturing." *Brookings Papers on Economic Activity* 1 (1994): 1–84.
Empirical examination of the relationship between trade and wages; intermediate and advanced.

Samuelson, Paul A. "International Factor-Price Equalization Once Again." *Economic Journal* (June 1949): 181–197.
Clarified version of the original demonstration of the factor price equalization theorem. With the exception of a brief mathematical section, the paper is appropriate for students of all levels.

Schonhardt-Bailey, Cheryl. "Specific Factors, Capital Markets, Portfolio Diversification, and Free Trade: Domestic Determinants of the Repeal of the Corn Laws." *World Politics* 43 (1991): 545–569.
A new look at the repeal of the Corn Laws by a political scientist; for all students.

Stolper, Wolfgang, and Paul A. Samuelson. "Protection and Real Wages." *Review of Economic Studies* 9 (November 1941): 58–73.
Original presentation of the Stolper-Samuelson theorem; accessible to intermediate students.

Wood, Adrian. "How Trade Hurt Unskilled Workers." *Journal of Economic Perspectives* 9 (Summer 1995): 57–80.
Argues trade has hurt unskilled U.S. workers; for all students.

World Bank. *World Development Report: Workers in an Integrating World.* New York: Oxford University Press, 1995.
Examines the effects of international economic integration on workers; for all students.

CHAPTER FIVE

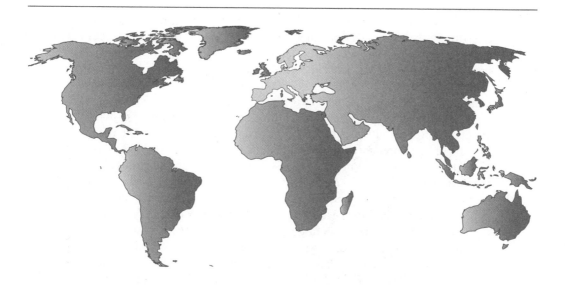

Beyond Comparative Advantage:
Empirical Evidence and New Trade Theories

5.1 Introduction

Chapters Two through Four explored a range of questions, including why nations trade, the direction and volume of trade, and the impact of opening trade on output prices, factor prices, and the distribution of income. Economists have suggested several theories to explain international trade patterns, including the Ricardian, Neoclassical, and Heckscher-Ohlin models. It is now time to confront the question of which (if any) of these theories is *the* model that explains observed trade patterns. First, we shall review just what we are trying to explain. Must we adopt a single theory of trade, or might different theories best explain various aspects of trade? Next, after a brief discussion of the role of empirical testing, we shall review the empirical evidence concerning the various models. Finally, we shall discuss some suggested modifications and important recent extensions of international trade theories.

5.2 Questions to Be Answered

The models presented in Chapters Two through Four focus on the determinants of trade patterns. Why does Colombia export coffee, Taiwan color televisions, the

United States soybeans, Japan automobiles, or Brazil steel? Is one explanation sufficient for all these observations? This chapter argues that the answer to the second question probably is *no*: Different types of international trade likely require different explanations. For example, unique political and strategic considerations may dictate government imports and exports of military equipment. Trade in manufactured goods may respond to influences different from those that affect trade in primary products. The importance of relative factor endowments in determining trade patterns in oil or diamonds seems much more obvious than in the case of bicycles or shoes. Differences in relative labor productivity probably play a larger role in U.S. exports of computer software than in Saudi exports of oil.

A large share of trade in many sophisticated manufactured goods is **intra-industry trade**–trade in which each country both imports and exports products from the same industry. Explaining this component of trade requires modifying the basic trade model. Countries tend to engage in trade largely with countries of similar income levels, particularly in manufactured goods; this provides the basis for an alternate theory of trade. The United States and a few other industrialized countries typically produce and export new or high-technology products; this observation gives rise to yet another theory of trade. All these considerations are important to a full explanation of international trade patterns. Simple extensions of the model already introduced can incorporate some of these; others require complementary models.

A second question concerns not the pattern of trade at a given time but how that pattern *changes* over time. In the case of the preceding export examples, Colombia has exported large amounts of coffee for a long time, but all the other exports are recent. Steel, color televisions, and automobiles now produced in Brazil, Taiwan, and Japan were, not long ago, produced primarily in the United States. The huge international market in soybeans is relatively new, and computer software did not even exist until a few years ago. As Case One highlights using the semiconductor industry as an example, trade patterns can change significantly over time. This carries important implications for trade policy because, as we saw in Chapter Four, such changes can result in significant policy controversy and in pressures for protection.

5.3 Empirical Testing of Trade Theories

In the previous section, we argued intuitively that some considerations are likely more important than others in explaining various aspects of world trade patterns. In some cases these intuitive arguments seem very persuasive, for example, the importance of relative factor endowments in explaining trade patterns in primary products such as oil or diamonds. In other cases, the arguments seem less immediately relevant. To strengthen our arguments about the important influences on various types of trade, we must turn to empirical tests of the various possible explanations.

Empirical work in international trade theory, both formal and informal, has a long and distinguished history. Adam Smith used the historical observation that income levels tended to be higher in coastal cities (which engaged actively in trade) than in inland areas (which engaged in little trade) to support his argument that trade can increase income. David Ricardo used his observations of differing opportunity costs in the production of wine and cloth in Portugal and England to argue that unrestricted trade between the two countries could increase the output of both wine and cloth. Certainly these early examples do not satisfy the rigorous standards by which economists conduct empirical work today. With the development of the science of statistics, the speed of today's computers, and the vast amount of available data on production, consumption, and world trade, the empirical testing of trade theories has grown into a highly technical and exacting field.[1] Nonetheless, the Smith and Ricardo examples serve to remind us that the vital interaction between trade theory and empirical observation has been going on for centuries.

Empirical testing helps economists separate theories with real explanatory power from those that, although plausible, lack the power to explain observed phenomena. However, we must keep in mind the difficulties inherent in such testing. That the available empirical evidence appears to support a theory cannot prove the theory true. A second and yet undiscovered explanation may be the true one despite apparent empirical support for the existing theory. Empirical testing can never prove a theory true, but repeated testing can increase our confidence in the theory. Similarly, empirical results that contradict a theory's implications cannot prove the theory false. Such contradictions may weaken our confidence in the theory and lead us to consider alternatives, but there always is a chance that the test itself was faulty in either design or execution. Compromises are necessary in translating a theory's implications into a form suitable for empirical implementation, and these compromises may introduce logical flaws that invalidate the test. Often the most useful outcome of an empirical test is neither validation nor invalidation of the theory in question but refinement of both the theory and the test.

Case One in Chapter Two presented the results of early tests of the Ricardian model. The model's assertion—that differences in relative labor productivity across countries help explain the pattern of trade—appeared strongly supported in tests for several countries and time periods. In the next section, we discuss attempts to test the Heckscher-Ohlin or factor-endowment theory of trade.

5.4 Tests of the Heckscher-Ohlin Model: The Leontief Paradox

5.4.1 Hurdles to Empirical Testing

For several decades after the development of the Heckscher-Ohlin model, it was impossible to test the theory empirically using anything more than the simplest observations. England does not specialize in growing wheat, or the United States in growing bananas, or France in mining diamonds. All these observations are, of course, consistent with Heckscher and Ohlin's proposal of relative factor endowments as the basis of comparative advantage; but the observations hardly comprise definitive evidence in the theory's favor.

[1]Section 4.6 of Chapter Four outlines one recent development, computable general-equilibrium models.

There were several barriers to obtaining more precise and demanding tests. The major hurdle was lack of sufficient data on the production interrelationships among industries. A simple example clearly illustrates the problem. Suppose you need to estimate the capital intensity of the steel industry. An obvious first step is to go to a representative steel mill and find out how much capital and labor it uses to produce steel. This step can give a crude approximation of the capital intensity, or capital-labor ratio, in the steel industry; but this estimate will have serious shortcomings. The most severe of these is that each item used in the production of steel is also produced using capital and labor. To obtain an acceptable approximation of the capital intensity of the steel industry, you must know how much capital and labor go into making each item that in turn is used in making steel. In other words, it is not only the *direct* capital and labor inputs that are relevant but also the *indirect* usage of capital and labor.

Until the pioneering work of Wassily Leontief in 1941, the means for generating this complex set of information did not exist. Leontief developed **input-output tables** for the U.S. economy that calculate how much output from each industry is used as input in each of the other industries. For this contribution to our understanding of the economy's structure, Leontief received the Nobel prize in 1973. By facilitating computation of capital-labor ratios for many different industries, Leontief's input-output tables made possible the first systematic tests of Heckscher and Ohlin's model.

5.4.2 The Leontief Tests

The key testable implication of the Heckscher-Ohlin model is that a country will export those goods whose production involves intensive use of its relatively abundant factor and import those goods whose production involves intensive use of its scarce factor. This implies that exports as a group should be more intensive in use of the abundant factor than imports as a group. Leontief first tested this proposition using 1947 data for the United States. With no data available on the factor intensity of actual imports (because they were produced outside the United States), Leontief had to use data on **import substitutes** (the U.S.-produced versions of the import goods) as a proxy.

During the period immediately following the Second World War, when Leontief performed these tests, no one seriously questioned the relative capital abundance of the United States. The United States had had a highly developed, capital-intensive manufacturing sector before the war, and the war's destruction of much of the rest of the world's capital stock made the United States even more relatively capital abundant. This implied that the goods exported by the United States should be capital intensive relative to goods imported (as measured by the factor intensity of import substitutes).

Much to everyone's surprise, Leontief found the opposite result: The United States exported labor-intensive goods and imported capital-intensive goods! In fact, Leontief's calculations showed U.S. exports to be about 30 percent more labor intensive than U.S. import substitutes, as Table 5.1 reports. This result was so puzzling that it became known as the **Leontief paradox.** A flurry of research activity emerged to explain the paradox, and the work continues today. Economists performed tests for different countries and for different time periods. Several economists suggested that the use of 1947 data was potentially misleading because the post-Second World War world economy was still in a highly disrupted state. Later tests using data for the early

Table 5.1 □ **The Leontief Paradox**

Given the country's apparent capital abundance, everyone expected the United States to export capital-intensive goods. Instead, Leontief found U.S. exports to be about 30 percent more labor intensive than U.S. imports. The numbers reported are inputs per $1 million of exports and import substitutes.

	Exports	Import Substitutes
Capital (1947 dollars)	2,550,780	3,091,339
Labor (person-years)	182	170
Capital-labor ratio (dollars per person-year)	14,015	18,184

Source: W. W. Leontief, "Domestic Production and Foreign Trade," *Proceedings of the American Philosophical Society,* 1953. Reprinted in *Readings in International Economics,* ed. R. E. Caves and H. G. Johnson (Homewood, Ill.: Irwin, 1968), pp. 503–527.

1950s did reduce the magnitude of the paradox; U.S. exports still were labor intensive but by a much smaller margin than 1947's 30 percent. Data for Canada, Japan, East Germany, and India also were examined, with mixed results. For some countries and periods, the implications of the Heckscher-Ohlin model seemed consistent with observed patterns of trade. In other cases, the Leontief paradox recurred.

In general, it seems fair to say that the simplest version of the Heckscher-Ohlin model does a poor job of explaining trade patterns, particularly in manufactured goods. These results have prompted some analysts to abandon the basic notions of factor abundance and factor intensity as explanations for trade. Others have retained the basic Heckscher-Ohlin framework, incorporated extensions, and relaxed assumptions to produce a more general model of trade still very much in the spirit of Heckscher-Ohlin. The continuing empirical work on these questions suggests that slightly modified versions of the Heckscher-Ohlin model can explain many aspects of trade quite well. Other aspects, however, seem to require more radical changes and the introduction of considerations outside the Heckscher-Ohlin framework and, in fact, beyond comparative advantage.

In the next section, we present several modifications of the Heckscher-Ohlin model and evaluate their ability to explain trade patterns. Later we consider alternate and complementary theories that explain aspects of trade poorly explained by the Heckscher-Ohlin model.

5.4.3 Modifications of the Heckscher-Ohlin Model

The primary modifications of the Heckscher-Ohlin model suggested as possible explanations of the Leontief paradox include the roles of tastes, barriers to trade, the categorization of inputs, and technology and productivity differences (à la Ricardo).[2]

---

[2]A fifth possible explanation—factor intensity reversals—occur when a good is labor intensive in one country but capital intensive in the other. Evidence indicates such reversals are not an empirically important phenomenon.

The Role of Tastes

Recall from Chapter Three that Heckscher and Ohlin assumed tastes were identical across countries to focus on relative factor endowments' role in determining comparative advantage. When tastes are identical, the production bias from different factor endowments implies that a country will have a comparative advantage in the good that uses its abundant factor intensively. Section 3.4.2 of Chapter Three showed that large differences in tastes among countries can introduce a taste bias that, in principle, can dominate the production bias. Should this occur, a country will have a comparative advantage in production of the good that uses its scarce factor intensively.

Logically, taste bias can explain the Leontief paradox. If residents of the United States had tastes very strongly biased toward consumption of capital-intensive goods relative to tastes in the rest of the world, the price of capital-intensive goods would be high in the United States; the country would import capital-intensive goods and export labor-intensive ones. Such a finding would not violate the spirit of the Heckscher-Ohlin model, which merely states that different factor endowments create a production bias toward the good intensive in the abundant factor.

Given that taste bias can logically explain the Leontief paradox, how likely is it to be the true source of the paradox? The available evidence suggests that this type of taste bias probably is not the explanation. The primary reason for this verdict is evidence that tastes are remarkably similar across countries. There is little support for the idea that tastes for labor- or capital-intensive goods differ to such an extent that they would prevail over factor-endowment-based production biases. A second consideration is that the taste bias explanation—at least in the case of the United States—could well work in the "wrong" direction for explaining the Leontief paradox. For taste bias to explain U.S. imports of capital-intensive goods, tastes in the United States would have to be strongly oriented toward such goods. However, to the extent that any differences in tastes exist across countries, residents of high-income countries such as the United States tend to consume more labor-intensive goods (such as handmade or luxury items) rather than more capital-intensive mass-produced goods.

Some evidence does exist for a "home bias" in consumption; that is, consumers in a given country tend to consume more domestically produced goods and fewer imports than we might expect. But, for most countries, the observed home bias in consumption probably is small relative to the factor-endowment-based production bias.

In conclusion, it is theoretically possible to explain the Leontief paradox by the presence of taste biases. There is little evidence, however, that strong biases for labor- or capital-intensive goods exist—and, in the case of the United States, they could work in the wrong direction. Home bias in consumption may be more important, but is unlikely to overwhelm factor-endowment-based differences in production possibilities.

The Role of Trade Barriers

Comparative advantage determines trade patterns in the absence of trade barriers or other government restrictions. Heckscher and Ohlin explained the source of comparative advantage by differences in relative factor endowments. When trade is *not* unrestricted but subject to barriers such as tariffs and quotas, the observed pattern of trade does not reflect the pattern of comparative advantage. Because of this, data

---

Table 5.2 □ Average Tariff Rates, Pre- and Post-Uruguay Round

Despite reductions during the postwar period, tariffs remain high enough to make the observed pattern of trade differ significantly from the pattern predicted by comparative advantage without trade restrictions.

Country or Country Group	Trade-Weighted Average Tariffs (Percent)	
	Pre-Uruguay Round	Post-Uruguay Round
Developed countries	6.3	3.9
Canada	9.0	4.8
European Union	5.7	3.6
Japan	3.9	1.7
United States	4.6	3.0
Developing countries	15.3	12.3
Economies in transition	8.6	6.0

Source: Jeffrey J. Schott, *The Uruguay Round: An Assessment* (Washington, D.C.: Institute for International Economics, 1994), p. 61.

---

consisting of observed trade flows cannot answer accurately the question of whether factor endowments explain comparative advantage and, thus, trade.

One approach to dealing with this problem is to measure the various trade restrictions and use that information to estimate what trade patterns would be in their absence. The "corrected" data could then be used to test the predictive ability of the Heckscher-Ohlin model. Unfortunately, most countries employ such complicated sets of tariffs, quotas, and other barriers to trade that this technique proves impossible.

Table 5.2 illustrates the average tariffs (taxes on imports) imposed by several countries and groups of countries. Although average tariff levels have fallen significantly since the postwar period, they remain high enough to indicate that the observed pattern of world trade does not correspond to the pattern that would be observed without tariffs. In addition, tariff levels vary greatly across industries. The opportunities to measure trade restrictions and correct for them in testing trade theories have grown even more remote recently due to changes in the types of trade restrictions used. The use of more easily identifiable and measurable barriers such as tariffs has largely given way to much more complex, subtle, and difficult to measure restrictions (we shall discuss this change further in Chapter Seven). In evaluating the reliability of the results of empirical tests, it is important to keep in mind that the data used come from a world full of restrictions on the volume and direction of trade. This fact poses a serious problem for testing of the Heckscher-Ohlin as well as other trade models.

Classification of Inputs

Attempts to test the Heckscher-Ohlin model of trade have revealed the shortcomings of the traditional two-way classification of inputs as capital or labor.[3] Most modern production

---

[3]Table 3.2 reports estimates of countries' factor endowments using the capital/labor breakdown.

processes involve many inputs, some not easily grouped into the capital or labor category. A five-way categorization of inputs can capture the major differences among the factor endowments of various countries much more successfully than can the capital-labor breakdown. Authors have classified inputs in several ways, but the most common includes arable farmland, raw materials or natural resources, human capital, man-made or nonhuman capital, and unskilled labor. Given this more precise categorical breakdown, the United States' factor abundance exists in human capital and arable farmland.[4] This explains U.S. export success in high-technology and research and development-intensive industries such as large-scale computers and in agricultural products, a seemingly peculiar combination.

Once we incorporate this more realistic breakdown of inputs, Heckscher and Ohlin's fundamental notion of comparative advantage based on differing factor endowments and factor intensities does a good job of explaining trade patterns for many goods. Two aspects of this modification of the simple model are especially important in the case of the United States: the separate consideration of natural resources and the separation of human from nonhuman capital.

Soon after publication of Leontief's surprising results, analysts noticed the industries that seemed most out of line with Heckscher and Ohlin's predictions included those in which natural resources such as minerals played a substantial role. The United States imports a number of these products because many key minerals are not found in significant amounts in the United States. When these resource-oriented industries were omitted from the tests, the Leontief paradox seemed to disappear or at least greatly diminish in magnitude.

The crucial aspect of these mineral resources turns out to be their interrelationship with capital. The production of minerals and related products tends to be very capital intensive; mining is one obvious example. When the United States imports minerals or other natural resource-intensive products, it in effect also imports capital-intensive goods; but the importation occurs because the United States has a scarcity of the mineral and *not* because of a scarcity of capital. Nonetheless, two-factor tests that classify inputs simply as capital and labor pick up mineral-intensive imports as capital intensive. This phenomenon appears to explain a significant portion of the Leontief paradox. When mineral-intensive imports are reported as such rather than as capital-intensive imports, much of the paradox disappears.[5]

The fact that labor is not a homogeneous input can explain another portion of the Leontief paradox. Labor varies widely in skill, education, training, health, and other attributes. Investments in skill, education, and training, which improve an individual's productive capacity, create **human capital** in much the same way investments in machinery create a stock of **physical capital.** The United States is rich in this human capital, including

---

[4]Most international trade models assume, as we have, that all areas within a country possess equivalent factor endowments; that is, that endowments of each factor are spread evenly across the country's territory. Violation of this assumption creates interesting possibilities; see Courant and Deardorff, listed in the chapter references.

[5]Recent work suggests the role of nonreproducible natural resources in U.S. trade may be underappreciated. Before the Second World War, the United States possessed unique access to many natural resources that, in turn, supported U.S. technological superiority based on resource-intensive technologies. Since, U.S. resource abundance relative to the rest of the world has diminished considerably, and U.S. strength has shifted to its educated labor force and scientific leadership. See the article by Wright, included in the chapter references.

Table 5.3 □ **The U.S. Workforce Embodies a Large Amount of Human Capital Relative to Those of Many Other Countries**

Education captures only one dimension of this human capital, but it is the easiest dimension to measure.

	Number Enrolled in Primary School as Percentage of Age Group, 1991	Number Enrolled in Tertiary Education as Percentage of Age Group, 1991	Adult Illiteracy Rate (Percent), 1990
United States	104	76	<5
Norway	100	45	<5
Israel	95	34	n.a.
Spain	109	36	5
Japan	102	31	<5
Ireland	103	34	n.a.
Mexico	114	15	13
Saudi Arabia	77	13	38
Iran	112	12	46
Bangladesh	77	4	65
China	123	2	27
Nigeria	71	4	49
Kenya	95	2	31
Indonesia	116	10	23

Source: *World Development Report 1994*, pp. 162–163, 216–217.

a workforce well educated and trained relative to those of other countries, as the inter-country comparisons in Table 5.3 show. As a result, the United States exports goods (such as computer software) that use this highly skilled work force intensively. When tests use a simple capital-labor classification, these exports show up as labor intensive and contribute to the Leontief paradox. The exportation occurs not because of an abundance of labor *per se* but because of an abundance of human capital. With this human-capital component of exports properly categorized, the measured labor intensity of U.S. exports declines.

A more realistic classification of inputs than the simple capital/labor breakdown appears to play a large role in explaining the Leontief paradox. In the case of the United States, separate treatment of certain natural resources, such as minerals, and human capital is particularly important.

Technology, Productivity, and Specialization

Recall that Heckscher and Ohlin assumed not only identical tastes, but also identical technologies across countries when they predicted countries would export goods that used their abundant factors intensively. The identical-technology assumption implies that, with completely unrestricted trade, equalized output and factor prices would lead firms in all countries to adopt identical production processes. *(Why?)*

But we clearly observe technology differences across countries. Some are easy to understand. Warm, sunny countries have access to a technology for producing tropical fruits that colder, less sunny countries cannot match. Firms that undertake the research-

and-development expenditures necessary to discover an innovative production process typically apply for patents that restrict other firms' abilities to use that process.

Other sources of technological differences across countries, while just as important, are harder to explain. The former Soviet Union trained many talented scientists and engineers. Yet, those highly skilled individuals failed to attain the levels of productivity in the Soviet Union that they have since emigrating to the West. One likely reason is that the incentive system in the Soviet Union and other centrally planned economies failed to encourage individual productivity. When considerations such as these result in different countries using different technologies of production, the simple predictions of Heckscher and Ohlin, based on identical technologies, may not follow directly, but must be amended to take account of the cross-country differences in production processes.

The preceding modifications to the Heckscher-Ohlin model appear to produce a framework capable of explaining a significant portion of world trade. Some aspects of trade, however, require alternate, complementary models—including some not based on comparative advantage—to which we now turn.

5.5 Intra-Industry Trade

5.5.1 Definition and Measurement

Intra-industry trade—trade in which a single country both imports and exports products in the same industry—comprises a significant share of world trade, particularly in manufactures. How can we estimate the extent of intra-industry trade in a given industry? The most commonly used technique is an *intra-industry* trade (IIT) index,

$$IIT_X = 1 - \frac{|Exports_X - Imports_X|}{Exports_X + Imports_X}, \qquad [5.1]$$

where the vertical bars in the numerator denote absolute value.[6] The IIT index varies from 0 to 1 as intra-industry trade in industry X increases. If a country only imports or only exports the good in question (no intra-industry trade), the index equals 0. *(Why?)* If a country's imports and exports of the good are equal (maximum intra-industry trade), the IIT index takes a value of 1.

One warning is appropriate concerning the interpretation of measures of intra-industry trade: The measures are extremely sensitive to the definitions of products or industries used. For example, Grubel and Lloyd found that about 66 percent of trade in chemicals was intra-industry. The chemical industry is large and diverse; thus, it is not surprising that most industrialized countries import some types of chemicals and export others. In general, the more narrowly defined the industry classifications used, the lower the resulting estimates of intra-industry trade.

---

[6]Strictly speaking, if the country's trade is not balanced (in other words, if total imports do not equal total exports), each export and import term in Equation 5.1 should be replaced by industry exports or imports as a share of total exports or imports.

The index can be useful despite the warning about its sensitivity to industry definitions. It is particularly valuable for measuring changes in the extent of intra-industry
trade over time; here the warning presents less of a problem. The index also is useful for
comparing levels of intra-industry trade across various industries. In this case, one must
use consistent industry classifications; it would be inappropriate to compare the value
of the index for a narrow class of goods such as gasoline-powered automobile engines
with that for a very broad class of goods such as miscellaneous manufactures. *(Why?)*

Besides the intra-industry trade index for a particular industry, we can define an
analogous index for a country's trade as a whole. This involves calculating the ratio
on the right-hand side of Equation 5.1 for each industry, summing the ratios across
industries, and using the summation in place of the industry ratio, as indicated in
Equation 5.2 where the symbol Σ represents summation across industries.

$$ \text{IIT} = 1 - \frac{\Sigma \, |\text{Exports} - \text{Imports}|}{\Sigma(\text{Exports} + \text{Imports})} . \qquad [5.2]$$

Calculating the IIT index for a country's overall trade allows comparison across
countries of the degree of intra-industry trade. Table 5.4 reports intra-industry trade
indexes for a large sample of countries.

Intra-industry trade represents a growing share of total trade, especially among
the high-income industrial economies. But why would a country choose to export
and import similar goods?

5.5.2 Intra-Industry Trade in Homogeneous Goods

Transportation costs and seasonal trade patterns can explain intra-industry trade in
nondifferentiated, or **homogeneous,** products. Figure 5.1 illustrates the transportation-
cost case. Homogeneous goods most likely to be involved in intra-industry trade
include items that are heavy or for some other reason expensive to transport. In Figure
5.1, firm F^A in country A and firm F^B in country B, spatially located as shown, produce
such a product. Consumers C^A and C^B buy the product. Because of the firms' and
consumers' locations, it may be the case that consumer C^A deals with firm F^B and
consumer C^B with firm F^A. As a result, countries A and B both import and export the
good. Later in this chapter, we shall look in more detail at the issues of transportation costs and the location of industry as possible explanations for the pattern of trade.

Seasonal considerations also can cause intra-industry trade in homogeneous
goods. Agricultural growing seasons provide a clear example. A country in the northern hemisphere might export agricultural products during the summer and import
those same goods from a southern-hemisphere trading partner during the winter.
Because governments report most trade statistics on an annual basis, summer exports
and winter imports would appear in the statistics as simultaneous exports and
imports of the same goods—intra-industry trade.

5.5.3 Intra-Industry Trade in Differentiated Products

The most obvious explanation of intra-industry trade is product differentiation.
Consumers have a variety of tastes, some best served by domestically produced goods and

Table 5.4 □ Intra-Industry Trade Indexes

Developing Countries	IIT Index	Newly Industrializing Countries	IIT Index	Industrial Countries	IIT Index
Algeria	.01	Argentina	.42	Australia	.25
Cameroon	.06	Brazil	.38	Austria	.74
Central African Rep.	.01	Greece	.21	Belgium-Lux.	.79
Chile	.10	Hong Kong	.41	Canada	.67
Colombia	.20	India	.37	Denmark	.67
Costa Rica	.32	Israel	.62	Finland	.45
Dominican Republic	.07	South Korea	.35	France	.80
Egypt	.07	Mexico	.32	West Germany	.63
El Salvador	.33	Portugal	.33	Ireland	.61
Ghana	.04	Singapore	.67	Italy	.59
Guatemala	.33	Spain	.52	Japan	.26
Guyana	.20	Taiwan	.35	Netherlands	.74
Haiti	.46	Yugoslavia	.51	New Zealand	.26
Ivory Coast	.13	Average	.42	Norway	.44
Jamaica	.14			Sweden	.68
Jordan	.15			Switzerland	.60
Kenya	.14			United Kingdom	.81
Malawi	.06			United States	.59
Malaysia	.32			Average	.59
Morocco	.11				
Nigeria	.00				
Pakistan	.15				
Peru	.10				
Philippines	.15				
Senegal	.19				
Sri Lanka	.05				
Sudan	.01				
Thailand	.17				
Trinidad	.14				
Tunisia	.17				
Turkey	.08				
Average	.15				

Source: Nigel Grimwade, *International Trade: New Patterns of Trade, Production and Investment* (London: Routledge, 1989), p. 127.

others by imports. Standard trade theory assumes goods are homogeneous; this is one of the assumptions required for perfectly competitive markets. Homogeneity implies (at least in the presence of transportation costs) that a single good would not be both imported and exported by the same country. Rather than import units of the good from abroad, a country would choose to consume more of its domestic production and reduce its exports.

Figure 5.1 ▫ **Intra-Industry Trade in Homogeneous Products**

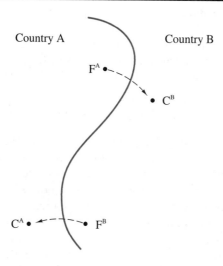

The product is both imported and exported by each country because of the greater proximity of consumers to the foreign than to the domestic producer.

However, many manufactured goods do not satisfy the homogeneity assumption very well.[7] The example most often cited is automobiles. Throughout the world, firms produce a variety of types and models of automobiles. American-made automobiles differ from Japanese-made automobiles, which differ from German-made automobiles. All the major industrialized economies both import and export cars.[8] American consumers buy Mercedes and Hyundais, while German consumers buy Chryslers and Saabs. The English drive Chevrolets, and Americans drive Jaguars. Obviously firms incur substantial costs to ship automobiles back and forth among countries. This situation is worthwhile only because consumers do not view the various types of cars as perfect substitutes. An American who buys a BMW, Toyota, or Fiat is not indifferent between that car and a Ford. A satisfactory explanation of trade in many manufactured goods requires taking into account such **product differentiation** and the intra-industry trade it produces.

---

[7]Markets with differentiated products but that otherwise satisfy the requirements for perfect competition are called *monopolistically competitive markets.*

[8]The automobile industry, as well as other industries, engages in two types of intra-industry trade. The first—the focus here—is bidirectional trade in differentiated but similar goods such as automobiles. The second, explored later, is trade in component parts; for example, a car may be assembled in the United States from parts produced in 15 different countries. Since the components typically are classified within the automotive industry category, such trade in components shows up along with bidirectional trade in finished automobiles as intra-industry trade. Some intra-industry trade also is due to an aspect of transportation costs called *cross-hauling*—the fact that once a loaded ship carries goods from country A to country B, the cost of shipping goods back from B to A rather than sending an empty ship is low (see Case Two in this chapter).

Product differentiation takes us one step toward understanding intra-industry trade, but a true explanation of the phenomenon requires an additional step. Suppose that most Italians are content to drive Fiats, while most Germans are happy with their Volkswagens and BMWs. Nonetheless a few Italians want BMWs, and a few Germans want Fiats. Why don't the Italians produce a few good BMW substitutes and the Germans a few good Fiat substitutes? To explain why this adjustment to minority tastes does not occur and intra-industry trade occurs instead, we need to incorporate the idea of increasing returns to scale, the subject of section 5.6.

5.5.4 Implications of Intra-Industry Trade

Unlike trade based on comparative advantage, intra-industry trade occurs in greatest volume between developed industrial economies with similar factor endowments, skill levels, and levels of development. The industries most likely to report high intra-industry trade include sophisticated manufactured goods that exhibit product differentiation and whose production processes are characterized by economies of scale.

Intra-industry trade based on transportation costs, seasonal trade, or product differentiation often presents fewer pressures for protection and less controversy than does inter-industry trade based on comparative advantage. Recall that the redistribution of income caused by inter-industry trade occurs because the *different* factor intensities of industries imply that opening trade alters relative demands for different factors and thereby changes their relative prices. Intra-industry trade, on the other hand, involves trade in goods in the same industry and produced using *similar* factor intensities. Therefore, the changes in factor demands and relative factor prices from such trade tend to be smaller. This may provide one explanation for the pattern of observed trade liberalization since the Second World War. The greatest success in lowering trade barriers has occurred in manufactured-goods industries in which the developed industrial countries engage in large amounts of *intra*-industry trade. In contrast, barriers to trade in agriculture, primary products, and other sectors in which we would expect resource-based comparative advantage to result in *inter*-industry trade between developed and developing countries have been slow to come down.

5.6 Trade with Economies of Scale

For some goods, the average cost of production depends on the scale of output, or the number of units of the good produced. If the average cost per unit of a good falls as the scale of production increases, production exhibits **decreasing costs, increasing returns to scale,** or **economies of scale.** Some types of economies of scale can make it difficult for small firms to compete with large ones. Whether economies of scale give an advantage to large firms depends on whether the scale economies are internal or external to the firm.

Internal economies occur when the firm's average costs fall as the *firm's* output rises, as in panel (a) of Figure 5.2. The primary sources of internal economies of scale are large fixed costs that can be spread over all the firm's output; examples include research-and-development expenditures and advanced assembly-line production techniques such as

Figure 5.2 □ Internal and External Economies of Scale

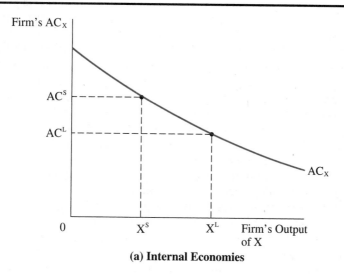

(a) Internal Economies

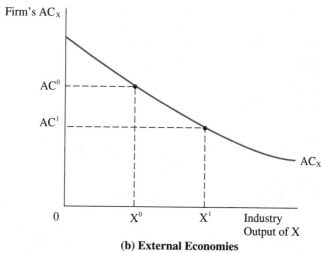

(b) External Economies

In an industry characterized by internal economies of scale, the firm's average costs fall with increases in the firm's level of output. In an industry characterized by external economies of scale, the firms' average costs fall with increases in industry output.

robotics. In an industry characterized by such economies, a firm that produces a small output, X^S in Figure 5.2, faces relatively high average costs of AC^S. A *large* firm in the same industry produces more output, X^L, can spread its fixed costs over more units, and therefore achieves lower per unit costs, AC^L. These lower costs allow the large firm to sell its product at a lower price, so we would not expect the small firm to survive in the long run.[9] The automobile industry provides a classic example of an industry characterized by internal economies of scale. Most studies suggest that a small automobile plant that produced only a few cars per year would have much higher average costs per car than would a giant firm such as General Motors or Toyota.[10] If economies of scale in a particular industry are internal to the firm, large firms have an obvious cost advantage over small ones. The perfectly competitive market structure, in which many small firms take the market price as given, tends to give way to an imperfectly competitive one, in which each firm is large and acts as if it has some control over the price of its product.

External economies, on the other hand, occur when the firm's average costs fall as the *industry's* output rises, as in Figure 5.2 panel (b). When the output of the computer industry rises, for example, computer firms' costs fall because the industry becomes large enough to support a pool of skilled labor along with input suppliers such as semiconductor chip manufacturers. Therefore, AC^0 represents the average costs of a typical computer firm when the industry is small (industry output X^0), while AC^1 denotes the typical firm's average costs when the industry reaches output level X^1. *(How might this phenomenon explain why so many computer-related firms concentrate in California's "Silicon Valley" and along Boston's Route 128?)*

Economies of scale, both internal and external, have important implications for international trade. Such economies create an additional incentive for production specialization. Rather than producing a few units of each good domestic consumers want to buy, a country can specialize in producing large quantities of a small number of goods (in which the industries achieve scale economies) and trade for the remaining goods. Therefore, economies of scale provide a basis for trade *even between countries with identical production possibilities and tastes.* (Recall from Chapters Two and Three that under constant or increasing costs, mutually beneficial trade requires that two countries *differ* in production possibilities, tastes, or both, to generate a pattern of comparative advantage.)

Figure 5.3, which assumes countries A and B are identical in tastes and production possibilities, shows the potential of mutually beneficial trade based solely on economies of scale rather than comparative advantage. Gains from trade occur because the presence of scale economies places a special premium (in the form of cost reductions) on specialization. Just as increasing opportunity costs produced a concave production possibilities frontier in Chapter Three, decreasing opportunity costs result in a *convex* or bowed-in production possibilities frontier. At each point, the (absolute) slope of the frontier reflects the opportunity cost of good X; along a convex frontier such as that in Figure 5.3, this cost *decreases* as more good X is produced. Without trade, the two identical countries would produce and consume at their autarky equilibria, A^* and B^*, placing them on indifference curves U_0^A and U_0^B. Each industry in each country fails to achieve economies of scale because domestic consumers demand some of *both* goods. Alternatively, each country can take advantage of economies of scale by specializing in

---

[9]In the long run, with entry and exit, a firm's price must equal its average costs, implying that the firm earns zero economic profits.

[10]Internal economies of scale can include plant economies, which take the form of declining average costs as production in a given *plant* rises, or firm economies, which imply declining average costs as the production of a given *firm* rises, perhaps in multiple plants.

Figure 5.3 □ **Mutually Beneficial Trade Based Solely on Economies of Scale**

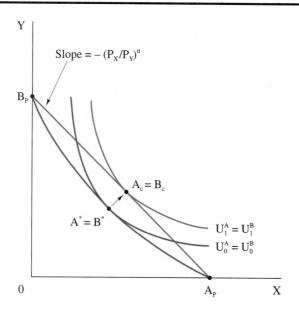

Productive specialization provides an additional benefit with economies of scale.

production of one of the goods. Note an important difference from trade based on comparative advantage: Because the two countries are identical, it does not matter which country produces which good. Suppose A specializes in good X (at point A_p) and B in good Y (at point B_p). The two countries can then trade along the terms-of-trade line to points A_c and B_c, reaching indifference curves U_1^A and U_1^B—a clear improvement over the autarky equilibria. Consumers in each economy can have a variety of goods to consume while still enjoying the cost-saving from specialized large-scale production.

We shall see that whether trade in the presence of economies of scale will be unambiguously beneficial depends on whether the economies are internal or external to the firm and on the presence or absence of comparative advantage.

5.6.1 Internal Economies of Scale

With internal economies of scale, trade allows consumers to consume a larger variety of goods at lower prices.[11] Generally, we associate more varieties with higher

---

[11]We shall demonstrate that opening trade reduces average costs. As long as entry and exit into and out of the industry remain unrestricted, price will equal average costs in the long run because any differential between the two would reflect either positive economic profits (causing entry) or negative economic profits (causing exit).

levels of consumer welfare or satisfaction for one of two reasons. For some goods, individual consumers may want to consume several varieties; clothing provides one obvious example. If trade increases the number of styles and fabrics available, most consumers enjoy the expanded choices for variety in their wardrobes. For other goods, each individual may consume a single variety, but different individuals may prefer different varieties. Although an individual may own only one car at a time, some individuals prefer BMWs while others prefer Fiats, so the availability of many different varieties improves welfare.

But why should trade increase variety? Without trade, firms produce only for the domestic population. That population may value variety; but because of the limited size of the population, firms may produce a limited number of variations to achieve economies of scale. For example, if the domestic population buys a million cars per year, domestic firms may choose to produce, say, a half million each of two varieties, not a hundred thousand each of ten varieties. To produce ten varieties for such a small population would result in high per unit cost—because of the failure to achieve economies of scale. Trade can help by expanding the consuming population for any firm's product. Firms in one country specialize in one set of varieties, and firms in the other in another set. Consumers then have access to all the varieties through trade, and each firm achieves economies of scale by specializing.

Figure 5.4 illustrates. The four panels represent the markets for goods X and Y in countries A and B. We assume that the costs of producing each good do not vary across countries, so the average costs curves for good X in panels (a) and (c) match, as do those for good Y in panels (b) and (d). In other words, we assume the two countries do *not* exhibit a pattern of comparative advantage. To focus on the effect of economies of scale, we also assume that demands for the two goods in the two countries are identical. Curve D_X^A shows country A's demand for good X in panel (a), and D_X^{A+B} shows the total demand for good X, including both countries A and B.[12]

With no international trade, firms in each country would produce for domestic consumers only. Outputs would be X_0^A, Y_0^A, X_0^B, and Y_0^B in the four markets, respectively, where domestic demand intersects the average cost curve in each case (because long-run equilibrium requires that price equal average cost). The relatively small levels of output would cause firms to fail to achieve economies of scale, so average costs would be relatively high (with superscript zeroes in Figure 5.4); and consumers would pay correspondingly high prices. If the two countries opened trade, each could specialize in producing just one of the two goods. Because the countries are identical, which country produces which good does not matter. Assume country A specializes in good X and country B in Y. Country A would produce X_1^A and serve the entire market for X; its average costs and price would fall to AC_X^1. Country B would produce Y_1^B, serve the entire world market for Y, and achieve economies of scale that lower average cost and price to AC_Y^1. *(Explain why, if country A specialized in Y and B in X rather than vice versa, average costs would be AC_X^2 and AC_Y^2.)* Note that the smaller the home market relative to the world market, the bigger the gain from opening trade in goods whose production exhibits internal economies of scale.

---

[12]The horizontal distance between the two demand curves at any price gives country B's quantity demanded.

Figure 5.4 □ **Internal Economies of Scale as a Basis for Trade between Identical Countries**

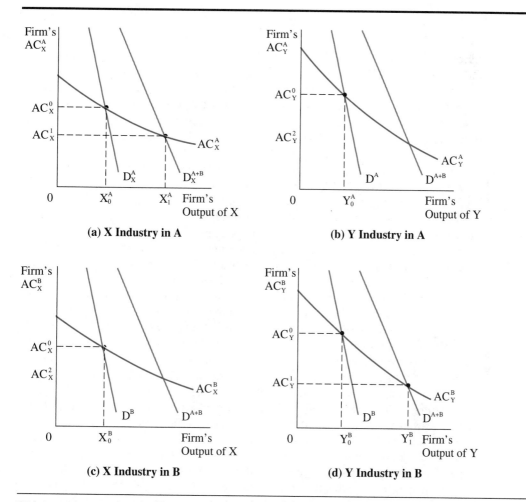

(a) X Industry in A

(b) Y Industry in A

(c) X Industry in B

(d) Y Industry in B

With internal economies of scale and no comparative advantage, international trade permits production of higher levels of output (X_1^A and Y_1^B) at lower costs (AC_X^1 and AC_Y^1) than autarky (X_0^A, Y_0^A, X_0^B and Y_0^B at costs AC_X^0 and AC_Y^0). Consumers enjoy both a variety of goods and the cost-saving that accompanies production specialization.

Economies of scale contribute to our understanding of intra-industry trade in differentiated products. In industries that exhibit such economies, domestic firms have an incentive to produce for the majority or mass domestic market and to ignore small domestic consumer groups with tastes for different types of products. The costs of small-scale production to satisfy minority tastes would result in very high-priced products. However, if minority tastes in country A match majority tastes in country B, then imports from country B, produced with economies of scale, can satisfy those tastes. At the same time, a few consumers in country B probably will have "type A" tastes that imports from country A can satisfy at low cost.

5.6.2 External Economies of Scale

External economies of scale can help explain the widely observed phenomenon of industrial agglomeration, or the tendency of firms in an industry to cluster geographically. Examples include the watch industry in Switzerland, the high-fashion apparel industry in Italy, and the financial industry in New York and London. Recall that external economies arise when a firm's average costs fall as the *industry's* output rises. Such a scenario typically happens when the clustered industry reaches a size adequate to support specialized services such as skilled labor markets and makers of specialized inputs. *(Suppose you own a computer software firm, and your star programmer just quit to start her own firm. Do you think you could find a suitable replacement more quickly if you were located in Palo Alto, California, or in Peoria, Illinois? Why? How would this affect your costs?)* Small firms can remain viable in industries characterized by external economies, unlike the internal economies case, because industry rather than firm output generates the cost reductions. Even the tiniest computer firm in Silicon Valley can benefit from the rich pool of specialized workers and components available nearby as a result of the industry's agglomeration.

The agglomeration effects produced by external economies of scale can give "historical accident" an important role in determining production and trade patterns. It is easy to see why. Suppose that a few high-fashion firms just happen to locate in Italy. Then the next few firms will have lower average costs if they also locate in Italy—where they can take advantage of the specialized input markets supported by the earlier firms. This location pattern becomes self-perpetuating and reinforcing. Eventually, no one may even remember the details of how or why the cluster got started.

The interaction between external economies of scale and international trade can be either beneficial or harmful, depending on the presence or absence of comparative advantage. Consider first the pure case in which an industry's costs exhibit external economies but are identical in two countries (that is, there is no comparative advantage). Then the analysis in Figure 5.4 of the benefits from opening trade carries over; we just need to relabel the horizontal axes to measure industry rather than firm output. In this case, external economies provide the *only* basis for trade because no comparative advantage exists; and trade benefits both countries by providing more output at lower costs.

However, things are not always so simple. Consider Figure 5.5. Now, external economies of scale characterize industry X *and* country A has a comparative advantage in X—in the sense that the average costs of producing good X, *at any given level of industry output*, are lower in country A than in country B. To keep things simple, we continue to assume that the two countries' demands for good X are identical. If the two countries begin in autarky, they will produce X_0^A and X_0^B at average costs of AC^A and AC^B, respectively. *(Why?)* From the autarky starting point, opening trade would benefit each country. Country A, with its cost advantage, would produce X_1 units at cost AC_1, at the point where the total demand curve (D^{A+B}) intersects A's average cost curve (AC^A). Consumers in both

Figure 5.5 □ **External Economies of Scale and Comparative Advantage**

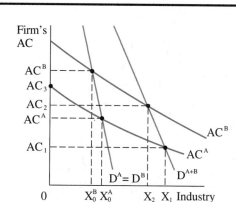

In autarky, country A produces X_0^A at cost AC^A and country B produces X_0^B at cost AC^B. International trade will be mutually beneficial if the country with comparative advantage (A) gets a head start in the industry; firms in country A would produce X_1 at cost AC_1. However, if the comparative-disadvantage country (B) gets a head start, firms in the comparative-advantage country will not be able to enter because of their high costs (AC_3), and country B firms would produce X_2 at cost AC_2.

countries benefit from lower prices and more good X to consume. *(Would consumers in A or B gain more? Why?)*

What if the two countries start out, not in autarky, but trading with each other? If, for some historical reason, country A got started in the X industry first, the outcome would be the same as in the case where the countries move from autarky to trade. Country A will produce X_1 units at cost AC_1. Here, external economies of scale reinforce country A's comparative advantage, and both countries benefit from trade.

However, if the industry's history is such that country B got an early start, firms from B would end up servicing the entire market, producing X_2 at cost AC_2, under unrestricted trade. In this case, firms from country A would have a hard time breaking into the market *despite their lower average cost curve* because B's head start gives it the advantage of large scale. A firm in A, wanting to enter the industry, would incur initial average costs of AC_3 and could not compete with established firms from country B. This presents a case in which trade may be harmful—in the sense that it has allowed country B firms to achieve economies of scale and foreclose entry to country A firms, which have a comparative advantage. Consumers in both countries pay a higher price (AC_2 versus AC_1) for a smaller quantity of good X (X_2 versus X_1) as an unfortunate result. Historical accident, in the form of country B's head start in the X industry, has combined with external economies of scale to dominate comparative advantage in determining the pattern of trade.

Might protection help in cases such as the one in Figure 5.5 where economies of scale result in trade running counter to comparative advantage? Maybe, and maybe

Figure 5.6 □ Interaction of External Scale Economies and Comparative Advantage

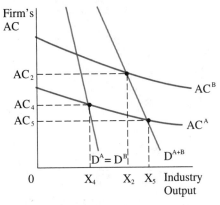

**(a) Small Scale Economies,
Large Comparative Advantage**

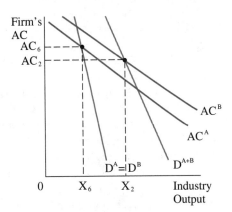

**(b) Large Scale Economies,
Small Comparative Advantage**

Panel (a) combines weak scale economies and strong comparative advantage. Temporary protection of A's market could allow country A firms to capture the market even if country B firms enjoyed a head start. Panel (b) combines strong scale economies and weak comparative advantage. Temporary protection of A's market would not allow country A firms to capture the market from already-established B firms, despite A's comparative advantage.

not. Figure 5.6 illustrates the two cases. In panel (a), if country A's government prohibited imports of X and kept A's market for domestic firms, those firms could achieve partial economies of scale and produce X_4 at AC_4. This would allow them to undersell the country B firms (who under free trade sell at a price equal to AC_2) and cap-

Figure 5.7 □ Dynamic External Economies and the Learning Curve

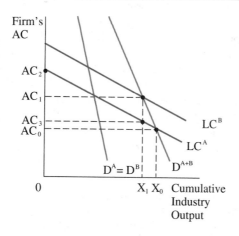

With a learning curve based on the output of the domestic industry, country A firms can be shut out of the market if country B firms get a head start, despite A firms' comparative advantage. The outcome would be output X_1 produced at cost AC_1. However, if domestic firms can learn from foreign firms' experience, the learning curve will not block entry by firms from country A, whose initial average cost will equal AC_3. The outcome then will be output X_0 at cost AC_0.

ture the rest of the market from the initially advantaged country B firms. Consumers in both countries eventually might benefit from lower prices and increased availability of good X (at AC_5 and X_5).[13] But in some cases such a strategy may not work. Panel (b) shows why. There, even a completely protected home market in good X may not allow country A firms to move far enough down their average cost curve to undersell country B firms; the best A firms can do is output X_6 at a price equal to AC_6, which may not be good enough to displace the B firms, whose initial price equals AC_2. Eventually, the loss of A's market will push B firms upward and to the left along their average cost curves as industry output falls. The extent to which this occurs and the time horizon over which it happens depend on the exact source of the industry's external economies. In general, existing skilled-labor pools or specialized input markets probably would not disappear very quickly in B, so any increase in B firms' costs due to A's protection of its home market could be slow in materializing. The smaller and slower the increase in B firms' costs, the less likely A's protection would be to allow A firms to capture the market and realize their comparative advantage.

Which case occurs, (a) or (b), depends on a combination of the strength of external economies in the industry (that is, how *steep* are the AC curves?) and the extent of comparative advantage (that is, how large is the *vertical distance* between the two countries' average cost curves?). With small economies of scale and a strong pattern of comparative

---

[13]In Chapter Eight, we shall discuss some potential problems with these protectionist policies.

advantage, as in Figure 5.6 panel (a), protection of A's home market can permit country A firms to displace the already-established country B firms. But, with large economies of scale and a weak pattern of comparative advantage, as in panel (b), even protection of their home market may not allow country A firms to catch up with their country B rivals.

In some cases, firms' average costs depend not on the industry's *current* output but on its *cumulative* output, that is, the total of all past industry production. This occurs when the learning process plays a large role in achieving cost reductions. In fact, the downward sloping curve that captures the negative relationship between cumulative industry output and firms' average costs, illustrated as LC in Figure 5.7, is called the **learning curve,** and the associated economies are called **dynamic external economies.** When these dynamic effects are present, they can reinforce or work against comparative advantage, just like other external economies of scale. In Figure 5.7, where country A has a comparative advantage, learning and comparative advantage could work together under free trade to give consumers the most output at the best price (X_0 and AC_0), but only if the industry got underway first in country A. If a quirk of history gave the B industry a head start, free trade would generate X_1 at price AC_1, definitely an inferior outcome. Despite their comparative advantage, country A firms, with no history of production to let them generate dynamic external economies, could not break into the B-dominated market because of their high initial costs (AC_2), even though they could eventually produce more at lower cost that country B firms. *(Show that trade must be beneficial with a learning curve and no comparative advantage.)*

Note that all our discussion of external economies of scale has assumed that the industry output of relevance is the *domestic* industry. The other possibility is the case in which the firm's costs depend on the output of the *worldwide* industry, either current or cumulative. If this were the case, arguments for protection based on external economies of scale, like the one in Figure 5.6 (a), would disappear. To see why, look at Figure 5.7, and assume country B has captured the market through historical accident. If country A firms can learn from country B firms' production experience as well as they could learn from domestic firms' experience, then A firms can start producing at cost AC_3, not AC_2. *(Why?)* This allows A firms to undersell their B rivals and capture the market, building on their comparative advantage. They then produce X_0 at a price equal to AC_0.

Because policy recommendations can hinge on whether dynamic economies of scale depend on output of the domestic or the worldwide industry, answering this question is a high priority. Unfortunately, external economies have proven very difficult to identify and measure. However, in one industry thought to be characterized by strong external economies, the semiconductor industry, recent evidence suggests effective learning may take place based on foreign as well as domestic production experience.[14] If so, any case for protection disappears.

In summary, economies of scale can provide a basis for trade, even in the absence of comparative advantage. In markets characterized by internal economies of scale, international trade allows consumers to enjoy a greater variety of goods while still achieving the cost-saving that comes with large-scale production. The resulting trade is intra-industry and may generate fewer pressures for protection than inter-industry trade because of its smaller impact on relative factor demands, factor prices, and the distribution of income.

---

[14]See the Irwin book and the Irwin and Klenow paper in the chapter references.

Trade based on external economies of scale can be beneficial or harmful depending on (1) the importance of scale economies relative to comparative advantage, (2) whether historical production patterns follow or run counter to comparative advantage, and (3) whether domestic or worldwide industry output provides the basis for the economies.

Economies of scale as basis for trade is just one of several ways in which the characteristics of the available production technologies affect international trade. The next section introduces the idea that changes in technology over time can change the pattern of imports and exports by various countries.

5.7 Technology-Based Theories of Trade: The Product Cycle

The Heckscher-Ohlin trade model assumes all countries have access to and use the same productive technologies. Remember that this implies the isoquant map for each industry is the same across countries. Even though the isoquant maps are identical, firms in different countries may use different capital-labor ratios in their production processes because of different factor prices that reflect differences in factor endowments. However, with unrestricted trade, factor prices equalize across countries, and all firms use identical production techniques. (The reader may want to review Chapter Three, section 3.2.1 and Chapter Four, section 4.4.)

Some industries probably satisfy the assumption of identical technologies across countries reasonably well. For others, the assumption seems less viable. Consider, for example, the electric-power industry. Countries endowed with large and swiftly flowing rivers have access to a technology for production of electric power not feasible for desert countries. The natural endowment of resources such as rivers is just one possible source of differences in technologies available in various countries. Other sources include technologies kept secret for security reasons (nuclear power and some computer capabilities) and legal restrictions such as patents that limit imitation of proprietary technologies. History provides many examples of technological innovations that allowed firms in one country to make significant advances over others at least in the short run, most notably England's industrial revolution of the late eighteenth century, the "second industrial revolution" in late nineteenth- and early twentieth-century America, and the late twentieth-century "computer revolution."

Economists have suggested a number of ways cross-country differences in technology affect international trade. Here we shall concentrate on one particular technology-based explanation for temporal changes in the observed pattern of trade: the **product cycle hypothesis,** first articulated by Raymond Vernon in the mid-1960s.[15] The basic idea underlying the product cycle is that certain countries tend to specialize in producing new products based on technological innovation, and others in producing already well-established goods. The primary implication of the theory is that as each product moves through its life cycle, it will experience changes in the geographical location of its production. From the viewpoint of the innovating country, Figure 5.8 represents the relationship among domestic production, consumption, and exports through a good's product cycle.

---

[15]Raymond Vernon, "International Investment and International Trade in the Product Cycle," *Quarterly Journal of Economics* (May 1966), 190–207.

Figure 5.8 □ **The Product Cycle**

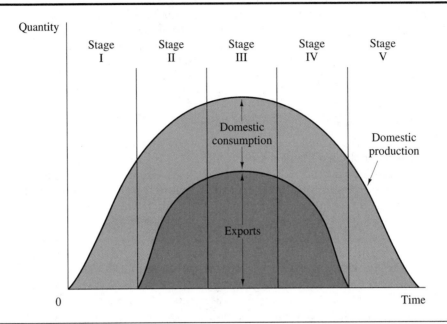

The product cycle hypothesis suggests that the relationship among domestic production, consumption from domestic production, and exports varies over the life cycle of the typical manufactured good. A few countries specialize in innovation and development of new products (stages I and II), while others specialize in producing goods with standardized technologies (stages III, IV, and V).

Vernon argued that technological innovation and new-product development tend to occur in major industrialized economies, particularly the United States. This reflects factors such as the highly educated and skilled workforce and the relatively high level of expenditure on research and development. Early production of a new product typically occurs on a small scale as the innovating firm works out problems and refines the product and production process. Firms usually aim this early, small-scale production at the domestic rather than the export market. At first, actual production needs to be located close to consumers so they can provide feedback on its refinement. Only the domestic firm owns the new technology, so production occurs only in the technologically innovative firm's home country. This can be thought of as stage I of the product cycle.

Stage II of the cycle begins when the firm perfects the product and production accelerates, first for the domestic market and then for export. Domestic consumption and domestic production rise, but production rises more rapidly to accommodate growing export demand. The innovating firm still controls the new technology.

As the production technology becomes standardized (no longer a matter of trial and error and experimentation), the innovating firm may find it profitable to license the technology to other firms both domestically and abroad. It then becomes feasible to relocate production to other countries in which the cost of standardized production is lower. The cost of such production in the innovating country remains relatively high because of its highly skilled labor force. Once production no longer requires the research and development and engineering skills of that labor force, relocation of production becomes economical. This is stage III of the product cycle. Some domestic production of the good continues in the innovating country, but exports level off as new, low-cost producers licensed by the innovating firm capture export markets.

Stage IV begins when imports rather than domestic production begin to serve the domestic market of the innovating country. The technology has diffused completely, and any patents or other proprietary restrictions that once limited its use have expired. Domestic production falls rapidly as the domestic industry loses both its domestic and export markets.

Finally, in stage V the product has moved through its cycle. Although domestic consumption of the good continues, imports satisfy that consumption. Attention in the innovating country concentrates on new technological innovations, leading to new products in the early stage of their product cycles. Examples of products that appear to have experienced a typical product cycle include radios, black-and-white and color televisions, and semiconductor chips (see Case One at the end of the chapter).

The textile industry provides a long-term example of the product cycle scenario at work. The industrial revolution gave England a huge technological advantage in production of textiles. As the new technologies spread, textile production moved to the United States (first to New England, then to the South) and then on to other countries where abundant low-skilled labor permitted production of low-cost textiles using a standardized technology. Today the major centers of textile production are in the labor-abundant countries of Asia. The industry's migration continues; as wages rise in established textile centers such as Hong Kong and Singapore, production shifts to new Asian centers including Malaysia, the Philippines, and China.

The product cycle hypothesis and other related explanations of trade focus on characteristics of the production process. An alternate theory focuses on the importance of demand characteristics in various countries.

5.8 Overlapping Demands as a Basis for Trade

The Ricardian and Heckscher-Ohlin theories of trade imply a country will find it most beneficial to trade with countries very different from itself. Differences in production possibilities, tastes, or both can form a basis for trade, as demonstrated in Chapter Three. This would lead us to expect large volumes of trade between dissimilar countries, particularly between the capital- and human-capital-abundant developed countries and the mineral- and unskilled-labor-abundant developing countries. World trade figures, however, do not bear out this expectation. The largest share of world trade, particularly in manufactured goods, occurs among the group of developed countries. One explanation of this phenomenon focuses on economies of scale (section 5.6) rather than comparative advantage as the source of trade.

Alternatively, economist Staffan Linder has suggested that similarities in *demand* between two countries also can form a basis for trade, especially for manufactured

Figure 5.9 □ The Overlapping-Demand Hypothesis

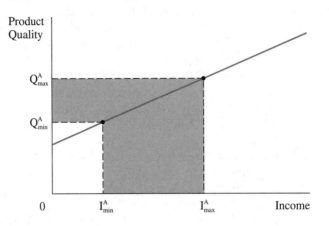

Linder hypothesizes a positive relationship between a country's level of income and the quality of manufactured goods demanded by its residents.

goods.[16] Linder's argument rests on the idea that firms typically do not produce goods solely for export; most produce for the domestic market as well. If a country develops only those industries for which a viable domestic market exists, trade will occur in those products for which domestic consumers and foreign consumers share similar tastes.

To formulate empirically testable implications, we must state the Linder hypothesis more precisely. Linder argues that for many manufactured goods, the *quality* of the good that consumers in a particular country demand depends primarily on their income levels. Consumers with higher incomes tend to demand manufactured goods of higher quality. Figure 5.9 represents this hypothesized relationship as an upward-sloping line. Of course, the income levels of consumers in any given country vary. In Figure 5.9, *i*ncomes for country A range from a low of I_{min}^A to a high of I_{max}^A. Given these income levels, consumers in country A demand goods of *quality* range Q_{min}^A to Q_{max}^A. If, as Linder suggests, a domestic market is necessary for an industry to develop, country A will produce manufactured goods in the Q_{min}^A to Q_{max}^A quality range.

Figure 5.10 introduces a second country with income range I_{min}^B to I_{max}^B and demand for goods in quality range Q_{min}^B to Q_{max}^B. Industries in country B will develop to provide goods in the quality range demanded by B consumers. The overlap in the quality ranges demanded by consumers in countries A and B (Q_{min}^B to Q_{max}^A in Figure 5.10) represents the goods in which trade between the two countries might occur. The more similar the ranges of income, the larger the overlap in the demanded qualities and the greater the potential for trade.

---

[16]Staffan B. Linder, *An Essay on Trade and Transformation* (New York: Wiley, 1961).

Figure 5.10 □ **According to the Overlapping-Demand Hypothesis, Countries Trade Goods in the Range of Qualities in Which the Demands Overlap**

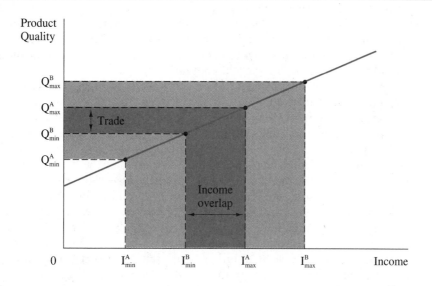

Countries A and B exchange goods in quality range Q^B_{min} to Q^A_{max} determined by the overlap in their ranges of income.

Empirical evidence on the validity of the Linder hypothesis is mixed. As mentioned earlier, the large share of trade that occurs among the developed countries provides informal evidence in support of Linder's view. More precise tests have been less encouraging. In evaluating the results of tests of the model, we must remember the problems introduced by differences in the distribution of income across countries. Consider an extreme example. Let all but one consumer in country A have income level I^A_{min} and the remaining individual income level I^A_{max} and all country B individuals but one have income level I^B_{max} and the remaining individual income level I^B_{min}. The potential for trade is much lower than the illustrated range of overlap in qualities suggests. Because of this problem, tests of the Linder hypothesis require careful corrections for the distribution of income, and good data on the distribution of income are difficult to obtain. An additional problem in testing Linder's hypothesis arises because the model's predictions closely match that of a model of intra-industry trade based on economies of scale—high levels of trade between similar trading partners. The similarity of the models' predictions presents a problem for empirical researchers trying to sort out the relative merits of the two for explaining the pattern of trade observed in the world economy.

Besides theories of trade based on the characteristics of production or of demand, several rely heavily on characteristics of the trade process itself. One consideration we have ignored so far is the role of transportation costs.

5.9 Transportation Costs as a Determinant of Trade

Some goods typically are not traded internationally. Called **nontraded goods,** the reason for their special status usually involves a prohibitive cost of transporting them from one country to another. The classic example is haircuts. Although substantial differences may exist in the prices of haircuts across countries, trade does not develop by shipping haircuts from low-price to high-price countries. The cost of transporting either the barber or the customer to take advantage of the low prices in another country would far outweigh the price differential.

For other classes of goods, **transportation costs** may not be prohibitive (that is, high enough to prevent any trade) but still may be high enough to have a significant impact on the pattern of trade. Very heavy goods tend to be more costly to transport. For these goods, the relationship between the item's weight and value is important. Automobiles, which are relatively heavy and of comparatively high value, are traded; gravel, on the other hand, typically is not traded internationally because its low value does not warrant the high transportation costs implied by its weight. Perishable items must be moved quickly, and rapid means of transportation usually are more expensive than slower means. We saw in section 5.5.2 that transportation costs could generate intra-industry trade in heavy homogeneous goods when the placement of national boundaries puts consumers in one country near producers in the other.

Traditionally, economists devoted little attention to the effects of transportation costs on trade. The volume of trade in the world economy certainly is smaller than would be the case without transportation costs or if goods could be transported magically and instantaneously from country to country. However, as long as transportation costs remain fairly constant over time, their incorporation adds little explanatory power to some of the models already developed.

When sudden *changes* occur in transportation costs, things become interesting. Often the changes result from an advance in technology. One example is the development of refrigerated truck and ship transportation. These innovations reduced spoilage by enough to make international trade in many food products feasible for the first time. In the northeastern United States, many of the fresh fruits and vegetables available in stores during the winter come from Latin America. Before invention of refrigerated transport, the spoilage cost of such trade would have been prohibitive. Containerized cargo shipping provides another example. By prepacking goods in very large, uniformly sized containers that machines can load quickly and efficiently onto ships, the cost of hauling many large items long distances has been substantially reduced.

Transportation costs also play an important role in trade with external economies of scale. High transportation costs contribute to the agglomeration effects common in industries characterized by external economies. Also, past transportation costs may have caused an industry to spring up in a particular location, and external economies of scale may perpetuate that pattern long after the initial transportation-cost reason for it disappears.

Another interesting issue concerning transportation costs is the question of which country will pay them—the importer or the exporter. In general, the two countries share the costs. Other things being equal, the less price responsive the demand for the good by the importing country, the larger the share of transportation costs the importer will bear, and the less price responsive the supply of the good by the exporting country, the greater the share of transportation costs the exporter will bear.

Figure 5.11 □ **The International Market for Good X without Transportation Costs**

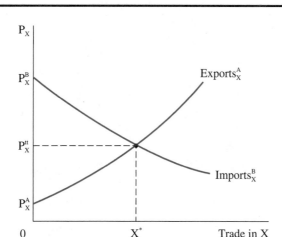

Figure 5.11 illustrates the international market for good X. Country A is assumed to have a comparative advantage in production of X and is willing to export X at any price above the autarky price, P_X^A.[17] Country B has a comparative disadvantage in production of good X and is willing to import X at any price below the autarky price, P_X^B. The demand curve for imports, $Imports_X^B$, shows how many units of good X country B is willing to import at various prices. The supply curve for exports, $Exports_X^A$, shows how many units of good X country A is willing to export at various prices. The equilibrium outcome without transportation costs involves X^* units of good X traded at international terms of trade P_X^{tt}.

Next, consider the effect of transportation costs of T per unit of good X transported between countries A and B, as shown in Figure 5.12. T could include the actual cost of packing and transporting the good as well as insurance premiums for the trip and related expenses. The price paid for good X by consumers in country B must cover *both* the price paid to producers in A and the transportation costs. If $T = P_X^0 - P_X^1$, the new equilibrium volume of good X traded is X_T^*. Consumers in country B pay price P_X^0, and producers in country A get price P_X^1. The difference of T per unit, or $T \cdot X_T^*$ in total, goes to pay the costs of transportation. Transportation costs have reduced the volume of trade in good X between the two countries, just as we would expect.

Producers in country A pay a share of the transportation costs by accepting the lower price P_X^1 rather than the price P_X^{tt} that prevailed without these costs; the area of rectangle HGJM in Figure 5.12 shows producers' contribution toward the costs.

---

[17]To simplify notation, we show the price of good X simply as P_X rather than as the relative price, P_X/P_Y, as in Chapters Two and Three.

Figure 5.12 □ **Effect of Transportation Costs on International Trade**

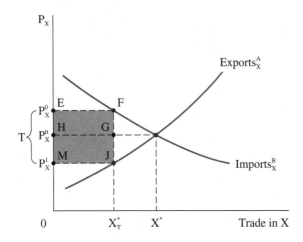

Transportation costs of T per unit cause the quantity of good X traded to fall from X^* to X_T^*. The price consumers pay rises from P_X^{tt} to P_X^0, and the price producers receive falls from P_X^{tt} to P_X^1.

Consumers in country B share in the burden of the transportation costs by paying the higher price P_X^0; the area of rectangle EFGH represents their contribution. The graphical demonstration that the division of the total transportation costs, area EFJM, between the share borne by producers and that borne by consumers depends on the particular shapes of the demand and supply curves is left to the reader. *(Hint: Draw two graphs with identical demand curves, one with a very steep supply curve and the other with a very flat supply curve.)*

If transportation costs are an important determinant of the pattern of international trade, the choices of firms and industries concerning where to locate also must be significant. The field of urban and regional economics, which focuses on locational decisions, is a separate, fascinating area of study. Here we suggest a few basic industry characteristics that may play a role in the choice of location.

5.10 Location of Industry

An industry's decision about where to locate depends on, among other things, the characteristics of the production process in the industry.[18] Many industries can be classified as resource oriented, market oriented, or footloose.

---

[18]International trade theory and location theory have evolved separately. For a recent attempt to integrate the two using economies of scale and transportation costs, see Krugman (1991) in the chapter references.

Resource-oriented industries tend to locate near the sources of inputs or raw materials. One obvious example is mining operations. Once the mineral is out of the ground, the location of each stage of the refining process must be decided. Should the mineral be refined into its final form at a location next to the mine, or should the raw material be shipped to another location for refining? The answer to such a question largely depends on how the ore's weight changes as it moves through the various stages of refining. Because transportation costs tend to increase with a good's weight, firms have an incentive to avoid moving the good long distances until it is refined to a lighter form. Consider a hypothetical mining operation in which each 100 pounds of ore pulled from the ground contains 1 pound of the valuable mineral and 99 pounds of worthless soil and rock. By locating the industry that separates the mineral from the soil and rock near the mine, it becomes possible to transport only the 1 pound of mineral rather than the entire 100 pounds of ore. Industries in which the good becomes lighter as it moves through the production stages tend to locate near the source of raw materials to avoid having to move the good until it is in its lighter form.

Other industries tend to be **market oriented** in their location. One example is retail sales operations. It would make little sense to locate all bakeries in Iowa to be close to the inputs, corn and wheat. Bakeries locate near their customers. Other industries may be market oriented because they involve goods that become heavier or otherwise more difficult to move during the production process. It generally is less costly to gather the inputs to construct a building on the building site and then assemble the parts than to build the building and then move it to its site (some small modular buildings provide an exception to the rule); hence, the construction industry locates near its markets. The soft-drink industry provides another example. Most soft-drink companies manufacture a highly concentrated syrup in a centralized location and ship it to local bottling companies, which add carbonated water and distribute the soft drinks to retailers. Shipping the small volume of concentrated syrup is less costly than shipping the much larger volume of soft drink.

A third category of industry has no need for location near either input sources or markets; these industries often are characterized as **footloose** or **light industries.** Their products typically neither gain nor lose a significant amount of weight or volume as they move through the stages of production. Goods such as semiconductor chips and electronic components fall into this category because of their high value-to-weight ratios. Footloose or light industries are free to move around the world in response to changes in the prices of inputs. The product-cycle idea may be important in determining the location of footloose industries. As a product matures, the type of labor and other resources required to produce it may change, causing the industry to relocate. Both the semiconductor and electronics industries have tended to follow this pattern.

Economies of scale also play a role in determining firms' and industries' locations. A firm with substantial internal economies needs a large market to achieve its scale economies. If transportation costs are low, the firm can serve a large dispersed market and be flexible in its location. But if transportation costs are high, a geographically dispersed market becomes prohibitively expensive, and the firm needs to locate near a large concentration of its customers. We have already seen how external economies of scale can dictate that firms concentrate geographically. High transportation costs for the firms' final product may counteract the tendency toward agglomeration if the good's final consumers are spread over a large area.

Case One
Conducting Semiconductor Trade

Engineers at Texas Instruments and Fairchild invented integrated circuits, or semiconductor chips, in 1958. Since then, the industry has maintained a rapid rate of change. U.S. firms dominated the industry in the early years, but during the late 1970s and 1980s, foreign producers, especially Japanese firms, made rapid gains in manufacturing technology. Japanese firms' total worldwide sales of semiconductor chips passed those of U.S. firms in 1986, and U.S. firms did not regain the sales lead until 1993. Figure 5.13 represents regional market shares in the three major semiconductor markets, North America, Japan, and Europe. Total chip sales in Japan surpassed those in the United States during 1986–1992, but the United States once again represented the single largest chip market in 1993, when the total worldwide market reached $60 billion in sales. Of the top ten semiconductor companies in the world in 1994, ranked by worldwide revenue, five were Japanese, four U.S. owned, and one South Korean, as documented in Table 5.5.

Viewing the semiconductor industry as a single entity can be misleading. Relatively early in its life cycle, the industry split into two branches, each with distinct production and trade characteristics. The first branch, highly research-and-development intensive, emphasizes technological innovation and continual introduction of more powerful and self-contained chip designs. This technologically innovative branch of the industry has moved beyond ever-bigger memory chips into so-called designer chips, including microprocessors, microcontrollers, and custom-logic chips. The industry's second branch focuses on standardizing and lowering the cost of large-scale production for existing memory-chip designs (a process known as *commoditization*). Memory chips of a given design are a

Table 5.5 □ **Top Ten Chip Makers, 1994**

Company	Chip Sales (Billion $)
Intel (U.S.)	10.9
NEC (Japan)	7.9
Toshiba (Japan)	7.5
Motorola (U.S.)	7.2
Hitachi (Japan)	6.6
Texas Instruments (U.S.)	5.5
Samsung (South Korea)	4.8
Fujitsu (Japan)	3.8
Mitsubishi (Japan)	3.7
IBM (U.S.)	3.0

Source: *The Wall Street Journal*, July 11, 1995, p. A12.

Figure 5.13 □ **Suppliers to Major Chip Markets**

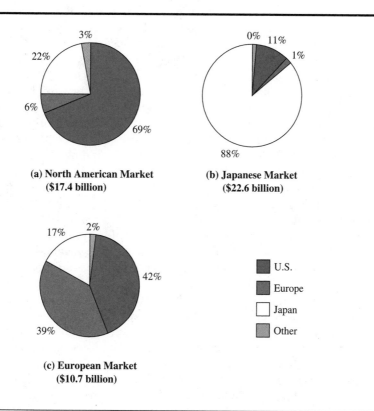

(a) North American Market
($17.4 billion)

(b) Japanese Market
($22.6 billion)

(c) European Market
($10.7 billion)

- U.S.
- Europe
- Japan
- Other

Source: *Fortune,* May 6, 1991, p. 92.

largely homogeneous product, and the primary consideration in capturing market share is lowering manufacturing cost.

The first branch of the industry remains active in the United States, while the second has moved increasingly to other areas, first Japan and now South Korea. In 1991 the United States chip industry experienced an increase in worldwide market share from 34.9 to 36.5 percent, the first such increase since 1979. This reflects the growth of the designer end of the chip industry, the area of U.S. comparative advantage, as opposed to memory-chip production, where Japan's and South Korea's manufacturing techniques give them the edge. In 1992, the United States held about 48 percent of the designer-chip market, as opposed to only 23 percent of the memory-chip market. Among the top five firms in memory-chip sales in 1992, two were South Korean, Samsung and Hyundai.

The United States and Europe responded to increasing Japanese dominance of chip production as well as to Japan's entry into the more technologically innovative branch of the industry. In 1986, the United States pressured Japan to join a five-year trade pact in chips aimed at raising the price of Japanese chips in both U.S. and foreign markets and improving access to the Japanese market for U.S. chip producers.[19] The agreement succeeded in raising chip prices, much to the dismay of the U.S. computer industry (the major buyer of chips); but U.S. chip makers expressed frustration over lack of progress in increasing their sales in Japan. Under pressure from domestic chip makers, the United States imposed retaliatory 100 percent tariffs against U.S. imports of Japanese televisions, power tools, and laptop computers in 1987.

In 1991, the United States removed the retaliatory tariffs when the two countries extended the chip pact for five more years. The renewed agreement reduced its earlier emphasis on keeping the U.S. price of Japanese chips high (a concession to the U.S. computer industry) and increased its emphasis on increasing the market share of foreign chips sold in Japan, including a controversial 20 percent foreign market-share target by the end of 1992. The two countries have trouble even agreeing on how to calculate the market share of foreign chips in Japan. The United States wants to count only sales on the open market, while Japan wants to include sales by U.S. companies such as IBM to their Japanese subsidiaries and sales of Japanese chips under foreign labels. As of mid-1992, foreign chip sales represented about 13 percent of the Japanese market under the U.S. calculation method and about 16 percent under the Japanese method, far enough below the 20-percent target to generate threats of U.S. sanctions against Japan. Since, foreign chip sales in Japan have fluctuated around 20 percent, and trade tensions fluctuate with the sales figures.

Besides trade in chips themselves, controversy surrounds trade in the machinery used to manufacture chips, including chemical-vapor deposition and photolithography tools. Japan's share of the world market in this equipment rose during the 1980s, and the U.S. share fell (from 73 percent in 1981 to 43 percent in 1990). U.S. chip makers argued that if Japan came to dominate the production of chip-making machinery, they would delay shipment of new technology to the United States, thereby giving Japanese chip makers a jump on their U.S. competitors in new technology chips. As of 1993, six of the top ten firms in the equipment industry are based in the United States and four in Japan, as reported in Figure 5.14.

In 1987, 14 U.S. firms joined in a government-supported consortium called Sematech to improve semiconductor manufacturing techniques and bolster U.S. firms that manufacture the equipment used to produce chips. Half of Sematech's annual $200 million budget comes from government sources. Many analysts have expressed disappointment with Sematech's results, but Congress extended the group's funding in September 1992 for five more years. In 1993, the Department of Energy signed a five-year, $103 million dollar deal with Sematech to develop new chip equipment. Japanese firms have expressed interest in joining Sematech which, so far, has been restricted to U.S.-based firms. Sematech announced in 1994 that when its currently promised funding expires in 1997, it will cease to take government funds and become a strictly industry-funded research group.

---

[19]On the chip pact's protectionist effects, see the Irwin book in the chapter references and section 7.7 on voluntary import expansions.

Figure 5.14 □ Top Semiconductor Equipment Manufacturers (Million $)

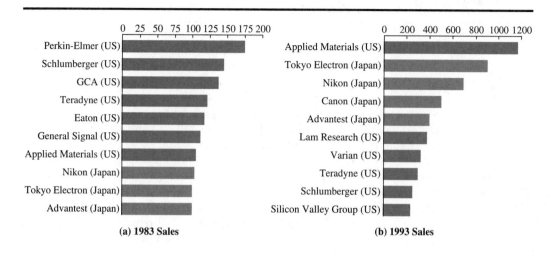

(a) 1983 Sales

(b) 1993 Sales

Source: *The Economist*, April 2, 1994, p. 79; data from VLSI Research.

In 1991, U.S. semiconductor tool makers did increase their worldwide market share by about 3 percent, the first increase in a decade, while Japanese manufacturers lost market share; and U.S. firms gained in their share of the Japanese market. From 1990 to 1993, the U.S. share of the market for chip-making machinery rose from 44 percent to 54 percent.

Other attempts to aid the U.S. chip industry included a request by seven U.S. producers for permission to form US Memories, a commercial consortium to improve U.S. production of DRAMs (a particular kind of semiconductor chip); but the consortium died in early 1990 due to members' unwillingness to contribute adequate funding to the research.[20] Europe's reaction to Japanese moves in the industry has been the Joint European Submicron Silicon project (JESSI), a $4 billion, eight-year, government-funded consortium created to develop the European chip industry. Increasingly, the enormous research and development expenditures required to produce a new generation of chips have forced firms to join together in these efforts, often across national boundaries. For example, in 1992, American IBM, German Siemens, and Japanese Toshiba announced a joint project to produce the new 256-megabit DRAM chip.

---

[20]The consortium required government permission to avoid the possibility of antitrust actions.

Case Two
Cross-Hauling[21]

Honda Trading America Corporation ships Honda automobiles from Japan to the United States, mostly in its own ships. In the early 1970s, when Honda sold more motorcycles than cars in the United States, most of the ships returned to Japan empty. Then the trading company started trying to fill the ships on the return trip. Early U.S. exports included golf clubs, towels, fruit, and coffee.

Now Honda Trading America handles over $200 million annually in U.S. exports. Most, such as auto parts, machine tools, steel, and plastics, go to Honda's own production facilities in Japan. A few exports are unusual. For example, Honda converted the top decks of two ships into cattle pens and became one of the largest cattle exporters to Japan. Once the cattle arrive at Honda's cattle ranch in northern Japan—where performance tests on Honda power equipment are conducted—the cows munch on compressed chunks of hay also exported from the United States. *(Illustrate, in a diagram similar to Figure 5.12, how cross-hauling might generate trade that otherwise would not occur.)*

Since Honda's early back-hauling ventures in exporting, much of the firm's auto and motorcycle production has moved to the United States. In 1995, Honda was named Exporter of the Year by the state of Ohio for exporting 105,000 Ohio-built automobiles and 20,000 motorcycles to 43 countries in 1994.

Case Three
Laser Lace[22]

The industrial revolution in the late eighteenth century allowed Britain to capture the world market in textiles. Soon, however, knowledge of the new technologies spread; and, by the late nineteenth century, the textile industry had shifted to the mills of New England. Britain's textile industry shrunk, losing most of its export markets and much of its domestic market to imports from lower cost producers, first in the United States, then in Asia.

Recently, another technological advance, while hardly on the scale of the industrial revolution, promises to resurrect a small segment of the British textile industry. A new computer-controlled laser device allows lace of much higher quality to be produced using much less labor. The old lace technology involves rotating knives that cut the holes to make lace and produce the lace's scalloped edges. Unfortunately, the knives tend to catch on the net material used as a backing, so the procedure

[21]Kathryn Graven, "Japan's Major Exporters Are Striving to Balance U.S. Trade by Filling Ships Going the Other Way," *The Wall Street Journal,* April 9, 1993.
[22]"Knicker Frills," *The Economist,* November 27, 1993, 93.

requires constant monitoring, which raises labor costs and gives labor-scarce Britain a comparative disadvantage. The new technique uses lasers to cut holes and scallop edges. Unlike the older rotating knives, the lasers exert no pressure on the fabric, so the net backing does not catch on the machines, and much less monitoring is required. In addition, the laser's heat seals the fabric edges as it cuts, leaving a smooth surface. The laser also can cut more intricate patterns than the mechanical knives. The process reduces labor requirements and may allow Britain to regain a comparative advantage in lace.

Case Four
Global Sourcing in the Apparel Industry[23]

The overlapping demands hypothesis suggests that consumers in different countries *demand* different levels of quality in manufactured goods. Data for some industries suggest that producers in different countries also specialize in *supplying* different levels of quality. The apparel industry provides one example. Figure 5.15 divides apparel exporting countries into five rings. Moving from the inner rings to the outer ones, costs, the sophistication of the manufacturing process, and the speediness of product delivery all tend to fall.

High-fashion clothing producers buy primarily from the inner two rings. Factories in these countries turn out designer-quality products showing a high level of craftsmanship. They handle orders in small lots and on custom terms, including the ability to deliver products quickly, as dictated by the fashion seasons. Department and specialty stores buy their clothing in the second-, third-, and fourth-ring countries. Here, orders tend to be large and delivery times a bit slower, but quality is still high. Mass merchandisers also buy in those same countries, but provide larger orders and tolerate slower delivery times in exchange for lower prices. Discount chains buy from suppliers in the third, fourth, and fifth rings. These orders are huge, and slow delivery times allow the discounters to obtain the lowest possible prices.

Summary

International trade is too complex a phenomenon to be explained based on one simple theory. This chapter explored the ability of the Heckscher-Ohlin model to explain observed trade patterns, along with several alternate theories useful for understanding particular aspects of trade. The Heckscher-Ohlin model does a fair job of explaining a large share of trade once refined definitions of inputs account for complex modern production processes. However, growing intra-industry trade in

---

[23]Eileen Rabach and Eun Mee Kim, "Where is the Chain in Commodity Chains? The Service Sector Nexus," in *Commodity Chains and Global Capitalism,* edited by Gary Gereffi and Miguel Korzeniewic (Westport, Conn.: Praeger), 1994, 111.

Figure 5.15 □ **Global Sourcing by U.S. Apparel Retailers**

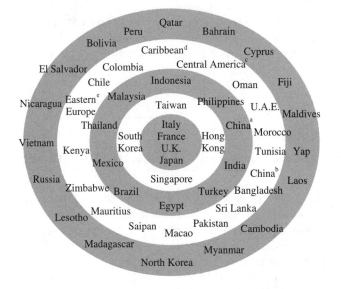

[a] Southern China
[b] Interior provinces of China
[c] Guatemala, Honduras, Costa Rica
[d] Dominican Republic, Jamaica, Haiti
[e] Poland, Hungary, Czechoslovakia, Bulgaria

Source: Eileen Rabach and Eun Mee Kim, "Where is the Chain in Commodity Chains? The Service Sector Nexus," in *Commodity Chains and Global Capitalism*, edited by Gary Gereffi and Miguel Korzeniewicz (Westport, Conn.: Praeger, 1994), p. 111.

manufactures requires that we move beyond comparative advantage and add economies of scale to our list of bases for mutually beneficial trade. Alternate, complementary explanations include the product cycle, overlapping demands, transportation costs, and location of industry.

Looking Ahead

Chapter Six examines the simplest form of trade restriction: the tariff. By altering relative prices, tariffs change consumption and production decisions as well as redistribute income. The overall welfare effect of a tariff in a small country is negative, but a large country may be able to gain at the expense of its trading partners by imposing a tariff on imports. International negotiations since the Second World War have significantly lowered overall tariff levels, but high tariffs still distort trade in many industries.

Key Terms

intra-industry trade	internal scale economies
input-output tables	external scale economies
import substitutes	learning curve
Leontief paradox	dynamic external economies
human capital	product cycle hypothesis
physical capital	nontraded goods
homogeneous good	transportation costs
product differentiation	resource-oriented industries
decreasing costs	market-oriented industries
increasing returns to scale	footloose (light) industries
economies of scale	

Problems and Questions for Review

1. Explain why the data in Table 5.1 present a paradox.

2. (a) Write the formula for the intra-industry trade index. Explain why the index takes a value of 0 in industries with no intra-industry trade and a value of 1 in industries with maximal intra-industry trade.

   (b) If country A exports $10 million worth of semiconductor chips per year and imports $20 million worth of semiconductor chips per year, what is country A's intra-industry trade index for semiconductor chips? Suppose you had data to calculate the IIT index for 256K DRAMs. How would you expect the two IIT indices to compare? Explain.

3. Use a figure similar to Figure 5.4 to show that international trade is particularly important for small countries in the presence of economies of scale. *(Hint: Alter Figure 5.4 so that country A's demand for each good is half the size of country B's demand.)* Explain.

4. How can international trade theory explain intra-industry trade?

5. The product-cycle theory of trade argues that the economically efficient geographic location of production changes as a good moves through its life cycle. In what sense is this consistent with the Heckscher-Ohlin theory of trade? Why might the kinds of locational shifts suggested by the product-cycle theory result in pressures for protectionist policies?

6. Assume (1) the computer software industry exhibits external economies of scale, (2) India has a comparative advantage over the United States in producing computer software, (3) the Indian market for software is one-tenth the size of the U.S. market, and (4) the United States has a head start in the industry and currently produces for both the U.S. and Indian markets. Illustrate in a diagram similar to Figure 5.5. What would happen if India protected its software market? On what does your answer depend?

7. Economies of scale provide a second basis (in addition to comparative advantage) for gains from trade. Explain.

8. For what types of countries and what types of goods would you expect trade based on comparative advantage to be important relative to trade based on economies of scale? For what types of countries and what types of goods would you expect trade based on economies of scale to be important relative to trade based on comparative advantage? Explain. What are the implications of your answers for policy controversies related to international trade?

References and Selected Readings

Abernathy, Frederick H., et al. "The Information-Integrated Channel: A Study of the U.S. Apparel Industry in Transition." *Brookings Papers on Economic Activity: Microeconomics* (1995): 175–246.
Adjustment of the apparel industry to competition; intermediate.

Baily, Martin Neil, and Hans Gersbach. "Efficiency in Manufacturing and the Need for Global Competition." *Brookings Papers on Economic Activity: Microeconomics* (1995): 307–358.
Effects of foreign competition on firms' technology and productivity; intermediate and advanced.

Balassa, Bela. "Intra-Industry Specialization: A Cross-Country Analysis," *European Economic Review* 30 (February 1986): 27–42.
Empirical tests of hypotheses related to intra-industry trade.

Baldwin, Robert E. "Are Economists' Traditional Trade Policy Views Still Valid?" *Journal of Economic Literature* 30 (June 1992): 804–829.
Survey of the literature incorporating imperfect competition and economies of scale and their implications for international trade policy.

Brander, James A. "Strategic Trade Policy." In *Handbook of International Economics,* Vol. 3, edited by G. M. Grossman and Kenneth Rogoff, 1395–1456. Amsterdam: North-Holland, 1995.
Advanced, up-to-date survey of the literature on strategic aspects of trade policy.

Caves, Richard E. "International Differences in Industrial Organization." In *Handbook of Industrial Organization,* Vol. 2, edited by Richard Schmalensee and Robert Willig. Amsterdam: North-Holland, 1989.
Advanced survey of how industrial organization varies across countries.

Courant, Paul N., and Alan V. Deardorff, "International Trade with Lumpy Countries." *Journal of Political Economy* 100 (February 1992): 198–210.
Effect on international trade when factors are distributed unevenly within countries.

Deardorff, Alan V. "Testing Trade Theories and Predicting Trade Flows." In *Handbook of International Economics,* Vol. 1, edited by Ronald W. Jones and Peter B. Kenen, 467–518. Amsterdam: North-Holland, 1984.
Advanced survey of the issues that arise in empirically testing implications of theoretical trade models.

Feenstra, Robert, ed. *Empirical Methods for International Trade.* Cambridge, Mass.: MIT Press, 1988.
Collection of advanced papers on testing various aspects of trade models.

Feenstra, Robert C. "Estimating the Effects of Trade Policy." In *Handbook of International Economics,* Vol. 3, edited by G. M. Grossman and Kenneth Rogoff, 1553–1596. Amsterdam: North-Holland, 1995.
Advanced, up-to-date survey of the empirical literature on the economic effects of various trade policies.

Gray, H. Peter. "Non-Competitive Imports and Gains from Trade." *International Trade Journal* 1 (Winter 1986): 107–128.
Incorporates trade in goods that cannot be produced domestically; for intermediate students.

Grimwade, Nigel. *International Trade: New Patterns of Trade, Production and Investment.* London: Routledge, 1989.
Readable survey of recent developments in trade theory and policy, especially intra-industry trade.

Grossman, Gene M., ed. *Imperfect Competition and International Trade.* Cambridge, Mass.: MIT Press, 1992.
Collection of important papers on international trade under imperfect competition. Level of papers varies from intermediate to advanced.

Grossman, Gene M., and Elhanan Helpman. "Technology and Trade." In *Handbook of International Economics,* Vol. 3, edited by G. M. Grossman and Kenneth Rogoff, 1279–1338. Amsterdam: North-Holland, 1995.
Advanced up-to-date survey of technology-related aspects of international trade and trade theory.

Helpman, Elhanan. "Increasing Returns, Imperfect Markets, and Trade Theory." In *Handbook of International Economics,* Vol. 1, edited by Ronald W. Jones and Peter B. Kenen, 325–366. Amsterdam: North-Holland, 1984.
Advanced treatment of trade under imperfect competition and increasing returns to scale.

Helpman, Elhanan, and Paul R. Krugman. *Market Structure and Foreign Trade.* Cambridge, Mass.: MIT Press, 1985.
Advanced discussion of many models presented in the chapter, especially trade with imperfect competition and economies of scale.

Helpman, Elhanan, and Paul R. Krugman. *Trade Policy and Market Structure.* Cambridge, Mass.: MIT Press, 1989.
Advanced discussion of many models presented in the chapter, especially trade with imperfect competition and economies of scale.

"International Location of Economic Activity." *American Economic Review Papers and Proceedings* 85 (May 1995): 296–316.
Collection of short papers on the interaction between location and international trade; intermediate to advanced.

Irwin, Douglas A., *Managed Trade: The Case Against Import Targets.* Washington, D.C.: The Brookings Institution, 1994.
Excellent, readable analysis of trade agreements such as the U.S.-Japan chip pact.

Irwin, Douglas A., and Peter J. Klenow. "Learning-By-Doing Spillovers in the Semiconductor Industry." *Journal of Political Economy* 102 (December 1994): 1200–1227.
Empirical estimation of learning curves in the semiconductor industry. Advanced.

Kemp, Murray C., and Ngo Van Long. "The Role of Natural Resources in Trade Models." In *Handbook of International Economics,* Vol. 1, edited by Ronald W. Jones and Peter B. Kenen, 367–418. Amsterdam: North-Holland, 1984.
Advanced discussion of modeling natural resources in trade.

Komiya, Ryutaro, and Motoshige Itoh. "Japan's International Trade and Trade Policy, 1955–1984." In *The Political Economy of Japan, Vol. 2: The Changing International Context,* edited by Takashi Inoguchi and Daniel I. Okimoto, 173–224. Stanford, Calif.: Stanford University Press, 1988.
Accessible survey of Japanese postwar trade policy.

Krugman, Paul R. *Geography and Trade.* Cambridge, Mass.: MIT Press, 1991.
How increasing returns affect locational choice; for all students.

Krugman, Paul R. "Industrial Organization and International Trade." In *Rethinking International Trade,* 226–268. Cambridge, Mass.: MIT Press.
Advanced survey of the growing overlap in industrial organization and international trade theory.

Krugman, Paul R. "Increasing Returns, Imperfect Competition and the Positive Theory of Trade." In *Handbook of International Economics,* Vol. 3, edited by G. M. Grossman and Kenneth Rogoff, 1243–1278. Amsterdam: North-Holland, 1995.
Advanced up-to-date survey of recent developments in trade theory.

Leamer, E. E. *Sources of International Comparative Advantage.* Cambridge, Mass.: MIT Press, 1984.
Empirical study of factor endowment-based trade theory; advanced.

Leamer, Edward, and John Levinsohn. "International Trade Theory: The Evidence." In *Handbook of International Economics,* Vol. 3, edited by G. M. Grossman and Kenneth Rogoff, 1339–1394. Amsterdam: North-Holland, 1995.
Advanced up-to-date survey of empirical evidence on international trade theories.

Leontief, Wassily. "Domestic Production and Foreign Trade: The American Capital Position Reexamined." *Economia Internazionale* 7 (February 1954): 3–32.
Presents the empirical evidence that became known as the Leontief paradox. For introductory or intermediate students.

Richardson, J. David. "Empirical Research on Trade Liberalization with Imperfect Competition: A Survey." *OECD Economic Studies* 12 (Spring 1989): 7–50.
Overview of the literature, theoretical and empirical, that examines the potential for gains from trade in a world characterized by imperfect competition. For intermediate and advanced students.

Tharakan, P. K. M., ed., *Intra-Industry Trade.* Amsterdam: North-Holland, 1983.
Collection of papers on intra-industry trade; level of difficulty varies.

Trefler, Daniel. "International Price Differences." *Journal of Political Economy* 101 (December 1993): 961–987.
Empirical test of the factor price equalization theorem emphasizing productivity differences. Advanced.

Vernon, Raymond. "The Product Cycle Hypothesis in a New International Environment." *Oxford Bulletin of Economics and Statistics* 41 (November 1979): 255–267.
Updated perspective on the product cycle from its original proponent; for introductory or intermediate students.

Westhoff, Frank H., Beth V. Yarbrough, and Robert M. Yarbrough. "Complexity, Organization, and Stuart Kauffman's *The Origins of Order.*" *Journal of Economic Behavior and Organization* 29 (January 1996): 1–25.
Application of complexity theory to the role of "historical accident" in economic history; advanced.

"What Do We Know About the Long-Term Sources of Comparative Advantage?" *American Economic Review Papers and Proceedings* 83 (May 1993): 431–449.
Collection of short papers summarizing recent empirical evidence on the sources of comparative advantage. Intermediate.

Wright, Gavin. "The Origins of American Industrial Success, 1879–1940," *American Economic Review* 80 (September 1990): 651–668.
Emphasizes the role of natural resources in the evolution of American trade; for intermediate and advanced students.

Yarbrough, Beth V., and Robert M. Yarbrough. "International Contracting and Territorial Control: The Boundary Question," *Journal of Institutional and Theoretical Economics* 150 (March 1994): 239–264.
Application of the new economics of organization to the problem of why national boundaries change. For all students.

CHAPTER SIX

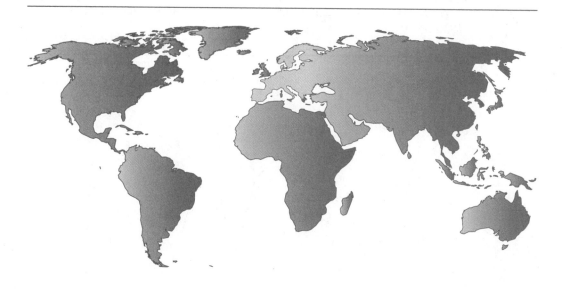

Tariffs

6.1 Introduction

Up to this point, we have explored the benefits of unrestricted international trade. Although the methods used come from the modern economist's tool kit, the benefits of trade have been known for several centuries, at least since the work of David Hume, Adam Smith, and David Ricardo. Nonetheless, in no period of history has international trade been free of a complicated array of restrictions. Chapter Four presented several reasons for the controversial nature of trade, particularly its effect in redistributing income within each participating country. The policies countries use to restrict trade are called **barriers to trade,** one of the most common of which is the tariff. In this chapter, we explore tariffs' effects on production, consumption, prices, trade volume, and welfare.

A **tariff** is simply a tax imposed on a good as it crosses a national boundary. Historically, tariffs have been the most commonly used type of trade restriction. In recent years, however, the level of tariffs in the world economy has declined and use of a variety of other restrictions has increased. Figure 6.1 documents the average tariff level in the United States over the last 160 years. Average tariff levels have fallen in other countries as well, largely as a result of international negotiations conducted under the General Agreement on Tariffs and Trade (GATT), created after the Second World War to provide a forum for international discussion of trade issues.

Figure 6.1 □ **Tariff Revenue as a Percentage of Total Dutiable Imports and Total Imports, 1830–1990**

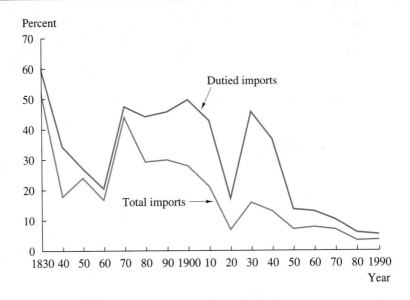

Sources: U.S. Department of Commerce, *Historical Statistics of the United States,* Part 2, p. 888; U.S. Department of Commerce, *Statistical Abstract of the United States,* 1994, p. 828.

6.2 Reasons for Imposing a Tariff

A country might choose to impose a tariff for four basic reasons. First, a tariff, like any other tax, can discourage consumption of a particular good. Placing a tariff on an imported good makes it relatively more costly to consumers. During the OPEC oil price increases of the 1970s, many policy makers proposed a tariff on oil imports. They argued that the United States needed to reduce its consumption of oil, particularly foreign oil, and that a tariff presented one possible solution. Some developing countries tariff items most often bought by foreigners. For example, China recently imposed tariffs on 20 such luxury goods, including a 130 percent tariff on air conditioners, an item foreign firms often purchase when they establish ventures in China.[1]

A second reason for imposing tariffs is to generate revenue for the government of the tariff-imposing country. Developed countries rarely impose tariffs specifically to raise revenue, because those countries have the infrastructure necessary to administer other types of taxes, such as personal and corporate income taxes. Figure 6.2

---

[1]Kathy Chen, "Beijing Imposes Substantial New Taxes and Duties on Imports by Foreigners," *The Wall Street Journal,* January 12, 1995, A10.

Figure 6.2 □ **Tariff Revenue as a Share of Total U.S. Federal Government Receipts, 1830–1990**

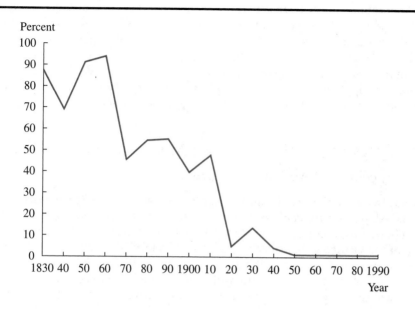

Sources: U.S. Department of Commerce, *Historical Statistics of the United States,* Part 2, pp. 1105–1106; U.S. Department of Commerce, *Statistical Abstract of the United States,* 1994, p. 331.

traces the historical decline in tariffs' share of U.S. government revenue. However, many developing countries still use tariffs to raise a significant share of the revenue required to finance their governments' activities. Successful administration of an income tax requires a well-developed bureaucracy as well as a literate and settled population. Countries lacking these prerequisites find it much easier to administer tariffs by patrolling ports and national borders. Tunisia, for example, collected three-quarters of its government revenues from tariffs in 1990.[2]

A third reason for imposing import tariffs is to discourage imports to decrease a deficit in the balance of trade (that is, a situation in which payments to foreigners for imports exceed receipts from foreigners for exports). A country designing a tariff to reduce a trade deficit would apply the tariff to all imports, or at least to a wide range of goods, rather than to a single good or a narrow range of goods. We have not yet developed a framework for analyzing this motive because it involves tariffs as a tool of *macro*economic rather than *micro*economic policy. In Part Two, we shall see that proper use of other policy tools typically makes the use of tariffs for balance-of-trade purposes unnecessary.

---

[2]International Monetary Fund, *Government Finance Statistics Yearbook* (Washington, D.C.: International Monetary Fund), 1991.

The fourth—and most common—purpose of tariffs, and the one on which our discussion will focus, is that of a **protectionist policy**—a way to "protect" or insulate a domestic industry from competition by foreign producers of the same good. Such a tariff on imports allows domestic producers both to capture a larger share of the market and to charge a higher price than would be possible in the tariff's absence.

Countries impose many more tariffs on imports than on exports, especially developed countries that do not use tariffs as a major source of revenue. In fact, the U.S. Constitution makes export taxes illegal in the United States. We shall focus our discussion on import tariffs and, at the end of the chapter, briefly examine the effects of export taxes and the history behind the U.S. prohibition on them.

6.3   Types of Tariffs and Their Measurement

6.3.1   Specific and Ad Valorem Tariffs

Like any tax, tariffs can be classified as specific or ad valorem.[3] **Specific tariffs** charge a specified amount for *each unit* of the tariffed good imported, for example, $60 per imported television set. **Ad valorem tariffs** charge a specified percentage of the *value* of the tariffed good, such as 6 percent of a television set's value. The fundamental economic effects of tariffs apply to both specific and ad valorem ones. For most of our analysis, specific tariffs will be more convenient because they are easier to depict graphically. From a policy maker's perspective, both types have advantages and disadvantages.

The primary advantage of a specific tariff is ease of administration. Customs officials need only monitor, for example, the number of television sets coming into the country to calculate the tariff. Of course, the tariff law may make portable black-and-white and big-screen color television sets subject to different tariff rates, making customs officials' jobs more difficult. In general, however, a specific tariff is the easier type to administer.

One disadvantage of specific tariffs becomes apparent during periods of inflation. A specific tariff instituted in the United States in 1960 would have only about one-fifth the effect today, in real terms, that it did in 1960. This deterioration in the tariff's effect is due to the U.S. price level having nearly quintupled since 1960. A consumer good that cost $150 in 1960 would cost about $750 today. In 1960, the $60 specific tariff would have been equivalent to a 40 percent ad valorem tariff ($60 = $150 \cdot 0.40$), while today the same $60 specific tariff would be equivalent to only an 8 percent ad valorem rate ($60 = $750 \cdot 0.08$). Under a specific tariff, keeping the real tariff constant when the price level rises (inflation) or falls (deflation) requires adjusting the **nominal tariff rate** (the tariff measured in current dollars). (*What new nominal specific tariff rate would have the same real effect the $60 tariff had in 1960?*)

A second disadvantage of specific tariffs is their tendency to place higher tariff burdens on lower-quality items than on higher-quality items within each class of

---

[3]Compound tariffs combine a specific and an ad valorem tariff on the same good.

tariffed goods. For example, a $60 tariff on imported television sets would be equivalent to a 50 percent ad valorem tariff for portable black-and-white sets that sell for $120 and to a 10 percent ad valorem tariff for big-screen color sets that sell for $600. Of course, a country could set different specific tariff rates for the two types of television sets, but this approach would at least partially eliminate the advantage of specific tariffs: ease of administration.

The primary advantage of an ad valorem tariff is that its nominal amount rises and falls automatically with the price of the good, keeping the tariff's real effect constant. In times of inflation, if the price of the good doubles, so does the dollar amount of the tariff, although the tariff *rate* remains the same. The same automatic adjustment occurs over goods of different quality. For example, with all television sets subject to a 6 percent ad valorem tariff, $120 portable black-and-white sets will incur a $7.20 tariff and $600 color sets a $36.00 tariff.

The major disadvantage of ad valorem tariffs is their difficulty of administration. Collecting a tariff of 6 percent on a television set requires determining the "value" of the set. This **customs valuation** could equal the cost of producing the set, the price for which the set would sell in the country in which it was produced, the wholesale price in the importing country, or the price to the final consumer. In practice, customs valuations typically equal either f.o.b. (*free on board*) or c.i.f. (*costs, insurance, freight*) prices.[4] A good's **f.o.b. price** is the price once loaded for shipment at its port of origin. The **c.i.f. price** equals the f.o.b. price plus transportation costs, insurance premiums for the trip, and freight charges.

The country imposing the tariff and the firm paying it obviously have reason to disagree on the appropriate customs valuation. The customs official, acting on behalf of the tariff-imposing country, collects more tariff revenue by declaring a high customs valuation. The firm paying the tariff negotiates for the lowest possible valuation to lower its tariff bill. Customs valuations have been a frequent source of trade disputes between countries. The Tokyo Round of GATT negotiations, completed in 1979, produced a Customs Valuations Code aimed at establishing a uniform set of valuation rules. The Uruguay Round, completed in 1994, expanded the code, which currently has about 45 signatory countries.[5]

Even before customs officials can establish a customs valuation, they must classify a good into a customs category. The U.S. tariff code contains 8,753 categories, on which tariffs vary from 0 percent to 458 percent, so the classification task is not trivial.[6] Disputes over classification are at least as common as disputes over customs valuation. In 1988, the U.S. Customs Service raised the tariff on a shipment of 33,000 girls' ski jackets from 10.6 percent to 27.5 percent plus 17 cents per pound because the jackets had little corduroy strips on the sleeves. The Customs Service claimed the strips (approximately 2 percent of the jacket) shifted the product's tariff category from "garments designed for rainwear, hunting, fishing, or similar uses" to "other girls' wearing apparel, not ornamented." The jacket importer sued in the U.S. Court of International

---

[4]The United States historically used f.o.b. prices; and most other countries used c.i.f. prices.

[5]Case Three in the chapter provides an example of the kind of dispute that can arise over customs categories.

[6]James Bovard, "The Customs Service's Fickle Philosophers," *The Wall Street Journal*, July 31, 1991.

Trade and got the tariff increase refunded.[7] In 1989, Hasbro, Inc. took the U.S. Customs Service to court, claiming the company's G.I. Joe toy is not a doll, as the Customs Service claimed, but rather an action figure or toy soldier. At stake was a 12 percent tariff that applies to dolls but not to the other two categories. The U.S. Customs Service won, and G.I. Joes from Hong Kong now pay the 12 percent doll tariff.[8]

Customs operations also present an additional administrative problem—the potential for graft, corruption, and smuggling. Several countries, including Indonesia and the Philippines, use a private Swiss firm, Societe Generale de Surveillance, to run their customs operations. In the firm's first year in Indonesia, revenue from import tariffs rose 58 percent despite a 9 percent decline in imports and a reduction in tariff rates, an indication that the corruption and smuggling problem had been significant.[9]

6.3.2 Measuring Tariffs

Most countries apply tariffs on a product-by-product basis, as demonstrated by the 8,753 U.S. tariff categories. However, economists and policy makers often want a measure of a country's *overall* tariff level. That is, we often want to know about the general level of trade restriction a country imposes in the form of tariffs rather than the amount of the tariff on a narrow product category such as "other girls' wearing apparel, not ornamented." This appears simple enough, but measuring a country's overall tariff level turns out to be less simple than it seems.

Because tariff rates differ across goods (for example, over 200 separate U.S. tariff rates apply to different kinds of watches and clocks), characterizing the overall level of a country's tariff protection requires combining these separate rates into some type of average. There are two basic approaches, each of which has advantages and disadvantages.

The first technique involves a simple unweighted average of industry tariff rates. Consider country A, which imports two goods, X and Y, with imports of X subject to a 25 tariff and imports of good Y to a 50 percent tariff. The unweighted average tariff for the country equals $(0.25 + 0.50)/2 = 0.375$ or 37.5 percent. The unweighted-average technique works reasonably well for countries that import approximately equal amounts of different goods, for example, if country A imported $50 worth of X and $50 worth of Y.

But what if country A imported $80 worth of X and $20 of Y? In this case, simply averaging the two tariff rates without taking into account the goods' relative importances in overall imports seems less desirable. This is why the more common measure of tariffs is a weighted-average measure. It involves weighting the tariff rate for each industry by that industry's share of total imports. If country A imported $50 of X and $50 of Y, then A's weighted-average tariff rate would equal $(\$50/\$100) \cdot 0.25 + (\$50/\$100) \cdot 0.50 = 0.375 = 37.5$ percent. Note that with equal imports in both industries, the unweighted and weighted tariff measures give the same result. However, if A imports $80 worth of X and $20 worth of Y, the weighted-average measure equals

---

[7]Ibid.

[8] "G.I. Joe's a Real Doll," *USA Today,* July 20, 1989.

[9]Steven Jones, "Indonesia Curbs Graft, Boosts Revenues by Letting Swiss Firm Handle Customs," *The Wall Street Journal,* October 1, 1987.

($80/$100) · 0.25 + ($20/$100) · 0.50 = 0.30, considerably below the unweighted figure of 0.375. This occurs because the more prevalent import, X, has the low tariff rate. In this case, the weighted-average tariff appears to give a more accurate picture of country A's overall tariff situation than does the unweighted measure.

For the purpose of measuring a country's overall level of protection, the main problem with both kinds of average tariffs is that they ignore trade prevented by the tariff. In other words, the measures do not take into account that the country might have imported $100 *million* (rather than $100) of the two goods with no tariff. The easiest way to see this problem is to consider the extreme case of a **prohibitive tariff,** that is, one high enough to halt trade in the product. Consider again the case where country A imports $50 each of goods X and Y. Now suppose country A raises its tariff on good Y from 50 percent to 100 percent, high enough to cause imports of Y to fall to zero. Total imports fall to $50, all good X. The average tariff (whether weighted or not) now equals 25 percent because the tariff on good Y disappears from the calculation. Ironically, the *increase* in the import tariff on good Y caused a *decrease* in country A's average tariff. But, as a policy maker, we certainly would not want to conclude that country A's trade has become more open!

Despite the cautions about interpreting average tariff figures, average tariff levels have declined significantly. Table 6.1 uses unweighted average tariffs to support this claim.

Particularly since the Second World War, many countries have made great progress in reducing import tariffs through international negotiations sponsored by the GATT. The last completed round of trade liberalization talks, the Uruguay Round, ended in 1994, and the tariff cuts negotiated in those talks will be phased in gradually and most completed by 2000. Table 6.2 reports average Uruguay Round tariff cuts and the remaining trade-weighted average tariffs.

Despite the impressive liberalization summarized in Table 6.2, many products remain subject to much higher-than-average tariff rates. In the markets for these products, tariffs (and, in some cases, nontariff barriers as well) continue to distort trade. Even after the Uruguay Round results, approximately 5 percent of developed country imports remain subject to "peak" tariffs in excess of 15 percent. For example, the United States cut its average tariffs on apparel imports as part of the Uruguay Round, but only from 19.3 to 17.5 percent.[10] In addition, the United States does not grant the negotiated tariff reductions, either from the Uruguay Round or from earlier GATT rounds, to some countries. Regions that do not receive most-favored-nation status, which grants access to the lower tariffs, include Afghanistan, Azerbaijan, Cuba, Cambodia, Laos, Montenegro, North Korea, Serbia, and Vietnam.

Because most of the tariff reductions since the Second World War have taken place in the context of GATT rounds, nonmember countries often retain high tariffs relative to the GATT members. China, for example, has expressed interest in joining the GATT, but an acceptable plan for its accession to the group has yet to be worked out, primarily because of the continuing roles of central planning and nonmarket activity in its economy.[11] Table 6.3 reports China's tariffs on selected goods as of August 1993.

---

[10]Jeffrey J. Schott, *The Uruguay Round: An Assessment* (Washington, D.C.: Institute for International Economics, 1994), 62.

[11]See Case Four in Chapter Eight.

Table 6.1 □ Tariff Rates in Industrial Countries, 1820–1987 (Unweighted Average Percentages)

Kinds of Goods and Country	1820	1875	1913	1925	1930–1	1950	1987
Manufactures							
Austria	n.a.	15–20	18	16	24	18	9
Belgium	7	9–10	9	15	14	11	7
Denmark	30	15–20	14	10	n.a.	3	n.a.
France	n.a.	12–15	20	21	30	18	7
Germany	10	4–6	13	20	21	26	7
Italy	n.a.	8–10	18	22	46	25	7
Netherlands	7	3–5	4	6	n.a.	11	7
Spain	n.a.	15–20	41	41	63	n.a.	n.a.
Sweden	n.a.	3–5	20	16	21	9	5
Switzerland	10	4–6	9	14	19	n.a.	3
United Kingdom	50	0	n.a.	5	n.a.	23	7
United States	40	40–50	25	37	48	14	7
Average	22	11–14	17	19	32	16	7
All Goods							
Australia	n.a.	n.a.	16	18	14	17	n.a.
Canada	n.a.	14	17	14	13	9	6
Japan	n.a.	4	20	13	19	4	8
United States	45	41	40	38	45	13	6
Average	n.a.	6	23	21	23	11	7

Source: World Bank, *World Development Report 1991* (Oxford: Oxford University Press), p. 97.

6.4   Effects of Tariff Imposition by a Small Country

In analyzing the effects of a tariff, the size of the country imposing it matters. We begin with the case of a small country. Remember that *small* refers not to geographic size but to economic size in world markets. A small country is a price taker in world markets; that is, it forms such a small share of total purchases and sales of a good that its actions have no perceptible impact on the world price. In other words, a small country's terms of trade are determined exogenously (outside the country), and the country makes its production decision based on those terms of trade.

6.4.1   Partial-Equilibrium Effects on Production, Consumption, and Price

We begin by analyzing the partial-equilibrium effects of a small country's imposition of an import tariff. The analysis is a partial-equilibrium one because it focuses on the tariff's effects in the market for the tariffed good and in the country imposing the tariff. Let D^d

Table 6.2 □ **Tariffs and the Uruguay Round**

Country or Group	Post-Uruguay Round Trade-Weighted Average Tariff (percent)	Average Tariff Cut in Uruguay Round (percent)
Developed countries	3.9	38
Canada	4.8	47
European Union	3.6	37
Japan	1.7	56
United States	3.0	34
Developing countries	12.3	20
Economies in transition	6.0	30

Source: Jeffrey J. Schott, *The Uruguay Round: An Assessment* (Washington, D.C.: Institute for International Economics), 1994, p. 61; data from A. Hoda, "Trade Liberalization Results of the Uruguay Round."

and S^d in Figure 6.3 represent *domestic demand* and *domestic supply*, respectively, of good Y in the small country. (We omit country superscripts because the analysis refers to a single country.) In autarky, point E represents equilibrium in the market for Y, with Y^0 units produced and sold at price P_Y^0. With unrestricted trade, the equilibrium world price of good Y equals P_Y^1, which is less than P_Y^0. This relationship between the autarky and world prices implies that good Y is the country's comparative-disadvantage good. This is consistent with good Y being the country's imported good.

Table 6.3 □ **Chinese Import Tariffs, 1993 (Percent)**

Product	Tariff Rate
Beer	120
Chocolate	15
Cigarettes	150
Coffee	20
Cosmetics	120
Jewelry	90
Record and cassette players	100
Refrigerators	100
Telephones	20
Facsimile machines	12
Color television sets	100
Video games	100

Source: *The Wall Street Journal*, December 10, 1993; data from *Import and Export Tariff Schedule of the People's Republic of China*; Hong Kong Trade Development Council.

Figure 6.3 □ **Effects of an Import Tariff by a Small Country**

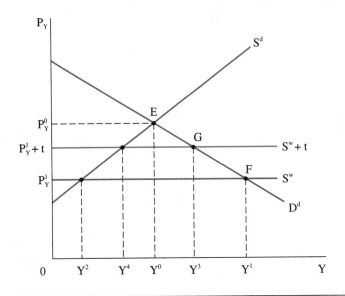

The tariff increases the price of the good by the amount of the tariff, reduces domestic consumption, increases domestic production, and decreases imports.

Because the country is small, it can buy as many units of good Y as it chooses on the world market at price P_Y^1. The perfectly elastic (horizontal) world supply curve, S^w, represents graphically the country's smallness. Under unrestricted trade, the economy would locate at point F, consuming Y^1 units of good Y, producing Y^2 units domestically, and importing $Y^1 - Y^2$ units, all at price P_Y^1. Even though residents consume more good Y at a lower price under unrestricted trade than in autarky, domestic producers can sell fewer units and only at the lower price. This effect of trade on domestic producers of the imported good creates pressure for protection from foreign competition. Unrestricted trade does not eliminate the domestic Y industry, but it lowers the industry output and the price the industry can charge for its product. The cost of domestic production is such that domestic firms can produce units of good Y up to Y^2 more cheaply than they can be imported. Figure 6.3 reflects this, because the domestic supply curve (representing the domestic cost of production) lies below the world supply curve (representing the foreign cost of production or the domestic cost of importing) out to Y^2. For all units of good Y beyond Y^2, foreign production is less costly than domestic production; thus, the country imports those units under unrestricted trade.

Suppose the country imposes a specific tariff of amount t per unit on imported Y to improve the position of domestic producers of good Y. A horizontal line at $P_Y^1 + t$ illustrates the new world supply curve the country faces. Because the small country cannot affect its terms of trade, the tariff is simply an addition to the domestic price of imports.

Figure 6.4 □ **Consumer Surplus**

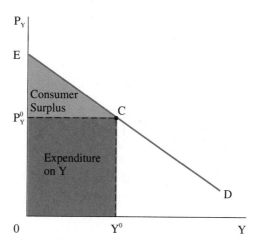

The consumer surplus generated by consumption of a good equals the value of the satisfaction from that consumption over and above the expenditures necessary to obtain the good. Graphically, consumer surplus can be represented as the area under the demand curve out to the level of consumption and above the good's price.

To obtain a unit of imported Y, domestic consumers now must pay P_Y^1 to the foreign producer plus t to the domestic government. Point G represents the new equilibrium. Consumers demand Y^3 units of Y at price P_Y^1 + t; domestic producers supply Y^4 units; and $Y^3 - Y^4$ units are imported. By raising the good's effective domestic price, the tariff discourages consumption of good Y by $Y^1 - Y^3$, encourages domestic production by $Y^4 - Y^2$, and discourages imports by $(Y^1 - Y^2) - (Y^3 - Y^4)$. Domestic producers of good Y now produce more and can sell at a higher price, but domestic consumers consume less and must pay a higher price.

6.4.2   Partial-Equilibrium Effects on Welfare

The impact of a tariff on production, prices, and consumption translates into an effect on the welfare of the small country. In analyzing the change in welfare caused by the tariff, it is useful to separate the effects on consumers from those on producers. For each group we need a measure of welfare, called *consumer surplus* and *producer surplus*, respectively.

Consumer Surplus
Consumer surplus measures the satisfaction consumers receive from a good over the amount they must pay to obtain it. In Figure 6.4 the shaded triangle under the demand curve and above the effective price of the good illustrates the concept of consumer surplus.

Figure 6.5 □ **Producer Surplus**

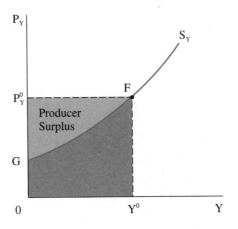

Producer surplus equals the revenue producers receive over and above the minimum necessary for production. Graphically, producer surplus is reflected in the area above the supply curve and below the good's price.

Recall that the height of a demand curve measures the maximum amount consumers are willing and able to pay for each successive unit of the good. Because no one would pay more for a good than the satisfaction gained by its consumption, the height of the demand curve represents the satisfaction derived from consumption of each unit. If consumers demand Y^0 units, the total satisfaction must equal the area under the demand curve for good Y out to Y^0, or the sum of the satisfactions generated by each unit. But consumers must pay P_Y^0 for each unit; in other words, total expenditures on Y equal the area of rectangle $0P_Y^0CY^0$. This implies that the net satisfaction from consumption of Y^0 units over their cost is the area under the demand curve out to Y^0 and above P_Y^0, or triangle P_Y^0EC.

Producer Surplus
Producer surplus measures the revenue producers receive over the minimum required to induce them to supply the good.[12] In Figure 6.5, producer surplus is the area above the supply curve and below the good's price. The height of the supply curve represents the minimum price at which producers would willingly supply each unit of the good. The minimum price rises with the level of production because of increasing opportunity costs. If the market price equals P_Y^0 and firms supply Y^0 units, producer surplus is given by the area above the supply curve out to Y^0 and below P_Y^0. Producers receive total revenue equal to area $0P_Y^0FY^0$. The minimum revenue they must receive to produce Y^0 is area $0GFY^0$. The difference, GP_Y^0F, captures producer surplus.

---

[12]The minimum revenue required to induce production is a short-run concept; that is, it includes variable but not fixed costs.

Figure 6.6 □ **Welfare Effects of an Import Tariff by a Small Country**

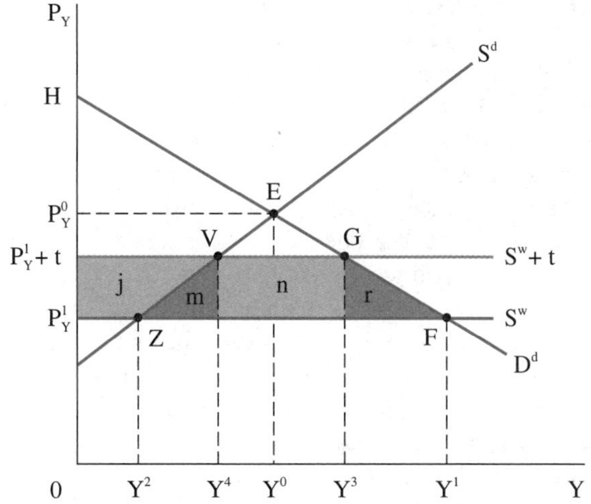

Areas j and n represent transfers of consumer surplus to domestic producers and the domestic government, respectively. Areas m and r represent deadweight losses due to production and consumption inefficiencies generated by the tariff.

Effects of a Tariff on Consumer and Producer Surplus

Figure 6.6 shows the welfare effects of a tariff on imports by a small country as changes in consumer and producer surplus. In autarky, area $P_Y^0 HE$ represents consumer surplus. Under unrestricted trade, consumer surplus rises to $P_Y^1 HF$. When the country imposes a tariff, consumer surplus falls to $(P_Y^1 + t)HG$. Therefore, imposition of the tariff reduces consumer surplus by the area bounded by $P_Y^1(P_Y^1 + t)GF$. We can divide this loss of consumer surplus into revenue, redistribution, production, and consumption effects.

In Figure 6.6, rectangle n is the tariff's **revenue effect,** a transfer from consumer surplus to the government that collects the tariff revenue. The total amount of revenue equals the quantity of imports in the presence of the tariff, $Y^3 - Y^4$, times the tariff rate per unit, t. Although the tariff transfers this revenue from consumers to the government, most analyses assume the government uses the revenue to finance spending it otherwise would finance with some kind of domestic tax. Therefore, the revenue effect of the tariff represents not a net welfare loss to the country but merely a transfer.[13] Consumers of good Y suffer a loss of consumer surplus, but they also enjoy a reduction in their tax bills made possible by the tariff revenue.

[13]One branch of international trade theory suggests this assumption may not be realistic. Rent-seeking or directly unproductive profit-seeking (DUP) analysis argues that individuals and groups in society lobby to capture the available revenue. Resources will be spent in lobbying up to an amount equal to the reward from lobbying (the tariff revenue), making the revenue a loss to society rather than a transfer. Good surveys of the literature on rent-seeking behavior appear in the Tollison and Magee, Brock, and Young references at the end of the chapter.

Area j in Figure 6.6 is the tariff's **redistribution effect**—the loss of consumer surplus transferred to domestic producers as an increase in producer surplus. *(What area in Figure 6.6 represents domestic producer surplus in autarky? With unrestricted trade? With the tariff?)* Like the revenue effect, the tariff's redistribution effect is not lost to society, but merely transferred from consumers to domestic producers. The transfer takes place through the higher prices consumers pay and domestic producers receive with the tariff. Under unrestricted trade, the revenue domestic Y producers receive is $0P_Y^1ZY^2$. With the tariff, producers receive $0(P_Y^1 + t)VY^4$ in revenue. Increased costs offset a portion of the increased revenue as production rises from Y^2 to Y^4; these increased costs are measured by the area under the domestic supply curve between Y^2 and Y^4. The excess of increased revenue over increased cost is area j, the increase in producer surplus.

Triangle m in Figure 6.6 is the tariff's **production effect.** Units Y^2 through Y^4 are now (with the tariff) produced domestically rather than imported. Each unit is produced domestically at a cost (represented by the height of the domestic supply curve) that exceeds the cost of importing it (represented by the height of the world supply curve, S^w). Area m is a **deadweight loss** to the small country, that is, a loss of consumer surplus *not* transferred to another group in the country but lost through inefficient domestic production. Domestic production of units Y^2 through Y^4 is inefficient because the small country is the high-opportunity-cost producer; foreign firms can produce the good at a lower opportunity cost abroad. Efficiency requires each unit of a good to be produced by the low-opportunity-cost producer. This condition was satisfied under unrestricted trade (at point F) but is not satisfied under the tariff. By causing inefficiently high domestic production of good Y, the tariff reduces welfare in the small country by an amount equal to the area of triangle m. The high opportunity cost of domestic production of units Y^2 through Y^4 signals that the resources could be used more productively elsewhere in the economy.

Triangle r in Figure 6.6 represents another deadweight loss to the small country. This **consumption effect** is the loss of consumer surplus that occurs because consumers no longer can obtain units Y^3 through Y^1 at price P_Y^1 with the tariff. For each unit of Y between Y^3 and Y^1, consumers value the good by an amount (measured by the height of the demand curve, D^d) greater than the cost of importing (measured by the height of the world supply curve, S^w). Efficiency requires that each good be consumed to the point at which the marginal benefit from consuming an additional unit just equals the marginal cost of producing it. The unrestricted trade equilibrium (point F) satisfied this condition. The tariff causes consumption to be inefficiently low, thereby lowering welfare.

Net Welfare Effects of a Tariff

The net welfare loss to the small country as a whole from the import tariff equals the sum of areas m and r in Figure 6.6. The remainder of the loss of consumer surplus (areas j and n) is a transfer from domestic consumers to domestic producers and to the government. The small country enjoys no gain in welfare from the tariff to offset the loss of areas m and r. The tariff clearly benefits domestic producers of good Y—but at the direct expense of domestic consumers.

The tariff taxes trade, encourages domestic production, and discourages domestic consumption and imports. The volume of trade falls under the tariff. From this point of view, imposition of a tariff wipes out a portion of the potential gains from trade by artificially limiting the extent to which a country can specialize production according to its comparative advantage and import goods in which it has a comparative disadvantage. In fact, a tariff set at a high enough rate can stop trade completely, returning countries to autarky and eliminating all the gains from trade. Such a prohibitive tariff would equal $P_Y^0 - P_Y^1$ in Figure 6.6.

Notice that in our analysis of the welfare effects of a tariff, we have implicitly used the compensation criterion from section 4.7.3. Domestic producers gain area j from a tariff, and the government gains area n. Domestic consumers lose area j + m + n + r. Can the gainers compensate the losers and still be better off? Clearly the answer is *no:* The gainers from a tariff gain less than the losers lose, making compensation impossible. This is just another way of saying the tariff imposes a *net* welfare loss on the country equal to area m + r.

Under some circumstances, residents of a country may want to create a transfer from consumers to producers and the government. Chapter Eight contains a discussion of this possibility as a potential justification for tariffs. In general, however, if a society wants to make such a transfer, there are more efficient ways to do so than through tariffs. This is because a tariff not only creates the transfer but causes deadweight losses (m + r). We shall see in Chapter Eight that other means of accomplishing the transfer avoid the inefficient production and consumption that create the deadweight losses and, therefore, can effect the desired transfer at a lower cost to society.

6.4.3   Tariffs, Specific Factors, and the Stolper-Samuelson Theorem

Imposition of an import tariff by a small country raises the domestic price of the imported good by the tariff amount. If one or more of the factors cannot move among industries in the short run, the factor specific to the import-competing industry will gain from the tariff, while the factor specific to the export industry will lose, as suggested by the specific-factors model of section 4.5.3. The effect on any factor able to move among industries will depend on the factor owner's consumption pattern. The tariff's welfare effect will be positive if he or she consumes mainly the now cheaper export good and negative if he or she consumes mainly the now more expensive import good.

In the long run, when all factors are mobile among industries, the tariff has the effects predicted by the Stolper-Samuelson theorem (see section 4.3). That theorem states that a rise in the price of a good will cause a (more than proportional) rise in the price of the input used intensively in that good's production and a fall in the price of the other input. Under the assumptions of the Heckscher-Ohlin theorem, production of the import good will involve intensive use of the scarce factor. Therefore, a tariff, by raising the domestic price of the import good, tends to raise the reward to the scarce factor and lower the reward to the abundant factor.

6.4.4   Tariffs and Economies of Scale

Thus far, our analysis of tariffs' effects has assumed that comparative advantage—differences in production possibilities or in tastes—forms the basis for trade. In this case, tariffs interfere with the allocation of production to low-cost locations, causing a loss of gains from trade. Recall from section 5.6 of Chapter Five that economies of scale provide another potential basis for mutually beneficial trade, one applicable even if two countries are identical in their production possibilities and tastes. Tariffs also can interfere with this type of trade. With widespread tariffs, each country must produce small quantities of all the goods domestic consumers want to consume, instead of specializing in the export good and producing a large quantity of it, thereby achieving economies of scale. This implies that the costs of tariffs can be even higher in industries characterized by economies of scale. Recent empirical work suggests a large share of the actual gains from international trade come from exploiting economies of scale, a point of great importance to countries with domestic markets too small to allow their industries to achieve economies of scale without access to foreign markets.[14]

6.4.5 Summary of Effects of an Import Tariff in a Small Country

A small country lowers its overall welfare by imposing an import tariff. The tariff generates no positive effects to offset the deadweight losses from inefficient production and consumption. Producer surplus rises, but the increase is merely a transfer from domestic consumers. Even if the society deemed it desirable to redistribute income from consumers to producers, alternate policies could accomplish this with no deadweight losses from the price-distorting effects of a tariff, as we shall see in Chapter Eight.

6.5 Effects of Tariff Imposition by a Large Country

A *large* country constitutes a share of world markets sufficient to enable it to affect its terms of trade. When this condition is satisfied, the country may be able to use an import tariff to improve its terms of trade. Therefore, a large country can in some cases improve its welfare by imposing a tariff, an outcome impossible for a small country. The United States plays a large enough role in many markets to affect world prices through its trade policy. However, many other countries are also large in a few markets. Some developing countries, for example, produce a large share of the world total of some products and therefore possess some market power.

6.5.1 Partial-Equilibrium Effects on Production, Consumption, and Price

The supply curve of good Y facing the large country is the summation of domestic supply and supply from the rest of the world. In Figure 6.7, S^d represents the *domestic* supply, S^w the supply from the rest of the *world*, and S^{d+w} the total supply. At each price for good Y, we find the total quantity supplied by adding the quantity supplied domestically (read off the domestic supply curve) to the quantity supplied in the rest of the world (read off the world supply curve). The total supply curve slopes upward because the large country, as it buys more Y in world markets, pushes up the world price.

---

[14]See section 5.6 and Chapter Eight's discussion of strategic trade policy in section 8.4.3.

Figure 6.7 □ **The Total Supply of Good Y Equals the Sum of Domestic Supply and Supply by the Rest of the World**

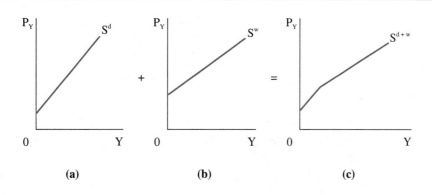

$$P_Y \quad S^d \qquad + \qquad P_Y \quad S^w \qquad = \qquad P_Y \quad S^{d+w}$$

| 0 | Y | 0 | Y | 0 | Y |

(a)   (b)   (c)

A large country faces an upward-sloping total supply curve.

Figure 6.8 combines the total supply curve, S^{d+w}, with the domestic demand curve, D^d, to determine the unrestricted trade equilibrium at point C. Domestic residents consume Y^0 units of good Y, of which Y^1 units are produced domestically and $Y^0 - Y^1$ units imported, at the equilibrium price of P_Y^0. For the first Y^1 units of output, domestic production involves a lower cost than importing; beyond Y^1, the domestic country becomes the high-cost producer. Consumer and producer surplus under unrestricted trade equal the areas $P_Y^0 EC$ and $GP_Y^0 F$, respectively.

Now the country imposes an import tariff of t per unit on good Y. The total supply curve shifts upward by t to $S^{d+w} + t$. For each unit imported, domestic consumers must pay the price charged by foreign producers *plus* the tariff. Point H represents the new equilibrium. The domestic price of good Y rises to P_Y^1; Y^2 units are consumed, Y^3 produced domestically, and $Y^2 - Y^3$ imported. Consumer surplus now is $P_Y^1 EH$, and producer surplus $GP_Y^1 I$. Areas j, m, n, and r represent, respectively, the transfer from consumer to producer surplus (redistribution effect), the deadweight loss from inefficiently high domestic production (production effect), the tariff revenue transferred from domestic consumers to the government (revenue effect), and the deadweight loss due to inefficiently low domestic consumption (consumption effect). Thus far, the analysis exactly parallels that of the small-country case from section 6.4.2.

Notice, however, that area n cannot represent the full amount of tariff revenue. Total tariff revenue must equal the number of imports $(Y^2 - Y^3)$ times the amount of the tariff (the vertical distance between the S^{d+w} and $S^{d+w} + t$ supply curves). The revenue effect, area n, is only a portion of the total revenue—the share paid by domestic consumers in higher prices for good Y (that is, P_Y^1 rather than P_Y^0). Area s represents the remainder of the revenue, the portion of the tariff borne by foreign producers of good Y in the form of lower prices for their products. Before imposition of the tariff, foreign producers received P_Y^0 for each unit of good Y exported. With the tariff, they

Figure 6.8 ▫ **Effects of an Import Tariff by a Large Country**

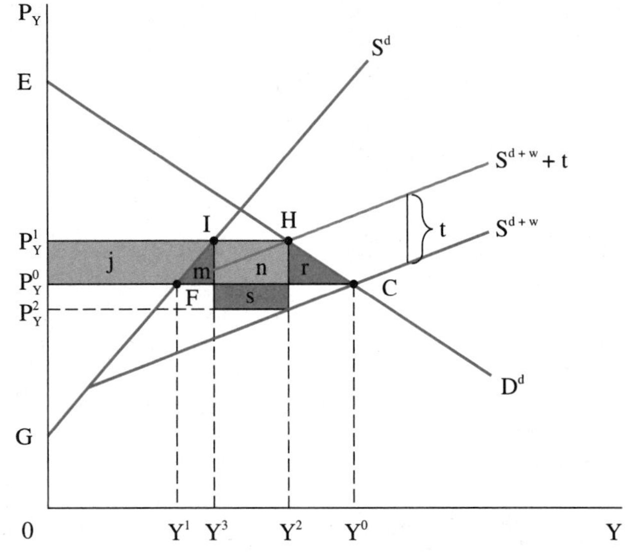

The tariff reduces consumption from Y^0 to Y^2, increases domestic production from Y^1 to Y^3, and decreases imports. The price domestic consumers pay rises from P_Y^0 to P_Y^1, and the price foreign producers receive falls from P_Y^0 to P_Y^2. Area j is a transfer from domestic consumers to domestic producers. Areas m and r are deadweight losses reflecting inefficient production and consumption, respectively. Area n is a transfer from domestic consumers to the government. Area s is a transfer from foreign producers to the domestic government.

receive only P_Y^2, or the price paid by domestic consumers (P_Y^1) *minus* the tariff, because the tariff goes to the domestic government, not to foreign producers.

Why does the tariff force foreign producers to accept a lower price for good Y? The tariff raises the price paid by domestic consumers, lowering the quantity of good Y demanded. The tariff-imposing country is large enough, by assumption, for this decline in quantity demanded to have a significant impact on the market. When foreign producers face a substantially lower quantity demanded for their product, opportunity costs of production fall, and so does price. This effect of the tariff is called the **terms-of-trade effect.**

The analyses of the welfare effects of areas j, m, n, and r are precisely the same as in the small-country case. Areas j and n represent transfers within the country, and m and r are deadweight welfare losses caused by inefficient domestic production and consumption. The large-country case introduces a gain to the tariff-imposing country in the form of tariff revenue paid by foreign producers, area s. If the deadweight losses (the production and consumption effects) exceed this revenue gain (the terms-of-trade effect), the tariff harms the large country. If the revenue gain from foreign producers exceeds the deadweight losses, the country may improve its welfare by imposing the import tariff. Table 6.4 summarizes these results. Of course, the tariff still affects the

Table 6.4 □ **Summary of Possible Net Welfare Effects of an Import Tariff by a Large Country**

If:	Then:
m + r = s	No net effect on domestic welfare Negative net effect on world welfare
m + r < s	Positive net effect on domestic welfare Negative net effect on world welfare
m + r > s	Negative net effect on domestic welfare Negative net effect on world welfare

domestic distribution of income. Domestic producers of good Y gain relative to consumers. In the long run, when resources are free to move among industries, the Stolper-Samuelson theorem implies that owners of resources used intensively in production of good Y gain, while owners of resources used intensively in production of other goods lose (see section 4.3).

The tariff also exerts a redistributive effect among countries. Even if conditions are such that the tariff-imposing country gains, all gains come at the expense of the trading partner, which must accept lower prices for its exports. In other words, *a tariff has a negative impact on world welfare regardless of the size of the countries involved.* Tariffs cause inefficient production and consumption patterns and a loss of part of the gains from trade. If the industries involved exhibit economies of scale, tariffs can impose an additional cost on the economy by limiting firms' abilities to specialize and capture those scale economies.

6.5.2 Optimal Tariffs and the Threat of Retaliation

We have seen that imposition of an import tariff by a large country has two effects on the country's welfare. The first, called the *volume-of-trade effect,* occurs when the tariff lowers welfare by discouraging trade. Second, by lowering the price foreign producers receive, the tariff causes a terms-of-trade effect that enhances welfare in the tariff-imposing country. The tariff's net effect on the large country's welfare depends on the relative magnitudes of the volume-of-trade and terms-of-trade effects. The tariff rate that maximizes the net benefits to the country is called the **optimal tariff.** Note that the optimal tariff for a small country always equals zero because of the absence of any terms-of-trade effect. For a large country beginning from unrestricted trade, increasing the tariff raises welfare up to a point beyond which welfare begins to decline.

The concept of an optimal tariff deserves some skepticism. Imposition of a tariff reduces total *world* welfare regardless of the size of the countries involved. The source of a large country's ability to affect its terms of trade is simply its ability to force its trading partners to accept lower prices for their exports. Any improvement in the terms of trade that a large country generates by imposing an import tariff also causes a deterioration in the terms of trade of the country's trading partner. The trading partner's losses exceed the tariff-imposing country's gains, because the tariff causes an inefficient pattern of production and consumption. Policies such as optimal tariffs that try to improve the welfare of the domestic country at the expense of others are called **beggar-thy-neighbor policies.**

The beggar-thy-neighbor characteristic of tariffs implies that they risk retaliation by trading partners. The optimal tariff is the one that maximizes the imposing country's welfare *assuming* the trading partner does nothing in response to having its exports tariffed and its terms of trade harmed. This seems like a rather unrealistic assumption, since the tariff definitely reduces the exporting country's welfare. A tariff by one country invites retaliation, which invites counter-retaliation, and so on. A tariff war that progressively lowers the volume of trade and welfare for all combatants may result. Such a war eventually could drive the participants all the way back to autarky, eliminating all the potential gains from trade.

6.6   The Effective Rate of Protection

It is tempting to assume that domestic producers in all industries with high import tariffs receive high degrees of protection. However, such a simple relationship between tariff rates and degrees of protection does not necessarily hold. To determine the actual degree of protection for any domestic industry, we must consider not only tariffs within the industry itself but also any tariffs on inputs the industry uses. The relationship among tariffs in related markets and industries is called **tariff structure.**

Although tariff structure differs across sectors of the economy, tariff rates generally rise as products move through various stages of production, as illustrated in Figure 6.9. Raw materials tend to have lower tariff rates than the manufactured products ultimately produced with them, a phenomenon known as **cascading tariffs.** The Uruguay Round tariff cuts reduced the difference in tariffs applied to processed and nonprocessed versions of industrial goods by about 37 percent. When the negotiated cuts take effect, cascading tariffs will disappear in paper, jute, and tobacco products and be reduced substantially in wood and metal products.[15]

Considering the importance of tariff structure, clearly the tariff rate on a final good may provide an inaccurate measure of the effective protection provided to domestic producers of the good. An alternative measure that accounts for the importance of tariff structure is the **effective rate of protection (ERP).** To illustrate, suppose a domestically produced television set sells at the world price of $500 under unrestricted trade. The domestic producer uses $300 worth of imported inputs (picture tube, chassis, tuner, and various electronic components). The $200 difference between the world price of the finished television set and the cost of the imported components represents **domestic value-added (V).** Domestic value-added includes the payments made to domestic labor and capital inputs (for example, for assembling the imported components into a finished television set). Under unrestricted trade, domestic value-

---

[15]Jeffrey J. Schott, *The Uruguay Round: An Assessment* (Washington, D.C.: Institute for International Economics, 1994), 63.

Figure 6.9 □ **Average Tariffs in Industrial Countries for Selected Primary and Processed Commodities, 1986**

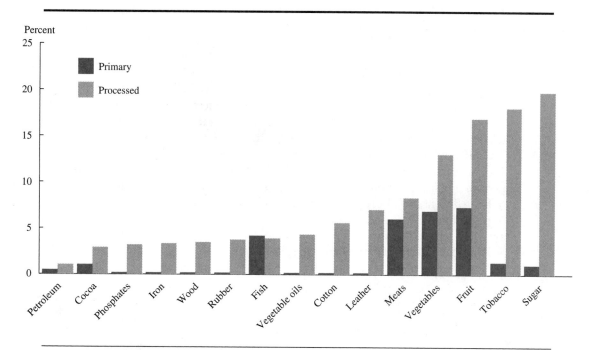

Source: The World Bank, *Global Economic Prospects and the Developing Countries 1991* (Washington, D.C.: The World Bank), p. 25

added cannot exceed $200, or the price of domestically produced television sets will exceed that of imported ones and the domestic sets will not sell.

An ad valorem tariff of 10 percent on imported television sets would raise the domestic price of an imported TV to $550 (= $500[1 + 0.10]). The price of the domestically produced set then could rise as high as $550 and still compete against imported sets in the domestic market. The nominal tariff rate is 10 percent—but is this the effective rate of protection? The ERP answers the question "What percentage increase in domestic value-added does the tariff make possible?" Domestic value-added under unrestricted trade (V_0) was $200; a higher level of value-added would have rendered domestically produced television sets noncompetitive by raising their price above the $500 world price. Domestic value-added with a 10 percent tariff on imported television sets (V_1) can rise to $250 (or $550 − $300 worth of imported inputs) and still allow domestic TVs to compete. The effective rate of protection provided for domestic television producers by the 10 percent tariff on imports of finished television sets is ERP = $(V_1 - V_0)/V_0$ = ($250 − $200)/$200 = 25%. The 10 percent nominal tariff allows domestic value-added to rise by 25 percent, and this measures the degree of protection for domestic producers.

A 10 percent nominal tariff does not always imply an effective rate of protection of 25 percent. The relationship between the nominal tariff rate and the effective rate of protection depends on (1) the share of imported inputs in the production process and (2) the presence or absence of tariffs on imported inputs. To examine the impact on the effective rate of protection of a tariff on imported inputs, consider the 10 percent tariff on finished television sets accompanied by a 5 percent tariff on imported components used in domestic production of TVs. The 5 percent tariff on inputs implies that domestic producers now must pay $300(1 + 0.05) = $315 for their inputs. Domestic value-added with the tariff package can be as high as $V_1 = \$500(1 + 0.10)$ − $300(1 + 0.05) = $550 − $315 = $235 before domestic sets become noncompetitive. This new value-added is the difference between the tariffed price of imported television sets and the tariffed price of imported inputs used in domestic production. The effective rate of protection is ERP = $(V_1 - V_0)/V_0$ = ($235 − $200)/$200 = 17.5%. Imposition of the 5 percent tariff on imported inputs lowers the ERP of a 10 percent nominal tariff on finished television sets from 25 to 17.5 percent. The tariff on finished TVs taxes imports of both inputs and assembly costs (foreign value-added). If imported inputs used domestically do not face a tariff, domestic value-added can absorb all the differential, as columns 1 and 2 of Figure 6.10 illustrate.

The general formula for calculating the effective rate of protection is

$$ERP = \frac{t_f - at_i}{1 - a},$$

where t_f is the nominal tariff rate on the imported *finished* good (imported television sets), a is the value of imported inputs as a share of the value of the final good under free trade ($300/$500 = 0.6), and t_i is the tariff on imported *inputs* used by domestic producers.[16] From the general expression for ERP, we can see that whenever the tariff rate on finished goods exceeds the rate on imported inputs $(t_f > t_i)$, the ERP is greater than the tariff on finished goods (ERP > t_f). When imported finished goods and imported inputs are tariffed at the same rate $(t_f = t_i)$, that rate accurately measures the extent of protection provided for the domestic industry (ERP = $t_f = t_i$). When a country tariffs imported inputs at a rate exceeding that on finished goods $(t_f < t_i)$, the effective rate of protection is lower than the tariff rate on finished goods (ERP < t_f). In fact, the ERP can be negative even though t_f is positive! A negative ERP implies that the tariff structure makes it more difficult for domestically produced goods to compete against foreign ones. Other things being equal, the effective rate of protection is higher (1) the higher the nominal tariff rate on finished goods, (2) the lower the tariff rate on imported inputs, and (3) the larger the share of imported inputs in the value of the good (if $t_f > t_i$).[17]

---

[16]With more than one input, the sum of the shares and tariff rates for all inputs replaces the at_i term. It is easy to show that $(V_1 - V_0)/V_0 = (t_f - at_i)/(1 - a)$. Letting P denote the price of the finished product, $(V_1 - V_0)/V_0 = [P(1 + t_f) - Pa(1 + t_i) - P(1 - a)]/P(1 - a) = (t_f - at_i)/(1 - a)$.

[17]Results (1) through (3) can be verified by taking the partial derivative of the ERP equation with respect to t_f, t_i, and a, respectively.

Figure 6.10 □ **Calculating the Effective Rate of Protection**

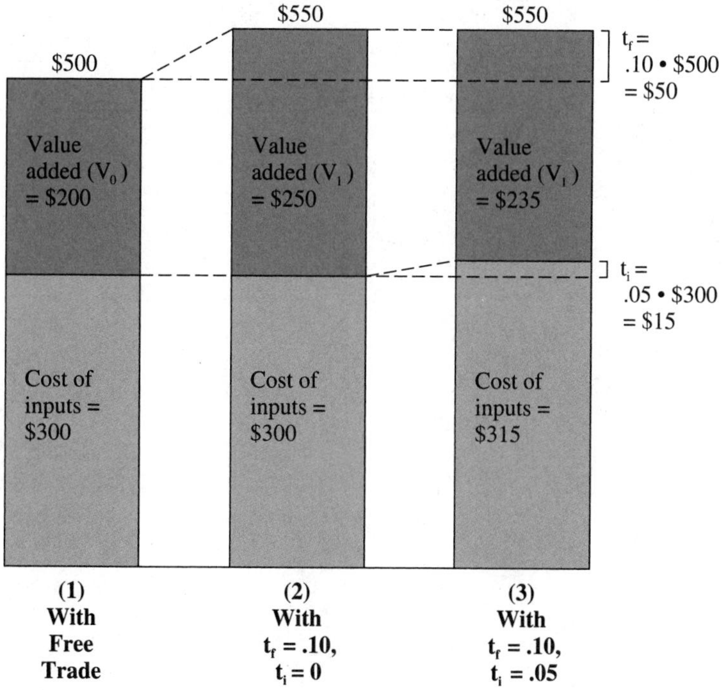

The effective rate of protection measures the amount by which a given tariff structure allows domestic value-added to rise, expressed as a percentage. A tariff of 10 percent on finished TVs with no tariff on imported inputs allows domestic value-added to rise by $50, or 25 percent. A tariff of 10 percent on finished TVs along with a 5 percent tariff on inputs allows domestic value-added to rise by $35, or 17.5 percent.

Effective rates of protection differ greatly from actual or nominal tariff rates for many industries, as Table 6.5 reports. Actual tariff rates significantly underestimate the effective protection received by many industries in the United States as well in other countries. The effective-rate-of-protection idea carries over to nontariff barriers as well; trade barriers on inputs always lower the effective protection given to finished-goods producers.

Notice that Table 6.5 includes several instances of negative rates of effective protection. Leather products and wood products in Japan exhibit high negative rates, results of Japan's high tariffs on the leather and wood that comprise those industries' main inputs.

6.7 Off-Shore Assembly Provisions

We already have seen that tariff rates typically differ by industry and by country, making measurement difficult. However, many countries including the United States

Table 6.5 □ **Post-Tokyo Round Effective Rates of Protection and Nominal Tariff Rates in the United States, the European Community, and Japan (Percent)**

Industry	United States		European Community		Japan	
	Tariff	ERP	Tariff	ERP	Tariff	ERP
Agriculture, forestry, and fishing	1.8	1.9	4.9	4.1	18.4	21.4
Food, beverage, and tobacco	4.7	10.2	10.6	17.4	25.4	50.3
Textiles	9.2	18.0	7.2	8.8	3.3	−2.4
Wearing apparel	22.7	43.3	13.4	19.3	13.8	42.2
Leather products	4.2	5.0	2.0	−2.2	3.0	−14.8
Footwear	8.8	15.4	11.6	20.1	15.7	50.0
Wood products	1.7	1.7	2.5	1.7	0.3	−30.6
Furniture and fixtures	4.1	5.5	5.6	11.3	5.1	10.3
Paper and paper products	0.2	−0.9	5.4	8.3	2.1	1.8
Printing and publishing	0.7	0.9	2.1	−1.0	0.1	−1.5
Chemicals	2.4	3.7	8.0	11.7	4.8	6.4
Petroleum and related products	1.4	4.7	1.2	3.4	2.2	4.1
Rubber products	2.5	2.0	3.5	2.3	1.1	−5.0
Nonmetallic mineral products	5.3	9.2	3.7	6.5	0.5	−0.5
Glass and glass products	6.2	9.8	7.7	12.2	5.1	8.1
Iron and steel	3.6	6.2	4.7	11.6	2.8	4.3
Nonferrous metals	0.7	0.5	2.1	8.3	1.1	1.7
Metal products	4.8	7.9	5.5	7.1	5.2	9.2
Nonelectrical machinery	3.3	4.1	4.4	4.7	4.4	6.7
Electrical machinery	4.4	6.3	7.9	10.8	4.3	6.7
Transport equipment	2.5	1.9	8.0	12.3	1.5	0.0
Miscellaneous manufactures	4.2	5.8	4.7	6.6	4.6	7.3

Source: Alan V. Deardorff and Robert M. Stern, "The Effects of the Tokyo Round on the Structure of Protection," in R. E. Baldwin and A. O. Krueger, eds., *The Structure and Evolution of U.S. Trade Policy* (Chicago: University of Chicago Press, 1984), pp. 370–375. Reprinted with permission.

have special tariff provisions that make things even more complicated. The most common are **off-shore assembly provisions (OAPs),** which allow reduced tariffs on goods assembled abroad from domestically produced components. Suppose, for example, that the U.S. imposes a tariff of 50 percent on imported luggage and that the Bahamas develops an industry that assembles luggage from U.S.-made components. With no off-shore assembly provision, a Bahamian suitcase with a free-trade price of $200 would sell for $300 in the United States, since $300 = $200(1 + 0.50); in other words, the tariff would equal $100. The simplest form of off-shore assembly provision would state that suitcases imported into the United States from the Bahamas must pay the 50 percent tariff *only* on Bahamian value-added, not on the full value of the suitcase. If we assume each $200 suitcase uses $150 worth of U.S.-

made components, making Bahamian value-added $50 per suitcase, then the suitcases would sell in the United States for $200 + ($50)(0.50) = $225. The OAP reduces the tariff from $100 to $25 per suitcase (although the tariff *rate* remains 50 percent) by restricting the tariff to foreign value-added and allowing U.S.-made components to re-enter the United States tariff free. The United States maintains such OAP arrangements with many countries, among them the 28 members of the Caribbean Basin Initiative that includes the Bahamas.

6.8   Taxes on Exports

In some cases, countries place trade restrictions such as taxes on exports as well as on imports. Export taxes violate the Constitution in the United States, although other export restrictions are legal. During the framing of the Constitution, southern states, fearful that protectionist-minded northern interests would tax the South's massive exports of cotton and tobacco, successfully pressured for the export-tax ban.

The goal of an export tax obviously would not be to protect domestic producers from foreign competition. Why might a country tax its own exports? There are two basic reasons.[18] The first is in response to pressure by domestic consumer groups to keep the domestic price of a good low; goods such as food are particularly susceptible to political pressure. For example, pressure for export taxes and other restrictions has arisen several times in response to U.S. exports of grain to the former Soviet Union that put upward pressure on U.S. grain prices. The second possible reason for an export tax applies only to large countries. Such countries may endeavor to exploit their power in a world market by using export taxes to raise the prices foreign buyers pay for their exports. Such a mechanism allowed the Organization of Petroleum Exporting Countries (OPEC) to engineer the famous oil price increases of the 1970s.

6.8.1   Export Tax Imposition by a Small Country

Consider the effect of an export tax imposed by a small country, that is, a country that can export all it wants without lowering the world price. In Figure 6.11, point E represents equilibrium under unrestricted trade in the market for good X. The small country produces X^1 units, consumes X^2 units, and exports $X^1 - X^2$ at the world price P_X^1. Note that the world price of good X lies *above* the country's autarky price (P_X^0) because X is the export good in which the country has a comparative advantage.

The country levies a specific tax of t per unit on exports of good X. For each unit exported, domestic producers still receive the world price (P_X^1) from consumers; but the producers must pay t to the domestic government, leaving a *net* price to the producer of $P_X^1 - t$. Domestic production falls from X^1 to X^3, and domestic consumption rises from X^2 to X^4. Exports fall to $X^3 - X^4$.

---

[18]A third set of reasons, which underlie the bulk of U.S. export restrictions, include national security, weapons nonproliferation, and foreign policies. For an excellent summary of U.S. export restrictions, including economically and politically motivated ones, see the Richardson book in the chapter references.

Figure 6.11 □ **Effects of an Export Tax by a Small Country**

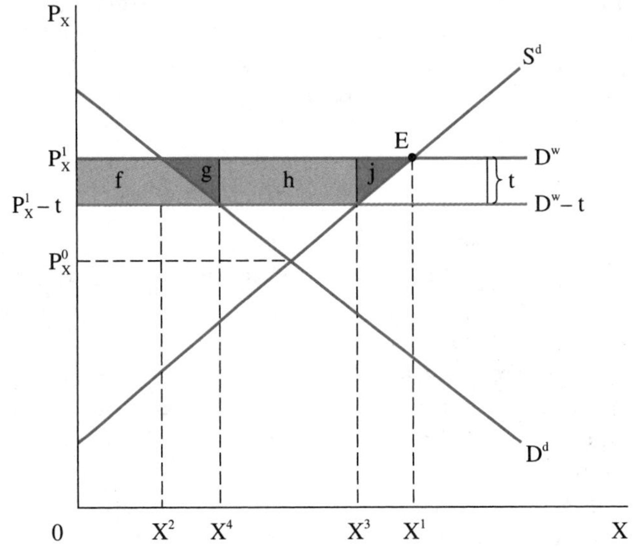

The export tax encourages domestic consumption and discourages domestic production and exports. Consumers gain at the expense of domestic producers.

Domestic producers of good X lose producer surplus equal to f + g + h + j because of the export tax. Area f is a transfer to domestic consumers, who now can buy good X at price $P_X^1 - t$ rather than P_X^1. Area g is a deadweight loss from the inefficient increase in domestic consumption of good X caused by the tax. Too much X is consumed domestically because the marginal benefit of domestic consumption at X^4 (given by the height of D^d) is less than the marginal benefit of foreign consumption of X (measured by the world price foreign consumers are willing to pay for the country's exports). Foreign consumers value the units of good X between X^2 and X^4 more highly than do domestic consumers. Area h is a transfer from producer surplus to the domestic government in the form of tax revenue. Area j is the deadweight loss from curtailment of domestic production to X^3. For all units of good X between X^1 and X^3, the cost of producing domestically is less than the cost of producing elsewhere. So long as consumers somewhere in the world are willing to pay P_X^1 for good X, efficiency requires that domestic production be X^1, not X^3.

Some small, very open economies use export taxes primarily as a revenue-generating mechanism; but the most common reason for export taxes is to "protect" domestic consumers from competition by foreign consumers. The discussion of Canadian energy exports in Case Two of Chapter Four provides one example. A second example involves a recent trade dispute between Argentina and the United States. In this case, "consumers" actually were firms that buy soybeans for refining. The U.S. National Soybean Producers Association argued that Argentina's export

Figure 6.12 □ Effects of an Export Tax by a Large Country

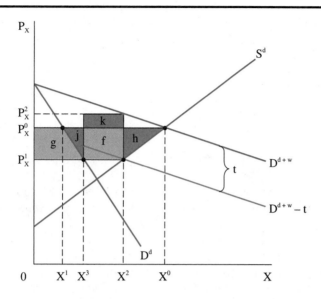

The tax-imposing country suffers deadweight losses equal to area h + j and enjoys a gain in revenue from foreign consumers equal to area k. If (h + j) > k, the country suffers a net welfare loss from the tax. If (h + j) < k, the country enjoys a net welfare gain. The export tax reduces world welfare regardless of the relative sizes of h, j, and k.

tax on soybeans allowed Argentine soybean processors to pay artificially low prices for soybeans, providing an unfair advantage to the refiners.

The effect of an export tax by a small country is to transfer welfare from domestic producers to domestic consumers. Because the tax causes inefficient production and consumption decisions, there is a net welfare loss. Domestic producers lose more than domestic consumers gain, so export taxes fail the test of whether gainers can compensate losers.

6.8.2 Export Tax Imposition by a Large Country

The second reason for export taxes applies only to countries large in the market for the export good under consideration. An export tax may allow such countries to exploit their market position by charging higher prices for their exports than otherwise would be possible. Consider the case of a country that produces a large share of total world output of a particular product, good X. In Figure 6.12, S^d represents the country's supply curve, D^d the country's domestic demand curve, and D^{d+w} the total world demand curve for good X. The distance between D^d and D^{d+w} at each price measures the rest of the world's demand for good X. Under unrestricted trade, the country would produce X^0 units, of which X^1 would be sold domestically and $X^0 - X^1$ exported; price P_X^0 would apply to both domestic sales and exports.

Table 6.6 □ **Summary of Possible Net Welfare Effects of an Export Tax by a Large Country**

If:	Then:
$h + j = k$	No net effect on domestic welfare Negative net effect on world welfare
$h + j < k$	Positive net effect on domestic welfare Negative net effect on world welfare
$h + j > k$	Negative net effect on domestic welfare Negative net effect on world welfare

Now suppose the country imposes a tax of t per unit on X exports; units sold domestically are exempt from the tax. The new world demand curve shifts down by the amount of the tax to $D^{d+w} - t$. Production falls to X^2, with X^3 sold in the domestic market and $X^2 - X^3$ exported. Producers receive price P_X^1 for each unit sold, and the government receives t for each unit exported. Domestic consumers pay P_X^1, but foreign consumers pay P_X^2, with P_X^1 going to producers and t to the exporting-country government.

Domestic consumer surplus rises by area g as domestic consumers can buy the good at P_X^1 rather than P_X^0. Domestic producer surplus falls by area f + g + h + j, of which f is a transfer to the government (revenue effect), g is a transfer to domestic consumers (redistribution effect), h is a deadweight loss from the inefficient reduction of production (production effect), and j is a deadweight loss caused by the inefficient expansion of domestic consumption (consumption effect). However, area f, the transfer from domestic producers to the domestic government, cannot capture all the revenue from the tax. Total tax revenue must equal area f + k, whose length is the number of units exported and whose height is the per-unit export tax. Area k is paid to the domestic government by *foreign* consumers, who now must pay P_X^2 for each unit of good X. Thus, k is a gain to the country imposing the export tax that comes at the expense of trading partners. If this transfer from abroad exceeds the deadweight losses (h + j) from the tax, the tax-imposing country will enjoy a net welfare gain, as Table 6.6 summarizes. The magnitude of the tax that maximizes the net gain (k − [h + j]) is the optimal export tariff.

Because any net gain comes from foreign consumers, the export tax's effect on world welfare is always negative. Attempts to use beggar-thy-neighbor export taxes can backfire. Such policies create an incentive for foreign consumers to find new suppliers who have an enhanced incentive (the higher world price) to enter the market. Ghana and Nigeria suffered such a fate in the cocoa market, and Nigeria and Zaire in palm oil.[19] OPEC's use of export taxes spurred a dramatic decrease in the growth of petroleum use as well as increased production by non-OPEC suppliers such as Britain (from its North Sea reserves) and the United States (from Alaska's north slope). OPEC produced almost half of the world's oil in 1975 but less than one-third in 1988.

---

[19]World Bank, *World Development Report, 1988* (New York: Oxford University Press), 91.

Case One
Fleeing Tariffs[20]

We have seen that import tariffs cause consumption of the tariffed good to fall and domestic production of it to rise. In today's world economy, where firms increasingly are footloose and spread their production facilities around the world, tariffs can exert even wider influence. For example, firms can alter their production locations to avoid a tariff. Sometimes a tariff's effects turn out quite differently from what policy makers in the tariff-imposing country intended.

In August 1991, the United States imposed a 63 percent tariff on imports of Japanese active-matrix flat-panel computer screens, used on laptop and notebook computers.[21] The tariff did not apply to imports of finished computers, just to screens imported as components. The screen comprises a major share of the total cost of a computer, up to 50 percent in some models. A spokesperson for IBM estimated the tariff could increase the cost of the company's personal computers by as much as $600 and called the tariff "an eviction notice to the fastest-growing part of the computer industry." *(What would be the effective rate of protection for computer manufacturers if finished computers have a zero tariff and imported screens that make up 50 percent of the value of the computer are tariffed at 63 percent?)*

Computer manufacturers responded by moving their laptop production abroad. Within a month of the tariff action, Toshiba announced it would begin exporting its laptops from Japan to the United States in finished form instead of assembling them in Irvine, California, from imported components. Apple moved production from Colorado to Ireland. The major Japanese screen exporter, Hosiden, announced it would continue to sell to Apple Computer abroad, but it no longer would sell its screens in the United States.

Computer manufacturers' claims that there was no real U.S. screen industry to protect made the computer-screen decision even more controversial. A handful of U.S. firms do manufacture screens, but most operate on a small scale, inadequate to supply computer giants such as Apple and Compaq, and concentrate on government and military contracts for small orders of highly specialized products. U.S. computer firms sued in the U.S. Court of International Trade to have the screen tariff removed. The court ruled against the government, concluding the International Trade Commission had improperly defined the industry. Before the court's ruling could take effect, Optical Imaging Systems, the only U.S. maker of active-matrix displays, asked the government to remove the tariff.

---

[20]This case uses material from G. Pascal Zachary, "Duty on Screens Could Lift Price of U.S. Laptops," *The Wall Street Journal,* February 11, 1991; "Toshiba Shifts Output of Some Laptop PCs from U.S. Over Tariff," *The Wall Street Journal,* September 26, 1991; "Did Washington Lose Sight of the Big Picture?" *Business Week,* December 2, 1991; "U.S. Court Rules Against Tariff on Japanese Screens," *The Wall Street Journal,* January 4, 1993; and G. Pascal Zachary, "Road Toward Success at 'Flat Scree is Full of Bumps," *The Wall Street Journal,* April 29, 1994.

[21]The United States imposed the tariff on computer screens as an antidumping duty in response to Japan's allegedly selling screens below cost in the U.S. market. We shall examine dumping and antidumping duties in Chapter Seven; for now, the duty can be treated like any other tariff.

In April 1994, the Pentagon announced plans to spend $600 million over the next five years to boost U.S. producers of active-matrix displays and encourage entry by large electronics producers such as Motorola, IBM, AT&T, and Xerox. Critics of the proposal claim that existing small U.S. specialty producers already satisfy the military's needs for displays and that the proposal's military link disguises the project's true protectionist motivation.

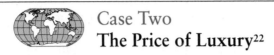

Case Two
The Price of Luxury[22]

For years, the U.S. auto industry has complained about lack of access to the Japanese market. U.S.-based auto firms claim that Japanese auto producers refuse to buy U.S. parts, that the auto-safety inspection system biases the spare-part market in favor of Japanese parts, and that Japanese auto firms refuse to allow their dealers to carry U.S. car lines. The long simmering dispute flared in 1995 when Japanese auto firms refused U.S. demands that they make voluntary pledges to increase their purchases of U.S. auto parts.[23]

In response, the United States threatened to impose 100 percent tariffs on imports of 13 Japanese luxury car models, priced from $26,000 to more than $50,000. Total sales of Japanese luxury cars in the United States totaled $5.9 billion in 1994. The selection of these cars for retaliation promised to win political support for the Democratic Party from key auto-producing states—Michigan, Missouri, and Ohio. Policy makers decided against including minivans on the retaliatory tariff list, fearing adverse political repercussions from the middle class.

The U.S. trade representative announced the tariffs would take effect on June 28, retroactive on all cars entering the United States after May 20, if the two countries failed to reach a compromise. The affected Japanese auto producers stopped production to avoid building backlog inventories in the event of prolonged retaliatory tariffs. European luxury car producers expected big gains in sales, because the young affluent market for the tariffed cars seemed more likely to switch to Jaguars, BMWs, Mercedes, Volvos, and Saabs than to U.S.-made Lincolns and Cadillacs, which typically appeal to older buyers. Experts estimated that many of the over 2,000 U.S. dealerships for the luxury Japanese lines would go out of business, leaving approximately 87,000 employees out of work. Many of the dealerships earned very low profits even before the tariff, so industry analysts concluded that even a 20 percent tariff would kill sales and close the dealerships. The dealers would have no legal recourse for their economic loses, nor would their employees for their lost jobs. The Japanese government put together a list of products for counter-retaliation tariffs, including autos and auto parts, aircraft, and food products.

[22]See "U.S., Europe Face Win-Win Situation in Auto Trade Battle With Japanese," *The Wall Street Journal,* May 10, 1995, A4; and Robert L. Simison and Neal Templin, "Battle Begins for Luxury Imp Market," *The Wall Street Journal,* May 18, 1995, A2.

[23]Case One in Chapter Five reports on one such "voluntary" agreement in semiconductors.

Some observers question the U.S. auto industry's claims about the closed nature of the Japanese market and attribute low U.S. auto sales in Japan to the fact that U.S. producers have refused to supply either right-hand-drive vehicles or vehicles with engines of less than 3,000 cubic centimeters (a class that includes nine out of every ten new cars sold in Japan). German car manufacturers, without these self-imposed handicaps, have expanded their car sales in Japan. Even some U.S. auto parts producers opposed the tariffs, citing their own successful sales efforts in Japan.

Perhaps the most controversial aspect of the U.S. announcement was the unilateral nature of the action. Just months before, both the United States and Japan participated in the inauguration of the World Trade Organization (WTO), successor to the GATT, which includes elaborate new trade-dispute mechanisms to handle such disagreements. Rather than filing a case alleging Japanese closure of its automotive markets and allowing the WTO to rule according to the specified procedures, the United States chose to act unilaterally and only then file a WTO case. Japan retaliated with its own appeal to the WTO, alleging that the U.S. action violated WTO rules, but the United States vetoed Japan's request to have the case heard on a special expedited basis before the American tariffs took effect.

Just hours before the punitive U.S. tariffs were to take effect, the two countries announced an agreement. Japan's five major auto producers said they would increase their U.S. auto production by 25 percent by 1998, plans already underway before the dispute arose. U.S. negotiators announced, based on their own calculations, that the Japanese firms' added U.S. production would lead to more demand for U.S. auto parts, but neither the firms nor the Japanese government either confirmed or denied the numbers cited. Japan's Ministry of International Trade and Industry pledged to send letters to all Japanese car dealerships noting the dealers' legal right to sell U.S.-made cars, even over the objections of the dealers' Japanese manufacturers. And the Japanese government reiterated its plans to deregulate the car repair and safety-inspection systems, again plans that already were in place before the dispute.

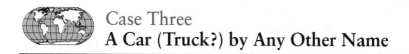

Case Three
A Car (Truck?) by Any Other Name

Since 1981, U.S. imports of Japanese automobiles (but *not* trucks) have been subject to voluntary export restraints under which Japan "voluntarily" limited the number of cars exported annually to the United States.[24] Light trucks, on the other hand, pay a 25 percent tariff in place of the 2.5 percent tariff on automobiles.[25] In the early 1980s, when the United States imposed the restriction on autos, the definition of an automobile seemed clear. A small, separate quota category covered station wagons

---

[24]Section 7.3 analyzes voluntary export restraints.

[25]The 25 percent tariff on trucks is a leftover from a 1963 trade dispute with the European Community. The United States imposed the tariff on light trucks (often called the "chicken" tariff) in retaliation after alleging that Europe unfairly curtailed imports of U.S. frozen chickens.

Table 6.7 □ **Japanese-Made Sport Utility Vehicles**

	Imported in 1987 as		
	Cars	Trucks	Total
Suzuki Samarai	3,000	78,349	81,349
Isuzu Trooper	2,100	40,212	42,312
Toyota 4Runner	3,635	31,423	35,058
Dodge Raider[a]	0	19,539	19,539
Mitsubishi Montero	2,013	8,912	10,925
Nissan Pathfinder	5,314	0	5,314
Total	16,062	178,435	194,497

[a]Made by Mitsubishi for Chrysler Corporation.

Source: Melinda Grenier Guiles, "U.S. Says Car, Japanese Auto Makers Say Truck, Customs Isn't about to Call the Whole Thing Off," *The Wall Street Journal*, March 24, 1988.

and the few Jeep-like sport-utility vehicles (SUVs) that contained rear-passenger seats. Most of the Japanese SUVs sold were spartan, off-road designs without rear seats and with few of the amenities of the typical passenger car; these were classified as trucks, thereby escaping the voluntary export restraints.

Producers gradually upgraded the SUVs to include amenities such as carpeting, air conditioning, and stereo sound systems. But as long as they lacked rear seats when they entered the United States, the vehicles were still "trucks," even though dealers typically added rear seats before sale. Table 6.7 reports classifications for SUVs entering the United States in 1987.

As SUV sales grew, politicians from the U.S. automobile-producing region began to complain, claiming that the vehicles should be reclassified as "cars" subject to the import restrictions. In response, the U.S. Customs Service ruled that "absence of rear-passenger seating is not conclusive evidence of classification," but customs agents should also look for rear-passenger amenities such as carpeting, insulation, windows that open, ventilation ducts, speakers, ashtrays, armrests, and other signs of a "vehicle designed for transport of persons rather than cargo."[26] Japanese producers immediately protested the change, and some temporarily stopped shipments. Suzuki and Isuzu stood to lose the most because of their very small share of the automobile quotas; if their vehicles could no longer gain entry as trucks, they would be shut out of the U.S. market entirely. In early 1988, the U.S. Customs Service ruled on the Japanese protest by declaring the SUVs trucks subject to the 25 percent tariff even if they had rear-passenger amenities. Both Japanese producers and U.S. auto firms saw the ruling as a victory for the Japanese. However, things were to change.

---

[26]Melinda Grenier Guiles, "U.S. Says Car, Japanese Auto Makers Say Truck, Customs Isn't about to Call the Whole Thing Off," *The Wall Street Journal*, March 24, 1988.

In the early 1980s, when the voluntary export restraints on Japanese automobiles were tight and strictly enforced, classification as a truck was desirable—even though it implied paying a 25 percent tariff—because the alternative was to be subject to the auto voluntary export restraints. By 1989, the export restraint on automobiles, while nominally still in effect, was much looser. The once-desired truck classification had become a burden to the Japanese, and U.S. producers liked the truck classification because the high truck tariff effectively limited the foreign competition. Under pressure from the American automobile producers, the U.S. Customs Service ruled in 1989 that SUVs were trucks for tariff purposes, but the Department of the Treasury overturned the ruling and allowed the Japanese to import SUVs as cars and pay the 2.5 percent auto tariff instead of the 25 percent truck tariff. As the import restraint on cars became less binding, the auto classification became more appealing to Japanese producers and more of an irritant to U.S. producers. The car-truck classification issue took on new importance in 1992 when Chrysler petitioned to have one of its most successful products, minivans, reclassified as trucks so that import versions would face the 25 percent truck tariff. At the time of the request, Chrysler held over 50 percent of the minivan market, and U.S. manufacturers as a group held over 90 percent of the market.[27]

In early 1993, the new Clinton administration faced strong pressure from the U.S. auto industry to reclassify SUVs as trucks subject to a 25 percent tariff. Economists estimated such a move would cost U.S. consumers $1 billion per year and raise the price of vehicles by $1,000 to $3,500 depending on the model. But a case brought by Nissan to the U.S. Court of International Trade weighed against reclassification. In the case, Nissan asked that its two-door Pathfinders, which had been classified as trucks while the four-door versions were classified as cars, be reclassified as cars based on their predominant use carrying passengers rather than cargo. The court held in Nissan's favor and ordered that the 25 percent truck tariff that had been charged on two-door Pathfinders during 1989 and 1990 be refunded by U.S. Customs. The U.S. government appealed the ruling, but a federal appeals court upheld it in 1994. The high tariff had caused Nissan to stop importing the two-door Pathfinder to the United States, but the company announced that it might once again import the vehicle, now subject to a 2.5 percent tariff.

Summary

This chapter analyzed tariffs' effects on the allocation of resources and distribution of income. Tariffs have a negative effect on welfare in a small country, although a large country may be able to improve its terms of trade and produce an increase in welfare through an import tariff. Even when imposed by a large country, however, a tariff reduces total world welfare and invites retaliation by trading partners.

When imported inputs as well as imports of finished products are considered, nominal tariff rates fail to measure accurately the degree of protection a particular tariff

---

[27]Neal Templin and Asra Q. Nomain, "Chrysler to Curb Minivan Price Rises if Japanese Vehicles Get a 25% Tariff," *The Wall Street Journal*, March 3, 1993.

structure provides. The effective rate of protection corrects this problem by taking into account the relationship between tariffs on inputs and those on finished products.

Looking Ahead

The international negotiations sponsored by GATT since the Second World War have produced significant reductions in tariff rates, although trade in certain industries remains subject to high tariffs. During the last decade, other types of trade barriers—so-called nontariff barriers—have received increasing attention. These barriers have effects at least as harmful as those of tariffs and have proven much less amenable to international liberalization efforts. The "new protectionism" and its increasing use of nontariff restrictions are the subjects of Chapter Seven.

Key Terms

barriers to trade	redistribution effect
tariff	production effect
protectionist policy	deadweight loss
specific tariff	consumption effect
ad valorem tariff	terms-of-trade effect
nominal tariff rate	optimal tariff
customs valuation	beggar-thy-neighbor policy
f.o.b. price	tariff structure
c.i.f. price	cascading tariff
prohibitive tariff	effective rate of protection (ERP)
consumer surplus	domestic value-added (V)
producer surplus	off-shore assembly provision (OAP)
revenue effect	

Problems and Questions for Review

1. If the world price of automobiles is $10,000 under free trade and if domestic producers of automobiles use $5,000 worth of imported inputs, what is domestic value added under free trade?
   (a) What rate of effective protection would be provided to the domestic auto industry by a 25 percent tariff on imported autos with no tariff on inputs?
   (b) What rate of effective protection would be provided to the domestic auto industry by a 25 percent tariff on imported autos with a 25 percent tariff on inputs?
   (c) What rate of effective protection would be provided to the domestic auto industry by a 25 percent tariff on imported autos with a 50 percent tariff on inputs?
   (d) What rate of effective protection would be provided to the domestic auto industry by a 25 percent tariff on imported autos with a 100 percent tariff on inputs?

2. (a) What position would you expect U.S. apparel manufacturers to take on U.S. import tariffs on textiles (that is, fabrics)?

(b) What position would you expect U.S. computer manufacturers to take on U.S. import tariffs on semiconductor chips?

3. This question asks you to analyze the effects of *removal* of a tariff on imported oranges. The table below summarizes situations in the orange market with and without the tariff. The first column describes the situation with a $4.00 per bushel tariff on oranges. The second column represents the situation after the tariff is removed. You may assume that transportation costs are zero and that the supply and demand curves are straight lines.

	With $4.00 Tariff	With Free Trade
World price of oranges ($/bushel)	$12.00	$12.00
Tariff per bushel ($/bushel)	$4.00	0
Domestic price of oranges ($/bushel)	$16.00	$12.00
Oranges consumed domestically (million bushels/year)	24	28
Oranges produced domestically (million bushels/year)	8	6

(a) Illustrate the effects of *removal* of the tariff. (You may find graph paper useful.) Label the free-trade and tariff equilibria in terms of consumption, domestic production, imports, and domestic and world prices.

(b) Estimate the amount domestic consumers gain from removal of the tariff. Show and explain your work.

(c) Estimate the amount of the *net* effect on the country's welfare from removal of the tariff. Show and explain your work.

(d) In this case, would the optimal import tariff on oranges be negative, zero, or positive? Why? Under what assumptions is the "optimal" tariff really optimal?

4. Country A is labor abundant and practices unrestricted trade with the rest of the world. The country's new minister for trade proposes an import tariff, claiming such a policy would raise wages relative to the return to capital. Do you agree? Why, or why not?

5. Explain why the commonly used empirical measures of average tariff levels tend to *underestimate* actual tariffs.

6. Briefly explain why the welfare effects of an export tax depend on the size of the country imposing the tax.

7. Assume that small country Usia, because of its abundant endowment of forests, has a comparative advantage in producing both logs and lumber (that is, processed logs).

(a) Usia imposes a *prohibitive* export tax on logs. Illustrate the effects of such a tax. Label the effects on consumption, production, exports, world and domestic prices, consumer and producer surplus, and economic efficiency. Explain.

(b) Usia's lumber industry uses logs as its major input. Illustrate the effect of the prohibitive export tax on *logs* on Usia's *lumber* industry. What will happen to consumption, production, price, and exports of lumber because of the tax on log exports? Explain.

References and Selected Readings

Bovard, James. *The Fair Trade Fraud.* New York: St. Martin's Press, 1991.
A treasure trove of examples of protectionist policies written by an outspoken advocate of free trade.

Feenstra, Robert C. "Estimating the Effects of Trade Policy." In *Handbook of International Economics,* Vol. 3, edited by G. M. Grossman and Kenneth Rogoff, 1553–1596. Amsterdam: North-Holland, 1995.
Advanced, up-to-date survey of the empirical literature on the economic effects of various trade policies.

Grubel, Herbert G. "Effective Tariff Protection: A Non-Specialist Introduction to the Theory, Policy Implications, and Controversies." In *Effective Tariff Protection,* edited by Herbert G. Grubel and Harry G. Johnson, 1–15. Geneva: GATT, 1971.
Analyzes the theory and policy implications of the effective rate of protection; for all students.

Hansen, John Mark. "Taxation and the Political Economy of the Tariff." *International Organization* 44 (Autumn 1990): 527–552.
Historical relationship between government revenue and tariffs; for all students.

Hufbauer, Gary Clyde, Diane T. Berliner, and Kimberly Ann Elliott. *Trade Protection in the United States: 31 Case Studies.* Washington, D.C.: Institute for International Economics, 1986.
Empirical studies of 31 U.S. industries and how protection affects them. Excellent source of paper or project topics for all students.

Hufbauer, Gary Clyde, and Jeffrey J. Schott. *NAFTA: An Assessment.* Washington, D.C.: Institute for International Economics, 1993.
Comprehensible and readable survey of the North American Free-Trade Agreement; for all students.

Magee, Stephen P., William A. Brock, and Leslie Young. *Black Hole Tariffs and Endogenous Policy Theory.* Cambridge: Cambridge University Press, 1989.
Path-breaking contribution to analysis of tariffs as the outcome of special-interest-group politics; for intermediate students.

Richardson, J. David. *Sizing Up U.S. Export Disincentives.* Washington, D.C.: Institute for International Economics, 1993.
Readable survey of policies that discourage U.S. exports, along with empirical estimates of the policies' importance.

Rodrik, Dani. "Political Economy of Trade Policy." In *Handbook of International Economics,* Vol. 3, edited by G. M. Grossman and Kenneth Rogoff, 1457–1494. Amsterdam: North-Holland, 1995.
Advanced, up-to-date survey of the literature on distributional aspects of trade policy and their implications for the policy process.

Sazanami, Yoko, Shujiro Urata, and Kiroki Kawai. *Measuring the Costs of Protection in Japan.* Washington, D.C.: Institute for International Economics, 1995.
Attempt to quantify the cost to Japanese consumers and the Japanese economy as a whole of the structure of protection. Intermediate.

Schott, Jeffrey J. *The Uruguay Round: An Assessment.* Washington, D.C.: Institute for International Economics, 1994.
Excellent, accessible survey of the issues and results of the Uruguay Round, including tariff reductions.

Subramanian, Arvind. "The Case for Low Uniform Tariffs." *Finance and Development* 31 (June 1994): 33–35.
Recommends tariff simplification for developing countries that still use tariffs to raise government revenue. For all students.

Tollison, Robert D. "Rent Seeking: A Survey." *Kyklos* 35 (1982): 575–602.
Introduction to rent-seeking analysis and a survey of its major results; for intermediate students.

Vousden, Neil. *The Economics of Trade Protection.* Cambridge: Cambridge University Press, 1990.
Excellent survey of the effects of protection for advanced students.

Warr, Peter G. "Export Processing Zones and Trade Policy." *Finance and Development* 26 (June 1989): 34–36.
Introduction to the effects of special trade zones, in which goods are exempt from tariffs.

Westhoff, Frank H., Beth V. Yarbrough, and Robert M. Yarbrough. "Harassment versus Lobbying for Trade Protection." *International Trade Journal* 9 (Summer 1995): 203–224.
Examines use of protection to harass foreign producers; intermediate.

Chapter Six Appendix A

Offer Curves and Tariffs

The effect of an import tariff on the terms of trade (or the lack of effect in the case of a small country) is easily seen using offer curves. Recall from Chapter Three Appendix B that an offer curve represents how many units of the export good a country is willing to give up to obtain a given quantity of the import good. A straight line from the diagram's origin through a point on the offer curve represents the terms of trade. The slope of a straight line through the origin and the intersection of two countries' offer curves captures the equilibrium, or market-clearing, terms of trade.

Figure 6A.1 illustrates an offer curve (denoted A) for country A assuming unrestricted trade. Country A has a comparative advantage in production of good X and exports X to country B in exchange for good Y. Point C, for example, illustrates A's willingness to export X_0 units of X in exchange for Y_0 units of Y. Now suppose country A imposes a tariff on imports of good Y. The effect on A's offer curve is shown by the shift from curve

Figure 6A.1 □ **Effect of an Import Tariff on Country A's Offer Curve**

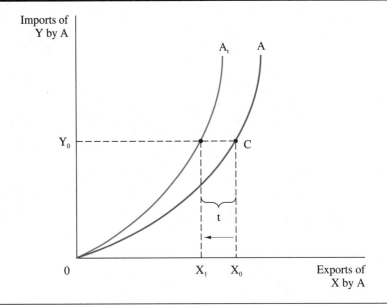

An import tariff of t percent imposed by country A reduces the volume of trade in which A wants to engage and shifts A's offer curve inward to A_t. In exchange for Y_0 units of imports, country A reduces the amount of good X it is willing to export from X_0 to X_1. The difference, $X_0 - X_1$, goes to the government as tariff revenue.

Figure 6A.2 □ **Effect of an Import Tariff by a Small Country**

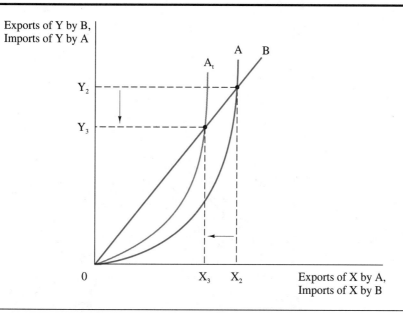

Country A's smallness is represented by the straight-line shape of trading partner B's offer curve. The slope of B's offer curve determines the equilibrium terms of trade regardless of A's action. The tariff imposed by A reduces the volume of trade from X_2 and Y_2 to X_3 and Y_3 but has no effect on the equilibrium terms of trade.

A to curve A_t, where the t subscript denotes *tariff*. The offer curve drawn for a tariff-imposing country often is called a *tariff-ridden offer curve*.

Why does A's offer curve shift inward toward the origin as a result of the tariff? One way to answer this is to recall from the analysis of tariffs in Chapter Six that a tariff *reduces* the volume of trade in which the tariff-imposing country wants to engage. This implies country A will be willing to export a smaller quantity of X in exchange for any given quantity of Y (for example, only X_1 rather than X_0 units in exchange for Y_0).

A second way to consider the shift in A's offer curve caused by the tariff is to note that consumers of Y in country A now must pay *both* the producers of Y in country B and the domestic government for each unit of Y imported. To consume Y_0 units of Y, consumers must pay X_1 units of X to country B and $X_0 - X_1$ to the domestic government. Thus, in total, the price consumers in A are willing to pay for Y_0 units of Y is still X_0 units of X, but now that price is divided between foreign producers and the government. The tariff reduces the amount of good X country A is willing to offer to country B by the amount of the tariff; the new offer curve reflects this new lower quantity of goods traded. Therefore, country A's offer curve shifts inward, or to the left, by a proportion equal to the tariff rate.

Now that we know the effect of a tariff on the offer curve, we can use it to examine the effect of a tariff on the equilibrium terms of trade and the importance of country size

Figure 6A.3 □ Effect of an Import Tariff by a Large Country

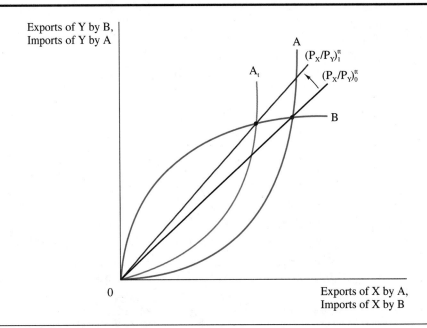

Exports of Y by B, Imports of Y by A

$(P_X/P_Y)_1^{tt}$

$(P_X/P_Y)_0^{tt}$

A

A_t

B

0

Exports of X by A, Imports of X by B

Country A's large size is represented by the curved shape of trading partner B's offer curve. The imposition of a tariff by A raises the relative price of good X, A's export good, as shown by the increased slope of the straight line from the origin through the new intersection of the two countries' offer curves. Country A's tariff worsens country B's terms of trade and reduces the volume of trade.

in determining that effect. First, we assume that country A is small in the markets for goods X and Y and that it possesses no market power. In an offer-curve diagram, A's smallness is represented by drawing the trading partner's (country B's) offer curve as a straight line, as in Figure 6A.2. The slope of B's offer curve measures the equilibrium terms of trade that, by assumption, A can do nothing to affect. If A imposes an import tariff, shifting its offer curve to A_t, the volume of trade declines (trade in X from X_2 to X_3 and trade in Y from Y_2 to Y_3) but the terms of trade are unaffected. Since the decline in the volume of trade has a negative welfare effect on country A (as well as on B), the overall welfare effect of a tariff by a small country is negative.

Next, we assume country A is large enough to possess some degree of market power in the markets for goods X and Y. In this case, the trading partner's (B's) offer curve no longer is a straight line but is curved, as in Figure 6A.3. The imposition of an import tariff by A improves A's terms of trade, as shown by the increase in the slope of the relative price line. Since the slope of the price line gives the relative price of good X, country A's export good, an increase in the line's slope is an improvement in A's terms of trade (and a deterioration in B's). The imposition of a tariff reduces the volume of trade, just as in the small-country case, but now the terms of trade are affected as well. The net effect of the tariff on the country's welfare depends on the relative magnitudes of the two effects.

Figure 6A.4 □ **Tariff Retaliation**

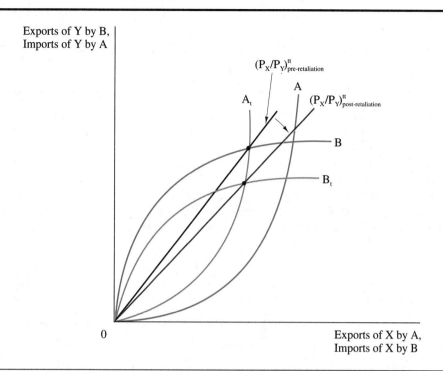

In response to the damage caused by A's tariff, B may choose to impose an import tariff, shifting its offer curve to B_t. The retaliation further reduces the volume of trade. The net effect on the terms of trade depends on the relative sizes of the two countries' tariffs and on the shapes of their offer curves. As drawn, B's retaliatory tariff is too low to restore the terms of trade to their original, pre-tariff level.

It is important to note that the improvement in country A's terms of trade through the tariff is synonymous with a deterioration in country B's. Country B is unambiguously harmed by the tariff and may retaliate by imposing an import tariff of its own on country A's exports.

Figure 6A.4 illustrates the possibility of retaliation by B. Should this occur, B's offer curve shifts inward to B_t, further reducing the volume of trade and shifting the terms of trade in B's favor. Whether the *net* effect on the terms of trade favors A or B depends, of course, on the magnitudes of the original and retaliatory tariffs and on the precise shapes of the countries' offer curves. As drawn, the terms of trade following B's retaliation remain more favorable to A than the pre-tariff terms of trade (omitted from the figure). Country B could restore the original terms of trade by imposing a slightly higher retaliatory tariff. However, the stronger retaliation would reduce further the volume of trade. If a trade war of retaliation and counter retaliation erupted, the countries could be driven back to autarky (represented by the origin in Figure 6A.4).

Chapter Six Appendix B

General-Equilibrium Tariff Effects in a Small Country

General-equilibrium analysis allows a tariff's effects on consumption and production of both goods to be investigated. In addition, it illustrates more directly the tariff's negative impact on the imposing country's welfare. We continue to assume the country is small, has a comparative advantage in production of good X, and uses the tariff revenue to lower domestic taxes.

In Figure 6B.1, the *production* and *consumption* points under free trade are p^0 and c^0, respectively. We omit the autarky equilibrium and the country superscripts for simplicity. The equilibrium terms of trade are given by the *world* price ratio,

Figure 6B.1 □ **General-Equilibrium Effects of an Import Tariff by a Small Country**

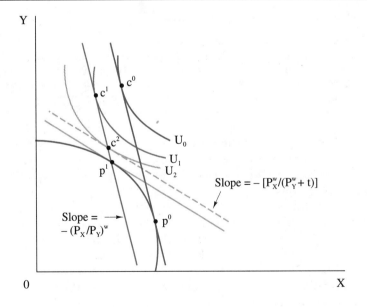

The tariff shifts production from p^0 to p^1, causing a loss of efficiency and a decrease in welfare represented by the move from indifference curve U_0 to U_1. Consumption is based on the domestic price ratio ($P_X^w/[P_Y^w + t]$) and also is inefficient, causing a further reduction in welfare from U_1 to U_2.

$(P_X/P_Y)^w$, and the country's utility level is U_0. Now suppose the country imposes a tariff of t on each unit of good Y imported. The world price of good Y, P_Y^w, is unaffected because of the country's small size. The domestic price of Y in the small country rises to $P_Y^w + t$. The new relative price ratio relevant for individual domestic producers is $[P_X^w/(P_Y^w + t)]$, which is less than $(P_X/P_Y)^w$. We know production occurs at the point where the production possibilities frontier is tangent to the price line relevant for domestic producers; this production point with the tariff is p^1 in Figure 6B.1.

As always, the country can trade on world markets to obtain the combination of goods its residents want to consume. At which price ratio does this trade occur? It must occur at $(P_X/P_Y)^w$, because that is the only price ratio at which trade occurs in world markets; the small country's tariff cannot affect world prices. Another way to see that $(P_X/P_Y)^w$ is the relevant price ratio for international trade is to note that out of the new domestic price of good Y, only P_Y^w goes to the foreign country while t goes to the domestic government as tariff revenue. Thus, for the importing country as a whole, the price of the import still is only P_Y^w.

At first glance, we would expect the country to trade along the price line going through the tariff production point p^1 to the point tangent to the highest attainable indifference curve (U_1). If consumption point c^1 were the final equilibrium, there would be only one source of welfare loss from the tariff: the loss caused by inefficient production (p^1 rather than p^0) and represented by the downward move from utility level U_0 to U_1. However, the actual outcome involves a second welfare loss due to inefficient consumption. The price ratio relevant for individual domestic consumers is $P_X/(P_Y^w + t)$ because for each imported unit of good Y, a consumer must pay P_Y^w to the producer *and* t to the domestic government. The final equilibrium involves trading along the world price line to a point where an indifference curve is tangent to the domestic price line. The final consumption point with the tariff is c^2 on indifference curve U_2. The move from U_1 to U_2 represents the welfare loss due to inefficient consumption.

CHAPTER SEVEN

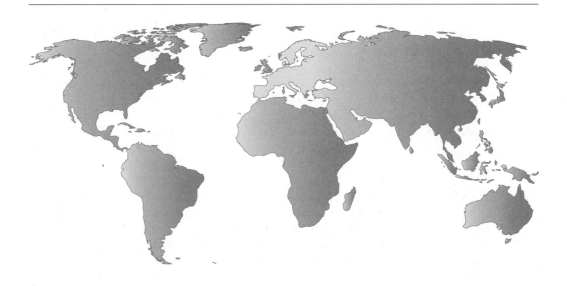

Nontariff Barriers and the New Protectionism

7.1 Introduction

Nontariff barriers (**NTBs**) include quotas, voluntary export restraints, export subsidies, and a variety of other regulations and restrictions covering international trade. International economists and policy makers have become increasingly concerned about such barriers in the last few years, for three reasons. First, postwar success in international negotiations for reduction of tariffs has made nontariff barriers all the more visible. (See Figures 6.1 and 6.2 for the historical decline in U.S. average tariff rates.) Nontariff barriers have proven much less amenable to reduction through international negotiations; and, until recently, agreements to lower trade barriers more or less explicitly excluded two industry groups most affected by NTBs, agriculture and textiles. Second, many countries increasingly use these barriers precisely because the main body of rules in international trade, the General Agreement on Tariffs and Trade, does not cover many NTBs. The recent tendency to circumvent GATT rules by using loopholes in the agreements and imposing types of barriers over which negotiations have failed has been called the **new protectionism.**[1] The fears aroused by the

---

[1]For a survey of current NTB disputes involving the United States, see the U.S. International Trade Commission's annual, *The Year in Trade: Operation of the Trade Agreements Program.*

new protectionism reflect not only the negative welfare effects of specific restrictions already imposed but also the damage done to the framework of international agreements when countries intentionally ignore or circumvent the specified rules of conduct. Third, countries often apply NTBs in a discriminatory way; that is, the barriers often apply to trade with some countries but not others. In particular, exports from developing countries appear particularly vulnerable to restriction through nontariff barriers. NTBs by the European Union, the United States, and Japan apply to a higher percentage of exports from developing countries than from industrial countries. Such barriers can only make the development process more difficult.

7.2 Quotas

The simplest and most direct form of nontariff trade barrier is the import **quota,** a direct quantitative restriction on the number of units of a good imported during a specified period. Countries impose quotas for the same reasons as those for imposing import tariffs (see section 6.2). The two most common policy goals of quotas are to protect a domestic industry from foreign competition and to cut imports to reduce a balance-of-trade deficit. As in the case of tariffs, we shall focus on the protection issue and postpone balance-of-trade questions until Part Two. Developed countries (for example, Japan, the United States, and the members of the European Union) have used import quotas primarily to protect agricultural producers. Cases One and Two in this chapter trace the role of U.S. import quotas in the international market for raw sugar and other restrictive policies in agricultural markets. Developing countries, on the other hand, have used quotas to try to stimulate growth of manufacturing industries; but we shall see in Chapter Eleven that protection's repeated failure to stimulate manufacturing has persuaded many developing countries to move toward more open trade policies.

The Uruguay Round agreement contains two major developments concerning quotas. First, the accord requires countries to convert their quotas to equivalent tariffs, which then fall subject to the agreement's phased-in tariff reductions. Second, countries agreed to establish minimum market access for products, mostly agricultural, previously subject to prohibitive trade barriers. The most notable products subject to the minimum-access rule include Japanese and South Korean rice imports (see Case Two).

Partial-equilibrium analysis of an import quota's effects closely resembles that for a tariff. In Figure 7.1, D^d and S^d represent, respectively, the *domestic demand and supply* for good Y, the import good of the country considering imposition of a quota. For simplicity, the figure omits the total world supply curve of good Y. Assume the unrestricted trade equilibrium is at point C. Residents consume Y^0 units of good Y, of which Y^1 units are produced domestically and $Y^0 - Y^1$ imported. The price of the good, both domestically and in world markets, is P_Y^0.

Now suppose the country decides that availability of low-cost imports is limiting sales by domestic producers to Y^1. One method to protect the domestic industry from foreign competition is to impose a quota on imports. To determine the quota's effect, we define a horizontal line whose length represents the quota (for example, 1 million tons of sugar per year). Then we "slide" the line representing the quota up until it fits between the domestic demand and supply curves. Point E in Figure 7.1

Figure 7.1 □ **Effects of an Import Quota of $Y^2 - Y^3$ Units on Good Y**

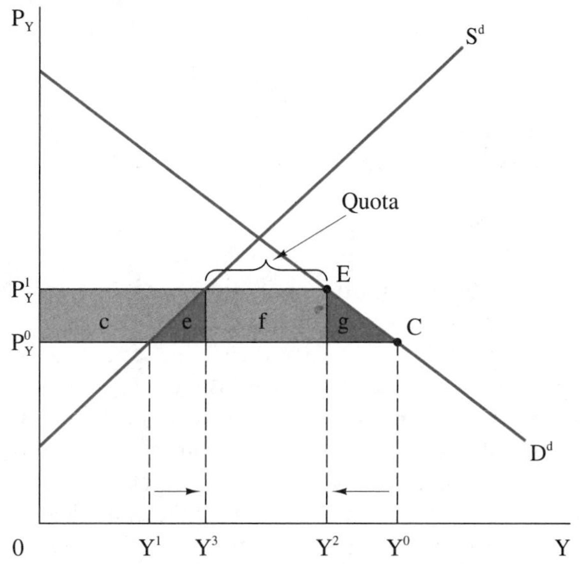

By restricting imports, a quota increases domestic production from Y^1 to Y^3 and decreases domestic consumption from Y^0 to Y^2. The net welfare loss from the quota is shown as the sum of the areas of triangles e and g. Area c represents a transfer from domestic consumers to producers; area f represents the revenue or rents from the quota.

denotes equilibrium with the quota. The domestic price of good Y is P^1_Y; at this price, the quantity produced domestically (Y^3) plus the imports allowed under the quota ($Y^2 - Y^3$) equals the quantity demanded by domestic consumers (Y^2).

Area c + e + f + g represents the loss of consumer surplus due to the quota, much as in the case of an import tariff. (The reader can review the concepts of consumer and producer surplus in section 6.4.2.) The basic interpretations of areas c, e, f, and g are the same as the analogous areas in the tariff analysis. Area c is a transfer from domestic consumers to domestic producers able to sell more of their product at higher prices with the quota. Consumers pay the amount represented by c in a higher price (P^1_Y rather than P^0_Y). Triangle e is a deadweight welfare loss. The quota causes the country to produce units between Y^1 and Y^3 domestically rather than importing them; however, each unit costs more to produce domestically (represented by the height of the domestic supply curve) than to import (represented by P^0_Y). Triangle g is the other deadweight loss, this one caused by inefficient consumption. The quota reduces domestic consumption of good Y from Y^0 to Y^2. For each unit of consumption forgone, the value to consumers (represented by the height of the demand curve) exceeds the cost of importing the good (represented by P^0_Y). Therefore, the reduction in consumption caused by the quota is inefficient.

Area f symbolizes a type of "revenue" generated by the quota, usually called the **quota rents.** For each unit of good Y imported under the quota ($Y^2 - Y^3$), consumers now pay a higher price. But to whom do the rents go? Under a tariff, the answer is clear: The tariff revenue goes to the tariff-imposing government.[2] Under a quota, the answer is less certain; rents generated by the quota may go to any of several groups, depending on their relative bargaining strengths and the institutional arrangements the government uses to administer the quota. Importers or exporters, foreign producers, or the quota-imposing government may capture the rents; or they may become an additional deadweight loss.

The rents will go to importers if they have the bargaining power to buy $Y^2 - Y^3$ units on world markets at price P_Y^0 and sell them domestically at P_Y^1. This likely will occur only if importers have some degree of monopoly power. If importing is a competitive industry, importers will bid against one another to buy good Y, and the price producers or exporters charge will rise above P_Y^0. In that case, the sellers of good Y, either producers or exporters, will capture at least a portion of the quota rents represented by area f in Figure 7.1.

Administration of an import quota typically is less simple than it first appears. The government issues a statement that no more than $Y^2 - Y^3$ units of good Y may be imported. To enforce the restriction, the government must devise a scheme to both keep track of how many units of Y enter the country and allocate the quota among competing importers. The government may choose to auction import licenses. Under such a system, the rents from the quota would go to the government. An importer able to buy Y on the world market for P_Y^0 would willingly pay approximately $P_Y^1 - P_Y^0$ for a license to import 1 unit of Y. *(Why?)* The total amount for which the government could sell the import licenses would equal the area of rectangle f. Quotas administered under such a scheme are called *auction quotas*.[3] The U.S. government's budget deficits during the 1980s led many analysts to recommend auctioning all U.S. quotas. Proponents estimate auctions could raise as much as $10 billion per year in revenue. Table 7.1 reports revenue estimates for changing six of the major U.S. import quotas to an auction system. Auction plans resurfaced in the United States in 1994, but were withdrawn when trade-law experts found such arrangements illegal under both the GATT and the Multifiber Agreement covering trade in textiles and apparel.

A third possibility is that area f may end up as an additional deadweight loss; that is, the rents may go to no one. Suppose, for example, the government does not sell import licenses but gives them away on a first-come, first-served basis. Importers then have an incentive to lobby to obtain licenses and otherwise spend resources to obtain them; for example, importers might be willing to wait in line for hours, an allocation method economists refer to as *queuing*. Because the value of a license to import 1 unit

---

[2]Traditional economic analysis assumes governments use tariff revenue in place of domestic taxes. However, rent-seeking behavior by producers may use up the revenue, adding an additional deadweight loss due to trade restrictions (see footnote 13 in Chapter Six).

[3]See C. Fred Bergsten et al., *Auction Quotas and United States Trade Policy* (Washington, D.C.: Institute for International Economics, 1987). Kala Krishna, "The Case of the Vanishing Revenues: Auction Quotas with Monopoly," *American Economic Review* 80 (September 1990), 828–836, demonstrates that auction quotas do not raise revenue under monopoly. Chapter Eight (section 8.4.2) treats tariffs and quotas under monopoly.

Table 7.1 □ **Estimated Maximum Revenue from Auctioning U.S. Import Quotas ($ Billions)**

Industry	Annual Auction Revenue
Steel	2.8
Shipping	2.7
Automobiles	2.1
Textiles and apparel	1.5
Sugar	0.6
Dairy products	0.3

Source: Monica Langley, "The Idea of Auctioning Import Rights Appeals to Lawmakers Faced with Trade, Budget Gaps," *The Wall Street Journal,* February 6, 1987; data from the Institute for International Economics.

of Y is approximately $(P_Y^1 - P_Y^0)$, importers would be willing to expend resources equal to that amount to obtain a license. The total resources spent on lobbying or waiting in line equal area f. The process of competition for licenses "uses up" the quota rents which, in this case, represent an additional deadweight loss from society's viewpoint.

The final possibility is that foreign producers or exporters will capture the rents from the quota. A quota in the form of a voluntary export restraint makes this outcome more likely.

7.3 Voluntary Export Restraints

Major world industries—automobiles, steel, and textiles/apparel—are among those subject to trade restrictions known as **voluntary export restraints** (VERs). As the term suggests, importing and exporting countries negotiate these agreements for the exporter to "voluntarily" restrict the volume of exports. The voluntarism may be more apparent than real, because the exporting country often faces the choice of agreeing to the VER, facing a tariff, or, most likely, facing a quota on its exports. U.S. imports of steel products have been subject to VERs off and on since 1968.[4] The United States negotiated a VER on Japanese automobile imports in 1981 and extended it annually until 1985, after which Japan unilaterally kept the VER in place. Several European countries also negotiated informal agreements with Japan to limit automobile imports. Some of the agreements were quite restrictive; for example, Italy allowed only 2,200 Japanese automobiles into the country per year. In 1992, as part of the economic integration among members of the European Union, a single EU-wide VER with Japan replaced the member countries' separate national quotas and VERs on Japanese cars. That agreement will last until December 31, 1999, when all barriers to Japanese auto sales in Europe are scheduled to fall.

---

[4]Case Four summarizes the recent history of U.S. protection in the steel industry.

The Uruguay Round achieved notable success in restricting use of VERs, one of the fastest growing types of protection. Under the new rules, countries cannot impose new VERs in response to escape-clause claims of injury by domestic industries. Existing VERs must be phased out within four years, except for the EU-Japan auto agreement, which can run until its scheduled close in 1999.

A VER has effects similar to those of a quota. The primary difference lies in the method of administration. In the case of a quota, the importing or quota-imposing country typically handles the administration; under a VER, the exporting country enforces the agreement.[5] This distinction carries important implications for the allocation of the quota rents (area f in Figure 7.1). Administration by the exporting country increases the likelihood that foreign producers or exporters will capture a large share of the rents. Usually the exporting-country government administers the VER by assigning export limits to each firm. This prohibits competition among the firms and facilitates their charging a higher price (P_Y^1 rather than P_Y^0). As a result, exporters much prefer VERs to tariffs or quotas. Because VERs require negotiations between exporting and importing countries, they typically restrain exports from some but not all suppliers. Exporters not included in a VER agreement sometimes can expand exports to fill the gap left by restrained exporters; often, this results in further expansion of the VER as additional exporters become restrained.[6]

The effects of quotas and voluntary export restraints include a tendency for exporters to raise the average quality of their exported goods. In 1981, Japan agreed under U.S. pressure to restrict its exports of passenger cars to the United States to 1.68 million per year. Japanese automobile companies responded by stopping shipments of plain, low-priced models in favor of higher priced ones with more optional features. This implies that quotas and VERs impose especially high welfare costs on low-income individuals, because the imports such policies eliminate often include the low-cost items bought primarily by low-income families. These quality responses by suppliers are more likely when quotas or VERs state import limits in quantity terms (for example, 1.68 million cars) than in value terms (for example, $10.68 billion worth of cars). *(Why?)*

Like tariffs, administering quotas or VERs requires defining the categories of goods to be restricted. Product categories tend to be very specific, and exporters can use definitional loopholes to circumvent the restrictions. For example, one clothing exporter got around a quota on two-piece suits by sewing the tops and bottoms together and importing them as jumpsuits. Another circumvented a quota on ski jackets by cutting off the sleeves, importing the sleeveless jackets as vests, then reattaching the sleeves with zippers once the items reached the United States.[7] In 1994, the European Union placed a $81.7 million import quota on "nonhuman dolls" from China, while leaving "human dolls" with no quota. So far, EU officials have ruled teddy bears and two popular European dolls, Noddy and Big Ears, subject to the quota. Batman, Robin, and *Star Trek's*

---

[5]In this sense, most U.S. quotas operate like VERs, because most are administered by the exporting country. The major exception is the dairy product program.

[6]The Multifiber Agreement (MFA), described in Case One in Chapter Eleven, represents the classic case. It began in the early 1960s restricting Japanese exports of cotton shirts to the United States. Today, the MFA restricts exports of textiles and apparel from virtually all developing countries and to almost all developed countries

.[7]"The Warp and Weft of Anti-Dumping," *The Economist*, November 23, 1991, 72.

Captain Kirk have escaped the quota by an affirmative ruling on their humanity. The biggest controversy surrounded *Star Trek* hero Mr. Spock. Spock's mother was human, which some aficionados claimed should win him exemption, but customs officials used the size of his ears to rule him nonhuman and subject to the quota.[8]

Thus far, with the exception of the rents issue, the effects of quotas appear identical to those of tariffs. Nonetheless, economists generally believe quotas cause larger losses of welfare than do equivalent tariffs. Section 7.4 further examines quotas to uncover the reasoning behind this belief.

7.4 Comparison of Tariffs and Quotas

We have seen one major difference between the effect of an import tariff and that of an import quota: The revenue from a tariff goes to the tariff-imposing government, but it is unclear who receives the quota rent. Several other, more subtle differences matter in evaluating the overall effects of the two policies.

Domestic firms in an industry seeking protection typically prefer a quota to other types of import restrictions. One explanation for this preference is the greater certainty associated with the protective effects of a quota. A quota assures the domestic industry a ceiling on imports *regardless of changing market conditions*. Even if the domestic industry's comparative disadvantage grows more severe, the quota prohibits consumers from switching to the imported good. Note, however, that the quota does cause a decline in the total quantity demanded by raising the good's domestic price. Therefore, a quota cannot keep the domestic industry from facing a shrinking market. Some quotas do attempt to shelter domestic firms from a shrinking market by guaranteeing them a fixed share of the domestic market. Under such a system, if the domestic market shrinks, the import quota automatically falls to maintain domestic firms' market share; for example, the Australian Car Plan assures Australian car makers 80 percent of their domestic market.

Beyond increasing their market share, domestic firms seek protection from competition by foreign firms to gain and exploit monopoly power in the domestic market. Suppose an industry following this strategy gains protection in the form of an import tariff. Firms in the industry can raise their prices. However, if they raise prices too much, consumers will switch to the imported good even though they have to pay the tariff. In particular, if domestic firms try to charge a price that exceeds the world price plus the tariff, consumers will not buy from domestic firms and the attempt at monopolization will fail. If the industry's protection takes the form of a quota, however, the attempt to monopolize by restricting foreign competition will more likely succeed. Under a quota, domestic consumers do *not* have the option of switching to the imported good. If domestic firms try to exploit a monopoly position by raising prices, the only choice consumers face is to pay the higher prices or consume less of the good. Because successful monopolization of an industry reduces

---

[8]Dana Milbank, "British Customs Officials Consider Mr. Spock Dolls to be Illegal Aliens," *The Wall Street Journal*, August 2, 1994.

Figure 7.2 □ **Comparison of Response to Increased Demand under a Tariff and under a Quota**

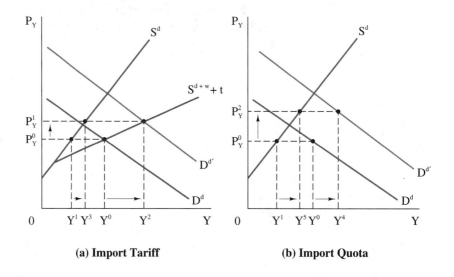

(a) Import Tariff   **(b) Import Quota**

A quota on imports is more restrictive than an equivalent tariff in the face of an increase in demand. Under a tariff, imports serve a portion of the increased demand; in panel (a), increased demand causes a larger increase in consumption than in domestic production. A quota forces any increased demand to be matched by increases in (inefficient) domestic production, as panel (b) illustrates. An equal increase in demand causes a larger price increase under a quota than under a tariff.

the efficiency of the economy, economists believe the tendency of quotas to facilitate monopolization makes quotas more damaging than tariffs.[9]

Setting aside the issue of who gets the associated rents, it is possible, given any tariff, to define a quota with precisely the same effects on prices, production, consumption, and trade at any moment. Similarly, given any quota, it is possible to set a tariff with exactly the same effects. This result is referred to as the **equivalence of tariffs and quotas**.[10] We have hinted, however, that as market conditions change, tariffs and quotas cease to have identical effects. Figure 7.2 illustrates this more rigorously for a large country. Panel (a) analyzes an increase in demand for good Y under a tariff; panel (b) examines the effect of the same increase in demand under a quota. We define the tariff and quota such that given the initial level of demand (D^d), Y^0 units are consumed under both systems, Y^1 units are produced domestically, and $Y^0 - Y^1$ units imported at price P_Y^0.

---

[9]Monopolization reduces efficiency by allowing firms to restrict output and charge prices that exceed marginal costs.

[10]This result provides the basis for the process of *tariffication,* through which countries replace their quotas with equivalent tariffs, as required by the Uruguay Round. Equivalence also underlies one technique for measuring or quantifying NTBs; see section 7.9.

Table 7.2 □ **Global and Country-Specific U.S. Import Quotas**

Global	Long-staple cotton (1939–present)
	Peanuts (1953–present)
	Canned tuna (1956–present)
Country specific	Sugar (off and on since 1937)
	Meat[a] (off and on since 1965)
	Short-staple cotton (1939–present)
	Machine tools[a] (1986–present)
	Carbon steel[a] (1969–1974; 1982–1992)
	Specialty steel (1976–1980; 1983–1992)
	Textiles and apparel[a] (1957–present)
	Dairy products (1953–present)

[a]Voluntary export restraints.

Source: C. Fred Bergsten, et al., *Auction Quotas and United States Trade Policy* (Washington, D.C.: Institute for International Economics, 1987), pp. 34, 206–217.

In panel (a), with an increase in demand to $D^{d'}$, the quantity of good Y consumed rises to Y^2, of which firms produce Y^3 units domestically under a tariff. Note that domestic production rises by *less* than domestic consumption; part of the increased consumption comes from increased imports. The tariff allows increased imports by permitting consumers to either buy domestically or import at a price equal to the world price plus the tariff.

In panel (b), the same increase in demand raises consumption of Y to Y^4 and domestic production to Y^5 under the quota. Increased domestic production exactly *matches* increased consumption, because the quota prohibits any increase in imports. The increased domestic production is inefficient (that is, more costly than increased imports); therefore, the domestic price of good Y rises more under the quota (to P_Y^2) than under the tariff (to P_Y^1). The quota forbids additional imports no matter what price domestic consumers are willing to pay for them. *(Compare the effects of a fall in domestic supply under a tariff and under a quota.)*

Quotas also present more administrative problems than tariffs. In imposing a quota, a country must decide between a **global quota** (limiting overall imports of a good regardless of country of origin) and a **country-specific, or country-of-origin, quota** (restricting imports from a particular country). Some quotas combine the two: They set an overall global import limit and allocate the limit among supplier countries. Table 7.2 classifies U.S. import quotas as global or country specific.

Country-specific quotas create problems of definition and administration. The country of origin of a product is not always apparent. Suppose firms in South Korea cut cloth into a shirt pattern. The firms then send the pieces to Hong Kong, where other firms assemble the shirt, add buttons and labels, and inspect and package the shirt. Is the shirt's country of origin South Korea or Hong Kong? Because the United States has separate country-specific quotas on clothing imports from South Korea and Hong Kong, against which country's quota should the shirt count?[11] What if imports from Hong Kong were subject to a quota but not those from South Korea? Should the shirt be subject to the quota? Any answers to these questions must be somewhat arbitrary, but successful administration of a quota requires they be codified.[12] This process has gotten more complicated as products' nationalities have become murkier due to firms' abilities to produce products globally. The European Union, for example, tightened its country-of-origin rules so goods made in the United States by Japanese firms no longer can enter the EU as "Made in America."

An additional, related problem arising in administration of import quotas is **transshipment,** which involves use of a third country to circumvent a country-specific quota. Suppose quotas cover U.S. shirt imports from both Hong Kong and South Korea. It may be possible to circumvent the quota by having the shirt appear to come from a third, nonquota country. For example, once assembly of the shirt is complete, the shirt can be shipped to Venezuela, boxed for shipment to the United States, and shipped as a Venezuelan shirt, not subject to the quota. The welfare effect of such schemes is ambiguous, although the possibility of transshipment clearly raises the costs of enforcing a quota. Transshipment uses scarce resources (for example, the resources used in shipping the shirt from Hong Kong to the United States by way of Venezuela rather than directly); however, if Hong Kong is the most efficient producer of shirts, the quota itself causes inefficiency and reduces world welfare. If transshipments make the quota less effective, they reduce this welfare loss. For a quota to have its full trade-restricting effect, the quota-imposing government must bear substantial enforcement costs. For example, the U.S. Customs Service conducted a major investigation ("Operation Q-Tip") in 1991 following allegations that China exceeded its apparel quotas by transshipping through Egypt, Macao, Honduras, Hong Kong, the Philippines, and Singapore. Analysts estimate transshipped Chinese textiles and apparel at about $2 billion annually. China's current quota for exports to the United States under the Multifiber Agreement equals $4.6 billion per year, so illegal goods could represent a 40 percent increase in China's exports to the United States. Many recently concluded bilateral agreements under the Multifiber Agreement, including China's, give the United States the right to deduct from the exporting country's quota three times the value of any goods illegally transshipped.

Until recently, most attention devoted to trade barriers focused on tariffs and quotas. In the last few years, a number of subtler, more complex restrictions have proliferated. In the following sections, we briefly examine several of these barriers, including export subsidies and countervailing duties, dumping, voluntary import expansions, domestic-content rules and rules of origin, government procurement, and technical standards.

---

[11]The United States restricts textile and apparel imports from Hong Kong to just under $4 billion and those from South Korea to just under $2.5 billion. The Uruguay Round agreement requires the phaseout of textile and apparel quotas, as discussed in Case One in Chapter Eleven.

[12]Under rules in effect since 1984, the United States had counted the shirt in the example against South Korea's quota, because the shirt was cut there; see Eduard Lachica, "Apparel Firms and Asian Suppliers Join In Fight to Stave Off New Customs Rules," *The Wall Street Journal*, August 15, 1994. The Uruguay Round agreement requires items to be charged according to the location of assembly, not cutting.

7.5 Export Subsidies and Countervailing Duties

An **export subsidy** is a financial contribution from a government to a firm for export of a commodity; the firm receives the government subsidy along with the price paid by foreign consumers. Note that this definition restricts subsidies to *exports* rather than the country's *export good*. For example, if American Steel Company produces 5 million tons of steel per year of which it exports 2 million tons, a subsidy of $10 per ton on *exports* implies a total subsidy of $20 million, while a $10-per-ton subsidy on *production* (regardless of whether sold domestically or exported) implies a total subsidy of $50 million. Both types of subsidies are important in international trade, but more controversy surrounds export subsidies because they involve differential or discriminatory treatment of domestic sales versus exports. Such subsidies create incentives for firms to export larger shares of their production and sell smaller shares domestically, since the latter do not receive the subsidy payment.

7.5.1 The Importing-Country View

Given the jealousy with which industries guard their domestic markets from foreign competition, it is not surprising that government subsidization of exports is one of the most controversial issues in international trade policy. Domestic industries often argue they face unfair competition from rivals subsidized by foreign governments.

Our initial examination of the effects of export subsidies takes the perspective of the importing country, which we assume to be small in the market for good Y. (Note that desirability of subsidies from the exporting country's standpoint also is an issue, the subject of section 7.5.2.) The importing country's trading partners subsidize exports of good Y by s per unit.[13] Because a subsidy is just a negative tax, it lowers the price at which importing-country consumers can buy the good.

In Figure 7.3, the total supply curve for good Y, the country's import good, shifts down by the amount of the subsidy from S^{d+w} to $S^{d+w} - s$. The overall effect is to increase consumption of good Y from Y^0 to Y^2, decrease importing-country production from Y^1 to Y^3, and increase imports from $Y^0 - Y^1$ to $Y^2 - Y^3$. The price of good Y falls from the free-trade price, P_Y^0, to P_Y^1; exporting-country producers willingly sell at lower prices because they now receive the subsidy in addition to the price received directly from consumers. Importing-country consumers gain an amount represented by area e + f + g + h in consumer surplus. *(Why?)* The subsidy harms importing-country producers, as lower-priced imports reduce sales by domestic firms and dictate lower prices. Area e captures this loss of producer surplus, which is transferred to domestic consumers. The remainder of domestic consumers' gains (area f + g + h) come at the expense of taxpayers in the exporting countries, who must finance the subsidy.

---

[13]We assume all exporting countries subsidize, so an importing country can purchase all the good Y it wants at the subsidized price. If a single small country subsidized, buyers would compete for the country's exports, driving the price back up to the initial world price and allowing the subsidizing country's exporters to earn the world price *plus* the subsidy for each unit exported.

Figure 7.3 □ Effects of an Export Subsidy: Importing-Country Perspective

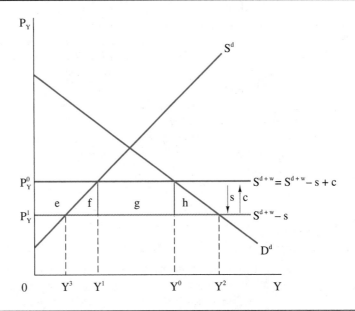

An export subsidy of s per unit increases domestic consumption from Y^0 to Y^2 while reducing domestic production from Y^1 to Y^3. The difference is made up by increased imports now available at a lower price (P_Y^1 rather than P_Y^0). Importing-country producers are harmed (area e), but by less than the gains to importing-country consumers (area e + f + g + h) in the form of lower prices and increased availability of imports. A countervailing duty (c) can offset the subsidy's effects on trade and consumption but will not eliminate a transfer (area g) from exporting-country to importing-country taxpayers.

Importing-country producers of good Y are likely to lobby for protection from subsidized exports to prevent the loss of area e. GATT rules allow for **countervailing duties (CVDs)**, or import taxes designed specifically to offset the competitive advantage provided by trading partners' export subsidies.[14] A countervailing duty of c (= s) per unit in Figure 7.3 eliminates the subsidy's effect on trade. Importing-country consumption returns to Y^0 and production to Y^1. Note, however, that one important effect of the subsidy remains even with the countervailing duty: The importing country continues to gain area g at the expense of exporting countries, who still pay a subsidy of s per unit on units Y^1 through Y^0. With the countervailing duty, importing-country consumers do not reap the subsidy directly through lower prices, but the importing-country government collects the duty and can lower domestic taxes accordingly. Therefore, area g represents a transfer from exporting-country

---

[14]The U.S. International Trade Commission's annual report, *The Year in Trade,* contains a summary of current subsidy investigations and countervailing duties in effect. Case Five examines a subsidy case concerning Canadian lumber exports.

Table 7.3 ▫ **U.S. Countervailing Duty Investigations**

Status	1991	1992	1993
Petitions filed	8	4	3
Final Commerce determinations:			
Negative	2	2	0
Affirmative	4	4	36
Suspended	0	0	0
Final Commission determinations:			
Negative	2	0	18
Affirmative	1	2	18
Terminated	0	3	0

Source: U.S. International Trade Commission, *The Year in Trade 1993* (Washington, D.C.: ITC, 1994), p. 129.

taxpayers (who finance the subsidy) to importing-country taxpayers (who enjoy lower domestic taxes).

Analysis of Figure 7.3 makes clear the importing country as a whole loses from a countervailing duty. The duty imposes costs on importing-country consumers (area e + f + g + h) that outweigh the gains to producers (area e) and the government (area g). From the importing-country perspective, countervailing duties represent a victory of protectionist pressures by domestic producers. From a worldwide view, imposition of a countervailing duty improves total welfare because the cost of the subsidy to exporting countries outweighs the benefits to the importing country. The countervailing duty cancels the inefficiencies in production and consumption introduced by the subsidy; only the transfer from taxpayers in the exporting countries to those in the importing country remains.

U.S. law requires firms alleging foreign subsidies to file complaints with the Department of Commerce and the International Trade Commission. Commerce investigates to determine whether a subsidy in fact exists, and the Commission determines whether the subsidy, if any, harms or threatens to harm domestic firms. If both findings are affirmative, a countervailing duty is imposed. Table 7.3 summarizes recent investigations. As of the end of 1993, the United States had 95 countervailing duties in effect, covering goods ranging from carnations to ball bearings and trading partners from Argentina to Zimbabwe.

7.5.2 The Exporting-Country View

From the perspective of the importing country, foreign export subsidies produce a net welfare gain but impose losses on importing-country producers who must compete with the subsidized products. The situation in the exporting country is quite different. There, subsidized producers gain at the expense of exporting-country consumers and/or taxpayers, depending on how many countries in the market subsidize exports.

Figure 7.4 represents the market for good Y in the exporting country. We continue to assume the country is small in the world market. Point C represents the unrestricted-

Figure 7.4 □ **Effects of an Export Subsidy: Exporting-Country Perspective**

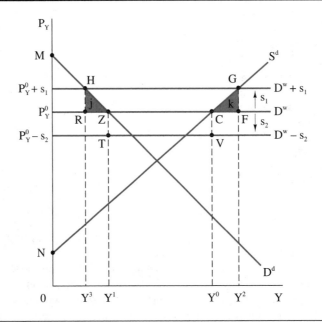

If the small country is the only exporter subsidizing (Scenario 1), export firms receive the world price *plus* the subsidy ($P_Y^0 + s_1$), and the net welfare effect on the exporting country is a loss equal to areas j and k. If all exporters subsidize (Scenario 2), the world price is bid down by the amount of the subsidy (s_2). Exporting firms receive only P_Y^0, and the net welfare loss to the exporting country is area TZCV.

trade equilibrium. The country produces Y^0 units, consumes Y^1, and exports $Y^0 - Y^1$. Domestic consumer surplus is $P_Y^0 MZ$, and domestic producer surplus is $NP_Y^0 C$.

Scenario 1: Subsidization by a Single Exporting Country

Assume first the country under consideration is the *only* one providing export subsidies in the market for good Y. The small country's subsidy will not affect the world price of the good, P_Y^0.[15] Exporting firms receive P_Y^0 from foreign consumers *plus* the subsidy, s_1. Point G in Figure 7.4 represents the new equilibrium. Exporting-country production rises to Y^2 because of the higher total price received for exports. The higher price also creates an incentive for producers to sell more abroad ($Y^2 - Y^3$) and less domestically (Y^3). Domestic consumer surplus falls to $(P_Y^0 + s_1)MH$. Domestic producer surplus rises to $N(P_Y^0 + s_1)G$. In addition, taxpayers pay RHGF to finance the subsidy. Note that import barriers must accompany export subsidies; otherwise foreign producers will bring in the good and re-export it to take advantage of the subsidy. *(Why?)*

---

[15]See footnote 13.

The sum of triangles j and k measures the net deadweight loss to the exporting country. Area j is "lost twice"—once in the form of lost consumer surplus and again in the form of subsidy payments by taxpayers—and only "gained once"—in increased producer surplus. Taxpayers pay area k as part of the subsidy, but it does not go to producer surplus because of the high cost of producing units Y^0 through Y^2. Overall, exporting-country producers gain at the expense of exporting-country consumers and taxpayers. The welfare losses exceed the gains; thus, the export subsidy fails the compensation test from the exporting country's perspective.

Scenario 2: Subsidization by All Exporting Countries

Now we assume the country under consideration is not the only one providing an export subsidy on good Y; *all* exporting countries subsidize. In this case, a subsidy of s_2 ($= s_1$) dollars per unit on exports of Y shifts down the price exporting-country producers require for sales in the export market.[16] The downward shift represents the amount of the subsidy. Producers are willing to sell abroad at $P_Y^0 - s_2$ in Figure 7.4 because they also receive s_2 from their government for each unit sold abroad; therefore, the total price producers receive, including both the price paid by foreign consumers *and* the subsidy, continues to equal P_Y^0. Exporting-country production does not change, nor do domestic producer and consumer surplus. However, taxpayers pay TZCV to finance the subsidy. *(Why?)* The net loss to the country is simply area TZCV, transferred to importing-country consumers in the form of a lower price.

7.5.3 The Controversy over Export Subsidies

Export subsidies raise an obvious question: Why would any country choose to subsidize its exports, thereby providing artificially low-priced imports to foreign consumers? One possible answer lies in the redistribution of income that subsidies generate in the exporting country. If the country is alone in subsidizing (Scenario 1), export-country producers gain and therefore have an incentive to lobby for export subsidies. But if many countries subsidize in the same market (Scenario 2), the subsidies drive down the world price. Producers then cease to gain from the subsidy, but they still cannot ask their governments to stop the subsidies. A producer whose government stopped subsidizing while other governments continued could not sell any output in the world market. *(Why?)* This explains the importance of Uruguay Round negotiations for all member countries to lower export subsidies in agricultural products simultaneously; no single country wanted to lower its subsidies while other countries continued theirs, because that country would lose its export markets.

The clustering of export subsidies in markets for agricultural products provides a clue to a second motivation for the subsidies.[17] Most industrial economies (including the United States, the European Union, and Japan) administer agricultural price-support

---

[16]When many countries subsidize exports, they drive down the world price by the amount of the subsidy (see footnote 13).

[17]Cases One and Two provide examples.

systems that keep prices for those products and farmers' incomes artificially high. When a country imposes a price floor above the equilibrium price of a good—say, wheat—the good's quantity supplied exceeds the quantity demanded. Under a simple price-support program, the government prevents the natural fall in price by buying the surplus wheat. Were the government to turn around and sell that wheat domestically, the sales would undermine the domestic price-support system. However, export sales do not undermine the artificially high domestic price. The difference between the high price paid to domestic farmers and the lower world price obtained by the government for export sales represents the subsidy. U.S. export subsidies of this type (under the Export Enhancement Program, or EEP) grew from $280 million in 1986 to $995 million in 1988. Wheat subsidies alone grew from $209 million to $744 million, and approximately 20 percent of the corn crop and 50 percent of the wheat crop were exported. Recent studies suggest the costs of the wheat subsidies have been so high (about $4.08 per bushel) that simply destroying the surplus wheat (at a cost of about $3.16 per bushel) would have provided a more cost-effective method of disposal than subsidized exports.[18] Similar subsidies under the European Union's Common Agricultural Program grew from $4.7 billion in 1982 to about $12.9 billion in 1988.[19]

The Uruguay Round agreement requires member countries to cut their agricultural export subsidies, to reduce the volume of agricultural exports receiving subsidies, and to refrain from granting new subsidies to additional agricultural products. As we shall see in Chapter Nine, reaching this compromise between demands for agricultural trade reform and farmers' demands for protection almost derailed the Uruguay Round talks and delayed the agreement for almost four years.

A more complex reason for export subsidies involves the possibility that temporary export subsidies in markets with certain characteristics may allow a country to capture a larger share of the world market that it can then exploit by charging monopoly prices for the good. A full examination of this argument, part of a branch of international trade called *strategic trade policy*, must wait until Chapter Eight.

Export subsidies rarely take the form of explicit and direct payments from a government to exporting firms. As mentioned earlier, GATT guidelines, even before the Uruguay Round, ruled out such payments on industrial products. Actual subsidies take less direct and visible forms. Defining precisely which actions do and do not comprise subsidies was one of the most difficult issues facing negotiators in the Uruguay Round of GATT talks. One of the most common types of subsidy involves provision of low-cost government loans to firms in certain industries. By lowering the cost of borrowed funds, such loans reduce production costs and allow goods to be sold at lower prices than otherwise would be feasible. It often is difficult to prove the

---

[18]On U.S. wheat export subsidies, see Cletus C. Coughlin and Kenneth C. Carraro, "The Dubious Success of Export Subsidies for Wheat," Federal Reserve Bank of St. Louis *Review* 70 (November–December 1988), 38–47.

[19]One purpose of increased U.S. agricultural subsidies was to raise the cost to the EU of its subsidies, thereby pressuring the EU to support multilateral talks for reduction and eventual elimination of subsidies, a goal partially accomplished in the Uruguay Round.

loans are subsidies because of problems involved in determining whether the interest rates charged are "artificially" low.[20]

In the United States, the Commodity Credit Corporation (CCC) and the Export-Import Bank provide export-related loans. The CCC guarantees private bank loans to finance agricultural exports. The laws governing both agencies state that they should provide loans for economic rather than foreign-policy reasons, but political controversy surrounds the programs. For example, they guaranteed $5 billion in loans to Iraq in the period leading up to Iraq's invasion of Kuwait. Once the Gulf War started, Iraq stopped payments on the loans, leaving almost $2 billion unpaid. Another controversial issue relates to loans to the former Soviet Union. On the one hand, political forces pressure for assistance to the republics; on the other hand, fears of nonrepayment of loans suggest caution.

A second type of subsidy is provision of favorable tax treatment for firms involved in exporting. The Uruguay Round agreement clarifies that forgone or uncollected government tax revenue, that is, tax credits, do constitute a subsidy under GATT rules.

Government subsidies have been a source of increasing controversy over the past decade. During the Tokyo Round of talks, which ended in 1979, a subset of GATT member countries agreed to a Code on Subsidies and Countervailing Duties. The signatory countries agreed that if one country's subsidized exports injured another signatory's domestic industry, the injured party could either impose a countervailing duty or request that the exporting country eliminate the subsidy. A signatory country also could seek redress when one country's subsidized exports displaced its own exports in third-country markets. However, failure to adopt a clear definition of subsidies continued to hamper the functioning of the Code, which made little progress on domestic (nonexport) subsidies. The subsequent Uruguay Round succeeded in reducing agricultural export subsidies, clarifying the definition of industrial export subsidies, providing discipline on domestic subsidies if they distort trade, and reforming rules on implementation of countervailing duties. A closely related problem is the frequent charge of dumping in international markets, discussed next.

7.6 Dumping

Perhaps no phenomenon in international trade generates as much controversy and as many calls for protection as does dumping. **Dumping** can be defined in one of two ways.[21] According to the "price-based" definition, dumping occurs whenever a firm sells a good in a foreign market at a price below that for which the same good sells in the domestic market. Under the "cost-based" definition, sale of a good in a foreign market at a price below its production cost constitutes dumping. Historically, both

---

[20]To limit interest-rate-based export subsidies, the Organization for Economic Cooperation and Development (a forum of developed countries) sets minimum interest rates member countries can charge on export loans. The permissible rates vary with the economic status of the borrowing country, the length or term of the financing, and the current level of market interest rates.

[21]Many economists agree that rules against dumping should be restricted to predatory dumping (defined in section 7.6.3); the original 1916 U.S. law was so restricted.

the economic literature on dumping and actual dumping charges used the price-based definition. In the last few years, the cost-based definition has become more widely used, as evidence on any disparity between sales price and production cost has been accepted in some U.S. dumping cases. The definitional distinction is important, because dumping under one definition is not necessarily dumping under the other. In particular, whenever the domestic price of a good differs from its cost of production, the requirements for dumping differ under the two definitions.

7.6.1 Sporadic Dumping

Economists classify dumping into three categories. The first is **sporadic dumping**, which involves sale of a good in a foreign market for a short time at a price below either the domestic price or the cost of production. This short-lived variety of dumping resembles an international "sale." Stores sometimes sell goods for short periods at prices below their regular prices, often to eliminate undesired inventories. Sale prices may even fall below the average total cost of production in the short run. Sporadic dumping is the international equivalent of such sales.

Sporadic dumping may disrupt the domestic market because of the uncertainty generated when foreign supply changes suddenly. However, it is unlikely to cause permanent and serious injury to a domestic industry, just as a store's market position is unlikely to be damaged irrevocably by a competitor's occasional sales. During the brief period of dumping, domestic consumers benefit from availability of the imported good at an unusually low price.

7.6.2 Persistent Dumping

Persistent dumping, as the term suggests, is continued sale of a good in a foreign market at a price below either the domestic price or production cost, a practice that provides the basis for many calls for protection. The distinction between the price-based and cost-based definitions is crucial in analyzing persistent dumping.

The major cause of persistent dumping according to the price-based definition is international price discrimination. Any firm able to separate its customers into two or more groups with different elasticities of demand for its product and to prevent resale of the good among them can increase profit by charging the groups different prices.[22] This practice is called **price discrimination.** Often a firm serving both a domestic and an export market can charge a higher price to domestic consumers, who typically exhibit a lower elasticity of demand than foreign consumers. Other things being equal, the more and better the substitutes for a good, the higher the elasticity of demand; good substitutes allow consumers to be very responsive to changes in the good's price. In most industries, a firm has more competitors in export markets than in the home-country market; this implies that the elasticity of demand facing the

---

[22]The elasticity of demand for a good is the percentage change in quantity demanded resulting from a 1 percent change in price (elasticity of demand = % change in quantity demanded/% change in price).

Figure 7.5 □ **Persistent Dumping as International Price Discrimination**

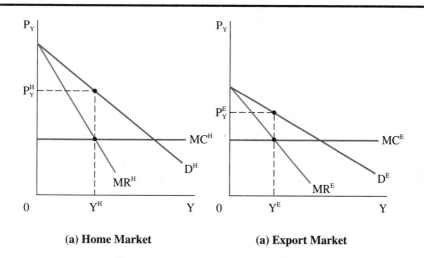

(a) Home Market   **(a) Export Market**

If a firm can prevent resale of its product between domestic and foreign customers, price discrimination based on differing elasticities of demand will increase the firm's profits. Because of the greater number of competitors in export markets, the firm generally will charge a higher price in the home market than in the export market (that is, $P_Y^H > P_Y^E$), generating dumping by the price-based definition.

firm in the export market typically exceeds that in the home market and creates an incentive for price discrimination.[23]

Figure 7.5 illustrates the relationship between international price discrimination and persistent dumping. A firm producing good Y faces the situation in panel (a) in the home market and the situation in panel (b) in the export market. The demand curves reflect a higher elasticity of demand for good Y in the export market at any given price; in other words, the firm possesses more market power in the home market than in the world market—an intuitively plausible assumption.

The firm maximizes profit in each market by producing the level of output at which *marginal cost* (denoted by MC and assumed for simplicity to be constant at all levels of output and equal across markets) equals *marginal revenue* (MR).[24] The height of the corresponding demand curve at the profit-maximizing level of output

[23]In Chapter Eight (section 8.4.2), we discuss the case of two monopolists charging high prices in their respective home markets and dumping (under the price definition) to capture part of the rival's market, a practice known as *reciprocal dumping.*

[24]Marginal revenue is defined as the change in total revenue when the firm changes its level of output by one unit. Under the assumption that the firm has some market power and must charge the same price for all units sold in a given market, marginal revenue at any level of output is less than price. To sell an additional unit of output in any market, the firm must lower its price, and the lower price must apply t all units sold in that market. Therefore, the marginal revenue from sale of the additional unit is less than the price for which the unit itself is sold.

gives the profit-maximizing price. The price in the *home* market (P_Y^H) exceeds that in the *export* market (P_Y^E) because of the relative inelasticity of home-country demand. The firm dumps by the price-based definition, with a **dumping margin** of $P_Y^H - P_Y^E$. However, such price discrimination produces ambiguous welfare effects. The market power reflected in the firm's ability to charge prices above marginal cost (especially in the home market) reduces economic efficiency and harms consumers, as with any case of monopoly. However, the effect of restricting the firm to charge equal prices in the two markets cannot be ascertained without further information about the market in question. Hence, international trade theory provides no clear rationale for policies that prohibit international price discrimination.

What about persistent dumping under the cost-based definition? Would we expect to observe continual sales of a good below cost? The answer depends on what one means by *cost*. If *cost* is defined as the firm's marginal cost of production, economists believe the general answer to the question is *no:* Firms will not sell a good persistently at a price below its marginal cost of production. Although many industries in many countries ask for protection from foreign competition by pointing to alleged persistent dumping, there are few cases in which such behavior has been observed.[25] There is, however, one major exception to this rule.

As noted earlier, most developed countries (notably the United States and the members of the European Union) maintain complex systems of price supports in agriculture to keep farmers' incomes above the market-determined level. The artificially high prices for agricultural products create an excess of quantity supplied of many products above the quantity demanded. Most governments enforce their price-support systems by using tax revenues to buy the excess agricultural products at the supported prices. Once the government has bought the surplus, selling the good at any positive price brings in revenue that helps finance the price-support system. However, selling the surplus in the domestic market would undermine the price support by putting downward pressure on the domestic price. Exporting provides an obvious alternative. Because it is worthwhile to sell the agricultural surplus abroad at prices not only below the (artificially high) domestic price but perhaps below the marginal cost of production as well, these sales are a case of persistent dumping even under the cost-based definition. Such sales are a continuing source of ill will in the international trading system. The similarity of the agricultural price-support systems among the major developed economies implies that foreign sales by one country often undercut the price supports of another. The United States defends its policies while it attacks those of Japan and the European Union by pointing out that the United States is a low-cost producer of many major agricultural commodities.[26]

Outside agricultural markets, charges of dumping under the cost-based definition often use a concept of cost other than the exporting firm's *marginal* cost. For example, firms may sell in the short run at prices below their *average* total cost. In fact, we expect firms with significant fixed costs to do so in periods of low demand.

[25]See Appendix A in the Congressional Budget Office volume in the chapter references.
[26]See Case Two.

As long as producing brings in revenue sufficient to cover variable cost, the profit-maximizing firm will choose to produce rather than shut down in the short run—even if price falls below average total cost. This holds regardless of whether the firm sells domestically or internationally.[27]

Another problem arises because foreign production costs often are difficult to determine, presenting a temptation to use indirect measures of those costs. Careless use of the cost-based definition of dumping could allow domestic producers to accuse any foreign rival who undersold them. Assume American Steel Company loses business to Brazilian Steel Company, which sells steel products at lower prices. American Steel accuses Brazilian Steel of dumping. Since neither American Steel nor U.S. trade-policy makers know Brazilian Steel's true cost of production, American Steel argues that Brazilian Steel's prices are below *American Steel's* production cost. Acceptance of such an argument as evidence of dumping sets a dangerous precedent. Domestic producers in *any* comparative-disadvantage industry could accuse foreign rivals of dumping. Recall that a country with a comparative advantage always can sell the industry's product for less than a country with a comparative disadvantage. Disallowing trade based on dumping charges that involve careless use of the cost-based definition of dumping could eliminate all trade based on comparative advantage!

In practice, use of the cost-based definition in dumping cases is not yet quite as disastrous as the previous example might suggest. When a domestic firm files dumping charges, trade law requires an effort to determine their validity using the price-based definition. If domestic-country prices of the good in question are not available (for example, if the foreign firm produces only for export), investigators must make an effort to determine the price of the good in a third market. When this fails, investigators seek production costs in the country of origin, followed by production costs in third markets.

The most famous example of this situation involved a 1974 U.S. charge that Poland dumped golf carts in the U.S. market. Since Poland sold no golf carts domestically, the price-based definition of dumping proved useless. No one knew the true cost of production by Polish firms because Poland, as a centrally planned economy, did not use market-determined prices for its inputs. To resolve the case, investigators evaluated the inputs the Polish firm used to make a golf cart at input prices from Spain. The estimated cost turned out to be very close to the price Poland charged for golf carts sold in the United States. Rapid changes in nonmarket economies raise interesting issues for the calculations in dumping investigations. In dumping charges against China, another centrally planned economy, the United States historically used prices from third countries including Germany, Japan, France, Canada, Switzerland, the Netherlands, India, Pakistan, and Thailand to substitute for missing Chinese prices. However, as China has increased the role of market prices in its economy, U.S. dumping-investigation procedures have adjusted. In recent cases regarding sparkler fireworks, lug nuts used to attach wheels to cars, and electric fans, investigators used some Chinese prices. The policy change generated controversy because

---

[27]If sales at high prices in a protected domestic market cover the firm's fixed cost, sales in export markets can occur at any price that covers the variable cost of production (a strategy often attributed to Japan during the 1950s and 1960s).

the two procedures can lead to very different dumping margins (for example, 4 percent using third-country prices versus 69 percent using Chinese prices in the case of lug nuts).

Another recent controversial U.S. dumping case involved uranium exported from six former Soviet republics. The charges alleged the Soviet Union had dumped uranium between June and October of 1991, before the republics even existed as independent states. U.S. investigators computed a dumping margin of 115 percent. James Bovard characterized the third-country data used to arrive at that figure by saying, "[The Department of] Commerce took the unproven assertions it received from U.S. producers, juggled the numbers, and then announced that, if Soviet uranium had been mined with Canadian efficiency, Portuguese electricity, and Namibian labor costs, it would have cost 115 percent more than it actually did."[28] In other words, the Department of Commerce, lacking data on Soviet prices and costs, which would have been meaningless anyway given the centrally planned structure of the Soviet economy, substituted Canadian productivity figures, Portuguese electricity prices, and wages from Namibia to calculate whether the Soviet Union dumped uranium.

7.6.3 Predatory Dumping

Domestic firms often claim foreign firms sell in the domestic market at prices below production cost to drive domestic firms from the industry. The alleged purpose behind this strategy of **predatory dumping** is to eliminate domestic competitors and then exploit the newly created monopoly power by raising prices. Although intuitively appealing, several aspects of this story stand up poorly to scrutiny.

First, foreign firms—if indeed they sell at prices below their production cost—suffer losses while dumping. The prospective monopoly power they hope to gain must promise future rewards high enough to compensate for current losses. Second, domestic firms would know predatory dumping could be only temporary because of the losses it would create for its instigators. If the "unfair competition" is only temporary, domestic firms should be able to borrow funds with which to hold out until the foreign firms give up on the attempt to drive rivals out of business. Third, even if predatory dumping drove domestic firms from the industry, the strategy would prove worthwhile only if foreign firms could then exploit their monopoly power by charging higher prices. However, once this occurred, what would prevent domestic firms (either old or new) from re-entering the industry and underselling the foreign monopolist? If domestic firms did this, foreign firms would have suffered losses during the dumping for little or no reward. Finally, the predatory dumping story requires a firm to perceive an opportunity to monopolize the industry. But large groups of firms often file dumping charges against dozens of competitors; the large number of firms involved on both sides of the typical dumping case implies a low probability of monopolization.

The United States' first antidumping law, passed in 1916, applied only to predatory dumping. In the 80 years since, no firm has been convicted under that statute.

---

[28]James Bovard, "U.S. Protectionists Claim a Russian Victim," *The Wall Street Journal,* June 8, 1992.

Current dumping cases use statutes that embody much broader definitions of dumping to include that with no predatory intent.[29]

7.6.4 Policy Responses to Dumping

Under U.S. trade law, when a domestic firm charges its foreign counterpart with dumping, the U.S. International Trade Commission and the U.S. Department of Commerce conduct investigations. Those investigations must determine (1) whether dumping is occurring, and (2) if so, whether it materially injures or threatens to materially injure the domestic industry. If both questions are answered affirmatively, the government imposes an **antidumping duty,** an import tariff equal to the dumping margin.

Despite rules written into antidumping laws, many analysts argue that U.S. procedures in dumping investigations almost guarantee guilty findings for foreign firms charged with dumping. The computation of dumping margins involves many complex issues, and trading partners complain with some justification that U.S. procedures bias findings toward high dumping margins and, therefore, high antidumping duties.[30]

Historically, the United States used antidumping policies much more extensively than other countries. However, in recent years, trading partners have been catching up. Twenty member countries reported to the GATT having taken antidumping actions in 1993. By one estimate, 77 percent of trade disputes during the 1980s involved dumping charges.[31] The United States ranks high, along with EU members and China, as a target of trading partners' dumping accusations. For example, in 1993, trading partners found U.S. firms guilty of dumping sodium cyanide, gypsum wallboard, and several classes of steel. But the United States continues to file the most dumping charges; recent examples include semiconductor chips from South Korea, fresh flowers from Colombia, European coated ground-wood paper, Taiwanese sweaters, and Japanese power tools.[32] At the end of 1993, the United States had 290 antidumping orders in effect, covering goods from pears to shop towels to bicycle speedometers and involving trading partners as varied as Canada and Uzbekistan. Table 7.4 reports the number of U.S. dumping cases in recent years, along with the number of negative and affirmative findings by both the Department of Commerce and the International Trade Commission.

Trading partners complain about the U.S. practice of demanding extraordinary amounts of detailed information on short notice from firms accused of dumping. If a firm cannot or chooses not to provide any piece of the requested information, the U.S. investigators can use their own "best information available" to substitute for the missing data. In practice, the "best information available" consists of data provided by the domestic firms seeking protection and, as a result, might be expected to contain a bias toward a large dumping margin.

---

[29]The Congressional Budget Office volume in the chapter references contains a useful history of U.S. dumping legislation.

[30]John H. Jackson provides an excellent overview of dumping rules in Chapter Ten of the book cited in the chapter references. See also the books by Finger and by Boltuck and Litan.

[31]*The Economist,* June 15, 1991, 20.

[32]The U.S. International Trade Commission, *The Year in Trade* summarizes current dumping cases.

Table 7.4 □ U.S. Antidumping Investigations

	1991	1992	1993
Petitions filed	24	24	21
Final Commerce determinations:			
Negative	0	2	1
Affirmative	28	24	76
Terminated	1	2	0
Suspended	0	7	0
Final Commision determinations:			
Negative	13	4	32
Affirmative	19	16	41
Terminated	0	1	0

Source: U.S. International Trade Commission, *The Year in Trade 1993* (Washington, D.C.: ITC, 1994), p. 128.

One interesting dumping dispute involved two-way dumping allegations between long-time rivals Brother and Smith-Corona, producers of typewriters and word processors. U.S.-owned Smith-Corona charged Japanese-owned Brother with dumping word processors. The case succeeded, and the United States imposed a 59 percent antidumping duty. Soon after, Brother accused Smith-Corona of dumping typewriters in the U.S. market. How can this be—since Brother is Japanese and Smith-Corona is American? Although Japanese owned, Brother maintains production facilities in the United States making the firm the largest U.S. producer of typewriters; and, while Smith-Corona is U.S. owned, it imports its typewriters from Singapore, making it the largest importer of typewriters. Nonetheless, the U.S. government refused to pursue Brother's charge against Smith-Corona.

The Uruguay Round elaborated on antidumping rules negotiated as a code during the Tokyo Round. However, progress in dealing with dumping fell far short of that in many other areas. The new agreement does require countries to remove antidumping duties that have been in place for five years unless they can demonstrate that doing so would reinstitute the damage to the domestic industry that led to the initial finding. This provision should help curtail the current practice of more-or-less permanent protection in the form of antidumping duties.

7.7 Voluntary Import Expansions

A **voluntary import expansion (VIE)** requires a country to import a specified quantity of foreign goods in a given industry. The mandated imports typically are stated as a minimum market share. Failure to achieve the target usually leads to retaliation with tariffs.[33] The exporting country pushing a trading partner to accept a VIE

---

[33]See Case One in Chapter Five on the U.S.–Japan semiconductor pact, and Case Two in Chapter Six on U.S. threats to tariff Japanese luxury cars unless Japan increased its auto and auto-part imports. Chapter Eight (section 8.12) treats more generally the use of protectionist policies to force trade liberalization on trading partners.

often alleges that foreign trade barriers block exports and necessitate the agreement. On the surface, VIEs appear different from other protectionist policies. After all, VIEs aim to increase, not decrease, trade and claim to offset or break through foreign trade barriers.

VIEs form a key part of "results-oriented" trade policies, that is, policies that focus on generating specific trade *outcomes* rather than on establishing a framework of *rules* under which trade is market determined. Japan has been a particular target of results-oriented policies, because of the widespread perception that the structure of the Japanese economy embodies many "informal" or "invisible" trade barriers, such as a preference on the part of Japanese firms for long-term business relationships that favor domestic partners. These informal barriers present problems for the international trading system for three reasons. First, their very informality makes substantiating their existence, much less measuring their magnitude or impact, difficult.[34] Second, the complexity of the barriers, if indeed they exist, makes multilateral or even bilateral negotiations for their reduction difficult. Finally, the barriers are embedded in the structure of the economy and culture in such a way that international pressures for change encounter resistance. Proponents of VIEs claim these factors, taken together, render traditional rules-oriented trade policy ineffective in reducing Japan's informal barriers.

Despite first appearances, VIEs can act as powerful tools of protection. They ignore the possibility that the observed outcome in a particular industry simply reflects comparative advantage rather than foreign trade barriers.[35] The agreements allocate specific market shares to foreign and domestic firms, allowing the firms to act as an informal cartel and charge higher prices than would be feasible under market competition. VIEs often allocate the required foreign market share to the country powerful enough to force the import country to negotiate the VIE; again, competition is restricted rather than encouraged, as the VIE itself shuts potential exporters from other countries out of the market. Finally, any industry that potentially could export has an incentive to push for VIEs—even if the industry has a comparative disadvantage. Policy makers tend to measure the "success" of a VIE in increased export sales, regardless of whether those sales coincide with the international pattern of comparative advantage. More trade, however, is not necessarily better than less trade. Trade produces gains only if it is based on either comparative advantage or economies of scale. VIE-induced exports that run counter to comparative advantage damage foreign producers, may damage consumers, and reduce the efficiency of the world economy, even though they help exporting firms.

7.8 Administrative and Technical Standards

Most countries subject international trade to a variety of regulatory standards, some protectionist by design and others unintentionally so. A few of the more common classes of restrictions include domestic-content requirements and rules of origin,

---

[34]See, for example, the articles by Lawrence and Saxonhouse in the chapter references.

[35]The quotation in problem 4 in the "Problems and Questions for Review" provides one vivid example.

government procurement policies, technical product standards, and regulatory standards. Such policies constitute a continuing source of controversy within the international trading system because of the inherent difficulty in sorting intentionally protectionist policies from those pursued for legitimate domestic reasons but having unintended negative effects on international trade.

7.8.1 Domestic-Content Requirements and Rules of Origin

Domestic-content requirements mandate that a specified percentage of a product's inputs and/or assembly have domestic origins in order for the good to be sold domestically. Such requirements have three main constituencies. One consists of domestic input producers. For example, most U.S. auto parts producers support rules to require all cars sold in the United States, especially those produced by Japanese-based firms, to include high percentages of U.S.-made parts. A second constituency includes workers in the domestic industry. A U.S. domestic-content rule on cars, for example, could require Japanese auto producers to perform a high percentage of assembly tasks in the United States, increasing demand for the services of U.S. auto workers. Finally, domestic producers of the good typically support domestic-content requirements because such rules can raise foreign firms' costs and make them less competitive. If U.S.-made labor and auto parts cost more than their Japanese counterparts, then forcing Japanese producers to use more U.S. parts and perform more assembly tasks in the United States could raise Toyota's, Nissan's, and Honda's costs and shift sales toward domestic auto producers.

Worldwide, domestic-content requirements have received most attention in the automobile industry, which in recent years has sponsored almost every type of trade restriction imaginable. The United Auto Workers union has pressured U.S. policy makers to pass domestic-content legislation. The original UAW-supported legislation would have required 90 percent value-added produced in the United States or Canada for all manufacturers selling 500,000 or more cars in the United States. The reasons for this pressure are twofold. First, domestic-content requirements would limit imports of foreign-produced automobiles. Second, the requirements would limit **outsourcing,** in which U.S.-based automobile manufacturers buy inputs and perform assembly functions abroad. Many "American" cars—that is, cars sold by U.S.-based automobile companies—now are built abroad, much to the dismay of American automobile workers. Auto makers have adopted Japan's high-technology assembly methods and use them in factories around the world. Cars built outside the United States from mostly foreign parts include the Dodge Colt and Stealth, Ford Festiva, Plymouth Colt, and Pontiac LeMans. Also, many car parts, including engines and transmissions, now are built in Canada, Mexico, and Brazil, imported into the United States, and placed in "American" cars. U.S. companies are not the only ones taking advantage of low-cost production in developing countries; Volkswagen and Nissan, for example, maintain assembly operations in Mexico. Foreign-based auto producers also build cars in the United States, including the Honda Accord and some Mazda models. For cars sold in the United States, the vehicle-identification number (VIN) provides information about the country where the car was assembled. Cars assembled in the United States have VINs beginning with 1 or 4, while cars assembled in Japan begin with J and in Sweden with Y, for example. *(Where was your car assembled?)*

Modern worldwide production makes it difficult or impossible to determine the "nationality" of a product. A car may be assembled in England from parts produced in Brazil and sold by a firm owned primarily by Germans. One U.S. pro-protection interest group wants to require all goods to carry labels listing how much of the goods' value-added comes from each country. The South Dakota legislature carried the idea further by proposing all goods be labeled with three flags denoting the countries of the producing firm's ownership, the product's manufacture, and the parts used in the product. Since 1994, cars sold in the United States have required stickers stating the percentage of parts from U.S. and Canadian sources. The stickers, designed by U.S. auto producers, understate the domestic content of cars produced in the United States by foreign-based companies. Under the new rules, the Toyota Camry's measured domestic content was expected to fall from 75 percent to 30 percent.[36]

Direct political pressure from protectionist-oriented special-interest groups is not the only reason for increased domestic-content requirements. When groups of countries negotiate reductions in their barriers to trade, those reductions sometimes apply *only* to members of the group. Recent examples include the European Union's 1992 removal of trade barriers among its members and the North American Free-Trade Agreement. These agreements require a version of domestic-content rules, often called **rules of origin;** otherwise, nonmember countries could use the agreements to circumvent tariffs. For example, if Canada's import tariffs exceed those of the United States, countries exporting to Canada would like to ship their goods to the United States, pay the low U.S. tariff, and then ship to Canada duty-free from the United States under the NAFTA. To prevent this, agreements such as the NAFTA must contain provisions that limit duty-free access to goods "originating" in the member countries.[37] In practice, this involves complicated and politically sensitive issues, as members of the European Union and the NAFTA have discovered.

Nissan recently built an auto plant in Britain, intending to use the plant to serve the EU market. But France and Italy, with domestic auto industries to protect, wanted to count Nissan Bluebirds imported from Britain as Japanese cars subject to the auto VER negotiated between Japan and the EU. Similarly, France tried unsuccessfully to count Honda Accord wagons (called Aerodecks in Europe) as Japanese cars—even though they were designed in America and built in Marysville, Ohio. In an even more bitter dispute, the United States ruled Honda Civics built in Alliston, Ontario, ineligible to enter the United States duty-free because they contained less than 50 percent North American content, the cutoff for duty-free treatment under the Canada–U.S. Free-Trade Agreement, the precursor to the NAFTA. Canadians were furious, especially since engines the United States claimed contained too much foreign content were cast in Ohio from U.S. aluminum and had been accepted into Canada duty-free, placed in finished Civics, and re-exported to the United States. The case involved $17 million in back tariff duties and about $180 in tariff for every Honda Civic shipped from Ontario to the United States. A binational review panel considered

---

[36]"Rules Redefine Origin," *USA Today,* June 29, 1994, B2.

[37]The alternative is to form a customs union with a common external tariff on trade with nonmembers; we shall discuss this option in section 9.4.1

the dispute, as specified under the dispute-settlement procedures of the Canada–U.S. Free-Trade Agreement, and ruled in favor of Canada. The Civics qualified for duty-free entry in the United States because they satisfied the agreement's rules of origin.

Under the NAFTA, most goods qualify for duty-free treatment if they *either* contain a specified percentage of North American content *or* are sufficiently "transformed" in North America to change tariff classification.[38] For goods in sensitive sectors (autos, computers, and textiles and apparel), *both* conditions must be satisfied. Autos, in particular, must contain 62.5 percent North American content; the United States insisted on the high percentage after its loss in the Honda Civic case.

The Uruguay Round agreement set in motion a three-year process to develop harmonized rules of origin for GATT member countries. Suggested disciplines include requiring rules to be consistent and impartial, prohibiting retroactive application of rule changes, and restricting the frequency of rule changes to every three years, since frequent changes in rules disadvantage exporters.

Domestic-content rules and rules of origin discourage production of goods in the countries where opportunity costs are lowest. Thus, such rules reduce the gains from trade. The potential losses may be particularly large in industries, such as the automobile industry, that involve many diverse manufacturing and assembly tasks. A single country is unlikely to have a comparative advantage in every aspect of the automobile production process, from research and development-intensive design to labor-intensive assembly. Arrangements such as outsourcing reflect attempts to perform each manufacturing and assembly stage in the country of comparative advantage. As a result, outsourcing not only contributes to efficient production of automobiles but also may support developing countries' attempts to build manufacturing sectors. A developing or newly industrializing country finds it difficult to build a complete automobile industry that can compete with the established industries in the developed economies. An alternative is to specialize in particular stages of the production process appropriate for its factor endowment, but domestic-content rules and rules of origin can restrict such specialization.

7.8.2 Government Procurement Policies

Our analyses of international trade have relied on profit-maximizing motives of firms and utility maximization by consumers. We have assumed consumers and firms try to buy at the lowest and sell at the highest available prices. The interaction of buyers' and sellers' decisions in each market determines the prices of goods and of factors of production. A large amount of trade, however, is undertaken by entities that may not respond to these motives of profit and utility maximization, at least in the simple terms in which we have defined them. Governments are foremost among the trading entities with unique goals.

We have seen several effects of government involvement in international trade: agricultural price supports and the resulting surpluses as an explanation for persistent dumping, and the role of government subsidization of exports. Two other areas

---

[38]On tariff classification, see section 6.3.1 and Case Three in Chapter Six.

involve even more direct government roles in international trade. First, governments actually buy and sell many goods and services in international markets. Second, government-owned industries and government-run monopolies make purchases and sales. These phenomena are called **government procurement policies.**

Most countries have **buy-domestic requirements,** which either legally or informally require governments to purchase domestically made goods on a preferential basis. The strength of the requirements varies considerably. Some prohibit government purchases of certain imports outright; for example, laws require many governments to use the domestic airline exclusively and to patronize only domestic insurance firms. Other laws mandate strict guidelines for giving preference to domestic over foreign producers. The Buy American Act of 1933 required a 6 percent margin of preference for domestic producers of goods bought by the government. In other words, a foreign firm would have to sell at a price more than 6 percent below the domestic firm's price to win the contract.[39] For military or defense-related goods, the margin of preference expanded to 50 percent. The U.S. government spent $81 billion on military equipment in 1989, much of it restricted to U.S. firms.

Many of the most controversial government procurement practices are much more subtle and informal than the provisions of the Buy American Act and its foreign counterparts. For example, governments may keep their bidding practices secret so foreign firms will have little or no information concerning the procedure and timing for submission of bids for government contracts. Government agencies may advertise contracts in media unlikely to be available to foreign firms, and bids may be kept secret to prevent scrutiny of the award process. The Tokyo Round of trade negotiations addressed some of these problems with a government procurement code, and the Uruguay Round built on this effort. The code has only 22 signatory countries and applies only to specified government agencies and projects; but it represents a step forward in recommending that government bidding procedures be well specified and open. The Uruguay Round rules apply to procurement of services as well as goods, and to some purchases by subfederal governments and public utilities. However, governments still can practice many forms of preference for domestic firms.

Even more controversy arises when the government owns sizable industries, as in the cases of postal, telephone, and telegraph services (PTTs) in Japan, Europe, and most developing economies. The governments involved often claim to maintain these monopolies for purely domestic reasons, including national security and protection of domestic consumers from exploitation by private monopolies. The complex web of restrictions on imports of goods used in these industries suggests that protection of the domestic industry from foreign competition may be another government goal. The scope of the problem varies widely across countries with the extent of public ownership of industry. National policies typically restrict imports of telecommunications equipment, data processing, and computer-oriented technology by PTTs. One result is telephone calls from Germany to New York that cost three times as

---

[39]Many U.S. states have gone even further with "buy in the state" legislation, which gives preference to in-state firms for goods purchased by state and local government agencies. Los Angeles requires a specified percentage of *local* value-added for purchases related to its mass-transportation system.

much as similar calls in the opposite direction.[40] Japanese restrictions on telecommunications equipment for Nippon Telephone and Telegraph became the focus of a wide range of trade complaints between the United States and Japan during the 1980s. Most governments have recognized the need to privatize or deregulate their utilities, both to improve the industries' efficiency and to avoid trade disputes, but progress in this reform has varied widely across countries.

7.8.3   Technical, Administrative, and Regulatory Standards

Governments regulate various aspects of activity within their economies and carefully guard their rights to do so. Regulations may include health, safety, and product-labeling requirements, as well as controls over entry into certain professions and access to certain types of mass media. Domestic considerations motivate many of these **technical barriers to trade.** Governments require imported foods to meet hygienic standards, toys and autos to meet safety standards, and products to conform to labeling laws to prevent fraud and provide consumer information.

As in the case of government-owned telecommunications monopolies, some of the observed restrictions clearly have protectionist effects. In some cases, these effects are so strong that one must suspect the proclaimed domestic goals of the restrictions as mere covers for protectionist intent. The European Union has a quota of television air time for European-produced programs. Japan makes it difficult for non-Japanese to practice law. The United States, except for Alaska, bans Mexican avocados. Japanese road taxes penalize large-engine automobiles; but recently the tax was lowered (perhaps because Japanese auto makers themselves now make larger cars). The United States imposes financial penalties on car manufacturers whose fleets fail to meet fuel-economy standards, and the penalties have fallen mainly on European producers Mercedes and BMW. France reserves 40 percent of prime-time radio programming for French songs. For several years, the Japanese Ministry of Posts and Telecommunications maintained technical standards that rendered U.S.-made car phones unusable in the Tokyo-Nagoya corridor, which encompasses most of Japan's industrial and financial activity; the standards were altered only after a U.S. threat to impose retaliatory tariffs. For 471 years (until 1987), Germany's "beer purity law" decreed that beer sold in Germany could contain only water, hops, yeast, and barley, effectively ruling out imported beers, most of which contain chemical additives, rice, corn, soy, or millet. Germany is not alone in protecting its beer industry. In 1992, the GATT ruled in favor of Canada that U.S. federal excise-tax rules and tax and distribution rules in 41 states discriminated against foreign brewers.

China requires firms wanting to sell cars in China to provide the Chinese government with two free samples, pay $40,000 for testing, and pay for Chinese officials to visit and inspect factories where the cars are produced. South Korean customs procedures delay perishable products such as oranges and strawberries for periods of five days to four months, enough time for them to perish. Japan resists changing its

---

[40]John Diebold, "The Information Technology Industries: A Case Study of High Technology Trade," in William R. Cline, ed., *Trade Policy in the 1980s* (Washington, D.C.: Institute for International Economics, 1983), 667.

building codes to allow construction with imported lumber, claiming Japanese earthquakes are too severe to allow such construction. Many analysts suggested the destruction caused by the 1994 earthquake would have been substantially less had state-of-the-art construction techniques, developed in California, been used in Kobe.

Because of the difficulties in sorting legitimate domestic policy goals from protectionist ones, efforts at international negotiations to lower technical barriers to trade have met with relatively little success. Taken individually, the rules may seem small and rather insignificant in terms of cost. When taken together, however, the costs become substantial. Eliminating these costs by removing technical barriers to trade provided a major stimulus to the European Union's efforts to develop a completely open market for trade among its members.

7.9 Measuring Nontariff Barriers

Nontariff barriers present major hurdles to analysts interested in measuring the range and magnitude of those barriers. As the discussion of technical barriers to trade makes clear, deciding exactly what should count as a nontariff barrier can be difficult in itself. Once we decide which barriers to include, at least four measures can be calculated.

The most common empirical measure of NTBs is the **coverage ratio,** or the value of imports subject to NTBs, divided by total imports. Consider a simple example. Country A imports $60 worth of good X and $40 worth of good Y, so A's total imports equal $100. Imports of X are subject to a quota under which a maximum of $60 worth of X can be imported, and imports of Y are free of any NTBs. NTBs affect $60 out of the country's $100 worth of imports, so country A's NTB coverage ratio equals ($60/$100) = 0.6. The major problem with the coverage ratio is that incipient trade, shut off by the trade restriction, is not counted. With no quota on good X, perhaps country A would have imported $5,000 worth of X; but the loss of the additional $4,940 worth of trade does not enter the coverage-ratio calculation. Another problem involves measuring changes in NTBs. Suppose, beginning with the situation just outlined, country A tightens the quota on good X until no imports can enter, while good Y remains unrestricted. Now none of country A's imports are covered by NTBs, so the new coverage ratio is $0/$40 = 0. Counter-intuitively, *tightening* the quota, by stopping all trade in the restricted good, *lowered* the NTB coverage ratio![41]

An alternative measure, called the **implicit tariff,** uses the equivalence between tariffs and quotas (see section 7.4). The idea is to calculate the tariff rate that would have the same effect on trade as the existing quota or other nontariff barrier. For example, the U.S. International Trade Commission estimated that the U.S. import quota on cheese in 1990 had effects equivalent to those of a tariff of 172 percent.

The most comprehensive measures of nontariff barriers are producer- and consumer-subsidy equivalents. An industry's **producer-subsidy equivalent (PSE)** measures the difference between the income that industry producers receive *with* their NTBs

---

[41]Average tariff measures exhibit the same weakness; see section 6.3.2 in Chapter Six.

Table 7.5 □ **Producer-Subsidy Equivalents in Agriculture, 1990**

	Net PSE as Percent of Value of Production
Japan	68
European Community	48
Canada	41
United States	30
Australia	11
New Zealand	5

Source: *The Economist*, June 8, 1991; data from Organization for Economic Cooperation and Development.

and the income that producers would receive *with no* such barriers, and expresses that difference as a percentage of the income-without-barriers figure. If producers earn $2 million with a quota but would earn only $1 million under free trade, the producer-subsidy equivalent is ($2 million − $1 million)/$1 million = 1.0 or 100 percent. Economists have calculated producer-subsidy equivalents for many agricultural products because those products are subject to so many NTBs. Table 7.5 reports one set of estimates that compares agricultural PSEs for several major agricultural producers. Over the last few years, PSEs have risen in Japan and the European Union, but have fallen in Canada, the United States, Australia, and New Zealand.

The **consumer-subsidy equivalent** (CSE) performs the same exercise for an industry's consumers. If, because of an import quota, consumers must pay $5 million for a good they could get for $4 million without the quota, the quota's consumer-subsidy equivalent is ($4 million − $5 million)/$4 million = −0.25 or −25 percent. Note the negative sign; the quota forces consumers to pay higher prices, hence in effect they receive a *negative* subsidy. Generally, protectionist policies including NTBs affect producers and consumers in an industry in opposite ways. Therefore, the producer- and consumer-subsidy equivalents for an industry usually have opposite signs. *(Name a trade policy with a negative PSE and a positive CSE, and vice versa.)*

Case One
U.S. Sugar Quotas: Sweet for Whom?

The international sugar market provides a good example of the interaction of domestic and international economic policies. Policies pursued by developed countries toward sugar (particularly by the United States and the European Union) have distorted the market, imposed high costs on debt-burdened developing countries, and spurred technological advances in sugar substitutes that greatly reduced world demand for sugar.

The United States has protected the sugar industry since 1816. U.S. policies in the sugar market consist of two main elements: price supports currently set at about 18

Table 7.6 ▫ **U.S. Import Quota on Raw Sugar (Million Tons)**

Year	Quota
1983	3.10
1984	3.20
1985	2.55
1986	1.70
1987	1.00
1988	0.75
1989	1.10
1990	2.65
1991	2.00
1992	1.30
1993	1.13
1994	1.23

cents per pound and quotas restricting sugar imports (along with a tariff of just under 3 cents per pound). Since 1982, the combination of price supports and import quotas has resulted in U.S. sugar prices ranging from two to seven times world levels.

Government price supports led to imposition of the quotas. In 1981, the world price of sugar fell to about 9 cents per pound. The U.S. domestic price-support program obligates the government to accept sugar as repayment of government loans to domestic sugar producers at the support price of approximately 18 cents per pound. In addition to writing off the loans, the government would have to store the sugar at significant costs. The United States imposed an import quota to push the domestic price above the support price and prevent the government from being forced to accept sugar in repayment of loans. The quota persisted, as Table 7.6 reports, with periodic adjustments for changing market conditions.

Whenever a poor domestic crop places upward pressure on already high domestic prices, sugar refiners and users such as soft-drink manufacturers push for relief from the high prices and often succeed in having the quota loosened. As soon as domestic supply recovers, the price falls close to the support price, recreating the danger that the government might be forced to accept sugar in repayment of loans, and policy makers respond by tightening the quota. There appears to be a "balance of power" between sugar growers, who desire tight quotas and high sugar prices, and sugar refiners and users, who want loose or no quotas and low sugar prices. This scenario suggests policy makers will not allow domestic sugar prices to deviate far from current levels.

Artificially high U.S. sugar prices have encouraged development of improved sugar substitutes. Industries that use large amounts of sugar, particularly the soft-drink industry, increasingly turn to less expensive sweeteners. In 1984, Coca-Cola and Pepsi announced they would switch from sugar to corn sweeteners. Analysts have estimated the share of the U.S. sweetener market held by corn sweeteners grew from 4 to 50 percent in ten years. The decrease in sugar demand related to availability of new and better substitutes certainly contributed to the 15-year low in world sugar prices recorded in 1985. U.S. corn growers have become a major constituency for the sugar quotas, because high sugar prices increase demand for corn to make corn sweeteners. The political support of corn growers is important to continuation of the costly sugar program, because U.S. sugar producers themselves number only about 11,000, although they are politically powerful and have a large stake in continuation of the quotas. The annual gain to each domestic grower amounts to about $170,000, and recent Department of Agriculture figures indicate more than 50 percent of domestic producers' revenues come from the price supports and quota.

The quotas have harmed many developing countries that rely on sugar export revenues, especially Brazil, the Philippines, Argentina, and Mexico, all of which need those revenues to help pay off large external debts. Each year's sugar quota is allocated among approximately 40 exporting countries. Countries that receive large shares of the quota gain, because they are able to sell large amounts of sugar in the United States at the artificially high price. But countries that receive small quota allocations, or none at all, suffer from loss of their U.S. market. Reports from several Caribbean countries suggest unemployed sugar workers now grow illegal drug crops for export to the United States.

The NAFTA required a special provision for Mexican sugar exports to the United States. Mexico holds a very small share of the U.S. quota, but over the next ten years the agreement provides for substantial expansion of Mexican exports. Unless the overall level of U.S. protection to its sugar industry declines, the increased imports from Mexico will come at the expense of other sugar-exporting countries.

The quotas also have defined a new crime in the United States: illegal sugar importing. Several dozen individuals have been convicted under the U.S. Customs Service's "Operation Bittersweet" of illegally importing sugar for sale at the artificially high domestic price. Sentences range from 200 hours community service to two years in jail and a $250,000 fine. Operation Bittersweet brought in $16 million in fines, a minuscule amount compared to the cost the quotas themselves impose on U.S. consumers.

The total cost to U.S. consumers of the sugar policy package has been estimated at $1.4 billion per year. In addition, by making sugar-using firms such as candy producers less competitive, high sugar prices destroyed an estimated 9,000 jobs in food manufacturing during the 1980s. Besides the direct cost of the price-support and quota policies, the distortions in the sugar market introduced a growing web of restrictions on other markets as well. Import restrictions were extended to sugar/sweetener blends in 1983 and 1984. The huge price differential between domestic and world markets makes it profitable to import goods that contain sugar but are not subject to the quota, extract the sugar, and sell it at the artificially high domestic price. Because of fears of such activity, sugar growers pressured President Ronald Reagan, who issued an emergency proclamation on January 28, 1985, that placed quotas on such products as lemon curd, kosher pizzas, chocolate sprinkles, mussel salad, and chocolate-covered ants![42]

---

[42]Trish Hall, "Why Israeli Pizzas and Korean Noodles Find Door Slammed," *The Wall Street Journal*, April 23, 1985, A1.

Trading partners, including the EU and Australia, have filed complaints with the GATT over U.S. sugar policy and won. The GATT declared the U.S. policy counter to international trade rules. The United States responded in late 1990 by replacing the old system with a barely modified combination of quotas and tariffs.

How can a program persist that imposes such high costs on so many U.S. consumers? Lobbyists from the sugar industry contributed approximately $3 million to members of Congress between 1984 and 1989. The millions of sugar consumers, each with a relatively small stake in U.S. sugar policy, find it difficult to organize and compete with such a lobby.[43] A new controversy, however, may help end the sugar industry's protection. The industry is one of the largest polluters of the Florida Everglades, the most endangered U.S. national park. Fertilizer from cane fields flows into the glades, encourages growth of plants such as cat-tails that choke out native plants, and kills fish and birds.[44] Recent proposals call for taxes on sugar firms to help pay for cleanup. The proposed taxes, however, are tiny when compared to the enormous benefits the industry receives from price supports and import quotas. The removal of the protectionist policies would go a long way toward slowing the Everglades' environmental decay.

Case Two
Peanuts, Rice, and the CAP on Dollar Bananas

We have seen that most developed countries maintain price-support systems that keep farmers' incomes above their market-determined level. The United States, Japan, and the European Union all fit this classic pattern. In each case, the artificial price systems require import restrictions; otherwise, imports would flood in to take advantage of the high prices.

As an example, the United States has since 1953 restricted annual peanut imports to 1.7 million pounds, about two-thirds of which come from Argentina. Annual U.S. peanut consumption comes to 3.3 billion pounds, so legal imports account for less than 1 percent of consumption. In 1992, the peanut restrictions resulted in a domestic price of $700 per ton for nuts that sold in world markets for $300 per ton. U.S. policies toward peanuts restrict domestic production as well as imports. Approximately 44,000 growers in the United States own licenses to sell peanuts domestically. Families pass the licenses down from generation to generation as a valuable asset—valuable because they convey the right to sell peanuts at prices far exceeding the world price.

In 1990 a drought in Georgia, where most domestic peanuts grow, cut supply and doubled prices. Peanut-butter and candy producers protested as the price of their major input rose. Finally, nine months after the drought, an emergency government proclamation allowed increased imports above the quota for three weeks to

---

[43]Section 9.2 examines reasons why producer interests often dominate consumer interests in the formation of international trade policy.

[44]Chapters Eight and Eleven, in discussions of the relationship between international trade and the environment, note that protection often causes overuse of fertilizers and thereby damages the environment.

moderate the price increase; 18 million pounds, over ten times the annual quota, flowed into the United States. At the end of the three weeks, the import door closed again, leaving U.S. consumers paying prices far above world levels for peanuts.

The Uruguay Round agreement implies long-run changes for the U.S. peanut market. First, United States must convert the quotas into their tariff-rate equivalents (155 percent for shelled nuts and 193 percent for in-shell nuts). Then, over the next six years, the tariff must be reduced by at least 15 percent.

Halfway around the world, Japanese consumers pay approximately eight times the world price for rice. Rice farmers hold a special place in the traditional culture of Japan, and imports have been forbidden since 1965. The government has argued that Japan's national security depends on self-sufficiency in rice. In March 1991, rice farmers even tried to have Americans at a trade show arrested because their display included a ten-pound bag of U.S. rice! Approximately 3 million rice farmers remain in Japan, many of them elderly. The younger generation increasingly has left farming or maintained it only as a second, part-time occupation. Fewer than 500,000 farmers grow rice full time. Along with forbidding all imports, the Japanese government until recently controlled the domestic rice market and forced consumers to buy even inferior varieties. The price differentials resulting from Japan's rice policies are so large that is profitable for Japanese to import frozen sushi from California to circumvent the rice prohibition; sushi qualifies as "processed seafood" rather than rice as long as fish constitutes at least 20 percent of the product's weight.[45]

Political pressure (gaiatsu) from the United States and other potential rice exporters such as Australia and Thailand, combined with Japanese consumers' desires for lower prices (naiatsu), have had an effect. The Japanese government no longer fixes the price of domestic rice, and farmers growing inferior varieties no longer have their sales guaranteed. A domestic crop failure in 1993 forced Japan to allow emergency imports to moderate price increases.

The Uruguay Round brought a modest breakthrough in Japanese rice policy. Under the agreement's "minimum access" requirements for import markets, Japan will allow annual rice imports equal to 4 percent of domestic consumption, rising to 8 percent by the year 2000. At that time, the rice quotas must be converted to tariffs. The U.S. rice market has its version of government intervention as well. The U.S. government promises to cover any gap between the world price that growers receive for their crop and a target, or support price, set by policy makers.

The most complex and controversial agricultural trade policies in the world comprise the European Union's Common Agricultural Policy, or CAP. In 1991, the EC—European Community, the predecessor to the EU—paid $49 billion in direct subsidies to farmers, and EC consumers paid $85 billion more in the form of higher food prices. Half the total EU budget goes to agriculture. Although 30 percent of European farmers have other jobs, the agriculture issue evokes strong political pressure. EU refusal to lower its farm subsidies caused a breakdown in GATT talks in December 1990 and again in 1992. Not until December 1993, seven years after the launching of the Uruguay Round, did the United States and the European Union reach an accord on agricultural trade

---

[45]"Sushi Chain Owner Fights for Imports," *Daily Hampshire Gazette,* September 18, 1992; and Toru Takanarita, "Rice Market Debate Heats Up," *Asahi Evening News,* October 15, 1992.

reform. Still, the agreement allows governments to continue direct payments to farmers. It does, however, require cuts in agricultural export subsidies and mandate eventual conversion of all agricultural quotas to tariffs, which are subject to a schedule of cuts.

Europe's CAP causes internal as well as external disputes. Prior to the 1992 completion of Europe's internal market, Britain, France and Spain imported small, expensive bananas from a group of African, Caribbean, and Pacific (ACP) exporters (mostly former colonies) with a special trade agreement with the European Union. Other EU members bought larger, cheaper "dollar bananas" grown in Central America. As a result, banana prices varied widely within the EU, from $125 per ton in Portugal to $700 per ton in Spain. Dollar bananas paid a 20 percent tariff except in Germany, the biggest per capita banana-consuming country in the world, which imposed no tariff.

The 1992 program required free movement of bananas within the EU member countries, a plan that would destroy the market for expensive non-dollar bananas. The EU responded by replacing member countries' individual trade restrictions on bananas with an EU-wide policy. Two million tons of dollar bananas could enter the EU with a tariff of 20 percent; any imports beyond that faced a 170 percent tariff. When dollar-banana producers Costa Rica, Colombia, Nicaragua, and Venezuela complained to the GATT, the EU offered them the Framework Agreement, which promised to raise the EU quota against those countries' banana exports in exchange for the countries dropping their complaint. Germany took a case to the European Court of Justice, insisting on its right to free trade in bananas, but lost. The fight holds particular significance to East Germans, for whom access to bananas (unavailable during the Communist years) became a symbol of new freedom. Since the fall of the Berlin Wall, residents of former East Germany have consumed approximately 60 pounds of bananas per capita annually, almost three times the rate of U.S. consumption, despite having prices rise by 50 percent because of the EU's import restrictions on dollar bananas.

The CAP faces pressure for reform beyond that exerted by angry trading partners, food consumers, and Uruguay Round negotiators. Eastern European countries, several with a comparative advantage in agricultural products, are eager to join the European Union. Experts have estimated that providing CAP benefits to farmers in those countries would cost the EU an additional $15 billion to $45 billion annually.

Case Three
The Making of U.S. Trade Policy in the Footwear Industry[46]

Section 201 of the Trade Act of 1974 permits the United States temporarily to "escape" its trade-liberalization obligations under the GATT when increased imports

---

[46]The passage quoted comes from Official Transcript Proceedings before the U.S. International Trade Commission, Meeting of the Commission, June 12, 1985, Washington, D.C. Additional information in the case comes from James Bovard, *The Fair Trade Fraud.*

of a particular product substantially cause serious injury or threat of serious injury to a domestic industry.[47] Section 201 often is called the "escape clause" or a "safeguard provision." If a domestic industry brings a 201 case, the U.S. International Trade Commission investigates whether such a situation in fact exists. The Commission submits its findings to the president, who may impose tariffs, quotas, VERs, adjustment assistance, or other measures for up to five years to provide the domestic industry with relief from its injury. Section 201 cases have become rare recently, because domestic industries find protection easier to obtain under other trade laws, especially dumping and subsidy rules and voluntary export restraints. Since 1979, the United States has invoked the GATT escape clause only four times, and the European Union has invoked it fewer than 20 times.

The following reproduces an excerpt from the Commission's hearing on a famous 1985 case brought under Section 201 by the U.S. footwear industry.

I.T.C. Chairwoman Paula Stern: We turn now to investigation TA-201-55 regarding non-rubber footwear. Staff has assembled. Are there any questions? Vice Chairman Liebeler has a question. Please proceed.

I.T.C. Vice Chairman Liebeler: My questions are for the Office of Economics, Mr. Benedick. Do foreign countries have a comparative advantage in producing footwear?

Mr. Benedick (of the I.T.C. Office of Economics): Yes, foreign producers generally have a comparative advantage vis-à-vis the domestic producers in producing footwear. Footwear production generally involves labor intensive processes which favor the low wage countries such as Taiwan, Korea, and Brazil, which are the three largest foreign suppliers by volume. For instance, the hourly rate for foreign footwear workers in these countries ranges from about one-twelfth to one-fourth of the rate for U.S. footwear workers.

Vice Chairman Liebeler: Is it likely that this comparative advantage will shift in favor of the domestic industries over the next several years?

Mr. Benedick: It is not very likely. There seems to be little evidence that supports this. The domestic industry's generally poor productivity performance over the last several years, which includes the period 1977 to 1981, roughly corresponding to the period of OMAs (Orderly Marketing Arrangements) for Taiwan and Korea, suggests that U.S. producers must significantly increase their modernization efforts to reduce the competitive advantage of the imported footwear.

Vice Chairman Liebeler: Have you calculated the benefits and costs of import relief using various assumptions about the responsiveness of supply and demand to changes in price?

Mr. Benedick: Yes. On the benefit side, we estimated benefits of import restrictions to U.S. producers, which included both increased domestic production and higher domestic prices. We also estimated the terms of trade benefits resulting from import restrictions. These latter benefits result from an appreciation of the U.S. dollar as a result of the import restrictions. On the cost side, we estimated cost to consumers of the increase in average prices on total footwear purchases under the import restrictions and the consumer costs associated with the drop in total consumption due to the higher prices.

Vice Chairman Liebeler: In your work, did you take into account any retaliation by our trading partners?

Mr. Benedick: No.

Vice Chairman Liebeler: What was the 1984 level of imports?

---

[47]Chapter Seven of the Jackson book cited in the chapter references contains a useful overview of escape-clause rules.

Mr. Benedick: In 1984, imports of nonrubber footwear were approximately 726 million pairs.

Vice Chairman Liebeler: If a 600-million-pair quota were imposed, what would the effect on price of domestic and foreign shoes be, and what would the market share of imports be?

Mr. Benedick: At your request, the Office of Economics estimated the effects of the 600 million pair quota. We estimate that prices of domestic footwear would increase by about 11 percent, and prices of imported footwear would increase by about 19 percent. The import share, however, would drop to about 59 percent of the market in the first year of the quota.

Vice Chairman Liebeler: What would aggregate cost to consumers be of that kind of quota?

Mr. Benedick: Total consumer cost would approach $1.3 billion in each year of such a quota.

Vice Chairman Liebeler: What would be the benefit to the domestic industry of this quota?

Mr. Benedick: Domestic footwear production would increase from about 299 million pairs for 1984 to about 367 million pairs, or by about 23 percent. Domestic sales would increase from about $3.8 billion to about $5.2 billion, an increase of about 37 percent.

Vice Chairman Liebeler: How many jobs would be saved?

Mr. Benedick: As a result of this quota, domestic employment would rise by about 26,000 workers over the 1984 level.

Vice Chairman Liebeler: What is the average paid to those workers?

Mr. Benedick: Based on questionnaire responses, each worker would earn approximately $11,900 per year in wages and another $2,100 in fringe benefits, for a total of about $14,000 per year.

Vice Chairman Liebeler: So what then would be the cost to consumers of each of these $14,000-a-year jobs?

Mr. Benedick: It would cost consumers approximately $49,800 annually for each of these jobs.

Vice Chairman Liebeler: Thank you very much, Mr. Benedick.

I.T.C. Commissioner Alfred Eckes: I have a question for the general counsel's representative. I heard an interesting phrase a few moments ago, "comparative advantage." I don't recall seeing that phrase in Section 201. Could you tell me whether it is there and whether it is defined?

Ms. Jacobs (of the I.T.C. General Counsel's Office): It is not.

On July 1, 1985, the commission found that increased footwear imports were a substantial cause of serious injury, or threat thereof, to the domestic industry. A majority of the commission recommended that the president impose a quota of 474 million pairs on nonrubber footwear valued over $2.50 per pair for a five-year period. *(How do you think Vice Chairman Liebeler voted? Commissioner Eckes? Why?)* On August 28, 1985, the president refused to impose a quota, ruling it was not in the national interest due to the burden on consumers and the fact that such protection would not promote industry adjustment to increased foreign competition. In place of the quota, the president ordered a program of retraining and relocation assistance for workers in the domestic nonrubber footwear industry. The footwear industry also is covered by tariffs, some as high as 67 percent. Unfortunately for low-income consumers, low-cost footwear carries substantially higher tariffs than high-cost footwear. For example, the tariff on shoes with outer soles of rubber or plastic is 48 percent if the shoes' value is less than $3 and 20 percent on shoes with a value of more than $12.

Case Four
The Steel Industry Has It All: Subsidies, Dumping, and VERs

The U.S. steel industry has enjoyed protection from foreign competition for many years, beginning with a three-year voluntary export restraint in 1969. Seven years later, the United States imposed import quotas on specialty steel. The next year U.S. steel firms filed dumping charges, resulting in a complicated protectionist scheme called the trigger-price mechanism, which amounted to minimum-price rules for foreign steel sold in the United States. In 1983, stainless steel became subject to quotas, and in 1984 more VERs and quotas were enacted. Specialty steel received further quota protection in 1987.

The industry's latest episodes involve subsidies, dumping, and VERs. U.S. firms claim that foreign governments subsidize competitors' exports. In early 1992, voluntary export restraints that had protected the U.S. industry expired. Under industry pressure, the United States tried to negotiate a multilateral steel agreement with trading partners to outlaw subsidies, but the talks failed. In response, U.S. steel firms filed 84 charges against 21 trading partners, including 48 dumping charges and 36 cases alleging foreign subsidies. The trading partners involved included Japan, South Korea, Germany, Brazil, France, Canada, and Finland. Ironically, five of the six U.S. firms filing the charges had Japanese partners in joint ventures, and some U.S. firms refused to participate in the charges because of their foreign partnerships. Canadian steel producers responded promptly with dumping charges of their own against U.S. firms. Canadian investigators found dumping margins of 5 to 125 percent on various U.S. steel products, but Canada did not impose antidumping duties after finding the Canadian steel industry suffered no injury.

Filing large numbers of trade complaints has two effects that support an industry's desires for protection. First, the sheer number of cases pressures the domestic government to seek an alternate solution to avoid getting bogged down in investigating the cases.[48] Second, fear of the cases, especially given the bad reputation of U.S. procedures in dumping and subsidy cases, pressures foreign firms and governments to seek a negotiated settlement by "voluntarily" restricting their exports. Similar episodes of mass case filings in 1977 and 1982 led to negotiation of the trigger-price mechanism and a VER, after U.S. steel firms made clear they would drop all pending cases once a system of protection was negotiated.

Government investigations into the 1992 steel cases produced mixed findings. The Department of Commerce found dumping margins of up to 109 percent and subsidies of up to 73 percent; but the International Trade Commission found a lack of injury to the domestic industry in 42 of 74 cases.

---

[48]Dumping and subsidy cases under U.S. trade law are very complex and typically last a year or more; on the details, see Cletus C. Coughlin, "U.S. Trade-Remedy Laws," cited in the chapter references, as well as the Bovard, Finger, and Boltuck and Litan books, and the Congressional Budget Office volume.

The major result of 30 years of steel-industry protection has been higher prices and periodic shortages for many of the more than 500 steel products covered. Higher prices for steel make all U.S. steel-using industries (for example, automobiles) *less* competitive in world markets. Estimates place the cost of steel protection to the U.S. economy at over $6 billion per year.

Not all the U.S. steel industry has trouble competing and seeks protection. Steel minimills are thriving, and large integrated producers are beginning to imitate the minimills' new technologies. Minimills use electric furnaces rather than coke ovens and blast furnaces, require approximately one-fifth as much labor as integrated mills, produce their products very quickly, and generate much less air and water pollution than integrated mills. Even in Japan, home of the world's largest steel mill (Nippon Steel's Kimutsu Works), minimills with their 30 percent cost advantage are gaining at the expense of big integrated producers.

Meanwhile, international talks continue in an effort to reach a multilateral steel agreement. U.S. government priorities for such an agreement include constraining government subsidies to the industry, eliminating nontariff barriers to trade (the Uruguay Round agreement included a timetable for eliminating tariffs), and instituting a dispute-settlement mechanism for trade-related steel disputes. Given the record of trade policy in the world's steel industry, many economists wonder whether an agreement would constitute anything but an informal cartel among international steel producers.

 ## Case Five
Hard Feelings over Soft Lumber

Canada exports to the United States 12 billion board feet of lumber, valued at $3.1 billion per year, comprising 26 percent of the U.S. softwood lumber market. In 1986, the United States ruled that Canada subsidized exports of lumber products because Canadian provinces charged artificially low stumpage (or cutting) fees to firms cutting timber on provincially owned land. Canadian lumber firms able to cut logs with low stumpage fees could, in turn, sell their lumber at lower prices. With U.S. consent, Canada responded to the subsidy ruling by imposing a 15 percent export tax on lumber exports to the United States, in place of a possible U.S. countervailing duty.

Late in 1991, Canada announced it would end the export tax because previously low stumpage fees had increased to a level sufficient to rule out existence of a subsidy. Under pressure from the lumber industry, the U.S. administration itself initiated a subsidy/countervailing duty case instead of waiting for the lumber industry to file a formal complaint; this unusual procedure angered Canadians. The U.S. Department of Commerce's findings ruled Canadian stumpage fees still amounted to a subsidy, and the U.S. International Trade Commission ruled the subsidy injured the U.S. industry, resulting in countervailing duties of 6.51 percent. Canada appealed the decision through a binational panel review, part of the dispute-settlement procedure instituted by the Canada–U.S. Free-Trade Agreement. U.S. firms claimed

Canada's ban on Canadian log exports contributed to the lumber subsidy by keeping Canadian log prices low, an advantage for Canadian lumber-product companies that use logs as an input. Canadians expressed particular indignation over this argument, quickly pointing out that the United States similarly bans the export of U.S. logs cut from federal land.

The binational review panels established under the Canada–U.S. Free-Trade Agreement ruled that both the U.S. Department of Commerce's calculation of the subsidy and the U.S. ITC's finding of injury to the U.S. industry failed to correspond to the facts of the case and should be withdrawn. The United States appealed to a binational Extraordinary Challenge Committee (the "court of last resort" under the trade agreement's dispute-settlement procedure), which refused to hear the appeal. The finding required the United States to refund to Canada nearly $500 million collected in tariffs under the overturned subsidy decision.

Case Six

L'affaire du Sang Contaminé (The Case of the Contaminated Blood)[49]

Occasionally, a country's scheme of protection imposes costs far beyond the obvious loss of consumer surplus. One such episode occurred in the mid-1980s when France's efforts to use protectionist policies to dominate the European market for blood products led to widespread sale of blood and blood products contaminated with the human immunodeficiency virus, which causes AIDS.

The French state-run blood monopoly, the Centre National de Transfusion Sanguine, refused to import tested virus-free products (offered at a price 30 percent *below* the price of untested French products), as well as foreign technology to heat plasma and thereby kill any virus present. French doctors and bureaucrats insisted AIDS was "the American disease." In the United States, dispensers of blood products began heating in mid-1983, as soon as they realized blood's role in transmission of the virus, and the U.S. medical community notified French doctors and researchers of the importance of heating. Despite the warnings, widespread heating of blood products in France was delayed until French researchers could develop their own heating equipment and then delayed further because the state-owned Centre has just completed a huge factory that could produce only unheated blood products. In the meantime, several hundred French hemophiliacs died of AIDS, and over 70 percent of Paris's hemophiliac community became infected with HIV. Individual doctors and patients who demanded heated blood products could not obtain them because the Centre maintained a monopoly over any imported blood plasma and plasma products.

---

[49]Jane Kramer, "Bad Blood," *The New Yorker*, October 11, 1993, 74–95

During the same period, France also refused to import from the United States the available HIV test for blood donors. French doctors and bureaucrats insisted on "scientific self-sufficiency." France's prestigious Pasteur Institute was working on its own test, which did not become available until five months after the U.S. test. As soon as the French test was approved, the government ordered mandatory testing of all blood donors. Estimates suggest that the five-month delay in testing caused between 4,000 and 5,000 French residents to become infected with HIV. As one writer put it, "It added up to a choice between buying foreign tests and saving lives, or saving an annual market estimated at 91 million francs ($11 million) for a French company."[50]

In the end, four doctors were tried in *l'affaire du sang contaminé*, and several received prison sentences. Government bureaucrats and policy makers used their immunity to avoid trial. The Centre National de Transfusion Sanguine changed its name but continues in business. Despite the tremendous cost of its earlier protectionism, France has since passed even stricter laws to curb commercial imports of blood plasma.

Summary

In this chapter, we examined the effects of import quotas, voluntary export restraints, export subsidies and countervailing duties, dumping, voluntary import expansions, domestic-content rules and rules of origin, government procurement policies, and technical standards. For a variety of reasons, these restrictions have been much more difficult to deal with in the context of international negotiations than the tariffs discussed in Chapter Six. Economists have dubbed the failure to eliminate these barriers to trade and increased reliance on nontariff forms of trade restriction the *new protectionism*, which restricts trade in goods ranging from automobiles to legal services to blood plasma to chocolate-covered ants.

Looking Ahead

Despite arguments that unrestricted trade maximizes welfare for the world as a whole, pursuit of free trade as a policy clearly is the exception rather than the rule. The effect of trade on the distribution of income and the adjustment costs incurred when resources must move from a comparative-disadvantage industry to one of comparative advantage provide two explanations for the existence of trade restrictions. In Chapter Eight, we examine in more detail arguments presented in favor of tariffs, quotas, and other barriers to trade.

Key Terms

nontariff barrier (NTB)	dumping margin
new protectionism	predatory dumping
quota	antidumping duty
quota rents	voluntary import expansion (VIE)

---

[50]Mark Hunter, "Blood Money," *Discover*, August 1993, 76.

voluntary export restraint (VER)
equivalence of tariffs and quotas
global quota
country-specific (country-of-origin)
   quota
transshipment
export subsidy
countervailing duty (CVD)
dumping
sporadic dumping
persistent dumping
price discrimination

domestic-content requirements
outsourcing
rules of origin
government procurement policies
buy-domestic requirements
technical barriers to trade
coverage ratio
implicit tariff
producer-subsidy equivalent (PSE)
consumer-subsidy equivalent (CSE)
Section 201

Problems and Questions for Review

1. Imports of peanuts into the United States are subject to a quota, currently set at about 1.7 million pounds per year.
   (a) Illustrate the free-trade equilibrium in the market for peanuts. Then show the quota's effects on domestic consumption, domestic production, imports, and price. Label carefully.
   (b) What are the quota's welfare effects, including both the distributional effects and the overall (net) effect on the United States? Relate the effects to your diagram in part (a).
   (c) In 1990, a severe drought hit Georgia, where most U.S. peanuts are grown. Illustrate the effects of the drought, assuming policy makers do not change the quota. What happens to domestic production, domestic consumption, imports, and price as a result of the drought?
   (d) Assume the United States is a small country in the peanut market. Now suppose that the peanut market is subject to an import tariff *instead* of the quota. *The tariff is set at a level that results in the same pre-drought level of production, consumption, and price as under the quota in part (a).* Illustrate the effects of the tariff *before* the drought.
   (e) Compare the effects of the drought under the tariff with those under the quota. What are the similarities and differences?

2. This question asks you to address several issues related to dumping, using as an example U.S. accusations that Japanese firms dumped laptop-computer screens in the United States in 1991.
   (a) A lawyer for Compaq, a U.S. computer manufacturer, was quoted in *The Wall Street Journal* (February 11, 1991), asserting, "There are no U.S. suppliers for these products [the screens for laptop computers], and therefore there can be no dumping." Is the lawyer correct or incorrect, and why?
   (b) According to *The Wall Street Journal,* the Department of Commerce has "decided that display prices set by Japanese companies in their home market may be artificially low. Rather than comparing U.S. prices with Japanese prices, Commerce is now coming up with its own 'fair' price based on a formula

accounting for the costs of materials, research, and return on investment." Do you think this procedure is more or less likely to result in imposition of antidumping duties than one in which prices charged for Japanese displays in the United States are compared with actual prices for the same displays in Japan? Why? As an economist, which procedure would you prefer to see used? Why?

3. Country A is a small country with a comparative advantage in good X. The government of country A provides X producers with a subsidy of $10 for each unit of X exported. The governments of all other X-exporting countries also subsidize exports of X by $10 per unit. Evaluate the following statement: "Producers of good X in country A don't really gain from the subsidy. Nevertheless, they are unwilling to have their government stop the subsidy."

4. Do you agree or disagree with the argument in the following letter to the editor from *The Wall Street Journal* (February 14, 1985)? Support your answer with a brief economic analysis. You may take the numbers reported in the letter as factual for purposes of your argument.

   [A recent letter to the editor] claims that the [United Auto Workers'] request for continued auto restraints on the part of Japanese auto manufacturers is protectionist and anti-competitive. At present, the UAW wants to limit imports of Japanese autos to 17 percent of the U.S. market. This seems fair enough after one examines auto sales in Japan during 1984. According to *The Japan Times,* 5,471,982 cars were sold in Japan last year, of which only 41,982 were foreign. American auto sales totaled 2,382—or less than one-half of 1 percent! These figures show that a much higher degree of protectionism exists in Japan than in the U.S., a fact that should be remembered by both American policy makers and Japanese who accuse the U.S. of being anti-competitive and protectionist.

5. What is the major weakness of the coverage ratio as an empirical measure of nontariff trade barriers? Explain the concept of a producer-subsidy equivalent.

6. This question continues problem 7 from Chapter Six. The country of Usia has a prohibitive export tax on logs. Both Usia and Themia export lumber made from logs. Usia files a complaint against Themia alleging that the government of Themia subsidizes lumber exports and that Themia's subsidized exports steal markets from Usia's lumber producers. The government of Themia is angered by Usia's accusation and counter-charges that Usia's prohibitive export tax on *logs* amounts to an export subsidy for Usia's *lumber* producers. Briefly evaluate Themia's charge.

References and Selected Readings

Boltuck, Richard, and Robert E. Litan, eds. *Down in the Dumps*. Washington, D.C.: The Brookings Institution, 1991.
Collection of accessible papers on the economics, law, and politics of U.S. unfair trade laws.

Bovard, James. *The Fair Trade Fraud*. New York: St. Martin's Press, 1991.
An irreverent look at U.S. trade policy including numerous NTB examples; for all students.

Congressional Budget Office. *How the GATT Affects U.S. Antidumping and Countervailing Duty Policies*. Washington, D.C.: Congressional Budget Office, 1994.
Excellent, up-to-date survey of U.S. law and policy related to dumping and export subsidies.

Coughlin, Cletus C. "U.S. Trade-Remedy Laws: Do They Facilitate or Hinder Free Trade?" Federal Reserve Bank of St. Louis *Review* (1991): 3–18.
Accessible treatment of trade-remedy laws, including those covering dumping and subsidies.

Coughlin, Cletus C., and Geoffrey E. Wood. "An Introduction to Non-tariff Barriers to Trade." Federal Reserve Bank of St. Louis *Review* 71 (January–February 1989): 32–46.
Accessible introduction to the use and effects of nontariff barriers.

Deardorff, Alan V., and Robert M. Stern, eds. *Analytical and Negotiating Issues in the Global Trading System.* Ann Arbor, Mich.: University of Michigan Press, 1994.
Collection of papers on many NTBs; for intermediate and advanced students.

de Melo, Jaime, and David Tarr. *A General Equilibrium Analysis of U.S. Trade Policy.* Cambridge, Mass.: MIT Press, 1992.
Estimates the costs of U.S. protection; for intermediate and advanced students.

Feenstra, Robert C. "Estimating the Effects of Trade Policy." In *Handbook of International Economics,* Vol. 3, edited by G. M. Grossman and Kenneth Rogoff, 1553–1596. Amsterdam: North-Holland, 1995.
Advanced, up-to-date survey of the empirical literature on the economic effects of various trade policies.

Fieleke, Norman S., "The Soaring Trade in 'Nontradables'." Federal Reserve Bank of Boston *New England Economic Review* (1995): 25–36.
Overview of one of the fastest growing segments of international trade; for all students.

Finger, J. Michael, ed. *Antidumping.* Ann Arbor, Mich.: University of Michigan Press, 1993.
Collection of papers on dumping and antidumping policies; level of papers varies.

Hufbauer, Gary C., Diane T. Berliner, and Kimberly Ann Elliott. *Trade Protection in the United States: 31 Case Studies.* Washington, D.C.: Institute for International Economics, 1986.
Excellent source of references and data on trade restrictions in various U.S. industries.

Hufbauer, Gary C., and Kimberly A. Elliott. *Measuring the Costs of Protection in the United States.* Washington, D.C.: Institute for International Economics, 1994.
Estimates the costs of protection to the U.S. economy; for all students.

Hufbauer, Gary C., and Joanna Shelton Erb. *Subsidies in International Trade.* Washington, D.C.: Institute for International Economics, 1984.
Detailed study of subsidies in trade; for all students.

Hufbauer, Gary Clyde, and Jeffrey J. Schott. *NAFTA: An Assessment.* Washington, D.C.: Institute for International Economics, 1993.
Comprehensive and readable survey of the North American Free-Trade Agreement; for all students.

Irwin, Douglas A. *Managed Trade: The Case Against Import Targets.* Washington D.C.: American Enterprise Institute, 1994.
Accessible analysis of the protectionist effects of voluntary import expansions.

Jackson, John H. *The World Trading System: Law and Policy of International Economic Relations.* Cambridge, Mass.: MIT Press, 1989.
Excellent and readable treatment of legal aspects of trade, including subsidies and dumping.

Jones, Kent A. *Export Restraint and the New Protectionism.* Ann Arbor, Mich.: University of Michigan Press, 1994.
Analysis of negotiated export restraint agreements; intermediate.

Lawrence, Robert Z. "Japan's Different Trade Regime." *Journal of Economic Perspectives* 7 (Summer 1993): 3–20.
How the structure of Japan's economy affects its trade policy; for all students.

Leidy, Michael. "Antidumping: Unfair Trade or Unfair Remedy?" *Finance and Development* 32 (March 1995): 27–29.
Introductory overview of the protectionist effects of antidumping policies.

Rodrik, Dani. "Political Economy of Trade Policy." In *Handbook of International Economics,* Vol. 3, edited by G. M. Grossman and Kenneth Rogoff., 1457–1494. Amsterdam: North-Holland, 1995. *Advanced, up-to-date survey of the literature on distributional aspects of trade policy and their implications for the policy process.*

Saxonhouse, Gary R. "What Does Japanese Trade Structure Tell Us About Japanese Trade Policy?" *Journal of Economic Perspectives* 7 (Summer 1993): 21–43. *Relationship between Japanese trade policy and trade flows; for all students.*

Sazanami, Yoko, Shujiro Urata, and Kiroki Kawai. *Measuring the Costs of Protection in Japan.* Washington, D.C.: Institute for International Economics, 1995. *Attempt to quantify the cost to Japanese consumers and the Japanese economy as a whole of the structure of protection. Intermediate.*

Schott, Jeffrey J. *The Uruguay Round: An Assessment.* Washington, D.C.: Institute for International Economics, 1994. *Excellent, accessible survey of the issues and results of the Uruguay Round.*

Skeath, Susan E. "Input Tariffs as a Way to Deal with Dumping." Federal Reserve Bank of Boston *New England Economic Review* (November–December 1993):45–55. *Advanced analysis of antidumping duties, focusing on the computer-screen case (see Case One in Chapter Six).*

Staiger, Robert. "International Rules and Institutions for Cooperative Trade Policy." In *Handbook of International Economics,* Vol. 3, edited by G. M. Grossman and Kenneth Rogoff, 1495–1552. Amsterdam: North-Holland, 1995. *Advanced, up-to-date survey of the literature on how rules and institutions at the international level affect national trade policies.*

Staiger, Robert W., and Frank A. Wolak. "Measuring Industry-Specific Protection: Antidumping in the United States." *Brookings Papers on Economic Activity: Microeconomics* (1994): 51–118. *Empirical investigation of the purposes and effects of dumping cases; intermediate.*

Sykes, Alan O. *Product Standards for Internationally Integrated Goods Markets.* Washington, D.C.: The Brookings Institution, 1995. *Excellent treatment of the role for and protectionist potential for product standards.*

Trefler, Daniel. "Trade Liberalization and the Theory of Endogenous Protection." *Journal of Political Economy* 101 (February 1993): 138–160. *Empirical study of the determinants and effects of U.S. import restrictions; advanced.*

Vousden, Neil. *The Economics of Trade Protection.* Cambridge: Cambridge University Press, 1990. *Theoretical analysis of many types of protection; for intermediate to advanced students.*

Westhoff, Frank H., Beth V. Yarbrough, and Robert M. Yarbrough. "Harassment versus Lobbying for Trade Protection." *International Trade Journal* 9 (Summer 1995): 203–224. *Examines use of protection to harass foreign producers; intermediate.*

CHAPTER EIGHT

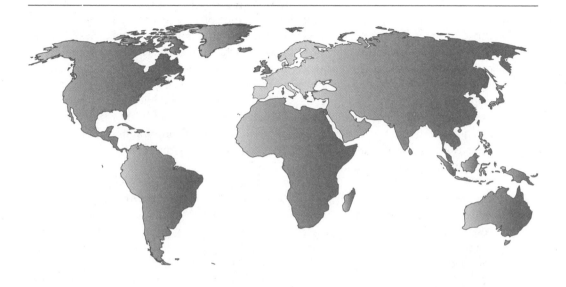

Arguments for Restricting Trade

8.1 Introduction

Chapters Six and Seven showed how international trade restrictions reduce world welfare by distorting the relationship between a good's price and its opportunity cost, causing inefficient production and consumption decisions. Efficiency requires that each good be produced at the level at which the value consumers place on the good (price) just equals the opportunity cost of producing it (marginal cost).

In this chapter, we probe the results of Chapters Six and Seven for weaknesses. Are there circumstances in which unrestricted trade is not efficient or does not maximize world welfare? Can protection ever increase welfare, not just for some groups at the expense of others, but for the country or the world as a whole? Are there major aspects of the world economy that we ignored in the earlier chapters? In particular, might goals other than efficiency justify the use of protection?

8.2 Categories of Arguments for Trade Restrictions

In policy debates over international trade, many arguments for protection emerge. It is useful to categorize the arguments into three major groups.

Arguments that question the assumptions we used to develop our model of international trade comprise the first group. Assumptions frequently challenged include those of perfect competition, no economies of scale, and no externalities in either production or consumption. The situation in which all these assumptions are met is called **optimal market conditions.**[1] The presence of a violation of one of the assumptions—for example, a monopolized industry or an externality—is referred to as a **domestic distortion.** In Chapters Two through Seven, we demonstrated that under optimal market conditions, unrestricted trade produces an efficient result and trade restrictions reduce world welfare. Once we relax the assumption of optimal market conditions, the efficiency of unrestricted trade may or may not continue to hold. This chapter examines these issues.

The second category of arguments for trade restrictions focuses on the distributional effects of trade. International trade affects the distribution of income both within each country and among countries. Both effects generate constituencies for restricting trade. Proponents of arguments in this category often couch them in somewhat deceptive terms. An explicit argument to tax domestic consumers and give the proceeds to producers in a certain industry would have scant political appeal; but an argument phrased in nationalistic terms that emphasizes preventing "them" (foreign producers) from taking something from "us" (a domestic industry) tends to meet with more success. Therefore, domestic groups seeking protection do not claim to seek to improve their own welfare at the expense of other domestic groups; instead, groups seek to identify their own interests with those of the country as a whole to make their calls for protection seem more patriotic and less self-interested.

The third group of justifications for protection includes so-called *noneconomic arguments.* The term does not imply that the arguments have nothing to do with economics or that economic theory has nothing to say about their relative merits. This group of arguments does, however, emphasize elements beyond the narrow scope of economics by pointing out that a society typically values things such as national security and equity along with economic efficiency. The primary role for an economist in evaluating these justifications for protection is to provide information about the tradeoff between economic efficiency and other societal goals, so an informed policy decision can be made. If a society desires (as all do) to pursue goals in addition to economic efficiency, what kinds of policies will best achieve those goals with a minimum cost in terms of lost efficiency?

8.3 The Infant-Industry Argument

The **infant-industry argument** makes a case for short-term protection of a new industry temporarily unable to compete with experienced rivals in other countries. Advocates of infant-industry protection admit that trade restrictions cause welfare losses along the lines discussed in Chapters Six and Seven. But, they argue, those

---

[1]Among other assumptions included under "optimal market conditions" are absence of factor market distortions such as minimum wages.

Figure 8.1 □ **The Infant-Industry Argument for Protection**

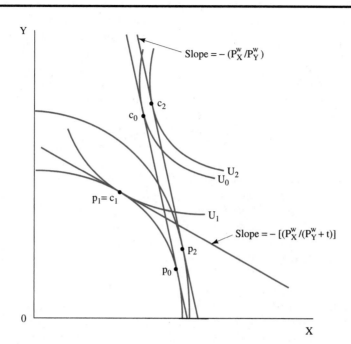

A prohibitive tariff on imports of good Y imposes a welfare loss in the short run due to inefficiently high domestic production of Y (p_1 rather than p_0) and inefficiently low domestic consumption (c_1 versus c_0). If the infant industry matures and becomes capable of competing in world markets without protection, the country's production possibilities frontier will expand beyond the frontier that would have existed without the temporary protection afforded the Y industry. The economy then will be able to produce at p_2 and consume at c_2, a previously unattainable outcome.

short-term losses will be more than offset when the industry matures and can compete in world markets. Figure 8.1 illustrates the short- and long-run effects of infant-industry protection for the Y industry, where we assume for simplicity that protection takes the form of a prohibitive import tariff imposed by a small country.

Without protection, domestic production initially occurs at p_0 and consumption at c_0. (*Why?*) A prohibitive import tariff on good Y shifts production and consumption to p_1 and c_1, reducing welfare from U_0 to U_1.[2] If temporary protection allows the Y industry to perfect its production techniques, train its work force, and develop management skills, the improved productivity will shift the production possibilities frontier outward.[3] At this

---

[2]A prohibitive tariff shifts the country back to its autarky equilibrium. A lower tariff would place the country at some point between the free-trade and prohibitive-tariff outcomes.

[3]This process often is called *learning by doing* (see section 5.6.2).

point, policy makers remove the protection (theoretically), and the industry should be capable of competing with its rivals in other countries. Because the country is assumed to be small, development of the new industry does not affect world prices. The new long-run equilibrium involves production at point p_2 and consumption at c_2. Welfare has increased (to utility level U_2) from U_0 before the protection of the infant Y industry.

Economists generally are rather skeptical of calls for protection of infant industries. The first and perhaps foremost reason is the difficulty in spotting good candidates for protection. Many firms and industries are born each year, and many do not survive. A policy of infant-industry protection requires policy makers to recognize *in advance* those industries that could, on maturing, compete successfully in world markets. A wrong decision could prove very costly, involving years of inefficiency with no reward.[4] The challenge of picking winners becomes even harder once we realize that patterns of comparative advantage change over time.

Suppose a certain industry is recognized widely as an excellent prospect. In this case, why would the industry need even temporary protection? If private investors expected the industry to succeed, they would willingly invest in it and suffer short-run losses in return for the promise of future profits. The infant-industry argument must assume government policy makers somehow are better able than private investors to spot "winners." Because private investors have a sizable economic incentive to search out good prospects, economists doubt policy makers' ability to do better. Even if government policy makers somehow became aware of a new industry likely to succeed but overlooked by private investors, an alternative to infant-industry protection would be for the government to provide investors with information about the industry to encourage them to take advantage of the opportunity.

The second problem with evaluating infant-industry protection is that early support of an industry that turns out successful provides insufficient evidence that the protection itself constituted a wise policy. For the protection to provide *net* benefits, the industry must be successful enough to more than offset the efficiency losses incurred during the protection period. Perhaps the industry would have succeeded without protection, implying that the costs incurred were wasted. Also, the resources spent in developing the infant industry could have been spent on another industry, one that might have been even more successful.

The third problem is based on the politics of the policy-making process. The infant-industry argument justifies only *temporary* protection. Historically, removal of protection has proven very difficult. Even if changing conditions allow an industry to become able to compete successfully without protection, maintaining that protection still permits the industry to gain at the expense of domestic consumers and foreign producers. This creates an incentive for producers in the industry to lobby strongly for continuing protection even after any true infant-industry justification fades.

---

[4] Even Japan, whose rapid growth and industrialization during the 1950s and 1960s is attributed by many to successful use of infant-industry policies, made a number of costly blunders along these lines. See Richard Beason and David Weinstein, "Growth, Economies of Scale, and Targeting in Japan (1955–90)," Harvard Institute of Economic Research Discussion Paper 1644.

Voluntary export restraints on imports of Japanese automobiles into the United States provide one recent example of the tendency of protection to linger. The United States instituted the restrictions for one year in May 1981, after U.S. auto makers suffered record losses. Yet, the restraints extended well into the 1990s, even though U.S. auto makers reported record profits (and record bonuses for their executives) in the interim. Although the automobile export restraints were not an explicit infant-industry policy, since the U.S. automobile industry hardly is an infant, the rationale behind them was similar. Domestic automobile manufacturers argued they needed temporary protection to allow them to modernize and change their product lines to smaller cars following the 1970s oil price increases, which had caused consumers to demand cars with better fuel economy. The U.S. steel industry has made similar pleas for temporary protection to finance modernization. These pleas have succeeded in increasing protected industries' profit positions, but they hardly have been temporary. The steel industry's protection has persisted in one form or another since 1968![5] These two instances are not unique; for more examples of the persistence of protectionism once instituted, see Table 7.2.

The final basis for economists' skepticism toward infant-industry protection is the availability of superior policies for dealing with the problem. Assume an industry exists that could develop successfully if it received short-run assistance (that is, ignore the problems of sorting potential winner industries from losers and whether future gains will exceed current welfare losses). Assume also that private investors are unwilling to invest in the industry despite its promise. The policy that will allow the industry to develop at minimal efficiency cost to the economy is a production subsidy. This represents the first example of what will emerge in this chapter as a general rule: The least-cost policy is the one that attacks the problem directly rather than indirectly. In the case of an infant industry, the goal is to encourage production in the industry to facilitate learning and the perfection of productive techniques. If increasing production is the goal, the direct policy is to temporarily subsidize production, not even temporarily to restrict trade.

Figure 8.2 illustrates the superiority of a direct policy, a production subsidy, over an indirect policy, an import tariff. Panel (a) repeats the effects of a prohibitive tariff on imports of good Y, and panel (b) shows the effects of a subsidy to Y producers. Both policies generate equal increases in domestic production. The tariff operates by artificially raising the price of imports from P_Y^0 to P_Y^1 (where $P_Y^1 = P_Y^0 + t$), which allows domestic producers to raise their price to P_Y^1 and encourages domestic production to expand from Y^0 to Y^1. By raising the price of good Y, the tariff also discourages consumption of Y, and consumption falls from Y^2 to Y^1. The sum of the areas of triangles c and e captures the total loss of welfare to the country from the *two* inefficiencies caused by the tariff.[6]

The production subsidy of s (= t) per unit in panel (b) of Figure 8.2 encourages domestic producers to produce a higher level of good Y at each price paid by consumers because firms receive the subsidy payment along with those prices. Domestic production rises from Y^0 to Y^1. The subsidy to producers does not affect the price

[5]See Case Four in Chapter Seven.

[6]Section 6.4 presents a more detailed treatment of the effects of an import tariff.

Figure 8.2 □ Comparison of an Import Tariff and a Production Subsidy in an Infant Industry

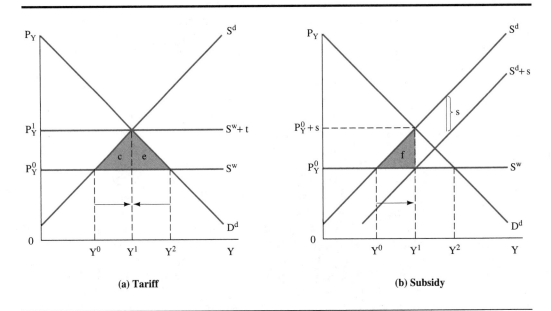

(a) Tariff   (b) Subsidy

The import tariff both increases domestic production of good Y from Y^0 to Y^1 (the desired goal) and decreases domestic consumption of Y from Y^2 to Y^1 (an additional source of inefficiency). The production subsidy increases domestic production while leaving consumption unaffected

consumers face (P_Y^0) and leaves consumption of good Y unchanged. The area of triangle f measures the net welfare loss due to the subsidy; for each unit of Y between Y^0 and Y^1, the opportunity cost of domestic production exceeds the cost of imports. Of course, domestic taxpayers must finance the subsidy, but the full amount of the subsidy, with the exception of area f, is transferred to domestic producers. Therefore, only area f represents a deadweight loss to society.

Because the two policies have identical impacts on domestic production of good Y, an import tariff and a production subsidy are equally effective in helping the infant industry develop. The production inefficiencies, represented by triangle c in the case of the tariff and by triangle f in the case of the subsidy, are identical. The tariff involves a second inefficiency, represented by triangle e, in the form of a distortion of the consumption decision caused by the change in P_Y. The production subsidy, by attacking the problem more directly, can encourage domestic production at a lower cost in lost economic efficiency.

Brazil's Informatics Law provides the most famous recent example of an infant-industry protection policy that backfired.[7] Since 1975, Brazil informally prohibited

---

[7]Thomas Kamm, "Brazil Set to Lift Electronics Import Ban," *The Wall Street Journal, August 8, 1991,* A9.

imports of electronics products, including microchips, fax machines, and especially personal computers. In 1984, the extremely restrictive Informatics Law replaced the informal prohibitions. As Brazil's secretary for science and technology put it, "It was enough for a Brazilian company to say that it was planning to develop the same thing eventually and imports were banned." The law was designed to build a domestic electronics industry by creating "market reserves," that is, reserving the domestic market for domestic firms by prohibiting imports and banning foreign companies wanting to build local electronics manufacturing facilities.[8] The law had unintended but predictable results: an uncompetitive and technologically outdated Brazilian electronics industry, and electronics products that cost two and a half times the products' world prices. Even Brazilian electronics firms—the supposed beneficiaries of the law—complained that it made reasonably priced, high-quality parts unavailable, thereby making it impossible for Brazilian firms to produce goods that could compete in world markets. Finally, growing opposition to the law produced change. New policies eliminated the market reserve (but replaced it with high tariffs) and allowed foreign firms to own up to 49 percent stakes in joint ventures with Brazilian partners.

8.4 Monopoly-Based Arguments

8.4.1 The Optimal Tariff: Monopoly in a World Market

One argument for protection based on monopoly power is the optimal tariff argument we saw in section 6.5.2. When a single country comprises a large enough share of the world market in a good to obtain some market power, that country may be able to gain at the expense of its trading partners by imposing a tariff.

Figure 8.3 presents the graphical analysis of the optimal tariff. The country is large enough that its imposition of a tariff on imports of good Y forces exporting countries to accept a lower price (P_Y^2 instead of P_Y^0). As a result, foreign producers pay a portion of the tariff revenue in lower prices for their product. If the revenue gained from foreign producers (area s in Figure 8.3) exceeds the deadweight efficiency losses caused by the tariff (the sum of triangles m and r), the tariff-imposing country enjoys a net welfare gain *at the expense of the exporting country*. The optimal tariff rate is the one that maximizes this net gain or (area s − area [m + r]).

Note that, unlike some arguments for protection discussed in this chapter, the optimal tariff argument takes a national perspective; that is, the imposing country gains but total world welfare suffers from the imposition of an optimal tariff. Use of an optimal tariff, like any other exploitation of monopoly power, is a beggar-thy-neighbor policy. Gains come only at the expense of others, and the gains to the monopolist are smaller than the losses imposed on others (in the case of the optimal tariff, domestic consumers and foreign producers). In addition, use of an optimal tariff invites retaliation by trading partners, which would further reduce the gains from trade.

---

[8]Case Six in Chapter Seven provides a dramatic example of the potential cost of such policies.

Figure 8.3 □ **A Tariff on Imports by a Large Country**

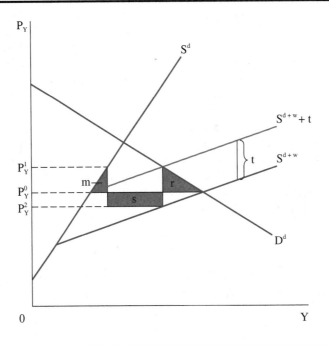

By exploiting its monopoly power, the country can gain the equivalent of area s in revenue from foreign producers. The areas of triangles m and r measure the deadweight welfare losses due to the tariff. The optimum tariff maximizes the net gain to the country from the tariff (area s − area [m + r]).

8.4.2 Protection and Monopolized Industries

Another monopoly-based argument for protection focuses not on the monopoly power of a *country* in a world market, as in the case of the optimal tariff, but on the monopoly power of *firms* in a domestic industry. Recall the mechanism by which trade expands world output under perfect competition. In autarky, the opportunity cost of producing a good differs across countries. Under perfect competition, the price of a good equals its opportunity cost; thus, the relative price of a good also varies across countries in autarky. Unrestricted trade equalizes the relative price of a good by allowing productive specialization and exchange. Under unrestricted trade, the relative prices of a good equalize across countries, as do the good's opportunity costs of production. Unrestricted trade satisfies the criteria for efficiency: Each good is produced at the lowest possible opportunity cost and to the point at which price equals marginal cost. The equality of relative prices and opportunity costs that follows from the assumption of perfect competition generates this efficiency result.

Figure 8.4 □ **Pricing and Output Decision by a Monopolist**

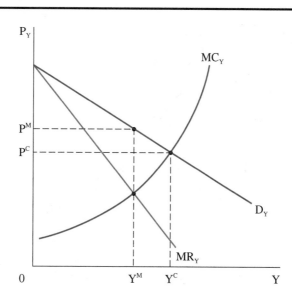

A monopolist maximizes profit by producing where marginal revenue (MR) equals marginal cost (MC). The monopolist's level of output (Y^M) is lower and price (P^M) higher than the perfectly competitive outcome (Y^C and P^C). Because marginal revenue is less than price, price exceeds marginal cost. Consumers value the marginal unit produced by the monopolist by more than the opportunity cost of producing it; thus, output is inefficiently low.

Price and Opportunity Cost for a Monopolist

When we relax the perfect-competition assumption and allow a firm to monopolize an industry, the price of the good the monopolist produces no longer will equal its marginal cost. A monopolist will produce the level of output at which marginal revenue equals marginal cost, as in Figure 8.4. Because price exceeds marginal revenue for a monopolist (see footnote 24 in Chapter Seven), marginal cost is less than price in a monopolized industry. The *m*onopolist produces a smaller level of output and charges a higher price (Y^M and P^M in Figure 8.4) than if the industry were organized *c*ompetitively (Y^C and P^C).

More important from the standpoint of international trade, monopoly power in output markets causes relative output prices to fail to reflect the true opportunity costs of production. If both the X and Y industries are perfectly competitive in country B, then $P_X^B = MC_X^B$ and $P_Y^B = MC_Y^B$, implying

$$P_X^B/P_Y^B = MC_X^B/MC_Y^B, \qquad [8.1]$$

or that relative prices accurately reflect opportunity costs.

Figure 8.5 □ **Production and Consumption in Autarky**

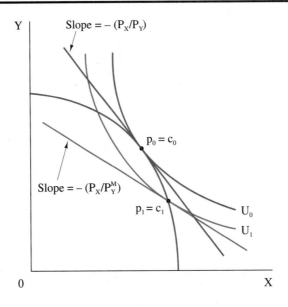

With two perfectly competitive industries, production and consumption occur at $p_0 = c_0$. The relative production costs of the two goods (represented by the slope of the production possibilities frontier) equal the goods' relative prices (represented by the slope of the price line) and consumers' marginal rate of substitution between the goods (represented by the slope of the indifference curve). The introduction of a monopoly in Y raises the relative price of good Y to P_Y^M, which is above its opportunity cost. Production and consumption occur at point $p_1 = c_1$, where the slope of the production possibilities frontier exceeds those of the price line and indifference curve. The monopoly lowers the level of utility attainable in autarky from U_0 to U_1.

Graphically, the autarky production and consumption decision in a country in which both industries are perfectly competitive appears as in Figure 8.5. The autarky price ratio just equals the marginal rate of substitution along the indifference curve and the marginal rate of transformation, or relative opportunity costs, of the two goods. (For a review, see section 3.2.2.) Production and consumption occur at point $p_0 = c_0$ on indifference curve U_0. This outcome is efficient in the narrow sense that U_0 represents the highest level of utility attainable without trade.

If one industry—say, Y—is monopolized in country A, then $P_X^A = MC_X^A$ but $P_Y^A > MC_Y^A$; thus,

$$P_X^A/P_Y^A < MC_X^A/MC_Y^A,$$ [8.2]

and relative output prices do not reflect opportunity costs. Inefficiency results. In Figure 8.5, monopolization of the Y industry causes country A to locate at point $p_1 = c_1$ on indifference curve U_1. The monopoly price charged for good Y restricts both production and consumption of that good. Not only does country A fail to realize the potential gains available through international trade; the monopoly causes utility even in autarky to be lower than if both industries were competitive.

Trade with a Monopolized Industry in Both Countries

Suppose monopolies characterize the Y industry in both countries A and B. In autarky, both countries suffer from the monopoly-induced inefficiency illustrated in Figure 8.5. Allowing international trade can improve the welfare of both countries. Forced to compete with its foreign rival, each firm, formerly a domestic monopolist, lowers its price and increases its output.

Actual international trade may or may not occur. If the two countries are identical and the monopolized industry produces a homogeneous good, there is no need for actual trade. The important point is that just the *possibility* of trade forces the firms to compete by lowering price and expanding output. A firm that failed to respond in this way to the opening of trade would find itself undersold in its domestic market by its foreign rival.[9] Lowering barriers to international trade in a monopolized industry can produce gains even greater than those from opening trade in a competitive industry; gains come from undermining monopoly power in the market as well as from the usual specialization and exchange. Although the welfare of each country improves as trade enhances efficiency, the new rivalry harms the former monopolists.

Trade with a Monopolized Industry in One Country

Now suppose the Y industry is monopolized in country A but competitive in country B. Intra-country competition among the country B firms results in a price of good Y equal to Y's opportunity cost in country B. The monopoly in A, however, charges a price for good Y above the opportunity cost of production. Therefore, if the cost of producing good Y is the same in both countries, B firms will offer the good for sale at a lower price than the A firm. With no restrictions on trade in good Y, the B firms will be able to export to A, breaking the A firm's monopoly. So, given similar costs of production, countries tend to export goods produced by industries that are structured competitively compared to their foreign rivals.

Maintaining a domestic monopoly in an industry competitively structured in other countries requires import barriers to prevent the monopoly, with its artificially high price, from being undersold. This provides a useful explanation for long-standing trade disputes between the United States and the European Community over trade in utility-related goods, such as telecommunications and power-generating equipment. In the late 1970s and 1980s, the United States deregulated many of its utilities industries, making them more competitive; the most famous example was the breakup of the telephone monopoly, AT&T. Prices fell in the United States following deregulation. Although European economies have engaged in some utility deregulation, the

---

[9] A monopolist's efforts to maintain the monopoly price in the domestic market and capture a share of the rival's market by cutting price there can result in dumping charges. Such behavior is called *reciprocal dumping*.

Figure 8.6 □ International Trade Can Cause a Monopolist to Behave as if the Industry Were Competitive

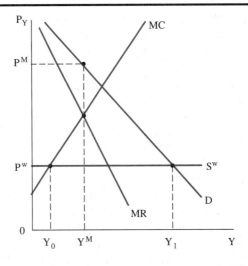

A monopolist in a small country cannot ignore the competitive nature of the worldwide industry under free trade. With no trade, the monopolist produces Y^M and charges P^M. With trade, the monopolist produces Y_0 and charges the world price, P^W.

pace of the process has been far slower than in the United States, so prices remain high in Europe. The trade disputes involve U.S. firms' complaints about trade barriers that European economies maintain to block access of the now-cheaper U.S. goods.

More generally, unrestricted international trade, along with antitrust policy or regulation, can be a powerful tool in limiting monopoly power. The size of the domestic market in a single country may support only a small number of firms and, as a result, allow them a significant degree of monopoly power. By allowing foreign firms to compete in the domestic market, international trade can limit domestic firms' ability to raise price above marginal cost. In fact, free trade can force a monopolist to act as if its industry were perfectly competitive.

Figure 8.6 illustrates the situation facing a domestic monopolist producing good Y in a small country. With no trade, the firm would choose to produce the level of output, Y^M, at which marginal revenue equals marginal cost and to charge the monopoly price P^M. But, if the small country allows international trade in Y, foreign producers will undersell the monopolist. The importing country is small, so consumers can import as much good Y as they want at the world price of P^W, which is not affected by the monopolization of the small country's industry. With trade, if the monopolist tries to charge any price above P^W, it cannot sell any of its product. Therefore, the monopolist will charge P^W and produce Y_0, the output at which the firm's marginal cost equals the world price. Consumers will import $Y_1 - Y_0$.

Figure 8.7 □ **A Monopolist Behaves Differently under a Tariff and a Quota**

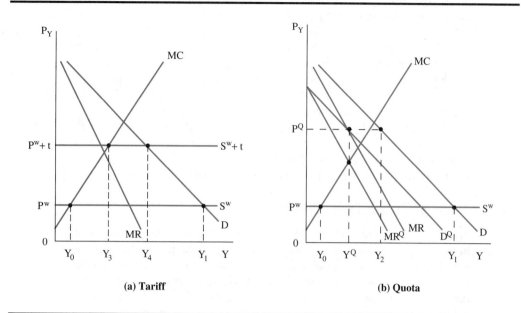

(a) Tariff   **(b) Quota**

The quota allows the monopolist more market power. The firm produces less output and charges a higher price under a quota than under a tariff.

Unrestricted trade has forced the monopolist to behave as if the industry were perfectly competitive. This occurs because trade makes the scope of the relevant industry worldwide, and the worldwide industry *is* competitive, despite the small country's monopoly firm.

Tariffs and Quotas with Monopoly

Panel (a) in Figure 8.7 illustrates that a tariff on a good produced by a small country's monopoly firm generates exactly the same effects as if the industry were competitive. The tariff raises the price the monopolist can charge by the amount of the tariff, t, to $P^W + t$. The monopolist produces a higher level of output, Y_3, and consumption falls to Y_4. Unless the tariff is prohibitive, the possibility of international trade still limits the monopolist from charging the full monopoly price.

Panel (b) shows the monopolist's price and output choices when protection takes the form of a quota rather than a tariff. The quota shifts the demand curve facing the monopolist to the left by the amount of the quota, from D to D^Q. The new marginal revenue curve corresponding to D^Q is MR^Q. The monopolist produces the level of output at which marginal cost equals this new marginal revenue, or Y^Q in panel (b), and charges price P^Q, which we read off the quota-adjusted demand curve. Consumers purchase Y_2 units, of which they import $Y_2 - Y^Q$.

Comparing panels (a) and (b) in Figure 8.7, note that the tariff and the quota cause the monopolist to behave differently, even when we define the two policies to allow the same quantity of imports. The tariff allows the monopolist to produce more and charge a higher price than under unrestricted trade. But, the monopolist knows that raising price above $P^W + t$ will cause consumers to buy from foreign suppliers. This constraint evaporates under the quota. No matter how high the monopolist raises price, consumers cannot shift to imports. Quotas allow monopolists to act more like monopolists. They produce less and charge higher prices than under tariffs. This represents a major cause of concern given the recent shift away from tariffs and toward nontariff barriers in international trade policy.

When domestic firms sell in export markets, any monopoly power they may have allows them to raise prices at the expense of foreign rather than domestic consumers. This idea of capturing monopoly profits on foreign sales provides the basis for a relatively new branch of international trade theory known as strategic trade policy.

8.4.3   Strategic Trade Policy

Strategic trade policy focuses on trade policy among small groups of players—firms and governments—in which any action brings a reaction, leading to games of strategy. For example, when can a firm deter a foreign rival from entering a profitable export market; or when can country A, through its choice of trade policy, cause country B to pursue a policy more favorable to A than the policy B otherwise would follow? Here we examine the strategies firms use and whether government policies can or should be used to help domestic firms fare well in international markets. There are two basic types of strategic trade policy models, based on the concepts of *profit-shifting* and *the learning curve*. We shall examine each and then address practical problems and dangers related to strategic trade policy.

Profit-Shifting Strategic Trade Policy

Firms behave strategically in international markets in which the number of firms is small enough to confer on them some degree of market power. Then, firms treat one another as rivals and respond to one another's actions. If the world market for a good is one in which economic profits exist, individual firms will enact strategies designed to capture the largest possible share of those profits.[10] In designing its strategy, each firm will take account of rivals' reactions.

From a national perspective, each country wants its firms in the international market to capture the largest possible share of available profits.[11] This goal coincides with the goal of the firms themselves. Typically, when the goal of individual firms matches that of policy makers, there is little need for active government policy; individual firms, acting in their own self-interest, accomplish the policy makers' goal as

---

[10]Recall that economic profits can exist only in markets characterized by some degree of monopoly power, at least in the long run. In perfectly competitive markets, any positive economic profits lead to entry by additional firms, which eventually drives economic profit to zero.

[11]Of course, monopoly profits come at the expense of consumers. The perspective taken in the strategic trade policy literature is that, assuming an international monopoly exists along with its burden on con-

well. In situations involving games of strategy, however, this intuitively plausible result can break down. Even though firms and policy makers have the same goal in mind (maximizing the country's share of the profits available in an international market), there may be a role for an active policy to accomplish the **profit shifting.** In other words, government policy may be able to accomplish something domestic firms, either individually or as a group, cannot do.

Assume a market consists of one firm in country A and one firm in country B.[12] Now suppose the A firm wants to capture a larger share of the international market and its profits. If the A firm expands production with no reduction in output by the B firm, the market price will fall and both firms will be worse off. Obviously, what the A firm wants is for the B firm to cut production and allow the A firm to expand its market share; however, the B firm has no incentive to go along.

One possibility is for the A firm to try to bluff the B firm into reducing output; for example, the A firm might announce, "If you do not cut production by 20 percent, I shall expand production and drive the price of the product so low that you will suffer losses." From the B firm's perspective, the question is whether the threat is credible; that is, should the B firm expect the A firm to carry out the threat? The answer is *no*. The threat is not credible, because carrying it out obviously would impose losses on the A firm. Thus, the B firm, unimpressed with the threat, carries on business as usual, thwarting the A firm's effort to capture a larger share of the market.

Now enter the country A government. Can it devise a policy that will make the country B firm take the A firm's threat seriously? If so, the A firm can force the B firm to cut production, allowing the A firm to take up the slack and the accompanying profits. Suppose, for example, the government of country A promises its domestic firm an export subsidy so the firm will find it still profitable to export even if the market price of the good falls to a very low level (as it would if the A firm carried out its threat to increase production). Then the A firm's threat becomes credible; carrying it out no longer will impose losses on the A firm but still will do so on the B firm. Without any retaliatory intervention by the government of country B, the B firm will respond by cutting production, allowing the A firm to expand its market share. The promised export subsidy facilitates the A firm's success by giving it the ability to credibly threaten the B firm.

The country A firm clearly gains; it captures a larger share of the world market and is able to charge a higher price thanks to the foreign rival's retreat. Whether country A as a whole gains is a more complicated question. Domestic taxpayers must pick up the tab for the subsidy. But, depending on the number of firms in the market and on consumption patterns, the increased monopoly profits earned by the domestic firm in foreign markets may outweigh the cost to domestic taxpayers of the subsidy. If so, the subsidizing country enjoys a net gain from its profit-shifting policy.

---

sumers, each country will want its firms to capture the largest possible share of worldwide profits. The only alternative is to allow foreign firms to capture the profits.

[12]Markets consisting of two firms are called *duopolies,* a special case of oligopoly.

The Learning Curve and Strategic Trade Policy

Learning-curve models of strategic trade policy are similar to infant-industry models.[13] The basic idea is that firms in some industries learn by producing, a phenomenon known as *moving down the learning curve* or *learning by doing*. As the firm accumulates production experience, its production costs fall, making it more competitive in world markets. If the industry is one in which the presence of economic profits characterizes the world market, the ability of domestic firms to capture a larger share of export markets means an ability to capture a larger share of those profits. The goal of government policy in such a scenario is to provide domestic firms in these industries with large enough markets to allow the firms to move down their learning curves.[14]

One obvious way to provide domestic firms in an industry with a large market is to restrict imports to reserve the entire domestic market for domestic firms. Tariffs, quotas, or a variety of other import restrictions can be used. If the domestic market is large enough to allow domestic firms to move down their learning curves, protection of the domestic market may, by making the domestic firms *more* competitive, allow those firms to capture larger shares of export markets. Such a policy will have the secondary effect of making foreign rivals *less* competitive by reducing their scale of production and raising their costs. Protection of the domestic market thus becomes a tool for expanding export markets. Domestic firms clearly gain from the export-promotion policies. Domestic consumers, however, must pay higher prices in the protected market. Thus, the country as a whole enjoys a net gain only if the domestic firm sells a large share of its output abroad so that foreign rather than domestic consumers bear most of the burden of the high prices.

Problems and Precautions

What are the practical problems and possible dangers in using strategic trade policies? One of the most basic problems in trying to apply such a policy is difficulty in defining the nationalities of firms. Given the spread of multinational enterprises, joint ventures, partnerships, and foreign stock ownership, the nationalities of firms have become much less clear in recent years. Determining exactly which firms a government would want to assist with the tools of strategic trade policy becomes problematic. If the U.S. government wanted to shift economic profits toward "American" firms, exactly which firms would it assist? Firms whose stock is owned primarily by U.S. citizens, firms with production plants located in the United States, or firms that use inputs manufactured in the United States?

A second problem centers on the sensitivity of strategic trade policy recommendations to the precise assumptions of the model. For example, in profit-shifting models, if we assume firms practice their rivalry by setting prices (and allowing quantities to be determined by market conditions) rather than by setting quantities (and allowing prices to be determined by market conditions), the optimal

---

[13]Section 5.6.2 develops graphical analyses of learning-curve models.

[14]The learning-curve argument for protection applies only if firms can learn from domestic but not foreign firms' production. Some evidence suggests this is not the case, at least in some industries; see section 5.6.2.

strategic policy recommendation switches from an export subsidy to an export tax.[15] Similarly, changes in assumptions about the number of domestic firms in the industry can shift the policy prescription from an export subsidy to an export tax, similar to the optimal export tax of section 6.8.2. Monopoly profits—the competition for which forms the basis for all strategic trade policies—may disappear if entry occurs in response to the policies; thus, strategic trade policies prove useless in industries without substantial entry barriers. All these considerations contribute to the difficulty of pinpointing industries that satisfy the requirements for successful strategic trade policy. Studies by many researchers suggest that the commercial aircraft industry probably satisfies the criteria as well as any existing industry. Case Three in this chapter uses the rivalry between U.S.-based Boeing and Europe-based Airbus to highlight some of the issues involved in strategic trade policies.

Like all beggar-thy-neighbor policies, strategic trade policies rely on the assumption that rival governments do not retaliate. If, in the profit-shifting case, both governments subsidize their respective firms, both countries end up worse off than in the case of no subsidies. Taxpayers in both countries bear the burden of the subsidies, but neither firm can enjoy the increased monopoly profits that come with increased market share, because neither firm will back down in the face of the other firm's government-backed threats.

Another issue concerns the distributional effect of such policies. As noted earlier, the pool of profits over which firms and governments fight the strategic-trade-policy battle comes from higher prices paid by consumers. Therefore, even though some may see it as preferable for "domestic" rather than "foreign" firms to capture those profits, the issue of government-assisted redistribution from consumers to (large, profitable, multinational) firms remains.

Finally, but perhaps most importantly, when a government chooses to become involved in an active policy of trade intervention, the system is subject to abuse by special-interest groups. In spite of stringent industry-characteristic requirements for successful strategic trade policy, producers in virtually all industries have an incentive to lobby for trade restrictions, in the guise of strategic trade policy, to gain protection from foreign rivals.

8.5 Externalities as a Basis for Protection

Among the assumptions used in deriving the result that unrestricted trade maximizes world welfare was the absence of externalities in either production or consumption. An **externality** exists whenever production or consumption of a good generates effects not taken into account in the production or consumption decision.

Pollution provides the most common example of an externality. Without anti-pollution laws, a chemical firm may dump its waste materials into a river. The resulting pollution imposes costs on individuals outside the firm (such as families who live

---

[15]In the formal language of strategic trade, price-setting behavior characterizes models having Bertrand assumptions and quantity-setting behavior models having Cournot assumptions.

near the river or want to use it for recreation, or firms downstream that want clean river water to use in their plants). The chemical firm, meanwhile, has no incentive to take these external costs into account in making its decisions. Pollution generates a **negative externality**, or one that imposes *costs* on others. When production of a good involves negative externalities, output of that good tends to be inefficiently high from society's point of view. The chemical firm produces too much output because it fails to consider a portion of the cost of producing the chemicals, that is, pollution.

Production also may involve **positive externalities** by generating *benefits* for third parties not considered in the decision-making process. In this case, a firm will tend to produce too little of the good from society's perspective. Suppose a firm, in the process of producing its output, teaches workers skills also useful in other firms. The other firms get benefits from the original firm's production. The original firm has no incentive to weigh the benefits of its training to other firms in deciding how much to produce or how many workers to train.

Consumption also can involve either negative or positive externalities. Consumption of cigars or cigarettes, for example, imposes costs on nonsmokers. As long as smokers do not consider these costs in their decision concerning how much to smoke, too much smoking occurs from society's perspective. Education is a good whose consumption generates positive externalities. An education clearly benefits the individual obtaining it; but by producing a more informed voter and citizen, it also provides benefits to others. If individuals ignore these external benefits, they will choose inefficiently low levels of education.

Efficiency requires that each activity be conducted to the point where its marginal benefit equals its marginal cost. The relevant benefits and costs include those enjoyed or suffered by individuals *other than* the consumers or producers of the good. Because externalities represent costs and benefits ignored in the decision-making process, they can cause inefficient outcomes. Many types of government policies aim at eliminating inefficiencies caused by positive and negative production and consumption externalities. Proponents of protectionism or trade-restricting policies often cite externalities as justifications for the policies they propose. The next two sections examine trade restrictions as ways to deal with externalities.

8.5.1 Production Externalities

Increasing (decreasing) production in industries that involve positive (negative) production externalities can raise welfare. We begin by considering the case of a positive production externality where the policy goal is to increase production to capture the external benefits associated with a higher level of output. Chapters Six and Seven explored several restrictions on international trade that have the effect of increasing domestic production.

Suppose production in the Y industry provides valuable worker training that benefits firms outside the industry. The country under consideration has a comparative disadvantage in production of Y and therefore imports a large percentage of the Y consumed. Imposing a restriction on imports of Y, such as a tariff or quota, would allow the country to increase domestic production of Y and capture the external benefits of the additional training. Figure 8.8 assumes the (small) country

Figure 8.8 □ An Import Tariff and a Production Subsidy by a Small Country in Response to a Positive Production Externality

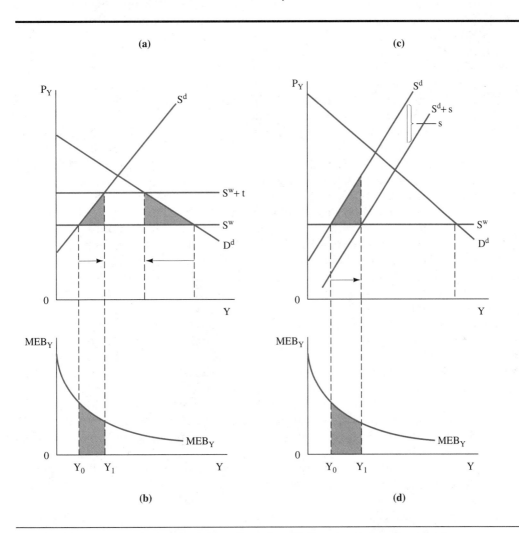

(a)

(c)

(b)

(d)

Panel (a) represents the standard analysis of the effects of a tariff. Here the Y industry is assumed to generate positive production externalities measured by the height of the marginal external benefit curve in panel (b). By increasing domestic production of good Y from Y_0 to Y_1, the tariff allows the country to capture external benefits equal to the shaded area in panel (b). The shaded triangles in panel (a) represent the standard deadweight welfare losses from the tariff. The difference between the shaded area in panel (b) and the sum of the shaded areas in panel (a) gives the tariff's net welfare effect in the presence of the production externality. The production subsidy in panel (c) increases domestic production without distorting prices and consumption. The country captures the same external benefits as under the import tariff, but avoids the loss caused by inefficient consumption.

chooses to impose a tariff on imports.[16] Panel (a) reproduces the effects of an import tariff in a small country. Panel (b) represents the external benefits from the worker training involved in producing good Y. The height of the *marginal external benefit* (MEB) curve in panel (b) measures the extra benefit to third parties (for example, firms able to hire workers trained in the Y industry) for each unit of good Y produced domestically. At each level of Y output, the total area under the MEB curve gives the total external benefits generated by that production level. The tariff increases domestic production of Y, which leads to an increase in external benefits equal to the shaded area in panel (b). The tariff also imposes the standard welfare losses represented by the shaded triangles in panel (a).

The net welfare effect of the import tariff depends on the relative sizes of the shaded areas in the two panels. If the standard welfare losses from the tariff exceed the external benefits of expanded production, the tariff reduces welfare. If the external benefits of increased domestic production are great enough to more than offset the welfare losses in panel (a), the tariff increases net welfare.

Although we cannot be certain whether a tariff would improve welfare compared with the case in which policy makers simply ignore the positive production externality, we can be sure that a superior policy for dealing with the externality exists. The tariff confronts the production externality *indirectly* by restricting imports. A policy that *directly* encouraged increased production of Y would be an improvement. One such policy would be a production subsidy to the Y industry. Just as in the infant-industry case, the direct production subsidy would encourage production without introducing a distortion of prices affecting consumption.

Panel (c) of Figure 8.8 shows the effect of a subsidy to Y producers. The domestic supply curve shifts down by the amount of the subsidy, and domestic production rises from Y_0 to Y_1. The amount of the subsidy (s) is chosen to have precisely the same effect on domestic Y production as the tariff in panel (a); therefore, the external benefits (in panel (d)) generated by the increased production are identical to those in panel (b). The welfare losses are smaller under the production subsidy than under the import tariff. The tariff causes domestic consumption of good Y to fall, while the production subsidy leaves the consumption decision unaffected. The efficiency loss from the subsidy consists of the single shaded triangle in panel (c). By creating the same external benefits at lower welfare cost than with the tariff, the subsidy constitutes a superior policy for handling the positive production externality.

In the preceding example, we assumed the positive production externality takes the form of worker training. If this is the case, an even better and more direct policy involves a subsidy on employment in the Y industry. A subsidy to employment rather than production will have a greater effect on employment. A production subsidy gives firms an incentive to increase output by increasing use of both labor and capital. An employment subsidy creates a more direct incentive for firms to hire and train more workers, thereby producing more external benefits. The superiority of an employment subsidy over a production subsidy for dealing with this particular type of externality

---

[16]Neither the assumption that the country is small nor that the trade restriction takes the form of a tariff affects the general result; the assumptions are for simplicity only.

is just another application of the general rule that direct policies generate more efficient outcomes than indirect ones. A production subsidy increases employment indirectly by increasing output; an employment subsidy increases employment directly.

Production of a country's import good also may result in negative rather than positive externalities. In this case, the industry's output will be too high from society's point of view because firms ignore part of the cost of production. One policy for discouraging production is a subsidy on imports, but this is indirect and alters the consumption as well as the production decision. A better policy would be a domestic production tax that would reduce domestic production and the associated external costs without altering consumption. *(Draw diagrams similar to those in Figure 8.8 that compare an import subsidy and a production tax as responses to a negative production externality.)*

The good a country exports also may involve either positive or negative production externalities. Trade-oriented solutions, such as export subsidies (to encourage production in cases of positive externalities) or export taxes (to discourage production in cases of negative externalities), introduce a new source of inefficiency by distorting prices and interfering with consumption. Direct production subsidies or taxes avoid these effects and take account of the externality at a smaller cost in lost efficiency.

8.5.2 Consumption Externalities

When consumption of a good generates positive or negative externalities, consumption subsidies or taxes lead to more efficient outcomes than do trade restrictions. The reason is analogous to the production externality case: If the problem concerns the level of consumption, the best policy is one that alters consumption directly without interfering with production decisions. Consumption subsidies or taxes accomplish this; trade restrictions do not.

Consider a case of a negative consumption externality: consumption of cigarettes. Panel (a) of Figure 8.9 represents conditions in the market for cigarettes. Panel (b) illustrates the external cost imposed on nonsmokers by cigarette consumption. The height of the *marginal external cost* curve (MEC) measures the additional cost imposed on third parties by each unit of cigarettes smoked. We assume cigarettes are the country's import good. The small country can discourage consumption of cigarettes by imposing an import tariff as in panel (a). The society suffers the usual deadweight welfare losses from altered consumption *and* production. In panel (b), the society avoids the costs represented by the shaded area underneath the MEC curve. Whether the tariff improves welfare depends on the relative magnitudes of these effects.

Again, a superior policy exists in the form of a consumption tax. Such a tax could reduce consumption of cigarettes by the same amount as does the tariff in Figure 8.9 without creating the inefficient increase in domestic production the tariff causes. *(Demonstrate this result with a diagram.)*

When a country's import good creates a positive consumption externality, policy makers can choose between an import subsidy and a consumption subsidy. The import subsidy lowers domestic production, while the more direct policy leaves production unaffected.

The same logic applies when a country's export good exhibits externalities in consumption. In the last few years, controversy has surrounded U.S. export policy

Figure 8.9 ▫ **Effect of a Tariff as a Policy Response to a Negative Consumption Externality**

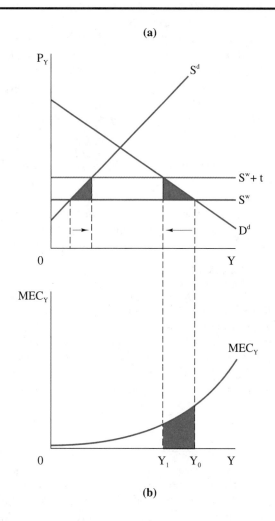

(a)

(b)

An import tariff reduces consumption, allowing the country to avoid the external costs represented by the shaded area in panel (b). The tariff also imposes the welfare losses associated with the two triangles in panel (a). The tariff's net welfare effect is uncertain. However, a consumption tax would be a superior policy, since it could reduce consumption by the same amount as the tariff without leading to inefficient production.

regarding tobacco and cigarettes. Policy makers, as we shall see later in the chapter (see section 8.11), have taken aggressive steps to open foreign markets to U.S. products in these industries. The markets in question include those in the former Soviet Union, Eastern Europe, and Asia. Anti-smoking activists charge policy makers with hypocrisy for forcing open export markets at the same time that they discourage smoking at home for health-related reasons. Policy makers respond that foreigners already smoke cigarettes, usually those produced by foreign governments' tobacco monopolies, and that aggressive U.S. market-opening efforts merely allow U.S. firms to capture their fair share of those markets.

Externalities on a larger scale lead to one of the hot topics in current international trade policy debates: the environment.

8.5.3 International Trade and the Environment

Growing concerns about the environment have made environmental issues a source of increasing controversy in international trade policy.[17] There are three basic problems or issues: how to conduct international trade while allowing individual countries to choose their own preferred levels of environmental protection, how to encourage international cooperation in safeguarding and improving the environment, and how to prevent feigned concern over the environment from becoming a thin excuse for protectionism.

The General Agreement on Tariffs and Trade does not contain explicit rules concerning environmental policy. The GATT does require countries' environmental policies to apply equally to domestic and foreign products. For example, the GATT would not permit a country to exclude foreign automobiles on pollution grounds while allowing sale of equally polluting domestically produced cars. Countries are free to exclude *products* that fail the import country's environmental standards; for example, the GATT permits countries to ban food products if they fail to meet hygienic standards that apply to both domestic and imported foods. However, the GATT has ruled that countries cannot exclude imports based on the environmental consequences of the *process* used to produce them. Thus, a country could not exclude food products by claiming that the foreign factories where the products were packed generated air pollution exceeding the import country's standards.

The most famous recent case revolving around the "product versus process" distinction involved the United States, Mexico, and tuna. The United States banned tuna imports from Mexico, Venezuela, and Vanuatu, claiming those countries used purse-net fishing techniques that resulted in unacceptably high rates of dolphin deaths. Mexico protested to the GATT, which ruled the U.S. ban illegal. Nothing about the tuna product itself violated U.S. environmental standards, and the GATT does not allow one country to impose its regulations concerning production processes, such as fishing techniques, on other countries. The ruling outraged many U.S. environmentalists, who were never fans of the GATT or an open international trade regime. Eventually, the countries involved agreed to a five-year moratorium on purse-net fishing in the Pacific Ocean.

Many environmentalists claim trade liberalization harms the environment by encouraging commercial development and facilitating firms' moves to countries of least stringent regulation. For example, opponents of the North American Free-Trade

---

[17]Jagdish Bhagwati, "The Case for Free Trade," *Scientific American,* November 1993, 42–49; and Herman E. Daly, "The Perils of Free Trade," *Scientific American,* November 1993, 50–57 provide two diverse perspectives.

Agreement claim it will erode U.S. progress on the environment by allowing firms to serve the U.S. market by producing in Mexico, where some regulations are less strict. However, there are strong counter-arguments. Primary among them is evidence that the primary determinant of demand for environmental protection is income level; the wealthy can afford it while the poor cannot.[18] Hence, supporters claim free trade, by raising income, increases demand for environmental protection. Trade also spreads newer, cleaner technologies, both directly and by raising income to pay for them. Growing evidence also suggests that the price-support schemes and elaborate protection granted to agriculture by most developed countries have led to over-clearing of land, overuse of fertilizers, and negative environmental consequences.

The arguments for a positive relationship between trade openness and the environment received new empirical support in the early 1990s when revolutions swept Eastern Europe and revealed the environmental messes the Iron Curtain had concealed. The centrally planned economies of Eastern Europe had isolated themselves from the trading system, denied firms access to new and clean technology, and provided firms with artificially cheap energy. The result was massive environmental problems that the countries' poorly performing economies could not afford to clean up.

Some types of environmental problems call more strongly for international cooperation than others. Many types of pollution have primarily local effects and, thus, reasonably are subject only to domestic rules. Other types, such as air pollution, release of greenhouse gases with climatic consequences, acid rain, and deforestation, have international or even global effects and are more reasonably subject to mutually agreed international rules. Often, what is needed is not so much new environmental rules but changes in existing domestic or international policies that have adverse environmental consequences. For example, Borneo is a prime offender in rapid cutting of its tropical rain forest. Part of the reason is its policy of short-term logging concessions that give a firm rights to log a piece of land for only 20 to 25 years. With no future rights to the land's productivity, concessionaires have little incentive to manage the forest with environmentally responsible techniques; instead, they cut as much as possible as quickly as possible and move on to the next piece of land.[19] These issues, particularly deforestation, often pit richer industrialized countries (many of whom cut most of their forests years ago) against poorer developing countries. One proposed solution is for developed countries to pay developing nations for the carbon-absorbing services of their forests, providing a financial incentive for poor countries to maintain rather than cut their forests.

Sound environmental policy requires insulating it from protectionists who disguise their self-interested arguments as concern for the environment. In the guise of environmentalism, Germany recently passed legislation (the "Töpfer Law") requiring firms that sell in Germany to collect their used packaging and recycle it. While such a policy may provide some environmental benefits, it clearly discriminates

---

[18]For example, urban pollution appears to decline sharply with income after a country attains an income level of approximately $5,000 per capita per year (*The Economist,* February 15, 1992, 78). Chapter Eleven contains a discussion of environmental issues between developed and developing countries.

[19]*The Economist,* August 8, 1991, 36.

against foreign firms who, because of transportation costs and lack of established local distribution networks, have a much harder time complying with the regulation. To cite another example, South Korea recently passed a Toxic Substances Control Act. Under the law, any firm selling a chemical product in South Korea must provide a list of components, their proportions, and the manufacturing process used to produce the chemical. Foreign chemical companies are highly suspicious of the law's true intent because South Korea has a rapidly growing chemical industry and endeavors to move into specialty chemicals, where technologies the country does not have are needed. U.S. chemical firms claim the new disclosure rules use environmentalism to disguise an attempt by South Korean chemical firms to obtain trade secrets from foreign firms.

8.6   Trade Restrictions as a Source of Government Revenue

For many years, tariffs and sales of import licenses comprised a major source of government revenue. As most developed countries now generate their revenue primarily through personal or corporate income taxes, the revenue-generating role of trade restrictions has diminished greatly. Many developing countries, however, still resort to trade-related mechanisms for revenue, because they lack the infrastructure required to administer a comprehensive income tax. Low-income countries, particularly those in sub-Saharan Africa, use import and export taxes most heavily.

Use of trade restrictions as a source of revenue often conflicts with other goals of such policies. Suppose, for example, that a country imposes a tariff on imports with two goals: protection of the domestic industry and collection of tariff revenue by the government. A prohibitive tariff—that is, one that reduces imports to zero—maximizes the protection the domestic industry receives. But a prohibitive tariff produces no revenue precisely because it drives the imports on which revenue is collected to zero.

8.7   The Scientific Tariff

Explicit calls for a prohibitive tariff are rare, but policy debates resound with arguments for a "scientific" tariff, which has the same effect as a prohibitive tariff. A **scientific tariff** is specifically designed to offset the cost advantage enjoyed by foreign producers of the tariffed good. For example, if Japanese auto makers can produce a subcompact car for $1,718 less than the cost of an equivalent American car, the scientific tariff on each imported Japanese subcompact car will be $1,718.[20]

Proponents of scientific tariffs argue international trade is inherently unfair whenever domestic producers must compete with foreign producers who enjoy lower production costs. They argue that trade can be fair only when all producers begin on an equal footing by having equal costs. Domestic producers seeking protection often cite the need for a "level playing field."

---

[20]Robert B. Cohen, "The Prospects for Trade and Protectionism in the Auto Industry," in *Trade Policy in the 1980s*, ed. William R. Cline (Washington, D.C.: Institute for International Economics, 1983), 553.

The primary fallacy in the argument for a scientific tariff lies in its failure to recognize across-country cost differentials as a reflection of comparative advantage. Every country will be the low-cost producer of some goods—those in which it has a comparative advantage—and the high-cost producer of other goods—those in which it has a comparative disadvantage. International trade's potential to increase world output and welfare comes from exploitation of these cost differences. Across-the-board scientific tariffs would eliminate all trade based on comparative advantage. The result would be a return to autarky and a significant reduction in world welfare.

8.8 Competition with Low-Wage Countries

In high-wage developed countries such as the United States, one of the most commonly heard justifications for protection is labor's supposed inability to compete with low-wage foreign labor. How can it be fair to expect goods produced in the United States to compete with those produced in developing countries using labor paid subsistence wages for work in sweatshop conditions? Proponents of this argument assert that American labor can compete under these conditions only by accepting a significantly lower standard of living.[21]

The fact is that products in many U.S. industries do compete successfully in world markets against goods produced using foreign labor paid only a small fraction of the wages earned by U.S. labor. High wages do not render an industry uncompetitive *so long as labor's productivity justifies them.* German workers may earn wages 20 times the level of Polish wages (see Figure 4.4), yet German products still will outcompete Polish ones if German labor in those industries is 20 times as productive as Polish labor.

The United States, with its highly skilled labor force and abundant capital stock relative to the rest of the world, has a comparative advantage in industries that involve intensive use of human capital and research and development skills. By world standards, U.S. workers in these industries are highly paid but also highly productive. On the other hand, the United States suffers a comparative disadvantage in goods involving intensive use of unskilled labor, relatively scarce in the United States. Trade according to comparative advantage moves these industries to low-wage countries with abundant unskilled labor. The result is a higher level of world output and a higher standard of living for residents of both the United States and labor-abundant countries.

As productivity rises in a country, so do wages. In a world where production facilities are increasingly mobile, firms are attracted to countries with workers highly productive relative to the wages they earn. As firms relocate to take advantage of the high ratio of productivity to wages, they bid up those wages.[22] Four Asian countries, often referred to as the "Four Tigers" because of their

---

[21]See Case Four in Chapter Four.
[22]See Chapter Four, Case Three.

Table 8.1 □ **Increases in Asian Labor Costs**

| | Average Industrial Monthly Wage | | |
	1984	1988	Percent Increase
South Korea	$302	$633	110
Taiwan	325	598	84
Hong Kong	363	544	50
Singapore	416	547	32

Source: *Business Week*, May 15, 1989, 46.

impressive success in industrialization and exporting, provide an outstanding recent example. As Table 8.1 documents, wages in the Four Tigers have begun to rise rapidly. As recently as ten years ago, wage rates in these four economies were very low by world standards, and firms from all over the world moved labor-intensive tasks there. That movement slowed with the rising wages; firms now shift instead to Indonesia, Malaysia, Thailand, China, the Philippines, and other countries where wages still are low.

High wages not justified by high productivity can make industries uncompetitive. The U.S. automobile and steel industries, for example, lost their ability to compete in world markets largely because of increases in union wage rates far in excess of productivity gains.[23] When workers in an industry succeed in raising wages above the value of the productivity of labor, the industry loses its ability to export and also must have protection from foreign competition in the domestic market. Although firms and workers in such industries typically rationalize protection on the grounds of saving domestic jobs, evidence from the steel and auto industries does not support this view. The increased profitability based on protectionism in those industries tended to go to even higher wages; hence, layoffs continue. The United Auto Workers union membership, for example, fell by almost half during the 1980s and early 1990s, from 1.5 million members in 1979 to 800,000 in 1995. Stringent union work rules that hinder flexibility and productivity, combined with high wages, continue to hamper the domestic industry even after more than a decade of protection.

Recently, a new U.S. industry has sought protection using a wage-based argument: the nanny industry. Nanny agencies, which provide individuals to take care of children, claim they cannot compete with *au pairs*, young European women who come to the United States under a cultural program to learn about the country and improve their English while taking care of an American family's children. *Au pairs* work about 45 hours per week in child care and light housekeeping, in return for

[23]Mordechai E. Kreinin, "Wage Competitiveness in the U.S. Auto and Steel Industries," *Contemporary Policy Issues* 4 (1984), 39–50. The same argument has been made about the compensation of management in the two industries.

which they are paid room and board and $100 per week. Nannies, on the other hand, charge room and board plus $175 to $400 per week.[24]

8.9 National Security and Defense

Some industries have particular strategic importance, making countries hesitant to depend on imports for supply. Two examples are the food and steel industries. The strategic importance of food is obvious, and the military applications of steel make that industry crucial during periods of conflict. Another industry in which the United States has used a national security argument to limit imports is petroleum.

The national security and defense argument for protectionist policies has several weaknesses. First, in the event of war or other catastrophe, it may be more effective to build new capacity for production of some needed goods than to rely on outdated and inefficient plants. During the Second World War the United States developed many new plants, including some to produce goods previously supplied by Germany. During the Gulf War, the United States chartered on the world market half the ships used to carry equipment to the Gulf—despite the Jones Act, which has protected the U.S. shipping industry since 1920 by requiring that all domestic maritime trade be conducted on ships that are U.S. owned, built, and manned.[25] Even in cases requiring continuous maintenance of productive capacity, trade restrictions represent inefficient means for doing so. Production subsidies can encourage domestic production of strategic goods without altering consumption patterns. Why should consumers have to pay higher prices for all goods containing steel to maintain capacity for steel production in the event of war? A direct production subsidy to the steel industry can avoid the effect of higher prices on consumers, although taxpayers must finance the subsidy.

Another fallacy in the national security argument is best illustrated using U.S. policy toward the petroleum industry. When imported oil was easily available at low cost from the Persian Gulf (before 1974), the United States chose to limit imports. The logic behind the action was to avoid becoming dependent on imported petroleum, whose supply could be cut off in time of war. The import restrictions kept U.S. petroleum prices artificially above world prices with the stated goal of encouraging the search for oil reserves in the United States. The strategy worked, but it had unfortunate consequences. The United States searched for, found, and used a large share of its oil reserves during a period when low-cost imports were freely available. When the OPEC embargo of 1974 ended the availability of low-cost imports, the previously used U.S. reserves were sorely missed. A better strategy—and one that several countries gradually have adopted—would have been to buy imported oil and stockpile it for emergencies. Not only would the stockpiles have been relatively inexpensive, but also domestic reserves would have been saved for the day when imports ceased to be available.

---

[24]Brent Bowers, "Nanny Agencies Say Threat from 'Au Pairs' Isn't Kid Stuff," *The Wall Street Journal,* May 28, 1992, B1.
[25]"Ruling the Waves," *The Economist,* March 23, 1991, 81.

Japan, which imports all its oil, has been trying to raise the percentage of its imports from Japanese-owned or leased oil fields to 30 percent because of national security concerns. The government grants tax deductions to firms buying existing oil fields and reimburses up to 80 percent of exploration costs for new fields. The program has its costs, however. Besides the taxes necessary to support the new drive for oil reserves, Japanese consumers pay approximately $5 a gallon for gasoline, due partly to extensive government regulation of the refining, distribution, and retailing sectors of the industry.

A wide range of industries, including some surprises, use the national security argument for protection. Of course, industries have an incentive to use any politically successful argument to obtain protection. The U.S. footwear industry, for example, has argued that national security dictates protection in shoes because in time of war, soldiers must have boots for combat.[26] The national security argument's vulnerability to special interests asking for self-interested protection represents a serious problem. In a particularly blatant example, one of two U.S. producers of depleted uranium persuaded law makers to mandate Pentagon purchases of 36 million pounds ($200 million worth) of the material—*for which the Pentagon claims it has no use since it has enough supply for 100 years of war*.[27] The same military stockpile to which the depleted uranium was added also contains an 84-year supply of watch jewels (not used since the arrival of digital watches), which continue to be produced by a government-owned plant built in 1952 at the urging of Bulova Watch Company, then a major user of jewels.

8.9.1 National Defense and the Changing World Political Economy

Regardless of the strength or weakness of their economic logic, for much of the post-Second World War period, national defense arguments for restricting trade were relatively straightforward. The two primary aspects of the resulting policies were (1) avoiding dependence for key imports on unfriendly countries, particularly the Soviet Union and its allies and satellite states, and (2) prohibiting exports of high-technology and military goods that might enhance the economic or military capabilities of those countries. With the waning of the Cold War in the 1990s, national defense arguments have grown more complex and less distinct from debates over other international trade policies. Several recent controversies highlight these changes.

The relationship between Japanese industry and the U.S. defense industry has become a source of controversy. On the one hand, the United States and other industrial economies pressure Japan to take on a larger share of the responsibilities of world leadership, including defense of itself and its allies. On the other hand, Japan's efforts to build its own fighter jet or early warning airspace monitoring system either

---

[26]Art Pine, "Footwear Industry Tells Congress 'Shoe Gap' Threatens U.S. Defense," *The Wall Street Journal,* August 24, 1984.

[27]Bob Davis, "Law Forces Pentagon to Purchase and Store Metal It Doesn't Want," *The Wall Street Journal,* June 10, 1991, A1.

alone or as a joint venture with U.S. defense contractors, rather than buying from U.S. firms, set off a flurry of protectionist and national security concerns.

As the world has moved from a situation of prolonged conflict between two super-powers to one of periodic regional conflicts between changing allies and enemies, the export-control side of national security policies has become more difficult. During the early postwar period, it was relatively simple to decide which countries not to provide with high-technology and military goods. More recently, those decisions have become more controversial, particularly in volatile regions such as the Middle East. For example, the United States and Western Europe provided extensive weaponry and technology to Iraq during the 1980s, largely because of Iraq's enmity with Iran, a U.S. enemy. In 1991, Iraq invaded Kuwait, and the United States intervened against an Iraqi military supplied in large part by the United States and its allies.

8.9.2 Government Intelligence and Industrial Spying

With the decline of the military rivalry between the United States and the Soviet Union, policy makers commonly pronounce that national rivalries in the future will be more economic than military. If so, should countries' intelligence services (for example, the U.S. Central Intelligence Agency and the former Soviet KGB) gather information useful to firms in their global competition for markets and technology? Such information includes data on rival firms' technological innovations and strategies for bidding on contracts. Evidence suggests many countries do use their security services in this way, intercepting telexes, fax transmissions, phone calls, and satellite signals as well as searching briefcases left in hotel rooms by traveling executives. Needless to say, such policies are controversial. The U.S. intelligence services describe their policies as striking a middle ground. They claim not to seek information for commercial purposes deliberately. They turn over such information that they uncover during their other activities to government policy makers (for example, trade negotiators) but not to private U.S. businesses. In addition, the CIA monitors foreign intelligence operations that might steal secrets from U.S. companies.[28]

8.10 Goods versus Goods and Money

The "goods versus goods *and* money" argument for protection appeals to intuition and "common sense." When a consumer buys a domestic good, both the good and the money paid for it remain in the country, but when a consumer buys an import, the good comes into the country and the money leaves. Proponents of the argument claim that surely it must be better to keep both the good and the money than just the good. If so, a country must be better off producing all goods domestically than engaging in international trade.

The fallacy in this argument lies in its failure to recognize that the country loses something when a consumer buys a domestically produced good—even though both the good and the money remain in the country. It loses the resources used in producing

---

[28]Gerald F. Seib, "Some Urge CIA to Go Further in Gathering Economic Intelligence," *The Wall Street Journal,* August 4, 1992, A1.

the good. Whenever these resources have a higher value than the price that would have been paid for importing the good, the country is better off importing. This is just another way of stating the principle of comparative advantage. *(Why?)* Also, as we shall see in Part Two of the book, money spent on imported goods does not disappear forever; it returns in the form of foreign demand for domestically produced goods or foreign capital flows into the domestic economy.

8.11 Protectionist Threats and Trade Liberalization[29]

An argument heard with increasing frequency (especially in the United States) supports protectionism, or, more precisely, the threat of protectionism, as a means of lowering trade barriers. If domestic special-interest groups in a foreign country succeed in winning protection from competition, how can trading partners overcome the influence of those interest groups to achieve liberalization? One possible answer is "with the threat of retaliation."

A recent case involving the Japanese tobacco and cigarette industry illustrates this idea. For years, import tariffs and marketing restrictions closed the industry to foreign competition. Japan Tobacco, Inc., a government-owned monopoly, held 98 percent of the Japanese market for cigarettes (the second largest market in the world at 300 billion cigarettes per year, where 60.5 percent of men and 14.3 percent of women smoke). In 1987 the United States threatened to restrict Japanese exports in retaliation, using Section 301 of the 1974 Trade Act, which provides for retaliation against "unfair" trade practices by U.S. trading partners. The threat worked: Japan removed the tariffs and other restrictions on imported cigarettes. In the first two years following the liberalization, U.S. tobacco sales in Japan rose by about 500 percent. Japan Tobacco, forced by continuing Japanese restrictions on imports of raw tobacco to buy domestically grown tobacco at two to three times world prices, found it increasingly difficult to compete.[30]

Similar stories apply in other Asian cigarette markets, the world's fastest growing ones as smoking continues to decline in the United States and Western Europe.[31] Taiwan, under U.S. pressure, opened its cigarette market in 1986. The government monopoly still holds about 80 percent of the market, and the country now bans some types of cigarette advertising. Although the United States also restricts cigarette advertising, U.S. policy makers have resisted other countries' efforts to limit advertising, which is viewed as essential to successful introduction of new foreign brands into a market.[32]

Thailand formerly banned imported cigarettes as well as cigarette advertising. The United States filed a case with the General Agreement on Tariffs and Trade, claiming the Thai bans violated GATT rules. The GATT investigating panel ruled the import

---

[29]See section 7.7 on voluntary import expansions, as well as Case One in Chapter Five and Case Two in Chapter Six.

[30]Gale Eisenstodt and Hiroko Katayama, "A Trade Threat That Worked," *Forbes,* April 3, 1989, 38–39.

[31]Stan Stesser, "Opium War Redux," *The New Yorker,* September 13, 1993, 78–89.

[32]Because of advertising's information content, bans favor the existing domestic government monopolies over their foreign rivals—even if the bans apply equally to advertising of both domestic and foreign cigarettes.

ban illegal because it discriminated between foreign and domestic cigarettes (thereby making Thailand's claimed public-health justification implausible), but upheld Thailand's right to ban cigarette advertising for health reasons so long as the ban applied equally to domestic and foreign products.

The United States now exports 200 billion cigarettes annually. In addition, U.S.-based firms Philip Morris and R. J. Reynolds produce millions more cigarettes abroad, particularly in Eastern Europe, where the firms have purchased most of the formerly state-owned tobacco monopolies. The biggest market currently under dispute is China's. The country has 300 million smokers (61 percent of men and 7 percent of women), and they consume 1.8 trillion cigarettes each year. All tobacco products must be sold through the China National Tobacco Company, a state-owned monopoly. Tariffs of 450 percent bring in $6 billion a year in revenue to China's central government. China banned cigarette advertising in 1994, but the new law contains many loopholes, such as allowing cigarette firms to sponsor sporting events and rock concerts.

Cigarette export policies remain controversial for two reasons. First, they represent cases of the United States using its size and power to threaten other countries into changing policies that run counter to U.S. commercial interests. Second, many individuals argue that the U.S. government should not aid U.S. firms' tobacco sales abroad at the same that time public policies in the United States increasingly discourage smoking for health reasons.

Despite apparent "success" stories such as the cigarette cases, many economists remain skeptical of protectionist threats as a tool for trade liberalization. Supporters insist threats are the only way to eliminate foreign trade barriers supported by deeply entrenched and politically powerful special-interest groups. Detractors insist the United States should concentrate on reducing its own trade barriers before issuing threats to trading partners about theirs. Skeptics also point out the danger of introducing a world trading system based on who has the power to issue effective threats rather than on the multilateral, nondiscriminatory framework of the General Agreement on Tariffs and Trade and its successor, the World Trade Organization.

The Omnibus Trade and Competitiveness Act of 1988 increased the scope for protectionist threats by the United States, especially in the form of so-called **super-301 cases.** Under this provision, the U.S. International Trade Commission must issue an annual list of countries that maintain unfair trade barriers against U.S. exports. Once named, the countries must negotiate to lower the cited "priority" barriers or face retaliation. The first annual list, issued in 1989, included Japan, India, and Brazil, but the United States never retaliated against any of the three. The super-301 provision of the law expired after only two years, but Congress reinstated a similar provision.

A related provision of the 1988 trade act, called **special-301,** provides a framework for the United States to threaten retaliation against countries that do not enforce copyrights, patents, trademarks, and other intellectual property rights. Many countries do not have or enforce laws that limit firms' ability to copy other firms' inventions or products without paying fees to the innovating firm. U.S. firms, especially producers of computer software, movies, and books, claim to lose millions of dollars in sales each year because illegal copies produced abroad replace those sales. In 1993, the United States named Brazil and Thailand as the worst violators of intellectual property rights. Being named to the annual list of "priority countries" triggers investigations and compulsory negotiations after which import tariffs and other retaliatory measures can be taken if the parties fail to reach a satisfactory outcome.[33]

Another tool the United States has used is the Structural Impediments Initiative (SII) talks with Japan. Under pressure from the United States, including threats of retaliation, Japan agreed in 1990 to enter talks designed to make the two economies more compatible for trade and to lower structural barriers that may contribute to the trade imbalance between the two countries. At the beginning of the talks, Japan requested that the United States lower its federal government budget deficit and cut management compensation levels to make U.S. firms more competitive. The United States requested that Japan strengthen its antitrust policies against monopoly business practices, especially those by Japanese corporate groupings called *keiretsu*, increase public spending on infrastructure projects in Japan, and facilitate opening of larger stores in Japan that would carry more foreign-produced goods. Evaluations of the talks were mixed. In 1993, the Clinton administration combined two sets of trade talks with Japan, those on structural trade issues and those on sectoral issues such as government procurement and auto trade, into a single effort called the "Framework Talks."

Supporters of protectionist policies use many variations of the arguments presented in this chapter. Our primary aim has been to look logically at the arguments and evaluate the merits and demerits of each. The general conclusion must be that protectionism is not the best policy response to most of the problems discussed in the chapter. Regardless of the guise in which the argument appears, it is wise to approach any demand for trade-restricting policies as a request for protection from foreign competition. The most common motive underlying such requests, whether stated or not, is an effort to improve the welfare of the industry seeking protection at the expense of other groups both in the domestic economy and abroad.

We turn now to several cases that illustrate the contexts in which arguments for protection appear. Case One examines international trade in weapons. Case Two highlights the effect of trade restrictions on the distribution of income. Case Three uses the commercial aircraft industry to illustrate the uses and possible abuses of strategic trade policy. Case Four explores recent U.S. decisions to renew most-favored-nation trade status for China, despite many tensions between the two countries. Case Five analyses the fight between the United States and the European Union over trade in oilseeds.

Case One
The Arms Trade[34]

International trade in arms has received increased attention since the 1991 Gulf War and the demise of the Soviet Union. Arms trade grew during the late 1980s,

---

[33]Case Three in Chapter Eleven reports on an intellectual-property dispute between the United States and China.

[34]Much of the information in this section comes from Norman S. Fieleke, "A Primer on the Arms Trade," Federal Reserve Bank of Boston *New England Economic Review* (November/December 1991), 47–63.

Table 8.2 □ **Leading Conventional Weapons Exporters, 1988–1992**
              ($ Billions at 1990 Prices)

	1988	1989	1990	1991	1992
United States	12.20	11.85	10.82	11.67	8.43
USSR/Russia	14.66	14.31	9.72	4.45	2.04
France	2.40	2.85	2.13	0.82	1.15
West Germany	1.24	0.81	1.68	2.53	1.93
China	2.16	1.01	1.25	1.71	1.54
Britain	1.70	2.71	1.46	0.80	0.95

Source: "Ask Me No Questions, I'll Tell You No Lies," *The Economist*, February 12, 1994, p. 57.

but less rapidly than overall trade. On average, military expenditures comprise about 5 percent of the world's annual output. More than 120 countries imported arms in 1989, of which 47 also exported weapons. About three-quarters of the participants were developing countries, and they accounted for about 75 percent of arms imports and 10 percent of exports. Countries of the Middle East imported the most, while the members of the (then) Warsaw Pact led exporters. Table 8.2 lists the top six conventional weapons exporters with their annual sales for 1988 through 1992. The United States leads the list by a wide margin since the demise of the Soviet Union.

Table 8.3 reports the top ten arms importers for 1989. Imports were spread more evenly across countries than exports, heavily dominated by the former Soviet Union and the United States. However, because of those two nations' large economies, their arms trade—though large in absolute terms by world standards—represented relatively low shares of their total economic activity. Several small countries, including Israel and North Korea, devote much larger shares of their economic activity to arms.

Of course, measuring trade in arms requires defining them. The U.S. Arms Control and Disarmament Agency defines arms as military equipment, "including weapons of war, parts thereof, ammunition, support equipment, and other commodities designed for military use." For the United States, military aircraft lead both arms exports and arms imports. Japan is the leading customer for U.S. arms exports; the United States buys primarily from the United Kingdom and Canada, two longtime allies. There is some evidence of growing illegal arms shipments from the United States. The value of U.S. Customs Service seizures of shipments with invalid or deficient export-license documentation rose about 36 percent in real terms between 1982 and 1990. Worldwide, experts estimate covert trade in arms at between $2 billion and $10 billion per year.

During most of the period after World War II, the United States took a more restrictive stand than its trading partners concerning arms trade and high-technology trade with unfriendly countries. U.S. firms frequently argued that they lost business as a result, since goods the United States restricted often could be obtained elsewhere. In 1994, the Clinton administration announced it would begin to consider the effect on domestic weapons-producing industries, as well as foreign-policy and security concerns, in its decisions on permitting and prohibiting arms sales.

Table 8.3 □ **Leading Arms Importers, 1989**

	Arms Imports ($ Millions)	Arms Imports as Percent of World Total
Saudi Arabia	4,200	9
Afghanistan	3,800	8
India	3,500	8
Greece	2,000	4
Iraq	1,900	4
United States	1,600	4
Japan	1,400	3
Iran	1,300	3
Vietnam	1,300	3
Cuba	1,200	3

Source: Norman S. Fieleke, "A Primer on the Arms Trade," Federal Reserve Bank of Boston *New England Economic Review,* November–December 1991; data from U.S. Arms Control and Disarmament Agency.

The top five arms exporters (the Soviet Union, United States, United Kingdom, France, and China) agreed in 1991 to nonbinding guidelines for conventional weapons exports; the agreement included a promise to inform each other about large sales in volatile regions such as the Middle East. However, countering pressure for restraint in arms exports is political pressure to maintain jobs and profits in weapons industries in the face of reduced domestic weapons demand.

Case Two
More on the Costs of Protectionism: Who Pays?

In earlier chapters, we saw that international trade and protectionism affect the distribution of income. In this chapter, we saw that proponents of protectionism often claim to be protecting domestic jobs or wages.

One legitimate question for policy makers to consider in evaluating calls for protection is the effect on low-income families. Are the welfare costs of protection distributed evenly across the population, or do some groups systematically bear more of the burden? In a 1985 study, Susan Hickok set out to answer these questions.[35]

Protection penalizes low-income families. Tariffs often apply to goods at the lower end of the price and quality spectrum. The United States subjects basic goods such as clothing and shoes to tariffs and quotas, and these goods comprise large shares of the expenditures of low-income families.

---

[35]Susan Hickok, "The Consumer Cost of U.S. Trade Restraints," Federal Reserve Bank of New York *Quarterly Review* (Summer 1985), 1–12.

Figure 8.10 □ **Income-Tax-Surcharge Equivalent of the Cost of U.S. Protection, 1984**

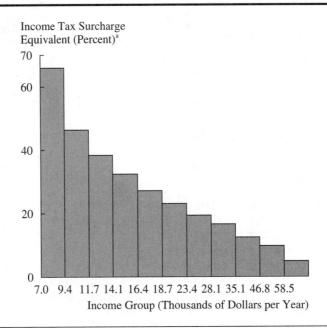

Income Tax Surcharge
Equivalent (Percent)[a]

Income Group (Thousands of Dollars per Year)

[a]Cost of protection as a percentage of income divided by the applicable federal income tax rate.

Source: Susan Hickok, "The Consumer Cost of U.S. Trade Restraints," Federal Reserve Bank of New York *Quarterly Review* (Summer 1985); reproduced in World Bank, *World Development Report 1986*, p. 22.

Hickok estimated the price increases caused by protection on clothing, sugar, and automobiles. She then used these figures to calculate the income-tax-surcharge equivalent of the protection for different income groups in the U.S. economy. In other words, how much of a tax does protection in the three industries place on different income groups? Figure 8.10 summarizes the dramatic results. For high-income families (above $50,000 per year), the price increases from protection are equivalent to an income-tax increase of less than 10 percent. But for low-income families (below about $9,000 per year), the same price increases are equivalent to a 65 percent income-tax increase!

Few voters or policy makers would support a change in the income-tax system with the effects just noted. However, many individuals recommend protectionism with the claim of protecting low-income workers. Unfortunately, protectionist policies generate effects quite different from those claimed. Estimates suggest protection in the three industries studied by Hickok cost U.S. consumers $39,000 (clothing), $60,000 (sugar), and $105,000 (automobiles) *per job saved* each year, much of it borne by low-income consumers.[36]

---

[36]Estimates of cost per job saved come from Gary Clyde Hufbauer, Diane T. Berliner, and Kimberly Ann Elliott, *Trade Protection in the United States: 31 Case Studies* (Washington, D.C.: Institute for International Economics, 1986).

Case Three
Playing Games in the Aircraft Industry[37]

Most analysts agree that if any industry fits the requirements for strategic trade policy as discussed in section 8.4.3, the commercial aircraft industry does. Worldwide, the number of new commercial aircraft demanded in any given year amounts to only a few hundred. Models are designed for specific distance ranges and numbers of passenger seats, as Table 8.4 illustrates, so the number of any particular type of aircraft sold is even smaller.

The bulk of the cost of a new family of commercial aircraft comes in the early research, development, and design stages. A firm incurs these costs regardless of how many planes actually are produced, so cost per plane declines significantly as the firm produces more planes of a given model, spreading the fixed cost over a larger number of units. Analysts estimate the break-even (that is, zero profit) number of planes

Table 8.4 □ **Commercial Aircraft Market Niches**

	Boeing	Airbus
Short range (up to 1,500 nautical miles)		
60–135 seats	—	—
Medium range (1,500–3,500 nautical miles)		
Up to 175 seats	727	A319
	737	A320
176–225 seats	727	A321
	767	—
Long range (over 3,500 nautical miles)		
Up to 225 seats	757	A310
	767	—
226–310 seats	767	A300
	777	A340
311–475 seats	747	A330
	777	—
Very long range (over 7,000 nautical miles)		
550–800 seats	?	?

Sources: *Fortune,* July 17, 1989, 42; *USA Today,* October 30, 1991, 3E; "Airbus Industrie Begins Marketing for New Plane," *The Wall Street Journal,* May 26, 1992; "Boeing, Four Members of Airbus to Study Jointly Developing Jet," *The Wall Street Journal,* January 28, 1993.

---

[37]This case draws on Richard Baldwin and Paul Krugman, "Industrial Policy and International Competition in Wide-Bodied Jet Aircraft," in *Trade Policy Issues and Empirical Analysis,* ed. Robert Baldwin (Chicago: University of Chicago Press, 1988), 45–78.

Table 8.5 □ **Hypothetical Profits or Losses for Boeing and Airbus**

		Airbus	
		Enter	Don't Enter
	Enter	−100, −100	500, 0
Boeing			
	Don't Enter	0, 500	0, 0

of a given model at around 500; selling fewer means revenues fail to cover the large research and development costs. The combination of limited demand, high research and development costs, and economies of scale or learning curve means that the worldwide aircraft industry can support only a few firms, probably two and perhaps only one.

The major firms are Boeing, a Seattle-based company holding about 60 percent of the market, and Airbus, a European consortium with about 30 percent.[38] France's Aerospatiale, German Daimler-Benz, British Aerospace, and Spain's Construcciones Aeronauticas head the Airbus consortium. Boeing and the United States claim that Airbus exists only through government subsidies. The European governments involved deny this, claiming they fully expect Airbus to repay all its borrowing, making the aid loans rather than subsidies. Under the terms of the government loans to Airbus, the firm must repay only if it earns a profit—something the firm claimed to do for the first time in 1990. Although Airbus entered the market in 1970, many initial years of losses would not be unusual given the cost structure of the industry, especially the high up-front research and development costs.

Current tensions surround the possible introduction of a "super-jumbo" jet to carry 550 to 800 passengers over 7,000 miles. If Airbus decides to produce such a plane, should Boeing also enter the market? How might government subsidies to Airbus, if indeed they exist, affect Boeing's decision? A hypothetical strategic, or game theory, model helps highlight the issues.

Table 8.5 represents how the two firms' hypothetical profits depend on their decisions whether to enter the new market. Each of the two rows in the table corresponds to a decision by Boeing and each of the two columns to a decision by Airbus. Each of the four decision combinations represents a possible outcome of the game (one on the lower right, where neither firm enters; one on the upper left, where both enter; and two where one enters but the other does not). For each outcome, the first numerical entry in the table reports the profit (or loss, if negative) earned by Boeing and the second the profit (or loss) earned by Airbus.

Table 8.5 assumes either firm can profitably enter the new market if the other firm does not; but if both enter, both will incur losses of 100 because each firm's sales will be too small to cover its large fixed cost. If Airbus already is committed to entry,

---

[38]The other producers are McDonnell Douglas, British Aerospace, and Fokker, each of which produces planes for a special market niche and encounters little direct competition with Boeing or Airbus.

Table 8.6 □ **Hypothetical Profits or Losses for Boeing and Airbus with a Subsidy to Airbus**

		Airbus	
		Enter	Don't Enter
	Enter	−100, 100	500, 0
Boeing			
	Don't Enter	0, 700	0, 0

Boeing will choose not to enter, thereby earning zero rather than the losses of 100 that would come from joining Airbus in the market.

But what if Airbus were not already committed to entry? Each firm would want to enter the market and would want to do so alone. Airbus would enter only if it believed that Boeing would not, and similarly for Boeing. *(Why?)* This is where strategic trade policy might play a role. Suppose European governments commit themselves to subsidize Airbus by 200 if Airbus enters the market, regardless of what Boeing does.

Table 8.6 captures the new game. With the subsidy, Airbus is better off entering no matter what Boeing does.[39] Equally as important, since Boeing now knows Airbus *will* enter, Boeing will choose not to, giving Airbus its most favorable outcome. The subsidy, by confirming that Airbus will enter no matter what, deters entry by Boeing and allows Airbus to capture all the profits in the market (here, 500) plus the subsidy.[40]

But the United States could play the subsidy game too, offering Boeing a subsidy of 200 for entry regardless of what Airbus does. *(How would the new table look?)* If this happens, both firms will enter and both will earn profits of 100 (actually a loss of 100 plus the 200 subsidy). Both countries make themselves worse off in this case, since taxpayers bear the burden of the subsidies that induce the two firms to enter an unprofitable market. Efforts to restrict such subsidies are difficult to negotiate. Each country has an incentive to force its trading partners to stop subsidizing and then continue its own subsidies. *(Why?)* Besides the problem of retaliation or "competitive subsidies," this type of strategic trade policy poses another problem: The success of the policy depends critically on the precise configuration of the numbers in the table. Most analysts see little evidence that the benefits to Europe of Airbus have exceeded the costs of the subsidies provided.

The dispute between the United States and Europe over subsidies to Airbus Industrie started in 1987. The United States demanded that subsidies (which it claimed totaled $26 billion over Airbus' 20-year life) be capped at 35 percent of research and development cost per airplane model. Europe responded with charges that Boeing and McDonnell Douglas benefit from implicit subsidies in the form of military contracts that aid their production of civilian planes. The dispute proved difficult to settle in part because of poor information. Airbus, as a special type of firm

---

[39]In the formal language of game theory, Airbus has a dominant strategy—enter.

[40]Of course, the subsidy simply transfers income from European taxpayers to Airbus.

incorporated in France *(groupements intérêt économique),* does not have to disclose financial information; thus, Boeing's and the United States government's estimates of Airbus subsidies necessarily involve guesswork, and perhaps exaggeration. Similarly, the military and government contracts between Boeing and the United States face limited disclosure requirements, leading Europeans to suspect the worst. Interrelationships among firms in the American and European aerospace industries complicate matters even further; Airbus planes contain many U.S.-made components, including engines, and Boeing planes commonly use European parts.

In 1991 negotiations with the United States, the owners of Airbus tentatively agreed to halt government aid for aircraft production but not aid for research and development. The dispute died down, but flared again in 1992 when lease terms that were unusually generous by industry standards convinced Delta Airlines to contract with Airbus instead of Boeing for a major aircraft purchase. Further negotiations followed; and a 1992 agreement barred government subsidies for production and marketing, capped subsidies for product development at 33 percent, increased transparency and reporting requirements, and limited indirect subsidies of the type arising from military contracts to 4 percent of a firm's sales. Both sides seemed content with the agreement until United Airlines entered a huge contract (100 planes for $3 billion) with Airbus in 1992—its first non-Boeing purchase in 14 years.

Boeing, in a surprise move in 1993, announced a joint study with the four Airbus member firms for joint development of the 550- to 800-seat super-jumbo jet, a project expected to cost between $10 billion and $15 billion. Each plane likely would cost over $200 million; and only major airlines flying long international routes—Japan Airlines, Lufthansa, British Airways, Singapore Airlines, and United Airlines—would buy them. The total market has been estimated at 500 planes, so at most one producer could profitably produce such a plane. While its member firms considered joint production with Boeing, the Airbus consortium announced it would consider designing an A3XX-100 super-jumbo jet to compete with Boeing's 747.[41] In 1995, after two years' study, Boeing and the European firms temporarily suspended their joint development plans, citing weak potential demand for a super-jumbo jet.

Case Four
Hard Choices:
China, MFN Status, and the WTO

One of the United States' fastest growing trade relationships is with China. In 1993, U.S. merchandise exports to China totaled almost $9 billion and U.S. imports from China over $31 billion, making the United States China's largest export market. Major U.S. exports include airplanes, grain, automobiles, and fertilizer. Leading imports include footwear, toys, and apparel.

---

[41]"A Paper Dart Against Boeing," *The Economist,* June 11, 1994, 61.

Despite the large volume and rapid recent growth of U.S.–China trade, the relationship has not been without its problems. For countries with Communist governments, U.S. law requires annual reviews to determine whether the country in question should have **most-favored-nation (MFN) status.** This status means the country receives the favorable tariff rate that the United States provides to most trading partners on their exports. Without such status, a country's exports are hampered by very high U.S. tariffs that date back to the early 1930s, before the postwar tariff reductions through the GATT. As of 1994, the United States denied MFN status to only nine countries: Afghanistan, Azerbaijan, Cuba, Cambodia, Laos, Montenegro, North Korea, Serbia, and Vietnam.

During the early 1990s, reviews of China's MFN status generated more controversy than usual. Concern surrounded China's human rights record (particularly vis-à-vis political prisoners following the 1989 Tiananmen Square incident and use of prison labor to produce for export); reported Chinese arms sales to Syria, Libya, Iran, and Pakistan; and the country's growing trade deficit with the United States. Proponents of revoking China's MFN status argued the country's leaders must pay for their behavior at Tiananmen Square and their arms trade.

Supporters of maintaining MFN status for China pointed to the political dangers of isolating it from the benefits of world trade. Loss of MFN status would affect most adversely the southern coastal areas of China that are most politically and economically open, Guangdong and Fujien.[42] Hong Kong, which processes most of China's trade, would also suffer, along with U.S. consumers who would pay more for many goods now imported from China. To cite just a few examples, tariffs on cotton T-shirts would rise from 21 percent to 90 percent, on toys from 6.8 to 70 percent, and on cotton petticoats from 17 to 90 percent. As we learned in Chapter Six, these tariff increases would directly affect prices to consumers.

Critics allege China exports products—including rubber boots, diesel engines, textiles, hand tools, and chain and lever hoists—produced with prison labor. U.S. law prohibits importing such products. However, supporters of China's MFN status point out the difficulty of documenting the prison-labor claims, which have been made by competitors (who have an incentive to make allegations that might gain them protection). Also, many U.S. prison products, besides the famous license plates, are sold to private firms and exported. About 65,000 inmates in the United States work for wages between 20 cents and 90 cents per hour.[43] In fact, the same firms and labor unions that allege China's use of prison labor complain about having to compete with the U.S. government's $400 million annual purchases from U.S. prisons; these groups say prisons should restrict themselves to tasks such as recycling that involve little private competition.[44]

---

[42]Some analysts argue that a more effective way to punish those responsible for arms sales and Tiananmen Square would be to block loans from the World Bank, the United Nations, and the Asian Development Bank, all of which aid Beijing policy makers more directly than trade policy, which aids individuals in the relatively open coastal regions.

[43]*Business Week,* February 17, 1992, 42.

[44]*The Wall Street Journal,* August 10, 1993, A1.

Giving in to U.S. pressure regarding its arms trade, China recently endorsed the Nuclear Non-Proliferation Treaty and agreed to abide by the rules of the Missile Technology Control Regime, which limits sales of missiles suitable for carrying nuclear weapons. However, repeated violations have been alleged, especially missile sales to Pakistan that violate nonproliferation agreements.

During the early 1990s, Congress repeatedly passed bills requiring Chinese progress on human rights and arms sales as a requisite for continued MFN status. Then-President Bush vetoed the bills, calling instead for continued engagement with the Chinese as a way of supporting the desired progress. As a presidential candidate, Bill Clinton harshly criticized the Bush approach and vowed to "get tough" with China. In 1993, President Clinton renewed China's MFN status, but with an executive order requiring human-rights progress with a one-year deadline. By 1994, most analysts agreed little actually had changed since 1993, but Clinton had become convinced of the wisdom of the Bush approach. He renewed MFN status and "delinked" trade policy decisions from human-rights concerns, but banned Chinese guns and ammunition exports from the U.S. market.

An additional major trade issue between the United States and China concerns the latter's desire to join the GATT's successor, the World Trade Organization (WTO). China helped found the GATT in 1947, but the Taiwan-based government withdrew in 1950 after the Communists took power on the mainland. In 1986, China applied to "resume" its membership. Other GATT members ruled that membership could not be resumed, but that China could negotiate to apply for accession as a new member. The negotiations have been long and acrimonious because of the nonmarket-based nature of China's economy. China wanted to complete an accession agreement before January 1, 1995, so it could be a founding member of the WTO, which took effect on that date, but negotiators failed to make the deadline.

The United States made five demands on China to gain WTO membership: (1) implement a single national trade policy for all regions,[45] (2) make the trading system transparent, (3) continue to remove nontariff barriers, (4) commit to move to a full market economy, and (5) agree to special procedures to protect industries in other WTO member countries from surges in Chinese exports. Predictably, the fourth demand has proven a major sticking point. China has committed itself to become a "socialist market economy;" but policy makers seem unsure quite what the term might mean.

The Chinese government did cut tariffs on more than 3,000 products in 1992, but the average tariff rate still is about 35 percent (see Table 6.3). And Beijing raised tariffs in early 1995 on a list of goods bought primarily by foreigners. Another sticking point in the negotiations is China's insistence on entering as a "developing economy," a status that grants a longer timetable for meeting WTO rules. Trading partners insist that China, as the world's eleventh largest trader, no longer deserves "developing" status as a trading nation. The results of the Uruguay Round enhanced China's incentive to achieve WTO membership. Member countries will phase out the restrictive Multifiber Agreement, which severely restricts China's textile and apparel exports, by 2004, but the change applies only to trade with member countries.

---

[45]Section 9.5.2 reports on China's special economic zones, which allow more liberal international trade than the rest of the country.

Case Five
The Oilseed Dispute

Oilseeds are agricultural products such as rapeseed, soybeans, and sunflowers, whose seeds produce edible oils. The European Community agreed in 1962 to bind its tariffs on such products at zero. In 1987, the American Soybean Association claimed that EC policies in oilseed markets harmed U.S. exporters and, in particular, denied them the benefits they should receive from the EC's 1962 removal of tariffs. This dispute dragged on for seven years and almost derailed the Uruguay Round agreement.

The European Community had replaced the tariffs on oilseeds with production subsidies. U.S. producers claimed these subsidies encouraged EC production and limited access to the market by non-EC producers. *(Draw a diagram comparing an import tariff and a production subsidy in the EC oilseed market. What effects are similar? Different?)* GATT panels, responding to U.S. complaints, ruled in 1990 and again in 1992 that EC oilseed subsidies did in fact have the effects the United States alleged. The EC offered minor reforms and compensation packages, none of which satisfied U.S. concerns. The United States threatened to retaliate with 200 percent tariffs on European exports after the EC refused to comply with the GATT rulings. The chief tariff target was France's white wines, because France was the most intransigent EC member in supporting European agricultural protectionism.

In late 1992, the United States and the Community agreed to a plan under which the EC would take at least 10 percent of oilseed crop land out of production. *(Draw a diagram illustrating the effects of such a policy.)* France later tried to force the EC to back out of the agreement, but other EC members made concessions to France to hold the agreement together.

Summary

In this chapter we analyzed the merits of many arguments for international trade restrictions, including those based on infant industries, monopolies, strategic trade policy, externalities, government revenue raising, optimum and scientific tariffs, competition with low-wage foreign suppliers, adjustment costs, national security, "goods versus goods and money," and protectionist threats to open markets. Several of the arguments contain valid elements, but more direct policies (such as production or consumption taxes or subsidies) generally produce results superior to those from restricting international trade. Restrictions on trade are not the most effective policies for dealing with domestic distortions.

Looking Ahead

A tension between the self-interested, nationalistic policies pursued by individual interest groups and countries and the broader perspective of the gains from an open and liberal trading system dominates the history of international trade. In Chapter

Nine we explore this tension, focusing on the history of international trade policy and on the development of regional trading groups that extend beyond the boundaries of a single country. We also examine the role of national borders and the differences between interregional and international trade.

Key Terms

optimal market conditions
domestic distortion
infant-industry argument
strategic trade policy
profit shifting
learning-curve models
externality

negative externality
positive externality
scientific tariff
super-301 cases
special-301
most-favored-nation status (MFN)

Problems and Questions for Review

1. Small country Dismalia "imports" education by sending its students to school abroad. Education generates positive consumption externalities for Dismalia, and the marginal external benefits decline with the quantity of education. As the new minister of education for Dismalia, you must develop policy proposals for dealing with this issue.
   (a) First, present to the minister of trade a proposal for how trade policy might be applied to the problem. Explain the economic logic of your proposal and illustrate graphically the policy's effects.
   (b) For the minister of the budget, you must present a proposal for how domestic policy might be applied to the problem. Explain the economic logic of your proposal and illustrate graphically its effects.
   (c) Given the choice of policies outlined in (a) and (b), what is your recommendation, and why?

2. In evaluating economic policies, we typically are concerned with not only the overall or net welfare effects, but with the distribution of those effects across different income groups in society. What does the empirical evidence suggest about protection in this regard? Examples of industries you might think about include footwear, clothing, and automobiles.

3. Analyze the following statement: "If an American buys a car produced in the United States, both the car and the money stay in the United States. If an American buys a car produced in Japan, then the car comes to America, but the money goes to Japan. Clearly, the first case is better for America because Americans get both the car and the money."

4. (a) Define "strategic trade policy." How does the strategic trade policy literature differ from more traditional international trade policy models?
   (b) Explain the profit-shifting argument for strategic trade policy. In what kinds of industries might such a policy work? What would the policy entail?

(c) Explain the learning-curve argument for strategic trade policy. What would the policy entail?

(d) What are the potential practical difficulties with implementing a strategic trade policy?

5. Briefly explain why a policy other than a trade restriction generally can handle a domestic distortion at lower cost than can a trade restriction.

6. For each of the justifications for protection below, propose an alternate policy:
    (a) An infant industry.
    (b) National defense reasons for not wanting to rely on imports.
    (c) A negative production externality in the country's export good.
    (d) A negative consumption externality in the country's import good.

7. Name two channels through which international trade may improve environmental quality.

8. Small country Alpha exports lumber products obtained by cutting Alpha's forests. Cutting the forests creates negative external effects in Alpha (soil erosion, loss of wildlife habitat, and so forth). The marginal external costs rise with the level of production of lumber products. As the new minister for the interior of Alpha, you are charged with devising policy proposals for dealing with the problem.
    (a) First, you must present to the minister of trade a proposal for how trade policy might be applied to the problem. Explain the economic logic of your proposal and use graphs to illustrate.
    (b) For the minister of domestic agriculture, you must present a proposal for how domestic policy might be applied to the problem. Explain your proposal, and use graphs to illustrate.
    (c) Given the choice of policies you outlined in (a) and (b), what is your recommendation, and why?
    (d) Suppose now that Alpha's cutting of its forests has negative externalities abroad as well as domestically (for example, the worldwide climatic effects of destruction of forests). What are the implications for the economic efficiency of free trade from a worldwide perspective? What policy problems might such a situation present? Why?

References and Selected Readings

Baily, Martin Neil, and Hans Gersbach. "Efficiency in Manufacturing and the Need for Global Competition." *Brookings Papers on Economic Activity: Microeconomics* (1995): 307–358.
Effects of foreign competition on firms' technology and productivity; intermediate and advanced.

Baldwin, Robert E. "Are Economists' Traditional Trade Policy Views Still Valid?" *Journal of Economic Literature* 30 (June 1992): 804–829.
Assesses free trade considering strategic trade policy arguments; for all students.

Bayard, Thomas O., and Kimberley Ann Elliott. *Reciprocity and Retaliation in U.S. Trade Policy.* Washington, D.C.: Institute for International Economics, 1994.
Empirical examination of the efficacy of reciprocity as a basis for trade policy; for all students.

Bhagwati, Jagdish. *Protectionism.* Cambridge, Mass.: MIT Press, 1988.
An entertaining look at the roots of protectionism; for all students.

Bhagwati, Jagdish, and Hugh T. Patrick, eds. *Aggressive Unilateralism: America's 301 Trade Policy and the World Trading System.* Ann Arbor, Mich.: University of Michigan Press, 1990.
Analysis of Section 301 as a means of opening foreign markets.

Bhagwati, Jagdish, and V. K. Ramaswami. "Domestic Distortions, Tariffs, and the Theory of Optimum Subsidy." *Journal of Political Economy* 71 (February 1963): 44–50.
A classic paper comparing tariffs with other policies as responses to domestic distortions; for intermediate students.

Brander, James A. "Strategic Trade Policy." In *Handbook of International Economics,* Vol. 3, edited by G. M. Grossman and Kenneth Rogoff, 1395–1456. Amsterdam: North-Holland, 1995.
Advanced, up-to-date survey of the literature on strategic aspects of trade policy.

Burtless, Gary. "International Trade and the Rise of Earnings Inequality." *Journal of Economic Literature* 33 (June 1995): 800–816.
Review of recent books on the relationship between trade and wages.

Cline, William R. *The Economics of Global Warming.* Washington, D.C.: Institute for International Economics, 1992.
Analysis of one of the more controversial aspects of environmental policy; for all students.

Coughlin, Cletus, K. Alec Chrystal, and Geoffrey E. Wood. "Protectionist Trade Policies: A Survey of Theory, Evidence, and Rationale." Federal Reserve Bank of St. Louis *Review* 70 (January–February 1988): 12–29.
An excellent, accessible survey of the causes and effects of protectionism.

Esty, Daniel. *Greening the GATT.* Washington, D.C.: Institute for International Economics, 1994.
Good overview of issues involved in extending international trade rules to cover the environment; for all students.

Feenstra, Robert C. "Estimating the Effects of Trade Policy." In *Handbook of International Economics,* Vol. 3, edited by G. M. Grossman and Kenneth Rogoff, 1553–1596. Amsterdam: North-Holland, 1995.
Advanced, up-to-date survey of the empirical literature on the economic affects of various trade policies.

Fieleke, Norman S. "A Primer on the Arms Trade." Federal Reserve Bank of Boston *New England Economic Review* (November–December 1991): 47–63.
Introduction to an increasingly controversial type of trade.

Grossman, Gene M., and Elhanan Helpman. "Technology and Trade." In *Handbook of International Economics,* Vol. 3, edited by G. M. Grossman and Kenneth Rogoff, 1279–1338. Amsterdam: North-Holland, 1995.
Advanced, up-to-date survey of technology-related aspects of international trade and trade theory.

Irwin, Douglas A. *Managed Trade: The Case Against Import Targets.* Washington D.C.: American Enterprise Institute, 1994.
Accessible analysis of the protectionist effects of voluntary import expansions, or threatened protection to force down foreign trade barriers.

Irwin, Douglas A. "Mercantilism as Strategic Trade Policy: The Anglo–Dutch Rivalry for the East India Trade." *Journal of Political Economy* 99 (December 1991): 1296–1314.
Argues that the seventeenth-century Dutch East India Company practiced strategic trade; parts are accessible to all students.

Irwin, Douglas A., and Peter J. Klenow. "Learning-By-Doing Spillovers in the Semiconductor Industry." *Journal of Political Economy* 102 (December 1994): 1200–1227.
Empirical examination of the application of learning-curve models to the semiconductor industry; intermediate and advanced.

Johnson, Harry G. "Optimal Trade Intervention in the Presence of Domestic Distortions." In *Trade, Growth, and the Balance of Payments,* edited by Richard Caves, Harry Johnson, and Peter Kenen. New York: Rand McNally, 1965.
The classic paper on the theory of protection with domestic distortions; for intermediate students.

Krueger, Anne O. *American Trade Policy.* Washington, D.C.: American Enterprise Institute, 1995. *Analysis of recent protectionist trends in U.S. trade policy; for all students.*

Krugman, Paul R. "Is Free Trade Passé?" *Journal of Economic Perspectives* 1 (Fall 1987): 3–12. *An accessible introduction to the implications of imperfect competition and economies of scale for international trade theory and policy.*

Krugman, Paul R. "The Narrow and Broad Arguments for Free Trade." *American Economic Review Papers and Proceedings* 83 (May 1993): 362–366. *Consideration of the merits of free trade in light of many of the issues raised in this chapter; for all students.*

Lawrence, Robert Z. "Protection: Is There a Better Way?" *American Economic Review Papers and Proceedings* 79 (May 1989): 118–122. *Alternatives to protectionism; for all students.*

McCulloch, Rachel. "The Optimality of Free Trade: Science or Religion?" *American Economic Review Papers and Proceedings* 83 (May 1993): 367–371. *Consideration of the merits of free trade in light of many of the issues raised in this chapter; for all students.*

Mussa, Michael. "Making the Practical Case for Freer Trade." *American Economic Review Papers and Proceedings* 83 (May 1993): 372–376. *Consideration of the merits of free trade in light of many of the issues raised in this chapter; for all students.*

Richardson, J. David. *Sizing Up U.S. Export Disincentives.* Washington, D.C.: Institute for International Economics, 1993. *Readable survey of policies that discourage U.S. exports, along with empirical estimates of the policies' importance.*

Rodrik, Dani. "Political Economy of Trade Policy." In *Handbook of International Economics,* Vol. 3, edited by G. M. Grossman and Kenneth Rogoff, 1457–1494. Amsterdam: North-Holland, 1995. *Advanced, up-to-date survey of the literature on distributional aspects of trade policy and their implications for the policy process.*

Srinivasan, T. N. "The National Defense Argument for Government Intervention in Foreign Trade." In *U.S. Trade Policies in a Changing World Economy,* edited by Robert M. Stern, 337–376. Cambridge, Mass.: MIT Press, 1987. *An up-to-date examination of many aspects of the defense or security argument for protection; most of the article is accessible to intermediate students.*

Tyson, Laura D'Andrea. *Who's Bashing Whom?* Washington, D.C.: Institute for International Economics, 1993. *The case for strategic trade policy, made by one of President Clinton's top advisers.*

Vousden, Neil. *The Economics of Trade Protection.* Cambridge: Cambridge University Press, 1990. *Excellent review of literature on arguments for protection; intermediate and advanced students.*

World Bank. *World Development Report 1995: Workers in an Integrating World.* New York: Oxford University Press, 1995. *The effect of international trade on wages.*

Zaelke, Durwood, et al., eds. *Trade and the Environment.* Washington: D.C.: Island Press, 1993. *Collection of readable papers representing diverse views on the relationship between trade and the environment.*

CHAPTER NINE

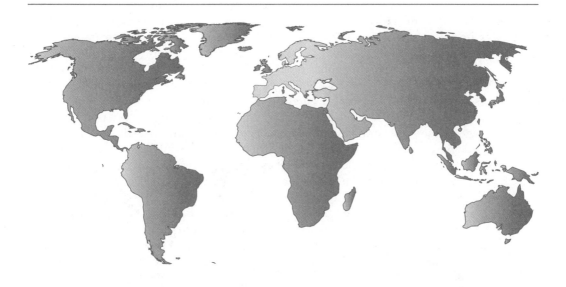

The Political Economy of Trade Policy and Borders

9.1 Introduction

The history of international trade and trade policy perhaps is best characterized as the outcome of countries' ambivalent feelings toward free trade. Since the decline of mercantilism in the early nineteenth century, many countries have perceived free trade in goods and services as an ideal toward which trade policy should aim. During the same 200 years, however, actual policies have been littered with relics of mercantilist thought and with protectionist policies won by inefficient domestic industries in the lobbying battles that determine policy in most countries. Within each country, political processes interact to determine the country's stance on international trade. Once domestic political institutions produce an outcome, policy toward trade with other countries stands as nationally determined.

From the viewpoint of the welfare of the world economy as a whole, the national character of international trade policy has advantages and disadvantages. On the positive side, the constitutional prohibition against tariffs among states in the United States, examined in Case One, undoubtedly has contributed to the remarkable growth and stability of the United States over the last 200 years. On the negative side, the national character of trade policy tends to perpetuate the mercantilist view of trade as a zero-sum game—that one country's gains must come at the expense of its trading partners rather than from improved efficiency.

The fact that most trade policy is nationally determined draws our attention to the existence, definition, and economic significance of national borders, as well as to cases in which policy making occurs at levels other than a national one. First, we recognize that sometimes countries form themselves into groups and determine jointly a range of economic policies. The European Union and the North American Free-Trade Agreement represent the best-known of many examples. By extending beyond the boundaries of a single country, these groups internationalize both economic activity and decision making. Trade among group members takes on some, but not all, the characteristics of a country's internal trade.

Second, regions within a single country may differ in their factor endowments, market sizes, or economic policies. Differences between the northern and southern United States, for example, have played an important role throughout the country's economic history. The same holds true for Italy, Mexico, and many other countries. In other cases, policy makers subject subnational regions to different policies, as in the special economic zones along the southern coast of China, where economic activity follows a more market-oriented path than in the country's interior. Trade between distinct regions, called *interregional trade,* exhibits similarities to and differences from international trade. Understanding these similarities and differences helps illuminate the role of international trade and highlights more precisely the economic significance of national borders.

Finally, recent events in the world economy remind us that even the definition of nations can change. At the same time that some groups of countries join to coordinate their economies and trade policies, other nations disintegrate. Examples of the first trend include the former East and West Germanies, the members of the European Union, and Canada, Mexico, and the United States. The demise of the Soviet Union, civil war in the former Yugoslavia, the breakup of Czechoslovakia, and tensions between Quebec and the rest of Canada represent just a few examples of the tendency of nation-states to break into smaller policy-making units. Trade between East Germany and West Germany constituted inter*national* trade, while trade between the Czech and Slovak regions of Czechoslovakia was inter*regional* trade. Now, the situation has reversed; trade in the Czech and Slovak case crosses a national border while German trade does not.

In this chapter, we address the domestic political processes that determine national trade policies, the history of the world trading system, and cases of supranational and subnational trade policies.

9.2 The Political Economy of National Trade Policy

In Chapter Eight, we saw that despite the many guises of arguments for protection, almost all could be met with a superior policy that would not sacrifice the gains from trade. The problems best solved by trade protection are few.

Nonetheless, protectionist policies are numerous, diverse, and widespread. Thus far, we have explained the overwhelming presence of protection in the world economy based on the distributional effects of trade. International trade alters relative prices, thereby helping some groups, hurting others, and creating a natural constituency for protectionist policies. Chapters Two and Three, however, demonstrated that the benefits of unrestricted international trade outweigh the costs—in the sense that the winners can compensate the losers and still enjoy net gains. Therefore, why does unrestricted trade remain the exception rather than the rule? The keys to solving the puzzle lie in understanding the distribution of the costs and benefits of trade and its implications for the political process through which countries make trade-policy decisions.

The costs of international trade (for example, the decline of comparative-disadvantage industries) tend to be concentrated on a relatively small number of individuals. The benefits of international trade, on the other hand, come primarily in the form of lower prices for consumers and are spread over a large group, with each individual capturing only a small portion. This implies that in a direct referendum in which individuals costlessly voted on the question "Should the country impose a tariff on imports of good X?" the vote should be a resounding *no*, because consumers of X typically outnumber producers of X by a wide margin. If it were costly to vote (because each voter must gather information on the issue and go to the polling place), the referendum's outcome would be less certain. Each of the few producers of good X would have a large stake in the issue, making them likely to vote. Consumers, although they would have an even larger stake as a group, might find as individuals that the cost of voting would exceed the potential benefits from avoiding the tariff.

But countries rarely make trade policy decisions by direct referendum. In a direct referendum, each individual votes on a specific issue, not on a list of candidates, one of whom then "represents" the voter on a number of questions. This turns out to be an important distinction. Rarely is a voter lucky enough to find a candidate who perfectly represents that voter's views on all issues; typically, picking a candidate requires tradeoffs. Each voter has a priority regarding issues. For producers of good X, the tariff question is likely to decide which candidate gets their vote. For consumers of good X, the small effect the tariff would have on each individual makes the tariff a lower priority issue. As a result, a vote-maximizing candidate will more likely follow the wishes of X producers and support the tariff.

A related phenomenon that also pushes policy in a protectionist direction concerns the costs of organization. The fact that a small number of individuals bear the costs of international trade while the benefits are much more widely dispersed implies that pro-protectionist supporters will be more successful in organizing an effective lobbying force than will supporters of unrestricted trade. Suppose Congress holds a hearing in Washington, D.C. that will influence the vote on the tariff. Who will undertake the inconvenience and expense to go to Washington to make their feelings known—workers and producers in the X industry or consumers? Workers and producers will, because failure to get a tariff will impose a cost on each individual high enough to justify the expense of the trip. An individual consumer, on the other hand, has too small a stake in the issue to make the trip. Members of Congress see a biased sample of their constituents and become more likely to vote for the tariff.

This systematic pro-protection bias in the policy-making process carries over to the laws governing the making of international trade policy. One of the clearest examples is **Section 201** of the Trade Act of 1974, the "escape clause" that allows the United States to abandon its tariff-reduction obligations under the GATT whenever imports are a substantial cause of serious injury or threat to a domestic industry. Under the law, the U.S. International Trade Commission investigates an industry's claim of injury. If the ITC finds imports indeed injure or threaten to injure the domestic industry, the commission must recommend to the president relief in the form of a tariff, quota, or Trade Adjustment Assistance eligibility for the industry.[1] Nowhere does the law require that the ITC take the interests of consumers into account. The president, having instructions to weigh a broader set of considerations, may accept the ITC's recommendation or reject it in the national economic interest.[2]

Of course, opening trade injures a country's industries of comparative disadvantage, as predicted by the specific-factor model and the Stolper-Samuelson theorem derived in Chapter Four. But the benefits of trade in terms of lower prices and improved efficiency more than offset these losses. The wording of Section 201, by limiting ITC consideration to the interest of domestic producers, biases trade policy toward protectionism. This bias has become stronger as successive amendments to the original Section 201 have restricted the freedom of the ITC and the president to refuse to recommend or implement import relief, part of an overall tendency by Congress to acquire more control over the making of international trade policy.

Given the pro-protection bias in the policy-making process, how does trade liberalization ever get accomplished? One way is by informing voters of the often-hidden costs of protection. Even though an individual consumer loses a relatively small amount from a single protectionist measure, such as the U.S. sugar quota or antidumping duties on foreign steel, such measures taken together impose enormous costs on consumers, particularly low-income ones.[3] Laws that require the hidden costs of protection to be spelled out can help voters make more informed decisions. For example, as we saw in Chapter Eight, most arguments for protection can be met with alternate policies that provide equivalent benefits at lower efficiency costs.

Since the Second World War, international negotiations through the GATT have persuaded many countries to lower their trade barriers. One reason negotiations may succeed in cases where countries are not willing to liberalize unilaterally is that the reciprocity involved in negotiations creates another pro-liberalization constituency: export industries. In the context of reciprocal negotiations such as those conducted within the GATT, a country lowers its trade barriers in exchange for trading partners lowering theirs. Therefore, the opposition of import-competing producers can be balanced by support from exporters who would benefit from increased openness of foreign markets.

---

[1]Before the Uruguay Round, escape-clause cases often culminated in negotiation of a voluntary export restraint; but the Round agreement rules out this source of proliferation of VERs.
[2]See Chapter Seven, Case Three for the ITC debate over import relief in the U.S. footwear industry.
[3]Case Two in Chapter Eight contains examples.

9.3   A Brief History of International Trade Policy

9.3.1   Before Smith, Ricardo, and Hume: The Doctrine of Mercantilism

The first dominant theory of international trade was **mercantilism,** which prevailed from the Renaissance until the early nineteenth century. This was the era of nation-building and consolidation of power by emerging nation-states. Rulers raised armies, built navies, and went to war to protect their newly formed dominions—an expensive process. These rulers viewed international trade primarily as a way to finance the expenditures involved in building nations.

The use of paper money (dollar bills, pound sterling notes, and paper yen) had not yet spread during the mercantilist era. "Money," or the means of payment, consisted of precious metals, primarily gold and silver, called **specie.** Because ownership of gold and silver provided the wherewithal to pay armies and build ships, policy makers' goal for international trade was to accumulate as much specie as possible. Policies that encouraged exports and restricted imports contributed to the accumulation. Whenever a nation exported more than it imported vis-à-vis another country, the deficit country (the one for which the value of imports exceeded the value of exports) paid the balance of its account to the surplus country (the one for which the value of exports exceeded the value of imports) in gold or silver.[4]

Mercantilism dominated thought on international trade for a remarkably long period. Eventually the Classical economists in England began to point out critical weaknesses in the mercantilist view.[5] One important point was that all nations could not conduct successful mercantilist policies simultaneously. Because one country's exports are by definition another's imports, one country's success necessarily implied the failure of another. In fact, mercantilists viewed international trade as a zero-sum game: Whatever specie one nation accumulated necessarily came at the expense of another. As we learned in Chapter Two, the work of Adam Smith and David Ricardo on absolute and comparative advantage transformed the perspective on trade into a positive-sum view.

David Hume continued the critique of mercantilism by arguing that even when one country succeeded from the mercantilist viewpoint, the success could not continue in the long run. The accumulation of specie or money had the effect of raising prices in the successful mercantilist country.[6] As prices rose relative to those in other countries, imports became relatively cheaper and more attractive while the desirability of the country's exports waned due to price increases. The very success in accumulating specie caused imports to rise and exports to fall, eliminating the surplus that had facilitated the accumulation process. So any mercantilist "success" was short-lived at best.

---

[4]Section 2.2 discusses mercantilism in more detail.

[5]Section 2.3 contains more discussion.

[6]Part Two discusses the relationship between the supply of money and prices.

Finally—and perhaps most importantly—specie was useful only insofar as it represented **purchasing power,** or the ability to buy goods and services that produce satisfaction. If a country exported to the limits of its ability and imported nothing, it would accumulate specie but would have little in the way of goods and services.

9.3.2 Britain and the Rise of the United States

At the close of the eighteenth century, world events and the effect of the Classical economists' work moved trade policy away from mercantilism and toward liberalization. In Britain the Industrial Revolution created textile, iron, and steel industries that, because of their technological superiority and scale economies, could serve the entire world. Opening export markets and locating foreign sources of raw materials became policy priorities. Invention of railroads and steamships provided the inexpensive land and sea transport needed to expand world trade. All these events edged Britain toward a policy of relatively unrestricted international trade throughout the first half of the nineteenth century, although wars and recessions interjected temporary periods of renewed trade restrictions.[7]

Before the American Revolution, the colonies used tariffs to generate government revenue. The protection of domestic industries was not a major issue, since British law prevented the colonies from developing manufacturing to compete with British industry. During the Revolution, American manufacturing grew to replace British imports that were no longer available. In what has become a common historical pattern, the end of the war coincided with demands for protection by the new American industries that had been insulated from foreign competition during the Revolution. The protection of domestic manufacturing joined revenue generation as a major reason for the tariffs instituted by the United States, whose first comprehensive trade legislation passed in 1789.

Strong disagreement over the proper course of international trade policy characterized the first half of the nineteenth century in the United States. The North, with its dominant manufacturing interests, favored protective tariffs. The South, on the other hand, was still a largely agricultural economy and favored unrestricted trade. The South exported raw materials, primarily cotton and tobacco, in exchange for manufactures from Britain and Europe. The North might have pushed for tariffs on exports as well as imports, but the South had inserted a clause into the Constitution prohibiting such taxation. The disagreement continued until the Civil War of the 1860s, when the North used tariffs to finance its victorious war effort and then continued to impose tariffs to protect its manufacturing interests after the South's defeat.

During the late 1800s, tariffs rose in both Britain and the United States. Germany and France were growing and industrializing rapidly, eroding Britain's

---

[7]See Chapter Four, Case One for a related discussion of the British Reform Bill of 1832 and the repeal of the Corn Laws that protected British agriculture. On Britain's mid-nineteenth-century trade liberalization, see Beth V. Yarbrough and Robert M. Yarbrough, *Cooperation and Governance in International Trade* in the chapter references.

Figure 9.1 □ **World Trade, 1929–1933 ($ Millions)**

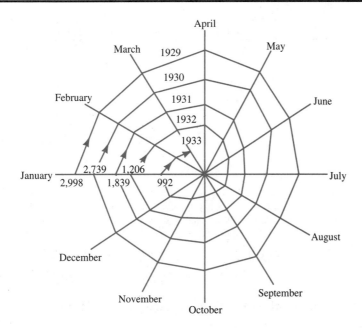

Source: Charles Kindleberger, *The World in Depression* (Berkeley, Calif.: University of California Press, 1973), p. 170.

technological advantage from the Industrial Revolution. During the first decade of the twentieth century, the negative effects of tariffs on world growth and trade were gaining recognition. Policy makers laid plans for tariff reductions, but the First World War intervened before any serious liberalization could take place. As usual, the war and its aftermath created renewed demands for protection in most countries, and tariff levels continued to rise. The U.S. economy enjoyed phenomenal growth relative to the rest of the world during this period, and U.S. trade policy became increasingly important as a worldwide model.

Unfortunately, the model set by the United States rested on the **Smoot-Hawley tariff bill of 1930,** which raised tariffs to an average level of 53 percent. Other economies retaliated by raising their own barriers, and the volume of world trade plummeted as the world economy entered the Great Depression. Figure 9.1 summarizes the pattern of world trade during 1929–1933. Countries attempted to "export" their unemployment problems by blocking imports, a classic example of a beggar-thy-neighbor policy. Analysts disagree over the precise degree of blame for the Great Depression that rests on the Smoot-Hawley bill, but clearly the bill did not help solve the severe economic problems of the time.

Table 9.1 □ **Tariff Duty Reductions, 1934–1994**

GATT Conference	Average Cut in All Duties	Remaining Duties as a Proportion of 1930 Tariffs	Number of Participants
Pre-GATT (1934–1947)	33.2%	66.8%	23
First Round (Geneva, 1947)	21.1	52.7	23
Second Round (Annecy, 1949)	1.9	51.7	13
Third Round (Torquay, 1950–1951)	3.0	50.1	38
Fourth Round (Geneva, 1955–1956)	3.5	48.9	26
Dillon Round (Geneva, 1961–1962)	2.4	47.7	26
Kennedy Round (Geneva, 1964–1967)	36.0	30.5	62
Tokyo Round (Geneva, 1974–1979)	29.6	21.2	99
Uruguay Round (Geneva, 1987–1994)	38.0	13.1	125

Source: Real Phillipe Lavergne, "The Political Economy of U.S. Tariffs" (Ph.D. thesis, University of Toronto, 1981); reproduced in Robert E. Baldwin, "U.S. Trade Policy Since World War II," in R. E. Baldwin and A. O. Krueger, eds., *The Structure and Evolution of Recent U.S. Trade Policy* (Chicago: University of Chicago Press, 1984), p. 6; updated to include the Uruguay Round.

9.3.3 The Reciprocal Trade Agreements Act of 1934

Despite the dubious value of U.S. leadership in the Smoot-Hawley episode, the United States soon recognized the need for liberalization of international trade as a way to emerge from the Great Depression. In 1934, a radical change in U.S. policy toward trade produced the **Reciprocal Trade Agreements Act (RTAA)**, which set the stage for trade liberalization for the next half-century. Not only did the act reduce the Smoot-Hawley-level tariffs, but it also changed the institutional arrangements for making U.S. trade policy.[8] Previously Congress had sole responsibility for tariffs and determined, on a unilateral and product-by-product basis, U.S. tariff levels. The Reciprocal Trade Agreements Act switched authority over tariffs to the executive branch of government and authorized negotiations with other countries over tariff levels. For the first time, countries could negotiate, coordinate, and cooperate in their (still nationally determined) international trade policies.

The RTAA remained the backbone of U.S. trade policy through 11 revisions and extensions until the Trade Expansion Act of 1962 replaced it 28 years later. Table 9.1 documents the success in tariff reduction under the RTAA and summarizes the reductions achieved in negotiations between 1934 and 1962 as well as more recent events.

Another innovative aspect of the RTAA was its recognition of the interdependence of trade policies by the United States and its trading partners. The argument

---

[8]Political scientist I. M. Destler argues in *American Trade Politics* that this institutional change was a key element in the liberalization that followed.

that U.S. tariff reductions would encourage reciprocal reductions by other countries and thereby stimulate U.S. exports (important to agricultural interests) was critical to passage of the 1934 act.[9]

9.3.4 Post-Second World War Trade Policy

Soon war again interrupted world trade. Emerging from the Second World War as the only major industrial economy with its capital stock intact, the United States took a strong leadership position in pushing for postwar trade liberalization.[10] The policy resulted from a combination of economic and political factors. Clearly the dominant country in technology and industrial strength, the United States had vast export opportunities it could exploit only in a relatively open trading environment. American intellectual and political leaders also believed that building economic linkages through trade could promote world peace. A related concern was the desire to help Europe reunite and rebuild quickly, to limit the spread of Soviet influence through Europe.

The U.S. commitment to open trade was reflected primarily in the development of a strong institutional framework for international economic and political interaction. This framework included the **International Monetary Fund (IMF)**, responsible for helping member countries with short-run balance-of-payments problems; the **World Bank** to deal with economic development issues; and the **General Agreement on Tariffs and Trade (GATT)**, the survivor of an unsuccessful attempt to form the International Trade Organization (ITO). These institutions continue to form the basic structure for international economic relations in the monetary, development, and trade spheres, although each has evolved and others have emerged in the intervening years.

Even in the postwar heyday of trade liberalization, the United States continued to exhibit ambivalence toward trade. The GATT was meant as a preliminary to formation of the more extensive and formal ITO, but the U.S. Congress refused to ratify the ITO because of fears of losing control over the nation's trade policy to an international organization. As a result, the GATT became the basis for international trade-policy negotiations.[11] Congress repeatedly authorized the president to seek further reciprocal tariff reductions through negotiations with trading partners, but at the same time imposed increasing restrictions on the liberalization process. Perhaps the clearest example of these restrictions was the insistence in 1947 that a

---

[9]Calls for "reciprocity" in U.S. trade policy continue. Often a mask for protectionism, reciprocity is given one possible pro-trade interpretation in Beth V. Yarbrough and Robert M. Yarbrough, "Reciprocity, Bilateralism, and Economic 'Hostages': Self-Enforcing Agreements in International Trade," *International Studies Quarterly* (March 1986), 7–21.

[10]Analyses of the U.S. role in the postwar trading system appear in Beth V. Yarbrough and Robert M. Yarbrough, "Free Trade, Hegemony, and the Theory of Agency," *Kyklos* (1985), fasc. 3, 348–364; "Cooperation in the Liberalization of International Trade," *International Organization* 41 (Winter 1987) 1–26; and "Institutions for the Governance of Opportunism in International Trade," *Journal of Law, Economics, and Organization* (Spring 1987), 129–139.

[11]The Jackson book in the chapter references includes an excellent treatment of the history of the GATT.

formal escape clause be included in all tariff treaties. The **escape clause** permits cancellation of tariff reductions shown to cause injury to a domestic industry. As earlier chapters of this book show, the sources of gains from international trade are increased specialization and exchange according to comparative advantage and exploitation of economies of scale. The process of specialization inherently involves the shrinkage or elimination of some industries. The idea of an escape clause, if carried to its logical limit, could eliminate trade, since trade always injures a nation's comparative-disadvantage industries. The escape clause represents just one example of a number of *safeguards* imposed in an effort to avoid the adjustment costs involved in trade's reallocation of resources.

In the United States, Congress has alternately tightened and loosened safeguard provisions with evolving perceptions of international trade. We can see these changing views by briefly examining the main trade acts passed since the 1950s: the Trade Expansion Act of 1962, the Trade Act of 1974, the Trade Agreements Act of 1979, the Trade and Tariff Act of 1984, the Omnibus Trade and Competitiveness Act of 1988, and the Uruguay Round Agreements Act of 1994.[12] Each act attempted to reclaim for Congress a portion of the control over international trade policy delegated to the president during the Depression and the Second World War.

9.3.5   Trade Policy in the 1960s and 1970s

The Trade Expansion Act and the Kennedy Round

The trade policies of the 1940s and 1950s involved extensions of the Reciprocal Trade Agreements Act. Congress had authorized the president to negotiate tariff reductions with trading partners, but throughout the period it gradually tightened the restrictions on the president's actions, particularly through changes in the safeguard provisions. Partly as a result of this increased protectionist sentiment, President Kennedy sought to regain momentum in trade liberalization by designing a comprehensive trade bill to replace, rather than merely revise and extend, the RTAA. The result was the **Trade Expansion Act of 1962 (TEA)**.

In addition to granting the president authority to negotiate reductions of up to 50 percent in tariffs through the GATT, the TEA contained three provisions important for their lasting effect on world trade policy. The first resulted not from the bill itself but from the political process necessary to obtain its passage. To gain the political support of representatives from the southern states (site of the U.S. textile industry), Kennedy agreed to impose quotas on cotton textile imports and to partially exempt textiles from the negotiations to take place under the proposed bill. These quotas and exemptions grew through the years, in the form of the **Multifiber Agreement (MFA)**, into one of the world's most far-reaching and restrictive sets of trade barriers.

---

[12]Robert E. Baldwin, *The Political Economy of U.S. Import Policy* provides an excellent account of the ebb and flow of support for pro-trade and protectionist policies and the reflections of those sentiments in the postwar trade bills. Most provisions of each bill take the form of amendments of earlier bills; thus, U.S. trade law is cumulative. For example, Section 201 of the Trade Act of 1974, as amended by the Trade Agreements Act of 1979, the Trade and Tariff Act of 1984, the Omnibus Trade and Competitiveness Act of 1988, and the 1994 Uruguay Round Agreements Act, still forms the basis of U.S. escape-clause law.

The Trade Expansion Act also introduced two rather sweeping changes into the institutional arrangements for tariff negotiations. The form of negotiations shifted from a *product-by-product format* to an *across-the-board*, or *linear, format*. Before the TEA, countries had negotiated tariffs for each product separately. The process was slow and tedious, and countries often proved unwilling to consider reductions on a large number of goods. Under the TEA, a single negotiated tariff-cutting formula would apply to all products. Each country then could submit a list of exceptions, or products on which it would not cut tariffs. The new approach speeded up the negotiation process somewhat; however, arrival at the tariff-cutting formula was slow as each country tried to fine-tune the formula to its own advantage. In the end, the **Kennedy Round** of tariff reductions conducted under the GATT by authority granted to the president by the TEA achieved a tariff cut of approximately 36 percent by the major industrial countries (see Table 9.1).

The other institutional innovation introduced in the Trade Expansion Act was the addition of the Trade Adjustment Assistance (TAA) program to U.S. safeguard provisions. Before the act, if imports resulting from a tariff reduction injured an industry, the only remedy was reinstitution of the tariff. Trade Adjustment Assistance constituted an alternate way to deal with injury: directly compensate injured firms and workers for their losses. Compensation could take the form of extended unemployment benefits, retraining, and relocation assistance for workers; low-interest loans and other assistance to help firms move into new product lines; and even restitution to whole communities harmed by an industry's decline. Trade Adjustment Assistance provided a way to capture the benefits from unrestricted trade while assisting those harmed by it; in other words, the program attempted to provide the compensation discussed in earlier chapters on the distributional effect of trade.[13]

Following the success of the TEA and the accompanying Kennedy Round talks, protectionist pressures rose in the United States. U.S. industries claimed other countries, especially members of the European Community, violated the spirit if not the letter of the GATT agreement by replacing their tariffs with nontariff barriers. The Trade Adjustment Assistance program, which many expected to reduce pressure by domestic industries for protection, had little actual effect during the 1960s, due to the stringency of eligibility requirements. For eligibility, an industry had to prove a tariff reduction had injured it and had been the primary cause of injury (that is, had caused at least 51 percent of the industry's problems). These requirements were interpreted strictly, and essentially no assistance was paid under the TAA program until 1969. The powerful AFL-CIO labor group, dissatisfied with the adjustment assistance program, reversed its historical support of trade liberalization in favor of import restrictions. Not until 1974 was Congress willing to pass another trade bill authorizing a further round of tariff negotiations.

The Trade Act of 1974, the Tokyo Round, and the 1979 Trade Agreements Act

The **Trade Act of 1974** resembled the 1962 TEA in several respects. The 1974 bill granted the president an impressive 60 percent tariff-reduction authority, but at the

---

[13]See the discussion of Trade Adjustment Assistance in section 4.7.4.

same time placed numerous additional constraints on the president's liberalization efforts and continued Congress's campaign to reclaim its power over trade policy from the president. As in 1962, obtaining adequate support for the trade bill required large concessions to the textile industry. The United States extended the existing set of import quotas from cotton textiles to cover wools and synthetics. Congress specifically excluded several items from the president's tariff-cutting authority, including footwear, an industry of particular interest to the developing countries.

The bill strengthened the role of the International Trade Commission, then known as the Tariff Commission, relative to the president in the interpretation and enforcement of safeguards against injury to domestic industries. Rules requiring stronger enforcement against "unfair" foreign trade practices such as subsidies and dumping were included. The president received authority to negotiate reductions in nontariff trade barriers as well as tariffs, but only with the specific approval of Congress.

Finally, the act loosened eligibility requirements for compensation under the Trade Adjustment Assistance program in two important ways. Injury to a domestic industry no longer had to be directly linked to a government policy (the reduction of tariffs) but only to increased imports. And increased competition from imports had to represent an "important" cause of the injury but no longer the "primary" one.

These rules set out in the Trade Act of 1974 laid the groundwork for U.S. participation in the **Tokyo Round** of GATT talks, which lasted from 1974 to 1979. The tariff cuts took the across-the-board, or linear, form initiated in the Kennedy Round. The formula for cuts proved even more controversial this time. The controversy finally was resolved in favor of a tariff-cutting formula suggested by the Swiss: $T_1 = 14T_0/(14 + T_0)$, where T_1 represents the after-cut tariff and T_0 the pre-cut tariff. Applied to a 5 percent tariff, the formula reduced the rate to 3.7 percent, a decline of 26 percent; applied to a 20 percent initial tariff, it cut the rate to 8.2 percent, a drop of 59 percent. Overall, the major industrial economies' tariff rates fell by approximately 30 percent.

The Tokyo Round, which was more ambitious than earlier talks in addressing problems associated with nontariff barriers, had mixed success. Because of the price-support systems discussed in the context of export subsidies and dumping (see sections 7.5 and 7.6), trade barriers on most agricultural products proved immune to progress. The Tokyo Round made some advances in defining export subsidies and outlining acceptable procedures for the imposition of countervailing duties when one country's export subsidies injured another country's industry. Agreement on a definition of subsidies, beyond those on exports, eluded negotiators. The concerns of developing countries received somewhat more attention than in earlier rounds of talks, but lack of progress in the crucial agricultural, textile, apparel, and footwear industries continued.

The Tokyo Round broke controversial ground by reaching several agreements accepted by only a subset of the more than 90 GATT member countries.[14] Nine such *codes* were negotiated, with additional signatories free to join. Areas covered by

---

[14]The members of the GATT are known formally as "contracting parties." For the codes accepted by only a subset of the contracting parties, the countries involved are called "signatories."

the codes included subsidies and countervailing duties, government procurement, standards or technical trade barriers, import licensing, customs valuation, antidumping, trade in civilian aircraft, trade in dairy products, and trade in bovine meat. Some of the codes proved more successful than others, but the idea of codes or mini-agreements remains controversial, because they represent a move away from the more traditional multilateral approach of the GATT.

The Tokyo Round left the international trading system with a number of unresolved issues, including developed-country barriers against developing-country exports, mutually acceptable interpretations of safeguard provisions, and procedures for settling disputes within the GATT. The United States ratified the results of the Tokyo Round negotiations in the **Trade Agreements Act of 1979.** That act also further limited the executive branch's discretion over trade policy by requiring more extensive monitoring of trade agreements and reporting to Congress.

9.3.6 Trade Policy in the 1980s and 1990s

The Trade and Tariff Act of 1984

The **Trade and Tariff Act of 1984** made minor changes in the U.S. escape clause and in provisions for antidumping and countervailing duties in response to foreign dumping and export subsidies. However, the act is best known for its approval of an historic shift in U.S. trade policy: It gave the president authority to negotiate *bilateral* trade treaties.[15] Since the Second World War, the United States had insisted that trade liberalization be accomplished *multilaterally* through the GATT to ensure that all member countries benefited from liberalization on a nondiscriminatory basis. Throughout the early 1980s, the United States promoted a new round of multilateral GATT trade talks and sought support from its trading partners. The world economy was mired in both a global recession, which was increasing protectionist pressures, and the developing-country debt crisis; this unfortunate combination of circumstances threatened to undermine the progress toward opening trade made in the Tokyo Round.[16] Other countries resisted U.S. appeals to support a new round of GATT talks. So U.S. policy makers turned to bilateral agreements for two reasons, as an alternate path to liberalization and as an attempt to pressure trading partners to support a new GATT round. However, the TTA of 1984 failed to give the president actual authorization to enter a new round of multilateral trade liberalization talks.

The Omnibus Trade and Competitiveness Act and the Uruguay Round Agreements Act

Finally, a 1986 meeting of trade ministers in Puente del Este, Uruguay, launched a round of GATT talks known as the **Uruguay Round.** Goals included complete elimination of tariffs by the major trading partners; extension of GATT rules to previously neglected areas such as trade in services and agriculture; clarification of

---

[15]Section 9.4.4 discusses the treaties with Israel and with Canada and Mexico.

[16]Chapters Eleven and Twenty-One cover the developing-country debt crisis, from microeconomic and macroeconomic perspectives.

GATT's institutional role, especially in dispute settlement; better enforcement of property rights in intellectual property such as computer software and movies; and limiting use of nontariff trade barriers, particularly voluntary export restraints.

Although the Uruguay Round talks began in late 1986, it was not until August 1988, in the **Omnibus Trade and Competitiveness Act of 1988,** that Congress actually granted the executive branch the formal authority to participate and to negotiate tariff reductions of up to 50 percent. The 1988 act also required domestic industries seeking import relief under the Section 201 escape clause to show they were prepared to make "positive adjustment" to import competition. Although subject to a range of interpretation, this change at least provided the opportunity to halt the trend toward long-term, permanent protection for the country's comparative-disadvantage industries.

Despite the provision for participation in the GATT talks and the modification of Section 201 to take some account of patterns of comparative advantage, the origin of many of the act's elements lay in concern over the U.S. trade deficit and in the often-cited decline in the country's "competitiveness." As a result, many parts of the 1,000-page bill represented a move in the direction of protectionism. Under the amended Section 301, domestic industries found it easier to claim (sometimes falsely) they were injured by imports facilitated by foreign unfair trade practices, thereby justifying relief or retaliation.[17] The 1988 bill transferred responsibility for initiating 301 cases from the president to the U.S. trade representative, a move many expected to help firms obtain affirmative findings in unfair trade cases.

The Uruguay Round talks were scheduled for completion by the end of 1990. If submitted to Congress by May 1991, the results of the round could have been approved under a special **fast-track** process that expedites congressional action by prohibiting amendments and limiting the time Congress has to consider the bill. However, a deadlock between the United States and the European Community over always-controversial agricultural export subsidies prevented agreement, and talks broke down in December 1990. The United States wanted the agreement to eliminate agricultural subsidies, and the EC wanted to keep intact its Common Agricultural Policy, which was based on subsidies. A group of 14 agricultural exporting countries, the Cairns group, refused to approve other parts of the tentative agreement unless the U.S.–EC deadlock over agriculture broke.

The Uruguay Round continued past its original deadline under a two-year extension of the president's negotiating authority granted by Congress in the spring of 1991. In December 1991, the director general of the GATT, Arthur Dunkel, put forward a 450-page draft agreement in an effort to hasten the negotiations to a conclusion. The "Dunkel draft" indicated that key countries had reached tentative agreement in many areas, including industrial subsidies, antidumping duties, foreign investment, dispute settlement, safeguards, and bringing textile trade into the GATT system. Negotiations within the GATT, however, follow a format in which no part of an agreement becomes final until the

---

[17]Recall that Section 301 of the Trade Act of 1974 is the foundation of U.S. trade law dealing with "unfair" trade practices of foreign countries. See also section 8.11.

entire agreement becomes final. Continuing disagreement between the EC and the United States over the depth of cuts in farm subsidies threatened the whole negotiation, after five years' work.

Congress extended fast-track authority for the Uruguay Round for the final time in the spring of 1993, but only until December 15 of that year. U.S. policy makers took a risk that, by signaling they would walk away from the entire venture if talks did not conclude by the end of the year, they could pressure recalcitrant Europeans to compromise on agriculture. The gamble paid off, and the Uruguay Round agreement was approved by GATT members in April 1994.

In the end, the Uruguay Round accomplished many of the tasks on its ambitious agenda. The major results included:

1. The agricultural provisions significantly reduce export subsidies and impose some discipline on domestic subsidies. The agreement also requires tariffication of existing nontariff barriers and makes the resulting tariffs subject to average 36 percent cuts. In agricultural markets completely closed to imports, the agreement requires reduction of trade barriers sufficient to allow minimum access for imports.

2. In textiles, the bilateral quotas that comprise the Multifiber Agreement must be removed by the end of a ten-year transition period. Most of the protection will remain in place until the end of that period, and high tariffs will remain in many textile and apparel sectors even after the quotas disappear.

3. Overall progress on tariffs includes an almost 40 percent average cut plus complete elimination of tariffs by industrial countries in several important sectors. A much higher percentage of world trade will occur duty free after the Uruguay Round, and many developing economies agreed to bind (that is, promise not to raise) tariffs on a large share of their imports.

4. The agreement clarifies the distinction between acceptable and unacceptable subsidies. Developing countries' subsidies are subject to discipline for the first time.

5. The new General Agreement on Trade in Services begins the task of developing a framework of rules for trade in services comparable to the GATT rules for trade in goods.

6. The agreement strengthens international rules for enforcement of intellectual property rights including patents, trademarks, copyrights, and industrial secrets. After specified transition periods, the rules will apply to developing as well as developed countries.

7. Most importantly, the agreement strengthened the structure of the GATT framework itself by establishing the World Trade Organization (WTO). The new organization brings together the 50-year accumulation of GATT rules and agreements under one umbrella. The WTO exists as a "single undertaking," so member countries now must subscribe to all rules and responsibilities, rather than picking and choosing as in the past. A much improved dispute-settlement procedure will handle all disputes and should significantly improve members' compliance with their obligations.

Given the Round's diverse accomplishments, estimating its overall effect on the world economy poses an impossible task. Economists have used computable general-equilibrium models to estimate the effects of the agreement's tariff-reduction provisions, because these are the most easily quantifiable policy changes.[18] Results suggest that, by the end of the ten-year phase-in period, total world GDP will be approximately 1 percent higher than had tariffs remained at their pre-Uruguay Round rates.

The GATT, culminating in the Uruguay Round and the creation of the WTO, is just one of the paths by which many of the economic goals expressed at the close of the Second World War have been met. As mentioned earlier, one of those goals was a quick rebuilding of Western Europe. The United States encouraged not only the rebuilding of individual European economies but also the economic and political unification, or *integration,* of Western Europe as a means of preserving the peace. Policy makers saw the nationalistic character of prewar political and economic policies as a cause of the war that devastated both sides. The integration of Europe greatly affected postwar trade policy, providing one example of institutions' role in transcending the strictly national character of economic policies. Ironically, some policy makers now cite Europe's integration as a danger sign for the world trading system. European success in moving toward an open market within the European Union, along with the formation of NAFTA, raise fears that the trading system will break into blocs, or regional areas within which trade is relatively free but between which protectionism dominates. To understand and evaluate these concerns, we must analyze the impact of economic integration on the world trading system.

9.4   Economic Integration and Regional Trading

The combination of countries' variation in economic size and the importance of economic size in determining a country's role in world markets provides a powerful incentive for nations to form themselves into groups. At the same time, the unique situation each country faces forms a barrier to smooth coordination and cooperation within such groups. Each country wants to retain its national economic goals and its power over policies for pursuing them, while capturing the ability to make decisions that transcend national boundaries. One attempt to obtain the benefits of both nationalism and supranationalism involves the creation of groups of countries that explicitly agree to coordinate certain aspects of their policies.

9.4.1   Stages of Integration

Integration, or the formation of countries into groups, can be either political or economic, although the distinction between the two often blurs. Five types or stages of economic integration represent increasing degrees of unification as illustrated in Figure 9.2.

---

[18]Section 4.6 describes computable general-equilibrium models.

Figure 9.2 □ **Levels of Economic Integration**

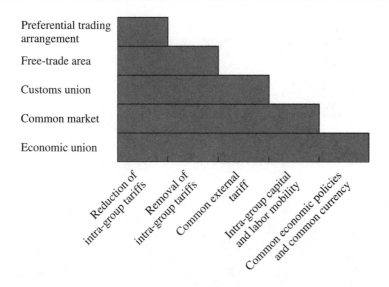

Moving from a preferential trade arrangement to an economic union involves successively higher degrees of integration.

The lowest level of integration is the formation of a **preferential trading arrangement (PTA)**.[19] Under this system, member countries agree to erect lower barriers to trade within the group than to trade with nonmember countries. Each country continues to determine its own policies, but the trade policy of each includes preferential treatment of group members. One simple example of such an arrangement would be a differential tariff whereby each member places a tariff on imports from member countries equal to half its tariff on imports from nonmembers. Panel (a) of Figure 9.3 illustrates such an arrangement in a three-country world where A and B form a PTA while C remains a nonmember.

The next stage of integration is a **free-trade area,** which involves eliminating all barriers to intra-group trade while allowing each country to maintain its own nationally determined barriers to trade with nonmembers; the NAFTA is an example of such a group. A free-trade area may apply to all goods or to only a specified list of goods.[20] Free-trade areas have the advantage of requiring agreement among member countries on only a narrow range of issues. The disadvantage of this limited form

---

[19]In the literature on economic integration, the term *preferential trade arrangement* (PTA) also is used as a generic name for all five stages of integration.

[20]In order not to violate the GATT nondiscrimination requirement, a free-trade area or customs union (discussed shortly) must remove the barriers to all or almost all trade between members.

Figure 9.3 ▫ **Tariffs under Different Stages of Integration**

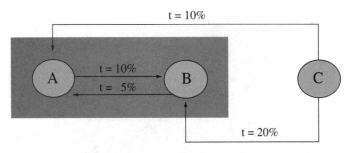

(a) Preferential Trade Arrangement

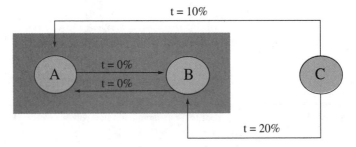

(b) Free-trade Area

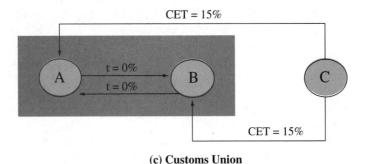

(c) Customs Union

Countries maintain their own tariffs under preferential trade arrangements and free-trade areas, but adopt a common external tariff under a customs union. The CET rules out transshipment to avoid tariffs.

of integration lies in the area of enforcement. Panel (b) in Figure 9.3 outlines a free-trade area in which country A maintains a 10 percent tariff on imports from C, and country B imposes a 20 percent tariff on goods from C. This situation produces an incentive for C to ship goods ultimately destined for B through A, paying the 10 percent tariff and then shipping duty free from A to B, thereby avoiding B's 20 percent tariff. Transshipment problems arise whenever member countries try to maintain different tariff levels on trade with nonmembers.[21]

One way to ameliorate the transshipment problem involves moving to the next level of integration by forming a **customs union.** With this arrangement, intra-group trade faces no barriers and members maintain a **common external tariff (CET)** on trade with nonmembers. If countries A and B from the previous example formed a customs union, the tariff against goods from C would be uniform; it could be 10 percent, 20 percent, or a compromise, perhaps 15 percent, as in panel (c) of Figure 9.3. In the case of the most successful economic integration, the European Union, CET levels equal the average of the members' pre-integration tariff rates. The CET eliminates the incentive for transshipments.

The fourth stage of economic integration is a **common market,** which extends free trade among members to factors of production (labor migration and capital flows) as well as to goods and services. In addition, common-market members typically maintain fixed exchange rates among their national currencies.[22] The European Union refers to the "four freedoms" that make it a customs union: free intra-group movement for labor, goods, services, and capital.

The most extensive form of economic integration, an **economic union,** means common, group-determined economic policies as well as a common currency or unit of money. Economic union proves very difficult to achieve and maintain, because it requires member countries to agree on a very wide range of issues, including micro- and macroeconomic policies. Even countries that are politically, economically, and culturally similar find differences in their individual situations that make such agreement elusive. Historically, countries have been extremely reluctant to forgo the exercise of their national sovereignty in the interest of an economic union. The European Union has taken steps toward a full economic union, as outlined in the 1991 Maastricht treaty, but achievement of this goal inevitably proves elusive. It appears that while political boundaries have economic significance, economic barriers have some political implications as well.

9.4.2 Trade Creation and Trade Diversion: Integration and Welfare

The overall welfare effects of economic integration are ambiguous and require case-by-case judgment. We can see the reason for this ambiguity by recognizing integration as both a policy of protection (against nonmembers) and a move toward free trade (with members). The effect of the protectionist element of integration is called **trade diversion.** This refers to the diversion of trade from nonmembers to members caused by the discrimination inherent in integration. The effect of the trade liberalization element of integration is called **trade creation.** Integration eliminates protection

---

[21]The U.S.–Israel and Canada–U.S. free-trade agreements seek to avoid the transshipment problem by restricting tariff-free treatment to goods produced in the partner country. These restrictions require rules of origin (see section 7.8.1).

[22]Chapter Twelve and later chapters examine the implications of fixed exchange rates.

Figure 9.4 ▫ **Welfare Effects of Economic Integration: Formation of a Free-Trade Area in Good X**

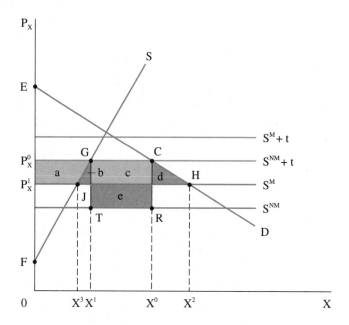

S^M denotes the supply of good X by member countries and S^{NM} the supply by nonmember countries. Formation of a free-trade area causes a move from point C to point H. Trade increases as imports rise from $X^0 - X^1$ to $X^2 - X^3$. Trade also is diverted from nonmember countries toward member countries, causing an efficiency loss represented by the area of rectangle e.

among member countries and allows them to specialize and trade according to comparative advantage and to exploit potential economies of scale. In cases in which trade creation exceeds trade diversion, economic integration increases member countries' welfare. If trade diversion dominates trade creation, welfare falls.

Figure 9.4 illustrates the trade-creating and trade-diverting effects of integration. We take the point of view of a small country considering elimination of trade barriers on good X with a group of countries (that is, the formation of a free-trade area in good X). D and S, respectively, represent the country's domestic demand for and supply of good X. S^M denotes the supply of good X from the other countries that would be *member*s of the free-trade area; S^{NM} is the supply of X by countries that would be *nonmember*s.

Before integration, imports of good X from all countries are subject to a tariff of t per unit; thus, $S^M + t$ and $S^{NM} + t$ represent the effective supply curves of imports from the two possible sources. Point C represents the initial equilibrium. Residents of the country consume X^0 units of X at price P_X^0, of which X^1 are produced domestically and $X^0 - X^1$ are imported from countries that, if integration occurred, would be nonmembers. No imported X comes from would-be members, because nonmembers supply the good at a lower price than do members. Graphically, this is reflected by the fact that S^{NM} lies below S^M, or $S^{NM} + t$ lies below $S^M + t$. Consumer surplus is given by the area of triangle $P_X^0 EC$, and the surplus of domestic producers by $FP_X^0 G$. The government collects the equivalent of the area of rectangle TGCR in tariff revenue.

After formation of a free-trade area, the relevant supply curves are S^M (because imports from member countries no longer are subject to the tariff) and $S^{NM} + t$ (because imports from nonmembers remain subject to the tariff). The new equilibrium is at point H. Residents consume X^2 units of X at price P_X^1, and X^3 units are produced domestically. The remainder $(X^2 - X^3)$ are imported, but now from member countries. *(Why?)* Consumer surplus rises by $a + b + c + d$, and domestic producer surplus declines by area a. The government no longer collects any tariff revenue, since all imports come from member (tariff-free) countries. Area c, which previously went to the government as tariff revenue, now goes to consumers in the form of reduced prices for good X. Area b is a net gain from increased efficiency; the units of X between X^3 and X^1 were previously produced domestically at relatively high costs (represented by the height of the domestic supply curve) but now are imported at lower costs (represented by the height of S^M). This efficiency gain captures one part of the trade-creation effect of integration. Area d denotes the other trade-creation effect. As lower-cost imports become available, consumption increases from X^0 to X^2. For each additional unit of consumption, the value to consumers (represented by the height of the demand curve) exceeds the opportunity costs of production (represented by the height of S^M). The total trade-creating effect of the elimination of the tariff on imports from member countries equals the sum of areas b and d.

Area e in Figure 9.4 shows the trade-diverting effect of integration. Notice that before integration, all imports came from nonmember countries, the low-cost producers of good X. After integration, all imports come from higher-cost member country producers. This switch from low-cost to high-cost sources of imports represents trade diversion. Before integration, area e was a portion of the tariff revenue going to the domestic government. After formation of the free-trade area, e becomes a deadweight loss. Each unit of imports between X^1 and X^0 now is being produced at an opportunity cost represented by the height of S^M rather than the lower opportunity cost given by the height of S^{NM}.

The free-trade area's overall effect on welfare is determined by comparing the trade-creation and trade-diversion effects. If trade creation dominates, the formation of a free-trade area will enhance welfare; if trade diversion exceeds trade creation, the group reduces welfare. Note that if member countries are the low-cost producers of good X, there will be no trade-diversion effect and integration will unambiguously increase welfare. *(To see this, switch the labels of S^M and S^{NM} and of $S^M + t$ and $S^{NM} + t$ in Figure 9.4.)* Note also that if the tariff is low enough to make the tariff-inclusive price of nonmember imports lower than the price of member imports, the free-trade area will have no trade-creating or trade-diverting effects, since no trade will occur with member countries.

We can formulate some general rules about when trade creation will be likely to dominate trade diversion or vice versa. First, the higher member countries' initial tariffs, other things equal, the more trade creation induced by integration and, therefore, the more likely integration will improve members' welfare. Second, lower member barriers against trade with nonmembers translate into less trade diversion and make welfare-enhancing integration more likely. Finally, the more members the better, because the group will more likely include low-cost producers. As noted above, when the low-cost producers of the good are group members, no trade diversion occurs. Another way of viewing this last rule is to notice that a free-trade area that included *all* countries could not generate any trade diversion, because the good's lowest cost producers would, by definition, be members.

Economists estimate of the overall impact of integration by calculating the effects corresponding to areas a, b, c, d, and e in Figure 9.4 for each major good traded. In the case of the European Union, most analysts agree that trade creation outweighs trade diversion; estimates suggest the EU's trade-creating effect has been about four times that of its trade-diverting impact.

9.4.3 Additional Considerations

The analysis of economic integration in Figure 9.4 is static, focusing on a single time period and on the reallocation of resources caused by elimination of barriers to intra-group trade. Integration may also have dynamic effects—that is, it may cause the member economies to evolve differently over time. For this reason, a complete analysis of the welfare effects of integration must include an examination of the effects of dynamic changes.

Economic integration increases the size of the "domestic" market. In industries that exhibit economies of scale, the increased size of the market may allow firms to achieve the economies necessary for them to become competitive in export markets, as we saw in Chapter Five.

Increased market size also may allow a group of countries to exercise some monopoly power in world markets. A group of "small" countries may, by banding together, be able to act as a "large" country and impose an optimal tariff or export tax (see sections 6.5 and 6.8). This pooling of power also may be important within international organizations and in other bargaining situations. One often-cited reason for the formation of the European Community in 1957 was to present the United States with a more nearly equal partner in terms of bargaining strength.

An additional source of dynamic benefits from economic integration takes the form of increased competitive pressures on industries within the integrated group. Once intra-group trade barriers fall, industries face competition from their counterparts in other member countries. If the group allows market forces to determine success and failure, intra-group specialization will develop along the lines of comparative advantage. Monopolization and the associated inefficiencies will be less likely to develop and persist. Groups forgo these potential benefits if the group "assigns" industries to the various members or otherwise prohibits competition within the group. The question of distribution of industries across member countries has proven troublesome, especially among groups of developing countries whose members are eager to industrialize.

Besides the static and dynamic welfare effects of any particular integration group, any trend toward the formation of such groups affects the fundamental ideals and norms of the international trading system. The GATT system of the postwar years rests on a foundation of multilateral nondiscriminatory liberalization that treats all trading partners equally, in principle if not in practice. Many policy makers and economists express concern that the GATT system may lose out to a system based on bilateral arrangements and discriminatory treatment of trading partners, in which regional trading blocs threaten to partition the world trading system into a small number of groups, each practicing discriminatory protection against nonmembers.

Supporters of regional trading groups point out that more progress on difficult issues may be possible when participants are a small group of like-minded countries.[23] As the GATT membership has grown from 23 members to well over 100 (see Table 9.1) and has become more diverse, negotiations there have become more unwieldy. At the same time, changes in the nature of trade policy and of protection complicate the negotiation process. Tariffs have fallen substantially, and the most important issues in the world trading system include much more complex policies— subsidies, antidumping policies, informal protectionism, and voluntary import expansions. These developments, taken together, may suggest a growing role for small-group trade agreements.

9.4.4 Efforts at Integration: Success and Failure

Since the Second World War, attempts at economic integration have come in two waves. The first, in the 1960s, included numerous groups of developing economies that attempted to follow the European Community model. The definition and goals of economic integration suggest that groups of small developing countries might be most likely to choose integration as a policy. However, most early attempts at integration among developing countries met with only mediocre success, and many arrangements throughout Africa and Latin America collapsed within a decade of initiation.

The second wave of economic integration began in the mid-1980s. The United States, for the first time, entered bilateral trade arrangements, and the European Community expanded its membership and its integration agenda. Developing countries also are participating in this second wave of integration. Some groups that formed earlier have been revived, and new groups have formed in Africa, Latin America, the Middle East, and Asia. Outside of the EU and NAFTA, the groups that have received the most attention, because of their rapidly growing and industrializing economies, are the Association for South East Asian nations (ASEAN) and the Southern Common Market (MERCOSUR), which includes Argentina, Brazil, Paraguay, and Uruguay.

GATT member countries forming integration groups must report their actions to the GATT, because such groups do not apply the most-favored-nation and nondiscrimination principles that underlie the GATT. Article 24 of the GATT agreement does permit economic integration so long as (i) trade liberalization

---

[23]See Beth V. Yarbrough, "Preferential Trade Arrangements and the GATT: EC 1992 as Rogue or Role Model?" in the chapter references.

applies to "substantially all" intra-group trade and (ii) group barriers to trade with nonmembers are no higher than before the group formed. Since 1948, many integration groups have notified the GATT of their existence, but only a handful have had a substantial and sustained impact on trade. Table 9.2 reports the only groups whose share of intra-group exports in total exports reached 4 percent, certainly a modest goal. Several groups on the list have made little progress toward integrating their economies.

The history of failed and only moderately successful attempts at economic integration testifies to the strong desire for national sovereignty in economic policy making—even though political boundaries are largely arbitrary from the standpoint of the organization of economic activity. Generally speaking, integration efforts among developed economies have enjoyed more success than those among developing economies. Some reasons for this pattern emerge from the simple graphical analysis of a free-trade area in Figure 9.4. Several African integration groups, for example, included economies with highly similar factor endowments and trade stemming almost exclusively from factor-endowment-based comparative advantage. Prior to integration, members imported largely the same goods from the same nonmember countries. Such a pattern provides little scope for trade creation. *(Why?)* In addition, the first wave of integration attempts among developing economies coincided with the height of import-substitution development strategies based on extensive import restrictions.[24] Therefore, much of the trade liberalization envisioned in the integration treaties never actually occurred.

Among developed economies, especially in the European Union, beneficial effects of integration came largely from intra-industry trade based on economies of scale. So trade creation was possible despite the similarities of members' factor endowments.

The second historical wave of integration differs from the first in its inclusion of groups whose members encompass countries at widely divergent levels of development. The NAFTA provides one example, as does the expansion of the EU to include countries less developed than the original members. Developing economies can achieve two major benefits from integration with developed ones. The first is market access on a preferential basis. The "Europe Agreements," for example, grant the Czech and Slovak Republics, Hungary, Poland, Romania, and Bulgaria extensive access to the markets of the European Union, although sensitive industrial sectors and agriculture remain restricted; all those economies hope to qualify eventually for full EU membership. The second benefit is a means of credibly committing the developing country government to market-oriented reforms and open economic institutions. Mexico, eager to guarantee it would not reverse its dramatic economic reforms of the 1980s, saw the NAFTA as a way of making a public commitment to that effect.

The developed members of developed-developing integration groups, on the other hand, hope to discourage labor migration and to support the developing economies' commitments to market-oriented reforms. Both these elements play a large role in the relationships between the EU and the transitional economies of Eastern Europe and between Mexico and the United States.

---

[24]Section 11.5.1 compares import-substitution and export-oriented development strategies.

Table 9.2 □ Economic Integration Groups

Group (Year Formed)	Level of Integration	Members
Australia–New Zealand Closer Economic Relations Trade Agreement (1983)	Free-trade area	Australia, New Zealand
Andean Pact (1969)	Common market	Bolivia, Colombia, Ecuador, Peru, Venezuela
ASEAN (1967)	Preferential trading arrangement	Brunei, Indonesia, Malaysia, Philippines, Singapore, Thailand
Central American Common Market (1961)	Common market	Costa Rica, El Salvador, Guatemala, Honduras, Nicaragua
Economic Community of West African States (1975)	Preferential trading arrangement	Benin, Burkina Faso, Côte d'Ivoire, Mali, Niger, Nigeria, Senegal, Liberia, Sierra Leone, Mauritania, Upper Volta, Gambia, Ghana, Guinea, Guinea-Bissau, Togo
European Community/European Union (1957)	Common market	Belgium, Luxembourg, Netherlands, France, Germany, Italy, Britain, Ireland, Denmark, Greece, Spain, Portugal, Austria, Finland, Sweden
European Free Trade Association (1960)	Free-trade area	Austria, Finland, Iceland, Liechtenstein, Norway, Sweden, Switzerland
Latin American Integration Association (1960, 1980)	Free-trade area	Argentina, Bolivia, Brazil, Chile, Colombia, Ecuador, Mexico, Paraguay, Peru, Uruguay, Venezuela
North American Free-Trade Agreement (1994)	Free-trade area	Canada, Mexico, United States
Preferential Trade Area for Eastern and Southern Africa (1981)	Preferential trading arrangement	Kenya, Zimbabwe, Burundi, Comoros, Djibouti, Ethopia, Malawi, Lesotho, Mauritius, Rwanda, Somalia, Swaziland, Uganda, Tanzania, Zambia, Zaire, Sudan, Namibia, Mozambique
U.S.–Canada Free-Trade Agreement (1989)	Free-trade area	Canada, United States

Source: Jaime de Melo and Arvind Panagariya, "Introduction," in *New Dimensions in Regional Integration* (Cambridge: Cambridge University Press, 1993), p. 13; updated to include the NAFTA.

The European Union

The 1957 Treaty of Rome established the European Community, consisting of six member states (the first six countries listed under the EC in Table 9.2). The goals of the treaty included formation of a common market with shared agricultural policies and aid programs to facilitate development of the less-developed areas within the Community. More fundamentally, the goal was a unified Europe, both to prevent the intra-European rivalries that had resulted in two world wars in a 30-year period and to present the United States with a more equal economic and political rival.

The group satisfied its customs-union goals within about a decade of the original treaty, but efforts at further integration stalled. In 1971, the EC agreed to a ten-year plan to achieve a full economic union. An incomplete common market evolved; however, many nontariff barriers and impediments to labor and capital flows remained, most of them intimately connected to issues of national sovereignty over economic policy making. Decision-making complexity grew as membership expanded to 12 after Spain and Portugal joined in 1986. With that phase of increased membership, the EC became the world's largest market in terms of population (over 345 million) and the second largest in terms of GDP (over $6 trillion).

In 1987, the EC passed the Single Europe Act, an amendment to the Treaty of Rome designed to recapture momentum toward integration and to complete the open internal market by 1992. The act facilitated achievement of these goals by limiting the ability of a single member country to veto EC proposals. It also expanded the EC bureaucracy based in Brussels and the scope of EC policy making in areas such as the environment, monetary policy, health and safety standards, and foreign policy.

In 1991, the EC made another major commitment toward moving to an economic union and changed the group's name from the European Community to the European Union. The Maastricht Treaty pledged member countries to coordinate their monetary, foreign and security, and immigration and policing policies. Most important, the treaty outlined a schedule and procedure by which the members would move to a common currency (the *Euro*) and a common European central bank to conduct monetary policy for the group.[25] Reaction to the Maastricht proposals has been mixed; but plans remain in place.

In 1994, the EU and the European Free Trade Association (EFTA), minus Switzerland and Liechtenstein, signed an accord forming the European Economic Area (EEA), which grants all members free trade in goods, services, capital flows, and labor flows, except for agriculture. Since, three EFTA members—Austria, Finland, and Sweden—have moved to full EU membership.

Many of the most controversial issues that face Europe's integration efforts also face the world trading system: trade in services, agricultural policy, government procurement, technical barriers to trade, and capital mobility. These issues present difficulties because they involve a delicate balance between international cooperation and national sovereignty. Although *EC92* became a buzzword for regional economic

---

[25]Chapter Twenty contains an examination of the monetary aspects of the EU, including the common currency proposal.

integration, analysts and policy makers now realize that integration is a continuing process, not a goal achievable by a set date such as December 31, 1992.

From the standpoint of the rest of the world, the major question concerns European barriers to trade with nonmembers. Some predict that the liberalizing spirit of the open internal market will carry over to trade with nonmembers. Others fear the formation of a "Fortress Europe" in which freer intra-group trade is accompanied by higher barriers to trade with nonmembers. This uncertainty led non-European firms, especially those from the United States and Japan, to expand their presence in Europe to ensure access to the huge market after 1992, a trend captured in Figure 9.5. Recent studies suggest that these capital inflows potentially represent a major source of EU economic growth; if so, the eventual benefits to Europe of 1992 could far exceed earlier estimates.

The threat of an EU trade fortress raises additional fears as the prospect of a larger Union grows. The democratization of Eastern Europe and its move toward markets suggest there may be even more members of the EU.[26]

Europeans have promised their overall level of protection will not rise as a result of the 1992 program; but the member states remain divided on the protection issue. Germany, Britain, Denmark, and the Netherlands generally support relatively open trade, while other members, especially France and Italy, lean more toward protection. The protection question is just one issue on which members' interests differ.

One major goal of the European Union has always been its regional policy aimed at development of the declining or less-developed areas within the Union. As Figure 9.6 shows, large areas of Greece, Italy, France, Spain, Portugal, Britain, and Ireland qualify for "structural" aid to areas with per capita GDPs less than 75 percent of the EU average. The Union allocates more than $30 billion in such aid annually. The Maastricht Treaty provided for additional "cohesion funds" to go to poorer areas of the Union. Controversy arises over the design and selection of projects for funding and over the division of power between the individual countries and the Union bureaucracy. Intra-group development aid will become even more controversial when Eastern European countries, which face major development tasks, attain membership.

In general, the issues facing the European Union highlight the fundamental dilemma confronting the world economy: how to capture the gains from international cooperation and trade while maintaining politically acceptable levels of national control over economic, political, and social policy making. This dilemma becomes even more apparent as EU members attempt to move beyond a common market toward the goal of an economic and political union, with a common currency and common macroeconomic policies.

The United States–Israel Free-Trade Area Agreement

In 1985, the United States entered its first bilateral free-trade agreement. A beneficiary of the Generalized System of Preferences and the leading recipient of U.S. development aid, Israel wanted a still closer and more certain trade relationship with the

---

[26]Section 11.9 treats the experience of economies in transition.

Figure 9.5 □ **U.S. and Japanese Foreign Direct Investment in the EC ($ Billions)**

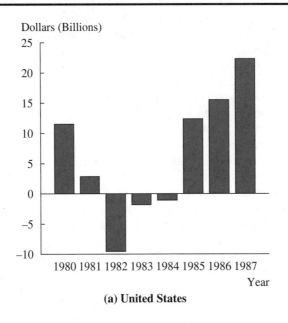

(a) United States

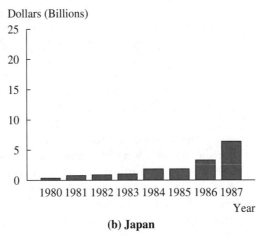

(b) Japan

Source: *The Economist,* July 8, 1989, p. 24; data from U.S. Department of Commerce and Japanese Ministry of Finance.

Figure 9.6 □ **Regions Eligible for Intra-EC Development Aid**

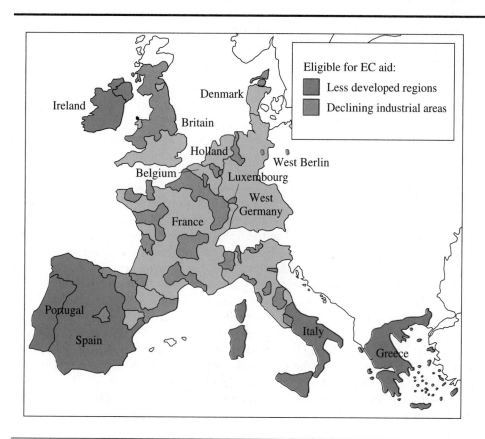

Source: *The Economist,* July 15, 1989, p. 45.

United States.[27] Although most analysts agree the special political relationship between the United States and Israel limits the usefulness of the agreement as an example for future negotiations among other countries, the agreement is notable in several respects.[28]

Unlike other trade agreements, this one removes tariffs on *all* goods; there is no list of exceptions or industries that will maintain protection. The agreement provides for the possibility of exemption for Israel from U.S. escape-clause actions. If a U.S. industry claims injury from imports and the U.S. International Trade Commission finds Israeli exports are not the source of the injury, Israel can be exempted from any

[27]Under the Generalized System of Preferences, the United States grants preferential access to the U.S. market for exports from qualifying developing countries.

[28]Israel also entered a free-trade agreement with the European Community.

tariffs or quotas imposed by the United States to provide relief for the domestic industry. The most interesting part of the agreement from the perspective of the larger world economy was its pioneering effort to extend its coverage to trade in services (such as banking, financial services, insurance, engineering, and consulting), an issue that GATT tackled in the Uruguay Round and faces increasing pressure to address more adequately.

The Canada–United States Free-Trade Agreement

The United States and Canada have the largest bilateral trading relationship in the world, totaling over $200 billion in 1993. A free-trade agreement effective in 1989 negotiated the elimination of all tariffs between the two countries by 1998. Canada's primary goal in seeking the agreement was to secure continued access to the U.S. market.[29] Much of Canadian industry has long depended on protection from U.S. firms, especially in sectors subject to economies of scale but unable to achieve those economies because of the relatively small Canadian market (27 million persons). Other sectors of the Canadian economy, such as steel, newsprint, and aluminum, compete well in world markets. The free-trade agreement exempted relatively few sectors, including unprocessed fish, logs, beer, and the maritime industry.

Besides eliminating tariffs on trade in goods, the agreement provided for a freer flow of investment, business travel, and services and for an innovative process for settling trade disputes.[30] However, Canada and the United States discovered that a free-trade agreement, even between countries with close and friendly political and economic relations, does not end disputes. Recent disagreements include treatment of Canadian lumber exports, U.S. interpretation of the agreement's domestic-content rules for automobiles, Canadian taxation of beer, and U.S. charges of Canadian steel dumping.[31] The Canada–U.S. Free-Trade Agreement was superseded on January 1, 1994, by the North American Free-Trade Agreement, which includes Mexico as a third partner.

North American Free-Trade Agreement

The North American Free-Trade Agreement (NAFTA), linking the United States, Canada, and Mexico, exhibits several unique characteristics. First, the process leading up to the agreement was unusual. Mexico approached the United States about a free-trade agreement after launching a series of economic reforms, including the elimination of its long-standing program of import substitution, in 1987.[32] Shortly thereafter, the United States signed the Canada–United States Free-Trade Agreement. When the United States consented to talks with Mexico, Canada asked to join in a three-way

[29]Beth V. Yarbrough and Robert M. Yarbrough, *Cooperation and Governance in International Trade* treats Canadian and U.S. motivations behind the agreement.

[30]The U.S. International Trade Commission, *Operation of the Trade Agreements Program 1987*, 1-5–1-12, provides historical background on the origins and passage of the bill as well as details of its provisions. Later annual issues of the same publication detail disputes under the agreement.

[31]Details of some of these disputes can be found in section 7.8 and in Cases Four and Five in Chapter Seven.

[32]Section 11.5.1 examines import-substitution development strategies.

Figure 9.7 □ **Trade Flows among the NAFTA Countries, 1992 ($ Billions)**

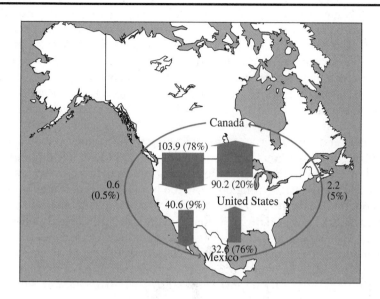

Figures in parentheses report exports as a percent of the originating country's total exports.

Source: *The Economist,* November 13, 1993, p. 26.

---

agreement to reach "from the Yukon to Yucatan." Talks began in February 1991, and the three countries initialed a 2,000-page agreement in August 1992, subject to legislative approval in each country. After a long and controversial approval process, the agreement took effect on January 1, 1994. Figure 9.7 illustrates the pattern of trade among the three NAFTA members.

The NAFTA breaks ground for free-trade agreements because of the very different levels of economic development of its members. Mexico had two primary reasons for desiring such an agreement with the United States. Over 75 percent of Mexican exports come to the United States, so assured access to the market of its large neighbor plays a big role in the long-run viability of the Mexican trade liberalization program. Economic reforms in Mexico have an erratic history; and many such attempts have failed. The agreement with the United States helps demonstrate the Mexican government's commitment to reform and to open trade; such government credibility improves Mexico's ability to attract foreign investment and reestablish creditworthiness after the debt problems of the 1980s. In return for these benefits, Mexico made politically difficult concessions, including opening its markets for financial services, securities, and insurance as well as many parts of its oil industry—a politically sensitive move because the oil industry's nationalization coincided with Mexico's revolution. Mexico also improved the transparency of its trade laws, which, like those in many developing countries, have tended to be ad hoc and arbitrary.

As a large economy, the United States had a substantially smaller stake in an agreement than Mexico, because the bulk of the gains from trade between a large and a small economy go to the smaller economy, as we learned in Chapters Two and Three. Nonetheless, over 80 percent of U.S. exports to Mexico are subject to Mexican tariffs (at an average rate of 10 percent), which will be eliminated by the agreement. With the worst of its debt problems now behind it, Mexico promises to continue to be an important trading partner, especially if its economic reforms take hold and increase per capita incomes, as most analysts predict.

Under the terms of the NAFTA, tariffs on approximately half of members' trade were removed immediately. The remaining tariffs will be removed during a 15-year period. The most sensitive items, on which some tariffs will remain for 15 years, include sneakers, ceramic tile, household glassware, orange juice concentrate, peanuts, broccoli, asparagus, and melons. In agriculture, all existing quotas were converted to equivalent tariffs, and those tariffs will be reduced over 15 years.

One of the stickier negotiating points in the NAFTA involved rules of origin that specify how much North American content a product must contain to qualify for duty-free treatment, especially in automobile, textile and apparel, and television industries.[33] The U.S. auto industry pressed for very high (70 percent) content rules. Canada and Mexico resisted, fearful that such rules would inhibit Japanese auto producers from investing in plants in Canada and Mexico to serve the U.S. market—since such plants typically import many auto parts from Japan. A last-minute compromise set the rules of origin for autos at 62.5 percent of value. In textiles and apparel, textiles must be woven and processed in North America to qualify for duty-free movement; apparel made from qualifying textiles also qualifies.

These stringent rules of origin probably represent the biggest threat for substantial trade diversion from the NAFTA, because they exclude low-cost Asian suppliers of textiles and auto parts. If the Uruguay Round agreement succeeds in dismantling the Multifiber Agreement, freer worldwide trade in textiles will reduce the NAFTA's trade-diversion impact in textiles, but high textile tariffs that will remain after the Uruguay Round imply a residual potential for substantial trade diversion. *(Why?)*

In any free-trade agreement, procedures for settling disputes and escape-clause provisions are two of the key elements. The NAFTA creates the North American Trade Commission, consisting of three cabinet-level officials, to hear disputes. If a member country claims another member's exports injure one of its industries, it can stop its tariff reduction or return to the most-favored-nation (pre-NAFTA) tariff rate for that industry. Each country can do this only one time per industry, and for a maximum period of three years.

Opposition to the NAFTA from pro-protection forces in the United States centered on three issues: the agreement's environmental impact, the effects of differences between labor standards and wages in the United States and Mexico, and the possibility of sudden large import surges from Mexico, particularly in a few agricultural products. To gain the domestic political support necessary for passage through Congress, the United States negotiated three "side agreements" to cover some of these concerns. The environmental

---

[33]Section 7.8.1 introduces domestic-content rules and rules of origin.

and labor-standard side agreements provide mechanisms to monitor members' compliance with their respective national laws and regulations and procedures for disputes. The side agreements encourage transparency and voluntary compliance and allow fines and trade sanctions only as last resorts and only for certain classes of violations. In the case of sudden and large import surges, the side agreement provides a monitoring system to allow governments to anticipate problems in import-competing industries.

The NAFTA's success, like that of the European Union, has created a waiting list of would-be members throughout the Western Hemisphere. Talks began in mid-1995 for Chile's accession to the agreement. Some analysts expect a free-trade arrangement eventually to include the entire hemisphere.[34]

9.5 Interregional Trade

National boundaries distinguish inter*regional* from inter*national* trade. When boundaries change, formerly interregional trade becomes international, or vice versa. Trade between Russia and Ukraine, interregional during the Soviet Union's existence, now is international trade. And, in 1997, when Hong Kong becomes part of China, the trade between the two will switch from international to interregional. Historically, most periods of widespread changes in national boundaries have coincided with major wars; for example, the end of the Second World War brought dramatic changes to the map of Europe. More recently, an unusual number of border adjustments have occurred peacefully, including the unification of Germany and the breakup of Czechoslovakia.

National boundaries are somewhat arbitrary from the perspective of the organization of economic activity.[35] Economic interaction between Toronto and Detroit dwarfs that between Toronto and Vancouver, or between Detroit and Seattle. Although economic activity across national borders sometimes exceeds the level of activity within borders, political boundaries do have major economic significance, as we shall see in Case Two. Economic policies, laws, tastes, currencies, and economic and political systems are just a few of the dimensions on which political borders matter.

Trade barriers, in particular, influence the spatial organization of economic activity. Regions within a country (that is, areas within which relatively free trade prevails) typically exhibit greater specialization than do countries themselves, in part because national trade barriers preclude countries' further specialization.

9.5.1 The Role of Factor Mobility

Another dimension of economic policy that distinguishes interregional from international trade patterns is factor mobility.[36] Labor and capital move more easily within than between countries because of both natural and policy-induced barriers

---

[34]See Case Four.

[35]Sometimes, however, economic considerations help explain changes in national boundaries; see, for example, Beth V. Yarbrough and Robert M. Yarbrough, "International Contracting and Territorial Control: The Boundary Question," in the chapter references.

[36]Jacob Viner, writing in 1937, emphasized the role of factor immobility in distinguishing international trade.

to inter-country mobility. The high rate of factor mobility within a national economy carries an important implication: Because factors tend to flow out of the low-productivity regions within an economy, reduced wages or returns to capital cannot offset low factor productivity.

Consider a simple example in which labor is the only input. There are two geographical areas, A and B. First, assume A and B represent countries between which labor cannot move. Labor in country A is more productive than labor in country B. This results in a situation identical to Chapter Two's Ricardian model. B's relatively unproductive labor still can compete with country A's more productive labor, at least in some goods, by accepting lower wages that reflect the lower productivity.[37] This is just comparative advantage again. Even if B's labor is less productive than A's in every industry, B still can export those goods in which B's labor is *relatively* productive.

Now, introduce one change. Areas A and B now represent regions within a single country, so labor can move easily between the two. But labor in A remains more productive than labor in B. A wage differential no longer will allow area B to produce and export goods to area A, because labor flows from B to A in response to the higher wages. Factors migrate from the low-productivity to the high-productivity area, instead of remaining in the low-productivity area and accepting a lower wage. This mobility improves efficiency because the labor moves to the area where it can be more productive, but less productive regions are abandoned.

Of course, factors of production are neither perfectly immobile between countries nor perfectly mobile within countries. Given a pattern of productivity differences across two geographic areas, the higher the factor mobility between the two, the more equal the wages and the more unequally dispersed the population. The lower the degree of factor mobility, the bigger the wage differential and the more equally dispersed the population.

9.5.2 The Role of Economic Policy

The majority of government policies with greatest relevance for trade are defined at the national level. U.S. imports pay the same tariff whether they land at New York or at San Francisco. Occasionally, however, governments show their ambivalent feelings toward trade by applying different trade rules in different regions of a country. Such policies are used most often by policy makers with histories of relatively closed, inward-looking economic policies who recognize the need to allow more trade to improve economic performance but are hesitant to give up the control that closed borders imply.

The most common forms of subnational trade policy are special economic zones or export-processing zones. **Special economic zones (SEZ)** typically allow more generous rules for trade and for inward foreign direct investment than apply in the rest of the country. The goal is to encourage such investment, which brings access to foreign technology, manufacturing expertise, and knowledge of world export markets.

---

[37]On the role of wage differentials in Ricardian comparative advantage, see sections 2.5.3 and 2.6.3.

Foreign firms investing in such zones may receive exemption from certain taxes or minimum wage laws, as well as reduced site-rental charges and other inducements. **Export-processing zones** concentrate on attracting firms that assemble products for export. These zones provide low-cost infrastructure such as port facilities, power supplies, and rail connections. Tariff exemptions, particularly on imported inputs, also play an important role. Mexico's *maquiladora* program, which provides duty-free export processing sites along the United States–Mexico border (examined in Case Three of Chapter Ten), is one example.

Some of the most dramatic examples of special economic zones come from China. They are particularly interesting because they link particular provinces of China economically with more open nearby economies such as Taiwan and Hong Kong. Fujian and Guandong provinces, on China's south coast, received designation as experimental reform regions in 1978, when China first began opening up to the world economy. Since, the Chinese government has created several additional zones; their economic success, along with rapidly rising incomes, has created pressure to allow the trade reforms to spread to the rest of the economy.

The most successful zone is the Greater South China Economic Region, which encompasses Guandong and Fujian provinces, Hong Kong, and Taiwan. Businesses in the zone combine China's cheap labor and land with Hong Kong's marketing links and transportation network, and with Taiwan's capital, manufacturing technology, and management skills. Shoes and toys comprise large shares of production in the region.

Latin American and other Asian economies also created many special economic zones and export-processing zones during the 1980s. The zones played an important role in demonstrating the potential of open international trade for raising incomes and allowing developing economies to move into manufacturing. As we mentioned in the case of China, the success of open regions within the economy typically creates political pressure for national policy reform. As many developing and transitional countries open their economies to international trade, the significance of their special zones declines. For example, the liberalization of Mexico's trade policy and the provisions of the NAFTA eliminate the special role for the *maquiladora* program.

 ## Case One
Is the United States a Common Market?

The U.S. Constitution specifies: "No State shall, without the consent of the Congress, lay any imposts or duties on imports or exports, except what may be absolutely necessary for executing its inspection laws." This provision of the Constitution makes the United States a common market as defined in section 9.4.1. The writers of the provision were careful to permit policies that might be necessary to enforce safety and health standards. The most common use of such standards is by the fruit- and vegetable-producing states to prevent the transport of pests and diseases that could cause extensive crop damage or endanger public health. One recent example was the temporary prohibition on Florida citrus exports during that state's citrus canker epidemic.

Although many such policies reflect legitimate health and safety concerns, a number appear to contain elements of protectionism as well. For almost 50 years (1925–1973), California residents could not buy Florida-grown avocados because a California law required avocados to contain at least 8 percent oil, more than most Florida avocados contain. Texas residents could not buy grapefruit from Florida, which Texas growers claimed contained insufficient sugar.[38] The main effect of these laws was to protect in-state growers from "foreign" (out-of-state) competition.

South Dakota, Nebraska, and Iowa recently sought to ban all imports of hogs from Canada, a major supplier of pork to those states, on grounds that the hogs were treated with an unapproved antibiotic. During the same period, farmers in the three states complained about the price-depressing effect of Canadian hog exports. The protectionist interpretation of the import restriction received support when certification by veterinarians that the Canadian hogs did not contain the antibiotic was rejected as grounds for ending the ban.

The Canadian hog case is just one example of a number of instances in which states have sought to institute their own independent trade policies, either international or interstate. Most states have professional licensing requirements (for doctors, dentists, beauticians, lawyers, and so forth) that effectively restrict interstate competition. Banking and insurance industries historically have been subject to laws prohibiting interstate expansion, although these laws have been relaxed in the last few years. A number of states maintain "buy within the state" laws, which give in-state companies preference in bidding for state contracts.

In all, trade within the United States is subject to much less restriction than is international trade. Nonetheless, the constitutional prohibition on trade policies by individual states has not made the United States a perfect common market.

Case Two
The Economic Significance of Political Boundaries

The United States and Canada enjoy strong similarities in language, culture, and economic, legal, and political institutions. The two countries trade more with each other than with any other partner. Figure 9.8 reports the location of economic activity in the two countries. The size of each circle represents the GDP of the corresponding

---

[38]Steven G. Craig and Joel W. Sailors, "Interstate Trade Barriers and the Constitution," in the chapter references.

Figure 9.8 □ **Economic Map of North America**

Canadian province

U.S. state

Area of circle proportional to GDP

Source: John McCallum, "National Borders Matter: Canada–U.S. Regional Trade Patterns," *American Economic Review* 85 (June 1995), p. 618.

province or state. Much of each country's manufacturing capacity is centered in the east, northeast in the United States and the southeast in Canada. If a person unfamiliar with the two countries were asked to sketch in a national border on the map, he or she probably would guess that the border ran north-south, placing the entire eastern seaboard economic cluster in one country.

However, a careful study of Canada–U.S. trade suggests that the national border continues to exert a strong influence on patterns of imports and exports. Holding constant incomes and distance, trade between two Canadian provinces averages more than 20 times the level of trade between a province and an American state. The provinces exhibit significant differences in the orientation of their trade, as Table 9.3 reports. Ontario has the highest level of economic interaction with the United States. This reflects, in large part, the close integration of the automobile industry, which spans Toronto and Detroit. The 1965 Auto Pact encouraged trade and foreign investment in the auto industry and predated the Canada–U.S. Free-Trade Agreement by over 20 years. British Columbia, far from Canada's eastern economic center, has the highest level of trade with the rest of the world.

Evidence also suggests, however, that integration agreements affect the pattern of trade across national borders. Since the Canada–U.S. Free-Trade Agreement took effect, Canadian exports to the United States in industries liberalized by the agreement increased 33 percent between 1989 and 1992. Canadian exports of those same products to the rest of the world rose by only 2 percent over the same period. Canadian imports from the United States in liberalized industries grew by 28 percent, compared with 10

Table 9.3 □ **Canadian Goods Shipments by Destination, 1988**

Provincial Origin	Shipments ($ Billions)	Destination (Percent of Total Shipments)			
		Own Province	Other Provinces	United States	Rest of World
Canada	387	44	23	24	9
Atlantic provinces	18	37	29	19	15
Quebec	85	47	27	19	7
Ontario	179	45	21	29	5
Prairie provinces	67	41	28	18	13
British Columbia	37	43	13	19	25

Source: John McCallum, "National Borders Matter: Canada–U.S. Regional Trade Patterns," *American Economic Review* 85 (June 1995), p. 618.

percent for imports from other countries. And a U.S. Department of Commerce study found that in 45 of 98 product categories in which the agreement cut tariffs, U.S. exports to Canada increased by over 100 percent between 1987 and 1991.[39]

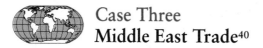

Case Three
Middle East Trade[40]

Since the Israeli occupation in 1967, most of the economic growth in the West Bank and Gaza has come from earnings of Palestinian workers employed in Israel and in the Persian Gulf countries, especially Kuwait. Recently, the influx of immigrants to Israel from other areas such as the former Soviet Union, continued security concerns, and the aftermath of the Gulf War have curtailed these employment possibilities and created a need for alternate sources of economic growth and development. The West Bank and Gaza economies are tiny, so inward-looking policies that focus on the domestic market offer poor prospects. A 1993 report by 30 Israeli, Jordanian, and Palestinian economists recommended free trade among Israel, Jordan, and the West Bank and Gaza as a basis for economic development and improved prospects for peace.

For almost 30 years, Israeli goods entered the occupied territories duty-free, while agricultural products, especially vegetables, from the territories faced strict Israeli import barriers. Extensive Israeli subsidies to its domestic agriculture limited still fur-

---

[39]*The Economist,* January 14, 1995, 26.

[40]Material for this case comes from the Nashashibi and Kanaan article in the chapter references.

ther Palestinian products' access to the Israeli market.

A 1994 peace accord between Israel and Jordan granted Palestinians free trade with Israel and the potential for free trade with Jordan. The 1994 Protocol on Economic Relations between Israel and the West Bank and Gaza sets Palestinian tariffs on most goods at rates equal to Israeli tariffs; so the U.S.–Israel and EU–Israel Free-Trade Agreements mean Palestinians have duty-free access to nonagricultural imports from the United States and the European Union. However, the protocol limits Palestinian imports from Arab countries, restricts Arab sources for some goods to Egypt or Jordan, and fails to eliminate Israeli nontariff trade barriers and domestic subsidies.

Case Four
Free Trade in the Americas

In December 1994, leaders of 34 countries met at the Summit of the Americas in Miami to proclaim interest in building a free-trade area throughout the Americas, including over 800 million consumers, by the year 2005.[41] The region already contains numerous regional groupings, the most active of which are illustrated in Figure 9.9; and countries throughout the hemisphere made a dramatic move during the 1980s from inward-looking protectionist trade regimes to openness to the world economy. The Andean Group and the Central American Common Market date from the 1960s, when most members still followed protectionist policies that emphasized industrialization at any cost and regardless of comparative advantage. Predictably, under such circumstances, the groups failed. Recent relaunches of the groups, whose members now pursue much more open trade policies, hold more promise. The NAFTA, MERCOSUR, and the Group of Three are new groups created in the context of members' trade liberalization and policy reform.

The United States already grants duty-free or reduced-duty access to many products from 24 Caribbean countries under the 1984 Caribbean Basin Economic Recovery Act. And in 1991, the United States agreed to provide duty-free access to a subset of imports from Bolivia, Colombia, Ecuador, and Peru in order to encourage economic development as an alternative to illegal narcotics production. U.S. exports to Latin America more than doubled between 1985 and 1993, from $30 billion to almost $80 billion.

Among the many road blocks facing a potential Free-Trade Area of the Americas will be how to harmonize the various groups' diverse rules, procedures, and exceptions into a workable whole.

---

[41]Only Cuba, the Western Hemisphere country without a democratically elected government, was excluded.

Figure 9.9 □ **Integration Groups in the Americas**

Source: *The Economist*, June 18, 1994, p. 47.

Summary

Within each economy, a complex political bargaining process determines national trade policy. The history of international trade relations chronicles the interaction of nations' political and economic self-interests. Despite the dominance of nations in the world economy, political boundaries remain somewhat arbitrary from the standpoint of organization of economic activities. This has resulted in the evolution of economic institutions, such as economic integration groups, that extend beyond the boundaries of a single nation.

Looking Ahead

In Chapter Ten, we relax the assumption that each country contains a fixed quantity of capital and labor to be allocated among industries. We examine the implications of economic growth, international labor migration, and capital flows. Free movement of factors of production generates distributional effects similar to those of free movement of goods and services. These distributional consequences create pressures for policies that restrict the international mobility of both capital and labor.

Key Terms

Section 201
mercantilism
specie
purchasing power
Smoot-Hawley tariff bill of 1930
Reciprocal Trade Agreements Act
    (RTAA)
International Monetary Fund (IMF)
World Bank
General Agreement on Tariffs and
    Trade (GATT)
escape clause
Trade Expansion Act of 1962 (TEA)
Multifiber Agreement (MFA)
Kennedy Round
Trade Act of 1974
Tokyo Round
Trade Agreements Act of 1979

Trade and Tariff Act of 1984
Uruguay Round
Omnibus Trade and Competitiveness Act
    of 1988
fast track
integration
preferential trading arrangement (PTA)
free-trade area
customs union
common external tariff (CET)
common market
economic union
trade diversion
trade creation
special economic zone (SEZ)
export-processing zone

Problems and Questions for Review

1. We have seen that trade policy has predictable distributional effects. In particular, protection of a domestic industry tends to help domestic producers in that industry at the expense of domestic consumers. In almost any industry, the number of consumers outweighs the number of producers; and we know that the loss in consumer surplus as a result of protection outweighs the gain in producer surplus. How, then, can we explain the success of domestic producers in winning protection through the political process?

2. What is fast-track authority? Using the political economy of trade policy argument, why might fast-track authority be important to the process of trade liberalization?

3. What are the five levels or stages of economic integration? What are some of the costs and benefits of moving from each stage to the next?

4. Country A is a small country considering joining a free-trade area for trade in good X. The cost of importing a unit of good X from countries that would *not* be members of the potential group is $10 per unit. The cost of importing a unit of good X from countries that would be members of the potential group is $20 per unit. Currently, country A applies a $5 per unit tariff on imports of good X from all sources. If the free-trade group forms, will there be any trade creation? Any trade diversion? Why?

5. Use the illustration of trade creation and trade diversion in Figure 9.4. Under what conditions is trade creation likely to outweigh trade diversion? Under what conditions is trade diversion likely to outweigh trade creation?

6. Several Eastern European transitional economies that hope to gain admission to the European Union have a comparative advantage (relative to current EU members) in agriculture. What are the implications for trade creation and trade diversion if these countries gain admission? What groups would you expect to support and oppose such a move? Why?

7. Suppose a labor-abundant economy that does *not* engage in international trade creates a special economic zone with free trade with the rest of the world. If labor were immobile geographically within the country, what would you expect to happen? If labor were mobile geographically within the country, what would you expect to happen? Why?

8. What was the immediate effect of the breakup of the Soviet Union on measured world exports? What was the immediate effect of the unification of Germany on measured world exports? Explain.

References and Selected Readings

Baldwin, Richard E., and T. Venables. "Regional Economic Integration." In *Handbook of International Economics,* Vol. 3, edited by G. M. Grossman and Kenneth Rogoff, 1597–1644. Amsterdam: North-Holland, 1995.
Advanced, up-to-date survey of the literature on the causes and implications of regional trade groups.

Baldwin, Robert E. *The Political Economy of U.S. Import Policy.* Cambridge, Mass.: MIT Press, 1985.
The institutions involved in the trade policy process in the United States; for all students.

Baldwin, Robert E. "The Political Economy of Trade Policy." *Journal of Economic Perspectives* (Fall 1989):119–136.
More on political economy explanations for protection; for all students.

Blanchard, Olivier, and Lawrence F. Katz. "Regional Evolutions." *Brookings Papers on Economic Activity* 1 (1992): 1–76.
Examination of differential regional performance within the United States; intermediate and advanced.

Collins, Susan M., and Barry P. Bosworth. *The New GATT.* Washington, D.C.: The Brookings Institution, 1994.
Introductory overview of Uruguay Round changes to the GATT system.

Craig, Steven G., and Joel W. Sailors. "Interstate Trade Barriers and the Constitution." *Cato Journal* 6 (Winter 1987): 819–835.
The history of beggar-thy-neighbor policies by states and the Commerce Clause of the Constitution; for all students.

Dadush, Uri, and Dong He. "China: A New Power in World Trade." *Finance and Development* 32 (June 1995): 36–38.
Introduction to China's growing role in trade, including the effect of its special economic zones.

Deardorff, Alan V., and Robert M. Stern, eds. *Analytical and Negotiating Issues in the Global Trading System.* Ann Arbor, Mich.: University of Michigan Press, 1994.
Collection of papers on current international trade issues, many of which played key roles in the Uruguay Round; for intermediate and advanced students.

de Melo, Jaime, and Arvind Panagariya, eds. *New Dimensions in Regional Integration.* Cambridge: Cambridge University Press, 1993.
Excellent collection of intermediate and advanced papers on the recent integration phenomenon.

de Melo, Jaime, and Arvind Panagariya. "The New Regionalism." *Finance and Development* 29 (December 1992): 37–40.
Introductory overview of recent trends in the formation of regional trade groups.

Destler, I. M. *American Trade Politics.* Washington, D.C.: Institute for International Economics, 1995.
A political scientist's analysis of American institutions that make trade policy and how their evolution has affected policy outcomes; for all students.

Federal Reserve Bank of Kansas City. *Policy Implications of Trade and Currency Zones.* Kansas City, Mo.: Federal Reserve Bank of Kansas City, 1991.
Collection of accessible papers on recent trends toward regional free-trade zones.

Feenstra, Robert C. "Estimating the Effects of Trade Policy." In *Handbook of International Economics,* Vol. 3, edited by G. M. Grossman and Kenneth Rogoff, 1553–1596. Amsterdam: North-Holland, 1995.
Advanced, up-to-date survey of the empirical literature on the economic effects of various trade policies.

Fieleke, Norman S. "The Uruguay Round of Trade Negotiations: An Overview." Federal Reserve Bank of Boston *New England Economic Review* (May–June 1995): 3–14.
Accessible overview of the main accomplishments of the Uruguay Round.

Fieleke, Norman S. "The Uruguay Round of Trade Negotiations: Industrial and Geographic Effects in the United States." Federal Reserve Bank of Boston *New England Economic Review* (July–August 1995): 3–12.
Economic effects of the Uruguay Round by industrial sector and state; for all students.

Frankel, Jeffrey, and Miles Kahler, eds. *Regionalism and Rivalry: Japan and the United States in Pacific Asia.* Chicago: University of Chicago Press, 1993.
Collection of papers on Asian economies; intermediate to advanced.

Harmsen, Richard. "The Uruguay Round: A Boon for the World Economy." *Finance and Development* 32 (March 1995): 24–26.
Accessible three-page summary of the Uruguay Round.

Hoekman, Bernard, and Michael Kostecki. *The Political Economy of the World Trading System: From GATT to WTO.* Oxford University Press, 1995.
Excellent introduction to the GATT and WTO, both history and current issues; for all students.

Hufbauer, Gary Clyde, and Jeffrey J. Schott. *NAFTA: An Assessment.* Washington, D.C.: Institute for International Economics, 1993.
Issue-by-issue assessment of NAFTA; for all students.

Hufbauer, Gary Clyde, and Jeffrey J. Schott. *Western Hemisphere Economic Integration.* Washington, D.C.: Institute for International Economics, 1994.
Prospects for extending NAFTA-like agreements to other countries; for all students.

Irwin, Douglas A. "The GATT in Historical Perspective." *American Economic Review Papers and Proceedings* 85 (May 1995): 323–328.
Excellent short article on the role of the GATT in trade liberalization.

Irwin, Douglas A. "The Political Economy of Free Trade: Voting in the British General Election of 1906." *Journal of Law and Economics* 37 (April 1994): 75–108.
Empirical test of political-economy theories of voting; intermediate.

Jackson, John H. *The World Trading System.* Cambridge, Mass.: MIT Press, 1989.
Introduction to the history and structure of the GATT by a leading legal scholar of that institution.

Krugman, Paul. "Growing World Trade: Causes and Consequences." *Brookings Papers on Economic Activity* 1 (1995): 327–377.
Essay on recent trends in world trade; intermediate.

Lipsey, Richard. "The Theory of Customs Unions: A General Survey." *Economic Journal* 70 (1960): 496–513.
A survey of the classic papers that developed the theory of customs unions; for intermediate students.

Low, Patrick. *Trading Free: The GATT and U.S. Trade Policy.* New York: Twentieth Century Fund Press, 1993.
Comprehensive overview of the relationship between the GATT and U.S. trade policy.

Lustig, Nora, et al., eds. *North American Free Trade.* Washington, D.C.: The Brookings Institution, 1992.
Collection of papers on the NAFTA; introductory to intermediate.

Magee, Stephen P., William A. Brock, and Leslie Young. *Black Hole Tariffs and Endogenous Policy Theory.* Cambridge: Cambridge University Press, 1989.
A recent classic on the political economy of protection; for intermediate and advanced students.

Nashashibi, Karim, and Oussama Kanaan. "Which Trade Arrangements for the West Bank and Gaza?" *Finance and Development* 31 (September 1994): 10–13.
Introduction to economic aspects of Middle East peace.

Panagariya, Arvind. "East Asia: A New Trading Bloc?" *Finance and Development* 31 (March 1994): 16–19.
Introduction to the growth of intra-Asian trade.

Panagariya, Arvind. "What Can We Learn from China's Export Strategy?" *Finance and Development* 32 (June 1995): 32–35.
Introduction to China's growing world trade, including the role of special economic zones.

Rodrik, Dani. "Political Economy of Trade Policy." In *Handbook of International Economics,* Vol. 3, edited by G. M. Grossman and Kenneth Rogoff, 1457–1494. Amsterdam: North-Holland, 1995.
Advanced, up-to-date survey of the literature on distributional aspects of trade policy and their implications for the policy process.

Schott, Jeffrey J. *The Uruguay Round: An Assessment.* Washington, D.C.: Institute for International Economics, 1994.
Issue-by-issue assessment of the round's accomplishments and shortcomings; for all students.

Shiells, Clinton. "Regional Trading Blocs: Trade Creating or Diverting?" *Finance and Development* 32 (March 1995): 30–32.
Introductory overview of the arguments for and against regional integration groups.

Staiger, Robert. "International Rules and Institutions for Cooperative Trade Policy." In *Handbook of International Economics,* Vol. 3, edited by G. M. Grossman and Kenneth Rogoff, 1494–1552. Amsterdam : North-Holland, 1995.
Advanced, up-to-date survey of the literature on how rules and institutions at the international level affect national trade policies.

Westhoff, Frank H., Beth V. Yarbrough, and Robert M. Yarbrough. "Preferential Trade Agreements and the GATT: Can Bilateralism and Multilateralism Coexist?" *Kyklos* 47 (1994): 179–195.
Interaction of bilateral and multilateral trade-liberalization agreements; intermediate.

Yarbrough, Beth V. "Preferential Trade Arrangements and the GATT: EC 1992 as Rogue or Role Model?" In *The Challenge of European Integration,* edited by Berhanu Abegaz, et al., 79–117. Boulder, Colo.: Westview Press, 1994.
Overview of the effects of preferential trade agreements on the world trading system; for all students.

Yarbrough, Beth V., and Robert M. Yarbrough. *Cooperation and Governance in International Trade: The Strategic Organizational Approach.* Princeton: Princeton University Press, 1992.
An analysis of bilateralism, minilateralism, and multilateralism in trade policy; for all students.

Yarbrough, Beth V., and Robert M. Yarbrough. "International Contracting and Territorial Control: The Boundary Question." *Journal of Institutional and Theoretical Economics* 150 (March 1994): 239–264.
Examines the role of economics in disputes over national boundaries; for all students.

CHAPTER TEN

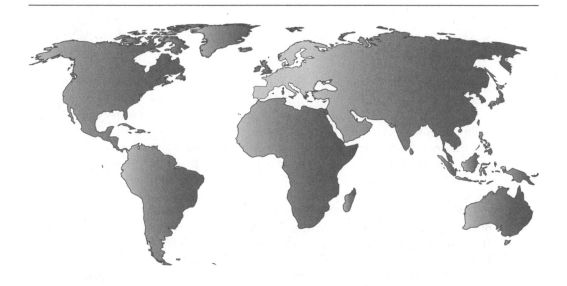

Economic Growth and Factor Mobility

10.1 Introduction

Chapters Two through Nine examined international trade's effects on production, consumption, output and input prices, and the distribution of income under the assumptions of fixed factor endowments and fixed technology. In terms of the schematic diagram in Figure 4.9, factor endowments and technology, along with tastes, form the "given" foundation on which the basic trade model rests. These assumptions seem appropriate for many countries and time periods in which endowments and technology, while not perfectly constant, change slowly. For other periods and countries, changes in endowments and technology lie at the very heart of events in the international economy. The many examples that come to mind include the Industrial Revolution in late eighteenth-century Britain, the massive European immigration to America during the nineteenth century, the worldwide spread of multinational corporations since the Second World War, the increased pace of foreign investment in the United States in the 1980s, and recent immigration waves to the United States and Western Europe. In this chapter, we extend the basic trade model to consider issues related to economic growth and factor mobility.

Thus far, we have viewed trade only in static terms—that is, comparing a country's situation under unrestricted trade with its situation at the same time and in the same circumstances but without trade. When we introduce dynamic considerations such as economic growth, the basic characteristics of the world economy, including the pattern of comparative advantage, change over time.[1] These changes can dramatically alter the pattern of trade and governments' policies toward trade. For example, Britain, which came to dominate the world textile industry through the technological advances of the Industrial Revolution, lost that industry to the United States because of changing patterns of comparative advantage. The United States, in turn, lost the textile industry to the labor-abundant countries of Asia. More recently, many U.S. industries now asking for protection from the rigors of foreign competition once were industries of U.S. comparative advantage—not just textiles, but steel, automobiles, televisions, and semiconductor chips.

Economic growth is a complex phenomenon, particularly when viewed as an objective of economic policy making. The debate among economists and policy makers over what types of policies promote economic growth has been long and lively. In this chapter, our perspective differs from that of a policy maker interested in promoting economic growth. We are interested primarily in the *effects* of growth rather than how to bring it about; in fact, we shall discover that some kinds of economic growth may not be desirable. In Chapter Eleven, we shall examine the pursuit of growth from the viewpoint of developing countries.

For our purposes, we can define **economic growth** as any shift outward in a country's production possibilities frontier. Any change that allows the economy to produce a larger quantity of goods (that is, more of one good and no less of any other) represents economic growth. Recall from the discussion of production possibilities frontiers in Chapters Two and Three that the position of a country's frontier depends on the endowment of productive resources and on the technology with which those resources can be transformed into goods. The major sources of economic growth, then, are (1) increases in the quantities of inputs or resources available to the country and (2) technical progress, or improvements in available production technology. Empirical evidence suggests increases in resources have accounted for somewhat less than half of economic growth in the modern period, and technical progress for somewhat more than half.

Early economic growth theories focused on increases in stocks of labor and capital, but more recent work emphasizes the role of knowledge and education in the technical progress that generates economic growth.[2] Called **endogenous growth theory**, these new approaches to growth recognize knowledge as an input, along with capital and labor, in an economy's ability to produce goods and services. An economy

---

[1] The analysis of economic growth provides an example of comparative-static rather than dynamic analysis. Comparative-static analysis involves a comparison of the pre-growth and post-growth equilibria in the economy. A true dynamic analysis also would examine the path along which the economy moves from the old equilibrium to the new one. Dynamic analysis lies beyond the scope of this book.

[2] The key citations are Robert M. Solow, "A Contribution to the Theory of Economic Growth," *Quarterly Journal of Economics* 70 (1956), 65–94; and Paul M. Romer, "Endogenous Technological Change," *Journal of Political Economy* 98 (1990), S71–S102, respectively.

Figure 10.1 □ **Growth Rates for 114 Countries, 1960–1985**

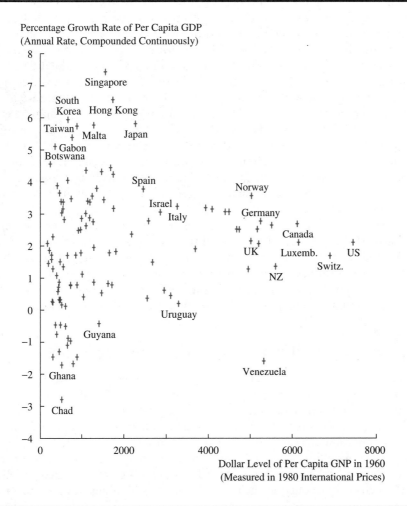

Source: Gene M. Grossman and Elhanan Helpman, *Innovation and Growth in the Global Economy* (Cambridge, Mass.: MIT Press, 1991), p. 3; data from Robert Summers and Alan Heston, "A New Set of International Comparisons of Real Product and Price Levels: Estimates of 130 Countries," *The Review of Income and Wealth* 34 (1988), pp. 1–25.

produces knowledge by investing in education and research, which requires forgoing current consumption, just as investing in physical capital does. Unfortunately, economists' understanding of the growth process, especially the role of knowledge creation, still has a long way to go. Growth rates among countries differ dramatically (see Figure 10.1) for reasons not fully understood, although many economists agree that governments' policy choices play a major role in explaining differential growth rates.

As noted in Chapters One and Nine, the assumption that factors of production move much more freely within than among countries seems realistic. Although a significant amount of inter-country factor movement does occur, it remains small relative to intra-country movement. This holds true for two basic reasons. First, most governments maintain some restrictions on flows of both capital and labor across their national boundaries. The United States, for example, restricts immigration of labor, and Mexico imposes limits on foreign-owned production facilities. Second, even without such government restrictions, the differences in costs involved in inter-country versus intra-country mobility would produce a differential rate of movement. In the case of labor, some of the additional costs of inter-country mobility might include the costs—both financial and psychological—of overcoming language and cultural barriers. In the case of capital, additional costs could take the form of risks associated with owning capital in a foreign country (such as the risk of nationalization or expropriation). The important point is that, as long as political boundaries continue to have economic significance, inter-country mobility will remain less than intra-country mobility.

Factor mobility among countries raises issues similar to those surrounding economic growth. We can view factor mobility as simultaneous positive growth in one country (the country of immigration, or host) and negative growth in another (the country of emigration, or source). Because factor mobility raises additional distributional issues, we shall separate the discussions of growth (sections 10.2 and 10.3) and factor mobility (section 10.4), despite the close relationship between the two.

10.2   Factor Endowment-Based Economic Growth

Economists classify economic growth resulting from increased factor endowments according to the relative changes in the endowments of capital and labor. A country's labor endowment can grow in three ways. First, the *population* can grow because of an increase in the birth rate relative to the death rate. Second, *immigration* can lead to population changes (to be considered in section 10.4.1). Third, available labor can increase due to a rise in *labor-force participation,* or the proportion of the population in the labor force. A nation's capital stock is its accumulation of durable factors of production such as machines and buildings. Capital accumulates whenever a country's residents choose to consume less than the total amount of current production, setting a portion of output aside for increasing future production capacity.

10.2.1   Effects of Balanced Growth

Economists refer to a proportional increase in a country's endowments of both capital and labor as **balanced growth.** Such growth generates an outward shift of the production possibilities frontier that maintains its original shape, as Figure 10.2 illustrates. The country in the figure is assumed to be small in the sense that it cannot alter the international terms of trade. When both goods exhibit constant returns to scale, the production possibilities frontier shifts outward in the same proportion as

Figure 10.2 □ **Effects of Balanced Growth**

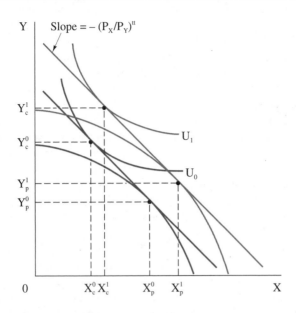

Production and consumption of each good, imports, exports, and the volume of trade all increase in the same proportion as the factor endowments. The country superscript is omitted for simplicity. Subscript p refers to *production*, c to *consumption*, 0 to pre-growth, and 1 to post-growth.

the increase in the factor endowments, because constant-returns-to-scale production means that output increases proportionally with a proportional increase in all inputs. For example, after a doubling of the endowments, the new frontier intersects both axes at points twice as far from the origin as the original frontier.

Balanced growth increases production of both goods, consumption of both goods, imports, and exports proportionally with the endowments. Balanced growth has a neutral **production effect,** because output of each good increases proportionally at unchanged relative output prices or terms of trade. The **consumption effect** of balanced growth also is neutral, because consumption of each good increases in equal proportion. The combination of neutral production and consumption effects implies that balanced growth also exhibits a neutral **volume-of-trade effect.** In other words, balanced growth increases the volume of imports and the volume of exports in the same proportion as the increased endowments.

How does balanced growth affect welfare? It is tempting to answer quickly that welfare increases—based on the rise in consumption of both goods. Such a reply, however, would ignore that the country's population also may have increased. *Total* consumption of both goods has risen, but now that total may be spread across a larger population. If the increased availability of labor that led to growth was due to an increase in population, *per capita* consumption (that is, total consumption divided by population) would not change under balanced growth with constant terms of trade. *(Why?)* But if the increased availability of labor resulted from increased labor-force participation, per capita consumption would rise. Individuals who previously had consumed but not produced (nonparticipants in the labor force) now would produce as well as consume, allowing per capita consumption to rise. Economists call growth's effect on per capita consumption at unchanged terms of trade the **income effect** of growth. The income effect of balanced growth equals zero if labor growth comes from population growth and is positive if labor growth comes from increased labor-force participation.

For a small country, the income effect captures the entire impact of growth. For a country large enough to affect the international terms of trade, the income effect is only one of two components of growth's effect on welfare. The second component, the **terms-of-trade effect,** captures the effect of changes in relative output prices. A country's terms of trade just equal the price of its export good(s) relative to the price of its import good(s). If country A exports X and imports Y, its terms of trade are $(P_X/P_Y)^{tt}$. Decreases in this ratio represent deterioration in the terms of trade, while increases represent improvement in the terms of trade. If country B exports Y and imports X, its terms of trade are $(P_Y/P_X)^{tt}$, or the reciprocal of A's terms of trade. Deterioration in a country's terms of trade reduces the country's total consumption, because the country receives fewer units of the import good in exchange for each unit of the export good. Because balanced growth causes a country to want to engage in a larger volume of trade at the original terms of trade, the relative price of the country's import good rises (because of increased demand) and that of its export good falls (because of increased supply). This change in relative prices represents a deterioration in the terms of trade from the growing country's perspective and an improvement in the terms of trade for the trading partner. Note this implies that balanced growth in a large country improves the welfare of its trading partner. The trading partner experiences no income effect and a positive terms-of-trade effect.

Figure 10.3 shows the effects of a deterioration in the growing country's terms of trade. At constant terms of trade, given by $(P_X/P_Y)^{tt}_0$, balanced growth would move the country from U_0 to U_1. Note that the increase in total consumption does not necessarily translate into an increase in per capita consumption because U_0 and U_1 may be drawn for different population sizes. For a large country, balanced growth increases the desired volume of trade at the original terms of trade and causes the terms of trade to deteriorate to $(P_X/P_Y)^{tt}_1$. This terms-of-trade effect moves the country to U_2. Thus, the welfare effects of balanced growth are less encouraging for a large country than for a small one. The net effect of balanced growth on per capita consumption in a large country depends on (1) the source of the growth in the labor endowment (population versus labor-force participation), and (2) the relative magnitudes of the income and terms-of-trade effects.

10.2.2 Effects of Labor Endowment Growth

An increase in the labor endowment with a constant capital endowment shifts the production possibilities frontier asymmetrically. The shift exhibits a bias

Figure 10.3 □ **Effect of Deterioration in the Terms of Trade**

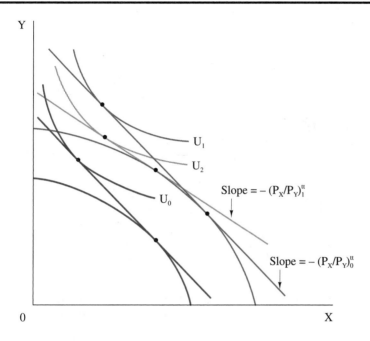

Balanced growth shifts the production possibilities frontier outward, increasing utility from U_0 to U_1 at unchanged output prices. The increased volume of trade deteriorates the terms of trade from $(P_X/P_Y)_0^{tt}$ to $(P_X/P_Y)_1^{tt}$ and lowers utility to U_2.

toward production of the labor-intensive good, assumed in Figure 10.4 to be good X. The intersection of the new production possibilities frontier with both axes shifts outward, reflecting the fact that the additional labor could be used to produce more of the capital-intensive good, Y, but the shift along the X axis is larger. The economy's overall capital-labor ratio falls. The effect on the economy of a decline in the capital-labor ratio depends on whether the country imports or exports the labor-intensive good and on the impact on the international terms of trade.

First, consider the effect on a small country. In Figure 10.4, the increased labor endowment causes such a country to increase production of the labor-intensive good and reduce production of the capital-intensive good, as represented by the move from point I to point II. This somewhat peculiar-sounding result provides an example of the **Rybczynski theorem.** The theorem states that when the terms of trade are held constant (as in a small country), an increase in the endowment of one factor with the other factor endowment held constant increases production

Figure 10.4 □ Effect of Labor Endowment Growth on the Production Possibilities Frontier

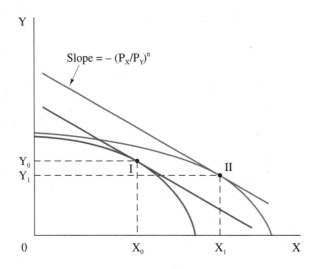

Good X is assumed to be the labor-intensive good. With a constant capital endowment, output of the labor-intensive good rises more than proportionally with the labor endowment and output of the capital-intensive good falls.

of the good intensive in the increased factor and decreases production of the good intensive in the constant factor.[3]

Why would economic growth cause a country to reduce production of one of the two goods? To take advantage of the increased availability of labor and increase output of the labor-intensive good, the labor-intensive industry must obtain some additional capital, because even the labor-intensive industry uses some capital along with labor. With the country's endowment of capital held constant, the only source of additional capital is that employed in the capital-intensive industry. Therefore, the capital-intensive industry must reduce its output somewhat to facilitate the expansion of the labor-intensive industry made possible by the increased endowment of labor.

---

[3]Using more advanced techniques, we could demonstrate a much more general form of the Rybczynski theorem. For any change in factor endowments at unchanged output prices, the output of the labor-intensive commodity always changes proportionally more than the endowment of labor. If the endowment of labor increases, the output of the labor-intensive good increases by a larger percentage. If the endowment of labor decreases, output of the labor-intensive industry shrinks by a larger percentage. Similarly, output in the capital-intensive industry changes proportionally more than the capital endowment. In Figure 10.4, output of good Y must shrink because the rate of growth of the capital endowment is zero. This phenomenon provides another example of the magnification effect discussed in Chapter Four.

Growth of the labor endowment creates a production effect biased toward the labor-intensive good; output of the labor-intensive good rises relative to output of the capital-intensive good. If the labor-intensive good is the country's export good, the production effect tends to increase the volume of trade and is referred to as *export expanding*. If the labor-intensive good is the country's import good, increased domestic production reduces desired imports and the production effect is *import replacing*.

The pattern of domestic consumption of the two goods also influences the net effect of labor growth on trade. When domestic consumption of the import good rises relative to that of the export good, the consumption effect is export expanding—that is, it represents a force that tends to increase the volume of trade. If consumption of the export good rises relative to that of the import good, the volume of trade falls and the consumption effect is import replacing. The total effect of labor endowment growth on the volume of trade depends on the combination of the production and consumption effects; the volume of trade can rise, fall, or remain unchanged.

Economic growth based on an increased population coupled with a constant endowment of capital generally creates a negative income effect. The increased population implies that each worker now has less capital with which to work, so the marginal product of labor falls. Total consumption rises, but at a lower rate than the population growth; thus, per capita consumption falls. As in the case of balanced growth, the income effect changes if the increased availability of labor comes from greater labor-force participation rather than increased population. Population increases produce negative income effects, that is, declines in per capita consumption at unchanged terms of trade. In contrast, increased labor-force participation results in positive income effects, or increases in per capita consumption.

For a large growing country, the impact of labor endowment growth on the terms of trade is uncertain. If the volume-of-trade effect is export expanding, growth tends to worsen the terms of trade by increasing the supply of the export good and demand for the import good. On the other hand, if the volume-of-trade effect is import replacing, the terms of trade improve as the supply of the export good falls along with the demand for imports. Therefore, the total effect of labor growth on per capita consumption in a large country is ambiguous for three reasons: (1) The income effect of growth depends on whether the labor growth comes from a growing population or increased labor-force participation; (2) the effect of labor growth on the volume of trade, and therefore on the terms of trade, is ambiguous; and (3) if the income and terms-of-trade effects work in opposite directions, either effect may dominate. When a large country grows, its trading partners experience a terms-of-trade effect but no income effect. Therefore, export-expanding growth in one country helps its trading partners, while import-replacing growth harms them.

10.2.3 Effects of Capital Endowment Growth

The overall effects of growth due to an increased endowment of capital in a large country are ambiguous, as in the case of labor-based growth. The major change in the analysis is a definitely positive income effect on per capita consumption in the case of capital-based growth. Total consumption rises, and, because the population does not change, a rise in per capita consumption follows. In a small country, in which growth generates no terms-of-trade effect, capital-based growth must increase per capita consumption. In a large country, the terms-of-trade effect can be either positive or negative, making the overall effect of growth uncertain. If both the production and consumption effects are import replacing, the terms of trade improve and the overall effect of growth on welfare is positive.

10.2.4 Immiserizing Growth

For many years, economists have recognized the possibility that increased production may lower welfare through its deteriorating effect on the terms of trade. In 1956, Jagdish Bhagwati rigorously analyzed this situation and named it **immiserizing growth.** Sections 10.2.1, 10.2.2, and 10.2.3 covered several cases in which economic growth lowers per capita consumption. We might expect such a result when growth takes the form of a growing population. The case of immiserizing growth as developed by Bhagwati is somewhat more surprising in its implication that growth may lower per capita consumption even if the population remains constant.

The source of immiserizing growth is a strongly negative terms-of-trade effect. Therefore, the problem can affect only large countries, which have some influence on international terms of trade. The word *large* can be somewhat deceptive, however. While many developing countries are small in most markets, they may dominate a few world markets, often in primary products. Such countries may be susceptible to immiserizing growth.

The possibility of immiserizing growth is illustrated in Figure 10.5, drawn under the assumption that growth does not result from an increase in population. The move from U_0 to U_1 represents the income effect of growth. Because growth is biased toward production of the export good (X), the country's terms of trade deteriorate sharply, from $(P_X/P_Y)_0^{tt}$ to $(P_X/P_Y)_1^{tt}$, reducing welfare from U_1 to U_2 and leaving the country worse off than in its pre-growth situation (U_0).

Many conditions must be satisfied for the immiserizing-growth result to emerge. First, growth must be relatively modest. If it is substantial, the positive income effect (represented in Figure 10.5 by the move from U_0 to U_1) swamps any negative terms-of-trade effect and growth enhances welfare. Second, the volume-of-trade effect must be strongly positive; growth must significantly increase the supply of a country's exports and demand for its imports. Third, the elasticity of trading partners' demand for the country's exports must be sufficiently low for increased exports to lower their price substantially. Finally, the country must depend heavily on foreign trade so changes in the terms of trade exert a large impact on its welfare. In Chapter Eleven, where we discuss problems facing developing countries, the possibility of chronic deterioration in the terms of trade will play a prominent role. Little evidence, however, suggests immiserizing growth actually occurs; the phenomenon appears more a theoretical possibility than an empirical reality.

Historical periods involving rapid economic growth based solely on increases in factor endowments have been rare. More commonly, periods of rapid growth

Figure 10.5 □ **Immiserizing Growth**

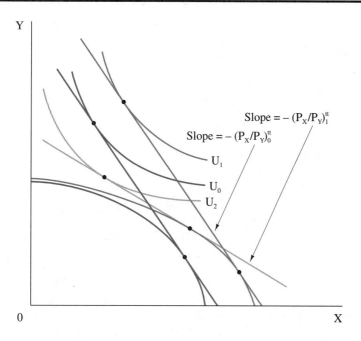

With unrestricted trade, growth at unchanged terms of trade shifts out the production possibilities curve, allowing the country to reach U_1 rather than the pre-growth U_0. If the increased volume of trade significantly worsens the terms of trade, the country may end up on U_2, which lies below U_0.

have followed technological advances or technical progress. Of course, one frequent outcome of technical progress is to turn something not viewed as an important resource into a valuable factor of production (for example, development of the internal combustion engine and the resulting importance of petroleum).

10.3 Economic Growth Based on Technical Progress

Defining and measuring technical progress is difficult. In general, **technical progress** occurs whenever a larger quantity of goods can be produced from a given quantity of resources or, equivalently, a given quantity of goods can be produced from a smaller quantity of inputs. Technical progress involves an increase in the productivity of capital, labor, or both. For small countries, technical progress generates an unambiguously positive welfare effect; per capita consumption rises. For large countries, the income effect of technical progress is unambiguously positive, but the terms-of-trade effect may be negative.

Figure 10.6 ▫ Neutral Technical Progress in the X Industry

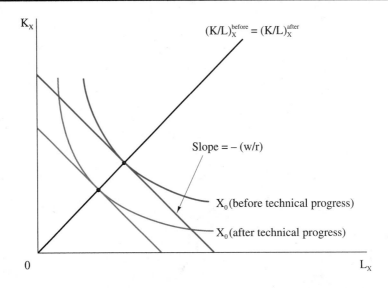

Technical progress shifts the isoquant representing production level X_0 in toward the origin. The isoquant retains its original shape, and firms' capital–labor ratio is unchanged at the old relative factor prices.

10.3.1 Types of Technical Progress

Nobel prize winner Sir John Hicks provided the classification system, known as **Hicksian technical progress,** commonly used by economists for the various types of technical progress. Hicks classified technical progress according to its effect on the cost-minimizing capital–labor ratio that firms choose to use at unchanged factor prices.

Neutral technical progress leaves the chosen capital–labor ratio unchanged. It increases the productivity of both capital and labor proportionally such that at any given capital–labor ratio (K/L) the marginal rate of technical substitution (MRTS) between the two inputs remains unchanged.[4] Figure 10.6 represents neutral technical progress in production of good X. (The reader may want to review the use of isoquants and the firm's choice of the cost-minimizing capital–labor ratio in section 3.2.1.) After the technical progress, smaller bundles of capital and labor than before can produce output X_0, and the new isoquant representing X_0 retains the same shape as the old one. At the same relative factor prices, the firm chooses the same capital–labor ratio as before.

---

[4]By definition, the marginal rate of technical substitution equals the ratio of the *marginal products* of the two inputs ($-[MP_L/MP_K]$), where an input's marginal product equals the increase in output made possible by use of one additional unit of the input with the quantity of the other input held constant. Neutral technical progress raises MP_L and MP_K proportionally, leaving MRTS unchanged.

Figure 10.7 □ **Capital-Saving Technical Progress**

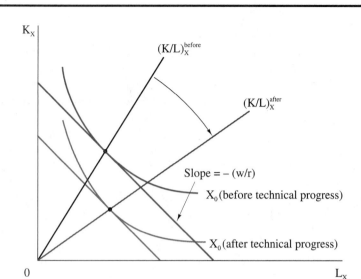

Capital-saving technical progress raises the marginal productivity of labor relative to that of capital. At unchanged factor prices, firms use a lower capital–labor ratio. Along any ray from the origin (for any given K/L), the new isoquant is steeper than the old one.

Capital-saving technical progress raises the marginal productivity of labor relative to the marginal product of capital. At unchanged factor prices, firms choose a lower capital–labor ratio (hence the term *capital-saving*). Graphically, such progress implies that for any given capital–labor ratio (along any ray from the origin), the new isoquant is steeper than the old one because the slope, given by $-(MP_{LX}/MP_{KX})$, is greater (see Figure 10.7).

Note two sources of potential confusion. First, capital-saving technical progress makes an industry more labor intensive. Second, capital-saving technical progress does not save just capital; it saves both capital and labor in the sense that good X now can be produced using less of both types of resources than before. The term *capital-saving* indicates only that firms will employ less capital per unit of labor.

Similarly, **labor-saving technical progress** involves an increase in the marginal product of capital relative to the marginal product of labor. The cost-minimizing capital–labor ratio rises. *(We leave construction of a diagram representing labor-saving technical progress to the reader.)*

10.3.2 Effects of Technical Progress

The fundamental effect of any kind of technical progress on the production possibilities frontier is clear: The frontier shifts outward. The precise nature of the shift, however, depends on several considerations. The frontier represents two industries, each of which can enjoy technical progress of any type and at any rate. For example, industry X might experience rapid capital-saving progress and industry Y slow neutral progress. Because of the many possible combinations, we shall restrict our attention to the case of neutral progress.

In the event that both industries enjoy neutral technical progress at precisely the same rates, the production possibilities frontier shifts out at the rate of the increased productivity while maintaining its original shape. Figure 10.2, drawn to represent balanced factor growth, also can represent neutral technical progress in both industries.

The welfare analysis of balanced growth also carries over, with one important exception. Remember that the income effect of balanced growth equaled zero because population grew at the same rate as output, leaving per capita consumption unchanged.[5] Because neutral technical progress involves productivity growth rather than population growth, the increased output raises per capita consumption. Therefore, neutral technical progress in both industries exerts a definitely positive income effect. For a small country, the income effect constitutes the only component of the welfare impact, and thus the overall impact is favorable. The welfare impact on a large country depends on the relative strengths of the positive income effect and the negative terms-of-trade effect, identical to that in the case of balanced growth.

What if neutral technical progress occurs in only one industry? The intersection of the production possibilities frontier with the axis representing the static industry remains unaltered, while the intersection with the axis representing the industry experiencing progress shifts outward at the rate of the increased productivity. A small country would reduce output in the static industry and increase output of the progressive industry.

Figure 10.8 captures the effect of single-industry neutral progress in a small country. The production point after technical progress must lie to the southeast of the original production point. The slope of the production possibilities frontier represents the opportunity cost of good X in terms of forgone good Y. Neutral technical progress in the X industry reduces the amount of resources required to produce a unit of good X and, therefore, the opportunity cost of good X in terms of good Y. At the point on the new frontier directly to the right of the original production point, the slope of the new frontier must be flatter than that of the old one, and the point on the new frontier with a slope equal to that at the original production point must lie to the southeast.

Again, the welfare effect on the small country is unambiguously positive. Total consumption has risen with an unchanged population, implying increased per capita consumption. For a large country, the total welfare effect is ambiguous because of the possibility of a deterioration in the terms of trade. In theory, technical progress can cause immiserizing growth in a large country. If the progress is strongly biased toward the export good, increased production of that good may lower its price sufficiently to offset the positive income effect on welfare. The conditions discussed in

---

[5]Balanced growth creates a positive income effect if increased labor availability comes from greater labor-force participation rather than population growth.

Figure 10.8 ▫ **Effect of Neutral Technical Progress in the X Industry**

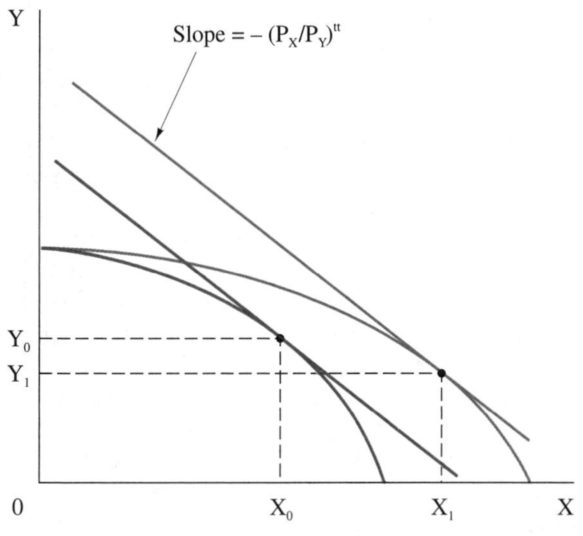

With neutral technical progress in industry X, a small country reduces production of good Y and increases production of good X.

section 10.2.4 as necessary to the immiserizing-growth result apply not only to factor endowment-based growth but to technical progress. Again, little empirical evidence documents actual occurrence of immiserizing growth.

For the trading partners of a large country experiencing technical progress, the welfare effect depends on what happens to the terms of trade. If the terms of trade turn in favor of the country experiencing progress, trading partners suffer. If the progressive country experiences a deterioration in its terms of trade, trading partners benefit from the technical progress.

Thus far, we have analyzed the effects of economic growth in one country by assuming the fundamental situation in the other country remains unchanged, although we have seen that factor endowment growth or technical progress in a large country affects trading partners through the terms-of-trade effect. When factors of production can move between countries, we must extend the analysis to include the direct impacts in both countries.

10.4 Factor Mobility

The basic trade model of Chapters Three and Four assumes factors of production are completely immobile between countries. Nonetheless, with unrestricted trade, factor prices tend to equalize across countries according to the factor price equalization theorem (see section 4.4). Trade in outputs substitutes for trade in factors, because exports of a capital-intensive output essentially are equivalent in their effects to exports of capital.

The link between factor mobility and international trade in goods and services lies at the center of several current international policy debates. Consider the North American Free-Trade Agreement (NAFTA), negotiated by the United States, Canada, and Mexico in 1994. Proponents argued the agreement would enlarge the U.S. market for Mexican goods, raise incomes in Mexico, and decrease Mexican migration, especially illegal migration, to the United States. This view presents trade in goods and services as a substitute for and a desirable alternative to factor mobility. On the other hand, opponents of the agreement claimed firms would move from the United States to Mexico to "exploit" its low-wage labor. Along similar lines, the governments of Western Europe debate whether to lower trade barriers and admit the cheaper products from Eastern Europe or to maintain trade barriers in goods and services and run the risk of massive migration from East to West.

Achievement of complete factor price equalization would remove the major incentive for inter-country factor movements: obtaining higher factor rewards. In this section, we shall see that some reasons for movement would persist for both labor and capital even with complete factor price equalization. The primary cause of factor movements, however, is differences in factor prices across countries. As long as capital or labor earns a higher reward in one country than in another, the incentive for factor movements exists.

Section 4.4 indicated the relatively stringent requirements for complete factor price equalization. For example, the presence of either trade barriers or nontraded goods (such as haircuts) can prevent complete equalization. Trade barriers play a particularly strong role in generating factor movements. The development of U.S. production facilities by Japanese automobile producers provides one outstanding recent example. The United States first subjected imports of Japanese automobiles to voluntary export restraints in 1981, and the Japanese feared even stronger trade restrictions. One way to guarantee continued access to the U.S. market was to build production facilities in the United States—and Japanese auto firms chose to do just that.

The welfare analysis of factor movements involves four questions. First, how does factor movement affect total world output; can factor mobility increase the efficiency of the world economy in a manner similar to trade in outputs? Second, how does factor movement affect the division of welfare between the two countries? Third, how does factor movement affect the distribution of income within each country? And fourth, how does the movement affect the factors that move? The answer to the fourth question is the easiest to predict: Assuming factor movements take place voluntarily, the owners of the factors that move must expect to be better off, or they would not move.

Inter-country movements of capital and movements of labor generate similar effects. However, the particular motivations for movement and some of the issues that arise in response to the movements differ between the two classes of factors. For this reason, we shall analyze separately the effects of labor mobility (section 10.4.1) and capital mobility (section 10.4.2). In recent years, the United States has imported both labor and capital, as summarized in Table 10.1.

Table 10.1 □ **Recent U.S. Factor Flows**

	Immigrants Admitted (Thousands)	Private Capital Flows ($ Millions)	
		U.S. Assets Purchased by Foreigners	Foreign Assets Purchased by U.S. Residents
1960	265	821	5,144
1965	297	607	5,336
1970	373	−550	10,229
1975	386	8,643	35,380
1980	531	42,615	73,651
1985	570	142,301	32,547
1990	1,536[a]	88,282	70,512
1991	1,827[a]	80,935	60,175
1992	974[a]	105,646	63,759
1993	880	159,017	146,213
1994	na	275,702	130,755

[a]Includes persons granted permanent resident status under the legalization program of the Immigration Reform and Control Act of 1986 (see "U.S. Immigration Policy" section below).

Sources: *Statistical Abstract of the United States;* Department of Commerce, *Historical Statistics of the United States: Colonial Times to 1970; Economic Report of the President;* and *Survey of Current Business.*

10.4.1 Inter-Country Mobility of Labor

Labor generally flows less easily than capital across national boundaries. This reflects the special character of labor as a factor of production: A unit of labor is embodied in a human being. The person has tastes and preferences, a culture, a language, and valued friends and family. Individuals do not feel indifferent about where they work or the conditions under which they work; many considerations other than the wage rate enter into the work decision. The owner of a machine, on the other hand, probably does not care about the machine's location or working conditions so long as the equipment is not abused in such a way as to reduce its productivity and value.

Despite the financial and personal costs involved, growing numbers of individuals have chosen to immigrate in recent years. During 1990 and early 1991, an average of 400 persons per day flowed from Romania into Hungary on their way to the West. North Africans comprise a growing share of the population in Europe, including 600,000 Algerians in France. Vietnamese continue to flock to Hong Kong despite the uncertainties associated with the colony's 1997 return to China. Germany took in 4.4 million immigrants in 1992, many of them from the former East Germany. The United States apprehends more than 1 million individuals illegally crossing the Mexican border each year, and experts estimate that only 10 to 50 percent of those who cross illegally are caught. In all these cases, immigration presents political

Figure 10.9 □ **Net International Migration, 1985–1990 (Thousands)**

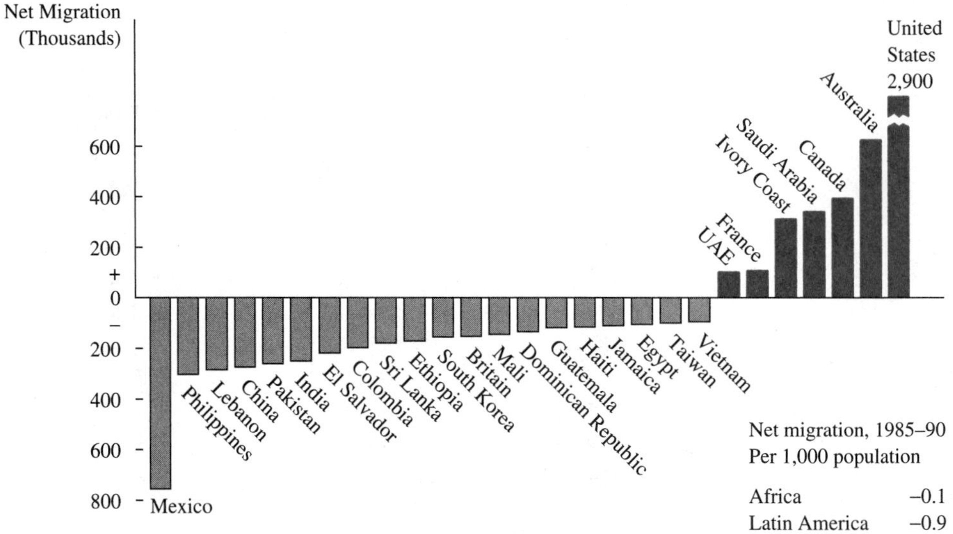

	Net migration, 1985–90 Per 1,000 population	
Africa	−0.1	
Latin America	−0.9	
North America	2.3	
Asia	−0.1	
Europe & USSR	0	
Oceania	4.3	

Source: Gerald Segal, *The World Affairs Companion* (New York: Simon & Schuster, 1991), p. 57; data from World Bank.

problems in the receiving country. Other countries, among them Brazil, Chile, Uruguay, and Paraguay, seek immigrants including those from newly opened countries of Eastern Europe and the former Soviet Union.

Sometimes countries change quickly from exporters of labor to importers, or vice versa. During the 1970s and 1980s, South Korea exported large quantities of labor, reaching a peak of 225,000 workers in 1983. Now, with rapid industrialization, a slowing population growth rate, and rapidly rising wages, South Korea imports workers from China, the Philippines, and Pakistan. Overall, between 1985 and 1990, the United States took in more immigrants than any other country, while Mexico lost the largest number of people (see Figure 10.9).

Incentives for Migration

When labor moves between countries, the reasons can be economic or noneconomic, and often the two are interconnected. The periods of mass migration to America during the nineteenth and twentieth centuries reflected immigrants' desires for religious and political freedom and for the economic freedom to better themselves and improve economic opportunities for their children. These motives remain important today; for example, the

Figure 10.10 □ Effects of Labor Mobility

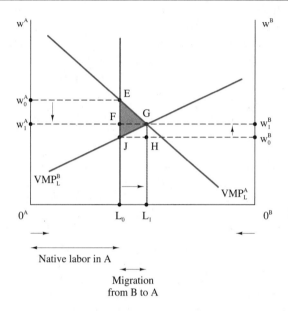

The ability of labor to move from country B to country A in response to a wage differential raises total world output by an amount represented by the area of triangle EGJ. Country A gains, and country B loses. In A capital owners gain relative to labor, and in B workers gain relative to capital owners.

United Nations estimated the worldwide total of refugees at 18 million persons in 1993. Although a complex web of influences determines an individual's decision to move to another country, we shall focus on economic motivations and assume an individual moves when the reward paid to labor is higher in the destination country.

Figure 10.10 provides a convenient guide for analyzing the effects of labor mobility. The world is assumed to be composed of two countries, A and B. The length of the horizontal axis (distance 0^A0^B) represents the total quantity of labor in the world. The two vertical axes measure the wage paid to labor in the two countries (w^A on the left axis and w^B on the right). L_0 represents the initial allocation of labor between countries A and B; so 0^AL_0 units of labor work in A, and 0^BL_0 in B.

In each country, labor earns a wage rate (w) equal to the value of the marginal unit of labor's productivity. The *value* of the *marginal product* of *labor* (VMP_L) equals the marginal product of labor (the number of units of additional output produced when 1 additional unit of labor is employed) multiplied by the price of the good produced. As the quantity of labor increases in a given country, the marginal productivity of labor declines and, with it, the value of that productivity and the wage rate.[6] The

_____

[6]For a review of the law of diminishing returns, see the discussion of Figure 4.6.

curves VMP_L^A and VMP_L^B represent the value of the marginal product of labor in countries A and B, respectively. With the initial allocation of labor between countries, workers in A earn a wage rate of w_0^A and workers in B earn w_0^B. The higher wage in A reflects labor's higher marginal productivity in A (point E) relative to B (point J).

Workers in country B will be tempted to migrate to A to obtain higher wages. This incentive will cause the workers represented by the distance between L_0 and L_1 to move. Once sufficient migration has occurred to reach the new labor allocation at L_1, wage rates in the two countries will equalize at $w_1^A = w_1^B$.

Effects of Labor Migration

Our first task is to determine how labor movements in response to wage differentials affect the efficiency of the world economy. Does such mobility increase or decrease total world output? The shaded area (triangle EGJ) in Figure 10.10 represents an increase in total world output from the mobility of labor. Each unit of labor between L_0 and L_1 produces more in country A than in country B; that the VMP_L^A curve is higher than the VMP_L^B curve throughout the L_0 to L_1 range reflects this productivity differential. Higher wages in A signal to workers the greater value of labor's marginal product in A, attracting them to the area where they will be more productive. As labor is used more efficiently, total output increases.

How are the gains represented by area EGJ divided between countries A and B? The extremely controversial nature of emigration and immigration policies leads us to suspect—correctly—that the gains are not divided equally among all interested parties. Country A as a whole gains from the immigration. The net gain is the sum of gains by capital owners in A, losses by native (pre-immigration) country A workers, and gains by the immigrants themselves. Country B as a whole loses from its emigration, but workers in B gain relative to owners of capital. As we predicted earlier, the immigrants themselves gain.

The net gain to country A equals the sum of the value of the marginal product of all labor units between L_0 and L_1, or area EGL_1L_0. The original work force from A loses area $w_0^A EFw_1^A$ because of the negative effect of immigration on the wage rate. Area FGL_1L_0 represents the income earned by immigrants in country A. Area JHL_1L_0 just replaces the income they could have earned in country B, but FGHJ shows the net increase in income that provided the incentive for migration. Owners of the fixed quantity of capital in A gain as the marginal product of capital rises because of the availability of more labor for use along with the capital.[7] Country B's output falls by JGL_1L_0 as a result of the emigration. Workers who remain in B gain area $Gw_1^Bw_0^BH$ in increased wages, but B's capital owners lose as the marginal product of capital falls. Table 10.2 summarizes these effects.

Opposition to Immigration Policies

The preceding analysis makes clear why labor groups typically favor strong limitations on immigration: Open immigration tends to lower wages of domestic workers

---

[7]Remember that the marginal product of an input measures the change in total output resulting from the use of one more unit of the input with the quantities of all other inputs held constant. The marginal product of an input is increased by availability of a larger quantity of other inputs used together with it; a reduction in the use of other inputs lowers the marginal product.

Table 10.2 □ **Effects of Labor Migration from Country B to Country A**

Effect on	
Capital owners in A	+
Native labor in A	−
Immigrants	+
Net effect on A	+ (area EGL_1L_0)
Capital owners in B	−
Labor remaining in B	+
Net effect on B	− (area JGL_1L_0)
Net effect on world	+ (area EGJ)

who compete with the immigrants in labor markets. When immigrant workers are unskilled, the negative impact on wages affects primarily unskilled domestic workers and other recent immigrants. Recent waves of immigrants to the United States, for example, possess skill levels considerably below those of earlier immigrants.[8] Empirical evidence suggests that in developed countries unskilled migrants sometimes fill jobs not wanted by domestic workers, minimizing the effect of immigration on overall wages. Of course, there also can be noneconomic reasons for opposing open immigration, including cultural prejudice or racism, but even these seemingly noneconomic arguments may reflect fear of the economic effects of immigration.

Another reason for opposition to open immigration has emerged in recent years as governments have taken larger roles in assuring residents minimal levels of food, housing, medical care, education, and income even if they are unable or unwilling to work. Countries that provide generous levels of such social benefits may fear an influx of immigrants who will not work and produce, as did the immigrants in Figure 10.10, but will live on government-provided benefits at the expense of domestic workers and working immigrants.[9] Immigrants to the United States during the 1950s and 1960s did not avail themselves of public assistance at rates exceeding those for domestic residents. However, this no longer is the case. Recent arrivals have drawn public assistance at high rates relative to earlier immigrant arrivals; and their use of public assistance appears to be growing over time.[10] The rate of dependence on public assistance varies widely across source countries. Table 10.3 lists the 21 countries from whom the United States accepted more than 10,000 emigrants each in 1993.

One other issue that adds controversy to immigration policies is developing countries' concerns about **brain drain,** the tendency of the most highly skilled, trained, and

---

[8]See the Borjas articles in the chapter references.

[9]Barry R. Chiswick, "Illegal Immigration and Immigration Control," *Journal of Economic Perspectives* 2 (Summer 1988), 101–115, analyzes of the importance of social welfare policies in evaluating the effects of immigration.

[10]See the Borjas articles in the chapter references.

Table 10.3 □ **Immigration to the United States by Source Country, 1993**

Country	Immigrants
Mexico	109,027
China	65,552
Philippines	63,189
Vietnam	59,613
Dominican Republic	44,886
India	40,021
Poland	27,729
El Salvador	25,517
United Kingdom	18,543
Ukraine	18,316
South Korea	17,949
Canada	17,081
Jamaica	16,969
Iran	14,700
Taiwan	14,309
Cuba	13,650
Ireland	13,575
Colombia	12,512
Russia	12,079
Guatemala	11,269
Peru	10,276

Source: Immigration and Naturalization Service.

educated individuals from developing countries to migrate to the industrialized countries. The developing countries argue they expend scarce resources on the education and training of these individuals only to lose the return on their investment to other nations, particularly the United States. Case One in this chapter examines the economic impacts of the brain drain as well as policy proposals for dealing with it.

U.S. Immigration Policy

Over the last century, U.S. immigration policy changed dramatically four times, affecting both the overall magnitude and the composition of immigration flows. In the late nineteenth century, the United States placed restrictions on many classes of immigration, including an almost total ban on persons from Asia. The 1920s brought a shift in policy; national-origin quotas severely restricted entry for persons from southern and eastern Europe by allocating visas to maintain the ethnic balance of the 1920 U.S. population. By 1965, the national-origin quotas became politically unacceptable, and the government abandoned them in favor of a system that provided easy entry primarily for persons with family ties to U.S. residents.

By the 1980s, immigration controversies in the United States centered squarely on Mexico. U.S. immigration policy vis-à-vis Mexico changed with the 1986 passage of the Immigration Reform and Control Act (IRCA), also known as the Simpson-Rodino bill. The act aimed to eliminate illegal foreign workers, especially those from Mexico, from the U.S. labor market. The Simpson-Rodino bill pursued this aim in two ways. First, the bill granted amnesty to foreign workers who (1) had been in the United States illegally since before 1982 and could document their residence, or (2) had worked in U.S. perishable-crop agriculture for at least 90 days during the previous year. By the end of the program, 3.2 million individuals, 90 percent from Mexico, had gained permanent resident status through the amnesty program. Second, to reduce the demand for illegal labor, the bill imposed penalties known as employer sanctions on firms that hire illegal workers. Agricultural interests incorporated provisions for temporary admission of foreign workers during the harvest season, since foreign workers, most from Mexico and other parts of Central America, harvest many U.S. crops. The bill also bars workers granted legal status under its amnesty provision from receiving welfare benefits for five years.

Although a significant number of illegal workers gained legal status through IRCA provisions, the bill represented an effort at long-run curtailment of labor flows into the United States. The high cost of enforcement, weak penalties imposed on employers found guilty of violations, and the absence of provisions for penalties on illegal workers themselves, however, made many analysts skeptical of the bill's curtailment effects.

Predictably, based on our graphical analysis in Figure 10.10 and on the results reported in Table 10.2, U.S. labor unions found the 1986 bill too weak, believing it allowed too much competition from foreign workers for jobs in the United States. U.S. firms, on the other hand, particularly in industries such as the Los Angeles-based garment industry, found their operations threatened by the reduction in the supply of illegal labor. Many leaders of the Hispanic community also opposed the bill's provisions for penalties on firms that hire illegal workers, fearing firms would choose to avoid the risk of hiring improperly documented workers by refusing to hire any Hispanics. The first few years after Simpson-Rodino saw a decline in the number of illegal entrants apprehended along the U.S.–Mexico border, but the decline was short lived.

In late 1990, the United States overhauled its immigration policy for the first time since 1965. The law increased the number of immigrants allowed in annually from about 500,000 to around 700,000. Of these, 140,000 visas went to workers with specific skills and their families. This almost tripled the number of skill-based visas available, reflecting a U.S. effort to compete for skilled immigrants who increasingly had chosen to go to Canada or Australia in recent years. A controversial aspect of the 1990 law allocated 10,000 visas annually for individuals who invested at least $1 million in a business to employ at least 10 workers (or $500,000 to employ at least five workers in a rural area). Many experts expected millionaires around the world would eagerly "buy their way" into the United States; but the first three months of the program drew only 225 applicants, of which only six were approved. Another immigration reform proposed in 1995 cut legal immigration back to 550,000 per year, of which 400,000 would go to family members of U.S. residents; 100,000 to individuals with special skills needed in U.S. labor markets; and the remainder to refugees.

The United States hardly is alone in its debate over immigration policy. Canada cut its legal immigration for 1995 by 24 percent to 215,000. The Canadian law gives preference to individuals with specific skills needed in Canada and to individuals who speak English or French.

With its well-publicized economic growth over the last two decades, Japan also has begun to attract illegal workers. Current estimates suggest 100,000 workers are in Japan illegally, filling jobs in restaurants, construction, and small factories. Japanese labor unions favor policing entry more carefully, while firms support the availability of cheaper foreign labor. Policy proposals under consideration include institution of a formal "guest worker" program that would admit foreign workers with skills needed in Japan for three- to five-year stays, increasing aid to developing countries to lessen incentives for illegal migration, and new laws penalizing firms that hire illegal workers.[11]

In addition to controversy that surrounds policy debates over permanent immigration, governments must face opposition to short-term arrangements in which firms hire foreign workers. Since 1990, the United States has admitted up to 65,000 workers with special skills each year on "H-1B" visas, which permit the individual to work in the United States for up to six years. Many firms brought engineers and software-development specialists into the country under the program. Domestic workers in these industries protested, claiming the foreign workers took their jobs and worked for far lower wages. In 1995, the United States cut the maximum H-1B visa length to three years and began investigations to require that foreign workers entering under the program be paid the same wages as domestic workers in equivalent jobs.

Until 1994, South Korea banned foreigners from starring in commercials on Korean television, allowing Korean stars to charge high rates. In 1994, as part of an overall trend toward opening its markets to international trade, South Korea dropped the prohibition on foreign stars. Now American television and movie stars, including Brooke Shields and Shannen Doherty, make television commercials for Korean products and earn wages far below those charged by Korean stars.

Japanese baseball teams, which often hire American baseball players, did so especially during the 1994–95 strike in the United States, when well-known players including Shane Mack, Julio Franco, and Kevin Mitchell signed contracts with Japanese teams. Japanese restrictions, however, limit the number of foreign players per team to three.

Japan Airlines was, until 1994, a quintessential Japanese firm. But, faced with high costs and declining business travel during Japan's prolonged recession, the airline has hired largely foreign workers. Thai flight attendants earn one-twentieth the wage earned by Japanese attendants, and Irish and Canadian pilots, co-pilots, and flight engineers charge about half the rates of Japanese workers. The airline overhauls its planes in Singapore and China, where costs are much lower.

Labor Mobility without Immigration?

Recently firms have begun to use several arrangements that amount to labor mobility without migration. The first arrangement is **outsourcing** or offshore assembly, in

---

[11]Kathryn Graven, "Japan Isn't Ready for Illegal Aliens, but It Has 100,000," *The Wall Street Journal,* June 23, 1988.

which a firm performs each step in a manufacturing process in the country with a comparative advantage in the particular stage. Components for a finished product may be produced in many countries, and labor-intensive assembly of the components often occurs in labor-abundant developing countries. Such offshore assembly operations make up a large share of manufactured imports into the United States from developing countries, especially Mexico. In many cases, including Mexico's, special tax and tariff arrangements have encouraged firms to use offshore assembly.[12] Case Three at the end of the chapter examines Mexico's *maquiladora* plants, which have grown up along the U.S.–Mexico border and specialize in assembly operations.

Sometimes technology makes possible even more innovative ways of accomplishing labor mobility without migration. A U.S.–India satellite linkup permits U.S. computer firms such as Texas Instruments to use Indian computer programmers for routine programming tasks.[13] The U.S. firms send software design specifications to India by satellite link; the Indian software engineers develop and test the software in India and then transmit it back to the United States. Some firms estimate the arrangement could cut programming costs in half. Indian programmers earn more than they would otherwise but less than programmers in the United States. Highly trained programmers remain in India (along with their earnings), instead of migrating to the United States as part of the brain drain.

10.4.2 Inter-Country Mobility of Capital

Capital mobility among countries exceeds labor mobility largely because it does not require persons to move; an owner of capital can stay in one place while the capital flows from country to country in response to differences in available returns and other relevant considerations. The term *capital mobility* is somewhat deceptive. In international trade, *capital* typically refers to durable productive inputs such as factories, machines, and tools. But capital mobility refers not to actual international movement of such inputs but to international borrowing and lending activity.

There are two major classes of capital mobility. The first is international **portfolio investment,** or the flow across national boundaries of funds for financing investments in which the lender does not gain operating control over the borrower. Whenever an individual, firm, or government agency buys the bonds of a foreign firm or government, funds are transferred and the transaction represents a portfolio investment. Because this type of transaction involves very low transaction and transportation costs, portfolio investment represents the most mobile component of capital. Often all that is involved is an electronic transfer of funds accomplished almost instantaneously at very little cost using modern computer technology. If a U.S. firm issues bonds (borrows) and sells some of those bonds to a resident of Germany (who thereby makes a loan to the U.S. firm), the transaction represents a **capital outflow** or an **international purchase of assets** from Germany's perspective and a

[12]See section 6.7.

[13]Udayan Gupta, "U.S.-India Satellite Link Stands to Cut Software Costs," *The Wall Street Journal,* March 6, 1989.

Figure 10.11 □ **World Stock of Foreign Direct Investment, 1960–1988 ($ Billions)**

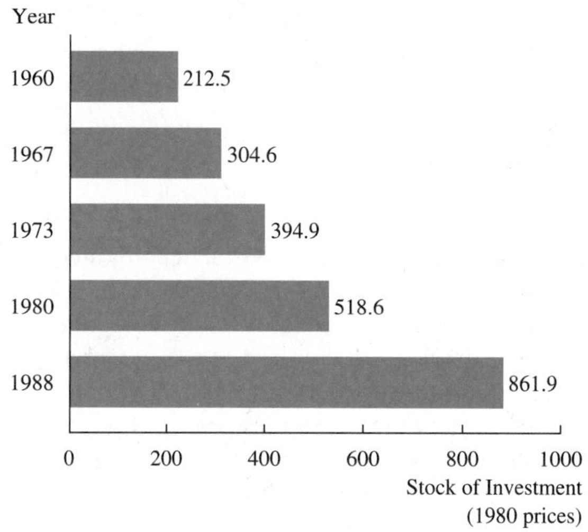

Year

1960	212.5
1967	304.6
1973	394.9
1980	518.6
1988	861.9

0   200   400   600   800   1000

Stock of Investment
(1980 prices)

Source: World Bank, *Global Economic Prospects and the Developing Countries 1991* (Washington, D.C.: World Bank); data from Department of Commerce and World Bank.

capital inflow or **international sale of assets** from the perspective of the United States. The U.S. firm typically uses the borrowed funds to buy a piece of physical capital; the U.S. stock of physical capital rises and the German stock of physical capital falls relative to what it would have been had the German resident lent his or her funds domestically to a German firm—even though no one packed up a factory and shipped it from Germany to the United States.

The other component of capital flows is **direct investment,** which gives the lender operating ownership of and control over the borrower. For example, if a U.S. firm buys or establishes a subsidiary in Germany, the transaction represents an outward foreign direct investment from the point of view of the United States and an inward foreign direct investment from the perspective of Germany. The line between portfolio and direct investment is somewhat fuzzy. If a Japanese firm buys stock in a U.S. corporation, it may or may not gain operating control—depending on the magnitude of the purchase relative to the U.S. firm's outstanding stock. U.S. government statistics assume that ownership of 10 percent or more of a firm's outstanding stock gives the holder operating control and therefore classifies the investment as a direct one.

Recent Patterns in International Capital Mobility

Worldwide, two trends characterize recent direct investment patterns. First, as illustrated in Figure 10.11, the stock of foreign direct investment increased by a factor of four between 1960 and 1988, including a 66 percent rise from 1980 to

Figure 10.12 □ **Source and Host Countries for World Stock of Foreign Direct Investment, 1988**

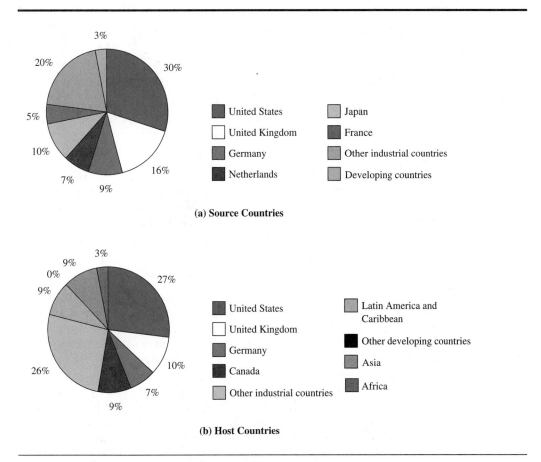

(a) Source Countries

(b) Host Countries

Source: World Bank, *Global Economic Prospects and the Developing Countries 1991* (Washington, D.C.: World Bank); data from Department of Commerce.

1988.[14] Between 1985 and 1989, foreign direct investment grew at three times the rate of growth of international trade.

The second notable trend is a diversification of the source countries. Although industrial countries still own 97 percent of foreign direct investment, the United States no longer is alone as the major source, as shown in Figure 10.12. In terms of host countries, a declining share of foreign direct investment goes to developing countries; their share fell from about a third to less than 20 percent during the 1980s.

---

[14]These data are measured in constant 1980 prices, so the noted increases are corrected for inflation.

Table 10.4 □ **Private U.S. Investment Abroad, Assets Held at Year End, 1950–1994 ($ Billions)**

Year	Direct Investment	Bonds	Stocks	Total[a]
1950	11.8	3.2	1.2	17.5
1960	31.9	5.5	4.0	44.4
1970	78.2	13.2	6.4	105.0
1980	396.2	43.5	18.9	701.0
1985	394.8	73.3	41.0	1,098.3
1990	620.0	118.7	110.0	1,809.7
1991	644.3	143.6	158.8	1,893.4
1992	657.9	155.8	178.1	1,914.0
1993	706.6	245.2	297.7	2,147.6
1994	761.0	224.7	313.9	2,233.0

[a]Total includes categories besides direct investment, bonds, and stocks; therefore, components do not sum to total.

Sources: William H. Branson, "Trends in United States International Trade and Investment since World War II," in Martin Feldstein, ed., *The American Economy in Transition* (Chicago: University of Chicago Press, 1980), p. 237; *Economic Report of the President; Survey of Current Business.*

Table 10.4 shows the relative sizes of the stocks of portfolio and direct investments held by private U.S. residents in recent years. As the table makes evident, direct investment dominated U.S. private international portfolio investment. This pattern contrasts with that of British investment during Britain's economic dominance in the late nineteenth century. Britain's investment consisted largely of portfolio investment, exemplified by British purchases of bonds to finance worldwide railroad construction, particularly in the United States. Note that Table 10.4 reports private investment; it does not include holdings of foreign assets by the U.S. government. In evaluating the overall investment position of the United States, government holdings as well as private holdings are important, but government borrowing and lending respond to different motivations than do private borrowing and lending. For now, we shall focus on the voluntary transactions undertaken by the private sector. In Part Two of the book, we shall explore in detail the role of government borrowing and lending and its impact on the economy.

During the 1980s, the rate of foreign investment in the United States exceeded that of U.S. investment abroad. The result was a net capital inflow, implying that the United States borrowed abroad more than it lent abroad, as a comparison of Table 10.4 and Table 10.5 illustrates. In 1986, the stock of U.S. assets held by foreigners surpassed the stock of foreign assets held by private parties in the United States. The United States became, for the first time in 71 years, a debtor nation.[15] As the

[15]This statement is not without controversy. Because of measurement difficulties and differences in accounting procedures, no single number can claim to represent the net investment position of the United States. In particular, measures are sensitive to how assets are valued—at historical cost, at current cost, or at market value. We shall see more about this controversy in Chapter Thirteen.

Table 10.5 □ **Nonofficial[a] Foreign Investment in the United States, Assets Held at Year End, 1950–1994 ($ Billions)**

Year	Direct Investment	Bonds	Stocks	Total[b]
1950	3.4	0.2	2.9	8.0
1960	6.9	0.6	9.3	18.4
1970	13.3	6.9	18.7	44.8
1980	125.9	25.6	64.6	367.7
1985	231.3	170.3	125.6	968.6
1990	467.3	408.1	221.7	1,942.2
1991	491.9	476.8	271.9	2,085.1
1992	498.6	544.7	300.2	2,215.2
1993	535.8	645.4	340.0	2,422.2
1994	580.5	683.4	337.9	2,613.3

[a]As reported by the Department of Commerce and reproduced in Tables 10.4 and 10.5, the U.S. and foreign investment positions are not precisely comparable, because foreign assets in the United States include nonofficial assets held by foreign governments while U.S. assets abroad exclude all government-held assets, whether official or nonofficial.

[b]Total includes categories besides direct investment, bonds, and stocks; therefore, components do not sum to total.

Sources: William H. Branson, "Trends in United States International Trade and Investment since World War II," in Martin Feldstein, ed., *The American Economy in Transition* (Chicago: University of Chicago Press, 1980), pp. 239, 245; *Economic Report of the President;* and *Survey of Current Business.*

comparison of Tables 10.4 and 10.5 reveals, the rapid change in U.S. status from creditor to debtor resulted not from a decline in U.S. investment abroad but from a rapid increase in foreign investment in the United States during the 1980s. Note that U.S. direct investment assets held abroad still exceed foreign direct investment assets in the United States.

The most politically controversial aspect of foreign investment in the United States involves direct investment by the Japanese. During the 1980s, Japanese invested heavily in the United States and made highly visible purchases such as Rockefeller Center in New York, Columbia Pictures, the Beverly Wilshire Hotel, Firestone Tire and Rubber, and, in 1992, the Seattle Mariners baseball team. Many analysts extrapolated that pace of investment into the future and concluded the United States soon would be owned and controlled by the Japanese. But, as happens with most economic trends, the 1990s brought a sharp decline in all foreign investment in the United States, including that by Japan.

Not only did the Japanese buying trend not last forever, but some of the transactions also turned out to be great deals for the U.S. sellers, because Japanese investors bought just before the plummet in U.S. real-estate values in the early 1990s. For example, a Japanese investor bought the Los Angeles Hotel Bel-Air in 1989 for $110 million and sold it in 1994 for $60 million. Similarly, the Japanese investor who bought the Pebble Beach Golf Links in Pebble Beach, California, paid $841 million in 1990 and sold the course in 1992 for $500 million. Even the Rockefeller Center purchase did not turn out well for the buyer. A Japanese firm paid $1.4 billion for 80 percent ownership of the complex between 1989 and 1991; the owners now are in bankruptcy.[16]

Incentives for International Capital Movements

Several incentives exist for capital owners to move that capital across national boundaries. We focus first on incentives for portfolio investment; section 10.4.4 will consider multinational enterprises as a vehicle of foreign direct investment. The primary incentive for capital movements, of course, is the opportunity to earn a higher rate of return or reward. Differential tax laws among countries also affect capital flows, as we shall see in section 10.4.3.

Another major reason for inter-country capital mobility is individuals' and firms' desire to diversify their asset portfolios to reduce risk. Evidence suggests that individuals are risk averse. This just means that given a choice between two assets, one with a certain return and the other with a return that is uncertain but expected to equal, on average, the certain return on the other asset, most individuals will choose the certain return.[17] Most investment decisions involve a tradeoff between the rate of return and the level of risk; by tolerating higher levels of risk, an investor often can earn higher rates of return.

To reduce the riskiness of a portfolio of assets, an investor need not hold only low-risk, low-return assets. One can do better by diversification. **Diversification** refers to holding a variety of assets, chosen such that when some perform poorly, others are likely to perform well. An owner of an orange grove in Florida and a hotel on a Florida beach would not be very well diversified. A severe freeze, for example, would both kill the orange trees and ruin the hotel business. Owning an orange grove in Florida and a New England ski resort would represent better diversification. A severe winter might kill the orange trees, but it would help the ski business; a warm winter, on the other hand, might mean no skiing but a bumper orange crop. Diversification generally means owning various assets that any given circumstance would affect differently.

The role of international capital mobility in diversification is obvious. Holding all one's assets in a single country heightens risk because it subjects all the assets to common events. A political disturbance in the country or an economic slump or recession could cause all the assets to perform poorly at the same time. Holding assets in several countries, on the other hand, can diversify these risks. If one country pursues a policy that turns out to be disastrous, the policy would harm only a subset of the assets. Asset holders' risk aversion creates a motivation for capital mobility even under conditions of full factor price equalization.

Yet another motivation for capital mobility focuses on mobility as a way of trading goods across time, called **intertemporal trade**. Without international borrowing and lending, each country must divide its current production between current consumption

---

[16]"Japan's U.S. Property Deals: A Poor Report Card," *The Wall Street Journal*, June 9, 1995.

[17]*If you were offered a choice between (1) $5 with certainty and (2) a 50 percent chance of winning $10 and a 50 percent chance of winning nothing, which would you choose? If you chose (1), you exhibited aversion to risk, because the expected value of the two offers are equal (at $5) while offer (1) involves no risk.*

and investment in machines and buildings to improve future output. The sum of consumption and investment must equal output each period for each country. Intertemporal trade, however, relaxes this constraint. A country with a net capital inflow borrows from the rest of the world. Residents of the country can consume and invest more than current production by borrowing, but they will have to consume and invest less than production later when the loans must be repaid. Such borrowing by a developing country, for example, might allow the country to take advantage of productive investment opportunities that its current low level of production could not accommodate. A country with a net capital outflow, on the other hand, lends to the rest of the world. Residents consume and invest less than current production, lend their savings to foreigners, and can consume and invest more than production in the future when borrowers repay the loans with interest. In the 1970s, oil-exporting countries suddenly found themselves with more current income than they could consume or invest profitably in their home economies; therefore, they used the savings to buy assets abroad.

Such intertemporal exchange in assets can be mutually beneficial in much the same way as ordinary trade in goods and services. In fact, we can phrase the story in terms of comparative advantage. Countries with an abundance of current production and a scarcity of domestic investment opportunities exhibit a comparative advantage in current goods relative to future goods. They can specialize in producing current goods by lending abroad and import future goods when the borrowers repay. On the other hand, countries with a scarcity of current production and an abundance of domestic investment opportunities hold a comparative advantage in future goods relative to current goods. They can import current goods by borrowing abroad and export future goods when they repay their loans.

Effects of Inter-Country Capital Mobility

Analysis of the effects of inter-country capital mobility is very similar to that for labor mobility. Figure 10.13 modifies the labor mobility diagram from Figure 10.10. From an initial allocation of capital between the two countries represented by K_0, capital flows from country B to country A in response to the higher rate of return, $r_0^A > r_0^B$. Area EGJ measures the positive effect on the output of the world economy from capital's shift from B to A. The gain comes from using the units of capital between K_0 and K_1 in the country with the higher value marginal product of capital (VMP_K).

The allocation of benefits from capital mobility differs from the case of labor mobility. With labor mobility, not only the labor power itself migrated but also the owner of the labor.[18] When capital migrates, its owner typically stays in country B. The migrant capital earns FGK_1K_0 in A, a gain of FGHJ over what it earned in B. This represents a gain to country B, which enjoys the income from the capital. Country A gains EGF, the productivity of the migrant capital above the return paid to it. The emigrant country lost in the case of labor mobility but gains from capital

---

[18]Worker remittances represent an exception to the assumption that migrant workers' incomes remain in the new country. Remittances are payments sent by migrant workers back to their country of origin, usually to family members. Such remittances represent significant sources of income for many developing countries, as we see in Case Two in this chapter.

Figure 10.13 □ **Effects of Capital Mobility**

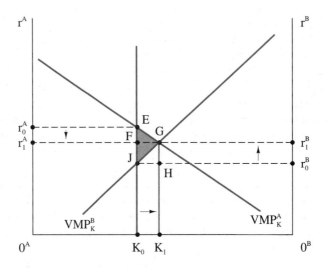

Beginning at point E, capital flows, in response to the higher rate of return in country A, improve efficiency and increase output by EGJ. Both countries gain because ownership of the migrant capital remains with country B. In A workers gain relative to capital owners, and in B capital owners gain relative to workers.

mobility, because it retains the ownership of and rights to the income from the migrant capital. Therefore, both countries enjoy a net gain; as usual, however, some groups within each country gain while others lose.

Owners of "native" capital in A suffer a reduction in their rate of return from r_0^A to r_1^A because of the capital inflow. Workers in A gain as the marginal productivity of labor rises from the availability of additional capital to use with labor. Owners of capital that remains in country B benefit from the rise in the return to capital that occurs after the capital outflow. Workers in B have less capital to work with, suffer reduced marginal products, and earn lower wages. Therefore, it is not surprising most labor groups favor restrictions not only on labor immigration but on capital outflows. Table 10.6 summarizes these results.

So far we have considered only factor mobility resulting from inter-country differentials in the rewards paid to factors of production. An additional consideration arises when governments tax the rewards paid to inputs.

10.4.3 Taxation and Inter-Country Mobility of Factors

Most governments levy taxes on income earned by both workers and owners of capital. The rates of taxation and the precise rules defining taxable income vary widely from country to country, creating additional incentives for inter-country mobility of factors of production. Ireland, for example, attracted many internationally known

Table 10.6 □ **Effects of Capital Flow from Country B to Country A**

Effect on	
Owners of native capital in A	−
Laborers in A	+
Net effect on A	+ (area EGF)
Owners of capital remaining in B	+
Laborers in B	−
Owners of migrant capital	+
Net effect on B	+ (area FGJ)
Net effect on world welfare	+ (area EGJ)

writers and poets by exempting from taxation all income earned from such activities. Several movie stars, rock stars, and athletes (including David Bowie, Michael Caine, Roger Moore, and Sean Connery) gained attention for leaving England to avoid its high tax rates. England responded by lowering its top income tax rate from 60 to 40 percent and lured its tax exiles home.

Our analysis so far suggests that inter-country mobility of factors increases world efficiency by drawing resources to those locations where they can be most productive. This conclusion does not apply, however, to mobility motivated by countries' differing tax rates and rules. Although such mobility clearly benefits the migrant labor or capital, it does not contribute to the efficiency of the world economy.[19] On the other hand, it does raise some interesting policy issues.

Taxation of wages and of income from capital have similar effects. The following discussion focuses on taxation of wages. The results carry over, with minor modifications, to taxation of capital. Figure 10.14 resembles Figure 10.10, which illustrates the effects of labor mobility. To keep the analysis simple, Figure 10.14 assumes the initial allocation of labor between countries A and B (represented by L_0) is efficient; that is, at L_0 the values of the marginal productivity of labor and the wage rates are equal in the two countries. Now suppose country A imposes a tax on wages at a rate denoted by t^A, where $0 < t^A < 1$.[20] For each dollar of wages earned, a worker must pay t^A in taxes, leaving a net reward to labor of $\$1(1 - t^A)$. At any wage rate w^A, labor suppliers get to keep only $w^A(1 - t^A)$.

---

[19]This statement ignores supply-side or incentive arguments that, for example, individuals work more when they face low marginal tax rates because the after-tax return to working is higher.

[20]For simplicity, we assume a constant tax rate; that is, the tax system is proportional. The tax liability equals a constant proportion (t^A) of the wage. Systems in which the tax rate rises with income are progressive, while those in which it falls with rising income are regressive. In Figure 10.14, we depict the tax, for simplicity, by a parallel shift of the VMP curve. In reality, the new curve would be steeper than the original one.

Figure 10.14 □ **Effect of Taxation of Wages by Country A**

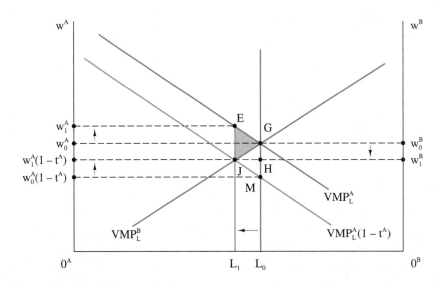

Beginning with an efficient allocation of labor between A and B, taxation of wages by A reduces total output by EGJ. Workers between L_1 and L_0 migrate to B in response to a differential in wages net of taxes; but gross returns reflect true labor productivity. Immigration harms workers in B. Workers in A are better off than they would be in the presence of the tax and with no labor mobility.

Workers no longer choose between countries A and B by comparing $VMP_L^A = w^A$ with $VMP_L^B = w^B$; now the relevant comparison from the individual worker's point of view is between net or after-tax wages in the two countries, or $VMP_L^A(1 - t^A)$ $= w^A(1 - t^A)$ and $VMP_L^B = w^B$. At L_0, $w_0^A(1 - t^A) < w_0^B$; thus, country A's taxation of wages causes the units of labor between L_1 and L_0 to migrate to country B to avoid the tax. Remember that L_0 represents the efficient, or output-maximizing, allocation of labor between the two countries. The workers who migrate in response to country A's tax are less productive in B than they were in A (reflected in the fact that VMP_L^A lies above VMP_L^B between L_1 and L_0); but because of the tax in A, workers earn higher *net* wages by working in B. Area EGJ measures the total *loss* of world output from the tax-migration effect.

Total output in A falls by EGL_0L_1. Workers who remain in A earn w_1^A but get to keep only $w_1^A(1 - t^A)$. They are worse off than before the tax (since $w_1^A[1 - t^A] < w_0^A$) but better off than if the tax had occurred with restrictions on labor mobility, in which case net wages would have fallen to $w_0^A(1 - t^A)$. *(Why?)* Capital owners in A earn less because their capital has less labor with which to work than before the imposition of the tax on wages. The government of country A collects $w_1^A EJ w_1^A(1 - t^A)$ in tax revenues. Note, however, that labor's ability to move across the national boundary to avoid the tax reduces the government's ability to raise revenue by taxing wages. With completely immobile labor, the same tax rate depicted in Figure 10.14 would raise $w_0^A G M w_0^A (1 - t^A)$ in revenue.

Total output in country B rises by JGL_0L_1. Native workers in B lose $Gw_0^B w_1^B H$ because of the inflow of workers, and owners of capital gain. The mobility of labor drives the wage rate in B down to equality with the *net* wage in A, even though wages in B go untaxed.

Country A's taxation of wages has caused a distortion in the labor market and resulted in inefficient labor migration from A to B. Workers flow to the country in which they can earn the higher net wage, but gross rather than net wages reflect true productivity.

Figure 10.14 assumes only country A imposes a tax on wages. In reality, most countries tax wages, and the size of the distortion created by those taxes depends on relative tax rates. If countries A and B tax wages at the same rate and use the same definitions for taxable income, the taxes create no incentive for labor migration; workers face taxes at the same rate no matter where they live and work. *(How would this case be represented in Figure 10.14?)* [21] As long as the only choice labor has is whether to live and work in country A or in country B, taxation has no net effect through migration when countries impose equal tax rates.[22]

Because of the importance of relative tax rates, governments worry about other countries' tax rates. During the 1980s, top income tax rates trended downward in the major industrial economies, as Figure 10.15 illustrates. That the trend was in the same direction for the various countries limited incentives for migration in response to the tax changes. Even with the downward trend, substantial differences in tax rates remain. Top marginal federal tax rates for 1991 range from Canada's 29 percent to France's 57 percent.[23] Such simple comparisons can be misleading, however. For example, much of Canada's taxation occurs at the provincial rather than the federal level, and overall tax liability depends on definitions of taxable income and allowable deductions as well as tax rates.

Figure 10.16 documents a pattern in corporate tax rates, or taxes on capital, similar to that in personal income taxes. Differences in tax rates remain a source of controversy, particularly among the members of the European Union as they try to harmonize their economies as part of the continuing 1992 open-market plan. Despite the distorting effects of difference in taxes on capital, top rates in Western Europe ranged from Britain's 33 percent to Germany's 56 percent in 1994.[24]

So far, our examination of the effect of taxation has maintained one subtle but important assumption: Income was subject to taxation by only one country at a time. By moving from A to B, workers could avoid paying the tax levied by A but became

---

[21]Add a $VMP_L^B(1 - t^B)$ curve to represent the net return to labor in country B. If $t^B = t^A$, the new curve will intersect $VMP_L^A(1 - t^A)$ at point M. No labor will migrate. Gross wages will be equal at $w_0^A = w_0^B$, and net wages will be equal at $w_0^A(1 - t^A) = w_0^B(1 - t^B)$.

[22]Taxation of wages may cause some individuals to choose not to work; in that case, taxation will lower the total quantity of labor available. Even if taxation has no effect on total world output, distributive effects remain. The revenue raised by the tax will be transferred from workers to the government, and the overall outcome will depend on how the government chooses to use the revenue.

[23]*The Economist,* June 8, 1991, 58.

[24]*The Economist,* July 30, 1994, 93.

Figure 10.15 □ **Top Marginal Personal Income Tax Rates, 1975, 1983, and 1989**

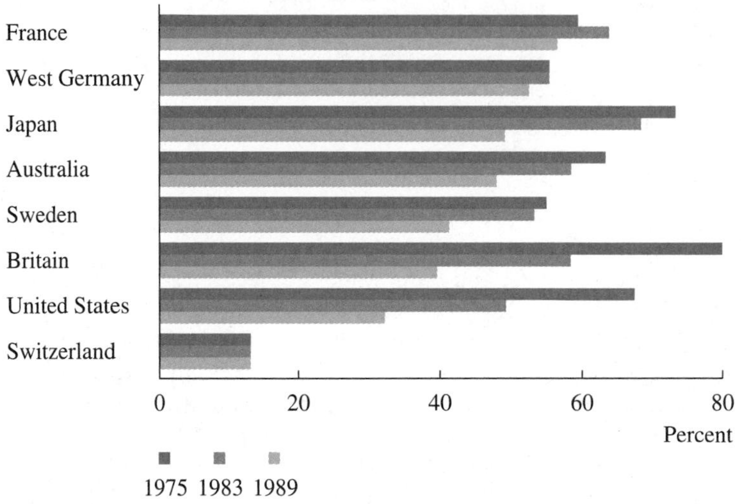

Source: *The Economist,* June 24, 1989, p. 15; data from Organization for Economic Cooperation and Development.

subject to any tax levied by B. The real-life situation is much more complex. A citizen working or investing abroad or a firm earning income abroad often faces taxation by both the domestic and foreign governments. This raises several policy issues.

Double taxation, or taxation of the same income by two governments, creates a strong disincentive for factor mobility. Most governments agree, through tax treaties, to reduce if not eliminate the problem by granting either tax credits or tax deductions for taxes paid to foreign governments. A tax credit reduces the tax liability to country A by the full amount of the tax paid to country B. A tax deduction reduces the income subject to taxation in A by the amount of the tax paid to B. The tax credit eliminates double taxation, and the total tax liability equals the higher of the two countries' tax rates. The tax deduction, on the other hand, reduces but does not eliminate double taxation. The negotiation of tax treaties reflects a delicate balancing of costs and benefits in terms of the revenue of the governments involved. Even with tax treaties, the international mobility of factors of production reallocates the world's tax base, providing another source of controversy over policies toward factor mobility.

Most industrial countries, including the United States, use a residence-based tax system that taxes U.S. residents' income even if earned outside the country but does not tax interest income paid to foreigners. Many developing countries, on the other hand, use a source-based tax system that taxes income originating in the domestic economy but not income of domestic citizens earned abroad. The combination of the two systems creates an incentive for capital flows from developing countries to industrial countries. *(Why?)*

Figure 10.16 □ **Top Corporate Tax Rates, 1994**

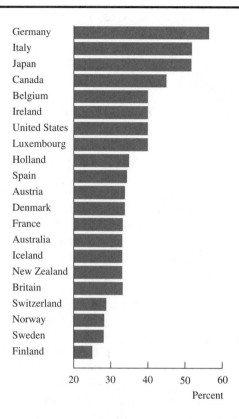

Source: *The Economist,* July 30, 1994, p. 93; data from KPMG.

10.4.4 Multinational Enterprises and the World Economy

Definition

One of the major economic trends of the postwar period has been the growth of firms across national boundaries, a source of both political and economic controversy. We can define **multinational enterprises** (**MNEs**) simply as enterprises that manage and control production facilities in at least two countries. This simple definition, however, does not clearly separate multinational enterprises from non-multinational enterprises; the main source of ambiguity is the meaning of "manage and control." Would a firm based in country A, which owns half the shares of stock of a firm in country B, be an MNE? From the standpoint of economic theory, the primary issue in establishing whether an enterprise qualifies as an MNE is the centralization of some functions—most commonly corporate finance decisions and research and development activity—in the *parent, home,* or *source country.* When an enterprise engages in production in several countries but administers some finance and research functions centrally, the enterprise becomes truly multinational. Decisions made in one country direct and allocate resources located in another. This transcending of national boundaries makes MNEs both economically important and controversial.

Multinational enterprises can be classified into three groups based on the pattern of organization of their production. Some MNEs produce basically the same or similar goods in several countries; these are called *horizontally integrated MNEs*. Other enterprises produce inputs in one country that they then use to produce another good in another country; these are referred to as *vertically integrated MNEs*. The third possibility involves production of different or even totally unrelated goods in various countries; such arrangements are called *diversified* or *conglomerate MNEs*. Early MNEs clustered in agricultural and mining sectors, but most are now in manufacturing.

The phenomenon of MNEs is not new, but the multinationalization of production has grown rapidly since the Second World War. Advances in both transportation and communications technologies have increased the feasibility of multinational production. MNE-associated merchandise trade accounted for 58 percent of U.S. exports and 41 percent of imports in 1992. Intra-MNE trade, that between U.S. parent firms and their foreign affiliates, comprised 23 percent of U.S. merchandise exports and 17 percent of imports.

Foreign MNEs' U.S. affiliates are concentrated in manufacturing, especially machinery and chemicals, and in real estate. Over half of foreign firms' direct investment outlays in the United States come from parent companies in Europe. U.S.-owned firms have affiliates throughout the world, but approximately 40 percent (in terms of value of assets) are located in Europe, especially the United Kingdom and Germany. In recent years, the pace of foreign direct investment in the United States has exceeded that of U.S. investment abroad, although the accumulated stock of U.S.-owned assets abroad still exceeds the stock of foreign-owned assets in the United States.

The central questions to be answered concerning multinational enterprises include the reasons for their existence, their welfare implications, and the policy issues they raise for both parent and host governments. We now turn to each of these issues in turn.

Why Multinationalism?

For many years, most analysts of multinational enterprises viewed MNEs as vehicles for spreading capital from one country to another, a perspective known as the **capital arbitrage theory of multinationals**. In capital-abundant countries, capital tends to earn a low return compared with that in capital-scarce countries. This difference in returns creates an incentive for owners of capital to shift their resources from low-return to high-return countries, as discussed in section 10.4.2. Such activity increases total world income because it moves capital from areas of low productivity to those of higher productivity. However, the capital arbitrage view seems inconsistent with at least three aspects of observed MNE behavior. First, MNE capital does not necessarily flow from capital-abundant to capital-scarce countries. Second, in many countries inflows and outflows of MNE capital occur simultaneously. Third, although MNEs often move capital from one country to another, such movements are not necessary because MNEs can borrow funds locally for their subsidiaries. Overall, the capital arbitrage hypothesis appears unsatisfactory as an explanation of the MNE phenomenon.

When seeking an explanation for the observed location of production facilities around the world, economists think first of the low-cost way to service markets. The theories of comparative advantage and trade based on economies of scale are, in a sense, theories of the location of production: Industries tend to locate where they can produce a product at the lowest possible opportunity cost. However, this rule alone cannot explain the existence of multinational enterprises, because all firms in each country could be locally owned and controlled. The fact that Honda sells automobiles in both Japan and the United States does not necessarily imply that the firm must own and control separate production sites in Japan and Marysville, Ohio, in such a way as to form an MNE. Alternatives include (1) production in Japan and export to the U.S. market, or (2) licensing by Honda in Japan (for a fee) of a U.S. company to produce and sell Hondas in the United States. That Honda now exports automobiles from its U.S. plants to Japan further complicates the puzzle!

A theory of the MNE phenomenon must explain why an enterprise would choose true multinationalism over exporting or licensing. In other words, why does the enterprise choose to have its decision making and control of resources cross national borders? Multinationalism clearly involves costs. The firm must move goods, employees, and information around the world as well as learn the laws and customs of a number of countries. The headquarters in the parent country must spend resources monitoring the activities of the foreign affiliates. Given these costs, a firm that chooses to become an MNE must expect significant benefits from the centralized control of foreign production facilities.

In choosing between exporting and producing abroad as alternative methods for serving a foreign market, the presence or absence of barriers to trade is probably the chief determinant of strategy. If the foreign market is protected by tariffs, quotas, or other restrictions on imports, exporting becomes less attractive relative to producing abroad "behind the tariff wall." Statistical studies have confirmed that barriers to trade encourage the development of MNEs. Even during the Great Depression, U.S. firms set up foreign production facilities behind the Smoot-Hawley retaliatory tariffs passed by many countries. More recently, several developing countries have used this response as a strategy for attracting foreign investment for development purposes. The tactic involves imposing import restrictions high enough to force foreign firms wanting to sell in the market to establish local production facilities. Other examples include increased investment in Europe to avoid the loss of those markets following completion of the European Community in 1992 (Figure 9.5) and recent Japanese investment in the United States to avoid actual or threatened protectionism.

The other alternative to forming an MNE is to license a foreign firm to serve the foreign market. Examination of this alternative takes us closer to the frontiers of research on MNEs. Empirically, multinational enterprises cluster in industries with large research and development or technological innovation components. The special character of information, technology, and other outputs of the research and development process provide a key to understanding the logic of the choice between licensing and multinationalism. Suppose an X-producing firm in country A, through a costly research and development program, has discovered a lower-cost technology for producing good X. The firm adopts the new technology in servicing the domestic market and wants to use it to sell in country B. The firm has no production facilities in B, and B's trade barriers against imports make exporting infeasible. The firm can either acquire or build production facilities in B, thereby becoming an MNE, or sell the right to use the new technology to an existing firm in B. Consider the second alternative, licensing. How much would the A firm charge for the license, and how much would the second firm (in B) be willing to pay for it? The character of new technology makes it difficult to arrive at mutually acceptable answers. The firm in B has no incentive to accept the A firm's word on the new technology's worth because of the A firm's incentive to exaggerate to obtain a high price for the license. But if the A firm reveals the technological secret to the firm in B to establish the innovation's value, the B firm may steal the design and use it without paying any license fee. The combination of the A firm's incentive to overstate the value of the new technology and the B firm's motive to steal the underlying information makes a licensing agreement difficult to achieve.

These problems may be particularly acute in developing countries that have weak or nonexistent systems of patent and trademark protection for inventions.[25] For these reasons, firms in technologically innovative or research and development-intensive industries tend to choose multinationalism over licensing. By forming an MNE, the firm maintains control over its technology while using it to serve foreign markets.

Effects of MNEs

The effect of multinational enterprises, both overall and on parent and host countries separately, is a subject of disagreement. Insofar as MNEs play a role in moving production to its least-cost locations and contribute to the spread of technological improvements, total world output increases. This makes possible an increase in total world welfare and potentially (though not necessarily) improves welfare in parent and host countries alike. MNEs may facilitate achievement of economies of scale by handling some functions (such as research and finance) centrally while continuing to adapt to local conditions in relevant areas of operation (for example, labor relations and marketing). By handling many transactions internally, the MNE may be able to guarantee supplies of raw materials (by owning its own) and to build more reliable distribution networks.

Most of the controversy surrounding multinationals relates to the division of benefits and costs between parent and host countries. U.S. labor organizations, for example, claim the multinationalization of production by U.S. firms "exports" jobs. Because of the scarcity and relatively high wages of unskilled labor in the United States, firms tend to move abroad production that involves intensive use of unskilled labor. Assembly tasks, such as those in apparel, consumer electronics, and some high-technology products, often are conducted for U.S. companies by operations in labor-abundant and low-wage countries.[26]

---

[25]See Chapter Eleven, Case Three.
[26]Case Three looks at one example—the *maquiladora* plants along the U.S.–Mexico border.

Claims by labor groups that this constitutes export of jobs that rightfully belong to U.S. workers are subject to several important qualifications. First, once short-run adjustment and relocation costs are overcome, the movement of production processes to areas of low-cost production maximizes total world output and income. Second, in many cases the firm faces a choice between moving abroad or stopping production completely; that is, solely domestic production may cease to be viable due to comparative disadvantage. Third, if foreign production operations make inputs cheaper for U.S. producers, the competitive positions of those producers improve. Increased foreign production also increases employment in management and research within the parent country. Finally, to the extent that foreign production raises foreign income levels, demand for U.S. exports increases, raising employment in export-oriented industries.

The proliferation of multinationals tends to spread the technology developed in parent countries to the rest of the world. Developing countries complain that this pattern of production keeps research and development operations clustered in the industrialized countries rather than spreading facilities that would allow developing countries to become more self-sufficient in research and development and in technological innovation. The issue of the appropriateness of technology (discussed in section 11.6) arises here, as developing countries claim that only they can arrive at the labor-intensive, small-scale technological innovations suited to their needs. On the other hand, proponents of multinationals point out that the growth of advanced research and development facilities in developing countries would be unlikely even without multinational production. With firms limited to producing within their parent countries, the developing countries would not only lack facilities to develop their own innovative technologies but also would be less able to borrow chosen aspects of the technology of the industrialized countries.

Developing countries also charge that the sheer size and economic strength of many MNEs allow them to exploit their host countries. This alleged exploitation takes a variety of forms: bargaining with the host government for excessive tax concessions, paying unfairly low prices for raw materials removed from the host country, and issuing deceptive financial statements to repatriate all the benefits from the operation to the parent country. An additional concern is the MNE's general domination of the host's economy and culture, which can cause a loss of indigenous values and damage to local enterprises. Local firms in the host country also have an incentive to block the entry of MNEs that would compete in the local market.

A final source of contention between MNEs and their parent and host governments arises not because of the multinationals themselves but rather because of governments' policies toward them. An MNE exists under the jurisdiction of several governments, and one of the most controversial questions surrounding these arrangements concerns the rights of those governments to tax the MNE.[27] By moving production facilities around the world, multinationals reallocate the tax base among countries, as we saw in section 10.4.3, sometimes with significant distributional consequences.

---

[27]The discussion of taxes and factor mobility in section 10.4.3 applies to multinational enterprises as well as to labor.

Government Policies toward MNEs

Historically, government policies toward multinationals have been erratic. Countries have vacillated between explicitly encouraging foreign investment and legally forbidding it. Current policies toward both inward investment (as viewed by the host country) and outward investment (as viewed by the parent country) differ widely across countries, although the last few years have seen a general move toward greater encouragement of foreign investment. Canada, for example, after several years of trying to limit foreign investment (particularly by the United States) through the Foreign Investment Review Agency (FIRA), moved in 1984 to a policy more amenable to such investment under the Investment Canada Act. The Latin American economies, including Argentina, Brazil, Ecuador, Mexico, and Venezuela, are actively trying to attract foreign investment, partly as a result of their debt situations' effect on their ability to borrow. Several formerly nonmarket economies, including the former Soviet Union and economies of Eastern Europe, have significantly liberalized opportunities for multinational enterprises, either independently or through joint ventures with local companies. China, while still centrally planned, has taken similar steps, particularly in its southern coastal provinces.

Despite the desire, particularly by developing countries, to attract foreign capital, many countries continue to impose a variety of restrictions on the entry and behavior of MNEs. The more common policies of host-country governments toward multinationals include bans from participation in certain industries, limits on dividend payments and repatriation of profits to the parent country, requirements that MNEs buy specified percentages of inputs locally, local ownership requirements, minimum export limits, and ceilings on royalty payments for technology owned by parent-country firms. Industries in which governments often restrict participation by multinationals include banking and insurance, telecommunications, pharmaceuticals, computers, and advertising.

At the same time restrictions make foreign investment less attractive, many host-country governments offer tax incentives to multinationals to locate in their countries. Other incentives include government provision of infrastructures such as roads, ports, railroads, and other facilities the MNE needs, as well as exemption from tariffs on imported inputs.

Parent-country governments generally place far fewer restrictions on the behavior of MNEs. As mentioned earlier, labor groups argue that multinationalization leads to job exportation. In the United States there have been efforts to pass domestic-content legislation for the automobile industry, but the attempts have failed so far, except for the NAFTA's stringent rules of origin.

Case One
The Brain Drain

One of the most controversial aspects of immigration and emigration policies between developed and developing nations is the brain drain. This refers to the tendency of many of the most highly educated, trained, and skilled individuals from developing countries to migrate to the industrialized countries, particularly the United Kingdom and the United States. A 1984 study by the United Nations estimated that about 500,000 professionals had left developing countries since the end of the Second World War. Most came from India, the Philippines, Iran, South Korea, Pakistan, Egypt, Greece, Turkey, Colombia, Argentina, and the Caribbean countries. Higher per capita incomes and better working conditions lure individuals to the industrialized nations. As in the case of labor mobility in general, migrants themselves gain from their mobility. To the extent the migrants are more productive in the industrialized countries, total world output rises, but perhaps at the expense of some developing countries.

Most industrialized nations have hesitated to adopt policies aimed at stopping the brain drain. Arguments against such policies contain both economic and political elements. First, to the extent the migrant workers have higher productivity in the industrialized countries, total world output rises (see Figure 10.10 and Table 10.2). If migrant workers such as doctors or scientists can make breakthroughs in the industrialized countries not possible in the countries of origin, the entire world, including the native countries, benefits. Second, a precedent of limits on immigration or emigration runs political risks in the sense that governments might later use such laws to limit political freedom or mobility in unacceptable ways. Third, migration does not necessarily imply the country of origin obtains no benefits from the migrant worker. Many workers send significant shares of their earnings back to their countries of origin, as we shall see in Case Two. Finally, many professionals eventually return home; for example, Taiwan's computer industry is growing rapidly thanks in part to engineers and scientists returning from the United States with valuable education and experience working in the U.S. computer industry.[28]

On the other hand, developing countries argue, they have invested in the workers' education, and emigration prevents the countries from earning a return on their investment. In most countries, government sources, rather than the family of the person receiving the education, fund early education. Figure 10.17 illustrates the cost per student of public education as a percentage of per capita GNP; for the higher education required for the professions, the cost per student equals almost four times per capita GNP in developing countries.

Society invests in the child in the hope of reaping future gains in the form of higher productivity and tax revenue, but when the skilled person emigrates, the destination country collects the higher productivity and tax revenue. Developing countries also argue the industrialized countries encourage the brain drain through laws that make immigration much easier for highly educated and skilled workers than for unskilled workers.

The flow of highly skilled workers from Eastern Europe and the former Soviet Union provides a large-scale current example of a brain drain. Scientists at elite Soviet research facilities no longer have funds for equipment to do their research.

---

[28]Andrew Tanzer, "Brain Drain in Reverse," *Forbes*, April 17, 1989, 114–115.

Figure 10.17 □ **Costs per Student of Public Education as a Percentage of Per Capita GNP, Early 1980s**

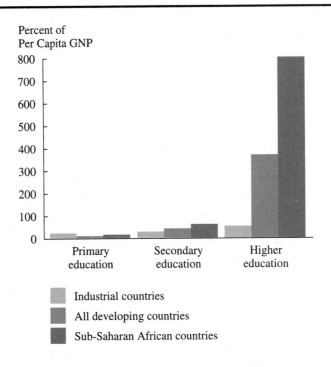

Percent of
Per Capita GNP

Industrial countries
All developing countries
Sub-Saharan African countries

Source: World Bank, *World Development Report 1988* (New York: Oxford University Press), 1988, p. 135; data from World Bank.

Increasingly, they emigrate, going primarily to Israel and to the United States where firms such as AT&T and Corning hire them at wages below those earned by U.S. scientists. However, because the end of the Cold War reduced demand for defense-related skilled workers in the United States, many of the immigrants remain unemployed or work in jobs that do not use their skills. Some experts fear that these individuals—including a small group knowledgeable in techniques for building nuclear weapons—will become discouraged in the United States and sell their defense- and weapons-related knowledge to countries that engage in military aggression or terrorism.

Economists have proposed several policies for dealing with the brain drain. The most common proposal involves a tax on skilled emigrants. Such a tax has three effects: lowering the number of individuals leaving the source country, sharing the gains of the immigrants' improved productivity with that country, and collecting from those who do leave a fee to help recover the cost of their earlier education. An alternate suggestion is that source countries change to a residence-based tax system so professionals earning abroad will pay taxes to their source governments.[29]

Case Two
Worker Remittances

This chapter's analysis of labor mobility assumes the incomes of immigrant workers remain in the host countries. For many groups of workers, this assumption is accurate. Some countries, however, tend to export labor, which in turn sends large shares of the earned income back to the countries of origin. These flows of funds are called **worker remittances.**

Historically, two labor flows accounted for the bulk of worker remittances. The first was the flow of so-called guest-workers, or *Gastarbeiter,* to northern Europe (Germany, France, and Switzerland) from southern Europe (Turkey and Portugal) during economic booms, especially before the mid-1970s. Estimates place the number of such workers at between 6 million and 7 million, or nearly 15 percent of Western Europe's labor force in 1975. Because of their explicitly temporary status, these workers were supposed to return home when unemployment became a problem in the host countries. As with most immigration policies, however, enforcement of the *Gastarbeiter* departure proved largely unsuccessful.

The other major remittance flow is from low- and middle-income countries (for example, Sudan, Jordan, Pakistan, India, and South Korea) to the oil-rich countries of the Middle East. This flow began in the mid-1970s, and worker remittances grew as a source of income during the 1970s largely as a result of the increased flow from the Middle East. In 1990, 3.5 million workers in the Middle East from Bangladesh, India, Indonesia, South Korea, Pakistan, the Philippines, Sri Lanka, and Thailand sent home $8.5 billion in official remittances, part of an estimated total of $10 billion to $12 billion in remittances. The 1991 Gulf War trapped many guest workers in Kuwait and the surrounding area. The war imposed heavy cost in lost remittances on several countries because Asians were sending $1.4 billion home from Kuwait and $120 million from Iraq when the war began.[30]

Table 10.7 reveals that, for some countries, exports of labor comprise the largest share of export earnings. For several countries, notably Egypt and Jordan, remittances represent a sizable share of per capita income. These figures are deceptive, however, since remittances typically are not spread evenly across the population, but concentrated among families with an emigrant member. Evidence

[29]See the discussion of alternate income tax systems in section 10.4.3, and Jagdish Bhagwati, "Global Interdependence and International Migration," in *Capital, Technology, and Labor in the New Global Economy,* ed. James H. Cassing and Steven L. Husted (Washington, D.C.: American Enterprise Institute 1988, especially pp. 171–178.

[30]"Iraq May Cost Parts of Asia $750 Million in Remittances," *The Wall Street Journal,* October 18, 1990.

Table 10.7 □ **Worker Remittances, 1989**

Country	Remittances ($ Billions)	Remittances as Percent of Exports	Remittances as Percent of GNP
Yugoslavia	6.3	47	9
Egypt	4.3	166	13
Portugal	3.4	26	8
Turkey	3.0	26	4
India	2.7	17	1
Pakistan	1.9	41	5
Morocco	1.3	40	6
Bangladesh	0.8	59	4
Jordan	0.6	61	11

Source: United Nations Development Program, *Human Development Report 1992* (New York: Oxford University Press, 1992).

suggests low-income emigrants, less likely to afford to take their immediate families with them, are most likely to remit large portions of their income.

Case Three
Maquiladoras and the NAFTA

U.S. trade policy includes several **offshore assembly provisions (OAPs)** that give favorable treatment to products assembled abroad from U.S.-made components.[31] One example is the *maquiladora* program in Mexico (*maquiladora* from the Spanish for "preparing goods for market"), began in 1965 under Mexico's Border Industrialization Program. Under the program, U.S. firms such as General Motors manufacture components and ship them to Mexico, where Mexican workers in *maquila* plants along the border assemble them into products that then re-enter the United States for packaging and distribution.

This arrangement attracts firms for two reasons. First, under sections 9802.00.60 and 9802.00.80 of the *Harmonized Tariff Schedule of the United States,* firms must pay tariffs on re-entry to the United States only on the difference between the value of the finished product and the sum of the values of its U.S.-made components, rather than on the full value of the finished product. Second, wages in Mexico are below those in the United States. In evaluating the importance of wage differences in the success of the *maquiladora* program, recall that firms respond to differences in wages

---

[31]See section 6.7.

Table 10.8 □ **Growth of *Maquiladoras*, 1975–1992**

Year	Number of Plants	Total Employment	Net Exports ($ Millions)	Average Hourly Compensation ($)
1975	454	67,213	332	1.44
1980	578	119,546	772	2.18
1985	789	211,968	1,268	1.58
1990	1,938	460,293	3,611	1.64
1991	1,925	467,454	4,122	1.95
1992	2,075	505,053	4,808	2.35

Source: Gary Clyde Hufbauer and Jeffrey J. Schott, *NAFTA: An Assessment* (Washington, D.C.: Institute for International Economics, 1993), p. 172.

relative to productivity. Currently, average U.S. wages are about eight times average Mexican wages; but U.S. productivity also runs about eight times Mexican productivity. Therefore, wage differences provide modest motivation for firms to move across the border.

The *maquiladora* program grew from only 12 plants in 1965 to well over 2,000 in 1992, providing jobs for over half a million Mexicans. Table 10.8 traces the growth of *maquiladoras,* their exports, and the wages they pay to Mexican workers. Many U.S. workers also are employed in production of the components used by *maquiladoras* and in the distribution and sale of the final goods they produce. Nevertheless, U.S. labor unions bitterly oppose the program, which they claim exports jobs rightfully belonging to American workers. Critics also point to overcrowding, pollution, and inadequate infrastructure in the *maquiladora* region. Until recently, Mexican law restricted the plants to a certain region along the border, but recent changes in Mexican law and provisions of the NAFTA will allow plants to spread farther from the border, which should alleviate the overcrowding and pollution problems.

Goods assembled under OAP programs include electronics, automobiles, televisions, electronic machinery, and apparel and textiles. The program applies not only to U.S. firms but also to foreign firms. A Japanese firm wanting to export a good to the United States can buy U.S.-made components, have them assembled in Mexico at a *maquila* plant, and ship them to the United States under the favorable tariff provisions.

Under the provisions of the NAFTA, the *maquiladora* program will change over the next few years in several ways. Ultimately, the program will lose its unique features and the plants will become just another piece of the Mexican economy. Originally, all *maquiladora* products had to be exported; Mexican law prohibited domestic sales. Rules changes in 1977 and again in 1989 allowed domestic sales of up to 50 percent of output. NAFTA rules raise the allowable percentage of domestic sales by 5 percent a year until, in the year 2000, *maquiladora* products can be sold on the domestic Mexican market without restriction. In addition, the *maquila* plants' inputs no longer will gain entry to Mexico tariff-free. They will face the same tariffs as any other goods: zero if they meet the NAFTA requirements for duty-free treatment and Mexico's regular tariff rates if they do not. This provision will adversely affect primarily the plants of Asian-based firms who, under the *maquiladora* program, imported inputs from Asia tariff-free. Firms may replace those inputs with ones produced in North America or may build capacity in Mexico to produce the inputs. However, three-quarters of the inputs imported for the *maquila* plants already originate in the United States.

 ## Case Four
Saving, Investment, and Intertemporal Trade

With no international capital mobility, each country's saving must equal its investment, because the only way to obtain funds to finance investment is to forgo current consumption, that is, to save. In such a world, a graph with national investment rates on the horizontal axis and national saving rates on the vertical axis would show countries as a series of dots on an upward-sloping 45-degree line. Countries with low saving and investment rates would appear as dots on the lower, left-hand end of the line, and those with high saving and investment rates on the upper, right-hand end of the line.

Of course, capital is not completely immobile. Most countries have removed many of their legal barriers to capital flows, at least in the industrialized world. But a graph of countries' actual saving and investment rates, in Figure 10.18, looks remarkably similar to the 45-degree line we just described. Of the 23 industrialized countries included, not a single one pairs low saving and high investment or high saving and low investment; the maximum difference between the two rates for any country equals about 4 percent.

Countries' savings rates differ for several reasons. Cultures place different levels of importance on thriftiness. A country's age, demographic, and labor-force participation patterns affect saving because individuals' saving behavior varies considerably over their life cycle. Tax systems can encourage or discourage saving. Countries with generous public and private retirement systems may experience lower levels of non-retirement saving than those in which individuals feel more responsible for their own retirement income.

Figure 10.18 has two possible interpretations. The first takes the figure as evidence of a lack of international capital mobility. Countries' saving and investment rates still match closely, just as we argued would be the case if mobility were zero. This suggests capital may not be flowing from countries with poor investment opportunities to those with good ones.

The second interpretation argues that perhaps countries with high savings rates happen to be the same countries that offer good investment opportunities, while countries with low saving rates offer few or poor investment opportunities. Countries that experience rapid economic growth, for example, tend to both save and invest at high rates. Countries whose economic policy makers follow policies that lead to stability

Figure 10.18 □ **Saving and Investment Rates, 1970–1992 Averages**

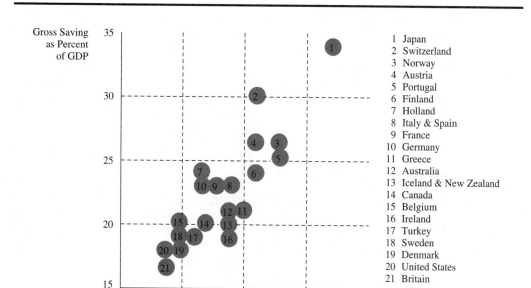

Source: Martin Feldstein, "Global Capital Flows," *The Economist,* June 24, 1995, p. 73.

foster both saving and investment in their economies. Other countries' policy makers cause uncertainty and instability that discourages both saving and investment.

Unfortunately, economists do not have enough information about the potential gains from intertemporal trade to choose confidently between Figure 10.18's two interpretations. We do know, however, that international capital mobility has risen in recent years and that countries' saving and investment rates diverge more now than in earlier years.

Summary

The effect of economic growth on welfare is more complex than a first glance suggests. The two components are the income effect (which applies to both small and large countries) and the terms-of-trade effect (which applies only to large countries).

When growth results from increased factor endowments, the direction of the income effect depends on the relative increases in total consumption and population. If total consumption rises at a faster rate than population, per capita consumption rises. The terms-of-trade effect can be either positive or negative, depending on growth's impact on the desired volume of trade at the original terms of trade. The overall effect of factor endowment-based economic growth on welfare is uncertain for both large and small countries.

Economic growth due to technical progress improves the welfare of small countries by raising per capita consumption. For large countries, the terms-of-trade effect can be either positive or negative. The possibility of a strongly negative terms-of-trade effect outweighing the positive income effect implies that growth can be immiserizing, although little empirical evidence supports this view.

International mobility of factors of production increases the efficiency of the world economy when it is based on differential productivity across countries. Mobility also alters the distribution of income in each country between capital owners and labor, making policies that promote or restrict mobility controversial. When artificial incentives such as differential tax rates cause migration of capital or labor, the migration reduces the efficiency of the world economy.

Looking Ahead

Chapter Eleven focuses on special problems facing developing countries. It examines the role of international trade in growth and development as well as the use of trade restrictions for dealing with the special problems of development. We also explore the experience of a new class of developing economies—those in transition from central planning.

Key Terms

economic growth
endogenous growth theory
balanced growth
production effect
consumption effect
volume-of-trade effect
income effect
terms-of-trade effect
Rybczynski theorem
immiserizing growth
technical progress
Hicksian technical progress
neutral technical progress
capital-saving technical progress
labor-saving technical progress

brain drain
outsourcing
portfolio investment
capital outflow
international purchase of assets
capital inflow
international sale of assets
direct investment
diversification
intertemporal trade
multinational enterprise (MNE)
capital arbitrage theory of multinationals
worker remittances
offshore assembly provision (OAP)

Problems and Questions for Review

1. Recent technological advances in computer hookups and satellite communications have allowed U.S.-based computer software development firms to use computer programmers in India for routine programming tasks. The firms send the program specifications to India via satellite; the Indian programmers do the programming (at wages below those of programmers in the United States) and transmit the completed programs back to the United States via satellite.

(a) Explain whether you expect the following groups to support or oppose the new arrangement and why: U.S. computer software development firms, U.S. computer programmers, computer programmers in India.

(b) What effect might such policies have on the brain drain?

2. Which of the following groups would you expect to support the policy of allowing U.S. offshore assembly provisions? For each group, briefly explain why.
(a) Workers in labor-abundant developing countries.
(b) Capital owners in labor-abundant developing countries.
(c) Labor in the United States.
(d) Capital owners in the United States.

3. U.S. automobile manufacturers have taken a variety of positions on U.S. limitations on auto imports from Japan. Ordinarily, we would expect domestic producers to favor such restrictions. What might explain the observation that some domestic producers have not favored the import restrictions?

4. (a) Illustrate an equilibrium situation with an efficient allocation of capital between two developing countries, A and B, and with no taxation of capital income in either country. Be sure to label carefully and explain.
(b) Illustrate the effects if developing country A imposes a tax (at rate t^A) on capital income. What are the tax's implications for capital mobility, for efficiency, and for the government budget of country A?
(c) Illustrate the effects if country B also imposes a tax (at rate $t^B = t^A$) on capital income. What are the tax's implications for capital mobility, for efficiency, and for the government budgets of country A and country B, compared with the situation in part (b)?
(d) Developing countries often grant tax concessions (that is, partial or complete exemptions) to multinational firms in an effort to attract capital inflows. What happens if country A grants tax concessions and country B does not? What happens if both countries grant tax concessions? Why might countries want to negotiate agreements that limit tax concessions they can grant to multinational firms?

5. Explain the similarities between balanced growth and neutral technical progress. Can the welfare effects of the two differ? Why, or why not?

6. How does foreign investment contribute to portfolio diversification? Why is diversification desirable?

7. Figure 10.9 reports large labor outflows from Mexico and large inflows into the United States. If the United States and Mexico eliminated barriers to trade in goods and services, would you expect the migration to increase or decrease? Why? Might your answer differ for the short run and the long run? Why?

References and Selected Readings

Baily, Martin Neil, and Hans Gersbach. "Efficiency in Manufacturing and the Need for Global Competition." *Brookings Papers on Economic Activity: Microeconomics* (1995): 307–358.
The effect of foreign competition on firms' technology and productivity; intermediate and advanced.

Baldwin, Richard E., and T. Venables. "Regional Economic Integration." In *Handbook of International Economics,* Vol. 3, edited by G. M. Grossman and Kenneth Rogoff, 1597–1644. Amsterdam: North-Holland, 1995.
Advanced, up-to-date survey of the literature on the causes and implications of regional trade groups.

Bhagwati, Jagdish N. "Immiserizing Growth: A Geometrical Note." *Review of Economic Studies* (June 1956): 201–205.
The original demonstration of immiserizing growth; for advanced students.

Borjas, George J. "The Economics of Immigration." *Journal of Economic Literature* 32 (December 1994): 1667–1717.
Excellent review of the recent literature and recent events; for all students.

Borjas, George J. "The Internationalization of the U.S. Labor Market and the Wage Structure." Federal Reserve Bank of New York *Economic Policy Review* 1 (January 1995): 3–7.
Short, up-to-date overview of recent trends in U.S. immigration and its impact on wages; introductory.

Corneliu, Wayne A., et al., eds. *Controlling Immigration.* Stanford, Calif.: Stanford University Press, 1995.
Collection of interdisciplinary papers on immigration; level of papers varies.

Coughlin, Cletus C. "Foreign Owned Companies in the United States: Malign or Benign?" Federal Reserve Bank of St. Louis *Review* 74 (May–June 1992): 17–31.
Examines the behavior of foreign firms in the United States and their effects on the U.S. economy; for all students.

Findlay, Ronald. "Growth and Development in Trade Models." In *Handbook of International Economics,* Vol. 1, edited by Ronald W. Jones and Peter B. Kenen, 185–236. Amsterdam: North-Holland, 1984.
Advanced review of the economic literature on growth.

Findlay, Ronald, and Harry Grubert. "Factor Intensities, Technological Progress, and the Terms of Trade." *Oxford Economic Papers* (1959): 111–121.
The classic paper on the effects of various types of technical progress; for intermediate students.

Graham, Edward M., and Paul R. Krugman. *Foreign Direct Investment in the United States.* Washington, D.C.: Institute for International Economics, 1995.
Measurement and implications of foreign direct investment in the United States; for all students.

Grossman, Gene M., and Elhanan Helpman. *Innovation and Growth in the Global Economy.* Cambridge, Mass.: MIT Press, 1991.
New theoretical approaches to growth; opening and closing chapters accessible, rest for advanced students only.

Grossman, Gene M., and Elhanan Helpman. "Technology and Trade." In *Handbook of International Economics,* Vol. 3, edited by G. M. Grossman and Kenneth Rogoff, 1279–1338. Amsterdam: North-Holland, 1995.
Advanced, up-to-date survey of technology-related aspects of international trade and trade theory.

Hufbauer, Gary Clyde. *Fundamental Tax Reform and Border Tax Adjustments.* Washington, D.C.: Institute for International Economics, 1996.
International-trade implications of alternative tax systems; for all students.

Hufbauer, Gary Clyde. *U.S. Taxation of International Income.* Washington, D.C.: Institute for International Economics, 1992.
Effects of U.S. tax system on capital flows; for all students.

Kodrzycki, Yolanda K. "Tax Reform in Newly Emerging Market Economies." Federal Reserve Bank of Boston *New England Economic Review* (November–December 1993): 3–17.
Examines the importance of newly created tax systems in integration of transitional economies into the world economy; for all students.

Mankiw, N. Gregory. "The Growth of Nations." *Brookings Papers on Economic Activity* 1 (1995): 275–326.
Overview of economic growth models; intermediate and advanced.

Markusen, James R. "The Boundaries of Multinational Enterprises and the Theory of International Trade." *Journal of Economic Perspectives* 9 (Spring 1995): 169–190.
Relationship between multinational firms and patterns of international trade; intermediate students.

Martin, Philip L. *Trade and Migration: NAFTA and Agriculture.* Washington, D.C.: Institute for International Economics, 1993.
Effects of the NAFTA on Mexican agriculture and implications for migration to the United States; for all students.

McCulloch, Rachel. "Foreign Direct Investment in the United States." *Finance and Development* 30 (March 1993): 9–12.
Short, accessible overview of issues related to foreign direct investment in the United States.

Mataloni, Raymond J., Jr. "A Guide to BEA Statistics on U.S. Multinational Companies." United States Department of Commerce *Survey of Current Business* 75 (March 1995): 38–55.
Detailed guide to U.S. government statistics on multinationals.

Pfefferman, Guy. "Facilitating Foreign Investment." *Finance and Development* 29 (March 1992): 46–47.
Policies that encourage or hinder foreign investment; for all students.

Razin, Assaf, and Efraim Sadka. "Resisting Migration: Wage Rigidity and Income Distribution." *American Economic Review Papers and Proceedings* 85 (May 1995): 312–316.
Distributional effects as a basis for opposing open immigration; intermediate and advanced.

"Recent Trends in Foreign Direct Investment for the Developing World." *Finance and Development* 29 (March 1992): 50–51.
Data on investment in developing countries; for all students.

Rodrik, Dani. "Political Economy of Trade Policy." In *Handbook of International Economics,* Vol. 3, edited by G. M. Grossman and Kenneth Rogoff, 1457–1494. Amsterdam: North-Holland, 1995.
Advanced, up-to-date survey of the literature on distributional aspects of trade policy and their implications for the policy process.

Ruffin, Roy J. "International Factor Movements." In *Handbook of International Economics,* Vol. 1, edited by Ronald W. Jones and Peter B. Kenen, 237–288. Amsterdam: North-Holland, 1984.
Advanced survey of the economic literature on factor movements.

Rybczynski, T. M. "Factor Endowment and Relative Commodity Prices." *Economica* 22 (November 1955): 336–341.
The original statement of the Rybczynski theorem; for intermediate students.

Session on "The Location of Economic Activity." *American Economic Review Papers and Proceedings* 85 (May 1995): 296–316.
Collection of papers on geographical patterns in production; level varies.

Siebert, Horst, ed. *Migration.* Ann Arbor, Mich.: University of Michigan Press, 1994.
Collection of papers on the causes and effects of labor migration; level of papers varies.

Smith, Alasdair. "Capital Theory and Trade Theory." In *Handbook of International Economics,* Vol. 1, edited by Ronald W. Jones and Peter B. Kenen, 289–324. Amsterdam: North-Holland, 1984.
Advanced survey of intertemporal issues in trade.

Symposium on "Immigration." *Journal of Economic Perspectives* 9 (Spring 1995): 3–62.
Collection of papers on immigration; level varies.

Van Ark, Bart, and Dirk Pilat. "Productivity Levels in Germany, Japan, and the United States: Differences and Causes." *Brookings Papers on Economic Activity: Microeconomics* 2 (1993): 1–70.
Empirical examination of across-country productivity differences; intermediate and advanced.

Whalley, John. "Taxes in Canada, Japan, and the United States: Influences on Trade and Investment Flows, and the Role of Tax-Based Irritants." In *Trade and Investment Relations Among the United States, Canada, and Japan,* edited by Robert M. Stern, 219–246. Chicago: University of Chicago Press, 1989.
The role of taxes in trade relations and disputes; for intermediate and advanced students.

World Bank. *World Development Report 1995: Workers in an Integrating World.* New York: Oxford University Press, 1995.
Implications of capital and labor mobility.

CHAPTER ELEVEN

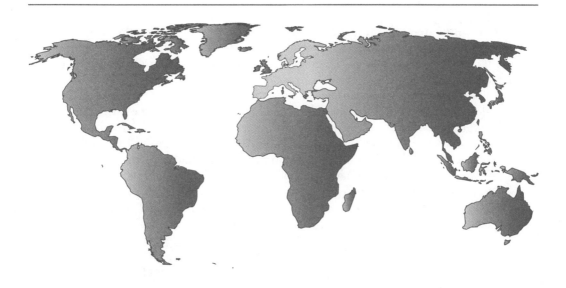

Development, Transition, and Trade

11.1 Introduction

In some of the earlier chapters, a country's economic size affected the results expected from a given policy, for example, the "optimal" tariff for a large country (section 6.5). In other cases, the feasibility of various policies depended on conditions within a country, such as the use of income taxes versus tariffs to obtain government revenue (section 8.6). Thus far, however, our basic analyses have applied to countries regardless of their individual economic circumstances. The gains from specialization and exchange exist for both the United States and Kazakhstan and for both Singapore and Ethiopia.

In this chapter, we focus on the international trade-related issues facing developing countries. First, we define and evaluate the magnitude of the development task. Next, we highlight several distinct subgroups of developing countries that face somewhat different sets of problems and concerns: low-income economies, newly industrializing economies, severely indebted countries, and economies in transition from central planning. We then turn to some concerns developing countries express related to their participation in the international trading system.

11.2 Defining Development

The ultimate goal of a country's development process is an improvement in the well-being of its residents, but there is neither an indisputable definition of economic development nor an unambiguous standard by which to measure a country's development status.

Per capita gross national product or income represents the most widely used single indicator of development. **Gross national product (GNP)** measures the value of output produced in a country in a year.[1] International organizations divide countries into several development groups based on per capita income. The World Bank classifies countries into high-income economies with annual per capita incomes above $8,626 in 1993, upper-middle-income economies with per capita incomes between $2,786 and $8,626, lower-middle-income economies with per capita incomes between $696 and $2,785, and low-income economies with per capita incomes below $696. That 3.1 billion people live in low-income countries, while only 812 million persons live in high-income economies, highlights the magnitude of the development task.

As an indicator of development, per capita gross national product is far from perfect, however. First, it fails to account for variation in the scope of market transactions in different economies. Economic transactions typically count in gross national product only if they occur in an organized market. As a country develops, an increasingly large share of its economic activity typically moves into organized markets; for example, commercially bought food and restaurant meals often replace home-grown and prepared food. Therefore, per capita GNP probably overestimates the gap between developing and developed countries. Nonetheless, very large income differences across countries persist. An additional cause for concern is the low growth rate of GNP in the low-income economies (0.1 percent annually during 1980 to 1993 for the group of low-income economies, excluding China and India) compared with that of the high-income economies (2.2 percent per year over the same period).

A second weakness of differences in per capita income as an indicator of development is that such differences, dramatic as they are, fail to capture many of the issues relevant to development. Average infant mortality and life expectancy at birth in low-income countries are 103 per thousand and 62 years, respectively, compared with nine per thousand and 77 years in the high-income countries. Individual countries sometimes fare quite differently in terms of different indicators of well-being. For example, Gabon's per capita income exceeds that of Jamaica by a factor of three, but Gabon's illiteracy rate is 20 times Jamaica's, its average life expectancy 20 years shorter, and its child mortality rate almost 10 times higher.[2] A final weakness of focusing exclusively on per capita income as an indicator of development is that the measure fails to indicate the distribution of income across the population.

---

[1]More precisely, gross national product is the sum of the current market values of all currently produced final goods and services over a specified time period, such as one year.

[2]World Bank, *World Development Report 1995* (New York: Oxford University Press, 1995), 162–163, 214–215.

Recently, the United Nations responded to the shortcomings of per capita GNP as an indicator by compiling a *human development index (HDI)*, which includes income, life expectancy, adult literacy, and average years of schooling. Table 11.1 reports country rankings by GNP per capita and by the HDI. Single asterisks denote countries classified by the International Monetary Fund as severely indebted in 1995, and double asterisks mark the economies classified as countries in transition. Notice that the ranking of individual countries differs significantly in some cases depending on whether the ranking is based solely on per capita income or on the more comprehensive index. *(Compare the situations of Oman and China.)* Overall, statistics indicate that even developing countries that suffered declines in per capita income during the 1980s did manage improvements in other indicators of well-being such as infant-mortality rates and life expectancy.

Another way of looking at the task of development focuses on disparities in the distribution of economic activity across countries, illustrated in Figure 11.1. The richest 20 percent of the world population account for 84.7 percent of GNP, 84.2 percent of world trade, 85.5 percent of domestic savings, and 85.0 percent of domestic investment. In contrast, the poorest 20 percent of the population comprises only 1.4 percent of GNP, 0.9 percent of trade, 0.7 percent of savings, and 0.9 percent of investment.

Lumping all low- and middle-income economies together under the rubric "developing countries" conceals important differences, both in the well-being of the countries' residents and in the trade-related issues of primary concern to policy makers in the various countries. Table 11.2 divides the low- and middle-income economies by region and reports their basic economic indicators.

Note the differences revealed in Table 11.2. Sub-Saharan Africa suffers low per capita GNP, negative growth rates, short life expectancy and high illiteracy. East Asia, on the other hand, although per capita GNP remains low, enjoys very rapid economic growth and life expectancy approaching that in high-income economies, but illiteracy remains high. Europe and Central Asia—encompassing most of the economies in transition from central planning—enjoy relatively high rates of income, life expectancy, and literacy compared with other developing countries; but their negative growth rate over the 1980s and early 1990s reveals the difficulties of shifting an economy to a market orientation and integrating it into the world economy after decades of isolation. The severely indebted countries include those hit hardest by external debt problems in the 1980s. They have relatively high levels of income but endured a "lost decade" in economic growth because of the debt crisis, the subject of section 11.7.

11.3 Development Issues

Since the 1950s, policies for fostering development have been an area of active research, both theoretical and empirical, by economists and other social scientists. Individual countries have followed a variety of policies in their efforts to develop themselves, and, as we have seen, the results have been mixed. Some economies, such as South Korea, Taiwan, Hong Kong, and Singapore, have achieved economic

Table 11.1 □ **Country Rankings by Per Capita GNP and Human Development Index, 1992 (1 = Highest; 173 = Lowest)**

Country	GNP Ranking	HDI Ranking	Country	GNP Ranking	HDI Ranking
Afghanistan*	169	171	France	10	6
Albania**	27	76	Gabon	42	114
Algeria	72	109	Gambia	144	166
Angola*	120	155	Georgia**	80	66
Argentina*	37	43	Germany	8	11
Armenia**	73	53	Ghana	133	134
Australia	15	7	Greece	21	25
Austria	11	12	Guatemala	106	108
Azerbaijan**	92	71	Guinea*	129	173
Bangladesh	159	146	Guinea-Bissau*	167	164
Belarus**	49	40	Haiti	141	137
Belgium	12	13	Honduras*	123	115
Benin	142	156	Hong Kong	22	24
Bhutan	165	162	Hungary**	23	31
Bolivia*	119	113	India	147	135
Botswana	58	87	Indonesia	121	105
Brazil*	52	63	Iran	64	86
Bulgaria*, **	25	48	Iraq*	59	100
Burkina Faso	153	172	Ireland	20	21
Burundi*	158	152	Israel	19	19
Cambodia	164	147	Italy	14	22
Cameroon*	111	124	Jamaica*	87	65
Canada	8	1	Japan	2	3
C. African Republic*	135	160	Jordan*	99	98
Chad	161	168	Kazakhstan**	71	61
Chile	66	38	Kenya*	146	125
China	143	94	Kuwait	28	51
Colombia	91	50	Kirgizstan**	95	82
Congo*	100	123	Laos*	157	133
Costa Rica	75	39	Latvia**	47	30
Côte d'Ivoire*	117	136	Lebanon	83	103
Denmark	6	15	Lesotho	124	120
Dominican Republic	107	96	Liberia*	130	144
Ecuador*	102	74	Libya	41	79
Egypt	122	110	Lithuania**	63	28
El Salvador	97	112	Madagascar*	162	131
Estonia**	43	29	Malawi	156	157
Ethiopia	171	161	Malaysia	61	57
Finland	5	16	Mali*	155	167

Table 11.1 ▫ *Continued*

Country	GNP Ranking	HDI Ranking	Country	GNP Ranking	HDI Ranking
Mauritania*	127	158	Singapore	21	43
Mauritius	65	60	South Africa	60	93
Mexico	51	52	South Korea	36	32
Moldova**	81	75	Spain	17	23
Mongolia**	103	102	Sri Lanka	128	90
Morocco*	101	111	Sudan*	137	151
Mozambique*	173	159	Sweden	3	4
Myanmar*	149	130	Switzerland	1	2
Namibia	84	127	Syria*	94	73
Nepal	166	149	Tajikistan**	116	97
Netherlands	13	9	Tanzania*	170	148
New Zealand	18	18	Thailand	82	54
Nicaragua*	139	106	Togo	136	145
Niger*	148	169	Trinidad and Tobago	46	35
Nigeria	145	139	Tunisia	85	81
Norway	4	5	Turkey	78	68
Oman	38	92	Turkmenistan**	88	80
Pakistan	140	132	Uganda*	168	154
Panama*	70	47	Ukraine**	68	45
Papua New Guinea	108	129	United Arab Emirates	10	62
Paraguay	90	84	United Kingdom	16	10
Peru*	98	95	United States	7	8
Philippines	113	99	Uruguay*	53	33
Poland*, **	26	49	Uzbekistan**	104	91
Portugal	22	42	Venezuela	55	46
Romania**	28	72	Vietnam*	150	116
Russia**	48	34	Yemen	126	142
Rwanda*	152	153	Zaire*	160	140
Saudi Arabia	31	67	Zambia*	134	138
Senegal	114	143	Zimbabwe	118	121
Sierra Leone*	163	170			

Source: United Nations, *Human Development Report 1995;* World Bank, *World Development Report 1995.*

successes that make even the high-income economies envious. Others, including many in sub-Saharan Africa, continue to suffer dramatic economic deprivation.

Nonetheless, developing countries as a group do share some commonalities. Historically, most followed policies that favored the industrialized sectors of their economies over primary-product production, for reasons we explore below. Policy

Figure 11.1 ▫ **Distribution of Economic Activity, 1991 (Percent of World Totals)**

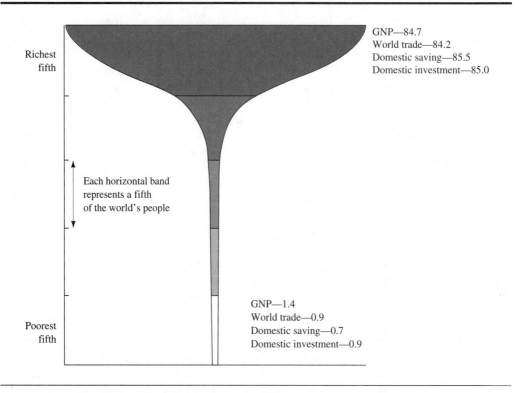

Source: United Nations, *Human Development Report 1994*, p. 63.

makers from most developing countries argued, especially during the 1960s and 1970s, that their undeveloped status warranted special assistance from the developed economies and fundamental changes in the international trading system. These calls for change became known as the **North–South debate,** because the majority of developing economies lie in the Southern Hemisphere and most developed economies in the Northern Hemisphere. The developing economies' divergent experience during the last 15 years, especially the impressive growth and industrialization of several Asian economies, has made the countries' policy concerns and interests more diverse, as the more successful economies have come to hold more in common with high-income developed economies than with the least developed.

Historically, developing countries have expressed discontent with five basic areas of the international trading system, outlined below. As the countries' experiences have diverged, some of the issues remain more salient for some countries than for others. We shall see later in the chapter that several of the items made their way onto the Uruguay Round agenda, and others are the subjects of active negotiations between developed and developing economies.

Table 11.2 □ **Low- and Middle-Income Economies' Indicators**

Country Group	GNP Per Capita		Life Expectancy, 1993	Adult Illiteracy, 1990 (Percent)
	1993 ($)	Annual Growth, 1980–93 (Percent)		
All low- and middle-income	1,090	0.9	64	33
Sub-Saharan Africa	520	–0.8	52	50
East Asia and Pacific	820	6.4	68	24
South Asia	310	3.0	60	54
Europe and Central Asia	2,450	–0.3	69	5
Middle East and North Africa	1,950[a]	–2.4	66	45
Latin America and Caribbean	2,950	–0.1	69	15
Severely indebted low- and middle-income	2,640	–1.1	67	23

[a]Data for 1992.

Source: World Bank, *World Development Report 1994, 1995.*

1. Until the 1970s, most developing countries specialized in **primary products,** including agriculture, metals, and minerals, and a large number still do. Primary-product producers often allege they are harmed by (i) the highly competitive and volatile nature of primary-product markets; (ii) developed countries' agricultural policies, especially price supports and subsidized exports; and (iii) developed countries' cascading tariff structures, which place higher tariffs on goods at higher stages of processing, resulting in very high effective rates of protection on manufactured goods.[3] Historically, most GATT negotiations excluded agricultural issues; as a result, many developing countries chose not to become actively involved in the GATT. To change this pattern, developed countries offered to include agricultural trade on the Uruguay Round agenda in exchange for developing countries' willingness to negotiate over trade in services. Issues of access to developed countries' agricultural markets took on new urgency with the opening of Eastern Europe, where several economies exhibit a comparative advantage in agricultural products heavily protected by the European Union, the United States, and Japan.

2. Most developing countries view economic development as synonymous with industrialization. In their attempts to industrialize, individual economies have followed two alternate strategies: import substitution and export promotion. One of the most dramatic events in the world economy during the 1980s was the shift of many developing countries from inward-looking import-substitution

---

[3]See section 6.6 for a review of the effective rate of protection.

policies to more outward-oriented export promotion. This change, undertaken to different degrees by different countries, explains in part the increasingly divergent economic performance among developing economies. However, the desire by many developing countries to become active participants in international trade has created tensions in the world trading system, again related to protection by developed economies. As developing countries attempt to industrialize, export markets in the developed countries play a vital role, but the industries most viable in the early stages of industrialization (labor-intensive industries such as textiles, apparel, and footwear) receive the strongest protection in industrialized countries, limiting access to those export markets.

3. Developing countries' low incomes limit the resources they can spend on research and development that leads to technological innovation. One possible shortcut involves borrowing and adapting technology from more advanced economies, but the international system of patents and the monopoly power held by some technologically innovative firms constrains such borrowing. Many developing economies do not have or enforce laws to protect technology from unauthorized copying. Industries in the industrialized economies—semiconductors, movies, computer software—claim they lose millions in revenues as a result. But some developing countries resist pressure to adopt and enforce rules that would limit their ability to borrow and copy technology.

4. The external debt of the developing world as a whole escalated rapidly in the 1980s, threatening the solvency of several countries. These debts complicated the development process and caused many countries to lose a decade of progress in their development efforts. By the mid-1990s, the crisis aspect of the debt had subsided, but its side effects lingered. Many developing countries continue to exhibit very low saving rates, making them dependent on foreign borrowing to finance investment. They still face the problem of how to maintain policies that create enough confidence in their economies' future performance to allow them to borrow to finance the investment required for development.

5. Developed and developing economies both have come to recognize a link between economic development and the environment. High-income developed economies press the developing economies to adopt more stringent environmental protections. Developing countries point out the disproportionate share of waste and pollution generated by the developed world with its high levels of consumption. Developing countries guard their right to exploit resources as they see fit, despite developed countries' wishes to restrict practices such as cutting of tropical rain forests that have global climatic consequences.

11.4 Primary-Product Markets: Opportunity or Dead End?

Historically, countries have viewed the process of economic development as synonymous with industrialization, or the move from a traditional agricultural society to a more urban one involved in manufacturing industries. Continued heavy reliance on agriculture and raw-material commodities has been one mark of an economy

Figure 11.2 □ **Relationship between GDP Per Capita and Share of Manufacturing Value-Added in GDP, 1984**

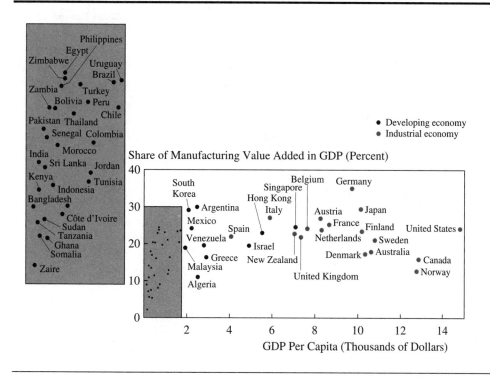

Source: World Bank, *World Development Report 1987*, p. 51. Reprinted with permission from The World Bank.

stalled in the early stages of development. As Figure 11.2 illustrates, there appears to be some relationship between gross domestic product (GDP) per capita and the share of manufacturing in GDP, but not a strong one.[4] Nonetheless, the 35 countries (26 in Africa) that the World Bank classifies as low-income commodity producers have average per capita incomes of only $420. These economies contain 31 percent of the world's population but produce only 3 percent of total world output.

Many developing countries strive to limit their concentration in primary products and move on to industrialization as a hallmark of successful development. In addition, primary product producers argue that markets for most primary products are highly competitive, resulting in prices equal to the marginal costs of production. On the other hand, they claim, the markets for manufactured goods often are monopolistic,

---

[4]GDP is a measure of a country's total output, similar to GNP. For a comparison of the two measures, see section 14.2.

Figure 11.3 □ **Sectoral Distribution of Working-Age Population by Country Income, 1995**

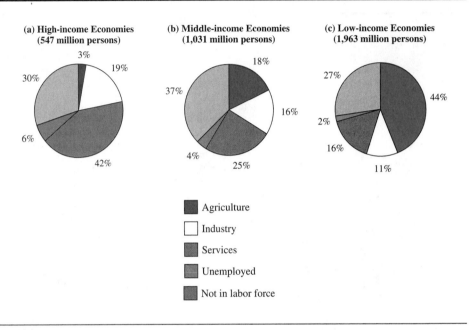

Source: World Bank, *World Development Report 1995*, p. 10.

resulting in monopoly profits. Because agriculture accounts for a much larger share of employment in developing than in developed economies, as illustrated in Figure 11.3, developing countries claim the inherent characteristics of primary-product markets foster their continued dependence on and low incomes relative to developed countries.

Extending this argument, developing countries claim their terms of trade deteriorate over time as prices of primary products fall relative to those of manufactured goods.[5] While the empirical evidence on this point is mixed, most economists agree there is little or no evidence of systematic long-term deterioration in developing countries' terms of trade. But even short-term periods of deterioration, such as that during the 1980s (see Figure 11.4), may interfere with development prospects.

During the 1970s, OPEC's example encouraged developing countries to believe concentration in primary products did not necessarily mean stagnant or deteriorating terms of trade. Demands for structural change in primary-product markets center on *stabilizing* prices and *raising* the prices paid by developed countries for imported primary products. The major policy tools suggested for accomplishing these goals include buffer stocks for stabilization and export restrictions or producer cartels to raise prices.

---

[5] A country's terms of trade consist of the price of the country's export good(s) relative to the price of its import good(s). A rise in this ratio is an improvement in the terms of trade and a fall is a deterioration.

Figure 11.4 □ **Developing Countries' Terms of Trade**

Barter terms of trade equal the weighted export unit values of primary commodities deflated by the weighted import unit values of each region. The barter terms of trade multiplied by the actual volume of exports yields the income terms of trade. Data are based on a sample of 90 developing countries.

Source: World Bank, *World Development Report 1991*, p. 106.

11.4.1 Buffer Stocks for Commodity Price Stabilization

Developing countries that specialize in and export primary commodities claim erratic prices in the markets for these goods make their export earnings extremely volatile. Although the prices of individual commodities, as well as price indices for primary products as a group, are quite volatile, careful empirical studies suggest the prices are only slightly more erratic than those of manufactured goods. Figure 11.5 outlines the recent historical pattern of changes in nonfuel commodities prices and oil prices relative to prices of manufactured goods.

Price volatility for individual commodities does not necessarily imply volatility of export earnings for producers. If the price of a commodity changes because of a shift in demand, both quantity sold and price move in the same direction, implying a positive relationship between price and revenue. *(Why?)* Shifts in demand caused by changes in the level of economic activity in the developed countries that make up the major markets often dominate markets for mineral and metal resources. The deep recession of the early 1980s, for example, drove prices in several mineral and metal markets to post-Second World War lows.

When shifts in supply cause changes in price, price and quantity sold move in opposite directions, and the effect on revenue depends on the elasticity of demand for the

Figure 11.5 □ **Price of Nonfuel Primary Commodities and Oil Relative to Price of Manufactures, 1982–1994 (Index, 1980 = 100)**

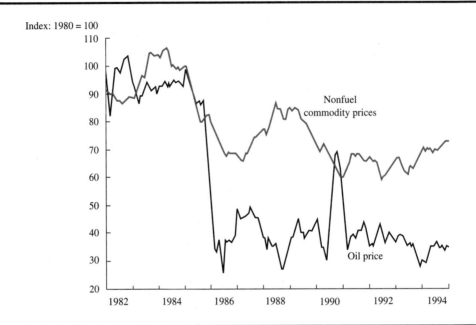

Source: International Monetary Fund, *World Economic Outlook*, May 1995, p. 36.

product. *(Why?)*[6] Markets for agricultural products often exhibit erratic shifts in supply because of uncontrollable influences such as weather. Because demand for many agricultural products is inelastic, supply-induced price increases cause increases in revenue to producers and decreases in price cause reductions in revenue. Because of this complex relationship between prices and revenues, the major policy tool suggested for dealing with price volatility—buffer stocks—would not necessarily stabilize revenue or export earnings and, in some cases, might even exacerbate their volatility.

One major reason for the volatility of export earnings among developing countries is their characteristic high degree of specialization in only a few commodities. As few as three export commodities typically comprise as much as 80 to 90 percent of a country's export revenue. Figure 11.6 illustrates this pattern in Africa. This situation becomes particularly acute when all three commodities are subject to the same shocks—for example, three minerals highly sensitive to business-cycle

---

[6]If demand is *inelastic*, any supply-induced change in price causes a *less* than proportional change in quantity demanded in the opposite direction; thus, revenue moves in the *same* direction as price. If demand is *elastic*, any supply-induced change in price causes a *more* than proportional change in quantity demanded in the opposite direction; hence revenue moves in the *opposite* direction from price.

Figure 11.6 □ **Share of Three Leading Commodity Exports in Total Exports, 1983–84**

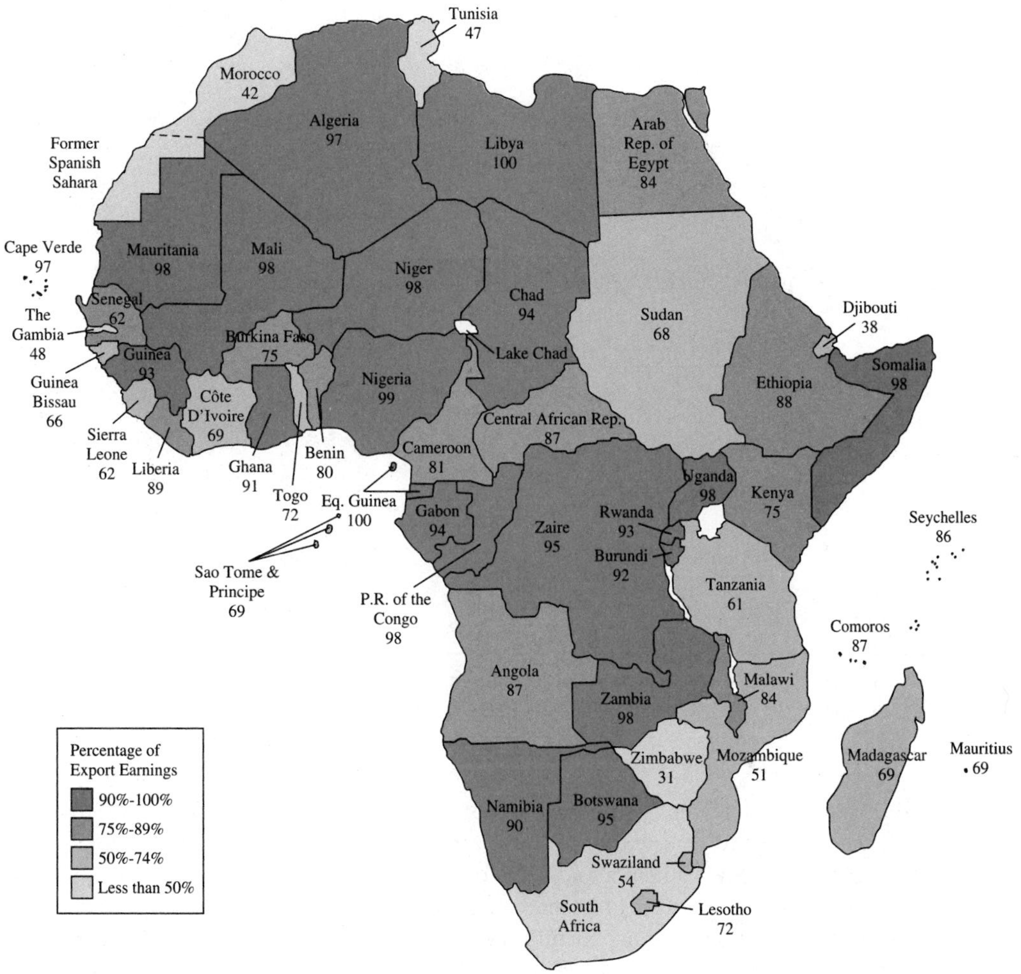

Tunisia 47
Morocco 42
Algeria 97
Libya 100
Arab Rep. of Egypt 84
Former Spanish Sahara
Cape Verde 97
Mauritania 98
Mali 98
Niger 98
Chad 94
Sudan 68
Djibouti 38
The Gambia 48
Senegal 62
Burkina Faso 75
Nigeria 99
Lake Chad
Ethiopia 88
Somalia 98
Guinea 93
Guinea Bissau 66
Côte D'Ivoire 69
Sierra Leone 62
Liberia 89
Ghana 91
Togo 72
Benin 80
Eq. Guinea 100
Cameroon 81
Central African Rep. 87
Uganda 98
Kenya 75
Seychelles 86
Gabon 94
Zaire 95
Rwanda 93
Burundi 92
Tanzania 61
Sao Tome & Principe 69
P.R. of the Congo 98
Comoros 87
Angola 87
Zambia 98
Malawi 84
Madagascar 69
Mauritius 69
Zimbabwe 31
Mozambique 51
Namibia 90
Botswana 95
Swaziland 54
South Africa
Lesotho 72

Percentage of Export Earnings
- 90%–100%
- 75%–89%
- 50%–74%
- Less than 50%

Source: World Bank, *Global Economic Prospects and the Developing Countries* (Washington, D.C.: The World Bank, 1991), p. 19.

conditions in developed countries or three agricultural commodities similarly affected by weather patterns.

One possible policy response, of course, is to save during good years to acquire a surplus for bad years. At the very low levels of income in some developing countries, saving is difficult even during good years. High inflation rates and the absence of well-developed financial institutions combine to discourage saving. In addition, many low-income

Figure 11.7 □ Buffer Stock to Stabilize Price of Commodity X

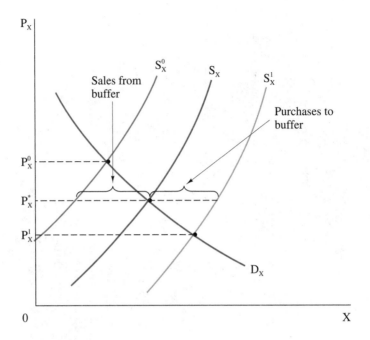

When short-run shocks push price above P_X^*, sales from the buffer stock lessen the upward pressure on price. When price falls below P_X^*, purchases are made and added to the buffer.

countries historically have suffered corrupt, shortsighted, unstable, and ineffective governments unable to deal with erratic export revenues. Policies that are international in scope offer one way to help avoid some of these problems. The major policy proposed for reducing price volatility in primary commodity markets involves buffer stocks.

A **buffer stock** is an arrangement to hold a stock of cash and a stock of the commodity to use to intervene in the market to offset any short-run volatility in the commodity's price. The major commodities with international buffer-stock arrangements in effect include cocoa and natural rubber.[7] Figure 11.7 illustrates the operation of a buffer stock as a means of stabilizing a commodity's price. Assume P_X^* is the long-run equilibrium price of good X in the world market, and the market for X is perfectly competitive. If supply and demand for X are subject to short-run shocks, P_X will fluctuate around P_X^* as supply and demand shift. With a buffer stock, whenever price rises above P_X^* (say, to P_X^0), X will be sold from the buffer stock, increasing quantity supplied and lowering the price back

---

[7]An agreement covering tin ceased to function when tin prices collapsed in 1985. For a summary of all international commodity agreements, see the annual U.S. International Trade Commission, *The Year in Trade.*

Figure 11.8 □ **Effect on Buffer Stock Arrangement When the Equilibrium Price is Over- or Underestimated**

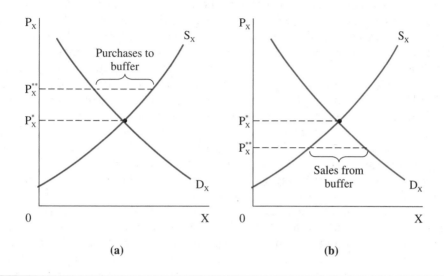

(a)   (b)

When the price at which purchases are made into the buffer stock is set above the true equilibrium price as in panel (a), the buffer stock grows and becomes expensive to maintain. When the price at which sales are made from the buffer stock is set below the true equilibrium price as in panel (b), the buffer stock is soon exhausted.

toward P_X^*. Similarly, when a shock in the market causes P_X to fall below P_X^* (say, to P_X^1), X will be bought and added to the buffer stock, raising the price back toward P_X^*.

Several problems arise in the use of buffer stocks. First, keep in mind from our earlier discussion that even if the buffer-stock arrangement stabilizes price, such success would not necessarily ensure stabilization of revenue or earnings. Beyond this, several additional considerations make operation of a buffer stock much more difficult than Figure 11.7 suggests. In the figure, the long-run equilibrium price, P_X^*, is known, so those in charge of administering the buffer stock know whenever price rises or falls *temporarily* above or below the long-run equilibrium level. In actual markets with continuously fluctuating supply and demand conditions, it is difficult, if not impossible, to determine the good's long-run equilibrium price.

Knowledge of the true equilibrium price is crucial to the viability of a buffer-stock arrangement. Figure 11.8 illustrates why. In panel (a), the true long-run equilibrium price of good X is P_X^*, but the administrators of the buffer stock mistakenly believe the equilibrium price is higher—at P_X^{**}. Price will chronically fall below P_X^{**}, causing purchases to be made and added to the buffer stock. This pattern will continue period after period as managers of the buffer stock try in vain to hold the price at P_X^{**}. Not only will their efforts fail, but the cost of continuous purchases and additions to the buffer stock also will become prohibitive.

Panel (b) of Figure 11.8 illustrates the opposite problem. Again the true long-run equilibrium is P_X^*, but managers of the buffer stock believe P_X^{**} is the equilibrium price. As price rises above P_X^{**}, sales will be made from the buffer stock. As the situation continues, the buffer stock eventually will be exhausted by the sales and price will rise to P_X^*.

Historically buffer stocks created with the stated goal of price *stabilization* have tended to take on a price-*support* role. The price that triggers purchases into the buffer stock is set artificially high (as in panel (a) of Figure 11.8), and the buffer stock of the commodity grows as the stock of cash shrinks. A new International Cocoa Agreement, negotiated in 1993, faced this problem. The International Cocoa Organization, which managed the buffer stock, had accumulated a 230,000-ton buffer stock of cocoa, to be liquidated; the new agreement was designed to rely more on promotion of cocoa consumption and less on buffer-stock purchases.

For a buffer-stock arrangement to remain viable in the long run, the "target" price (the price from which deviations trigger purchases or sales from the buffer stock) must approximately equal the long-run market equilibrium price, and deviations above and below that price must balance out so the size of the buffer stock does not change significantly over time. Purchases and sales must offset each other to prevent either the program's becoming prohibitively costly (as in panel (a) of Figure 11.8) or the exhaustion of the buffer stock (as in panel (b)).

An additional argument against widespread use of buffer stocks for price stabilization focuses on the role of private **speculation** in markets. An individual speculates in a market by buying (selling) the good when he or she expects its price to rise (fall) in order to subsequently sell (purchase) it and earn a profit. As long as private speculation is permitted, as in the markets for most primary products, it should perform much the same function outlined above for a buffer stock. When price rises above what speculators believe to be its long-run equilibrium level, they will expect price to fall, causing them to sell, just as sales would be made from a buffer stock. Similarly, price decreases below the perceived long-run level would lead to speculative purchases and a moderating upward pressure on price.

Because developing countries seek not only price stabilization for primary products but also increases in primary product relative prices, buffer-stock systems tend to suffer from the problem illustrated in panel (a) of Figure 11.8. The buffer stock is used not to stabilize price but to hold price above its true long-run equilibrium level. This requires continual purchases into the buffer stock and becomes enormously costly. The more successful commodity agreements include both producer and consumer countries, limiting the temptation to use the agreements to raise prices far above equilibrium levels. But producer- and consumer-country members of commodity agreements often disagree about appropriate policy, leading to breakdowns in the agreements.

It is also important to realize that the poor performance of some developing economies' agricultural sectors reflect poor policy choices more than inherent market characteristics. In many cases, import barriers restrict farmers' access to new agricultural technology and to productivity-enhancing improvements such as tractors. Governments maintain monopolies in farm products and force farmers to sell to the government monopolies at prices far below market levels, discouraging production. Government policies often favor the manufacturing sector with lower interest rates and easier access to credit, once again penalizing agriculture. Domestic politics contribute

Figure 11.9 □ Outcome of Collusion versus Competition

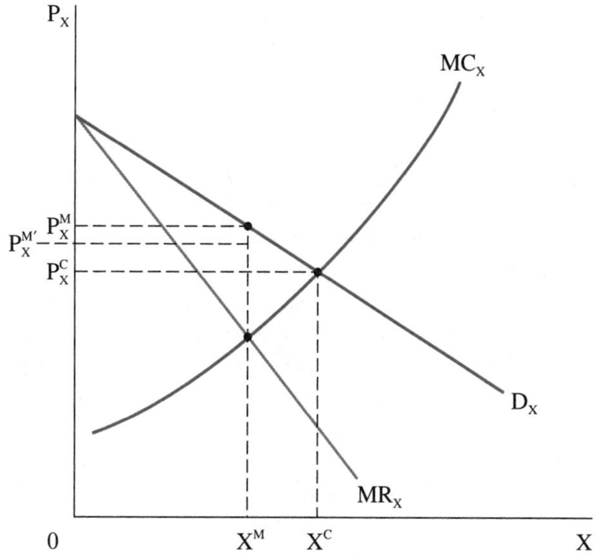

Collusion results in higher profits for the group of producers. However, each member has an incentive to cheat by charging a slightly lower price (such as $P_X^{M'}$) to increase the quantity sold.

to these counter-productive agricultural policies because small rural farmers in developing economies typically possess little political influence compared with urban elites who benefit from low food prices and government assistance to manufacturing.

11.4.2 Commodity Cartels for Raising Primary-Product Prices

Insofar as relative price increases for primary products, rather than price stabilization, are the goal, the most commonly proposed strategy involves producer cartels similar to the Organization of Petroleum Exporting Countries (OPEC). As noted previously, many primary products are produced under perfectly competitive conditions, implying that each seller makes up too small a portion of the world market to affect the market price. For some primary products, however, including several minerals, metals, and tropical agricultural products, production is clustered within a small number of countries. In such markets, producers may agree to act collectively as a monopolist rather than competing with one another. Such **collusion** produces increased profits available to share among the participants.

Figure 11.9 compares the outcome of producers competing with one another with that of producers colluding to act as a monopolist. Under competition, the marginal cost curve in Figure 11.9 represents the industry supply curve and output level X^C

would be produced at price P_X^C. By colluding, producers can agree to restrict output to the *monopoly* level, X^M, which will allow them to charge the monopoly price, P_X^M. Because the restriction in output is necessary to charge the monopoly price (that is, consumers are not willing to pay P_X^M per unit for each of X^C units), cartel arrangements among exporters sometimes are called **export restrictions**. The cartel arrangement can work only if producers can agree on an allocation of production that results in a total output of no more than X^M.

Two major problems exist with collusive export restrictions as a long-run strategy for raising the relative prices of particular products; one problem arises on the part of producers and the other on the part of consumers. Producers as a group are better off colluding than competing with one another. But each producer is better off cheating and charging a price below P_X^M so long as the others charge P_X^M. Suppose a single producer cheats by producing one unit more than its agreed-upon share of X^M and charging a price slightly below P_X^M—say, $P_X^{M'}$. The cheating producer will gain additional revenue equal to $P_X^{M'}$ and incur additional costs equal to MC_X, realizing a sizable profit from cheating on the cartel agreement. But each producer has the same incentive to cheat; thus, the agreement is likely to break down as individual producers lower their prices and raise their production levels in attempts to gain larger shares of the profitable market.

Even OPEC fell prey to the lure of cheating in the 1980s, resulting in a significant decline in oil prices.[8] The smaller OPEC producers cheated by selling at prices somewhat below the cartel's agreed-upon price; they counted on Saudi Arabia, the dominant producer, to absorb the cost of their cheating by cutting its own production to keep the total at X^M. Eventually Saudi Arabia tired of its thankless and unprofitable role and raised its own production in retaliation, causing a rapid fall in the market price. Price reductions by non-OPEC producers, including Mexico (which needed the additional revenues to service its debt), Egypt, Britain, and the United States, reinforced the price decline.

In 1995, the Association of Coffee Producing countries agreed to reduce their exports from 70 million bags per year to 60 million bags (a bag contains 132 pounds of coffee). Most analysts predicted widespread cheating would prevent the agreement from exerting much influence on price. Several major producers, including Mexico, do not belong to the association, further limiting the group's effectiveness.

The problem (from the colluding producers' point of view) arising on the consumers' side of the market involves development of new substitutes for the product in response to the high monopoly price; the more successful the cartel, the stronger the incentive to develop substitutes. Synthetic rubber, plastics, synthetic fabrics, and artificial sweeteners are a few of the products developed as substitutes. Even when development of a substitute is difficult, new producers outside the cartel arrangement often enter to take advantage of the high prices. Kenya's coffee industry, for example, grew in response to Brazil's attempts to raise export prices. International commodity agreements in coffee and sugar rely on export quotas to

---

[8]OPEC members include Kuwait, Ecuador, Indonesia, Venezuela, Nigeria, Iraq, Saudi Arabia, Qatar, Algeria, Libya, Iran, the United Arab Emirates, and Gabon.

achieve their price goals; unlike OPEC, both agreements include consumer as well as producer countries.

Even if cartel arrangements in commodity markets could achieve a permanent increase in the relative prices of primary products, the cartels' contribution to the long-term well-being of the developing countries would still be open to question. MacBean and Snowden point out the possibility of undesirable distributional consequences of cartels: "They raise revenues by imposing a regressive tax on consumers and may transfer these revenues to wealthy producers or exporters or to governments whose policies with regard to either growth or equity leave a great deal to be desired."[9] And, of course, monopolized markets cause inefficiency, so consumers lose more than the monopolists gain.

11.4.3 Agricultural Policies and the Uruguay Round

The agricultural policies of developed countries also limit developing countries' abilities to export primary products. These policies have primarily domestic goals, including raising agricultural prices and supporting domestic farmers' incomes in the developed countries. However, as we saw in Chapters Seven and Eight, the domestic policies often require trade-policy supplements, especially import quotas and export subsidies. One study, summarized in Figure 11.10, found that reduction of developed countries' barriers to agricultural imports could increase developing country exports by 2 to 40 percent. In a comical but revealing incident, European Community ministers argued for an hour over tariff reductions on artichokes from 66 developing countries—until the EC development commissioner told the ministers the countries did not even grow artichokes![10]

We saw in Chapter Six that the **effective rate of protection (ERP)** provided by a given nominal tariff on a finished product depends on the tariffs levied on inputs used in producing it. The lower the tariffs on inputs, other things equal, the higher the rate of protection on the finished good. The developed countries' **cascading tariff structures** impose increasing tariff rates as a good moves through the stages of production; tariffs are lowest on raw materials and highest on finished manufactures. The tariff reductions negotiated through the GATT prior to the Uruguay Round perpetuated this cascading structure (see Table 11.3 for examples). The result was often an effective rate of protection on processed and finished goods several times the nominal tariff rates. In reaching developed-country markets, developing countries faced increasingly high barriers as they attempted to move into processing and manufacturing. They perceived these barriers as deliberate attempts to relegate them to a role of supplying raw materials to the developed economies.

All these agriculture-related issues ranked high on developing countries' lists of concerns about the world trading system in the 1980s. The beginning of the Uruguay Round of GATT talks in 1986 involved special attempts to encourage

---

[9]A. I. MacBean and P. N. Snowden, *International Institutions in Trade and Finance* (London: George Allen & Unwin, 1981), 103.

[10]"The Art of Choking on Words," *Sacramento Bee*, October 30, 1989.

Figure 11.10 □ **Potential Increases in Agricultural Exports of Selected Developing Countries from Reducing Trade Barriers in OECD Countries**

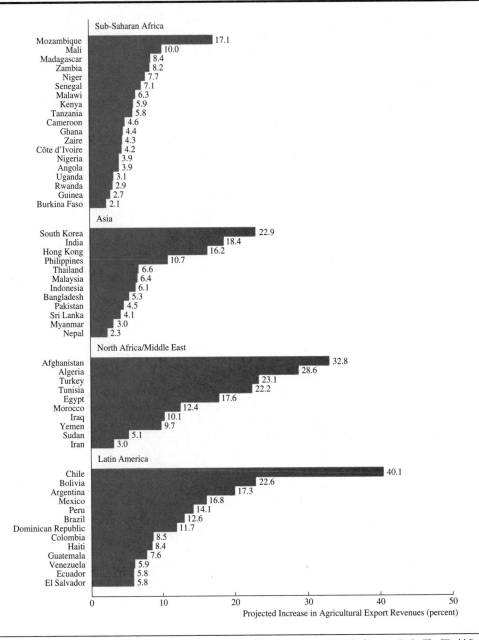

Source: World Bank, *Global Economic Prospects and the Developing Countries* (Washington, D.C.: The World Bank, 1991), p. 32; data from Samuel Laird and Alexander Yeats, *Quantitative Methods for Trade Barrier Analysis* (London: Macmillan, 1990).

Table 11.3 □ **Post-Tokyo Round Tariffs for 12 Processing Chains (Percent)**

Stage of Processing	Product Description	Post-Tokyo Tariff Rate
1	Fish, crustaceans, and mollusks	3.5
2	Fish, crustaceans, and mollusks, prepared	5.5
1	Vegetables, fresh or dried	8.9
2	Vegetables, prepared	12.4
1	Fruit, fresh or dried	4.8
2	Fruit, provisionally preserved	12.2
3	Fruit, prepared	16.6
1	Coffee	6.8
2	Processed coffee	9.4
1	Cocoa beans	2.6
2	Processed cocoa	4.3
3	Chocolate products	11.8
1	Oilseeds and flour	2.7
2	Fixed vegetable oils	8.1
1	Unmanufactured tobacco	55.8
2	Manufactured tobacco	81.8
1	Natural rubber	2.3
2	Semimanufactured rubber (nonvulcanized)	2.9
3	Rubber articles	6.7
1	Rawhides and skins	0.0
2	Semimanufactured leather	4.2
3	Travel goods, handbags, and so on	8.5
4	Manufactured articles of leather	8.2
1	Vegetable textiles and yarns (excluding hemp)	2.9
2	Twine, rope, and articles; sacks and bags	4.7
3	Jute fabrics	8.3
1	Silk yarn, but not for retail sale	2.6
2	Silk fabric	5.3
1	Semimanufactured wood	1.8
2	Wood panels	9.2
3	Wood articles	4.1
4	Furniture	6.6

Source: The World Bank, *World Development Report 1987*, p. 138. Reprinted with permission from The World Bank.

active participation by developing countries; and the debates over agricultural policy just described played a key role. Earlier GATT rounds had ignored agricultural trade, although it was a major concern of developing countries and a major source of trade disagreements, because the developed economies did not want to face the domestic political consequences of changing their agricultural policies. At the beginning of the Uruguay Round, developed countries promised to include agriculture in the talks in exchange for developing countries' active participation and their consent to include trade liberalization in services on the agenda as well.

At several points in the negotiations, most notably in late 1990 and 1992, disagreements between the United States and the European Union over agricultural policy threatened to kill the Uruguay Round after years of work. But a group of mostly developing agricultural exporting countries known as the Cairns group maintained pressure for agricultural reform.[11]

In the end, the Uruguay Round made substantial progress in agricultural reform. Several of the changes will enhance developing countries' access to export markets in the developed countries. GATT members no longer can grant new export subsidies to agricultural goods. For developed countries, existing export subsidies must be cut by 36 percent over the next six years, and each country's volume of subsidized exports must be reduced by 21 percent. Developing countries must institute similar changes, but at rates of 24 percent and 14 percent on the amount and volume of subsidies, respectively. Countries also must reduce their aggregate domestic subsidies provided to farmers by 20 percent.

The Uruguay Round agreement also requires developed member countries to convert all nontariff barriers into their tariff equivalents, which then become subject to the negotiated schedule of average tariff reductions of 36 percent over six years. Developing countries must follow a similar plan, but with cuts of 24 percent over ten years. For the least developed economies, the agreement requires binding agricultural tariffs at current levels, but no cuts. And markets subject to prohibitive quotas in the past, such as the Japanese rice market, must provide minimum access to imports. In addition, the agreement reduces cascading tariffs. For paper, jute, and tobacco products, it eliminates completely the differentials between tariffs on processed and unprocessed goods; overall, the agreement reduces the differential by 37 percent.

11.5 Efforts at Industrialization

Industrialization traditionally has been viewed as a crucial step in the process of economic development. The record of success in industrialization varies. The United States and Japan were, not too many years ago, developing countries and now are industrial giants in the world economy. More recent years have seen other success stories, including Taiwan, South Korea, and Brazil. The experiences of other countries, such as India, Argentina, and many of those in sub-Saharan Africa, have been much less encouraging, sometimes for obvious reasons and sometimes for less obvious ones. Overall the developing countries' shares of production and export of manufactures have increased significantly over the past two decades, but most of the growth has come in middle-income developing countries rather than in low-income ones.

International trade often has been called the "engine of growth." Historically, periods of rapid growth in international trade have corresponded with periods of rapid increases in world output. Nonetheless, developing countries differ widely in the role assigned to international trade in the development process. The two basic

---

[11]The group includes Argentina, Australia, Brazil, Canada, Chile, Colombia, Fiji, Hungary, Indonesia, Malaysia, New Zealand, the Philippines, Thailand, and Uruguay.

development strategies have come to be known as *import substitution* and *export promotion,* or *export-oriented growth.*

11.5.1 Industrialization Strategies

An **import-substitution** development strategy involves extensive use of trade barriers to protect domestic industries from import competition. The goal is to replace imports with domestically produced goods. Import substitution focuses primarily on eliminating imported manufactures and on encouraging the growth of domestic manufacturing. Many developing countries, using the infant-industry argument from Chapter Eight, followed import-substitution policies during the 1950s and 1960s, and some continue to do so. However, evidence suggests that forgoing gains from trade to develop often inefficient domestic manufacturing industries does *not* constitute a promising development strategy; in fact, the results of import substitution have been disappointing, exactly as the early chapters of the book would lead one to expect. Somewhat more surprising is that import substitution seemingly fails to decrease dependence on imports. By artificially encouraging industrialization even in areas of comparative disadvantage, import substitution can actually increase dependence on imported inputs and capital goods required to keep production going in the protected industries. Because of the inefficient nature of many of the manufacturing processes, the value of these imports often exceeds that of the manufactured goods imported before institution of an import-substitution policy. The inefficiencies of import-substitution policies multiply when the industries chosen exhibit economies of scale, because the domestic market typically is too small to support production at a level high enough to achieve those economies.

The other strategy for development, **export-oriented growth** or **export promotion,** is best characterized as outward looking. The strategy involves exploiting comparative advantage and economies of scale and importing goods costly to produce domestically. Industrialization for its own sake receives less emphasis here than under an import-substitution policy. Countries specialize production along the lines dictated by their comparative advantage, which may be resource based, and in sectors where export success can allow them to achieve economies of scale. Industrialization is a natural outcome of development rather than a goal pursued for its own sake.

Because of the critical importance of the import-substitution/export-promotion policy choice for world welfare, economists have devoted a great deal of time and effort to examining the implications of each. One of the world's leading authorities on economic development, Anne Krueger of Stanford University and formerly of the World Bank, completed one of the most thorough studies. The Krueger analysis suggests the evidence overwhelmingly favors export-oriented policies as a strategy for development. Countries that pursue such policies have higher average growth rates than countries that pursue import substitution. In addition, individual countries typically experience spurts in their growth rates when they switch from import substitution to export-oriented policies. Finally, despite its lower emphasis on industrialization, an export-oriented policy appears to promote higher growth rates in manufactured exports than does a policy that attempts industrialization through import substitution.

To understand the differential success of import-substitution and export-promotion development strategies, recall how early chapters of this book emphasized the importance of market-determined prices in guiding resources to their highest-valued use. An inward-oriented strategy, or import substitution, involves circumventing market forces to alter prices and encourage domestic manufacturing regardless of the pattern of comparative advantage and without regard to the prospects for achieving economies of scale. Such a strategy involves extensive use of tariffs, quotas, and import licensing schemes, often justified by appeals to the infant-industry argument for protection (see section 8.3). The second strategy, an outward-oriented one, stresses specialization according to comparative advantage and reliance on sectors where firms can achieve economies of scale rather than an attempt at artificially induced industrialization.

The World Bank study classified 41 developing countries, together accounting for two-thirds of the output of all developing countries in 1985, according to their development strategies in two periods, 1963–1973 and 1973–1985.[12] Table 11.4 lists the results of the classification.

Next, the study collected weighted averages of annual growth rates in GDP, GNP per capita, and real manufactured exports for each of the four groups of countries. Figure 11.11 reports these results. The figure suggests the economic performance of the outward-oriented economies has been superior to that of the inward-oriented economies. The trend is clear in both GDP and GNP per capita and for both time periods. Not only was overall growth of GDP higher, but manufactured exports also grew more rapidly in the outward-oriented economies. Given the models presented in Chapters Two through Eight, this finding is not surprising, since the industries supported under inward-oriented policies often are not industries of comparative advantage and therefore are poorly equipped to compete in world markets. With no ability to export, firms in industries subject to economies of scale suffer from their small scale, while import restrictions grant them monopoly positions in the domestic market.

Several explanations contribute to the apparent failure of many import-substitution programs. Most important, the infant-industry argument, as we saw in Chapter Eight, suffers from serious weaknesses. A period of temporary government support is no substitute for comparative advantage, and an industry without comparative advantage will remain an infant forever. In many developing economies, shortages of skilled labor, experienced management, clear and well-enforced property rights and contract law, and entrepreneurship hamper the emergence of successful industrial enterprises. Under these circumstances, an import-substitution policy based on import barriers simply guarantees the continued existence of an inefficient domestic industry—at the expense of domestic consumers and taxpayers. To make matters worse, many of the developing countries that pursued import substitution most aggressively were small, so their attempts to develop manufacturing based solely on the domestic market doomed firms to produce at inefficiently small scale.

---

[12]David Greenaway, "Characteristics of Industrialization and Economic Performance under Alternative Strategies," World Bank background paper.

Table 11.4 □ **Classification by Trade Orientation, 1963–1973 and 1973–1985**

Period	Outward Oriented		Inward Oriented	
	Strongly Outward Oriented	**Moderately Outward Oriented**	**Moderately Inward Oriented**	**Strongly Inward Oriented**
1963–1973	Hong Kong	Brazil	Bolivia	Argentina
	Singapore	Cameroon	El Salvador	Bangladesh
	South Korea	Colombia	Kenya	Burundi
		Costa Rica	Madagascar	Chile
		Côte d'Ivoire	Mexico	Dominican Republic
		Guatemala	Nicaragua	Ethiopia
		Indonesia	Nigeria	Ghana
		Israel	Philippines	India
		Malaysia	Senegal	Pakistan
		Thailand	Tunisia	Peru
			Yugoslavia	Sri Lanka
				Sudan
				Tanzania
				Turkey
				Uruguay
				Zambia
1973–1985	Hong Kong	Brazil	Cameroon	Argentina
	Singapore	Chile	Colombia	Bangladesh
	South Korea	Israel	Costa Rica	Bolivia
		Malaysia	Côte d'Ivoire	Burundi
		Thailand	El Salvador	Dominican Republic
		Tunisia	Guatemala	Ethiopia
		Turkey	Honduras	Ghana
		Uruguay	Indonesia	India
			Kenya	Madagascar
			Mexico	Nigeria
			Nicaragua	Peru
			Pakistan	Sudan
			Philippines	Tanzania
			Senegal	Zambia
			Sri Lanka	
			Yugoslavia	

Source: World Bank, *World Development Report 1987,* p. 83.

Figure 11.11 □ **Performance of 41 Developing Countries Grouped by Trade Orientation, 1963–1973 and 1973–1985**

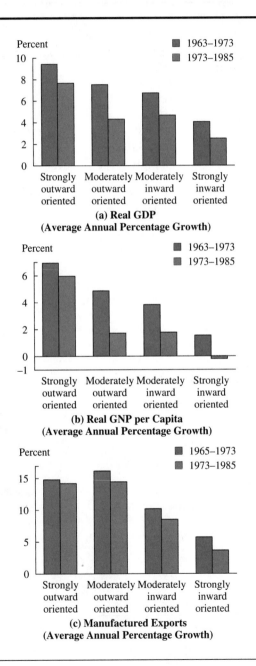

Table 11.5 □ **NIC Economic Indicators, 1993**

Country	Per Capita GDP ($)	Exports ($ Billions)	Imports ($ Billions)	Life Expectancy	Dispersed Foreign Aid ($ Millions)
Hong Kong	22,900	135.2	138.7	80	n.a.
Singapore	18,800	74.0	85.2	76	12.4
South Korea	10,100	82.2	83.8	70	176.0
Taiwan	10,600	84.7	77.1	75	61.0

Source: *The Wall Street Journal*, February 28, 1995.

Import substitution also failed for reasons having as much to do with politics as with economics. The strategy's emphasis on manufacturing tempted many developing economies to pour vast resources into building highly visible and symbolic national industries, such as steel, autos, chemicals, and national airlines, with no regard for comparative advantage or economies of scale. Active involvement by governments in favoring some sectors of the economy over others asks governments to predict which industries might succeed. Such predictions run a high risk of failure as patterns of comparative advantage change throughout the world economy. Even in Japan, a success story overall, the industries that proved most successful often were not the ones favored by the government during the years of import substitution in the 1950s and 1960s. Governments often fail in the task of choosing industries to support because they pick in part based on special-interest groups' political pressure for protection rather than analysis of the economic situation. Political factors also make the switch away from import substitution difficult, even after the strategy's failure becomes apparent. Capital owners and workers in industries created by import-substitution policies are potent political forces to block a shift toward other development strategies.

11.5.2 The Newly Industrializing Countries

Some developing economies switched away from import substitution early and opened their economies to trade. Many have enjoyed remarkable rates of economic growth and industrialization. Some, including South Korea, Hong Kong, Singapore, and Taiwan, earned the name **newly industrializing countries (NICs)** for their swift move along the development path. Most indicators suggest these economies now have substantially more in common with the developed countries than with the low-income developing ones, as Table 11.5 reports. They have built major export industries including steel, ship-building, chemicals, semiconductors, and computers. They are undertaking foreign investment projects in Vietnam and China, as well as the United States and Europe. They even have started financing foreign aid projects in less-developed economies.

Scholars and policy makers debate the precise reasons for these countries' success. Most analysts agree, however, that the countries did not ignore patterns of comparative advantage and the importance of achieving economies of scale.

11.6   Technology, Intellectual Property, and Development

Technology, viewed from the economist's perspective, is the set of rules that govern how inputs or factors of production can be transformed into goods and services. Improvements in technology allow more goods and services to be produced from the same quantity of inputs or the same quantity of goods and services to be produced from a smaller quantity of inputs. Technological improvement contributes to economic development by increasing the output a country can produce given its endowment of resources.[13]

The research and development (R&D) process that leads to technological innovations is very long, expensive, risky, and skill intensive. It also is subject to economies of scale, implying that R&D on a very small scale is inefficient. These characteristics of the R&D process make it difficult for developing countries to create their own indigenous technologies, resulting in dependence on the developed world for technological innovation.

11.6.1   Technology Transfer and Appropriateness

Developing economies point to two aspects of current technology arrangements they believe work to their disadvantage. The first is the terms on which firms in developing countries gain access to new technologies, often through multinational enterprises. The second issue concerns the nature of the technology itself and its appropriateness for developing countries.

In the industrial market economies, where most technological innovation takes place, private companies whose incentive is the promise of profit from any forthcoming innovations typically conduct most research. An international system of patents—legal restrictions on uncompensated use of technology developed by others—protects technology from being freely copied, a protection that allows companies engaged in research to capture the returns necessary to justify their efforts. If a newly developed innovation were available to all at no cost, research might slow as the incentive to innovate fell. However, experience suggests that competitive pressures from rival firms are at least as important as the prospect of future monopoly returns in inducing firms to innovate. The prices firms charge for licenses to use new technologies do slow the spread of technology from developed to developing countries. Multinational enterprises sometimes maintain their technologically innovative research and development divisions in their home countries and restrict the degree of **technology transfer** to their foreign subsidiaries.

Critics of multinationals claim these policies prevent developing countries from using the technologies to advance the rest of their economies. The more relevant question is not whether developing economies would benefit if given free access to all technology created by developed country firms (a scenario unlikely to happen), but whether developing countries that open themselves to trade gain access to useful technologies and grow faster than countries that insulate themselves from the world

---

[13]Section 10.3 analyzed the effect of technical progress on economic growth.

trading system. Recent experience provides a clear answer to this question. Although the most successful developing economies differ widely in the extent to which they have welcomed foreign direct investment by multinational enterprises, virtually all have imported and exported relatively freely and used their trade to learn about and master technologies created abroad.

Major technological advances tend to occur in physical-capital-abundant and human-capital-abundant countries, where firms' goals for technological improvement include substitution of abundant capital for relatively scarce unskilled labor. The technology often is designed for use on a large scale, in plants producing for the entire world market. Developing countries, however, often claim they need a different type of technology, because they tend to have abundant unskilled labor and little physical or human capital. The appropriate technologies in such situations typically would be labor intensive and perhaps small scale.

Firms, whether multinational or domestic, respond to the incentives they face in choosing technologies. In the past, many developing economies' import-substitution policies gave firms incentives to use highly capital-intensive technologies, because capital-intensive industries gave the illusion of successful industrialization. Without such artificial incentives, multinational firms producing in labor-abundant countries have an incentive to use technologies that take advantage of the availability of low-wage labor. Thus, labor-abundant developing countries must recognize that the production techniques that use their labor and, thereby, raise wages, may not correspond to the symbolically important capital-intensive industrialization typical of industries such as steel and chemicals.

11.6.2 Intellectual Property

Trade disputes over **intellectual property** involve trade in goods that infringe on foreign copyrights, trademarks, industrial secrets, and patents, including counterfeit goods. Industries in which intellectual-property issues play a large role include pharmaceuticals, computer software, music recordings, computers, books, and movies. These issues have only recently earned a prominent role in international trade negotiations. Earlier, developed economies tended to ignore whatever losses their firms sustained due to unauthorized copying, and developing economies claimed openly the right to copy at will in order to diffuse the benefits from technological advances and to avoid the monopoly prices charged by innovating firms for their technologies.

More recently, trade in goods containing important intellectual-property elements has grown much faster than trade overall. This trend has caused firms in developed economies to take their lost revenues more seriously, since the developed economies exhibit strong comparative advantage in most of the relevant industries. In addition, the growth of developing economies' markets has made innovating firms eager to sell there, but the developing countries' weak intellectual-property laws and enforcement have limited the profitability of doing so.

Several developing economies have moved unilaterally to strengthen their intellectual-property protection. Although this trend represents in part a response to pressure from developed countries, especially the United States, other reasons exist as well. Some of the more successful developing economies have begun to innovate and to shift into industries where they themselves desire intellectual-property protection. Other countries hope, by strengthening their rules, to encourage inward foreign direct investment and the willingness of foreign firms to share new technologies with their local affiliates.

Several factors complicate international negotiations over intellectual-property rules. One is the difficulty in determining the optimal level of protection. Any system of intellectual-property rules represents a tradeoff between the incentives to innovate (which rest on strong protection) and the benefits from rapid diffusion (which come from weak or nonexistent rules). Probably a more important impediment to successful negotiations is the obvious distributional consequence of rule changes. Unlike negotiations to lower most trade barriers, which produce gains for all countries, strengthening intellectual-property protection is likely to generate gains for some (developed and a few advanced developing economies) and losses for others (most developing economies), at least in the short run. Because each country knows into which group it falls, gaining consensus is difficult. Countries that expect to be technology importers for the foreseeable future have little incentive to accept stronger intellectual-property rules, and countries that are or expect to become technology exporters have every incentive to push for strong rules.

The Uruguay Round did produce an agreement on intellectual property. Members will grant *national treatment,* which means foreign intellectual property will receive equal protection to that granted domestic intellectual property. Countries must grant any protection given to one trading partner to all under the agreement's most-favored-nation provision. Members also agreed to respect copyrights, trademarks, industrial-design secrets, and patents, with rules to be phased in over a one-year period for developed countries, five years for developing countries and economies in transition, and 11 years for the least-developed economies. Since completion of the Uruguay Round, the United States has conducted investigations and bilateral negotiations with Mexico, Taiwan, South Korea, and China concerning alleged widespread intellectual-property violations by those countries. Case Three at the end of the chapter traces the U.S.–China dispute.

11.7 Debts for Development

In 1982, Mexico announced it could no longer afford to make the scheduled payments on its debt, and the debt owed by developing economies moved to the front page of newspapers worldwide. It was a full decade before policy makers declared the "end" of "the debt crisis." During that decade, developing countries' inability to make interest and principal payments on their debt periodically threatened the stability of the world financial system and continually strained relations between developed and developing countries. While the day-to-day crisis aspect of the developing-country debt may be over, its effects linger. Here we shall analyze the nature of developing-country debt, how it came about, its effects, and how it evolved from a trade-oriented, or microeconomic, perspective. In Part Two, we focus on the macroeconomic aspects of the debt.

11.7.1 Defining and Measuring the Debt

Historically, developing economies always have relied heavily on borrowing from abroad to finance the domestic investment that plays such a vital role in development. The extent and exact nature of the borrowing have varied through time. Before the First World War and again between the First and Second, British private investors financed much of the investment in the then-developing world (including the United States) by buying bonds. After the Second World War, the newly created international institutions, the International Monetary Fund and the World Bank, began making development-oriented loans. This lending continues, especially to the lowest-income economies. At the same time, investors in developed countries undertook large-scale foreign direct investment in the developing world, at first in mining and mineral industries and then in manufacturing. Newly independent developing economies in the 1960s often viewed foreign investors as exploiters and sought alternate sources of funding that would maintain more local control. They found such a source in the mid-1970s when members of OPEC lacked adequate domestic investment opportunities for their burgeoning revenues. The OPEC countries deposited their funds in banks, mostly in the United States, which then made bank loans to developing economies. The various sources of borrowing by developing economies vary greatly in their importance over time, but all four types continue to be used. All these sources of borrowing—bonds sold abroad to private investors, official lending, foreign direct investment, and foreign bank loans—together constitute **external debt,** that is, borrowing from abroad.[14]

The external debt of developing countries now totals well over $1.9 trillion, as shown in Figure 11.12. However, in analyzing debt, knowing the total quantities owed—even when the amounts are measured in trillions—is not sufficient; different types of debt carry different implications.

Figure 11.13 diagrams a useful taxonomy for the developing countries. Total debt can be divided into short-term debt, long-term debt, and use of credit from the International Monetary Fund. The bulk of developing-country debt (over 75 percent as of 1994) falls into the long-term category; this means the prinicipal need not be repaid until well in the future, and only interest payments are required in the short term. Long-term debt is classified by the identity of the debtor—the private sector or the public sector. Public-sector debt refers to amounts either owed by or guaranteed by the developing-country government; private-sector debt is owed by individuals and firms and not guaranteed by government. About 90 percent of total long-term developing-country debt is public or publicly guaranteed, so the debt problem is primarily one of public-sector debt. For short-term debt (loans with maturities of one year or less), available statistics do not distinguish between public- and private-sector debt.

Because governments owe or guarantee so much of the developing-country debt, the defaults feared during the debt crisis would have been **government** or **sovereign defaults** rather than defaults by private firms or individuals. This effectively ruled out the legal

---

[14]With the "end of the debt crisis," stock markets in developing economies have begun to attract investment funds from abroad. This represents a fifth component of external debt, but it was trivial during most of the crisis period; see Figure 11.16.

Figure 11.12 □ **Developing Countries' Nominal External Debt, 1982–1994**

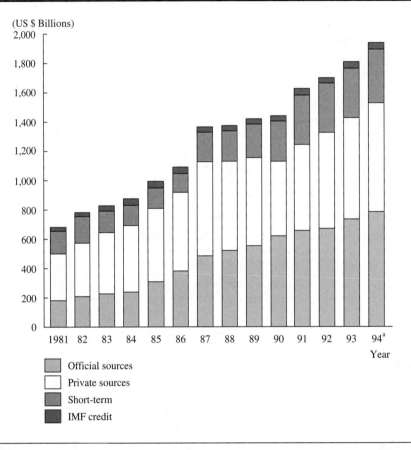

(US $ Billions)

Official sources
Private sources
Short-term
IMF credit

ªProjected.

Source: World Bank, *World Debt Tables Vol. 1, 1991–1992*, p. 4; *1994–1995*, p. 25.

remedies a bank normally would pursue against a firm or individual who failed to make loan payments. However, governments still had incentives not to default on their loans. The primary reason: Such behavior could result in inability to borrow in the future, at least for several years.[15] Loss of borrowing privileges, in turn, would limit access to trade by eliminating a major source of trade financing. An additional incentive rested on the threat of seizure by creditors of any assets that the debtor government owned abroad.

[15]History reveals that the punishment for debt repudiation does not last forever. Most of the countries of Latin America, for example, defaulted on loans during the 1930s. But by the early postwar years, those countries were able to borrow again in international capital markets. As we shall see below, capital flows already have resumed following the 1980s crisis.

Figure 11.13 □ **Taxonomy of Developing Country Debt**

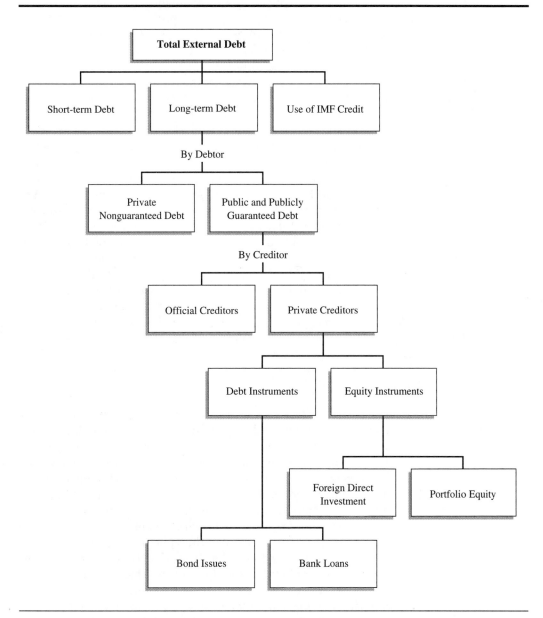

Source: World Bank, *World Debt Tables Vol. 1, 1991–1992*, p. ix; augmented.

Just as debt can be divided according to type of debtor, either public or private, it can be classified by type of creditor. The main classification distinguishes between **official debt,** owed to governments and international organizations, and **commercial,** or **unofficial,** or **market debt,** owed to private sources, primarily commercial banks. During the 1950s and 1960s, the bulk of development loans were of the official type. Throughout the 1970s, commercial banks became more involved in making loans to developing countries, with dramatic consequences.

We also can classify borrowing by the nature of the payments owed by debtors to creditors. The two main types are borrowing using **debt instruments** and borrowing using **equity instruments.** Debt instruments obligate the debtor to make payments of a fixed amount to the creditor at a specified date, regardless of the profitability of the financed project and regardless of economic circumstances. Borrowing by issuing bonds and through bank loans both fall into this category. The alternative is equity finance, in which debtor and creditor agree to share in the fortunes of a project, good or bad, with the shares determined in advance. Historically, equity finance in developing economies occurred primarily through foreign direct investment. Only recently have stock markets in some developing economies evolved to the point that they attract significant flows of equity finance from investors in developed economies. Borrowing through equity has the advantage that when an investment project turns out badly, the payments owed by the debtor to its creditors automatically fall, eliminating the risk of default. One reason developing countries encountered problems with their accumulation of borrowing in the 1980s was that most of the debt took the form of bank loans and bonds rather than equity. When investment projects failed and debtors' economic circumstances deteriorated, the same loan payments still came due. In fact, we shall see that, as matters got worse, the loan payments actually grew.

11.7.2 General Rules of Debt

That many developing countries face large external debts does not necessarily signal a problem. We have seen that intertemporal trade, in which countries with low current incomes and saving but plentiful investment opportunities borrow from countries with high incomes and saving but scarce investment opportunities, generates gains from trade. Therefore, borrowing by developing countries from developed countries would be expected to produce gains for both debtors and creditors. All borrowing, however, must conform to a few simple rules to avoid repayment and default problems.

To evaluate a particular country's debt situation, we must have information beyond just the amount of the debt, much of it the same information we would want to evaluate the debt facing an individual or firm. The economic implications of debt depend on the amount of funds borrowed, the use to which the funds are put, the terms of the borrowing, and the borrowing country's future prospects and general economic circumstances. Only when one considers all these aspects can one appraise a particular country's debt. Generally, a country's borrowing presents no problem as long as (1) the funds finance investment projects that produce returns sufficient to pay the interest on the loan (to "service the debt," in banking jargon); (2) the **maturity** of the loan, or the time over which the loan must be repaid, matches that of the financed investment projects; and (3) the possibility of unforeseen events is evaluated in calculating the total amount of acceptable debt. Unfortunately, much of the borrowing by developing countries during the 1970s broke at least one of these rules, and some of it violated all three.

Use of Funds

In evaluating any debt, whether individual, firm, or government, the most important question concerns the use of the funds. Did the developing-country governments use debt primarily to finance consumption in excess of income (in which case we would expect a crisis, because the borrowed funds would not produce the returns to cover repayment) or to finance investment projects that reasonably could be expected to support repayment? The answer to this question clearly differs over time and across countries, but the evidence suggests the borrowing went primarily for investment and not current consumption purposes. Why, then, did such serious problems arise?

In some countries, such as Mexico, the bulk of the investment funded by borrowing was undertaken by the public rather than the private sector, and a large portion went into publicly owned industries. Government allocation of investment funds often introduces inefficiency by failing to channel funds into areas in which they would be most productive. In many developing countries, public-sector industries sell their output to the public at highly subsidized prices to lower artificially the cost of living. As a result, investment in these enterprises does not generate a return sufficient to repay debt, almost as if the borrowed funds went to support the subsidies rather than actual production. Developing-country governments typically sell food, gasoline and other forms of fuel, and basic utility services such as electricity at artificially low prices. Insofar as borrowed funds go into investment to produce goods then sold at prices below their production costs, the funds actually pay for current consumption.

Venezuela (current external debt, $37 billion) tried to industrialize "overnight" using borrowed funds and, in the process, invested heavily in inefficient industries that produced no return. Peru (current external debt, $20 billion) also borrowed heavily and used the funds to subsidize highly inefficient state-run enterprises. Argentina (current external debt, $74 billion) spent a large share of its borrowed funds on military hardware. Because many of these investments produced zero, or even negative, economic returns, the borrowing countries could not even make interest payments as they came due, much less repay the loans' principal (the sum originally borrowed). The resulting inability to pay is called **insolvency.**

Maturity of Debt

A second source of the debt crisis concerns the relationship between the maturity, or time horizon, of the borrowing and the time frame of the investment projects undertaken with it. Many of the more productive investments undertaken in developing countries involved long-term projects that could not be expected to pay off for several years. Most borrowing from official lenders such as the World Bank and the IMF constituted long-term debt, requiring borrowers to make only interest payments and not payments on the principal. As borrowing moved to private sources of funds such as the recycled OPEC oil revenues, loans terms shortened. Loans that come due before the investment projects they fund become productive lead to a **liquidity problem;** the borrower can afford to repay eventually—but not on schedule.

One response to inability to service existing debt was to borrow more to cover the interest payments. Often these additional loans were short term. Because the funds went to pay interest on earlier loans or, in some cases, to finance consumption-oriented expenditures, they did not generate returns for repayment. The short-term nature of the additional debt aggravated an already bad situation, and default became a serious possibility. In other cases, countries used short-term loans to finance long-term investment projects that, even if successful, could not possibly produce returns in time to repay the loans. Venezuela, for example, incurred a large amount of short-term debt for long-term industrialization projects. When a borrower uses short-term debt to finance long-term projects, a liquidity problem arises regardless of how productive the projects are. If the loan must be repaid before the investment has generated returns, repayment will be impossible.

Unforeseen Contingencies

The final—and perhaps most serious—error by both borrowers and lenders was to assume the economic conditions prevailing at the time the loans were made would continue indefinitely. An individual analogy would be to borrow an amount based on current income with no regard for the possibility of unemployment, illness, or other causes of reduction in income. During the 1970s, when many of the loans that led to the crisis were made, commodity prices were booming. The boom led developing countries to guess wrong concerning the permanence of those price increases. Countries tended to assume their endowments of natural resources would always be worth as much as the then-prevailing market value. Those lucky enough to have stocks of minerals and other products enjoying rising prices chose to invest heavily in increased capacity designed to take advantage of the high prices. Unfortunately, by the time the investments got well under way, the high prices were a thing of the past. Investments that would have been very profitable at the price structure prevailing in 1974 turned out to be very unprofitable at the prices prevailing in 1979 and 1980, when the debt came due. Mexico, for example, invested heavily in its nationalized oil company, Pemex, only to experience a drop in the price it could get for its oil. Venezuela hoarded its oil when oil prices were high and borrowed based on projected future oil revenues to finance industrialization. When oil prices collapsed during the recession of the early 1980s, the country was left with its oil inventory (now worth much less), an enormous debt, and inefficient industries.

Along with faulty forecasts of future commodity prices, developing countries based their borrowing on the assumption that developed countries' economic policies would remain more or less unchanged. The 1970s was a period of high and rising inflation rates, and borrowers and lenders assumed these policies would continue into the 1980s. Instead, the 1980s opened with developed countries (particularly the United States and Britain) making determined efforts to reduce their inflation rates. The resulting recession cut deeply into their demand for developing countries' exports, but the debtors had counted on revenue from those exports as a way of meeting debt payments. Prices for primary products, the leading exports for many debtor economies, collapsed as demand in the developed economies fell. To make matters worse, the recession in the developed economies increased pressures by their domestic industries for protection from foreign competition, so developed-country markets became less open to developing-country exports.

The dramatic changes in economic policy by developed countries also caused real interest rates to rise, and much of the developing-country debt was subject to floating interest rates. Brazil, for example, had 70 percent of its debt at interest rates that floated with market conditions; each 1-percentage-point rise in the U.S. interest rate cost Brazil $650 million per year in additional interest payments.

The same economic forces that cut demand for their exports and raised interest rates on their outstanding loans also caused the value of many debtors' national currencies to fall (or *depreciate*) against the U.S. dollar. Most of the debt was denominated in dollars, so the amount of debt rose sharply when measured in the debtors' local currencies. Developing-country debtors hoped the painful combination of recession, reduced export demand, higher interest rates, and currency depreciations were temporary. In an effort to avoid the painful adjustment to these adverse circumstances, many borrowers simply borrowed more to finance spending at current levels. Such decisions contributed to both the liquidity and solvency problems facing debtors.

The burgeoning debt-service burdens faced by several middle-income developing countries began to dry up the sources of private borrowing. The OPEC oil revenue surpluses disappeared as OPEC fell victim to internal cheating; banks, so eager to lend in the 1970s, sharply curtailed their lending to developing-country governments. Additional loans were required to prevent default on existing loans, and official lenders, especially the International Monetary Fund, found themselves acting as lenders of last resort and playing an increasing role as arbitrators between debtor countries and creditor banks.

11.7.3 Responses to the Debt Crisis

Because the debt problem grew so large, differed so much across countries, and involved so many parties, the proposed solutions numbered in the hundreds. The plans differed in many respects, but each had to address several central questions. How much of the debt was to be rescheduled (where **rescheduling** refers to postponement of payment, as opposed to cancellation of the debt)? How much **new money** (additional lending) was required, and how would banks be persuaded to make additional loans to countries already on the brink of default? How much say in debtor-country policies should creditors or their representatives have? What role should the international organizations, primarily the World Bank and the International Monetary Fund, play? How much, if any, of the debt was to be forgiven?[16] If any debt was forgiven, who would bear the costs (creditor bank shareholders, taxpayers)? Should all debtor countries receive debt relief regardless of their individual economic circumstances? If not, then which ones?

---

[16]Debt forgiveness can reflect more than altruism. If debt is so high that it significantly reduces economic growth, the threat of default increases. Forgiving some of the debt can increase economic growth and the likelihood of repayment of the remaining debt. Therefore, creditors may actually benefit, but no simple rule exists for determining how large debt must be before creditors would benefit from forgiving a portion of the outstanding debt.

In the early stages of the crisis, shortly after Mexico announced in August 1982 that it could not meet its payments, most participants perceived the problem as one of liquidity. Banks responded by rescheduling debtor countries' payments. The largest banks with the greatest exposure to the debt crisis continued to issue loans to debtor countries and pressured other banks to do so, knowing that an abrupt halt to all lending would have a devastating impact on the debtors' economies and ruin any chance of eventual repayment.[17] The International Monetary Fund also made loans and monitored the policies that debtors formulated for handling the crisis. Policies the IMF required—cutting subsidies on consumer goods, cutting wages in government-owned industries, reducing government expenditure, and raising taxes—often proved unpopular with debtor-country citizens, and the IMF sometimes took the blame to alleviate political pressure on debtor governments. Meanwhile, banks tried to reduce their exposure to the crisis by increasing their capitalization-to-loan ratios and hoped an early end to the worldwide recession would allow the debtors to outgrow the problem.

By 1985, the recession had ended, interest rates had come down, and most debtor-country currencies had stopped depreciating against the dollar. But it had become clear that many debtors would not grow sufficiently to allow them to meet their payment obligations. Real output and wages were falling in debtor countries; in some cases, political unrest loomed. The U.S. government response was what became known as the Baker Plan, named after Treasury Secretary James Baker. It provided official support for debt rescheduling, but not debt forgiveness, and encouraged the IMF and the World Bank to provide additional resources to the indebted countries. To provide incentives for debtors to adjust their policies, the plan restricted rescheduling to countries that reached agreements with the IMF. Such agreements required debtors' commitments to structural reforms and economic policies aimed at contributing to long-term solutions.

Banks began to set aside reserves to cover their bad loans; this amounted to recognition that some of the debt would never be repaid. A fall in oil prices in 1986 added to debtors' problems. Residents of the big debtor countries continued to move their private assets abroad in the form of capital flight that totaled over $100 billion during 1984–1987.

With the realization that only a portion of the outstanding debt was likely to be paid, markets started to respond with innovative approaches. Secondary markets in developing-country debt emerged where creditors could sell their claims, accepting a fraction of the face value of the debt. Buyers in secondary markets purchased the debt at discounted prices that reflected the likelihood of payment. Prices varied with the evaluation of the situation in the particular country. Figure 11.14 documents the volatility over time of secondary-market prices and the wide range of prices across countries. For example, an investor could buy $1 million of Côte d'Ivoire's debt on the secondary market in March 1988 for about $355,000, but by late 1991, a deterioration in the outlook for Côte d'Ivoire's repayment so depressed prices that the same $1 million in debt could be bought for about $100,000. Several countries have bought back a portion of their own debt at secondary-market prices. In

---

[17]These essentially involuntary loans by banks became known as *concerted lending*.

Figure 11.14 □ **Secondary-Market Debt Prices as a Share of Face Value or Par, 1988–1991**

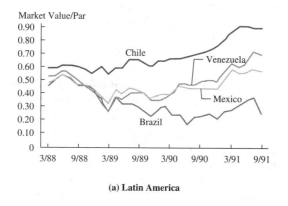

(a) Latin America

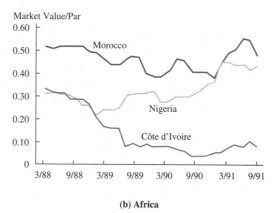

(b) Africa

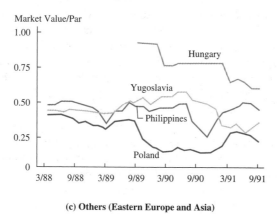

(c) Others (Eastern Europe and Asia)

Source: World Bank, *World Debt Tables Vol. 1, 1991–92,* p. 24.

1988, Bolivia bought almost half of its $670 million debt to foreign commercial banks. The buy-back of debt with a face value of $308 million cost the country $34 million, or about 11 cents on the dollar.

At the time, the Baker Plan received much criticism from all sides as too little, too late. However, the plan did forestall major defaults, pressure countries to undertake structural reform and policy changes, provide creditor banks time to lessen their financial vulnerability, and help spur innovative market-based responses such as the secondary market for debt.

That next stage of the official U.S. response involved the **Brady Plan,** named after then-Treasury Secretary Nicholas Brady, who outlined the plan in 1989. As originally presented, the Brady Plan was more a framework than a detailed proposal. It represented the first time the U.S. government officially supported the idea of debt relief, reduction, or forgiveness (in addition to rescheduling) for at least some of the indebted developing countries. Low prices for secondary debt revealed that capital-market participants believed the likelihood of repayment was low. Analysts suggested that the sheer size of the outstanding debt, or **debt overhang,** placed such a drain on the debtor economies that they could not undertake adequate domestic investment to support the growth required for repayment.

The Brady proposal called for direct negotiations between individual debtor countries and creditor banks and for funding from the IMF and World Bank to support debt reduction. Banks could receive collateral from the IMF, the World Bank, the Inter-American Development Bank, and the Japanese government in exchange for reducing their claims against developing economies. In essence, banks could exchange their status quo position—a low likelihood of repayment of a large debt—for a high probability of repayment of a smaller debt. The general strategy involved offering creditors a "menu" of options. One option (the *discount-bond option*) involved accepting large write-downs of the values of the outstanding loans, which amounted to forgiving the debt to the extent of the write-down, but continuing to charge market interest rates. Under a second option (the *par-bond option*), creditors granted interest-rate reductions but maintained the full amount of the debt. The third option, chosen by relatively few creditors, involved providing new money to debtors while maintaining the full value of current debt and market interest rates. The exact menu varied across debtors, but most creditors chose a combination of the discount-bond and par-bond provisions.

Mexico concluded the first Brady Plan agreement in early 1990. Other countries followed, culminating with Argentina and Brazil in late 1992—the basis of the proclaimed "end" of the debt crisis. By the end of 1994, 18 countries had made Brady Plan deals. Those countries' debt amounted to approximately 85 percent of the outstanding commercial bank debt of all severely indebted middle-income developing economies when the Brady Plan took effect. Judging from market responses, the Brady Plan agreements appear to have restored confidence, facilitated investment, and encouraged a return to "normalcy" in the debtor economies.

The keys to resolution included forced cooperation between debtors and creditors, each recognizing that no escape from the crisis was possible without the other's help. Many indebted countries bore substantial short-term political costs to put in place economic reforms that have the potential to support growth. Only time will tell whether those reforms will last. The indebted countries were not the only ones to suffer from the crisis; a handful of the largest U.S. banks lost $26 billion, not counting the administrative costs of a decade of negotiations.

Like the Baker Plan, the Brady Plan met strong criticism from many corners, especially for its late arrival and its generic, open character. In retrospect, these qualities might be viewed as strengths. Undertaken earlier, the debt-reduction plan might have discouraged or delayed the debtors' structural and policy reforms by giving the illusion of an international "bailout." The Brady Plan's generic character allowed different approaches with different debtors rather than a one-size-fits-all approach. The crisis ended with no major sovereign default, no major bank default, and no major panic in the world's financial system. As we shall see below, the reforms put in place have allowed many debtor countries to regain their borrowing privileges in private capital markets. The extent of debt forgiveness struck a balance by providing enough that the debtor economies could grow, but not providing so much that creditors would hesitate to engage in future lending.

11.7.4 Legacy of a Crisis: Is It Over, and What Was Learned?

The Brady Plan agreements ended the debt crisis in one sense: The day-to-day threat of major sovereign defaults by large developing countries no longer hangs over the international financial system in the 1990s as it did throughout the 1980s. Situations in some debtor countries have improved to the point that a new flow of much-needed private capital is under way, eloquent testimony to investors' confidence in the countries' economic stability. In 1991, two of the biggest debtors, Argentina and Brazil, successfully floated their first new international bond issues in years, and the pace of the capital inflows has accelerated dramatically since. Most of the early new capital inflows have taken the form of private bond issues or equity sales, not bank loans of the kind that caused so much pain in the 1980s, although bank loans are once again being made.

The debt problem remains in at least two senses. The crisis of the 1980s centered on middle- rather than low-income developing countries. This occurred for two reasons. First, low-income developing economies, because of their overwhelming development tasks, never gained access to the large-scale private commercial bank lending that played a key role in the crisis.[18] Figure 11.15 summarizes these countries' debt by type of creditor; they continued to borrow largely from official development agencies that provide loans at concessional (below-market) interest rates. As a result, low-income economies escaped the sudden inability to repay that hit the middle-income countries that borrowed from commercial banks during the years of plentiful OPEC funds. Second, because the low-income economies remain small relative to the world economy as a whole, their financial difficulties do not threaten the stability of the world financial system as difficulties in Brazil, Mexico, and Argentina did.

Because the crisis of the 1980s was a crisis of the middle-income economies, the responses focused on those economies as well. The severely indebted low-income economies continue to face huge external debts with little prospect of repayment; their external debt totaled $196 billion at the end of 1993. Nicaragua, Somalia, and Sudan each owe debt more than 2,000 times their respective annual export earnings. Moreover,

---

[18]See Case Two in this chapter.

Figure 11.15 □ **Severely Indebted Low-Income Country Debt, by Creditor, 1993**

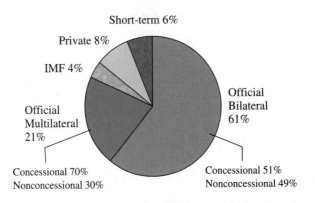

Source: World Bank, *World Debt Tables Vol. 1, 1994–95,* p. 38.

many of the severely indebted low-income economies lack the basic institutional structures essential for economic growth and development. Some have suffered government
policies that produced income insufficient to feed their populations, much less repay
debt. Most have stopped making payments on their medium- and long-term debt to
private creditors and fallen behind in payments to governments and international agencies. Much of these countries' debt has been forgiven ($6 billion just between 1990 and
1993), but debt forgiveness carries costs. It can adversely affect the debtors' future ability to borrow and can reduce the pressure on debtor governments to alter the policies that
led to debt problems of such magnitudes. In the long run, only fundamental policy
reforms to support economic growth, combined with continued support from creditors,
will allow these countries to overcome their debt. In this sense, the debt crisis continues.

A second, more general legacy of the 1980s debt crisis is developing countries' continued heavy reliance on capital flows from abroad to finance investment. As noted
earlier, the post-crisis renewal of capital flows into developing economies, summarized in Figure 11.16, represents the most often-cited basis for proclamation of the
debt crisis' end. However, a substantial portion of these inflows probably represents
the return of flight capital that flowed out during the crisis. This repatriation is a
one-time phenomenon and cannot be counted on as a permanent method of external
finance. As Mexico learned in 1994, foreign capital inflows are potentially reversible;
economies dependent on those flows face particular pressures to maintain policies that
support investor confidence.[19] Those same policies can encourage domestic saving
and provide a domestic source of funds for development-related investment.[20]

---

[19]See Case Three in Chapter Sixteen for an analysis of the Mexican financial crisis of 1994–1995.
[20]Case Four in Chapter Ten examines the continued correlation between domestic saving and investment.

Figure 11.16 □ **Capital Flows to Developing Countries, 1986–1994 ($ Billions)**

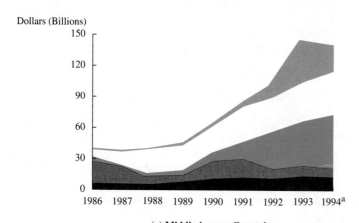

Dollars (Billions)

(a) Middle-income Countries

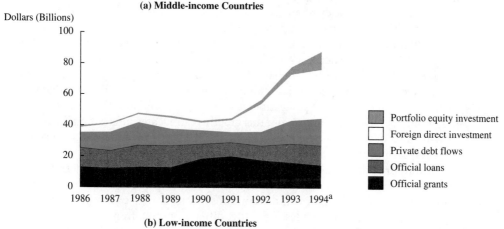

Dollars (Billions)

Portfolio equity investment

Foreign direct investment

Private debt flows

Official loans

Official grants

(b) Low-income Countries

Note: Flows are deflated by an import price index for developing countries in 1994 dollars.

[a]Projected.

Source: World Bank, *World Debt Tables Vol. 1, 1994–95*, p. 8.

Some of the legacies of the debt crisis take the form of even more general lessons about the world economy. The successful growth of many developing economies over the past three decades has rendered them an important force in the world economy. Trade and capital flows between developed and developing economies are substantial, so problems in either area no longer can be ignored in the other. The debt crisis forced recognition of this increased interdependence. The crisis also forced developing economies to undertake structural reforms and to support institutional structures such as the Uruguay Round and the NAFTA for codifying those reforms, thereby helping to ensure that they remain in place. The crisis reinforced the importance of the differing implications of various types of external borrowing. The large role of bank loans in the crisis reminded debtors and creditors of the appropriate roles for debt instruments and equity instruments in foreign borrowing. Finally, the crisis highlighted the futility of debtor–creditor deadlock once a crisis erupts. Only when debtors and creditors worked together, with support from other governments and international organizations, did the worst of the crisis end.

11.8 Economic Development and The Environment

Although scholars and policy makers long have recognized links between international trade and environmental policies, recent increased concern with environmental issues has moved the trade-environment link to center stage.[21] This applies especially to developing countries, because environmental quality represents an essential element in the improved quality of life that is the ultimate goal of the development process, and because some forms of environmental degradation hinder productivity and development prospects.

Several characteristics of environmental issues combine to produce controversy and difficulties in international policy making. First, a lack of scientific consensus on the physical effects of some classes of pollution (for example, the effect of "greenhouse gases" and any accompanying global warming) makes agreements difficult to reach because each side of the debate can point to reputable scientific studies supporting its position. Second, countries with different income levels demand different levels of environmental quality or protection, just as they demand different qualities of housing, food, or transportation. Again, this greatly complicates international agreements. Low-income developing countries fear having the high-income developed countries' relatively stringent environmental standards imposed on them. Third, environmental restrictions provide an easy disguise for protectionism. For example, a developed country wanting to protect its vegetable producers from competition by developing-country producers might ban imports and claim those producers use environmentally unacceptable chemicals or pesticides.[22] Finally, different population densities, geography, and past pollution levels imply that countries' *assimilative capacities* (that is, their abilities to absorb new pollution with minimal damage) vary widely. A factory whose air pollution might impose heavy health costs if placed in the Los Angeles basin might pose few costs in North Dakota. The Los Angeles basin has a relatively high population density, a geographical configuration in which sea winds trap pollution against the mountains that ring the basin, and a high existing level of many pollutants; North Dakota's situation, and hence its assimilative capacity, is quite different.

Differences among types of pollution also complicate the link between international trade and the environment. Some types (for example, water pollution) have primarily local effects and can be dealt with through domestically financed local policies.

---

[21]Chapter Eight contains a more general discussion of international trade and the environment. Here, we restrict our attention to issues of particular concern to developing economies.

[22]Section 8.5.3 outlines GATT rules on environmental protection through trade policy.

Others have cross-border, or even global, effects and require more international coordination of policies as well as more cooperative financing. For example, habitat destruction that reduces biological diversity and deforestation with global climatic consequences impose costs on the entire world. Solving these problems requires international cooperation. Potential approaches include payments by wealthy countries to developing countries for the "species-diversity services" and "carbon-absorption services" provided by their forests. Such payments would provide incentives for developing countries to conserve their habitat and forests.

The environmental priorities of developed and developing countries differ. If you were to ask an individual in a high-income, developed country about environmental problems, his or her response probably would deal with issues such as carbon dioxide emissions from automobiles, depletion of the ozone layer by chlorofluorocarbons, and hazardous wastes. The same question posed to a resident of a low-income developing country would more likely elicit concern over unsafe drinking water, lack of sanitation facilities, soil depletion, and indoor smoke from burning wood or dung for cooking. These understandable differences in priorities (along with inevitable controversy over who pays for cleanup) go a long way toward explaining the difficulties in international discussions about the environment.

Increasingly, specialists in the environment recognize that the first step toward improvement must involve curtailing policies that encourage environmental damage. Examples of such policies include subsidized use of fossil fuels and water, lack of private property rights for poor farmers in their land, insulation of state-owned industries (which tend to be heavy polluters) from competitive forces, and rewarding aggressive land clearing by awarding ownership of the land to those who clear it.[23] All these policies are prevalent in developing countries, and all take a heavy toll on the environment. Fortunately, elimination of these policies would improve economic efficiency, facilitate international trade liberalization, and raise incomes as well as improve the environment. Therefore, the commonly held idea that economic development and international trade necessarily come at an environmental cost clearly is wrong.

11.9 Developing Markets: Economies in Transition

Between 1989 and 1991, the breakup of the Soviet Union and the overthrow of the governments in its Eastern European satellite states revealed a new group of developing economies. Forty years of central planning had left a zone of outdated technology, environmental disasters, dilapidated factories, and frustrated citizens. Even areas such as East Germany, industrialized and modern before falling under Soviet domination at the end of the Second World War, had declined into backwardness compared with the Western market economies. Because the most fundamental task facing the formerly centrally planned countries is the shift to market-oriented economies, they typically are called **economies in transition.**[24] As a group, they have much in common with

---

[23]See section 8.5.3 for specific examples.

[24]Other economies throughout the world, including about 30 in Africa, also abandoned central planning during the 1980s and early 1990s. These countries typically are not included in "economies in transition."

other developing economies, but face some unique problems and opportunities. To understand the special character of the trade-related aspects of their development prospects, we must briefly turn back the clock and return to central planning.

11.9.1 International Trade and Central Planning

A **market-based economic system** relies on prices to allocate resources, signal trends, and provide incentives. If the price of a good rises, signaling increased scarcity, consumers have an incentive to consume less of the good and producers an incentive to make more of it. A **centrally planned economy** relies instead on government planning to decide what and how much to produce and how much to pay factors of production. When government bureaucrats rather than supply and demand determine prices, no automatic mechanism exists to equate quantity supplied with quantity demanded for various goods, and shortages and surpluses are more the rule than the exception.

Because market-determined prices play a central role in international trade theory (for example, as the basis for the definition of comparative advantage), the theory says little about how centrally planned economies conduct their international trade policies. In practice, autarky, or self-sufficiency, often was an explicit policy goal. Planners viewed international trade as a necessary evil whereby export goods were produced to obtain only those imports impossible to produce domestically. Like policy makers in many other developing economies, the central planners also placed great weight on industrialization as a policy goal.

The Soviet Union moved to a system of central planning in the 1920s, approximately a decade after the 1917 revolution brought the Communists to power. From the late 1920s until the end of the Second World War, the Soviet state pursued national self-sufficiency and industrialization, accompanied by a disastrous collectivization of agriculture. Following the Second World War, the Soviet Union extended its power into Eastern Europe and integrated those economies into its self-sufficient industrial system. The countries formed a group, the **Council for Mutual Economic Assistance (CMEA or COMECON)**, to manage and coordinate their intra-group trade. Original CMEA members were the Soviet Union, Poland, Hungary, Czechoslovakia, Bulgaria, and Romania; later, East Germany, Vietnam, Cuba, and (temporarily) Albania joined.

Trade within the CMEA grew rapidly, expanding from less than one-third of members' total trade to over three-fourths in just the first five years. The Soviet Union exported oil to other members in return for manufactured goods such as tractors. Although the policy makers did not believe in open international trade according to comparative advantage, they did believe in the importance of specialization and economies of scale. Many goods were produced in a single enormous plant that served the entire CMEA market.[25] Even steel and automobiles came from a mere handful of factories. As a result, the CMEA countries traded heavily with one

---

[25]In the Soviet Union, of 5,884 product lines, 77 percent were supplied by a single producer ("Remaking the Soviet Union," *The Economist*, July 13, 1991, 23).

another, even though they traded relatively little with the West, especially during periods of heightened Cold War tensions. The Soviet Republics were linked even more tightly; only the Russian Republic exported less than 30 percent of it output in 1988, and ten republics exported more than 50 percent.

The CMEA trading system, inefficient as it was (for reasons we shall see in a moment), allowed the centrally planned economies to escape some of the negative effects of their isolation from the rest of the world trading system.[26] Unfortunately, the pattern of trade established under the CMEA made the 1989–1991 revolutions more painful and continues to complicate the countries' transition to market economies. Bulgaria, for example, conducted approximately 80 percent of its trade with CMEA members, so the collapse of the Soviet Union abruptly halted most of Bulgaria's trade.

The isolation of the CMEA economies from the rest of the world was not just a matter of ideological refusal to accept the theory of comparative advantage or of political tensions with the West. To be feasible, a centrally planned system must be insulated from external contact with market economies; otherwise, trade at market-determined world prices will erode the government's ability to impose its artificial prices and centrally planned resource allocation. For example, the Soviet Union emphasized production of capital and military goods in its planning and left little productive capacity for consumer goods. The results were queues, waiting, rationing, and high black-market prices for consumer goods. If the Soviet government had allowed free trade, Soviet consumers would have purchased Western consumer goods and Western firms would have bought the capital goods on which the Soviet government kept prices artificially low (that is, a fraction of the opportunity cost of producing them). To avoid these disruptions, a centrally planned economy must prevent a free flow of goods and services between itself and market economies.

The primary mechanism by which CMEA countries achieved this separation was use of a state bureaucracy to handle all foreign trade.[27] Typically the state planning ministry worked with a ministry of foreign trade to decide which goods the country would need but be unable to produce domestically. To obtain these imports, they made plans to use other (surplus) goods as exports. The foreign trade ministry then informed official state trading corporations of the necessary imports and exports. This bureaucratic process greatly interfered with the efficiency of trade. Often goods failed to arrive as planned. Firms hoarded inputs so they could continue to produce when input shipments failed to appear. The result was an economy of enormous enterprises, each of which tried to maintain self-sufficiency to the extent possible within the central planning system.

The nature of the centrally planned economies imposed several other barriers to efficient international trade. First, policy makers did not allow the currencies of centrally planned economies to be traded in foreign exchange markets; in particular, they

---

[26]Ignoring the political barriers to East–West trade, most intra-CMEA trade represented trade diversion (see section 9.4.2). However, during the Cold War and the Soviet domination of Eastern Europe, trade with the West was severely limited. The choice was between no trade and intra-CMEA trade.

[27]Lenin imposed a state monopoly on foreign trade shortly after the 1917 revolution in Russia; most other socialist economies followed.

were not *convertible* into other currencies. If a Czechoslovakian firm exported machinery to the Soviet Union and received payment in rubles (the Soviet currency), Czechoslovakia could spend the proceeds only on imports from a country willing to accept rubles in payment, most likely the Soviet Union. If the ruble had been freely convertible, Czechoslovakia could, for example, have exchanged the rubles for French francs in the foreign exchange market and used the francs to import a desired good from France. But because the centrally planned economies maintained artificial values for their currencies just as they maintained other artificial prices, unrestricted trade in currencies had to be avoided. The result was trade that was largely bilateral. Each country found it necessary to import and export approximately equal amounts with each trading partner, because the proceeds from exports took the form of nonconvertible currencies useful only on imports from the issuing country. This bilateralism ignored patterns of comparative advantage and led to inefficient trade flows at prices that bore little resemblance to market-determined world prices.

The planning system presented an additional barrier to trade with market economies by giving producers weak incentives to make the types of high-quality goods demanded in world markets. Under central planning, the rewards producers earned were very weakly connected to the quality of their product. Because producers could not keep any profits resulting from production of a superior product, quality tended to be low and erratic. Such products could not compete with western-made goods in world markets, but traded in CMEA transactions at prices that ignored the manufactured goods' shoddy quality.

The CMEA amounted to a trading system that ignored comparative advantage, overemphasized regional specialization and economies of scale, channeled trade to group members at the expense of potential trade with the West, and ignored market prices and product quality. Needless to say, its historical legacy did not facilitate transition.

11.9.2 The Painful Transition from Central Planning

Even before the massive political and economic change that swept Eastern Europe and the Soviet Union between 1989 and 1991, some of the centrally planned economies liberalized their trade procedures to allow firms wanting to import or export to deal more directly with foreign firms. Most notably, as part of the Soviet Union's economic restructuring or *perestroika*, new trade laws allowed Soviet firms to trade directly with foreign firms as of 1989. The Soviet Union also expressed interest in joining the GATT, but Western nations were skeptical of the ability to apply GATT rules to an economy so insulated from the forces of world markets. In efforts to improve product quality, several countries including the Soviet Union started to encourage joint ventures with Western firms.

Between 1989 and 1991, economic and political reforms in Eastern Europe and the Soviet Union grew from a trickle to a torrent. One by one, authoritarian regimes fell, and new governments pledged themselves to the difficult task of transition to market-oriented economies. Each country faces unique problems and challenges, but there are elements common to all.

Although analysts agree the economies of the former Soviet Union and Eastern Europe will perform much better under market systems than under central planning, things got worse before they got better. With the threat of Soviet intervention gone, so was the incentive to accept the system's poor quality goods. Demand shifted to better, Western-made goods. The massive government-owned factories lost their only markets. The CMEA disbanded as its members shifted their trade to the West. Countries such as Hungary and Czechoslovakia that had relied on exports of manufactured goods saw the (artificial) prices of those goods collapse when confronted with prices in world markets. Some economies tried to shift exports to the West, but outdated technology and trade barriers in developed-country markets limited this ability in the short run. Coordination among the various economies to "stick together" during the painful transition might have helped, but the historical legacy of political, economic, and military domination by the Soviet Union made such coordination unlikely; each country was eager to escape from the system.

Several economies in transition instituted large-scale reforms early, signaling a dramatic shift to a market orientation. For these countries—including Albania, the Baltic republics, the Czech Republic, Mongolia, Poland, the Slovak Republic, and Slovenia—analysts believe the worst of the short-run shock of transition may be over, and growth rates are climbing. For others, late or overly timid reforms or special difficulties such as armed conflicts have their economies still mired in the downturn phase of transition.

One additional problem in evaluating the performance and prospects of the Eastern European economies is the lack of reliable data on key economic variables such as gross national product. Existing data have two problems. First, GNP calculations in centrally planned economies often include only the state-owned sector of large industries. Typically, this represents the least productive sector, especially as reforms remove the subsidies that allowed these "dinosaur" industries to survive. As reforms take hold and small, privately owned firms appear, this dynamic sector of the economy provides a growing share of income but fails to find its way into official income accounting. The second data problem reflects the effect of inconvertible currencies. Cross-country comparisons of gross national product figures require that data be "translated" from domestic currency units (the Soviet ruble, or the Polish zloty) to a common unit, usually the U.S. dollar. This translation process uses the exchange rate, or the value of one currency expressed in units of the other currency. But, as we have noted, until very recently the centrally planned economies maintained highly artificial exchange rates. This implies that economic data calculated using such rates were highly suspect at best. At least a portion of the dramatic declines in reported Eastern European income levels since 1989 reflects the move toward use of more realistic exchange rates for the calculations. Table 11.6 reports estimates of GNP per capita during transition for the former Soviet Republics and the Eastern European economies; however, the World Bank cautions that the figures, especially those for the former Soviet Union, must be regarded as tentative. As the transitional economies join the key international economic organizations (for example, all former Soviet republics joined the World Bank in April 1992), data quality and reliability should improve, because assistance with such tasks represents an important service provided by those organizations.

Table 11.6 □ **Per Capita GNP for the Economies in Transition, 1989–1993 ($)**

Country	1989	1990	1991	1992	1993
Albania	n.a.	n.a.	n.a.	n.a.	340
Bulgaria	2,320	2,250	1,840	1,330	1,140
Czechoslovakia	3,540	3,140	2,470	n.a.	n.a.
Czech Republic	n.a.	n.a.	n.a.	2,450	2,710
Slovak Republic	n.a.	n.a.	n.a.	1,930	1,950
Hungary	2,590	2,780	2,720	2,970	3,350
Poland	1,790	1,690	1,790	1,910	2,260
Romania	n.a.	1,640	1,390	1,130	1,140
Yugoslavia	2,920	3,060	n.a.	n.a.	n.a.
Soviet Union	n.a.	n.a.	n.a.	n.a.	n.a.
Armenia	n.a.	2,380	2,150	780	660
Azerbaijan	n.a.	1,640	1,670	740	730
Belarus	n.a.	3,110	3,110	2,930	2,870
Estonia	n.a.	4,170	3,830	2,760	3,080
Georgia	n.a.	2,120	1,640	850	580
Kazakhstan	n.a.	2,600	2,470	1,680	1,560
Kirgizstan	n.a.	1,570	1,550	820	850
Latvia	n.a.	3,590	3,410	1,930	2,010
Lithuania	n.a.	3,110	2,710	1,310	1,320
Moldova	n.a.	2,390	2,170	1,300	1,060
Russia	n.a.	3,430	3,220	2,510	2,340
Tajikistan	n.a.	1,130	1,050	490	470
Turkmenistan	n.a.	1,690	1,700	1,230	n.a.
Ukraine	n.a.	2,500	2,340	1,820	2,210
Uzbekistan	n.a.	1,340	1,350	850	970

Source: World Bank, *World Development Report;* United Nations, *Human Development Report.*

11.9.3   The Reform Agenda and Prospects

The list of major transition tasks includes eliminating price controls and introducing market-determined prices, cutting government subsidies to industry, removing restrictions on private ownership and market activities, cutting military spending and the role of government in the economy, assuring macroeconomic stability, providing incentives for improved productivity and quality, and creation of independent central banks to administer policies necessary for currency convertibility. In the former Soviet Union, even more fundamental reforms such as building a legal system to protect private property, a framework for enforcement of contracts, and a transparent accounting system are needed; some of the economies of Eastern Europe, with their shorter histories of central planning, are luckier in these regards.

Most analysts and policy makers agree on most items on the reform list. However, there are two controversies. The first concerns the proper speed and ordering of reforms. Faced with such a daunting list, should one attempt all the reforms simultaneously and as quickly as possible? Or, should one concentrate on a few elements at a time and allow for lengthy adjustment periods? History provides few models of such broad political and economic change; therefore, substantial disagreement remains on this question. Poland followed the sudden, or "big-bang" approach on January 1, 1990, when it cut tariffs and moved its zloty currency toward convertibility. Many economists argue that opening international trade supports the other needed reforms by providing information about market prices, putting competitive pressure on domestic firms to improve quality, and providing access to new technology, an area in which most of Eastern Europe lags seriously behind the West. The former Soviet Republics have, with some exceptions, taken more gradual approaches, but have met with only erratic success. Table 11.7 reports the progress of the economies in transition on the major margins of reform.

The second controversy concerns how (and how much) to cushion the effects of transition on individuals and firms. On the one hand, failure to provide social cushions generates social and political discontent that may threaten the reform process. On the other hand, too much cushioning removes the essential incentives to adjust and prolongs the inevitable pain of transition. As price controls are removed, particularly for key goods such as energy, food, and housing, citizens bring tremendous political pressure to raise wages to maintain their purchasing power. But the low productivity in many sectors does not justify those higher wages, so yielding to the political pressure prolongs the transitional period of increased unemployment.[28]

The short-run prospects for economic performance vary substantially across Eastern Europe and the former Soviet Union. In some countries, such as Hungary, central planning was never complete and substantial market expertise exists within the population. In others, such as the former Soviet Union, a longer and more exclusive history of socialism means that few citizens possess significant market experience. The share of the state sector in the economies varied substantially before reforms began. For example, in the mid-1980s, 97 percent of value-added originated in the state sector in Czechoslovakia, East Germany, and the Soviet Union, but only 65 percent in Hungary.[29] So the magnitude of the privatization task—often one of the slowest and most difficult aspects of reform—differs across countries. In some countries, the population strongly supports reform; other countries, such as Romania, face more troubling domestic political situations.

The economies' differential prospects for success are reflected in flows of foreign direct investment, illustrated in Figure 11.17. Two-thirds of all investment during 1990–1993 went to just four hosts: Hungary, Russia, the Czech Republic, and Poland. Most (71 percent) came from the European Union and the United States, went to the manufacturing sector (61 percent), and occurred in joint ventures with local firms.

---

[28]See Cases Three and Four in Chapter Four and section 8.8 on the relationship among wages, productivity, and competitiveness.

[29]*The Wall Street Journal,* July 23, 1991.

Table 11.7 ◻ **Reform in Transitional Economies, 1994**

| | Private Sector Share of GDP (Percent) | Score (4 = market economy, 1 = little progress) | | | | | |
| | | Privatization | | | | | |
		Large	Small	Firm Restructuring	Prices, Competition	Trade, Foreign Exchange	Banks
Albania	50	1	3	2	3	4	2
Armenia	40	1	3	1	3	2	1
Azerbaijan	20	1	1	1	3	1	1
Belarus	15	2	2	2	2	1	1
Bulgaria	40	2	2	2	3	4	2
Croatia	40	3	4	2	3	4	3
Czech Rep.	65	4	4	3	3	4	3
Estonia	55	3	4	3	3	4	3
Georgia	20	1	2	1	2	1	1
Hungary	55	3	4	3	3	4	3
Kazakhstan	20	2	2	1	2	2	1
Kirgizstan	30	3	4	2	3	3	2
Latvia	55	2	3	2	3	4	3
Lithuania	50	3	4	2	3	4	2
Macedonia	35	2	4	2	3	2	2
Moldova	20	2	2	2	3	2	2
Poland	55	3	4	3	3	4	3
Romania	35	2	3	2	3	4	2
Russia	50	3	3	2	3	3	2
Slovakia	55	3	4	3	3	4	3
Slovenia	30	2	4	3	3	4	3
Tajikistan	15	2	2	1	3	1	1
Turkmenistan	15	1	1	1	2	1	1
Ukraine	30	1	2	1	2	1	1
Uzbekistan	20	2	3	1	3	2	1

Source: *The Economist*, December 3, 1994, p. 27; data from European Bank for Reconstruction and Development.

Foreign direct investment plays many roles in the transition and development process, including revitalizing obsolete industries with new technology, injecting managerial know-how and worker training, and building marketing links to foreign markets.

The republics of the former Soviet Union face several additional problems. The breakup of the country severed long-standing supply relations, leaving factories without supplies and component producers without customers. Unlike most Eastern European economies, the Soviet planning system encompassed agriculture as well

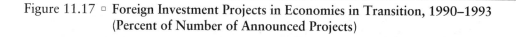

Figure 11.17 □ **Foreign Investment Projects in Economies in Transition, 1990–1993 (Percent of Number of Announced Projects)**

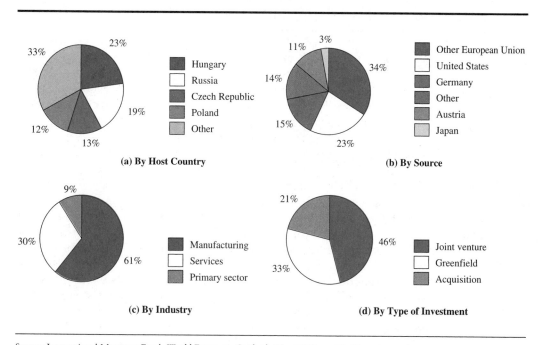

(a) By Host Country

Hungary
Russia
Czech Republic
Poland
Other

(b) By Source

Other European Union
United States
Germany
Other
Austria
Japan

(c) By Industry

Manufacturing
Services
Primary sector

(d) By Type of Investment

Joint venture
Greenfield
Acquisition

Source: International Monetary Fund, *World Economic Outlook*, May 1995, pp. 62, 64.

as industry, so both sectors must undergo the transition process. Separated from the national framework of the Soviet Union, the republics lack the institutions of a typical nation-state, including central banks and legal frameworks to deal with the bankruptcies that comprise an inevitable part of the transition process. The republics must decide how closely to cooperate and what functions to share within the Commonwealth of Independent States, a loose confederation joined by most of the former Soviet republics. Prospects for economic growth and development vary widely among the republics based on different size, resource endowments, international linkages, damage from broken supplier relationships, environmental problems, ethnic tensions, and degrees of political instability.

Like other developing countries, the economies in transition also face the hurdle of developed-country trade barriers. Industries in which the emerging economies have comparative advantage—such as agriculture, textiles, and steel—are precisely those industries in which many developed countries erect the highest trade barriers. The Uruguay Round reforms, once in full effect, will improve market access for the economies in transition. In addition, the reforms will require that those economies continue to dismantle their own trade barriers, although the agreement permits a slower liberalization schedule for developing and transitional economies than for developed ones.

Case One

U.S. Trade Policy, the Multifiber Agreement, and Bangladesh[30]

Bangladesh is one of the world's poorest countries, with a 1993 per capita GNP of $220 per year, and subject to floods, cyclones, and typhoons. During the 1980s, Bangladesh built a successful garment industry that earned much-needed export revenue. The Multifiber Agreement (MFA)—an elaborate system of quotas developed countries impose on textile and apparel imports from most developing countries—played a role in creating the industry but now limits its growth.

The MFA consists of a web of bilateral quota arrangements between exporting and importing countries. The United States maintains quotas on textile and apparel products from more than 40 countries that together supply approximately 70 percent of U.S. imports in these sectors. In the early 1980s, South Korean garment exporters began to exceed their U.S. quotas under the MFA and found their growth stymied. They responded by forming a joint venture in Bangladesh to circumvent the quota on exports from South Korea. Soon, more than 700 Bangladeshi garment factories earned over $100 million in export revenue. The garment industry relied on Bangladesh's large endowment of unskilled labor and hired mostly women, a potent source of social change in a largely Islamic country. The industry's success marked the country's first substantial exports of manufactured goods; earlier exports were jute and tea. Shipping companies, which began to serve Bangladesh because of its garment industry, also provided access to foreign markets for other potential industries.

In 1985, in response to the industry's success, the United States, Britain, Canada, and France imposed import quotas on Bangladeshi garments. The quotas spread across product categories, and by 1987, 13 classes of goods fell under the MFA system. Many factories closed, and others spent scarce resources to diversify into products not yet subject to limits. Besides the MFA quotas, U.S. textile giant Milliken & Co. accused the Bangladeshi "industrial wiping cloth" industry of dumping and receiving government export subsidies. A U.S. antidumping order against the Bangladeshi industry remains in effect.

A major accomplishment of the Uruguay Round agreement is its provision for a ten-year phase-out of MFA quotas for GATT member countries.[31] At the end of that period, trade in textiles and apparel, which comprises 7 percent of total world merchandise trade, will be subject to the same GATT rules as trade in other sectors, ending 30 years of market distortion and damage to developing-country interests. However, apparel markets in developed countries and textile markets in developing ones will remain subject to very high tariff rates, even after the Uruguay Round reforms end the MFA quotas.

---

[30]This case draws on the World Bank, *World Development Report 1990*, 123; William Lash, "U.S. Textile Industry Fears Bangladesh's Rags," *The Wall Street Journal*, June 19, 1991; and Marcus W. Brauchli, "Garment Industry Booms in Bangladesh," *The Wall Street Journal*, August 6, 1991.

[31]Two major producers, China and Taiwan, which together supply about 25 percent of U.S. imports, do not belong to the GATT. The MFA phase-out applies only to GATT members.

Case Two

Official versus Market Borrowing and the Debt Crisis

During the 1970s, patterns of external borrowing differed among subgroups of developing countries. In general, low-income countries continued to borrow primarily from official lenders such as the World Bank and the IMF and to engage in long-term borrowing at below-market interest rates. This reflected the unwillingness of private lenders such as banks to lend extensively to countries facing such massive development tasks. Middle-income developing countries, on the other hand, had greater access to private financial markets and found private lenders more accommodating. Several of these countries borrowed heavily in private capital markets, sometimes on a short-term basis and at floating, market interest rates. Initially these borrowers received attractive terms due to the easy availability of funds from OPEC revenues; and the use of private lenders allowed the countries to escape the domestic political consequences of the policy reforms demanded by the IMF.

The IMF classifies 124 debtor countries into market borrowers (22 countries that owed at least two-thirds of their external debt at the end of 1989 to private-sector creditors), official borrowers (69 countries with more than two-thirds of their total liabilities at the end of 1989 owed to official creditors), and diversified borrowers (33 countries that are indebted but neither market nor official borrowers under the preceding definitions). Of the 15 heavily indebted countries whose debt constituted the crux of the 1980s crisis, eight are market borrowers, two are official borrowers, and five are diversified borrowers (see Table 11.8).

Early in the debt-crisis decade, the set of countries with the most severe problems involved an even heavier share of market borrowers. In 1982, the 13 heavily indebted countries included 12 market borrowers, no official borrowers, and only one diversified borrower. The changes between 1982 and 1995 reflect the role of official lenders in making continuing loans to countries with debt problems, transforming those countries from market borrowers to diversified or official borrowers. Nonetheless, the debt crisis arose primarily from market borrowing.

Table 11.8 □ **Fifteen Heavily Indebted Countries by Class of Borrowing**

Market Borrowers	Official Borrowers	Diversified Borrowers
Argentina	Bolivia	Colombia
Brazil	Morocco	Côte d'Ivoire
Chile	Nigeria	Ecuador
Mexico		Philippines
Peru		Yugoslavia
Uruguay		
Venezuela		

Source: International Monetary Fund, *World Economic Outlook*, May 1995, pp. 117–118.

Case Three
Intellectual Property and Piracy in China

The rapid industrial development of Asian economies over the last decade has raised new trade issues with the United States. One of those issues is the protection of intellectual property, over which the United States has engaged in disputes with Taiwan, South Korea, Thailand, and China. Intellectual-property protection includes copyrights, patents, and trademarks. Goods commonly copied illegally include computer software, music recordings, movies, pharmaceuticals, clothing, video games, computer parts, laser videos, and even automobiles. Sometimes, the goods lose something in translation, as in the case of "Rambo" facial tissues produced in China, but many of the goods are of high quality and difficult to distinguish from their legitimate versions.

For music recordings, industrial analysts claim that over $2 billion of the industry's $30 billion in yearly sales consist of pirated goods. High-quality pirated compact disks sell in China for about 15 yuan, the equivalent of $1.75. Thirty Chinese factories can produce up to 80 million CDs per year, and many of the firms have political ties that have insulated them from earlier attempts at intellectual-property enforcement. Of music recordings sold in China, over 90 percent are thought to be illegal copies, along with over 90 percent of computer software sold in China. Damage to U.S. firms from Chinese copyright infringement alone is alleged to run about $800 million annually.

The "special 301" provision of U.S. trade law forms the basis of the U.S. government's response to intellectual-property trade disputes. Each year, the Office of the U.S. Trade Representative compiles a list of "priority countries" thought to violate intellectual-property rules in ways that damage U.S. firms' interests. Investigations of the alleged violations ensue, and, failing a satisfactory resolution of the dispute, the United States can impose punitive sanctions in the form of tariffs on a country's exports.

During the early 1990s, when the U.S.–China dispute began, China lacked laws against intellectual-property infringement. The first stages of the dispute involved the United States pressuring China to pass such laws and to agree to enforce international copyright laws, particularly for CDs. Later stages of the dispute have centered on China's inadequate enforcement of its existing laws. A 1994 investigation under special-301 law led to a U.S. threat to impose 100 percent tariffs on over $1 billion of Chinese exports (for example, cellular phones, sporting goods, and plastic items), to which China responded with a threat of counter-retaliation against U.S. exports, many of them the same goods the United States accused China of pirating.

A last-minute agreement avoided the sanctions. China promised to strengthen its intellectual-property enforcement and to open its markets to U.S. audiovisual and published products. The second part of the agreement is important because Chinese import restrictions on U.S. movies, music recordings, and computer software create a huge domestic market for pirated goods that then find their way into export markets as well. For example, before the 1995 agreement, China limited U.S. movie exports to ten films per year.

 Case Four
Reform and Growth in Transition

We saw in section 11.5.1 that developing countries that open their economies to trade appear to perform better than those that remain closed and attempt to develop through import substitution. But what about the newest set of developing countries—those in transition from central planning? They differ from many other developing countries in that several of the countries in transition industrialized prior to or during their years of socialism. Does openness to international trade still play an important role in their growth? The early evidence suggests the answer is *yes*. Recall that Table 11.7 reported the progress of each economy in transition on six margins of reform. Table 11.9 classifies the 25 economies in transition according to their trade reforms alone.

The evidence (admittedly early) suggests that economies with the strongest and earliest reforms of their trade regimes suffered smaller declines in GDP during their transitions and have now achieved positive growth. Countries with weak, late, or nonexistent reforms, on the other hand, suffered larger slumps and continue to endure negative GDP growth. Note, however, that the economies of Eastern Europe fall into the strong reform group, while most of the former Soviet republics comprise the other groups. Therefore, we cannot rule out the possibility that transition is simply more difficult, painful, and prolonged for the former Soviet states, for reasons discussed in section 11.9, especially the severing of such a large share of their trade. Another possibility is that economies facing easier transitions find it more feasible to institute reforms than do countries facing more serious transition problems.

Summary

The basic economic theory of international trade as developed in Chapters Two through Nine applies to developed and developing countries alike. But developing countries face special concerns regarding specialization in primary products, the desire for industrialization, access to new technologies, external borrowing to finance investment, environmental policies, and integration into the world economy. The process of economic development is long and difficult and offers few easy answers or quick fixes. But active participation in the world economy, based on comparative advantage and economies of scale, appears to offer a brighter future for the developing nations than the price-distorting and inward-looking policies prevalent in the past.

Looking Ahead

Thus far, we have ignored the fact that economic transactions across national borders involve use of more than one currency or unit of money. In Chapter Twelve, we explore the mechanics of dealing in different currencies and the policies open to governments for determining the value of their currencies relative to other currencies.

Table 11.9 □ Reform and Growth in Transitional Economies

Country	Year of Trade Reform	Cumulative GDP Growth, 1989–1994 (Percent)	GDP Growth, 1994 (Percent)
Strong Reforms			
Hungary	1990	–17.94	2.0
Poland	1990	–9.23	5.0
Bulgaria	1991	–26.41	1.4
Czech Republic	1991	–15.49	3.0
Slovak Republic	1991	–19.53	5.5
Slovenia	1991	–13.26	5.0
Albania	1992	–22.89	7.0
Estonia	1992	–29.15	5.0
Romania	1992	–30.79	3.0
Croatia	1993	–31.04	1.0
Latvia	1993	–39.52	3.0
Lithuania	1993	–55.44	2.0
Average		–25.89	3.5
Moderate Reforms			
Kirgizstan	1994	–42.30	–10.0
Russia	still closed	–47.29	–15.0
Average		–42.61	–12.5
Weak Reforms			
Macedonia	1994	–51.30	–7.0
Moldova	1994	–54.30	–25.0
Armenia	still closed	–61.60	0.0
Kazakhstan	still closed	–51.01	–25.0
Uzbekistan	still closed	–11.75	–3.0
Average		–45.99	–12.0
Weakest Reforms			
Belarus	1994	–35.93	–22.0
Azerbaijan	still closed	–54.32	–22.0
Georgia	still closed	–85.35	–35.0
Tajikistan	still closed	–70.37	–25.0
Turkmenistan	still closed	–38.29	–20.0
Ukraine	still closed	–51.36	–23.0
Average		–38.63	–24.5

Source: Jeffrey D. Sachs and Andrew Warner, "Economic Reform and the Process of Global Integration," *Brookings Papers on Economic Activity* 1 (1995), p. 62; data from European Bank for Reconstruction and Development.

Key Terms

gross national product (GNP)
North–South debate
primary products
buffer stock
speculation
collusion
export restrictions
effective rate of protection (ERP)
cascading tariff structure
import substitution
export-oriented growth
    (export promotion)
newly industrializing countries
    (NICs)
technology
technology transfer
intellectual property
external debt

government (sovereign) defaults
official debt
commercial (unofficial, or market)
    debt
debt instruments
equity instruments
maturity
insolvency
liquidity problem
rescheduling
new money
Brady Plan
debt overhang
economies in transition
market-based economic system
centrally planned economy
Council for Mutual Economic
    Assistance (CMEA, or COMECON)

Problems and Questions for Review

1. Developing countries often accuse developed countries of pursuing trade policies that impede the ability of developing countries to export to developed countries. Briefly describe two examples of trade policies that provide some support for the developing countries' position, including why the policies you cite might harm developing countries.

2. Suppose you have been called in as a consultant to a country trying to decide whether to take out a substantial amount of foreign bank loans. What basic questions would you ask the country to obtain information to evaluate the desirability of the borrowing? Briefly explain the importance of each of your questions and how the answer to each would affect your recommendation.

3. What are some of the weaknesses of per capita GNP (or GDP) as a measure of development? How has the United Nations responded to criticisms of its use of these measures?

4. Illustrate how a buffer stock could exhaust its stock of cash or its stock of the commodity. If producer countries organize the buffer stock, which of the two problems do you think would be more likely to arise, and why?

5. Explain why cascading tariffs provide high rates of effective protection for finished products.

6. Briefly describe several reasons why developing and developed countries often have difficulty reaching agreements in negotiations over environmental issues.

7. Explain why, using the theory from earlier chapters of the book, you might expect export-promotion development strategies to be more successful than strategies based on import substitution.

8. Explain two reasons why the successor states to the former Soviet Union experienced a more painful and prolonged economic downturn from the events of 1989–1991 than did most of the formerly centrally planned states of Eastern Europe.

References and Selected Readings

Bates, Robert H., et al. "Risk and Trade Regimes: Another Exploration." *International Organization* (Winter 1991): 1–18.
Relationship between export specialization and trade liberalization; for intermediate and advanced students.

Berkley, Seth, et al. "AIDS: Invest Now or Pay More Later." *Finance and Development* 31 (June 1994): 40–43.
The heavy cost of AIDS to developing economies, especially in Africa; accessible to all readers.

Boycko, Maxim, Andrei Schleifer, and Robert W. Vishny. "Privatizing Russia." *Brookings Papers on Economic Activity* 2 (1993): 139–192.
The politics and economics of privatization in the former Soviet Union; intermediate.

Bulow, Jeremy, Kenneth Rogoff, and Afonso S. Bevilaqua. "Official Creditor Seniority and Burden-Sharing in the Former Soviet Bloc." *Brookings Papers on Economic Activity* 1 (1992): 195–234.
Debt in the former Soviet Union; advanced.

Butler, Alison. "Environmental Protection and Free Trade: Are They Mutually Exclusive?" Federal Reserve Bank of St. Louis *Review* 74 (May–June 1992): 3–16.
Accessible introduction to the relationship between trade and the environment.

Butler, Alison. "The Trade-Related Aspects of Intellectual Property Rights: What Is at Stake?" Federal Reserve Bank of St. Louis *Review* 72 (November–December 1990): 34–46.
Introduction to the issues related to trade and intellectual property rights.

Chandrasekhar, Sandhya. "Cartel in a Can: The Financial Collapse of the International Tin Council." *Northwestern Journal of International Law and Business* (Fall 1989): 309–332.
History of the tin commodity agreement and its 1985 collapse; accessible to all students.

Chenery, H., and T. N. Srinivasan, eds. *Handbook of Development Economics*, Vols. I and II. Amsterdam: North-Holland, 1989.
The definitive source book for advanced students.

Deardorff, Alan V., and Robert M. Stern, eds. *Analytical and Negotiating Issues in the Global Trading System.* Ann Arbor, Mich.: University of Michigan Press, 1994.
Collection of papers on current trade issues, many relevant to developing countries; level of papers varies.

Dornbusch, Rudiger, and Holger Wolf. "Economic Transition in Eastern Germany." *Brookings Papers on Economic Activity* 1 (1992): 235–272.
The economics of transition in Eastern Germany. Intermediate; includes both microeconomic and macroeconomic aspects of transition.

Dornbusch, Rudiger. "The Case for Trade Liberalization in Developing Countries." *Journal of Economic Perspectives* (Winter 1992): 69–85.
Argues trade liberalization benefits developing economies; for all students.

Easterly, William, and Lant Pritchett. "The Determinants of Economic Success: Luck and Policy." *Finance and Development* 30 (March 1993): 38–41.
Why do some developing countries succeed and others fail? Accessible to all students.

Edwards, Sebastian. "Openness, Trade Liberalization, and Growth in Developing Countries." *Journal of Economic Literature* 31 (September 1993): 1358–1393.
Explanations for developing countries' differential success; intermediate and advanced.

Eichengreen, Barry. "Historical Research on International Lending and Debt." *Journal of Economic Perspectives* (Spring 1991): 149–170.
Compares recent debt problems and scholarship with that of earlier periods; for all students.

Fieleke, Norman S. "The Liberalization of International Trade and Payments in Eastern Europe." Federal Reserve Bank of Boston *New England Economic Review* (March–April 1991): 41–51.
Introduction to the process of reform in Eastern European economies.

Fieleke, Norman S. "The Terms on Which Nations Trade." Federal Reserve Bank of Boston *New England Economic Review* (November–December 1989): 3–12.
Importance of and historical data on the terms of trade; for all students.

Findlay, Ronald. "Growth and Development in Trade Models." In *Handbook of International Economics*, Vol. 1, edited by Ronald W. Jones and Peter B. Kenen, 185–236. Amsterdam: North-Holland, 1984.
Advanced treatment of growth and development issues.

Fischer, Stanley. "Stabilization and Economic Reform in Russia." *Brookings Papers on Economic Activity* 1 (1992): 77–126.
The economics of transition in the former Soviet Union; intermediate. Includes both microeconomic and macroeconomic considerations.

Greenaway, David, and Chris Milner. *Evaluating Trade and Industrial Policy in Developing Countries.* Ann Arbor, Mich.: University of Michigan Press, 1993.
Comprehensive study of developing country policies; level varies.

Grossman, Gene M., and Elhanan Helpman. "Technology and Trade." In *Handbook of International Economics,* Vol. 3, edited by G. M. Grossman and Kenneth Rogoff, 1279–1338. Amsterdam: North-Holland, 1995.
Advanced, up-to-date survey of technology-related aspects of international trade and trade theory.

Hewitt, Daniel P. "Military Expenditures in the Developing World." *Finance and Development* 28 (September 1991): 22–25.
Data on developing countries' weapons expenditures and their implications; for all students.

International Montary Fund. *World Economic Outlook.* Washington, D.C.: International Monetary Fund, annual.
Overview of economic events and prospects relevant to the developing economies, with data. The May 1995 issue focuses on global saving.

Keesing, Donald B., and Andrew Singer. "Why Official Export Promotion Fails." *Finance and Development* 29 (March 1992): 52–53.
Shortcomings of policies to promote exports; accessible to all students.

Klitgaard, Robert. *Tropical Gangsters.* New York: Basic Books, 1990.
A Harvard University economist's entertaining story of his experiences with corruption while working on a World Bank project in Equatorial Guinea.

Krueger, Anne O. *Economic Policies at Cross Purposes.* Washington, D.C.: The Brookings Institution, 1993.
A leading development expert argues that developed countries follow contradictory policies toward developing countries; for all students.

Krueger, Anne O. "Trade Policy in Developing Countries." In *Handbook of International Economics,* Vol. 1, edited by Ronald W. Jones and Peter B. Kenen, 519–570. Amsterdam: North-Holland, 1984.
Advanced treatment of trends in trade policies followed by developing countries.

Lipton, David, and Jeffrey D. Sachs. "Prospects for Russia's Economic Reforms." *Brookings Papers on Economic Activity* 2 (1992): 213–284.
The politics and economics of reform in the former Soviet Union; intermediate.

Meier, Gerald M. *Leading Issues in Economic Development*. New York: Oxford University Press, 1995.
Comprehensive collection of short articles on the many issues that comprise the development process; appropriate for all students.

Michalopoulos, Constantine, and David Tarr. "Energizing Trade of the States of the Former Soviet Union." *Finance and Development* 30 (March 1993): 22–25.
Integrating the former Soviet republics into the world trading system; for all students.

Pinto, Brian, Marek Belka, and Stefan Krajewski. "Transforming State Enterprises in Poland: Evidence on Adjustment by Manufacturing Firms." *Brookings Papers on Economic Activity* 1 (1993): 213–270.
Effects of transition on Polish firms; intermediate.

Pollard, Patricia. "Trade Between the United States and Eastern Europe." Federal Reserve Bank of St. Louis *Review* 76 (July–August 1994): 25–46.
Introduction to the growing economic relationship between the United States and the formerly centrally planned economies.

Rodrik, Dani. "Political Economy Trade Policy." In *Handbook of International Economics,* Vol. 3, edited by G. M. Grossman and Kenneth Rogoff, 1457–1494. Amsterdam: North-Holland, 1995.
Advanced, up-to-date survey of the literature on distributional aspects of trade policy and their implications for the policy process.

Rodrik, Dani. "The Limits of Trade Policy Reform in Developing Countries." *Journal of Economic Perspectives* (Winter 1992): 87–105.
Cautions against unrealistically high expectations about the benefits of trade liberalization for development; for all students.

Sachs, Jeffrey D., and Andrew Warner. "Economic Reform and the Process of Global Integration." *Brookings Papers on Economic Activity* 1 (1995): 1–118.
The role of openness in economic development and growth; intermediate.

Schiff, Maurice, and Alberto Valdés. "The Plundering of Agriculture in Developing Countries." *Finance and Development* 32 (March 1995): 44–47.
The negative side of developing countries' artificial support of manufacturing; for all students.

Summers, Lawrence H. "The Challenges of Development." *Finance and Development* 29 (March 1992): 6–9.
Summary of the problems and prospects of development; for all students.

Summers, Lawrence. "Research Challenges for Development Economists." *Finance and Development* 28 (September 1991): 2–5.
Survey of unsolved problems; accessible to all students.

"Sustainable Development." *Finance and Development* 30 (December 1993): 6–23.
Collection of short articles on development from different disciplinary perspectives; accessible to all students.

Symposium on "The State and Economic Development." *Journal of Economic Perspectives* (Spring 1990): 3–74.
Collection of papers examining the role of government policy in development; for all students.

United Nations Conference on Trade and Development. *The Outcome of the Uruguay Round: An Initial Assessment*. New York: United Nations, 1994.
Overview of the accomplishments and shortcomings of the Uruguay Round from the perspective of many developing economies; includes detailed discussions of most of the issues covered in this chapter.

Whalley, John, ed. *Developing Countries and the Global Trading System,* Vols. 1 and 2. Ann Arbor, Mich.: University of Michigan Press, 1990.
Results of a large-scale study of the interaction between development and the world trading system; level varies.

Williamson, John, ed. *Economic Consequences of Soviet Disintegration*. Washington, D.C.: Institute for International Economics, 1993.
The effects of the breakup of the Soviet Union on the former Soviet republics, satellite states, and the rest of the world economy; for all students.

Williamson, John. *International Debt Re-examined*. Washington, D.C.: Institute for International Economics, 1995.
A readable ex-post examination of the developing-country debt crisis and responses by the debtors, international capital markets, creditors, developed economies, and international organizations.

Williamson, John, ed. *The Political Economy of Policy Reform*. Washington, D.C.: Institute for International Economics, 1994.
A collection of papers on the different experiences of various developing countries undergoing political and economic reform; for all students.

World Bank. *World Debt Tables*, Vol. 1. Washington, D.C.: World Bank, annual.
Comprehensive survey of recent trends in developing-country debt, with data.

World Bank. *World Development Report*. New York: Oxford University Press, annual.
Devoted to examination of various aspects of development; accessible to all students. The 1994 issue examines "Infrastructure for Development," and the 1995 issue focuses on "Workers in an Integrating World." Also contains large collection of data.

PART TWO

International Macroeconomics

CHAPTER TWELVE

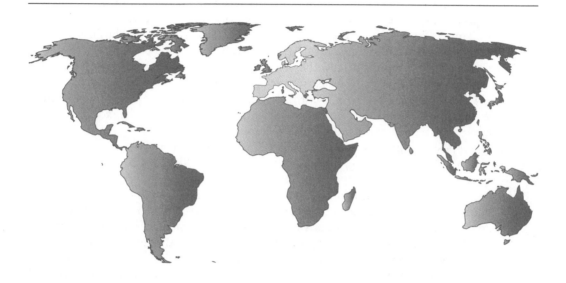

Currency Markets and Exchange Rates

12.1 Introduction

From a macroeconomic perspective, one fundamental characteristic distinguishes international trade from other transactions: international trade typically involves the use of more than one currency or monetary unit. Whether a German buys an Italian sports car, a Japanese airline buys a Boeing airplane, a citizen of Taiwan buys a U.S. Treasury bond, or an American buys stock in a Mexican firm, the transaction requires that one country's currency be exchanged for another's. Thus far, we have avoided the complications multiple currencies introduce by focusing on the effects of trade in real rather than monetary terms. In this chapter, we add another layer of realism to our analysis by examining the mechanics of currency markets and their role in international trade and financial activity.

12.2 Exchange Rates and Prices

12.2.1 Relative and Money Prices

In Chapters Two through Eleven, we examined the decisions individuals and firms make concerning goods to produce, consume, and trade. They use relative prices as guides for making these decisions. Relative prices convey information to consumers and producers concerning the opportunity costs of various goods. In day-to-day transactions, however, we rarely see relative prices directly. It would be unusual to walk into a store and find the price of a bushel of corn listed as two bushels of wheat or to shop for a car and find a sticker price of five personal computers. Instead, the prices used are **money prices**; they tell how many units of money (dollars in the United States, yen in Japan, Deutsche marks in Germany, pesos in Mexico, or yuan in China) we must pay to buy corn, wheat, a car, or a personal computer. If individuals and firms are to make everyday economic decisions according to comparative advantage, money prices must reflect relative prices or opportunity costs.

Suppose that good X sells in the United States for $10 per unit and good Y for $5 per unit. The *ratio* of these two money prices ($P_X/P_Y = \$10/\$5 = 2$ units of Y per unit of X) gives the opportunity cost or relative price of good X; to obtain an additional unit of good X, we must forgo 2 units of good Y. Similarly, $P_Y/P_X = \$5/\$10 = 0.5$ units of X is the opportunity cost of Y; a consumer must forgo 0.5 units of X to obtain an additional unit of Y. The **relative price** of a good is sometimes referred to as its real price; this means the price is measured in "real" units (other goods) rather than in monetary or "nominal" units such as dollars or yen. Because of the simple relationship between money prices and relative prices, individuals can enjoy the convenience of using money prices for everyday decisions without losing the information about opportunity costs that relative prices convey.

Notice that money prices can change while relative prices remain unchanged as long as all money prices change proportionally. If the money prices of goods X and Y doubled from the previous example to $P_X = \$20$ and $P_Y = \$10$, the relative prices of X and Y still would be 2 units of Y and 0.5 units of X, respectively. This will prove important in our analysis of inflation in Chapters Eighteen and Nineteen. After all, inflation is simply a persistent proportional rise in all money prices, so it should leave relative prices unchanged.

12.2.2 Prices in Different Currencies

We have solved the puzzle of the relationship between relative and money prices in a single country's currency. Now, we need an additional step to compare prices stated in different currency units. How can we compare the price of an item selling for 10 dollars in the United States ($P^{US} = \$10$) and for 5 pounds sterling in Britain ($P^B = £5$)? We need to know the exchange rate between pounds and dollars. We define the **exchange rate** (e) as the number of units of *domestic* currency required to purchase 1 unit of the *foreign* currency—in our example, the number of dollars required to buy 1 British pound sterling. In shorthand notation, e = $/£; for example, if the exchange rate (e) is 2, then buying 1 pound will require 2 dollars (e = $2/£1).

The exchange rate also can be defined as the number of units of *foreign* currency required to buy 1 unit of *domestic* currency, or e′ = £/$. Of course, e′ just equals 1/e. Writers use both definitions, and we shall see that the daily *Wall Street Journal* exchange rate quotations report both. To avoid confusion, form the habit of checking carefully when reading about exchange rates (as well as while traveling) to see which definition is being quoted. Buying 2 dollars with 1 pound (e = $2/£1) is quite a different matter than buying 2 pounds with 1 dollar (e′ = £2/$1). In this book, we shall define the exchange rate as the domestic currency ($) price of foreign currency unless specified otherwise.

Suppose an identical good is produced both in the United States and in Britain. At P^{US} = $10, P^B = £5, and e = $2/£1, individuals would be indifferent between buying the U.S. good and buying the identical British good, ignoring transportation costs. To obtain the £5 to buy the British good, an American would have to give up $10, or $2 for each pound; this makes the dollar price the same for both the British- and U.S.-made goods. Similarly, a British resident would have to give up £5 to buy the $10 necessary to buy the U.S. good; thus, the price of the two goods would also be the same when measured in pounds. If e > 2, at P^{US} = $10 and P^B = £5, individuals from both countries would have an incentive to buy the U.S.-made good. *(Why?)* If e < 2, individuals would have an incentive to buy the British good. *(Why?)*

Now consider goods produced uniquely in one country, say, tickets to the National Football League's Super Bowl, produced only in the United States and priced in dollars, and tickets to the Wimbledon tennis tournament, produced only in Britain and priced in pounds. Assume for simplicity that a Super Bowl ticket costs $125 and a ticket to Wimbledon costs £75. The exchange rate between dollars and pounds allows potential purchasers to compare the relative prices of the two tickets, even though their money prices are denominated in different currencies. In 1992, the exchange rate between dollars and pounds was e = $1.77/£. From an American's perspective, a Super Bowl ticket cost $125, while a ticket to Wimbledon cost an amount equal to the dollar price of a pound multiplied by the pound price of a Wimbledon ticket. So the relative price of the two sporting events was equal to $125/([$1.77/£] · £75) = $125/$132.75 = 0.94. A resident of Britain would compare the prices in pounds; and the pound price of a Super Bowl ticket equals the dollar price of the ticket divided by the dollar price of a pound; so ($125/[$1.77/£])/£75 = 0.94—the same result. From either nationality's perspective, the exchange rate in 1992 made the Super Bowl less expensive than Wimbledon, because the pounds necessary to buy a Wimbledon ticket were relatively cheap compared with the dollars necessary to buy a Super Bowl ticket. But by 1993, the dollar price of a pound had fallen from $1.77 to $1.50. The change in the exchange rate raised the Super Bowl's relative price from an American's perspective to $125/([$1.50/£] · £75) = $125/$112.5 = 1.11. Similarly, a British resident would find that a Super Bowl ticket now cost $125/($1.50/£) = £83.33, while a Wimbledon ticket cost £75; and £83.33/£75 = 1.11. The fall in the dollar price of pounds between 1992 and 1993 raised the price of Super Bowl tickets relative to Wimbledon tickets, from either an American or a British perspective.

From these examples, we can see that a change in the exchange rate between two currencies, other things equal, changes all foreign prices relative to all domestic prices. When the dollar price of the pound falls (e decreases), American goods become more expensive relative to British goods. If the dollar price of the pound rises (e increases), American goods become cheaper relative to British goods. This simple observation explains why individuals, firms, and governments care about the value of the exchange rate. Changes in the exchange rate can alter the relative prices of domestic and foreign goods, shifting demand away from the goods that become more expensive and toward the ones that become relatively cheaper.[1]

---

[1]Note that we have held the prices of the goods themselves constant; we shall relax this assumption later.

If exchange rates or the relative prices of various currencies never changed, there would be little reason to study the effects of using different currencies. Exchange rates would be merely a minor nuisance—like the fact that distances are measured in inches, yards, and miles in the United States and in centimeters, meters, and kilometers in Canada. But what if the "rate of exchange" between miles and kilometers were not just a constant (= 0.62 mile/1 kilometer) but varied over time? Travelers then would need a theory to explain the relationship. Similarly, because exchange rates are not constant but change over time, we need a theory to explain them. So we turn to an analysis of foreign exchange markets.

12.3   Foreign Exchange Markets

12.3.1   Definition

The **foreign exchange market** is the generic term for the worldwide institutions that exist to exchange or trade the currencies of different countries. Most of the approximately 200 countries in the world use a unique currency or monetary unit, from Afghanistan's afghani to Zambia's kwacha. As long as the nations of the world economy use different national currencies, international trade requires some mechanism for exchanging them. With so many different currencies, there are literally thousands of exchange rates, because each currency has a relative price in terms of every other.

In practice, the currencies of many smaller countries rarely are traded (professional foreign exchange traders call them "exotics"), and many nonmarket and developing economies do not allow their currencies to trade freely in foreign exchange markets. Figure 12.1 reproduces a recent set of daily exchange rate quotations from *The Wall Street Journal*. The daily lists include only about 50 of the most frequently traded currencies. The first two columns in Figure 12.1 report the exchange rate as this book defines it: the number of dollars required to buy a unit of the foreign currency (e). The two columns on the right report the number of units of the foreign currency required to purchase a dollar (e' = 1/e). *(Verify the relationship between e and e' for several of the currencies.)* The prices quoted in *The Wall Street Journal* are for the large commercial transactions ($1 million or more) that comprise the bulk of the market activity. For small transactions, such as those undertaken by individuals or small firms, higher prices prevail to cover banks' costs of handling them.

Each Monday, *The Wall Street Journal* publishes a more complete listing of exchange rates, including more than 200 currencies. This listing quotes rates for the previous two Fridays, so the change in a currency's value over the preceding week can be calculated. Figure 12.2 reproduces a recent listing. *(Are the quotations e or e'? Can you find currencies on the list for which e = e'? Why?)*

The primary participants in foreign exchange markets include banks (who execute almost 90 percent of foreign exchange market transactions), firms, foreign exchange brokers, and central banks and other official government agencies. Most transactions are made by telephone, cable, or electronic transfer and involve the exchange of large bank deposits denominated in different currencies. There are separate, much smaller markets for the exchange of actual cash or bank notes; this form of foreign exchange is more expensive to buy because of the costs of transporting the cash and guarding

Figure 12.1 □ Foreign Exchange Rate Quotations

Wednesday, August 16, 1995

EXCHANGE RATES

The New York foreign exchange selling rates below apply to trading among banks in amounts of $1 million and more, as quoted at 3 p.m. Eastern time by Bankers Trust Co., Dow Jones Telerate Inc. and other sources. Retail transactions provide fewer units of foreign currency per dollar.

Country	U.S. $ equiv. Wed	U.S. $ equiv. Tue	Currency per U.S. $ Wed	Currency per U.S. $ Tue
Argentina (Peso)	1.0000	1.0000	1.0001	1.0001
Australia (Dollar)	.7327	.7370	1.3649	1.3569
Austria (Schilling)	.09637	.09909	10.376	10.092
Bahrain (Dinar)	2.6525	2.6524	.3770	.3770
Belgium (Franc)	.03290	.03293	30.391	30.369
Brazil (Real)	1.0626	1.0628	.9411	.9409
Britain (Pound)	1.5435	1.5545	.6479	.6433
30-Day Forward	1.5399	1.5513	.6494	.6446
90-Day Forward	1.5375	1.5489	.6504	.6456
180-Day Forward	1.5333	1.5447	.6522	.6474
Canada (Dollar)	.7360	.7351	1.3587	1.3603
30-Day Forward	.7358	.7349	1.3590	1.3607
90-Day Forward	.7347	.7339	1.3611	1.3626
180-Day Forward	.7327	.7317	1.3648	1.3666
Chile (Peso)	.002536	.002582	394.25	387.25
China (Renminbi)	.1203	.1204	8.3094	8.3057
Colombia (Peso)	.001054	.001074	949.00	931.00
Czech. Rep. (Koruna) .	....	....	....	....
Commercial rate	.03695	.03745	27.063	26.700
Denmark (Krone)	.1747	.1748	5.7255	5.7220
Ecuador (Sucre)	....	....	....	....
Floating rate	.0003882	.0003889	2576.00	2571.50
Finland (Markka)	.2299	.2303	4.3496	4.3415
France (Franc)	.1975	.1978	5.0625	5.0560
30-Day Forward	.1974	.1977	5.0653	5.0577
90-Day Forward	.1974	.1977	5.0655	5.0579
180-Day Forward	.1975	.1978	5.0641	5.0560
Germany (Mark)	.6766	.6775	1.4780	1.4760
30-Day Forward	.6771	.6777	1.4770	1.4756
90-Day Forward	.6787	.6793	1.4733	1.4722
180-Day Forward	.6812	.6819	1.4680	1.4665
Greece (Drachma)	.004237	.004227	236.00	236.55
Hong Kong (Dollar)	.1291	.1292	7.7435	7.7420
Hungary (Forint)	.007577	.007663	131.98	130.50
India (Rupee)	.03164	.03178	31.610	31.465
Indonesia (Rupiah)	.0004445	.0004458	2249.50	2243.00
Ireland (Punt)	1.5825	1.5830	.6319	.6317
Israel (Shekel)	.3289	.3290	3.0408	3.0396

Country	U.S. $ equiv. Wed.	U.S. $ equiv. Tues.	Currency per U.S. $ Wed.	Currency per U.S. $ Tues.
Italy (Lira)	.0006161	.0006173	1623.00	1620.00
Japan (Yen)	.01023	.01034	97.750	96.750
30-Day Forward	.01026	.01036	97.479	96.509
90-Day Forward	.01035	.01045	96.637	95.702
180-Day Forward	.01048	.01059	95.435	94.460
Jordan (Dinar)	1.4006	1.4144	.7140	.7070
Kuwait (Dinar)	3.2927	3.3055	.3037	.3025
Lebanon (Pound)	.0006190	.0006195	1615.50	1614.08
Malaysia (Ringgit)	.4008	.4023	2.4953	2.4855
Malta (Lira)	2.8729	2.8729	.3481	.3481
Mexico (Peso)	....	....	....	....
Floating rate	.1621	.1626	6.1700	6.1500
Netherland (Guilder) ..	.6047	.6052	1.6538	1.6523
New Zealand (Dollar) .	.6504	.6562	1.5376	1.5240
Norway (Krone)	.1547	.1548	6.4630	6.4585
Pakistan (Rupee)	.03196	.03196	31.289	31.289
Peru (new Sol)	.4464	.4461	2.2400	2.2415
Philippines (Peso)	.03899	.03898	25.645	25.655
Poland (Zloty)	.4211	.4211	2.3750	2.3750
Portugal (Escudo)	.006540	.006517	152.90	153.45
Saudi Arabia (Riyal) ..	.2666	.2666	3.7508	3.7507
Singapore (Dollar)	.7032	.7060	1.4220	1.4165
Slovak Rep. (Koruna) .	.03301	.03337	30.290	29.970
South Africa (Rand) ...	.2735	.2733	3.6557	3.6592
South Korea (Won)	.001296	.001313	771.85	761.75
Spain (Peseta)	.007936	.007969	126.01	125.48
Sweden (Krona)	.1370	.1359	7.2996	7.3559
Switzerland (Franc) ...	.8130	.8137	1.2300	1.2290
30-Day Forward	.8147	.8143	1.2274	1.2280
90-Day Forward	.8188	.8182	1.2213	1.2222
180-Day Forward	.8245	.8239	1.2128	1.2137
Taiwan (Dollar)	.03639	.03665	27.478	27.287
Thailand (Baht)	.03982	.03997	25.110	25.020
Turkey (Lira)	.00002117	.00002139	47230.50	46740.00
United Arab (Dirham) .	.2723	.2723	3.6730	3.6728
Uruguay (New Peso) ..	....	....	....	....
Financial	.1536	.1538	6.5100	6.5000
Venezuela (Bolivar) ...	.005890	.005890	169.79	169.78
— — —				
SDR	1.4891	1.5085	.6716	.6629
ECU	1.2733	1.2724	....	....

Special Drawing Rights (SDR) are based on exchange rates for the U.S., German, British, French, and Japanese currencies. Source: International Monetary Fund.

European Currency Unit (ECU) is based on a basket of community currencies.

Source: *The Wall Street Journal*, August 17, 1995.

it from theft. Just as the domestic money supply of each country consists primarily of bank deposits rather than cash, activity in the foreign exchange market consists mainly of transactions in bank deposits denominated in the various currencies.[2] This is important to keep in mind in the discussion that follows: "Selling dollars and buying pounds" really means using funds from a bank deposit denominated in dollars to open or add to a bank deposit denominated in pounds.

---

[2]The bank deposits traded in the foreign exchange market consist of large time deposits or certificates of deposit, not part of the issuing country's money stock.

Figure 12.2 □ Extended Foreign Exchange Rate Quotations

World Value of the Dollar

The table below, compiled by Bank of America, gives the rates of exchange for the U.S. dollar against various currencies as of Friday August 11, 1995. Unless otherwise noted, all rates listed are middle rates of interbank bid and asked quotes, and are expressed in foreign currency units per one U.S. dollar. The rates are indicative and aren't based on, nor intended to be used as a basis for, particular transactions.

BankAmerica International doesn't trade in all the listed foreign currencies.

Country (Currency)	Value 8/11	Value 8/4	Country (Currency)	Value 8/11	Value 8/4
Afghanistan (Afghani -c)	3540.00	3540.00	Lesotho (Maloti)	3.6328	3.6173
Albania (Lek)	111.91	110.33	Liberia (Dollar)	1.00	1.00
Algeria (Dinar)	49.96	49.96	Libya (Dinar)	0.3555	0.3555
Andorra (Peseta -5)	121.74	119.34	Liechtenstein (Franc)	1.1871	1.1529
Andorra (Franc)	4.9199	4.8062	Lithuania (Litas)	4.06	4.00
Angola (Readjust Kwanza)	3224.00	2216.50	Luxembourg (Lux.Franc)	29.362	28.675
Antigua (E Caribbean $)	2.70	2.70	Macao (Pataca)	7.9985	7.9934
Argentina (Peso)	1.00	1.00	Madagascar DR (Franc)	4100.00	4100.00
Aruba (Florin)	1.79	1.79	Malawi (Kwacha)	15.08	15.36
Australia (Australia Dollar)	1.3428	1.3532	Malaysia (Ringgit)	2.4675	2.4625
Austria (Schilling)	10.0565	9.812	Maldive (Rufiyaa)	11.77	11.77
Bahamas (Dollar)	1.00	1.00	Mali Rep (C.F.A. Franc)	491.99	480.62
Bahrain (Dinar)	0.377	0.377	Malta (Lira *)	2.8409	2.8841
Bangladesh (Taka)	40.288	40.29	Martinique (Franc)	4.9199	4.8062
Barbados (Dollar)	2.0113	2.0113	Mauritania (Ouguiya)	128.99	128.99
Belgium (Franc)	29.362	28.675	Mauritius (Rupee)	17.89	17.60
Belize (Dollar)	2.00	2.00	Mexico (New Peso -1)	6.15	6.14
Benin (C.F.A. Franc)	491.99	480.62	Monaco (Franc)	4.9199	4.8062
Bermuda (Dollar)	1.00	1.00	Mongolia (Tugrik -o)	432.75	432.75
Bhutan (Ngultrum)	31.45	31.40	Montserrat (E Caribbean $)	2.70	2.70
Bolivia (Boliviano -o)	4.83	4.83	Morocco (Dirham)	8.385	8.3763
Bolivia (Boliviano -f)	4.82	4.82	Mozambique (Metical)	7300.00	7300.00
Botswana (Pula)	2.7816	2.7601	Namibia (Rand -c-11)	3.6328	3.6173
Bouvet Island (Norwegian Krone)	6.273	6.161	Nauru Islands (Australia Dollar)	1.3428	1.3532
Brazil (Real -3)	0.936	0.9351	Nepal (Rupee)	50.39	50.39
Brunei (Dollar)	1.399	1.3983	Netherlands (Guilder)	1.6013	1.563
Bulgaria (Lev)	68.108	66.88	Netherlands Ant'les (Guilder)	1.79	1.79
Burkina Faso (C.F.A. Franc)	491.99	480.62	New Zealand (N.Z.Dollar)	1.5114	1.4934
Burma (Kyat)	5.5754	5.4821	Nicaragua (Gold Cordoba)	7.6191	7.6026
Burundi (Franc)	236.1949	232.2397	Niger Rep (C.F.A. Franc)	491.99	480.62
Cambodia (Riel)	2300.00	2300.00	Nigeria (Naira -m)	80.00	79.90
Cameroon (C.F.A. Franc)	491.99	480.62	Nigeria (Naira -o)	22.00	22.00
Canada (Dollar)	1.3585	1.3566	Norway (Norwegian Krone)	6.273	6.161
Cape Verde Isl (Escudo)	82.97	82.97	Oman, Sultanate of (Rial)	0.385	0.385
Cayman Islands (Dollar)	0.8282	0.8282	Pakistan (Rupee)	31.33	31.27
Centrl African Rp (C.F.A. Franc)	491.99	480.62	Panama (Balboa)	1.00	1.00
Chad (C.F.A. Franc)	491.99	480.62	Papua N.G. (Kina)	1.3661	1.3569
Chile (Peso -m)	388.69	379.83	Paraguay (Guarani -d)	1966.00	1966.00
Chile (Peso -o)	411.51	406.35	Peru (New Sol -d)	2.245	2.245
China (Renminbi Yuan)	8.3025	8.3002	Philippines (Peso)	25.674	25.59
Colombia (Peso -o)	919.32	900.78	Pitcairn Island (N.Z.Dollar)	1.5114	1.4934
Commnwlth Ind Sts (Rouble -m)	4405.00	4415.00	Poland (Zloty -o-6)	2.4035	2.384
Comoros (Franc)	368.9925	360.465	Portugal (Escudo -4)	148.25	144.83
Congo, People Rp (C.F.A. Franc)	491.99	480.62	Puerto Rico (U.S. $)	1.00	1.00
Costa Rica (Colon)	182.71	182.11	Qatar (Riyal)	3.6392	3.6392
Croatia (Kuna)	5.1104	5.0248	Repub of Macedonia (Denar -8)	37.0047	36.9499
Cuba (Peso)	1.00	1.00	Republic of Yemen (Rial -a-12)	140.00	140.00
Cyprus (Pound *)	2.2384	2.2763	Republic of Yemen (Rial -12)	50.25	50.25
Czech (Koruna)	26.43	25.99	Reunion, Ile de la (Franc)	4.9199	4.8062
Denmark (Danish Krone)	5.535	5.409	Romania (Leu)	2043.00	2032.00
Djibouti (Djibouti Franc)	177.72	177.72	Rwanda (Franc -9)	220.00	220.00
Dominica (E Caribbean $)	2.70	2.70	Saint Christopher (E Caribbean $)	2.70	2.70
Dominican Rep (Peso -d)	14.02	13.93	Saint Helena (Pound Sterling *)	1.5848	1.6031
Ecuador (Sucre -2)	2554.00	2549.50	Saint Lucia (E Caribbean $)	2.70	2.70
Ecuador (Sucre -o2)	2580.00	2582.50	Saint Pierre (Franc)	4.9199	4.8062
Egypt (Pound)	3.3955	3.3955	Saint Vincent (E Caribbean $)	2.70	2.70
El Salvador (Colon -d)	8.76	8.75	Samoa, American (U.S. $)	1.00	1.00
Equatorial Guinea (C.F.A. Franc)	491.99	480.62	Samoa, Western (Tala)	2.5227	2.4685
Estonia (Kroon)	11.43	11.16	San Marino (Lira)	1588.25	1582.20
Ethiopia (Birr -o)	5.95	5.95	Sao Tome & Principe (Dobra)	1258.33	1258.33
Faeroe Islands (Danish Krone)	5.535	5.409	Saudi Arabia (Riyal)	3.7507	3.7507
Falkland Islands (Pound *)	1.5848	1.6031	Senegal (C.F.A. Franc)	491.99	480.62
Fiji (Dollar)	1.4025	1.3926	Seychelles (Rupee)	4.7406	4.6612
Finland (Markka)	4.233	4.193	Sierra Leone (Leone)	730.00	730.00
France (Franc)	4.9199	4.8062	Singapore (Dollar)	1.399	1.3983
French Guiana (Franc)	4.9199	4.8062	Slovak (Koruna)	29.465	29.26
French Pacific Isl (C.F.P. Franc)	89.4526	87.3854	Slovenia (Tolar)	115.79	113.42
Gabon (C.F.A. Franc)	491.99	480.62	Solomon Islands (Solomon Dollar)	2.9944	2.9944
Gambia (Dalasi)	9.55	9.55	Somali Rep (Shilling -d)	2620.00	2620.00
Germany (Mark)	1.4298	1.3949	South Africa (Rand -c-11)	3.6328	3.6173
Ghana (Cedi)	1200.00	1200.00	Spain (Peseta -5)	121.74	119.34
Gibraltar (Pound *)	1.5848	1.6031	Sri Lanka (Rupee)	50.59	50.53
Greece (Drachma)	229.94	225.36	Sudan Rep (Dinar)	52.08	52.08
Greenland (Danish Krone)	5.535	5.409	Sudan Rep (Pound -c)	520.83	520.83
Grenada (E Caribbean $)	2.70	2.70	Surinam (Guilder)	492.00	492.00
Guadeloupe (Franc)	4.9199	4.8062	Swaziland (Lilangeni)	3.6328	3.6173
Guam (U.S. $)	1.00	1.00	Sweden (Krona)	7.1138	7.0813
Guatemala (Quetzal)	5.7706	5.7765	Switzerland (Franc)	1.1871	1.1529
Guinea Bissau (Peso)	16748.00	16748.00	Syria (Pound)	41.65	41.65
Guinea Rep (Franc)	989.40	989.40	Taiwan (Dollar -o)	26.50	26.50
Guyana (Dollar)	143.80	143.80	Tanzania (Shilling)	585.00	605.00
Haiti (Gourde)	19.00	19.00	Thailand (Baht)	24.91	24.81
Honduras Rep (Lempira -d)	9.45	9.46	Togo, Rep (C.F.A. Franc)	491.99	480.62
Hong Kong (Dollar)	7.743	7.738	Tonga Islands (Pa'anga)	1.2569	1.2569
Hungary (Forint -7)	129.34	127.18	Trinidad & Tobago (Dollar)	5.705	5.7025
Iceland (Krona)	63.72	63.20	Tunisia (Dinar)	0.9273	0.914
India (Rupee -m)	31.45	31.40	Turkey (Lira)	46300.50	45721.50
Indonesia (Rupiah)	2229.25	2236.50	Turks & Caicos (U.S. $)	1.00	1.00
Iran (Rial -o)	3000.00	3000.00	Tuvalu (Australia Dollar)	1.3428	1.3532
Iraq (Dinar)	0.60	0.60	Uganda (Shilling -l)	975.00	975.00
Ireland (Punt *)	1.623	1.6425	Ukraine (Karbovanet)	147833.00	145747.00
Israel (New Shekel)	3.022	3.013	United Arab Emir (Dirham)	3.671	3.671
Italy (Lira)	1588.25	1582.20	United Kingdom (Pound Sterling *)	1.5848	1.6031
Ivory Coast (C.F.A. Franc)	491.99	480.62	Uruguay (Peso Uruguayo -m)	6.43	6.39
Jamaica (Peso -o)	32.90	32.90	Vanuatu (Vatu)	111.75	111.75
Japan (Yen)	93.65	91.04	Vatican City (Lira)	1588.25	1582.20
Jordan (Dinar)	0.703	0.701	Venezuela (Bolivar -d)	170.00	170.00
Kenya (Shilling)	55.01	57.47	Vietnam (Dong -o)	11043.50	11032.00
Kiribati (Australian Dollar)	1.3428	1.3532	Virgin Is, Br (U.S. $)	1.00	1.00
Korea, North (Won)	2.15	2.15	Virgin Is, US (U.S. $)	1.00	1.00
Korea, South (Won)	758.30	758.80	Yugoslavia (New Dinar)	1.4298	1.3949
Kuwait (Dinar)	0.3022	0.3006	Zaire Rep (New Zaire)	4750.00	4750.00
Laos, People DR (Kip)	729.00	729.00	Zambia (Kwacha)	915.00	942.50
Latvia (Lat)	0.52	0.52	Zimbabwe (Dollar)	8.60	8.6225
Lebanon (Pound)	1615.50	1616.00			

*U.S. dollars per National Currency unit. (a) Free market central bank rate. (b) Floating rate. (c) Commercial rate. (d) Free market rate. (e) Controlled. (f) Financial rate. (g) Preferential rate. (h) Nonessential imports. (i) Floating tourist rate. (j) Public transaction rate. (k) Agricultural products. (l) Priority rate. (m) Market rate. (n) Essential imports. (o) Official rate. (p) Exports. (n.a.) Not available.

(1) Mexico, 23 December 1994: Currency allowed to float. (2) Ecuador, 21 December 1994: Central Bank to implement a crawling peg technique. (3) Brazil, 7 March 1995: New Foreign Exchange Rate policy announced. (4) Portugal, 6 March 1995: Escudo devalued by approx 3 1/2%. (5) Spain, 6 March 1995: Peseta devalued by approx 7%. (6) Poland, 1 January 1995: Currency rebased. (7) Hungary, 13 March 1995: Forint devalued by approx 9%. (8) , 26 May 1995: Exchange rate now being quoted for Macedonia. (9) Rwanda, 9 March 1995: Franc devalued by approx 37.7%. (10) Angola, 3 July 1995: New currency called the Readjusted Kwanza introduced. (11) South Africa, 13 March 1995: Exchange rates unified. (12) Republic of Yemen, 30 March 1995: Rial devalued by approx 76%..

Further information available at BankAmerica International.

Source: Bank of America Global Trading, London

12.3.2 Transactions

We shall see that the decisions by actors in the foreign exchange market to buy and sell bank deposits denominated in different currencies combine to determine the equilibrium exchange rates between various pairs of currencies. But why do those actors buy and sell deposits in different currencies? The basic answer is that each bank, firm, or individual must choose how to allocate its available wealth among various assets. An **asset** is simply something of value, such as a house, a diamond, an acre of land, a bank deposit, a share of Microsoft stock, or a U.S. Treasury bond. An **asset portfolio** is simply a set of assets owned by a firm or individual. *Portfolio choice* refers to allocating one's wealth among various types of assets, some of which may produce pleasure from consumption (for example, houses, compact-disk players, National Basketball Association season tickets), and some of which produce income (for example, interest from bank deposits or capital gains from stock). We will assume that each firm or individual already has decided how to split the available wealth between pleasure-producing, consumption-oriented assets such as houses and income-generating wealth such as bank deposits; and we will focus on allocation *within* the second group. In particular, because the demand for bank deposits denominated in various currencies determines exchange rates, we need to examine what determines that demand.

The primary determinant of any particular asset's desirability is its expected rate of return, or the expected future change in its value expressed as a percent of its purchase price. Maximizing wealth requires that individuals and firms try to add to their portfolios those assets whose value will rise in the future and eliminate from their portfolios those assets whose value will fall. Of course, asset owners cannot know perfectly today what will happen to the value of different assets in the future, so portfolio choice requires collecting the available information on different assets and forming expectations about their future rates of return. Before we explore in detail the implications for the demand for bank deposits in different currencies, we can see that maximizing the rate of return from an asset portfolio could lead to four basic circumstances in which an individual or firm might choose to make transactions in the foreign exchange market. For now, we restrict our attention to the **spot foreign exchange market,** that is, the market in which participants trade currencies for current delivery, which actually means delivery within two business days.

Clearing

Suppose a firm in the United States decides to buy a bond issued by a firm from Britain.[3] The U.S. firm typically enters the spot foreign exchange market to buy the pounds in which the British firm issuing the bond wants to be paid. This happens when the U.S. firm instructs its bank to debit its dollar account and

---

[3] A bond is just an IOU. The U.S. firm lends funds to the British firm in return for a promise of repayment with interest.

credit the pound bank account of the British firm. In each international transaction, such a currency exchange occurs at some point. This type of transaction often is referred to as the **clearing** function of the foreign exchange market. The American firm demands foreign exchange (bank deposits denominated in pounds) in exchange for domestic currency (bank deposits denominated in dollars). In fact, it does not matter who (buyer or seller) actually conducts the foreign exchange transaction. At some point, a dollar deposit must be exchanged for a pound deposit. The location of the foreign exchange transaction is of little importance, because arbitrage links foreign exchange markets all over the world. This means that the rate at which dollar deposits exchange for pound deposits will be approximately the same whether the buyer makes the foreign exchange transaction in the United States or the seller makes the transaction in Britain.

Arbitrage

Arbitrage refers to the process by which banks, firms, or individuals (mainly banks in the case of foreign exchange) seek to earn a profit by taking advantage of discrepancies among prices prevailing simultaneously in different markets. For example, suppose $e^{NY} = \$2/\pounds1$ in New York and $e^L = \$2.20/\pounds1$ in London, and you have \$100 to use to arbitrage the foreign exchange market. You could use the \$100 deposit to buy a £50 deposit in New York and then use the £50 deposit to buy a \$110 deposit in London. You would make a profit of \$10 (or a 10 percent rate of return) ignoring transaction costs, which are close to zero in the foreign exchange market because most trading is done electronically in very large denominations. Of course, you would not be the only person doing this. Not only is the transaction very profitable, but it also involves no risk, since the New York and London transactions can be made simultaneously. In the process of making your profitable transaction, you increase the demand for pound-denominated deposits in New York (where you supplied \$100 to demand £50) and increase the demand for dollar-denominated deposits in London (where you demanded \$110 by supplying £50). This causes e^{NY} to rise and e^L to fall. Such arbitrage continues to be profitable until the two exchange rates (e^{NY} and e^L) equalize at some value between \$2.00 and \$2.20 per pound.

Arbitrage ensures not only that dollars and pounds exchange at the same rate in New York and London but also that exchange rates will be consistent across currencies. Suppose exchange rates are such that you can buy 4 Deutsche marks (DM) for 1 dollar, 1 pound for 8 Deutsche marks, and 3 dollars for 1 pound. Such a situation is referred to as *inconsistent* and would not persist in the presence of arbitrage. What if you again had \$100 to use in arbitrage? You could use your \$100 bank deposit to buy a DM400 deposit, use the marks to buy £50, and use the pounds to buy \$150—a 50 percent rate of return for your efforts! Of course, the example exaggerates the inconsistency of the rates, and you would not be fortunate enough to be the only one seeking to take advantage of the situation. Your efforts, along with those of others, would tend to raise the dollar price of Deutsche marks, the DM price of pounds, and the pound price of dollars, thereby eliminating the opportunity for profitable arbitrage and ending the **inconsistent**

Figure 12.3 □ Cross Exchange Rates

Key Currency Cross Rates Late New York Trading Aug 16, 1995

	Dollar	Pound	SFranc	Guilder	Peso	Yen	Lira	D-Mark	FFranc	CdnDlr
Canada	1.3587	2.0972	1.10463	.82156	.22021	.01390	.00084	.91928	.26839	....
France	5.0625	7.814	4.1159	3.0611	.82050	.05179	.00312	3.4252	....	3.7260
Germany	1.4780	2.2813	1.2016	.89370	.23955	.01512	.00091	....	.29195	1.0878
Italy	1623.0	2505.1	1319.51	981.38	263.05	16.604	....	1098.11	320.59	1194.5
Japan	97.75	150.88	79.472	59.106	15.843	....	.06023	66.137	19.309	71.94
Mexico	6.1700	9.5234	5.0163	3.7308	....	.06312	.00380	4.1746	1.2188	4.5411
Netherlands ..	1.6538	2.5526	1.3446	....	.26804	.01692	.00102	1.1189	.32668	1.2172
Switzerland ...	1.2300	1.8985	....	.74374	.19935	.01258	.00076	.83221	.24296	.9053
U.K.	.64788	....	.52673	.39175	.10500	.00663	.00040	.43835	.12798	.47684
U.S.	....	1.5435	.81301	.60467	.16207	.01023	.00062	.67659	.19753	.73600

Source: Dow Jones Telerate Inc.

Source: *The Wall Street Journal*, August 17, 1995.

cross rates. Because of the possibility of such **triangular** (three-currency) **arbitrage**, we expect that $/£ = $/DM · DM/£. *(Why?)*

Until recently, cross exchange rates rarely were reported. Most foreign exchange transactions took place through a two-step process with the dollar serving as an intermediary, or vehicle, currency. Someone who wanted to exchange Deutsche mark deposits for pound deposits would trade the marks for dollars and the dollars for pounds. However, with the acceleration of international trade and financial activity in the last few years, more transactions have begun to occur directly between nondollar currencies. *The Wall Street Journal* now prints a daily chart of cross exchange rates for ten major currencies, shown in Figure 12.3. The chart reports both e and e′ for each pair of currencies. *(Use the data in the chart to check the consistency of the cross rates for several currencies. Also, check the relationship between e and e′.)*

For the many currencies for which cross rates still are not reported, the best guess is the rate that would be consistent in the sense defined earlier. *(Use Figure 12.2 to predict the cross rates between the Panamanian balboa and the Belizian dollar and between the Mongolian tugrik and the Sudanese dinar.)* The degree to which consistency holds for a given currency depends on the extent of arbitrage activity allowed. If government policies restrict purchases and sales of a currency, inconsistent cross rates may persist.

Hedging

Another reason for making transactions in the spot foreign exchange market is hedging. **Hedging** is a way to transfer part of the **foreign exchange risk** inherent in all transactions, such as international trade, that involve two currencies. For example, suppose you are a U.S. importer who just purchased £1,000 of goods from a British exporter; payment is due in pounds in 30 days. You face at least two alternatives (we shall see an additional one later): (1) You can enter the spot foreign exchange market now, buy a £1,000 deposit at the current spot exchange rate and earn interest on it until the payment to the exporter is due in 30 days, or (2) you can hold your dollars in a deposit and earn interest for 30 days until the payment is due, at which time you enter the spot foreign exchange market and buy a £1,000 deposit at what is *then* the current spot exchange rate. In other words, you can choose whether to hold a pound deposit or a dollar deposit as an asset in your portfolio over the next 30 days.

If you choose the first option, you are hedging to avoid the risk that the dollar price of pounds could rise. If you wait (take option 2), the exchange rate might rise during the 30-day period, meaning you will have to pay more dollars for each of the £1,000 you must buy. During the 30-day period under option 2, you are said to be holding a **short position** in pounds—that is, you are short of pounds you will need at the end of the 30 days. Option 1 (buying now the pounds you will need in 30 days) allows you to avoid this short position and the associated foreign exchange risk. Once you have purchased the pounds, changes in the exchange rate no longer affect you. You are then said to be holding a **balanced,** or **closed, position** in pounds: You own just as many pounds as you need to cover your upcoming pound payment.

Entering the foreign exchange market to hedge is a way to avoid foreign exchange risk; it insulates your wealth from the effects of adverse changes in the exchange rate. But what if you decide to hedge and buy your pounds now and then, in 30 days, you happen to glance at *The Wall Street Journal* and find that the dollar price of pounds has fallen? You could buy the pounds now for less than you paid for them 30 days ago. Hedging allowed you to avoid the possibility that pounds would become more expensive, but it did not allow you to take advantage of the possibility of pounds becoming cheaper.[4]

Speculation
Speculation is yet another reason to make transactions on the spot foreign exchange market. In one sense, **speculation** is just the opposite of hedging: It means deliberately making your wealth depend on changes in the exchange rate by (1) buying a deposit denominated in foreign currency (taking a long position) in the hope that the currency's price will rise, allowing you to sell it later at a profit, or (2) promising to sell a foreign currency deposit in the future (taking a short position) in the hope that its price will fall, allowing you to buy the currency cheaply and sell it at a profit. When you speculate, changes in the exchange rate affect your wealth. Exchange rate movements in the direction you expected increase wealth, but those in a direction opposite to that anticipated reduce it. The line between hedging and speculation is a fuzzy one; choosing not to hedge is one kind of speculation. However, the term *speculation* often is reserved for cases in which someone buys

---

[4]For a small set of heavily traded currencies, a recently developed financial instrument known as an option contract provides still another alternative. Case One at the end of the chapter explains these contracts.

(sells) a bank deposit denominated in a currency solely because he or she expects the currency's price to rise (fall), with no link to another transaction, as in the case of the hedging decision.

12.3.3 Forward Markets

The major markets for foreign exchange other than spot markets are forward markets. Here participants sign contracts for foreign-exchange deliveries to be made at some specified future date (usually in 30, 90, or 180 days). The important thing is that the price of the foreign exchange is agreed on *now* for *future* delivery. The **30-day forward rate** for pounds is simply the dollar price at which you can buy a contract today for a pound deposit to be delivered in 30 days. The percentage difference between the 30-day forward rate (e^f) on a currency and the spot rate is called the **forward premium** if positive and the **forward discount** if negative.[5] If pounds sell at a 10 percent forward premium against dollars, the dollar price of a pound deposit to be delivered in 30 days is 10 percent higher than the dollar price of a pound deposit delivered today (that is, the spot rate). If a forward pound to be delivered in 180 days costs 5 percent less than a pound delivered today, the pound sells at a 5 percent 180-day forward discount against the dollar. Active forward markets exist in a relatively small number of currencies. Figure 12.1 reports 30, 90, and 180-day forward rates for the British pound (£), the Canadian dollar (Can$), the French franc (F), the German mark (DM), the Japanese yen (¥), and the Swiss franc (SF). *(In Figure 12.1, which currencies sell at a forward premium against the dollar? Which sell at a forward discount?)*

As we already have seen, every international transaction that does not occur instantaneously involves a foreign exchange risk for one of the parties because the spot exchange rate may change during the transaction's time horizon.[6] The existence of forward markets in foreign exchange allows these risks to be transferred.

Suppose you are a U.S. firm holding $1,000. What if you expect the dollar to lose value against the pound (that is, the dollar price of a pound to rise) over the next 30 days? You can buy a pound deposit now in the spot market, hold it for 30 days, and then sell it in the spot market in exchange for dollars; or you can buy a pound deposit now in the spot market *and* buy a dollar deposit in the 30-day forward market to "freeze" the price at which you can obtain dollars in 30 days; or you can simply hold dollars over the entire period. Which alternative will maximize your expected rate of return depends on (1) the forward exchange rate, (2) short-term interest rates available on deposits denominated in the two currencies, (3) the spot

---

[5]A forward premium or discount can be defined for any time horizon; 30 days is only one example. Note that for any two currencies a forward premium on one is equivalent to a forward discount on the other. If the pound sells at a forward premium against the dollar ($[e^f - e] > 0$), the dollar sells at a forward discount against the pound ($[e'^f - e'] < 0$). Therefore, when using the term *forward premium* or *forward discount,* one must specify the currency.

[6]The appropriate definition and measurement of foreign exchange risk is a matter of controversy. Here we mean simply that changes in the value of the exchange rate during a transaction may alter the rate of return anticipated by the parties at the time they agreed to the transaction.

rate you expect will prevail in 30 days, and (4) the current spot rate. If you choose to buy pounds now in the spot market and sell them in the future spot market, the current and future spot exchange rates and the interest rate on pound-denominated deposits will determine your rate of return. This is a risky strategy because the future spot rate cannot be known now; whether you would be willing to make this choice depends on your attitude toward risk and on your expectation about the future spot rate. If you buy pounds now in the spot market *and* buy dollars in the forward market, your rate of return will depend on the current spot rate, the forward rate, and the interest on the pound-denominated deposit you will hold for 30 days. If you simply hold a dollar-denominated deposit, your rate of return will depend on the interest rate available on dollar-denominated deposits.

The collective decisions of many individuals weighing the alternatives outlined above determine the relationships among the current spot rate, the forward rate, short-term interest rates on deposits denominated in the two currencies, and individuals' expectations of the future spot rate. The efforts of all individuals in the economy to maximize the expected rates of return on their asset portfolios result in two conditions—called *interest parity conditions*—that summarize the relationships between spot and forward exchange rates and short-term interest rates on assets denominated in the two currencies.

12.4 Interest Parity

Uncovered interest parity applies to transactions in which participants do not use forward markets to transfer foreign exchange risk, and covered interest parity applies to transactions in which they do. We examine each in turn.

12.4.1 Uncovered Interest Parity

Suppose the 30-day interest rate on dollar-denominated deposits is 1 percent, the 30-day interest rate on comparable pound-denominated deposits is 2 percent, and the spot exchange rate between dollars and pounds is e = \$2/£1. If you have \$1,000, should you buy a £500 bank deposit or keep the funds in a dollar deposit?

If you keep your initial \$1,000 in a dollar-denominated deposit at 1 percent interest, you will end up with \$1,010, or a rate of return of 1 percent (the interest rate on dollar-denominated deposits). If you use your \$1,000 in the spot foreign exchange market to buy a £500 deposit, it will mature in 30 days and earn 2 percent interest. Then, you can take your £510 (£500 of principal plus 2 percent interest) and convert them back into dollars at the then-current spot exchange rate. The rate of return on your deposit measured in dollars will depend on the spot exchange rate at the end of the 30-day period.[7] For example, if the spot rate does not change over the 30 days, you will end up with \$1,020. The rate of return will equal 2 percent, exactly the interest

---

[7]Note that investors generally care about rates of return in their *domestic* currency and that when comparing assets' rates of return, they must always be expressed in the *same* currency.

rate on pound-denominated deposits; and you will be glad you chose the pound deposit over the dollar deposit. But what if the spot rate during the 30-day period falls to e = $1.50/£1? Then, when you convert your £510 back into dollars, you will get only $765, a rate of return of *negative* 23 percent, consisting of the 2 percent interest on the pound deposit plus a *loss* of 25 percent from holding pounds which lost 25 percent of their value against the dollar over the 30 days (because [$1.50/£1 – $2.00/£1]/$2.00/£1 = –25%). In this case, you would have been much better off taking the 1 percent interest rate and rate of return on the dollar-denominated deposit.

Obviously, whether there is an incentive to buy the pound-denominated deposit depends not only on a comparison of the interest rates but also on what the individual expects to happen to the spot exchange rate during the life of the deposit. There is no way of knowing in advance (before making the decision about which deposit to purchase) what the future value of the spot rate will be. The individual must form an expectation about the future spot rate and base the asset decision on that. If the expectation turns out to be correct, the outcome of the decision will please the individual. If the expectation turns out to be wrong, the individual may regret the decision after the fact, even though it was made on the best information available at the time.

When all individuals in the economy choose between purchasing dollar- and pound-denominated deposits in a way to maximize expected rate of return, the result is a relationship among interest rates, the current spot rate, and individuals' expectations of the future value of the spot rate. As long as the interest differential in favor of dollar-denominated deposits is less than the expected increase in value of pounds against dollars over the life of the deposit, there is an incentive to sell dollar-denominated deposits and purchase pound-denominated ones, which promise a higher expected rate of return. Algebraically,

General Case:
If $i^\$ - i^£ < (e^e - e)/e$, purchase pound-denominated deposits.

[12.1]

Numerical Example:
1.5% – 1% < ($2.02/£1 – $2.00/£1)/($2.00/£1) = 1%;
therefore, purchase pound-denominated deposits,

where $i^\$$ is the interest rate on dollar-denominated deposits, $i^£$ is the interest rate on comparable pound-denominated deposits, e^e is the spot rate individuals *expect* to prevail at the end of the deposit's life, and e is the current spot rate.[8] The term on the left-hand side of Equation 12.1 is the **interest differential**; the term on the right-hand side is the expected increase (if positive) or decrease (if negative) in the value of pounds against dollars, expressed in percentage terms. In the numerical example,

[8]An alternative way of writing Equation 12.1 puts the rate of return on dollar-denominated deposits on the left-hand side and the rate of return on pound-denominated deposits on the right-hand side. The dollar rate of return on dollar-denominated assets simply equals the rate of interest on those deposits, or $i^\$$. The expected dollar rate of return on pound-denominated assets has two components: the rate of interest ($i^£$) and the expected rate of change in the value of pounds relative to dollars ([e^e – e]/e). Portfolio owners will buy more pound-denominated deposits if the total return on pound-denominated assets exceeds the rate of return on dollar-denominated assets, or if $i^\$ < i^£ + (e^e - e)/e$, which is equivalent to Equation 12.1.

the interest rate on dollar-denominated deposits exceeds that on pound-denominated deposits by 0.5 percent over the relevant time horizon. But the dollar price of pounds is expected to rise over the same period by ($2.02 – $2.00)/$2.00 = 1%. Therefore, the loss in the value of the dollar (1 percent) more than offsets the interest differential in favor of dollar-denominated deposits (0.5 percent), and portfolio owners will choose to buy pound-denominated deposits instead to earn a higher expected rate of return. *(What if $i^\$ = 1\%$, $i^\pounds = 2\%$, e = $2/£1, and e^e = $2/£1?)*

On the other hand,

> *General Case:*
> If $i^\$ - i^\pounds > (e^e - e)/e$, purchase dollar-denominated deposits.

[12.2]

> *Numerical Example:*
> 3% – 1% > ($2.02/£1 – $2.00/£1)/($2.00/£1) = 1%;
> therefore, purchase dollar-denominated deposits.

In this case, the interest differential in favor of dollar deposits (3% – 1% = 2%) is large enough to compensate for the expected loss (1%) in holding dollars. Therefore, the expected rate of return on dollar-denominated deposits exceeds that on pound-denominated ones. *(What decision would investors make if $i^\$ = 1\%$, $i^\pounds = 2\%$, e = $2/£1, and e^e = $1.50/£1?)*

From the rules in Equations 12.1 and 12.2, we can see that there will be no incentive to shift from one currency to the other when the expected gain or loss on the foreign-exchange transaction just offsets the interest differential, making the expected rates of return on the two types of deposits equal. This equilibrium condition is known as **uncovered interest parity.** Uncovered interest parity states that the difference in interest rates on deposits denominated in two currencies equals the percentage difference between the current spot exchange rate and the **expected future spot rate** (what people expect *today* about the spot rate that will prevail in the future) between those currencies.

> *General Case:*
> $i^\$ - i^\pounds = (e^e - e)/e$.

[12.3]

> *Numerical Example:*
> 2% – 1% = ($2.02/£1 – $2.00/£1)/($2.00/£1) = 1%.

The relationship in Equation 12.3 is an *equilibrium condition,* because when the condition does not hold expected rates of return on the two deposits differ and we expect portfolio owners and managers to reallocate their portfolios between deposits denominated in the two currencies. When the condition does hold, the two assets carry the same expected rates of return and we expect the allocation of deposits between the two currencies to be in equilibrium, with no tendency to change.[9]

---

[9]More precisely, uncovered interest parity requires $i^\$ - i^\pounds = ([e^e - e]/e) \cdot (1 + i^\pounds)$. The second term on the right-hand side appears because the interest earned on a pound-denominated asset, as well as the principal, must be reconverted into dollars and thus is subject to the premium or discount on foreign exchange. Because interest rates typically are less than 10 percent, at least in the major industrialized economies,

How do portfolio adjustments bring about this equilibrium? Suppose the condition in Equation 12.1 holds. The interest rate available on dollar-denominated deposits exceeds that on pound-denominated deposits ($i^\$ - i^\pounds > 0$), but by less than the percentage by which the pound is expected to gain value against the dollar ($[e^e - e]/e$). Portfolio owners will buy pound-denominated deposits because the expected gain in the form of increased value of pounds will more than offset the loss of interest; in other words, because the expected rate of return on pound deposits exceeds that on dollar-denominated ones. As many market participants try to buy pound deposits and few want to sell them, the price of pound deposits relative to that of dollar deposits rises. In other words, the current spot price of pounds rises.[10] *(Why?)* The increase in e lowers the right-hand side of Equation 12.1, leading toward interest parity as in Equation 12.3.

The portfolio choice activities discussed in this section clearly involve a foreign exchange risk. The total expected return on an asset includes the interest earned *and* the expected gain or loss on the value of the currency. Figure 12.4 illustrates these two components of total realized dollar return on assets denominated in ten foreign currencies during 1991. For example, the total dollar return of 15 percent on an asset denominated in yen included a 7 percent increase in value of the yen relative to the dollar plus a yen interest rate of approximately 8 percent. The total dollar return of 1 percent on Swiss franc assets included a franc interest rate of 8 percent plus a 7 percent loss in the franc's value relative to the dollar.

Individuals, firms, and banks make decisions based on what they *expect* to happen to the spot exchange rate in the future. If the expectations turn out to be incorrect, enormous losses can result. Many banks hesitate to take large open positions in foreign currencies because of the possibility of huge losses; most banks' foreign exchange activities focus on transactions central to their customers' day-to-day international trade and financial dealings. There are exceptions, however; Citicorp, Bankers Trust, and BankAmerica actively trade foreign exchange.

For those who want to speculate in foreign currencies beyond the extent of ordinary international trade and finance activities, the International Monetary Market (part of the Chicago Mercantile Exchange) has, for over a decade, provided a forum for the sale and purchase of foreign exchange futures contracts. Figure 12.5 presents *The Wall Street Journal* price quotations for the IMM.

Futures contracts are similar to, but distinct from, forward contracts. Both involve buying or selling currency deposits for delivery at a future date with the price determined today. Futures contracts are for uniform amounts and delivery dates (see Figure 12.5), while forward contracts can be negotiated for amounts and delivery dates tailored to the parties' specific needs. Because of their uniform nature, futures contracts are more liquid or tradable. Also, because the IMM imposes significant margin requirements (money put "up front" to guarantee the

---

the extra term is close to 1 and often is dropped, leaving the simplified expression for uncovered interest parity in Equation 12.3.

[10]In this simple, partial-equilibrium model of the foreign exchange market, we assume adjustment takes the form of changes in the exchange rate alone, not in interest rates. Later chapters will incorporate the foreign exchange market into a general-equilibrium model of the macroeconomy, which will allow interest rate adjustment as well.

Figure 12.4 □ **Total Return on Assets Denominated in Various Currencies, 1991**

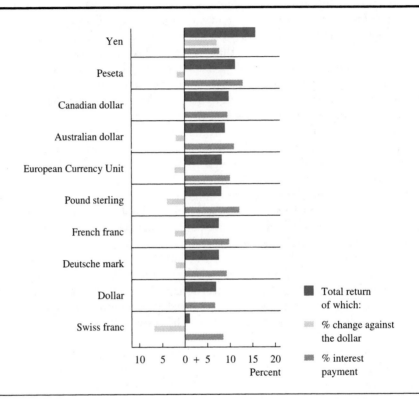

Two components comprise the total return on an asset: (1) the percentage change in the value of the currency in which the asset is denominated against the asset owner's home currency and (2) the interest earned on the asset.

Source: *The Economist*, January 11, 1992.

contract will be honored), speculators are free to use the IMM. Forward contracts, on the other hand, usually are arranged between a bank and a customer or between two banks. Most banks engage in forward contracts primarily to provide clearing and hedging services for customers, although in the process they can carry large short or long currency positions for brief periods.

12.4.2 Covered Interest Parity

Undertaking a transaction in the forward market for foreign exchange at the same time the portfolio decision is made can cover foreign exchange risk. A U.S. resident purchasing a pound-denominated deposit in the spot market could buy dollars (by selling pounds) in the forward market, thereby avoiding the risk that the price of dollars might rise during the deposit's life. For an individual using the forward market

Figure 12.5 □ International Monetary Market (IMM) Currency Futures Prices

	Open	High	Low	Settle	Change	Lifetime High	Lifetime Low	Open Interest
JAPAN YEN (CME)-12.5 million yen; $ per yen (.00)								
Sept	1.0384	1.0384	1.0150	1.0269	− .0095	1.2670	1.0150	52,697
Dec	1.0498	1.0504	1.0350	1.0398	− .0097	1.2813	1.0300	7,690
Mr96	1.0560	1.0560	1.0510	1.0525	− .0103	1.2990	1.0465	1,716
June	....	....	....	1.0648	− .0113	1.3130	1.0780	223
Est vol 27,024; vol 31,892; open int 62,361, +484.								
DEUTSCHEMARK (CME)-125,000 marks; $ per mark								
Sept	.6773	.6800	.6705	.6770	− .0005	.7450	.6347	60,083
Dec	.6782	.6851	.6744	.6794	− .0005	.7490	.6580	4,523
Mr96	.6835	.6842	.6830	.6819	− .0005	.7505	.6250	1,468
Est vol 26,833; vol 38,839; open int 66,074, +1,967.								
CANADIAN DOLLAR (CME)-100,000 dlrs.; $ per Can $								
Sept	.7355	.7360	.7336	.7355	+ .0006	.7438	.6920	31,747
Dec	.7334	.7343	.7325	.7338	+ .0007	.7401	.6895	3,389
Mr96	....	....	....	.7316	+ .0007	.7375	.6900	1,805
June	....	....	....	.7293	+ .0007	.7375	.6930	969
Sept	....	....	....	.7270	+ .0007	.7345	.7249	129
Est vol 3,570; vol 6,672; open int 38,040, +807.								
BRITISH POUND (CME)-62,500 pds.; $ per pound								
Sept	1.5514	1.5550	1.5368	1.5400	− .0108	1.6480	1.5368	35,073
Dec	1.5450	1.5510	1.5330	1.5364	− .0104	1.6440	1.5330	1,780
Est vol 14,232; vol 22,408; open int 36,871, +3,842.								
SWISS FRANC (CME)-125,000 francs; $ per franc								
Sept	.8153	.8188	.8045	.8147	+ .0003	.9085	.7605	27,836
Dec	.8200	.8244	.8150	.8203	+ .0003	.9145	.7834	2,568
Mr96	.8280	.8290	.8260	.8260	+ .0004	.9920	.8240	205
Est vol 17,262; vol 19,708; open int 30,609, +687.								
AUSTRALIAN DOLLAR (CME)-100,000 dlrs.; $ per A.$								
Sept	.7350	.7360	.7285	.7317	− .0043	.7442	.7055	10,588
Est vol 2,448; vol 2,667; open int 10,621, −1,899.								

Source: *The Wall Street Journal*, August 17, 1995.

to cover foreign-exchange risk, the relevant information for choosing between a dollar-denominated deposit and a pound-denominated asset includes a comparison of the interest differential and the forward premium or discount on foreign exchange (the percentage difference between the forward and spot exchange rates).[11] Letting e^f represent the *forward* rate,

General Case:
If $i^\$ - i^\pounds < (e^f - e)/e$, purchase pound-denominated deposits.

[12.4]

Numerical Example:
1.5% − 1% < ($2.02/£1 − $2.00/£1)/($2.00/£1) = 1%;
therefore, purchase pound-denominated deposits.

---

[11]Again, an alternative way of writing Equation 12.4 puts the rate of return on dollar-denominated deposits on the left-hand side and the dollar rate of return on pound-denominated deposits on the right-hand side. The rate of return on dollar-denominated assets simply equals the rate of interest on those deposits, or $i^\$$. The dollar rate of return on pound-denominated assets has two components: the rate of interest ($i^\pounds$) and the forward premium or discount on pounds relative to dollars ($[e^f - e]/e$). Portfolio owners will buy more pound-denominated deposits if the total return on pound-denominated assets exceeds the rate of return on dollar-denominated assets, or if $i^\$ < i^\pounds + (e^f - e)/e$, equivalent to Equation 12.4.

In this case, the interest differential in favor of dollar-denominated assets does not offset the forward premium on pounds, or the gain from converting dollars into pounds in the spot market and reconverting pounds into dollars in the forward market. Therefore, the rate of return on pound deposits exceeds that on dollar deposits; and portfolio owners shift toward pounds.

In Equation 12.5, the interest differential is negative; however, a negative interest differential does not necessarily rule out a decision to purchase dollar-denominated deposits. A sufficient rise in the value of the dollar over the period the deposit is held can offset the negative interest differential, as Equation 12.5 demonstrates.

General Case:
If $i^\$ - i^£ > (e^f - e)/e$, purchase dollar-denominated deposits.

[12.5]

Numerical Example:
$1\% - 2\% > (\$1.50/£1 - \$2.00/£1)/(\$2.00/£1) = -25\%$;
therefore, purchase dollar-denominated deposits.

In summary, both the interest differential and the forward premium or discount on foreign exchange must be taken into account in choosing among deposits denominated in different currencies based on their rates of return. When individuals in the economy make their decisions based on the relationships in Equations 12.4 and 12.5, the resulting equilibrium condition is **covered interest parity**.

General Case:
$i^\$ - i^£ = (e^f - e)/e$.

[12.6]

Numerical Example:
$2\% - 1\% = (\$2.02/£1 - \$2.00/£1)/(\$2.00/£1) = 1\%$.

When interest parity holds, the rates of return on dollar- and pound-denominated deposits are the same, and no incentive exists to alter the composition of asset portfolios. Therefore, currency markets are in equilibrium.

12.4.3 Empirical Evidence

Covered interest parity is one of the most frequently tested relationships in international macroeconomics.[12] The empirical support for the relationship is quite strong, but the results are sensitive to the testing technique. In particular, the parity relationship is much stronger when all deposits used in the test are issued in a single country. For example, a test using dollar-denominated and pound-denominated certificates of deposit (CDs) both issued by a Zurich bank typically will show a tighter parity relationship than a test using a dollar-denominated CD from a New York bank and a pound-denominated CD from a London bank. This is why, in our discussion of interest parity, we speak of the interest rates on deposits

---

[12]Testing uncovered interest parity is much more difficult, because the relationship involves the unobservable expected future spot exchange rate rather than the observable forward rate.

denominated in different *currencies* ($i^\$$ and $i^\pounds$) rather than the interest rates in different *countries* (i^{US} and i^B).

Why the difference? One factor in addition to the expected rate of return that influences individuals' portfolio decisions is the risk that a country will impose restrictions on the movement of funds across national boundaries. A high rate of return on a deposit issued by a London bank would be worth little to an American if Britain imposed controls that prevented the proceeds of the deposit from being reconverted into dollars and moved back to the United States. In comparing a dollar-denominated CD issued by a New York bank and a pound-denominated CD issued by a London bank, three things differ: (1) the currency, (2) the bank, and (3) the country. The interest parity relationship addresses factor 1. For major banks in industrialized countries, factor 2 is of little significance, because bank failures are rare and, when they occur, deposits usually are backed by government insurance such as that provided by the Federal Deposit Insurance Corporation (FDIC) in the United States. But factor 3 can interfere with interest parity, especially in times of uncertainty—when changes in government policy might be expected.

By performing tests of interest parity using deposits issued in the same country, the risk of government restrictions on movement of funds is equalized across currencies, allowing a purer test. Offshore currency markets provide the perfect opportunity for testing interest parity. **Offshore deposits** (or **Eurocurrencies**) are currencies held in deposit outside their country of issue; in other words, a dollar deposit held anywhere outside the United States is a Eurocurrency (or Eurodollar) deposit, regardless of who owns the deposit.[13] Among offshore deposits held in the same country but denominated in different currencies, interest parity holds so tightly and routinely that dealers actually use the relationship as a shorthand way to calculate the forward rates they offer.

12.5   The Demand for and Supply of Foreign Exchange

Up to now our reliance on the standard demand and supply framework in analyzing the market for foreign exchange has been implicit. In this section, we shall develop a simple model of the demand for and supply of foreign exchange based on the interest parity conditions. We shall see that equilibrium in the foreign exchange market and interest parity are equivalent conditions.

The demand for and supply of foreign exchange are similar in many respects to those for any other asset. The important thing to remember is that the demand for a currency is really the demand for bank deposits denominated in that currency, not demand for actual paper money. The **demand curve for a foreign currency** shows how many units of the currency individuals would want to hold in deposits at various exchange rates. In other words, the demand curve summarizes the relationship between the quantity demanded and the price of a foreign currency, holding constant the other economic variables affecting quantity demanded. Similarly, the **supply**

---

[13]Section 12.9 discusses Eurocurrency markets.

curve for a foreign currency shows how many units of foreign currency deposits are available for individuals to hold at various exchange rates.

The supply and demand model of the foreign exchange market is a partial-equilibrium model and, as such, ignores many of the interconnections among variables. Despite this limitation, the model is a useful first step in understanding the determination of exchange rates and their role in the international macroeconomy. Fuller elaboration of the relationships between exchange rates and the rest of the macroeconomy forms the basis of later chapters.

The interest parity relationships developed in section 12.4 suggest that individuals allocate their portfolios among deposits denominated in different currencies by comparing rates of return, which depend on interest rates, spot exchange rates, expected future spot exchange rates, and forward rates. When the interest parity conditions are satisfied (as in Equations 12.3 and 12.6), individuals are content to hold their existing portfolios; there is no incentive to shift from deposits denominated in one currency toward those denominated in another. So the foreign exchange market is in equilibrium when, given current interest rates, spot and forward exchange rates, and exchange rate expectations, individuals are content to hold in their portfolios the existing supply of deposits in each currency. In other words, interest parity and equilibrium in the foreign exchange market are two ways of looking at the same relationships.

12.5.1 The Demand for Foreign Exchange

The relationship between the quantity demanded of foreign exchange and the spot exchange rate (expressed as the domestic currency price of a unit of foreign currency) is a *negative* one: As the exchange rate rises, the quantity of foreign exchange demanded falls. It is easy to see why. As the spot exchange rate rises, each unit of foreign currency becomes more expensive in terms of domestic currency. Given existing interest rates, expected future spot rates, and forward rates, foreign-currency deposits become less attractive assets than domestic-currency deposits because the expected return on foreign-currency deposits falls. As a result, individuals choose to hold fewer foreign-currency deposits in their portfolios. *(Using the expressions for interest parity in Equations 12.3 and 12.6, verify that a rise in the value of e, holding the other values constant, changes the situation from interest-parity equilibrium to one in which individuals substitute away from foreign-currency deposits.)* On the other hand, a fall in the exchange rate makes foreign-currency deposits more attractive because their expected rate of return rises, causing individuals to want to hold a larger quantity in their portfolios. *(Use the expressions for interest parity in Equations 12.3 and 12.6 to verify that a fall in the value of e, holding the other values constant, changes the situation from interest-parity equilibrium to one in which individuals demand a larger quantity of foreign-currency deposits.)*

The negatively sloped line in Figure 12.6 illustrates the negative relationship between the quantity demanded of foreign exchange and the exchange rate. Just as in other goods or asset markets, the exchange rate is only one of several determinants of quantity demanded. Each demand curve is drawn for fixed values of the

Figure 12.6 □ **The Exchange Rate and the Quantity Demanded of Foreign Exchange**

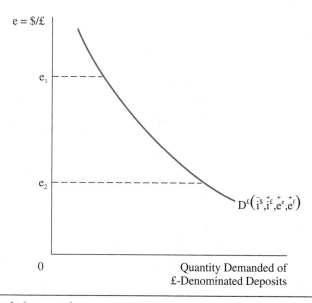

For given values of $i^\$$, $i^\pounds$, e^e, and e^f, a high exchange rate (such as e_1) makes foreign-currency-denominated deposits less attractive relative to domestic-currency deposits. The result is a low quantity demanded. A fall in the exchange rate from e_1 to e_2 makes foreign-currency deposits relatively more attractive to portfolio holders, increasing the quantity demanded. Increases in $i^\pounds$, e^e, or e^f shift the demand curve to the right; increases in $i^\$$ shift it to the left.

domestic interest rate ($i^\$$), the foreign interest rate ($i^\pounds$), the expected future spot rate (e^e), and the forward rate (e^f). Changes in any of these values cause individuals to demand different quantities of foreign-currency-denominated deposits at each value of the spot exchange rate; this causes the entire demand curve to shift.

If the domestic interest rate rises, the demand curve for foreign exchange shifts to the left. The higher rate of interest paid on domestic-currency deposits causes individuals to shift their portfolios away from foreign-currency deposits and toward domestic-currency ones whose rate of return has risen. A fall in the domestic interest rate shifts the demand curve for foreign exchange to the right. *(Use Equations 12.1 through 12.6 to verify.)* In Figure 12.6, the (−) sign over the domestic interest rate ($i^\$$) term represents this relationship; when the domestic interest rate changes, the demand curve for foreign exchange shifts in the *opposite* direction.

A rise in the interest rate on foreign-currency deposits raises the quantity of those deposits demanded at any given value of the exchange rate; the demand curve shifts to the right. *(Why?)* A fall in the foreign-currency interest rate lowers the rate of return on foreign-currency deposits and shifts the demand curve to the left.

The (+) sign over the foreign interest rate ($i^£$) term represents the positive relationship between the foreign interest rate and the quantity demanded of foreign-currency-denominated deposits; a change in $i^£$ shifts the demand curve in the *same* direction.

Using Equations 12.1 through 12.3, we can see that a rise in the expected future spot exchange rate increases the quantity demanded of foreign exchange. Such a change means that the dollar price of pounds is expected to rise; during the change, individuals want to hold pounds (which are becoming more valuable), not dollars (which are becoming less valuable). So the expected exchange rate term in Figure 12.6 has a (+) sign; the demand for pounds shifts in the same direction as any change in e^e.

Similarly, Equations 12.4 through 12.6 imply that a rise in the forward exchange rate causes an increase in the quantity demanded of foreign exchange. Converting the proceeds of pound-denominated deposits back into dollars brings more dollars when e^f rises, so holding pound-denominated deposits now becomes more attractive. The sign over e^f in Figure 12.6 is (+); when the forward rate changes, the demand for pounds shifts in the same direction.

The model of the demand for foreign exchange just developed is an *asset-oriented model*. It focuses on demand for foreign-currency deposits *as assets*. It may be tempting to ask, "What about international trade? Don't Americans demand yen to buy Toyotas, while Japanese demand dollars to buy Boeing 767s?" The answer, of course, is *yes*. Holding foreign-currency deposits for making trade transactions rather than as interest-bearing assets is called the *liquidity* or *transactions motive*. But in today's world economy, international financial activity dwarfs such considerations. Experts estimate that fewer than 5 percent of foreign exchange transactions reflect trade in goods and services. Foreign exchange transactions total about $1.3 trillion *per day*, representing about one-third of the value of all world merchandise trade *for an entire year!*[14] Also, as we have seen repeatedly in this chapter, an international trade transaction such as the purchase of an imported good typically involves an asset decision, since immediate payment usually is not required; the buyer must decide what currency to hold over the payment interval. Since asset-oriented financial transactions have come to dominate actual foreign exchange markets over the last few years, it is only appropriate that economists' models reflect this important change in the nature of the world economy. Case Five below will explore some of the implications of asset-price behavior for exchange rates.

12.5.2 The Supply of Foreign Exchange

Individuals determine the *demand* for foreign exchange through their efforts to earn the highest rates of return on their asset portfolios, as reflected in the interest parity conditions. In contrast, government policies, together with banks' loan decisions, determine the *supply* of deposits denominated in foreign currency. We shall explore this process in some detail later. For now, it suffices to point out that

---

[14]*The Economist*, September 23, 1995, 64.

private individuals' deposit transactions cannot create or destroy foreign-currency-denominated deposits.[15] An individual can only sell a deposit to another individual, firm, or bank or buy a deposit from another individual, firm, or bank.[16] In either case, the total stock of deposits denominated in the foreign currency remains unchanged; the total will simply have been reallocated among portfolio holders.

Because the stock of foreign-currency-denominated deposits available at any time is fixed, we can represent the supply of foreign exchange by a vertical line, $S^£$, in Figure 12.7. The supply curve is vertical because the supply of deposits in existence at any time does not depend on the exchange rate. We now are ready to combine the demand for and supply of foreign exchange to see how they determine exchange rates.

12.6 Exchange Rate Determination under a Flexible Rate Regime

Although we can draw demand and supply curves for foreign exchange, governments choose whether to allow the forces of demand and supply to determine the value of exchange rates for their respective currencies. In each country, the government decides the type of policy to follow regarding the exchange rate. The basic policy adopted usually is referred to as the **exchange rate regime.** There are four main types of regime: (1) flexible or floating exchange rates, (2) fixed or pegged exchange rates, (3) managed floating (a mixture of flexible and fixed), and (4) exchange controls. In the remaining chapters, we shall discuss all four systems.

We begin with the simplest: the **flexible** or **floating exchange rate.** Since the early 1970s, countries have moved toward the use of flexible exchange rates. Under such a regime, the demand for and supply of each currency in the foreign exchange market determine the exchange rate. The market for foreign exchange can be treated as a competitive one, because millions of individuals, firms, and banks participate, foreign exchange is a homogeneous commodity, information is good, and entry and exit are unrestricted. The market for foreign exchange under a flexible regime works much like the market for any other good: The price (the exchange rate) moves to the level that equates quantity demanded to quantity supplied. In the case of the foreign exchange market, the good in question is an asset in the form of bank deposits denominated in a foreign currency. The exchange rate adjusts until the quantity of foreign-currency-denominated deposits

---

[15]In the same sense, individual deposit transactions do not create or destroy domestic bank deposits. If an individual writes a $15,000 check for a new car, his or her account balance falls by $15,000, but the car dealer's account rises by the same amount. Total deposits remain unchanged; they merely have been reallocated between individuals. Cash transactions can affect total deposits but represent such a small share of activity that we can ignore them.

[16]We ignore for now the possibility that the individual will buy from or sell to a *central* bank (that is, the government monetary authority); we will cover this case in the forthcoming discussion of foreign exchange market intervention.

Figure 12.7 □ **The Supply of Foreign Exchange**

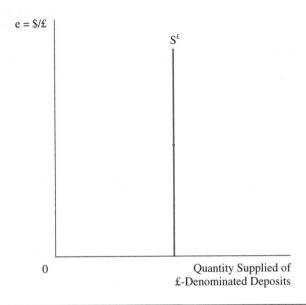

The quantity of pound-denominated deposits available is determined by government policies and banks' loan decisions. At each point in time, this quantity is independent of the exchange rate; therefore, a vertical line represents the supply of foreign-currency-denominated deposits.

individuals want to hold equals the quantity available, or equivalently, until the rates of return on domestic- and foreign-currency-denominated deposits are equal, or until interest parity holds.

Figure 12.8 shows the equilibrium exchange rate between the dollar and the pound. If the exchange rate were *above* the equilibrium (for example, at e_1), individuals would want to hold *less* than the existing quantity of pound-denominated deposits. A surplus of foreign exchange would cause the price to fall as individuals offered to sell pound-denominated deposits in exchange for dollar-denominated ones. If the exchange rate were *below* the equilibrium rate (for example, at e_2), individuals would want to hold *more* than the existing quantity of pound-denominated deposits. The shortage of foreign exchange would cause its price to be bid up as individuals offer to buy pound-denominated deposits in exchange for dollar-denominated ones. Only at e_3, where quantity demanded equals the quantity supplied of foreign exchange, is the market in equilibrium. At that exchange rate (given the values of $i^\$$, $i^£$, e^e, and e^f), individuals are content to hold exactly $S^£$ of pound-denominated deposits in their portfolios, and interest parity is satisfied because the rates of return on dollar-denominated and pound-denominated assets are equal.

Figure 12.8 ▫ Equilibrium in the Foreign Exchange Market under a Flexible Rate Regime

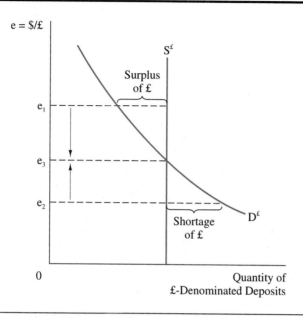

The exchange rate moves to equate the quantity demanded and the quantity supplied of pounds. The equilibrium exchange rate is e_3; at that exchange rate, portfolio owners willingly hold the existing quantity of pound-denominated deposits given the values of $i^\$$, $i^\pounds$, e^e, and e^f.

Under a flexible exchange rate regime, the price mechanism equates the total quantity demanded of each currency with the total quantity supplied; therefore, the foreign exchange markets clear. Later chapters will explore the arguments for using a flexible exchange rate regime as well as the implications of such a regime for various macroeconomic policies.

When the exchange rate is flexible, a rise in the market-determined rate is referred to as a **depreciation** of the currency whose price has fallen and an **appreciation** of the currency whose price has risen. A change in the rate from e_1 to e_3 represents a depreciation of the pound or, equivalently, an appreciation of the dollar. A move from e_2 to e_3 involves a depreciation of the dollar and an appreciation of the pound. Note that in discussing an appreciation or a depreciation we must always refer to a specific currency. Because a change in any exchange rate always involves an appreciation of one currency *and* a depreciation of another, saying "the exchange rate between yen and francs appreciated" conveys no information. *Either* the yen appreciated against the franc (implying that the franc depreciated against the yen) *or* the franc appreciated against the yen (implying that the yen depreciated against the franc).

Figure 12.9 ▫ Shifts in the Demand for Foreign Exchange Change the Exchange Rate

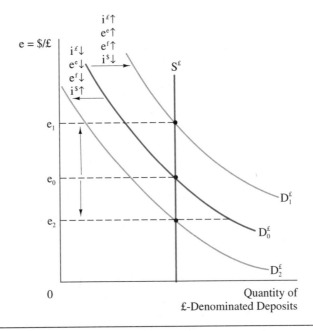

Increases in $i^£$, e^e, or e^f increase the demand for pound-denominated bank deposits and cause the pound to appreciate against the dollar. Increases in $i^\$$ decrease the demand for pound-denominated deposits and cause the pound to depreciate against the dollar.

Using the standard tools of supply and demand analysis, any change in economic conditions that increases the demand for pounds causes the pound to appreciate. Such changes could include a rise in $i^£$, a fall in $i^\$$, or a rise in e^e or e^f, as in Figure 12.9. A fall in the demand for pounds causes a depreciation of the pound. This might result from a fall in $i^£$, a rise in $i^\$$, or a fall in e^e or e^f.

12.7 Exchange Rate Determination under a Fixed Rate Regime

Exchange rates have not been flexible through most of modern economic history; in fact, flexible rates were rare until the early 1970s. Instead, the central banks of most countries used **fixed** or **pegged exchange rates** for their respective currencies. Such a practice works much like fixing the price of any good. The demand for and supply of foreign exchange still exist, but they do not determine the exchange rate as in a flexible rate system. Central banks (such as the U.S. Federal Reserve, the Bank of England, the German Bundesbank, the Bank of Japan, or Sweden's Riksbank) must

Figure 12.10 □ **A Pegged Exchange Rate above the Equilibrium Rate**

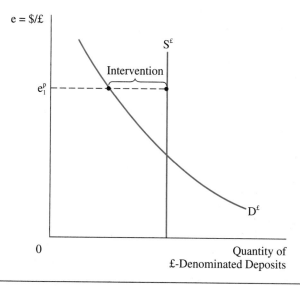

To maintain the exchange rate at e_1^P, the central bank must stand ready to absorb the excess quantity supplied of pounds. The U.S. central bank intervenes by buying pound-denominated deposits at a price of e_1^P; the horizontal distance between $D^£$ and $S^£$ at e_1^P represents the magnitude of the required intervention.

stand ready to absorb any excess demand for or supply of a currency to maintain the pegged rate.

Suppose the U.S. government decides to peg the exchange rate between dollars and pounds at e_1^P in Figure 12.10. At e_1^P, the quantity supplied of pounds exceeds the quantity demanded. The high dollar price of the pound makes dollar-denominated deposits attractive relative to pound-denominated ones; the quantity demanded of pounds therefore is low. The surplus of pounds in the foreign exchange market at e_1^P creates a tendency for the exchange rate to fall (that is, for the pound to depreciate against the dollar) as individuals try to sell pound-denominated deposits in return for dollars.

To hold the exchange rate at e_1^P, the U.S. government must step into the market and buy up the surplus pound-denominated deposits. This is called a policy of government **intervention** in the foreign exchange market. Individuals sell the pound-denominated deposits they no longer want to the U.S. central bank in return for dollar-denominated deposits at a rate of e_1^P per pound. The horizontal distance between $D^£$ and $S^£$ at e_1^P in Figure 12.10 represents the magnitude of the required intervention.

Alternatively, if the central bank chooses to adjust the pegged exchange rate downward from e_1^P, the policy is called a **revaluation** of the dollar. A revaluation under a pegged exchange regime is analogous to an appreciation under a flexible

Figure 12.11 □ A Pegged Exchange Rate below the Equilibrium Rate

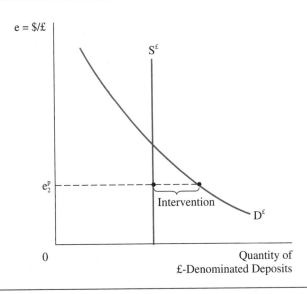

At e_2^p, the quantity demanded of pounds exceeds the quantity supplied. The rate can be maintained at e_2^p if the U.S. central bank intervenes by supplying pound-denominated deposits to the market from its foreign exchange reserves.

regime; that is, both revaluation and appreciation refer to a rise in the value of the currency (here, the dollar) relative to another currency (the pound).

Suppose, on the other hand, that the U.S. government decided to hold the exchange rate between dollars and pounds at e_2^p, below the equilibrium rate in Figure 12.11. At e_2^p, the quantity demanded of pounds exceeds the quantity supplied. The low value of the exchange rate makes pound-denominated deposits more attractive and dollar-denominated deposits less attractive. The forces of supply and demand in the foreign exchange market put upward pressure on the dollar price of pounds. If the exchange rate is to stay at e_2^p, the central bank must intervene in the foreign exchange market to supply enough pounds to make up the difference between the quantity individuals demand and the quantity supplied at e_2^p. For intervention purposes, governments hold stocks of deposits denominated in various foreign currencies, called **foreign exchange reserves**. In our example, the U.S. central bank would sell a portion of its pound reserves by buying dollar-denominated deposits with those pound-denominated deposits, thereby satisfying portfolio owners' demand.

For short periods, foreign exchange market intervention can occur on a massive scale. During September 1992, when European currency markets exhibited high volatility because of doubts about the future of European Community integration, reported intervention involved 24 billion Deutsche marks and 10 billion pounds. Also in September 1992, Canadian intervention to support the Canadian dollar—in the face of political uncertainty over the future of Quebec—totaled a record $4.26 billion. More recently, the U.S. Federal Reserve, along with central banks of several other countries, intervened several times in 1995 to lower the dollar price of other currencies, especially the Japanese yen.[17] For example, on March 2–3, 1995, the U.S. central bank bought $1.42 billion, and similar rounds of intervention followed in April, June, July, and August.

If a government tried to hold the exchange rate between its currency and another at a level below equilibrium for a long period, the country's central bank eventually would deplete its foreign exchange reserves. Then the policy choices would be to borrow reserves from other central banks or from the International Monetary Fund to continue the intervention, reset the pegged exchange rate at a level more consistent with equilibrium in the foreign exchange market, or allow the exchange rate to become flexible.[18] If the central bank chooses to reset the exchange rate at a level higher than e_2^p, the policy is called a **devaluation** of the dollar against the pound, analogous to a depreciation under a flexible exchange regime.

Later we shall discuss at length the implications of a fixed exchange rate regime for the conduct of macroeconomic policy. For now, note that the type of foreign exchange risk analyzed in our discussions of hedging arises from the possibility that the spot exchange rate will *change* over time. Were it possible for governments' monetary authorities to peg e such that everyone was certain the exchange rate would not change, there would be no foreign exchange risk of this type. There would be little need for a forward market, because everyone would know that foreign exchange could be bought in the future at the same price prevailing today. Unfortunately, history suggests no fixed rate system can provide that degree of certainty, since there always is a possibility that, due to shifts in the demand for and supply of a currency, the government may become unable or unwilling to maintain the pegged rate. Fixed exchange rates would eliminate many but not all the roles of private foreign exchange markets—if the exchange rate were fixed within very narrow bands that were permanent and dependable.

12.8 The Effective Exchange Rate

Because an exchange rate is merely the relative price of two currencies, reflecting the relative demands for and supplies of deposits denominated in those currencies,

---

[17]The currencies of some members of the European Union are fixed relative to one another and float as a group against other currencies in an arrangement known as the Exchange Rate Mechanism of the European Monetary System, discussed in Chapter Twenty. Canada and the United States operate under flexible exchange rate regimes, but still intervene occasionally to affect the exchange rate; Chapter Twenty also discusses such "managed floats." Case Four in Chapter Thirteen examines recent U.S. foreign exchange market intervention.

[18]Central banks enter agreements, called swaps, to lend specified amounts of their currencies to one another for intervention. For example, if the U.S. Federal Reserve ran short of pounds while trying to hold the dollar price of pounds below the equilibrium rate, it could borrow pounds from the Bank of England, to be repaid at a later date after U.S. pound reserves were replenished. The Federal Reserve Bank of New York's quarterly publication, *Treasury and Federal Reserve Foreign Exchange Operations,* reports recent trends in exchange rates and activity in the U.S. swap accounts.

a currency may *appreciate* against some currencies at the same time it *depreciates* against others. This means it is impossible, based on **bilateral exchange rates,** to determine whether a currency generally is appreciating or depreciating in foreign exchange markets. Nonetheless, it often is useful to have an indicator of the trend of a currency's overall movement relative to other currencies "on average." **Effective exchange rates** serve this purpose. The effective exchange rate of the dollar, for example, provides a measure of the dollar's value relative to the currencies of the United States' major trading partners as a group.

Several government agencies, international organizations, and private financial institutions compute effective exchange rates for the U.S. dollar and other currencies. Table 12.1 reports one measure of the effective exchange rate of the dollar, calculated by the Federal Reserve Board, for the years since the dollar began to float.

Various measures of the effective exchange rate differ primarily in the weights attached to the bilateral exchange rates in the calculation. Over short periods, these differences in weighting procedures can cause substantial variation in measures of the effective exchange rate. For example, during the depreciation of the dollar during 1985 and 1986, measures that weighted heavily Japanese and European currencies tended to show a larger depreciation of the dollar, because the dollar declined particularly sharply against the currencies belonging to those major trading partners. Other measures included the currencies of more developing-country trading partners; and because the bilateral depreciation of the dollar against the currencies of those countries was small (and in some cases the dollar actually appreciated), the effective exchange rate by such measures showed a much smaller decline.

Regardless of the weighting technique used in the calculation, a currency's effective exchange rate is more stable than its exchange rates against individual currencies. This reflects the fact that in any period, the currency typically appreciates against some currencies and depreciates against others. The bilateral appreciations and depreciations are "averaged out" in the effective exchange rate.

12.9 Offshore Currency Markets

Recall that an offshore deposit is simply a bank deposit denominated in the currency of a country *other than* the one in which the deposit is located. A deposit denominated in dollars in a London bank or a deposit of pounds sterling in a Hong Kong bank both constitute offshore deposits, regardless of their owners' nationalities. What makes a deposit part of the offshore currency market is the combination of the bank's geographical location and the deposit's currency of denomination.

One obvious question about offshore currency markets concerns why they exist at all. Why would anyone want to hold a deposit in a country other than the one issuing the currency? There are three answers to this question, two primarily economic and the other political; they comprise the reasons most often cited for the emergence and rapid growth of offshore currency markets.

Most countries heavily regulate banking within their borders. The United States, for example, imposes reserve, disclosure, and insurance requirements and many other restrictions on U.S. banks. Similar regulatory patterns exist in many

Table 12.1 □ **Effective Exchange Rate of the U.S. Dollar, 1973–1994**

The index reports the trade-weighted value of foreign currencies in terms of the U.S. dollar. Therefore, an increase in the index represents a depreciation of the dollar against other currencies.

Year	Effective Exchange Rate (Index: March 1973 = 100)
1973	101.0
1974	98.6
1975	101.5
1976	94.6
1977	96.7
1978	108.2
1979	113.5
1980	114.4
1981	96.7
1982	85.8
1983	79.8
1984	72.3
1985	69.9
1986	89.1
1987	103.2
1988	107.9
1989	101.4
1990	112.2
1991	111.4
1992	115.5
1993	107.3
1994	109.5

Source: *Economic Report of the President, 1995*, p. 402.

other countries, although the details vary considerably. Several reasons explain the heavy regulation of the industry. Because of the links between banking and the money-creation process (see section 15.2.3), the smooth functioning of the banking system constitutes an important element in the successful conduct of monetary policy. Confidence in the banking system is critical; the reserve, insurance, and disclosure requirements that governments impose on banks help ensure stability in banking and promote the public's confidence.

While the various government regulations imposed on domestic banks provide benefits, they also raise banks' costs of doing business. Because banks—at least those in the United States—are privately owned, profit-maximizing businesses, the costs of regulation imply that banks must pay lower interest rates to depositors and charge higher ones to borrowers to operate profitably. Any bank that can partially escape the costly national regulations can lower its operation costs and thus afford to pay higher interest rates to depositors and charge lower rates to borrowers. Offshore markets achieve this goal. The U.S. government, for example, has little control over a bank that accepts deposits denominated in dollars in other countries. Even for overseas branches or subsidiaries of a U.S. bank, a foreign location reduces the government's power to impose restrictions on it. Countries that choose not to regulate banking heavily within their borders attract international banking activity. By escaping regulation, banks operating in these countries can offer more attractive interest rates to both depositors and borrowers. Countries that have deliberately fostered the growth of offshore banking include Britain, Switzerland, Panama, Bahrain, the Cayman Islands, Singapore, and Hong Kong.

Other countries, including the United States, Germany, and Japan, historically have used regulation to discourage borrowing and lending in foreign currencies within their borders. However, with the rapid growth of the offshore segment of the banking industry (most estimates place the total volume at well over $6 trillion), the United States has adjusted its regulations to allow U.S. banks to capture a larger share of the growing business. The primary change came in 1981, when the U.S. government granted approval for international banking facilities (IBFs) to operate within the United States. IBFs accept deposits and make loans in any currency, including dollars, but only to foreigners. In return for reduced regulation, the IBFs agree not to compete with standard commercial banks for domestic business.

With the rapid growth of international trade and financial activity, firms' demand for offshore banking services has grown as well. When a firm buys and sells in many countries around the world, the ability to hold bank deposits in different currencies and locales becomes an important part of minimizing the costs of doing business. Firms' increased needs for international financial services help explain the rapid growth of offshore markets.

We can trace the third—and political—reason for offshore deposits to the Cold War tensions between the United States and the Soviet Union during the 1950s. As part of its efforts to modernize and develop its economy, the Soviet Union entered into growing trade relations with the Western economies, which meant dealing in dollars. However, the Soviet Union and the other Eastern European nonmarket economies were reluctant to hold dollar deposits in the United States, fearing that if hostilities suddenly escalated, the United States would seize or "freeze" their assets. To avoid the possibility of having their assets frozen, the Soviets searched for a bank outside the United States that would accept dollar-denominated deposits and located one in Paris.

Foreign branches and subsidiaries of the largest U.S. banks dominate the now huge offshore currency market. About two-thirds of all offshore deposits are denominated in dollars. Other currencies widely held abroad include Deutsche marks, yen, pounds sterling, French francs, and Swiss francs. In the market's early years, the bulk of activity consisted of dollar deposits held in Europe, which explains why offshore deposits often are called *Eurocurrencies* or *Eurodollars*. As a larger number of currencies have come to be used actively in offshore currency markets, the markets themselves have proliferated throughout the world. Because of the desire to escape regulation, offshore banking activity tends to move to areas of least regulation. Such activity originally centered in Europe, with London the dominant location. More recently it has expanded to a number of Asian centers, such as Singapore and Hong Kong, making the term *Eurocurrency* less descriptive of the entire phenomenon of offshore banking.

The primary effect of offshore currency markets has been to increase the mobility of financial capital. Previously it was difficult to buy short-term assets denominated in foreign currencies. Investment abroad took the form of direct investment, purchases of common stock or equity in foreign firms, or purchases of foreign bonds. Now, offshore bank deposits provide a way to hold assets denominated in foreign currencies for very short periods, often only a few days. Most deposits in the offshore market are time deposits with maturities ranging from overnight to a few years.

Now, we turn to five cases related to exchange rates. Case One examines the effects of movements in exchange rates on firms and some of the ways they deal with the uncertainties generated. Case Two focuses on the role of the Japanese yen in international markets. Case Three highlights a new player in foreign exchange markets: Russia. Case Four traces Sweden's dramatic policy response to growing expectations that the government would devalue the krona in September 1992. Case Five emphasizes the chapter's asset-oriented approach to exchange rates by exploring its implications for rate volatility and exchange-rate forecasting.

Case One
Handling Foreign Exchange Risk

The analysis in this chapter makes clear that any noninstantaneous transaction involving more than one currency also involves a foreign exchange risk. If the exchange rate between the relevant currencies changes significantly during the transaction, the terms of the transaction will deviate *ex post* from those originally negotiated. As reductions in transportation and communication costs have encouraged firms to become more international in their production, finance, and marketing operations, the firms' exposure to foreign exchange risk has grown. The result has been the development of several techniques firms use to deal with these risks.[19]

For large multinational firms, internal hedging (that is, offsetting one division's long position in a currency against another division's short position) provides the most common way of handling exchange risk. The costs involved in internal hedging often prove less than the cost of hedging using a bank's forward foreign exchange services. If a firm's chemical division expects to be paid 1 million Deutsche marks in 30 days for goods exported to Germany while the plastics division owes 1 million Deutsche marks for imported raw materials, an internal transfer of the marks from chemicals to plastics can provide a hedge against foreign exchange risk while avoiding the cost of a forward contract.

---

[19]These techniques cannot eliminate foreign exchange risk, but they transfer the risk from one party to another.

For smaller, less international firms, the most widely used method of minimizing foreign exchange risk is the use of forward markets for foreign exchange. By allowing a firm to contract to buy or sell a currency in the future at a prespecified price, forward markets facilitate planning by eliminating uncertainty about the domestic-currency value of future revenues earned in foreign currencies and costs owed in foreign currencies.

Another strategy for avoiding losses due to currency fluctuations is the design of contracts that allow flexibility in the timing of receipts and payments. A U.S. firm importing ¥1 million of goods from Japan may request contractual terms allowing payment at any time within a 180-day period following the delivery date. If the U.S. firm expects the dollar to appreciate against the yen, the firm may choose to postpone payment as long as possible to obtain the best expected price on the yen. If, on the other hand, the dollar is expected to depreciate, the firm may pay the bill right away to avoid the possibility that the dollar price of yen will rise. The same idea can be used to alter the timing of foreign-currency-denominated export receipts.

A newly available strategy involves holding domestic bank deposits denominated in foreign exchange. As of 1990, U.S. firms can hold such accounts, insured by the Federal Deposit Insurance Corporation. The accounts, with minimum deposits of $20,000–$25,000, are invested in foreign time deposits (CDs) with maturities of three months to one year. A relatively small number of currencies are available—typically marks, yen, pounds, Swiss francs, Canadian dollars, and Australian dollars.

Still another possibility is a relatively new financial tool called an *option contract*. Buying an option contract guarantees the buyer the right to purchase (or sell) a specified quantity of a currency at a future date for a predetermined price (called the *strike price*). The contracts are called *options* because the buyer has the option to exercise or not exercise the contract. Option contracts for future purchases of a currency are *calls,* and option contracts for future sales of a currency are *puts*. Figure 12.12 illustrates a recent set of price quotations for currency options.

A call option guarantees that the holder of the contract will not have to pay a price higher than the contract's strike price, because the owner will exercise the call if the spot price exceeds the strike price. *(Why?)* Note in Figure 12.12 that option prices rise for contracts with lower strike prices. A put option guarantees that the holder will not have to sell currency for a price below the strike price; the owner will exercise the put if the spot price is below the strike price. *(Why?)* For puts, note that prices rise for contracts with higher strike prices. Option contracts therefore provide the possibility of combining hedging and speculation. The holder of an option contract can still enjoy the benefits of favorable movements in the exchange rate (the speculative element) while limiting the effects of unfavorable movements (the hedging element). The Philadelphia Stock Exchange and Chicago Mercantile Exchange dominate currency options markets in the United States; each sells over 10 million contracts a year. The Philadelphia market enjoys popularity among firms interested in hedging, while the Chicago market draws professional currency traders.[20]

---

[20]Jeffrey Taylor, "Europe Boosts Philadelphia's Currency Options Market," *The Wall Street Journal,* October 4, 1993.

Figure 12.12 □ Quotations on Foreign Exchange Option Contracts

OPTIONS — PHILADELPHIA EXCHANGE

Left section

Strike	Month	Calls Vol.	Calls Last	Puts Vol.	Puts Last
Australian Dollar					**73.33**
50,000 Australian Dollar EOM-cents per unit.					
73	Aug	...	...	20	0.28
50,000 Australian Dollars-cents per unit.					
72	Sep	...	...	70	0.30
74	Dec	10	0.89	...	...
British Pound					**154.16**
31,250 British Pounds-European Style.					
152	Sep	...	...	5	0.80
157	Sep	20	1.02	...	...
31,250 British Pounds-cents per unit.					
150	Oct	...	...	200	1.04
152½	Sep	...	...	20	1.00
155	Sep	29	1.80	...	...
156	Dec	...	...	3	4.20
157	Sep	44	0.81	...	...
157	Oct	5	1.53	...	...
157½	Dec	2	2.55	...	...
160	Sep	10	0.25	...	...
170	Dec	1400	0.24	...	0.01
British Pound-GMark					**227.77**
31,250 British Pound-German Mark cross.					
226	Dec	...	...	1	3.94
228	Sep	40	2.60	...	...
230	Sep	...	...	16	2.80
230	Oct	40	2.24	...	...
31,250 British Pound-German mark EOM.					
226	Aug	800	2.90	...	...
228	Aug	800	1.62	4	0.74
228	Sep	270	3.18	...	...
Canadian Dollar					**73.59**
50,000 Canadian Dollars-cents per unit.					
68	Dec	...	0.01	30	0.07
69	Dec	...	...	39	0.12
72	Sep	4	1.62	...	...
73	Sep	...	...	30	0.32
74	Sep	50	0.34	...	...
French Franc					**197.75**
250,000 French Francs EOM-10ths of a unit per unit.					
20	Aug	...	...	40	3.40
250,000 French Francs-10ths of a cent per unit.					
19½	Sep	...	...	5	4.10
19¾	Sep	...	...	122	3.14
20	Dec	...	...	10	6.62
20½	Sep	...	...	60	7.62
250,000 French Francs-European Style.					
18¾	Dec	...	...	200	1.70
German Mark					**67.69**
62,500 German Marks EOM-cents per unit.					
55	Aug	...	...	20	0.28
67½	Aug	...	...	10	0.68
69½	Aug	3544	0.24	210	2.30
70½	Aug	...	...	20	2.80
71	Aug	...	...	10	3.27
62,500 German Marks-European Style.					
64	Dec	1	4.70	...	...
66	Sep	...	...	60	0.67
67	Sep	...	...	30	1.05
68	Sep	...	...	48	1.36
68½	Sep	...	...	60	1.78
69	Sep	48	0.74	...	...
69½	Sep	48	0.60	30	2.53
70	Oct	5	0.74	...	...
70½	Sep	...	...	600	2.95
71½	Sep	...	...	300	3.80
73	Dec	1	0.56	...	...

Middle section

Strike	Month	Calls Vol.	Calls Last	Puts Vol.	Puts Last
62,500 German Marks-cents per unit.					
60	Sep	2	7.86	...	...
60	Dec	2	8.11	...	...
61	Sep	2	6.90	...	...
61	Dec	2	7.20	...	...
62	Sep	2	5.89	...	...
62	Dec	2	6.30	2100	0.34
64	Sep	...	...	87	0.16
64	Dec	...	...	18	0.69
65	Dec	...	...	230	0.93
66	Sep	...	...	17	0.53
66	Dec	...	...	102	1.30
67	Sep	...	...	82	0.82
67	Dec	...	...	504	1.67
68	Sep	159	1.10	163	1.23
68	Dec	...	...	280	2.08
69	Sep	50	0.70	88	1.95
69	Oct	6	1.10	62	2.13
69	Dec	175	1.74	1	2.58
69½	Sep	20	0.47	...	...
70	Sep	2	0.35	6	2.48
70	Oct	1000	0.73	1	2.88
70	Dec	3	1.39	1	3.50
70½	Sep	43	0.34	...	...
71	Sep	10	0.25	18	3.32
71	Oct	...	...	6	3.52
71	Dec	233	1.04	21	3.95
72	Sep	...	...	41	4.24
72	Dec	1	0.70	4	4.61
73	Dec	2100	0.60	...	...
74	Sep	1	0.04	3	6.28
74	Dec	...	...	2	6.34
75	Oct	500	0.10	...	...
Japanese Yen					**102.30**
6,250,000 Japanese Yen -100ths of a cent					
107	Sep	1	0.64	20	4.98
107	Oct	...	...	1	5.25
107	Dec	...	...	2	5.72
108	Sep	8	0.58	...	...
108	Dec	2	2.32	1	6.40
109	Sep	...	...	1	6.58
109	Dec	548	1.95	...	...
110	Sep	...	...	34	7.65
110	Oct	...	...	402	7.58
110	Dec	...	...	2	8.05
111	Sep	...	...	1	8.45
111	Oct	...	...	3	8.55
111	Dec	1	1.50	...	...
113	Sep	5	0.06	4	10.32
113	Dec	5	1.12	4	10.61
115	Sep	5	0.07	3	12.70
117	Sep	...	...	5	15.10
117	Dec	...	...	4	14.50
118	Sep	...	...	100	15.80
118	Dec	...	...	101	15.80
120	Dec	...	...	50	17.60
121	Sep	...	...	50	18.60
6,250,000 Japanese Yen EOM-100ths of a cent per unit.					
108	Aug	...	...	20	6.05
109	Aug	30	0.08	...	...
6,250,000 Japanese Yen-100ths of a cent per unit.					
93	Dec	...	0.01	300	0.73
94	Dec	...	0.01	4	0.80

Right section

Strike	Month	Calls Vol.	Calls Last	Puts Vol.	Puts Last
95	Sep	...	...	13	0.22
95	Dec	...	...	108	1.04
97	Dec	...	...	10	1.65
98	Dec	...	...	14	1.70
100	Sep	10	3.60	163	1.10
100	Dec	...	...	570	2.22
101	Sep	10	3.14	...	...
102	Sep	...	...	44	1.80
102	Oct	...	...	2	2.35
102	Dec	...	...	114	2.90
103	Sep	5	2.20	29	2.20
103	Oct	...	...	405	2.70
103	Dec	...	...	6	3.40
104	Dec	200	3.90	263	3.90
105	Sep	400	1.30	104	3.43
105	Oct	...	...	2	3.96
105	Dec	...	...	10	4.60
106	Sep	...	...	6	4.20
106	Oct	27	1.66	11	4.44
6,250,000 Japanese Yen-European Style.					
108	Sep	...	...	36	5.86
111	Dec	...	...	36	8.30
6,250,000 Japanese Yen-European Style.					
100	Sep	...	...	36	1.39
100	Dec	...	...	3	2.20
105	Sep	40	1.22	...	...
Swiss Franc					**81.32**
62,500 Swiss Francs-European Style.					
73	Sep	40	8.72	...	...
74	Sep	50	7.74	...	...
76	Sep	25	5.84	...	...
76	Oct	25	6.10	...	...
77	Sep	115	4.95	...	...
79	Sep	480	2.81	20	0.72
80	Sep	480	2.15	...	...
82	Sep	...	...	80	1.96
83	Sep	240	0.94	...	...
83½	Sep	400	0.77	...	...
84	Sep	...	...	3	2.97
84½	Sep	...	...	600	3.37
86	Sep	...	...	300	4.60
87	Sep	160	0.16	...	...
88	Sep	320	0.09	...	...
62,500 Swiss Francs-cents per unit.					
76	Oct	...	...	15	0.55
77	Sep	...	...	25	0.95
78	Sep	...	...	10	0.36
78	Dec	...	...	23	1.18
79	Sep	...	...	3	0.58
80	Dec	...	...	214	1.85
81	Sep	13	1.74	24	1.23
81	Dec	...	...	40	2.05
82	Sep	10	1.33	49	1.82
82	Dec	80	2.86	...	...
82½	Oct	160	1.65	...	...
83	Sep	...	...	4	2.42
83	Dec	80	2.42	120	3.20
84	Oct	3	1.15	6	3.90
85	Sep	...	...	3	3.75
86	Sep	5	0.29	160	4.75
86	Oct	...	...	20	5.42
87	Oct	20	0.46	...	...
87	Dec	20	1.11	...	...

Call Vol 51,982   Open Int ... 244,118
Put Vol 50,890   Open Int ... 296,182

Source: *The Wall Street Journal*, August 17, 1995.

A 1992 survey of U.S. banks revealed that their foreign exchange transactions consisted of 51 percent spot transactions, 10 percent futures or options contracts, and 6 percent forward contracts. The remaining 33 percent were swaps—agreements between banks to convert currencies and reconvert them later, allowing each bank to obtain the currencies needed to service its customers. Swaps involve simultaneous spot and forward transactions in the same currencies.

Some firms follow the ultimate strategy to avoid foreign exchange risk. They insist on being paid in their own currencies even on foreign sales, forcing customers to handle the risk. Such arrangements occur primarily in markets where the selling firm has substantial market power; otherwise, customers can threaten to go to a competitor with more willingness to take on the risk.[21]

 Case Two
Exporting the Yen

In the 50 years since the devastation of the Second World War, Japan has grown into the second largest market economy in the world; only the United States has a higher GDP. Rapid increases in Japan's participation in world trade accompanied this growth. Merchandise imports grew at a 4.9 percent annual rate from 1965 to 1980 and at 6.3 percent from 1980 to 1993, while exports grew at annual rates of 11.4 and 4.2 percent, respectively, over the two periods. Despite this impressive pattern of growth and success in international economic activity, regulations in Japan's financial markets have limited the use of the yen as a currency for financing international trade and investment. These restrictions have become increasingly troublesome to some in the Japanese banking and financial community and to non-Japanese as well. Pressures have intensified for relaxation of restrictions and for financial deregulation that would allow the yen to become a more "international" currency.

Among the restrictions most effective in limiting international use of the yen have been government policies that kept interest rates in Japan artificially low, thereby reducing the attractiveness of yen-denominated assets; limitations on the range of short-term investment instruments (for example, until the mid-1980s no yen equivalent of dollar-denominated Treasury bills existed); and restrictions on the participation of non-Japanese banks and firms in Japanese financial markets. Since the early 1980s the United States has called for elimination of these rules in the hope that use of the yen along with the dollar as an international currency in trade and finance would help eliminate some of the dollar's fluctuation relative to other currencies.

Since 1985, Japan has allowed interest rates to approach market-determined levels by removing requirements that Japanese banks purchase government-issued bonds at artificially low rates. Rates on bank deposits held by corporations now are unrestricted. To encourage foreign holdings in yen, rules limiting certificates of

---

[21]Leslie Scism, "U.S. Firms Ride Shifting Waves of Currency," *The Wall Street Journal,* August 6, 1993.

deposit to very large sums (approaching the yen equivalent of $1.5 million) have been relaxed, allowing certificates for amounts as low as $400,000 that appeal to individual portfolio holders. Beginning in 1986, the Japanese government issued six-month Treasury bills, providing a much-needed short-term yen asset.

Limitations on the issuance outside Japan of bonds issued in yen and of yen-denominated bonds by foreigners also have been phased out. Non-Japanese firms and governments now issue bonds denominated in yen and sell them in Europe (Euro-yen bonds) and in Japan itself (samurai bonds). Examples include yen-denominated bonds issued by the Canadian province of Ontario, a New Zealand electric utility, and the Italian government. During June 1995, Japanese investors bought $20.2 billion in foreign-issued bonds, about half of which were samurai bonds, denominated in yen. In 1995, after a long decline in the yen price of the dollar (from ¥264/$1 in early 1985 to ¥80/$1 in early 1995), Japanese officials suggested that the U.S. government offer Treasury bonds denominated in yen to shield Japanese investors from more losses from the declining value of the dollar. Such bonds, however, would place the exchange risk on the United States, a move that could prove more costly to the United States than simply paying Japanese investors an interest premium to buy dollar-denominated debt.

Case Three
Russia Enters the World of Foreign Exchange Trading[22]

Reformers in the Soviet Union long recognized that a major element in any successful transformation of the Soviet economy would involve making the ruble a convertible currency, that is, allowing it to trade in foreign exchange markets at rates determined at least in part by market forces of supply and demand. During the reform period under Mikhail Gorbachev and since the demise of the Soviet Union, progress toward the goal of convertibility has come erratically.

The Moscow Currency Exchange represents Russia's attempt to develop a foreign exchange market. Because of its simplicity, the Exchange, perhaps the most primitive functioning official foreign exchange market, provides useful insights into the mechanics of exchange rate determination. To buy or sell foreign exchange, traders go to the ornate Russian central bank building, fill out sheets of paper detailing their desired transactions, and leave the sheets with the secretary at the door. The Exchange's broker stands at a lectern, sums the buy orders and the sell orders, and announces the differential. Most days, buy orders for foreign exchange greatly outweigh sell orders. The official broker then takes the steps necessary to eliminate the differential. He announces a higher ruble price for foreign exchange (mostly dollars).

---

[22]Laurie Hays, "As Ruble Slides in Moscow Trading, The Dollar Finds Takers at Any Price," *The Wall Street Journal*, November 7, 1992. Chapter Twenty-One examines the currency experiences of the economies in transition, including Russia.

Buyers and sellers fill out new sheets informing the broker of their quantities demanded or supplied at the new rate. The process continues, with the price of dollars rising in five-ruble and then three-ruble increments.

In the back of the auditorium, the dealer for the Russian central bank sits. He can choose to intervene by selling dollars from the central bank's foreign exchange reserves to support the price of the ruble. On a given day in late 1992, the market opened at 309 rubles per dollar. When the announced rate reached 342 rubles per dollar, traders wanted to sell a total of $58 million and to buy a total of $62 million. The central bank intervened to cover the difference, and the Moscow Currency Exchange's broker announced, "The official rate of the central bank of Russia is 342 rubles to the dollar of the United States of America."

By mid-1995, erratic reform efforts and macroeconomic policy in Russia had raised the ruble price of a dollar to over 5,200, a depreciation of over 1,400 percent in less than three years.[23] A single day in October 1994 saw the Russian currency lose 21.5 percent of its value against the dollar. Chapter Twenty-One explores the macroeconomic challenges facing economies in transition.

Case Four
Sweden Defends Its Krona

In September 1992, a wave of uncertainty and volatility swept markets for European currencies. Members of the European Community were in the midst of deciding whether to integrate their monetary systems by moving to a common currency and central bank for the (then) 12 member countries. The result was great political and economic uncertainty. Market participants began to expect devaluations of several European currencies, including the Swedish krona. Such changes in expectations can become a self-fulfilling prophecy—because they reduce demand for the currency that is expected to be devalued, thereby requiring either foreign exchange market intervention to maintain the current rate or an actual devaluation.

Swedish central bank officials acted quickly; they raised a key overnight interest rate from 12 percent to 75 percent! *(Use the interest parity conditions and the demand and supply model of the foreign exchange market to illustrate the effects of the change in e^e and of the rise in i^k.)* The rise in interest on krona-denominated deposits relative to the interest rates available on assets denominated in other currencies convinced portfolio owners and managers to continue to hold krona deposits in their portfolios. Five days later, after the Swedish government's strong stance convinced market participants that a devaluation of the krona was not imminent after all, the Swedish central bank lowered the interest rate back to near its original level.

[23]In 1989, the official Soviet exchange rate—insulated completely from market forces—was 0.6 rubles per dollar!

Two months later, market participants again began to expect a devaluation. The Swedish Riksbank intervened to support the price of the krona, selling $26.3 billion worth of its foreign exchange reserves. The Swedish government also raised the interest rate on krona deposits from 11.5 percent to 20 percent. But this time the strategy failed. Expectations of a krona devaluation persisted, and eventually the Riksbank allowed the krona to float. It immediately depreciated by approximately 10 percent against trading partner currencies.[24]

Case Five
Exchange Rates as Asset Prices

Since the move to more flexible exchange rates in the early 1970s, two major aspects of exchange rate behavior have emerged. First, exchange rates have exhibited more volatility than most analysts predicted. Second, the exchange rate movements often have been unpredictable—even for professionals who earn their livelihoods by forecasting rates. Foreign exchange market participants, professional forecasters, and economists alike have been unable to predict exchange rate movements successfully.

These two characteristics—volatility and unpredictability—also are common in markets for assets such as precious metals and shares of common stock or equity. The explanation is quite simple: Any event that affects the future value of an asset affects the wealth of the individual who owns it. Obviously the object of the game is to hold assets whose values rise and to avoid those whose values fall. For durable assets, this requires forming expectations about future events and their effects on asset values.

The key to understanding the asset view of exchange rates lies in realizing why expectations about the *future* affect the value of the spot rate *today*. Suppose a widespread belief exists that the peso will be devalued against the dollar six months from today. What will be the effects—present and future—on the spot exchange rate and on the 180-day forward exchange rate, the price at which foreign exchange can be bought today for delivery in six months? (See section 12.3.3 for a review of forward markets for foreign exchange.)

Individuals will be willing to pay prices for pesos in the 180-day forward market equal to the prices they expect will prevail in the spot market six months from now. If the forward dollar price of pesos exceeded the expected future spot exchange rate, individuals would not make forward peso purchases and the forward rate would fall. If the forward dollar price of pesos were lower than the expected future spot rate, individuals would make more forward peso purchases and the forward rate would rise.

These links between purchases in the present and purchases in the future imply that the forward rate will reflect currently available information about the future

---

[24]"Sweden Decides to Float Krona After Speculators Drive It Down," *The Wall Street Journal,* November 20, 1992.

spot rate. When individuals come to expect the spot rate to rise in six months, the 180-day forward rate will rise to reflect this. Market participants will willingly pay a higher forward price for dollars (or a lower forward price for pesos), because of the expected price of the alternative (using the future spot market).

The next key point is that today's *spot* rate also will change to reflect those expectations. Individuals will want to decrease their holdings of the peso before its devaluation to avoid losses. This creates an incentive to sell pesos *now,* causing a decline in demand for peso-denominated deposits and pressure for an actual devaluation. Expectations about something to happen in six months can cause an immediate devaluation. This phenomenon helps explain the volatility observed in foreign exchange markets. Changes in expectations concerning anything that would affect exchange rates in the future cause movements in today's spot and forward exchange rates. The list of possible events is long: government personnel changes that could affect policy, elections, political tensions, or the course of international trade policy.

The asset-oriented view of exchange rates also can explain the unpredictability of exchange rate movements. Jacob Frenkel, a leading expert on exchange rate behavior, has estimated that market participants can predict only about 5 percent of the movement in exchange rates.[25] This is exactly what we would expect if exchange rates already reflected all currently available information (including market participants' expectations). The only thing that would *change* exchange rates is new information that is, by definition, unpredictable. "News" provides additional, previously unknown information; and this new information affects exchange rates.

Summary

This chapter outlined the role of foreign exchange markets in the world economy. Transactions involving more than one currency are a hallmark of international trade and finance. Activities in the foreign exchange market include clearing, arbitrage, hedging, and speculation, as portfolio owners choose assets with the highest expected rates of return. These activities create relationships among interest rates, spot and forward exchange rates, and expected exchange rates called *covered* and *uncovered interest parity*. The chapter used a partial-equilibrium demand and supply framework based on interest parity to examine the determination of the spot exchange rate along with the mechanics of the two simplest exchange rate regimes— a flexible rate system and a fixed rate system.

Looking Ahead

Chapter Thirteen introduces the balance of payments as the summary of all transactions of domestic individuals, firms, and governments with their foreign counterparts. It examines the various accounts of the balance of payments and explores some popular but misleading misconceptions.

---

[25]Jacob A. Frenkel, "Flexible Exchange Rates, Prices, and the Role of 'News': Lessons from the 1970s," *Journal of Political Economy* 89 (August 1981), 665–705.

Key Terms

money price
relative price
exchange rate
foreign exchange market
asset
asset portfolio
spot foreign exchange market
clearing
arbitrage
inconsistent cross rates
triangular arbitrage
hedging
foreign exchange risk
short position
balanced (closed) position
speculation
30-day forward rate
forward premium
forward discount

interest differential
uncovered interest parity
expected future spot rate
covered interest parity
offshore deposits (Eurocurrencies)
demand curve for a foreign currency
supply curve for a foreign currency
exchange rate regime
flexible (floating) exchange rate
depreciation
appreciation
fixed (pegged) exchange rate
intervention
revaluation
foreign exchange reserves
devaluation
bilateral exchange rate
effective exchange rate

Problems and Questions for Review

1. Assume a fixed exchange rate regime is in effect.
   (a) Countries A and B have agreed to peg the exchange rate between their currencies (the alpha, α, and the beta, β, respectively) at $\alpha 1/\beta 2$. Initially, this exchange rate corresponds to equilibrium in the foreign exchange market. Illustrate the initial situation in the market for beta-denominated deposits; be sure to label your graph carefully.
   (b) Country A undertakes an economic policy that lowers the interest rate on alpha-denominated deposits (i^{α}). Explain and illustrate the effects of the policy in the market for beta-denominated deposits.
   (c) If the two countries want to maintain the original exchange rate of $\alpha 1/\beta 2$, what must Alphabank (country A's central bank) do?
   (d) Time passes, and the situation remains as described in part (c). Individuals in the two countries begin to anticipate a change in the pegged exchange rate. What type of change (that is, in which direction) would they be likely to expect? Why?
   (e) Illustrate how the change in expectations described in part (d) would affect the market for beta-denominated deposits. Would the expectations make a change in the actual exchange rate more likely or less likely? Would the expectations be likely to make any change in the exchange rate larger or smaller? Why?
   (f) Can your answers to parts (d) and (e) help explain the observation that policy makers and central bankers in countries facing likely currency devaluations often publicly deny that any devaluation is forthcoming? Why? Might there be a long-run cost to repeated such denials that turn out to be false? Why?

2. Firms and governments frequently issue bonds in currencies other than their home currency. Explain in what sense issuing bonds in the purchaser's home currency transfers the foreign exchange risk to the seller.

3. You have $2,000. The current interest rates on dollar- and pound-denominated deposits for 180-day maturity are $i^\$ = 0.02$ (2 percent) and $i^£ = 0.03$ (3 percent), respectively. The current spot exchange rate is e = $2/£1.
   (a) What are your three basic choices of strategy over the next 180 days?
   (b) If you (and everyone else) were certain that the exchange rate between dollars and pounds would not change over the next 180 days, what would you do? What would you have at the end of 180 days?
   (c) Assume you do not mind bearing foreign exchange risk. You expect the spot rate in 180 days to be $1.90/£1. What strategy would you follow, and why? After 180 days, the actual spot rate turns out to be $1.80/£1. Are you pleased with your decision? Why, or why not?
   (d) Now assume you are highly risk averse. The 180-forward rate is $2.02/£1. What strategy do you follow?

4. Assume for simplicity that Germany and the United States are the only two countries in the world.
   (a) Illustrate equilibrium in the foreign exchange market, using Deutsche marks (DM) as the foreign currency. Label your graph carefully.
   (b) Suddenly, because of costs associated with unifying (formerly) East and West Germany, everyone expects the Deutsche mark to appreciate against the dollar. Illustrate and explain the effect of the change in expectations on the foreign exchange market, including the equilibrium exchange rate.
   (c) What is the relationship between what everyone thought would happen and what actually happens? What might this imply about exchange rate volatility?

5. Suppose wheat sells for $3.00 per bushel in the United States and for 15,000 rubles in Russia. Ignoring transportation costs, what exchange rate between the dollar and the ruble would make consumers indifferent between buying U.S. and Russian wheat? Explain.

6. What is the relationship between the effective exchange rate and bilateral exchange rates? Why can there be more than one value of the effective exchange rate for a currency?

7. As of September 8, 1992, the exchange rate between the krona and the dollar was $1/k5.5. The interest rate on krona-denominated deposits was 0.12 (or 12 percent), and the interest rate on dollar-denominated deposits was 0.03 (or 3 percent).
   (a) Assume the foreign-exchange market is in equilibrium given the situation described above. Is the *expected* spot exchange rate between the krona and the dollar closer to $1/k5.0, $1/k5.5, or $1/k6.0? *(Hint: There's no need for complicated numerical calculations.)* Explain how you know, and provide the equation for equilibrium in the foreign exchange market that you used to arrive at your answer. Illustrate the equilibrium in a graph of the foreign exchange market between the dollar and the krona. Be sure to label your graph.

(b) On September 9, 1992, the expected future spot rate fell. Illustrate the effects of the change in expectations on the graph of the foreign exchange market. If policy makers did nothing, what would happen to the exchange rate? Explain why.

(c) Instead of doing nothing, Swedish policy makers raised interest rates on krona-denominated deposits. Use the equation for equilibrium in the foreign exchange market and your graph of the foreign exchange market to explain and illustrate the effect of the Swedish policy.

(d) After several days, Swedish policy makers reduced interest rates on krona-denominated deposits back to about 0.12 (or 12 percent), their original level. Yet, the exchange rate between the krona and the dollar remained approximately unchanged in the short run. What could account for this scenario? *(Hint: What effect, if any, might the temporary rise in interest rates have on exchange rate expectations? Why?)*

8. Comment on the following statements.

(a) "In 1993, short-term Mexican bonds paid an interest rate of over 17 percent, Argentine bonds over 23 percent, Indonesian certificates of deposit over 15 percent, and Philippine Treasury bills over 12 percent. U.S. interest rates on dollar-denominated assets during the same period ranged from 3 to 6 percent, depending on the type of asset. This is proof that portfolio owners don't pursue high rates of return. Otherwise, no one would have held any dollar assets in 1993."

(b) "During 1992, Brazil's currency depreciated by 95 percent against the dollar, Turkey's lira by 46 percent, Peru's new sol by 41 percent, Poland's zloty by 34 percent, and Russia's ruble by 100 percent. Surely no one holds deposits denominated in these currencies, because of their volatility."

References and Selected Readings

Abken, Peter A. "Globalization of Stock, Futures, and Options Markets." Federal Reserve Bank of Atlanta *Economic Review* 76 (July–August 1991): 1–22.
Assessment of the globalization of asset markets; for all students.

Batten, Dallas S., and Mack Ott. "What Can Central Banks Do about the Value of the Dollar?" Federal Reserve Bank of St. Louis *Review* 66 (May 1984): 16–25.
The mechanics of foreign exchange market intervention; for all students.

Branson, William H., and Dale W. Henderson. "The Specification and Influence of Asset Markets." In *Handbook of International Economics*, Vol. 2, edited by Ronald W. Jones and Peter B. Kenen, 749–806. Amsterdam: North-Holland, 1985.
An advanced discussion of the microeconomics of portfolio choice.

Chrystal, K. Alec. "A Guide to Foreign Exchange Markets." Federal Reserve Bank of St. Louis *Review* (March 1984): 5–18.
A handy summary of the mechanics and economic roles of foreign exchange markets; for all students.

Chrystal, K. Alec, and Cletus C. Coughlin. "How the 1992 Legislation Will Affect European Financial Services." Federal Reserve Bank of St. Louis *Review* 74 (March–April 1992): 62–77.
Assessment of the effects of the 1992 internal market program on the financial services industry; for all students.

Destler, I. M., and C. Randall Henning. *Dollar Politics: Exchange Rate Policymaking in the United States.* Washington, D.C.: Institute for International Economics, 1990.
The domestic politics involved in the making of exchange-rate policy; for all students.

Dominguez, Kathryn M., and Jeffrey A. Frankel. *Does Foreign Exchange Intervention Work?* Washington, D.C.: Institute for International Economics, 1993.
Examination of the ability of intervention to affect exchange rates; intermediate.

Feldman, Robert A. "Foreign Currency Options." *Finance and Development* 22 (December 1985): 38–41.
A review of one of the recent developments in financial markets; for all students.

Fieleke, Norman S. "The Rise of the Foreign Currency Futures Market." Federal Reserve Bank of Boston *New England Economic Review* (March–April 1985): 38–47.
The rise of the IMM market in foreign currency futures; for all students.

Frankel, J. A., and A. K. Rose. "Empirical Research on Nominal Exchange Rates." In *Handbook of International Economics,* Vol. 3, edited by G. M. Grossman and K. Rogoff, 1689–1730. Amsterdam: North-Holland, 1995.
Up-to-date survey of what economists know from empirical work on foreign exchange markets; intermediate to advanced.

Giddy, Ian H. *Global Financial Markets.* Lexington, Mass.: D. C. Heath, 1994.
Textbook covering international financial markets; intermediate.

Gilbert, R. Alton. "Implications of Netting Arrangements for Bank Risk in Foreign Exchange Transactions." Federal Reserve Bank of St. Louis *Review* 74 (January–February 1992): 3–16.
Techniques banks use to limit their foreign exchange risk; for all students.

Isard, Peter. *Exchange Rate Economics.* Cambridge: Cambridge University Press, 1995.
Excellent survey for advanced students.

Levich, Richard M. "Empirical Studies of Exchange Rates: Price Behavior, Rate Determination and Market Efficiency." In *Handbook of International Economics,* Vol. 2, edited by Ronald W. Jones and Peter B. Kenen, 979–1040. Amsterdam: North-Holland, 1985.
An advanced survey of the empirical evidence on exchange rate behavior, focusing on asset models.

Lewis, K. "Puzzles in International Financial Markets." In *Handbook of International Economics,* Vol. 3, edited by G. M. Grossman and K. Rogoff, 1913–1972. Amsterdam: North-Holland, 1995.
Up-to-date survey of unsolved puzzles concerning international financial markets, including foreign exchange markets; intermediate to advanced.

Lum, Yin-Fun, and Calvin McDonald. "Interbank Foreign Exchange Markets in Africa." *Finance and Development* 31 (June 1994): 14–18.
Development of foreign exchange markets in Africa; for all students.

Melvin, Michael. *International Money and Finance.* New York: Harper and Row, 1989.
A text covering the institutions of international finance; for all students.

Quirk, Peter, and Viktor Schoofs. "Forward Foreign Exchange Markets in LDCs." *Finance and Development* 25 (September 1988): 36–39.
The importance of forward foreign exchange markets' ability to transfer foreign exchange risk in integrating LDC firms into world markets; for all students.

Rangan, Subramanian, and Robert Z. Lawrence. "The Responses of U.S. Firms to Exchange Rate Fluctuations: Piercing the Corporate Veil." *Brookings Papers on Economic Activity* 2 (1993): 341–379.
Empirical examination of firms' pricing responses to changes in the value of the dollar; intermediate and advanced.

Tavlas, George. "International Currencies: The Rise of the Deutsche Mark." *Finance and Development* 27 (September 1990): 35–38.
Requirements for a currency to become an international currency and an assessment of the DM; accessible to all students.

Tavlas, George, and Yuzuru Ozeki. "The Internationalization of the Yen." *Finance and Development* 28 (June 1991): 2–5.
Progress and bottlenecks in the growth of the yen as an international currency; for all students.

Thornton, Daniel L. "Tests of Covered Interest Rate Parity." Federal Reserve Bank of St. Louis *Review* 71 (July–August 1989): 55–66.
Empirical tests of CIP and discussion of the issues that arise in performing such tests; for intermediate and advanced students.

CHAPTER THIRTEEN

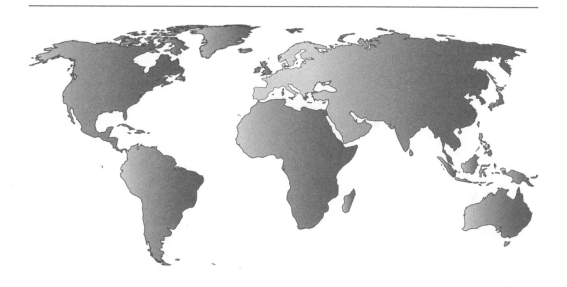

The Balance-of-Payments Accounts

13.1 Introduction

The countries of the world differ widely in their degree of *openness*, or the extent to which their economic activity occurs across international boundaries. The United States is, by world standards, a relatively closed economy, as measured by its ratio of exports or imports to gross domestic product (GDP), although the degree of openness has increased rapidly in recent years.[1] Between 1965 and 1993, U.S. **merchandise exports** (exports of physical goods) rose from 4 to 7 percent of GDP and merchandise imports from 3 to 10 percent. The trade percentages remain small, but fewer than a dozen countries have GDPs as large as U.S. merchandise exports!

Table 13.1 provides a perspective on openness by reporting merchandise exports as a share of GDP for a sample of countries. Merchandise exports range from 7 percent of GDP in the United States to 150 percent of GDP in Hong Kong, a small economy specializing in assembly and trade.

---

[1]Gross domestic product is a measure of a country's output. GDP differs from GNP in its treatment of production that occurs using the country's factors of production but outside the country's geographical borders. Section 14.2 presents the details of the distinction, as well as a numerical comparison between GNP and GDP for the United States.

Table 13.1 □ **Merchandise Exports as a Percentage of GDP, 1993 (Percent)**

Country	Exports as Percent of GDP
United States	7
Japan	9
India	10
Central African Republic	11
Russia	13
France	16
Ghana	17
Malawi	18
China	22
United Kingdom	22
Hungary	23
Canada	30
Belgium	53
Malaysia	73
Singapore	134
Hong Kong	150

Source: The World Bank, *World Development Report 1995.*

Although important, trade in goods comprises only one of many types of economic activities that occur internationally. Another significant dimension of openness is trade in **services**—banking, insurance, travel, transportation, consulting, and other economic activities in which the item traded is not a physical good. Trade in services represents one of the fastest-growing areas in the world economy, although data are difficult to obtain because of measurement problems. As we saw in Chapter Seven, nontariff barriers and regulatory restrictions also plague trade in services. Because of its highly developed markets in banking and insurance and its population of highly skilled consultants, the United States traditionally has been a net exporter of services; that is, the value of U.S. service exports exceeds the value of U.S. service imports. Table 13.2 reports U.S. *net* service exports, or the excess of exports over imports.

Financial and investment activities such as purchases and sales of stocks, bonds, and other financial assets and of physical capital such as factories, machines, and land comprise a third major category of international transactions. Reductions in transportation and communication costs have resulted in growing internationalization of both production and financial markets. It no longer is unusual for a U.S.-based firm to buy a plant in Europe financed with bonds sold worldwide and denominated in several currencies. Table 13.3 summarizes the magnitude of international investment flows.[2]

---

[2]Table 13.3 excludes U.S. and foreign purchases and sales of official assets, discussed below.

Table 13.2 □ **U.S. Net Trade in Services, 1960–1994 ($ Millions)**

Year	Net Travel, Transportation, and Other Services
1960	−1,382
1965	200
1970	292
1975	2,042
1980	7,915
1985	4,468
1990	37,789
1994	59,994

Source: *Economic Report of the President 1995; Survey of Current Business,* March 1995.

A set of accounts called the country's **balance-of-payments accounts** summarizes all the transactions by individuals, firms, and governments of one country with their counterparts in the rest of the world. Like any single set of numbers, the balance of payments cannot capture the full extent of the complex economic interactions among countries. In addition, a number of misconceptions that cause both confusion and bad economic policy surround the balance-of-payments accounts. This chapter introduces the fundamental definitions and mechanics of the balance-of-payments accounts, explores the associated misconceptions, and relates the balance of payments to the currency markets and exchange rates examined in Chapter Twelve.

Table 13.3 □ **International Investment, 1960–1994 ($ Millions)**

Year	Net U.S. Purchases of Assets Abroad (Increase or Capital Outflow [−])	Net Foreign Purchases of U.S. Assets (Increase or Capital Inflow [+])
1960	−6,244	821
1965	−6,941	607
1970	−11,818	−550
1975	−38,854	8,643
1980	−78,813	42,615
1985	−35,368	142,301
1990	−68,205	88,282
1994	−131,033	275,702

Source: *Economic Report of the President 1995; Survey of Current Business,* March 1995.

13.2 Components of the Balance-of-Payments Accounts

Because the balance-of-payments accounts merely summarize all the transactions undertaken by residents of one country with the rest of the world, we can divide them into subaccounts that correspond to the various categories of international transactions in which individuals, firms, and governments participate. The actual balance-of-payments accounts, as reported quarterly for the United States by the Department of Commerce, are quite complex, involving 70 categories of transactions. Table 13.4 reproduces a recent report.

For our purposes, a much simpler classification will suffice. Individuals and firms engage in international transactions when they buy or sell goods or services abroad, borrow or lend abroad (that is, sell or buy financial assets), or buy or sell buildings, equipment, or land located abroad. Government agencies also can engage in any of these transactions plus other "official" transactions outside the province of private individuals and firms. We can use this simple classification to define three basic accounts: the current account, the (nonofficial) capital account, and the official settlements account.

As we shall see, the balance-of-payments accounts consists of a **double-entry bookkeeping system.** This means that any international transaction is entered twice, because every transaction has two sides. For example, when the United States exports wheat to Russia, Russia also makes a payment to the United States. The wheat flows in one direction, while the payment flows in the other; *both* enter the double-entry bookkeeping system of the balance-of-payments accounts of both the United States and Russia. Or, when a Japanese bank buys a U.S. Treasury bill, the bill flows from the United States to Japan *and* payment for the bill flows from Japan to the United States; two entries are made in the balance-of-payments statistics for each country. Often the two entries reflecting the two sides of a single transaction will occur in different accounts. But before we can analyze the dual entries for various types of transactions, we must understand the differences among the current, capital, and official settlements accounts.

13.2.1 The Current Account

The major categories of transactions within the **current account** are (1) exports and imports of goods, called *merchandise,* (2) imports and exports of military services, travel and transportation, and other services, (3) current income received and paid on international investments, and (4) unilateral transfers, including worker remittances and pension payments.[3] Table 13.5 reports the status of the various current-account components for the United States during the postwar period.

Each category of current-account transactions includes both exports by the United States (referred to as **credits** in the bookkeeping sense because they generate *receipts* from foreigners to U.S. residents) and imports by the United States from the rest of the world (known as **debits** because they generate *payments* from U.S. residents to

---

[3]Case Two in Chapter Ten examines worker remittances.

Table 13.4 □ **U.S. International Transactions, 1994 ($ Millions)**[a]

Line		1994
1	Exports of goods, services, and income	832,871
2	Merchandise, adjusted, excluding military	502,729
3	Services	195,287
4	Transfers under U.S. military agency sales contracts	10,845
5	Travel	60,001
6	Passenger fares	17,651
7	Other transportation	24,733
8	Royalties and license fees	22,823
9	Other private services	58,453
10	U.S. Government miscellaneous services	782
11	Income receipts on U.S. assets abroad	134,855
12	Direct investment receipts	66,585
13	Other private receipts	64,232
14	U.S. Government receipts	4,038
15	Imports of goods, services, and income	−954,422
16	Merchandise, adjusted, excluding military	−669,093
17	Services	−135,293
18	Direct defense expenditures	−10,577
19	Travel	−43,059
20	Passenger fares	−12,558
21	Other transportation	−25,718
22	Royalties and license fees	−5,926
23	Other private services	−34,791
24	U.S. Government miscellaneous services	−2,663
25	Income payments on foreign assets in the United States	−150,036
26	Direct investment payments	−25,188
27	Other private payments	−77,829
28	U.S. Government payments	−47,019
29	Unilateral transfers, net	−34,121
30	U.S. Government grants	−14,532
31	U.S. Government pensions and other transfers	−4,246
32	Private remittances and other transfers	−15,343
33	U.S. assets abroad, net (increase/capital outflow[−])	−125,687
34	U.S. official reserve assets, net	5,346
35	Gold	—
36	Special drawing rights	−441
37	Reserve position in the International Monetary Fund	494
38	Foreign currencies	5,293

continued

Table 13.4 □ *continued*

Line		1994
39	U.S. Government assets, other than official reserve assets, net	−278
40	U.S. credits and other long-term assets	−5,156
41	Repayments on U.S. credits and other long-term assets	4,923
42	U.S. foreign currency holdings and U.S. short-term assets, net	−45
43	U.S. private assets, net	−130,755
44	Direct investment	−58,422
45	Foreign securities	−60,621
46	U.S. claims on unaffiliated foreigners reported by U.S. nonbanking concerns	n.a.
47	U.S. claims reported by U.S. banks, not included elsewhere	−2,033
48	Foreign assets in the United States, net (increase/capital inflow [+])	314,614
49	Foreign official assets in the United States, net	38,912
50	U.S. Government securities	36,429
51	U.S. Treasury securities	30,441
52	Other	5,988
53	Other U.S. Government liabilities	2,514
54	U.S. liabilities reported by U.S. banks, not included elsewhere	2,317
55	Other foreign official assets	−2,348
56	Other foreign assets in the United States, net	275,702
57	Direct investment	60,071
58	U.S. Treasury securities	32,925
59	U.S. securities other than U.S. Treasury securities	58,562
60	U.S. liabilities to unaffiliated foreigners reported by U.S. nonbanking concerns	n.a.
61	U.S. liabilities reported by U.S. banks, not included elsewhere	106,189
62	Allocations of special drawing rights	—
63	Statistical discrepancy (sum of above items with sign reversed)	−33,255
63a	Of which seasonal adjustment discrepancy	—
	Memoranda:	
64	Balance on merchandise trade (lines 2 and 16)	−166,364
65	Balance on services (lines 3 and 17)	59,994
66	Balance on goods and services (lines 64 and 65)	−106,370
67	Balance on investment income (lines 11 and 25)	−15,181
68	Balance on goods, services, and income (lines 1 and 15 or lines 66 and 67)	−121,551
69	Unilateral transfers, net (line 29)	−34,121
70	Balance on current account (lines 1, 15, and 29 or lines 68 and 69)	−155,673

[a]Credits (+), debits (−).

Source: *Survey of Current Business,* March 1995.

foreigners). A net value entered with a negative sign means that imports or payments by U.S. residents exceeded exports or receipts in that category; a positive value represents exports or receipts in excess of imports or payments.

Table 13.5 ▫ **U.S. Current Account, 1960–1994 ($ Millions)**

Year	Net Merchandise Trade	Net Services Exports	Net Investment Income	Net Unilateral Transfers	Current-Account Balance
1960	4,892	−1,382	3,379	−4,062	2,824
1965	4,951	−287	5,350	−4,583	5,431
1970	2,603	−349	6,233	−6,156	2,331
1975	8,903	3,503	12,787	−7,075	18,116
1980	−25,500	6,093	30,073	−8,349	2,317
1985	−122,173	78	19,673	−22,950	−125,372
1990	−109,033	30,222	20,725	−33,663	−91,748
1994	−166,364	59,994	−15,181	−34,121	−155,673

Source: *Economic Report of the President 1995*; *Survey of Current Business*, March 1995.

The final column in Table 13.5 reports the **balance on the current account.** This equals the sum of all the other entries and represents the difference between total exports or receipts (credits) by U.S. residents for current transactions and total imports or payments (debits) by U.S. residents for current transactions. Again a negative value implies that debits exceed credits. To better understand the various categories in Table 13.5, we can illustrate each with examples of typical entries.

Merchandise Trade

The largest source of credits in the U.S. current account is the export of merchandise. This category includes shipments abroad of a variety of items: agricultural products, high-technology goods such as the computers exported by IBM, and the aircraft exported by Boeing, the United States' largest industrial exporter. The sum of the value of all the goods exported by American individuals, firms, and government agencies (excluding the military) equals merchandise exports. Imports of goods include the value of all U.S. purchases: automobiles from Japan, coffee from Brazil, crude oil from Saudi Arabia, VCRs from South Korea, and apparel from China.

Since the mid-1970s, the value of U.S. merchandise imports has exceeded the value of U.S. merchandise exports; this is called a **deficit** on the **merchandise trade balance.** During the 1950s and 1960s, the United States ran a **surplus** in its merchandise trade balance; that is, the value of exports exceeded the value of imports. For the last few years, the large U.S. merchandise trade deficit (reaching well over $150 billion in 1987 and again in 1994) has received much attention. Many policies have been proposed for reducing the deficit, which often is claimed to cause the "exportation of jobs" and "deindustrialization of America." Unfortunately, many of the policy proposals amount to protectionism, as they attempt to restrict imports from countries with a comparative advantage in the production of items such as steel, automobiles, apparel, and footwear. We shall explore some misconceptions surrounding the effects of a trade deficit later. For now, note that the merchandise trade balance is only one of several components of the current account, which in turn is only one of several components of the balance-of-payments accounts. A deficit in the merchandise trade balance is *not* the same as a balance-of-payments deficit (a concept we have not yet defined), although the popular press often confuses the two.

Services

The services category of transactions includes military transactions, travel and transportation, royalties, education, accounting, banking, insurance, and consulting. A U.S. resident vacationing in France or attending Oxford University imports a service; and that import enters the U.S. balance-of-payments accounts as a debit because it involves a payment to foreigners. When Saudi Arabia hires a U.S. petroleum engineering consultant to work in its oil industry, the United States, in effect, exports the consultant's services to Saudi Arabia, a credit in services from the U.S. point of view. The United States typically runs a surplus (credits > debits) in the services account, primarily because large shares of the insurance and banking activities that comprise integral parts of international trade are conducted by U.S. firms.

Net merchandise trade and net services trade often are combined to report the **balance on goods and services,** or the difference between the value of U.S. exports of goods and services (credits) minus the value of U.S. imports of goods and services (debits).

Investment Income

The third category of items in the current account captures interest, dividends, and other forms of income Americans receive from investments they own abroad (credits) and payments by Americans to foreigners as income earned on foreign-owned investments in the United States (debits). This account does *not* include new investments but merely the current income from those made previously. Included would be receipts by Exxon of profits from its overseas operations and payments by Seagram and Sons to its Canadian parent company. Also included as credits would be all interest, dividends, and other income earned by American residents on the $2.5 trillion of foreign assets they own. To remember that these receipts are credits, it helps to recall that they involve payments *to* U.S. residents *from* foreigners, just as U.S. merchandise exports do. Debit entries include all the interest, dividends, and other income paid to owners of the $3 trillion of foreign-owned assets in the United States. Like U.S. merchandise imports, these represent debits on the U.S. current account because they involve payments *from* U.S. residents *to* foreigners. Despite the fact that the value of U.S. assets owned by foreigners exceeds the value of foreign assets owned by U.S. residents, the United States continued to run a surplus in the net investment income subaccount until 1994, when for the first time since the Second World War foreigners earned income on their investments in the United States that exceeded the current income Americans received on their investments abroad.

Unilateral Transfers

The final category of current-account transactions, unilateral transfers, includes transactions that are not purchases or sales of either goods or services. Unilateral debits include U.S. nonmilitary aid to foreign countries (government aid or private

Table 13.6 □ **Analogy between Transactions in the Current Account and Typical Economic Transactions of an Individual**

Current-Account Transaction	Analogous Individual Economic Transaction
Merchandise exports	Value of goods produced and sold by the individual
Investment income	Income from assets (stock dividends, bond interest, etc.)
Service exports	Value of services sold (wages, etc.)
Unilateral receipts	Gifts, pension payments, etc. received
Merchandise imports	Value of goods purchased (food, clothing, etc.)
Investment payments	Payments on loans, mortgages, etc.
Service imports	Services purchased (insurance, medical care, etc.)
Unilateral payments	Gifts, etc. given
Sum of current-account receipts or credits	Current individual income
Sum of current-account payments or debits	Current individual expenditures
Current-account surplus	Current income > current expenditures
Current-account deficit	Current expenditures > current income

charity); worker remittances, or funds sent back to the home country by individuals working in the United States; and pensions paid to former U.S. residents now living abroad. The United States consistently runs a deficit in unilateral transfers.

Current-Account Balance

The sum of the current-account components—merchandise trade, services, investment income, and unilateral transfers—gives the country's current-account balance. As Table 13.5 reports, in most years between the Second World War and the late 1970s the United States had a current-account surplus, although in isolated years current-account debits exceeded current-account credits. Since the late 1970s, however, a persistent and growing deficit has characterized the current account, reaching $155 billion in 1994.

The Current Account and Individual Transactions: An Analogy

When studying the balance-of-payments accounts for the first time, the greatest danger is missing the forest (the logic and meaning of the balance-of-payments accounts) for the trees (the details about the types of transactions in each account). Now that we have examined each tree in the current account, we can use an analogy to visualize the forest. The analogy is between the economic transactions undertaken by an individual and those recorded in a country's balance-of-payments accounts. Table 13.6 suggests a correspondence between the entries in the current account and the economic transactions of a typical individual.

Credits in the current account correspond to current receipts or income for the individual. This income could come from production and sale of a good (in which case it would be like a merchandise export in the current account), from the return on a previously made investment in a stock or bond (like investment income in the current account), from the sale of a service (like service exports in the current account), or from some sort of gift or pension (analogous to a unilateral transfer receipt in the current account). Debits in the current account correspond to current expenditures by an individual. The individual may make expenditures on goods (like a merchandise import), make interest payments on a loan (analogous to investment payments in the current account), pay for a service (corresponding to a service import), or give a gift (a unilateral transfer payment).

The sum of a country's credits in its current account is analogous to the total of an individual's current income, and the total of current-account debits corresponds to the total of an individual's current expenditures. A current-account surplus (credits > debits) is similar to a situation in which an individual's current income exceeds current expenditures. A deficit on the current account (debits > credits) matches the situation of an individual whose current expenditures exceed current income.

Just as current income and expenditures fail to capture all the relevant dimensions of an individual's economic situation, the current account gives an incomplete record of a country's transactions with the rest of the world. In both cases, the primary items missing include borrowing and lending activity, purchases and sales of assets, and changes in the stock of cash or money balances. For an individual, if current income exceeds current expenditures, the "excess" income must be used to make new loans, pay off old loans, buy an asset (such as a house or shares of stock), or increase money balances (for example, a checking account). On the other hand, if an individual's current expenditures exceed current income, the difference must be covered by borrowing, selling an asset, or running down money balances. A similar logic applies for a country and carries us beyond the current account to the other balance-of-payments accounts.

13.2.2 The Capital Account

The **capital account** records international borrowing and lending and purchases and sales of assets. When a U.S. resident (individual, firm, or government agency) purchases a foreign asset or makes a foreign loan, the asset or IOU is imported into the United States and enters as a debit in the U.S. capital account, known as a **capital outflow**. The asset could be a bond issued by a British firm, a house in France, or shares of stock in a Japanese company. The way to remember that a capital outflow is a debit (like the *import* of a good) is to think of it as the *importation* of the title to the asset or of the IOU in the case of a loan. Capital outflows from the United States represent *increases* in U.S. ownership of foreign assets. The figure reported in the capital account of the balance-of-payments accounts is a net value; it equals sales by U.S. residents of foreign assets minus purchases by U.S. residents of foreign assets. The reported figure therefore reflects the net increase (if negative) or decrease (if positive) in U.S. ownership of foreign assets, because debits (payments to foreigners) enter the balance-of-payments accounts with a negative sign and credits (receipts from foreigners) with a positive sign.

One effect of using the net figure is to make the volumes of capital flows appear much smaller than they actually are. For example, if one U.S. resident purchases $10 million worth of bonds from a British firm and another individual sells $9 mil-

Table 13.7 □ **U.S. Nonofficial Capital Account, 1960–1994 ($ Millions)**

Year	Net U.S. Purchases of Assets Abroad (Increase or Capital Outflow [–])	Net Foreign Purchases of U.S. Assets (Increase or Capital Inflow [+])	Capital-Account Balance
1960	–6,244	821	–5,423
1965	–6,941	607	–6,334
1970	–11,818	–550	–12,368
1975	–38,854	8,643	–30,211
1980	–78,813	42,615	–36,198
1985	–35,368	142,301	106,933
1990	–68,205	88,282	20,077
1994	–131,033	275,702	144,669

Source: *Economic Report of the President 1995; Survey of Current Business,* March 1995.

lion worth of Japanese bonds, the figure in the U.S. capital account will report a net capital outflow of $1 million ($9 million – $10 million), even though $19 million of bonds have changed hands. Also, annual balance-of-payments accounts do not reflect purchases of foreign assets resold within the same year.

Credit transactions in the capital account occur when foreign residents buy assets such as bonds, stocks, or land in the United States. It may help to think of the United States as *exporting* the titles to the assets or IOUs for the loans; thus, these **capital inflows** are credits in the U.S. balance-of-payments accounts, as are *exports* of goods. Capital inflows also are reported in net terms, so the figure reflects the net increase (or decrease, if negative) in foreign ownership of U.S. assets.

The difference between net capital inflows and net capital outflows is the capital-account balance: a surplus if inflows (= credits) > outflows (= debits) and a deficit if inflows < outflows.[4] Until recently, the United States consistently ran a capital-account deficit, buying more assets abroad than the rest of the world bought in the United States. The 1980s, however, brought a change in the pattern: The pace of U.S. investment abroad slowed dramatically, while the growth of foreign investment in the United States accelerated. Table 13.7 reports the U.S. capital-account balance.[5]

As with the various categories of current-account transactions, an analogy with an individual helps clarify the role of capital-account transactions in the world economy.

[4]The capital account as reported by the Department of Commerce includes all borrowing/lending and purchases/sales of assets by individuals, firms, and governments. For our purposes, we exclude transactions by central banks—changes in official reserve assets—from the nonofficial capital account and report them separately as the official settlements account (to be discussed in the next section). Other borrowing/lending and purchases/sales of assets by governments are part of the nonofficial capital account.

[5]Official transactions are not included but are discussed separately in the next section under the official settlements account; therefore, the figures in Table 13.7 refer to the nonofficial capital account.

Table 13.8 □ **Analogy between Transactions in the Capital Account and Typical Economic Transactions of an Individual**

Capital-Account Transaction	Analogous Individual Economic Transaction
Net capital outflows	(New loans made) minus (receipts for loans paid off) plus (purchases of assets) equals (net change in amount of lending outstanding and increase in assets owned)
Net capital inflows	(New loans taken out) minus (old loans paid off) plus (sales of assets) equals (net change in amount of borrowing outstanding and decrease in assets owned)
Capital-account balance	(Net change in amount of borrowing outstanding) minus (net change in amount of lending outstanding) minus (net change in assets owned) equals net decline (if +) or increase (if −) in ownership of assets
Capital-account surplus	Net change in borrowing plus sales of assets > net change in lending plus purchases of assets equals decline in net ownership of assets
Capital-account deficit	Net change in borrowing plus sales of assets < net change in lending plus purchases of assets equals increase in net ownership of assets

Table 13.8 suggests correspondences between typical transactions undertaken by an individual and capital-account transactions. At the individual level, net capital outflows represent the net change in the individual's lending plus purchases of other assets. Net capital inflows represent the individual's net change in borrowing plus sales of assets. A surplus in the capital account occurs when net capital inflows exceed net capital outflows. The capital account is in deficit when the overall flow of capital out of a country exceeds the flow coming in. Note the somewhat counterintuitive terminology here: A capital-account *surplus* denotes a *decline* in the net domestic ownership of foreign assets, while a capital-account *deficit* corresponds to an *increase* in such ownership.

13.2.3 The Official Settlements Balance

Unlike the current and capital accounts, all transactions within the official settlements account are conducted by "official" government authorities, usually central banks, rather than by individuals or firms. The **official settlements balance** reports the net change in a country's stock of foreign exchange reserves (see section 12.7) and official government borrowing.[6] Increases in the level of U.S. reserves or decreases in the level of reserves held by foreign central banks in the United States enter as debits in the U.S. official settlements account. (It may help to think of increases in U.S. foreign exchange

---

[6]For simplicity, we assume that all transactions in the official settlements account represent changes in the levels of official foreign exchange reserves resulting from intervention in foreign exchange markets. In reality, several other types of transactions show up in the account. For example, if a foreign central bank (say, the Bank of Japan) reduces its reserve holdings of a currency (such as the Italian lira) by selling the currency and buying U.S. Treasury bills, the transaction will appear as an increase in foreign official holdings in the United States (a credit in the U.S. official settlements account) even though the purpose was not to intervene in foreign exchange markets to affect the exchange rate between yen and dollars. In addition, government agencies other than the central bank, for example the U.S. Treasury Department through its Exchange Stabilization Fund, occasionally intervene in foreign exchange markets; but we can ignore such cases.

Table 13.9 □ **U.S. Official Settlements Balance, 1960–1994 ($ Millions)**

Year	Net U.S. Official Reserve Assets (Increase [–])	Net Foreign Reserve Assets in U.S. (Increase [+])	Official Settlements Balance
1960	2,145	1,473	3,618
1965	1,225	134	1,359
1970	2,481	6,908	9,389
1975	–849	7,027	6,178
1980	–8,155	15,497	7,342
1985	–3,858	–1,119	–4,977
1990	–2,158	33,910	31,752
1994	5,346	38,912	44,258

Source: *Economic Report of the President 1995; Survey of Current Business,* March 1995.

reserves as *imports* of foreign exchange.) Decreases in U.S. reserves or increases in foreign reserves held in the United States represent credits (think of decreases in U.S. reserves as *exports* of foreign exchange and, therefore, as a credit).[7] Table 13.9 reports the transactions on the U.S. official settlements balance. We shall see later in the chapter that whether governments undertake these transactions depends on whether the exchange rate is fixed or flexible.

The easiest way to see the relationship between the official settlements balance and the rest of the balance-of-payments accounts is through the analogy developed earlier with the transactions of an individual. The balance on the current account represents the relationship between the individual's current income and current expenditures. The capital account represents changes in the individual's borrowing and lending or purchases and sales of assets. Suppose the sum of the individual's current income, borrowing, and revenue from sales of assets exceeds the sum of current expenditures, loans made, and purchases of assets. What will happen to the difference? It will go into the individual's stock of money or cash balances.[8] On the other hand, how does an individual handle a situation in which the sum of current expenditures, loans made, and purchases of assets exceeds the sum of income, borrowing, and revenue from sales of assets? This is possible only if the individual possesses cash balances that can be depleted to cover the shortfall.

---

[7] Over recent years, it has become increasingly common for foreign central banks to hold a portion of their dollar reserves outside the United States. When central banks undertake intervention using these reserves, the U.S. official settlements account does not capture the activity. Because of this phenomenon, changes in the level of reserve assets as reported in the official settlements account have become somewhat less reliable as measures of the extent of intervention to affect the value of other currencies relative to the dollar.

[8] Consider a simple numerical example. Suppose that in a given month an individual earns a salary of $2,000, takes out a new-car loan from the bank for $15,000, and sells a used car for $5,000. During the same month, the individual buys a new car for $15,000 and spends $3,000 on routine expenses (rent, food, clothing, and so on). What must be true about the individual's cash balances? They rise by $4,000, or the difference between $22,000 and $18,000.

Table 13.10 □ **A Country's Current, Capital, and Official Settlements Balances Must Sum to Zero Just Like an Individual's Total Receipts and Total Payments**

Balance-of-Payments Accounts	Individual Transactions
Current-account balance	Current income − current expenditures
+ Capital-account balance	+ Net new borrowing + net revenue from sales of assets
+ Official settlements balance	+ Change in cash balances
Zero	Zero

The transactions on the official settlements account play the same role as increases or decreases in the individual's cash balances: They *compensate* for any differences between total payments and total receipts in the other accounts, as illustrated in Table 13.10. For the individual, the sum of income minus expenditures, borrowing minus lending, revenue from sales minus purchases of assets, and changes in cash balances *must* sum to zero. *(Why?)* In the balance-of-payments accounts, the sum of the current-account balance, the capital-account balance, and the official settlements balance must sum to zero. If the combined balance on the current and capital accounts is in deficit (debits > credits), there must be an offsetting surplus (credits > debits) in the official settlements account. With a surplus in the current and capital accounts, the official settlements account must be in deficit.

When the U.S. Department of Commerce collects the data for the balance-of-payments accounts, many transactions are missed or unreported. This occurs for a variety of reasons. The United States does not monitor closely tourism and imports brought into the United States by travelers, so many goods enter and exit the country unreported. Tax avoidance provides an incentive for some types of capital flows to go undisclosed (and therefore untaxed). These imperfections in data collection are reflected in the **statistical discrepancy,** or the amount by which the sum of the current, capital, and official settlements balances as actually calculated fail to total to zero. The magnitude of the statistical discrepancy has grown over the last few years along with international trade and financial activity. The discrepancy now ranges yearly from several hundred million dollars to around $40 billion, as shown in Table 13.11.

From one perspective, these numbers are quite large; in fact, in nine years since 1960, the U.S. statistical discrepancy was larger than the current-account balance! From another perspective, the statistical discrepancy is remarkably small given the task of accounting for all transactions between U.S. residents and the rest of the world.[9] Once we take the existence of the statistical discrepancy into account, the fundamental relationship that must hold for U.S. transactions with the rest of the world becomes:

---

[9]Case Two at the end of the chapter examines the statistical discrepancies in balance-of-payments statistics more closely.

Table 13.11 □ U.S. Statistical Discrepancy, 1960–1994 ($ Millions)

Year	Current-Account Balance	Capital-Account Balance	Official Settlements Balance	Statistical Discrepancy
1960	2,824	–5,423	3,618	–1,019
1965	5,431	–6,334	1,359	–457
1970	2,331	–12,368	9,389	–219[a]
1975	18,116	–30,211	6,178	5,917
1980	2,317	–36,198	7,342	25,386[a]
1985	–125,372	106,933	–4,977	23,415
1990	–91,748	20,077	31,752	39,919
1994	–155,673	144,669	44,258	–33,255

[a]Small allocations of special drawing rights in 1970 and 1980 are omitted.

Source: *Economic Report of the President 1995*; *Survey of Current Business*, March 1995.

$$\underset{\text{balance}}{\underset{\text{account}}{\text{Current-}}} + \underset{\text{balance}}{\underset{\text{account}}{\text{Capital-}}} + \underset{\text{balance}}{\underset{\text{settlements}}{\text{Official}}} + \underset{}{\underset{\text{discrepancy}}{\text{Statistical}}} = 0. \qquad [13.1]$$

Next, we must address a question that probably has occurred already to the careful reader: If the components of the balance-of-payments accounts always sum to zero, what do we mean by a balance-of-payments surplus or deficit? As a first step toward answering this question, we must recall that each international transaction has two sides and is, therefore, entered *twice* in the double-entry bookkeeping system that comprises the balance-of-payments accounts. This guarantees that Equation 13.1 holds, because any credit entry automatically generates an equal debit entry somewhere in the accounts. The easiest way to see the logic of the double-entry system is to look at some hypothetical transactions.

13.2.4 Double-Entry Bookkeeping: Some Illustrative Transactions

The simplest international transaction from a balance-of-payments perspective is barter, or the exchange of two goods without use of money. Suppose Coca-Cola exports $1 million worth of Coke to Poland in exchange for $1 million worth of Polish beer.[10] How would the Department of Commerce record the transaction in the U.S. balance-of-payments accounts? The soft-drink export is a $1 million credit in the merchandise category of the current account, and the beer import is a $1 million debit in the merchandise category. Note that although trade has increased, the merchandise trade balance and the current-account balance are unaffected—because both debits and credits have risen by the same amount. This occurs whenever both

---

[10]Such transactions are called *countertrade*.

the debit and credit entries for a given transaction occur in the same account. *(How would the transaction appear in Poland's balance-of-payments accounts?)*

Now suppose Coca-Cola exports $1 million worth of Coke to Britain and the British importer pays with a check for the pound equivalent of $1 million, which Coca-Cola deposits in a bank in London. The Coke export is again a $1 million credit entry in the merchandise category of the U.S. current account. But the payment for the Coke—the check—is a capital outflow, a debit in the U.S. capital account because a U.S. resident now owns an asset (the pound bank deposit in London) previously owned by the British importer.[11] The U.S. merchandise trade balance (as well as the current account) shows a $1 million credit entry *(Why?)*, while the U.S. capital account shows a $1 million debit entry *(Why?)*. *(How would the transaction appear in Britain's balance-of-payments accounts?)*

Now consider a third possibility. A private charity in the United States ships $1 million worth of Coke to a foreign country as aid following an earthquake that destroyed the sources of pure drinking water. What happens to the U.S. balance-of-payments accounts? The export of Coke is still a $1 million credit in the merchandise subaccount of the U.S. current account, but the United States expects no payment in return for the aid. So what is the second side of the transaction? This is where the unilateral transfer subaccount comes in; the second entry is a $1 million debit under unilateral transfers. The net effect is an increase of $1 million in the merchandise trade balance but no effect on the current-account balance *(Why?)*. *(Show the effect of the transaction on the recipient country's balance-of-payments accounts.)*

Now consider a transaction that occurs solely in the capital account. Suppose Coca-Cola buys a $1 million building in London to open a production facility there. The firm pays the building's owner with a check for $1 million drawn on a New York bank. The U.S. capital account shows a debit and a credit of $1 million. The debit represents Coca-Cola's "import" of the title to the building, and the credit Coke's "export" of ownership of the funds represented by the check. *(Show the entries in Britain's balance-of-payments accounts.)*

As these transactions illustrate, every transaction creates *both* a credit *and* a debit entry in each country's balance-of-payments accounts, and the two entries always are equal in magnitude. Therefore, total credits must always equal total debits (as in any double-entry bookkeeping system), although the debit and credit entries from any given transaction do not necessarily occur within the same account. But if total credits equal total debits, what do we mean by a balance-of-payments surplus or deficit?

13.3 Surpluses and Deficits in the Balance of Payments

The balance-of-payments accounts must always "balance" in the sense that total credits equal total debits. Just as for an individual, total receipts must equal total payments once changes in asset holdings and cash balances are taken into account.

---

[11]Alternatively, Coca-Cola could exchange the pound deposit for a dollar deposit at a New York bank. In this case, the New York bank would now be holding $1 million worth of pounds. For our purposes, this would not affect the way the transaction is recorded in the balance-of-payments accounts.

This type of balance in the balance-of-payments accounts is trivial and arises more from accounting and bookkeeping conventions than from the theory of international trade and finance. The fact that an individual's total receipts must equal total payments tells us very little about the individual's economic circumstances. Likewise, the fact that total receipts from the rest of the world must equal total payments to the rest of the world reveals little about a country's economic circumstances.

Examination of the balance (or lack of balance) in the balance of payments in the *nontrivial* sense requires distinguishing between two types of transactions: autonomous and accommodating ones. We refer to transactions that individuals, firms, or government agencies undertake for their own purposes (such as utility maximization by individuals, asset portfolio decisions, profit maximization by firms, and foreign policy goals by government) and whose goals are unrelated to the balance of payments as **autonomous, or independently motivated, transactions.** These transactions represent a routine part of the international trade and finance that comprise world economic activity. A U.S. resident buying a pair of Italian shoes, a U.S. firm selling a bond to a German resident, and the U.S. government sending foreign aid to Israel constitute actions taken for their own interests and independently of their effects on the balance of payments. The transactions may affect the balance of payments, but the effects are unintentional and not the goal of the transaction itself.

For our purposes, we can identify the sum of the current-account balance, the capital-account balance, and the statistical discrepancy as the balance on autonomous transactions.[12] The current and nonofficial capital accounts include all the trade and finance activities undertaken by individuals, firms, and governments without regard for the balance-of-payments effects. The statistical discrepancy measures current- and capital-account transactions that have been mismeasured or omitted.[13] The sum of autonomous transactions is the country's balance of payments (BOP) with the rest of the world:

$$\begin{matrix} \text{Current-} \\ \text{account} \\ \text{balance} \end{matrix} + \begin{matrix} \text{Capital-} \\ \text{account} \\ \text{balance} \end{matrix} + \begin{matrix} \text{Statistical} \\ \text{discrepancy} \end{matrix} = \text{Balance of payments.} \qquad [13.2]$$

If total autonomous credits exceed total autonomous debits, a **balance-of-payments surplus** (BOP > 0) exists. An excess of autonomous debits over credits is a **balance-of-payments deficit** (BOP < 0). The balance of payments shows whether a country's trade and finance activities (that is, its autonomous transactions) involve receipts from foreigners in excess of payments to foreigners (a surplus) or payments to foreigners in excess of receipts from foreigners (a deficit).

---

[12]As noted in footnotes 2, 4, and 5, official transactions actually are recorded in a separate subaccount *within* the capital account. We treat official transactions separately; when we speak of the capital accoun we mean the nonofficial capital account.

[13]We attribute the statistical discrepancy to mismeasurement in the current and capital accounts rather than in the official settlements account because the last includes only official government transactions subject to few measurement errors or omissions.

In each of the illustrative transactions discussed above, the net effect on the balance of payments is zero. In the first, the Coke-for-beer barter transaction, both the debit and the credit sides of the current account rise by $1 million, leaving the current-account balance unchanged. The capital account and the statistical discrepancy remain unaffected; therefore, Equation 13.2 implies that the transaction does not change the country's balance of payments. In the second transaction, in which the exported Coke is paid for by a check deposited in a London bank, the current-account balance rises by the $1 million credit while the capital-account balance falls by a $1 million debit; again the two parts of the transaction offset, leaving the overall balance (the left-hand side of Equation 13.2) unaffected. In the third transaction, the charity shipment of Coke is recorded as a $1 million credit in merchandise exports and a $1 million debit in unilateral transfers within the current account, leaving the current account and the balance of payments unaffected. In the fourth transaction, the purchase of a factory abroad appears as a $1 million debit and the payment by check as a $1 million credit, both in the U.S. capital account. For all four transactions, *both* the debit and credit entries occur on the left-hand side of Equation 13.2. All the entries are independent or autonomous, undertaken by private parties for reasons unrelated to the balance of payments.

The second class of transactions is **accommodating, or compensatory, transactions.** These are official government actions taken primarily for balance-of-payments purposes; they correspond to the transactions in the official settlements account—changes in the stocks of central banks' foreign exchange reserves. A comparison of Equations 13.1 and 13.2 reveals the relationship between the official settlements balance and the balance of payments. Rearranging Equation 13.1, the sum of the current-account balance, the capital-account balance, and the statistical discrepancy equals the *negative* of the official settlements balance:

$$
\begin{array}{l}
\text{Current-} \\
\text{account} \\
\text{balance}
\end{array}
+
\begin{array}{l}
\text{Capital-} \\
\text{account} \\
\text{balance}
\end{array}
+
\begin{array}{l}
\text{Statistical} \\
\text{discrepancy}
\end{array}
=
\begin{array}{l}
-\text{Official} \\
\text{settlements} \\
\text{balance.}
\end{array}
\qquad [13.3]
$$

Combining this with Equation 13.2, the balance of payments just equals the negative of the official settlements balance:

$$
\text{Balance of payments} = -\text{ Official settlements balance.} \qquad [13.4]
$$

The balance of payments represents the difference between credits and debits for autonomous transactions undertaken by individuals, firms, and governments. Any deficit or surplus must be "accommodated," or "compensated for," by official transactions on the official settlements account because a country's total receipts from foreigners must equal its total payments to foreigners (that is, the balance-of-payments accounts must balance in the trivial, double-entry bookkeeping sense). To highlight this point, we can rewrite Equation 13.4 as the explicit relationship between autonomous and accommodating transactions:

$$
\text{Balance on autonomous transactions} + \text{Balance on accommodating transactions} = 0. \quad [13.5]
$$

To understand better the significance of the distinction between autonomous and accommodating transactions in defining and interpreting the balance of payments, it is useful to relate the ideas and definitions developed in this chapter back to Chapter Twelve's model of the demand for and supply of foreign exchange.

13.4 The Balance of Payments and the Foreign Exchange Market

Before more explicitly introducing the demand for and supply of foreign exchange as a way to view the balance of payments, we need to distinguish between the overall, or multilateral, balance-of-payments accounts and the bilateral balance-of-payments accounts. The **overall, or multilateral, balance-of-payments accounts** are the ones discussed so far; they record all the transactions between U.S. residents and the rest of the world as a whole. The **bilateral balance-of-payments accounts** report receipts and payments between the United States and one other country; so there is one set of bilateral balance-of-payments accounts for each country with which the United States trades. The multilateral balance-of-payments accounts simply aggregate the bilateral ones. In relating the balance-of-payments accounts to demand and supply in foreign exchange markets, it is convenient to assume initially that there are only two countries (such as the United States and Britain) to be able to give specific names to the currencies involved.

Recall from Chapter Twelve that the foreign exchange market is in equilibrium when the quantity of foreign-currency-denominated deposits individuals want to hold in their asset portfolios just equals the quantity of foreign-currency-denominated deposits available. Figure 13.1 reproduces Figure 12.8, the graphical representation of such an equilibrium, using pounds as the foreign currency.

The supply of foreign-currency deposits, represented by the vertical line $S^{£}$, is determined by government policies and the lending decisions of banks, independently of the exchange rate. The demand for foreign-currency deposits reflects the asset-portfolio decisions of individuals and firms based on the interest parity conditions from section 12.4. The higher the value of the exchange rate (for given values of $i^{\$}$, $i^{£}$, e^{e}, and e^{f}), the higher the expected rate of return on domestic-currency deposits and the more attractive those become relative to foreign-currency deposits. *(Why? For a review, see section 12.5.1.)* Therefore, we represent the demand curve for foreign-currency deposits as a negatively sloped line. Changes in interest rates, the expected future spot rate, or the forward rate shift the demand curve in the directions indicated by the (+) and (–) signs in Figure 13.1, as portfolio owners respond to changes in the expected rates of return on the two types of deposits.

When quantity demanded and supplied of a good are not equal, what usually happens to bring a market back into equilibrium? Given no interference with the forces of supply and demand, price adjusts to equate quantity demanded and quantity supplied. This is the case in foreign exchange markets when the exchange rate (the domestic-currency price of foreign currency) is flexible. If the quantity supplied of foreign exchange exceeds the quantity demanded (as at e_1), the domestic currency appreciates (e falls); if the quantity demanded of foreign exchange exceeds the quantity supplied (as at e_2), the domestic currency depreciates. *(Explain why, using the interest parity conditions.)* In

Figure 13.1 □ Equilibrium in the Foreign Exchange Market under a Flexible Exchange Regime

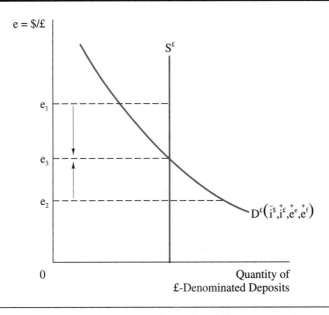

The exchange rate moves to equate the quantity demanded and supplied of pound-denominated deposits. The equilibrium exchange rate is e_3. At e_1, individuals are unwilling to hold the existing supply of pound-denominated deposits. As individuals try to exchange their excess pound-denominated deposits for deposits denominated in dollars, the dollar price of pounds falls toward e_3. At e_2, individuals want to hold more than the existing supply of pound-denominated deposits. Individuals enter the market trying to exchange dollar-denominated for pound-denominated deposits, thereby bidding up the dollar price of pounds to e_3.

contrast, under a fixed exchange rate regime, some other mechanism must equilibrate the foreign exchange market. In the next two sections, we examine the relationship among the balance of payments, demand and supply in foreign exchange markets, and exchange rates, first under a flexible and then under a fixed exchange rate regime.

13.4.1 The Balance of Payments, Foreign Exchange Markets, and a Flexible Exchange Rate

The demand for foreign exchange as developed in Chapter Twelve reflects autonomous transactions in the balance of payments. In these transactions, individuals and firms exchange goods, services, and financial assets, paid for with deposits denominated in various currencies.[14] Portfolio owners hold foreign-currency-denominated deposits to buy foreign goods and services, to earn interest on the deposits,

---

[14]Of course, some transactions are arranged using barter and others using actual currency rather than payment by check, but the overwhelming majority of international transactions are financed by check or bank deposit.

Figure 13.2 ▫ **Balance-of-Payments Equilibrium under a Flexible Exchange Rate**

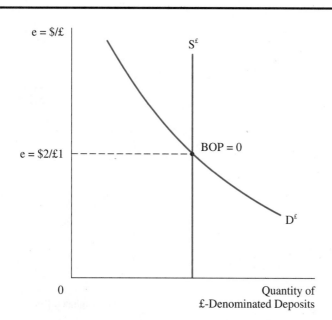

At $e = \$2/£1$, individuals willingly hold the pound-denominated deposits they receive in payment for exports and other transactions. Autonomous debits match autonomous credits in the balance of payments (BOP = 0).

to purchase other foreign assets (bonds, factories, and so forth), and to speculate by holding foreign exchange in the hope of an appreciation against the dollar. These transaction categories correspond to the various categories of autonomous transactions in the current and capital accounts of the balance of payments. The balance of payments is in equilibrium when individuals are willing to hold as assets any foreign-currency-denominated deposits received in payment for international transactions.

Consider a hypothetical transaction. A resident of Britain uses a £1,000 check to purchase a bond issued by a U.S. firm. The foreign exchange market is in equilibrium at $e = \$2/£1$ as in Figure 13.2. If the firm selling the bond is content to hold the £1,000 in its asset portfolio and deposits the check in a London bank, the total demand for pound-denominated deposits remains unchanged. The total of those deposits simply has been reallocated from the individual who purchased the bond to the firm that sold it.

The transaction appears in the U.S. balance-of-payments accounts as a capital-account credit of $2,000 (= £1,000 · \$2/£1) and a capital-account debit of $2,000. *(Why?)*[15] But suppose the seller of the bond does not want to hold the pounds and

---

[15]The bookkeeping for each country's balance-of-payments accounts is conducted in the domestic currency.

Figure 13.3 □ **Appreciation of the Domestic Currency**

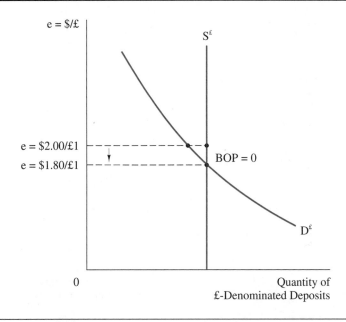

The dollar appreciates from $2/£1 to $1.80/£1 to encourage individuals to hold more pound-denominated deposits in their asset portfolios. The balance of payments is in equilibrium at e = $1.80/£1, where autonomous debits equal autonomous credits.

instead sells the pound-denominated deposit to the firm's New York bank in return for a $2,000 deposit. If e = $2/£1 is the equilibrium exchange rate, by definition someone *will* be content to hold the pound-denominated deposit, perhaps the New York bank or one of its customers. *(Why?)* Again the total demand for pound-denominated deposits remains unchanged. Portfolio owners are content to hold $S^£$ pound-denominated deposits (including the £1,000 involved in our hypothetical transaction) at e = $2/£1. The autonomous demand for pound-denominated deposits equals the quantity available. The British resident makes available the £1,000 deposit, and the U.S. firm or its bank is willing to hold that deposit. The current- and capital-account balances sum to zero.

If, given current interest rates and expected and forward exchange rates, *no one* wants to hold the pound-denominated deposit, e = $2/£1 is *not* the equilibrium exchange rate. The firm that received the pound-denominated deposit in payment for the bond will be willing to sell it for *less* than $2,000, receiving less than $2 for each £1. The pound depreciates against the dollar (see Figure 13.3). If the equilibrium value of the exchange rate is, say, $1.80/£1, the U.S. balance of payments reports the transaction as a $1,800 capital-account credit for "export" of the bond (= £1,000 · $1.80/£1) and a capital-account debit of $1,800 for "importing" ownership of the

Figure 13.4 □ **Depreciation of the Domestic Currency**

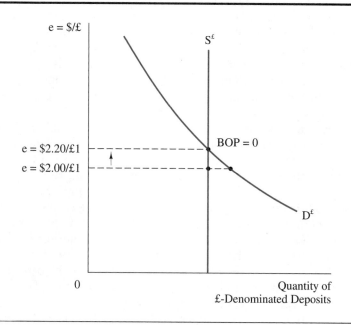

The dollar depreciates from $2/£1 to $2.20/£1 to discourage individuals from holding pound-denominated deposits in their asset portfolios. At e = $2.20/£1, autonomous debits equal autonomous credits and the balance of payments is in equilibrium.

deposit. Again autonomous debits equal autonomous credits; the balance of payments is in equilibrium at e = $1.80/£1.

On the other hand, if at current interest rates and expected and forward exchange rates, many portfolio owners want to purchase the pound-denominated deposit at a price of e = $2/£1 to add to their portfolios, the price of the deposit will be bid up. Each pound will bring the firm more than $2; and the pound will appreciate against the dollar as in Figure 13.4. If the equilibrium exchange rate turns out to be $2.20, the transaction appears in the U.S. balance-of-payments accounts as a $2,200 capital-account credit and a $2,200 capital-account debit. Autonomous debits and credits in the current and capital accounts remain equal, so the balance of payments is in equilibrium at $2.20/£1.

In both cases (Figures 13.3 and 13.4), the exchange rate adjusts until someone becomes willing to hold the pound-denominated deposit at current interest rates, although not necessarily the same firm that originally received it in payment for the bond exported to Britain.

Under a flexible exchange rate regime, governments allow the market forces of supply and demand to determine the price of foreign exchange, or the exchange rate between dollars and pounds. The exchange rate adjusts until individuals willingly hold the existing supply of pound-denominated deposits in their asset portfolios. As long as individuals and firms are willing to hold the existing supply of deposits at the current exchange rate, autonomous credits equal autonomous debits and the balance of payments balances (BOP = 0). A flexible exchange rate guarantees that the equality between autonomous debits and credits will hold and, therefore, that the balance of payments will be neither in surplus nor in deficit. This adjustment process occurs in each foreign exchange market where the dollar exchanges for the currency of a trading partner. Often the dollar appreciates against some currencies (to eliminate a bilateral U.S. balance-of-payments surplus) and depreciates against others (to eliminate a bilateral U.S. BOP deficit).

Another perspective on the balance of payments under a flexible exchange regime focuses on the official settlements account. Recall that the balance of payments equals the negative of the official settlements balance (see Equation 13.4). The transactions on the official settlements account represent changes in the central bank's stock of foreign exchange reserves. The cause of changes in the level of these reserves is intervention in foreign exchange markets to maintain the exchange rate at a level away from equilibrium (see section 12.7).[16] Under a flexible rate regime, authorities make no effort to hold the exchange rate away from its equilibrium level and, therefore, engage in no foreign exchange intervention that would lead to changes in the stocks of foreign exchange reserves. With no changes in the official stocks of reserves, the official settlements balance equals zero—another way of saying that the balance of payments is in equilibrium (BOP = 0).

Under a perfectly flexible exchange rate regime, the balance-of-payments concept is not very meaningful, at least in the long run, since the exchange rate always will move to keep the balance of payments balanced or in equilibrium. "Balance" in the balance of payments is just another way of looking at equilibrium in the market for foreign exchange. Since a perfectly flexible exchange rate, by definition, guarantees foreign exchange market equilibrium, equilibrium in the balance of payments also follows.

This does *not* imply that either the merchandise trade balance or the current account necessarily will be in balance under a flexible exchange rate regime. A current-account deficit (or surplus) merely requires an offsetting surplus (or deficit) on the capital account. There is a widespread misconception, often repeated in the popular press, that the theory of flexible exchange rates claims such a system will balance either the merchandise trade account or the current account. Since the move away from a fixed exchange rate regime in the early 1970s, deficits and surpluses have been observed widely in the merchandise trade and current accounts of many countries. This is the basis of frequently heard claims that flexible exchange rates do not work the way economic theory suggests. This argument reveals two misunderstandings. First, as we have noted, the theory of flexible exchange rates does *not* claim that deficits or surpluses in the merchandise trade or current accounts will disappear under flexible exchange rates, only that balance-of-payments deficits or surpluses will. Second, the exchange rate regime in use since the early 1970s,

---

[16]See footnote 6 above.

Figure 13.5 □ A Fixed Exchange Rate above the Equilibrium Rate

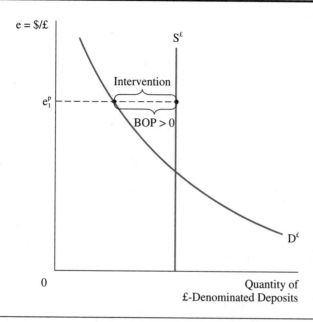

At e_1^p, individuals are unwilling to hold the existing supply of pounds. To maintain the exchange rate at e_1^p, a central bank must stand ready to absorb the excess supply of pounds. Individuals holding unwanted pound-denominated deposits can exchange them with the central bank for dollar-denominated deposits at a rate of e_1^p. The intervention is recorded in the U.S. balance-of-payments accounts as an accommodating debit in the official settlements account, accommodating the surplus (BOP > 0) in the autonomous current and capital accounts.

although much more flexible than the earlier system, is *not* a purely flexible exchange rate regime. Monetary authorities still intervene in foreign exchange markets to affect exchange rates, although the extent and frequency of intervention differ widely over time and across countries.

13.4.2 The Balance of Payments, Foreign Exchange Markets, and a Fixed Exchange Rate

Under a fixed exchange rate regime, the demand for and supply of foreign exchange still reflect the autonomous transactions in the balance of payments. However, governments do not allow the forces of demand and supply to determine the exchange rate; instead, policy makers *peg*, or fix, the exchange rate at a certain level by intervening in foreign exchange markets to buy and sell assets denominated in various currencies (for a review, see the discussion in section 12.7).

Figure 13.5 reproduces Figure 12.10, showing an exchange rate pegged above the equilibrium rate. Consider again a U.S. firm that sells a £1,000 bond to a resident of

Britain and receives payment by a check for £1,000. At the fixed exchange rate, e_1^P, the firm will not want to hold the pound-denominated deposit in its portfolio. Overall, the quantity supplied of pounds in the foreign exchange market exceeds the quantity demanded. Portfolio owners are not willing to hold the existing supply of pound-denominated deposits because the expected rate of return on dollar deposits is higher than that on pound deposits. Because the exchange rate is pegged, market forces cannot restore equilibrium by bidding down the value of pound-denominated deposits, as happened under a flexible rate regime in section 13.4.1. If the dollar price of pounds is to remain at e_1^P, either the U.S. or British central bank, or both, must intervene to eliminate the excess supply of pounds. The intervention consists of permitting those holding unwanted pound-denominated deposits to exchange them for dollar-denominated deposits with the central bank at a rate of e_1^P.

Under the rules of the fixed exchange rate system that governed the international monetary system from the end of the Second World War until 1971—called the **Bretton Woods system**—each central bank was responsible for intervening to maintain the value of its currency relative to the U.S. dollar. In other words, with the situation depicted in Figure 13.5, the Bank of England, the British central bank, intervened. Anyone holding unwanted deposits denominated in pounds could take them to the Bank of England and exchange them for deposits denominated in dollars, receiving e_1^P dollars per pound. To purchase the pounds, the Bank of England would use dollar-denominated deposits from its stock of foreign exchange reserves held in the United States. The size of the purchase would equal the difference between the quantity demanded and the quantity supplied of pounds at e_1^P. The result would be a decrease in the Bank of England's stock of dollar reserves held in the United States. Recall that such a decrease in British reserves would appear as a debit in the U.S. official settlements balance because that account records changes in *both* U.S. official reserves and foreign official reserves held in the United States (see section 13.2.3). The debit in the official settlements balance just matches the surplus (BOP > 0) in the U.S. balance of payments, as suggested by Equation 13.4.

Consider our hypothetical transaction in which a U.S. firm receives a £1,000 check in payment for a bond sold in Britain, and assume that e_1^P = $2.50/£1. The firm sells the pound-denominated deposit to the Bank of England in return for a $2,500 dollar-denominated deposit. The net effect on the U.S. balance-of-payments accounts is an autonomous capital-account credit of $2,500 for "export" of the bond (= £1,000 · $2.50/£1) and an official settlements debit of the same amount for the Bank of England's sale of $2,500 of its dollar reserves. *(Why?)* Using Equation 13.4, the result is a U.S. balance-of-payments surplus of $2,500. *(What is the corresponding situation in Britain's balance-of-payments accounts?)*

The analysis of a balance-of-payments deficit under a fixed exchange rate proceeds similarly. Figure 13.6 repeats Figure 12.11's depiction of an exchange rate fixed below the equilibrium level. At the relatively low dollar price of pounds represented by the fixed exchange rate, e_2^P, portfolio owners want to hold more than the existing stock of pound-denominated deposits. Individuals wanting to buy pound-denominated deposits are unable to do so at the current exchange rate. The U.S. balance of payments with Britain shows a deficit. With no intervention, the dollar will depreciate against the pound. To prevent depreciation of the dollar, one of the central

Figure 13.6 □ **A Fixed Exchange Rate below the Equilibrium Rate**

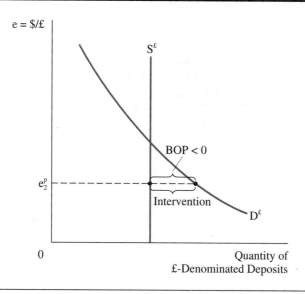

At e_2^P, the quantity demanded of pounds exceeds the quantity supplied. The exchange rate can be maintained at e_2^P only if a central bank supplies pounds to the market through intervention. Individuals wanting pound-denominated deposits can purchase them at the central bank at a price of e_2^P. The U.S. balance-of-payments accounts record the intervention as an accommodating official settlements credit, reflecting the BOP deficit (BOP < 0).

banks must intervene to supply pound-denominated deposits to the foreign exchange market. The Bank of England may sell pound-denominated deposits in exchange for dollar-denominated deposits and add the dollars to its foreign exchange reserves in the United States (a credit in the U.S. official settlements account), or the U.S. Federal Reserve may sell pound-denominated deposits from its foreign exchange reserves (also a credit in the U.S. official settlements account). In either case, the balance-of-payments deficit at e_2^P reflected in the excess demand for pounds is just matched by a credit on the official settlements balance of the U.S. balance of payments, as suggested by Equation 13.4.

Suppose a U.S. resident buys £5,000 worth of stock in a British firm. At the pegged exchange rate (say, $1.50/£1), the individual is unable to buy a pound-denominated deposit with which to pay for the stock because the quantity demanded of such deposits exceeds the quantity available. But the Bank of England can prevent appreciation of the pound by selling a £5,000 deposit to the individual at the pegged exchange rate (at e = $1.50/£1, the £5,000 deposit will exchange for a $7,500 deposit). The transaction's final effect on the U.S. balance of payments will consist of a $7,500 autonomous capital-account debit for the "imported" ownership of the stock and an accommodating $7,500 official settlements credit for the increase in dollar reserves held by the Bank of England. From Equation 13.4, the United States has a $7,500 balance-of-payments deficit (BOP < 0) with Britain. *(How would the transaction affect Britain's balance-of-payments accounts?)*

Earlier we noted that under flexible exchange rates a currency may simultaneously appreciate against some currencies and depreciate against others. With a fixed exchange regime, a similar phenomenon occurs when the quantity demanded of some currencies exceeds the quantity supplied while for other currencies the opposite holds true. A central bank may find it necessary to intervene by simultaneously purchasing one currency and selling another from its reserves. Suppose, for example, that the United States wants to maintain fixed exchange rates between the dollar and the pound and between the dollar and the Deutsche mark. If demand and supply in the two foreign exchange markets create pressure for the dollar to depreciate against the mark (excess demand for marks) and to appreciate against the pound (excess supply of pounds), the Federal Reserve can intervene by selling DM deposits from its reserves and purchasing pound-denominated deposits. The balance on the official settlements account will represent the net change in U.S. reserves (assuming the Bank of England and the Bundesbank undertake no intervention).

Case One
Capital Flight

As the transportation and information costs involved in foreign investments have fallen, the volume of worldwide capital flows has increased. This growing internationalization can increase the efficiency of the world economy as capital becomes better able to flow to areas where it will be most productive. For countries in economic crisis, however, the ability of investors to move funds abroad can aggravate an already bad situation. When asset holders fear political instability, currency devaluation, or tax increases, sudden and large capital outflows can result. For example, during the 1980s several countries in Latin America suffering from severe debt problems, high unemployment, and astronomical rates of inflation also endured enormous capital outflows in response to the dismal outlooks for their domestic economies.

Such capital flows are called **capital flight.** Defining and measuring capital flight can be difficult, especially separating it from the "normal" capital flows associated with international trade and financial activity. Table 13.12 reports estimates of capital flight from 15 indebted countries, along with estimates of the countries' external debt. The estimates probably considerably underestimate actual capital outflows. Many techniques used to accomplish capital flight are illegal; therefore, much of the activity is unreported and conducted in cash to make tracing difficult.

How do the mechanics of capital flight work when capital outflows are illegal? One of the most common techniques involves under-invoicing of exports. Suppose a Brazilian manufacturer exported 100,000 cruzados worth of goods, but reported

Table 13.12 □ **Capital Flight and External Debt, 1988 ($ Billions)**

Country	Total External Debt	Capital Flight (Stock of Assets Abroad)	Capital Flight/ External Debt
Argentina	56.8	46	.81
Bolivia	5.5	2	.36
Chile	21.2	2	.09
Côte d'Ivoire	13.5	0	.00
Morocco	20.7	3	.14
Nigeria	28.7	20	.70
Peru	18.0	2	.11
Philippines	29.9	23	.77
Yugoslavia	23.5	6	.26
Brazil	124.0	31	.25
Colombia	17.0	7	.41
Uruguay	4.3	4	.93
Mexico	108.0	84	.78
Venezuela	36.5	58	1.59
Ecuador	10.5	7	.67

Source: *The International Economy* 3 (July–August 1989), p. 12; data from World Bank and Morgan Stanley.

only 75,000 cruzados on the invoice.[17] The foreign buyer paid the unreported portion in dollars, which the exporter easily placed in a foreign bank. Other techniques are even simpler: for example, carrying suitcases of foreign currency abroad on trips when border checks are lax.

The relationship between external debt and capital flight became a matter of some controversy during the 1980s. Some observers of the indebted countries feared that loans made to the countries were being misappropriated by individuals and transferred back to the industrial countries in the form of capital-flight deposits rather than going toward debt payments or economic improvements. Note that for 7 of the 15 countries in Table 13.12, capital flight amounted to over half the value of the country's total external debt.

The economies in transition share capital-flight problems with other developing countries. World Bank officials estimated that between $10 billion and $15 billion (about 15 percent of the economy's GDP) left Russia in flight capital in 1992 alone. The existence of such funds—much of it belonging to ex-Communist Party officials—creates Western resistance to aiding Russia by rescheduling or forgiving its foreign debt. The fact that the capital flight from Russia exceeds the cash aid that foreign governments and multilateral agencies have provided Russia makes it easy for donors to argue that the aid is not needed or not well used.

[17]Brazil now uses a currency unit called the *real*, but during the 1980s the country used the cruzado.

Obviously, capital flight can impose heavy costs on an economy. On the other hand, it acts as a symptom that economic policies need to be altered to make the domestic economy more attractive. Unfortunately, governments of countries suffering from capital flight tend to attack the symptom (by instituting tighter rules and enforcement over capital outflows) instead of the cause (by fixing the policies that cause pessimism about the domestic economy). Economies that have overcome capital flight problems have done so by creating a stable monetary environment so asset owners feel safe holding domestic-currency assets, conducting macroeconomic policies in a way to foster domestic saving through attractive domestic interest rates, and making sure taxes and trade regulations are not punitive to savers and exporters.

Case Two
Why Don't the World Current and Capital Accounts Balance?

We have seen that there is no reason to expect a country's current account always to balance. If the exchange rate is flexible, the balance of payments will balance, but a current-account surplus or deficit can be offset by a corresponding deficit or surplus on the capital account. However, if we consider the current account for the world economy *as a whole,* the current account should equal zero. After all, one country's exports must be another country's imports, and vice versa; so worldwide debits on the current account should equal worldwide credits. Of course, errors occur in gathering and compiling statistics, but until the early 1970s discrepancies were relatively small. Since then, the size of the discrepancy has grown in size, and the world current-account balance consistently has shown a deficit. Apparently the deficits of individual countries are being overestimated and/or countries with surpluses are underestimating those surpluses.

Very large statistical discrepancies concern policy makers, because economic policies based on faulty estimates can damage rather than improve the functioning of the world economy. The International Monetary Fund set up a panel in the 1980s to study the problem and suggest improved data-gathering techniques. The panel found that the increasing integration of international financial markets allowed more transactions, especially capital flows, to slip through the cracks of data collection. In addition, illegal activities such as drug trafficking and tax evasion were creating incentives for concealment. The particular transactions that appeared most responsible for the discrepancy were unreported shipping income (especially by Greece, Hong Kong, and Eastern Europe) and unreported portfolio and direct investment income (especially by U.S. investors). The IMF panel made a number of recommendations for improvement. The size of the discrepancy fell during the late 1980s, but then started to grow again.

Similar problems apply to the balance-of-payments statistics for individual countries. In 1986, U.S. and Canadian figures for U.S. exports to Canada differed by

$12 billion, about half of the U.S. trade deficit with Canada and about 7 percent of the entire U.S. trade deficit at the time. Investigators found that U.S. truckers carrying exports into Canada often did not stop to file export declarations with U.S. customs officials but did record their cargoes with Canadian officials. As a result, U.S. officials reported a $23.3 billion trade deficit with Canada while Canada reported an $11.3 billion trade surplus with the United States. How have government officials solved the problem? The United States now gets its data on exports to Canada from Canadian figures on imports from the United States.[18]

Case Three
The United States as a Debtor

A country's **net foreign wealth,** or **net international investment position,** equals the difference between the value of foreign assets the country's residents own and the value of domestic assets owned by foreigners. Unlike the purchases and sales of assets recorded in a country's capital account, net foreign wealth or international investment position represents the accumulation of asset ownership over time; in other words, while transactions in the capital account are flows, net foreign wealth or international investment position is a stock. A country's net foreign wealth is negative whenever foreigners own more assets in the country than the country's residents own abroad. This seems straightforward. However, controversy surrounds the measurement of U.S. net foreign wealth. What is the value of U.S. assets owned by foreigners, and what is the value of foreign assets owned by Americans? When did the United States become a debtor in the sense of having a negative net foreign wealth? And how big is the debt?

There are at least three ways of valuing assets. Until recently, U.S. Department of Commerce statistics valued assets at historical cost, or their original purchase price. In other words, if a U.S. firm bought a factory in Britain in 1950, government statistics still reported the value of that asset in 1990 at the original 1950 purchase price. Most economists agree this is a poor way to measure the value of assets. And because most U.S. purchases of foreign assets occurred in years prior to the bulk of foreign purchases of U.S. assets, measuring at historical cost tends to understate the value of U.S.-owned foreign assets relative to foreign-owned U.S. assets.

The two alternate methods of valuing assets attempt to estimate current values rather than relying on values at the time of purchase. One current-valuation method estimates assets' current cost, or the cost of purchasing them now. The other method estimates market value, or the price for which each asset could be sold now. Both measures are difficult to estimate, but conceptually superior to the old historical-cost

---

[18]John Urquhart, "Canada Estimates U.S. Trade Deficit in 1986 Was Overstated by $12 Billion," *The Wall Street Journal,* March 10, 1987. For evidence that U.S. exports generally are under-reported, see the Ott article in the chapter references.

Table 13.13 □ U.S. International Investment Position ($ Billions)

Year	Historical Cost			Current Cost			Market Value		
	U.S. Assets Abroad	Foreign Assets in U.S.	U.S. Net Foreign Wealth	U.S. Assets Abroad	Foreign Assets in U.S.	U.S. Net Foreign Wealth	U.S. Assets Abroad	Foreign Assets in U.S.	U.S.Net Foreign Wealth
1976	347.2	263.6	83.6						
1977	379.1	306.4	72.7						
1978	447.8	371.7	76.1						
1979	510.6	416.1	94.5						
1980	606.9	500.8	106.1						
1981	719.6	576.5	143.1						
1982	838.1	688.6	149.5	1,100.6	736.6	364.0	954.9	696.4	258.5
1983	887.5	781.5	106.0	1,169.2	1,068.3	337.4	831.8	800.7	267.6
1984	895.9	892.6	3.3	1,177.5	1,081.8	232.9	944.7	905.9	175.9
1985	949.7	1,061.1	−111.4	1,296.4	1,171.1	125.3	1,288.3	1,159.8	128.5
1986	1,073.3	1,341.1	−267.8	1,468.8	1,434.2	34.6	1,566.4	1,441.3	125.1
1987	1,167.8	1,536.0	−368.2	1,625.4	1,648.2	−22.8	1,709.0	1,650.9	58.1
1988	1,253.7	1,786.2	−532.5	1,773.0	1,917.8	−144.8	1,935.9	1,935.0	0.9
1989				1,979.0	2,230.4	−251.4	2,236.7	2,328.5	−91.8
1990				2,066.9	2,318.3	−251.4	2,165.7	2,389.8	−224.1
1991				2,137.0	2,486.5	−349.5	2,300.2	2,668.9	−368.7
1992				2,149.6	2,657.5	−507.9	2,267.3	2,857.3	−590.0
1993				2,370.4	2,926.2	−555.7	2,647.4	3,155.1	−507.7

Source: *Economic Report of the President*, various issues.

method. When U.S. net foreign wealth became negative and by how much depend on the measure used, as reported in Table 13.13.

Although the U.S. international investment position has been negative since some point during the 1980s by all three measures reported in Table 13.13, the United States continued to earn positive current net income on its foreign investments until 1994. That is, U.S. owners of foreign assets earned more income from those assets than foreign owners of U.S. assets earned each year until 1994 (see Table 13.5).

The United States' negative net foreign wealth position often is compared with the debt of developing countries. U.S. external debt is equivalent in size to just over one-fourth of the total external debt of all developing economies ($1.9 trillion)—making the United States by far the world's largest debtor. If the developing country debt threatened the stability of those economies and the world financial system, as we saw in Chapter Eleven, must not the same be true of the U.S. external debt? Not necessarily. First, the U.S. debt, though large in absolute terms, remains relatively small compared with the U.S. economy, while several developing countries' debts equal many times their respective annual GDPs. Second, the U.S. debt is denominated in dollars, the country's domestic currency, while the developing countries' owe debt denominated in foreign currencies, meaning those economies must run current-account surpluses to earn the foreign exchange to make their debt payments. Finally, whether or not debt presents a problem depends on the uses to which borrowed funds are put. For countries with a comparative advantage in future production (that is, low current income but plentiful investment opportunities), borrowing provides a way to use those opportunities. The projects funded by such borrowing earn returns sufficient to repay the loans and make both debtors and creditors better off by creating gains from intertemporal trade. Borrowing to finance consumption beyond a country's income, on the other hand, fails to generate returns to repay the loans and leads to debt problems.

Case Four
U.S. Foreign Exchange Intervention, April–June 1995

Each quarter, the U.S. Federal Reserve Bank of New York publishes a report, "Treasury and Federal Reserve Foreign Exchange Operations," that outlines U.S. intervention activity in foreign exchange markets over the preceding quarter. The following excerpts summarize that activity over the second quarter of 1995.

> The U.S. monetary authorities intervened in the foreign exchange markets on three occasions during the period—April 3, April 5, and May 31—purchasing a total of $3.6 billion against the German mark and the Japanese yen. On each occasion, the U.S. monetary authorities' purchases of dollars were divided evenly between the Federal Reserve System and the U.S. Treasury Department's Exchange Stabilization Fund (ESF).[19] In other operations, the Mexican authorities drew a total of $5 billion on their medium-term swap facility with the ESF. The Bank of Mexico also renewed its short-term swaps with the Federal Reserve and the ESF, each for $1 billion, for an additional ninety days. . . .
>
> On April 3, with the dollar trading at ¥86.50, the Federal Reserve Bank of New York's Foreign Exchange Desk entered the market in Asian trading on behalf of the U.S. monetary authorities, purchasing $500 million against the yen from dealers in Tokyo, Singapore, Hong Kong, and Sydney. The dollar rallied briefly following the intervention, but gave up all of its gains by the New York open. Later that day, at about 11:20 A.M. in New York, the Desk entered the market again, buying $750 million against the mark and $250 million against the yen. The dollar-yen operation was coordinated with the Bank of Japan. . . . Overall, the U.S. monetary authorities purchased $1.5 billion during the course of the global trading day. However, the official purchases met sustained selling on any rally and the dollar ended the day slightly lower, at DM1.3722 and ¥86.10.

---

[19]The Destler and Henning book in the chapter references details the relationship between the Federal Reserve and the Treasury's Exchange Stabilization Fund in intervention.

On behalf of the U.S. monetary authorities, on April 5 the Desk again entered the market, at about 10:20 A.M., with the dollar trading at DM1.3737 and ¥86.00. The Desk was joined in this operation by the Bundesbank and the Bank of Japan. . . . During the day, the U.S. monetary authorities purchased $850 million against the mark and $250 million against the yen. The dollar initially rallied on the intervention, reaching intraday highs of DM1.3860 and ¥86.63, before drifting lower in thin afternoon trading to close essentially unchanged at DM1.3720 and ¥86.01. . . .

On the morning of Wednesday, May 31, with the dollar trading at DM1.3850 and ¥82.70, the Desk entered the market in concert with the central banks of the other G-10 countries, purchasing dollars against marks and yen in an operation initiated by the U.S. monetary authorities. The U.S. monetary authorities' purchases totaled $500 million against the mark and $500 million against the yen. . . . Market participants interpreted the operation as a signal of increased coordination by the major central banks and a reflection of their mutual desire for a stronger dollar. The dollar closed the day at DM1.4135 and ¥84.40. . . .

At the end of the [April–June 1995] period, the current values of the foreign exchange holdings of the Federal Reserve System and the ESF were $24 billion and $29.1 billion, respectively. The U.S. monetary authorities regularly invest their foreign currency balances in a variety of instruments that yield market-related rates of return and have a high degree of liquidity and credit quality. A portion of the balances is invested in foreign-government-issued securities. As of June 30, the Federal Reserve System and the ESF held, either directly or under repurchase agreement, $9.8 billion and $13.5 billion, respectively, in foreign-government securities.

Table 13.14 reports U.S. official sales of marks and yen, along with the swap of dollars to Mexico, and other minor changes in U.S. monetary authorities' foreign currency holdings.

Summary

The balance-of-payments accounts record transactions between the residents, firms, and government agencies in one country and those in the rest of the world. Goods, services, loans, and a variety of assets are traded internationally, and a country's balance-of-payments accounts reflect all these transactions.

One of the simplest and most useful schemes for examining the balance-of-payments accounts divides transactions into current, capital, and official settlements accounts. Because, by accounting convention, the accounts must "balance" in the trivial sense, the sum of the balances on the current and capital accounts (plus the statistical discrepancy) just equals the negative of the balance on the official settlements account. The current account, capital account, and statistical discrepancy represent autonomous transactions; and when these three entries sum to zero, payments balance in the nontrivial sense. Transactions for which both entries occur in the current account or the nonofficial capital account exert no effect on the net balance of payments. The official settlements account records changes in the level of official foreign exchange reserves (accommodating transactions) and captures the effects of government intervention in foreign exchange markets when

Table 13.14 □ U.S. Monetary Authorities' Foreign Currency Holdings ($ Millions)

	Balances as of March 31, 1995	Quarterly Changes in Balances by Source				Balances as of June 30, 1995
		Net Purchases and Sales[a]	Impact of Sales[b]	Investment Income	Currency Valuation Adjustment[c]	
Federal Reserve						
Deutsche marks	14,877.3	(1,050.0)	(0.1)	163.4	(54.6)	13,936.0
Japanese yen	9,416.9	(750.0)	1.1	45.5	217.9	8,931.4
Mexican pesos	865.1	(14.3)	0.0	14.3	102.4	967.5
Subtotal	25,159.2	(1,814.3)	1.0	223.2	265.7	23,834.8
Interest receivables	127.3					126.0
Total	25,286.5					23,960.8
U.S. Treasury Exchange Stabilization Fund						
Deutsche marks	8,148.8	(1,050.0)	(0.1)	85.6	(31.1)	7,153.2
Japanese yen	13,196.3	(750.0)	1.1	85.9	310.5	12,843.9
Mexican pesos	4,000.0	4,842.0	0.0	158.0	0.0	9,000.0
Subtotal	25,345.2	3,042.0	1.0	329.5	279.4	28,997.1
Interest receivables	88.0					72.8
Total	25,433.2					29,069.9

Note: Figures might not sum because of rounding.

[a] Purchases and sales for the purpose of this table include foreign currency sales and purchases related to official activity, swap drawings and repayments, and warehousing.

[b] This number is calculated using marked-to-market exchange rates: it represents the difference between the sale exchange rate and the most recent revaluation exchange rate.

[c] Foreign currency balances are marked-to-market monthly at month-end exchange rates.

Source: Federal Reserve Bank of New York, "Treasury and Federal Reserve Foreign Exchange Operations," April–June 1995, p. 11.

exchange rates are not completely flexible. Transactions for which one entry occurs in the official settlements balance do alter the net balance of payments. Figure 13.7 summarizes the balance-of-payments accounts and the effect of various classes of transactions.

A number of popular misconceptions surround the balance of payments. Two of the most widespread concern the relationship between the merchandise trade balance and the balance of payments. First, a balance-of-payments deficit (or surplus) is *not* the same as a merchandise trade deficit (or surplus). The merchandise trade balance reflects trade in goods only, while the balance of payments records trade in goods and services as well as borrowing/lending and purchases/sales of assets. Second, a perfectly flexible exchange rate assures balance-of-payments

Figure 13.7 □ Transactions in the Balance-of-Payments Accounts

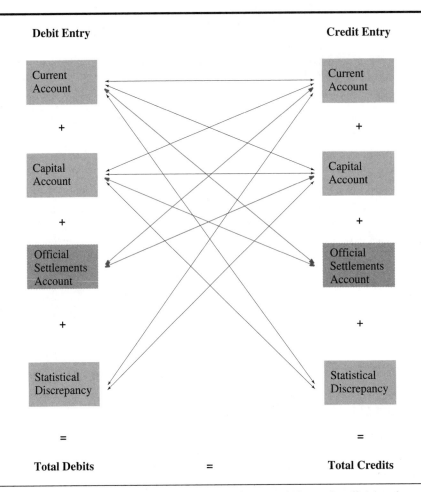

The sum of the current-account balance, the capital-account balance, the official settlements balance, and the statistical discrepancy must equal zero. Transactions for which both the debit and the credit entry appear in the (autonomous) current or capital accounts do not affect the net balance of payments (BOP = CAB + KAB = –OSB). Such transactions are represented by solid lines in the figure. Transactions for which either the debit or credit entry occurs in the (accommodating) official settlements balance do affect the net balance of payments and are represented by the colored elements in the figure.

equilibrium, but not balance in either merchandise trade or the current account. A flexible exchange rate moves to equate the quantity demanded and supplied of a currency in the foreign exchange markets. Like the balance-of-payments equilibrium, the demand for a currency reflects not only trade in goods but trade in services, assets, and loans.

Looking Ahead

A country's international economic relations, including its balance of payments, matter primarily because they affect and are affected by domestic economic performance. The various components of the balance-of-payments accounts can affect domestic output, employment, prices, and interest rates as well as exchange rates. Chapter Fourteen begins the process of integrating international considerations— foreign exchange markets and the balance of payments—into a simple model of the macroeconomy.

Key Terms

merchandise exports

services

balance-of-payments accounts

double-entry bookkeeping system

current account

credit

debit

balance on the current account

deficit

merchandise trade balance

surplus

balance on goods and services

capital account

capital outflow

capital inflow

official settlements balance

statistical discrepancy

autonomous (independently motivated)
  transactions

balance-of-payments surplus

balance-of-payments deficit

accommodating (compensatory)
  transactions

overall (multilateral) balance-of-
  payments accounts

bilateral balance-of-payments accounts

Bretton Woods system

capital flight

net foreign wealth (net international
  investment position)

Problems and Questions for Review

1. Country A has a current-account balance of −1,000 and a (nonofficial) capital-account balance of +1,500 (measured in units of country A's currency).
   (a) What is the status of A's balance of payments?
   (b) What would happen under a flexible exchange regime? Why?
   (c) What would happen under a fixed exchange rate regime? Why?

2. State whether each of the following represents a debit or a credit on the U.S. current account (for now, ignore the "second side" of each transaction).
   (a) Purchase of a Boeing aircraft by a Chinese airline
   (b) Expenditures by an American on vacation at EuroDisney
   (c) Purchase by a U.S. automaker of Brazilian steel
   (d) A U.S. telecommunications company hires a French firm to launch a new space satellite
   (e) A resident of Spain spends two weeks in Atlanta at the Olympic games
   (f) A Hong Kong-based corporation pays its annual dividend to its U.S. stockholders

3. Under the Bretton Woods system of pegged exchange rates in effect from the end of the Second World War to the early 1970s, suppose that (then West) Germany had a balance-of-payments deficit with the United States. According to the rules of the Bretton Woods system and ignoring other countries, what would have happened, and how would it have been reflected in the U.S. balance-of-payments accounts?

4. Evaluate the following statements:
   (a) "The theory of flexible exchange rates doesn't work. Otherwise, the United States couldn't have a $67 billion merchandise trade deficit with Japan."
   (b) "Look at Tables 13.7 and 13.13. The U.S. capital-account balance and net international investment position never show the same number for any given year. Obviously, the statistics can't be trusted."

5. Assume the United States operates under a flexible exchange rate regime. Comment on the following statement: "The U.S. current-account deficit provides a measure of how much the United States must borrow abroad."

6. For each of the following transactions, show the entries in the balance-of-payments accounts for each of the two countries involved and the overall effect on each country's balance of payments.
   (a) In the 1980s, Pepsico (a U.S.-owned firm) sold $3 billion worth of Pepsi syrup to the Soviet Union in exchange for $3 billion worth of Stolichnaya vodka and ships. The exchange rate between dollars and rubles was $1/ruble0.5.
   (b) A U.S. book publisher sells $20,000 of books to China and is paid with a check for 80,000 yuan that the publisher holds in an account in Beijing. The equilibrium exchange rate is $1/yuan4.
   (c) A U.S. firm imports DM5,000 worth of goods from Germany. In the foreign exchange market, the firm is unable to purchase a DM deposit (with which to pay for the goods) at the pegged exchange rate of $1/DM2. The firm buys a DM5,000 deposit from the U.S. central bank.
   (d) General Motors issues $10 million of new bonds, sells them to residents of Germany, and uses the proceeds to buy an automobile factory in Germany. The equilibrium exchange rate is $0.25/DM1.
   (e) Seagram sells Can$1 million worth of liquor to a U.S. distributor, who pays Seagram with a Can$1 million deposit in a New York bank. Seagram decides to keep the deposit. The equilibrium exchange rate is U.S.$1/Can$1.
   (f) A British firm purchases a U.S. supercomputer and pays with a £100,000 deposit in a New York bank. The computer seller doesn't want to hold the pounds and sells them to the U.S. central bank at a pegged rate of $2/£1.
   (g) Nissan (a Japanese auto firm) buys a factory in England and pays the British seller for the land and building with a ¥1 billion account in a Tokyo bank. The British seller decides to keep the yen deposit. The exchange rate is £1/¥200.
   (h) A German firm hires a British attorney as a consultant. The attorney is paid with a DM1,000 deposit in a Frankfurt bank, which she sells to the Bank of England (the British central bank) in exchange for a deposit of £350.

7. Briefly explain why equilibrium in the foreign exchange market and equilibrium in the balance of payments are two ways of looking at the same phenomenon.

8. Can a country have
   (a) a current-account deficit, a capital-account surplus, and a flexible exchange rate? Why, or why not?
   (b) a current-account deficit, a capital-account deficit, and a flexible exchange rate? Why, or why not?
   (c) a merchandise trade deficit, a capital-account deficit, and a flexible exchange rate? Why, or why not?
   (d) a current account-surplus, a capital-account surplus, and a fixed exchange rate? Why, or why not?
   (e) a current account-surplus, a capital-account surplus, an official settlements balance surplus, and a fixed exchange rate? Why, or why not?

References and Selected Readings

Carlson, Keith M. "The U.S. Balance Sheet: What is It and What Does it Tell Us?" Federal Reserve Bank of St. Louis *Review* 73 (September–October 1991): 3–18.
An introduction to national accounting; for all students.

Destler, I. M., and C. Randall Henning. *Dollar Politics: Exchange Rate Policymaking in the United States.* Washington, D.C.: Institute for International Economics, 1990.
The politics of exchange-rate policy, and the relationship between the Federal Reserve System and the U.S. Treasury; for all students.

Fieleke, Norman S., "The Soaring Trade in 'Nontradables'." Federal Reserve Bank of Boston *New England Economic Review* (November–December 1995): 25–36.
Accessible overview of the rapidly growing trade in previously nontraded goods.

Fieleke, Norman S. "The United States in Debt." Federal Reserve Bank of Boston *New England Economic Review* (May–June 1990): 19–33.
Assessment of the magnitude and implications of U.S. foreign debt; for all students.

Graboyes, Robert F. "International Trade and Payments Data: An Introduction." Federal Reserve Bank of Richmond *Review* 77 (September–October 1991): 20–31.
Outline and assessment of data on international trade and finance.

Hooper, Peter, and J. David Richardson, eds. *International Economic Transactions.* Chicago: University of Chicago Press, 1991.
Collection of papers on the problems of measuring international transactions; level of papers varies.

International Monetary Fund. *Report on the Statistical Discrepancy in World Current Account Balances.* Washington, D.C.: International Monetary Fund, 1987.
Report on the measurement problems summarized in Case Two.

Khan, Mohsin S., and Nadeem Ul Haque. "Capital Flight from Developing Countries." *Finance and Development* 24 (March 1987): 2–5.
Presents estimates of the magnitude of and causes behind capital flight from developing countries; for all students.

Nawaz, Shuja. "Why the World Current Account Does Not Balance." *Finance and Development* 24 (September 1987): 43–45.
The empirical problems that produce statistical discrepancies in the balance-of-payments accounts of individual countries and the world as a whole.

Obstfeld, M., and K. Rogoff. "The Intertemporal Approach to the Current Account." In *Handbook of International Economics,* Vol. 3, edited by G. M. Grossman and K. Rogoff, 1731–1800. Amsterdam: North-Holland, 1995.

Up-to-date survey of the current account as intertemporal trade; intermediate to advanced.

Ott, Mack. "Have U.S. Exports Been Larger Than Reported?" Federal Reserve Bank of St. Louis *Review* 70 (September–October 1988): 3–23.
Argues that U.S. exports are systematically underestimated, distorting balance-of-payments statistics.

Rosensweig, Jeffrey A. "Exchange Rates and Competition for Tourists." Federal Reserve Bank of Boston *New England Economic Review* (July–August 1986): 57–67.
An empirical study of the effect of exchange rate changes on vacation destinations; for all students.

U.S. Department of Commerce Bureau of Economic Analysis. *The Balance of Payments of the United States.* Washington, D.C.: U.S. Government Printing Office, 1990.
Detailed report on the presentation of U.S. government statistics on international transactions.

CHAPTER FOURTEEN

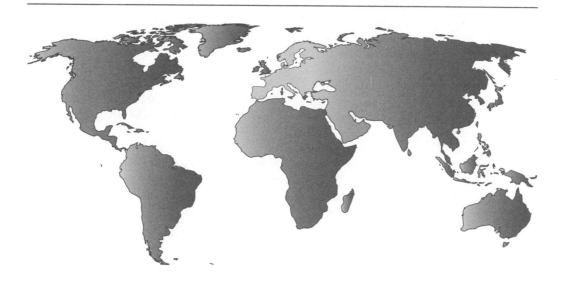

The Market for Goods and Services in an Open Economy

14.1 Introduction

Thus far, we have examined foreign exchange markets (Chapter Twelve) and the balance-of-payments accounts (Chapter Thirteen) in relative isolation from other elements of the international macroeconomy. The next few chapters integrate exchange rate and balance-of-payments considerations into a simple model of the macroeconomy. Our goal is to understand better the complex interaction between international and domestic elements in determining macroeconomic performance and the effectiveness of macroeconomic policy.

This is an area in which one hears many claims and counterclaims in the popular press. Critics of international openness claim merchandise trade deficits reduce economic growth and "deindustrialize" the U.S. economy. Government budget deficits allegedly cause U.S. export industries, such as agriculture, to lose their competitiveness in world markets. Analysts disagree whether the U.S. trade deficit reflects unfair trade practices abroad, an attractive investment environment in the United States, or simply the interplay of domestic and foreign macroeconomic policies.

These complex issues involve the interaction of many economic variables, including output, the price level, the rate of inflation, employment, exchange rates, and interest rates. Therefore, the perspective of this and subsequent chapters will alternate between partial-equilibrium analyses, which focus on a small subset of the interactions, and more general-equilibrium analyses, which, although more complicated, permit a broader view. We shall see that many disagreements and contradictory statements concerning international macroeconomics stem from ignoring or misunderstanding the relationship between partial- and general-equilibrium analyses. Statements that are true when we consider only one market in isolation may be completely false once we introduce a more complete set of economic interactions.

Our investigation of the international macroeconomy will focus attention on three markets: that for domestically produced goods and services (the subject of this chapter) and those for money and for foreign exchange (the subjects of Chapter Fifteen). Along the way, we shall mention several common sources of confusion and disagreement that have important effects on public opinion and on the policy-making process.

14.2 Some Definitions

The market for goods and services produced by the domestic economy provides the first building block of our model of an open macroeconomy. The most commonly used measures of an economy's output of goods and services are **gross national product (GNP)** and **gross domestic product (GDP)**. Both measure the sum of the market values of all final goods and services produced by the economy in a given period (typically a year, although the government reports figures quarterly). Several features of this definition deserve note.

First, GNP and GDP exclude most goods and services not transacted through markets. Thus, both measures fail to reflect items such as home-grown food and housekeeping by family members—even though those goods and services contribute to society's welfare. Both measures also ignore the economy's production of many "bads," such as pollution and congestion, because these costs are not transacted in markets. Therefore, GDP and GNP need not accurately reflect residents' welfare.

Second, calculation of GNP or GDP involves adding the *values* of all goods and services produced in the economy, evaluated at market prices. This is necessary to facilitate the aggregation of many diverse goods and services into a single measure. We cannot simply add in *physical units* (bushels, dozens, and so forth) the automobiles, bananas, computers, and dynamite produced, because each good and service is measured in different units. But market prices can translate the quantity of each good and service into a dollar value; and we can add the dollar values because they are measured in a common unit.

Third, GNP and GDP include only production of *final* goods and services; this convention helps avoid double-counting. If we included the values of silicon production, semiconductor-chip production, and computer production in GNP, we would count the value of the silicon three times, because the values of both chips and computers include the value of the silicon used as an input.

Table 14.1 □ **U.S. GDP and GNP, 1960–1993 ($ Billions)**

Year	GDP	Plus: Receipts of Factor Income from the Rest of the World	Less: Payments of Factor Income to the Rest of the World	Equals: GNP
1960	513.3	5.0	1.8	516.6
1965	702.7	8.1	2.7	708.1
1970	1,010.7	13.0	6.6	1,017.1
1975	1,585.9	28.2	14.9	1,599.1
1980	2,708.0	80.6	46.5	2,742.1
1985	4,038.7	97.3	82.4	4,053.6
1990	5,546.1	168.6	146.9	5,567.8
1993	6,343.3	136.6	132.1	6,347.8

Source: *Economic Report of the President 1995.*

Finally, GNP and GDP refer to production within a specified period. For example, consider an economy with a GDP of $6,737 billion. With no time period specified, this figure conveys little information. If the figure were a daily one, the economy would be enormous (approximately 365 times the size of the U.S. economy in 1994). If the figure referred to a decade, the economy would be much smaller (approximately one-tenth the size of the 1994 U.S. economy).

The difference between GNP and GDP lies in the definition of "the economy." Gross *national* product refers to the output produced by a country's factors of production—regardless of where in the world the production takes place. Gross *domestic* product refers to output produced within a country's geographical boundaries. The output of a U.S. resident temporarily working in Germany, for example, is a part of U.S. GNP but not U.S. GDP, and a part of German GDP but not German GNP. Beginning with a country's GDP, we can arrive at GNP by adding the country's receipts of factor income from the rest of the world and subtracting the country's payments of factor income to the rest of the world. Table 14.1 performs this exercise for the United States for a sample of years.

Until recently, most countries emphasized GDP in their economic reporting, while the United States emphasized GNP. In late 1991, the U.S. Department of Commerce announced it would begin to focus more attention on GDP as the primary measure of output, although both figures would continue to be collected and reported. For the United States in 1993, GNP and GDP differed by less than one-tenth of 1 percent. The change from GNP to GDP caused a rather small difference in the numbers reported, but it does make U.S. reporting more consistent with that of the rest of the world. For countries with a greater divergence between factor-income receipts from the rest of the world and factor-income payments to the rest of the world, the GNP versus GDP distinction makes a bigger difference. For example, during the late 1980s, GNP was 35 percent greater than GDP for Kuwait, but 14 percent less than GDP for Brazil. Countries, such as Kuwait, that are net providers of factor services to the rest of the world have GNPs that exceeds their respective GDPs. Countries, such as Brazil, that are net importers of factor services have GNPs smaller than their GDPs. International factor payments include not only wages and salaries, but also interest and dividends and firms' profits.

Given the volumes of economic data available today—primarily from government sources—it is difficult to imagine the scarcity of information available until relatively recently. Simon Kuznets published the first systematic calculations of GNP for the United States in 1934. The development of the **national income accounts** from which estimates of GNP are derived won Professor Kuznets one of the first Nobel prizes awarded in economics. More than a decade later another economist, Sir Richard Stone of Great Britain, also won a Nobel prize for contributions to national income accounting.

The depression of the 1930s almost certainly would have proven less severe had policy makers possessed better information concerning the state of the economy. No matter how high the quality of economists' theoretical models, policy makers can do little to improve the economy's performance without reasonably accurate and timely data. We must remember, however, that the figures reported for GDP and GNP, as well as other economic statistics, represent only estimates calculated by fallible individuals from imperfect data. We must adjust the degree of faith placed in them accordingly. It makes little sense to worry over small year-to-year changes in GDP when the statistical discrepancy in the calculation runs to several billion dollars per year.

14.3   Output and Income in an Open Economy

As in any other market, equilibrium in the market for goods and services requires that the total quantity supplied or produced equal the total quantity demanded or purchased. One useful way to think of this market at the macroeconomic level is to imagine the entire economy as composed of one giant firm, Nation Inc. The firm earns revenue by producing output that it sells at market prices. This revenue just equals the economy's GDP (the value of output) and, in turn, goes to pay the inputs used in production. Households in the economy own these inputs (labor services, raw materials, factories, and so on); thus, the revenue earned by Nation Inc. ends up being paid out as income to households. Therefore, the economy's GDP (represented by Nation Inc.'s revenue) equals the total income of the households in the economy (represented by Nation Inc.'s payments to inputs).[1] This equality between the value of output or GDP and the value of **national income** is important for understanding the determination of the equilibrium level of GDP.

The next step involves analyzing the sources of demand for Nation Inc.'s output. There are four basic groups to which Nation Inc. can sell its output: individuals; the firm Nation Inc. itself; government agencies; and residents of foreign countries.

---

[1]In the national-income accounts, two entries preclude exact equality between GNP and national income: the capital consumption allowance, or depreciation, and indirect business taxes. Neither is a part of national income. For simplicity, we assume both to be zero to create exact equality between GNP and national income. This simplification does not affect the results of the analysis. We use GDP rather than GNP because GDP figures are more widely reported.

When individuals buy goods and services such as food, automobiles, books, and medical care, the expenditure is referred to as **consumption (C)**. When Nation Inc. retains a portion of the goods and services it produces (for example, machine tools, hammers, and personal computers) to use to produce next year's output; this spending is **investment (I)**.[2] Local, state, and federal government agencies purchase a variety of goods and services (such as file cabinets, missiles, and telephone service); these purchases are called **government purchases (G)**. Government purchases refer only to government spending on goods and services and exclude government spending that simply transfers income between groups within the economy, such as social security benefits and welfare payments. Finally, **exports (X)** represent expenditures by residents of foreign countries on the domestic economy's output.

We must make one adjustment before we can add consumption, investment, government purchases, and exports to arrive at total demand for Nation Inc.'s output. Total consumption expenditure by individuals, investment expenditure by firms, and government purchases each typically include some purchases of foreign-produced goods, or **imports (imp)**, which we must subtract to obtain a measure of total demand for the output of the *domestic* economy. After this adjustment, we can write total *expenditures* (E) on Nation Inc.'s output as

$$E = C + I + G + X - \text{imp}. \qquad [14.1]$$

Equilibrium occurs in the market for domestically produced goods and services when this demand or expenditure just equals GDP, or the value of the economy's output of goods and services (denoted by Y):

$$Y = C + I + G + X - \text{imp}. \qquad [14.2]$$

In words, the value of the economy's output (the left-hand side of Equation 14.2) must equal total demand or total expenditures made on that output (the right-hand side of 14.2).[3] Thinking of the economy as a single firm, the value of Nation Inc.'s output must equal the amount of revenues it takes in from selling that output. Table 14.2 reports GDP, consumption, investment, government expenditure, exports, and imports for the United States for a sample of years, illustrating the relationships from Equations 14.1 and 14.2.[4]

Equation 14.2 provides the basic framework for our analysis of the market for goods and services, but it can reveal little until we understand how its various terms

---

[2]If we relax our simplifying assumption of only one firm, investment includes one firm's purchases of other firms' outputs.

[3]Equation 14.2 can be either an identity (a relationship that always is true—by definition) or an equation true only in equilibrium. If we define expenditure as including even unplanned changes in inventories (that is, accumulations of unsold output by firms), Equation 14.2 holds as an identity. If we define expenditure as excluding unplanned changes in inventories, Equation 14.2 holds only when no such changes occur. We use the second interpretation here.

[4]In Table 14.2, the categories of expenditure include unplanned changes in firms' inventories such that the equality of income and expenditure holds as an identity in each period (see footnote 3).

Table 14.2 □ **Components of U.S. GDP, 1960–1994 ($ Billions)**

Year	Y	=	C	+	I	+	G	+	X	–	imp
1960	513.3		332.4		78.7		99.8		25.3		22.8
1965	702.7		444.6		118.0		136.3		35.4		31.5
1970	1,010.7		646.5		150.3		212.7		57.0		55.8
1975	1,585.9		1,024.9		226.0		321.4		136.3		122.7
1980	2,708.0		1,748.1		467.6		507.1		279.2		293.9
1985	4,038.7		2,667.4		714.5		772.3		302.1		417.6
1990	5,546.1		3,761.2		808.9		1,047.4		557.1		628.5
1994	6,736.9		4,627.0		1,037.5		1,174.5		716.1		818.2

Source: *Economic Report of the President 1995.*

are determined as well as which economic variables are held constant in the analysis. Remember that the Y on the left–hand side of Equation 14.2 represents the value of the economy's output, or GDP; however, Y also represents the total income of the individuals in the economy (also known as *national income*).[5] This must hold true because Nation Inc. pays out the total value of its revenues in payments to owners of the resources it uses; these payments represent income to the recipients.

The amount of consumption expenditure (C) depends on income. In the case of one individual, the proposition that consumption depends positively on that individual's income seems intuitively appealing. The same relationship holds for the economy as a whole: Higher incomes coincide with higher consumption expenditures, and lower incomes with lower consumption expenditures. We can represent this relationship in shorthand form with $C(\overset{+}{Y})$, where the plus sign represents the positive relationship between income and consumption. When income rises, consumption rises, but by less than the increase in income; the remainder of the additional income goes into saving. The share of the increase in income consumed is called the **marginal propensity to consume (mpc)**, a fraction between 0 and 1. For example, if a $1,000 increase in national income causes consumption to rise by $800, the marginal propensity to consume equals $\Delta C/\Delta Y = \$800/\$1,000 = 0.8$.[6]

Investment includes firms' purchases of new capital equipment (machines, factories, and so on) for use in producing future output, along with changes in firms' inventories. The level of investment expenditure in the economy depends primarily on the interest rate, i, which measures the opportunity cost of using funds in a particular investment project.[7] If a firm borrows funds to finance an investment project, it is easy

---

[5]GDP excludes factor income earned abroad, but includes payments to foreign factors employed in the domestic economy.

[6]Recall that Δ denotes "change in"; ΔC represents the change in consumption expenditures.

[7]If individuals in the economy expect inflation, we must distinguish between real and nominal interest rates, with real rates determining investment behavior. We assume temporarily that expected inflation equals zero so that real and nominal rates of interest are equal.

to see that the interest rate represents the opportunity cost of the borrowed funds. At first, it may seem less obvious that the interest rate also measures the relevant opportunity cost when the firm uses internal (nonborrowed) funds. But remember that opportunity cost always measures forgone opportunity. A firm that undertakes an investment project using $1,000 of its own funds forgoes the opportunity to lend out those funds and earn interest. Therefore, the interest rate measures the opportunity cost of the funds used for investment regardless of whether the funds are borrowed or nonborrowed. When the interest rate in the economy is low, the opportunity cost of funds with which to undertake investment projects is low, and firms undertake a relatively large number of projects. With a higher interest rate, the higher opportunity cost of funds makes fewer investment projects worthwhile. We can represent this negative relationship between the rate of interest and investment by $I(\bar{i})$.

Explaining the determinants of the level of government expenditure is an important but complex and elusive goal. Two subareas within economics, public finance and public-choice theory, address this question directly. For our purposes, it is sufficient to assume that the level of government purchases of goods and services is determined exogenously, that is, outside our model. We shall take government expenditure as a given quantity, although we shall examine the effects of changes in the spending level.

Exports, or purchases of domestically produced goods and services by residents of foreign countries, depend primarily on income in trading-partner countries and on the relative prices of domestic and foreign goods. To keep things simple by examining one country at a time, we assume that foreign income is just a constant, Y^*. (Whenever possible, we shall let a * denote a magnitude for the foreign country; for example, if Y refers to domestic income, Y^* refers to foreign income.) Higher levels of foreign income imply higher levels of foreign spending on all goods and services, including imports from the domestic economy. Therefore, foreign income and the domestic economy's exports are positively related. As in the case of government expenditure, we can investigate the effects of changes in the level of foreign income even though we shall not build an explicit model of its determinants.

Demand for exports also depends on their prices relative to the prices of their foreign-produced counterparts. The price of domestically produced goods is P, the overall domestic price level, measured in the domestic currency.[8] The domestic-currency price of foreign-produced goods equals their foreign-currency price (P^*) multiplied by the exchange rate, or the price of foreign currency measured in units of domestic currency. *(Why?)*[9] Therefore, we can define R, the relative price of domestically produced goods and services, as

$$R \equiv P/eP^*. \qquad [14.3]$$

---

[8]The price level measure that takes into account prices of all the goods and services included in GDP is the *GDP deflator*. The deflator measures changes in prices over time by comparing the value of a given level of production at two sets of prices, one from a base year and the other from the current year.

[9]Whenever we compare two prices, we must express them in a common currency. This is why we compare P with eP^*, not P with P^*. For a review, see section 12.2.

The higher the relative price, R, the more expensive are domestic goods relative to foreign goods and the lower the economy's ability to export. The lower the relative price, the less expensive are domestic goods compared with foreign ones and the higher the level of exports. In other words, exports depend positively on foreign income and negatively on the relative price of domestic goods, or $X(\overset{+}{Y^*}, \overset{-}{\bar{R}})$.

The relative price of domestic and foreign goods, R, also is known as the **real exchange rate.** The domestic country's currency undergoes a real appreciation whenever R rises and a real depreciation when R falls. A real appreciation decreases the country's ability to export, and a real depreciation increases that ability. Note that a nominal appreciation of a country's currency (that is, a fall in e) leads to a real appreciation *if* there is no offsetting change in the domestic or foreign price level. Similarly, a nominal depreciation (that is, a rise in e) with no change in either price level implies a real depreciation as well.

The determinants of imports are simply the mirror image of the determinants of exports. Imports depend on domestic income and on the relative prices of domestic and foreign goods, or the real exchange rate. Imports rise with domestic income and with the relative price of domestic goods, $\text{imp}(\overset{+}{Y}, \overset{+}{R})$. *(Why?)* The share of any rise in income that goes to increased imports is known as the **marginal propensity to import (mpi)**, which, like the marginal propensity to consume, is a fraction between 0 and 1. If an increase in income of $1,000 leads to a $100 increase in imports, the marginal propensity to import equals $\Delta\text{imp}/\Delta Y = \$100/\$1,000 = 0.1$.

We now have the tools for depicting graphically the relationship between income in the economy and total expenditure on the economy's output of goods and services. The panels of Figure 14.1 combine consumption, investment, government expenditure, exports, and imports to give total expenditure. Panel (a) illustrates the positive relationship between consumption and income; the slope of the consumption line equals the marginal propensity to consume, or $\Delta C/\Delta Y$. The consumption line does not go through the origin but has a positive vertical intercept. This intercept captures the fact that if some disaster reduced income to zero in one period, consumption would not fall to zero but would continue at a positive level financed out of accumulated savings.

Panel (b) shows a horizontal line because we have assumed, for simplicity, that investment is independent of income. The height of the investment line depends on the interest rate. The government purchase and export lines (panels (c) and (d), respectively), also are horizontal, since we assume both spending categories are independent of income. Panel (e) exhibits a positive slope to capture the positive relationship between domestic income and expenditures on imports; the slope of the line measures the marginal propensity to import.

Total expenditure (panel (f)) is simply the sum of the various expenditure components (note that imports enter with a *negative* sign). The slope of the total expenditure line gives the effect of a change in income on total expenditure ($\Delta E/\Delta Y$). A rise in income causes two of the expenditure components to increase: consumption by the marginal propensity to consume and imports by the marginal propensity to import. The slope of the expenditure line equals the sum of these effects,

Figure 14.1 □ **Total Expenditure on Domestically Produced Goods and Services Depends on Domestic Income**

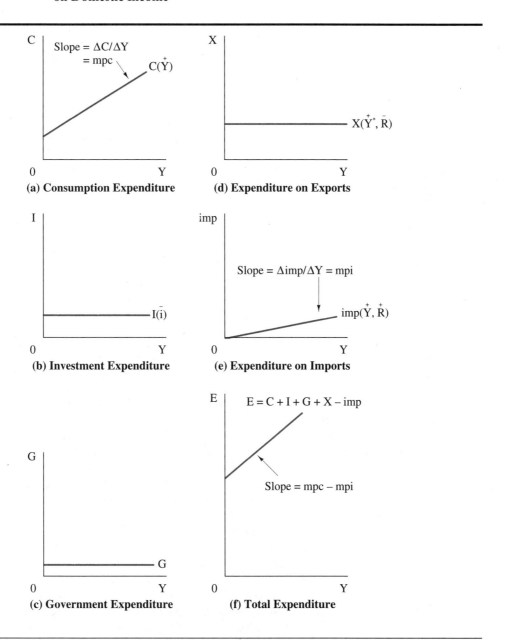

(a) Consumption Expenditure

(b) Investment Expenditure

(c) Government Expenditure

(d) Expenditure on Exports

(e) Expenditure on Imports

(f) Total Expenditure

Total expenditure includes consumption, investment, government purchases, and the current account or net exports (exports minus imports). Income affects consumption and imports by the marginal propensities to consume and import, respectively.

Figure 14.2 □ Equilibrium in the Market for Domestically Produced Goods and Services Requires That National Income or GDP Equal Total Expenditure

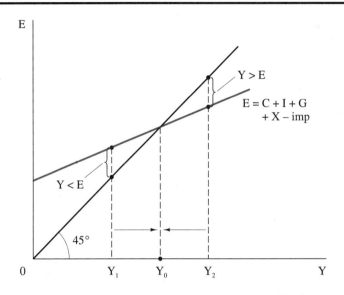

The market for goods and services is in equilibrium at Y_0. At incomes below Y_0 (such as Y_1), expenditure exceeds income, inventories decline, production increases, and income rises. At incomes greater than Y_0 (such as Y_2), income exceeds expenditure, inventories accumulate, production decreases, and income falls.

where the change in imports again enters with a negative sign. Therefore, the slope of the total expenditure line equals (mpc − mpi).

Panel (f) of Figure 14.1 illustrates the relationship between the economy's national income or GDP (measured on the horizontal axis) and total expenditure on domestically produced goods and services (measured on the vertical axis). The market for goods and services will be in equilibrium when national income or GDP just equals total expenditure (see Equation 14.2). We can easily find the point that satisfies this condition—by sketching in a 45-degree line as in Figure 14.2. Recall that along any 45-degree line, the quantity measured on the horizontal axis equals the quantity measured along the vertical axis; here this implies that national income equals total expenditure. The equilibrium level of income or GDP is Y_0.

At income levels below Y_0 (such as Y_1), expenditure exceeds the value of the economy's output of goods and services. When firms sell more goods and services than they produce, they see their inventories declining unexpectedly and respond by producing more. As a result, the value of output rises, moving Y toward Y_0. On the other hand, at levels of income above Y_0 (such as Y_2), income exceeds expenditure. The value of goods and services produced exceeds the expenditures made to buy them. Inventories begin to accumulate, and firms respond by reducing their production. Income falls toward Y_0. The equilibrium at Y_0 is based on the assumption that i, Y^*, G, and R are fixed at the levels in Figure 14.1. A change in any of these variables will *shift* the expenditure line, resulting in a different equilibrium income; we shall explore the details of such changes later.

Now that we have seen how to determine the equilibrium level of income or GDP, we turn to investigations of international trade's effects and of events that alter the economy's equilibrium income.

14.4   International Trade and the Market for Goods and Services

The current account comprises one component of the market for domestically produced goods and services.[10] The other balance-of-payments accounts discussed in Chapter Thirteen do not enter directly into the market for goods and services. Although simple, this point is important to remember to avoid confusion and to spot common errors. The model of the market for goods and services presented in section 14.3 often is used to draw sweeping conclusions concerning the relationship between a country's income or output and its balance of payments. This is obviously inappropriate, since the model contains only a small subset of the transactions recorded in the balance-of-payments accounts. The model does, however, produce some useful insights into the interaction between the current account and national income.

The most important lesson to be learned is that the relationship between national income and the current account is an interactive one; that is, income affects the current account, *and* the current account affects income. We can see this interaction clearly in Figure 14.3, which combines the export and import panels from Figure 14.1. Recall that exports are independent of the level of domestic income, while imports rise with income.

Holding constant foreign income (Y^*) and the relative prices of domestic and foreign goods or real exchange rate (R), the *current account* will be in balance (neither in surplus nor in deficit) at only one income level, denoted Y_{ca} in Figure 14.3. When income falls below Y_{ca}, the resulting decline in imports produces a current-account surplus (X > imp). When income rises above Y_{ca}, imports rise and the current account moves into deficit (imp > X). No correspondence necessarily exists between the level of income at which the market for goods and services is in equilibrium (Y_0 in Figure 14.2) and the level of income at which the current account balances (Y_{ca} in Figure 14.3). Only an unlikely coincidence would produce a situation in which the two income levels coincided.

So far we have focused on the effect of income on the current account: *Other things equal,* higher incomes are associated with current-account deficits and lower incomes with current-account surpluses. But other things are not always equal. We must also consider the effect of changes in the current account on income. Suppose, for example, that an increase in foreign income from Y_0^* to Y_1^* increases the demand

---

[10]In fact, the market for domestically produced goods and services includes only part of the current account—net exports of goods and services.

Figure 14.3 □ **The Current Account and National Income**

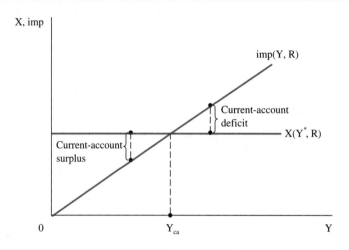

Because imports increase with income, other things equal, increases in income lead to current-account deficits and decreases in income lead to surpluses. Income Y_{ca} represents the income at which the current-account balance equals zero. There is no necessary relationship between Y_{ca} and the level of income at which the market for goods and services is in equilibrium.

for exports, shifting up the total expenditure line as in panel (a) of Figure 14.4. (You may want to review the effect of a change in exports on total expenditure in Figure 14.1.) The increased expenditures on domestic output run down inventories and cause firms to increase their production. The equilibrium level of domestic income rises from Y_0 to Y_1. The current account moves toward a surplus, but by *less* than the initial increase in exports would indicate. The increased exports lead to increased domestic income, which in turn raises imports and partially offsets the initial positive effect on the current account.[11] Once adjustment is complete, income is higher than in the initial equilibrium, and the current account will have moved toward a surplus. Similarly, a decrease in exports will move the current account toward a deficit and lead to a decrease in income that partially offsets that deficit. *(Illustrate the effects of a decrease in exports in a graph similar to Figure 14.4.)*

---

[11]You may wonder whether imports might rise by more than exports, leading to a deficit on the current account. The answer is *no,* and the logic goes like this: Suppose Y^* rises by \$1, causing foreign imports to rise by $mpi^* \cdot \Delta Y^* = mpi^* \cdot \$1$. With only two countries in the world, foreign imports equal domestic exports, so $\Delta X = mpi^* \cdot \$1$. Domestic income rises by the increase in domestic exports multiplied by the spending multiplier (defined in section 14.5.1), so $\Delta Y = mpi^* \cdot \$1 \, [1/(1 - mpc + mpi)]$. This causes domestic imports to rise by $mpi \cdot \Delta Y = mpi \cdot mpi^* \cdot \$1 \, [1/(1 - mpc + mpi)]$. Because the marginal propensity to consume must lie between zero and one, we can show that the increase in domestic exports ($\Delta X = mpi^* \cdot \$1$) exceeds the increase in domestic imports ($mpi \cdot mpi^* \cdot \$1 \, [1/(1 - mpc + mpi)]$). Therefore, the rise in Y^* must move the domestic current account toward a surplus.

Figure 14.4 □ **Interaction between Changes in the Current-Account Balance and Changes in Income**

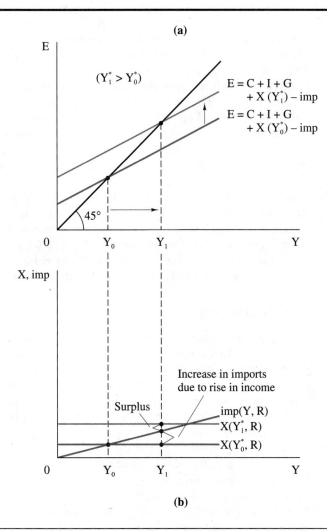

(a)

$(Y_1^* > Y_0^*)$

$E = C + I + G + X(Y_1^*) - \text{imp}$

$E = C + I + G + X(Y_0^*) - \text{imp}$

45°

X, imp

Increase in imports due to rise in income

Surplus

$\text{imp}(Y, R)$
$X(Y_1^*, R)$
$X(Y_0^*, R)$

(b)

The net effect of an increase in exports (caused here by an increase in foreign income) on the current account is smaller than the original increase in exports. Domestic income rises, producing a partially offsetting increase in imports.

These results are simple but important, because they point out a common error. Earlier we argued that, other things equal, an increase in income leads to a current-account deficit (through an increase in imports) and a decrease in income to a current-account surplus (through a decrease in imports). But Figure 14.4 illustrates a rise in income accompanied by a move toward a surplus in the current account.

There is no contradiction between the two lines of reasoning; in Figure 14.4, we can illustrate them by distinguishing between *movements along* the expenditure curves and *shifts* in the curves.

A change in income (represented by a horizontal *movement along* the curves in Figure 14.4) changes imports in the same direction. As a result, any rise in income causes a move toward a deficit in the current account, while a fall in income causes a move toward a current-account surplus. But a change in exports or imports caused by something *other than* a change in domestic income (such as a change in foreign income) *shifts* the expenditure curve in panel (a) of Figure 14.4 and changes the equilibrium level of income. The new level of income is reflected in panel (b) in a new current-account value read off the intersection of the import line and the *new* export line at the new equilibrium income. The increase in imports causes the current-account surplus to be smaller than it would be otherwise; but the rise in income nonetheless accompanies a move toward a surplus in the current account.

Because of the two-way interaction between income and the current account, we must draw conclusions with care. In some situations, income may rise while the current account moves toward a deficit; in others, income may rise while the current account moves toward a surplus. The relationship depends on what causes the initial change. We shall see in Case One in this chapter that increases in income historically have coincided with changes in both directions in the current account.

14.4.1 A Note on Terminology

A move toward a surplus in the current account commonly is referred to as an *improvement* and a move toward a deficit a *deterioration* or *worsening* of the current account. Although this terminology is convenient in the sense that it is easier to say "the current account improved" than to say "the current account moved toward a surplus" or that "the current-account deficit declined," it also is potentially misleading. Speaking of a move toward a surplus as an improvement implies such a move is desirable—which is not necessarily the case.

Surpluses are not necessarily "good," just as deficits are not necessarily "bad." In fact, economies that grow rapidly relative to the rest of the world and provide many profitable investment opportunities tend to run current-account deficits. Those deficits are matched by capital inflows (capital-account surpluses) as foreign investors take advantage of the profitable opportunities provided by the growing economy. Similarly, a surplus may (but not always) reflect a stagnant economy in which imports fall with declining income and foreign investors see no profitable investment opportunities. The desirability of a surplus or a deficit can be judged only in light of the country's overall economic situation.

There is another reason to avoid words with positive or negative connotations when describing economic phenomena: such phenomena typically affect different individuals or groups in the economy differentially. An editorial in *The Economist* noted this problem.

> It is bound to end in tears: some economists are trying to give their dismal science sex appeal. To make dry numbers more alluring, economic and financial

commentators add emotive adjectives or nouns: gloom, worsening, cheer, improved. But the next time you spot the word gloom in a headline or read that a trade balance has deteriorated, ask this question: gloom for whom? The answer may be surprisingly cheery.... Economic commentators take note. Trade surpluses and deficits increase, rise, grow, widen or swell, but they never improve.[12]

For these reasons, we attempt to avoid terminology with inappropriate positive or negative connotations.

14.5   Changes in the Market for Goods and Services

So far, variables held constant in the analysis include government expenditure (G), the relative prices of domestic and foreign goods or the real exchange rate (R), and the interest rate (i). We can determine the effects of each of these variables on income and the current account using the graphical framework developed in the preceding sections.[13] When we refer to "the" equilibrium level of income in the economy, we really mean the particular level of income that represents equilibrium *given* the values of a number of other variables, including G, i, Y^*, P, P^*, and e, as well as the marginal propensities to consume and import. A change in any one of these variables will change the income at which the value of goods and services produced (Y) equals expenditure on goods and services (E).

14.5.1   Fiscal Policy and the Spending Multiplier

A change in government purchases of goods and services provides one example of a **fiscal policy**, a policy that uses changes in government spending or taxation to affect the economy's performance. Because government purchases comprise one category of total expenditure on domestically produced goods and services, the initial effect of a change in government purchases is an equal change in total expenditure. Figure 14.5 depicts such a change as an increase from G_0 to G_1. Equilibrium income rises as a result, and the current account moves toward a deficit.

The magnitude of fiscal policy's effect on income depends on the **spending multiplier**. A \$1 increase in government purchases generates an income increase of \$1 times the spending multiplier. The value of the multiplier is given by $1/(1 - mpc + mpi)$, where mpc denotes the marginal propensity to consume and mpi the marginal propensity to import. A high marginal propensity to consume increases the value of the multiplier by causing a larger share of the rising income to be passed along in the form of increased consumption expenditure. A high marginal propensity to import decreases the value of the multiplier, because income spent on imports "leaks" out of the domestic economy.

Suppose, for example, that the initial increase in government purchases $(G_1 - G_0)$ equals \$1,000. Income immediately rises by \$1,000. The \$1,000 rise in income

---

[12]*The Economist*, August 31, 1991, 16.

[13]Other variables also can be changed, including the marginal propensities to consume and import; we leave these analyses to the reader.

Figure 14.5 □ **A Rise in Government Purchases Raises Equilibrium Income and Moves the Current Account toward a Deficit**

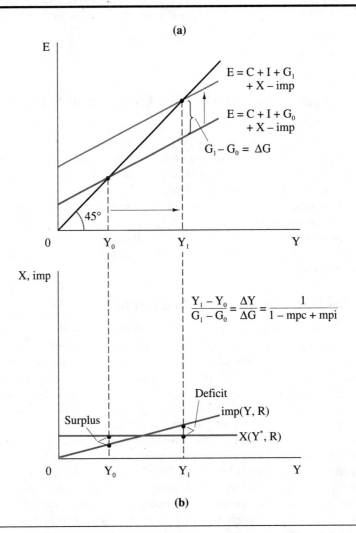

(a)

(b)

The amount of the increase in income per unit increase in government expenditure is known as the spending multiplier and is equal to $1/(1 - mpc + mpi)$.

increases spending on domestic output by $1,000(mpc - mpi)$. *(Why?)* This second round of increased spending is passed on as additional income out of which the recipients spend $1,000(mpc - mpi)(mpc - mpi)$ on domestic output. This process—often called the **round-by-round effect,** since additional spending gets passed on in the next "round" as an increase in income—continues until the initial $1,000 in government purchases has increased income by $1,000(1/[1 − mpc + mpi]).[14] Therefore, the change in the equilibrium level of income caused by a change in government purchases is given by

$$Y_1 - Y_0 = [1/(1 - mpc + mpi)] (G_1 - G_0).$$ [14.4]

Because a rise in government purchases increases income, imports rise and the current account moves toward a deficit, as represented in panel (b) of Figure 14.5.

14.5.2 Relative Prices of Domestic and Foreign Goods: The Real Exchange Rate

Changes in the relative price of domestic and foreign goods or real exchange rate, R, also alter equilibrium income and the current account. A real appreciation of the domestic currency, or a rise in R, reflects domestic goods becoming more expensive relative to foreign goods. Exports fall (shown as a downward shift in the export line in Figure 14.6), and imports rise (shown as an upward shift in the import line).[15] These responses result from individuals shifting their purchases from now more expensive domestic goods to now relatively less expensive foreign goods.

Total expenditure on domestically produced goods and services falls, and the total expenditure line shifts down. As expenditure on domestically produced goods declines, inventories accumulate and domestic firms cut their production. Income falls by an amount equal to the magnitude of the shift down in total expenditure multiplied by the spending multiplier, (1/[1 − mpc + mpi]). Because of the decline in income, individuals curtail their spending, including spending on imports. The current account moves toward a deficit, but by somewhat less than the initial impact of the change in R because of the partially offsetting effect of the decline in income and imports.[16]

Relative price or real exchange rate changes sometimes stem from deliberate economic policies. These policies, designed to alter the allocation of expenditure between domestic and foreign goods, are called **expenditure-switching policies.** Because the nominal exchange rate enters into the relative price of domestic and foreign goods or real exchange rate ($R \equiv P/eP^*$), changes in the nominal exchange

[14]This follows from the fact that $1 + $1(mpc − mpi) + $1(mpc − mpi)(mpc − mpi) + $1(mpc − mpi)(mpc − mpi)(mpc − mpi) +... = $1/(1 − [mpc − mpi]) = $1/([1 − mpc + mpi]). Each term corresponds to an increase in income of which a share equal to (mpc − mpi) is spent on domestic goods and therefore passed on as an increase in income to another individual in the economy.

[15]For simplicity, we assume the demands for imports and exports are price elastic. A rise in the relative price of domestic goods increases the quantity of imports and decreases the quantity of exports. The effects on the *value* of imports and exports depend on the cause of the change in relative price (P, e, or P^*) and on the elasticities of demand. See the section on the J curve and footnote 18.

[16]We know the *net* effect on the current account is a move toward a deficit because, otherwise, a net move toward a surplus would *increase* expenditure on domestically produced goods and services and *raise* income. But it is the *fall* in income that causes the secondary move toward a surplus on the current account to begin with. Hence, a net surplus on the current account from a rise in R produces a contradiction. We can show this algebraically using the technique from footnote 11.

Figure 14.6 ▫ **Changes in the Relative Prices of Domestic and Foreign Goods Affect Both Income and the Current-Account Balance**

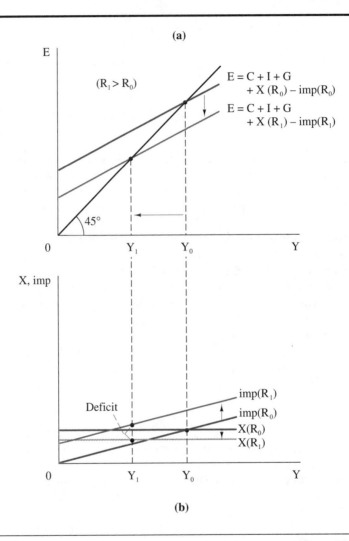

(a)

(b)

If domestic goods become relatively more expensive, demand shifts to imports, income falls, and the current account moves toward a deficit.

rate under either fixed or flexible exchange rate regimes can alter relative prices, at least in the short run. Under a fixed exchange rate regime, a nominal devaluation (a rise in the domestic currency price of foreign currency, e) will lower the relative price of domestic goods (or, equivalently, generate a real devaluation) so long as price levels, P and P^*, do not respond to offset completely the effect of the rise in e on R.

A similar statement is true for a depreciation under a flexible exchange rate regime. We shall see later that there are reasons to doubt that a devaluation or depreciation will leave P and P* unaffected, at least in the long run.

This effect of the exchange rate on relative prices historically has played an important role in international economic policy making. During the Depression of the 1930s, countries desperately tried to increase export markets for their goods as a means of combating unemployment. Country after country devalued its currency in an effort to achieve a real devaluation and a competitive advantage at the expense of its trading partners. Like other policies designed to benefit one country at the expense of others, such **competitive devaluations** are known as **beggar-thy-neighbor policies.** The nominal devaluations often failed to achieve the desired results because as soon as one country devalued its currency against its trading partners', the trading partners retaliated by devaluing their own currencies, leaving the initial exchange rate (and relative prices) unchanged. At the same time, protectionist policies such as the Smoot-Hawley tariff in the United States were on the rise, effectively eliminating the possibility that international trade could help pull the world economy out of its depression.

More recently, the real appreciation of the dollar against other major currencies during the early 1980s generated calls for policies designed to depreciate the dollar in an effort to reduce the U.S. current-account deficit and raise U.S. income. Traditional U.S. export industries, such as agricultural producers, blamed the dollar appreciation for their inability to export.[17] Import-competing industries, such as automobiles and footwear, found imports on the rise, which domestic producers blamed on the dollar's appreciation. Just as in the 1930s, political pressure for protection from competition by foreign rivals mounted.

Movements in exchange rates, unless accompanied by offsetting movements in price levels, always have distributive consequences within the domestic economy. Export-oriented and import-competing industries lose and domestically oriented (nontradable) industries gain from currency appreciations. Domestic consumers also gain as the domestic-currency price of imported goods falls, lowering the cost of living. Currency depreciations have the opposite effects, helping industries involved in international trade at the expense of nontrade industries and domestic consumers. These distributive effects help explain why the exchange rate never is perceived by everyone as being at the "right" level. During the 1970s, the dollar depreciated heavily against other major currencies, and the politicians seen as responsible lost public support. The early 1980s provided an example of the opposite phenomenon: The dollar appreciated substantially against other currencies, and support grew for policies designed to depreciate the dollar as well as for protectionism aimed at reducing the U.S. current-account deficit. The late 1980s and early 1990s have produced substantial depreciations of the dollar against trading-partner currencies, especially the yen and Deutsche mark, a trend policy makers sought to interrupt through foreign exchange market intervention, as we saw in Case Four of Chapter Thirteen.

---

[17]See Chapter Seven for a discussion of the special problems involved in international trade in agricultural products, particularly those caused by the agricultural price-support programs of the major industrial economies.

A Caveat: J-Curve Effects

We just argued that a real depreciation (or real devaluation) of the domestic currency lowers the relative price of domestically produced goods and services, increases exports, reduces imports, and thus moves the current account toward a surplus. This adjustment process, however, may not occur immediately. In fact, in the short run, a depreciation or devaluation of the domestic currency can even push the domestic current account toward a further *deficit*. To see why, it helps to write out the expression for the U.S. current-account balance, as in Equation 14.5:

$$\text{U.S. current-account balance} = (\text{Price of U.S. exports} \cdot \text{Quantity of U.S. exports})$$
$$- (\text{Price of U.S. imports} \cdot \text{Quantity of U.S. imports}) \quad [14.5]$$
$$= (P \cdot Q_X) - ([e \cdot P^*] \cdot Q_{imp}),$$

where Q_X and Q_{imp} represent the *q*uantities of U.S. exports of goods and services and imports of goods and services, respectively. When e rises, the price of imports rises immediately, but the quantity of imports may take some time to adjust downward in response to the price change, because current imports and exports typically occur based on orders placed months in advance—before the devaluation or depreciation. If so, the *value* of U.S. imports will rise in the short run. Similarly, the dollar depreciation makes U.S. exports more attractive to foreign buyers, but those buyers may not adjust immediately to the price change. The result of quantities' slow adjustment to the relative price changes caused by a dollar depreciation or devaluation can be a short-run move toward a further deficit in the U.S. current account. *(Use Equation 14.5 to explain why.)*

As time passes, import and export quantities do adjust. The quantity of U.S. imports falls, and the quantity of U.S. exports rises. This distinction between the short-run and long-run effects of a real depreciation or devaluation is called the **J-curve** phenomenon. Figure 14.7 makes clear the logic behind the name. The horizontal axis measures time; the vertical axis measures the U.S. current-account balance. As the story opens, the current account is in deficit. The devaluation or depreciation of the dollar occurs at time t_0. Initially the current-account deficit grows because the dollar price of imports rises. *(To test your understanding, explain what would happen to the J-curve analysis if contracts for U.S. imports were written in dollars, that is, if the prices paid for imports were set in terms of dollars, rather than in foreign currency.)* As time passes, export and import quantities begin to adjust. Export receipts rise, and expenditures on imports fall. The deficit stops growing, and the current account moves toward a surplus. The time path of the current account following the rise in e traces out a shape similar to the letter *J*.

Is the J curve just a theoretical curiosity, or is there evidence that it accurately describes the effects of exchange rate changes? Unfortunately, this question does not have a simple or definitive answer. The presence or absence of the J curve hinges on the demand elasticities for imports and exports.[18] Because these elasticities differ across historical periods and countries, we observe the J curve in some cases and not in others. Recent experience suggests that industrial countries often experience J-curve

---

[18]Letting ϵ_{imp} and ϵ_X represent the *e*lasticities of demand for U.S. *imports* and *exports*, respectively, the effect of a dollar depreciation on the U.S. current-account balance equals $\epsilon_X + \epsilon_{imp} - 1$. Therefore, the more elastic

Figure 14.7 □ **The J Curve**

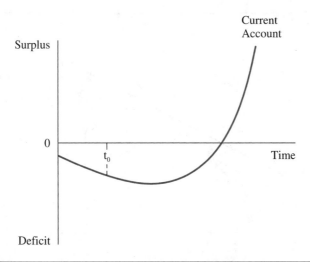

Policy makers devalue the domestic currency at time t_0. The devaluation immediately raises the domestic-currency price of imports. If the quantities of imports and exports do not adjust right away, the current-account deficit grows in the short run. As time passes, the quantity of imports falls and the quantity of exports rises. If the sum of the elasticities of demand for exports and imports exceeds 1, the current account moves toward a surplus. The time path of the devaluation's effect on the current-account balance traces out a pattern similar to the letter *J*.

effects for six months to a year following currency devaluations or depreciations. But even in cases with a pronounced J curve caused by low short-run elasticities, evidence shows long-run elasticities high enough for real currency depreciations or devaluations to move the current account toward a surplus.

14.5.3 Changes in Interest Rates

Changes in interest rates alter equilibrium income by changing investment expenditure. A rise in interest rates discourages investment (see section 14.3). Because investment expenditure comprises one component of total expenditure on the economy's output, a fall in investment reduces total expenditure and causes a decline in income. This is illustrated in Figure 14.8, in which the interest rate rises from i_0 to i_1. The decline in income equals the change in investment expenditure multiplied by the spending multiplier $(1/[1 - \text{mpc} + \text{mpi}])$. The decline in income reduces imports and moves the current account toward a surplus. We do not yet have a theory of what causes changes in the interest rate but will develop one in Chapter Fifteen, where we add the money market to our model of the macroeconomy.

the demands, the more likely a depreciation will shift the current account toward a surplus. If $(\epsilon_X + \epsilon_{\text{imp}}) > 1$, the current account does move toward a surplus; this is known as the *Marshall-Lerner condition.*

Figure 14.8 □ **Effect of a Rise in the Interest Rate on Income and the Current-Account Balance**

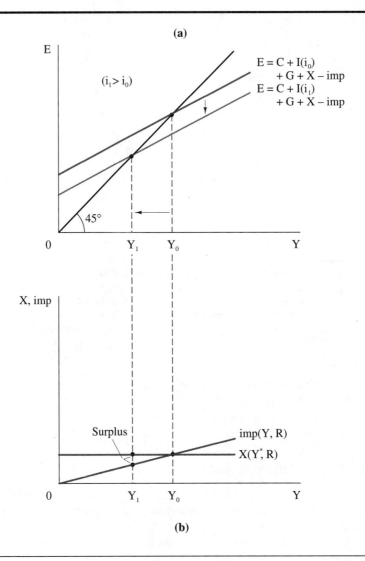

A rise in the interest rate raises the opportunity cost of funds available for investment. Investment expenditure falls, reducing total expenditure and the equilibrium level of income. The fall in income reduces imports, and the current account moves toward a surplus.

Table 14.3 □ Variables' Effects on Equilibrium Income and the Current Account

Variable	Effect on Equilibrium Income	Effect on Current-Account Balance
Increase total expenditure (E):		
Increase in G	+	−
Increase in Y^*	+	+
Decrease in R	+	+
Decrease in P	+	+
Increase in P^*	+	+
Increase in e	+	+
Decrease in i	+	−
Decrease total expenditure (E):		
Decrease in G	−	+
Decrease in Y^*	−	−
Increase in R	−	−
Increase in P	−	−
Decrease in P^*	−	−
Decrease in e	−	−
Increase in i	−	+

14.5.4 Summary of Effects on Income and the Current Account

Changes in variables that increase total expenditure on domestically produced goods and services increase the income consistent with equilibrium in the market for goods and services. Such changes include increases in government purchases or foreign income and decreases in the relative price of domestic goods and services or in the domestic interest rate. Table 14.3 summarizes these effects.

Increases in government purchases and decreases in interest rates move the current account toward a deficit. Increases in foreign income or decreases in the relative price of domestic goods and services (whether caused by a fall in P, or a rise in P^* or e) move the current account toward a surplus.

14.6 Interdependence: Protectionism, Income, and the Current Account

Despite protectionism's popularity as a response to a current-account deficit, economic analysis suggests such a response is ineffective at best and damaging to the world economy at worst. Problems with protection include repercussions from the adverse effect of U.S. protectionism on trading partners' economies, the possibility of retaliation, and the economic inefficiencies introduced by trade barriers.

Just as exports provide a source of demand for U.S.-made products, exports to the United States provide a source of demand for trading-partner economies. Protectionism by the United States, to the extent it succeeds in reducing U.S. demand for foreign goods, reduces foreign incomes. The reduction in foreign incomes then feeds back into the U.S. economy through a reduction in foreign demand for U.S. exports. Because of these linkages among economies, artificial reductions in imports through protectionism result in reductions in exports.[19]

The history of protectionist legislation makes clear that protectionism by one country in the world trading system leads to similar protectionism by other countries. Beggar-thy-neighbor policies of any type, by their very nature, spread quickly from one country to another. Since each country's exports comprise its trading partners' imports, successful efforts by one country to alter its current account always produce consequences for the current accounts of trading partners. Retaliation adds one more reason why the belief that protectionism can reduce imports while leaving exports unchanged is naive. In fact, if protectionism simultaneously switches expenditure from foreign- to domestically produced goods for all countries, current-account balances remain unchanged, other things equal, since exports decline by the same amount as imports.

Finally, the most important reasons for avoiding protectionist policies formed the basis of Chapters Two through Eleven. Unrestricted international trade allows the world's scarce resources to produce the maximum quantity of goods and services. By interfering with the efficient allocation of resources, barriers to trade reduce the world economy's ability to produce goods and services. The result: higher prices and fewer goods available for consumption.

14.7 The "Twin Deficits"

In the popular or business press coverage of the U.S. economy during the 1980s and early 1990s, one of the most commonly encountered subjects has been the **"twin deficits."** The term refers to the combination of a government budget deficit and a current-account deficit, both of which grew substantially during the 1980s in the United States. In what sense are the two deficits "twins"? After all, the government budget deficit equals the amount by which government purchases of goods and services exceed the net tax revenues government takes in $(G - T)$, while the current-account deficit refers to the amount by which the value of a country's imports of goods and services exceeds the value of its exports.[20] Given these definitions, a direct connection between the two is not immediately obvious.

Repeating the information from Equation 14.2, we know that national income equals the sum of consumption expenditure, investment expenditure, government purchases, and the current-account balance or net exports of goods and services $(CA = X - imp)$:

$$Y = C + I + G + X - imp = C + I + G + CA. \qquad [14.6]$$

Rearranging Equation 14.6, we can see that $Y - (C + I + G) = CA$, or that a country's current account just reflects the difference between the country's national

---

[19]This interdependence generalizes to other changes in spending.

[20]Note the other components of current account discussed in section 13.2.1.

income (Y) and its residents' spending on goods and services (C + I + G). If residents buy more goods and services than the country produces, the country runs a current-account deficit (imports more goods and services than it exports), and the country must borrow from foreigners to cover its excess spending. From a balance-of-payments perspective, this is just another way of saying that a current-account deficit must be covered by a capital-account surplus, or a decline in the country's net foreign wealth. A country that produces more goods and services than its residents buy, on the other hand, runs a current-account surplus, and lends the excess to foreigners. The current-account surplus is matched by a capital-account deficit, or an increase in the country's net foreign wealth.

From the standpoint of the households receiving national income, there are three outlets for that income: It can be spent on consumption (C), paid out in taxes (T) to the government, or saved (S):[21]

$$Y = C + T + S. \qquad [14.7]$$

Combining and rearranging Equations 14.6 and 14.7, we get an expression that highlights the relationship between the government budget deficit and the current account:

$$S - I = (G - T) + (X - \text{imp}) = (G - T) + CA. \qquad [14.8]$$

The difference between saving and investment in the economy (S − I) must equal the sum of the government budget surplus (G − T < 0) or deficit (G − T > 0) and the current-account surplus (CA > 0) or deficit (CA < 0). The two terms on the right-hand side of Equation 14.8 are "twins" in the sense that, for given values of saving and investment, a change in one of the deficits necessarily accompanies an offsetting change in the other; the larger the budget deficit (that is, the larger G − T), the larger the current-account deficit. Given private saving and investment in the economy, when government spends more than the revenue it takes in, the country must borrow abroad to finance that spending. (Recall that a current-account deficit implies a capital-account surplus or net borrowing from abroad.)

We can rearrange Equation 14.8 to note that

$$I = S - (G - T) - CA. \qquad [14.9]$$

An open economy has three sources of funds to finance investment: domestic saving, a government budget surplus, or borrowing from abroad. Saving represents individuals in the economy forgoing current consumption and using the income not consumed to fund investment projects that increase future consumption. A government budget surplus occurs when government does not spend all the tax revenue it takes in (G − T < 0); we can think of this as saving by the government, and the excess funds can finance investment projects. Finally, the country can import more

---

[21]By definition, saving equals income minus consumption expenditures and taxes.

goods and services than it exports (CA < 0), use some of the net imports for invest-ment purposes, and borrow from foreigners.

To take yet another perspective, we can rearrange Equation 14.8 to focus on pri-vate saving in the economy:

$$S = I + (G - T) + CA. \qquad [14.10]$$

When individuals in the economy save, that saving can go into any one of three chan-nels: domestic investment projects (I), purchases of the bonds issued by the domes-tic government to cover its spending in excess of tax revenues (G − T), or purchases of foreign assets and loans to foreigners (CA).

Equation 14.10 also suggests why many analysts have proposed policies to increase domestic saving as a means of reducing the twin deficits. Higher saving raises the left-hand side of Equation 14.10, allowing any given budget deficit to coin-cide with a smaller current-account deficit (or, equivalently, allowing any given cur-rent-account deficit to be associated with a smaller budget deficit). But evaluating policy proposals for dealing with the twin deficits requires more than the information provided in Equation 14.10. In particular, we need to understand *how* the variables in the equation are related, both to each other and to other important macroeco-nomic variables—tasks for the next three chapters. Before undertaking those tasks, we can summarize this chapter's results in a form handy for later use.

14.8 The IS Curve

Our goal is to combine the insights from this chapter's examination of the market for goods and services with an understanding of the markets for money and foreign exchange. To help accomplish that goal, a graphical technique called an IS curve will prove useful. An **IS curve** summarizes the relationship between income and the inter-est rate that must hold for the market for goods and services to be in equilibrium. When we use IS curves, we will assume that the price level P is fixed so that changes in nominal GDP (or Y, in our notation) translate directly into changes in real GDP, which we denote as Q, where $Y \equiv Q \cdot P$.

In section 14.5.3, we argued that a rise in the interest rate would, by discouraging investment, lower the income at which the market for goods and services was in equi-librium. Figure 14.9 repeats panel (a) of Figure 14.8, showing the effect of an increase in the interest rate on the income (now real GDP) at which the market for goods and services is in equilibrium. When the interest rate rises from i_0 to i_1, firms face an increased opportunity cost of funds for investment and investment expenditure falls from $I(i_0)$ to $I(i_1)$. Because investment expenditure is one component of total expendi-ture on the goods and services produced by the domestic economy, total expenditure falls. Firms find their inventories accumulating and respond by cutting their output, so GDP falls from Q_0 to Q_1. Similarly, a fall in the interest rate would require an increase in income for the market for goods and services to remain in equilibrium.

We can summarize the *negative* relationship between income and interest rates nec-essary to maintain equilibrium in the market for goods and services by a downward-

Figure 14.9 □ **The IS Curve**

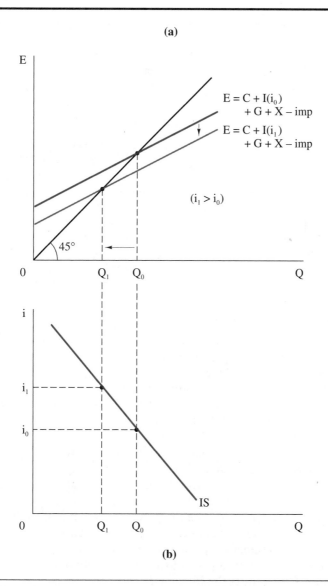

(a)

$E = C + I(i_0)$
$\quad + G + X - imp$

$E = C + I(i_1)$
$\quad + G + X - imp$

$(i_1 > i_0)$

45°

Q_1 Q_0

(b)

An increase in the interest rate raises the opportunity cost of funds for investment, discourages investment, and lowers total expenditure on goods and services. The IS curve in panel (b) represents all combinations of domestic income and interest rate that result in equilibrium in the market for goods and services. The IS curve is negatively sloped; a rise in the interest rate lowers investment expenditure and the equilibrium level of income.

Figure 14.10 □ **Changes in Variables That Shift the Total Expenditure Line Also Shift the IS Curve**

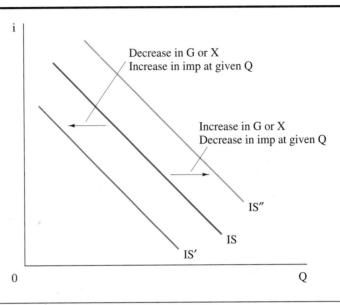

sloping line as in panel (b) of Figure 14.9. We call this an *IS curve,* so named because in a closed economy the market for goods and services is in equilibrium when *invest*ment equals *saving.* In an open economy the relationship becomes more complex, making the IS terminology less descriptive. Nevertheless, we shall use the standard term, keeping in mind that the IS curve shows the combinations of income and interest at which the market for goods and services is in equilibrium.

An IS curve is drawn assuming that government expenditure (G), exports (X), and quantity of imports at each income level are fixed. Changes in any of these variables shift the entire IS curve. In fact, a change in any variable, *other than the interest rate,* that shifts the total expenditure line also shifts the IS curve.[22] Any change that shifts the total expenditure line up shifts the IS curve to the right, and any change that lowers the total expenditure line shifts the IS curve to the left. For example, a rise in either government expenditure or exports raises total expenditure and therefore raises income at each level of the interest rate (see Equation 14.1). An increase in G or X thus shifts the IS curve to the right. An exogenous increase in imports reduces total expenditure and, given the interest rate, reduces income, shifting the IS curve to the left. Figure 14.10 summarizes these changes. The IS curve summarizes the requirements for equilibrium in the market for goods and services in a

---

[22]Changes in the interest rate cause movements along an IS curve rather than shifts in the curve, because the interest rate is the variable graphed on the diagram's vertical axis.

single line, a convenient way to carry this chapter's results forward and to integrate them with other elements of the world macroeconomy.

We now turn to three cases that explore issues raised in the chapter: the relationship between income and the current account, the link between the real exchange rate and the current account, and German unification as an example of fiscal policy's impact on income and the current account.

Case One
Changes in Income and the Current Account

The model developed in section 14.4 highlighted the need for caution in drawing conclusions about the relationship between a country's income or GDP and its current account. Although a rise in income, other things equal, tends to lead to a current-account deficit through increased imports, any independent changes in the current account also will affect the equilibrium level of income. Because of this interaction, the often-heard statement that current-account deficits lower income is potentially misleading; in fact, such deficits may result from rising incomes. Table 14.4 reports that although U.S. GDP rose each year between 1970 and 1994, the current-account balance underwent changes in both directions during the same period.

Case Two
The Real Exchange Rate and the Current Account

Figure 14.11 reports the paths of the real effective U.S. exchange rate and the U.S. current-account balance since the United States moved from a fixed to a flexible exchange rate regime in the early 1970s. The real effective exchange rate is defined as $R \equiv P/eP^*$, where P denotes the U.S. price level, e the dollar price of a basket of trading-partner currencies, and P^* the average price levels in those trading partners. Increases in R reflect U.S.-produced goods and services becoming more expensive relative to foreign-produced ones, while decreases in R imply U.S. goods and services becoming relatively cheaper. As enough time passes for consumers to respond to the changes in relative prices, we expect increases in R to shift the U.S. current-account balance toward a deficit and decreases in R to shift the current account toward a surplus.

The data in Figure 14.11 appear to support the hypothesized relationship between changes in a country's real exchange rate and its current-account balance. Periods such as the late 1970s and late 1980s, during which the dollar depreciated against trading partner currencies, led to moves toward a surplus on the U.S. current-account balance. The early 1980s and 1990s, by contrast, when the dollar appreciated, corresponded to growing current-account deficits.

Table 14.4 □ Changes in U.S. GDP and Current-Account Balance, 1970–1994

Increases in U.S. GDP have been associated with both increases and decreases in the country's current-account balance.

Year	Change in GDP from Previous Year (Percent)	Change in Current-Account Balance from Previous Year ($ Billions)
1970	+5.1	+1,932
1971	+9.0	−3,764
1972	+10.4	−4,362
1973	+11.0	+12,935
1974	+8.4	−5,178
1975	+7.6	+16,154
1976	+12.6	−13,821
1977	+12.8	−18,630
1978	+13.1	−808
1979	+11.2	+14,858
1980	+8.4	+2,602
1981	+11.8	+2,713
1982	+4.1	−16,473
1983	+9.0	−33,017
1984	+12.2	−55,313
1985	+7.1	−25,599
1986	+5.9	−25,829
1987	+6.4	−15,896
1988	+6.9	+38,903
1989	+6.4	+25,374
1990	+5.4	+11,072
1991	+2.3	+84,796
1992	+5.3	−60,934
1993	+5.9	−36,010
1994	+6.7	−51,777

Source: *Economic Report of the President 1995; Survey of Current Business,* March 1995.

Figure 14.11 □ **U.S. Current-Account Balance and the Dollar, 1973–1994**

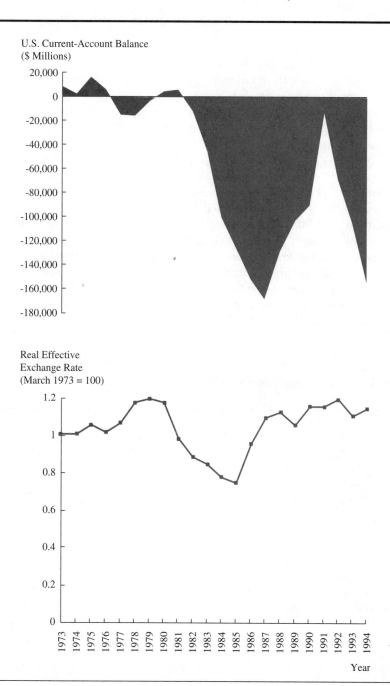

Case Three
The Macroeconomics of Unification

In 1990, the Federal Republic of Germany (West Germany) and the German Democratic Republic (East Germany) unified themselves into a single economic and political entity. The act carried dramatic macroeconomic implications, as we shall see at several points over the next several chapters. Table 14.5 highlights a few key macroeconomic variables for Germany and how they were affected by unification and the policies that accompanied it.

Prior to unification the Federal Republic of Germany ran a surplus on its current account, and the Deutsche mark price of a U.S. dollar stood at e = DM1.88/$1.[23] Fiscal policy exerted little net effect on the macroeconomy as the government budget surplus equaled less than one-half of 1 percent of GDP. With unification in 1990, government spending soared, the Deutsche mark appreciated dramatically against the dollar as well as many other currencies, and the interest rate rose.[24] The current-account surplus shrank, and the growth rate of real GDP accelerated, just as this chapter's model would lead us to expect. The expansionary fiscal policy continued for several years, and the DM price of the dollar remained low. The current account shifted into deficit, reducing demand for German goods and services. At the same time, the rising interest rate reduced

Table 14.5 □ German Macroeconomic Indicators, 1989–1994[a]

Year	Current-Account Balance ($ Billions)	Structural Fiscal Balance (Percent of GDP)[b]	e = DM/$	Percent Change in Real GDP	Interest Rate (Percent)
1989	57.3	−0.4	1.88	3.6	6.6
1990	46.9	−3.5	1.62	5.7	8.0
1991	−19.2	−5.3	1.66	2.9	8.9
1992	−21.0	−3.6	1.56	2.2	9.4
1993	−14.8	−2.0	1.65	−1.1	7.4
1994	−22.6	−1.0	1.62	2.3	5.3

[a]Figures through 1990 refer to Federal Republic only.

[b]Government budget surplus (+) or deficit (−) evaluated at potential output and expressed as a percent of GDP.

Source: International Monetary Fund, *World Economic Outlook*, May 1995; *Economic Report of the President 1995*.

[23]Since we focus in this case on the German economy, we report the exchange rate, e, as the domestic (German) currency price of foreign (U.S.) currency.

[24]We shall see in later chapters that there are reasons to expect a currency appreciation and a rise in the interest rate to follow expansionary fiscal policy.

domestic investment in Germany. The combination of these two forces pushed the German economy into recession, and real output actually fell in 1993.

German policy makers' responses included reducing the government budget deficit and lowering the interest rate by pursuing somewhat more expansionary monetary policies (the subject of Chapter Fifteen). By 1994, real GDP was growing again; but the DM had not reversed its appreciation relative to the dollar, and the German current account remained in deficit.

Summary

The current account's effect on equilibrium in the market for goods and services is one avenue by which international trade affects the performance of the domestic economy. But the relationship between income and the current account is more complex than is often recognized. Changes in the current account do affect national income, but changes in national income affect both the current account and the incomes of trading-partner countries. Other important considerations determining equilibrium in the market for goods and services include fiscal policy, the relative prices of domestic and foreign goods or real exchange rate, and interest rates.

Looking Ahead

In section 14.5.3, we saw that for every possible interest rate there exists a different equilibrium income. This implies that to determine equilibrium income, we need to know the interest rate. Because this chapter focused solely on the market for goods and services, we do not yet have a way to determine the interest rate. In Chapter Fifteen, we shall combine the market for goods and services developed here with the markets for money and foreign exchange. Using a general-equilibrium approach with all three markets will allow us to examine income, the interest rate, and the balance of payments (or the exchange rate) simultaneously.

Key Terms

gross national product (GNP)
gross domestic product (GDP)
national income accounts
national income
consumption (C)
investment (I)
government purchases (G)
exports (X)
imports (imp)
marginal propensity to consume
    (mpc)

real exchange rate
marginal propensity to import (mpi)
fiscal policy
spending multiplier
round-by-round effect
expenditure-switching policy
competitive devaluation
beggar-thy-neighbor policy
J curve
"twin deficits"
IS curve

Problems and Questions for Review

1. Beginning from a position of equilibrium in the market for goods and services and in the current account, government expenditure rises by 100. The marginal propensity to consume is 0.6, and the marginal propensity to import is 0.1. *Ignoring the effects on other countries,* by how much will equilibrium GDP change? What happens to exports? To imports? To the current account?

2. During the mid-1980s, a Democratic congressman from the Midwest was quoted as saying of the protectionist proposals then before Congress, "the effect of this bill on the [current-account] deficit will hardly be noticeable."
   (a) Based on the model in the chapter, briefly explain two reasons why import-limiting protection might not move the current-account balance toward a surplus.
   (b) Use Equation 14.8 to explain why import restrictions might not reduce a current-account deficit.

3. Assume the United States and Japan are the only countries in the world. Beginning from a position of equilibrium in the U.S. and Japanese markets for goods and services, suppose Japan cuts government spending by 1,000.
   (a) If the Japanese marginal propensity to consume equals 0.7 and the Japanese marginal propensity to import equals 0.2, what will happen to Japanese income (Y^J) as a result of the fiscal contraction?
   (b) What will happen to U.S. exports of goods and services because of the Japanese fiscal contraction?
   (c) Assume the U.S. marginal propensity to consume is 0.9 and the U.S. marginal propensity to import is 0.1. What will happen to U.S. income (Y^{US}) as a result of the Japanese fiscal contraction?
   (d) What is the net effect of the Japanese fiscal policy on the U.S. current-account balance?
   (e) Illustrate the U.S. results of the Japanese policy. (Don't worry about the numerical precision of your graph; just illustrate the qualitative effects.)

4. Give an example (either hypothetical or real) of a case in which a current-account deficit might be taken as good news and a current-account surplus as bad news about the overall state of the economy.

5. State how you would expect each of the following groups to feel about a real depreciation of the U.S. dollar. Briefly explain your reasoning.
   (a) Boeing (one of the largest U.S. exporters)
   (b) The United Auto Workers Union
   (c) The owner of a small shop selling foreign-made handicrafts
   (d) A dedicated consumer of fine French wines

6. Explain: "Other things equal, a high marginal propensity to import reduces the macroeconomic impact of fiscal policy."

7. Explain how the fact that one country's imports comprise its trading partners' exports can lead to international business cycles; that is, to situations in which trading partners experience simultaneous economic booms or simultaneous recessions.

8. Why might changes in the real exchange rate (or the relative price of domestic and foreign goods and services) have a greater macroeconomic impact in a very open economy than in a relatively closed one?

References and Selected Readings

Baxter, M. "International Trade and Business Cycles." In *Handbook of International Economics,* Vol. 3, edited by G. M. Grossman and K. Rogoff, 1801–1864. Amsterdam: North-Holland, 1995.
Up-to-date survey of research on the relationship between international trade activity and macroeconomic cycles; intermediate and advanced.

Butler, Alison. "Trade Imbalances and Economic Theory: The Case for a U.S.–Japan Trade Deficit." Federal Reserve Bank of St. Louis *Review* 73 (March–April 1991): 16–31.
Reasons why the economies of the United States and Japan make the recent trade deficit unsurprising; for all students.

Chrystal, K. Alec, and Geoffrey E. Wood. "Are Trade Deficits a Problem?" Federal Reserve Bank of St. Louis *Review* 70 (January–February 1988): 3–11.
An analysis of the circumstances in which trade deficits are and are not symptomatic of economic problems; for all students.

Cullison, William E. "Is Saving Too Low in the United States?" Federal Reserve Bank of Richmond *Economic Review* 76 (May–June 1990): 20–35.
Empirical comparison of saving rates across countries; for intermediate and advanced students.

Dornbusch, Rudiger, and Jeffrey A. Frankel. "Macroeconomics and Protection." In *U.S. Trade Policies in a Changing World Economy,* edited by Robert M. Stern, 77–144. Cambridge, Mass.: MIT Press, 1987.
A detailed study of the relationship among macroeconomic performance, the trade balance, and protectionism; for intermediate students.

Frenkel, Jacob A., and Assaf Razin. *Fiscal Policies and the World Economy,* Chaps. 2–4. Cambridge, Mass.: MIT Press, 1987.
An advanced treatment of models similar to the one presented in this chapter.

Goldstein, Morris, and Mohsin S. Khan. "Income and Price Effects in Foreign Trade." In *Handbook of International Economics,* Vol. 2, edited by Ronald W. Jones and Peter B. Kenen, 1041–1106. Amsterdam: North-Holland, 1985.
Advanced treatment of models similar to the one presented in this chapter.

Little, Jane Sneddon. "Exchange Rates and Structural Change in U.S. Manufacturing Employment." Federal Reserve Bank of Boston *New England Economic Review* (March–April 1989): 56–70.
The effect of changes in the exchange rate on sectoral employment patterns within the U.S. economy; accessible to intermediate students.

Obstfeld, M., and K. Rogoff. "The Intertemporal Approach to the Current Account." In *Handbook of International Economics,* Vol. 3, edited by G. M. Grossman and K. Rogoff, 1731–1800. Amsterdam: North-Holland, 1995.
Up-to-date survey of research on the current account from the perspective of intertemporal trade; intermediate and advanced.

Tatom, John A. "The Link Between the Value of the Dollar, U.S. Trade and Manufacturing Output." Federal Reserve Bank of St. Louis *Review* 70 (November–December 1988): 24–37.
The relationship between changes in the value of the dollar and U.S. economic performance; for all students.

CHAPTER FIFTEEN

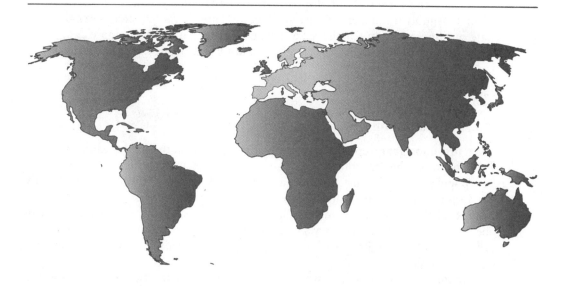

Money and Foreign Exchange

15.1 Introduction

This chapter constructs the second and third building blocks of our model of an open macroeconomy: the markets for money and foreign exchange. Chapter Fourteen explored the impact of openness on the market for goods and services. We saw that an economy that engages in international trade has an additional source of demand for its output (exports) and an additional leakage of domestic expenditure out of the domestic economy (imports). The current account, or the difference between the value of goods and services exported and the value of goods and services imported, provides one avenue through which events in trading-partner economies and the exchange rate affect the domestic economy.

An economy's openness also affects the money market, but in a more subtle way than it does the market for goods and services. At first glance the money market appears identical to that in a closed economy, which you may remember from introductory economics or other courses in macroeconomics. Later in the chapter, we shall see that the effect of openness on the money market, though subtle, is perhaps the most important key to understanding policy options in the world macroeconomy.

Of course, the most obvious effect of openness on the macroeconomy involves the introduction of a foreign exchange market, absent in a closed economy. We examined the essentials of the foreign exchange market in an asset-oriented demand/supply framework in Chapter Twelve. Later in this chapter, we shall translate our findings from Chapters Twelve and Thirteen into a form more convenient for combining with the market for goods and services from Chapter Fourteen.

15.2 Money

15.2.1 Definition

As a first important step in studying the role of money in the world macroeconomy, we must recall the definition of money economists use, which differs somewhat from the popular usage. To an economist, **money** is an asset that its owner can use directly as a means of payment. Currency (coins and paper bank notes in various denominations) held by the public and checkable deposits, or deposits on which checks can be written, constitute a country's money stock.[1] Either form of money, currency or checks, can be used directly (that is, without an intermediate exchange) to pay for goods and services.

Nonmoney assets, such as stocks, bonds, real estate, certificates of deposit, and diamonds, also represent purchasing power to their owners, but they typically cannot be used directly as a means of payment. If the owner of Microsoft stock, a U.S. Treasury bond, or a diamond ring decides to use the asset's purchasing power to buy a new car, the transaction requires two steps, or exchanges. First, the individual must find someone to buy the asset; this involves exchanging the asset for money. Second, the individual uses the money obtained in the first step to buy the car. Only an unlikely coincidence would find two individuals directly exchanging Microsoft stock for an automobile. Such **barter** exchanges—transactions that do not use money as an intermediate step—are rare, because they require a *double coincidence of wants*. The owner of Microsoft stock may find it difficult to locate an individual who both has the desired type of automobile for sale and wants to buy Microsoft stock. Money eliminates the need for this coincidence by allowing monetary exchange to separate the two transactions.

Note that the economist's definition of money is considerably narrower than the popular one, which identifies money with purchasing power or income. A statement such as "I want to go to the basketball game tonight, but I don't have enough money" usually means that the individual has chosen not to spend a portion of his or her limited income or purchasing power on a ticket. The individual might have a $50 bill in his or her wallet or in a checking account (more than enough *money* for a ticket, by the economist's definition) but have higher priority uses for it. The shortage, then, is really not one of money but one of purchasing power or income. Another way to view the distinction between money and income is to realize that a shortage of money, by the economist's definition, rarely is a problem. As long as an

---

[1]Traveler's checks also are included; see Figure 15.15. The large time deposits transacted in the foreign exchange market do *not* constitute part of a country's money stock.

Table 15.1 □ **U.S. Money Stock (M1), 1960–1994**

Year	M1 ($ Billions)
1960	140.7
1965	167.9
1970	214.4
1975	287.5
1980	408.5
1985	619.9
1990	826.4
1991	897.7
1992	1,024.8
1993	1,128.4
1994	1,147.6

Source: *Economic Report of the President 1995.*

individual owns some nonmoney assets, he or she will find it relatively easy to obtain more money by selling a nonmoney asset. In discussing the market for money, we must keep in mind the distinction between money and purchasing power or income.

Money serves its purpose primarily because individuals believe it will continue to do so. A storekeeper does not hesitate to accept a $20 bill in payment for a compact disk, because the storekeeper believes that he or she, in turn, can use the $20 to buy a good or service. It is this faith in money's acceptability as a means of payment—rather than any intrinsic value of the paper itself—that allows it to facilitate transactions effectively. Historically many curious items have functioned as money, including beads, seashells, beer, and cigarettes. The specific physical form of money is relatively unimportant as long as it is commonly accepted as payment.[2]

We denote a country's **nominal money stock,** or the money stock measured in current dollars, as M. The term *stock* denotes the quantity of dollars existing *at a point in time* in the same way the term *housing stock* refers to the existing number of houses at a given time.[3] Table 15.1 reports the U.S. money stock from 1960 through 1994. The reported measure, called *M1,* includes currency and transaction deposits as well as minor items such as traveler's checks.[4] The federal government also reports several broader measures of money, but for our purposes M1 will suffice.

U.S. M1 has increased by a factor of about 8 since 1960. Although it rose in every year, the rate of increase has been erratic, ranging from less than 1 percent per year in 1960 and in 1989 to about 17 percent in 1986.

---

[2]It is helpful if the form of money is durable and easily measured and transported, conditions satisfied by paper currency.

[3]Recall that the alternative type of measure is a *flow,* referring to a quantity (such as GDP) per unit of time.

[4]Case Three at the end of the chapter reports the composition of the U.S. money stock.

Table 15.2 □ U.S. Real Money Stock, 1960–1994

Year	M1/P (1987 $ Billions)
1960	545.3
1965	595.4
1970	617.9
1975	584.3
1980	561.9
1985	660.2
1990	728.7
1991	764.0
1992	849.0
1993	917.4
1994	915.9

Source: *Economic Report of the President 1995.*

Before going on to discuss money demand, we shall make one adjustment. Because economists traditionally analyze money demand in real rather than nominal terms, it is convenient to translate the money stock into real terms as well. As always, we can accomplish this translation easily by dividing the nominal money stock by a price index. The **real money stock** at any time equals the nominal money stock divided by a price index, represented here by the GDP deflator, P:

$$\text{Real money stock} = \text{Nominal money stock/Price index} = M/P. \qquad [15.1]$$

The real money stock is measured in constant dollars or at the price level in effect during the base year on which the price index is calculated. Over periods of rising prices, the nominal money stock grows faster than the real money stock. During periods of falling prices, the real money stock grows faster than the nominal money stock.

Table 15.2 reports the U.S. real money stock for 1960–1994. Because prices rose each year, the nominal money stock exceeds the real money stock for each year after the base year—here 1987—and the real money stock stated in 1987 dollars exceeds the nominal money stock for each year before 1987. *(Verify these relationships by comparing Tables 15.1 and 15.2.)* Unlike the nominal money stock over the same period, the real money stock increased in some years between 1960 and 1994 and decreased in others; annual growth rates ranged from −4 percent to +14 percent.

15.2.2 The Demand for Money

Because money is defined as a group of assets that can be used directly to make purchases, individuals choose to hold a portion of their total wealth in the form of money primarily for its convenience in making transactions. The demand for money reflects the quantity of cash and transaction deposits the public wants to hold to make purchases.[5] In 1994, money holdings in the United States averaged over $4,400 per person (including children), with over $1,350 per person in the form of currency.[6]

Studies of money demand behavior suggest that individuals care primarily about how many goods and services they can buy with their money balances. In other words, individuals appear to choose not the number of dollars to hold in the form of money but the amount of purchasing power over goods and services to hold in that form. This explains why economists usually formulate their models of money demand in terms of **real money balances,** or nominal money balances divided by the price level. These models imply that if the price level in the economy suddenly doubled while all other variables remained unchanged, individuals would choose to double the number of dollars held in money balances, keeping the purchasing power of money balances unchanged.[7]

If individuals choose to hold money for its convenience in making economic transactions, the quantity of money held should reflect the volume of transactions. We can incorporate this relationship into our model by assuming that the demand for real money balances depends on real income, Q.[8] When their real income is high, individuals undertake a large number of transactions and therefore demand a large quantity of real money balances. Low levels of real income, on the other hand, are associated with lower volumes of transactions and correspondingly lower real money balances. Letting L represent the demand for real money balances, we can express the positive relationship between real income and money demand as $L(\overset{+}{Q})$.

If money is convenient for making transactions, why do individuals choose not to hold all their assets in this form? The answer is that an individual choosing to hold money incurs a cost: the forgone interest that the individual could have earned on other assets, such as bonds. Generally, money balances earn no interest, although financial innovations such as NOW accounts partially relaxed this rule.[9] Even though some forms of money, such as NOW and other interest-bearing checking accounts, do earn interest, the rates paid remain lower than those on nonmoney

---

[5]This discussion concentrates on the transactions demand for money, that is, the demand for money resulting from its convenience as a means of payment. Other reasons suggested for holding money include a precautionary motive and a speculative motive. Standard macroeconomics texts discuss these motives at length; including them here would add little to the discussion. Empirically it is difficult to clearly separate money held for the various purposes.

[6]In fact, no one really knows the location of a large portion of the currency in circulation. Case Three at the end of the chapter explores the puzzle of the missing cash.

[7]If a portion of the goods and services that individuals purchase are imported, real money balances are more appropriately measured as nominal balances divided by a price level that is a weighted average of the domestic and foreign price levels, with the weights reflecting the shares of domestic goods and services and imports in total spending. Nonetheless, the real money stock typically is reported as the nominal money stock divided by the domestic price level.

[8]Real income, Q, equals nominal income or GDP divided by the price level: $Q \equiv Y/P$.

[9]NOW accounts are *n*egotiable *o*rders of *w*ithdrawal, basically interest-paying checking accounts. The government's measure of M1 includes such accounts, since they are transaction deposits. The holder of a NOW account does earn interest, but less than that on alternative assets such as bonds.

Figure 15.1 □ **The Demand for Real Money Balances Depends Negatively on the Interest Rate and Positively on Real Income**

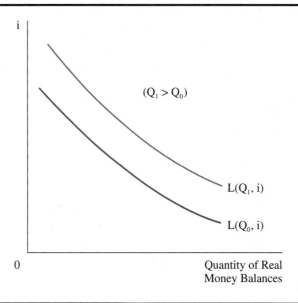

The negative slope of each demand curve (drawn for a fixed level of income) represents the negative relationship between the interest rate and the quantity demanded of real money balances. Changes in income shift the demand curve for real money balances. Here a rise in income from Q_0 to Q_1 shifts the demand curve to the right.

assets. Therefore, the differential between the interest paid on NOW accounts and the interest paid on bonds still represents an **opportunity cost of holding money.**

When the interest rate is high, the opportunity cost of holding money assets also is high, and individuals choose to hold a small fraction of their assets in money; in other words, they demand a relatively small quantity of money. At a lower interest rate, the opportunity cost of holding money is smaller and the quantity demanded of money higher. The negative relationship between money demand and the interest rate can be combined with the earlier result for income and written as $L(\overset{+}{Q}, \overset{-}{i})$.

Figure 15.1 depicts the relationship among the quantity of real money balances, the interest rate, and income. We measure the interest rate, representing the opportunity cost of holding money, on the vertical axis and the quantity of real money balances on the horizontal axis. The downward-sloping demand curve for money shows the negative relationship between the interest rate and the quantity demanded of money. A single demand curve for money assumes a fixed level of real income, for example, Q_0. Changes in real income shift the demand curve for money, just as a change in income shifts the demand curve for other goods. An increase in real income to $Q_1 > Q_0$ shifts the money demand curve to the right, implying that at any given interest rate individuals demand a larger quantity of money than before. The higher real income is associated with a desire to undertake more economic transactions, making it worthwhile to forgo interest on more funds in order to have money for convenience in making those additional transactions.

15.2.3 Money-Stock Creation

In a modern economy, the nominal money stock is the outcome of a process involving the central bank (often called a nation's **monetary authority**), commercial banks, and the public. While this process seems a bit mysterious at first, it will become more obvious if you keep the nature and definition of money in mind: Money is simply a type of asset that can be used directly as a means of payment.

The central bank or monetary authority creates the basis for a country's money stock by buying nonmoney assets (in particular, government bonds or foreign exchange) from the public, using checks written by the central bank and drawn on itself.[10] These checks are unique because they *create* money rather than merely *transfer* money from one person to another. When a party other than the central bank writes a check, that check transfers funds from the person writing the check to the person receiving it, leaving no net effect on the total quantity of transaction deposits and, therefore, no net effect on the money stock. In contrast, when the central bank buys a $1,000 government bond from an individual using one of its special checks, the individual exchanges a $1,000 nonmoney asset (the bond) for $1,000 of money. The $1,000 check written by the central bank represents money because the recipient can either cash the check at his or her bank and receive $1,000 in currency or deposit it in a checkable bank deposit. In either case, the $1,000 represents a part of the country's money stock because, by definition, the money stock includes both currency and checkable deposits (see section 15.2.1).

The central bank's purchase of a $1,000 bond from the public actually increases the money stock by considerably more than $1,000. This happens because modern economies operate under a **fractional reserve banking system.** Under such a system, banks can lend funds from their deposits because government regulation requires banks to hold only a fraction (say, 10 percent) of their deposits on hand to cover withdrawals. When the seller of the government bond deposits the $1,000 central bank check in a commercial bank, the bank must hold $100 (10 percent of $1,000) in reserves in case the depositor wants to make a withdrawal.[11] The bank may hold the $100 of reserves either in vault cash or in a deposit in the commercial bank's

---

[10]It is important to distinguish between (1) issuance of a new government bond that may be sold to the public and (2) the central bank's purchase of an outstanding (previously issued) bond from the public. Since bonds are just IOUs, the issuance of a new government bond essentially constitutes a loan from the bond purchaser to the government. In the United States, the Department of the Treasury handles this type of transaction. The central bank (the Federal Reserve in the United States) does not issue new bonds (that is, borrow from the public); rather, it either purchases bonds from the public that the public had purchased earlier from the Treasury or purchases bonds directly from the Treasury. In so doing, the central bank exchanges monetary for nonmonetary assets, thereby "creating money."

[11]Unfortunately, both the funds banks hold to cover withdrawals and the central bank's stock of foreign currencies are called "reserves." To minimize confusion, we will refer to the foreign currencies as *foreign exchange,* or *international, reserves.*

name at the central bank. The commercial bank can use the remaining $900 to make a loan, but the $900 loan eventually ends up as another deposit.

To see why, suppose an individual borrows the $900 to buy a stereo. Upon purchase, the $900 moves into the stereo dealer's bank account as a deposit. The stereo dealer's bank must then hold 10 percent, or $90, in reserves and can lend the remaining $810, which in turn ends up as an additional deposit. This "round-by-round" process, called **deposit expansion,** ends when the commercial banking system can no longer make additional loans because it is required to hold all available funds as reserves. When the process is completed, the money stock will have grown by a multiple (called the **money multiplier**) of the original $1,000 central bank purchase of the government bond. The money multiplier, or the relationship between the size of the original central bank purchase and the size of the total change in the money stock, depends on the fraction of deposits banks hold as reserves and on how much money the public chooses to hold in currency rather than in deposits.[12]

Policies by which the central bank changes the nominal money stock by buying or selling government bonds are called **open market operations.** A central bank purchase of bonds increases the money stock. The same type of policy can decrease the money stock, in which case the central bank sells government bonds to the public rather than buying them. These sales cause deposits in the economy to shrink as individuals exchange their deposits (money) for bonds (nonmoney assets).

The central bank can obtain exactly the same effects on the money stock in another way: It can purchase or sell foreign exchange rather than domestic government bonds.[13] Suppose the quantity supplied of foreign-currency-denominated assets exceeds the quantity demanded in the foreign exchange market. Individuals currently hold foreign exchange in excess of the amount they desire to hold in their asset portfolios; they want to exchange the excess foreign exchange for domestic-currency assets. The central bank can buy the excess foreign-currency-denominated assets from the public just as it did the government bond in the earlier example. It purchases the assets with its special check. The deposit-expansion process operates again, increasing the money stock by a multiple of the central bank's original purchase. In fact, the central bank's purchase of $1,000 of foreign-currency-denominated assets from the public has exactly the same effect on the money stock as did the $1,000 open market purchase of a government bond. If the quantity demanded of foreign exchange in the economy exceeds the quantity supplied, the central bank can sell foreign exchange from its international reserves. The effect is identical to that of the central bank's open market sale of government bonds; that is, the money stock falls by the amount of foreign exchange reserves sold times the money multiplier.

---

[12]We can write the *money multiplier* as $mm = (c + 1)/(c + d)$, where c denotes the ratio of currency to deposits held by the public and d the reserve-to-deposit ratio of banks. For a more extensive discussion of the money multiplier and the money creation process, see any introductory, intermediate macroeconomics, or money and banking text.

[13]Other policy options through which the central bank can alter the money stock include changes in the required reserve ratio for banks and changes in the discount rate, or the interest rate at which the central bank lends reserves to commercial banks.

Table 15.3 □ **Money Stock Expansion and Contraction**

Central Bank Operation	Effect on Money Stock
Open Market Operations	
Purchases of government bonds from the public	Rises by mm · ΔGB
Sales of government bonds to the public	Falls by mm · ΔGB
Foreign Exchange Market Intervention	
Purchases of foreign-currency deposits	Rises by mm · ΔFXR
Sales of foreign-currency deposits	Falls by mm · ΔFXR

A country's entire money stock is the outcome of the processes just outlined. Because the stock rises whenever the central bank purchases either government bonds or foreign exchange and falls whenever it sells either government bonds or foreign exchange, the money stock at any moment is determined by the quantity of government bonds and foreign exchange currently held by the monetary authority. We have seen, however, that each purchase or sale has a multiplier effect on the money stock, so the current money stock (M) equals the money multiplier (mm) times the government bonds (GB) and foreign exchange reserves (FXR) held by the central bank:[14]

$$M = mm(GB + FXR). \qquad [15.2]$$

Table 15.3 summarizes the effects of central bank open market operations and foreign exchange intervention on the domestic money stock.

15.2.4 Money Market Equilibrium

Equilibrium in the money market requires that the real money stock, the outcome of the central bank operations just described, equals the quantity of real money balances demanded by the public:

$$M/P = L(\overset{+}{Q}, \overset{-}{i}). \qquad [15.3]$$

The nominal money stock, M, depends on the actions of the central bank, as we just saw. In the remainder of this chapter, we shall assume that the price level, P, is fixed. (Later chapters will explore at length the importance of price flexibility.) Other

---

[14]With minor adjustments, the term in parentheses in Equation 15.2 represents what is known as *high-powered money,* or the *monetary base.* This is the determinant of the money stock that the central bank can affect directly through its policy choices. The money multiplier depends on the willingness of banks to lend, the central bank's regulated minimum reserve requirement imposed on banks, and the public's currency/deposit ratio (see footnote 12). Together, high-powered money and the money multiplier determine the money stock. In Equation 15.2, foreign exchange reserves are measured in units of domestic currency.

Figure 15.2 ▫ Money Market Equilibrium

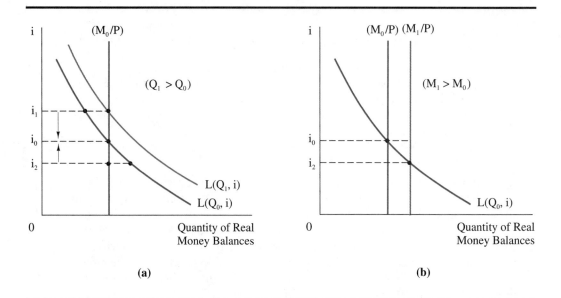

The equilibrium interest rate is the opportunity cost of holding money at which individuals are willing to hold the existing stock of real money balances. Increases in income raise the demand for money and increase the interest rate, as in panel (a), where a rise in income from Q_0 to Q_1 raises the interest rate from i_0 to i_1. Increases in the money stock produce a fall in the interest rate, inducing individuals to hold the new higher level of real money balances, as in panel (b), where the nominal money stock rises from M_0 to M_1 and reduces the equilibrium interest rate from i_0 to i_2.

variables, particularly the interest rate and income, must adjust to equate the quantity demanded of money (the right-hand side of Equation 15.3) to the stock of money in existence (the left-hand side of Equation 15.3).

Panel (a) of Figure 15.2 combines the money demand curves from Figure 15.1 with a vertical money supply curve that represents the size of the money stock (M_0/P) created by the monetary authority. If the current level of income in the economy is Q_0, the money market will be in equilibrium only if the interest rate equals i_0, the rate at which the quantity of real money balances individuals want to hold equals the quantity of real money balances the monetary authority has created.

What would happen at other interest rates? Suppose the interest rate were i_1. Panel (a) suggests that, at that relatively high interest rate, individuals choose to hold little of their wealth in money because of the high opportunity cost of holding it. The quantity of money individuals want to hold falls short of the quantity the monetary authority has created. Individuals try to eliminate their undesired money balances by buying other assets such as interest-bearing bonds. This process bids up the price of bonds or, equivalently, pushes down the interest rate to i_0.[15] Once the rate falls to i_0, individuals in the economy are content to hold (M_0/P) in real money balances, because the opportunity cost of doing so is less than at i_1.

Suppose the interest rate initially were i_2. At such a low interest rate, individuals want to hold a large portion of their wealth in the form of money—more money than the central bank has created, because money provides convenience for making transactions and the opportunity cost of not holding bonds is low. As individuals sell bonds to increase their money holdings, the price of bonds falls, or the interest rate rises. When the rate reaches i_0, the opportunity cost of holding money has risen sufficiently to make individuals content to hold only (M_0/P) in real money balances.

Changes in income shift the demand for money, as we saw in section 15.2.2. When income rises from Q_0 to Q_1, individuals in the economy undertake more transactions and need more real money balances to do so conveniently. The demand curve shifts to the right as in panel (a). At the old equilibrium interest rate, i_0, individuals now want to hold more than the existing quantity (M_0/P) of real money balances. They sell bonds to reach the desired level of money balances and push up the interest rate to i_1 in the process.

The demand for money also can shift for other (exogenous) reasons. For example, the widespread availability of automatic teller machines probably reduces the demand for money (that is, currency and checking deposits) by providing easier access to nonmoney assets such as savings accounts. Such an institutional innovation shifts the demand for money to the left and, other things being equal, results in a lower interest rate in the economy.

Panel (b) of Figure 15.2 illustrates the effect of a change in the size of the money stock. If the central bank buys government bonds or foreign-currency assets, the money stock rises from (M_0/P) to (M_1/P). At the old equilibrium interest rate, i_0, the existing money stock now exceeds the quantity of real money balances individuals want to hold given their income, Q_0. To reduce their money holdings, individuals purchase bonds, and the interest rate falls to i_2. If the central bank were to cut the money stock by selling government bonds or foreign-currency assets, individuals would respond by selling bonds, and the interest rate would rise. For now, we continue to assume the price level remains unchanged, but note that a rise in the price level reduces the real money stock, while a decline in the price level raises the real money stock.

---

[15]The simplest form of bond is an IOU promising to pay the owner (lender) the face value (say, $1,000) on a certain future date. Such a bond sells for less than its face value, because the purchaser (lender) must wait until the future date to receive the $1,000, and $1,000 received in the future has a value today of less than $1,000 even if future receipt is certain. The seller of the bond (borrower) willingly pays the difference between the face value and the purchase price to borrow funds over the bond's life. In other words, the seller willingly pays, and the purchaser demands, interest on the loan. When the demand for bonds is high (such as when individuals are holding a larger portion of their assets in money than is desired), the purchase price of bonds is bid up. The mirror image of this price increase is the fact that bond sellers need pay only a relatively low rate of interest because individuals are eager to lend (buy bonds). When the demand for bonds falls, so does the purchase price. Sellers must then pay higher rates of interest (that is, accept lower purchase prices for a given face value of a bond).

Table 15.4 □ **Summary of Money Market Effects on the Interest Rate**

Variable	Effect on Equilibrium Interest Rate
Income (Q)	
Increase	+
Decrease	−
Nominal Money Stock (M)	
Increase	−
Decrease	+
Price Level (P)	
Increase	+
Decrease	−
Demand for Money (L)	
Exogenous increase	+
Exogenous decrease	−

Table 15.4 summarizes the key relationships required for money-market equilibrium. An increase in income, a decrease in the nominal money stock, a rise in the price level, or an exogenous increase in money demand raises the equilibrium interest rate. A fall in income, an increase in the nominal money stock, a fall in the price level, or an exogenous decline in money demand lowers the interest rate at which individuals in the economy are content to hold the existing money stock.

To make it easier to combine our insights from the money market with those from the markets for goods and services and foreign exchange, we can summarize the money-market results in an LM curve.

15.2.5 The LM Curve

Panel (a) of Figure 15.3 illustrates one point of equilibrium in the money market, point I. The real money stock equals M_0/P. Real money demand is given by $L(Q_0, i_0)$, since income equals Q_0 and the interest rate equals i_0. Panel (b) marks the combination of income (Q_0, measured on the horizontal axis) and interest rate (i_0, measured on the vertical axis) that corresponds to the equilibrium at point I.

Now suppose income rises to Q_1. Panel (a) shows that at the original interest rate (i_0) and the new, higher level of income (Q_1), the new quantity demanded of money exceeds the unchanged money stock; that is, $M_0/P < L(Q_1, i_0)$. In panel (b), the (Q_1, i_0) point to the right of the line corresponds to a quantity demanded of money that exceeds the money stock. Given this situation, individuals attempt to obtain the additional desired cash balances by selling other assets, particularly bonds. Increased bond sales lower the price of bonds, and a fall in the price of bonds is equivalent to a rise in the interest rate. The interest rate will continue to rise until individuals are content to hold the quantity of money available (M_0/P). Point II represents the new equilibrium, and we mark the corresponding combination of

Figure 15.3 □ **The LM Curve Represents Equilibrium in the Money Market**

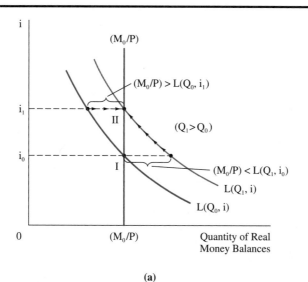

(a)

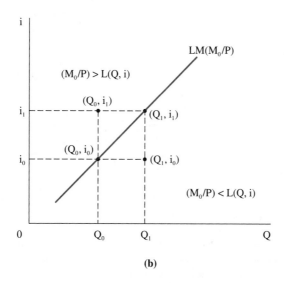

(b)

A rise in income from Q_0 to Q_1 increases the demand for money. For demand to be reequated with the fixed stock of money, a rise in the interest rate is necessary. Similarly, a rise in the interest rate lowers the quantity demanded of money. With the stock of money fixed, income must rise for the demand for money to increase. Therefore, the interest rate and income combinations consistent with equilibrium in the money market are *positively* related. The curve summarizing this positive relationship between i and Q is called an LM curve, because at each point on it the quantity demanded of money (L) equals the money stock (M/P). To the right of the LM curve, the quantity demanded of money exceeds the money stock; to the left of it, the quantity demanded of money is less than the money stock.

income and interest, (Q_1, i_1), in panel (b). The original rise in income required a rise in the interest rate for the quantity demanded of money to be reequated with the money stock. The rise in income increased the demand for money, and the rise in the interest rate raised the cost of holding money, causing an offsetting decline in quantity demanded. Note that throughout the process, the stock of money remained unchanged at M_0/P.

Beginning again at the original equilibrium, point I, suppose events in the economy cause the interest rate to rise from i_0 to i_1. With income at Q_0, the rise in the interest rate causes the quantity demanded of money to fall below the level of the money stock. In panel (b) of Figure 15.3, the point (Q_0, i_1) to the left of the line corresponds to a situation in which the quantity demanded of money is less than the money stock. The money market can be in equilibrium at an interest rate of i_1 only if income rises to Q_1, raising the demand for money and restoring equilibrium at point II. Again, the money stock does not change between points I and II.

The upward-sloping curve in panel (b) of Figure 15.3, called an **LM curve**, shows the various combinations of income and interest at which the money market is in equilibrium. The term *LM curve* refers to the fact that, at every point along the curve, the quantity demanded of money (L) equals the fixed money stock (M/P). At points to the right of the LM curve, the quantity demanded of money exceeds the money stock; at points to the left, the opposite holds. *(Why?)*

When the real money stock changes, the LM curve shifts. Since we assume the price level is fixed, only a change in the nominal money stock, M, can cause a change in the real money stock. As illustrated in Figure 15.4, increases in the nominal money stock shift the LM curve to the right. In panel (a), the nominal money stock rises to M_1, shifting the money stock line to the right. At income Q_0, equilibrium now requires an interest rate of i_2 at point III. A lower interest rate $(i_2 < i_0)$ induces individuals to hold the larger stock of money.

The same argument holds at income Q_1. The interest rate must fall from i_1 to i_3 for the quantity demanded of money to rise. At i_1, the opportunity cost of holding money is too high for the public to willingly hold the new, larger money stock. Panel (b) of Figure 15.4 marks the new combinations of income and interest that result in money market equilibrium given the new money stock. (As a reminder, we label each LM curve according to the real money stock on which it is based.)

15.2.6 Money in Open versus Closed Economies

As mentioned in section 15.1, the money market in an open economy at first glance appears identical to that in a closed economy. Money demand depends on domestic income and the interest rate, which must adjust to keep money demand equal to the money stock prevailing at each point in time. The effects of openness enter through the additional mechanism by which the central bank can create or destroy money, that is, purchases or sales of foreign exchange. In fact, the nature and extent of a central bank's ability to control the money stock hinge on the nature of the country's international linkages, particularly the exchange rate regime under which it operates. Before exploring the details of the interaction between the exchange rate regime and the money stock, we need to translate our knowledge of the foreign exchange market and balance of payments into a more convenient form.

Figure 15.4 □ **Effect of an Increase in the Real Money Stock on the LM Curve**

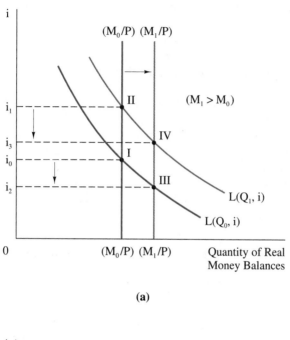

(a)

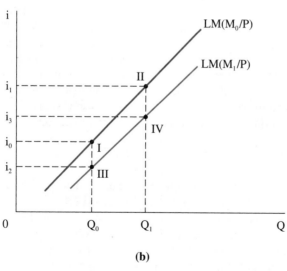

(b)

An increase in the real money stock (caused here by an increase in the nominal money stock from M_0 to M_1 with the price level held constant) shifts the LM curve to the right. Any given level of income now requires a lower interest rate for money market equilibrium.

15.3 Foreign Exchange[16]

15.3.1 Introduction

Recall from Chapter Thirteen that the balance-of-payments accounts classify autonomous foreign exchange transactions (that is, those arising in the course of day-to-day economic transactions by individuals, firms, and government agencies) into two major subaccounts: the *current account,* composed mainly of purchases and sales of goods and services, and the *capital account,* which reflects international borrowing and lending or purchases and sales of financial assets and direct investment.

When the sum of the current- and capital-account balances equals zero, the quantities demanded and supplied of foreign exchange are equal and the balance of payments is in balance. When the sum of the current- and capital-account balances is negative, the quantity demanded of foreign-currency-denominated deposits exceeds the quantity available and the domestic balance of payments is in deficit. A positive sum of the current- and capital-account balances corresponds to a quantity of available foreign-currency-denominated deposits that exceeds the quantity demanded and a balance-of-payments surplus.

15.3.2 Equilibrium in the Foreign Exchange Market

Because the current and capital accounts reflect different classes of economic transactions (purchases/sales of goods and services versus borrowing/lending and direct investment), each account responds to different economic variables. The current account depends on domestic and foreign incomes and on the relative prices of domestic and foreign goods and services (also called the real exchange rate). A rise in foreign income increases exports and moves the current-account balance toward a surplus. Increased domestic income has the opposite effect by raising imports. A rise in the relative price of domestic goods or real exchange rate ($R \equiv P/eP^*$) reduces exports and increases imports, moving the current account toward a deficit. (For a review, see sections 14.4 and 14.5.) Letting CAB denote the *current-account balance,* a plus sign denote a move toward a surplus, and a minus sign denote a move toward a deficit, we can summarize the effects on the current account as

$$CAB(\overset{+}{Q^*}, \overset{-}{Q}, \overset{-}{R}).$$ [15.4]

The capital account depends on relative interest rates on domestic and foreign assets and on the spot exchange rate, the forward rate, and the expected future spot exchange rate. Other things being equal, a rise in the foreign interest rate, i^*, makes foreign assets more attractive, resulting in a capital outflow and a move toward a deficit in the domestic capital account. A rise in the domestic interest rate, i, has the opposite effect, generating a capital inflow and a capital-account surplus. A rise in the spot rate lowers the expected return on foreign assets and causes a capital inflow, while a rise in the forward rate raises the

---

[16]The following discussion assumes that the reader is familiar with the material covered in Chapter Twelve; if not, we suggest a review at this point.

Figure 15.5 ▫ Balance-of-Payments Equilibrium Requires That the Sum of the Current-Account Balance (CAB) and the Capital-Account Balance (KAB) Equal Zero

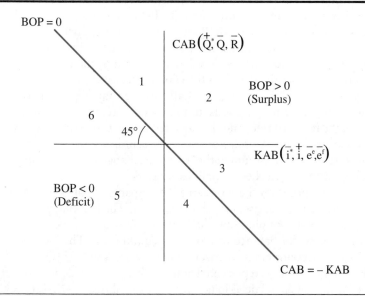

Along the negatively sloped 45-degree line, the balance of payments is in equilibrium. Below and to the left of the line, there is a deficit; above and to the right of the line, the balance of payments is in surplus.

expected return on foreign assets and produces a capital outflow. Given domestic and foreign interest rates, an expectation that the domestic currency will depreciate in the future makes foreign assets more attractive and produces a capital-account deficit. Letting KAB denote the capital-*account balance* (since K has symbolized capital throughout this book),

$$KAB(\bar{i}^*, \overset{+}{i}, \overset{+}{e}, \overset{-}{e}^f, \overset{-}{e}^e). \qquad [15.5]$$

When the sum of the current- and capital-account balances equals zero, the overall balance of payments (BOP) is in equilibrium. The market for foreign exchange also is in equilibrium, since the quantity demanded of foreign-currency-denominated assets equals the quantity available:

$$CAB + KAB = 0 \text{ for BOP equilibrium.} \qquad [15.6]$$

We can rearrange Equation 15.6 slightly to read

$$CAB = -KAB \text{ for BOP equilibrium.} \qquad [15.7]$$

Figure 15.5 represents graphically this requirement for equilibrium in the balance of payments or the foreign exchange market by a negatively sloped 45-degree line along which Equation 15.7 holds. At points above and to the right of the line, the balance of payments shows a surplus (BOP > 0) because either (1) the current-account surplus exceeds the capital-account deficit (in area 1), (2) both the current and capital accounts are in surplus (in area 2), or (3) the capital-account surplus exceeds the current-account deficit (in area 3). Below and to the left of the line, the balance of payments is in deficit (BOP < 0). In area 4, the current-account deficit exceeds the capital-account surplus. Area 5 represents combinations at which both the current and capital accounts are in deficit. In area 6, the current-account surplus is too small to offset the deficit in the capital account.

In the remainder of this section, we shall assume that foreign income, relative prices of domestic and foreign goods and services, foreign interest rates, the spot exchange rate, the forward rate, and the expected future spot exchange rate are fixed, so we can concentrate on the relationship between domestic income and interest rate that must hold for equilibrium in the foreign exchange market. Figure 15.6 panel (a) repeats Figure 15.5 with these simplifications.

Beginning at any point on the 45-degree line in panel (a) of Figure 15.6 (such as point I), let domestic income rise, say, from Q_0 to Q_1. The fact that point I lies on the balance-of-payments line implies that the interest rate equals i_0 such that $CAB(Q_0)$ = $-KAB(i_0)$, as required for balance-of-payments equilibrium. The increase in income moves the current-account balance toward a deficit, because $CAB(Q_1) < CAB(Q_0)$ as Equation 15.4 implies. This is represented graphically as a move downward to point II, at which the balance of payments is in deficit because $CAB(Q_1) < -KAB(i_0) = CAB(Q_0)$. Restoring balance-of-payments equilibrium requires that the interest rate rise by enough to generate an increased capital inflow sufficient to offset the current-account move toward a deficit.[17] We denote the new interest rate as i_1, where $CAB(Q_1)$ = $-KAB(i_1)$. Point III in panel (a) of Figure 15.6 represents this new equilibrium.

Generally, any rise in domestic income moves the CAB toward a deficit; therefore, maintaining foreign exchange market equilibrium requires a rise in the interest rate to generate an offsetting move toward a surplus in the KAB. Similarly, a fall in the interest rate moves the KAB toward a deficit (as individuals want to hold more foreign-currency-denominated assets) and requires a fall in income to reduce imports and move the CAB toward a surplus.

15.3.3 The BOP Curve

We can summarize the relationship among income, the interest rate, and the balance of payments by stating that the various combinations of domestic income and interest rates that result in foreign exchange market equilibrium lie along an upward-sloping line as illustrated in panel (b) of Figure 15.6. We label this line a **BOP curve,** because it reflects all combinations of income and interest rates that correspond to *balance-of-payments* (and foreign exchange market) equilibrium.

---

[17]We shall see that the magnitude of the rise in interest rates depends on the degree of capital mobility. The more mobile is capital, the smaller the rise in i required to generate capital inflows sufficient to restore balance-of-payments equilibrium.

Figure 15.6 □ **Effects of Domestic Income and Interest on the Market for Foreign Exchange**

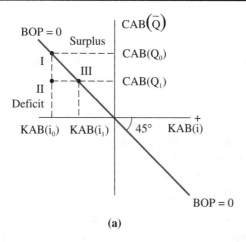

(a)

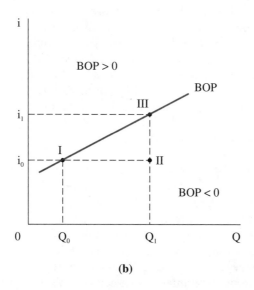

(b)

Starting from a point of balance-of-payments equilibrium (point I) in panel (a), an increase in domestic in-come from Q_0 to Q_1 moves the current-account balance toward a deficit, resulting in a balance-of-payments deficit at an unchanged interest rate (point II). To cause increased capital inflows with which to offset the decreased current-account surplus, the interest rate must rise from i_0 to i_1 (point III). At point III, the bal-ance of payments is again in equilibrium, but with a smaller current-account surplus and capital-account deficit than at the original equilibrium, point I. The BOP curve in panel (b) represents the various combi-nations of domestic income and interest rates at which the balance of payments and the foreign exchange market are in equilibrium. Because increases in income move the CAB toward a deficit while increases in interest rates move the KAB toward a surplus, the BOP line is upward sloping. Points I and III in panel (b) refer to those combinations of income and interest resulting in equilibrium points I and III in panel (a).

Although the balance of payments is in equilibrium at every point along the BOP curve, each point reflects a different situation for the current and capital accounts. Points on the lower left end of the BOP curve correspond to low levels of income and interest, implying current-account surpluses and capital-account deficits. At the upper right end of the BOP curve, high income results in a current-account deficit and a high interest rate produces an offsetting capital-account surplus. The BOP curve alone cannot determine at which point the economy will operate; once we combine the markets for goods and services, money, and foreign exchange, however, we can determine the point at which all three markets are in equilibrium. First, we discuss the causes of shifts in the BOP curve.

The BOP curve is drawn for given values of foreign income (Q^*), relative foreign and domestic prices or real exchange rate (R), foreign interest rates (i^*), the forward rate (e^f), and the expected exchange rate (e^e). Changes in any of these variables shift the entire BOP curve. At any given level of domestic income, a rise in foreign income or a decline in the relative price of domestic goods moves the CAB toward a surplus. Balance-of-payments equilibrium then requires a lower interest rate to produce an offsetting KAB move toward a deficit. Since BOP equilibrium requires a lower interest rate at any given level of income, the BOP curve shifts to the right. A similar analysis in the other direction implies that a fall in foreign income or a rise in the relative price of domestic goods shifts the BOP curve to the left; each level of domestic income requires a higher interest rate for balance-of-payments equilibrium.

Increases in foreign interest rates, an expected depreciation of the domestic currency, or a rise in the forward rate cause increased capital outflows, moving the KAB toward a deficit. An offsetting move toward a surplus in the current account requires a fall in domestic income to reduce imports. Because a lower level of domestic income is required at each domestic interest rate, the BOP curve shifts to the left. Figure 15.7 summarizes these results and lists the causes of shifts to the left and to the right of the BOP curve.

Two Special Cases: Capital Mobility and the BOP Curve

We just argued that balance-of-payments equilibrium requires a *positive* relationship between income and the interest rate; because a rise in income increases imports and moves the current account toward a deficit, a rise in the interest rate is required to generate an offsetting move toward surplus in the capital account. How big an increase in the interest rate is required depends on how sensitive international capital flows are to changes in interest rates. If asset owners do not respond strongly to slight changes in international interest rate differentials, then a large increase in the interest rate may be necessary to induce a capital inflow sufficient to offset the current-account deficit. In such circumstances, the BOP curve will be steeply upward sloping. *(Why?)* On the other hand, asset owners may be highly sensitive to even tiny changes in the international pattern of interest rates. If so, only a minute rise in the domestic interest rate will be necessary to bring about a capital inflow sufficient to restore balance-of-payments equilibrium. Graphically, this implies that the upward-sloping BOP curve will be relatively flat. *(Why?)* In other words, the slope of the BOP curve indicates the degree of capital mobility, or how sensitive international capital flows are to changes in domestic and foreign interest rates. Low capital mobility implies a steep BOP curve, and high capital mobility a flat one.

Figure 15.7 □ **Changes in Foreign Income, Relative Prices, Foreign Interest Rates, the Forward Rate, or the Expected Exchange Rate Shift the BOP Curve**

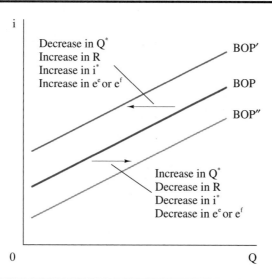

We shall see in the next two chapters that the degree of capital mobility exerts an important influence on the macroeconomy and on the effectiveness of macroeconomic policies. To examine the effects of differing degrees of capital mobility, it often proves useful to focus on two extreme cases: that of perfect capital immobility (or zero mobility) and that of perfect mobility.

Under perfect capital *im*mobility, the nonofficial capital account as described in Chapter Thirteen does not exist, because both capital inflows and outflows equal zero by definition. No autonomous international borrowing and lending occurs regardless of the interest rate differentials existing among countries. With no capital-account transactions, the balance of payments (normally BOP = CAB + KAB) consists solely of the current account (BOP = CAB). If the current account is in deficit, the balance of payments is in deficit; with a current-account surplus, a balance-of-payments surplus exists. The requirement for balance-of-payments equilibrium reduces to the requirement that the current-account balance equal zero.

Recall from section 14.4 that there exists only one level of income at which the current-account balance equals zero. The interest rate becomes irrelevant to balance-of-payments equilibrium with no capital mobility; thus, the BOP line becomes vertical, as in Figure 15.8 panel (a). To the right of the BOP line, the balance of payments lies in deficit; to the left of the line, a BOP surplus exists. A rise in foreign income (Q^*) or a fall in the relative price of domestic goods and services (R) increases exports at each level of domestic income and causes the income consistent with balance in the current account to rise, so the BOP curve shifts to the right. A decline in foreign income or a rise in the relative price of domestic goods and services decreases exports at each level of income and shifts the BOP curve to the left. *(Why?)*

Figure 15.8 □ **The Degree of Capital Mobility Determines the Slope of the BOP Curve**

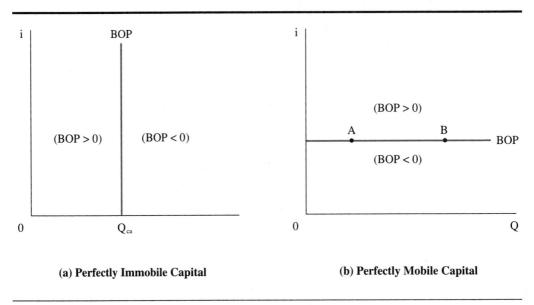

(a) Perfectly Immobile Capital   **(b) Perfectly Mobile Capital**

Perfectly immobile capital means no transactions occur in the nonofficial capital account. The balance of payments includes only the current-account balance, which equals zero at a single level of income, Q_{ca}, in panel (a). Perfectly mobile capital means that infinitesimal changes in interest rates generate large international capital flows, implying a horizontal BOP curve as in panel (b).

We now move to the opposite assumption, that of perfect capital mobility. The assumption of perfect capital mobility simply means that investors, in deciding which assets to hold, consider only interest rates and exchange rates (including the forward rate and the expected future spot rate). In other words, investors have no built-in preferences for assets denominated in one currency versus those denominated in another, and government policies do not restrict capital flows. Under perfect capital mobility, the balance-of-payments line becomes completely horizontal, as illustrated in panel (b) of Figure 15.8. Recall that in the presence of an active capital account we draw each BOP line for given values of foreign interest rates, the exchange rate, and forward and expected spot exchange rates. This implies that any rise in the domestic interest rate causes a capital inflow and a move toward a surplus on the capital account. (For a review, see the discussion of interest parity in section 12.4.)

How does the assumption of perfect capital mobility produce a horizontal BOP line? In Figure 15.8 panel (b), the balance of payments is in equilibrium at point A; this is true because A lies on the BOP line, which, by definition, represents points of balance-of-payments equilibrium. Beginning at A, suppose a disturbance in the economy raises income. Imports rise with income, and the current account moves toward a deficit. To maintain balance-of-payments equilibrium, the capital account must generate an offsetting move toward surplus. With perfectly mobile capital, how large an increase in the domestic interest rate is required to generate this capital-account surplus? The answer is that an infinitesimal (essentially zero) rise in the interest rate will suffice. The reason is that investors will respond immediately to the slightest rise in domestic rates by moving their funds into the domestic economy.

In terms of the interest parity condition discussed in Chapter Twelve, massive capital flows in response to even minute changes in relative interest rates maintain the equilibrium or parity condition. Therefore, the balance of payments is in equilibrium at B—with a larger current-account deficit and capital-account surplus than at A. All points above the BOP line correspond to situations of balance-of-payments surplus, and those below the line represent balance-of-payments deficits. *(Why?)* An increase in the foreign interest rate, the forward exchange rate, or the expected future spot rate raises the expected rate of return on foreign-currency-denominated assets and shifts the BOP line up, because a higher domestic interest rate is required to induce asset owners to hold domestic-currency assets. A fall in the spot exchange rate has a similar effect. *(Use interest parity to explain why a fall in i^*, e^e, or e^f, or a rise in e would shift the BOP curve down.)*

Our models of the goods and services, money, and foreign exchange markets are now complete and summarized in the IS, LM, and BOP curves, respectively, each of which represents the combinations of domestic income and interest rates at which quantity demanded equals quantity supplied in the respective market.

15.4 Bringing It All Together

Recall that *general equilibrium* refers to simultaneous equilibrium in several related markets. General-equilibrium analysis of an open macroeconomy examines the interaction of the goods and services, money, and foreign exchange markets in determining the economy's performance. Because we have summarized the requirement for each market's equilibrium with a curve relating domestic income and interest rates, we can combine the three markets easily to facilitate a general-equilibrium analysis.

Figure 15.9 brings together the IS, LM, and BOP curves representing equilibrium in the market for goods and services, money, and foreign exchange, respectively. The IS curve is downward sloping and the LM and BOP curves are upward sloping, reflecting our assumption of an intermediate degree of capital mobility.

A point at which all three curves intersect represents a general equilibrium in the economy. No such intersection occurs in Figure 15.9, illustrating that there appears to be no reason to expect such an intersection to occur. In fact, in the figure it appears that only a coincidence would result in a common intersection and general equilibrium. This somewhat pessimistic-sounding situation disappears, however, once we recognize several linkages among the three markets. These linkages guarantee that (in the absence of interference) the IS, LM, and BOP curves will move to a point of common intersection and that the economy will (eventually) reach a general equilibrium. This is an important and somewhat surprising result, especially since we have assumed throughout this chapter that the price level is fixed, thereby ruling out one of the economy's most powerful self-adjustment mechanisms.

The exact nature of the linkages among the three markets depends on the exchange rate regime under which the economy operates. Flexible exchange rates imply linkages that are somewhat easier to see than those under fixed rates. Thus, we begin with a flexible rate regime and then move on to adjustment under a fixed rate regime.

Figure 15.9 □ **Combining the IS, LM, and BOP Curves**

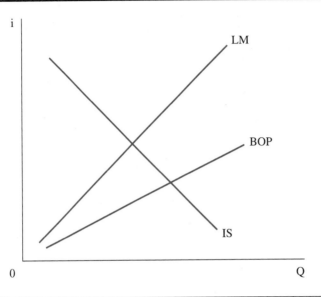

A general equilibrium in the economy requires that the three curves share a common point of intersection. At such a point, the markets for goods and services, money, and foreign exchange are all in equilibrium simultaneously at the given combination of Q, i, and e.

15.5 Automatic Adjustment under a Flexible Exchange Rate Regime

Under a perfectly flexible exchange rate regime, the exchange rate continually adjusts to keep the balance of payments in equilibrium and, equivalently, to keep the quantity demanded of foreign exchange equal to the quantity supplied. These changes in the exchange rate shift both the IS and BOP curves until they reach a general equilibrium on the LM curve.

Note that because of the negative slope of the IS curve and the positive slopes of the LM and BOP curves, the IS curve will always intersect each of the other two, but not necessarily at the same point. Point I in Figure 15.10 illustrates a case in which the markets for goods and services and for money are in equilibrium, but with a balance-of-payments surplus with the exchange rate at e_0.[18] The surplus in the BOP at point I is evident from I's position above and to the left of the BOP curve drawn with $e = e_0$ (see section 15.3.3). Because the quantity supplied of foreign exchange exceeds the quantity demanded (by the definition of a balance-of-payments surplus), the domestic currency appreciates, or

---

[18]We would never actually observe a point such as I under a perfectly flexible exchange rate, because the exchange rate adjusts instantaneously. Nonetheless, an examination of point I proves useful for understanding the nature of the adjustment process.

Figure 15.10 □ **Automatic Adjustment from a Position of Balance-of-Payments Surplus under a Flexible Exchange Rate**

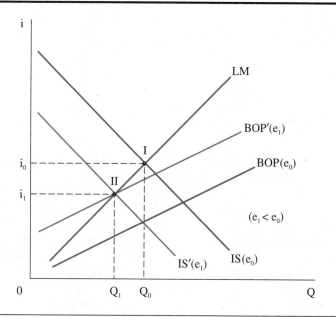

The balance-of-payments surplus at point I causes the domestic currency to appreciate, shifting the BOP and IS curves to the left. Point II represents equilibrium with income equal to Q_1, the interest rate at i_1, and the domestic-currency price of foreign currency at e_1.

the domestic currency price of foreign currency falls from e_0 to e_1. The appreciation raises the relative price of domestic goods, since $R \equiv P/eP^*$. Exports fall and imports rise, shifting the IS curve to the left from IS to IS'.[19]

An appreciation of the domestic currency also shifts the BOP curve to the left. The currency appreciation affects both balance-of-payments accounts. The current-account balance moves toward a deficit as exports fall and imports rise. *(Why?)* The capital account also moves toward a deficit. (If you have forgotten why the exchange rate has this effect on the capital account, you may want to review section 12.4 on interest parity.) Since the balance of payments originally was in surplus at point I, the changes in both accounts move it toward equilibrium. The new BOP line (BOP') represents the combinations of income and interest that place the balance of payments in equilibrium given the new, lower value of the exchange rate, e_1. The IS and BOP curves come to a rest once they share a common intersection with the LM curve. At that point (point II in Figure 15.10), all three markets are in equilibrium simultaneously at income Q_1, interest rate i_1, and exchange rate e_1. Table 15.5 reports the automatic adjustments in response to the balance-of-payments surplus.

[19]Recall from section 14.8 that events that lower total expenditure on domestic goods and services also shift the IS curve to the left.

Table 15.5 □ **Adjustment from a BOP Surplus under a Flexible Exchange Rate**[a]

Variable	
Domestic income (Q)	Falls
Domestic interest rate (i)	Falls
Exchange rate (e)	Falls (domestic currency appreciates)
Money stock (M/P)	None

[a]Here we assume an intermediate level of capital mobility. Chapter Seventeen will focus on the implications of different degrees of capital mobility for the adjustment process and for macroeconomic policy.

We can use a similar analysis to show that if the IS and LM curves intersect below and to the right of the BOP curve, indicating a BOP deficit, the domestic currency will depreciate. The IS curve will shift to the right *(Why?)*, as will the BOP line *(Why?)*. Again general equilibrium will occur when income, the interest rate, and the exchange rate have adjusted such that all three markets are in equilibrium simultaneously, as reported in Table 15.6.

In the process of shifting the IS, LM, and BOP curves, it is important to keep in mind the major results obtained so far. First, a general equilibrium in the economy requires a combination of income, interest rate, and exchange rate such that all three markets are in equilibrium simultaneously.

Second, even with prices held fixed, the economy contains self-adjusting mechanisms for bringing the three major markets into equilibrium. We call these mechanisms *self-adjusting,* or *automatic,* because they require no explicit policy actions. Under a flexible exchange rate regime, the currency appreciates in response to a balance-of-payments surplus and depreciates in response to a deficit as a result of market forces, not government action. Once the exchange rate adjustment begins, individuals respond by altering their relative purchases of foreign and domestic goods, services, and assets. This process brings income, the interest rate, and the exchange rate to levels that clear all three markets, although the adjustment may be gradual.

Third, the model highlights the pitfalls of drawing conclusions from analysis of only one market. If we consider only the market for goods and services or only the

Table 15.6 □ **Adjustment from a BOP Deficit under a Flexible Exchange Rate**[a]

Variable	
Domestic income (Q)	Rises
Domestic interest rate (i)	Rises
Exchange rate (e)	Rises (domestic currency depreciates)
Money stock (M/P)	None

[a]See note in Table 15.5.

market for money, point I in Figure 15.10 will appear to be an equilibrium point. Imagine a situation in which output Q_0 corresponds to an acceptable level of employment (or unemployment) such that policy makers want the economy to operate at point I. If we ignore the balance of payments, the tendency of the economy to move to point II will be difficult to understand. By taking into account the balance of payments, however, it becomes easy to see why the economy ends up at point II. If point II is unacceptable, moving the economy away from it may require some type of active macroeconomic policy. We shall analyze such policies in Chapters Sixteen and Seventeen. There we shall see that a general-equilibrium framework is essential not only for understanding where the economy tends to move independently but also for predicting accurately the effects of the various economic policies available. Just as a model that includes only the market for goods and services can wrongly imply that the economy will be in equilibrium at Q_0 and i_0, so can it produce misleading results concerning the effects of economic policies in an open economy.

15.6 Automatic Adjustment under a Fixed Exchange Rate Regime

It may seem obvious that the economy can adjust to reach a general equilibrium under a flexible exchange rate regime, since the exchange rate provides an automatic adjustment mechanism. But what about an economy under a completely fixed exchange rate regime in which even policy-induced changes in the pegged rate (that is, devaluations and revaluations) are ruled out? Do we have any reason to expect the economy to self-adjust and reach general equilibrium under such circumstances? The answer is *yes,* because there is a direct link between the nominal money stock and the balance of payments under a fixed rate regime.

With a flexible exchange rate, a currency appreciation or depreciation corrects any balance-of-payments surplus or deficit. In terms of the IS-LM-BOP graph, the change in the exchange rate shifts the IS and BOP curves until they intersect on the LM curve (which remains unchanged throughout the adjustment process). Under a fixed exchange rate regime, the IS and BOP curves no longer handle the adjustment. Instead, the LM curve moves to the intersection of the stationary IS and BOP curves, because surpluses or deficits in the balance of payments automatically cause changes in the money stock. (It may prove useful to review Figure 15.4's analysis of the effect of a change in the nominal money stock on the LM curve.) To understand this process, we need to examine the link between the balance of payments and the money stock under a fixed exchange rate.

15.6.1 Fixed Exchange Rates and the Nominal Money Stock

Recall that within a fixed exchange rate regime, the central bank maintains the pegged exchange rate by intervening to buy any excess supply of foreign exchange or to sell foreign exchange to cover any excess demand. As we shall see, such intervention by the central bank restores foreign exchange market equilibrium at the pegged exchange rate. The mechanics of foreign exchange market intervention are quite simple. When the balance

Figure 15.11 ▫ **Effect of Foreign Exchange Market Intervention on the Money Stock under a Fixed Exchange Rate**

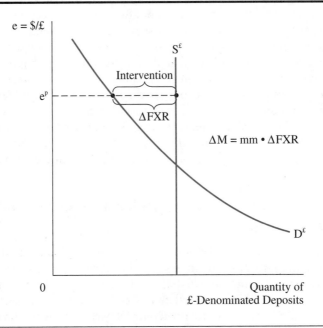

At the pegged rate, e^P, the quantity of foreign exchange supplied exceeds the quantity demanded. To prevent the dollar from appreciating, the U.S. central bank must buy the excess pounds. The purchased pounds are added to the central bank's foreign exchange reserves. The central bank check with which the pounds are bought creates the basis for an expansion of the U.S. money stock. The money stock rises by mm · ΔFXR.

of payments is in surplus, the central bank must purchase from the public the excess of quantity supplied over quantity demanded of foreign exchange. These purchases raise the central bank's stock of foreign exchange reserves. As Equation 15.2 suggests, the money stock rises by the amount of the FXR purchase times the money multiplier.

Figure 15.11 ties Chapter Twelve's analysis of the foreign exchange market to the effect on the money stock, using pounds to represent foreign exchange. To maintain the exchange rate at e^P, the central bank must buy the excess supply of foreign exchange at that rate. It makes this purchase with one of its special checks. The central bank's foreign exchange reserves rise by ΔFXR; and the money stock rises by mm · ΔFXR through the money creation process discussed in section 15.2.3.[20]

---

[20]In Chapter Sixteen, we shall see that this result hinges on an assumption that the central bank does not *sterilize* or engage in open market operations designed to offset the effect of intervention on the domestic money stock. As Equation 15.2 makes clear, if central bank purchases or sales of government bonds cancel out the effect of purchases or sales of foreign exchange (ΔGB = –ΔFXR), the money stock will remain unchanged.

Figure 15.12 □ Effect of Intervention on the Money Market and Foreign Exchange Market

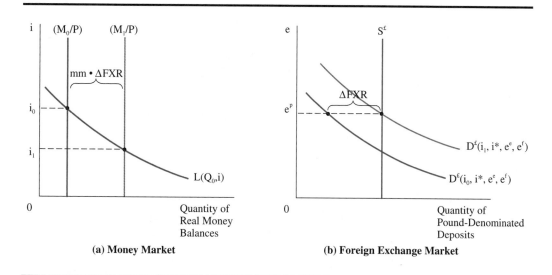

When the central bank intervenes by buying the excess supply of foreign-currency-denominated deposits in the foreign exchange market (panel (b)), the domestic money stock rises (panel (a)). The high domestic money stock pushes down the equilibrium interest rate, lowers the rate of return on domestic-currency deposits, and raises the demand for foreign-currency deposits. The intervention restores interest parity at the original exchange rate (e^P) and a lower domestic interest rate.

Figure 15.12 illustrates how the rise in the money stock restores foreign exchange market equilibrium at the pegged exchange rate, e^P. Panel (a) traces events in the money market. Prior to the central bank's intervention, the money stock is (M_0/P) and the equilibrium interest rate is i_0. Panel (b), representing the foreign exchange market, shows that the foreign exchange market is *not* in equilibrium at e^P and i_0. Given those values of the exchange rate and the domestic interest (along with i^*, e^e, and e^f), portfolio owners want to hold less than the existing stock of pound-denominated assets. The central bank must step in to buy up the excess supply, adding to its international reserves and expanding the domestic money stock by $mm \cdot \Delta FXR$. The rise in the domestic money stock shifts the money supply line in panel (a) to the right, from (M_0/P) to (M_1/P), where $(M_1/P) = (M_0/P) + (mm \cdot \Delta FXR)$. At the old equilibrium interest rate, i_0, individuals do not want to hold the new, higher level of real money balances. They buy bonds to lower real money balances to the desired level and, in the process, push the interest rate down to i_1. At i_1, individuals are content to hold the new, larger domestic money stock. The lower interest rate also affects the foreign exchange market. Because i has fallen, asset owners want to shift their portfolios toward more pound-denominated deposits, which now pay a higher expected rate of return. This shifts the demand for pound deposits to the right, achieving interest parity at e^P.

To retrace the argument, the initial excess supply of pound deposits at e^P and i_0 necessitated central bank intervention to buy foreign-currency assets. The intervention increased the domestic money stock and lowered the domestic interest rate, thereby making asset owners content to hold the existing quantity of foreign-currency assets.

If the exchange rate is fixed at a level below the equilibrium rate, the quantity demanded of foreign exchange exceeds the quantity supplied (see, for example, Figure 12.11). The central bank intervenes to sell foreign exchange from its reserves. Because the central bank's foreign exchange reserves fall by the amount of the excess demand at e^P, the domestic money stock falls by mm · ΔFXR. The decline in the domestic money stock pushes up the equilibrium domestic interest rate and restores equilibrium in the foreign exchange market by decreasing the demand for foreign-currency-denominated deposits. Interest parity holds at the pegged exchange rate and the new, higher domestic interest rate.

15.6.2 The Money Stock and Automatic Adjustment

As long as a balance-of-payments surplus exists, the central bank's foreign exchange market intervention will cause the money stock to expand, shifting the LM curve to the right. A balance-of-payments deficit, on the other hand, will shrink the money stock, shifting the LM curve to the left. These adjustments ensure that the LM curve will move to the point of intersection with the IS and BOP curves, resulting in a general equilibrium in the economy.

Figure 15.13 traces the economy's adjustment from a position of surplus in its balance of payments. At the intersection of the IS and LM curves (point I), the balance of payments is in surplus, because the point lies above and to the left of the BOP curve. In the foreign exchange market, there is an excess supply of foreign-currency-denominated deposits. To restore balance-of-payments equilibrium, the central bank must buy the excess foreign exchange, causing the domestic money stock to rise from M_0 to M_1 and shifting the LM curve to the right. The adjustment process is complete when the LM curve reaches to a point of intersection with both the IS and BOP curves (point II). There, all three markets are in simultaneous equilibrium at the existing income, interest rate, and exchange rate. Table 15.7 summarizes the economy's automatic adjustment from a point of balance-of-payments surplus under a fixed exchange rate regime.

Figure 15.14 illustrates the adjustment from a position of balance-of-payments deficit. At the intersection of the IS and LM curves (point I), the balance of payments is in deficit. To restore balance-of-payments equilibrium, the central bank must sell foreign exchange, causing the money stock to fall from M_0 to M_1 and shifting the LM curve to the left. The adjustment process is complete when the LM curve has shifted to a point of intersection with both the IS and BOP curves (point II). Table 15.8 lists each variable's contribution to the adjustment process.

We have demonstrated that linkages among the goods and services, money, and foreign exchange markets ensure that the economy can reach a point of general equilibrium even if prices are fixed. The exact mechanism by which the adjustment occurs

Figure 15.13 ▫ A Surplus in the Balance of Payments Causes the Money Stock to Rise, Shifting the LM Curve to the Right

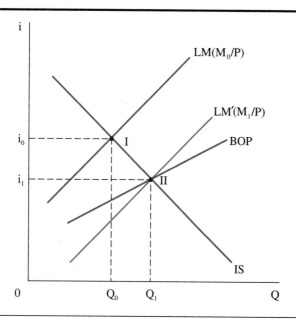

The balance-of-payments surplus corresponds to an excess supply of foreign exchange. To maintain the pegged exchange rate, the central bank must intervene, buying foreign exchange and adding it to the bank's reserves. The increase in reserves raises the domestic money stock from M_0 to M_1.

depends on the exchange rate regime in operation. Under a flexible rate regime, the *exchange rate* adjusts to equilibrate the balance of payments. Graphically, changes in the exchange rate shift the IS and BOP curves to a common intersection with the LM curve. Under a fixed exchange rate regime, the *money stock* adjusts through

Table 15.7 ▫ Adjustment from a BOP Surplus under a Fixed Exchange Rate[a]

Variable	
Domestic income (Q)	Rises
Domestic interest rate (i)	Falls
Exchange rate (e)	None
Money stock (M/P)	Rises

[a]Here we assume the degree of capital mobility to be intermediate. In Chapter Sixteen, we shall look in detail at the importance of the extent of capital mobility for the automatic adjustment process and for fiscal and monetary policies.

Figure 15.14 □ **A Deficit in the Balance of Payments Causes the Money Stock to Fall, Shifting the LM Curve to the Left**

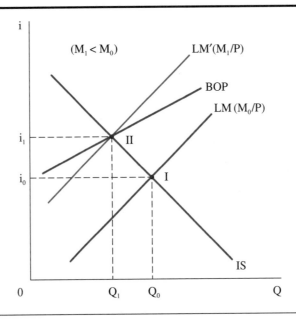

The deficit corresponds to an excess demand for foreign exchange. To maintain the pegged exchange rate, the central bank must intervene, supplying foreign exchange from its reserves. The loss of reserves lowers the domestic money stock from M_0 to M_1.

the central bank's foreign exchange intervention policies. Graphically, this is reflected in a shift of the LM curve to a common intersection with the IS and BOP curves. Note that the mechanism by which adjustment occurs carries important implications for the macroeconomy. For example, comparing Tables 15.5 and 15.7,

Table 15.8 □ **Adjustment from a BOP Deficit under a Fixed Exchange Rate[a]**

Variable	
Domestic income (Q)	Falls
Domestic interest rate (i)	Rises
Exchange rate (e)	None
Money stock (M/P)	Falls

[a]See note in Table 15.7.

we can see that automatic adjustment from a balance-of-payments surplus reduces income under a flexible exchange rate (because the currency appreciation raises the relative price of domestic goods and services relative to foreign ones) but increases income under a fixed exchange rate (because the money-stock growth lowers the interest rate and encourages investment).

Under either exchange rate system, the adjustment is automatic in the sense that the only policy required is that the central bank follow the "rules" of the exchange regime in effect. The rules of a flexible rate regime are to allow the forces of demand and supply to determine the exchange rate. The rules of a fixed regime are to intervene to buy and sell foreign exchange from international reserves to maintain the pegged exchange rate.

Case One
The Money Multiplier, Intervention, and the Money Stock

Under a fixed exchange rate, purchases or sales of foreign exchange by the central bank cause changes in the money stock equal to the money multiplier (mm) times the change in the bank's foreign exchange reserves (FXR).[21] Because of this linkage, the money multiplier plays an important role in determining the magnitude of any balance-of-payment surplus's or deficit's effect on the money stock. We can obtain a very simple estimate of the value of the money multiplier by dividing the money stock (measured here by M1) by the monetary base, or (GB + FXR) from Equation 15.2. Table 15.9 reports the result of such an exercise for recent years in the United States. The money multiplier can change over time as the public's preference for currency vis-à-vis deposits and banks' lending behavior change, although the simple estimate in Table 15.9 appears quite stable over the 20-year period.[22]

The United States has not operated under a fixed exchange rate regime since 1973; however, the central bank does still intervene periodically in foreign exchange markets to affect the exchange rate. The values of the money multiplier suggest that such intervention causes a money stock change of just under $3 for every $1 worth of foreign exchange bought or sold by the Federal Reserve.

We can use this rule of thumb to examine the effect of recent U.S. intervention episodes on the domestic money stock. We reported in Case Four of Chapter Thirteen that the Federal Reserve sold $1,814.3 million worth of foreign-currency-denominated assets between April and June 1995 in an effort to slow the dollar's depreciation against the Japanese yen and the Deutsche mark (see Table 13.14). Applying our estimate of a money multiplier of approximately 3, the intervention's net impact on the U.S. money

---

[21]We continue to assume away the possibility of sterilization as discussed in footnote 20.
[22]Footnote 12 above includes the formula for the money multiplier.

Table 15.9 ▫ The U.S. Money Multiplier, 1975–1994

Year	Money Multiplier
1975	3.1
1976	3.0
1977	3.0
1978	3.0
1979	2.9
1980	2.9
1981	2.9
1982	3.0
1983	3.0
1984	2.9
1985	3.0
1986	3.2
1987	3.1
1988	3.1
1989	3.0
1990	2.8
1991	2.8
1992	2.9
1993	2.9
1994	2.8

Source: *Economic Report of the President 1995.*

stock would be a decline of approximately $5.5 billion, or one-half of 1 percent of the total 1994 U.S. money stock of $1,147.6 billion.[23]

Case Two
The Case of the Missing Cash[24]

Actual cash or bank notes comprise only about 31 percent of the U.S. money stock; the remainder consists of checkable bank deposits, as illustrated in Figure 15.15. However, currency's share of the money stock has risen in recent years, contrary to

[23]This rule-of-thumb calculation assumes the intervention was unsterilized; see footnote 20.
[24]Background material for this case comes from Case M. Sprenkle, "The Case of the Missing Currency," *Journal of Economic Perspectives* 7 (1993), 175–184.

Figure 15.15 □ **Components of U.S. M1, 1960–1994 ($ Billions)**

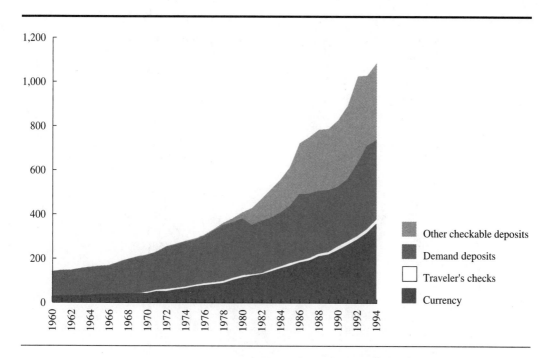

popular predictions of moves to a "cashless" economy based on credit cards, debit cards, and computerized transactions. Even more remarkably, experts estimate that of the approximately $350 billion in circulating cash in 1994, over 80 percent, or almost $300 billion, cannot be accounted for! Surveys indicate that households in the United States hold about 13 percent of the stock of outstanding dollar currency. U.S. businesses hold approximately 3 percent. The precise location of the rest isn't known.

How can $300 billion in U.S. currency go missing? Undoubtedly some resides in the "underground economy," used to finance drug trafficking, gambling, and organized-crime activities; but experts believe this probably accounts for only about 5 percent of the total stock of currency, or less than one-tenth of the missing sum. A second hiding place is the black markets for currency in Eastern European, Latin America, and other developing countries—where domestic currencies often are unreliable and inconvertible. When the domestic currency trades at highly artificial rates set by the government, or when inflation eats away at the value of the domestic monetary unit, U.S. dollars provide an alternate medium of exchange always much in demand.[25] The same restrictions and policies that make the domestic currency undesirable usually make it illegal

---

[25]In Angola, U.S. dollars and beer serve as the primary media for exchange in the country's thriving black markets. A certain brand of beer depreciated by 50 percent against the dollar and other beer brands because rumors suggested consumption of the brand caused impotence. See Roger Thurow, "In Marxist Angola, Capitalism Thrives, Using Beer Standard," *The Wall Street Journal,* September 19, 1988.

Table 15.10 □ **Currency Holdings per Capita, 1992 ($)**

Country	Currency per Capita
New Zealand	191
Iceland	232
Finland	406
Portugal	475
United Kingdom	537
Greece	600
Australia	655
Ireland	666
Canada	677
Denmark	817
France	880
Italy	1,076
United States	1,096
Norway	1,171
Sweden	1,222
Spain	1,278
Netherlands	1,308
Belgium	1,365
Austria	1,368
Germany	1,763
Japan	2,228
Switzerland	3,116

Source: Case M. Sprenkle, "The Case of the Missing Currency," *Journal of Economic Perspectives* 7 (1993), p. 177.

to hold bank deposits denominated in foreign currencies. Therefore, much of the black-market activity in foreign currencies uses cash rather than checks, even though cash runs the risk of loss or theft and forgoes the modest interest payments available on checkable bank deposits.

Some experts estimate that almost three-quarters of U.S. cash circulates abroad rather than within the United States. As much as $5 billion to $7 billion has been estimated to circulate in Argentina alone. Exporting U.S. currency is not illegal, but transactions in excess of $10,000 require a report to the Internal Revenue Service, a law that proves difficult to enforce.

The United States is not the only developed economy to experience sudden increases in use of cash and large sums of "missing" cash. Germany, long known for the stability and reliability of its Deutsche mark, noticed a substantial increase in the number of Deutsche marks in circulation during crises in the nearby Soviet Union and Yugoslavia. For most developed economies, actual per capita holdings of cash, as reported in Table 15.10 (calculated as cash outstanding divided by population), far exceed survey estimates of per capita demand for money balances. This suggests that a large portion of the money stocks of many developed economies may circulate abroad.

Case Three
The Dollarization of Cuba

The U.S. government has prohibited trade with Cuba since 1962, shortly after the revolution that brought Fidel Castro's Communist government to power. During the 1960s, 1970s, and 1980s, the Cuban economy ran largely on aid from the former Soviet Union, including subsidized energy imports and a lucrative market for the island's sugar crop. The demise of the Soviet Union brought Cuba's simmering economic crisis to a boil. By 1993, Fidel Castro sought economic help wherever he could find it—including foreign investment from the United States and increased help from the Cuban émigré community centered in Miami.

The aspect of Castro's policy change that received most attention was the 1993 legalization of the dollar in Cuba. Previously, possession of dollars was a crime. During periods of severe shortages of goods and services, supplies were available only from "hard currency" shops, which required payment in dollars and did not accept Cuban pesos. In theory, this meant that only foreigners and Cubans well connected to the government, which maintained a monopoly over all foreign exchange on the island, had access to the stores. In practice, black markets in dollars flourished, where dollars sold for 100 Cuban pesos rather than the official government rate of one peso per dollar (see Figure 12.2). Law required all Cubans who received dollars to turn the U.S. currency over to the Cuban government, from which they received approximately 25 pesos per dollar.

Now, Cubans can legally own dollars. The change has generated some interesting effects. For example, the new high-prestige professions are those that provide the opportunity to earn dollars from tourists: hotel bellhops, waiters, and taxi drivers. In contrast, doctors, lawyers, and other white-collar employees have little access to dollars and the plentiful goods and services they can buy.[26] Experts estimate that $450 million in U.S. currency now circulates in the Cuban economy.

Summary

An economy is in general equilibrium when the markets for goods and services, money, and foreign exchange all clear at a common income and interest rate. The economy contains self-adjusting mechanisms for reaching a general equilibrium under both fixed and flexible exchange rate regimes.

Under a flexible regime, imbalances in the balance of payments cause *exchange rate* changes. These changes alter the relative prices of domestic and foreign goods, affecting both the market for goods and services and the current account. Under a fixed exchange regime, imbalances in the balance of payments cause changes in the *money stock*. The monetary authority must intervene in foreign exchange markets to maintain

---

[26]"Cuba's Underground Dollar Economy Turns Class Structure Upside Down," *The Wall Street Journal,* October 13, 1994.

the pegged exchange rate in the face of a deficit or a surplus. This intervention causes changes in the stock of foreign exchange reserves and in the money stock. Since 1973, the major currencies have operated under a mixed exchange regime involving some flexibility of rates in response to market forces and some intervention by central banks.

Looking Ahead

This chapter argued that an economy contains self-adjusting mechanisms that bring the markets for goods and services, money, and foreign exchange into equilibrium under either a fixed or flexible exchange rate regime. However, these automatic mechanisms may operate slowly or produce side effects that conflict with other goals. For this reason, policy makers may choose to conduct a variety of policies that attempt to either speed up or hinder the adjustment process. These policies are the subject of Chapter Sixteen.

Key Terms

money	fractional reserve banking system
barter	deposit expansion
nominal money stock	money multiplier
real money stock	open market operation
real money balances	LM curve
opportunity cost of holding money	BOP curve
monetary authority	

Problems and Questions for Review

1. Explain the mechanics of the money-creation process in an open economy, focusing on differences from the closed economy case. Be sure your answer includes an equation for the money stock in an open economy and a discussion of the relationship between foreign exchange intervention and the domestic money stock.

2. Explain the following statement: "Macroeconomic policy makers can control either the money stock or the exchange rate, but not both."

3. Briefly explain how the IS, LM, and BOP curves represent the conditions for equilibrium in the markets for goods and services, money, and foreign exchange, respectively.

4. Explain the following statement: "The central bank can have the same effect on the domestic money stock by buying (or selling) either government bonds or foreign exchange."

5. Use a diagram similar to Figure 15.12 to predict the effect of an increase in the domestic money stock on the exchange rate under a flexible exchange rate regime. Explain.

6. Periodically, Japan considers "redenominating" its currency because the yen is such a "small" currency unit (for example, it takes about ¥100,000 to buy a color television

and about ¥2,500,000 to buy a new automobile). Would such a "redenomination" have effects equivalent to those of a devaluation of the yen? Why, or why not?

7. (a) Draw a diagram of the domestic money market in equilibrium.
   (b) Draw a diagram of the foreign exchange market in which the quantity demanded of foreign exchange exceeds the quantity supplied at the current fixed exchange rate.
   (c) Illustrate the effects of intervention by the central bank to supply foreign exchange.
   (d) Explain how the intervention restores interest parity at the original exchange rate.

8. Using the framework from problem 7, explain the following comment: "Central bank intervention is more successful when it affects market participants' expectations."

References and Selected Readings

Batten, Dallas S., and Mack Ott. "What Can Central Banks Do about the Value of the Dollar?" Federal Reserve Bank of St. Louis *Review* 66 (May 1984): 16–25.
The fundamentals of foreign exchange market intervention; for all students.

Destler, I. M., and C. Randall Henning. *Dollar Politics: Exchange Rate Policymaking in the United States.* Washington, D.C.: Institute for International Economics, 1990.
The mechanics and politics of exchange-rate policy making; for all students.

Dominguez, Kathryn M., and Jeffrey A. Frankel. *Does Foreign Exchange Intervention Work?* Washington, D.C.: Institute for International Economics, 1993.
Examines intervention's ability to affect exchange rates and the money stock; intermediate.

Frenkel, Jacob A., and Michael L. Mussa. "Asset Markets, Exchange Rates, and the Balance of Payments." *Handbook of International Economics,* Vol. 2, edited by Ronald W. Jones and Peter B. Kenen, 679–748. Amsterdam: North-Holland, 1985.
Advanced presentation of the material in this chapter.

Garber, P., and L. Svensson. "The Operation and Collapse of Fixed Exchange Rate Regimes." In *Handbook of International Economics,* Vol. 3, edited by G. M. Grossman and K. Rogoff, 1865–1912. Amsterdam: North-Holland, 1995.
Up-to-date survey of research on fixed exchange rate regimes, including the money stock-balance of payments link; intermediate and advanced.

Heller, H. Robert. "Money and the International Monetary System." Federal Reserve Bank of St. Louis *Review* 71 (March–April 1989): 65–71.
The role of money in the economy; for all students.

Hume, David. "On the Balance of Trade." In *Essays, Moral, Political, and Literary,* Vol. 1. London: Longmans, Green, 1898 [1752].
The classic work on automatic adjustment of the balance of payments, including the original statement of the specie-flow mechanism; for all students.

Humpage, Owen F. "Institutional Aspects of U.S. Intervention." Federal Reserve Bank of Cleveland *Economic Review* 30 (1994): 2–19.
Institutional details of U.S. foreign exchange market intervention practices.

Kemp, Donald S. "Balance of Payments Concepts—What Do They Really Mean?" Federal Reserve Bank of St. Louis *Review* (July 1975).
The implications of foreign exchange market intervention for balance-of-payments statistics as reported by the U.S. government; for all students.

Kenen, Peter B. "Macroeconomic Theory and Policy: How the Closed Economy Was Opened." In *Handbook of International Economics,* Vol. 2, edited by Ronald W. Jones and Peter B. Kenen, 625–678. Amsterdam: North-Holland, 1985.
Advanced analysis of the distinctions between closed-economy and open-economy macroeconomics.

Neumann, Manfred J. M. "Seignorage in the United States: How Much Does the U.S. Government Make from Money Production?" Federal Reserve Bank of St. Louis *Review* 74 (March–April 1992): 29–40.
Basic definitions and empirical estimates of seignorage for the United States.

Russell, Steven. "The U.S. Currency System: A Historical Perspective." Federal Reserve Bank of St. Louis *Review* 73 (September–October 1991): 3–18.
A brief and readable history of currency in the United States.

Spero, Joan Edelman, and Jeffrey A. Hart. *The Politics of International Economic Relations.* New York: St. Martin's Press, 1996.
A history of international monetary relations since World War II; for all students.

CHAPTER SIXTEEN

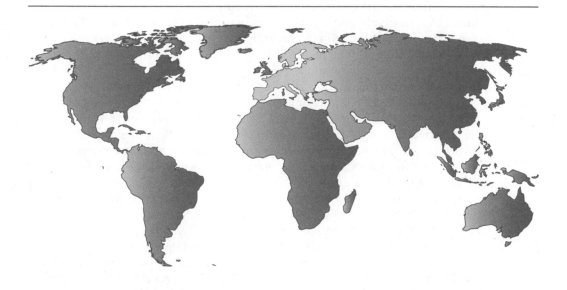

Short-Run Macroeconomic Policy under Fixed Exchange Rates

16.1 Introduction

Among the many purposes of studying the structure of an open macroeconomy is to understand better the implications of openness for conducting macroeconomic policy. The effectiveness of various policies depends, often in crucial ways, on the nature and extent of the linkages between a single economy and the larger world economy. These linkages include the magnitude of trade in goods and services, the integration of financial markets reflected in capital flows, and the type of exchange rate regime used for facilitating currency transactions.

Because these linkages vary across countries as well as over time, the effectiveness of different macroeconomic policies in dealing with certain problems may also vary across these dimensions. For example, during the 1950s and 1960s the degree of international capital mobility and the magnitude of capital flows were limited. Most governments regulated international borrowing and lending, limiting the flows of funds into and out of their economies. The absence of highly developed institutions through which to facilitate international capital flows (such as Eurocurrency markets[1] and bonds issued in multiple currencies) also contributed to a relatively low degree of international capital mobility. During the past quarter-century, the growth of a truly international capital market has been one of the major developments on the world scene. Governments of the major industrial economies have loosened their regulation of capital flows, and elaborate institutions have evolved to handle the resulting transactions.

These developments carry major implications for businesses, which can now conduct production, marketing, and borrowing and lending operations on a worldwide scale. Less recognized but equally important are the implications for formulating macroeconomic policy. For example, changes in capital markets, along with the move to more flexible exchange rates, have made fiscal policy a less effective tool for managing the domestic economy than in the 1950s. In general, changes in either the degree of capital mobility or the exchange rate regime will alter the expected effectiveness of the basic tools of macroeconomic policy.

This chapter examines the goals of macroeconomic policy in an open economy; defines some general principles useful in designing policies to meet those goals; and explores the effectiveness of three major types of macroeconomic policy: fiscal, monetary, and exchange rate policy, under a fixed exchange rate using the IS-LM-BOP model from Chapter Fifteen. Why analyze a fixed exchange rate regime when the United States and most other industrial economies shifted to more flexible rate regimes in the early 1970s? First, exchange rates for most currencies have been fixed throughout most of modern macroeconomic history. To understand that history, including its lessons for today and the future, we must understand the basic functioning of a fixed exchange rate system. Second, as reported in Table 16.1, two important groups of countries continue to maintain fixed exchange rates. Most members of the European Union maintain fixed exchange rates relative to other EU member currencies (albeit within wide bands) and float against nonmember currencies, and many developing economies continue to fix their exchange rates relative to the U.S. dollar or some other anchor. Thus, policy decisions by EU members and by developing economies remain bound by the structure and rules of a fixed-rate regime.

Third, even the governments of economies such as the United States, which operate under flexible exchange rates, engage in foreign exchange market intervention on occasion. When they do so, knowledge of how a fixed exchange rate system works is an important prerequisite to understanding the intervention's likely impact on the macroeconomy.

16.2 Macroeconomic Goals in an Open Economy

16.2.1 Internal and External Balance

A complete list of economic goals would constitute a book in itself. The main goals for an economic system include the efficient allocation of resources for producing goods and services desired by society, an acceptable rate of economic growth, and

---

[1]Eurocurrencies are offshore deposits denominated in the currency of a country other than the one in which the deposits are located. Section 12.9 discusses Eurocurrencies.

Table 16.1 □ IMF Member Countries Maintaining a Fixed Exchange Rate, June 30, 1995

| | | Currency Pegged To | | |
U.S. Dollar	French Franc	Other Currency	SDR	Other Composite
Antigua and Barbuda	Benin	Bhutan (Indian rupee)	Libya	Bangladesh
Argentina	Burkina Faso	Estonia (Deutsche mark)	Myanmar	Botswana
Bahamas	Cameroon	Kiribati (Australian dollar)	Seychelles	Burundi
Barbados	Central African Republic	Lesotho (South African rand)		Cape Verde
Belize	Chad	Namibia (South African rand)		Cyprus
Djibouti	Comoros	San Marino (Italian lira)		Czech Republic
Dominica	Congo	Swaziland (South African rand)		Fiji
Grenada	Côte d'Ivoire			Iceland
Iraq	Equatorial Guinea			Jordan
Liberia	Gabon			Kuwait
Lithuania	Mali			Malta
Marshall Islands	Niger			Mauritania
Micronesia	Senegal			Morocco
Nigeria	Togo			Nepal
Oman				Slovak Republic
Panama				Solomon Islands
St. Kitts and Nevis				Thailand
St. Lucia				Tonga
St. Vincent and the Grenadines				Vanuatu
Syrian Arab Republic				Western Samoa
Turkmenistan				
Venezuela				
Yemen, Republic of				

Source: International Monetary Fund, *International Financial Statistics*, September 1995.

an acceptable distribution of income. The study of each of these goals and the interrelationships among them constitutes economics as a discipline. We examined the efficient allocation of resources for producing the goods most desired by society in Part One. We briefly explored the effect of international trade on economic growth in Chapter Ten and its impact on the distribution of income in Chapters Four and Ten.

Here we focus on the two primary macroeconomic goals of an open economy—usually referred to as *internal* and *external balance*. **Internal balance** involves the full utilization of the economy's resources, or full employment, along with a stable price level. We shall examine directly not the level of employment or unemployment but the corresponding level of output or income. At income levels "too low" from the perspective of internal balance, the employment rate is too low or the unemployment rate too high. Unemployed resources indicate that the economy fails to produce as many goods and services as it can, a situation that clearly makes society worse off. However, if the unemployment level falls too low to attain the internal-balance goal, prices begin to rise and inflation may emerge as a problem in the economy.[2]

But what exactly does a "too low" or "too high" rate of unemployment mean? We cannot define the notion of full employment as a given percentage of unemployment measured by governments' official statistics (for example, 2, 4, or 6 percent). The percentage of measured unemployment properly identified with "full employment" depends on factors such as the pattern of wages in the economy, demographics (the age, gender, health, and educational characteristics of the population), and citizens' tastes for income versus leisure. We can, however, rule out a zero rate of unemployment as a reasonable or desirable policy goal. If an economy is to function efficiently, workers must sometimes spend time searching for the type of employment in which they will be most productive. During the search period workers may be unemployed, but such unemployment ultimately results in higher productivity through a better match between workers and jobs. In the remainder of this chapter, we shall assume that there exists a desired output level for the economy that corresponds to "full" employment, given the society's resources, technology, and tastes for leisure, and that the goal of internal balance consists of maintaining that level of output.

At first glance, the goal of external balance appears more easily definable. We might argue that an economy achieves **external balance** when the quantity demanded of foreign exchange equals the quantity available; that is, when the foreign exchange market is in equilibrium. Under a fixed exchange rate regime, such external balance occurs when the balance of payments is neither in surplus nor in deficit. The analogous definition of external balance under a flexible exchange rate regime corresponds to a situation in which the domestic currency neither appreciates nor depreciates against other currencies. However, we shall see that in reality the goal of external balance is subtle and complex.

Policy makers often have preferences for the status of particular subcategories within the balance-of-payments accounts (for example, a balanced merchandise trade account or current account) along with a goal of overall balance. But those preferences may differ across time and across countries. The current account provides no clear value to serve as a policy goal, such as full employment or zero inflation. A current-account balance of zero, for example, may make sense as a policy goal in some circumstance, but not as a general rule. We have seen at several points in the book that international borrowing and lending (or intertemporal trade) can provide gains from trade to both the borrowing and the lending country by allowing them to be net importers and net exporters, respectively, of current goods and

---

[2]So far, we have ignored inflation, or a sustained rise in the price level, through our assumption of fixed prices. Chapter Eighteen will relax that assumption, raising questions concerning the ability of macroeconomic policies to alter real income, at least in the long run. For now, we merely note that attempts to use macroeconomic policy to increase real output above a level sustainable given the availability of resources will promote inflation. Because of the problems inflation poses for an economy, avoidance of inflation constitutes a major goal of macroeconomic policy making, as does avoidance of unemployment.

services. In such circumstances, policy makers needlessly forgo the gains from intertemporal trade if they pursue a current-account balance of zero. Temporary disasters, such as earthquakes or wars, provide a second reason for tolerating current-account imbalances. A country that suffers a sudden but temporary reduction in its productive capacity can borrow from foreigners to "smooth" or spread the disaster's negative effect on consumption over several years rather than bearing the entire burden in a short period.

Nonetheless, large and persistent current-account deficits or surpluses cause policy makers concern. Large deficits, which imply large-scale foreign borrowing, raise the risk that some of the borrowed funds may go not to fund worthwhile investment projects but to excessive current consumption or "white-elephant" investments. If this happens, the funds will fail to earn a rate of return sufficient to repay the loans, and the debtor may be forced to either default or undergo costly adjustment policies to avoid default. Countries that borrow heavily abroad also must worry about foreigners' perceptions of their economic policies and economic performance. If foreign investors begin to suspect unwise use of borrowed funds, they may become unwilling to lend, forcing the debtor to suffer through a sudden reduction in its ability to borrow to finance its current-account deficit.[3]

Large and persistent current-account surpluses pose more subtle concerns for policy makers. They correspond to large and persistent capital-account deficits, or the accumulation of foreign assets, and to lower levels of domestic investment than would occur in the absence of the current-account surplus. Policy makers must wonder why foreign investments appear so much more attractive than domestic ones, when a higher rate of domestic investment might foster faster domestic economic growth, as well as a larger tax base to collect government revenue. In addition, the accumulation of foreign lending runs the risk that borrowers may be unable to repay some of their obligations. Countries with large current-account surpluses also often feel intense political pressure from the corresponding deficit countries to reduce their exports, accept protectionist policies against their exports, or endure accusations of unfair trade practices, as we saw in Chapter Eight.

Market forces, combined with governments following the rules of the exchange rate regime in effect, will produce external balance in the sense of balance-of-payments equilibrium, but not necessarily other definitions of external balance governments may have in mind, such as target levels for the current account. Therefore, in our analysis of the effect of macroeconomic policies, we shall track not only their impact on the macroeconomy as a whole, but also their effects on the current-account balance.

16.2.2 Targets and Instruments

The overall goal of macroeconomic policy making in an open economy is to help the economy achieve the desired performance. We have defined this objective as simultaneous achievement of internal and external balance. The word *objective* is

---

[3]Mexico's situation in 1994, reported in Case Three, provides one example.

subtly deceptive here, because there actually are two objectives: internal balance *and* external balance. In the terminology of the theory of economic policy, these objectives are **targets,** that is, the desired consequences of policy.

Instruments, on the other hand, are the policy tools available for use in pursuing the targets. Possible policy instruments include fiscal policy (changes in government expenditure or taxation), monetary policy (changes in the money stock), and exchange rate policy (devaluation or revaluation). However, not all these instruments will always be accessible to the policy maker; for example, according to the discussion of automatic balance-of-payments adjustment under fixed exchange rates in section 15.6, monetary policy vanishes as an instrument under a fixed rate regime. One of the major tasks of open-economy macroeconomics is to determine under what circumstances each potential instrument will be both available and effective.

The definitions of targets and instruments appear very straightforward and may seem to do little more than give labels to common sense. However, further examination reveals that the targets and instruments concepts yield important insights and that the distinction between targets and instruments is less clear than common sense suggests.

The major insight gleaned from the introduction of the targets and instruments view concerns the important relationship between the number of targets and the number of available instruments. A rule of successful policy making is that at least one instrument must be available for each target. Simple physical analogies prove useful in considering this point. The game of bowling, for example, involves aiming at multiple targets (10 pins) with a single instrument (a bowling ball). The object of the game, to hit multiple targets with a single instrument, is feasible only because the arrangement of the pins makes it possible (but not easy!) to hit them all with a single ball. Only when multiple targets are closely related—so that the requirement for achieving one is similar to that for achieving another—is the multiple target/single instrument game possible; the game of bowling would not work if the 10 pins were scattered randomly over an area the size of a football field rather than arrayed in the usual tight pattern. Macroeconomic policy makers rarely are lucky enough to have their multiple targets placed in such a prearranged pattern. As a result, reaching N macroeconomic targets typically requires at least N instruments.

Despite its useful insights, the distinction between targets and instruments is less neat than it first appears. Additional targets tend to appear on closer examination. For example, exchange rate policy is one of the above-mentioned possible instruments. Under a flexible exchange rate regime, exchange rate changes automatically achieve external balance in the sense of balance-of-payments equilibrium. In the United States, this process produced a substantial appreciation of the dollar against most other currencies in the early 1980s. The flexibility of the exchange rate facilitated external balance; however, many individuals in the United States and abroad expressed dissatisfaction with the dollar's value relative to other currencies. U.S. farmers blamed the high value of the dollar for their inability to export the desired quantities of agricultural products. U.S. automobile producers and firms in other import-competing sectors of the economy blamed the dollar for a "flood of imports" that "exported jobs." Some commentators worried that large-scale capital inflows meant foreign investors were "buying up" the United States. Debt-ridden developing countries blamed the worsening of their already severe debt problems on the depreciation of their currencies against the dollar.

Each of these elements of dissatisfaction reflects an additional target. For farmers, it is a value of the dollar that will enhance their ability to export; for import-competing industries, it is a value of the dollar that will lessen imports; for opponents of foreign investment in the United States, it is a value of the dollar that will discourage such investment; and for debtor countries, it is a stable value of their currencies against the dollar, because of their largely dollar-denominated debts. To achieve these four targets along with internal and external balance would require a total of six instruments; in other words, the exchange rate, because of its distributional effects, can itself become a target rather than an instrument.

In spite of these problems, the terminology of targets and instruments proves very useful in examining the prospects for macroeconomic policy in an open economy. Achievement of any number of targets requires at least an equal number of instruments. This means that policy makers must be on the lookout for hidden targets and for instruments that may be unavailable or ineffective in some circumstances.[4] Additional targets and missing instruments can present problems for policy makers. The primary determinants of effective instruments for the policy maker include the degree of international capital mobility and the nature of the exchange rate regime. We shall explore the effects of each combination in turn, beginning with macroeconomic policy under a fixed exchange rate and immobile capital.

16.3 Macroeconomic Policy with Immobile Capital

Economists developed their early analyses of macroeconomic policy in an open economy using the assumption of capital *im*mobility, that is, the absence of private international capital flows. From a 1990s perspective, this assumption seems quite unrealistic; however, until the 1960s capital immobility was a more reasonable supposition than a glance at today's active capital markets suggests. Most governments regulated private capital flows heavily, because policy makers viewed such flows as a source of instability in foreign exchange markets and therefore something to be avoided under the fixed exchange rate regime in effect at the time. Further, many of the institutions that facilitate private capital flows today had not yet developed. The markets for Eurocurrencies did not exist, nor did today's extensive international linking of bond and stock markets.

Under perfect capital immobility, no private capital flows exist to enter into the nonofficial capital account as described in Chapter Thirteen. Since both private capital inflows and outflows equal zero, the capital-account balance simply equals a constant, which we can set arbitrarily at zero for simplicity. There is no autonomous private international borrowing and lending regardless of the interest rate differentials existing among countries. With no capital account (KAB = 0), the balance of

---

[4]For example, for monetary and fiscal policy to comprise two instruments, the monetary authority must pursue a policy *independent* of the expenditure and taxing patterns of the fiscal authority. This is not the case in countries whose monetary authorities are expected to expand the money supply to offset any interest rate rise generated by expansionary fiscal policies.

Figure 16.1 ▫ Equilibrium with Internal and External Balance with Immobile Capital

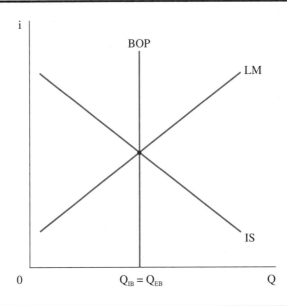

The economy is in equilibrium at the intersection of the IS, LM, and BOP curves representing the three major markets: goods and services, money, and foreign exchange. As drawn, the equilibrium income satisfies both internal balance (full employment, represented by Q_{IB}) and external balance (balance-of-payments equilibrium, represented by Q_{EB}).

payments (BOP = CAB + KAB) consists solely of the current account. If the current account is in deficit, the balance of payments is in deficit; with a current-account surplus, a balance-of-payments surplus exists. The requirement for external balance reduces to the requirement that the current-account balance equal zero. The variables that ordinarily affect the capital account, domestic and foreign interest rates and forward and expected future exchange rates (i, i^*, e^f, and e^e), no longer play a role in determining the state of the country's balance of payments, because private capital flows are prevented from responding to changes in those variables.

Recall from section 14.4 that there exists only one level of income at which the current-account balance (and, with no capital mobility, the balance of payments) equals zero. We shall denote that level of income as Q_{EB} for *external balance*. Capital immobility renders the interest rate irrelevant to balance-of-payments equilibrium; so, the BOP line becomes vertical, as in Figure 16.1, rather than upward sloping, as we saw in section 15.3.3. The degree of capital mobility does not affect the IS and LM curves, which represent equilibrium in the markets for goods and services and for money, respectively.

In Figure 16.1, Q_{IB} denotes the level of income consistent with *internal balance*, or full employment. The economy is in equilibrium at the intersection of the IS, LM, and BOP curves; the equilibrium income satisfies the requirements of both internal and external balance (that is, $Q_{IB} = Q_{EB}$). But so far, we have no reason to expect the incomes consistent with internal balance (full employment) and external balance (balance-of-payments equilibrium) to coincide.[5] If the lucky coincidence illustrated in Figure 16.1 held, there would be little need for macroeconomic policy.

We have seen that the economy does contain a self-adjustment mechanism for reaching external balance under a fixed exchange rate regime (see section 15.6). If the balance of payments is in deficit (at a point to the right of the BOP curve), the quantity demanded of foreign exchange exceeds the quantity available. To prevent the domestic currency from depreciating, the monetary authority must intervene to supply foreign exchange from international reserves. The resulting loss of reserves, which form a portion of the monetary base or high-powered money, causes the money stock to fall and the domestic interest rate to rise. Graphically, the reduction in the money stock shifts the LM curve to the left until it intersects the IS and BOP curves at Q_{EB}. The new equilibrium level of income is lower, because the higher interest rate has discouraged investment expenditure; the reduction in income curtails imports and eliminates the current-account deficit. The higher interest rate also reduces the quantity of real money balances individuals in the economy choose to hold, making them content with the new lower money stock. Similarly, a balance-of-payments surplus (at any point to the left of the BOP curve) causes intervention to buy foreign exchange. Reserves rise, and the money stock increases. The LM curve shifts to the right until it intersects IS and BOP at Q_{EB}. The lower rate of interest in the economy produces greater investment and higher income, as well as making portfolio owners content to hold the larger stock of money balances now available in the economy. The increased income encourages imports and eliminates the balance-of-payments surplus.

With the price level fixed (an assumption we have not yet relaxed), no analogous mechanism exists to enable the economy to self-adjust to reach internal balance if the income required for internal balance differs from that for external balance, as is generally the case. The primary role of macroeconomic policy under such circumstances would be to bring the economy into internal balance. The list of policy instruments to be considered includes fiscal, monetary, and exchange rate policies. We now consider each in turn. For each analysis, we begin with the economy in external balance at a level of income below that required for internal balance, or full employment. *(In each case, the reader should test his or her understanding by constructing the reasoning that would apply if the economy found itself in external balance at an income level above that required for internal balance, thereby creating a threat of inflation.)*[6]

16.3.1 Fiscal Policy with Immobile Capital

Expansionary fiscal policy can take the form of increased government spending on goods and services or of decreased taxes. The expansionary impact of a cut in taxes

---

[5]Once we introduce price flexibility in Chapter Eighteen, the economy will contain an adjustment mechanism with which to equate the incomes required for internal and external balance, at least in the long run.
[6]See footnote 2.

Figure 16.2 □ **Short-Run Effect of Fiscal Policy with Immobile Capital**

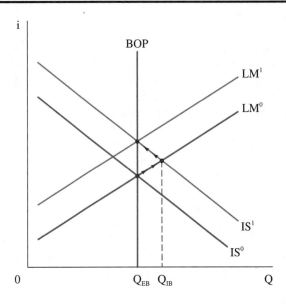

An increase in government expenditures raises total expenditure and shifts the IS curve to the right. Initially income rises as the economy moves to the intersection of the new IS curve with the LM curve. The rise in income increases imports, producing a balance-of-payments deficit. The central bank must intervene to supply foreign exchange, reducing the monetary base and the money stock. The LM curve shifts to the left and restores equilibrium at the original income level, but at a higher interest rate. Complete crowding out renders fiscal policy ineffective in achieving internal balance.

works through the effect on consumption: Lower taxes leave a larger share of income available for consumption.[7] Either form of expansionary fiscal policy shifts the IS curve to the right (for a review, see section 14.8).

In Figure 16.2, we selected the magnitude of the policy to shift the IS curve from IS^0 to IS^1—just enough to cause it to intersect the LM^0 curve at the income corresponding to internal balance. Initially the economy moves into internal balance. The interest rate rises because the increased income raises the demand for money, requiring a rise in interest rates to lower money demand to match the (constant) money stock. The rise in income also causes a current-account deficit as imports rise with income. The deficit requires intervention by the monetary authority to maintain the fixed value of the exchange rate; and the money supply falls, shifting the LM curve back to LM^1. Income falls back to the original level, eliminating the current-account deficit, but with a higher interest rate at the new equilibrium.

---

[7]Tax reductions may also encourage increased production if they take the form of lower marginal tax rates. These effects are referred to as the *supply-side impact* of tax cuts.

Although income ultimately remains unchanged by the fiscal policy, the pattern of spending in the economy does change. The new equilibrium involves a higher level of government spending. The overall level of spending cannot be higher, however, since output both begins and ends at Q_{EB}; therefore, the higher interest rate has curtailed the level of private investment spending, a phenomenon known as **crowding out.** When capital is immobile, increased government spending completely crowds out private investment; that is, private investment spending falls by the full amount of the rise in government purchases. This outcome follows from the rise in the interest rate caused by the combination of the increased government spending and the reduction in the money stock due to the current-account deficit. Fiscal policy proves unsuccessful in expanding the economy to achieve internal balance; in fact, it leaves income completely unaffected.

16.3.2 Monetary Policy with Immobile Capital

Monetary policy also turns out to be incapable of achieving internal balance under fixed exchange rates and capital immobility. The reason for the failure here is even more apparent than in the case of fiscal policy. Under fixed exchange rates, the monetary authority must commit to intervention in the foreign exchange market to maintain external balance; otherwise, the fixed exchange rate cannot be maintained. This intervention alters the domestic money stock. In other words, policy makers must allow the domestic money stock to grow and shrink according to the requirements for external balance.

Figure 16.3 illustrates the basic problem. Beginning from equilibrium at the intersection of IS^0, LM^0, and BOP, expansionary monetary policy shifts the LM curve to LM^1 in an effort to reach internal balance at Q_{IB}. The increase in the money stock lowers interest rates; investment rises, and the increase in total expenditure raises income. But the rise in income increases imports and causes a balance-of-payments deficit. Intervention in the foreign exchange market to maintain the pegged value of the exchange rate then causes a loss of reserves, shrinking the money stock and shifting the LM curve back to its original position. The interest rate returns to its original level, the temporary increases in investment and income disappear, and imports fall. These adjustments restore external balance but leave the goal of internal balance unachieved.

16.3.3 Sterilization

The monetary authority's primary means for bringing about an expansion of the money stock involves open market operations, or purchases of government bonds from the public (see section 15.2.3). The money stock equals the product of the money multiplier (mm) and the monetary base, or stock of high-powered money. The monetary base, in turn, equals the monetary authority's stock of government bonds (GB) accumulated through open market operations plus its foreign exchange reserves (FXR). The central bank accomplishes the move from LM^0 to LM^1 in Figure 16.3 by a purchase of government bonds that increases the money stock by $\Delta M = mm \cdot \Delta GB$. The resulting balance-of-payments deficit and intervention then cause the money stock to fall by $\Delta M = mm \cdot \Delta FXR$.

Figure 16.3 □ **Short-Run Effect of Monetary Policy with Immobile Capital**

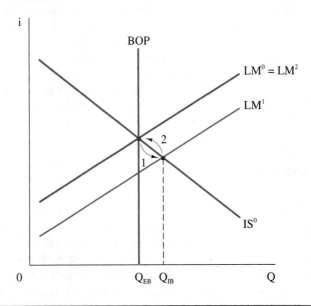

Monetary policy is ineffective in achieving internal balance under a fixed exchange rate and perfect capital immobility. Any attempt to increase the money stock (from LM^0 to LM^1) temporarily raises income and imports, causing a balance-of-payments deficit. The deficit requires intervention in the foreign exchange market to supply foreign exchange. Reserves fall, offsetting the initial increase in the money stock (from LM^1 to LM^2).

Since only one income level coincides with external balance with completely immobile capital, the money stock must fall all the way back to its original level—the only one consistent with Q_{EB}. Therefore, the loss of foreign exchange reserves must fully offset the purchase of government bonds so that

$$\text{Total } \Delta M = mm \, (\Delta GB + \Delta FXR) = 0,$$

or [16.1]

$$-\Delta FXR = \Delta GB.$$

The only lingering effect of monetary policy is a change in the portfolio of assets held by the central bank. After its intervention, the bank holds a larger quantity of government bonds and a smaller quantity of foreign exchange reserves, but the monetary base and the money stock remain unchanged.

Policy makers hardly can expect monetary policy to succeed in achieving internal balance if it cannot even succeed in increasing the money stock. Income rises only temporarily following an expansionary monetary policy, before the loss of reserves completely offsets the initial increase in the money stock. A policy that appeals to many central bankers under these circumstances is a **sterilization policy.** The idea is to prevent the loss of foreign exchange reserves from affecting the money stock, thereby maintaining LM^1 and Q_{IB} (see Figure 16.3). To sterilize, the central bank buys government bonds to offset any loss of foreign exchange reserves, or:

$$\Delta GB = -\Delta FXR. \qquad [16.2]$$

The incentive to pursue sterilization is obvious. Policy makers typically are much more sensitive to problems of internal imbalance (that is, unemployment) than to those of external imbalance. Sterilization represents an (ultimately unsuccessful) attempt to prevent the realities of external requirements from interfering with domestic priorities.

Equations 16.1 and 16.2 make clear the mechanics of sterilization policy: As the loss of foreign exchange reserves lowers the monetary base, the monetary authority offsets the loss with additional open market operations that raise GB. But such a policy is not viable in the long run.[8] As long as the government pursues sterilization policy, the economy fails to reach external balance because sterilization blocks the necessary downward adjustment in the size of the money stock. A balance-of-payments deficit persists, requiring continued sales of foreign exchange reserves to maintain the exchange rate. However, the central bank's stock of such reserves is finite, and eventually the reserves will run out. Then, policy makers face a choice: cease sterilization and allow the money stock to shrink back to LM^2 or alter the exchange rate with a devaluation, the policy to which we now turn.

16.3.4 Exchange Rate Policy with Immobile Capital

Under fixed exchange rates with capital immobility, exchange rate policy has the power to remove the fundamental barrier to simultaneous internal and external balance: the fact that each target requires a unique level of income, that is, Q_{IB} for internal balance and Q_{EB} for external balance. If the two income levels differ, as they generally do, the two targets must conflict. Neither fiscal nor monetary policy, alone nor used together, can resolve this conflict. The advantage of exchange rate policy is that it can *change* the level of income required for external balance; in other words, changes in the exchange rate can alter Q_{EB}, making it equal to Q_{IB}.

Recall that a government fixes its exchange rate by announcing the price at which it will buy and sell foreign exchange and then following through on the promise to exchange foreign for domestic currency at that price as demanded by participants in the foreign exchange market. To devalue or revalue its currency, the government simply announces a change in the price at which it will trade foreign exchange.

Figure 16.4 illustrates the use of exchange rate policy—in particular, a devaluation—to effect a solution to the same problem we have been examining: $Q_{EB} < Q_{IB}$.

---

[8]In the case of mobile capital, sterilization may affect the perceived riskiness of foreign and domestic assets, thereby altering portfolio decisions and rendering sterilization somewhat effective, at least in the short run. See section 16.4.2.

Figure 16.4 □ **Short-Run Effect of a Devaluation with Immobile Capital**

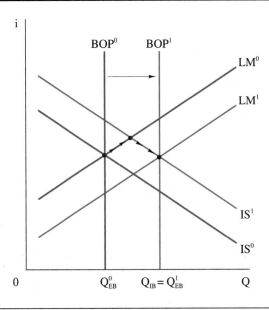

A devaluation of the domestic currency lowers the relative price of domestic goods and services. Exports rise relative to imports, shifting the IS and BOP curves to the right. The initial effect is to create a balance-of-payments surplus. Intervention in the foreign exchange market then increases the money stock. Equilibrium is restored at a point that satisfies both internal and external balance. The key to this result is the ability of the devaluation to alter the income level consistent with external balance to match that required for internal balance.

With fixed domestic and foreign price levels, a devaluation of the domestic currency lowers the relative price of domestic goods ($R \equiv P/eP^*$) and encourages exports while discouraging imports.[9] The devaluation shifts both the IS and BOP curves to the right. By lowering the relative price of domestic goods, the devaluation raises exports relative to imports at each level of income. Therefore, the income at which exports equal imports (Q_{EB}) rises, shifting the BOP curve to the right.[10] The increase in net exports due to the devaluation also shifts the IS curve to the right by raising total expenditure on domestic goods and services. To achieve the goal of simultaneous

---

[9]The assumption of fixed domestic and foreign price levels proves important because, once we relax it, changes in the exchange rate may not affect the relative prices of foreign and domestic goods. Since $R \equiv P/eP^*$, it remains unaffected if P rises proportionally with e or P^* falls proportionally with a rise in e. In other words, changes in the nominal exchange rate (e) imply corresponding changes in the real exchange rate (R) only if price levels are somewhat rigid.

[10]Recall that the change in the exchange rate exerts no influence on the capital account when capital is completely immobile.

internal and external balance, the devaluation must be just enough to shift the BOP curve such that $Q_{IB} = Q_{EB}$.

The devaluation shifts the BOP curve from BOP^0 to BOP^1 and the IS curve to IS^1. Initially the economy moves to the intersection of the new IS curve with the original LM curve, LM^0. The effect on income is positive, but income remains below the full-employment level. The balance of payments moves into surplus temporarily, causing central bank intervention to buy foreign exchange. The money stock rises with the stock of foreign exchange reserves, shifting the LM curve to the right. The new equilibrium occurs at the intersection of IS^1, LM^1, and BOP^1, which satisfies both the internal and external balance goals. By shifting the income required for external balance from Q_{EB}^0 to Q_{EB}^1, the level consistent with internal balance, the devaluation eliminates the basic policy conflict that prevented both fiscal and monetary policies from achieving the two targets.

Our analysis makes clear why governments might choose to devalue their currencies. The policy is simple in the sense that it requires merely an announcement of the government's intention to buy or sell foreign exchange at a different price; therefore, the policy change can be accomplished quickly. We have seen that governments with fixed exchange rates and immobile capital cannot use fiscal or monetary policy to influence the economy's performance. Exchange rate policy, by generating changes in the size of the money stock indirectly, provides an alternative policy.

16.3.5 Summary of Policy Effects with Immobile Capital

Under conditions of perfectly immobile capital and a fixed exchange rate, exchange rate policy is policy makers' only effective tool for altering domestic income. Neither fiscal nor monetary policy are effective, because attempts to use either generate offsetting changes in the money stock through foreign exchange market intervention. The money stock must adjust to achieve external balance (equivalent to current-account balance). Only exchange rate policy has the power to change the income consistent with external balance to match the income consistent with internal balance, thereby permitting policy makers to achieve both targets. Table 16.2 summarizes these results.

16.4 Macroeconomic Policy with Perfectly Mobile Capital

As mentioned earlier, the assumption of international capital immobility has become increasingly unrealistic in recent years. We now move to the opposite assumption: that of perfect capital mobility. The assumption of **perfect capital mobility** simply means that investors, in deciding which assets to hold, consider only interest rates and exchange rates (including the forward rate and the expected future spot rate). In other words, investors have no built-in preferences for assets denominated in one currency versus those denominated in another, and government policies do not restrict capital flows.

Under perfect capital mobility, the capital account plays the dominant role in foreign exchange markets. The balance-of-payments line depicts all the combinations of income and interest rate consistent with foreign exchange market equilibrium, or

Table 16.2 □ **Policy Effects with Immobile Capital**

Policy	Effect on Q	Effect on Current-Account Balance	Effect on Money Stock
Fiscal Policy			
Increase in G	0[a]	0[b]	−
Decrease in G	0[a]	0[b]	+
Monetary Policy			
Increase in M	0	0[b]	0[c]
Decrease in M	0	0[b]	0[c]
Exchange Rate Policy			
Devaluation	+	0[b]	+
Revaluation	−	0[b]	−

[a]Effect completely crowded out by offsetting impact of interest rate on investment.

[b]With completely immobile capital, only a current-account balance of zero is consistent with balance-of-payments equilibrium.

[c]Effect of initial monetary policy completely offset by foreign exchange market intervention.

the combinations consistent with interest parity. Recall that we draw each BOP line for given values of foreign interest rates, the exchange rate, and forward and expected spot exchange rates.[11] This implies that any rise in domestic interest rates causes a capital inflow and a move toward a surplus on the capital account.[12]

How does the assumption of perfect capital mobility produce a horizontal BOP line? In Figure 16.5, the balance of payments is in equilibrium at point A; this is true because A lies on the BOP line, which, by definition, represents points of balance-of-payments equilibrium. Beginning at A, suppose a disturbance in the economy raises income. Imports rise with income, and the current account moves toward a deficit. To maintain balance-of-payments equilibrium, the capital account must generate an offsetting move toward surplus. With perfectly mobile capital, how large an increase in the domestic interest rate is required to generate this capital-account surplus? The answer is that an infinitesimal (essentially zero) rise in the interest rate will suffice.[13] The reason is that investors will respond immediately to the slightest rise in domestic rates by moving funds into the domestic economy.

In terms of the interest parity condition discussed in Chapter Twelve, massive capital flows in response to even minute changes in relative interest rates maintain the equilibrium or parity condition. Therefore, the balance of payments is in equilibrium at B with a larger current-account deficit and capital-account surplus than at A. All

---

[11]See section 15.3.3.

[12]For a review, see the discussion of interest parity in section 12.4.

[13]This assumes that the country cannot affect world interest rates through its monetary policy. Although called the *small-country assumption,* this condition holds true for most countries.

Figure 16.5 □ **Effect of Perfect Capital Mobility on the BOP Line**

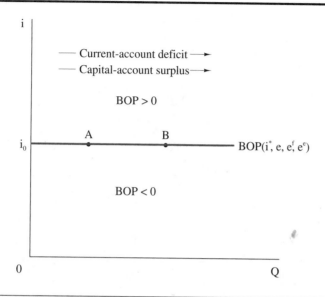

The BOP line is horizontal in the case of perfect capital mobility. A BOP line is drawn for given values of foreign interest rates and of spot, forward, and expected spot exchange rates. Given these values, even a tiny increase in the domestic interest rate causes massive capital inflows. Moving to the right along the BOP line (such as from point A to point B), the current account moves toward a deficit as a result of rising incomes and imports, and the capital account moves toward a surplus. Above the BOP line, the balance of payments is in surplus; below it, the balance is in deficit.

points above the BOP line correspond to situations of balance-of-payments surplus, and those below the line represent balance-of-payments deficits. *(Why?)*

We now turn to the question of the ability of fiscal, monetary, and exchange rate policies to achieve internal and external balance with perfect capital mobility. We shall continue to assume that the problem the economy faces is one of unemployment.

16.4.1 Fiscal Policy with Perfectly Mobile Capital

The change in assumption from perfectly immobile to perfectly mobile capital carries radical implications for the effectiveness of fiscal policy under fixed exchange rates. Recall that with no capital mobility, fiscal policy results in complete crowding out and leaves income unaffected. However, with perfect capital mobility in response to international interest differentials, fiscal policy is highly effective in raising income and achieving simultaneous internal and external balance.

Figure 16.6 traces the effects of an expansionary fiscal policy. Beginning in equilibrium at the intersection of IS^0, LM^0, and BOP, an increase in government spending

Figure 16.6 □ **Short-Run Effect of Fiscal Policy with Perfectly Mobile Capital**

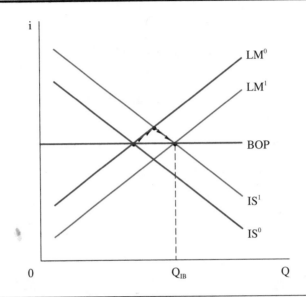

An expansionary fiscal policy, by initially raising income, causes the interest rate to rise. The response is a capital inflow that more than offsets the move toward deficit on the current account. Because the balance of payments is in surplus, foreign exchange market intervention raises the domestic money stock. The increase in the money stock prevents a crowding-out effect; thus, the expansionary fiscal policy raises total expenditure and income. This contrasts with the case under immobile capital, in which expansionary fiscal policy causes a balance-of-payments deficit and a decline in the domestic money stock.

shifts the IS curve to IS^1. Initially the economy moves to the intersection of the new IS curve with LM^0. The rise in income increases the demand for money, and, because the money stock does not change, the interest rate must rise to bring the quantity demanded of money back down to equality with the existing money stock. The rise in the domestic interest rate generates capital inflows and a balance-of-payments surplus. Note that the balance of payments is in surplus even though imports have risen with income; this occurs because, under perfect capital mobility, the capital flows made in response to interest rate changes dominate changes in the current account. To maintain the fixed exchange rate in the face of the BOP surplus, the central bank must purchase foreign exchange; this intervention raises the domestic money stock and shifts the LM curve to LM^1. A new equilibrium occurs at the intersection of IS^1, LM^1, and BOP.

Internal balance has been achieved (assuming the fiscal policy shifts the IS curve to the right by an amount sufficient to ensure that the new IS curve intersects BOP at Q_{IB}). The interest rate remains at its original level; the balance of payments is again in equilibrium, but with a larger current-account deficit and capital-account surplus. *(Why?)* The central bank also holds a larger stock of foreign exchange reserves, acquired through its intervention.

The key to understanding capital mobility's crucial role in determining the success of fiscal policy is the policy's effect on the balance of payments. With no capital mobility (see Figure 16.2), expansionary fiscal policy causes a balance-of-payments *deficit*. It (temporarily) raises income, moving the current account into deficit, and there is no possibility of offsetting capital flows. The balance-of-payments deficit, through the automatic adjustment mechanism, *reduces* the money stock. The fall in the money stock counteracts the expansionary effect of the initial fiscal policy (see fiscal policy's impact on the money stock in Table 16.1).

Perfectly mobile capital reverses the effect of fiscal policy on the balance of payments. Although an expansionary policy still moves the current account toward a deficit, this effect is more than offset by the capital inflow in response to the rise in the domestic interest rate. The net effect is a balance-of-payments *surplus,* which, through the automatic adjustment mechanism, results in an *increase* in the money stock. Thus, capital mobility causes expansionary fiscal policy to generate an accompanying increase in the money stock, rather than a decrease as under capital immobility. The expansion of the money stock prevents interest rates from rising and short-circuits the crowding-out mechanism. The increase in government spending does not cause an offsetting decrease in private spending (that is, investment), and total expenditure and income rise.

An alternative way to view the success of fiscal policy with mobile capital focuses more directly on the requirements for internal and external balance. With no capital mobility, external balance requires a unique income—the one consistent with a balanced current account. With capital mobility, *any* income can be consistent with external balance (represented graphically by a horizontal BOP line). Since capital mobility guarantees that external balance can occur at any income level, the policy problem reduces to one of reaching internal balance.

16.4.2 Monetary Policy with Perfectly Mobile Capital

Capital mobility greatly enhances the ability of fiscal policy to alter the equilibrium level of income in the economy. However, this is not true for monetary policy. Monetary policy cannot affect income under a fixed exchange rate regardless of the degree of capital mobility.

Expansionary monetary policy (represented by Figure 16.7's shift from LM^0 to LM^1) initially lowers the domestic interest rate and raises income, resulting in capital outflows as well as a current-account deficit. The balance-of-payments deficit requires sales of foreign exchange reserves until the money stock falls back to its original level.

Sterilization, Once Again
Recall that to sterilize, the central bank simply buys government bonds to offset any loss of foreign exchange reserves caused by intervention (see section 16.3.3). As the loss of foreign exchange reserves reduces the monetary base (GB + FXR), the monetary authority offsets the loss with additional open market operations that raise GB.

Could policy makers prevent the shift of LM back to LM^2 in Figure 16.7 through sterilization? Given the model developed so far, the answer is *no*. Sterilization is not viable in the long run, because so long as the central bank pursues such a policy, the

Figure 16.7 ▫ **Short-Run Effect of Monetary Policy with Perfectly Mobile Capital**

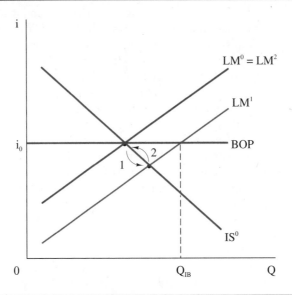

Beginning from a point of equilibrium, expansionary monetary policy causes a fall in the interest rate and a capital outflow. The resulting balance-of-payments deficit requires intervention to sell foreign exchange from reserves. The loss of reserves produces an offsetting fall in the money stock.

interest rate remains below the rate consistent with interest parity and the economy cannot reach external balance. The persistent balance-of-payments deficit requires continuing sales of foreign exchange reserves to maintain the fixed exchange rate. But each central bank's stock of such reserves is finite and eventually would be depleted, forcing policy makers to choose between a currency devaluation and a reduction in the money stock represented by the leftward shift of the LM curve to LM^2 in Figure 16.7.

An alternate way to recognize sterilization's futility is to recall that a balance-of-payments deficit reflects excess demand for foreign-currency deposits in the foreign exchange market, such as the one depicted in panel (a) of Figure 16.8. A fall in the domestic money stock, through foreign exchange market intervention to supply foreign currency, can eliminate such excess demand because, as the money stock falls, the domestic interest rate rises (shown in panel (b)). The increase in the domestic interest rate raises the expected return on domestic-currency-denominated deposits, reduces the demand for foreign-currency-denominated ones in panel (a), and restores equilibrium in the foreign exchange market.[14] Sterilization, by preventing the decline in the money stock and the increase in the interest rate,

---

[14]Figure 15.12 illustrates the corresponding case of monetary adjustment to eliminate a balance-of-payments surplus.

Figure 16.8 □ Sterilization Blocks Monetary Adjustment to Cure a BOP Deficit

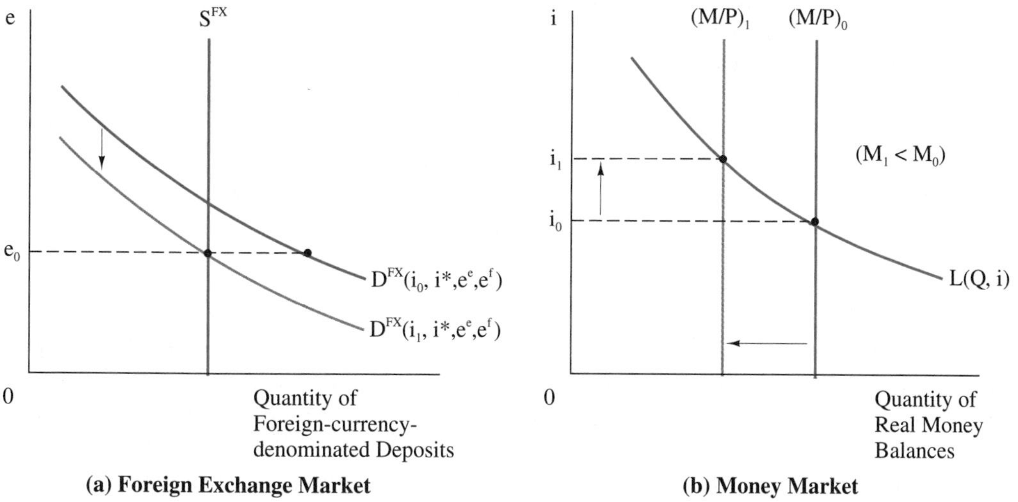

(a) Foreign Exchange Market   **(b) Money Market**

With a balance-of-payments deficit, intervention reduces the money stock and raises the domestic interest rate in panel (b) and reduces demand for foreign-currency-denominated deposits in panel (a). Sterilization uses open market operations to offset intervention's effect on the money stock. The domestic interest rate fails to rise, and the balance-of-payments deficit persists.

blocks this adjustment process and keeps the economy out of external balance because the excess demand for foreign-currency deposits at the fixed exchange rate persists.

Empirical evidence, however, suggests that central banks often do engage in sterilization policies. In fact, popular discussions of monetary policy often ignore completely the link between a country's balance of payments and its money stock, because they assume sterilization automatically accompanies any foreign exchange market intervention. Questions regarding the viability of sterilized intervention have become the subject of active research by both academic economists and policy makers.[15] Two considerations, when integrated into the model developed so far, suggest channels through which sterilized intervention—that is, intervention that leaves the money stock unchanged—might alter the demand for foreign-currency-denominated deposits to restore equilibrium in the foreign exchange market at the fixed exchange rate.

Suppose that in allocating their asset portfolios between foreign-currency- and domestic-currency-denominated deposits, investors care about the perceived riskiness

[15]See the citations by Catte et al., Dominguez and Frankel, Jurgensen, and Obstfeld in the chapter references; see also Case Four in this chapter.

of each type of deposit as well as its expected return.[16] To hold an asset perceived as risky, investors will demand a higher expected rate of return in compensation, and they will be willing to hold an asset carrying little risk at a lower expected rate of return. If assets denominated in different currencies vary in riskiness, the interest parity condition will contain a **risk premium, σ,** representing the extra return investors require to compensate for the additional risk in holding a particular currency.[17] In Equation 16.3, σ will be positive if domestic-currency assets require a risk premium, implying that domestic assets must carry a higher interest rate to compensate investors for their risk. The domestic interest rate can be lower relative to the foreign interest rate if σ is negative, that is, if foreign-currency assets require a risk premium.

$$i - i^* = [(e^e - e)/e] + \sigma. \qquad [16.3]$$

The existence of a risk premium in the interest parity condition carries several important implications. The most important is that, as the quantity of the domestic government's bonds held by the public rises, the risk premium on domestic assets is likely to rise because a large share of such bonds in an investor's portfolio makes the investor's wealth more vulnerable to changes in the exchange rate. Under such conditions, expansionary domestic monetary policy (that is, central bank purchases of government bonds that expand the domestic money stock) reduces the risk premium because it reduces the number of domestic government bonds held by the public. Similarly, contractionary monetary policy (that is, central bank sales of government bonds that reduce the domestic money stock) increases the risk premium.

A risk premium that changes with domestic monetary policy implies that sterilized foreign exchange market intervention may affect the demand for foreign-currency-denominated deposits and, therefore, the exchange rate. Recall that a government sterilizes its intervention by purchasing or selling government bonds to offset the effect of the intervention on the domestic money supply, as summarized in Equation 16.2. With no risk premium, sterilized intervention leaves the domestic money stock and interest rate, and therefore the exchange rate, unchanged. However, with a risk premium, if the central bank sterilizes a sale of foreign exchange by buying bonds, the quantity of government bonds that the public must hold falls, and this may cause the risk premium on domestic-currency assets to fall. If so, the domestic interest rate consistent with interest parity must fall, as indicated in Equation 16.3.

Figure 16.9 illustrates the implications for a country with a balance-of-payments deficit. To hold the exchange rate fixed, the central bank intervenes to supply foreign exchange but also sterilizes by buying government bonds so that the money stock remains unchanged. The central bank's bond purchase leaves fewer bonds to be held by the public, reduces the perceived riskiness associated with holding domestic bonds, and lowers the risk premium, σ. The reduction in risk makes investors more

[16]This condition is known as *imperfect asset substitutability,* in contrast to *perfect asset substitutability,* in which investors care only about expected rates of return in choosing among assets.

[17]In the economics literature, the lowercase Greek letter *sigma* (σ) constitutes the standard notation for variability or risk in a variable.

Figure 16.9 □ Sterilized Intervention with a Risk Premium

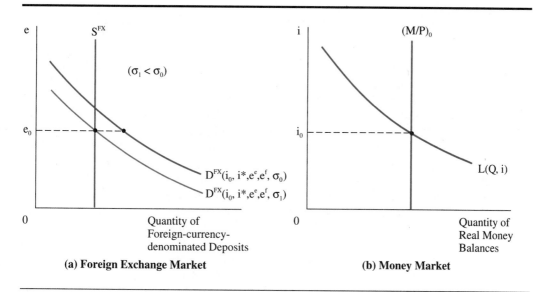

With a balance-of-payments deficit, sterilized intervention reduces the quantity of government bonds held by the public. If this reduces the risk premium (σ) demanded by market participants, the demand for foreign-currency deposits falls, and the balance-of-payments deficit is eliminated in panel (a), even though sterilized intervention fails to alter the size of the money stock in panel (b).

willing to hold domestic-currency-denominated assets and less willing to hold foreign-currency-denominated ones at any given interest rate. The demand for foreign-currency assets shifts to the left and restores balance-of-payments equilibrium at the fixed exchange rate of e_0. Because of the risk premium, sterilization does not block foreign exchange market equilibrium, as it does in the absence of a risk premium. In other words, a risk premium allows even sterilized intervention to shift the demand for foreign-currency assets.

The second channel through which sterilized intervention may be able to shift the demand for foreign-currency assets, even in the absence of a risk premium, relies on market participants using intervention as a source of information, or a **signal,** about future macroeconomic policies. When a government intervenes, even on a sterilized basis, market participants may interpret the intervention as a sign that future government policies will push the exchange rate in the direction indicated by the intervention. For example, if a central bank sells foreign exchange and buys domestic bonds, market participants may expect future macroeconomic policies aimed at reducing the domestic-currency price of foreign currency. If so, the expected future exchange rate (e^e) may fall, which would shift the demand for foreign-currency-denominated assets to the left, even though the domestic money stock remained unchanged.

Governments that attempt to use such signaling effects too often, however, will suffer a loss of credibility. Unlike the risk-premium effect, the signaling effect of sterilized intervention requires that market participants take such intervention as a credible indication of future government policies. Too many episodes of faulty signals lead market participants to ignore future signals.

Empirical studies of the effectiveness of sterilized intervention lead to mixed results for several reasons. First, detailed intervention data often are kept secret by central banks, so many studies rely on somewhat unreliable data. Second, the risk-premium and signaling hypotheses rest on effects that might be expected to vary across time and across countries. Investors may demand risk premiums for some currencies and not others or in some periods and not others; some risk premiums may respond to factors other than the quantity of government bonds held by the public. Similarly, market participants may accept sterilized intervention as a policy signal from some governments and not from others. Therefore, there may be no single correct answer to whether sterilized intervention "works."

Several existing studies find that sterilized intervention can alter the demand for foreign-currency-denominated assets, but often only insignificantly. These statistical studies suffer from observers' lack of knowledge of what would have happened in the absence of intervention. Economists remain somewhat divided on the correct interpretation of the findings. However, most agree that sterilized intervention, while it may exert some small short-run influence in foreign exchange markets in some circumstances, *cannot* be used to overcome trends in the foreign exchange market or to avoid the fundamental monetary adjustment necessary to achieve external balance under a fixed exchange rate.

16.4.3 Exchange Rate Policy with Perfectly Mobile Capital

As with fiscal policy, changes in the exchange rate can achieve internal balance under a fixed rate regime with perfect capital mobility. The devaluation does not affect the BOP curve as long as the forward and expected future spot exchange rates move in tandem with e. This will be the case when foreign exchange market participants expect the devaluation to be permanent, but do not expect it to lead to further devaluations. When these assumptions are met, the forward premium (or discount) on foreign exchange and the expected rate of future depreciation (or appreciation) remain unchanged during the devaluation. Therefore, for any given value of the foreign interest rate, the same domestic interest rate that was consistent with balance-of-payments equilibrium before the devaluation is still consistent with equilibrium after the devaluation.

A devaluation shifts the IS curve in Figure 16.10 to the right by lowering the relative price of domestically produced goods and services. The economy moves to the intersection of the new IS curve with LM^0. The interest rate rises because the rise in income raises money demand; and the rise in the interest rate reequates the quantity demanded of money with the money stock. The balance of payments moves to surplus because of increased capital inflows brought on by the higher interest rate.

The BOP surplus requires intervention to buy foreign exchange, swelling the money stock and moving the LM curve from LM^0 toward LM^1. Equilibrium is

Figure 16.10 □ **Short-Run Effect of a Domestic Currency Devaluation with Perfectly Mobile Capital**

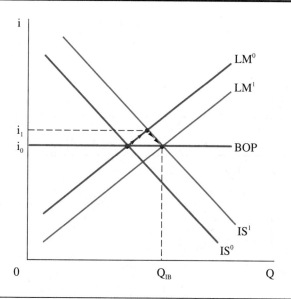

A devaluation shifts the IS curve to the right. At first, the balance of payments moves to a surplus because of an increased capital inflow. Intervention in the foreign exchange market raises the domestic money stock and shifts the LM curve from LM^0 to LM^1. The interest rate returns to i_0.

restored at the intersection of IS^1, LM^1, and BOP. The devaluation raises income by generating an increase in the money stock through the automatic adjustment mechanism. The devaluation also moves the current account toward a surplus and raises the central bank's stock of foreign exchange reserves. While devaluations can serve as an important tool of macroeconomic policy, they do run certain risks. In particular, a devaluation may lead market participants to anticipate further devaluations. If so, a devaluation can precipitate a balance-of-payments crisis, along the lines suggested in the following section.

16.4.4 Changes in Exchange Rate Expectations with Perfectly Mobile Capital

Even under a pegged exchange rate, participants in foreign exchange markets may come to believe that the government will be unwilling or unable to maintain the current pegged value. For example, individuals might come to expect a devaluation of the domestic currency because the central bank is running short of foreign exchange reserves, because of prolonged domestic unemployment, or because of a large or chronic current-account deficit. Figure 16.11 depicts the effects of such a

Figure 16.11 □ **Short-Run Effect of an *Expected* Devaluation with Perfectly Mobile Capital**

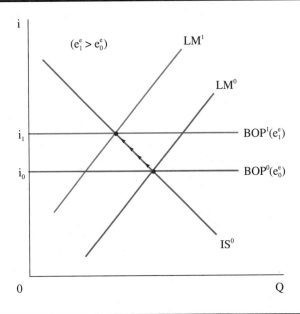

An expected devaluation (a rise in e^e) shifts the BOP line from BOP^0 to BOP^1. At i_0, the domestic balance of payments is in deficit. As the central bank intervenes to supply foreign exchange, the domestic money stock falls and the LM curve shifts from LM^0 to LM^1. A new equilibrium is restored at the intersection of IS^0, LM^1, and BOP^1.

change in expectations. Initially the economy is in equilibrium at the intersection of IS^0, LM^0, and BOP^0. Suddenly e^e rises from e_0^e to e_1^e, causing the BOP line to shift up to BOP^1. Because the actual exchange rate has not changed, the rise in e^e requires a higher domestic interest rate to make portfolio owners content to hold the existing stock of domestic-currency-denominated deposits in the face of the expected devaluation. *(Explain why, using the interest parity condition from section 12.4.1.)*

At the intersection of IS^0 and LM^0, the balance of payments is in deficit with $e^e = e_1^e$ because of the low domestic interest rate. Intervention by the central bank to hold the exchange rate at its peg lowers the domestic money stock and shifts the LM curve to the left to LM^1. The capital flight in response to the expected devaluation requires a rise in the domestic interest rate, thereby reducing investment and income. Maintaining the exchange rate in the face of the expected devaluation also causes the central bank to expend part of its foreign exchange reserves. This loss of reserves may cause foreign exchange market participants to anticipate a further devaluation, which sets the entire process in motion again. The result can be a vicious circle in which the loss of reserves creates expectations that require further central bank intervention to protect the exchange rate, further reducing its reserves. The possibility of such vicious circles had led many analysts to question the viability of

Table 16.3 □ **Policy Effects with Perfectly Mobile Capital**

Policy	Effect on Q	Effect on Current-Account Balance	Effect on Money Stock
Fiscal Policy			
Increase in G	+	−	+
Decrease in G	−	+	−
Monetary Policy[a]			
Increase in M	0	0	0[b]
Decrease in M	0	0	0[b]
Exchange Rate Policy			
Devaluation	+	+	+
Revaluation	−	−	−

[a]Foreign exchange market intervention assumed to be unsterilized.

[b]Effect of initial monetary policy completely offset by foreign exchange market intervention.

fixed but adjustable exchange rates under perfect capital mobility, especially for governments that lack a reputation for keeping their promises.

16.4.5 Summary of Policy Effects with Perfectly Mobile Capital

With perfectly mobile capital, fiscal policy and exchange rate policy can alter the level of income in the domestic economy. Monetary policy, in contrast, remains ineffective, as in the immobile-capital case. Fiscal policy and exchange rate policy work through their abilities to generate changes in the domestic money stock, as reported in Table 16.3.

16.5 Macroeconomic Policy with Imperfectly Mobile Capital

The two assumptions we have used so far concerning the capital market—zero capital mobility and perfect capital mobility—represent extremes. Although such extremes rarely are observed in the world economy, they do provide useful benchmarks in understanding capital mobility's role in determining the effectiveness of macroeconomic policies. We now turn to the case in which the degree of capital mobility falls between the two extremes. Investors do respond to international changes in interest rates by altering the compositions of their portfolios. However, the responses may not be instantaneous, investors may prefer assets denominated in certain currencies, and government policies may partially restrict mobility. In addition, the imperfect capital mobility case provides the analysis appropriate for an economy that plays a dominant enough role in international financial markets that its macroeconomic policies affect worldwide, not just domestic, interest rates.

Figure 16.12 □ **Short-Run Effect of Fiscal Policy with Imperfectly Mobile Capital**

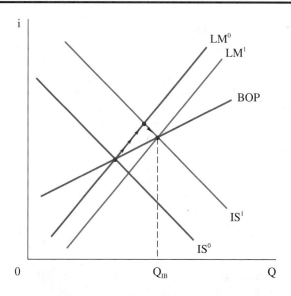

Expansionary fiscal policy shifts the IS curve to the right. The rise in the interest rate generates capital inflows, and foreign exchange market intervention increases the money stock. The new equilibrium occurs at a higher income and interest rate.

In this section, we examine the effectiveness of fiscal, monetary, and exchange rate policy in achieving internal balance under this intermediate degree of capital mobility. As we might expect, the results lie between those of the two extreme cases. Fiscal policy is effective in raising income (as in the perfect capital mobility case), but some degree of crowding out occurs (as in the perfect capital immobility case). Monetary policy remains ineffective, and a devaluation can still achieve internal balance.

When capital is imperfectly mobile, a question arises concerning the relative slopes of the LM and BOP curves. The more mobile is capital, the flatter the BOP curve. *(Why?)* We shall examine the case in which the BOP curve is flatter than the LM curve: that of high capital mobility. *(For each policy discussed, the reader should test his or her understanding by constructing a similar analysis under the assumption that capital is somewhat less mobile and the BOP curve thus is steeper than the LM curve.)*

16.5.1 Fiscal Policy with Imperfectly Mobile Capital

Fiscal policy raises income through the following chain of events, illustrated in Figure 16.12. The initial expansionary policy shifts the IS curve from IS^0 to IS^1 and raises income, increasing the demand for money. Because the money stock does not change, the interest rate must rise to cause an offsetting decline in the quantity demanded of money. The rise in the interest rate implies increased capital

Figure 16.13 □ **Short-Run Effect of Monetary Policy with Imperfectly Mobile Capital**

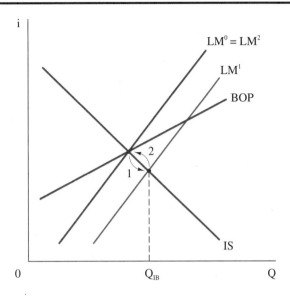

Expansionary monetary policy shifts the LM curve to the right and lowers the interest rate. Capital out-flows cause a balance-of-payments deficit; the central bank must intervene to sell foreign exchange. The decline in foreign exchange reserves cuts the money stock to its original level. The new equilibrium is at the original income and interest rate.

inflows and a balance-of-payments surplus. The surplus raises the money stock through the automatic adjustment mechanism under a fixed exchange rate. The rise in the money stock shifts the LM curve to the right, from LM^0 to LM^1.

The new equilibrium involves a higher income and a higher interest rate. The two must occur together because the higher income moves the current account toward a deficit. External balance, then, requires an increased capital inflow, which occurs with imperfect capital mobility only in response to a higher domestic interest rate.

16.5.2 Monetary Policy with Imperfectly Mobile Capital

Regardless of the degree of capital mobility, monetary policy cannot raise the income level under a fixed exchange rate regime. This is because the money stock must vary with the requirements of external balance through foreign exchange market intervention.

The more mobile capital is, the more futile are attempts to use expansionary monetary policy to raise income, even in the short run. The more sensitive capital flows are to interest rate changes, the larger and more rapid is the capital outflow in response to the temporary drop in the domestic interest rate following an open market purchase (see arrow 1 in Figure 16.13). A larger and more rapid

Figure 16.14 □ **Short-Run Effect of a Devaluation with Imperfectly Mobile Capital**

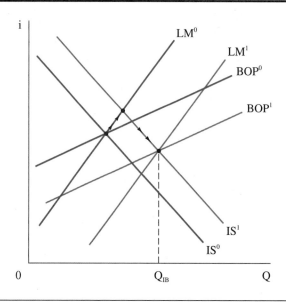

A devaluation of the domestic currency shifts both the IS and BOP curves to the right by lowering the relative price of domestic goods and services. The balance-of-payments surplus results in an increase in the domestic money stock. The new equilibrium occurs at a higher income level and a lower interest rate.

capital outflow implies a larger, more immediate balance-of-payments deficit and greater, more rapid losses of foreign exchange reserves (represented by arrow 2 in Figure 16.13).

16.5.3 Exchange Rate Policy with Imperfectly Mobile Capital

A devaluation raises income when capital is imperfectly mobile. The change in the exchange rate lowers the relative price of domestically produced goods and services, which shifts both the IS and BOP curves to the right.[18] The resulting balance-of-payments surplus leads to a rise in the stock of foreign exchange reserves and in the domestic money stock, shifting the LM curve from LM^0 to LM^1 (see Figure 16.14). The devaluation succeeds in permanently raising income to a level consistent with internal balance.

---

[18]If the devaluation is expected to be permanent, but does not generate expectations of further devaluations, then e and e^e move together, the original interest rate remains consistent with interest parity, and the BOP line shifts solely because of e's impact on the current account through the relative price of domestic goods and services ($R \equiv P/eP^*$). If the devaluation alters market participants' expectations of the future exchange rate, those changes must be taken into account in shifting the BOP line. Devaluation-induced changes in expectations can have dramatic consequences, as in Mexico in 1994; see Case Three.

16.6 A Special Case: The Reserve Country

Thus far, we have examined the case of a single country that fixes the value of its currency against the currency of a single trading partner by intervening in the foreign exchange market to exchange domestic-currency deposits for foreign-currency ones as demanded by participants in the foreign exchange market. In practice, hundreds of currencies exist in the world economy (see Figure 12.2), but fixed exchange rate regimes typically do not involve each country intervening in hundreds of separate foreign exchange markets to fix their respective currencies against each of the other currencies. Instead, countries agree, either implicitly or explicitly, on a single currency to act as the **reserve currency.** Each central bank announces a fixed exchange rate between its domestic currency and the reserve currency, which it holds as its foreign exchange reserves. The system of fixed rates between each nonreserve currency and the reserve currency indirectly produces fixed exchange rates between each pair of nonreserve currencies as well.

Under the **Bretton Woods** system of fixed exchange rates, in effect from the end of the Second World War until 1973, the U.S. dollar served as the reserve currency. Foreign (non-U.S.) central banks held most of their international reserves in the form of dollars, and each bank intervened as required to hold the exchange rate between its currency and the U.S. dollar at the agreed rate.[19] Private arbitrage kept cross exchange rates between nondollar currencies fixed, because whenever an exchange rate became inconsistent with the respective dollar exchange rates, the situation created a profitable arbitrage opportunity.[20] Suppose, for example, that in 1967 the fixed exchange rates between the dollar and the pound and between the dollar and the mark were $2.75/£1 and $0.275/DM1, respectively, and that the Bank of England and Bundesbank bought or sold dollars from their reserves to maintain those rates. The consistent exchange rate between pounds and marks would be DM10/£1. Any other exchange rate would lead to profitable arbitrage. Consider what would happen if the cross exchange rate fell to DM9/£1. Arbitrageurs could use $2.75 to buy DM10, use the 10 marks to buy £1.11, and turn those pounds into $3.05. The impact of the arbitrage would raise the mark price of a pound back toward the consistent rate, DM10/£1, earning a riskless profit of $0.30.

Existence of a reserve currency creates a special situation for policy makers in the reserve-currency country, the United States in the case of the Bretton Woods system. The reserve-currency country never has to intervene in the foreign exchange market, because each nonreserve central bank handles the task of keeping its exchange rate fixed relative to the reserve currency. Another way of noting the special situation is to realize that a world of N countries and N currencies has N – 1 exchange rates against the reserve currency. For example, if Britain, Germany, and the United States comprised the entire world economy (N = 3), there would be only two (N – 1 = 3 – 1 = 2) exchange rates relative to the dollar ($2.75/£1 and $0.275/DM1).

---

[19]Under Bretton Woods, exchange rates could fluctuate within bands of plus or minus 1 percent of the central rate.

[20]The same logic applies to the case of triangular arbitrage in section 12.3.2.

Figure 16.15 □ Monetary Policy by a Reserve-Currency Country

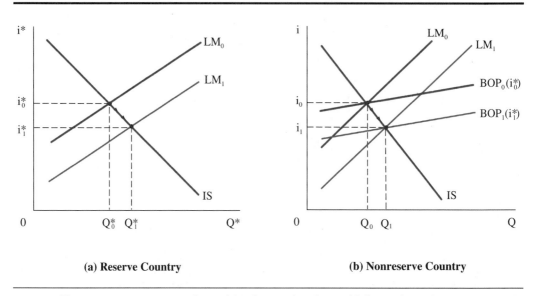

(a) Reserve Country   **(b) Nonreserve Country**

The reserve-currency country, in panel (a), does not face the usual balance-of-payments constraint on its monetary policy. Expansionary monetary policy by the reserve country shifts its LM curve to the right and lowers its interest rate. In the nonreserve country (panel (b)), the decline in the reserve country interest rate shifts the BOP line down, because the fall in i^* lowers the expected return on deposits denominated in the reserve currency and makes portfolio owners content to hold domestic-currency deposits at a lower interest rate than before. At i_0, the nonreserve country has a balance-of-payment surplus. It intervenes by purchasing reserve-currency deposits in the foreign exchange market. The domestic money stock rises and shifts the LM curve to the right. Expansionary monetary policy by the reserve country expands not only its own money stock, but that of the nonreserve country as well.

This asymmetry carries an important implication: the reserve-currency country *can* use monetary policy to pursue internal balance even under a fixed exchange rate. Recall that monetary policy fails for nonreserve countries because they must intervene to cover any balance-of-payments surpluses or deficits and such intervention offsets the effect of the initial monetary policy. The reserve country, in contrast, never has to intervene, so it can use monetary policy. In fact, it can conduct monetary policy not only for itself, but also for the entire set of countries in the fixed exchange rate system. Figure 16.15 shows why. Panel (a) represents the situation in the reserve country. We omit the BOP line from the diagram because, as we just argued, the central bank need not intervene to offset any balance-of-payments surplus or deficit that might arise. The reserve country is not constrained by external balance, because other countries adjust to keep the reserve country in balance-of-payments equilibrium. Panel (b), which illustrates events in a representative nonreserve economy, does contain a BOP line, because the central bank has the responsibility to intervene to keep its currency's exchange rate fixed against the reserve currency.

Suppose the reserve country conducts an expansionary monetary policy that shifts its LM curve to the right. The domestic interest rate falls, and the balance of payments moves into deficit. In the nonreserve country, the BOP line shifts down. This occurs because the lower interest rate in the reserve country generates a capital outflow from the reserve country into the nonreserve country and makes a lower interest rate in the nonreserve country consistent with interest parity. As the nonreserve country's BOP line shifts down, the economy experiences a balance-of-payments surplus from the capital inflow. To prevent its currency from appreciating against the reserve currency, the nonreserve central bank must buy foreign exchange (that is, reserve-currency deposits) in the foreign exchange market. This increases the money stock of the nonreserve country and shifts its LM curve to the right. At the new equilibrium, both the reserve and nonreserve economies have higher levels of income and lower interest rates.

Policy makers in the reserve country clearly enjoy an advantage from their ability to conduct monetary policy under a fixed exchange rate regime. Put another way, the reserve country avoids responsibility for financing its own balance-of-payments surpluses or deficits; other countries must do so. Other countries will view the spillover effects of reserve-country policy as a mixed blessing. If reserve and nonreserve countries tend to experience similar economic situations (for example, simultaneous booms or recessions), then the across-border effects of reserve-country policy may cause no problem and may even be welcomed. However, if economic situations in the two countries differ, making expansionary policy appropriate for one and contractionary policy appropriate for the other, tensions are likely to rise as the nonreserve country inherits the effects of the reserve-country policy. We shall see in Chapters Seventeen and Twenty that tensions such as these contributed to the demise of the Bretton Woods system of fixed exchange rates, as countries became unwilling to absorb the impact of U.S. policies during the late 1960s.

 Case One
More on German Unification

The unification of the Federal Republic of Germany and the former German Democratic Republic in 1990 occurred in the context of a fixed exchange rate regime among the (then 12) member countries of the European Community, now the European Union. Within the group, the German Deutsche mark served as the unofficial reserve currency; and other member countries adjusted their policies to maintain the values of their currencies relative to the mark. This implies that Germany could conduct effective monetary policy while other member countries could not, as we saw in section 16.6. This exchange rate regime played an important role in determining the economic effects of German unification on other EC members. In particular, the fixed-rate system caused Germany's unification-based economic boom to exert a contractionary effect on the country's European trading partners.

Figure 16.16 □ The Macroeconomics of German Unification

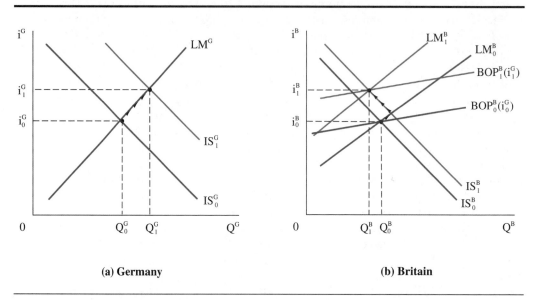

(a) Germany   **(b) Britain**

The accelerated expenditure and tight monetary policy that accompanied unification in Germany (panel a) exerted two influences on trading partners (panel b). First, increased demand for their exports shifted IS to the right and exerted an expansionary influence on trading-partner economies. Second, the increased German interest rate shifted trading partners' BOP lines upward. To keep their currencies from depreciating against the mark, trading partners had to intervene to supply marks, shifting their LM curves to the left and exerting a contractionary influence on the economy. The net effect on trading-partner economies—expansionary or contractionary—depends on the relative sizes of the two effects.

To keep our analysis simple, we let Britain represent all non-German EC members. Figure 16.16 illustrates the pre-unification economic conditions in Germany and Britain, where all three markets in both countries are in equilibrium. Recall that the absence of a BOP^G curve reflects Germany's monetary independence as the reserve-currency country. The unification process caused German consumption, investment, and especially government expenditure to rise, so the IS^G curve shifted substantially to the right. German central bankers, fearful that too much expansion might cause inflation to rise, kept the money stock constant. Upward pressure on German interest rates shifted BOP^B up and caused a capital flow from Britain to Germany, resulting in a British balance-of-payments deficit and a German surplus. Increased German demand for imports also shifted the IS^B curve to the right.

To prevent the pound from depreciating against the mark, the Bank of England had to supply marks to the foreign exchange market. This shifted the LM^B curve to the left until it intersected the new BOP_1^B and IS_1^B. Note that the net effect of German unification on Britain depends on the relative sizes of the shifts in IS^B and LM^B. The greater the increase in German demand for foreign goods and services, the bigger the shift in Britain's IS curve and the more likely Germany's unification boom would be transmitted as a boom to Germany's European trading partners. The smaller the increase in German demand for foreign goods and services, the smaller the shift in Britain's IS curve and the more likely German unification would push its European partners into economic slumps.

How did the scenario actually play out? Following unification, Germany pursued tight monetary policy to avoid unification-induced inflation. As the German LM curve shifted to the left, European trading partners were forced to do likewise to maintain their exchange rates against the mark. *(Illustrate in a diagram similar to Figure 16.16.)* Germany entered a recession along with most of the other economies of Europe. By late 1992, Germany's ability to force its partners to follow the Bundesbank's monetary policy threatened the whole process of monetary integration within the European Community. We shall see in Chapter Seventeen that Britain removed the pound from the EU's fixed exchange rate system and allowed the currency to depreciate against the mark, permitting a more expansionary British monetary policy than would otherwise have been feasible. *(Illustrate in a diagram similar to Figure 16.16.)*

Case Two
The French Franc in Africa[21]

Since 1948, 14 African countries, most former French colonies, have used the CFA franc (from "Communauté Financière Africaine") as their currency; the second column of Table 16.1 lists them. The countries maintained a fixed exchange rate of 50 CFA francs per French franc for over 45 years with no realignments. For example, on November 20, 1992, the French franc traded against the dollar at FF5.36/$1, and the CFA franc at CFAF268/$1. *(Why does this imply an exchange rate of 50 CFA francs per French franc?)*

Until the 1980s, the CFA franc system appeared to function relatively well. The fixed exchange rate, tied to the currency of a major industrial trading partner, prevented the CFA countries from pursuing the excessively expansionary (and therefore inflationary) policies typical of many developing countries, particularly in Africa. *(How does a fixed exchange rate discipline policy makers from following an excessively expansionary monetary policy?)*

Starting in the mid-1980s, the system worked less well for the countries involved. The French franc appreciated against other major currencies, carrying the CFA franc with it. As a result, the CFA countries found the relative price of their goods and services rising. Increasing imports and falling exports led to large current-account deficits— and balance-of-payments deficits, since most of the countries lack active capital accounts. The various countries in the system experienced different economic shocks, and most

---

[21]Information in this case comes from "Time to Devalue," *The Economist*, July 21, 1990, 82, and the Boughton and Clément articles from the chapter references.

analysts agreed the exchange rates needed adjustment. Between 1985 and 1992, per capita real GDP in the CFA countries fell by more than 20 percent. A devaluation seemed inevitable. One possibility was to allow one-time devaluations by the different countries before fixing the rates again, both relative to one another and relative to the French franc. Another possibility would simply devalue the CFA franc relative to the French franc and, therefore, relative to all other currencies, while leaving exchange rates between CFA countries unchanged. *(Explain why devaluation represents the primary macroeconomic policy tool for a country with a fixed exchange rate and immobile capital.)*

On January 12, 1994, the CFA countries devalued their franc from CFAF50/FF1 to CFAF100/FF1. Anticipated effects included improved performance of export and import-competing industries relative to the bloated civil-service sector. Early evidence suggests that the devaluation has shifted domestic consumption toward domestically produced goods and services. In addition, export industries such as cocoa, coffee, lumber, minerals, textiles, and tourism have grown. But the policy was controversial; the devaluation forced urban elites in the CFA countries to pay sharply higher prices for French wines, vacations in France, European cars, and other imported luxury goods.

Since the devaluation, some CFA countries have enjoyed much better economic performance than others for two reasons. First, policy makers in some countries have followed policies more conducive to economic growth, investment, and development. Second, the devaluation, although it realigned currencies relative to the French franc and all non-CFA currencies, failed to realign the CFA currencies relative to one another.

 ## Case Three
Pesos and Tequila

In 1988, after years of ineffective economic policies, failed efforts at reform, and a major external debt crisis, Mexico instituted a set of economic reforms that promised growth, stable prices, open trade, reduction of government's intrusive role in the economy, and a stable peso. Policy makers in other countries and participants in world markets viewed the reforms as evidence of Mexico's strong commitment to shift to a market-based economy as a means of supporting economic growth and development.

In 1994, events external and internal to Mexico interfered with the reforms. U.S. monetary policy shifted from expansionary to contractionary and pushed U.S. interest rates sharply higher. Capital flows, which had rushed into Mexico in response to the country's reforms and growth prospects, slowed. Policy makers had to intervene to supply dollars from their foreign exchange reserves to keep the peso within its promised exchange-rate band against the dollar. *(Illustrate using an IS-LM-BOP diagram for Mexico.)* Internal political disturbances—an uprising in Chiapas and the assassination of a leading presidential candidate—added to the political and economic uncertainty. Expectations of a pending devaluation mounted. *(Illustrate the impact of such expectations.)* By late December 1994, the Bank of Mexico's foreign exchange reserves had fallen by almost two-thirds from their March level. On December 22, after a devaluation failed to stabilize the currency, the new government abandoned its promise to peg the peso and allowed the currency to float. Market participants took the government's reneging on its peso commitment as a signal that the country's economic reforms and ability to make payments on its external debt were at risk. By the end of January, the peso had depreciated by more than 40 percent.

Economists and policy makers have performed many "autopsies" on the Mexican crisis in hopes of understanding what went wrong and how it could have been avoided. A complete verdict is not yet in, but most analysts agree several factors contributed to Mexico's rapid descent from promising emerging market to developing country on the verge of economic collapse. First, Mexico routinely sterilized its intervention in early 1994 in an attempt to prevent a contraction in the domestic economy. But, as we have seen, sterilized intervention can interfere with necessary macroeconomic adjustments, leading to a crisis. As foreign interest rates rose, especially those in the United States, a decline in the Mexican money stock could have facilitated international adjustment, but sterilization foreclosed that adjustment. Second, Mexico by 1994 ran a current-account deficit of almost $30 billion because of the real peso appreciation caused by continuing inflation in excess of the nominal peso depreciation. The deficit required financing by private capital inflows (that is, a capital-account surplus) or by intervention (that is, an official settlements balance surplus), which reduced the Bank of Mexico's reserves. At least part of the current-account deficit and associated international borrowing, no doubt, produced intertemporal gains from trade, but a large portion went to consumption expenditure rather than investment. And, the size of the deficit and the associated international borrowing rendered the Mexican economy vulnerable to a loss of confidence by international investors. The Chiapas rebellion and the assassination contributed to just such a loss of confidence. Note, however, that Mexicans faced the same incentives as foreign investors to move funds out of the country in response to an expected devaluation.

Mexico and its foreign investors were not the only ones affected by the peso experience. In what came to be known as the *tequila effect*, financial markets throughout Latin America, recently recovered from the 1980s debt crisis, became more volatile. Governments throughout the region, especially those of Argentina and Brazil, had to intervene to prevent their currencies from depreciating in foreign exchange markets, the result of market participants' expectations of potential devaluations similar to Mexico's.

As of late 1995, the Mexican peso continued to float against the U.S. dollar, against which the peso had depreciated by more than 80 percent since the initial December 1994 devaluation.

Case Four
Does Intervention Work?

Much of the foreign exchange intervention by central banks is sterilized. Such intervention leaves the money stock unchanged and must rely on other channels if it is to affect the exchange rate. When central banks intervene in foreign exchange markets, the quantities of currencies they buy or sell typically are small compared to total activity in foreign exchange markets. Even major intervention episodes by the largest

Table 16.4 □ Federal Reserve-Bundesbank Intervention and the Dollar Price of DM

Intervention Dates	Percent Change in $/DM, Month after Intervention	Central Bank Purchases (+) or Sales (−) of Dollars ($ Billions)		Percent Change in $/DM, Month prior to Intervention
		U.S. Federal Reserve	German Bundesbank	
January 11–March 4, 1985	2.3	−0.6	−3.5	−8.3
September 23–November 12, 1985	4.5	−3.3	−1.1	−3.5
March 11–June 3, 1987	1.3	4.8	0.7	0.8
October 19, 1987–January 21, 1988	−0.5	4.6	3.1	2.0
May 31–October 7, 1988	2.5	−5.1	−7.9	−3.7
October 31–December 2, 1988	−5.8	2.6	0.4	3.0
December 8, 1988–February 6, 1989	−1.3	−2.2	−0.2	−0.9
March 8–October 12, 1989	−0.9	−19.7	na	−1.5
February 23–April 9, 1990	−1.1	−1.8	na	−2.0
May 29–July 17, 1990	−0.2	1.0	na	−5.1
February 4–February 12, 1991	−2.6	1.3	na	8.0

Source: *The Economist*, September 18, 1993, p. 84; data from Dominguez and Frankel.

central banks involve only a few billion dollars, while approximately a trillion dollars worth of foreign exchange is transacted in foreign exchange markets around the world *every day*. The smallness of intervention transactions relative to the markets in which they occur has led some to question whether sterilized intervention can, in fact, exert any significant effect on exchange rates.

A recent study of daily intervention data from the U.S. Federal Reserve and Germany's Bundesbank by Kathryn Dominguez and Jeffrey Frankel suggests that sterilized intervention by the two central banks does alter exchange rates in the direction predicted by economists' models of the foreign exchange market. Dominguez and Frankel examined 11 intervention episodes in detail and compared movements in the exchange rate in the month following the intervention with those in the month prior to the central bank activity, as reported in Table 16.4. In 10 of the 11 cases, the exchange rate moved in the direction indicated by the intervention, and in six cases this involved reversing the rate's earlier trend.

The study also found that only a small portion of intervention's effect on the exchange rate comes directly from central banks' purchases or sales of foreign exchange. The rest comes from intervention's signaling effect on market participants' expectations of the future spot exchange rate (e^e). As we saw in section 16.4.2, if central banks intervene to halt a depreciation of the dollar, market participants may infer that monetary authorities would act in the same way again in the future; if so, e^e falls, and asset owners will choose to hold fewer foreign-currency-denominated deposits and more dollar-denominated ones. If intervention causes a decline in the

Table 16.5 □ **Short-Run Policy Effectiveness under Fixed Exchange Rates**

Policy	Ability to Affect Income under a Fixed Exchange Rate		
	Immobile Capital	Imperfectly Mobile Capital	Perfectly Mobile Capital
Fiscal	0	Effective	Effective
Monetary	0	0	0
Exchange rate	Effective	Effective	Effective

expected future spot rate, the demand curve for foreign-currency-denominated deposits shifts to the left, and the domestic currency appreciates more than in the absence of the expectation effect.

Many economists, however, remain skeptical for several reasons of sterilized intervention's ability to alter the exchange rate.[22] First, they point out that intervention is most likely when exchange rates reach extreme values; such episodes, however, correspond to times when exchange rate trends are most likely to reverse themselves even without intervention. Therefore, attributing such trend reversals to sterilized intervention runs the risk of interpreting something that would have happened anyway as an effect of intervention. Second, central banks may choose to intervene only when they believe market conditions are such that intervention can alter the path of the exchange rate. Finally, if central banks continue intervention until the exchange rate trend changes, then intervention will, by definition, be followed by trend reversal and will appear to "work."

Summary

With the price level and the exchange rate fixed, self-adjustment mechanisms exist for reaching external balance (balance-of-payments equilibrium) but not for attaining internal balance (full employment). The effectiveness of short-run macroeconomic policy in achieving internal balance under fixed exchange rates depends on the degree of international capital mobility.

With completely immobile capital, neither fiscal nor monetary policy can bring the economy into internal balance. A change in the exchange rate is required to alter the income consistent with external balance to match the income required for internal balance if both goals are to be reached.

Increased capital mobility enhances the ability of fiscal policy to alter income. Monetary policy remains ineffective even in the presence of capital mobility, and exchange rate policy retains its ability to affect income. Table 16.5 summarizes these results.

---

[22]The Obstfeld article in the chapter references contains a useful discussion.

Looking Ahead

Capital mobility strongly influences the effectiveness of various tools of macroeconomic policy. Likewise, a change in the exchange rate regime alters the ability of fiscal and monetary policy to achieve simultaneous internal and external balance. Since policy makers can choose the type of exchange rate regime under which the world economy operates (in fact, individual countries can—and do—choose different systems), understanding the implications of the type of exchange rate regime for macroeconomic policy is particularly important. Chapter Seventeen explores the move to a more flexible exchange rate system made by the major industrial economies in the early 1970s and its implications for fiscal and monetary policy and for internal and external balance.

Key Terms

internal balance	perfect capital mobility
external balance	risk premium
targets	signal
instruments	reserve currency
crowding out	Bretton Woods
sterilization policy	

Problems and Questions for Review

1. Consider an open market *sale* of 500 under a fixed exchange rate regime. Assume the money multiplier is 10 and the economy is at a general equilibrium before the policy.
   (a) Explain carefully what action by the central bank would constitute such a policy.
   (b) *Ignoring the foreign exchange market for a moment*, what would be the initial or direct effect of the open market sale on the domestic money stock (that is, by how much would M increase or decrease)? Explain.
   (c) What would be the effect of such a policy on the domestic balance of payments? Why? Does your answer depend on the extent of capital mobility? Explain.
   (d) To maintain the pegged exchange rate, what action would the central bank need to undertake, if any? What would be the effect on the domestic money stock (that is, by how much would this action increase or decrease M)?
   (e) What is the total net effect of the open market operation on the domestic money stock (taking into account the effects in (b) and (d))?
   (f) What are the implications of your answer to (e) for discretionary or activist monetary policy under a fixed exchange rate?

2. Assume the exchange rate is fixed and capital is perfectly mobile.
   (a) *Scenario 1:* Country A's central bank devalues the domestic currency, the alpha (α), but the citizens of A do *not* expect the devaluation to be permanent. Illustrate the effect of the exchange rate policy on income and the interest rate.

(b) *Scenario 2:* Country A's central bank devalues the domestic currency, the alpha (α), by the same amount as in Scenario 1, but the citizens of A *do* expect the devaluation to be permanent. Illustrate the effect of the exchange rate policy on income and the interest rate.

(c) Explain why you drew the graphs in (a) and (b) as you did, and compare the policy effects in the two scenarios.

3. Comment on the following statement by the head of a central bank of a small country that has a fixed exchange rate and strict capital controls that prohibit capital inflows and outflows: "The reason for our capital controls is to prevent external events from affecting our domestic economy. For the same reason, we will not alter the pegged value of our currency by devaluing or revaluing, but rather we will rely on domestic monetary and fiscal policies to achieve our economic goals."

4. Consider the case of country A, a small country operating under (i) a fixed exchange rate regime, (ii) a comprehensive set of capital controls that prohibit both nonofficial capital inflows and outflows, and (iii) an unacceptably high rate of unemployment. Trading partners of countries like the one just described often complain that such countries maintain their currencies at values that are too low (that is, their domestic currency price of foreign exchange is too high) and that the countries place too much emphasis on running a current-account surplus. Explain why countries like A might choose current-account surpluses and low values for their currencies. *(Hint: What are the prospects for fiscal and monetary policy in country A?)*

5. It is common for countries to complain about one another's interest rates. Assume the domestic country operates under a fixed exchange rate regime, and capital is completely mobile. Illustrate and explain the effect on the domestic economy of a *decline* in the *foreign* interest rate (i^*), beginning from a point of general equilibrium, using the IS-LM-BOP framework.

6. Answer the following questions about foreign exchange market intervention and sterilization policy.

(a) What is foreign exchange market intervention? Under what circumstances, and how, do central banks intervene in foreign exchange markets?

(b) What is sterilization policy? Under what circumstances, and how, do governments sterilize? What are the likely long-run effects of sterilization?

(c) If you wanted to determine whether a central bank is intervening in foreign exchange markets, what evidence would you look for? Why? If you wanted to determine whether a government is engaging in sterilization policy, what evidence would you look for? Why?

(d) Outline two channels through which sterilized intervention may affect the foreign exchange market.

7. Historically, it has been common for a country to pressure its trading partners to follow expansionary macroeconomic policies. Assume the domestic country operates under a fixed exchange rate regime, and capital is completely mobile. Illustrate and explain the effect on the domestic economy of an *increase* in *foreign* income, beginning from a point of general equilibrium, using the IS-LM-BOP framework.

8. Explain the role of the following in Mexico's December 1994 currency crisis.
   (a) The rise in U.S. interest rates.
   (b) Mexico's decision to sterilize its foreign exchange market intervention.
   (c) Declining confidence by market participants in the credibility of the Mexican government's commitment not to devalue the peso.

References and Selected Readings

Batten, Dallas S., and Mack Ott. "What Can Central Banks Do about the Value of the Dollar?" Federal Reserve Bank of St. Louis *Review* 66 (May 1984): 16–25.
The mechanics of foreign exchange market intervention; for all students.

Baxter, M. "International Trade and Business Cycles." In *Handbook of International Economics*, Vol. 3, edited by G. M. Grossman and K. Rogoff, 1801–1864. Amsterdam: North-Holland, 1995.
Up-to-date survey of research on the relationship between international trade activity and macroeconomic cycles; intermediate and advanced.

Boughton, James. "The CFA Franc: Zone of Fragile Stability in Africa." *Finance and Development* 29 (December 1992): 34–36.
Background material for Case Two.

Catte, Pietro, et al. "Concerted Interventions and the Dollar: An Analysis of Daily Data." In *The International Monetary System,* edited by Peter B. Kenen, et al., 201–254. Cambridge: Cambridge University Press, 1994.
Argues that sterilized intervention can influence foreign exchange markets; intermediate.

Clément, Jean A. P. "Striving for Stability: CFA Franc Realignment." *Finance and Development* 31 (June 1994): 10–13.
Background material for Case Two.

Clément, Jean A. P. "Aftermath of the CFA Franc Devaluation." *Finance and Development* 32 (June 1995): 24–27.
Background material for Case Two.

Dominguez, Kathryn M., and Jeffrey A. Frankel. *Does Foreign Exchange Intervention Work?* Washington, D.C.: Institute for International Economics, 1993.
Study of the effect of sterilized intervention; intermediate.

Dornbusch, Rudiger, et al. "Currency Crises and Collapses." *Brookings Papers on Economic Activity* 2 (1995): 219–293.
Lessons from four currency crises; intermediate.

Dornbusch, Rudiger, and Alejandro Werner. "Mexico: Stabilization, Reform, and No Growth." *Brookings Papers on Economic Activity* 1 (1994): 253–315.
Analysis of Mexico's macroeconomic prospects on the eve of the December 1994 crisis; intermediate.

Fieleke, Norman S. "International Capital Transactions: Should They Be Restricted?" Federal Reserve Bank of Boston *New England Economic Review* (March–April 1994): 27–39.
The pros and cons of restricting capital mobility; for all students.

Fleming, J. M. "Domestic Financial Policies under Fixed and Floating Exchange Rates." *IMF Staff Papers* 9 (November 1962): 369–380.
A classic paper on macroeconomic policy effectiveness in an open economy; for advanced students.

Frankel, Jeffrey A. "Measuring International Capital Mobility: A Review." *American Economic Review Papers and Proceedings* 92 (May 1992): 197–202.
Summary of different measures of capital mobility and recent experience; for all students.

Frenkel, Jacob A., and Michael L. Mussa. "Asset Markets, Exchange Rates, and the Balance of Payments." In *Handbook of International Economics*, Vol. 2, edited by Ronald W. Jones and Peter B.

Kenen, 679–748. Amsterdam: North-Holland, 1985.
Advanced presentation of asset models of the balance of payments.

Garber, P., and L. Svensson. "The Operation and Collapse of Fixed Exchange Rate Regimes." In *Handbook of International Economics,* Vol. 3, edited by G. M. Grossman and K. Rogoff, 1865–1912. Amsterdam: North-Holland, 1995.
Up-to-date survey of research on fixed-rate systems; intermediate and advanced.

Hume, David. "On the Balance of Trade." In Essays, *Moral, Political, and Literary,* Vol. 1. London: Longmans, Green, 1898 [1752].
The original statement of the automatic adjustment process under fixed exchange rates; for all students.

International Monetary Fund. *World Economic Outlook, May 1995.* Washington D.C.: International Monetary Fund, 1995.
Focuses on the role of domestic saving in the macroeconomy; includes a chapter on the Mexican crisis; for all students.

Isard, Peter. *Exchange Rate Economics.* Cambridge: Cambridge University Press, 1995.
Excellent survey of the literature on fixed exchange rates for intermediate and advanced students.

Johnson, Harry G. "Towards a General Theory of the Balance of Payments." In *International Trade and Economic Growth: Studies in Pure Theory,* 153–168. Cambridge, Mass.: Harvard University Press, 1961.
One of the early and classic criticisms of the traditional model of macroeconomic adjustment presented in the chapter; for intermediate and advanced students.

Jurgensen, Philippe. *Report of the Working Group on Exchange Market Intervention.* Washington, D.C.: U.S. Department of the Treasury, 1983.
Report of a group commissioned by central banks to study the effects of sterilized intervention.

Kenen, Peter B. "Macroeconomic Theory and Policy: How the Closed Economy Was Opened." In *Handbook of International Economics,* Vol. 2, edited by Ronald W. Jones and Peter B. Kenen, 625–678. Amsterdam: North-Holland, 1985.
Differences between open- and closed-economy macroeconomics; for advanced students.

Marston, Richard C. "Stabilization Policies in Open Economies." In *Handbook of International Economics,* Vol. 2, edited by Ronald W. Jones and Peter B. Kenen, 859–916, Amsterdam: North-Holland, 1985.
Advanced treatment of many of the models presented in the chapter.

Meade, James E. *The Balance of Payments.* London: Oxford University Press, 1951.
The definitive early work on the balance of payments; for advanced students.

Meltzer, Allan H. "U.S. Policy in the Bretton Woods Era." Federal Reserve Bank of St. Louis *Review* 73 (May–June 1991): 53–83.
Excellent, readable survey of the functioning of the Bretton Woods system of pegged exchange rates.

Mundell, Robert A. "Capital Mobility and Stabilization Policy under Fixed and Flexible Exchange Rates." *Canadian Journal of Economics and Political Science* 29 (November 1963): 475–485.
The original presentation of capital mobility's impact on macroeconomic policy effectiveness in an open economy; for intermediate and advanced students.

Obstfeld, Maurice. "International Currency Experience: New Lessons and Lessons Relearned." *Brookings Papers on Economic Activity* 1 (1995): 119–220.
Excellent survey of the current state of knowledge on exchange rates; intermediate.

Obstfeld, M., and K. Rogoff. "The Intertemporal Approach to the Current Account." In *Handbook of International Economics,* Vol. 3, edited by G. M. Grossman and K. Rogoff, 1731–1800. Amsterdam: North-Holland, 1995.
Up-to-date survey of research on the current account from the perspective of intertemporal trade; intermediate and advanced.

Persson, T., and G. Tabellini. "Double-Edged Incentives: Institutions and Policy Coordination." In *Handbook of International Economics,* Vol. 3, edited by G. M. Grossman and K. Rogoff, 1973–2030. Amsterdam: North-Holland, 1995.
Up-to-date survey of research on interactions between countries' macroeconomic policies; intermediate and advanced.

Spero, Joan Edelman, and Jeffrey A. Hart. *The Politics of International Economic Relations.* New York: St. Martin's Press, 1996.
The politics of the postwar international monetary order; for all students.

Tinbergen, Jan. *On the Theory of Economic Policy.* Amsterdam: North-Holland, 1952.
An early, influential work on the theory of macroeconomic policy making in an open economy; for advanced students.

Zurlinden, Martha. "The Vulnerability of Pegged Exchange Rates: The British Pound in the ERM." Federal Reserve Bank of St. Louis *Review* (September–October 1993): 41–56.
Uses the British ERM experience to outline the potential hazards of fixed but adjustable exchange rates with highly mobile capital; intermediate.

CHAPTER SEVENTEEN

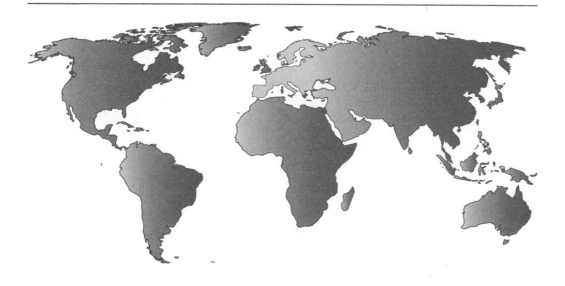

Short-Run Macroeconomic Policy under Flexible Exchange Rates

17.1 Introduction

During most of the post-Second World War period, the world economy operated under the **Bretton Woods system** of fixed, or pegged, exchange rates. The Bretton Woods agreement consisted of a commitment by each member country's central bank to intervene in foreign exchange markets to keep the value of its currency, in terms of U.S. dollars, within a certain range or band. If a currency's value threatened to rise above the upper limit of its band, the central bank would sell the currency in the foreign exchange market. If a currency's value sank to the lower limit of its band, the central bank would use dollars from its foreign exchange reserves to buy the excess supply of the domestic currency from the foreign exchange market. These intervention activities pegged the value of each currency within its agreed-upon band relative to the U.S. dollar.[1]

By the late 1960s, the Bretton Woods system came under stress and threatened to disintegrate for two basic reasons. First, governments of the major industrial economies faced increasing domestic political pressure to pursue macroeconomic

---

[1]Chapter Twenty provides more detail on the mechanics of the Bretton Woods system.

policies that maintained full employment; as we saw in Chapter Sixteen, however, fixed exchange rates prevented countries other than the United States from conducting independent monetary policies aimed at domestic goals such as full employment. A second, related problem hinged on the special role of the United States as the reserve country under Bretton Woods. As we saw in section 16.6, the reserve country under a fixed exchange rate regime conducts monetary policy not only for itself, but for all the other countries in the system. During the 1960s, the United States pursued increasingly expansionary monetary policies that generated inflation at home; and the rules of the Bretton Woods system transmitted that inflation to other countries.

By early 1973, after several years of gradual disintegration, the Bretton Woods system collapsed, and the major industrial countries allowed their currencies to float against the dollar.[2] The move to flexible exchange rates, viewed as unthinkable by most economists and policy makers only a decade before, occurred primarily as a response to the collapse of the former system and a lack of agreement on an alternative. The move was met with relief in some circles and dismay in others. Gradually the idea of a flexible exchange rate system gained support, though never unanimous. Since the early 1970s, each disruption to the world macroeconomy has generated renewed skepticism regarding a flexible rate regime, and a vocal constituency continues to support a return to some type of fixed exchange rate system. The arguments on both sides of this issue form the subject of Chapter Twenty. Before we can evaluate those arguments, though, we must understand how a flexible exchange rate system works and its implications for macroeconomic policy.

We shall continue to assume, as we did in Chapter Sixteen's analysis of fixed exchange rates, that the policy makers' goal is to bring the economy into internal balance, and that domestic and foreign price levels are fixed.[3] With flexible exchange rates, the economy contains an automatic adjustment mechanism for effecting external balance.[4] The adjustment takes the form of currency appreciations with which to relieve balance-of-payments surpluses and depreciations for relieving BOP deficits. However, policy makers may not be content with this outcome for two reasons. First, we have seen that changes in the nominal exchange rate with fixed price levels cause changes in the real exchange rate, or the relative price of domestic goods and services. This implies that different values of the nominal exchange rate carry different implications for the fortunes of various sectors of the economy—exporters, import-competing industries, consumers of imported goods, and users of imported

---

[2]In the post-Bretton Woods world, most central banks still intervene occasionally in foreign exchange markets. In other words, the current system is not a perfectly flexible one but a "managed" float (pejoratively called a "dirty" float). The extent of "management" or intervention varies over time and across countries. We shall examine the strengths and weaknesses of such a system later; for now, we focus on the effectiveness of macroeconomic policy under a perfectly flexible exchange rate regime, first without and then with capital mobility.

[3]In Chapter Eighteen, we shall relax the fixed price level assumption. Price flexibility has two important implications. First, the economy will contain an automatic adjustment mechanism for reaching internal as well as external balance. Second, attempts to use macroeconomic policy to alter the path of the economy may result in price level changes rather than changes in real income or employment.

[4]The economy also contains an automatic adjustment mechanism for reaching external balance under fixed exchange rates: changes in the money stock through foreign exchange market intervention

inputs—as well as for the current-account balance. Therefore, the value of the exchange rate consistent with external balance or balance-of-payments equilibrium may prove unacceptable because of its distributional ramifications or its implications for the current account. Second, the income at which the automatic adjustment mechanism produces external balance may prove unacceptable in terms of policy makers' internal balance goal; for example, the unemployment rate may be unacceptably high. We begin our analysis of each policy at a point of external balance that reflects the outcome of the automatic adjustment mechanism. The question then becomes whether the policy under scrutiny can bring the economy into internal balance while allowing exchange rate changes to continue maintaining external balance. We also must track the policies' implications for the current account.

A perfectly flexible exchange rate regime allows the supplies of and demands for different currencies to determine exchange rates. Central banks do not intervene in the foreign exchange market. The exchange rate moves to equate the quantity demanded and the quantity supplied for each currency; therefore, external balance is achieved through automatic adjustment in the form of exchange rate movements. The fact that achieving external balance with a flexible exchange rate does not require foreign exchange market intervention has important implications for macroeconomic policy.

Recall from Chapter Sixteen that under fixed exchange rates, a major determinant of the effectiveness of any macroeconomic policy is that policy's consequence for the balance of payments and, through intervention, for the domestic money stock. A flexible exchange rate breaks this link between a country's balance of payments and its money stock. By giving up the power to determine the exchange rate, the central bank gains the ability to affect the nominal money stock without causing offsetting changes through international reserves. Graphically, under a flexible exchange rate, the central bank's monetary policies, primarily open market operations, determine the position of the LM curve.[5] As long as the central bank does not purchase bonds from or sell bonds to the public, the money stock remains unchanged and the LM curve remains stationary.[6]

The role of exchange rate flexibility in breaking the link between the balance of payments and the domestic money stock was the primary argument used by the few early supporters of a move to flexible exchange rates. Proponents of flexible rates argued that freeing the domestic money stock from the constraint imposed by the balance of payments would allow policy makers to use monetary policy more effectively in pursuing internal balance, or full employment.[7] We shall see in Chapter Twenty that after the inflationary 1970s, opponents of flexible exchange rates reversed the argument and claimed that freeing monetary authorities to pursue

---

[5]Open market operations refer to central bank sales of government bonds to the public or purchases of government bonds from the public. Other tools of monetary policy include changes in the required reserve ratio, the percentage of their deposits that banks are required to hold in reserves, and changes in the discount rate, the interest rate that the central bank charges banks for borrowing reserves.

[6]For now, we ignore the possibility of changes in the level of money demand other than those arising from changes in Q or i.

[7]Note, however, that policy makers lose their ability to dictate the exchange rate. A fixed exchange rate regime allows control of the exchange rate but not the money stock. A flexible exchange rate allows control of the money stock but not the exchange rate.

internal balance permitted overly expansionary monetary policies that caused a dramatic increase in inflation rates.[8]

17.2 Macroeconomic Policy with Immobile Capital

Recall that with zero capital mobility, the balance of payments simply equals the current-account balance. For each value of the exchange rate, a unique income level coincides with a zero current-account balance. Because the income that corresponds to external balance varies with the exchange rate, any policy capable of affecting the exchange rate has the potential to bring the economy into simultaneous internal and external balance by altering the income required for external balance to match that required for internal balance.

17.2.1 Fiscal Policy with Immobile Capital

In Figure 17.1, a rise in government expenditure or a cut in taxes shifts the IS curve from IS^0 to IS^1 by raising total expenditure on domestically produced goods and services (see section 14.8 for a review). The initial effect raises income, because total expenditure has risen, and the interest rate. The rise in the interest rate is necessary to offset the effect of increased income on the demand for money, since the stock of money remains fixed at all points along LM^0 (see section 15.2.5). At the new, higher income, imports rise and the balance of payments shifts into deficit.[9] The exchange rate responds to the excess demand for foreign exchange by a domestic currency depreciation. The rise in the exchange rate lowers the relative price of domestic goods and services ($R \equiv P/eP^*$) and, therefore, raises the current-account balance at each income level. Because the current-account balance now equals zero at a higher income, the BOP curve shifts to the right from BOP^0 to BOP^1. The same fall in the relative price of domestic goods and services shifts expenditure toward those goods and moves the IS curve still further to the right to IS^2. In other words, the depreciation shifts both the BOP and IS curves to the right until they intersect at a point on the unchanged LM curve.

At the new equilibrium, income, the interest rate, and the exchange rate are all higher than at the original equilibrium. The rise in the interest rate that accompanies an expansionary fiscal policy prevents an even larger rise in income by crowding out a portion of private investment expenditure. In terms of Figure 17.1, crowding out causes income to rise to Q_{EB}^1 rather than to Q_{EB}^2.

Fiscal policy brings the external-balance requirement into harmony with that for internal balance *by generating a depreciation of the currency*.[10] However, governments

---

[8]These arguments will play prominent roles in Chapters Eighteen and Nineteen.

[9]To work step by step through the policy's effects, we say that the balance of payments moves into deficit, which causes the currency to depreciate. In fact, the depreciation of the currency prevents the deficit from actually arising; such a deficit is called *incipient*. An incipient surplus would be a balance-of-payments surplus that would arise in the absence of a currency appreciation.

[10]Of course, internal balance does not happen automatically in response to *any* expansionary fiscal

Figure 17.1 □ **Short-Run Effect of Fiscal Policy with Immobile Capital**

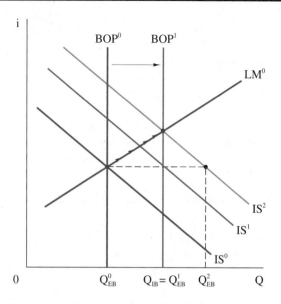

An expansionary fiscal policy shifts the IS curve from IS^0 to IS^1, raising income and the interest rate. The current-account balance moves into deficit, and the domestic currency depreciates. The depreciation raises the income consistent with external balance (shifting the BOP curve to the right) and lowers the relative price of domestic goods (shifting the IS curve from IS^1 to IS^2). At the new equilibrium, income, the interest rate, and the exchange rate are higher. The crowding-out effect of the rise in the interest rate prevents income from rising to Q_{EB}^2.

often seem reluctant to permit their currencies to depreciate. This reluctance has at least two sources. First, a currency depreciation raises the price of imported goods to consumers and the cost of imported inputs to domestic firms. Both groups will lobby against policies that would produce a currency depreciation, although exporters and import-competing firms will lobby for them. Second, an increase in the exchange rate often is called a "weakness" of the currency and thus interpreted as a sign of weakness of the economy.[11] The combination of these two factors may cause governments to intervene in foreign exchange markets to prevent a currency depreciation even under a supposedly flexible rate regime. Should this occur, the expansionary effect of fiscal policy with immobile capital disappears, and the appropriate analysis becomes that under a fixed exchange rate as discussed in section 16.3.1.

_____

policy. The magnitude of the policy must be calibrated to the increase in income required to reach internal balance.

[11]See section 14.4.1 for a discussion of the dangers of identifying a balance-of-payments surplus (deficit) or a currency appreciation (depreciation) with improvement (deterioration) of the economy.

Note that the results in Figure 17.1 will be temporary if the increase in government expenditure is a one-time policy. Sustaining the rise in income would require a permanently higher level of government spending, but analysis of the long-run effects of such a policy must await the introduction of price flexibility in the next chapter.

A second cautionary note in evaluating the effect of fiscal policy centers on the assumption of capital immobility. We shall see that the effectiveness of fiscal policy under flexible exchange rates hinges on the immobility of capital. As capital becomes more internationally mobile, the prospects for fiscal policy restoring internal balance fade because such a policy tends to cause a currency appreciation rather than depreciation. As the world economy becomes more integrated, capital tends to become more mobile. Efforts to achieve capital immobility often take the form of capital controls that are costly to administer, interfere with the efficient allocation of capital, lead to black markets and other means of circumvention, and tend to be ineffective at least in the long run.

17.2.2 Monetary Policy with Immobile Capital

The major effect of a move to a flexible exchange rate is the elimination of foreign exchange market intervention and its effect on the domestic money stock. Once changes in the central bank's foreign exchange reserves are eliminated, the monetary base and the money stock change only in response to open market operations:[12]

$$\Delta M = mm \cdot (\Delta GB + \Delta FXR); \qquad [17.1]$$

thus, $\Delta FXR = 0$ implies that

$$\Delta M = mm \cdot \Delta GB. \qquad [17.2]$$

The requirements of external balance no longer constrain the size of the domestic money stock, although its size will affect the exchange rate. The central bank can choose any value for the money stock, but it must be willing to accept the implied exchange rate.[13]

The initial effect of a money stock expansion through an open market purchase is a drop in the domestic interest rate and a rise in income, as illustrated in Figure 17.2 by the shift from LM^0 to LM^1. The lower interest rate encourages private investment spending, which raises total expenditure and income. The change in the interest rate has no direct effect on the balance of payments, because capital is assumed to be completely unresponsive to changes in the international pattern of interest rates. The higher income leads to more imports and a current-account deficit,

---

[12]The central bank can also alter the money stock by using other policy tools, including changes in the discount rate and in the required reserve ratio. The introduction of these additional tools would not alter the basic conclusion that the move to a flexible exchange rate breaks the link between the balance of payments and the money stock and places control over the nominal money stock in the hands of the central bank.

[13]Note that under a fixed exchange rate, the central bank could choose the level at which to peg the exchange rate but would have to accept the implied money stock.

Figure 17.2 ▫ **Short-Run Effect of Monetary Policy with Immobile Capital**

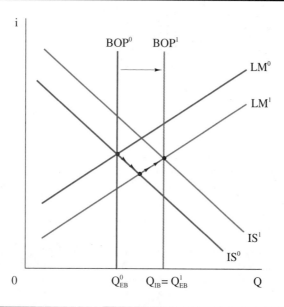

An increase in the money stock causes income to rise and interest rates to fall to equalize the quantity of money demanded with the new, higher stock. As income rises, the current account moves toward a deficit and the currency depreciates. The depreciation lowers the relative price of domestic goods, shifts spending toward domestic and away from foreign goods, and raises the income consistent with external balance.

and the domestic currency depreciates. The depreciation shifts both the BOP and IS curves to the right, to BOP^1 and IS^1 *(Why?)*, until they intersect on the new LM curve at a higher income.

In fact, monetary policy raises income precisely *because* it generates a currency depreciation that lowers the relative price of domestically produced goods and services. Again, depreciation may prove unpopular with consumers, who face higher prices for imported goods, and with producers who face higher prices for imported inputs. On the other hand, exporters and firms that sell import-competing products tend to view a currency depreciation favorably. Monetary policy therefore not only changes the level of income but also redistributes income among domestic industries. As in the case of fiscal policy, the impact of a temporary increase in the money stock is only temporary; income remains at Q_{IB} only so long as the money stock remains at the new higher level.

17.2.3 Summary of Policy Effects with Immobile Capital

With a flexible exchange rate and immobile capital, either fiscal or monetary policy can raise the economy's level of income or GDP. Both expansionary policies work through their ability to depreciate the domestic currency and shift expenditure

Table 17.1 □ **Policy Effects with Immobile Capital**

Policy	Effect on Q	Effect on Exchange Rate[a]	Effect on Current-Account Balance
Fiscal Policy			
Increase in G	+	+	0[b]
Decrease in G	−	−	0[b]
Monetary Policy			
Increase in M	+	+	0[b]
Decrease in M	−	−	0[b]

[a]A plus sign denotes a rise in e (currency depreciation); a minus sign denotes a fall in e (currency appreciation).

[b]With completely immobile capital, only a current-account balance of zero is consistent with balance-of-payments equilibrium.

toward domestically produced goods and services. Table 17.1 summarizes fiscal and monetary policies' effects on income, the exchange rate, and the current account. *(Compare Table 17.1 with Table 16.2, and make sure you can explain the reasons behind any differences.)*

17.3   Macroeconomic Policy with Perfectly Mobile Capital

The years since the move to more flexible exchange rates have also brought increased integration of world capital markets. The world's major trading economies now engage in extensive trade in stocks, bonds, and other financial assets as well as in goods and services. Because of these trends, the analysis of macroeconomic policies under flexible exchange rates and mobile capital is particularly important. Of course, a number of smaller economies remain largely outside the growing world capital market and have tended to remain under some form of fixed exchange rate system (see Table 16.1 in Chapter Sixteen).

17.3.1   Fiscal Policy with Perfectly Mobile Capital

Highly mobile capital reduces the effectiveness of fiscal policy under flexible exchange rates.[14] Recall that fiscal policy works to alter income with immobile capital because of the accompanying currency depreciation. With highly mobile capital, expansionary fiscal policy no longer causes a depreciation of the domestic currency but an appreciation. The appreciation causes a second form of the **crowding-out** phenomenon.[15]

---

[14]Capital is highly mobile when small changes in international interest rate differentials generate large capital flows.

[15]The first form of crowding out is the decline in private investment spending caused by a rise in the interest rate.

Figure 17.3 □ **Short-Run Effect of Fiscal Policy with Perfectly Mobile Capital**

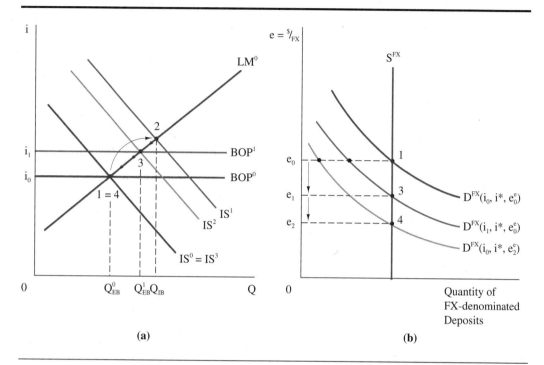

In panel (a), the initial direct effect of an expansionary fiscal policy (illustrated by the movement of the IS curve from IS^0 to IS^1) is to raise income and interest rates. Higher domestic interest rates (at point 2) generate a capital inflow and an appreciation of the domestic currency. If the fiscal policy is perceived as temporary, the BOP line shifts to BOP^1. As the exchange rate falls, domestic goods and services become more expensive relative to foreign ones. Individuals respond to the change in relative prices by shifting expenditure to foreign goods. The fall in private expenditure shifts the IS curve back to IS^2, at point 3. If the policy is perceived as permanent, the appreciation does not shift the BOP line but shifts the IS curve all the way back to IS^3, and equilibrium is restored at the original income level at point 4. Panel (b) traces events in the foreign exchange market.

As the domestic currency appreciates (e falls), the relative price of domestic goods rises because $R \equiv P/eP^*$, and individuals shift their expenditures toward the now relatively cheaper foreign goods. The decline in private expenditure on domestic goods partially or totally offsets the increased government expenditure, depending on whether asset holders perceive the fiscal policy as temporary or permanent.

Policy Expected to Be Temporary

In Figure 17.3 panel (a), expansionary fiscal policy initially raises expenditure on domestic goods and services and shifts the IS curve from IS^0 to IS^1. Income rises, and the interest rate must rise to keep the quantity demanded of money equal to the fixed money stock. As the domestic interest rate rises, capital flows into the economy and the balance of payments moves into surplus at point 2. The surplus causes the domestic currency to appreciate. If participants in the foreign exchange market perceive the increased government spending as temporary, they also will expect the currency appreciation to be temporary, leaving their expected future exchange rate, e^e, unaffected. The spot appreciation coupled with an unchanged expected future exchange rate shifts the BOP line up to BOP^1. *(Explain why, using uncovered interest parity.)*[16]

The currency appreciation also shifts the IS curve leftward to IS^2 as the relative price of domestic goods and services rises. The temporary rise in government spending moves the economy to the intersection of IS^2, LM^0, and BOP^1 at point 3, with income and the interest rate higher than before the policy was put into effect. The domestic currency has appreciated, and the current-account balance has shifted toward a deficit.

Panel (b) of Figure 17.3 allows us to view more explicitly events in the foreign exchange market. In the diagram, we denote the foreign currency simply as *FX*. We saw in panel (a) that the initial shift to the right in the IS curve due to increased government expenditure on domestic goods and services pushes up the domestic interest rate from i_0 to i_1. This raises the expected rate of return on domestic-currency-denominated deposits relative to that on foreign-currency (FX) ones. In the foreign exchange market in panel (b), the demand for foreign-currency deposits shifts to the left in response to the decline in their expected rate of return. At the original exchange rate of e_0, market participants now want to hold fewer foreign-currency deposits in their asset portfolios. Market participants' efforts to rid themselves of the extra foreign-currency deposits bids down the domestic price of foreign currency; that is, the domestic currency appreciates to e_1 at point 3.

Policy Expected to Be Permanent

If participants in the foreign exchange market expect the rise in government expenditure to be permanent, they also will expect the accompanying appreciation of the domestic currency to persist, so e^e will fall with e. In panel (a) of Figure 17.3, the currency appreciation no longer shifts the BOP curve because, as long as $e = e^e$, i_0 is consistent with foreign exchange market equilibrium for the given foreign interest rate. *(Show why, using the interest parity condition.)* With the BOP line remaining unchanged at BOP^0, the balance-of-payments surplus at point 2 is larger than in the case of a temporary policy just discussed. The larger surplus requires a larger currency appreciation to restore balance-of-payments equilibrium on BOP^0. The larger appreciation shifts the IS curve further to the left, since the appreciation raises the relative price of domestic goods and shifts spending toward imports.

Equilibrium is restored when the IS and BOP curves again intersect at a point on the LM curve, but this cannot happen until income falls all the way back to its original level. As long as income remains above Q_{EB}^0, the demand for money exceeds

---

[16]The currency appreciation is expected to be reversed; in other words, a depreciation of the domestic currency is anticipated. To compensate them for holding deposits denominated in the domestic currency during the expected depreciation, asset holders require a higher domestic interest rate (i_1 rather than i_0).

the money stock at i_0; thus, the interest rate must be above i_0. Perfect capital mobility implies that capital will flow into the economy, causing the currency to appreciate as long as the interest rate remains above i_0. The IS curve continues to shift to the left until the appreciation stops. This can happen only when the interest rate has fallen back to i_0, restoring balance-of-payments equilibrium at point 4 in Figure 17.3 panel (a).

Panel (b) of Figure 17.3 focuses on adjustments in the foreign exchange market. When the expected future exchange rate drops below e_0^e, the demand for FX-denominated deposits shifts further to the left as their expected rate of return falls. The result is a larger spot appreciation of the domestic currency than occurred in the case in which fiscal policy was expected to be temporary; e_2 denotes the new equilibrium exchange rate at point 4.

Because it generates a large appreciation of the domestic currency, fiscal policy that is expected to persist cannot bring the economy into internal balance when capital is very responsive to interest rates. The currency appreciation crowds out enough private expenditure on domestic goods and services to offset the expansionary effect of the increased government expenditure. Although the expansionary fiscal policy leaves total income unchanged, it does reallocate spending toward the public sector. It also reallocates income away from export-oriented and import-competing sectors of the economy and toward sectors insulated from the effects of foreign trade, such as construction and retailing. Just as depreciations prove unpopular with consumers and with firms that use imported inputs, currency appreciations are unwelcome in sectors of the economy tightly linked to international trade. For example, the appreciation of the dollar in the early 1980s (see Case One and Figure 17.10) proved unpopular with trade-oriented sectors of the U.S. economy and led to increased pressure for protectionism. What was the most commonly cited reason for the dramatic rise of the dollar? The expansionary fiscal policy of the United States, dramatically represented by the federal government's rapidly growing budget deficit.[17]

17.3.2 Monetary Policy with Perfectly Mobile Capital

Although fiscal policy is largely or completely ineffective under a flexible exchange rate with mobile capital because of the resulting exchange appreciation, monetary policy becomes effective in the same circumstances because it produces a currency depreciation. The depreciation lowers the relative price of domestic goods, which stimulates spending and income. Also unlike the fiscal policy case, expectations that monetary policy changes are permanent rather than temporary enhance the policy's effectiveness.

Policy Expected to Be Temporary
An open market purchase of government bonds increases the money stock by an amount equal to the money multiplier times the magnitude of the purchase (from

---

[17]Case Four in this chapter investigates the relationship between the government budget deficit and the exchange rate.

Figure 17.4 □ **Short-Run Effect of Monetary Policy with Perfectly Mobile Capital**

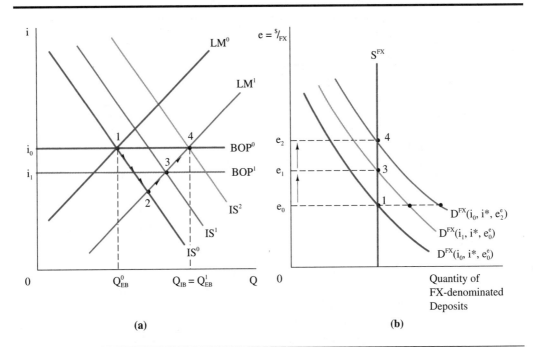

(a)   **(b)**

An open market purchase of government bonds by the central bank moves the LM curve from LM^0 to LM^1. Income rises and the interest rate falls to make individuals willing to hold the new, larger stock of money. Because capital flows are very sensitive to interest rate changes, the fall in the domestic interest rate causes a large capital outflow at point 2. The resulting balance-of-payments deficit causes the domestic currency to depreciate. As the exchange rate rises, domestic goods become relatively less expensive compared to foreign ones and spending shifts in favor of domestic goods. The IS curve moves to the right. If the monetary policy is perceived as temporary, e^e is unchanged and the depreciation shifts the BOP line down to BOP^1; the new equilibrium is at point 3. If the policy is perceived as permanent, e^e rises with e and the BOP line does not shift in response to the (now larger) depreciation, but the IS curve shifts further to IS^2, restoring equilibrium at point 4. Panel (b) illustrates adjustment in the foreign exchange market.

Equation 17.2) and shifts the LM curve in Figure 17.4 panel (a) from LM^0 to LM^1. As the money stock rises, income and the interest rate must adjust to keep the quantity demanded of money equal to the growing stock.[18] Income rises, and the interest rate falls, both of which increase the quantity of money that individuals in the economy choose to hold at point 2. The fall in the interest rate causes

---

[18]Recall that each point along an LM curve represents a combination of income and interest rate at which the quantity demanded of money equals the money stock. Changes in the money stock shift the LM curve.

capital to flow out of the country and moves the balance of payments toward a deficit. The deficit depreciates the domestic currency.[19]

If the expansionary monetary policy is expected to be temporary, the depreciation will be perceived as temporary as well, implying that e^e remains unchanged at e_0^e. The spot depreciation shifts the BOP line down to BOP^1. *(Why?)*[20] The depreciation also lowers the relative price of domestic goods and shifts the IS curve to the right (to IS^1) until it intersects the new BOP^1 curve on the new LM^1 curve at point 3. The overall effect of the expansionary monetary policy is to raise income, depreciate the currency, and move the current-account balance toward a surplus.

Panel (b) of Figure 17.4 highlights adjustments in the foreign exchange market. Beginning from point 1, the increase in the money stock puts downward pressure on the domestic interest rate, originally at i_0. The decline in the interest rate to i_1 lowers the expected rate of return on domestic-currency-denominated deposits and, therefore, increases demand for foreign-currency ones. At the original exchange rate, e_0, market participants now want to hold more than the existing quantity of foreign-currency deposits. As portfolio owners try to accumulate such deposits, they bid up their price. In other words, the domestic currency depreciates from e_0 to e_1, the new exchange rate at which participants in the foreign exchange market willingly hold the existing stock of deposits in each currency. As the exchange rate rises, the expected future exchange rate does not change from e_0^e, because market participants perceive the current depreciation as temporary. The new equilibrium occurs at point 3.

Policy Expected to Be Permanent

If participants in the foreign exchange market expect the expansionary monetary policy to be permanent, they will expect the depreciation to be permanent as well. The expected exchange rate then rises with e. In this case, in panel (a), the depreciation does *not* shift the BOP curve, which remains at BOP^0. *(Why?)* The large balance-of-payments deficit at point 2 (larger than in the case of the temporary monetary policy) causes a larger currency depreciation, shifting the IS curve further to the right to IS^2. At the new equilibrium at point 4 in panel (a), income is high enough to make individuals willing to hold the higher stock of money balances at the old interest rate. Only when this is true can the interest rate return to its original level at i_0, halting capital outflows and the currency depreciation.

In panel (b) of Figure 17.4, when the expected future exchange rate rises above e_0^e, the demand for FX-denominated deposits shifts to the right as their expected rate of return increases. *(Why?)* The result is a larger spot depreciation of the domestic currency than occurred in the case in which monetary policy was expected to be temporary; e_2 denotes the new equilibrium exchange rate at point 4.

---

[19]Recall that the deficit is an incipient one. The actual deficit is prevented by the depreciation, but it is helpful in understanding the logic of the adjustment process.

[20]This follows directly from uncovered interest parity. If the currency depreciates with no change in e^e, the currency is expected to appreciate. Because of the expected appreciation, portfolio owners are content to hold the existing quantity of domestic-currency deposits at a lower interest rate (i_1) than they would if the currency were not expected to appreciate (i_0).

Table 17.2 □ **Policy Effects with Perfectly Mobile Capital**

Policy	Effect on Q	Effect on Exchange Rate[a]	Effect on Current-Account Balance
Fiscal Policy			
Perceived as temporary			
Increase in G	+	−	−
Decrease in G	−	+	+
Perceived as permanent			
Increase in G	0[b]	−	−
Decrease in G	0[b]	+	+
Monetary Policy			
Perceived as temporary			
Increase in M	+	+	+
Decrease in M	−	−	−
Perceived as permanent			
Increase in M	+	+	+
Decrease in M	−	−	−

[a]A plus sign denotes a rise in e or currency depreciation; a minus sign denotes a decline in e or currency appreciation.
[b]Completely crowded out through change in the real exchange rate.

Monetary policy—temporary or permanent—succeeds in raising income because it causes the domestic currency to depreciate; and the depreciation again alters the distribution as well as the level of income. Export and import-competing sectors of the economy tend to gain relative to nontraded-goods sectors, consumers of imported goods, and firms that are heavy users of imported inputs. The current-account balance moves toward a surplus.

17.3.3 Summary of Policy Effects with Perfectly Mobile Capital

Table 17.2 summarizes fiscal and monetary policies' effects on the macroeconomy. Perfectly mobile capital reduces fiscal policy's effectiveness under flexible exchange rates. With highly mobile capital, expansionary fiscal policy causes a currency appreciation, rather than a depreciation as in the zero capital mobility case. The currency appreciation generates a second type of crowding out. As the domestic currency appreciates, the relative price of domestic goods rises, and expenditure shifts toward foreign goods that are now cheaper. This expenditure shift away from domestic goods partially or totally offsets the increased government expenditure, depending on whether participants in the foreign exchange market perceive the fiscal policy as temporary or permanent. *(Compare Table 17.2 with Table 16.3.)*

Although fiscal policy generates partial or complete crowding out because of the resulting appreciation, monetary policy becomes highly effective in the same circumstances because it produces a currency depreciation. The depreciation stimulates spending on domestic goods by lowering their relative price. Also unlike the fiscal policy case, expectations that monetary policy changes are permanent rather than temporary enhance the policy's effectiveness because they generate a larger currency depreciation.

17.4 Macroeconomic Policy with Imperfectly Mobile Capital

Most countries operate under an intermediate degree of capital mobility represented by an upward-sloping BOP curve. If income rises, the current account moves into deficit, and a rise in the domestic interest rate is needed to bring about an offsetting capital inflow. The more sensitive capital flows are to the interest rate, the smaller the required rise in the interest rate and the flatter the BOP curve. As in Chapter Sixteen, we shall concentrate on the case in which capital is very sensitive to interest rates and the BOP curve thus is flatter than the LM curve. *(A good way to test your understanding of the following analyses: construct analogous analyses for the low-mobility case in which the BOP curve is steeper than the LM curve.)*

17.4.1 Fiscal Policy with Imperfectly Mobile Capital

Fiscal policy may raise income with imperfectly mobile capital, but the expansionary effect is at least partially offset by an appreciating currency that induces a shift toward foreign goods and away from domestic ones. In Figure 17.5, the initial effect of an expansionary fiscal policy is a shift of the IS curve from IS^0 to IS^1. Income rises because of the increased spending on domestic output. The interest rate too must rise to keep the quantity demanded of money equal to the unchanged money stock. In response to the rise in the domestic interest rate, capital flows into the economy.

The balance of payments moves into surplus, and the currency appreciates. The BOP curve shifts to the left (BOP^0 to BOP^1) as a result of the appreciation. Because of the movement from domestic to foreign goods, at each interest rate balance-of-payments equilibrium requires a lower income. *(Why? For a review, see section 15.3.3.)* The IS curve also shifts to the left as individuals respond to the fall in e by switching spending from domestic to foreign goods. The new equilibrium occurs where the IS^2 and BOP^1 curves intersect on the LM curve.

The precise effects on income, the interest rate, and the exchange rate depend on whether the policy is perceived as temporary or permanent. If temporary, the leftward shift of the BOP line is relatively large because of the expected future depreciation, and the leftward shift of the IS curve is relatively small because of the relatively small BOP surplus; expansionary fiscal policy can then substantially raise income. However, if the policy is perceived as permanent, the leftward shift of the BOP line is small and that of the IS line is large *(Why?)*, leaving income largely unaffected by the fiscal policy.

Regardless of whether the fiscal policy is perceived as temporary or permanent, income rises by less than it would were the policy not accompanied by a currency

Figure 17.5 □ **Short-Run Effect of Fiscal Policy with Imperfectly Mobile Capital**

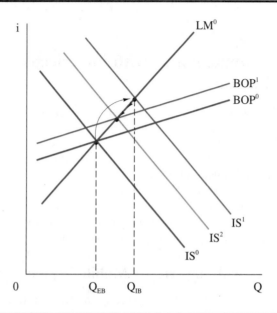

A rise in government expenditure shifts the IS curve to the right and raises income and the interest rate. With high capital mobility, capital flows into the economy and the currency appreciates. As the exchange rate falls, the relative price of domestic goods rises. A shift in expenditure to now relatively cheaper foreign goods at least partially offsets the policy's initial expenditure-increasing effect by shifting IS back to the left. Perceptions that the policy is permanent rather than temporary make the policy less effective in raising income.

appreciation. The appreciation makes domestically produced goods more expensive relative to foreign goods; and the resulting shift away from spending on domestic goods at least partially offsets the expansionary effect of the fiscal policy. The more mobile capital, the larger the currency appreciation and the smaller the policy's impact on income. Likewise, the more permanent the policy is perceived as being, the larger the currency appreciation and the smaller the effect on income.

The crowding-out effect through the real exchange rate was the center of much attention in the United States in the early 1980s. Fiscal policy was expansionary, and the dollar appreciated dramatically against a number of trading partners' currencies.[21] The dollar's appreciation, in turn, contributed to rising imports in industries such as steel, automobiles, textiles, and footwear, and to reduced exports of agricultural products. The net effect of the expansionary fiscal policy was to increase income, but the accompanying appreciation dampened the policy's impact on income and adversely altered the performances of trade-sensitive U.S. industries.

---

[21]See Case One.

Figure 17.6 □ **Short-Run Effect of Monetary Policy with Imperfectly Mobile Capital**

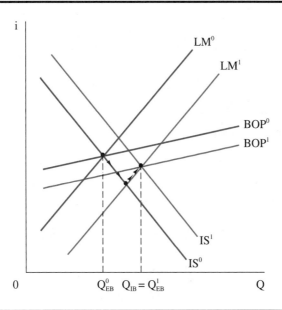

An increase in the money stock raises income and lowers the interest rate. A capital outflow depreciates the currency, lowering the relative price of domestic goods. Spending switches to domestic goods, and the IS curve shifts to the right. The depreciation of the currency makes monetary policy an effective instrument for reaching internal balance. Perceptions that the policy is permanent rather than temporary (resulting in a smaller shift in the BOP curve and a larger shift in the IS curve) make it more effective in raising income.

17.4.2 Monetary Policy with Imperfectly Mobile Capital

Capital mobility contributes to monetary policy's effectiveness in raising income under a flexible exchange rate regime. This follows from the fact that the currency depreciation that accompanies an expansionary monetary policy gives the economy an extra boost through its effect on domestic and foreign relative prices. The more mobile is capital, the larger the depreciation that follows a given monetary expansion and the greater the fall in the relative price of domestic goods. Similarly, the more permanent the expansionary monetary policy is perceived to be, the larger is the currency depreciation.

Figure 17.6 traces the effect of an expansionary monetary policy. The initial rightward shift of the LM curve from LM^0 to LM^1 lowers the domestic interest rate and creates a capital outflow. The outflow moves the balance of payments toward a deficit and generates a depreciation of the domestic currency. The depreciation shifts the BOP curve to the right to BOP^1. The more permanent the policy is perceived as being, the smaller will be the rightward shift in the BOP line and the larger will be the depreciation. *(Why? See footnote 20.)* As a result of the depreciation, the relative price of domestic goods falls and demand shifts toward domestic goods, moving the IS curve to the right to IS^1. Again, the more permanent the policy, the larger the deficit and the depreciation and the larger the shift in the IS curve. The new equilibrium occurs at the income level at which the IS^1 and BOP^1 curves intersect on the LM^1 curve. Through the accompanying currency depreciation, the expansionary monetary policy favors export and import-competing sectors of the domestic economy.

17.5 The Policy Mix

The analysis in the preceding section suggests that fiscal and, to a greater extent, monetary policy can be useful in pursuing internal balance under a flexible exchange rate with imperfectly mobile capital. Which combination of the two available policies should policy makers use, or does it matter? The choice of fiscal and monetary **policy mix** does matter, because each combination will result in a different domestic interest rate and exchange rate, which as we have noted all along can dramatically affect distribution in different sectors of the domestic economy.

17.5.1 Examples of Policy Mixes

Figure 17.7 illustrates three policy mixes that policy makers can use to reach internal balance beginning from a point of external balance with unemployment, $Q_{EB} < Q_{IB}$. The economy begins at an identical point in each case. In panel (a), fiscal policy alone is used; panel (b) represents the use of monetary policy alone; and panel (c) illustrates the use of one of many possible combinations of fiscal and monetary policy. Each scenario is designed to achieve the same level of output: the one corresponding to internal balance, Q_{IB}. However, each policy mix has different implications for the allocation of expenditure between the private and public sectors, for the performance of various industries within the economy, and for the status of the current and capital accounts of the balance of payments.

In panel (a) of Figure 17.7, expansionary fiscal policy raises both income and the interest rate and appreciates the domestic currency. The rise in the interest rate reduces private spending in those sectors most sensitive to interest rates—consumer durables such as automobiles and appliances, firms' investment in new plants and equipment, and construction. The currency appreciation switches a portion of expenditure from domestically produced to foreign-produced goods by causing a change in relative prices. Export and import-competing industries suffer most from this change in the expenditure pattern. Both effects of fiscal policy—crowding out by a rise in the interest rate and crowding out by currency appreciation—reduce private expenditure on domestic output, partially offsetting the policy's expansionary effect on income. The net effect is an increase in income, a rise in the share of spending accounted for by the public rather than the private sector, and a decline in both interest-sensitive and trade-oriented sectors of the economy.

Panel (b) of Figure 17.7 represents an expansionary monetary policy intended to have the same net effect on income as the fiscal policy illustrated in panel (a). The other effects

Figure 17.7 □ **Use of Various Policy Mixes to Achieve Internal Balance**

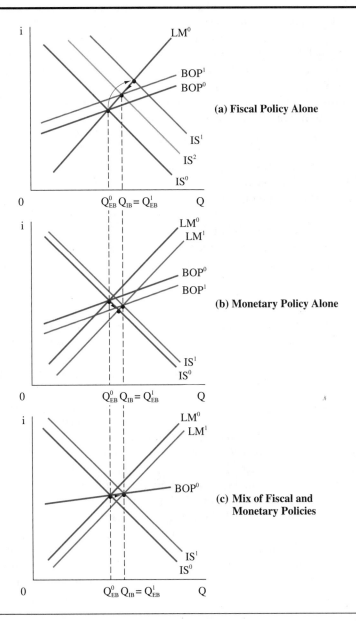

(a) Fiscal Policy Alone

(b) Monetary Policy Alone

(c) Mix of Fiscal and
Monetary Policies

Policy makers can use many fiscal/monetary policy combinations to increase income to Q_{IB}. Each combination results in different values for the interest rate and the exchange rate. Expansionary fiscal policy alone produces the highest interest rate, monetary policy alone the lowest, and a policy mix an intermediate value. Expansionary fiscal policy appreciates the domestic currency; monetary policy alone depreciates it; and the illustrated policy mix leaves the exchange rate unchanged.

of the two policies are quite different, however. The expansionary monetary policy lowers the domestic interest rate, and private investment expenditure rises. Interest-sensitive sectors, particularly consumer durables and construction, may benefit. The domestic currency depreciates, and trade-oriented sectors may find their performances improved. Consumers with a taste for imported goods and firms that use imported inputs, on the other hand, will face higher prices as a result of the rise in the exchange rate.

The use of either expansionary fiscal policy or expansionary monetary policy obviously has important domestic implications. Each allows some groups to gain at the expense of others. One way to limit the extent of these distributional effects is to use a combination of both types of expansionary policy. A large number of such mixes exist that would move the economy to Q_{IB} in Figure 17.7.

Panel (c) illustrates a policy mix that leaves the exchange rate unchanged. The interest rate rises slightly, causing a small amount of crowding out of interest-sensitive industries. But teaming the expansionary fiscal policy with an expansionary monetary policy moderates the rise in the interest rate and reduces the magnitude of crowding out from the fiscal-policy-only case in panel (a). The accompanying monetary policy also keeps the currency from appreciating; this prevents a rise in the relative price of domestically produced goods. At the same time, the combination keeps the exchange rate from depreciating and prevents a rise in the domestic price of imported goods and inputs.

17.5.2   Responding to Disturbances

The policy mix with which policy makers choose to pursue internal balance depends on, among other things, the nature of the disturbance that pushed the economy below full employment.[22] Such disturbances fall into two broad categories: shifts in tastes away from domestically produced goods and increases in the demand for real money balances.

Beginning from a position of internal balance (point 1 in Figure 17.8), suppose the economy experiences a shift in consumer tastes away from domestically produced goods and services. Potential causes of such a shift could include pessimism about the future leading to an overall reduction in consumption or investment spending or a shift in consumer preferences in favor of foreign goods and services.[23] We can represent such a spending disturbance by a shift to the left of the IS curve, from IS^0 to IS^1. Income falls below the level consistent with internal balance, and the domestic currency depreciates because of the decline in the domestic interest rate at point 2.

Policy makers might respond to the temporary shortfall in consumption or investment spending in one of two ways. An expansionary fiscal policy shifts IS back to the right to IS^2 and restores full employment at the same interest rate and exchange rate as before the disturbance (point 3). The alternative is an expansionary monetary policy. By shifting LM to the right to LM^1, such a policy puts further downward pressure on the interest

---

[22]Of course, the economy can experience expansionary disturbances that push income above the full-employment level. We concentrate on contractionary disturbances, which call for expansionary policy responses, because we have focused on the impact of expansionary policies.

[23]The exogenous spending disturbances under consideration here do *not* include changes in response to the domestic interest rate, domestic income, or the relative price of domestic goods and services, but rather shifts in spending for given levels of those variables.

Figure 17.8 □ **Policy Responses to a Spending Disturbance**

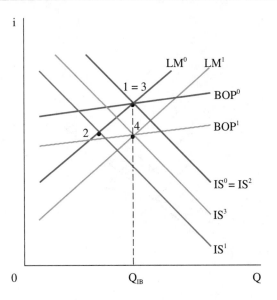

Policy makers can respond to a contractionary spending disturbance with an expansionary fiscal or monetary policy. A fiscal policy restores full employment at the original interest rate and exchange rate (point 3). A monetary policy restores full employment but magnifies the disturbance's effect on the interest rate and exchange rate (point 4).

rate and causes a further currency depreciation, which shifts the IS curve and BOP curve to the right, to IS^3 and BOP^1. Monetary policy restores full employment, but with a lower interest rate and a depreciated value of the domestic currency at point 4. As noted in section 17.5.1, the different values of the interest rate and the exchange rate implied by fiscal and monetary policies carry important implications for the performance of specific sectors of the economy, even though both can restore full employment.

A second type of contractionary economic disturbance consists of a rise in the demand for real money balances for a given value of income and the interest rate. Beginning from a point of full employment (point 1), such a shock shifts the LM curve to left, as in Figure 17.9.[24] Again, output falls below the full-employment level. The disturbance raises the domestic interest rate and causes a currency appreciation (at point 2).

If policy makers respond with an expansionary monetary policy, LM shifts back to the right, restoring full employment at the original interest rate and exchange rate (point 3). If, instead, policy makers respond with expansionary fiscal policy, the IS curve shifts to the right to IS^1. This puts further upward pressure on the interest rate

---

[24]Section 15.2.5 reviews why.

Figure 17.9 □ **Policy Responses to a Money-Demand Disturbance**

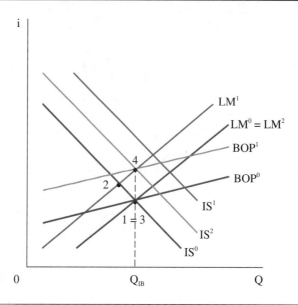

Possible policy responses to a contractionary monetary disturbance include expansionary fiscal or monetary policy. An expansionary fiscal policy restores full employment but exacerbates the rise in the interest rate and the currency appreciation (point 4). A monetary policy restores full employment at the predisturbance interest rate and exchange rate (point 3).

---

and causes further currency appreciation. As the domestic currency appreciates, the IS and BOP curves shift to the left to IS^2 and BOP^1. The economy returns to full employment at point 4, with a higher interest rate and a lower value of the exchange rate than prior to the disturbance to money demand.

17.5.3 Constraints on the Policy Mix

Several considerations not obvious in our analysis of Figures 17.8 and 17.9 considerably complicate policy makers' choice of policies. For example, we assumed that the level of output consistent with full employment is known, as is how the actual level of output compares with full employment. However, as we saw in Chapter Sixteen, defining the full-employment level of output for an economy is a complex task, as is judging whether the current level of output is consistent with, above, or below full employment. Policy makers may disagree among themselves or with the public about the current state of the economy and, therefore, about the need for macroeconomic policies and the appropriate magnitude of those policies.

We also assumed in our analysis that policy makers know the source of the disturbance to the economy, that is, whether the disturbance originates in the market for goods and services or in the money market. In fact, the nature of disturbances to the economy may be difficult to discern, particularly in the short run, during which policy makers must formulate their response. As Figures 17.8 and 17.9 make clear, responding to a spending disturbance with monetary policy or to a monetary disturbance with fiscal policy can exacerbate swings in the interest rate and the exchange rate and the accompanying distributional impacts on the economy.

Policy makers also must judge the time horizon of a disturbance in order to make an appropriate policy response. If the decline in spending or increase in money demand is short-lived, then no response may be required, as the economy will return to full employment automatically as soon as the disturbance ends. If policy makers respond too aggressively to a short-lived disturbance, they risk pushing output above the full-employment level and generating inflation. On the other hand, an overly passive response that relies too heavily on the temporary nature of the disturbance risks a prolonged period of unemployment. These timing decisions are complicated by the fact that macroeconomic policies typically affect the economy with a lag.

Finally, policy makers may face political pressures that constrain their ability to use some macroeconomic policy tools. We already have mentioned one source of such pressure: the distributional implications of changes in interest rates and exchange rates. A second source of pressure comes from policy targets beyond internal and external balance. For example, the ability to use expansionary fiscal policy may be constrained by concerns over the implications of existing government budget deficits. If a government accumulates a large budget deficit during times of economic prosperity, it may find itself constrained against using fiscal policy to respond to a slump. Along similar lines, a government facing reelection may find it difficult to cut spending even if macroeconomic considerations point to the appropriateness of a contractionary fiscal policy stance.

17.5.4 Transmission and the Policy Mix

Domestic political considerations are not the only constraints on macroeconomic policy makers. Different domestic macroeconomic policy mixes have different effects on trading-partner economies, a phenomenon known as **transmission,** so the governments of those economies often attempt to influence the course of domestic macroeconomic policy.

With a high degree of capital mobility, if domestic policy makers respond to a contractionary disturbance with an expansionary fiscal policy, trading-partner economies typically experience an expansion as well. This happens because the fiscal policy appreciates the domestic currency or, equivalently, depreciates the foreign currency. The depreciation makes foreign-produced goods and services relatively cheaper, so expenditure on them rises. In contrast, if domestic policy makers respond to a contractionary disturbance with an expansionary monetary policy, trading partners are likely to feel the contraction. The domestic currency depreciates, or the foreign currency appreciates. Foreign goods and services become more expensive relative to domestic ones, and consumers shift away from spending on foreign goods. Of course, how trading partners feel about these transmitted policy effects depends on the state of their economies. A country fighting inflation may welcome a contractionary effect initiated abroad, while a country suffering from excessive unemployment will resent the same effect.

Table 17.3 □ **Short-Run Policy Effectiveness under Flexible Exchange Rates**

	Ability to Affect Income under a Flexible Exchange Rate		
Policy	Immobile Capital	Highly Mobile Capital	Perfectly Mobile Capital
Fiscal	Effective (currency depreciates)	Somewhat effective[a] (currency appreciates)	Ineffective[a] (currency appreciates)
Monetary	Effective (currency depreciates)	Effective[b] (currency depreciates)	Very effective[b] (currency depreciates)

[a]Less effective if perceived as permanent than if perceived as temporary.

[b]More effective if perceived as permanent than if perceived as temporary.

17.6   Summary of Short-Run Policy Effectiveness under a Flexible Exchange Rate

The short-run effectiveness of fiscal and monetary policy in pursuing a goal of internal balance under a flexible exchange rate regime critically depends on the degree of capital mobility. As capital mobility rises, monetary policy becomes more effective than fiscal policy because of its different impact on the exchange rate. Policy-induced changes in the exchange rate are important because, with the assumption of fixed domestic and foreign price levels, they are reflected directly in changes in the relative prices of domestic and foreign goods. Any policy that can alter the exchange rate can change the allocation of expenditure between domestic and foreign goods.

Table 17.3 summarizes the effects of fiscal and monetary policy under flexible exchange rates with differing degrees of capital mobility. Because of the importance of changes in the exchange rate that accompany each policy, the table reports those as well.

Case One
Pity the Poor Dollar: A Historical Perspective

> Pity the poor dollar. It can't seem to do anything right. Just over a decade ago, it was blamed for being too weak. . . . And now the dollar is blamed for being too strong. . . . The dollar's strength, it's claimed, is such that U.S. goods can't compete in world markets and, as a result, millions of American jobs are being lost. . . .[25]

---

[25]Alfred L. Malabre, Jr., "Pity the Poor Dollar, It Can't Seem to Please," *The Wall Street Journal,* November 11, 1985, 11.

Figure 17.10 □ **Real Effective Exchange Rate of the Dollar against a Trade-Weighted Average of Several Major Currencies, 1980–1985 (Index: 1973 = 1.0)**

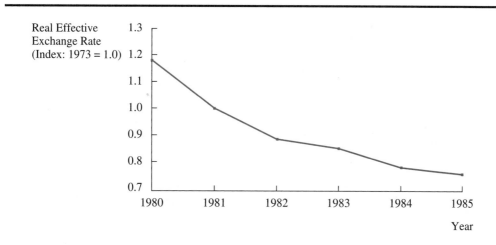

Source: *Economic Report of the President 1995.*

Probably no economic phenomenon received as much worldwide attention during the first half of the 1980s as the appreciation of the dollar against other major currencies. The popular press, politicians' speeches, and economists' writings abounded with analyses of the causes, cures, and implications. Those analyses typically were accompanied by charts showing the decline in the dollar price of other currencies between 1980 and 1985. Figure 17.10 illustrates the trade-weighted real effective exchange rate (see section 12.8 for a review of this concept), which shows a dollar appreciation of almost 50 percent between 1980 and 1985.

During the second half of the 1980s and the first half of the 1990s, on the other hand, the "weakness" of the dollar, or its tendency to depreciate against other currencies, became the focus of attention. Figure 17.11 illustrates this phenomenon using the same exchange rate measure as in Figure 17.10.

Whenever data such as those in Figures 17.10 and 17.11 are presented, an important question arises about the choice of starting and ending dates for the comparison—in other words, was 1980 (or 1985, or 1994) a representative year for the dollar's value relative to other currencies? In fact, the value of the dollar was near record lows against many currencies in 1980; that is, 1980 did *not* represent a typical year for the dollar, but rather the culmination of a period of unprecedented inflation and other economic problems in the United States. Neither was 1985 a representative year.

Figure 17.12 illustrates the real effective dollar exchange rate over the entire period since the switch to a more flexible exchange rate regime with the collapse of the Bretton Woods system in 1973. The larger historical context makes the exchange

Figure 17.11 ▫ **Real Effective Exchange Rate of the Dollar against a Trade-Weighted Average of Several Major Currencies, 1985–1994 (Index: 1973 = 1.0)**

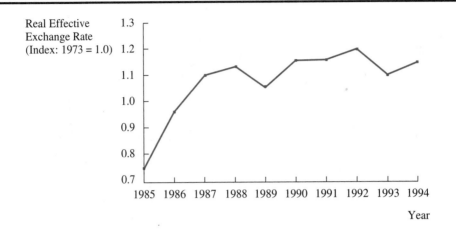

Source: *Economic Report of the President 1995.*

rates of both the early 1980s and the late 1980s to early 1990s seem less aberrant. Clearly the dollar exhibited two dramatic trends, but each comprises just part of the larger historical context.

Figure 17.12 ▫ **Real Effective Exchange Rate of the Dollar against a Trade-Weighted Average of Several Major Currencies, 1973–1994 (Index: 1973 = 1.0)**

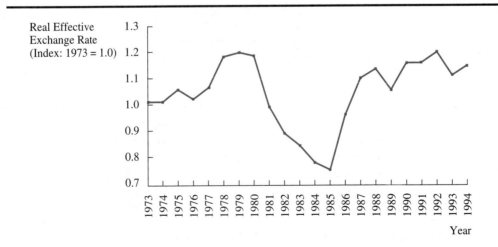

Source: *Economic Report of the President 1995.*

This interpretation problem arises when examining any type of economic data presented over an interval of time. Sometimes data availability or policy changes dictate the time interval presented. Nevertheless, when interpreting data such as those in Figure 17.10 or 17.11, it is advisable to investigate whether the chosen time period significantly affects the appearance of the phenomenon under study.

Case Two
The Trend toward Flexible Exchange Rates

In Table 16.1, we saw that a large number of countries remained under some form of fixed exchange rate system in 1995 despite the widely publicized move to more flexible rates since the early 1970s. Table 17.4 reports the groups of countries operating under various types of flexible exchange rates in 1995.

A general rule is that larger, more developed economies tend to operate under more flexible exchange rate regimes than do smaller, developing economies. However, throughout the 1980s, more and more economies moved toward more flexible exchange rate regimes, either managed floats or pure floats. Table 17.5 documents this trend.

Case Three
Floating the Pound

Case One in Chapter Sixteen analyzed the effect of German unification on Germany's European trading partners in the early 1990s. The combination of Germany's expansionary fiscal policies to finance unification and tight monetary policies to deter inflation kept the interest rate on Deutsche mark-denominated assets high and shifted trading partners' BOP curves upward. For fellow members of the European Union's Exchange Rate Mechanism of fixed exchange rates, preventing their currencies from depreciating against the Deutsche mark required intervention to buy marks. That intervention lowered trading partners' money stocks and placed contractionary pressures on their economies, where unemployment already was high.

In September 1992, a period of increased uncertainty about the future of monetary integration in Europe, participants in the foreign exchange markets started to expect devaluations of several EU currencies, including the British pound.[26] The expected devaluations implied that, to prevent actual devaluations, central banks would have to conduct even more intervention and monetary contraction. *(Why?)*

---

[26]Case Four in Chapter Twelve reports Sweden's reaction during the same period.

Table 17.4 ▫ **IMF Member Countries Maintaining a Flexible Exchange Rate, June 30, 1995**

Flexibility Limited in Terms of a Single Currency or Group of Currencies		More Flexible			
Single Currency	Cooperative Arrangements[a]	Adjusted According to a Set of Indicators	Other Managed Floating	Independently Floating	
Bahrain	Austria	Chile	Algeria	Afghanistan	Mozambique
Qatar	Belgium	Ecuador	Angola	Albania	New Zealand
Saudi Arabia	Denmark	Nicaragua	Belarus	Armenia	Norway
United Arab Emirates	France		Brazil	Australia	Papua New Guinea
	Germany		Cambodia	Azerbaijan	Paraguay
	Ireland		China	Bolivia	Peru
	Luxembourg		Colombia	Bulgaria	Philippines
	Netherlands		Croatia	Canada	Romania
	Portugal		Dominican Republic	Costa Rica	Rwanda
	Spain		Egypt	El Salvador	São Tomé and Príncipe
			Eritrea	Finland	Sierra Leone
			Georgia	Gambia	Somalia
			Greece	Ghana	South Africa
			Guinea-Bissau	Guatemala	Suriname
			Honduras	Guinea	Sweden
			Hungary	Guyana	Switzerland
			Indonesia	Haiti	Tajikistan
			Israel	India	Tanzania
			Laos	Iran	Trinidad and Tobago
			Latvia	Italy	Uganda
			Macedonia	Jamaica	Ukraine
			Malaysia	Japan	United Kingdom
			Maldives	Kazakhstan	United States
			Mauritius	Kenya	Uzbekistan
			Pakistan	Kirgizstan	Zaïre
			Poland	Lebanon	Zambia
			Russia	Madagascar	Zimbabwe
			Singapore	Malawi	
			Slovenia	Mexico	
			South Korea	Moldova	
			Sri Lanka	Mongolia	
			Sudan		
			Tunisia		
			Turkey		
			Uruguay		
			Vietnam		

aThe European Monetary System.

Source: International Monetary Fund, *International Financial Statistics,* September 1995.

Table 17.5 □ **Number of IMF Member Countries Using Exchange Rate Arrangements, 1980–1995**

Exchange Rate Arrangement	1980	1985	1990	1995
Currency Pegged to				
U.S. dollar	39	31	25	23
French franc	14	14	14	14
Other currency	4	5	5	7
Special drawing rights	15	12	6	3
Other composite	22	32	35	20
Flexibility Limited in Terms of a Single Currency or Group of Currencies				
Single currency	na	7	4	4
Cooperative arrangements[a]	8	8	9	10
More Flexible				
Adjusted according to set of indicators	4	6	3	3
Other managed floating	na	20	23	36
Independently floating	na	12	25	59
Other[b]	34	na	na	na
Total	141	148	154	179

[a]European Monetary System.

[b]Includes the headings "Flexibility limited in terms of single currency," "Other managed floating," and "Independently floating" for years in which those categories are not available separately.

Source: International Monetary Fund, *International Financial Statistics,* various issues.

But those policies posed political risks in countries such as Britain, already entering its third year of recession.

On September 16, 1992 (dubbed "Black Wednesday" by opponents of the move), rather than pursue further monetary contraction, the British government pulled the pound out of the fixed exchange rate system and allowed the pound to float against the Deutsche mark and other currencies. Britain's monetary policy became more expansionary, and interest rates on pound-denominated assets fell. The pound depreciated in foreign exchange markets from the fixed rate of DM2.85/£1 to a low of DM2.34/£1 in February 1993, lowering the relative prices of British goods and services, and the country's current-account deficit shrank. By 1994, the British economy was growing faster than the EU economies that remained in the Exchange Rate Mechanism.[27]

---

[27]An obvious question is why more countries did not abandon their fixed exchange rates. There are at least two reasons. First, several economies had histories of excessively expansionary monetary policies, inflation, and currency devaluations. Those countries feared that escaping the discipline imposed by the Exchange Rate Mechanism would generate expectations of further currency depreciations. Second, countries that pulled out of the system ran the risk of having less voice in the process of European monetary integration.

Case Four
The Budget Deficit and the Dollar

During the early 1980s, when the dollar *appreciated* dramatically against the currencies of most U.S. trading partners (see Figure 17.10), many commentators blamed the U.S. government budget deficit. Overly expansionary fiscal policy, they argued, placed upward pressure on U.S. interest rates, encouraged capital inflows, and caused the dollar to appreciate. *(Illustrate in the IS-LM-BOP framework.)* As Case One in this chapter reported, the period since 1985 has been one of substantial dollar *depreciation* (see Figure 17.11). Yet, commentators still blame the U.S. government budget deficit. The result has been a lively debate about the likely impact on the dollar of a reduction in the budget deficit.

The possible link between a budget deficit and currency *appreciation* shows up clearly in the model developed in this chapter. Why, then, would anyone link the deficit to the dollar *depreciation* since 1985? There are three possibilities. First, prolonged, large, and growing budget deficits may cause foreign exchange market participants to anticipate more expansionary future monetary policies to mitigate the deficit's effect on the interest rate. If so, a future currency depreciation might be expected to follow from the monetary expansion. Those expectations would reduce the demand for domestic-currency-denominated deposits and cause the currency to depreciate. A second possibility also relies on expectations, but in a more general way. If the persistent budget deficit weakens overall confidence in the U.S. economy, it might reduce the demand for dollar-denominated deposits. However, note that the resulting depreciation would increase demand for U.S. goods and services and thereby tend to offset the lack of confidence in the economy's future performance. The third possibility involves a risk premium.[28] Recall that portfolio owners may demand a risk premium to hold assets denominated in a particular currency if such assets comprise a large portion of their portfolios, making the portfolios' value vulnerable to exchange rate changes. If the government budget deficit, by requiring individuals to hold a large stock of dollar-denominated government bonds, generates a higher risk premium on dollar assets, then the U.S. BOP line would shift upward and the dollar would depreciate. As we noted in the earlier discussion of risk premiums, the empirical evidence on the importance of such premiums is mixed.

So, the basic model of an open macroeconomy suggests a currency appreciation would accompany budget deficits. But several expectations-based arguments may generate effects in the opposite direction. Figure 17.13 looks at the recent empirical evidence for the United States. Panel (a) reports the budget surplus (if positive) or deficit (if negative) of U.S. local, state, and federal governments as a percent of GDP. Panel (b) illustrates the real effective exchange rate, expressed as the dollar price of foreign exchange.

---

[28]See section 16.4.2.

Figure 17.13 □ **The U.S. Government Budget and the Exchange Rate, 1973–1994**

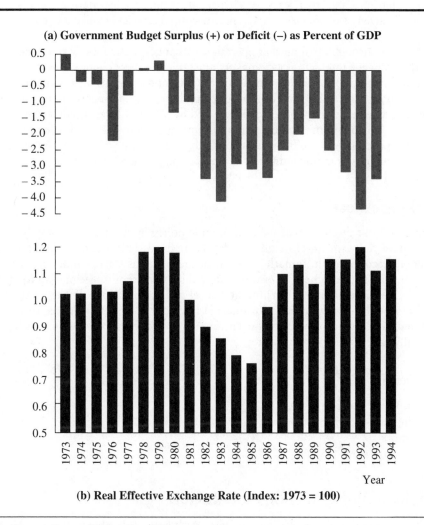

(a) Government Budget Surplus (+) or Deficit (–) as Percent of GDP

(b) Real Effective Exchange Rate (Index: 1973 = 100)

Year

Source: *Economic Report of the President 1995.*

The two dramatic trends in Figure 17.13 suggest a positive relationship between the size of the government budget deficit and the value of the dollar. During the early 1980s, the deficit grew dramatically and the dollar appreciated. During the late 1980s, the deficit shrank and the dollar depreciated. This supports the analysis based on the model presented in the chapter. However, the deficits of the 1980s were a relatively new phenomenon for the United States. It is possible that if the deficit grows, its impact on expectations may become more significant.

Summary

The switch from a fixed to a flexible exchange rate regime carries important implications for the effectiveness of various types of macroeconomic policy. Unlike a fixed exchange rate, a flexible rate allows the monetary authority to control the domestic nominal money stock through open market operations. Changes in the money stock, however, alter the exchange rate, and policy makers must tolerate these changes—with their distributional implications and their impact on the current-account balance—as a side effect of monetary policy. With high degrees of capital mobility, monetary policy becomes highly effective in altering domestic income and fiscal policy loses its effectiveness. The choice of fiscal and monetary policy mix for pursuing internal balance affects the allocation of spending between the private and public sectors as well as the relative performances of various domestic industries and of trading partners' economies.

Looking Ahead

Throughout our discussion of macroeconomic policy in an open economy, we have assumed the domestic and foreign price levels are fixed. This assumption implies that despite the economy's automatic adjustment mechanisms for reaching external balance, no analogous mechanism ensures internal balance; that is, the market for goods and services may be in equilibrium at a level of income above or below the level consistent with full employment or internal balance. In Chapter Eighteen, we relax the fixed-price assumption and concentrate on long-run macroeconomic behavior, especially that of the exchange rate.

Key Terms

Bretton Woods system
crowding out
policy mix
transmission

Problems and Questions for Review

1. Countries A and B are trading partners. Both have a flexible exchange rate and highly but not perfectly mobile capital. Both want to pursue expansionary policies to raise the level of income.
   (a) Country A pursues an expansionary fiscal policy and a tight monetary policy (that is, zero growth of the domestic money stock). Illustrate the effects of such a policy mix.
   (b) Country B pursues a tight fiscal policy (that is, no change in government purchases or taxes) and an expansionary monetary policy. Illustrate the effects of such a policy mix.
   (c) What would you expect to happen to the interest rate in country A relative to that in country B? What would happen to the exchange rate between country A's currency and country B's?

(d) What distributional effects would your results in part (c) have in the two economies?

(e) Use your answers to construct a brief argument in favor of international macroeconomic policy coordination (that is, for countries getting together to discuss and coordinate their macroeconomic policy actions).

2. A country hires you as its minister of macroeconomic policy. The country maintains strict capital controls that make any nonofficial capital inflows or outflows impossible. Up until now, the country has operated under a fixed exchange rate regime. The day you take office, exchange rate policy changes to a perfectly flexible exchange rate regime. Your first order of business is to give seminars for your subordinates, the assistant minister of fiscal policy and the assistant minister of monetary policy, to outline the implications of the change in exchange rate policy. Summarize the main points of your seminar presentations on the implications of the new policy, using the appropriate tools of analysis.

3. It is common for countries to complain about one another's interest rates. Assume the domestic country operates under a flexible exchange rate regime, and capital is completely mobile. Illustrate and explain the effect on the domestic economy of a *decline* in the *foreign* interest rate (i^*), beginning from a point of general equilibrium, using the IS-LM-BOP framework. (Compare your answer with that of Question 5 in Chapter Sixteen.)

4. Historically, it has been common for a country to pressure its trading partners to follow expansionary macroeconomic policies. Assume that the domestic country operates under a flexible exchange rate regime and that capital is completely mobile. Illustrate and explain the effect on the domestic economy of an *increase* in *foreign* income, beginning from a point of general equilibrium, using the IS-LM-BOP framework. (Compare your answer with that of Question 7 in Chapter Sixteen.)

5. How does the expectation that the policy is temporary affect the efficacy of fiscal policy under a flexible exchange rate and perfect capital mobility? Explain.

6. How does the expectation that the policy is temporary affect the efficacy of monetary policy under a flexible exchange rate and perfect capital mobility? Explain.

7. For countries with perfectly mobile capital, the choice between a fixed and flexible exchange rate determines whether fiscal policy can affect income. Explain why.

8. Country A operates under a flexible exchange rate regime and is characterized by a high degree of capital mobility. The country is beginning to experience inflationary pressure, and policy makers decide that a contractionary macroeconomic policy is appropriate. They consider three policy packages, all of which would be designed to generate the same overall effect on income:
Policy package 1: contractionary fiscal policy combined with neutral monetary policy;
Policy package 2: contractionary monetary policy combined with neutral fiscal policy;
Policy package 3: a combination of contractionary fiscal and contractionary monetary policy such that the exchange rate will remain the same.

(a) Suppose you own a residential construction firm. How might you rank your preferences for the three policy packages? Explain.

(b) Suppose you own a large soybean farm and typically export a large portion of your crop. How might you rank your preferences for the three policy packages? Explain.

(c) Suppose you own a small retail shop that sells handicrafts imported from developing countries. How might you rank your preferences for the three policy packages? Explain.

References and Selected Readings

Baxter, M. "International Trade and Business Cycles." In *Handbook of International Economics,* Vol. 3, edited by G. M. Grossman and K. Rogoff, 1801–1864. Amsterdam: North-Holland, 1995.
Up-to-date survey of research on the relationship between international trade activity and macroeconomic cycles; intermediate and advanced.

Bordo, Michael D., and Barry Eichengreen, eds. *A Retrospective on the Bretton Woods System: Lessons for International Monetary Reform.* Chicago: University of Chicago Press, 1993.
Collection of papers on the strengths and weaknesses of the Bretton Woods system; level of papers varies.

Destler, I. M., and C. Randall Henning. *Dollar Politics: Exchange Rate Policymaking in the United States.* Washington, D.C.: Institute for International Economics, 1989.
Readable examination of the distribution of international policy making responsibility in the United States.

Federal Reserve Bank of New York. *International Financial Integration and U.S. Monetary Policy.* New York: Federal Reserve Bank of New York, 1990.
Collection of studies of the effect of international linkages, especially those working through capital markets, on U.S. monetary policy; for intermediate students.

Fleming, J. M. "Domestic Financial Policies under Fixed and Floating Exchange Rates." *IMF Staff Papers* 9 (November 1962): 369–380.
A classic paper on macroeconomic policy effectiveness in an open economy; for advanced students.

Frankel, J. A., and A. K. Rose. "Empirical Research on Nominal Exchange Rates." In *Handbook of International Economics,* Vol. 3, edited by G. M. Grossman and K. Rogoff, 1689–1730. Amsterdam: North-Holland, 1995.
Up-to-date survey of research on the empirical behavior of exchange rates; intermediate and advanced.

Frankel, Jacob A., and Michael L. Mussa. "Asset Markets, Exchange Rates, and the Balance of Payments." In *Handbook of International Economics,* Vol. 2, edited by Ronald W. Jones and Peter B. Kenen, 679–748. Amsterdam: North-Holland, 1985.
An advanced treatment of the issues raised in the chapter.

Friedman, Milton. "The Case for Flexible Exchange Rates." In *Essays in Positive Economics,* 157–203. Chicago: University of Chicago Press, 1953.
One of the first serious calls for a change to flexible exchange rates; for all students.

Goldstein, Morris. *The Exchange Rate System and the IMF.* Washington, D.C.: Institute for International Economics, 1995.
Readable treatment of the current international monetary system and suggested reforms.

Kenen, Peter B. "Macroeconomic Theory and Policy: How the Closed Economy Was Opened." In *Handbook of International Economics,* Vol. 2, edited by Ronald W. Jones and Peter B. Kenen, 625–678. Amsterdam: North-Holland, 1985.
Advanced discussion of the important implications of openness for macroeconomics.

Kenen, Peter B., et al., eds. *The International Monetary System.* Cambridge: Cambridge University Press, 1994.
Collection of papers on the strengths and weaknesses of the current international monetary system; level of papers varies.

Kincaid, G. Russell. "Policy Implications of Structural Change in Financial Markets." *Finance and Development* 25 (March 1988): 2–5.
The influence of changes in capital mobility on macroeconomic policy; for all students.

Little, Jane Sneddon. "Exchange Rates and Structural Change in U.S. Manufacturing Employment." Federal Reserve Bank of Boston *New England Economic Review* (March–April 1989): 56–70.
The sectoral effects of changes in the exchange rate; for all students.

Marston, Richard C. "Stabilization Policies in Open Economies." In *Handbook of International Economics,* Vol. 2, edited by Ronald W. Jones and Peter B. Kenen, 859–916. Amsterdam: North-Holland, 1985.
Advanced analysis of macroeconomic policy in an open economy.

Meltzer, Allan H. "U.S. Policy in the Bretton Woods Era." Federal Reserve Bank of St. Louis *Review* (May–June 1991): 53–83.
Excellent survey of the Bretton Woods era; for all students.

Mundell, Robert A. "Capital Mobility and Stabilization Policy under Fixed and Flexible Exchange Rates." *Canadian Journal of Economics and Political Science* 29 (November 1963): 475–485.
The original presentation of capital mobility's impact on macroeconomic policy effectiveness in an open economy; for intermediate and advanced students.

Obstfeld, Maurice. "International Currency Experience: New Lessons and Lessons Relearned." *Brookings Papers on Economic Activity* 1 (1995): 119–220.
Excellent overview of lessons based on recent exchange rate experience.

Persson, T., and G. Tabellini. "Double-Edged Incentives: Institutions and Policy Coordination." In *Handbook of International Economics,* Vol. 3, edited by G. M. Grossman and K. Rogoff, 1973–2030. Amsterdam: North-Holland, 1995.
Up-to-date survey of interaction effects among countries' macroeconomic policies; intermediate and advanced.

Sachs, Jeffrey D. "The Dollar and the Policy Mix: 1985." *Brookings Papers on Economic Activity* 1 (1985): 117–197.
The macroeconomic policy mix of the early 1980s as a determinant of the value of the dollar; for advanced students.

Spero, Joan Edelman, and Jeffrey A. Hart. *The Politics of International Economic Relations.* New York: St. Martin's Press, 1996.
The politics of the postwar international monetary order; for all students.

Tatom, John A. "The Link between the Value of the Dollar, U.S. Trade and Manufacturing Output." Federal Reserve Bank of St. Louis *Review* 70 (November–December 1988): 24–37.
Sectoral effects of changes in the exchange rate; for intermediate students.

CHAPTER EIGHTEEN

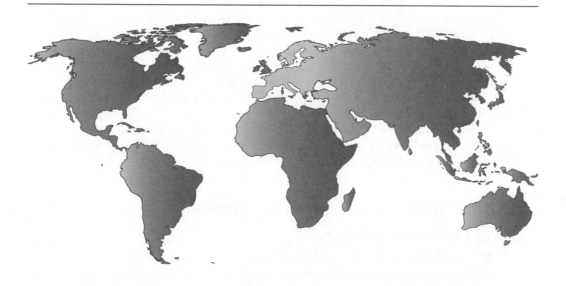

The Exchange Rate in Long-Run Equilibrium

18.1 Introduction

Exchange rates sometimes move dramatically in the very short run. For example, the Russian ruble depreciated by more than 20 percent against the dollar on October 11, 1994, falling from R3,081/$1 to R3,926/$1 in response to doubts about Russian economic and political reform. Thus far, in Chapters Fourteen through Seventeen, we have examined macroeconomic behavior in the short run, during which the price level remained fixed.

Longer-run trends in the world economy can be just as dramatic. In 1973, the dollar price of yen stood at $1/¥360; by early 1995, the price had risen to $1/¥80, a dollar depreciation of almost 80 percent. To understand such events, we must take into account the fact that in the long run prices *do* respond to macroeconomic policy, as well as to other events in the economy. This chapter and the next extend our model to incorporate those price-level changes. It is useful to proceed in two stages. In this chapter, we turn our attention to long-run equilibrium under a flexible exchange rate and explore the relationships we expect to observe among key macroeconomic variables *once the price level has adjusted completely to any change in the economy*. Chapter Nineteen focuses on the relationship between the short-run results from earlier chapters and the long-run results, or on what happens in the economy *as* the price level adjusts.

In **long-run equilibrium,** the economy satisfies two related conditions. First, output reaches its full-employment level, determined by how much capital and labor the economy contains, as well as by the available technology and by how much individuals in the economy choose to work. Second, all prices in the economy, including the wage rate and the exchange rate, reach levels consistent with equilibrium in their respective markets. We call this a long-run *equilibrium,* because once the economy attains it, economic variables will remain unchanged until some type of new shock to the system disturbs them.

In this chapter, we examine how the exchange rate behaves in long-run equilibrium. This requires an understanding of the long-run relationship among the country's money stock, its price level, and its exchange rate.

18.2   Money in Long-Run Equilibrium

18.2.1   Money and Output

What effect does a one-time permanent change in the money stock have on the economy's long-run equilibrium real output? The answer is *none,* and a simple thought experiment can help us see why. Suppose that, beginning from a position of long-run equilibrium, the U.S. government announced that, as of next January 1, the U.S. money stock would double. Each individual's bank balances would double, as would each worker's wage rate, and the money price of every good and service.

Such a policy would have no effect on real output. No one would be wealthier or poorer in real terms. And the relative prices of all goods in the economy would remain the same, because the relative price of two goods equals the ratio of the two goods' money prices, both of which would have doubled with the doubled money stock.[1] Output would remain at its full-employment level, determined by the economy's endowment of resources, its technology, and residents' tastes for income and leisure. Therefore, we can conclude that a one-time permanent change in the money stock has no effect on the economy's long-run equilibrium real output. This important result has a name: the **neutrality of money.**

18.2.2   Money and the Interest Rate

Just as a one-time change in the money stock leaves long-run output unaffected, such a change also has no effect on the long-run equilibrium interest rate. To understand why, recall that the equilibrium interest rate in the economy represents the rate of return a lender must receive to willingly lend funds to a borrower. A lender lends $1 today in return for a promised repayment of $1(1 + i) next year.

Suppose at the time the money supply doubled, the equilibrium interest rate in the economy equaled 5 percent, so that lending a dollar for one year brought a repayment of $1.05, or a rate of return of 5 percent. A bank willing to lend a firm

---

[1]Section 12.2.1 covers the relationship between money prices and relative prices.

$1 million to build a new factory (in return for $1,050,000) before the doubling of the money stock should still be willing to lend the firm $2 million for the same project after the doubling (in return for $2,100,000), because the bank's rate of return still would equal 5 percent. Because all borrowing and lending decisions in the economy should remain unchanged by a one-time permanent change in the money stock, we can conclude that such changes do not alter the long-run equilibrium interest rate.

18.2.3 Money and the Price Level

If one-time changes in the money stock do not change real output or the interest rate in long-run equilibrium, such changes in the money stock must cause proportional changes in the price level. For example, if the money stock doubles, the long-run equilibrium price level must double as well. We can see why by recalling from Chapter Fifteen the condition required for equilibrium in the money market.[2] The real money stock must equal the demand for real money balances, which depends positively on real income and negatively on the interest rate.

$$M/P = L(\overset{+}{Q}, \overset{-}{i}). \qquad [18.1]$$

If, in long-run equilibrium, one-time permanent changes in the nominal money stock, M, do not alter real income or the interest rate, Equation 18.1 implies that changes in M must generate proportional changes in P to maintain money-market equilibrium. In other words, if changes in the nominal money stock do not lead to changes in real money demand, then the price level must adjust to keep the *real* money stock (M/P) constant. So, in long-run equilibrium, one-time changes in the money stock lead to proportional changes in the price level. If the money stock doubles, for example, the price level must double as well.

We can examine empirically the relationship between changes in countries' money stocks and changes in their respective price levels. Our theory implies that changes in the money stock should lead to proportional changes in the long-run price level. Actual data, of course, come from a world economy constantly bombarded by shocks of various kinds, not from one constantly in long-run equilibrium; so we do not expect the predicted relationship to hold exactly. Nonetheless, countries with larger increases in their money stocks should experience larger increases in their price levels than countries whose money stocks exhibit smaller changes, especially if we focus on averages over a relatively long period to lessen the impact of short-run disturbances.

Figure 18.1 reports the average adjusted rates of money-stock growth (horizontal axis) and price-level growth (vertical axis) for a subset of industrial economies from 1980 through 1994.[3] If our predicted relationship held exactly, all points

---

[2]See section 15.2.4 for a review.

[3]To account for the fact that, over such a long period, the full-employment level of output grows, the money-stock growth rates have been reduced by 2.5 percent per year to cover real output growth.

Figure 18.1 ▫ **Money Stocks and Price Levels, 1980–1994**

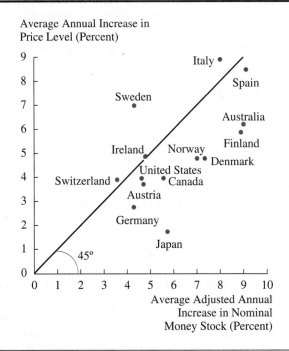

The horizontal axis measures the average annual percentage increase in each country's money stock, minus 2.5 percent to allow for increases in full-employment real output. The vertical axis measures the average annual percentage increase in each country's price level (CPI). In the long run, an increase in a country's nominal money stock leads to an approximately proportional increase in its price level, leaving the real money stock unchanged.

Source: Data from The World Bank, *World Development Report 1995.*

would fall along the upward-sloping 45-degree line in the figure. While few of the points actually lie on the 45-degree line, most are close to it, implying a close relationship between changes in countries' money stocks and their price levels.

We also can use the graph of money-market equilibrium from Chapter Fifteen to summarize the long-run equilibrium relationship among M, P, Q, and i, as in Figure 18.2. Equilibrium requires that the real money stock (M/P) equal the public's demand for real money balances (L[Q, i]). If changes in M fail to move Q or i from their long-run equilibrium values of Q_0 and i_0, the money demand function remains stationary. To maintain equilibrium, the money stock line must remain stationary as well, and this requires that the *real* money stock (M/P) not change. Therefore, the ratio of the new money stock and price level (M_1/P_1) must equal the ratio of the original money stock and price level (M_0/P_0). In other words, the nominal money stock and price level must change proportionally.

Figure 18.2 ▫ **Long-Run Equilibrium in the Money Market**

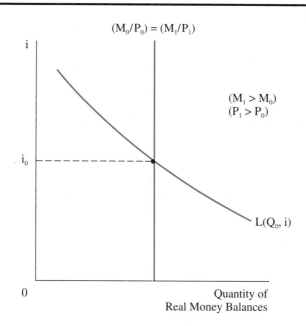

$(M_0/P_0) = (M_1/P_1)$

i

$(M_1 > M_0)$
$(P_1 > P_0)$

i_0

$L(Q_0, i)$

0

Quantity of
Real Money Balances

In long-run equilibrium, a change in the nominal money stock exerts no effect on real output or the interest rate. Money demand remains unchanged; and the price level must change proportionally with the nominal money stock to maintain equilibrium.

18.2.4 Money and the Exchange Rate

We have argued that in long-run equilibrium, all prices in the economy change proportionally with the level of the money stock, while real output and the interest rate remain unchanged. The nominal exchange rate, e, is just the domestic-currency price of a unit of foreign currency. Therefore, under a flexible exchange rate regime, we would expect the exchange rate to move proportionally with any change in the money stock.[4]

Returning to our thought experiment in which the U.S. money stock doubled, we would expect the dollar price of a unit of each foreign currency to double, implying that each foreign good or service would cost twice as many dollars as before. Again, individuals would be no better and no worse off. They would own and earn twice as many dollars, but every item they bought—including imports—would also cost twice as many dollars.

---

[4]Under a fixed exchange rate, monetary policy fails to alter the nominal money stock, because the necessary foreign exchange market intervention offsets the policy's impact.

Figure 18.3 □ Long-Run Equilibrium in the Foreign Exchange Market

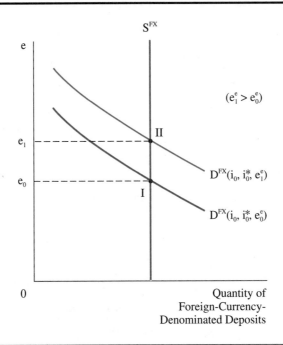

In long-run equilibrium, an increase in the nominal money stock does not change the interest rate. However, market participants anticipate proportional increases in all money prices, including the nominal exchange rate. The rise in e^e increases the demand for foreign-currency-denominated deposits and causes a proportional spot depreciation of the domestic currency.

Therefore, in long-run equilibrium, increases in the money stock lead to nominal depreciations of the domestic currency; and decreases in the money stock lead to currency appreciations. Figure 18.3 depicts equilibrium in the foreign exchange market. Beginning from a long-run equilibrium at point I, a rise in the nominal money stock leaves the domestic and foreign interest rates unchanged at i_0 and i_0^*. But the expected future exchange rate rises proportionally with M, because market participants expect a proportional increase in all money prices. The rise in e^e lowers the expected rate of return on deposits denominated in the domestic currency and shifts the demand for foreign-currency-denominated deposits to the right. This causes a spot depreciation of the domestic currency proportional to the original increase in the domestic money stock.

Note, however, that the *real* exchange rate, $R \equiv P/eP^*$, does not change. If a change in the money stock leads to proportional changes in both the domestic price level, P, and the nominal exchange rate, e, then the real exchange rate remains at its original value. This is simply another case of the long-run neutrality of money: one-time money stock changes do not change relative prices. After all, the real exchange

Table 18.1 □ **Summary of Monetary Effects in Long-Run Equilibrium**

Variable	Effect of One-Time Permanent Increase in Nominal Money Stock	Effect of One-Time Permanent Decrease in Nominal Money Stock
Real output (Q)	0	0
Interest rate (i)	0	0
Price level (P)	+[a]	−[a]
Nominal exchange rate (e)[b]	+[a]	−[a]
Real exchange rate (R)	0	0
Real money stock (M/P)	0	0

[a]Proportional to change in nominal money stock.

[b]A plus sign denotes a rise in e, or domestic currency depreciation; a negative sign denotes a fall in e , or domestic currency appreciation.

rate represents the relative price of domestic goods and services compared with foreign ones. Just as a rise in the price level fails to change relative prices because all money prices change proportionally, a proportional rise in both the price level and the nominal exchange rate leaves the real exchange rate unaffected.

18.2.5 Summary of Monetary Effects in Long-Run Equilibrium

A one-time permanent change in the nominal money stock changes all prices, including the nominal exchange rate, proportionally and leaves real output, the interest rate, relative prices, the real exchange rate, and the real money stock unchanged. Table 18.1 summarizes these results.

18.3 Purchasing Power Parity

We have seen that changes in countries' money stocks, in the long run, affect both price levels and nominal exchange rates. The interaction between these two relationships suggests a direct linkage between a country's price level and its nominal exchange rate. This linkage forms the basis for a view of long-run exchange rate behavior known as purchasing power parity (PPP), which focuses on exchange rates' role in determining the relative prices of domestic and foreign goods and services. The key building block for purchasing power parity is the law of one price.

18.3.1 The Law of One Price

The **law of one price** states that identical goods will sell for an equivalent price regardless of the currency in which the price is denominated. Arbitrage ensures that, with no transportation costs, barriers to trade, monopolies, or other restrictions, the law of one price will hold. Suppose, for example, that a stereo selling for £200 in London were priced at $500 in New York with the exchange rate equal to $2 per pound (e = $2/£). This would violate the law of one price, because the pound price of the stereo would be £200 in London and £250 in New York *(Why?)* or, equivalently, the dollar price would be $400 in London and $500 in New York *(Why?)*. Arbitrageurs would find it profitable to buy stereos in London and sell them in New York; in fact, their profit would equal £50, or $100, per stereo. Arbitrage would raise the price of stereos in London by increasing demand and lower the price of stereos in New York by increasing supply.

Algebraically, we can represent this scenario as follows, letting P_S^{NY} and P_S^{L} denote the price of *stereos* in *New York* and *London*, respectively. Initially,

$$P_S^{NY} > e \cdot P_S^{L},$$

or,

$$\$500 > (\$2/\pounds) \cdot (\pounds 200) = \$400.$$

Arbitrage causes P_S^{NY} to fall and P_S^{L} to rise until

$$P_S^{NY} = e \cdot P_S^{L}. \qquad [18.2]$$

Equation 18.2 states the law of one price: The dollar price of a stereo must equal the dollar price of a pound multiplied by the pound price of the stereo. *(State the law of one price for stereos in terms of pounds.)*[5]

Complications such as transportation costs, tariffs, or nontariff barriers to trade can prevent the law of one price from holding perfectly. Nevertheless, the possibility of arbitrage tightly links prices of identical traded goods expressed in different currencies. Even when we include a consideration such as transportation costs, the prices in different currencies of an identical good should differ by only a constant—equal to the amount of transportation cost involved in arbitrage. In other words, the prices still should move in tandem.

The degree to which the law of one price holds will differ depending on the characteristics of the good in question. Prices of identical, freely traded goods are the most tightly linked. Equation 18.2 will hold more closely if both stereos are identical than if their brands, qualities, or technical characteristics differ. For differentiated products (for example, three automobiles made by Chevrolet, Volkswagen, and Toyota), small differences among them can result in persistent price differences even with no transportation costs or trade barriers. We would not expect the dollar price of a Chevrolet to be equivalent to the dollar price of a Volkswagen or a Toyota—because consumers do not perceive the automobiles as identical.

Trade barriers introduce artificial price differences across countries and can cause the law of one price not to hold. Japan, for example, maintains strict import quotas

---

[5]If e' denotes the pound price of a dollar, we can write the law of one price as $e' \cdot P_S^{NY} = P_S^{L}$. This is simply Equation 18.2 divided through by e, because by definition $e' = 1/e$. In words, the pound price of a stereo must equal the pound price of a dollar times the dollar price of the stereo.

on rice to protect domestic rice farmers, who hold a special place in traditional Japanese culture. Imported rice would be much cheaper for Japanese consumers than domestically produced rice. *(Write out the relationship among the dollar price of rice imported from the United States, the yen price of Japanese-grown rice, and the dollar price of yen.)* But import quotas effectively rule out the kind of arbitrage we used to argue for Equation 18.2 in the stereo example.

For nontraded goods (that is, goods not traded internationally) the law of one price may hold even more loosely. Many services are traded only infrequently because the buyer and seller must be in the same location; examples include health-care services, haircuts, and retailing. Even if the dollar price of a tonsillectomy exceeded the pound price of a tonsillectomy multiplied by the dollar price of a pound, few Americans needing a tonsillectomy would choose to travel to London to get it. The inconvenience of some types of transactions limits the process of arbitrage in the case of these services. This implies that price differences among infrequently traded goods and services may persist for some time; that is, the law of one price does not hold for such items.

18.3.2 From the Law of One Price to PPP

Purchasing power parity carries the law of one price one step further by applying the logic not to the price of a single good such as stereos, but to countries' overall price levels. The simplest version of purchasing power parity states that the price level in one country (such as the *United States*) equals the price level in a second (for example, *Britain*) multiplied by the exchange rate between the countries' currencies:

$$P^{US} = e \cdot P^B. \qquad [18.3]$$

The U.S. price level measures the dollar price of a basket of goods and services, and the British price level measures the pound price a basket of goods and services. Therefore, purchasing power parity holds when the two countries' price levels are equal once translated into a common currency using the exchange rate.

Equations 18.2 and 18.3 appear similar. However, the apparently simple step from the law of one price's link between the prices of a good expressed in two currencies to purchasing power parity's link between the price levels of two countries actually entails a number of important considerations. If the law of one price held perfectly for every good and service, and if the baskets of goods and services used to compute the two countries' price levels were identical, then purchasing power parity would follow. But we have argued that considerations such as transportation costs, product differentiation, and trade barriers render the law of one price ineffective for some goods and services. And the baskets of goods and services produced or consumed in various countries differ.

Still, the forces of arbitrage that underlie the law of one price should keep price levels and exchange rates from deviating too far from the purchasing-power-parity relationship, at least in the long run. If goods and services in the United States become more expensive than those in Britain ($P^{US} > e \cdot P^B$), the demand for dollars and for U.S. goods and services should fall, while the demand for British goods and services should rise. This would lower P^{US} and raise both e and P^B, leading back to purchasing power parity. Similarly, if goods and services in the United States become cheaper than those in Britain, market forces should place upward pressure on the U.S. price level and downward pressure on Britain's price level, as well as generating a dollar appreciation against the pound.

18.3.3 Absolute and Relative PPP

Economists call the version of purchasing power parity in Equation 18.3 **absolute purchasing power parity.** Absolute parity represents the strongest form, because it requires a strict relationship between the price levels in the two countries to hold continually. In terms of the model of the macroeconomy we developed earlier, absolute purchasing power parity requires that the relative price of domestic and foreign goods or the real exchange rate ($R \equiv P/eP^*$) continually equal 1. Suppose R rose above 1. The dollar price of domestic (U.S.) goods would exceed the pound price of foreign (British) goods multiplied by the dollar price of pounds. Arbitrage would result in some combination of a fall in the dollar price of U.S. goods, a rise in the pound price of British goods, and a dollar depreciation. If the relative price of domestic and foreign goods fell below 1, the same types of adjustments would occur, but in the opposite direction. *(Why?)*

Under a weaker form of parity, **relative purchasing power parity,** the percentage change in the domestic country's price level equals the percentage change in the foreign country's *plus* the percentage change in the exchange rate between the two countries' currencies—or, letting "hats" over variables represent percentage rates of change in those variables,[6]

$$\hat{P} = \hat{e} + \hat{P}^*. \tag{18.4}$$

Equation 18.4 says that the rate of inflation in the domestic country (simply the percentage rate of increase in its price level) equals the rate of its currency's depreciation against that of the foreign country plus the latter's inflation rate. Relative PPP may hold even when absolute PPP fails. In particular, if the factors such as transportation costs and trade barriers that cause deviations from absolute PPP remain more or less constant across time, then the relative PPP relationship between inflation rates and changes in exchange rates will hold.

18.3.4 How Can PPP Not Hold?

We already have considered several factors that can cause purchasing power parity not to hold. The most obvious is the presence of transportation costs or trade barriers. These cause the law of one price—and therefore absolute purchasing power parity—not to hold, and they may do the same with relative PPP if transportation costs or trade barriers change over time.

---

[6]For example, an x with a "hat" equals the percentage change in x, or $\Delta x/x$.

Suppose two countries produced and consumed identical combinations of goods. We would then expect relative purchasing power parity to hold quite closely for them. But most countries produce and consume diverse combinations of goods, partly as a result of specialization according to comparative advantage and partly as a result of taste differences. Many goods are nontraded (such as the tonsillectomy discussed earlier); others are heterogeneous (such as the Chevrolet, Volkswagen, and Toyota). All these considerations imply that each country's price level, whether a production-based measure such as the GDP deflator or a consumption-based measure such as the consumer price index (CPI), measures the prices of a unique combination of goods. The goods produced and consumed in the United States differ from those produced and consumed in Britain, which can cause either version of PPP to fail to hold. After all, the logic of PPP rests ultimately on the arbitrage that leads to the law of one price. But if each country's basket of goods and services is different, we should not expect arbitrage to lead to equal prices for the various baskets.

Because PPP is more likely to hold for traded goods or services than for nontraded ones, the evidence in its favor tends to be stronger in tests conducted using wholesale rather than consumer prices. The wholesale (or producer) price index measures changes in the prices of goods bought by firms and includes mainly intermediate traded goods. The consumer price index, on the other hand, measures changes in the prices of items bought by the typical consumer. This includes many services, such as housing and health care, for which the law of one price is only a weak long-term tendency.

Relative purchasing power parity links inflation rates among countries. The implied relationship between inflation rates assumes that *relative* prices of various goods *within* each country do not change. When relative prices within countries do change, purchasing power parity may not hold, because the baskets of goods that countries produce and consume contain differing amounts of the goods whose relative prices have changed. An increase in the relative price of rice, for example, would raise the price levels of many Asian economies relative to the price levels of non-Asian economies, because rice constitutes the main staple of many Asian diets and is, therefore, weighted relatively heavily in the computation of those economies' price levels. Empirically, the PPP relationship holds more closely in periods of rapid inflation. This occurs because high inflation rates tend to overwhelm any changes in the pattern of relative prices that may occur simultaneously. During periods of little inflation, changes in relative prices may overwhelm any tendency toward PPP.

18.3.5 Empirical Evidence on PPP

Evidence from many countries and time periods shows conclusively that the absolute form of purchasing power parity does not hold reliably. Nor does the law of one price hold for many goods. The evidence provides somewhat more support for relative PPP. Generally it is true that when one country's rate of inflation exceeds another's, the first country's currency tends to depreciate against the second's. Of course, the precise relationship in Equation 18.4 does not always hold, but a trend

Figure 18.4 □ **Relative Purchasing Power Parity, 1973–1994 (Percent)**

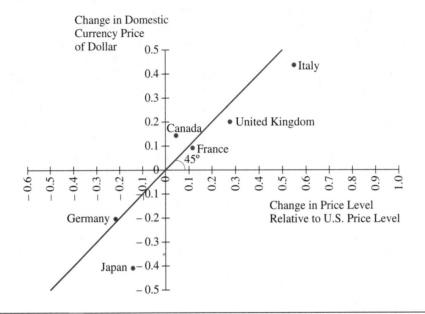

Relative purchasing power parity implies that the rate of change in the exchange rate between two countries' currencies equals the countries' inflation differential. The horizontal axis measures the percentage change in each country's price level minus the percentage change in the U.S. price level. The vertical axis measures the percentage change in the price of the dollar measured in each country's currency. If purchasing power parity held perfectly, all points would lie on the 45-degree line. Deviations from the 45-degree line represent real appreciations of the yen, franc, pound, and lira, along with real depreciations of the mark and Canadian dollar.

Source: Data from *Economic Report of the President 1995.*

toward relative purchasing power parity does hold, at least over the long run. For most country pairs, relative PPP held more closely prior to 1971, during the years of the Bretton Woods system of fixed exchange rates. Since 1973, and particularly since 1979, even relative PPP has failed to explain short- and medium-run movements in exchange rates and price levels.

However, for the post-1973 flexible exchange rate period as a whole, relative purchasing power parity performs reasonably well in explaining the long-run behavior of industrialized countries' exchange rates against the dollar. Figure 18.4 demonstrates this relationship, using changes in countries' consumer price indices to measure their rates of inflation relative to that of the United States. If relative purchasing power parity held perfectly, all points would lie on the upward-sloping 45-degree line, along which the currency's depreciation or appreciation relative to the dollar (measured along the vertical axis) equals the country's inflation rate relative to U.S. inflation (measured along the horizontal axis).

The countries below the 45-degree line in Figure 18.4, Japan, France, the United Kingdom, and Italy, experienced real currency *appreciations* relative to the dollar between 1973 and 1994. In the most dramatic case, Japan, the inflation rate fell short of the U.S. rate by approximately 1 percent per year, but the yen appreciated against the dollar by about 4 percent a year. Therefore, the price of Japan's goods and services relative to U.S. goods and services rose by about 3 percent per year ($\hat{R} \equiv [\hat{P}^J - \hat{P}^{US}] - (\widehat{¥/\$}) = -1 - [-4] = 3$). Real currency appreciations always make the foreign country's goods and services more expensive relative to U.S. goods and services. Note that in the cases of France, the United Kingdom, and Italy, the currencies depreciated in nominal terms but appreciated in real terms; in other words, the nominal depreciations were smaller than the amount by which the countries' inflation exceed the United States'.

Countries above the 45-degree line in Figure 18.4 experienced real currency depreciations, as changes in their nominal exchange rates more than offset any excess of their inflation rates relative to that of the United States. Canada, for example, experienced inflation approximately one-half of 1 percent above that in the United States, while the Canadian dollar depreciated by about 1.5 percent against its U.S. counterpart. Therefore, the relative price of Canadian goods and services fell by approximately 1 percent ($\hat{R} \equiv [\hat{P}^C - \hat{P}^{US}] - (\widehat{C\$/\$}) = 0.5 - [1.5] = -1.0$). Real currency depreciations always make the foreign country's goods and services cheaper relative to U.S. goods and services.

Now that we have defined the basic concepts of purchasing power parity and examined them empirically, we add a few cautionary notes about what purchasing power parity does and does not imply, for the concept often is misinterpreted.

18.3.6 Cautionary Notes on PPP

Economist Gustav Cassel elaborated the concept of purchasing power parity following the First World War. The gold standard of fixed exchange rates had broken down during the war, leaving economists and policy makers with the problem of choosing new rates at which to peg postwar currencies. Cassel suggested using purchasing power parity as a guide in selecting the new rates. Purchasing power parity, according to Cassel, would capture the underlying equilibrium level of exchange rates, even if shocks temporarily drove rates away from their PPP levels.

Today interpretation of purchasing power parity ranges from positive to normative.[7] Some economists perceive PPP as a positive statement of how the economy works. Others attach a more normative significance to PPP, arguing that it *should* hold and that, if it fails, policy makers should take actions to restore it. We have argued that the possibility of international arbitrage creates a linkage among various prices that drives them toward purchasing power parity, at least over the very long run. However, we have little reason to expect PPP to hold over the short or medium term, nor any justification for using PPP as a policy goal.

Arguments that a currency is under- or overvalued based on purchasing power parity rest on a misunderstanding of PPP. In fact, under a perfectly flexible exchange

---

[7]The Isard book in the chapter references contains a useful discussion.

rate regime, the terms *undervalued* and *overvalued* carry little meaning, since the forces of supply and demand in foreign exchange markets determine exchange rates. A currency can be "wrongly" valued only if intervention by central banks holds the rate away from its equilibrium level. This does not imply that individuals and firms in the economy will be happy with the value of the exchange rate. We have repeatedly discovered that different exchange rate values benefit different groups within the economy. Export and import-competing industries benefit from currency depreciations, while consumers and nontraded-goods industries prefer currency appreciations, at least over the short run when changes in the nominal exchange rate imply changes in the relative prices of domestic and foreign goods.

A second caution deals with the cause-and-effect implications of PPP. Purchasing power parity can be interpreted as a theory of exchange rate behavior that attributes changes in the nominal exchange rate between two currencies to differences in the countries' inflation rates. We can make this view of PPP more explicit by rewriting Equation 18.4 with the exchange rate on the left-hand side and the inflation rate differential on the right-hand side:

$$\hat{e} = \hat{P} - \hat{P}^{*}. \qquad\qquad [18.5]$$

This view of PPP treats inflation rates as exogenous and assumes they determine changes in the exchange rate. For example, if the domestic inflation rate equals 10 percent per year and the foreign inflation rate 5 percent per year, Equation 18.5 predicts the domestic currency will depreciate by 5 percent.

Alternatively, purchasing power parity sometimes is viewed as a theory of price-level determination. Given the foreign inflation rate and the rate of change in the exchange rate, we can solve the PPP expression for the domestic inflation rate. If the foreign inflation rate is 5 percent and the domestic currency is depreciating by 5 percent per year, the domestic inflation rate must equal 10 percent. *(Could you distinguish empirically between this case and the previous one, in which inflation rates determined the change in the exchange rate?)*

However, neither of these interpretations is correct. Purchasing power parity does not imply that inflation rates determine exchange rates *or* vice versa. Domestic and foreign price levels and the exchange rate all are determined jointly and simultaneously within the macroeconomy, as we shall see in Chapter Nineteen. All three values result from the interrelationships among many variables. Neither the price level nor the nominal exchange rate is under policy makers' direct control, although their macroeconomic policy choices certainly affect both prices and exchange rates.

Another caution concerns "tests" of PPP frequently reported in the popular press. Table 18.2 reproduces one of the most popular: the "hamburger standard" published each year since 1986 by *The Economist*. The *Economist* staff collects the local-currency price of a Big Mac in 32 foreign countries, as listed in the first two columns of the table. Each price is then divided by the dollar price of a Big Mac in the United States; the third column reports this ratio (called the *implied PPP of the dollar*). This is the value of the exchange rate that would make the foreign hamburger equivalent in price to an American one once both prices are expressed in a common currency. The fourth column in the table lists the actual foreign currency price of a dollar as of

Table 18.2 □ One Popular (but Flawed) Test of PPP: Big MacCurrencies

Country	Price of Big Mac in Local Currency	Implied PPP of the Dollar	Actual Foreign Currency Price of Dollar	Foreign Currency's Percent Over (+) or Under (−) Valuation
Argentina	Peso3.00	1.29	1.00	+29
Australia	A$2.45	1.06	1.35	−22
Austria	Sch39.0	16.80	9.72	+73
Belgium	BFr109	47.00	28.40	+66
Brazil	Real2.42	1.04	0.90	+16
Britain	£1.74	0.75	0.62	+21
Canada	C$2.77	1.19	1.39	−14
Chile	Peso9.50	409.00	395.00	+4
China	Yuan9.00	3.88	8.54	−55
Czech Republic	CKr50.0	21.60	26.20	−18
Denmark	DKr26.75	11.50	5.43	+112
France	FFr18.5	7.97	4.80	+66
Germany	DM4.80	2.07	1.38	+50
Holland	F15.45	2.35	1.55	+52
Hong Kong	HK$9.50	4.09	7.73	−47
Hungary	Forint191	82.30	121.00	−32
Indonesia	Rupiah3,900	1,681.00	2,231.00	−25
Israel	Shekel8.90	3.84	2.95	+30
Italy	Lire4,500	1,940.00	1,702.00	+14
Japan	¥391	169.00	84.20	+100
Malaysia	M$3.76	1.62	2.49	−35
Mexico	Peso10.9	4.70	6.37	−26
New Zealand	NZ$2.95	1.27	1.51	−16
Poland	Zloty3.40	1.47	2.34	−37
Russia	Ruble8,100	3,491.00	4,985.00	−30
Singapore	S$2.95	1.27	1.40	−9
South Korea	Won2,300	991.00	769.00	+29
Spain	Ptas355	153.00	124.00	+23
Sweden	SKr26.0	11.20	7.34	+53
Switzerland	SFr5.90	2.54	1.13	+124
Taiwan	NT$65.0	28.00	25.70	+9
Thailand	Baht48.0	20.70	24.60	−16

Source: *The Economist*, April 15, 1995, 74; data from McDonald's.

April 7, 1995.[8] The final column concludes that the foreign currency is overvalued or undervalued by the difference between column 4 (e′) and column 3 (P^*/P). The 55 percent under-valuation of the Chinese yuan relative to the dollar means that the actual exchange rate of yuan8.54/$1 makes Chinese goods and services inexpensive relative to U.S. goods. The Swiss franc's overvaluation of 124 percent, on the other hand, makes Swiss goods and services expensive relative to American ones.

Our discussion of the law of one price and purchasing power parity suggests at least two major problems with Table 18.2's purported PPP test. First, the use of a single good, the Big Mac, means that the test can at best evaluate the law of one price, *not* purchasing power parity. Second, even as a test of the law of one price, the Big Mac represents a poor choice, because as a restaurant meal it is not a traded good. The Big Mac market is difficult to arbitrage, although the availability of cheap restaurant meals might serve as a small inducement to tourism.[9] It may seem harsh to criticize the Big Mac survey, which was, after all, introduced as a joke. But many so-called tests of PPP use inappropriate goods. For example, another PPP test included a deluxe single hotel room, a hotel room-service American-style breakfast, the ubiquitous Big Mac, a one-mile taxi ride, a man's haircut, a drink of Johnnie Walker Black Label scotch on the rocks, a local phone call from a pay phone, and a first-run movie. *(Evaluate each good and service for inclusion in a test of PPP.)*[10]

We now are ready to combine our results on the long-run neutrality of money with those from purchasing power parity to develop a simple but useful theory of long-run exchange rate behavior, known as the *monetary approach* because the model focuses exclusively on the role of monetary factors in explaining long-run movements in exchange rates.

18.4   The Monetary Approach to the Exchange Rate

18.4.1   History and Intuition behind the Monetary Approach

The **monetary approach to the exchange rate** assumes that the primary role of the exchange rate in the macroeconomy is to equate the quantities supplied and demanded of various monies or currencies.[11] Any event that alters either the quantity of money balances demanded or the money stock will alter the exchange rate according to the monetary approach.

The modern version of this view of the exchange rate dates from the 1970s and work by University of Chicago economists Robert Mundell, the late Harry Johnson,

---

[8]In our notation, columns 2 through 4 of Table 18.2 represent P^*, P^*/P, and e′, respectively, and absolute purchasing power parity is written as e′ = P^*/P. *(Why?)*

[9]The *Economist* article that reports the test's results has in recent years included a discussion of these problems.

[10]Additional information you might find useful: A large portion of the price of liquor in most countries consists of taxes; phone service typically is either government owned or a regulated private monopoly; and most countries subject movies to import restrictions.

[11]The analogous theory under a fixed exchange rate regime is known as the *monetary approach to the balance of payments*.

and Jacob Frenkel, now governor of the Bank of Israel. Despite the relatively short modern history of the monetary approach, its roots reach back to David Hume's 1752 work on the specie-flow mechanism. Much of the monetary approach's renewed appeal rests on its simplicity. Unlike other models of exchange rate behavior, the monetary approach relies on the fundamental definition of an exchange rate as the relative price of two monies. Just as the supplies of and demands for, say, corn and wheat determine the relative price of those goods, so the supplies of and demands for two monies determine their relative price. When the quantity demanded of a money exceeds the quantity supplied, its relative price rises—that is, the currency appreciates. When the quantity supplied exceeds the quantity demanded, the money's relative price falls, or the currency depreciates.

The monetary approach assumes that real output equals its full-employment level and that output and input prices adjust quickly to their long-run equilibrium levels. Therefore, we take the monetary approach as a long-run theory of exchange rate behavior, with little to say about short-run exchange rate fluctuations that occur before prices in the economy have time to adjust to shocks.

18.4.2 A Simple Monetary Model of the Exchange Rate

Equilibrium in the money market requires that the real money stock, defined as the nominal money stock divided by the price level, equal the quantity demanded of real money balances. The demand for real money balances depends positively on real income and negatively on the nominal interest rate. Equation 18.6 repeats the money-market equilibrium condition for the domestic country:

$$M/P = L(\overset{+}{Q}, \overset{-}{i}). \qquad [18.6]$$

Equation 18.7 presents the corresponding condition for the foreign country:

$$M^*/P^* = L^*(\overset{+}{Q^*}, \overset{-}{i^*}). \qquad [18.7]$$

Because we are interested in the causes of *movements* in exchange rates rather than the particular *level* of the exchange rate at one instant, it is convenient to translate Equations 18.6 and 18.7 into relationships among the percentage rates of change of money stocks, price levels, and money demands. Letting "hats" continue to denote percentage rates of change,[12]

$$\hat{M} - \hat{P} = \hat{L} \text{ and } \hat{M}^* - \hat{P}^* = \hat{L}^*. \qquad [18.8]$$

Equation 18.8 says simply that the rate of growth of the real money stock (the left-hand side of the equation) must match that of the demand for real money balances (the right-hand side of the equation) for the money market to remain in equilibrium.

---

[12]The percentage rate of change of a ratio such as M/P equals the percentage rate of change of the numerator ($\hat{M}$) minus the percentage rate of change of the denominator ($\hat{P}$).

Subtracting the second expression in Equation 18.8 from the first and rearranging gives the fundamental relationship central to the monetary approach to the exchange rate:

$$\hat{P} - \hat{P}^* = (\hat{M} - \hat{M}^*) - (\hat{L} - \hat{L}^*).$$ [18.9]

The difference between the inflation rates in the two countries depends on the relative growth rates of the money stocks and of the demands for the two monies.

How can the monetary approach provide a theory of exchange rate behavior when the exchange rate does not even appear in Equation 18.9? The answer is that the monetary approach assumes relative purchasing power parity holds. This implies that, in the long run, the inflation differential on the left-hand side of Equation 18.9 will equal the percentage rate of change in the exchange rate from Equation 18.5, so that

$$\hat{e} = (\hat{M} - \hat{M}^*) - (\hat{L} - \hat{L}^*) = (\hat{M} - \hat{L}) - (\hat{M}^* - \hat{L}^*).$$ [18.10]

This statement makes a simple but powerful prediction about the exchange rate: *The relative rates of growth of the supplies of and demands for different monies determine movements in the exchange rate.* If the domestic money stock grows more rapidly than the foreign money stock and if money demands remain constant, the domestic currency will depreciate. If the stock of each money grows at the same rate as the demand for it, the exchange rate will remain stable. We can also use the simple monetary-approach expression for the exchange rate to highlight the inherent interdependence of exchange rate policies. Equation 18.10 makes clear that the exchange rate between two currencies depends on money supply and demand in *both* economies. Even a country with rapid money growth can experience an appreciation—if the other country's money stock grows more rapidly.

18.4.3 Implications of the Monetary Approach to the Exchange Rate

As a theory of long-run exchange rate behavior, the monetary approach summarized in Equation 18.10 predicts the long-term effects of changes in domestic and foreign money stocks, real outputs, and interest rates on the exchange rate. Table 18.3 summarizes these results. *Other things being equal,* a permanent rise in the domestic money stock causes a proportional increase in the domestic price level (from Equation 18.6) and, through PPP, a proportional depreciation of the domestic currency. Similarly, a permanent increase in the foreign money stock raises the foreign price level (from Equation 18.7) and appreciates the domestic currency proportionally in the long run.

The monetary approach in Equation 18.10 also predicts that economic events that raise the domestic demand for money ($\hat{L} > 0$) will cause a domestic appreciation; examples include a rise in domestic income or a fall in the domestic interest rate. If domestic real output rises, for given levels of the nominal money stock and the interest rate, Equation 18.6 implies that the domestic price level must fall. According to purchasing power parity, a decline in the domestic price level causes the domestic currency to appreciate.

Table 18.3 ▫ **Implications of the Monetary Approach to the Exchange Rate**

Variable	Effect on the Exchange Rate[a]
Domestic Nominal Money Stock (M)	
Increase	+
Decrease	−
Foreign Nominal Money Stock (M*)	
Increase	−
Decrease	+
Domestic Money Demand (L)	
Domestic real output (Q):	
Increase	−
Decrease	+
Domestic interest rate (i):	
Increase	+
Decrease	−
Foreign Money Demand (L*)	
Foreign real output (Q):*	
Increase	+
Decrease	−
Foreign interest rate (i):*	
Increase	−
Decrease	+

[a]Plus signs denote increases in e or domestic currency depreciations. Minus signs denote decreases in e or domestic currency appreciations.

A rise in the domestic interest rate lowers the domestic demand for money according to Equation 18.6 and, for given values of M and Q, raises the domestic price level. Therefore, the domestic currency must depreciate to maintain purchasing power parity. Note that this seems to contradict the predictions of our short-run model from Chapters Fifteen through Seventeen, in which a rise in the domestic interest rate always caused a currency *appreciation*. Here, the monetary approach argues instead that a rise in the domestic interest rate should cause a domestic currency *depreciation*. Despite first appearances, the two predictions do not contradict one another; they simply rest on different assumptions about the relevant time horizon.

The short-run model of earlier chapters assumes that the price level is fixed. This allows one-time changes in the money stock to alter the interest rate. The monetary approach, with its long-run equilibrium focus, assumes the price level adjusts immediately to any monetary disturbance. As we saw in section 18.2.2, this implies that one-time changes in the money stock do not alter the interest rate. Therefore, when the monetary approach makes predictions about the impact of an interest rate change on the exchange rate, the cause of the change in the interest rate must be something *other than* a simple one-time increase in the money stock. If the interest rate changes in the two models for different reasons, we should not be surprised that the interest rate's effect on the exchange rate also differs between the short-run

Table 18.4 □ **Annual Growth of Nominal Money Stocks, 1987–1993 (Percent)**

Country	1987	1988	1989	1990	1991	1992	1993
United States	6.3	4.3	0.6	4.2	7.9	14.3	10.5
Japan	4.8	8.6	2.4	4.5	9.5	3.9	7.0
Germany[a]	7.4	10.9	5.6	29.6	3.4	10.8	8.5
France	4.1	4.1	7.7	3.9	−4.7	−0.1	1.7
Italy	7.8	7.3	10.3	6.6	10.5	0.6	7.4
United Kingdom	4.8	6.8	5.7	5.2	2.4	2.4	4.9
Canada	8.2	7.5	3.2	−1.2	5.2	5.4	13.9

[a]Data through 1989 apply to Federal Democratic Republic only; 1990 figures reflect the extension of the Deutsche mark area to the former German Democratic Republic as part of the two countries' unification.

Source: International Monetary Fund, *World Economic Outlook,* May 1995, p. 144.

model and the long-run monetary-approach model. To understand better the relationship between the two models' predictions, we must find the fundamental cause of changes in the interest rate in long-run equilibrium.

18.4.4 Purchasing Power Parity and Long-Run Interest Parity with Inflation

If permanent one-time changes in the nominal money stock do not alter the interest rate in the long run, what kind of monetary disturbance would cause a change in the long-run equilibrium interest rate? The answer is a change in the *rate of growth* (as opposed to the *level*) of the money stock. Virtually all economies experience more or less continual growth in their money stocks. Actual monetary policy decisions typically concern the rate of growth of the money stock, not one-time increases or decreases in its level. Table 18.4 reports recent percentage rates of growth of the money stocks for the major industrial economies.

When the money stock grows continually, prices in the economy must continually adjust. The result is **inflation,** which by definition simply means a continuing rise in the price level. In long-run equilibrium, the money stock's growth rate does not affect real output, and the price level rises at the same rate as the money stock. We can incorporate the possibility of inflation into our theory of the long-run relationship among prices, interest rates, and the exchange rate simply by combining interest parity and purchasing power parity.

Recall that interest parity summarizes the relationship between interest rates and exchange rates that must exist in order for portfolio owners to hold the current quantities of deposits in various currencies.[13] The interest parity relationship, written as

---

[13]Section 12.4 develops the theory of interest parity.

$$i - i^* = (e^e - e)/e = \hat{e}^e, \qquad\qquad [18.11]$$

holds whenever the expected rates of return on deposits denominated in the domestic and foreign currencies are equal, so portfolio owners have no incentive to reallocate their portfolios between the two types of deposits.[14] This requires the interest differential (the left-hand side of Equation 18.11) to equal the expected rate of domestic currency depreciation (the right-hand side of Equation 18.11).

But, in the long run, what determines the expected rate of domestic currency depreciation? If relative PPP determines the behavior of the exchange rate in the long run, the *actual* rate of depreciation will equal the difference in the two countries' rates of inflation, as in Equation 18.5. And, if individuals in the economy know this is how the exchange rate behaves, they will *expect* the domestic currency to depreciate by whatever amount they *expect* domestic inflation to exceed foreign inflation. To summarize the argument algebraically, if relative purchasing power parity implies that

$$\hat{e} = (\hat{P} - \hat{P}^*),$$

then market participants will form their expectations using the same relationship, so

$$\hat{e}^e = (\hat{P}^e - \hat{P}^{*e}). \qquad\qquad [18.12]$$

Combining Equations 18.11 and 18.12 tells us that in the long run, if relative purchasing power parity holds and market participants expect it to hold, the interest differential between deposits denominated in two currencies equals the expected inflation differential between the two countries, or

$$i - i^* = (\hat{P}^e - \hat{P}^{*e}). \qquad\qquad [18.13]$$

This implies that changes in interest rates, in long-run equilibrium, reflect changes in expected inflation. If the domestic country's expected inflation rate rises relative to the foreign country's, the interest rate on deposits denominated in the domestic currency must rise proportionally to maintain interest parity.[15] To understand why, we need to distinguish between two measures of an asset's rate of return.

Real and Nominal Rates of Return
The interest rate, i, measures an asset's rate of return measured in units of the domestic currency. Suppose an individual purchases a $1,000 bond that promises to pay $1,100 in one year. The interest rate equals ($1,100 − $1,000)/$1,000 = 10%,

---

[14]The expected nominal rate of return on domestic-currency-denominated deposits equals the domestic interest rate minus the expected rate of domestic currency depreciation. The expected nominal rate of return on foreign-currency-denominated deposits equals the foreign interest rate. Equality between the two expected rates of return requires $i - \hat{e}^e = i^*$, an expression equivalent to Equation 18.11.

[15]The relationship between expected inflation and the interest rate is known as the *Fisher effect*, after Irving Fisher, an economist who did important work on interest rates and their role in the economy.

because the individual earns 10 percent in dollars on the funds invested in the bond. The interest rate gives the **nominal rate of return** on the investment, or the rate of return measured in dollars.

If the rate of inflation equals zero over the year, the individual's purchasing power, or ability to purchase goods and services, also will increase by 10 percent. This increase in purchasing power represents the bond's **real rate of return,** or its return measured in real terms (that is, goods and services) rather than in dollars. Whenever the price level remains constant or the rate of inflation equals zero, the nominal and real rates of return on any asset are equal.

Suppose instead that the rate of inflation is 10 percent during the year of the investment. At the end of the year, \$1,100 will buy the same quantity of goods and services that \$1,000 would buy at the beginning. The investment still earns a nominal return (i) of 10 percent measured in dollars but now earns a real return (r) of 0 percent measured in purchasing power over goods and services; the difference just equals the rate of inflation ($\hat{P}$). Generally, the real return on any asset equals the nominal rate of return minus the rate of inflation, a relationship known as the **Fisher equation:**

$$r = i - \hat{P}. \qquad [18.14]$$

Of course, an individual making an asset portfolio decision cannot know in advance what the actual inflation rate will be over the asset's life. Asset decisions must be made on *expected* real rates, or the difference between the observable nominal rate of return and the expected rate of inflation:

$$r^e = i - \hat{P}^e. \qquad [18.15]$$

To keep the expected *real* rate of return on domestic-currency-denominated deposits constant, Equation 18.15 makes clear that the domestic nominal interest rate must rise by the amount of any expected inflation. This is exactly what Equation 18.13 predicts will happen in the long run. In long-run equilibrium, any inflation-induced interest rate increase does not make portfolio owners any better off or any worse off in real terms; it simply compensates them for inflation's expected erosion of the domestic currency's purchasing power.

Interest and Exchange Rates in the Monetary Approach

We now can see more clearly the reasons for the monetary approach's surprising long-run prediction: that an increase in the domestic interest rate would cause a currency *de*preciation. In the long run on which the monetary approach focuses, the interest rate rises only in response to a rise in the money stock's rate of growth. Such grows causes inflation; and market participants expect that inflation. They demand higher *nominal* rates of return in order to maintain a constant *real* rate of return as inflation reduces the domestic currency's purchasing power. Because we know that money growth leads to currency depreciations, the monetary approach's link between increases in interest rates and currency depreciations makes perfect sense once we understand that increases in the long-run equilibrium interest rate come only from inflation-inducing increases in the rate of money growth.

The monetary approach's link between inflation, the exchange rate, and the nominal interest rate suggests that, other things equal, high-inflation countries should have higher nominal interest rates than low-inflation countries and that a single country's nominal interest rate should vary positively with the country's rate of inflation. We can investigate these relationships empirically by illustrating recent interest rates and inflation for a sample of three industrialized economies, as in Figure 18.5. Within each economy, periods of higher rates of inflation clearly are associated with higher nominal interest rates. Comparing across countries, the higher inflation rate in the United States than in Germany or Japan translates into a higher nominal U.S. interest rate as well.

18.4.5 What's Missing from the Monetary Approach?

Purchasing power parity and the monetary approach to the exchange rate provide only one piece of a complete explanation of exchange rate behavior. We have seen that even relative purchasing power parity does not hold in the short run, making the monetary approach, which relies on purchasing power parity, an inappropriate model for predicting short-run behavior of the exchange rate or any other macroeconomic variable. The fixed-price model from Chapters Fifteen through Seventeen provides a better guide to the macroeconomy in the short run, and in Chapter Nineteen we shall turn our attention to the economy's adjustment from short-run to long-run results.

But, even in long-run equilibrium, elements beyond PPP play an important role. Purchasing power parity explains how exchange rates respond to price level changes *caused by changes in the money stock*. Similarly, the monetary approach focuses exclusively on the long-run equilibrium effect of changes in the money stock or its rate of growth. When nonmonetary shocks hit the economy, the exchange rate may behave in ways not explained by purchasing power parity and the monetary approach, even in long-run equilibrium. In other words, the *real* exchange rate may change.

18.5 The Real Exchange Rate

18.5.1 Changes in the Real Exchange Rate

The monetary approach to the exchange rate does a reasonably good job of explaining exchange rate movements in the long run when the disturbances to the economy come from the money market. However, to understand exchange rates better, we must be able to analyze disturbances that are nonmonetary in nature. Such shocks cause purchasing power parity not to hold. In other words, they cause changes in the *real* exchange rate. Recall that the real exchange rate or, equivalently, the relative price of domestic goods and services, equals the ratio of the domestic price level to the foreign price level expressed in terms of domestic currency:

$$R \equiv P/eP^*. \qquad [18.16]$$

A decline in the real exchange rate constitutes a **real depreciation** of the domestic currency. When price levels are fixed, a nominal depreciation (a rise in e) leads directly

Figure 18.5 □ **Inflation and Nominal Interest Rates**

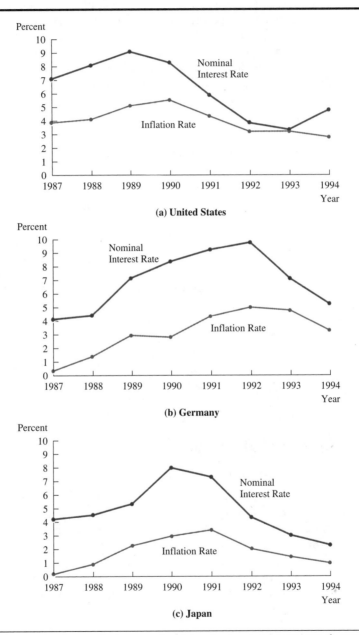

(a) United States

(b) Germany

(c) Japan

To maintain assets' real rates of return, nominal interest rates must incorporate changes in the rate of inflation. Within each country, nominal interest rates rise and fall with the country's inflation rate. Across countries, those with higher inflation exhibit higher nominal interest rates.

Source: Data from International Monetary Fund, *World Economic Outlook,* May 1995.

to a real depreciation. We saw in earlier chapters that a real depreciation causes consumers to shift their spending from foreign to domestic goods. A rise in the real exchange rate represents a **real appreciation** of the domestic currency. A real appreciation can be caused by, among other things, a nominal appreciation (a decline in e) with price levels fixed. The major impact of a real appreciation is a shift of expenditure from domestic to foreign goods and services. But, as we have seen, price levels cannot be assumed fixed in the long run.

If absolute purchasing power parity held continually in the long run ($P = e \cdot P^*$ from Equation 18.3), the real exchange rate would always equal 1. Or, if relative purchasing power parity held continually ($\hat{P} = \hat{e} + \hat{P}^*$ from Equation 18.4), the real exchange rate would be a constant, because expressing Equation 18.14 in rates of change shows that

$$\hat{R} = (\hat{P} - \hat{P}^*) - \hat{e}, \qquad [18.17]$$

so relative purchasing power parity implies that $\hat{R} = 0$. Or, we can rearrange Equation 18.17 to express changes in the nominal exchange rate in terms of two components as in Equation 18.18. The first component represents the inflation differential between the two countries as predicted by purchasing power parity, and the second captures changes in the real exchange rate or deviations from purchasing power parity.

$$\hat{e} = (\hat{P} - \hat{P}^*) - \hat{R}. \qquad [18.18]$$

Real exchange rates can change dramatically; and trends in real exchange rates can last for decades. The yen appreciation mentioned in the chapter opening, for example, has persisted since 1960 and has far exceeded the inflation differential between the United States and Japan during the same period; in other words, the yen has experienced a *real* appreciation against the dollar, with occasional interruptions, for decades. Such changes exert important influences on the international macroeconomy because they generate shifts in expenditure between domestic and foreign goods and services.

18.5.2 Causes of Changes in the Real Exchange Rate

Unfortunately, economists do not yet understand as well as we would like all the causes of real exchange rate movements. Work to understand real exchange rates is in its relatively early stages in part because real exchange rates have exhibited much more volatility during the flexible-exchange-rate years since 1973 than they did during the fixed-rate years between the Second World War and the early 1970s. A full understanding of real exchange rates presents a formidable task because they involve the interaction of many macroeconomic variables. However, we can gain substantial insight into several important causes of changes in real exchange rates by noting simply that the real exchange rate represents the relative price of domestic goods and services compared with foreign goods and services. Therefore, we should expect economic events that change the relative price of domestic and foreign goods and services to affect the real exchange rate. This focuses our attention on output markets, because

---

Figure 18.6 □ **Relative Output Demand Affects the Real Exchange Rate**

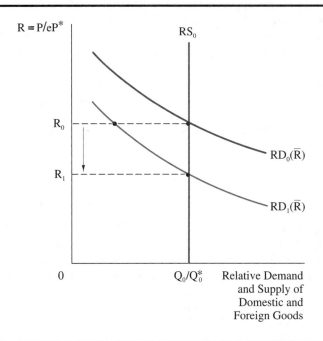

The real exchange rate ($R \equiv P/eP^*$) represents the relative price of domestic and foreign goods and services. When demand for foreign goods rises relative to demand for domestic goods, RD shifts to the left. At the old real exchange rate, R_0, there is excess supply of domestic goods and excess demand for foreign ones. The domestic currency depreciates in real terms to make domestic goods relatively cheaper, increase relative demand for domestic goods, and bring it back into equality with relative output supply at a real exchange rate of R_1.

---

the relative prices of domestic and foreign goods and services should be determined by the relative demands for and supplies of those goods and services.

Figure 18.6 illustrates how the relative demands for and supplies of domestic and foreign goods and services interact to determine the relative price of those goods and services, or the real exchange rate, in long-run equilibrium. Because we focus on the long run, the supplies of both domestic and foreign output are at their full-employment levels, Q_0 and Q_0^*, respectively. This implies a vertical long-run *relative supply* curve, RS_0. Relative demands for domestic and foreign goods and services depend on their relative price. At high values of R, expenditures shift toward foreign goods and services, so the relative demand for domestic goods is low. At low values of R, expenditure shifts toward domestic goods and services, so the relative demand is high. Therefore, the *relative demand* curve, RD_0, exhibits a negative slope in Figure 18.6. Just as in other product markets, the equilibrium price in Figure 18.6 is the one at which the relative supply of domestic goods equals the relative demand for them, or R_0.

Figure 18.7 ▫ **Relative Output Supply Affects the Real Exchange Rate**

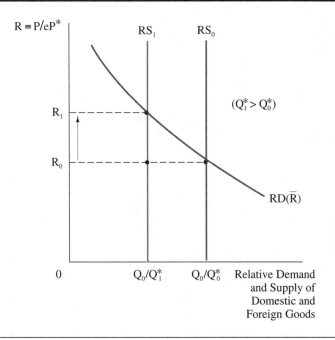

A rise in the long-run equilibrium level of foreign output (Q^*) relative to domestic output (Q) shifts RS to the left. At the original real exchange rate, R_0, there is excess demand for domestic goods and excess supply of foreign ones. The domestic currency appreciates to make domestic goods relatively more expensive, reduce relative demand for domestic goods, and bring it back into equality with relative output supply at a real exchange rate of R_1.

Disturbances that shift either the relative supply curve or the relative demand curve lead to changes in the real exchange rate. Suppose consumers' tastes shift in favor of foreign goods and services. RD shifts to the left, from RD_0 to RD_1 in Figure 18.6. At the original real exchange rate, excess relative supply of domestic goods and services exists, or, equivalently, excess relative demand for foreign ones. This causes the relative price of domestic goods and services to fall to R_1. The foreign currency appreciates in real terms, and the domestic currency depreciates. This makes foreign goods and services relatively more expensive, shifts expenditure toward domestic ones, and reequates relative demands to the unchanged relative supplies of the two countries' outputs. *(Illustrate and explain why an increase in relative demand for domestic goods would lead to a domestic real appreciation.)*

Changes in relative output supplies also influence the real exchange rate. Suppose the foreign economy enjoys an increase in its productivity due to a technological innovation. The long-run, or full-employment, level of foreign output rises relative to domestic output, shifting RS to the left to RS_1 in Figure 18.7. At the original real exchange rate,

Table 18.5 □ Long-Run Equilibrium Nominal and Real Exchange Rates

Shock	Effect on $\hat{e}$ [a]	=	Effect on $(\hat{P}-\hat{P}^*)$	−	Effect on $\hat{R}$ [b]
Relative Money Stock Levels (M/M)* [c]					
Increase	+		+		0
Decrease	−		−		0
Relative Money Growth Rates ($\hat{M}/\hat{M}^*$) [c]					
Increase	+		+		0
Decrease	−		−		0
Relative Output Demands (RD) [d]					
Increase	−		0		+
Decrease	+		0		−
Relative Output Supplies (RS = Q/Q)* [d]					
Increase	?		−		−
Decrease	?		+		+

[a] A plus sign denotes a nominal depreciation, and a minus sign a nominal appreciation.

[b] A plus sign denotes a real appreciation, and a minus sign a real depreciation.

[c] Purchasing power parity holds.

[d] Purchasing power parity does not hold.

R_0, excess relative demand now exists for domestic goods. Their relative price rises to R_1. This constitutes a real domestic currency appreciation, or a real foreign currency depreciation. The change in the real exchange rate makes domestic goods relatively more expensive, shifts expenditure away from those goods, and reequates relative demands to the new lower relative supply of domestic goods. *(Illustrate that a rise in domestic relative supply leads to a domestic real depreciation and a foreign real appreciation.)*

18.6 Long-Run Equilibrium Exchange Rates

We now have seen through the monetary approach how *monetary* disturbances affect nominal exchange rates and through our theory of the real exchange rate how *nonmonetary* disturbances determine real exchange rates. We can combine these two insights to see how the long-run equilibrium exchange rate responds to various shocks to the economy; Table 18.5 summarizes these responses.

To examine the effect of a one-time change in the size of the domestic money stock, we need only the monetary approach to the exchange rate. Changes in the level of the money stock do not affect long-run equilibrium real output or the interest rate. Therefore, our money market equilibrium condition in Equation 18.6 implies that the price level moves in proportion to the change in the money stock. The domestic currency depreciates (appreciates) in nominal terms in proportion to the increase (decrease) in the domestic money stock. All *relative* prices in the economy, including the real exchange rate, remain unaffected.

The monetary approach also suffices to understand the effect of a change in relative money growth rates. If the domestic money growth rate rises relative to foreign money growth, we saw in section 18.4.4 that the rate of domestic inflation rises proportionally. Purchasing power parity requires a proportional nominal domestic currency depreciation. Again, all relative prices remain unchanged, including the real exchange rate.

A change in relative demand for domestic output (RD) does not change the long-run equilibrium price level, which is determined by the money market equilibrium condition in Equation 18.6.[16] However, section 18.5.2 implies that changes in relative output demands do alter the *real* exchange rate. In particular, a rise in relative demand for domestic output causes a domestic real appreciation, and a fall in relative demand causes a domestic real depreciation. Because long-run price levels do not change, nominal currency appreciations and depreciations are the mechanisms through which the real exchange rate changes occur.

Unlike changes in relative output demands, changes in relative output supplies (RS) do lead to changes in the long-run equilibrium price level. Recall that the price level is determined by the money market equilibrium condition in Equation 18.6. If the relative supply of domestic output rises, the increase in full-employment Q generates an increase in the demand for domestic money. With a fixed nominal money stock, this requires a fall in the price level to maintain money market equilibrium. Through purchasing power parity, the fall in the domestic price level pushes the nominal exchange rate down (a nominal appreciation). But the change in relative output supplies also alters the equilibrium *real* exchange rate. The domestic currency depreciates in real terms. Therefore, the supply shock's effects through the money and output markets push the nominal exchange rate in opposite directions, and we cannot be sure of the net effect.

18.7 More on Why Interest Rates Differ

At any point in time, the nominal interest rates paid on assets denominated in different currencies generally differ substantially. We encountered one reason why back in Chapter Twelve's introduction of the foreign exchange market. Interest parity suggests that interest-rate differences reflect market participants' expectations about future currency appreciations and depreciations. To hold assets denominated in currencies expected to appreciate, portfolio owners willingly accept lower nominal interest rates. For assets denominated in currencies expected to depreciate, portfolio owners demand higher nominal interest rates as compensation.

The monetary approach to the exchange rate in section 18.4 carried us one step further toward understanding international interest rate differences. Purchasing power parity implies that long-run equilibrium nominal exchange rate movements reflect differences in countries' rates of inflation. Hence, in long-run equilibrium,

[16]Note that the Q term in Equation 18.6 is not affected by a rise in demand for domestic output because, in long-run equilibrium, real output must be at its full-employment level, as determined by the supply side of the economy.

expected exchange rate movements should equal *expected* inflation differentials. This implies that long-run equilibrium differences in nominal interest rates equal differences in countries' expected inflation rates (see Equation 18.13).

We can take a further step by building in what we now know about changes in real exchange rates, or deviations from purchasing power parity. If, in long-run equilibrium, the changes in the nominal exchange rate include both relative inflation rates (as in the monetary approach) *and* changes in real exchange rates, then changes in the *expected* nominal exchange rate should include both *expected* relative inflation rates and changes in *expected* real exchange rates:

$$\hat{e}^e = (\hat{P}^e - \hat{P}^{*e}) - \hat{R}^e. \qquad [18.19]$$

Because interest parity says that the interest differential equals the expected rate of change in the nominal exchange rate, or the left-hand side of Equation 18.19, we can conclude that

$$i - i^* = (\hat{P}^e - \hat{P}^{*e}) - \hat{R}^e. \qquad [18.20]$$

Now we can see that international nominal interest-rate differences contain two components. The first reflects expected inflation differentials. The second reflects changes in the real exchange rate. Higher expected domestic inflation, lower expected foreign inflation, or an expected real domestic depreciation leads to a higher nominal interest rate differential.

We distinguished earlier between nominal interest rates, which measure an asset's rate of return in nominal or currency units, and real interest rates, which measure an asset's rate of return in real units of purchasing power. Equation 18.15, repeated here, indicated that the expected real interest rate equaled the nominal interest rate minus any expected inflation,

$$r^e = i - \hat{P}^e.$$

We can combine the expressions for the domestic and foreign real interest rates to see what determines the difference between them:

$$r^e - r^{*e} = (i - i^*) - (\hat{P}^e - \hat{P}^{*e}). \qquad [18.21]$$

Simply plugging the expression for the nominal interest differential from Equation 18.20 into Equation 18.21 reveals that international differences in expected real interest rates reflect expected real currency appreciations or depreciations,

$$r^e - r^{*e} = (\hat{P}^e - \hat{P}^{*e}) - \hat{R}^e - (\hat{P}^e - \hat{P}^{*e}) = -\hat{R}^e. \qquad [18.22]$$

Note that Equation 18.22 is simply a *real* form of interest parity. While nominal interest parity equates the nominal interest differential to the expected change in the nominal exchange rate, **real interest parity** equates the real interest differential to the expected change in the real exchange rate. This suggests that when all disturbances are monetary, implying that purchasing power parity is expected to hold, real expected interest rates should be equal across countries. But if nonmonetary shocks are expected to cause deviations from purchasing power parity, real interest rates can differ, even in long-run equilibrium.

Case One
The Interest Rate and the Dollar

The flexibility of the price level in the long run carries important implications for the relationship between interest rates and exchange rates. Short-run fixed-price models, like the one developed in Chapters Fourteen through Seventeen, imply that the domestic interest rate and the exchange rate should move inversely: Increases in interest rates should be associated with currency appreciations and decreases in interest rates with currency depreciations. This reasoning rests the interest rate's impact on the capital account of the balance of payments. A rise in the domestic interest rate (with a fixed foreign interest rate) generates a capital inflow that causes an incipient balance-of-payments surplus and a currency appreciation. A fall in the domestic interest rate causes a capital outflow and a depreciation. As Figure 18.8 illustrates, this predicted negative relationship appeared to hold in the United States for some periods, such as the mid 1980s and early 1990s.

Most years, on the other hand, did not conform to the short-run fixed-price model's prediction of a negative relationship between the domestic interest rate and the exchange rate, according to Figure 18.8. The two were positively related during most years, rising interest rates with currency depreciations and falling interest rates with currency appreciations. Incorporating a role for changes in the price level and for expectations, we can easily explain this observation.

We now know from the Fisher equation that two components comprise the nominal interest rate (i): the real interest rate (r) and the rate of inflation ($\hat{P}$):

$$i = r + \hat{P}.$$

When an individual buys an asset, the actual rate of inflation that will prevail over the asset's life is unknown. Predicting the asset's real rate of return involves forming an expectation of the future inflation rate. Given a nominal interest rate (which is observable), the potential buyer must form an expectation about what portion of i will end up as part of the real return (r^e) and what part will be eroded through inflation ($\hat{P}^e$):

$$i = r^e + \hat{P}^e.$$

Changes in the nominal interest rate can reflect changes in the expected real interest rate, changes in the expected rate of inflation, or a combination of both. When inflation is low and stable, changes in the nominal interest rate reflect primarily changes

Figure 18.8 □ **The Interest Rate and the Exchange Rate, 1973–1994**

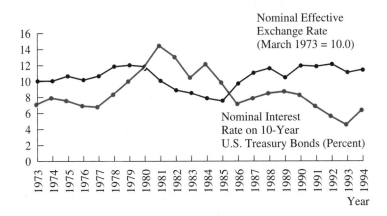

When changes in the nominal interest rate (i) reflect changes in the real interest rate (r) rather than changes in expected inflation ($\hat{P}^e$), the interest rate and the exchange rate tend to move in the same direction, as in the early 1980s in the United States. When changes in the nominal interest rate reflect changes in expected inflation rather than changes in the real interest rate, the interest rate and the exchange rate tend to move in opposite directions, as in the 1970s and since 1985 in the United States.

Source: Data from *Economic Report of the President 1995.*

in the real interest rate; when inflation is high and erratic, the expected inflation component of the nominal interest rate tends to dominate. Depending on which component of the nominal interest rate changes, the predicted relationship between the interest rate and the exchange rate will differ.

During the inflationary 1970s and the disinflationary early 1980s in the United States, changes in nominal interest rates reflected mainly changes in expected inflation. Rising nominal interest rates did not generate capital inflows in the 1970s, because those flows respond to expected real, not nominal, rates of return. Instead, the high nominal interest rates raised the opportunity cost of holding money balances and reduced the quantity demanded of money. With high money growth rates and a reduced quantity demanded of money, the dollar depreciated. As a result of the dominance of inflationary expectations, the domestic nominal interest rate and the exchange rate moved in the same direction, as predicted by the monetary approach to the exchange rate.

Early in the 1980s, the rate of inflation slowed dramatically and the interest rate and exchange rate both fell. During the early 1990s, inflation remained reasonably low and stable, and the interest rate and exchange rate began to move inversely, as our short-run fixed-price model predicted. Changes in the expected real interest rate rather than inflationary expectations have come to dominate changes in the nominal interest rate. When a rise in the nominal interest rate reflects an increase in the real interest rate rather than an expected rise in the price level, a capital inflow results and the domestic currency appreciates.

Case Two
Shoppers, Borders, and Exchange Rates

Along the 5,500-mile U.S.–Canada border, from Blaine, Washington, to Buffalo, New York, Canadian cars used to crowd U.S. shopping malls each weekend. The Canada–U.S. Free Trade Agreement reduced tariffs on many household items bought in the United States and carried into Canada. Many Canadian stores remained closed on Sundays, and the exchange rate between the two dollars (C$ and $) made U.S. shopping attractive. In 1989, with the U.S. dollar price of a Canadian dollar at $0.84, Canadians averaged 3.5 million same-day visits per month across the U.S. border. Grocery stores, liquor stores, gasoline stations, and factory outlets drew especially big crowds. Canada taxes gasoline heavily, so prices averaged about twice their U.S. levels. Some farm products, such as milk and cheese, enjoy higher price supports in Canada, making U.S. grocery stores attractive.

By 1991, the exchange rate had risen to $0.87, and cross-border shopping by Canadians totaled approximately C$3 billion = $2.54 billion annually. Canadian retailers and mail-order firms protested. The Canadian government responded by reducing by half the exemption from duties or taxes on mail-order packages received from outside Canada and by toughening Canadian customs inspections of returning vehicles. The Canadian government also agreed to begin to collect provincial sales taxes (which range up to 12 percent) on goods brought into the country from the United States. The Ontario government lifted its restrictions on Sunday store openings.

Since 1991, a decline of the Canadian dollar relative to the U.S. dollar has meant that shopping mall parking lots south of the border contain fewer cars bearing Canadian license plates. By 1994, the U.S. dollar price of a Canadian dollar had fallen to $0.72, and same-day car trips across the border fell to their lowest level in five years.

Canadians are not the only cross-border shoppers. Basque shoppers cross from Spain into France for groceries, avoiding Spain's small specialty retailers in favor of France's supermarkets and discount stores. Germans and Belgians save 40 to 50 percent on many consumer goods by buying in Luxembourg or the Netherlands. Britons can cut their liquor bills by half by traveling to France to avoid Britain's high liquor taxes.[17] And the yen's dramatic appreciation against the dollar has had its effect. Waikele, a 60-acre mall of discount stores in Waipahu, Hawaii, has become one of the most popular stops for Japanese tourists, who find prices on goods—from designer clothes to dog food—less than half those in Japan.[18]

---

[17]Cacilie Rohwedder, "Europeans Make Cross-Border Treks to Ring Up Savings on Shopping Bills," *The Wall Street Journal*, May 2, 1994, B5A.

[18]Jim Carlton, "Japanese Skip Waikiki, Head for KMart," *The Wall Street Journal*, June 29, 1995.

Figure 18.9 □ The Kobe Earthquake and the Yen

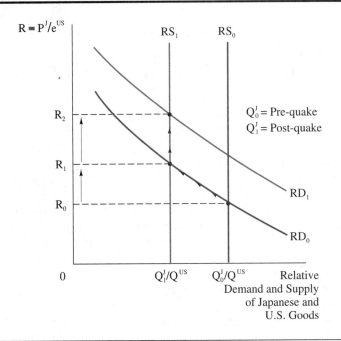

A disaster such as an earthquake reduces the full-employment level of output, shifting RS to the left. Reconstruction expenditures raise the demand for local goods and services and shift RD to the right. Both effects lead to a real appreciation of the currency of the country struck by the disaster.

Case Three
Disaster and the Real Exchange Rate

On January 17, 1995, a powerful earthquake struck the Japanese industrial port city of Kobe. The area around Kobe accounts for almost 5 percent of Japan's industrial output, and the port handles approximately 10 percent of all the country's foreign trade. Estimates indicated damage of about ¥6 trillion, or 1.25 percent of Japanese GDP. Estimates also suggested that the earthquake had destroyed about one-half of 1 percent of the country's capital stock.[19]

How might we expect the Kobe disaster to affect the real exchange rate between the yen and other currencies? Figure 18.9 traces the likely effects, using the United

---

[19]Estimates come from the International Monetary Fund's *World Economic Outlook*, May 1995, 16.

States as a representative trading partner. Initially, Japan's long-run equilibrium relative output supply falls because of the earthquake's destruction of capital. The relative output supply line shifts to the left, from RS_0 to RS_1. At the original real exchange rate, R_0, excess relative demand for Japanese goods and services exists; so the yen appreciates in real terms against the dollar to R_1. Later, reconstruction efforts begin. To the extent that this increased demand goes toward Japanese rather than U.S. goods, the relative demand curve, RD, shifts to the right. Again, the excess relative demand forces a real yen appreciation, this time to R_2.

Case Four
Purchasing Power Parity at Home?

Section 18.3 cited many possible reasons for the failure of purchasing power parity—trade barriers, nontraded goods, changes in relative prices, and differences in countries' production and consumption patterns among them. With so many possible causes of failure, it becomes difficult to sort out empirically which are genuinely important and which are not. A recent test took an unusual approach to testing purchasing power parity in order to circumvent this problem.[20]

The study tested whether purchasing power parity held among consumer price indices for Philadelphia, Chicago, New York, and Los Angeles. Because the four U.S. cities use the same currency, exchange rate fluctuations could be ruled out as the explanation of any deviation of prices across regions. Along the same lines, macroeconomic policies could be assumed to exert similar influences on the four cities. And, while consumption patterns differ somewhat regionally, the consumer-price-index data reflected the prices of similar consumption baskets.

The study found that purchasing power parity fails to hold when tests are based on cities' overall consumer prices indices. However, when nontraded goods are excluded, purchasing power parity holds. These results indicate that the presence of nontraded goods, such as housing, which contains a large real-estate component, provide the key to explaining deviations from purchasing power parity. We can apply these insights in an international context. Suppose, for example, that each country's price level includes two components: one captures prices of *traded* goods and services and one reflects prices of *nontraded* goods and services:

$$P = \alpha_T \cdot P_T + \alpha_{NT} \cdot P_{NT} \text{ and } P^* = \alpha_T^* \cdot P_T^* + \alpha_{NT}^* \cdot P_{NT}^*, \qquad [18.23]$$

where α_T and α_{NT} represent the weights of traded and nontraded goods in the domestic country's consumption basket, while α_T^* and α_{NT}^* denote the corresponding weights for the foreign country's consumption. If the law of one price holds for traded goods but not for nontraded ones, because arbitrage works for the former but

[20]Information for this case comes from the Tootell article in the chapter references.

not for the latter, then $P_T = e \cdot P_T^*$. This allows us to write the real exchange rate by plugging Equation 18.23 into the definition, $R \equiv P/eP^*$:

$$R = [\alpha_T \cdot e \cdot P_T^* + \alpha_{NT} \cdot P_{NT}]/[\alpha_T^* \cdot e \cdot P_T^* + \alpha_{NT}^* \cdot e \cdot P_{NT}^*]. \qquad [18.24]$$

Recall that absolute purchasing power parity holds if R equals 1, and relative purchasing power parity holds if R equals a constant. Equation 18.24 will equal 1 only if two conditions hold. First, the two countries' consumption weights for traded and nontraded goods must be equal ($a_T = a_T^*$ and $a_{NT} = a_{NT}^*$). Second, the prices of nontraded goods must be equal, or the law of one price must hold for those goods (that is, $P_{NT} = e \cdot P_{NT}^*$). Equation 18.24 will remain constant only if the two countries' weights remain constant relative to one another *and* if nontraded goods prices in the two countries remain constant relative to one another. The next case examines the importance of across-country changes in nontraded goods prices for purchasing power parity and real exchange rates.

Case Five
Nontraded Goods and the Real Exchange Rate

For most countries, workers exhibit higher degrees of mobility between industries within the domestic economy than across international borders. This characteristic of world markets played an important role in our study of international trade theory in Chapters Two through Four. If workers are more mobile within than across countries, then similarly skilled workers in different sectors of the same economy will tend to earn similar wages, while even similarly skilled workers in different countries may earn very different wages.[21] In such a world, differences in countries' rates of productivity growth can cause changes in real exchange rates, or deviations from purchasing power parity. This link between differential productivity growth and the real exchange rate constitutes the **Balassa-Samuelson effect.**

Suppose the domestic country enjoys rapid productivity growth limited to its traded-goods sector. Wages will rise with productivity in that sector. And, because workers are mobile between the domestic traded- and nontraded-goods sectors, wages will rise in the nontraded-goods sector as well, even though it has not shared in the productivity growth. The combination of rising wages and no productivity growth in the nontraded-goods sector leads to rising prices for nontraded goods (P_{NT}) relative to the prices of traded goods ($P_T = e \cdot P_T^*$) in the domestic economy. With no productivity growth in the foreign economy, the price of domestic nontraded goods rises relative to the price of foreign ones ($e \cdot P_{NT}^*$) as well. As Equation 18.24 indicates, such relative price changes cause purchasing power parity to fail in both its absolute and relative forms.

---

[21]Section 4.4 discusses the factor price equalization theorem.

The Balassa-Samuelson effect often is cited as one possible explanation for the yen's dramatic real appreciation relative to the U.S. dollar over the last 30 years. Suppose U.S. and Japanese nontraded-goods sectors enjoy productivity growth at about the same rate, but that productivity growth in Japan's traded-goods sector outpaces that in the U.S. traded-goods sector. Enhanced productivity in the traded-goods sector raises Japanese wages, and labor mobility within Japan transmits that wage increase to the nontraded-goods sector. The price of Japanese nontraded goods rises relative to the price of U.S. nontraded goods, and the yen appreciates in real terms against the dollar.

The Balassa-Samuelson effect also carries another potentially important implication: it may explain why nontraded goods tend to be much cheaper in relatively poor countries than in more affluent ones. If poor countries have lower labor productivity in traded goods than richer countries, but equal productivity in nontraded goods and services, then nontraded goods will be cheaper in poor countries. This follows because the low productivity in traded goods implies low wages in poor countries; and low wages imply low prices for nontraded goods. India may provide a classic example:

> A meal at a roadside diner costs the equivalent of about 35 U.S. cents, while lunch at a downtown Delhi cafeteria costs $1. A full-time housekeeper earns $25 a month; a private driver charges $80 a month. Monthly rent for a two-bedroom apartment in New Delhi is about $130.[22]

Summary

In long-run equilibrium, money has a neutral effect on the macroeconomy. In other words, changes in the money stock can affect the price level and the nominal exchange rate, but not real output, the real rate of interest, or the real exchange rate. The monetary approach to the exchange rate describes how the macroeconomy behaves in the long run when all shocks to the economy are monetary and purchasing power parity holds, at least in its relative form. When shocks can disturb the output market as well as the money market, even relative purchasing power parity can fail, resulting in real currency appreciations and depreciations.

Looking Ahead

In Chapters Sixteen through Eighteen, we have examined how the macroeconomy behaves in the short run and in long-run equilibrium. In Chapter Nineteen, we focus on how the economy adjusts as it moves from its short-run response to its new long-run equilibrium. We shall see that economic policies may generate short-run effects that differ substantially from their long-run ones.

---

[22]Miriam Jordan, "In India, Luxury Is Within Reach of Many," *The Wall Street Journal,* October 17, 1995.

Key Terms

long-run equilibrium
neutrality of money
law of one price
purchasing power parity (PPP)
absolute purchasing power
  parity
relative purchasing power
  parity
monetary approach to the
  exchange rate

inflation
nominal rate of return
real rate of return
Fisher equation
real depreciation
real appreciation
real interest parity
Balassa-Samuelson effect

Problems and Questions for Review

1. Suppose an automobile air conditioner (an intermediate good or input into automobile production) sells for 11,000 bolivar in Venezuela, while an identical air conditioner sells for $500 in the United States. If the exchange rate between the bolivar and the dollar is 20 bolivar per dollar, does the law of one price hold? Why, or why not? If not, what adjustments would you expect in the bolivar price of air conditioners and in the dollar price of air conditioners? How would your answer differ if the item in question were the price of having a car washed rather than the price of an air conditioner? Why?

2. The following data are for 1983–1991.

Country	Percent Increase in Price Level (CPI)	Percent Change in Exchange Rate (e = $/FX)
United States	36%	—
United Kingdom	57%	−16%
Canada	43%	+16%
France	37%	+26%
Germany	16%	+35%
Italy	70%	+18%

(a) Generally, do the data seem to support purchasing power parity? Be sure to define purchasing power parity.

(b) Briefly outline three reasons why purchasing power parity might not hold between a particular pair of countries over a particular period.

3. Suppose the law of one price held for all goods and services. Would purchasing power parity necessarily hold? Why, or why not?

4. For several decades in the United States, productivity grew more rapidly in traded-goods sectors such as manufacturing than in nontraded sectors such as services. Some analysts recently have argued that the "computer revolution" may be changing that trend, as automation raises productivity growth in many nontraded services.

(a) If increased productivity in the nontraded sector were unique to the United States, how would you expect it to affect the real exchange rate? Explain.

(b) Services (many of which are nontraded) typically comprise a larger share of economic activity in advanced industrial economies than in developing economies. If so, how might a worldwide rise in productivity in the service sector tend to affect real exchange rates between advanced industrial economies and developing economies?

5. According to the monetary approach to the exchange rate, what would happen to the nominal exchange rate if:

(a) The domestic money stock grew at 10 percent, the foreign money stock grew at 10 percent, the demand for domestic money balances grew at 10 percent, and the demand for foreign money balances grew at 10 percent?

(b) The domestic money stock grew at 10 percent, the foreign money stock grew at 10 percent, the demand for domestic money balances grew at 5 percent, and the demand for foreign money balances grew at 5 percent?

(c) The domestic money stock grew at 5 percent, the foreign money stock grew at 10 percent, the demand for domestic money balances grew at 5 percent, and the demand for foreign money balances grew at 10 percent?

6. In November 1992, the number of same-day automobile trips by Canadians to the United States declined almost 6 percent. Based on the information in Case Two, would you guess that the Canadian dollar appreciated or depreciated relative to the U.S. dollar during the period in question? Explain.

7. Case Three examines the likely effect of the 1995 Kobe, Japan, earthquake on the *real* exchange rate between the Japanese yen and the U.S. dollar. What would be the likely effect on the *nominal* exchange rate? Explain.

8. When policy makers in an economy with a history of high inflation rates attempt to change their macroeconomic policies to lower inflation, they often cite declining long-term nominal interest rates as evidence that the policy change is working. Explain. How might policy makers use changes in the exchange rate as an additional source of information about the success of their policy change? Explain.

References and Selected Readings

Bartolini, Leonardo. "Purchasing Power Parity Measures of Competitiveness." *Finance and Development* (September 1995): 46–49.
Dangers of interpreting deviations from purchasing power parity as indicators of a country's "competitiveness." Intermediate.

Coughlin, Cletus C., and Kees Koedijk. "What Do We Know About the Long-Run Real Exchange Rate?" Federal Reserve Bank of St. Louis *Review* (January–February 1990): 35–48.
Theory and evidence on changes in the real exchange rate, or R, the relative price of domestic and foreign goods and services.

Fielke, Norman S. "The Soaring Trade in 'Nontradables'." Federal Reserve Bank of Boston *New England Economic Review* (November–December 1995): 25–36.
Excellent overview of the growing trade in services and other "nontradables"; for all students.

Frankel, J. A., and A. K. Rose. "Research on Nominal Exchange Rates." In *Handbook of International Economics,* Vol. 3, edited by G. M. Grossman and K. Rogoff, 1689–1730. Amsterdam: North-Holland, 1995.
Review of theory and evidence on exchange rate behavior; intermediate and advanced.

Frankel, Jacob A., and Harry G. Johnson, eds. *The Economics of Exchange Rates.* Reading, Mass.: Addison-Wesley, 1978.
A classic collection on exchange rate theory's major developments during the 1970s, especially the monetary approach; for advanced students.

Frenkel, Jacob A., and Harry G. Johnson, eds. *The Monetary Approach to the Balance of Payments.* London: George Allen and Unwin, 1976.
The classic collection on the monetary approach; for intermediate and advanced students.

Frenkel, Jacob A., and Michael L. Mussa. "Asset Markets, Exchange Rates, and the Balance of Payments." In *Handbook of International Economics,* Vol. 2, edited by Ronald W. Jones and Peter B. Kenen, 679–748. Amsterdam: North-Holland, 1985.
Advanced treatment of asset-oriented models of the international macroeconomy.

Froot, K., and K. Rogoff. "Perspectives on PPP and Long-Run Real Exchange Rates." In *Handbook of International Economics,* Vol. 3, edited by G. M. Grossman and K. Rogoff, 1647–1688. Amsterdam: North-Holland, 1995.
Review of theory and evidence on long-run exchange rate behavior; intermediate and advanced.

Hafer, R. W. "Does Dollar Depreciation Cause Inflation?" Federal Reserve Bank of St. Louis *Review* 71 (July–August 1989): 16–28.
A careful examination of the subtle relationship between the price level and the exchange rate; for all students.

Hooper, Peter, and Catherine L. Mann. "Exchange Rate Pass-Through in the 1980s: The Case of U.S. Imports of Manufactures." *Brookings Papers on Economic Activity* (1989): 297–337.
The relationship between changes in exchange rates and prices; for intermediate and advanced students.

Johnson, Harry G. "The Monetary Approach to the Balance of Payments: A Nontechnical Guide." *Journal of International Economics* 7 (August 1977): 251–268.
An introduction to the monetary approach by one of its originators; for all students.

Isard, Peter. *Exchange Rate Economics.* Cambridge: Cambridge University Press, 1995.
Survey of the state of knowledge about exchange rates; level of different sections of the book varies.

Levich, Richard M. "Empirical Studies of Exchange Rates: Price Behavior, Rate Determination and Market Efficiency." In *Handbook of International Economics,* Vol. 2, edited by Ronald W. Jones and Peter B. Kenen, 979–1040. Amsterdam: North-Holland, 1985.
Advanced examination of empirical studies of exchange rate behavior.

Lewis, K. "Puzzles in International Financial Markets." In *Handbook of International Economics,* Vol. 3, edited by G. M. Grossman and K. Rogoff, 1913–1972. Amsterdam: North-Holland, 1995.
Review of theory and evidence on exchange rate behavior and interest rates; intermediate and advanced.

Marrinan, Jane. "Exchange Rate Determination: Sorting Out Theory and Evidence." Federal Reserve Bank of Boston *New England Economic Review* (November–December 1989): 39–51.
Survey of theories of exchange rate determination; for all students.

Marston, Richard C. "Stabilization Policies in Open Economies." In *Handbook of International Economics,* Vol. 2, edited by Ronald W. Jones and Peter B. Kenen, 859–916. Amsterdam: North-Holland, 1985.
Advanced treatment of many of the issues raised in this chapter, including the monetary approach to the exchange rate.

Meltzer, Allan H. "Real Exchange Rates: Some Evidence from the Postwar Years." Federal Reserve Bank of St. Louis *Review* (March–April 1993): 103–117.
Theoretical and empirical overview of real exchange rates; intermediate.

Obstfeld, Maurice. "International Currency Experience: New Lessons and Lessons Relearned." *Brookings Papers on Economic Activity* 1 (1995): 119–220.
Excellent survey of recent currency experience, including purchasing power parity. Intermediate.

Obstfeld, Maurice, and Alan C. Stockman. "Exchange-Rate Dynamics." In *Handbook of International Economics,* Vol. 2, edited by Ronald W. Jones and Peter B. Kenen, 917–977. Amsterdam: North-Holland, 1985.
Advanced discussion of theoretical developments in exchange rate dynamics.

Taylor, Mark P. "The Economics of Exchange Rates." *Journal of Economic Literature* 33 (March 1993): 13–47.
Survey of recent literature on exchange rates; intermediate and advanced.

Tootell, Geoffrey M. B. "PPP Within the United States." Federal Reserve Bank of Boston *New England Economic Review* (July–August 1992): 15–24.
Tests find purchasing power parity fails to hold within the United States; for all students.

CHAPTER NINETEEN

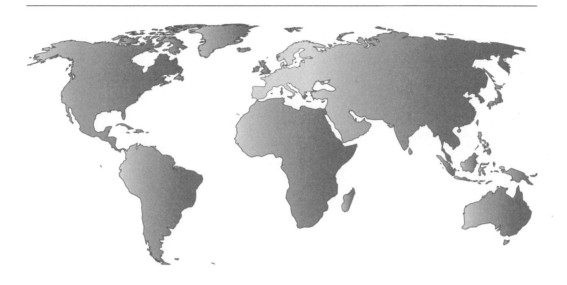

Prices and Output in an Open Economy

19.1 Introduction

In Chapters Fourteen through Seventeen, we examined how fiscal, monetary, and exchange rate policies affect an open macroeconomy in the *short run*—that is, the time horizon over which the price level remains fixed. In Chapter Eighteen, we turned our attention to the *long run,* when output reaches and maintains its full-employment level and the price level adjusts fully to any shocks or policy changes in the economy. Now it is time to explore how the economy behaves *between* the short run and the long run. In other words, what happens *as the price level adjusts* to economic shocks and policy changes?

A quick examination of basic macroeconomic data for a sample of countries reveals that this medium-run period—in which both output and the price level adjust—appears to fit the situation in which most economies find themselves most of the time. This should come as no surprise. After all, economic shocks of all kinds constantly impinge on economies, and policy makers continually adjust their policy instruments. Long-run equilibrium, when all macroeconomic variables have reached states of rest, provides a useful conceptual benchmark, but it is unlikely to be observed often in the world economy, where new shocks and policy changes occur before the economy has adjusted fully to earlier events.

Table 19.1 □ Annual Change in Consumer Prices, 1988–1994 (Percent)

Country	1988	1989	1990	1991	1992	1993	1994
United States	3.9	4.6	4.3	3.8	2.8	2.2	2.1
Canada	4.6	4.8	3.1	2.7	1.4	1.1	0.6
Japan	0.4	1.8	2.2	2.0	1.5	0.9	0.2
France	2.8	3.0	3.1	3.1	2.3	2.4	1.4
Germany[a]	1.6	2.4	3.2	4.9	5.5	3.9	2.2
Italy	6.6	6.2	7.6	7.7	4.5	4.4	3.5
United Kingdom	6.0	7.1	6.4	6.5	4.3	3.4	2.0
China	18.5	17.8	2.1	2.9	5.4	13.0	n.a.
Saudi Arabia	0.9	1.0	2.1	4.6	−0.4	0.8	n.a.
India	8.9	6.5	9.9	13.0	10.7	7.9	n.a.
Israel	16.3	20.2	17.2	19.0	11.9	10.9	n.a.
Mexico	114.2	20.0	26.7	22.7	15.5	9.8	n.a.
Uganda	180.1	61.5	33.1	63.0	−0.6	16.1	n.a.
Poland	60.2	251.1	585.8	70.3	43.0	35.3	n.a.
Yugoslavia	194.1	1,239.9	583.1	117.4	6,146.6	n.a.	n.a.
Argentina	343.0	3,080.5	2,314.7	171.7	24.9	10.6	n.a.
Peru	1,722.3	2,775.3	7,649.7	409.2	73.2	48.6	n.a.
Brazil	684.6	1,319.9	2,738.8	413.7	991.1	2,103.3	n.a.
Zaire	82.8	104.3	81.3	2,153.8	4,130.0	1,893.0	n.a.

[a]Data for West Germany through 1990 and for unified Germany thereafter.

Source: International Monetary Fund, *World Economic Outlook*, May 1995.

Countries rarely have a stable, unchanging price level. Typically, the price level rises in most years, but at variable and sometimes highly erratic rates. A sustained rise in the overall price level defines **inflation;** a sustained fall in the price level, rarely observed, represents **deflation.** Table 19.1 reports recent price-level behavior for a sample of countries. Note two patterns. First, inflation rates vary widely across countries. Second, inflation rates often change dramatically within a single country, even over a short period, confirming as we noted above that economies constantly are adjusting to shocks and policy changes that impact their price levels.

Just as changes in countries' price levels differ, both across countries and across time, so do changes in their outputs. If an economy were perpetually in long-run equilibrium, of the type we examined in Chapter Eighteen, we would expect its real output to grow fairly smoothly over time, at a rate determined by growth in the country's resource endowment and improvements in its technology. Instead, we see output growth speeding up and slowing down, as in Table 19.2, mirrored by changes in unemployment. This provides further evidence that we observe economies primarily in the process of adjusting to more-or-less constant economic shocks and policy changes.

Table 19.2 □ **Annual Change in Real GDP, 1988–1994 (Percent)**

Country	1988	1989	1990	1991	1992	1993	1994
United States	3.9	2.5	1.2	−0.6	2.3	3.1	4.1
Canada	5.0	2.4	−0.2	−1.8	0.6	2.2	4.5
Japan	6.2	4.7	4.8	4.3	1.1	−0.2	0.6
France	4.4	4.3	2.5	0.8	1.2	−1.0	2.5
Germany[a]	3.7	3.6	5.7	2.8	2.2	−1.1	2.9
Italy	4.1	2.9	2.1	1.2	0.7	−0.7	2.5
United Kingdom	5.0	2.2	0.4	−2.0	−0.5	2.2	3.8
China	11.3	4.3	3.8	8.2	13.1	13.7	n.a.
Saudi Arabia	6.6	0.5	9.3	9.9	2.2	0.5	n.a.
India	8.7	7.4	5.5	1.8	3.8	3.8	n.a.
Israel	3.1	1.3	5.8	6.2	6.6	3.5	n.a.
Mexico	1.2	3.3	4.4	3.6	2.8	0.6	n.a.
Uganda	6.1	6.0	5.4	3.6	8.6	5.1	n.a.
Poland	4.1	0.2	−11.6	−7.0	2.6	3.8	n.a.
Yugoslavia	−2.0	0.8	−7.5	−17.0	−34.0	n.a.	n.a.
Argentina	−1.9	−6.2	0.1	8.9	8.7	6.0	n.a.
Peru	−8.2	−11.8	−4.2	2.8	−2.3	6.5	n.a.
Brazil	0.3	3.3	−4.4	1.1	−0.9	4.3	n.a.
Zaire	0.5	−1.4	−2.3	−7.2	−11.2	−16.6	n.a.

[a]Data for West Germany through 1990 and for unified Germany thereafter.

Source: International Monetary Fund, *World Economic Outlook,* May 1995.

To augment our model of the macroeconomy to incorporate price-level adjustment, we need to distinguish between the *supply,* or production, side of the economy and the *demand,* or expenditure, side, and then to combine the two. Our fixed-price model of Chapters Fourteen through Seventeen focused on the demand side alone; in fact, the IS, LM, and BOP curves together comprise the demand side of the economy. We assumed implicitly that firms willingly supplied at unchanged prices all the output demanded. If this condition were met, the quantity of output demanded, or what we have called *total expenditure on domestic goods and services,* would determine the level of output, as it did in Chapters Fourteen through Seventeen. However, once we introduce an independent supply side of the economy, representing firms' production decisions and workers' labor-supply decisions, things become more complex.

19.2 Apples versus GDP: Supply in Micro- and Macroeconomics

A microeconomic analogy with a market for a single good, such as apples, is useful here. For the price of apples to remain fixed and for demand to determine completely

Figure 19.1 □ **Price and Supply in the Apple Market**

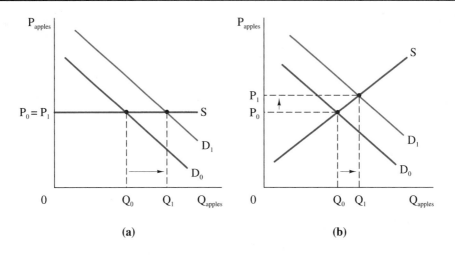

(a)   (b)

In panel (a), the supply curve for apples is perfectly horizontal. The price of apples is fixed, and the quantity is determined completely by demand. In panel (b), the supply curve for apples is upward sloping, reflecting the movement of resources into and out of apple production in response to price changes.

the quantity of apples requires a horizontal supply curve for apples, as depicted in panel (a) of Figure 19.1. Changes in the demand for apples would then cause quantity to change in the same direction and leave price unchanged. But the horizontal supply curve in panel (a) of Figure 19.1 does not depict how microeconomic markets typically function.

Changes in demand usually generate changes in both price and quantity. Figure 19.1 shows this in panel (b), where we draw the supply of apples as an upward-sloping line. The positive slope of the supply curve represents the role of price increases (that is, increases in the price of apples *relative* to the prices of other goods) in drawing resources into apple production and of price decreases in driving resources out of it. These resource movements in response to demand-induced price changes cause changes in the quantity supplied of apples. When the demand for apples rises, the relative price of apples rises and resources flow out of other endeavors (production of goods and services whose prices have declined relative to the price of apples) and into apple growing. This resource movement allows the quantity of apples supplied to fluctuate in response to changes in consumers' desire for apples.

Moving back to the macroeconomy, changes in the economy's overall output, or GDP, also require changes in the quantity of resources employed in production. Increased production requires more inputs. However, when we want to model changes in real GDP, or the economy's *total* output of goods and services, we cannot explain increases and decreases in the quantity of resources used in terms of movements among industries in response to relative price changes, as in the apple market example. For the quantity of real output supplied to increase, resources previously unemployed must come into use or resources must be used more intensively (such as workers' overtime, running machines two shifts per day rather than one, or cultivating previously idle land). *If* a rise in the price level causes these types of adjustments to occur, the economy's macroeconomic or aggregate supply curve (the relationship between the quantity of real output produced and the price level) will be upward sloping.

The relevant question then becomes: Will an increase in the price level cause resource utilization to rise? Economists' answer to this question has evolved with our understanding of the macroeconomy; in fact, the question represents one of the most fundamental and enduring issues of macroeconomics. A hundred years ago, most economists would have answered in the negative. Forty years ago, most would have answered with a resounding "Yes." Today only a few would give such an unequivocal reply. Most would answer, "Yes, but not in the long run, and only if the economy has not experienced continual increases in its price level," and a few would reply with an only slightly qualified "No."

With this introduction to the problems at hand, let us proceed to translate our model of an open macroeconomy into a form more convenient for analyzing the economy's adjustment from the short run to its long-run equilibrium. We must develop an aggregate demand curve and a more complete concept of an aggregate, or macroeconomic, supply curve. We shall continue to use the microeconomic concepts of demand and supply as analogies, but we must also distinguish the features that make an *aggregate* demand or supply curve unique to the study of macroeconomics.

19.3 Aggregate Demand under a Fixed Exchange Rate Regime

An economy's **aggregate demand curve** represents the relationship between the quantity demanded of domestic goods and services and the domestic price level. Note that this definition closely resembles that of a market demand curve for a single good in microeconomics. The differences in the case of the aggregate demand curve are that (1) the quantity examined represents the economy's total output of goods and services, or real GDP, rather than output of a single good or service, and (2) the relevant price represents the overall domestic price level (for example, the GDP deflator) rather than the relative price of a single good. Because the form of the aggregate demand curve differs slightly depending on whether the economy operates under a fixed or flexible exchange rate regime, we begin with the analysis under a fixed exchange rate.

19.3.1 The Slope of the Aggregate Demand Curve[1]

The aggregate demand curve slopes downward like a microeconomic demand curve, but for different reasons. Two reasons account for its negative slope. First, a rise in

---

[1]The appendix to this chapter outlines the derivation of the aggregate demand curve from the IS-LM-BOP framework of Chapters Sixteen and Seventeen.

the domestic price level, P (with the foreign price level, P^*, and the exchange rate, e, held constant), raises the price of domestic goods and services relative to that of foreign ones because $R \equiv P/eP^*$. Individuals respond by shifting expenditure from domestic to foreign goods; thus, the quantity demanded of domestic goods and services falls, resulting in a negative relationship between the domestic price level and the quantity demanded of domestic goods. *(To test your understanding, outline the effect of a* fall *in the price level on relative prices and on the quantity demanded of domestic goods.)*

The second reason for the aggregate demand curve's negative slope comes from the money market.[2] Recall that individuals demand real money balances for convenience in making transactions. The quantity demanded of real money balances (L) depends positively on real income (Q)—because the number and size of transactions depend positively on income—and negatively on the interest rate (i), which measures the opportunity cost of holding cash balances rather than interest-bearing bonds.

In equilibrium, the quantity of real money balances demanded by the public (L[Q, i]) must equal the stock of real money balances, which equals the nominal money stock (M) divided by the price level (P). Figure 19.2 illustrates such an equilibrium, along with the effects of a rise in the price level. Given a value for the nominal money stock (M_0), a rise in the price level from P_0 to P_1 reduces the real money stock and shifts the money stock line to the left. At the original interest rate (i_0), the quantity demanded of money exceeds the new, smaller stock. Individuals try to sell bonds to raise real money balances to their desired level. The price of bonds falls, which is reflected in a rise in the interest rate to i_1. At the new, higher interest rate, individuals are satisfied holding the new, smaller stock of real money balances.

The rise in the interest rate produced by adjustments in the money market discourages investment expenditure.[3] Total expenditure on domestic goods and services falls. This chain of events—from a rise in the price level to a decline in total expenditure—provides the second reason why the aggregate demand curve slopes downward. Again, a higher price level corresponds to a smaller quantity demanded of domestic goods and services. *(To test your understanding, go through the effects of a* fall *in the price level on the money market and total expenditure.)*

The effects of a change in the domestic price level on the relative price of domestic goods and the real money stock both contribute to the negative relationship between the quantity demanded of domestic goods and services and the domestic price level represented by the downward-sloping aggregate demand curve in an open economy.[4] Besides the slope, we need information on the variables that cause the entire aggregate demand curve to shift. Just as with a market demand curve in microeconomics, we draw an aggregate demand curve assuming that certain variables are held constant; when any of these variables changes, the entire demand curve shifts.

---

[2]See section 15.2 to review the demand for money and the money stock.

[3]For a review, see the discussion of investment in section 14.5.3.

[4]Note that the second effect, but not the first, exists in a closed economy; therefore, the aggregate demand curve in an open economy tends to be flatter than that in an otherwise comparable closed economy.

Figure 19.2 □ **Effect of a Rise in the Price Level in the Money Market**

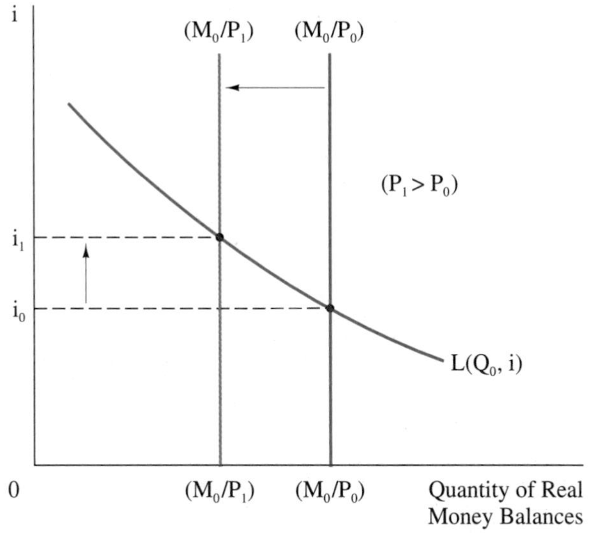

A rise in the price level from P_0 to P_1 reduces the real money stock (M/P), assuming that the nominal money stock (M) is held constant. The equilibrium interest rate rises to reduce the quantity demanded of real money balances to equal the new, smaller stock.

19.3.2 Shifts in the Aggregate Demand Curve

For our purposes, the important variables fixed along a given aggregate demand curve include the nominal money stock, fiscal policy variables such as government expenditures and taxes, the nominal exchange rate, and the foreign price level. A change in any one of these variables alters the demand for domestic goods *at each domestic price level* and, therefore, shifts the entire aggregate demand curve. Figure 19.3 summarizes the effects of changes in each variable on the aggregate demand curve.

Changes in the nominal money stock can arise through either open market operations or foreign exchange intervention in response to a balance-of-payments surplus or deficit (recall we are examining aggregate demand under a *fixed* exchange rate regime). In either case, an increase in the nominal money stock raises the real money stock for a given price level. The interest rate must fall to make individuals willing to hold the new, larger stock of real money balances. The fall in the interest rate raises the investment component of expenditure on domestic goods and services, and the aggregate demand curve shifts to the right. A decrease in the nominal money stock shifts the aggregate demand curve to the left, for the same reason. Note that a change in the real money stock can cause *either* a movement along a single aggregate demand curve *or* a shift of the entire curve, depending on

Figure 19.3 □ **Shifts in the Aggregate Demand Curve**

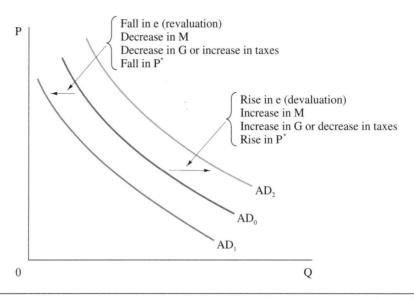

The demand for domestically produced goods and services is reduced at each domestic price level by a revaluation of the domestic currency, a decline in the domestic nominal money stock, a decrease in government expenditures, a rise in taxes, or a fall in the foreign price level. The demand for domestically produced goods and services increases at each domestic price level due to a devaluation of the domestic currency, a rise in the domestic money stock, an increase in government expenditures, a reduction in taxes, or a rise in the foreign price level. Changes in the domestic price level itself, other things equal, cause movements along a single aggregate demand curve rather than shifts in it.

whether that change was caused by a change in the price level or in the nominal money stock.[5]

By raising total expenditure on domestic goods and services, expansionary fiscal policy increases demand for them at each price level and shifts the aggregate demand curve to the right. Expansionary fiscal policy can consist of either increased government purchases of goods and services or tax cuts, which raise disposable income and increase consumption expenditure. Contractionary fiscal policy lowers demand and shifts the AD curve to the left.

A devaluation of the domestic currency (a rise in the nominal exchange rate, e) lowers the relative price of domestic goods ($R \equiv P/eP^*$) and raises demand for them at each level of domestic prices. The aggregate demand curve shifts to the right. A revaluation of the domestic currency has the opposite effect; it raises the relative price of domestic goods and shifts the aggregate demand curve to the left.

---

[5]This seemingly peculiar state of affairs arises because the price level is the variable plotted on the vertical axis in drawing an aggregate demand curve.

Changes in the foreign price level (P^*) also shift the aggregate demand curve because, for given values of the domestic price level and the nominal exchange rate, they alter the relative price of domestic goods. A rise in P^* switches expenditure toward domestic goods and shifts the aggregate demand curve to the right. A fall in the foreign price level switches spending toward now relatively cheaper foreign goods and shifts the domestic aggregate demand curve to the left. Note that changes in R can lead to either a movement along the AD curve (if R changes through P) or to a shift of the AD curve (if R changes through e or P^*).

19.3.3 Aggregate Demand Alone Cannot Determine Output

The models of an open macroeconomy we considered in Chapters Fourteen through Seventeen constitute models of aggregate demand. They tell us, *given* the price level, the quantity of domestic goods and services demanded by individuals, firms, government agencies, and foreigners. However, goods and services do not appear magically; they must be produced by firms, using labor and capital inputs and the available technology. The economy's aggregate supply curves contain information about this production process.

19.4 Long-Run Aggregate Supply in an Open Economy

Aggregate supply refers to the relationship between the price level in an economy and the total quantity of goods and services supplied or produced. As in a microeconomic context, the theory of aggregate supply reflects the use of inputs and technology to produce output and the responses by producers and input suppliers to changes in the domestic price level.

The quantity of available resources and the existing technology constrain the total quantity of output an economy can produce. Changes in employment, the capital stock, natural resource inputs, or technology alter an economy's ability to produce goods and services. Macroeconomists typically assume that a country's capital stock, natural resource inputs, and technology are fixed over the time horizon under analysis. Over a long period, capital stocks grow or shrink, natural resources are discovered or exhausted, and new technologies permit the same resources to produce larger quantities of output.[6] These changes usually, but not always, occur gradually and largely outside policy makers' control. For these reasons, macroeconomic analysis tends to focus on changes in the quantity of output produced holding constant the quantity of available resources and technology. Changes in output then must come from changes in employment or in the intensity with which firms use the given capital stock.

19.4.1 The Short, Medium, and Long Runs

When examining the supply or production side of the economy, we must distinguish among behavior in the short, medium, and long runs. Production inherently takes time,

---

[6]See Chapter Ten for a discussion of the sources of economic growth.

and firms cannot adjust instantaneously to changes in their economic environments. For example, firms often hire workers at wage rates fixed contractually for a set period, such as a year, and the cost of changing the wage rate within the contract period may be prohibitive. Firms also make contracts with raw-material suppliers, often well before actual input delivery. Toy makers must decide how many of the hottest toys to make for the Christmas season long before they can determine whether the toys' popularity will even last until Christmas. Auto makers must commit to produce a certain number and size of cars before knowing next year's gasoline prices. All these factors force firms to make hiring and production decisions based on less than perfect information and limit firms' ability to adjust quickly as new information becomes available.

The limited availability of information and firms' restricted ability to adjust speedily to new information create an important distinction between their medium- and long-run responses to changes in the price level. We define the **short run** as in Chapters Fourteen through Seventeen—the period during which the price level remains fixed in response to economic shocks or policy changes, so aggregate demand alone determines real output. The **medium run** is the period during which the price level begins to respond to shocks or policy changes, but individuals and firms may remain unaware of price changes or may find it too costly because of contracts or other rigidities to adjust their behavior in response to price changes. The **long run,** on the other hand, denotes the time over which everyone in the economy knows the price level and has had time to adjust production decisions accordingly.

Economists cannot attach concrete time periods, such as a month, six months, or a year, to the concepts of the short, medium, and long runs, because the time required to learn and adjust to price changes depends on the nature of the economy in which one functions and on the past history of the price level in that economy. Generally, the more volatile prices have been in the past, the shorter will be the short and medium runs. When price changes have been very dramatic, individuals have an economic incentive to learn to monitor and anticipate them to avoid the large losses that a drastic unexpected change in the price level could impose. On the other hand, when prices have been stable historically, individuals have less incentive to monitor prices closely and may be slow to perceive or react to changes when they do occur.

19.4.2 The Vertical Long-Run Aggregate Supply Curve

Because the theory of aggregate supply in the long run is somewhat simpler than that in the medium run, we begin with the long run. The **long-run aggregate supply curve** is a simple vertical line at the economy's full-employment output, implying that changes in the price level have no effect on the quantity of output supplied. Remember that along a *long-run aggregate supply* curve (LRAS in Figure 19.4), individuals and firms in the economy know about and have adjusted fully to any change in the price level.

The vertical long-run aggregate supply curve reflects the way economists think individuals and firms make economic decisions. Firms decide how much to produce and workers how much labor to supply in response to relative prices. If the price a firm receives for its product rises *relative to* the prices the firm must pay for its inputs, the firm increases production. But if the price a firm receives for its product rises while the prices

Figure 19.4 □ **Long-Run Aggregate Supply**

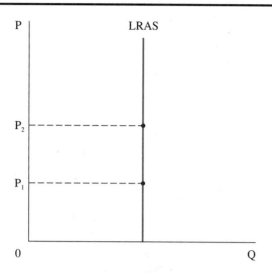

In the long run (when the price level is known and individuals and firms have time to adjust their decisions to changes in it), the quantity of output supplied is independent of the price level. The economy's quantity of resources and technology determine the horizontal placement of the LRAS curve.

of all the inputs it uses rise in the same proportion, the firm finds it not worthwhile to boost production. Similarly, if workers' wage rates rise *relative* to the prices of the goods workers buy, they will supply a larger quantity of labor to take advantage of the relatively higher wages. A similar wage increase would not encourage additional work if the prices of all the goods workers purchase rose in the same proportion as wages.

A change in the overall price level on the vertical axis of Figure 19.4 implies that *all* money prices in the economy (prices of all goods and services, nominal wages, and so on) change proportionally, leaving all relative prices unaffected. Because real economic decisions (that is, how much to produce or how much labor to supply) depend on relative prices, those decisions remain unaffected. Therefore, real output, on the horizontal axis in Figure 19.4, does not vary with the price level: *The long-run aggregate supply curve is vertical.*

Resource availability and technology determine the position of the long-run aggregate supply curve. As resource supplies increase over time or as technological progress allows given quantities of resources to produce larger quantities of output, the LRAS curve shifts to the right. As we noted earlier, this movement usually happens quite slowly and outside the direct control of macroeconomic policy makers; we shall ignore the effects of growth by assuming a fixed position for the LRAS curve through most of our analysis.[7]

---

[7]Section 19.10's analysis of supply shocks is an exception.

One final note about the LRAS curve is in order. The full-employment output corresponding to the position of the LRAS curve does *not* represent an absolute constraint on the output the economy can produce. In fact, more output can be (and often is) produced for brief periods. But, given the pattern of relative prices in the economy, the equilibrium output in the long run (when all firms and workers have made their chosen adjustments in response to price changes) is given by the LRAS curve. This represents full-employment output, or the output firms can produce without resorting to overtime for workers, overtime for machines (which raises maintenance costs), and other short-term arrangements.[8]

Consider an economy operating at full employment. Could it produce a still higher output? Yes—for example, workers could work 45 hours per week rather than the 35 to 40 hours typical in modern industrial economies, and output clearly would rise. Societies settle for a smaller output in order to work fewer hours per week, because individuals value leisure as well as income. Given the wage rate, individuals choose how to allocate their time between work (to earn income) and leisure, a decision reflected in the position of the LRAS curve. *(What would happen to the long-run aggregate supply curve if everyone in the economy suddenly wanted to take more leisure and to work less? If everyone suddenly wanted to take less leisure and work more?)* Similarly, firms could raise output by running machines for longer periods or using double shifts. When temporary considerations cause individuals to alter their decisions about how to divide time between work and leisure or firms to alter their decisions about how intensively to use their equipment, the economy temporarily moves off the LRAS curve.

19.5   Medium-Run Aggregate Supply in an Open Economy

The **medium-run aggregate supply curve** captures the behavior of individuals and firms when lack of information about the price level, stickiness of some prices, or inability to adjust quickly to a change in the price level causes behavior to differ from what it would be with full information and instantaneous adjustment. Since macroeconomic policy decisions tend to center on medium-run considerations, understanding supply behavior in the medium run is critical.

19.5.1   The Slope of the Medium-Run Aggregate Supply Curve

The medium-run aggregate supply curve slopes upward, somewhat like the letter *J*. When the price level rises while individuals and firms do not fully perceive or adjust to the event, output increases. Of course, at some output the economy reaches an absolute resource constraint (for example, when all workers are working 100 hours per week and all machines are running 24 hours per day) that prohibits further production. At that point, the *medium-run aggregate supply* curve (MRAS in Figure 19.5) becomes vertical, since further price increases cannot generate further production. However, the

[8]This long-run equilibrium level of real output often is called the *natural rate of output,* or *potential real output.*

Figure 19.5 □ **Medium-Run Aggregate Supply**

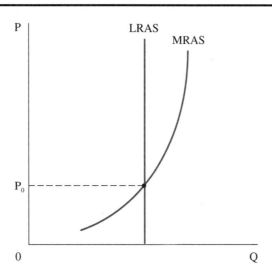

When individuals in the economy are not fully aware of increases in the price level or are unable to adjust quickly to them (due to contractual rigidities, for example), a rise in the price level causes an increase in the quantity of output supplied. This is captured by the upward-sloping portion of the MRAS curve. At some point the economy reaches the constraint of resources and technology, causing the medium-run aggregate supply curve to become vertical.

upward-sloping portion of the MRAS curve is of interest here; thus, we shall ignore the vertical section in the following discussion and figures.

Given the economic arguments for the vertical shape of the long-run aggregate supply curve, why would a rise in the price level ever cause output to increase? Economic theory and empirical evidence from many economies suggest several possible answers to this question. The key definitional differences between the medium-run and long-run supply curves are (1) the information available to individuals and firms within the economy and (2) their ability to adjust to that information; so we shall focus on the roles these two factors play in explaining the positive medium-run relationship between the price level and quantity supplied.

Even if firms and workers always had complete information about events throughout the economy, contractual rigidities still would prevent instantaneous adjustment. Consider, for example, the case of an industry that sets its wages in nominal terms in year-long contracts. If the overall price level in the economy rises during the year, the price the firm can charge for its product rises, while the contractually fixed wage rate stays constant. The firm responds to the rise in the price of its output relative to the price of its labor input by producing more. Graphically, we illustrate this response by a movement up along the economy's medium-run supply curve. We shall see later that once the firm's wage contract expires and must be renegotiated, the nominal wage will tend to rise to compensate workers for the higher prices of the goods they buy. When this happens, the firm's relative price falls back to its original level, as does its output. This places the economy back on the long-run aggregate supply curve. Before we see more about this adjustment process, we turn to the role of limited information in causing workers' and firms' medium-run behavior to differ from their long-run behavior.

Firms base production decisions on information about the prices received for their products relative to the prices of the inputs used in production. There are two major sources of information about these prices: government statistics and firms' own experiences in selling their products and buying inputs. Each of these sources is subject to lags. Governments publish some price statistics monthly and others quarterly; all are subject to periodic revision that can continue long after initial publication. Likewise, a firm's own experience cannot provide full, up-to-date information on the state of prices throughout the economy. Suppose an automobile producer sees its sales rise, signaling an increase in demand. How should the producer interpret this information? There are two basic possibilities, and the appropriate (that is, profit-maximizing) response by the firm depends on which one occurs. If the increase in demand occurs *only* in the automobile industry or *only* for the output of that particular automobile producer, the price of the firm's output rises *relative* to those of other goods in the economy (including the firm's inputs) and the firm should increase output. The second possibility is that the increase in demand for the firm's output is part of a general increase in demand for *all* products (that is, in aggregate demand). In this case, the firm can charge a higher price for its product but also must pay proportionally higher prices for its inputs. The firm's *relative* price remains unchanged, and the profit-maximizing response keeps output at its original level.

In the medium run, the firm may be unable to tell which of these two possibilities has occurred. If firms mistakenly interpret a rise in the overall price level as a rise in the relative prices of their respective outputs and respond by raising output, the economy moves up along the medium-run aggregate supply curve. A rise in the price level, if misperceived by firms, causes output to increase. But eventually firms will discover their mistake—for example, when they go to buy additional inputs and find that input prices have risen by the same percentage as the prices of their products. When this happens, output falls back to its original level and the economy moves back onto the long-run aggregate supply curve. We shall examine this adjustment from the medium run to the long run by considering the cause of shifts in the medium-run aggregate supply curve.[9]

19.5.2 Shifts in the Medium-Run Aggregate Supply Curve

Each medium-run aggregate supply curve is drawn for given values of input prices and of firms' expectations about prices other than those of their own products. If the price level rises but contractual rigidities keep some input prices constant and firms

---

[9]Several types of shifts in the medium-run aggregate supply curve can occur. We concentrate here on those caused by changes in input prices or perceptions of the price level. These shifts are vertical ones. Both the medium- and long-run supply curves may shift horizontally because of changes in the quantity of available resources or in technology, as we shall see in section 19.10.

Figure 19.6 □ **Vertical Shift in the Medium-Run Aggregate Supply Curve Due to a Rise in Input Prices or in the Expected Price Level**

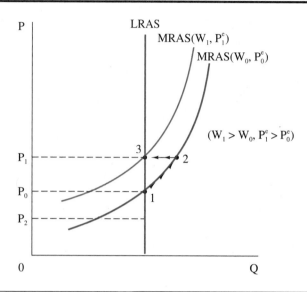

Each MRAS curve is draw for given input prices and expectations about the price level. A rise in input prices or in the expected price level shifts the MRAS curve upward.

do not immediately alter their expectations about other prices throughout the economy, firms will perceive that the relative prices of their outputs have risen and will increase output. This causes the economy to move up along a given MRAS curve.

Figure 19.6 depicts this situation, in which W denotes nominal wages and P^e denotes firms' expectations about the price level. Beginning at point 1, the price level rises but input prices and firms' price expectations do not adjust immediately. Output rises, and the economy moves to point 2. Gradually, input prices adjust upward, firms detect the rise in all prices, the expected price level rises, and the economy moves to point 3, back on the long-run aggregate supply curve. *(What would happen to output in the medium run if the price level suddenly fell to $P_2 < P_0$? In the long run?)*

Of course, not every rise in the price level leaves input prices temporarily untouched or fools firms into believing their relative prices have risen. If all input prices respond immediately and if firms immediately recognize a proportional rise in all prices, the economy moves directly from point 1 to point 3, leaving output completely unaffected by the rise in prices.

When the economy is at a point to the right of the LRAS curve, two things happen. First, output is above the full-employment level, so wages and other input prices tend to rise, shifting the MRAS upward. Second, if the actual price level exceeds the expected price level ($P > P^e$), the expected price level will rise, again shifting the MRAS curve upward. When the economy is at a point to the left of the LRAS curve,

Figure 19.7 □ **Medium-Run and Long-Run Equilibrium**

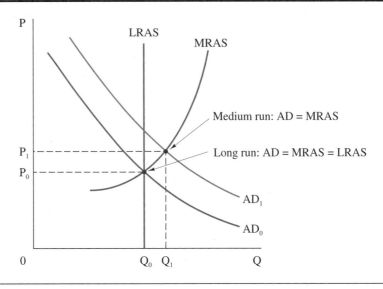

In the medium run, the economy must be at a point of intersection of an aggregate demand curve and a medium-run aggregate supply curve. In the long run, there is the additional requirement that the intersection of the aggregate demand and medium-run aggregate supply curves occur on the long-run aggregate supply curve.

output is below the full-employment level and the expected price level may be higher than the actual price level ($P^e > P$). As input prices fall and information about the lower-than-expected price level spreads, the expected price level falls and the medium-run aggregate supply curve shifts downward.

19.6 Combining Aggregate Demand and Aggregate Supply

The simultaneous determination of output and the price level requires that we combine the aggregate demand curve with the aggregate supply curves as in Figure 19.7. In the medium run, the economy can operate at any intersection of an aggregate demand curve and a medium-run aggregate supply curve. In the long run, there is the additional requirement that the aggregate demand and medium-run aggregate supply curves intersect at a point *on* the long-run aggregate supply curve. This means that individuals and firms must know the price level and must have adjusted all their pricing and output decisions accordingly.

To analyze various policies' effects on output and prices, we must make an assumption about the degree of capital mobility for the country in question. Since the degree of capital mobility has increased in recent years, especially for the industrial economies, we choose the assumption of **perfectly mobile capital.** Recall this means that portfolio owners, in deciding where to place their funds, consider only interest rates, exchange rates, and expected changes in exchange rates. They have no inherent preferences for investments in one currency over those in another, and no government regulations restrict capital flows among countries. With perfectly mobile capital, the interest parity conditions discussed in Chapter Twelve determine the pattern of international interest rates.

19.7   Macroeconomic Policy under Fixed Exchange Rates

Once we relax the assumption of a fixed price level, the economy contains **automatic adjustment mechanisms** (that is, mechanisms that do not require an active response from policy makers) for reaching a long-run equilibrium in which (1) the quantity demanded of domestic goods equals the quantity supplied at full employment and (2) balance-of-payments equilibrium prevails. Changes in input prices and in the expected price level move the economy onto the long-run aggregate supply curve by shifting the medium-run supply curve until it intersects the aggregate demand curve at a point on the long-run supply curve. Changes in the money stock due to intervention in the foreign exchange market handle any imbalance in the country's international payments. A balance-of-payments surplus (deficit) causes a rise (fall) in the money stock that shifts the aggregate demand curve to restore balance-of-payments equilibrium. Therefore, the economy reaches long-run equilibrium only when these adjustment mechanisms have resolved problems of output, employment, and balance of payments.

The primary shortcoming of the automatic adjustment mechanisms is their lack of speed. The price level, in particular, may adjust quite slowly, keeping the economy off the long-run supply curve for relatively long periods. Given this possibility, an obvious question arises whether macroeconomic policies can speed up the adjustment process. In Chapter Sixteen, we saw that, with a *fixed* price level, fiscal policy can affect domestic output with a fixed exchange rate and perfectly mobile capital. Monetary policy, on the other hand, proved completely incapable of affecting output. Before examining the impact of price flexibility on those results, we briefly review the results themselves, discussed in detail in section 16.4 and summarized in Table 16.3.

19.7.1   A Basis for Comparison: Policy Effects with Fixed Prices

When prices are fixed, an expansionary fiscal policy raises income by generating a capital inflow and an increase in the money stock. The initial rise in government purchases raises income and, therefore, the demand for money. The interest rate rises to lower the quantity demanded of money to equal the (initially fixed) money stock.[10] Because of the high degree of capital mobility, the rise in the

---

[10]Under perfectly mobile capital, the interest rate cannot *actually* rise, because any upward movement of the interest rate generates capital inflows that drive it back to its original level. Such interest rate movements are *incipient*; that is, they would occur if capital flows did not respond. Rather than explicitly referring to the incipient nature of interest rate movements in each case, we shall simply say that the interest rate rises and causes a capital inflow. However, we must remember that, in the new long-run equilibrium, the real interest rate will be unchanged.

domestic interest rate brings about a capital inflow and causes a balance-of-payments surplus. The monetary authority must intervene to purchase the excess supply of foreign exchange at the pegged exchange rate, and the rise in the stock of foreign exchange reserves increases the domestic money stock. As the money stock rises, it offsets the initial interest rate rise; so investment does not decline. The net result: an increase in income with no change in the interest rate, making fiscal policy a very effective tool for raising income.[11] Note that the mechanism through which fiscal policy works is its ability to generate a rise in the money stock.

Monetary policy, in contrast, cannot alter income in an economy with fixed prices and exchange rates and perfectly mobile capital. Any rise in the money stock from an open market operation lowers the domestic interest rate and causes a capital outflow and a balance-of-payments deficit.[12] The central bank must then intervene to supply foreign exchange. The stock of foreign exchange reserves and the money stock fall, completely offsetting the initial expansionary effect of the open market purchase. Monetary policy cannot affect income because policy makers cannot use open market operations to alter the money stock—because of the offsetting changes that occur through the balance of payments under a fixed exchange rate regime.

Fiscal policy works through its ability to change the domestic money stock. Monetary policy itself, however, cannot change the money stock because of the constraint imposed by balance-of-payments equilibrium. How does the introduction of price flexibility alter these results? The already pessimistic conclusion about monetary policy remains unchanged, but the previously optimistic view of fiscal policy becomes a bit more pessimistic. In the medium-run, fiscal policy can alter income, but monetary policy cannot. Neither policy can affect real output in the long run, although fiscal policy continues to affect the price level. Because price flexibility is important primarily in assessing a policy's medium- and long-run effectiveness, we focus on permanent changes in the level of government spending and the domestic money stock.[13]

19.7.2 Fiscal Policy, Prices, and Output

We begin our initial analysis of fiscal policy from a point of long-run equilibrium (point 1 in Figure 19.8). In long-run equilibrium, the markets for goods and services, money, and foreign exchange are in equilibrium and everyone in the economy has adjusted fully to the actual price level (P_1).[14] A one-time permanent expansionary fiscal policy shifts the aggregate demand curve to the right from AD_1 to AD_2 (see section 19.3.2). The price level begins to rise. If some input prices do not adjust quickly,

---

[11]Of course, a contractionary fiscal policy would prove similarly effective in reducing income. We shall continue to analyze each policy from the expansionary perspective and leave the contractionary case to the reader as an exercise.

[12]Once again, changes in the interest rate are incipient under perfect capital mobility (see footnote 10).

[13]Section 17.3 highlights the different effects of temporary and permanent fiscal and monetary policies.

[14]Recall that the AD curve incorporates the IS, LM, and BOP lines, as shown in more detail in the chapter appendix.

Figure 19.8 □ **Effect of Expansionary Fiscal Policy with Flexible Prices, Fixed Exchange Rates, and Perfectly Mobile Capital**

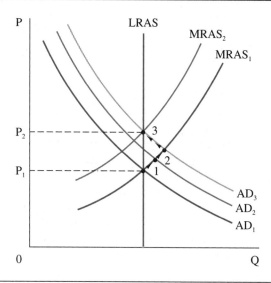

Beginning from a long-run equilibrium at point 1, an expansionary fiscal policy temporarily raises output. As firms and individuals adjust to the rise in the price level, the increase in output is offset, and the long-run effect is merely a rise in the price level.

or if some individuals or firms mistake the rise in all prices for a rise in a specific relative price, the quantity supplied of output increases, as illustrated by point 2. However, the economy cannot remain at point 2 in the long run for two reasons: (1) balance of payments disequilibrium, implying additional movement of AD, and (2) lack of full adjustment to the new price level, placing the economy off the long-run aggregate supply curve.

The balance of payments is in surplus at point 2, because the rise in income raised the demand for money with a fixed nominal money stock, implying a rise in the interest rate and a capital inflow. The resulting intervention increases the nominal money stock and shifts AD further to the right from AD_2 to AD_3. As individuals and firms in the economy gradually come to realize the price level has risen, and as input prices rise in response to output above full-employment level, the MRAS curve shifts upward until long-run equilibrium is restored on the LRAS curve at point 3. The net long-run effect of the expansionary fiscal policy is a rise in the price level (from P_1 to P_2) with no effect on real output.

If government purchases of goods and services increase while total output remains unchanged, some sectors of the economy must shrink. The growth of the public sector comes at the expense of other components of expenditure on goods and services. Because the rise in the domestic price level makes foreign goods relatively more attractive by raising the real exchange rate ($R \equiv P/eP^*$), export and import-competing industries in the domestic economy contract.[15]

Perhaps it is not surprising to find that an expansionary fiscal policy that begins from a point of long-run equilibrium and attempts to expand output beyond full employment fails in the long run. In fact, it is unclear why policy makers would pursue expansionary policies when output already is at full employment and can be raised further only by generating a rise in the price level that firms and individuals in the economy misinterpret or respond to slowly.[16] A more appropriate test of fiscal policy's effectiveness would be its ability to bring the economy into long-run equilibrium from a point of less than full employment. In other words, if an exogenous disturbance pushed the economy below full employment, could fiscal policy help restore output to its long-run equilibrium in a timely fashion?

Suppose policy makers executed an expansionary fiscal policy beginning at a point to the left of the LRAS curve to stimulate output. Could the policy then raise real output? The answer is *yes*, but the policy would still result in a rise in the price level. *(We leave the graphical demonstration to the reader.)* The domestic economy still experiences a real currency appreciation caused by the price-level increase, and the trade-oriented sectors still contract, but by less than the initial increase in government expenditure. This is important because the economy most needs expansionary fiscal policies during periods of below-full-employment output.

However, this more optimistic result requires a proviso. With flexible prices, the economy contains a mechanism with which to move *automatically* to the LRAS curve without using expansionary policies. At any point to the left of the LRAS curve, output is below its full-employment level. Less than full employment puts downward pressure on input prices. And as a lower-than-expected actual price level (including input prices) becomes known, the expected price level falls and the medium-run supply curve shifts downward to restore a long-run equilibrium on the LRAS curve. Unfortunately, this process may unfold quite slowly, leaving output and employment at a low level for extended periods. This presents a possible role for fiscal policy in speeding up adjustment by shifting AD upward rather than waiting for MRAS to shift downward.

Figure 19.9 compares the two alternative paths to long-run equilibrium. Beginning at point 1, with low output and employment, automatic adjustment through a reduction in input prices and the expected price level would gradually shift the MRAS curve down, bringing the economy into long-run equilibrium at point 2a. If, instead, policy makers pursue expansionary fiscal policy in an effort to speed up the return of output to its long-run level, the aggregate demand curve would shift upward to AD_2 and the price level would rise to P_2 at point 2b. Both scenarios

---

[15]The capital inflow maintains balance-of-payments equilibrium in the face of a move toward a deficit in the current account. Note that the real appreciation under a fixed exchange rate comes through a rise in P, with the nominal exchange rate and foreign price level fixed. We shall see later (section 19.9) that, under a flexible exchange rate, the real appreciation comes through a nominal currency appreciation with the domestic and foreign price levels fixed.

[16]Political business cycle theory suggests that politicians, prior to elections, have an incentive to engage in overly expansionary policies to generate higher employment and output in the short run. The long-run effect is inflation, but only *after* the election.

Figure 19.9 □ **Expansionary Fiscal Policy versus Automatic Adjustment**

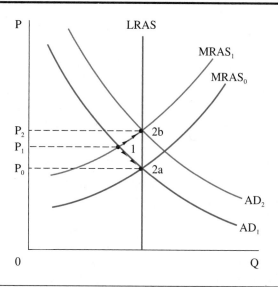

Beginning at point 1, expansionary fiscal policy brings the economy to a new long-run equilibrium at point 2b. Automatic adjustment leads to a long-run equilibrium at point 2a. In either case, the location of the long-run aggregate supply curve determines output. The equilibrium price level is higher in the case of expansionary fiscal policy (P_2) than in that of automatic adjustment (P_0).

would end with the same level of real output, but the final price level would be higher under the expansionary fiscal policy (P_2) than under automatic adjustment (P_0).

The primary reason for using expansionary fiscal policy in such a situation is that empirical evidence suggests that, at least sometimes, the automatic adjustment mechanism may work quite slowly, leaving output and employment low for a long period. The fiscal policy solution might be faster, at least ideally. However, as anyone who follows congressional debates on tax and spending policy knows, fiscal policy is hardly an instantaneous cure. In fact, many economists believe that by the time policy makers realize the need for an expansionary fiscal policy and implement it, the economy is likely to be well on the way to correcting itself through the admittedly slow process of price adjustment. If the expansionary policy arrives too late, the rightward shift of AD will push output above full employment and the price level will rise, as we saw in Figure 19.8.[17]

---

[17]We ignore some economists' even more fundamental argument that fiscal policy cannot shift the AD curve. The simplest version of this view is that increased government expenditures must imply eventual increased taxes to pay for them. If individuals in the economy realize that a rise in government spending means higher future taxes, they may reduce consumption expenditures to save to cover their expected tax liability. The reduction in consumption expenditures would offset the rise in government expenditures, leaving total expenditures and aggregate demand unchanged.

Although automatic adjustment and expansionary fiscal policy lead the economy to the same level of real output in Figure 19.9, the two alternatives imply different outcomes for other macroeconomic variables besides just the price level. Automatic adjustment lowers the price level to P_0, generates a real currency depreciation, improves the competitiveness of the country's export goods in world markets and its import-competing goods in domestic markets, and leads toward a surplus on the current account. Expansionary fiscal policy, on the other hand, raises the price level to P_2. The current account moves toward a deficit as the real currency appreciation makes domestic goods less competitive in world markets; and public expenditure rises to offset the decline in net exports of goods and services. These differential effects imply that various interest groups within the economy are likely to disagree about the appropriate policy.

19.7.3 Monetary Policy, Prices, and Output

Monetary policy cannot affect income with a fixed price level, a fixed exchange rate, and perfectly mobile capital. This conclusion continues to hold when we introduce price flexibility. Recall that the aggregate demand curve for the economy is drawn for a given value of the nominal money stock (see section 19.3.2). An open market purchase that attempts a one-time permanent expansion of the nominal money stock puts downward pressure on the interest rate and causes a capital outflow. The resulting balance-of-payments deficit requires foreign exchange market intervention by the central bank to supply foreign exchange. Foreign exchange reserves fall, and the money stock returns to its original level. Graphically, an open market purchase can shift the aggregate demand curve to the right (raising output and prices) only for the brief time interval between the initial expansionary policy and the offsetting loss of foreign exchange reserves.

Unlike the fiscal policy case, the pessimistic outlook for monetary policy with perfectly mobile capital does *not* depend on the output at which the policy experiment begins. Even if current output lies to the left of the LRAS curve, where the economy operates at less than full employment, the balance-of-payments constraint on the money stock still prevents monetary policy from affecting income. This does *not* mean, however, that the economy remains stuck at low levels of output and employment indefinitely.

Again, price flexibility eventually restores output to its long-run, full-employment level. Output remains below the long-run level only so long as input prices fail to decline or the actual price level remains below the expected price level. As information about the price level spreads and input-price adjustments occur, the medium-run aggregate supply curve shifts downward to restore a long-run equilibrium. Therefore, so long as the price level is flexible, the **price adjustment mechanism** pushes output toward its long-run level, though not necessarily quickly. As for the balance of payments, the fixed exchange rate implies that the money stock adjusts through changes in foreign exchange reserves to equate the balance of payments.

19.7.4 Exchange Rate Policy, Prices, and Output

A third type of possible macroeconomic policy under a fixed exchange rate involves a permanent change in the exchange rate, such as a devaluation. Figure 19.10 illustrates the medium- and long-run effects of a devaluation.

Figure 19.10 □ **Effect of a Devaluation with Flexible Prices, Fixed Exchanged Rates, and Perfectly Mobile Capital**

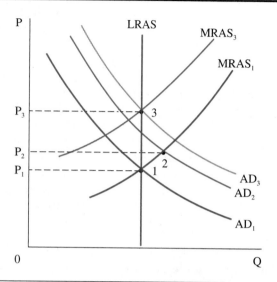

Beginning at point 1, a devaluation of the domestic currency lowers the relative price of domestic goods and services and switches expenditure toward them. The aggregate demand curve shifts to the right from AD_1 to AD_2. At point 2, the balance of payments is in surplus due to the devaluation. Intervention in the foreign exchange market increases the domestic money supply, and the aggregate demand curve shifts further to the right. The medium-run aggregate supply curve moves upward; long-run equilibrium is restored at point 3.

The story begins at point 1 with the economy in long-run equilibrium. A devaluation shifts the aggregate demand curve to the right from AD_1 to AD_2.[18] At point 2, the rise in the price level from P_1 to P_2 has reduced the real money stock, placing upward pressure on interest rates and generating a capital inflow. The combination of the capital inflow and the move toward a surplus on the current account due to the devaluation implies that the balance of payments exhibits a surplus at point 2. In the medium run, export and import-competing sectors gain from the decline in the relative price of domestically produced goods and services.

Under the fixed exchange rate regime, the central bank must intervene to buy foreign exchange, and the money stock rises with the accumulation of foreign exchange reserves. Aggregate demand shifts further to the right to AD_3. Output above full employment puts upward pressure on input prices, and the expected price level adjusts upward as information about rising prices spreads. These developments shift MRAS upward from $MRAS_1$ to $MRAS_3$. The new long-run equilibrium

---

[18]See section 19.3.2 for a review of the reasons why.

is at point 3. The domestic nominal money stock and the domestic price level have risen proportionally with the exchange rate. The real money stock remains unchanged *(Why?)*, as do the relative price of domestic and foreign goods *(Why?)* and the interest rate *(Why?)*. In the long run, distribution within the domestic economy as well as the overall level of output returns to its original configuration.[19]

What about the effects of a devaluation implemented when the economy's output has fallen below full employment? A devaluation can restore output to its full employment level, but only by generating a rise in the price level. The devaluation shifts the AD curve to the right by lowering the relative price of domestic goods and services, or causing a short-run real depreciation. As the price level begins to rise, the real money stock falls, putting upward pressure on the domestic interest rate. Capital inflows lead to a balance-of-payments surplus and require the central bank to intervene by buying foreign currency. The resulting increase in the domestic nominal money stock shifts the aggregate demand curve further to the right. The process ends when output is back at its full employment level, on the long-run aggregate supply curve. The devaluation's long-run effects include restoring full employment, increasing the domestic money stock, increasing the central bank's foreign exchange reserves, and a long-run real depreciation, because the price level rises less than proportionally with the initial devaluation.

The economy's response to a currency devaluation depends in part on the economy's history. When past policy has been overly expansionary and currency devaluations have been common responses to balance-of-payments crises, then a devaluation may cause foreign exchange market participants to expect further devaluations and further increases in the price level. If so, the medium-run aggregate supply curve may shift up following a devaluation, as input suppliers and firms try to protect themselves from losses due to future price increases. Then the response to the devaluation will be a bigger price increase and less growth in real output. However, if a country has a history of stable prices and if past devaluations have been rare events, a devaluation is likely to have less effect on price expectations, keeping the medium-run aggregate supply curve more stable. Such conditions lead to a longer-lasting effect on real output from a currency devaluation.

19.7.5 Summary of Long-Run Policy Effects

Table 19.3 summarizes the long-run effects of one-time permanent fiscal, monetary, and exchange rate policies under a fixed exchange rate with perfectly mobile capital. The table assumes the policies pursued are expansionary ones; switching the nonzero signs in the table would be appropriate to evaluate the effects of contractionary policies. Note that whether the policy is initiated from a point of full employment affects

---

[19] We shall see that devaluations and revaluations under a fixed exchange rate regime have identical effects, respectively, as increases and decreases in the nominal money stock under a flexible exchange rate regime (section 19.9). This should not come as a surprise, because a fixed exchange rate requires policy makers to surrender their ability to control the nominal money stock in order to control the exchange rate, while a flexible rate requires that they surrender control over the exchange rate to gain control over the nominal money stock.

Table 19.3 □ **Long-Run Effects of Expansionary Policies under a Fixed Exchange Rate**

Policy	Effect on					
	Q	P	i	e	R	CAB
Fiscal						
Initiated on LRAS	0	+	0	0	+	−
Initiated to left of LRAS	+	+	0	0	+	−
Monetary						
Initiated on LRAS	0	0	0	0	0	0
Initiated to left of LRAS	0	0	0	0	0	0
Exchange Rate						
Initiated on LRAS	0	+[a]	0	+	0	0
Initiated to left of LRAS	+	+	0	+	−	+

[a]Proportional to initial policy.

the long-run impact of fiscal and exchange rate policies. Monetary policies, in contrast, have no long-run impact on any economic variable reported in the table regardless of whether the economy is operating at full employment. This result reflects the fact that policy makers cannot alter the size of the domestic money stock under a fixed exchange rate regime.

19.8 Aggregate Demand under a Flexible Exchange Rate Regime

Just as it does under a fixed exchange rate regime, the aggregate demand curve under a flexible rate regime captures the negative relationship between the domestic price level and the quantity demanded of domestic goods and services.[20] Due to differences in how the economy adjusts to disturbances under the two types of regime, however, there are minor differences in the aggregate demand curve for each system, primarily in the variables held constant along a given aggregate demand curve. For simplicity, we continue to assume that capital is perfectly mobile among countries.

19.8.1 Slope of the Aggregate Demand Curve

The aggregate demand curve under a flexible exchange rate slopes downward for the same reasons that the aggregate demand curve under a fixed exchange rate

---

[20]In both cases, the aggregate demand curve incorporates the requirements for equilibrium in the goods, money, and foreign exchange markets; that is, the aggregate demand curve is derived from the IS, LM, and BOP curves. The chapter appendix illustrates the derivation.

does. First, a rise in the price level raises the relative price of domestic goods and shifts expenditure toward foreign goods. Second, a rise in the domestic price level (given the nominal money stock) lowers the real money stock, raises the domestic interest rate, lowers investment, and causes capital inflows and a currency appreciation.[21] Both mechanisms cause a rise in the price level to correspond with a fall in the quantity demanded of domestic goods and services. The difference in the aggregate demand curve under a flexible exchange rate arises because any change in the price level results in a change in the exchange rate.[22] Each aggregate demand curve is drawn taking these exchange rate changes into account; thus, the exchange rate is not held constant along an aggregate demand curve, as was the case under a fixed exchange rate system, but adjusts to maintain balance-of-payments equilibrium.

19.8.2 Shifts in the Aggregate Demand Curve

Although a number of variables are held constant along each aggregate demand curve, we shall focus on the effects of changes in the nominal money stock due to monetary policy and of changes in expenditure due to fiscal policy.

A one-time permanent increase in the nominal money stock (holding the price level constant) raises the real money stock and lowers the interest rate. The fall in the interest rate causes a capital outflow, which depreciates the domestic currency and lowers the relative price of domestic goods. This implies a larger quantity demanded of domestic goods *at each price level* when the nominal money stock rises, represented graphically by a rightward shift in the aggregate demand curve. *(Go through the logic in the opposite direction, beginning with a fall in the nominal money stock, to see why the result would be a leftward shift in AD.)*

It is tempting to conclude that a one-time permanent rise in government expenditure would shift the AD curve to the right in a manner similar to the effect of a rise in the money stock. However, this conclusion would be incorrect: Such changes in government expenditure have *no* effect on aggregate demand under a flexible exchange rate and perfect capital mobility. When government expenditure rises, any expansionary effect on income raises the quantity demanded of money. But because the money stock remains fixed, the interest rate must rise to make individuals content to hold only the available stock of real balances. With perfectly mobile capital, the rise in the interest rate brings in capital flows that appreciate the domestic currency and raise the relative price of domestic goods. Net exports respond to the rise in relative prices by falling enough to offset the initial increase in government expenditure. Total demand remains unchanged, but spending shifts from the trade-oriented sector (export and import-competing industries) to the public sector.

---

[21]Since we continue to operate under the assumption of perfectly mobile capital, changes in the interest rate are incipient just as under a fixed exchange rate.

[22]For details, see section 19A.2 in the chapter appendix.

19.9   Macroeconomic Policies under Flexible Exchange Rates

19.9.1   Automatic Adjustment Mechanisms

When both the price level and the exchange rate are flexible, the economy contains automatic adjustment mechanisms for bringing it into equilibrium on the long-run supply curve with balanced payments. The price level adjusts to equate the quantity demanded of domestic goods and services with the quantity supplied at full employment, and the exchange rate adjusts to bring the balance of payments into equilibrium.

As in the case of fixed exchange rates, the automatic adjustment mechanisms may work slowly, especially the price adjustment mechanism. This can be particularly troublesome when shocks push the economy to the left of the long-run aggregate supply curve, to low output and employment levels.[23] In such a situation, the question again arises whether an expansionary macroeconomic policy can speed up the economy's movement toward long-run equilibrium, minimizing the loss of output and the costs of unemployment.

19.9.2   A Basis for Comparison: Policy Effects with Fixed Prices

In the short-run, when the price level is fixed, fiscal policy cannot affect income but monetary policy can under a flexible exchange rate and perfectly mobile capital.[24] Fiscal policy fails in this case, because it generates movements in the real exchange rate that cause an *offsetting* shift between spending on domestic and foreign goods. For example, an expansionary fiscal policy generates a real domestic currency appreciation, raises the relative price of domestic goods, and shifts spending toward foreign goods. The overall level of output remains unchanged, although interest groups associated with trade (that is, export and import-competing industries) lose and spending shifts from the private to the public sector of the economy. The current account moves toward a deficit. Monetary policy, in contrast, succeeds because it generates a movement in the exchange rate that causes a *reinforcing* shift between spending on domestic and foreign goods. An expansionary monetary policy depreciates the domestic currency in real terms, lowering the relative price of domestic goods in the short run, and shifting expenditure toward them. The current account moves toward a surplus.

19.9.3   Macroeconomic Policy, Prices, and Output

Within the aggregate demand–aggregate supply framework, a policy clearly must shift the aggregate demand curve if it is to affect income.[25] Section 19.8.2 argued that

---

[23]The basic form of the aggregate supply curve is unchanged by the move from a fixed to a flexible exchange rate regime.

[24]Section 17.3 discusses these results at length, and Table 17.2 summarizes them.

[25]We ignore the possibility of "supply-side" policies that alter the position of the medium-run and/or long-run aggregate supply curve. Monetary and fiscal policy do not affect the supply curves directly, although they may shift the MRAS curve indirectly through their effects on the expected price level.

monetary but not fiscal policy can shift the aggregate demand curve under a flexible exchange rate and perfectly mobile capital. In fact, this is just another way of saying that with a fixed price level monetary policy can affect income but fiscal policy cannot. Recall that when the price level is fixed, aggregate demand completely determines income, so any policy that can shift aggregate demand can affect income as long as the price level is fixed. A one-time permanent fiscal expansion fails because it generates a nominal and real appreciation of the domestic currency that exactly offsets the policy's potential effect on output.[26]

Because fiscal policy is ruled out by its inability to shift the aggregate demand curve, we shall concentrate on the possibility of using monetary policy. Beginning from a point of long-run equilibrium, consider the impact of an open market purchase that raises the nominal money stock and shifts the AD curve to the right as illustrated in Figure 19.11. The rise in aggregate demand causes a rise in the price level. In the medium run, contractual rigidities may prevent some prices (for example, nominal wages) from adjusting quickly, and firms or individuals may mistake the price increase for a change in relative prices. Output climbs along $MRAS_1$.

What causes the quantity demanded of domestic goods to rise to match the temporarily higher output level? Domestic goods become temporarily cheaper relative to foreign goods even though the domestic price level has risen. This is caused by the depreciation of the domestic currency. Because the relative price of domestic goods is defined as $R \equiv P/eP^*$, a rise in e can more than offset a rise in P, lowering the relative price of domestic goods. We know that in the long run, P and e must rise proportionally with M, but in the short and medium runs, the price level lags behind, so the rise in e temporarily represents a real as well as a nominal depreciation.

The rise in output occurs either because of confusion over a change in the price level versus a change in the relative price that a firm receives for its output or because input prices fail to rise immediately. When firms and labor suppliers realize that the price level (including the prices of inputs) has risen and adjust their behavior accordingly, the medium-run supply curve shifts upward and output returns to its original level. As the price level rises to P_2, the relative price of domestic goods returns to its original level, with the total rise in P just matching the overall depreciation of the domestic currency and leaving R unchanged. The domestic interest rate also returns to its original level as the price level catches up with the increase in M. In the long run, the sole remaining effects of the expansionary monetary policy are a proportionally higher price level and a proportionally depreciated domestic currency. Note that these policy results match those of a currency devaluation under a fixed exchange rate.[27]

Exchange Rate Overshooting

The economy's adjustment to the new long-run equilibrium following an expansionary monetary policy reveals an interesting and important phenomenon known as

---

[26]Note that under a fixed exchange rate, the real appreciation caused by a fiscal expansion works through a rise in P with no change in e. Under a flexible exchange rate, the real appreciation caused by a fiscal expansion works through a nominal appreciation with no change in P. See footnote 15 above.

[27]See footnote 19 above.

Figure 19.11 ▫ **Effect of Expansionary Monetary Policy with Flexible Prices, Flexible Exchange Rates, and Perfectly Mobile Capital**

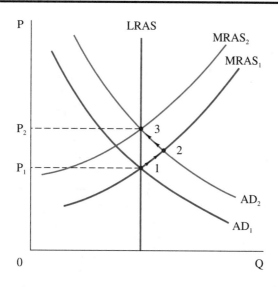

Beginning from a point of long-run equilibrium such as 1, expansionary monetary policy is able to raise output, but only temporarily. As the accompanying rise in the price level is recognized and adjusted to, output falls back to its original level. The long-run effect of the expansionary policy consists solely of a rise in the price level and a domestic currency depreciation.

exchange rate overshooting. **Overshooting** occurs when a variable responds to a disturbance more in the medium run than it does in the long run. Overshooting phenomena tend to occur whenever one variable adjusts more quickly to a disturbance than another variable. Our model of the macroeconomy suggests that the exchange rate and interest rate adjust more quickly than do prices, which tend to be somewhat sluggish because of incomplete information and long-term contracts. In the case of a one-time permanent monetary expansion under a flexible exchange rate regime with perfectly mobile capital, the domestic currency depreciates sharply in the medium run and then undergoes a partially offsetting appreciation as the price level adjusts.

To understand exchange rate overshooting, we must begin from the interest parity condition and trace the effect of the expansionary monetary policy on each of the relevant variables. Equation 19.1 repeats the uncovered interest parity condition from section 12.4:

$$i - i^* = (e^e - e)/e. \qquad [19.1]$$

For simplicity, we assume that the story begins at a point where $e^e = e$ and, therefore, $i = i^*$. The foreign interest rate, i^*, remains constant throughout the whole process.

Because the monetary policy is recognized as permanent, the expected exchange rate, e^e, moves immediately to its new long-run level, which equals the value that the actual exchange rate will have at the new long-run equilibrium (point 3 in Figure 19.11). In the medium run following the monetary expansion, i falls because P rises by less than M, resulting in a rise in the real money stock. But if $i < i^*$ at point 2, it must be true that $e > e^e$ at point 2. *(Why?)* Since e^e equals the new long-run equilibrium value of e at point 3, it follows that e is higher at point 2 than at point 3. The monetary expansion generates a medium-run depreciation of the domestic currency that exceeds the long-run depreciation. In other words, the domestic currency *appreciates* in the adjustment from point 2 to point 3!

Why does overshooting depend on the slow adjustment of the price level? If the monetary expansion caused the price level to rise immediately to P_2, the real money supply would not rise, even in the medium run. The domestic interest rate would not fall below the foreign interest rate, and a period of $e > e^e$ would not be necessary to maintain interest parity.

Again the outlook for expansionary monetary policy beginning from a point of long-run equilibrium is pessimistic. However, a more important issue concerns its ability to move the economy to equilibrium from a point of low output and employment (to the left of the long-run aggregate supply curve). Figure 19.12 demonstrates that expansionary monetary policy can move the economy into equilibrium, but only at the cost of a rise in the price level. At point 1, the economy suffers from low output and employment. An expansionary monetary policy shifts the AD curve to the right. The price level rises, and output returns to its long-run level at point 2a. The alternative course involves reliance on the economy's automatic adjustment mechanism. In that case, below-full-employment output eventually causes input prices to fall and individuals in the economy to adjust downward their price-level expectations. The medium-run supply curve shifts downward, restoring output to its long-run level at point 2b—at a price level lower than that in the case of expansionary monetary policy.

19.9.4 Summary of Long-Run Policy Effects

Table 19.4 summarizes the long-run effects of one-time permanent expansionary fiscal and monetary policies under a flexible exchange rate, flexible prices, and perfectly mobile capital.[28] Fiscal policy exerts no long-run effects on output, the price level, or the interest rate. An expansionary fiscal policy generates a nominal and real appreciation of the domestic currency that shifts the current account toward a deficit and reduces expenditure by the amount of the initial fiscal expansion.

Monetary policy, in contrast, can affect output, although only if instituted after some disturbance has pushed the economy away from long-run equilibrium. Otherwise, expansionary monetary policy leads only to a proportional increase in the price level and the nominal exchange rate, with no effect on output, the real exchange rate, or the current-account balance.

---

[28]For contractionary policies, simply switch the signs of all non-zero entries in the table.

Figure 19.12 ▫ **Expansionary Monetary Policy versus Automatic Adjustment**

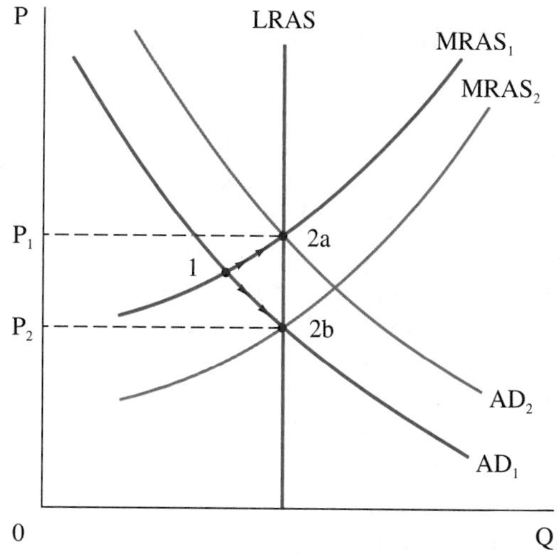

Beginning from point 1, expansionary monetary policy leads to a long-run equilibrium at point 2a with price level P_1. Automatic adjustment leads to a long-run equilibrium at 2b with price level P_2.

19.10 Supply Shocks

So far, we have considered how the macroeconomy responds to shifts in the aggregate *demand* curve, shifts that may reflect either exogenous shocks or policy makers' efforts to influence the economy. We have assumed the long-run aggregate supply curve remains stable throughout the adjustment process and that the medium-run aggregate supply curve shifts as input prices and price expectations adjust up or down in response

Table 19.4 ▫ **Long-Run Effects of Expansionary Policies under a Flexible Exchange Rate**

Policy	Effect on					
	Q	P	i	e	R	CAB
Fiscal:						
Initiated on LRAS	0	0	0	−	+	−
Initiated to left of LRAS	0	0	0	−	+	−
Monetary:						
Initiated on LRAS	0	+[a]	0	+[a]	0	0
Initiated to left of LRAS	+	+	0	+	−	+

[a]Proportional to initial policy.

to shifts in aggregate demand. Our discussion thus far has ignored the second major source of macroeconomic disturbances and the second major set of events to which policy makers must respond: **supply shocks.** Such shocks include any event that alters the economy's long-run equilibrium productive capacity.[29] Any newspaper suggests many possible examples, such as earthquakes, floods, and wars. The OPEC oil embargoes of the 1970s provide the cases most often examined by macroeconomists. For now, we focus on the effects of a generic supply shock.

Point 1 in Figure 19.13 represents an economy in long-run equilibrium at the intersection of AD_0, $MRAS_0$, and $LRAS_0$. Output is at its full employment level, Q_0; and all prices have adjusted fully to long-run equilibrium in their respective markets, with an overall price level of P_1. Now suppose an adverse supply shock hits the economy and reduces its ability to produce goods and services. Both the medium-run and long-run supply curves shift to the left, although the relative magnitudes of the two shifts depends on the exact nature of the shock.

If policy makers do not respond immediately to the decline in supply, the economy moves to point 2, at the intersection of the original aggregate demand curve and the new medium-run aggregate supply curve, $MRAS_1$. The price level rises sharply to P_2. The increase in price cuts the quantity demanded of domestic goods and services, along AD_0, to match the curtailed supply. This combination of rising prices and declining output often is called **stagflation.**

What happens next depends on how policy makers respond. We can outline four basic possibilities, ranging from the most passive to the most active responses. First, macroeconomic policy makers can choose to do nothing to alter aggregate demand. From point 2, to the left of the new long-run aggregate supply curve, $LRAS_1$, input prices would fall in response to the less than full-employment level of output. The medium-run aggregate supply curve eventually would shift down with input prices, and a new long-run equilibrium would occur at point 3a. Output would be lower than prior to the supply shock, but this is inevitable, and the price level (P_a) would be higher.

A more active response by policy makers would involve an expansionary policy to shift aggregate demand to the right to AD_1, rather than waiting for unemployment to shift the medium-run aggregate supply curve down. An expansionary policy would restore long-run equilibrium at point 3b. Again, real output is lower than before the shock; and the price level rises to P_b, more than in the case where policy makers chose to avoid an expansionary policy.

Policy makers also might follow an even more aggressively expansionary policy in an attempt to restore real output to its preshock value. By shifting aggregate demand all the way up to AD_2, policy makers could accomplish this goal at point 3c, but only temporarily. Because the new postshock, full-employment output is Q_1, not Q_0, their attempts to keep output at Q_0 eventually cause the price level to rise to P_c as the medium-run aggregate supply curve shifts up. Point 4c denotes the new long-run equilibrium under this scenario.

---

[29]Temporary supply shocks that shift the medium-run supply curve to the left but leave the long-run supply curve unaffected also are possible. We restrict our attention to supply shocks that impact the economy's long-run ability to produce goods and services.

Figure 19.13 ▫ **An Adverse Supply Shock and Potential Policy Responses**

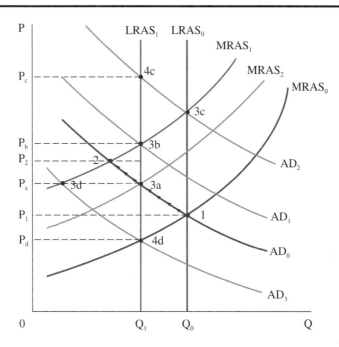

An adverse supply shock shifts the medium- and long-run aggregate supply curves to the left. Policy makers can choose from several policy options. First, they can leave AD unchanged at AD_0, so the new long-run equilibrium occurs at point 3a. Second, they can expand AD to AD_1 to speed the economy's return to full employment at point 3b, but such a policy raises prices. Third, policy makers can expand AD by more (to AD_2) and push output back to its preshock level, but only temporarily. The long-term cost of this aggressively expansionary policy is a much higher price level at point 4c. Finally, policy makers can contract AD to AD_3 and restore long-run equilibrium at point 4d. This keeps prices down but requires an extended period of exacerbated unemployment (at 3d). Regardless of policy makers' choice, the new long-run, full-employment output is at the lower Q_1.

A final possibility involves policy makers pursuing policies designed to prevent a rise in the price level. For example, beginning from point 2, they could *cut* aggregate demand to AD_3. In the medium run, output would fall even further, to point 3d. Eventually, as input prices and price expectations adjusted, the MRAS curve would shift down and the economy would reach a new long-run equilibrium at point 4d, with prices at P_d, slightly below the preshock value.

The four policy paths just outlined suggest the menu of possibilities facing policy makers in the aftermath of the OPEC oil embargoes of 1973–1974 and 1979–1980. The first shock, during which oil prices quadrupled, occurred shortly after the breakdown of the Bretton Woods system of pegged exchange rates. Many economists believe that the flexibility of exchange rates played an important role in facilitating adjustment to the shocks. Under a fixed-rate system, countries' abilities to choose among the various policy responses would have been constrained by the need to intervene in foreign exchange markets to prevent appreciations or depreciations of their currencies. Alternatively, a system of fixed exchange rates would have ruled out monetary policy as a tool for shifting aggregate demand in response to the supply shocks. But because exchange rates were flexible, most countries responded with monetary policies, although the degrees of expansion pursued by different countries varied substantially.

Case One
Recent Macroeconomic Performance in the United States

The theory developed in this chapter suggests that real output tends toward a long-run level represented by the long-run aggregate supply curve regardless of the behavior of the price level. Macroeconomic policies may cause medium-run movements off the long-run supply curve, but the automatic adjustment mechanism works, through price flexibility, to restore equilibrium. In this case, we briefly examine the recent macroeconomic performance of the United States to see whether the implications of the aggregate demand and supply framework appear to hold.

Recall that in developing the supply curves for an open economy, we ignored the process of growth through which increases in the quantity of resources available and in the production technology boost the economy's long-run equilibrium output. This simplifying assumption enabled us to draw a single long-run aggregate supply curve for the time horizon of a few years relevant for most macroeconomic policy making. When we take the growth process into account, the long-run supply curve drifts to the right as the economy's productive capacity grows, perhaps interrupted occasionally by adverse supply shocks of the type we examined in section 19.10.

To evaluate the recent macroeconomic performance of the United States, we must make an adjustment for economic growth to allow us to discern any fluctuations of output *around* its long-run upward trend. Recent historical evidence from a number of industrial economies has led economists to estimate the countries' long-run growth rates at an average of about 2 percentage points per year. Therefore, to obtain the real output data presented in Figure 19.14, we subtracted 2 percentage points from each year's annual growth in real gross domestic product. The remaining growth (which can be negative) roughly estimates the change in real GDP around its long-run upward trend. To facilitate comparison with the aggregate demand and supply framework developed in the chapter, Figure 19.14 presents real output, or real GDP, on the horizontal axis and the price level, or GDP deflator, on the vertical axis. We measure both real output and the price level as indices. The real output index equals 100 in 1973, and the price index equals 100 in 1987.

Once corrected for the growth trend, U.S. real output seems to fluctuate around a fairly stable output level despite increases in the price level. This evidence, though cursory,

Figure 19.14 □ **Macroeconomic Performance in the United States, 1973–1994**

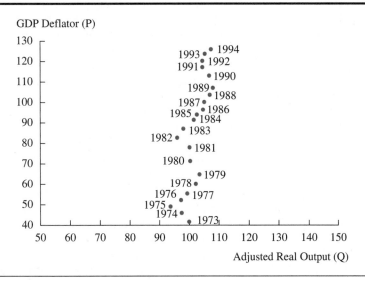

GDP Deflator (P)

Adjusted Real Output (Q)

In the long run, adjusted real GDP does not depend on the price level.

Source: *Economic Report of the President 1995.* Data were adjusted for the growth in potential output by subtracting 2 percentage points from the growth rate of real GDP.

appears to support the basic idea developed in the chapter: that various disturbances and policies may drive the economy away from its long-run output, but only temporarily.

Case Two
Inflation Culture in Brazil

Brazilian annual inflation in 1990 was 2,739 percent. After falling to a mere 414 percent in 1991, inflation reignited to 2,103 percent in 1993. During the last 15 years, by one account, Brazil has had eight monetary stabilization plans, four currencies, 11 inflation measures, five price and wage freezes, 14 wage policies, 18 changes in foreign exchange rules, 54 changes in price-control guidelines, 21 foreign-debt proposals, and 19 decrees on the need for fiscal austerity.[30] As of 1994, none had worked.

With the reported inflation rates, one might predict that stopping inflation would be economic priority number one in Brazil. However, the long history of failed policies makes trying for success painful and difficult. To understand why, recall that a rise in

[30]See Thomas Kamm, "Brazil's Efforts to Curb Inflation Face Hurdle: A Lot of People Like It," *The Wall Street Journal,* March 29, 1991.

the *expected* price level shifts the medium-run aggregate supply curve upward. Suppose policy makers began to follow through on one of their promises to curtail the excessive growth of aggregate demand. The long history of erratic policy and failed reforms implies that most individuals in the economy would continue to expect inflation. The result—a stationary aggregate demand curve combined with an upward shifting medium-run aggregate supply curve produces the painful combination known as stagflation, or falling real output and employment along with continued inflation. *(Use an aggregate demand–aggregate supply diagram to illustrate this phenomenon.)* Once inflationary expectations become embedded in an economy, eliminating inflation inevitably carries a higher cost in terms of reduced output.

Early in 1994, Brazil embarked on its sixth major anti-inflation policy in seven years, the Real Plan. It included reduced government spending, increased taxes, and a new currency, the real, pegged to the U.S. dollar. The role of reduced government spending and increased taxes is obvious; both represent contractionary fiscal policies that attempt to halt the continual rightward shift of the aggregate demand curve that leads to high and rising inflation. The new currency, with its fixed exchange rate, would provide discipline against overly expansionary monetary policy.

On its first anniversary, in mid-1995, most analysts judged the Real Plan the most effective of Brazil's many attempts at macroeconomic reform. The *monthly* inflation rate had fallen from 50 percent to 2 percent. But hard issues remained, in particular the need to reduce the role of **indexation** in the economy. Most wages, contracts, and tax payments are indexed in many countries with histories of inflation problems similar to Brazil's. This means the nominal amounts are adjusted automatically for inflation, keeping real values constant. Such indexation, while reducing some of the costs of inflation to individuals and firms, hampers the adjustment of relative prices within the economy. Indexation can also provide a mechanism for the wealthy and the politically influential, who are more likely to be able to negotiate attractive indexation provisions, to avoid many of the costs of inflation and, in some cases, even to profit from it. Other items on Brazil's reform agenda include institutional reform, to ensure that the cuts in government spending will not be reversed, and the privatization of a large state-owned sector of the economy.

Case Three
The History of Inflation[31]

In recent years, most countries have experienced some inflation, although a few such as Argentina, Brazil, Peru, (former) Yugoslavia, and Zaire stand out for their dramatic price increases. The price level in most industrial countries has risen in most years since the end of the Great Depression of the 1930s. Despite this recent experience, inflation is not the historical norm. Before 1933, prices fell in more years than they

---

[31]Information reported in this case comes from "A Short History of Inflation," *The Economist,* February 22, 1992, 68.

Figure 19.15 □ **British Consumer Prices, 1661–1990 (1661 = 100)**

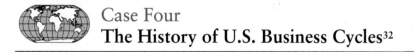

Source: *The Economist*, February 22, 1992, p. 68.

rose in both Britain and the United States. In the United States, prices fell by 40 percent between 1820 and 1900, more than doubled during the First World War, and by 1930 fell back to their 1820 level. In Britain from the late seventeenth century to the Great Depression, on only six occasions did prices rise for more than three years in a row. By 1933, prices had hardly changed from their 1660 levels. Figure 19.15 dramatizes the relative stability of prices in Britain before the Second World War.

Case Four
The History of U.S. Business Cycles[32]

Case Three suggests that inflation has become much more pronounced since the end of the Second World War—at least in the United States and Britain. Does the

---

[32]Background material for this case comes from "Taking the Business Cycle's Pulse," *The Economist,* October 28, 1995, 89–90.

Figure 19.16 □ U.S. Gross Domestic Product, 1875–1995 (Percent Change from Previous Quarter)

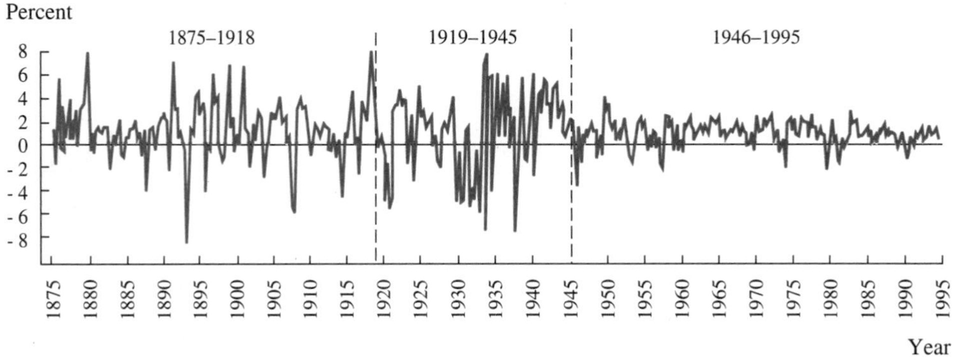

Source: *The Economist,* October 28, 1995, p. 89; data from Victor Zarnowitz, "Business Cycles," National Bureau of Economic Research.

same trend apply to output? At least for the case of the United States, the answer is *no.* Figure 19.16 traces changes in U.S. gross domestic product, measured as percent changes from the previous quarter, since 1875. As the figure makes clear, economic booms and busts come in many magnitudes and durations. But one trend stands out in the figure: Since 1945, the magnitude of swings in GDP has been substantially smaller than in the period prior to the First World War or in the period between the wars. In fact, the volatility of quarterly changes in U.S. GDP since 1945 has been only about a third the level that characterized 1919–1945.[33]

Why might business cycles have become less severe? Only since the Second World War have policy makers in the United States recognized management of the macroeconomy and the pursuit of full employment as major government responsibilities. While economists differ in their evaluation of how good a job policy makers have done in actively managing the economy, some innovations such as deposit insurance to avoid banking crises and automatic stabilizers (that is, tax and spending programs that adjust automatically to the state of the economy) no doubt deserve some credit for the economy's performance. Other possible contributing factors include the growing role that services, as opposed to goods, play in the economy, as well as the inventory-smoothing effects of improved transportation and communication technologies that allow firms to manage their inventories more effectively.

The National Bureau of Economic Research, an economic research institute in Cambridge, Massachusetts, officially designates periods of expansion and recession in the United States. Since the end of the Second World War, recessions have lasted 11 months on average and expansions 50 months. Figure 19.17 summarizes the post-war experience.

---

[33]Not all economists agree. Lack of data availability over long time horizons makes long-term comparisons notoriously difficult and unreliable.

Figure 19.17 □ **Postwar U.S. Business-Cycle Expansions and Recessions**

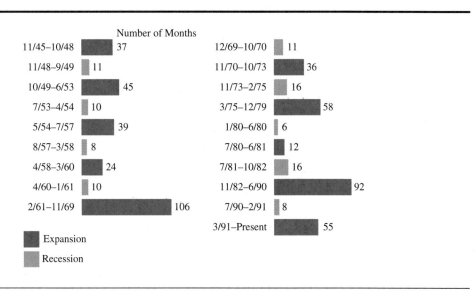

Number of Months

11/45–10/48 37	12/69–10/70 11
11/48–9/49 11	11/70–10/73 36
10/49–6/53 45	11/73–2/75 16
7/53–4/54 10	3/75–12/79 58
5/54–7/57 39	1/80–6/80 6
8/57–3/58 8	7/80–6/81 12
4/58–3/60 24	7/81–10/82 16
4/60–1/61 10	11/82–6/90 92
2/61–11/69 106	7/90–2/91 8
	3/91–Present 55

■ Expansion
▪ Recession

Source: Data from Victor Zarnowitz, "Business Cycles," National Bureau of Economic Research.

Summary

The introduction of price flexibility in this chapter has three major implications:

1. The economy now contains an automatic adjustment mechanism for bringing output to its long-run equilibrium level at full employment, unlike the situations of chronic internal imbalance in Chapters Sixteen and Seventeen.

2. The remaining effective tools of macroeconomic policy (fiscal policy and exchange rate under fixed exchange rates and monetary policy under flexible exchange rates) can permanently increase output *only* if the economy is operating temporarily to the left of the long-run aggregate supply curve and *only* by raising the price level.

3. Fiscal and monetary policy, if pursued beginning from a point of long-run equilibrium, can permanently affect only the price level and not the level of real output or employment.

Table 19.5 summarizes the policy results derived in the chapter.

Looking Ahead

We have seen that the effectiveness of various macroeconomic policies critically depends on the exchange rate regime under which the economy operates. Recall from Chapters Sixteen and Seventeen that countries manage their exchange rates in

Table 19.5 □ **Policy Effectiveness in Altering Output with Flexible Prices and Capital Mobility**

Policy	Fixed Rate Regime	Flexible Rate Regime
If Instituted Beginning at Point of Long-Run Equilibrium		
Fiscal		
Medium run	Effective[a]	Ineffective
Long run	Ineffective[a]	Ineffective
Monetary		
Medium run	Ineffective	Effective[a]
Long run	Ineffective	Ineffective[a]
If Instituted at Point to Left of Long-Run Equilibrium		
Fiscal		
Medium run	Effective[a]	Ineffective
Long run	Effective[a]	Ineffective
Monetary		
Medium run	Ineffective	Effective[a]
Long run	Ineffective	Effective[a]

[a]Results accompanied by changes in the price level.

a variety of ways, ranging from a fixed to a purely flexible exchange rate. Chapter Twenty traces recent macroeconomic history, considers the major arguments regarding the choice of exchange rate regime, and explores several possible arrangements other than a simple fixed or flexible rate.

Key Terms

inflation
deflation
aggregate demand curve
aggregate supply
short run
medium run
long run
long-run aggregate supply curve

medium-run aggregate supply curve
perfectly mobile capital
automatic adjustment mechanisms
price adjustment mechanism
overshooting
supply shocks
stagflation
indexation

Problems and Questions for Review

1. Use the aggregate demand–aggregate supply model to analyze the following policy dispute. The country involved is an open economy with perfectly mobile capital

and a fixed exchange rate. The economy currently operates at a long-run equilibrium, including the balance of payments.

(a) *Policy maker 1:* "We need to expand real output and lower the unemployment rate. If only we had a flexible exchange rate, we could undertake an expansionary monetary policy that would have the desired effect. But, since our exchange rate is fixed, there is no way we can expand our money stock."

(b) *Policy maker 2:* "There are two things wrong with your argument. First, it *is* possible to increase our money stock even though our exchange rate is fixed; all we have to do is devalue our currency. Second, if we follow such a policy, the increase in real output and decrease in unemployment will be a medium-run effect only. In the long run, all it will accomplish is a rise in the price level."

2. This question asks you to examine the relationship between an economy's openness and the effects of fiscal policy.

(a) Country A is a closed economy. It engages in no transactions with other countries, so its current-account and capital-account balances always equal zero. Country A pursues an expansionary fiscal policy of cutting taxes and increasing government purchases. Illustrate and explain the effects of the policy on real output and on the price level in the medium run and in the long run. What is the effect on the interest rate? What are the long-run distributional effects of the policy?

(b) Country B is an open economy. It engages in trade in goods, services, and financial assets. It operates under a flexible exchange rate regime and has perfectly mobile capital. Country B pursues an expansionary fiscal policy of cutting taxes and increasing government purchases. Illustrate and explain the effects of the policy on real output and on the price level in the medium run and in the long run. What is the effect on the interest rate? What are the long-run distributional effects of the policy?

(c) Compare the effects of expansionary fiscal policies in countries A and B. (Assume that the two follow identical, neutral monetary policies that can be ignored for purposes of this analysis.) As an economy becomes more open, how do the effects (especially the distributional effects) of fiscal policy change?

(d) In the early 1980s, the United States followed an expansionary fiscal policy of lower taxes and increased government purchases. Policy makers seemed surprised by two characteristics of the period, in comparison with earlier experience. First, the U.S. trade balance moved sharply into deficit. Second, private investment remained relatively high. Given your answers to parts (a), (b), and (c), can you explain the two observations? Should they have come as a surprise?

One of the major recent events in the international monetary system has been the unification of Germany and the accompanying macroeconomic adjustment. The next two questions ask you to analyze two aspects of that process.

3. One aspect of the unification that had to be dealt with was the East German currency, the ostmark, which had been nonconvertible. Black market prices suggested that the market value of the ostmark relative to other currencies was about 10 percent of its official (East German) price or exchange rate. As a part of unification, (West) Germany decided to intervene in the foreign exchange market to buy up the ostmarks. But policy makers had to decide at what price to purchase the currency. Consider three possibilities: (i) buy the ostmarks at the black market price of approximately DM0.08 per ostmark, (ii) buy the ostmarks at the official East German exchange rate of DM1.00 per ostmark, or (iii) buy the ostmarks at an intermediate value of DM0.50 per ostmark.

   (a) Write the expression for a country's money stock as a function of the assets held by the central bank.

   (b) What would be the effects of the three cases of intervention listed above on the German money stock? (Hint: Remember that the foreign exchange reserve component of the monetary base is expressed in units of the *domestic* currency (the DM in the case of West Germany). For example, if the U.S. Federal Reserve buys one pound sterling at an exchange rate of two dollars per pound, the foreign exchange reserve component of the U.S. monetary base rises by two dollars.)

   (c) Assume that Germany decided to go with option (ii) and exchanged ostmarks for Deutsche marks at a one-for-one exchange rate. This might raise serious questions about inflation in historically inflation-conscious Germany. Illustrate and explain the logic behind this concern. Assume that unified Germany uses a flexible exchange rate and has perfectly mobile capital.

4. A second aspect of German unification concerned the supply or production side of the economy. East German factories were notoriously inefficient after years of central planning. Before unification, East German workers were paid in ostmarks. After unification, those same workers were to be paid in Deutsche marks. Again, a decision had to be made how to translate ostmark-denominated wages into DM-denominated wages. This question asks you to analyze the macroeconomic effects of a decision to translate wages on a one-for-one basis; in other words, a worker who previously made 100 ostmarks per week now is paid 100 DM per week.

   (a) Remember that the real value of DM is much higher than the real value of ostmarks; therefore, the wage policy is equivalent to a large increase in real wages. Illustrate and explain the effects on real output and the price level of the change from ostmark wages to DM wages in the medium run. (Hint: How does a rise in real wages or other input prices affect the aggregate demand–aggregate supply model?)

   (b) Germany currently has unemployment, particularly in the "new states" of former East Germany. Is this surprising, or not, given your analysis in part (a)? Can you think of a wage policy (that is, an alternative to the one-for-one translation of ostmark wages into Deutsche mark wages) that might have resulted in less unemployment? Explain.

   (c) Given the one-for-one translation of wages, what adjustments would you expect to occur in the long run? Explain.

5. The countries of USia and Germania have flexible price levels, flexible exchange rates, and perfectly mobile capital.

   (a) The USia economy currently operates to the left of its long-run aggregate supply curve. USia has a large government debt, so policy makers decide to pursue expansionary monetary policy rather than fiscal policy. Illustrate, showing the initial position, the effect of the policy, and the new long-run equilibrium. Explain.

   (b) The Germania economy currently operates to the left of its long-run aggregate supply curve. Residents of Germania, for historical reasons, have an aversion to inflation. Germania has just undertaken political unification with a less-developed neighbor, and the unification involves substantial expansion of government expenditure on goods and services. Because of the expansionary fiscal policy, Germania's policy makers decide to hold the money stock constant rather than pursue expansionary monetary policy. Illustrate, showing the initial position, the effect of the fiscal policy, and the new long-run equilibrium. Explain.

   (c) Using your answers to parts (a) and (b), what would you expect to happen to the exchange rate between USia's currency (the dollie) and Germania's currency (the markie) in the medium run? What would you predict about the two countries' current and capital accounts? Explain.

6. In the early 1990s, the U.S. economy experienced a "shallow" or slow recovery from a recession. Discretionary policy took primarily the form of expansionary monetary policy—because of hesitancy to pursue further expansionary fiscal policy in the face of the already-large government budget deficit. However, the slow pace of the recovery put pressure on policy makers for expansionary fiscal policy. Which groups in the economy would you predict would support expansionary fiscal policy? Which groups would counsel against expansionary fiscal policy and favor continued reliance on monetary policy to support the recovery? Why?

7. This questions asks you to analyze the effects of a currency devaluation.

   (a) Trustia is a country with perfectly mobile capital and a history of price stability. The government pegs Trustia's currency to the currency of an important trading partner. Trustia's policy makers, especially its central bankers, always do exactly what they say they will do. Unfortunately, Trustia's economy has fallen into a recession. Policy makers decide the appropriate response is a permanent, one-time devaluation of Trustia's currency, and they announce and enact such a policy. Illustrate and explain the devaluation's likely effects on Trustia's economy.

   (b) Messia is another country with perfectly mobile capital but a history of high inflation. The government pegs Messia's currency to the currency of an important trading partner. Messia's policy makers, especially its central bankers, rarely do what they say they will do, and the country has a long history of failed economic reforms. Unfortunately, Messia's economy has fallen into a recession. Policy makers postpone a devaluation as long as possible and deny publicly that they are even considering a devaluation. Finally, the central bank runs short of foreign exchange reserves and is forced to devalue. Illustrate and explain the likely effects of the devaluation on Messia's economy.

(c) Based on your answers to parts (a) and (b), is devaluation an effective policy tool for an economy operating under a fixed exchange rate and a high degree of capital mobility? Why, or why not?

8. Mediate the following dispute between two macroeconomic policy makers. The economy they are discussing operates under a flexible exchange rate and has perfectly mobile capital.

(a) *Policy maker 1:* "To increase real output, we should use expansionary fiscal policy. After all, the primary problem with fiscal policy is crowding out. But, because our country has perfectly mobile capital, expansionary fiscal policy can't push up the interest rate and discourage investment. Therefore, any increase in government purchases or any cut in taxes will go directly into increased real output."

(b) *Policy maker 2:* "You need to review the notes from your undergraduate macroeconomics course. Fiscal policy never works under a flexible exchange rate with perfectly mobile capital—an ideal combination to generate complete crowding out."

References and Selected Readings

Baxter, M. "International Trade and Business Cycles." In *Handbook of International Economics,* Vol. 3, edited by G. M. Grossman and K. Rogoff, 1801–1864. Amsterdam: North-Holland, 1995.
Up-to-date survey of empirical evidence on the relationship between macroeconomic cycles and international trade; intermediate to advanced.

Dornbusch, Rudiger, and Alberto Giovannini. "Monetary Policy in an Open Economy." In *Handbook of Monetary Economics,* Vol. 2, edited by B. M. Friedman and F. M. Hahn. Amsterdam: North-Holland, 1990.
Advanced treatment of the implications of openness for monetary policy.

Dotsey, Michael. "An Examination of International Trade Data in the 1980s." Federal Reserve Bank of Richmond *Economic Review* 75 (March–April 1989): 21–27.
Tests alternative hypotheses as explanations for the international macroeconomic events of the 1980s; for intermediate students.

Frankel, J. A., and A. K. Rose. "Empirical Research on Nominal Exchange Rates." In *Handbook of International Economics,* Vol. 3, edited by G. M. Grossman and K. Rogoff, 1689–1730. Amsterdam: North-Holland, 1995.
Up-to-date survey of empirical evidence on exchange rate behavior; intermediate to advanced.

Froot, K., and K. Rogoff. "Perspectives on PPP and Long-Run Real Exchange Rates." In *Handbook of International Economics,* Vol. 3, edited by G. M. Grossman and K. Rogoff, 1647–1688. Amsterdam: North-Holland, 1995.
Up-to-date survey of the literature and empirical evidence on long-run exchange rate behavior; intermediate to advanced.

Garber, P., and L. Svensson. "The Operation and Collapse of Fixed Exchange Rate Regimes." In *Handbook of International Economics,* Vol. 3, edited by G. M. Grossman and K. Rogoff, 1865–1912. Amsterdam: North-Holland, 1995.
Up-to-date survey of how fixed exchange rate regimes work—and fail; intermediate to advanced.

Garfinkel, Michelle R. "What Is an 'Acceptable' Rate of Inflation?—A Review of the Issues." Federal Reserve Bank of St. Louis *Review* 71 (July–August 1989): 3–15.
Introduction to the impact of inflation on the macroeconomy.

Hafer, R. W. "Does Dollar Depreciation Cause Inflation?" Federal Reserve Bank of St. Louis *Review*

(July–August 1989): 16–28.
Accessible discussion of the subtle links between the exchange rate and the price level.

Isard, Peter. *Exchange Rate Economics.* Cambridge: Cambridge University Press, 1995.
Survey of the literature on exchange rates and the macroeconomy; intermediate.

Little, Jane Sneddon. "Exchange Rates and Structural Change in U.S. Manufacturing Employment."
Federal Reserve Bank of Boston *New England Economic Review* (March–April 1989): 56–70.
The sectoral impact of exchange rate changes; for all students.

Mills, T. C., and G. E. Wood. "Does the Exchange Rate Regime Affect the Economy?" Federal Reserve
Bank of St. Louis *Review* (July–August 1993): 3–20.
*Investigation of the extent to which macroeconomies perform differently based on the exchange rate
regime under which they operate; for all students.*

Obstfeld, Maurice. "International Currency Experience: New Lessons and Lessons Relearned." *Brookings
Papers on Economic Activity* 1 (1995): 119–220.
Useful survey of recent theory and evidence on exchange rate behavior; intermediate.

Persson, T., and G. Tabellini. "Double-Edged Incentives: Institutions and Policy Coordination." In
Handbook of International Economics, Vol. 3, edited by G. M. Grossman and K. Rogoff, 1973–2030.
Amsterdam: North-Holland, 1995.
*Up-to-date survey of strategic aspects of governments' macroeconomic policy choices; intermediate to
advanced.*

Pollard, P. S., "Central Bank Independence and Economic Performance." Federal Reserve Bank of St.
Louis *Review* (July–August 1993): 21–36.
*The links between countries' economic performances and the degrees of independence given their central
banks; for all students.*

Tatom, John A. "The Link between the Value of the Dollar, U.S. Trade and Manufacturing Output."
Federal Reserve Bank of St. Louis *Review* 70 (November–December 1988): 24–37.
*The differential impact of exchange rate changes across different sectors of the U.S. economy; for all stu-
dents.*

Chapter Nineteen Appendix

The Aggregate Demand Curve

In Chapter Nineteen, we used the aggregate demand curve to examine the effects of various macroeconomic policies on prices and output. This appendix demonstrates how to derive the aggregate demand curve from the IS-LM-BOP model of Chapters Sixteen and Seventeen. Because the aggregate demand curve differs slightly under fixed and flexible exchange rate regimes, we shall consider the two cases separately, beginning with the aggregate demand curve under a fixed exchange rate.

19A.1 Derivation of the Aggregate Demand Curve under a Fixed Exchange Rate

As in Chapter Nineteen, we assume that capital is perfectly mobile among countries. This implies that the BOP curve representing equilibrium in the balance of payments is horizontal. At points above the BOP line the balance of payments is in surplus; at points below it, the balance of payments is in deficit. With perfectly mobile capital, the economy will never actually be off its BOP line, but examining what would happen in such a case will help clarify the adjustment processes.

Panel (a) of Figure 19A.1 illustrates an initial equilibrium at the intersection of IS_0, LM_0, and BOP. The price level is P_0, and the equilibrium level of output is Q_0. Panel (b) represents that equilibrium price and output combination (P_0, Q_0) as a point on an aggregate demand curve.

Now suppose the price level rises from P_0 to P_1. The effects in the IS-LM-BOP diagram will include (1) a shift to the left of the IS curve because of the increase in the relative price of domestic goods and (2) a shift to the left of the LM curve due to the negative effect of the price rise on the real money stock. The more sensitive are the demands for imports and exports to changes in relative prices (that is, the higher are the price elasticities of the import and export demand curves), the larger will be the shift of the IS curve relative to that of the LM curve. IS_1 represents the low-elasticity case in which the IS shift is relatively small. In this case, the new equilibrium occurs at the intersection of IS_1 and LM_1, implying a point corresponding to (P_1, Q_1) on the aggregate demand curve labeled *AD(fixed, low elasticity)* in panel (b). IS_2 represents the high-elasticity case in which the IS shift is relatively large. In this case, the new equilibrium occurs at the intersection of IS_2 and LM_1, implying a point corresponding to (P_1, Q_2) on the aggregate demand curve labeled *AD(fixed, high elasticity)* in panel (b). As panel (b) demonstrates, the higher the elasticity values, the flatter the aggregate demand curve under a fixed exchange rate. *(To test your understanding, explain the points on the aggregate demand curve corresponding to a fall in the price level to $P_2 < P_0$.)*

Figure 19A.1 □ **Derivation of Aggregate Demand Curve from IS-LM-BOP with Perfectly Mobile Capital**

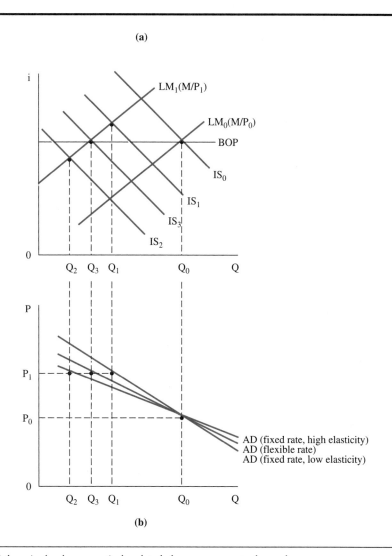

(a)

(b)

Real output and the price level are negatively related along an aggregate demand curve.

Note that at points (P_1,Q_1) and (P_1,Q_2) on the two fixed-exchange rate aggregate demand curves in panel (b) the balance of payments is not in equilibrium, but in surplus and deficit, respectively. *(Why?)* To restore balance-of-payments equilibrium given the fixed exchange rate, the central bank will have to intervene appropriately in each case. Intervention will alter the money stock and shift the aggregate demand curve.

19A.2 Derivation of the Aggregate Demand Curve under a Flexible Exchange Rate

The derivation of the aggregate demand curve from the IS-LM-BOP framework under a flexible exchange rate is quite similar to that under a fixed exchange rate. In fact, we can use Figure 19A.1 again. We continue to assume that capital is perfectly mobile internationally. In panel (a), the initial equilibrium is at the intersection of IS_0, LM_0, and BOP; the price level is P_0 and the equilibrium output Q_0. This initial equilibrium is represented in panel (b) of Figure 19A.1 as a point on the *AD(flexible rate)* curve.

A rise in the price level to $P_1 > P_0$ shifts the IS curve to the left, because the relative price of domestic goods rises and consumers switch to imports. The LM curve also shifts to the left (to LM_1), because the rise in the price level reduces the real money stock. The new equilibrium output at price level P_1 is Q_3. This new equilibrium forms a second point on the flexible-rate aggregate demand curve in panel (b).

But how do we know exactly how much the IS curve shifts as a result of the rise in the price level? In particular, how can we be sure that IS_3 and LM_1 intersect *on* the BOP curve at output level Q_3? If the IS curve (such as IS_2) intersects LM_1 below the BOP line, the balance of payments will be in deficit. Under a flexible exchange rate regime, the domestic currency will depreciate and the relative price of domestic goods will fall. The change in relative prices will shift the IS curve to the right to IS_3. On the other hand, if the IS curve (such as IS_1) intersects LM_1 at a point above the BOP line, the balance of payments will be in surplus. With a flexible exchange rate, the domestic currency will appreciate and domestic goods will become more expensive relative to foreign goods. The IS curve will shift to the left to IS_3. This exchange rate adjustment in response to the balance of payments will ensure that the new IS curve intersects LM_1 on the BOP line at output level Q_3. *(As an exercise, explain the shifts in the IS and LM curves in response to a fall in the price level to $P_2 < P_0$.)*

Note that, unlike the fixed exchange rate case, the balance of payments is in equilibrium at each and every point on the flexible rate aggregate demand curve. The slope of the flexible rate curve falls between the slopes of the fixed rate curves for the low- and high-elasticity cases.

CHAPTER TWENTY

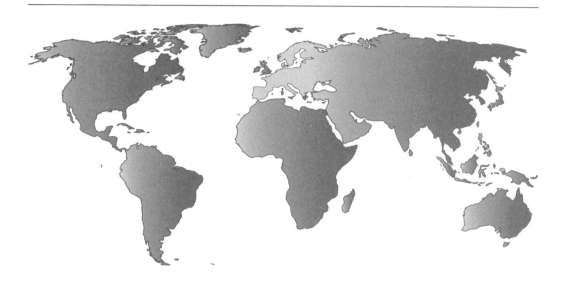

Alternative International Monetary Regimes

20.1 Introduction

Chapters Twelve through Nineteen provided numerous examples of how the adjustment process and the effects of macroeconomic policy depend on the exchange rate regime under which an economy operates. For the most part, we concentrated on differences between a fixed and a flexible exchange rate regime and assumed the regime was imposed exogenously. However, countries *choose* the systems to manage the interaction of their currencies with those of other countries, and the choices countries make in this regard differ widely, as indicated in Table 20.1.

The goals of this chapter are to (1) examine the considerations that go into the choice of monetary regime, (2) outline some of the available alternatives other than fixed or perfectly flexible exchange rates, and (3) evaluate the strengths and weaknesses of alternative regimes as well as the historical experience under each.

20.2 Goals of a Monetary Regime

Any country that engages in international trade must make some provision for handling transactions that involve more than one currency. Countries use a variety of arrangements, ranging from barter or countertrade that eliminates currencies

Table 20.1 □ **Number of IMF Member Countries Using Various Exchange Rate Arrangements, 1995**

Exchange Rate Arrangement	Number of Countries
Currency Pegged to	
U.S. dollar	23
French franc	14
Other currency	7
Special drawing rights	3
Other composite	20
Flexibility Limited in Terms of a Single Currency or Group of Currencies	
Single currency	4
Cooperative arrangements[a]	10
More Flexible	
Adjusted according to set of indicators	3
Other managed floating	36
Independently floating	59
Total	179

[a]Exchange Rate Mechanism of the European Monetary System.

Source: International Monetary Fund, *International Financial Statistics*.

altogether to flexible exchange rates that permit the unrestricted exchange of one currency for another at market-determined prices or exchange rates. That different countries choose different international monetary arrangements suggests that the decision involves many considerations. We begin our study of alternative monetary regimes by examining some desirable goals that a hypothetical "ideal" regime would achieve.

An international monetary regime should promote efficient functioning of the world economy by *facilitating international trade and investment* according to the patterns of comparative advantage. The regime also should support international borrowing and lending that produce gains from intertemporal trade. Under this criterion, regimes that depend on trade restrictions or capital controls do not perform well. Such restrictions reduce the output of the world economy by encouraging inefficient production or preventing resources and investment funds from flowing to their most productive uses. The ideal regime under this criterion would allow trade and finance to proceed just as if the entire world economy used a single currency.

A successful international monetary regime should also *promote balance-of-payments adjustment* to prevent the disruptions and crises associated with large and chronic BOP imbalances. This means that the system needs to either contain automatic adjustment mechanisms for restoring BOP equilibrium or encourage policy makers to take steps to correct any balance-of-payments problems that arise. A related requirement is that the system provide countries with liquidity sufficient for financing temporary balance-of-payments deficits. Under any arrangement other than a perfectly flexible exchange rate, some temporary imbalances are inevitable, and adequate provisions for handling them play a vital role in avoiding and resolving crises.

Individuals and firms that engage in international trade and financial transactions face many types of uncertainty due to the vagaries of the world economy. An ideal international monetary regime would *avoid adding to this uncertainty,* which may discourage international transactions and cause countries to forgo the gains from trade. Proponents of fixed exchange rates often present this criterion as an argument for using fixed rather than flexible exchange rates. As we shall see later in the chapter, however, fixed exchange rates do not necessarily involve less uncertainty than do flexible rates.

The choice of monetary regime interacts with the policy-making process to determine the effectiveness of various types of macroeconomic policies. The ideal monetary system would *enhance policy effectiveness* and provide policy makers with a number of instruments at least equal to the number of targets. In addition, the system would minimize the possibility of policy mistakes and cushion the negative impact of any that do occur. It would encourage policy makers to take correct and timely policy actions and shield the policy-making process from undue political pressure.

The definition of money itself demonstrates that confidence provides an essential ingredient in a successful world monetary system. Money can continue to function only as long as the public has confidence in the monetary unit and its acceptability as payment for goods and services. Because *expectations* of disruptions in the world monetary system can in themselves cause volatility, disorder, and poor economic performance, the ideal monetary system would *generate confidence in its stability and continuity.*

Finally, any international monetary system involves costs to operate. The relevant costs include those of negotiating international agreements, maintaining international organizations such as the International Monetary Fund, and holding stocks of foreign exchange reserves. Other things being equal, an international monetary system with *lower administrative and operating costs* is superior to one involving higher costs.

The list of attributes desirable for an international monetary regime is quite long. The following passage by Barry Eichengreen, a leading expert on international monetary history, summarizes the goals:

> The international monetary system is part of the institutional framework that binds national economies together. An ideally functioning system permits producers to specialize in goods in which the nation has a comparative advantage and savers to search beyond national borders for profitable investment opportunities. It does so by combining the virtues of stability and flexibility. Stability in the market for foreign exchange minimizes the volatility of import and export prices, permitting producers and consumers to exploit fully the advantages of international specialization. Flexibility in the operation of the international monetary system permits the divergent objectives of national economic authorities to be reconciled with one another.[1]

---

[1]Barry Eichengreen, "Editor's Introduction," in *The Gold Standard in Theory and History,* ed. Barry Eichengreen (New York: Methuen, 1985), 1.

No system satisfies all these attributes perfectly; rather, the choice of international monetary system implies tradeoffs among the various criteria.

We now turn to an examination of the major alternative monetary regimes and to the question of how each fares in terms of the above criteria. We begin with the gold standard, a monetary system with a controversial past that is struggling to have a future.

20.3   The Gold Standard, 1880–1913: Panacea or Rose-Colored Glasses?

20.3.1   History and Mechanics of the Gold Standard

The use of precious metals, especially gold, as money dates back many centuries. Gold's characteristics make it well suited for this purpose; it is scarce, durable, transportable (at least in the small quantities required for most economic transactions), easily measurable, and mintable into coins of uniform value.

The precise way gold has functioned as money has evolved as national governments have assumed larger roles in the money-supply process. At first, unminted gold circulated in the form of dust or bullion. Market forces determined the relative price between gold and goods. For example, gold discoveries led to a fall in the relative price of gold and a rise in the relative price of goods, as gold became more abundant relative to goods. Gradually, national governments or sovereigns began to mint gold into coins of a specified weight (for example, 1 troy ounce, or 1/12 of a pound) and to certify the coins' value. The value of these full-bodied coins equaled the value of the gold they contained. Coining gold offered clear advantages, because it eliminated the need to weigh and measure at each transaction.

As economies grew and the number and size of economic transactions increased, the use of currency or paper money as a substitute for gold began to spread. Paper money was lighter and easier to transport, and each unit of it could represent a unit of gold actually held by the issuer of the currency. Currency was **convertible;** that is, holders of currency could convert it into gold on request, and vice versa. This type of **gold standard,** in which currency backed by gold circulated as the money stock, evolved independently in many countries. While the gold standard involved no explicit international agreement, the major trading economies—including Britain, Germany, the United States, and Japan—operated under a gold standard by around 1880, providing the basis for an international monetary regime that would last until the outbreak of the First World War.

Simple rules governed the international gold standard. First, each government defined the value of a unit of its currency in terms of gold; for example, the United States defined the dollar value of an ounce of gold as $20.67, and Britain defined the pound price of gold as £4.24 per ounce. The U.S. government committed itself to buy or sell gold at $20.67 per ounce, while the British government likewise stood ready to exchange pounds for gold, and vice versa, at £4.24 per ounce. Each government held gold reserves to back its commitment. Together, the two governments' commitments defined an implicit or **mint exchange rate** between dollars and pounds of ($20.67/oz.)/(£4.24/oz.), or about $4.87/£1, as illustrated in Table 20.2.

Table 20.2 □ The Mint Exchange Rate under a Gold Standard

When each government buys and sells gold to keep the value of the country's currency fixed in terms of gold, the implicit exchange rate that holds between the two currencies is called the *mint exchange rate*.

	Guaranteed by United States	Guaranteed by Britain
	$20.67 = 1 ounce gold = £4.24	
	$20.67 = £4.24	
or, dividing by 4.24,		
	$4.87 = £1	

Under a gold standard, the mint exchange rate fixes the market exchange rate between two currencies, not by direct intervention by the countries' monetary authorities but by private arbitrage activities.[2] Suppose that the dollar price of pounds in the foreign exchange market rises above the mint exchange rate of $4.87/£1, say, to $5 per pound. Arbitrageurs then find it profitable to use dollars to buy gold in the United States at the official rate of $20.67 per ounce, ship it to Britain, sell it at the official rate of £4.24 per ounce, and exchange the pounds for (£4.24)·($5.00/£1) = $21.20 in the foreign exchange market. The arbitrageurs earn a profit of $21.20 – $20.67 = $0.53 on each ounce of gold, ignoring transportation and other transaction costs.

The arbitrage process raises the demand for dollars in the foreign exchange market and lowers the market exchange rate back toward the mint rate of $4.87 per pound. A fall in the dollar price of pounds to, say, $4.50 would cause arbitrageurs to ship gold from Britain to the United States at a profit of £0.35 per ounce. *(Why?)* Because of the transaction costs involved in shipping gold in response to deviations between the mint and market exchange rates, arbitrage cannot keep the two rates identical at all times. However, it will keep the market rate within a band around the mint rate. The costs of gold shipments determine the width of the band, and the boundaries of the band are called *gold points*.

The combination of (1) government purchases and sales of gold to keep the price of each currency fixed in terms of gold and (2) private arbitrage to keep the market exchange rate approximately equal to the mint exchange rate ensures a fixed exchange rate between each pair of currencies under a gold standard. The viability of the gold standard requires that each monetary authority issue no more currency than it can back with its stock of gold. If a central bank violates this rule, it faces the possibility of being unable to honor its promise to convert currency into gold.

We can see how the gold standard disciplines monetary policy by considering a country that pursues an open market purchase to expand its money stock. Initially, the domestic real money stock rises and the interest rate falls. The decline in

---

[2]Recall that arbitrage is an effort to make a profit by taking advantage of price differentials that exist in two submarkets at a given time.

domestic relative to foreign interest rates makes foreign-currency-denominated assets more attractive. Asset owners sell the now unattractive domestic-currency-denominated assets to the central bank for gold, a transaction the central bank is obligated to fulfill under gold-standard rules. New owners of gold then sell it to foreign central banks in exchange for foreign currency which they then use to purchase assets denominated in foreign currency—which pay higher interest rates. The net effect: The country that raised its money stock has a capital outflow, and other countries have a matching capital inflow.

These capital flows reequilibrate the foreign exchange market. The money stock of the country that conducted the expansionary monetary policy shrinks back to its original size as the country loses gold reserves. Other countries experience money-stock growth as they accumulate gold reserves. Once interest parity reestablishes itself, capital flows cease. The total world money stock remains unchanged. Note two important results. First, both countries take part in the adjustment process. This makes adjustment under the gold standard *symmetrical,* as opposed to the *asymmetrical* adjustment under other fixed exchange rate systems in which the reserve country controls its money stock and determines money growth for all members of the group.[3] Second, the rules of the gold standard link a country's money stock to its central bank's gold. This key characteristic of the gold standard—the tying of the money stock to the monetary authority's stock of gold—lies at the heart of arguments both in favor of and against the use of a gold standard as an international monetary regime.

20.3.2 Macroeconomic Adjustment under a Gold Standard: Theory

The primary arguments in favor of a gold standard rest on the belief that such a system contributes to price stability (particularly to avoiding inflation) and contains an automatic adjustment mechanism for maintaining balance-of-payments equilibrium. The price-stability argument stems from a gold standard's limitations on money stock growth. At the worldwide level, the world money stock can grow no faster than the total world stock of gold. At the national level, each country's money stock can grow no faster than that central bank's stock of gold, because gold must back all currency. The central bank cannot create gold but must either buy existing gold from the public or promote mining to enlarge the supply of available gold.[4] Insofar as this limitation on money stock growth works, the gold standard imposes **price discipline** on central banks, both individually and collectively. This discipline enjoins central banks from creating continual increases in the price level through excessively expansionary monetary policy.

The automatic adjustment mechanism for the balance of payments under a gold standard provides an example of David Hume's specie-flow mechanism, first discussed in Chapter Two. *Specie* is a term for money in the form of precious metals. In the **specie-flow mechanism,** international flows of gold (money) correct balance-of-payments disequilibria. Suppose, for example, that the United States has a balance-of-payments (or, more accurately, a current-account) deficit with Britain under a gold standard. The value of goods and services the United States imports from Britain exceeds that of U.S. exports to Britain. To cover the difference and settle its account, the United States must ship gold to Britain. This movement of gold reduces the U.S. money stock and raises the British money stock. The fall in the U.S. money stock causes prices in the United States to fall, while the rise in the British money stock causes prices in Britain to rise. The change in relative prices of American and British goods (or, equivalently, the real depreciation of the dollar) shifts demand away from now more expensive British goods and toward now cheaper American goods, correcting the original current-account imbalance. Under a gold standard, any such imbalance reduces the money stock of the deficit country and increases that of the surplus country. The resulting change in the relative prices of the two countries' products, or the real exchange rate between their currencies, raises the net exports of the deficit country and lowers the net exports of the surplus country, moving the balance of payments toward equilibrium.

Hume presented his specie-flow mechanism in 1752 as a counter to mercantilist arguments for restricting trade. Recall from Chapter Two that the mercantilists saw trade policy as a vehicle for the accumulation of specie, viewed as the source of wealth and power. The route to this accumulation involved policies designed to create balance-of-payments surpluses that would be settled in gold. Hume's logic, along with that of classical economists David Ricardo and Adam Smith, attempted to expose the fallacies of the mercantilist view. The specie-flow mechanism contributed by demonstrating the inherently short-term nature of balance-of-payments surpluses. When a country succeeded in creating such a surplus through mercantilist policies, it indeed experienced a gold inflow; but this swelled the money stock and raised prices, thereby encouraging imports, discouraging exports, and eliminating the surplus. On the basis of this automatic adjustment mechanism, Hume argued that mercantilist policies, *even if* they have been desirable, could not have succeeded in the long run.

The simple version of Hume's specie-flow mechanism emphasized price flexibility and focused on adjustment of the current-account balance rather than the overall balance of payments. However, we saw that a similar automatic adjustment mechanism works through the capital account. When the U.S. money stock falls and Britain's rises, U.S. interest rates rise relative to Britain's.[5] This causes the U.S. capital account to move toward a surplus and corrects the original deficit in the U.S. balance of payments. Thus, although Hume's treatment of the specie-flow mechanism analyzed the effect of price flexibility in promoting adjustment through the current account, the same basic idea can be applied to adjustment in the capital account.

In summary, a gold standard requires that individual governments peg the values of their currencies in terms of gold, that arbitrageurs keep the market exchange rate approximately equal to the mint exchange rate, and that adequate gold stocks back the money stock. The gold standard imposes a degree of price discipline on the monetary authority by limiting money stock growth to equality with gold stock growth. It also contains an

---

[5]A rise in the money supply could cause expectations of inflation and a rise in the long-term nominal interest rate. However, short-term interest rates are of primary concern here; section 18.4.4 treats the relationship between inflation and long-term interest rates.

Table 20.3 ▫ Annual Growth in the U.S. Monetary Gold Stock, 1880–1913 (Percent)

Year	Annual Growth in Domestic Monetary Gold Stock	Year	Annual Growth in Domestic Monetary Gold Stock
1880	43%	1897	13%
1881	33	1898	23
1882	7	1899	18
1883	6	1900	7
1884	2	1901	10
1885	6	1902	5
1886	4	1903	7
1887	9	1904	6
1888	7	1905	2
1889	−2	1906	9
1890	0	1907	10
1891	−3	1908	10
1892	−3	1909	1
1893	−7	1910	1
1894	0	1911	6
1895	−5	1912	9
1896	0	1913	3

Source: U.S. Department of Commerce, *Historical Statistics of the United States: Colonial Times to 1970.*

automatic adjustment mechanism in the form of Hume's specie-flow mechanism for solving balance-of-payments problems through symmetric changes in the relative sizes of individual countries' money stocks. As under any fixed exchange rate regime, the link between the balance of payments and the money stock plays an essential role in automatic adjustment. Given these proposed advantages of a gold standard, we can examine the historical evidence on actual operation of a gold-based international monetary regime.

20.3.3 Macroeconomic Performance under a Gold Standard

Because a gold standard links the growth of the domestic money stock to that of the gold stock, an accurate evaluation of its desirability depends on the pattern of growth in the gold stock, among other things. A fairly smooth pattern of growth, which keeps pace with output, would prevent shocks to the world economy. Consistently faster growth in gold than in output would put upward pressure on the price of goods relative to gold as countries accumulated gold reserves. Consistently slower growth in gold than in output would put downward pressure on the price of goods relative to gold and create a shortage of reserves for the growing economies. An erratic growth pattern in gold, on the other hand, could disrupt the world economy. Table 20.3 reports the growth rate of the U.S. monetary gold stock

Table 20.4 □ **Annual Changes in the U.S. Money Stock, 1880–1913 (Percent)**

Year	Annual Growth of M2	Year	Annual Growth of M2
1880	22%	1897	7%
1881	20	1898	13
1882	8	1899	16
1883	6	1900	8
1884	0	1901	13
1885	3	1902	9
1886	8	1903	6
1887	7	1904	6
1888	3	1905	11
1889	6	1906	8
1890	9	1907	5
1891	4	1908	−1
1892	9	1909	11
1893	−4	1910	5
1894	0	1911	6
1895	4	1912	7
1896	−2	1913	4

Source: U.S. Department of Commerce, *Historical Statistics of the United States: Colonial Times to 1970.*

during 1880 to 1913, when the major economies operated under a gold standard. The annual rates of change in the U.S. stock of monetary gold ranged from a low of −7 to a high of 43 percent during this period. Even if monetary authorities had closely followed the rule of creating no more money than they could back by gold, the rate of growth in the money stock would have been quite volatile.

But how closely did governments actually abide by the rules of the gold standard? Close studies suggest that policy makers often disregarded the rules. If the growth of the gold stock proved insufficient to support the growth of the money stock that policy makers desired, they could change the law to require less gold backing for each unit of currency issued or to exempt certain types of money creation (for example, bank deposits as opposed to currency) from gold backing. As under any fixed exchange rate regime, central banks could sterilize the effects of changes in the gold stock by engineering offsetting changes in domestic monetary policy.

In practice, the expediency of such policies limited the price discipline imposed by the gold standard, and the U.S. money stock grew erratically even by today's standards, as documented in Table 20.4. Comparison of Tables 20.3 and 20.4 reveals that changes in the gold stock explain most changes in the U.S. money stock during the gold-standard era. The years of the most rapid gold stock growth (1880–1881 and 1898–1899) correspond to those of greatest monetary growth. At the other extreme, during 1893 both the gold stock and the money stock suffered their greatest decline.

Table 20.5 □ **Annual Changes in U.S. Real GNP and Price Level under the Gold Standard, 1890–1913 (Percent)**

Year	Change in Real GNP (Q)	Change in GNP Deflator (P)	Year	Change in Real GNP (Q)	Change in GNP Deflator (P)
1890	7%	−2%	1902	1%	3%
1891	5	−1	1903	5	1
1892	10	−4	1904	−1	1
1893	−5	2	1905	7	2
1894	−3	−6	1906	12	2
1895	12	−1	1907	2	4
1896	−2	−3	1908	−8	−1
1897	9	0	1909	17	4
1898	2	3	1910	3	3
1899	9	4	1911	3	−1
1900	3	5	1912	6	4
1901	11	−1	1913	1	−1

Source: U.S. Department of Commerce, *Historical Statistics of the United States: Colonial Times to 1970.*

The gold standard in the United States did not appear to promote smooth, disciplined behavior of the money stock. However, the behavior of the money stock matters not in itself but for its implications for real output and the price level. Recall the ultimate goal of an international monetary system: smooth functioning of the world economy as reflected in steady growth of real output and stable prices. Table 20.5 reveals that wide variations in both real output and the price level matched the instability in the money stock, as the model of Chapter Nineteen would lead us to expect.[6]

Overall, the gold-standard era exhibited greater instability in terms of monetary growth, prices, and real output than some analysts admit. Apparently, rose-colored perceptions of the "good old days" filter popular views of the gold standard, as well as, perhaps, the views by some economists. Efforts to smooth and limit money growth by tying the money stock to gold had limited success, for two basic reasons. First, the gold stock itself grew erratically due to new discoveries, new extraction technologies, and changing incentives for mining. Second, unless inclined to abide by the restrictions placed on monetary growth by the gold stock, monetary authorities can circumvent the rules and eliminate much of the discipline credited to the gold standard. This second weakness of a gold standard seems likely to pose an even bigger problem for a gold standard today than during the early days of the twentieth century.

---

[6]See Cases Three and Four in Chapter Nineteen, on historical fluctuations in the price level and in real output, respectively.

A gold standard compels policy makers to focus on external balance; but, throughout the postwar period, governments have accepted increasing responsibility for internal-balance targets, such as full employment. A government committed by law to the pursuit of full employment (as is, for example, the United States as a result of the Humphrey-Hawkins bill passed after the Second World War) seems unlikely to abide by the rules of a gold standard when those rules require behavior that may come at high short-run costs in terms of domestic economic targets.

Despite evidence that the actual functioning of the gold standard fell considerably short of the ideal, a small group of economists and policy makers remain convinced that a return to the gold standard represents the only way to eliminate what they perceive as an inflationary bias in the international monetary system. In June 1981, the United States established the *Commission on the Role of Gold in the Domestic and International Monetary Systems* to study reinstitution of a monetary role for gold. The majority of the commission members recommended against returning to a gold standard, but a minority dissented vigorously.

A return to a gold-based international monetary system carries special political difficulties, because much of the world's unmined gold is concentrated in the former Soviet Union and in South Africa, a country with a difficult political and economic future because of its history of apartheid. Even if a return to gold seemed desirable on other criteria, the major industrial countries would hesitate to approve an international monetary system that concentrated control over a key element in the hands of former Soviet republics and South Africa.

20.4 The Interwar Years, 1919–1939: Search for an International Monetary System

The First World War disrupted all aspects of the world economy, including the gold standard. Financing the war emerged as the focus of economic policy in the large trading economies. Fiscal authorities borrowed to pay armies, buy arms, and later to finance reconstruction, and monetary policy makers printed money to cover the massive fiscal expenditures.[7] Except for the United States, countries abandoned the convertibility of their currencies into gold, ushering in a period of flexible exchange rates. The dollar remained convertible, but other governments ceased converting their currencies into either gold or dollars at fixed rates. Thus, the fixed mint exchange rates of the gold-standard era disappeared.

Few policy makers or economists viewed the flexible exchange rates as permanent, however. Discussion focused on when to reestablish the gold standard and how to choose the new rate at which to peg each currency to gold. Because the demands of financing the war and reconstruction had produced high rates of inflation in most economies (especially outside the United States), some policy makers recognized a return to prewar rates as infeasible. The war had shaken confidence in the gold standard, and the relative strengths of the United States and Britain in the world

---

[7]Other ways to finance government expenditures include raising taxes or borrowing from the public.

Table 20.6 □ Annual Changes in U.S. Real GNP and Price Level, 1919–1941 (Percent)

Year	Change in Real GNP (Q)	Change in GNP Deflator (P)	Year	Change in Real GNP (Q)	Change in GNP Deflator (P)
1919	−4%	14%	1931	−8%	−9%
1920	−4	14	1932	−15	−10
1921	−9	−17	1933	−2	−2
1922	16	−8	1934	9	7
1923	12	2	1935	10	1
1924	0	0	1936	14	0
1925	8	1	1937	5	4
1926	6	−2	1938	−5	−1
1927	0	−2	1939	9	−2
1928	1	2	1940	9	−2
1929	7	0	1941	16	8
1930	−10	−3			

Source: U.S. Department of Commerce, *Historical Statistics of the United States: Colonial Times to 1970.*

economy had changed. A handful of countries finally reestablished a partial gold standard in 1925, but with inappropriate exchange rates. British war-generated inflation, combined with the British government's determination to return the pound to gold convertibility at its prewar rate, led to severe monetary contraction, a dramatic real appreciation of the pound, and a prolonged British recession. Germany—saddled with a devastated economy and war reparations that it attempted to pay by printing massive quantities of money—suffered a hyperinflation in which the price level rose by a factor of almost 500 *billion* between 1919 and 1925.

Beginning in 1931, the brief return to a gold standard collapsed in the midst of the Great Depression. One by one, countries again suspended the convertibility of their currencies into gold. International monetary cooperation took a back seat to individual countries' self-interested attempts to regain control of their economies through competitive devaluations, tariffs, exchange and capital controls, and a variety of other desperate and often counterproductive policies.

Pervasive political and economic instability characterized the period between the First and Second World Wars. Table 20.6 summarizes the erratic macroeconomic performance during this time. The lack of a smoothly functioning international monetary system was but one symptom of the overall problem. Neither the breakdown of the gold standard nor the spread of trade restrictions can shoulder blame for all the economic problems, but narrowly nationalistic policies did little to alleviate them.

The interwar years left a historical record that for many years has served as a reminder of the interdependence of the world economy and of the costs of beggar-thy-neighbor policies. Only after the Great Depression did macroeconomic stability and internal balance become central goals of government policy. One result of the interwar and Depression experiences was the major economies' determination to unite to build a stable and open international trade and monetary system following the Second World War.[8]

20.5 Bretton Woods, 1945–1971: A Negotiated International Monetary System

In the 1940s, few scholars or policy makers viewed flexible exchange rates as a viable basis for an international monetary regime. The Bretton Woods system established after the Second World War reinstated fixed exchange rates, but with three major changes from the prewar system:

1. The new regime represented a gold-exchange standard rather than a gold standard. This meant that a national currency—the U.S. dollar—played a central role along with gold.

2. The new system was an adjustable-peg exchange rate system rather than a fixed rate system, because the Bretton Woods agreement explicitly introduced provisions for altering exchange rates under certain, albeit vaguely specified, conditions.

3. The Bretton Woods system, unlike the gold standard, represented the outcome of international bargaining, even though the United States and Britain dominated the negotiations. Those negotiations created a major international organization, the International Monetary Fund (IMF), as a multilateral body to facilitate the success of the new agreement.

20.5.1 The Mechanics of the Gold-Exchange Standard under Bretton Woods

The Bretton Woods system provides an example of a **gold-exchange,** or **gold-dollar, standard.** Nondollar currencies were not convertible directly into gold, but they were convertible, at a pegged exchange rate, into dollars, which in turn were convertible into gold at $35 per ounce.[9] That the U.S. dollar served as the key currency in the Bretton Woods gold-exchange standard implied a distinction between the policy rules followed by the United States and those followed by other countries.[10] The **key,** or **reserve, currency** was convertible into gold. Maintaining this convertibility (initially at $35 per ounce) defined the primary U.S. responsibility under Bretton Woods.

---

[8]This determination was evidenced by the negotiations for a postwar international monetary system that began in 1941 and continued throughout the war.

[9]At the war's end, most currencies were not convertible. The Bretton Woods agreement urged member countries to establish convertibility, at least for current-account transactions, as soon as possible. Most major economies accomplished this move by the late 1950s or early 1960s. In Chapter Twenty-One, we shall look into the costs nonconvertible currencies impose on economies.

[10]Section 16.6 discusses the special status of reserve-currency countries.

Table 20.7 □ Gold Exchange Rate under a Gold-Dollar Standard

The United States buys and sells gold to hold the dollar price of gold at $35 per ounce. Other central banks—represented here by the Bank of England—buy and sell dollars to hold the dollar prices of their currencies fixed. The combination of these two processes fixes the price of each nonreserve currency in terms of gold.

Guaranteed by United States	Guaranteed by Britain
1 ounce gold = $35 = £12.5	
1 ounce gold = £12.5	

Fulfillment of this responsibility required the United States to (1) stand ready to buy or sell gold in exchange for dollars at $35 per ounce on the request of other central banks and (2) create no more dollars subject to convertibility than the U.S. stock of monetary gold could support. Other countries' central banks held responsibility for intervening in foreign exchange markets to buy and sell dollars, thereby keeping the dollar values of their respective currencies at the agreed-upon pegged rates.

Table 20.7 represents the determination of exchange rates under a gold-dollar standard, a particular example of a gold-exchange standard. A comparison of Table 20.7 with Table 20.2 highlights the fundamental difference between a gold standard and a gold-exchange standard. Under a true gold standard, *each* currency is convertible into gold. Under a gold-exchange standard, *only* the reserve currency is convertible directly into gold. Other currencies, in turn, are convertible into the reserve currency at pegged exchange rates maintained through intervention by non-reserve-currency central banks.

20.5.2   Adjustment under Bretton Woods

The gold standard had collapsed when policy makers no longer could subordinate their domestic, internal-balance goals to the gold standard's externally oriented rules. To fight unemployment during the Great Depression, governments resorted to abandoning their exchange-rate pegs, competitively devaluing, and imposing trade barriers. Negotiators at Bretton Woods, fresh from the interwar experience, recognized that any new international monetary system, if it was to succeed based on fixed exchange rates, would have to provide governments with some flexibility to address the domestic macroeconomic priorities for which electorates increasingly held governments responsible. The Bretton Woods agreement contained three important elements that attempted to introduce this flexibility: an adjustable-peg exchange rate system, IMF lending facilities, and permission for countries to institute or continue to use exchange controls on some types of international transactions.

The Adjustable Peg

The designers of the Bretton Woods system recognized that the pegged exchange rates selected at the close of the Second World War would require periodic adjustment as the economic situations facing the various countries evolved. The major economies found themselves in widely divergent circumstances and pursuing diverse policies at the end of the war. Some economies were growing rapidly, while others struggled to reconstruct their basic productive capacities. For all these reasons, the negotiators at Bretton Woods recognized the need for periodic devaluations and revaluations to correct chronic balance-of-payments problems. Rather than fixing exchange rates at permanent levels, the Bretton Woods agreement explicitly left open the possibility of occasional currency realignments and allowed countries to devalue or revalue their currencies under specified conditions with the consent of the rest of the group.[11] The framers of the agreement hoped that by providing a cooperative framework for these changes, through the IMF, they could avoid future episodes of the destructive competitive devaluations that had occurred during the Great Depression. A system of fixed exchange rates that embodies rules for the periodic adjustment of rates as economic conditions change is called an **adjustable-peg system.**

Bretton Woods' adjustable peg allowed a central bank to intervene to buy or sell foreign exchange whenever short-run disturbances caused a temporary disequilibrium at the pegged rate of that central bank's currency. If, however, economic circumstances changed permanently or dramatically such that the pegged rate clearly differed from long-run equilibrium, intervention to maintain the rate could be undesirable or even infeasible. In such cases of **fundamental disequilibrium,** policy makers could change the pegged exchange rate, under the guidance of the International Monetary Fund, to a rate that corresponded more closely to the equilibrium level.

IMF Lending Facilities

A fixed exchange rate regime requires central banks to intervene in foreign exchange markets to maintain balance-of-payments equilibrium at the assigned exchange rates. This intervention alters the domestic money stock; in fact, intervention's effect on the money stock represents the key step in the mechanism through which intervention restores balance-of-payments equilibrium. However, these changes in the money stock may exacerbate problems of internal balance, particularly unemployment, and lead policy makers to circumvent the rules of the regime and cause crises. The Bretton Woods agreement recognized this possibility and incorporated provisions for lending reserves (either gold or foreign currencies) to governments who faced temporary balance-of-payments deficits but for whom immediate monetary contraction presented unacceptable domestic economic consequences.

The International Monetary Fund consists of member countries that promise to abide by the organization's Articles of Agreement, which define the rules, privileges, and obligations of membership. Each country joins the IMF by contributing a sum called the *quota,* which consists of gold (25 percent) and the country's domestic currency (75 percent). The IMF, in turn, could lend these funds to countries that needed its financial assistance to meet their Bretton Woods obligations. Countries could use their quotas to buy specific currencies they needed for foreign exchange

---

[11]Each exchange rate actually fluctuated in a band (of ±1 percent) around the pegged rate; minor exchange adjustments did not require consent.

market intervention. This allowed countries to maintain their exchange rate pegs while postponing monetary adjustment.

A country's economic size determined the size of its IMF quota and, therefore, of its routine borrowing privilege. Voting within the Fund also was determined by the size of a country's quota. The IMF divided each country's borrowing privileges into several classes called **tranches. Conditionality** referred to the Fund's requirement that countries follow certain policy prescriptions as a condition for borrowing. When a country borrowed small sums from the Fund, the borrowing came from the lower tranches subject to no conditionality requirements. As the country's borrowing rose into higher and higher tranches, which generally reflected increasingly serious and persistent economic problems, the number of conditions imposed by the Fund increased. The most common conditions included adjusting the exchange rate to make it more consistent with balance-of-payments equilibrium, lowering deficit spending by the public sector, and lowering money growth rates. These conditionality prescriptions were designed to eliminate the balance-of-payments problems that required borrowing from the Fund, while the IMF lending itself provided short-term relief to countries that had domestic unemployment and balance-of-payments deficits.

Exchange and Capital Controls

At the end of the Second World War, many national currencies were not convertible; that is, they could not be exchanged freely for other currencies. Nonconvertibility reduces the efficiency of the world economy by making international trade more costly, because it limits the usefulness or the liquidity of the foreign currency received in payment for exports. To encourage the reestablishment of international trade after the war, the Bretton Woods agreement urged member countries to restore currency convertibility quickly. However, the agreement limited the call for convertibility to current-account or international trade transactions and avoided requiring convertibility of capital-account or financial transactions.[12] The logic of the distinction was based on negotiators' perceptions that private capital flows, which could move quickly across national boundaries in response to expected changes in exchange rates, added instability to the world economy. If policy makers constantly had to worry about foreign exchange market participants' perceptions of their economy and policy, this might further constrain their ability to manage the economy while maintaining fixed exchange rates.

Currency nonconvertibility for capital-account transactions severely limited private capital flows in the years following the war. This implied that current-account deficits had to be financed in one of two ways: central banks' sales of foreign exchange, or official borrowing from other countries or the IMF.[13] At the same time, each government had to worry about keeping enough foreign exchange reserves to maintain the credibility of their exchange rate commitments.

---

[12]Chapter Thirteen covers the distinction between current- and capital-account transactions.

[13]Recall from Chapter Thirteen that BOP = CAB + KAB = −OSB. If capital controls limit the private capital flow portion of KAB, then CAB < 0 requires either OSB > 0 or official (noncontrolled) capital inflows such that KAB > 0.

As currencies gradually become convertible for capital-account transactions, private capital flows increased. This development enhanced the opportunity for countries to reap gains from intertemporal trade. For some countries, private capital flows could offset current-account deficits or surpluses and reduce the need for foreign exchange intervention. For others, capital-account deficits or surpluses exacerbated their current-account counterpart and required large-scale intervention that generated huge swings in governments' foreign exchange reserves—and in domestic money stocks. Hints of an impending devaluation could cause immediate capital outflows and necessitate an actual devaluation, often one larger in magnitude than would have been required in the absence of the expectation-based capital outflow.

20.5.3 Problems under Bretton Woods

Confidence in the international monetary system under Bretton Woods hinged on the credibility of two fundamental commitments: one tying individual currencies to the dollar and the other tying the dollar to gold. Unfortunately, requirements for meeting the two commitments sometimes conflicted.

Immediately after the Second World War, reconstruction meant that the European and Japanese economies ran large current-account deficits. With private capital flows constrained by capital controls and currency nonconvertibility, those deficits required central banks to intervene on a large scale to maintain the countries' fixed exchange rates against the dollar. Such large-scale intervention was possible only if the central banks held sufficiently large stocks of foreign exchange reserves. This implied that the United States had to make available enough dollars to provide adequate world **liquidity** or reserves, because countries held the bulk of their reserves in the form of U.S. dollars (the reserve currency).[14]

At the same time, continued confidence in the U.S. commitment to hold the price of gold at $35 per ounce required that the dollars in the hands of foreign central banks and therefore subject to requests for conversion into gold not exceed the value of the U.S. gold stock evaluated at the official price of $35 per ounce. The U.S. stock of gold reserves was large but finite. Figure 20.1 reports changes in the U.S. gold stock during the Bretton Woods period, along with the dollar liabilities that the United States could have been asked to convert into gold. As Figure 20.1 shows, dollar liabilities to foreign central banks surpassed the U.S. gold stock in the early 1960s. With dollars in the hands of foreign central banks exceeding the value of the stock of gold reserves (valued at $35 dollars per ounce), the United States clearly could no longer convert all dollars into gold on request.[15]

An obvious conflict exists between the need to *create large stocks of dollars* to provide adequate liquidity for intervention and the need to *limit the creation of dollars* so as not to jeopardize confidence in their convertibility into gold. If the United States created a large quantity of dollars for use as reserves, confidence in its ability to honor its commitment to convert dollars into gold at $35 per ounce on foreign governments' request weakened. Thus, it is not surprising that during much of the

---

[14]The remaining reserve stocks took the form of gold and a few other currencies, such as pounds.

[15]As long the Bretton Woods system enjoyed widespread confidence, the United States did not have to redeem all dollars at the promised rate, but the belief that it *could* do so was crucial.

Figure 20.1 □ **The U.S. Gold Stock and Dollars Eligible for Conversion into Gold During Bretton Woods (Gold Valued at the Official Rate)**

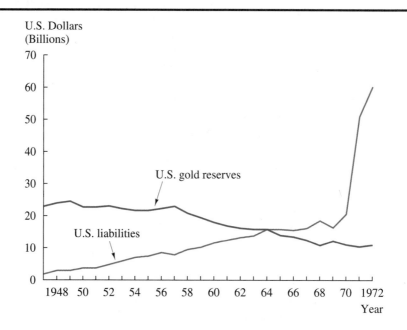

Sources: *Economic Report of the President 1973;* International Monetary Fund, *International Financial Statistics.*

Bretton Woods era failure to meet one or the other of these two goals was a source of concern. In fact, one can argue that the evolution and eventual demise of the Bretton Woods system resulted from the interplay of these two problems.

In the early postwar years, the first problem prevailed as other countries experienced large current-account deficits and a chronic "dollar shortage" as they sought dollars to supplement their gold reserves. The European economies maintained protectionist policies and controls on private capital flows in an effort to hold their balance-of-payments deficits at manageable levels.

In the mid-1960s, when the United States pursued more expansionary monetary policy and itself ran balance-of-payments deficits, the reserve-currency country obviously lost its ability to honor its commitment to convert dollars into gold.[16] The

---

[16]The classic explanation for U.S. expansionary macroeconomic policy during the mid-1960s goes as follows: The Lyndon Johnson administration incurred mounting fiscal expenditures as it financed both its Great Society programs (including the War on Poverty) and its defense buildup to support the expanding Vietnam War. Economists publicly warned Johnson of the need to raise taxes to finance the expenditures. But the president, aware of the growing unpopularity of the Vietnam conflict, insisted on printing money rather than raising taxes. The result was a succession of large increases in aggregate demand and, eventually, inflation and currency devaluation.

expansionary U.S. monetary policy meant that foreign central banks had to buy large quantities of dollars from the foreign exchange market to prevent their currencies from appreciating against the dollar. For a while, foreign central banks willingly accumulated dollar reserves, which, unlike gold, paid interest. So long as no one expected a dollar devaluation against gold, the United States, as the reserve-currency country, could continue to conduct expansionary monetary policy, relatively unconstrained by its gold stock.[17] Intervention by foreign central banks swelled their money stocks and spread the inflationary effects of U.S. expansionary policy abroad.

Eventually, many foreign governments and market participants began to anticipate a devaluation of the dollar (that is, a rise in the dollar price of gold). Foreign policy makers grew increasingly unwilling to hold large stocks of dollars, because they no longer viewed the dollar as "good as gold." The dollar shortage of the early postwar years had turned into a "dollar glut" by the mid-1960s. Some central banks hurried to exchange their dollars for gold before the expected devaluation, and pressures rose as the U.S. gold stock dwindled. France, in particular, insisted on converting portions of its dollar stocks into gold, further depleting the U.S. gold stock and eroding confidence in the $35 per ounce commitment. Countries strongly opposed to inflationary policies, particularly West Germany and Japan, ceased to support the Bretton Woods system, which had exported the inflationary effects of excessively expansionary U.S. policies (see Table 20.8).

Finally, in August 1971, the United States announced it no longer would convert dollars to gold at the official $35 rate on foreign central banks' request. By the end of 1971, a makeshift arrangement—the Smithsonian Agreement—had replaced Bretton Woods, fixing the price of gold at $38 per ounce (later to become $42 per ounce) and pegging foreign currencies against the dollar at higher rates. The shift from Bretton Woods to Smithsonian amounted to a dollar devaluation against all other member currencies imposed unilaterally by the United States. The Smithsonian Agreement also differed from Bretton Woods in that the United States made no promise to convert dollars into gold at the new $38 rate; in other words, the new system represented a **dollar standard** rather than a gold-dollar standard. The Smithsonian Agreement could not reestablish the stability and confidence enjoyed under Bretton Woods. High rates of U.S. money growth continued, and foreign exchange market participants dumped dollar-denominated assets in exchange for mark-denominated ones in anticipation of another dollar devaluation against the mark. By 1973, after several futile attempts to reestablish stable fixed exchange rates, the currencies of the major industrial economies floated against the dollar.

The Bretton Woods system met with difficulties for three basic reasons. First, as we have seen, U.S. responsibilities under the system sometimes conflicted, so at least some of them were not carried out. Second, the central banks of many countries faced a dilemma between their international responsibilities under the agreement and the macroeconomic policies acceptable to their domestic political constituencies.

---

[17]Gold's constraint on money expansion eroded further in 1968 when institution of a two-tier gold market allowed private traders to buy and sell gold at a market-determined price not linked to the official $35 per ounce price at which central banks continued to trade.

Table 20.8 ▫ **Inflation in the Major Industrial Economies, 1952–1973 (Percent Change in Consumer Prices)**

Year	U.S.	Canada	Japan	France	Germany	Italy	United Kingdom
1952	2%	2%	4%	12%	2%	4%	9%
1953	1	−1	7	−1	−2	2	3
1954	0	1	6	0	0	3	2
1955	0	0	−2	1	1	3	5
1956	1	1	0	2	3	3	5
1957	4	3	3	4	2	1	4
1958	3	2	0	15	2	3	3
1959	1	1	1	6	1	0	0
1960	2	1	4	4	1	2	1
1961	1	1	5	3	2	2	3
1962	1	1	7	5	3	5	4
1963	1	2	8	5	3	7	2
1964	1	2	4	3	2	6	3
1965	2	2	7	3	3	4	5
1966	3	4	5	3	4	2	4
1967	3	3	4	3	1	3	3
1968	4	4	5	5	2	1	5
1969	5	5	5	6	3	3	5
1970	6	3	8	5	4	5	6
1971	4	3	6	6	5	5	10
1972	3	5	5	6	6	6	7
1973	6	8	12	7	7	10	8

Source: *Economic Report of the President, 1986;* U.S. Department of Commerce, *Business Conditions Digest,* June 1985.

Finally, as capital mobility increased, potential conflicts between a country's international and domestic economic obligations could quickly trigger a capital outflow and a balance-of-payments crisis whenever market participants began to expect a devaluation.

20.5.4   Macroeconomic Performance under Bretton Woods

The Bretton Woods system clearly had imperfections: it implied potentially contradictory responsibilities for the United States and imposed the effects of U.S. policy on foreign economies. Although the underlying agreement allowed for exchange rate adjustments by design, actual devaluations or revaluations were rare, and chronic balance-of-payments deficits and surpluses common. Despite these problems, however, the world economy performed respectably during the Bretton Woods years.

Table 20.9 summarizes the behavior of U.S. real output and prices during the Bretton Woods era. Output grew, if not smoothly, and the increased openness of

Table 20.9 □ **Annual Changes in U.S. Real GNP and Price Level, 1946–1971 (Percent)**

Year	Change in Real GNP (Q)	Change in GNP Deflator (P)	Year	Change in Real GNP (Q)	Change in GNP Deflator (P)
1946	12%	12%	1959	6%	2%
1947	−1	12	1960	2	2
1948	4	7	1961	2	1
1949	0	−1	1962	7	1
1950	10	1	1963	4	1
1951	8	7	1964	5	1
1952	3	2	1965	6	2
1953	4	1	1966	7	3
1954	−1	1	1967	3	3
1955	8	1	1968	5	4
1956	2	3	1969	3	5
1957	1	4	1970	0	5
1958	−1	3	1971	3	5

Source: *Economic Report of the President, 1985.*

the international system led to rapid growth in world trade and investment. Inflation posed few problems during the early years once the immediate postwar adjustments passed, but it grew to be a bigger threat as U.S. expansionary policies produced growing balance-of-payments deficits and price increases.

20.6 Post-Bretton Woods, 1973– : Another Search for an International Monetary System

The breakdown of the Bretton Woods system of pegged exchange rates led less to a regime based on exchange rate flexibility than to a world in which individual countries unilaterally choose their own exchange rate arrangements. This represented less of a break with the past than is commonly acknowledged. Historically, the exchange arrangement used by the dominant economies has been treated as characteristic of each period, as though the entire world economy operated under a unified exchange regime. In fact, this rarely has been the case. During the gold-standard period, many countries never tied their currencies to gold, and others entered and exited the system according to prevailing domestic political constraints on economic policies. Under Bretton Woods, the regime was subject to negotiation, but the United States and Britain dominated those negotiations. Many countries, including large ones such as France, never liked the system. Many currencies never became fully convertible into dollars—a requirement for a true gold-exchange standard. Government leaders postponed exchange rate adjustments until balance-of-payments crises arose, actions that clearly violated the spirit, if not the letter, of the Bretton Woods agreement.

If economic history has taught any lessons, one is certainly that national governments are reluctant to relinquish sovereignty in any area, including international monetary relations and international trade policy. Nations jealously guard the prerogative to manage their respective currencies and never freely relinquish that prerogative to the dictates of an international monetary regime. Nor do countries easily relinquish power over other aspects of macroeconomic policy making.

Despite the problems inherent in characterizing a world monetary regime based on the policy choices of a handful of large countries, we examine today's system as a managed float, the arrangement in use by the major industrial economies. A **managed float** refers to a system in which the forces of supply and demand in foreign exchange markets determine basic long-term trends in exchange rates but central banks intervene when they perceive markets as "disorderly" or dominated by short-term disturbances. Some opponents call this arrangement a **dirty float,** referring to the fact that the intervention actions of central banks dirty, or interfere with, market forces.

20.6.1   Mechanics of a Managed Float: Theory

A managed float attempts, by combining market-determined exchange rates with some foreign exchange market intervention, to capture the best aspects of both fixed and flexible exchange rates. The fundamental idea is to use intervention to avoid short-term exchange rate fluctuations believed to contribute to uncertainty. At the same time, central banks avoid long-term intervention so that the supply of and demand for various currencies determine long-run movements in exchange rates, avoiding persistent fundamental misalignments.

Figure 20.2 illustrates the ideal working of a managed float. For simplicity, we maintain the simple two-country (Britain/United States) framework.[18] Each panel depicts the demand for pound-denominated deposits along with the supply of such deposits. Initially the demand for and supply of pounds are given by $D_0^{\pounds}$ and $S^{\pounds}$, respectively. With no central bank intervention, the exchange rate or dollar price of pounds equals e_0^*, at which the quantity demanded of pounds equals the quantity supplied. At that rate, portfolio owners willingly hold the existing stock of pound-denominated deposits in their asset portfolios.

In panel (a) of Figure 20.2, a permanent increase in the demand for pound-denominated assets disturbs the foreign exchange market. A number of events could cause such an increase, for example, an increase in the interest rate on pound assets. Once the demand for pounds shifts to $D_1^{\pounds}$, the old exchange rate, e_0^*, no longer represents an equilibrium. At e_0^*, the quantity demanded of pounds exceeds the quantity supplied. Individuals want to hold more than the available quantity of pound-denominated assets. How should the central banks react? Policy makers face two options: (1) allow the exchange rate to float in response to the forces of supply and demand, moving to a higher dollar price of pounds at e_1^*, or (2) intervene by selling pound-denominated assets from foreign exchange reserves to hold the exchange rate at e_0^*.

---

[18]Sections 12.5 through 12. 7 develop the basic demand and supply model of the foreign exchange market and apply the model under fixed and flexible exchange rates.

Figure 20.2 ▫ **Responses to Permanent and Temporary Changes in Demand under a
Managed Float**

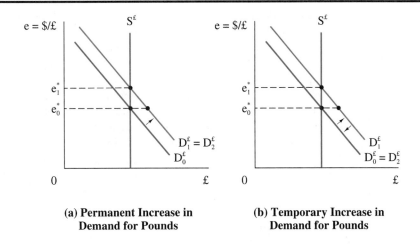

**(a) Permanent Increase in
Demand for Pounds**

**(b) Temporary Increase in
Demand for Pounds**

In panel (a), the demand for pounds increases permanently. The response under a managed float is to allow the exchange rate to move to a new equilibrium at e_1^*. In panel (b), the demand for pounds increases temporarily but then moves back down to its original level. Intervention would hold the exchange rate at its fundamental equilibrium level, e_0^*.

Under a managed float, the appropriate response to a *permanent* increase in the demand for pounds is to allow the exchange rate to move to a new equilibrium at e_1^*. Using intervention in an attempt to hold the exchange rate at e_0^* would require a fall in the U.S. money stock relative to Britain's to eliminate the payments imbalance. If the two countries are unwilling to allow balance-of-payments considerations to dictate their monetary policies, sterilization will result in a fundamental disequilibrium: a chronic U.S. balance-of-payments deficit and British balance-of-payments surplus.[19] The managed float breaks the link between the countries' BOPs and money supplies by allowing movements in the exchange rate to act as the adjustment mechanism when demand or supply conditions in the foreign exchange market change permanently.

Panel (b) of Figure 20.2 represents the case of a temporary increase in the demand for pounds (that is, demand shifts upward from $D_0^£$ to $D_1^£$ and then back down to the original level). Under a floating exchange regime, the dollar price of pounds would move upward from e_0^* to e_1^* and then back down. Many analysts view this type of short-term volatility in exchange rates as one of the primary drawbacks to a flexible exchange rate system. It can cause uncertainty about the profitability of international

---

[19]On the impact of sterilization, see sections 16.3.3 and 16.4.2, as well as Case Four in Chapter Sixteen.

trade and financial transactions, because the future value of the exchange rate partially determines that profitability. *(Why?)* Proponents of intervention argue that uncertainty about exchange rates discourages specialization and trade and thereby reduces the efficiency of the world economy. Under an ideal managed float, the appropriate response to the *temporary* disturbance would be temporary intervention to hold the exchange rate at its underlying equilibrium level, e_0^*. This would require a sale of pounds by central banks, but only for the brief period during which demand was at $D_1^£$. As soon as the disturbance ended, demand would return to $D_0^£ = D_2^£$ and intervention could cease.

A managed float aims to limit exchange rate uncertainty by using intervention in foreign exchange markets to eliminate short-run fluctuations in exchange rates, thereby achieving one of the proclaimed virtues of a fixed exchange rate. At the same time, a managed float allows market forces to determine long-run exchange rates, breaking the link between the balance of payments and the money stock and preventing chronic payments disequilibria, thereby achieving two virtues of a flexible exchange rate.

20.6.2 Criticisms of a Managed Float

The major criticism of the current system of managed floating exchange rates is practical rather than theoretical. Figure 20.2 makes clear the correct policy response to each disturbance in the foreign exchange market because the nature of the disturbance is obvious—we have labeled each up front as permanent or temporary. With this knowledge, a regime with rules that require intervention in the case of temporary disturbances and no intervention in the case of permanent disturbances performs satisfactorily. But in practice, of course, disturbances to the world economy have no clear-cut labels revealing their precise nature and time horizon.

Figure 20.3 illustrates the problem. Movement along the horizontal axis represents the passage of time, while the vertical axis measures the exchange rate. The jagged line to the left of t_0 depicts the historical movement of the exchange rate until today (denoted as time t_0). Let us assume that the dollar suddenly begins to appreciate rapidly against the pound just before t_0. Policy makers must decide whether to intervene to stop, or at least dampen, the appreciation. Under a managed float, intervention should occur only if the appreciation represents a short-term "blip" and not a fundamental change in the equilibrium exchange rate between dollars and pounds. But without knowing the future (that is, the path of the exchange rate line to the right of t_0), how can policy makers distinguish between the two?

If line I turns out to be the future path of the exchange rate, the dollar appreciation will have been temporary and intervention the correct policy under the rules of a managed float. On the other hand, if the future exchange rate ends up following line II, the appreciation will have signaled the beginning of a trend, or a permanent change in the equilibrium exchange rate between dollars and pounds; here the appropriate policy response will have been to allow the dollar to appreciate. In practice, central banks often intervene just enough to dampen or slow down the movement of the exchange rate but not enough to stop it completely. These types of policies are called **leaning-against-the-wind policies.**

Figure 20.3 □ **The Dilemma of a Managed Float: To Intervene or Not to Intervene?**

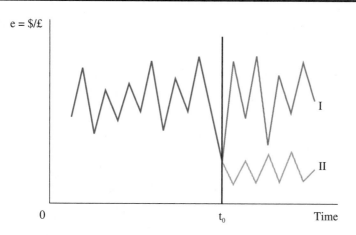

One interpretation of the "rules" of a managed float is to intervene in response to temporary disturbances in foreign exchange markets and to avoid intervention in response to permanent changes in the underlying equilibrium exchange rate. A practical difficulty arises because at the time of the disturbance (t_0), a policy decision must be made but the precise nature of the disturbance is unknown.

If central banks intervene often in foreign exchange markets, the heavily managed float will function much like an adjustable-peg exchange rate system. The primary advantage claimed for such active management of the exchange rate involves the greater reduction in exchange rate uncertainty than under a more flexible rate regime. For intervention to maintain the exchange rate successfully, monetary authorities must allow it to affect the money stock; that is, they must not sterilize.[20] If a currency depreciates in foreign exchange markets and the domestic central bank intervenes to stop the depreciation, the domestic money stock falls. This lowers domestic prices, raises interest rates, and may lower output. These changes help eliminate the balance-of-payments deficit that caused the initial currency depreciation. If the monetary authority sterilizes by making open market purchases to offset the intervention's impact on the money stock, the sterilization blocks the adjustment mechanism and the balance-of-payments deficit becomes chronic.

A managed float does not change the basic rule that correction of a payments imbalance requires a change in either the exchange rate or the money stock. When central banks engage in sterilized intervention to circumvent this basic rule, crises develop. Any advantage that pegged exchange rates may have in reducing uncertainty quickly disappears if they are accompanied by balance-of-payments crises due to interference with the economy's adjustment mechanisms. In other words, pegged exchange rates generate confidence and stability only if the chosen rates are sustainable.

[20]On sterilization, see sections 16.3.3 and 16.4.2, along with Case Four in Chapter Sixteen.

20.6.3 Macroeconomic Performance in the Post-Bretton Woods Years

For several years following the collapse of Bretton Woods in 1971, most policy makers and many economists considered the managed float a temporary measure. Gradually, alternatives faded as the world economy endured serious shocks, especially the OPEC oil embargo and price increase in 1973–1974, which brought rising price levels along with rising unemployment rates to most oil-importing countries.[21] Judging a return to fixed exchange rates not viable in the face of such shocks, policy makers turned their attention to defining specific rules as to when intervention should and should not occur or how "managed" the float should be. Eventually these attempts also failed. The *de facto* system, under which the major currencies floated subject to central banks' case-by-case intervention decisions, finally received official sanction at an economic summit in Rambouillet, France, in 1975 and in a revision of the IMF agreement in Kingston, Jamaica, in 1976.

The United States pursued expansionary policies in the mid-1970s in an effort to end its OPEC-induced economic slowdown. Other industrial countries, particularly West Germany and Japan, feared inflation more and waited several years before joining U.S. expansionary policies. The U.S. monetary expansion of the mid-1970s, unaccompanied by expansions by trading partners, produced a substantial depreciation of the dollar against other currencies. Even intervention by the United States, West Germany, and Japan proved unable to stop the depreciation because of the continuing rapid U.S. money growth. In 1979, President Jimmy Carter appointed Paul Volcker, a respected financier with a reputation for taking a tough stand against inflation, chairman of the U.S. Federal Reserve Board. The appointment resulted in new Fed policies of lower monetary growth as well as renewed confidence in the dollar among financial market participants.

The effects of the slowdown in U.S. monetary growth hit the economy at about the same time as a second round of OPEC oil price increases in 1979–1980. Fearful of encouraging the inflation they had worked so hard to eliminate, U.S. policy makers did not respond with expansionary monetary policies, as they had after the 1973–1974 oil shock, and the economy underwent a severe recession that lasted through 1983. Money growth rates remained low, but fiscal policy grew more expansionary as tax rates fell and government spending rose. The dollar appreciated dramatically, which had the effect of shifting demand away from U.S.-made goods and services toward foreign ones. *(Why?)* Gradually monetary policy loosened, but the dollar continued to appreciate into 1985, with virtually no intervention by the United States.

Although expansionary U.S. macroeconomic policies contributed to the recovery from the recession that opened the 1980s, the dollar appreciation also caused a significant redistribution of income. U.S. farmers found their overseas markets shrinking, while import-competing producers in U.S. industries such as automobiles, steel, and footwear endured increased competition from foreign rivals. Pressure mounted

---

[21]Section 19.10 examines supply shocks and policy responses to them under alternative exchange rate systems.

for protectionist policies, and Congress considered hundreds of bills ranging from import quotas for particular industries to across-the-board import tariffs.

Although the dollar began to depreciate in early 1985, protectionist pressures continued to grow. In September 1985, the Reagan administration responded with the Plaza Accord, named after the Plaza Hotel, where policy makers reached the agreement. The Group of Five nations (known as G-5—the United States, Britain, Japan, Germany, and France) agreed to intervene in foreign exchange markets to bring about a depreciation of the dollar. The dollar actually had begun to depreciate in March, several months before the Plaza meeting; in the months following the September accord, policy makers combined active intervention to lower the value of the dollar with public statements designed to "talk the dollar down" and with expansionary U.S. monetary policy, primarily cuts in the discount rate. The dollar continued to decline against trading-partner currencies, most notably those of Germany and Japan. By November 1986 it had reached postwar lows against the yen.[22]

By 1987, attention had turned to slowing the dollar's decline. Based on the Louvre Accord of February 1987, the Group of Seven countries (G-7 consists of the G-5 plus Canada and Italy) engaged in coordinated foreign exchange market intervention through 1987 and 1988, attempting to hold the dollar within (secret) bands.[23] The G-7 also explored possibilities for increased macroeconomic policy coordination in an effort to continue holding exchange rates within mutually agreed-on bands.

The extent of intervention in foreign exchange markets has varied since 1988. The dollar has experienced periods of both appreciation and depreciation against the currencies of most major trading partners. As the models of Chapters Seventeen and Nineteen would lead us to expect, strong U.S. export performance accompanied the depreciations. During the recession of the early 1990s, exports proved one of the few sectors of the U.S. economy to grow strongly, although that growth slowed in 1992 as Germany and Japan entered recessions of their own and bought fewer U.S.-produced goods and services. Germany's expansionary fiscal policy (related to unification of former East and West Germanies) and tight monetary policy caused both tensions between the United States and Germany and the near breakdown in 1992 of the European Union's efforts at monetary integration.[24]

By 1994, U.S. unemployment had fallen below many analysts' estimates of the full-employment level. Policy makers expressed concern about inflationary pressure, and the Federal Reserve tightened monetary policy. Most European economies experienced some recovery from their recessions, but European unemployment remained very high by U.S. standards. High government budget deficits continued to constrain fiscal policy both in the United States and in Europe.[25] Japan employed expansionary fiscal policy, beginning

---

[22]For a discussion of the differential depreciation of the dollar against various currencies, see section 12.8.

[23]The G-7 countries never announced the band parameters, and financial market participants spent much time guessing about their values. Observing intervention activity by the central banks provided the major clues to the exchange rate values acceptable or unacceptable to the Group of Seven.

[24]See Case One in Chapter Sixteen and Case Three in Chapter Seventeen, as well as the upcoming section 20.8.

[25]We shall see some of the reasons behind the constraints on European fiscal policy in section 20.8 on the European Monetary System.

Table 20.10 □ U.S. Intervention in Foreign Exchange Markets, 1989–1995

Year	Total Intervention	Frequency (Number of Days of Intervention)
1989	Sell $8.90 billion for DM; Sell $10.58 billion for ¥	97
1990	Sell $200 million for DM; Sell $2.18 billion for ¥	16
1991	Buy $1.34 billion with DM; Sell $520 million for DM; Sell $30 million for ¥	13
1992	Buy $1.27 billion with DM; Sell $250 million for ¥	8
1993	Buy $1.43 billion with ¥	5
1994	Buy $3.50 billion with DM; Buy $2.60 billion with ¥	5
1995[a]	Buy $3.25 billion with DM; Buy $3.10 billion with ¥	8

[a]Through September.

Source: Federal Reserve Bank of New York, *Treasury and Federal Reserve Foreign Exchange Operations Report.*

in 1992 and continuing through 1995, in an effort to emerge from its deepest recession since the Second World War. The Japanese economy began to recover by 1995, but the financial sector remained weak and vulnerable. Both Germany and Japan used expansionary monetary policy in 1995 in efforts to strengthen their recoveries.

Throughout most of the early 1990s, the dollar depreciated, especially against the Japanese yen and the German mark.[26] All three central banks intervened periodically to buy dollars. However, intervention occurred more rarely than during the Plaza-Louvre period of the late 1980s; and macroeconomic policy in the major countries appeared less directed toward exchange rates, even when those rates exhibited dramatic movements. Table 20.10 reports the frequency and scale of U.S. foreign exchange market intervention in recent years.

Policy makers and economists remain divided over the managed floating exchange rate system. On the one hand, many worry about exchange rate volatility, the resource-allocation effects of unpredictable changes in real exchange rates, and lack of effective policy coordination among the major players, especially the United States, Germany, and Japan. On the other hand, most acknowledge both the difficulties of returning to a fixed rate system in an environment of highly mobile capital and governments' reluctance to subordinate domestic economic interests to the requirements of external balance, as demanded by a fixed rate regime.

---

[26]Section 18.5 covers the long-run real depreciation of the dollar against the yen.

Table 20.11 □ **Annual Changes in U.S. Real GDP and Price Level, 1973–1994 (Percent)**

Year	Change in Real GDP (Q)	Change in GDP Deflator (P)	Year	Change in Real GDP (Q)	Change in GDP Deflator (P)
1973	5%	6%	1984	6%	4%
1974	−1	9	1985	3	4
1975	−1	10	1986	3	3
1976	5	6	1987	3	3
1977	5	7	1988	4	4
1978	5	8	1989	3	4
1979	3	9	1990	1	4
1980	−1	10	1991	−1	4
1981	2	10	1992	2	3
1982	−2	6	1993	3	2
1983	4	4	1994	4	2

Source: *Economic Report of the President, 1995.*

In summary, the years since 1973 represent a period of widely varying degrees of management of exchange rates. Table 20.11 presents the yearly performance of U.S. real output and prices under the managed float.

Unfortunately, our study of the history of international monetary regimes cannot answer the fundamental question of which arrangement is best. The answer depends in complex ways on an individual country's circumstances. We cannot even rely on a comparison of past macroeconomic performance under the various systems, because each historical period brought unique challenges and shocks to the world economy. We can, however, determine the facets of the different systems that worked well and those that apparently contributed to instability or other problems. In the next two sections, we summarize and briefly evaluate the main arguments for using fixed versus flexible exchange rates as a basis for the international monetary system.

20.7   The Fixed-versus-Flexible Debate

20.7.1   Pros and Cons of Fixed Exchange Rates

We came across two major arguments for using fixed exchange rates earlier in the chapter. Proponents of fixed exchange rates believe that they impose price discipline by preventing monetary authorities from engaging in excessively expansionary (and thus inflationary) monetary policies. Proponents also claim that fixed exchange rates reduce uncertainty over the future value of the exchange rate and thereby encourage international economic activity that enhances the world economy's efficiency.

Price Discipline

The price-discipline argument would be a solid one if a fixed exchange rate did indeed prevent inflationary monetary policies. Unfortunately, historical evidence suggests that central banks inclined to pursue overly expansionary policies tend to circumvent attempts at discipline. Under a fixed exchange rate, a country with a balance-of-payments deficit experiences a reduction in its money stock as the central bank intervenes to prevent a currency depreciation. Should the central bank be inclined to avoid this loss of control of the money stock (that is, the discipline of a fixed exchange rate), sterilization policies can offset the reduction in the money stock, resulting in a chronic deficit. In other words, a fixed exchange rate can impose price discipline only on central banks willing to submit to it. Also, a fixed exchange rate system based on a reserve currency, such as Bretton Woods, does not impose effective price discipline on the reserve-currency country, which conducts monetary policy for the entire system and exports any inflation it generates.[27]

Proponents of flexible rates counter the price-discipline argument by pointing out that voters can discipline governments that follow inflationary policies. Since the switch to flexible exchange rates, voters in the United States, Japan, and several countries of Western Europe have voted governments out of power for the inflation generated by their policies. Overall, experience suggests that avoiding inflation requires vigilance and discipline on the part of both voters and policy makers; a stable exchange rate regime can help, but it cannot substitute for sheer willpower and determination in avoiding inflation.[28]

Reduced Volatility and Uncertainty

Exchange rate volatility and/or uncertainty can cause two problems. First, they may discourage beneficial international economic activity, such as trade and foreign investment, by making the domestic-currency value of future receipts and payments less certain. Second, volatile exchange rates can cause costly movement of resources as hard-to-predict exchange rate changes alter relative prices and shift demand from domestic to foreign goods and vice versa. We have seen that such shifts in demand alter the performance of trade- and nontrade-oriented sectors of the economy, and resource reallocations can generate political pressures for protection and other beggar-thy-neighbor policies.

Empirical evidence suggests that real exchange rates have exhibited much more volatility since the shift to more flexible exchange rates. However, many analysts argue that exchange rate volatility actually exerts little negative effect on international trade and investment because of the availability of forward markets for hedging.[29] Proponents of fixed exchange rates counter by pointing out that forward contracts involve costs and may not be available for long-term economic activities

---

[27]On reserve-currency countries, see section 16.6.

[28]Recent evidence suggests that the design of policy-making institutions also plays a role; Case One examines one example—central bank independence.

[29]Section 12.3.2 explains hedging. The Obstfeld paper in the chapter references reviews the evidence on real exchange rate volatility. The annex in the Goldstein book (also in the chapter references) summarizes the evidence on links between exchange rate volatility, trade, investment, and economic growth.

such as foreign direct investment—although innovative financial instruments to provide long-term hedges are evolving. Numerous empirical studies that attempt to quantify the effect of exchange rate uncertainty on international trade, investment, or economic growth provide mixed rather than definitive results.

Real Exchange Rate Adjustment

We have seen that changes in real exchange rates play a vital role in macroeconomic adjustment to the shocks that constantly impinge on economies. Under a fixed exchange rate regime, changes in real exchange rates ($R \equiv P/eP^*$) can occur in one of two ways: changes in countries' price levels or currency realignments. Proponents of fixed exchange rates claim that, by preventing unilateral devaluations and revaluations, a fixed rate regime avoids the competitive devaluations that plagued the world economy during the Great Depression of the 1930s. Instead of such beggar-thy-neighbor policies, adjustment occurs when countries allow their price levels to adjust or alter their pegged exchange rate *in consultation with trading partners.* Opponents of fixed rates point out that devaluations occurred too infrequently under Bretton Woods, resulting in chronic failure to adjust to shocks, and that price levels adjust only very slowly, leaving economies to endure extended periods of unemployment. They also note that Bretton Woods required countries to hand the control of their money stocks over to the reserve-currency country—the United States.

Exchange Crises

Countries that operate under a fixed exchange rate regime can avoid crises only if central banks play by the rules and allow adjustments in the money stock to correct any balance-of-payments disequilibria. When a government intervenes, sterilizes, and refuses to adjust the exchange rate, pressures build and crises develop. Balance-of-payments crises hardly reduce uncertainty, and they discourage international trade and financial activities.[30] A fixed exchange rate regime builds confidence in the stability of exchange rates only when policy makers follow policies that facilitate adjustment. These policies include, first, not sterilizing the effects of the balance of payments on the money stock and, second, timely devaluations and revaluations when pegged exchange rates deviate too far from equilibrium. Both policies require a subordination of internal balance to external balance that may prove politically and economically painful in the short run. When market participants lose faith in a government's ability to withstand the domestic political pressures generated by this pain, a balance-of-payments crisis develops as portfolio owners' willingness to hold the domestic currency drops due to expectations of an impending devaluation.[31] Governments may attempt to avoid such crises by imposing capital controls that seek to limit the scale of payments imbalances, but such controls interfere with the world economy's efficiency and tend to lose their ineffectiveness as individuals learn to circumvent them.

---

[30]See sections 16.4.4 and 20.8, along with Cases One and Three in Chapter Sixteen and Three in Chapter Seventeen on recent crises within the Exchange Rate Mechanism of the European Monetary System.

[31]See Cases Four in Chapter Twelve, One in Chapter Thirteen, One and Three in Chapter Sixteen, and Three in Chapter Seventeen.

20.7.2 Pros and Cons of Flexible Exchange Rates

Crisis Avoidance

The primary benefits claimed for flexible exchange rates are essentially the same as those for market-determined prices in any market: smooth, automatic, and continuous adjustment to equate quantity demanded with quantity supplied. Such adjustment under a flexible exchange rate has several advantages. It avoids large balance-of-payments deficits and surpluses, because the exchange rate moves in response to any tendency for either to develop. Needed adjustments in the real exchange rate can occur quickly through changes in e rather than slowly through changes in countries' price levels.[32] Flexible exchange rates also render many policy decisions unnecessary, thereby avoiding the potential for policy errors or delays. These characteristics, taken together, imply that floating rates may help avoid the crises that occur under fixed rates when expectations of an impending devaluation or revaluation build.

The fact that flexible exchange rates respond to all disturbances in the foreign exchange market also is used as an argument *against* flexible rates on the grounds that they produce unacceptable levels of volatility. Of course, this need not be true; exchange rates, like any other price, will be volatile only if the demand and supply conditions in the foreign exchange market are volatile. However, because expectations are so important in asset markets, such as the foreign exchange market, the volatility of demand and supply conditions can be difficult to predict and to control.

Policy Independence and Symmetry

Flexible exchange rates allow each country to determine its monetary policy independently. Recall that a major problem during the final Bretton Woods years involved other countries' dissatisfaction with U.S. monetary policy, the inflationary effects of which were exported from the reserve-currency country through the rules of the adjustable-peg system. If one believes, as some economists do, that policy makers will misuse their ability to control the money stock by creating excessive monetary growth and inflation, one could view the ability of flexible exchange rates to give policy makers such power as a *minus* rather than a *plus* for flexible rates. Flexible exchange rates do free up the money stock for use in pursuing domestic targets; but as we saw in Chapters Eighteen and Nineteen, once we introduce price flexibility, monetary policy can affect only the price level in the long run and not real output.

On the other hand, floating rates do permit countries to determine their own inflation rates, rather than forcing them to "import" the inflation rate chosen by the reserve country. When the domestic and foreign inflation rates differ, the exchange rate adjusts in the long run in accordance with purchasing power parity.[33] This allows countries to pursue different rates of inflation, whereas a fixed exchange rate system such as Bretton Woods requires countries either to follow the same rate of inflation or to realign their currencies.

---

[32]On real exchange rate adjustment under fixed and flexible exchange rates, see sections 19.7.2 and 19.9.

[33]See Chapter Eighteen, especially sections 18.3 and 18.4, on purchasing power parity.

Consistency with Capital Mobility

A country operating under a fixed exchange rate can avoid crises only so long as its policies convince foreign exchange market participants that no devaluation is forthcoming, because this confidence makes portfolio owners willing to hold assets denominated in the domestic currency. A loss of confidence in the future value of the domestic currency causes portfolio owners to sell assets denominated in that currency and requires the central bank to sell foreign exchange reserves to maintain the fixed exchange rate. If the crisis is large enough in magnitude, the central bank may run short of reserves or ability to borrow and may be forced to devalue, leading to a further loss of confidence in the currency.

Economies become particularly sensitive to such crises when capital is highly mobile, because portfolio owners can move easily in and out of different currency holdings. Therefore, a common policy for governments seeking to avoid exchange crises under a fixed exchange rate involved controls on capital flows. But capital mobility serves an important economic function; it allows capital owners to move their resources to locations where those resources will be most productive. In other words, capital mobility allows countries to take advantage of the gains from intertemporal trade. Capital controls interfere with this capital-allocation process and can generate efficiency losses for the world economy. By eliminating the major source of crises—expected currency devaluations—flexible exchange rates can eliminate one of the most important reasons that governments institute capital controls.

Excessive Volatility and Real Exchange Rates

While a perfectly flexible exchange rate gives policy makers control over the money stock, it requires them to ignore movements in the exchange rate. Many economists doubt policy makers' ability to ignore the exchange rate because of its broad impact on the domestic economy. Evidence suggests that, in the short and medium runs, changes in the nominal exchange rate also affect the real exchange rate. This implies that movements in e lead to changing fortunes for the trade-sensitive sectors of the economy. Real appreciations, in particular, can cause dramatic increases in domestic political pressure for protectionism, as occurred in the United States in the early and mid-1980s.

The empirically demonstrated link between changes in real and nominal exchange rates in the short and medium runs also limits the ability of a flexible exchange rate to insulate an economy from foreign monetary disturbances. If changes in the foreign money stock, for example, lead to proportional changes in the foreign price level and in the exchange rate in the long run, then foreign monetary policy exerts no real influence on the domestic economy because it does not alter the real exchange rate. But in the short run, empirical evidence suggests that changes in the nominal exchange rate tend to alter the real exchange rate, as the foreign price level adjusts slowly to the change in the money stock, reducing the claimed insulation properties of a floating exchange rate.

As the preceding discussion makes clear, there is no "ideal" international monetary system. Both fixed and flexible exchange rate regimes have their advantages, and it is not surprising that various countries use different arrangements to manage their exchange rates. During periods of stability when countries pursue similar policy paths, either system can work quite well. During periods of instability in the world economy, both systems encounter problems and each has strengths and weaknesses in the face of different types of shocks.

20.7.3 Insulation from Economic Shocks

We have seen that three major classes of shocks disturb economies and require responses from policy makers: demand shocks that originate in the money market, demand shocks that originate in spending patterns, and supply shocks. Fixed and flexible exchange rates provide an economy with differing degrees of insulation and ability to adapt to these various shocks. For economies more prone to one type of shock than to others, these differences represent an important consideration in the countries' choice of exchange rate regime.

Shocks to the Domestic Money Market

Fixed exchange rates tend to provide more insulation than flexible ones to economies subject to frequent shocks originating in money markets. Consider what happens when the domestic money stock falls (or domestic money demand rises). Under a fixed exchange rate, the balance of payments moves toward a surplus, and the central bank must intervene by buying foreign exchange to prevent an appreciation. The money stock rises and reestablishes equilibrium in the domestic money market. *(Analyze the effects using an aggregate demand–aggregate supply diagram.)* If, instead, the economy operated under a flexible exchange rate, the monetary shock would appreciate the currency, shift demand toward foreign and away from domestic goods, and require a fall in the domestic price level to bring the economy back to internal balance. *(Analyze the effects using an aggregate demand–aggregate supply diagram.)* So, for economies prone to shocks to their domestic money market, fixed exchange rates provide an advantage over flexible ones in the form of this insulating property.

Shocks to Spending on Domestic Goods and Services

Flexible exchange rates tend to provide more insulation to economies subject to frequent shocks originating in output markets or spending patterns. Consider an economy that experiences a decline in demand for its exports. Under a fixed exchange rate, the decline in income reduces money demand, puts downward pressure on the interest rate, and causes a capital outflow. To keep the domestic currency from depreciating in response to the balance-of-payments deficit, the central bank must sell foreign exchange and reduce the domestic money stock. This accentuates the decline in aggregate demand and means that the price level must fall by more to restore full employment—a slow and painful adjustment process. *(Analyze the effects using an aggregate demand–aggregate supply diagram.)* Under a flexible exchange rate, the balance of payments deficit depreciates the domestic currency rather than reduces the money stock. This shifts demand away from foreign goods toward domestic ones and mitigates the shock's negative impact on employment and output. A flexible exchange rate allows the economy to return to long-run equilibrium more quickly (because the exchange rate adjusts more quickly than the price level) and minimizes the shock's short-run recessionary impact. *(Analyze the effects using an aggregate demand–aggregate supply diagram.)* This implies that a flexible exchange rate regime provides advantages to economies that face primarily spending shocks to their output markets.

Supply Shocks

As we saw in Chapter Nineteen, flexible exchange rates provide policy makers with more choices in their responses to supply shocks. When a country experiences a permanent negative supply shock, of the kind examined in section 19.10, no policy can restore output permanently to its preshock level. A permanent negative supply shock reduces the economy's ability to produce goods and services and shifts its long-run aggregate supply curve to the left. Different macroeconomic policies can, however, influence how long the economy takes to adjust to its new long-run equilibrium, the extent of unemployment and reduced output during the adjustment period, and the shock's final impact on the price level.

A fixed exchange rate constrains policy makers to pursue macroeconomic policies consistent with balance-of-payments equilibrium and rules out expansionary monetary policy as a temporary device to cushion a supply shock's impact on the economy. Many economists believe that, had the OPEC oil shock of 1973–1974 occurred while the major industrial economies still operated under the fixed exchange rates of Bretton Woods, the shock's short-term impact on unemployment could have been much more severe. The economies generally responded to the OPEC shock with expansionary monetary policy that, while it contributed to inflation, did mitigate the short- and medium-run rise in unemployment.[34] This experience, coming at a time when negotiations to replace the Bretton Woods system were underway, played a role in discouraging countries from committing themselves to another fixed exchange rate system.

In sum, different exchange rate regimes carry different implications for economies' adjustments to various types of economic shocks. Fixed exchange rates may mitigate domestic monetary shocks but exacerbate spending shocks. Flexible exchange rates may mitigate spending shocks but exacerbate monetary shocks. Floating rates provide policy makers with more flexibility in responding to supply shocks, but also give policy makers the option of following overly expansionary policies in vain attempts to avoid the inevitable decline in output following a permanent negative supply shock.

20.7.4 Lessons from Recent Experience

Since the collapse of Bretton Woods in 1971–1973, policy makers, economists, and myriad pundits have engaged in dialogue and debate over the history and future course of the international monetary system. Was Bretton Woods responsible for the economic growth and stability of the 1950s and 1960s? Or was it a flawed system that lasted as long as it did only because of the period's otherwise strong economic performance? Do flexible exchange rates doom the world economy to inflation and lack of policy coordination? Or does exchange rate flexibility free the world economy of the constraints and overemphasis on external balance imposed by a fixed rate regime? Even well-informed analysts

---

[34]Such a policy corresponds to following path "b" rather than path "a" or "d" in Figure 19.13. Of course, flexible exchange rates also allow policy makers to choose the very inflationary path "c."

and scholars differ in their answers to these questions. However, there are some observations, based on experience since 1971, upon which most economists agree.

1. Flexible exchange rates have allowed countries to choose more divergent money-growth and inflation rates.

2. Flexible exchange rates provide some insulation against foreign monetary disturbances, but only in the long run. In the short and medium runs, adjustment in the price level lags behind changes in money stocks, leading to changes in the real exchange rate that affect output in both the domestic and foreign economies.

3. Domestic political pressures from trade-oriented sectors of the economy make policy makers sensitive to changes in the real exchange rate and cause them to intervene in foreign exchange markets to maintain export competitiveness and domestic sectoral employment, even when the exchange rate is supposed to be flexible.

4. Flexible exchange rates speed the responsiveness of the price level to changes in the money stock, as currency depreciation raises import prices and causes workers to demand higher wages in compensation. Therefore, monetary policy influences real output and employment for shorter periods.

5. Inflation has risen during the floating period, but voters have disciplined many governments for inflation; and governments have learned to control, at least to some extent, their inflationary tendencies.

6. Flexible rates have helped economies adjust to supply shocks and other disturbances that require changes in real exchange rates.

7. Flexible rates, by removing the fear of crises caused by expected devaluations, have helped facilitate reduced governmental capital controls, allowing countries to capture the gains from intertemporal trade.

8. Exchange rates, both nominal and real, often have exhibited high short-term volatility, much of which economists cannot explain based on existing models. Longer run exchange rate movements, however, appear roughly consistent with relative purchasing power parity and with existing economic models' predictions concerning policy effects.

9. Increased exchange rate flexibility does not appear to have exerted a dramatic negative influence on the growth of international trade and investment.

10. The willingness and ability of governments to coordinate their macroeconomic policies appear to depend more on the state of the domestic economy than on the exchange rate regime.

20.8 The European Monetary System

20.8.1 Recent History

The major Western European currencies, as well as the U.S. dollar, have operated under a managed float since the early 1970s, but the European arrangement is somewhat more complicated. Since 1979, the currencies of most European Union members have been *fixed* relative to one another and have *floated* as a group against the dollar and other currencies, an arrangement called the **Exchange Rate Mechanism (ERM)** of the **European Monetary System (EMS)**.[35] A weighted basket or composite of the EU currencies called the **European Currency Unit (ECU)** floats against non-EU currencies. Within the ERM, each central bank intervenes in foreign exchange markets to keep the value of its currency fixed within a prescribed band against the ECU and, thereby, against other EU currencies.[36]

We have seen that attempts to maintain fixed but adjustable exchange rates among countries following highly divergent macroeconomic policies are fraught with difficulties, especially when capital is highly mobile, as is increasingly the case in Europe. When individual countries follow divergent policies, those policies create pressures for exchange rate realignments, because rates threaten to move outside their defined bands. Foreign exchange market participants begin to anticipate those realignments and start to buy currencies expected to face revaluation and to sell those subject to devaluation. Such speculative activity involves little risk because the official bands tell market participants which way the exchange rate adjustments must move; the process resembles buying or selling stock if you somehow knew the stock price could move only in one direction. Expectations become self-fulfilling prophecies as demand falls for already weak currencies and rises for already strong currencies.

Given what we know about the difficulties of maintaining fixed exchange rates among economies that follow divergent economic policies and encounter diverse economic shocks, why does the European Union persist in its efforts, and how has the system survived? Proponents of European monetary integration hope to accomplish several goals, some economic and some political. First, they hope to improve European economic performance and make Europe more "competitive" with other industrial areas, especially the United States and Japan. For 20 years, Europe has suffered much higher unemployment rates (an average of approximately 10 percent), lower rates of job creation, and deteriorating technological leadership compared with its rivals. Second, proponents hope to present the United States with a more nearly equal macroeconomic counterpart in terms of economic size and voice in international negotiations. Third, within Europe, proponents believe monetary integration will encourage intra-European trade and investment by lessening exchange rate fluctuations. Fourth, proponents want to use the policy credibility of governments and other institutions that have established policy making reputations (for example, Germany's Bundesbank) to help establish sound policies in countries that lack such credible institutions (for example, Italy and Greece).[37] Finally, supporters of European economic and political integration more generally hope that monetary integration will contribute to the momentum toward more unified policy making in Europe.

---

[35]All EU member countries join the EMS; however, not all join the ERM, which requires intervening to enforce the fixed intra-EU exchange rates. For example, Britain avoided joining the ERM until 1990 and dropped out in 1992 (see Case Three in Chapter Seventeen).

[36]Prior to 1993, the ERM bands allowed currencies to fluctuate up or down by 2.25 percent, or by 6 percent in some cases (Spain, Britain, Portugal, and Italy). Since the European currency crises of 1993 (discussed below), the bands have been widened to ±15 percent, and Italy and Britain have left the ERM.

[37]On Germany's reserve- or key-currency role within the EMS, see section 16.6.

Table 20.12 □ **EMS Exchange Realignments (Percent Changes in Bilateral Rates)**

Year	Date	German Mark	Belgian Franc	Danish Krone	French Franc	Irish Pound	Italian Lira	Dutch Guilder	Greek Drachma
1979	September 24	+2.00		−2.86					
	November 30			−4.76					
1981	March 23						−6.00		
	October 5	+5.50			−3.00		−3.00	+5.50	
1982	February22		−8.50	−3.00					
	June 14	+4.25			−5.75		−2.75	+4.25	
1983	March 21	+5.50	+1.50	+2.50	−2.50	−3.50	−2.50	+3.50	
1985	July 22	+2.00	+2.00	+2.00	+2.00	+2.00	−6.00	+2.00	−13.10
1986	April 7	+3.00	+1.00	+1.00	−3.00			+3.00	−25.80
	August 4					−8.00			−1.01
1987	January 12	+3.00	+2.00					+2.00	−9.11

Source: Michael T. Belongia, "Prospects for International Policy Coordination: Some Lessons from the EMS," Federal Reserve Bank of St. Louis *Review* 70 (July–August 1988), p. 21; data from Deutsche Bundesbank and International Monetary Fund.

Given this ambitious agenda and the problems that face fixed exchange rate systems, how has the European Monetary System survived? During most of the post-1979 period, the pegged bilateral exchange rates within the EMS were adjustable and, in fact, were subject to periodic realignments, usually one or two per year as reported in Table 20.12. The realignments involved revaluations of the Deutsche mark and the Dutch guilder, devaluations of the Italian lira and Greek drachma, and mixed changes in the other currencies. In addition, EU rules require that member countries with BOP surpluses lend to countries that encounter difficulties as a result of BOP deficits. Usually this involves Germany lending Deutsche marks to other central banks that, in turn, sell those marks in the foreign exchange market to support their respective currencies. Throughout much of the 1980s, many EU members maintained some degree of capital controls that limited the magnitude of BOP deficits and helped keep the required intervention and realignments manageable. But capital controls imposed costs on European economies as they prevented capital from flowing to its most productive location. The European program to complete an open internal market by 1992 required elimination of capital controls and made currencies more vulnerable to crisis under the adjustable-peg system of the ERM. The increased capital mobility limited the ability of European governments to realign their currencies without generating expectations-based crises. Beginning in 1987, facing the constraints of increasingly mobile capital, EU member countries began to place more emphasis on following convergent macroeconomic policies, resulting in less pressure for exchange rate realignments, and the deliberate periodic adjustments ceased. The period between 1987 and mid-1992 was one of relative quiet on the monetary front in Europe; but the quiet was not to last.

Table 20.13 □ **Maastricht Plan and Timetable for EU Monetary Unification (circa 1991)**

Stage	Dates	Tasks
Stage I	Ratification (November 1993)–December 1993	Remove all capital controls All EU member countries join ERM Accomplish policy convergence Establish interim European Monetary Institute to create framework for the European System of Central Banks
Stage II	January 1994–No later than January 1999	Make all national central banks independent (see Case One) Central banks cease direct finance of government debt Remove all technical barriers to monetary unification Determine which member countries satisfy convergence criteria (see below) Set date for initiation of Stage III
Stage III	January 1, 1997 *if* at least half of EU member countries meet convergence criteria No later than January 1999 for countries meeting convergence criteria	Liquidate interim European Monetary Institute Replace national currencies with a single European currency Begin operation of European System of Central Banks

20.8.2 Maastricht, Monetary Unification, and Crisis

The EMS is part of a long history of attempts to integrate the Western European economies.[38] Like the broader policy coordination efforts of the G-7 or of the world economy as a whole, integration efforts within the EMS encounter resistance when they threaten national sovereignty over macroeconomic policy. However, in 1991 at the Dutch town of Maastricht, the EU governments outlined an ambitious plan for a three-stage process of **economic and monetary union (EMU)** that included "the irrevocable fixing of exchange rates leading to the introduction of a single currency" and the goal of "definition and conduct of a single monetary policy and exchange rate policy the primary objective of both of which shall be to maintain price stability."[39] Table 20.13 outlines the timetable and strategy of Europe's plan for monetary unification. Proponents of the Maastricht plan hoped to accomplish two goals: (1) by creating a common currency, minimize transaction costs and establish a stable exchange rate system not susceptible to crises generated by expected currency realignments, and (2) by creating a European system of central banks, give other EU countries a voice in monetary policy, currently dictated largely by Germany's Bundesbank.

---

[38]For a discussion of integration in terms of international trade, see Chapter Nine.
[39]Europe's Werner Report made a proposal similar in many respects to Maastricht back in 1971.

The Maastricht plan turned out to be enormously controversial—in Europe and elsewhere. The timetable established at Maastricht required ratification by all 12 member countries—a process temporarily waylaid by Denmark's *no* vote in the summer of 1992. The political and economic uncertainty generated by the lengthy process of ratification contributed to buildups of speculative pressure against some member currencies. EU members refused to discuss any possible currency realignments, fearful of contributing to the growing expectations that devaluations of the Italian lira, Spanish peseta, Portuguese escudo, and British pound were inevitable.[40]

EU governments pressured German policy makers to expand the German money stock to lower German interest rates and ease the devaluation pressures. But German policy makers refused, not wanting to add monetary expansion to their dramatic fiscal expansion to cover the costs of unification.[41] This forced other EU members—some deep in recession—to continue to intervene to support their currencies against the Deutsche mark. In September 1992, rather than continue to intervene and contract their money stocks, Italy and Britain withdrew from the ERM and Spain devalued the peseta. [42] Denmark and Britain, in exchange for their ratification of Maastricht, won the right to "opt out" of its provisions for a common European currency.

A year of more or less constant crises followed. These crises forced several currency realignments, despite modest German monetary expansion. Ireland devalued the pound, and Spain and Portugal devalued their respective currencies several times. The EU reaffirmed each ERM member country's responsibility to intervene when its currency threatened to move outside the set trading band. Most European countries found themselves in recession and increasingly unwilling to constrain their monetary policies to maintain their exchange rates against the Deutsche mark. In August 1993, the exchange rate bands for ERM currencies were widened to ±15 percent except for the guilder-mark rate, making the system resemble more closely a floating exchange rate. By 1994, Europe showed signs of recovery from recession, and the exchange crises of 1992–1993 abated. The wide ±15 percent bands remained in place, but most currencies (with the exceptions of the pound and lira, which remained outside the ERM) returned to their earlier, narrower bands until March 1995, when the peseta and escudo were again devalued.

Historian Harold James, in his official IMF history, *International Monetary Cooperation since Bretton Woods,* summarizes the basic dilemma confronting European efforts at monetary integration:

> [Intervention] could not be a substitute for policy adjustment. In this case, central bank intervention could not counter the perception that two fundamentally opposed political pressures were pulling the system apart. Germany, threatened

---

[40]See section 16.4.4 on e^e.

[41]For various perspectives, see Case Four in Chapter Twelve, Case Three in Chapter Fourteen, Case One in Chapter Sixteen, and Case Three in Chapter Seventeen.

[42]See the cases cited in footnote 41.

Table 20.14 □ EU Monetary Unification Timetable (circa December 1995)

Date	Tasks
January 1, 1998	Determine which EU countries qualify for participation by applying convergence indicators (see below) to end-of-1997 data
January 1, 1999	Irrevocably fixed exchange rates between participating currencies Begin conduct of monetary policy by the European System of Central Banks
January 1, 1999–January 1, 2002	Conduct national government, bank, and some business transactions in the new Euro
No later than January 1, 2002	Issue Euro bills and notes for public usage (After six-month transition) Require exchange of all participating national currencies for Euros

by a large fiscal deficit as a consequence of the high costs of political unification, required monetary restraint. Tight money policies, however, elsewhere in Europe were blamed for the severity of the recession, and political pressure mounted for a relaxation. Germany's neighbors faced a dilemma: if they followed German monetary restraint, their recession would be intensified; if they failed to tighten, funds would flow out and lead to an exchange rate crisis.[43]

The early 1990s, especially the economic implications of Germany's unification, confronted the European Union with a dramatic economic shock originating in the system's reserve-currency country. That this shock seriously damaged the EU's fixed exchange rate system, just as U.S. policy during the late 1960s seriously damaged Bretton Woods, should not surprise us. But, having nominally survived German unification, the EU plan for monetary unification continues to face daunting challenges. How member countries adapt to these challenges will determine whether, how, when, and for whom monetary unification happens.

In December 1995, members of the European Union reconfirmed their intention to proceed with monetary unification. They announced the new European currency would be christened the **Euro**.[44] Table 20.14 summarizes the new post-crises timetable. As the countdown to the first key date began, attention focused on which countries would manage (or choose) to satisfy the economic criteria to participate.

Maastricht Convergence Indicators
Prior to participation in the planned common central bank, common monetary policy, and common currency, the Maastricht plan requires countries to conform to rules regarding exchange rate stability, inflation, interest rates, government budget

---

[43]Page 487.

[44]Throughout years of discussion of a common currency, the unofficial name most often used was the *ecu* (note the similarity to the European Currency Unit, or ECU). When a last-minute decision resulted in *Euro* instead, some commentators speculated that *ecu* had lost out because it sounded (especially to Germans) "too French."

deficits, and government debt.[45] These rules are known as **convergence indicators,** because they measure whether the EU economies follow policies similar enough to make a common currency viable. This raises a politically controversial issue: Should the subset of countries achieving policy convergence move ahead with plans for a common currency without the other EU members, an outcome known as *two-speed Europe?* The Maastricht plan's answer to this question is *yes.* All countries that do satisfy the criteria embark on unification as of January 1, 1999; other EU members may join later as they meet the convergence criteria.

The Maastricht treaty requires each EU member country to meet five economic convergence criteria before it can participate in monetary unification:

1. Currency must have remained within its ERM trading bands for at least two years with no realignment.

2. Inflation rate for the preceding year must have been no more than 1.5 percent above the average inflation rate of the three lowest-inflation EU members.

3. Long-term interest rate on government bonds during the preceding year must have been no more than 2 percent above the average interest rate of the three lowest-inflation EU members.

4. Budget deficit must not exceed 3 percent of the country's GDP.

5. Government debt must not exceed 60 percent of the country's GDP.

Table 20.15 demonstrates that the number of EU members satisfying the Maastricht convergence criteria has declined since 1990, when four countries met all five conditions. In 1994, only Germany and Luxembourg did. Other countries failed primarily on the exchange rate criterion (1), a legacy of the exchange crises of 1992–1993, and on the deficit (4) and debt criteria (5), because of increased government spending and reduced tax revenues associated with the recent recession.

If monetary unification proceeds according to plan, an EU conference in 1998 will determine, based on 1997 data, which countries meet the criteria. As of 1995, only Germany and Luxembourg seem certain to, hinting at the possibility of a very small European monetary union! Other countries are striving to meet the criteria in time as well as lobbying for relaxed and lenient interpretations of those criteria.[46]

Some economists and policy makers agree that a lenient interpretation is appropriate. They argue that any delay in monetary union because of EU members' failure to meet strict criteria merely provides opportunity for another period of instability to disrupt the schedule yet again. Proponents of leniency also argue that EU member countries will find it much easier to meet the criteria once monetary

---

[45]For more detail on the convergence criteria and their likely application, see the Pollard article in the chapter references.

[46]At first glance, the criteria appear rather specific; but, in fact, they embody quite a bit of "wiggle room." See the Pollard article in the chapter references.

Table 20.15 ▫ **EU Members' Status on Maastricht Convergence Indicators**

Country	Number of Criteria Met					
	1990	1991	1992	1993	1994	1995[b]
Belgium	2	3	3	3	3	3
Denmark	5	4	4	3	3	4
France	5	5	4	4	4	4
Germany	5	4	4	3	5	5
Greece	0	0	0	0	0	0
Ireland	4	4	4	3	3	4
Italy	0	0	0	0	0	0
Luxembourg	5	5	5	4	5	5
Netherlands	3	4	3	3	3	4
Portugal	0	0	0	0	0	1
Spain	1	1	1	1	0	1
United Kingdom	3	3	2	2	3	4
Austria[a]	4	4	3	2	3	3
Finland[a]	2	2	1	1	2	3
Sweden[a]	2	3	2	1	1	1
Number meeting all criteria	4	2	1	0	2	2

[a]Joined EU since 1991.

[b]Estimates. As of 1995, Finland, Greece, Italy, Sweden, and the United Kingdom did not participate in the ERM.

Source: Patricia S. Pollard, "EMU: Will It Fly?" Federal Reserve Bank of St. Louis *Review* 77 (July–August 1995), p. 6; updated with 1995 estimates from Thomas Kamm, "Monetary Chaos Precedes Europe's Single Market," *The Wall Street Journal,* July 28, 1995, p. A10, data from Deutsche Bank Research.

unification occurs and that a union including only Germany and Luxembourg would be hardly worth the trouble. Opponents of leniency argue that it threatens the monetary union because a single currency cannot possibly work among countries following divergent macroeconomic policies. In addition, countries with strong anti-inflation sentiment, particularly Germany, do not want to tie themselves to countries that lack the discipline to meet the strict convergence criteria.

Besides the obvious political or sovereignty-related arguments by politicians and policy makers against monetary union, there are economic arguments both in favor of and against such ventures. Those arguments attempt to shed light on the question, *how large is the optimal currency area?*

20.8.3 Optimal Currency Areas

Two geographic regions that use a common currency encounter both advantages and disadvantages compared with use of two separate and distinct currencies. As the area using a common currency grows, the costs tend to rise and the benefits to decline. The area that maximizes the benefits minus the costs of using a single currency is called an **optimal currency area.** Robert Mundell developed the theory of optimal currency areas in the early 1960s, but the issue has taken on new urgency and interest with recent events in the European Union.[47]

The potential benefits of using a common currency include reduced exchange rate volatility, reduced transaction costs, and enhanced policy credibility. As we noted earlier, uncertainty about future changes in exchange rates may discourage international trade and financial activity. A common currency—the ultimate fixed exchange rate—eliminates this uncertainty and allows firms to specialize according to comparative advantage and to plan imports and exports without worrying about losses due to exchange rate moves and without having to hedge in forward markets. *(What do you think would happen to trade between New York and California if the two states used different currencies?)* A common currency also allows individuals and firms to avoid the transaction costs of exchanging one currency for another when engaging in travel or cross-border transactions. Today in the European Union, if one begins with one currency and exchanges it step-by-step for each of the other EU currencies *without* buying any goods or services, the transaction cost of the currency exchanges alone reduces the original sum by approximately half. A single currency throughout Europe would eliminate these costs. The higher the share of intragroup trade and investment within a set of countries, the greater these benefits from a single currency.

A common currency also can provide an advantage to policy makers by allowing them to credibly commit to a future course for monetary policy. This argument proves particularly relevant for the European case. There, the German Bundesbank's strong anti-inflation reputation, if transferred to a European central bank with a common currency, would allow historically high-inflation countries such as Italy and Greece to commit themselves to noninflationary policies. For this reason, much of the monetary-union debate in Europe centers on the proposed European central bank's policy mandate; inflation-conscious citizens and policy makers want to ensure it would follow policies similar to those of the Bundesbank rather than the Banca d'Italia!

A common currency involves costs as well as benefits. Countries lose the ability to pursue independent monetary policies. After all, a common currency represents the ultimate fixed exchange rate ($e \equiv 1$), and we have seen that a fixed exchange rate eliminates monetary policy as a macroeconomic policy instrument. A common currency also eliminates exchange devaluations or revaluations as a policy tool within the currency area. The entire region using a common currency binds itself to follow the same monetary policy.

Given the list of costs and benefits, how does a region determine whether a currency area would provide net benefits? The literature on optimal currency areas suggests a region is likely to gain from a common currency if (1) the region is subject primarily to common shocks that affect the entire area similarly and not to shocks that affect subregions differentially, (2) labor is mobile within the region, and (3) a tax-transfer system exists to transfer resources from subregions performing strongly to those performing poorly.

---

[47]The Tavlas articles in the chapter references contain detailed but accessible discussions of optimal currency areas.

If different shocks buffet subregions, policy makers in those subregions may need to follow different monetary policies or to allow their exchange rate to move to offset the shocks' short-run effects. For example, suppose the German economy booms while Britain's languishes. Britain might follow an expansionary monetary policy relative to that of Germany, thereby depreciating (or devaluing) the pound and shifting demand toward British goods and services and away from German ones, at least in the short run. Such adjustment becomes impossible under a common currency.

When some subregions of a currency area grow quickly and others grow more slowly, labor flows across subregions represent another possible adjustment mechanism. If cultural or institutional factors restrict such labor flows, then differential monetary policies and exchange rate realignment may be necessary—ruling out a common currency. An alternative means of dealing with differential regional growth involves fiscal transfers from growing regions to stagnant ones. Suppose Florida booms while California suffers a recession. The U.S. federal tax and transfer system conducts an automatic transfer from Florida to California: Florida's tax payments rise with income, California's fall; Florida's transfer receipts (that is, unemployment benefits, welfare payments, and so forth) fall with rising income, and California's rise. These transfers partially offset the two states' differential economic performance and lessen the need for any exchange rate adjustment (impossible, of course, within the United States).

How does the European Union measure up to these standards for an optimal currency area? Most empirical studies have compared Europe to the United States, which, after all, operates under a common currency. Members of the EU appear more subject to differential shocks than are the regions of the United States. Labor is considerably less mobile between countries in Europe than between U.S. regions, perhaps because of greater language and cultural differences. Finally, the separate nation-states of the EU have no supranational tax and transfer system to reallocate resources across regions in response to differential shocks, although the EU does administer some development funds for less-developed or declining regions in the Union. All these findings have led many economists to question whether the EU really represents an optimal currency area, despite the relatively high level of intragroup trade. These questions take on even more significance as the EU extends its membership and announces plans to expand into Eastern Europe.

In the end, considerations such as countries' willingness to abandon their traditional national currencies and to subordinate their national policy-making sovereignty to the Union will determine the extent and pace of Europe's move to a common currency.

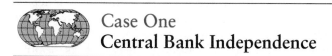

Case One
Central Bank Independence

Throughout this book, we have spoken of central banks conducting monetary policy. In fact, the degree of independence that central banks enjoy in deciding how contractionary or expansionary monetary policy should be differs greatly across

Figure 20.4 □ **Central Bank Independence and Average Inflation Performance**

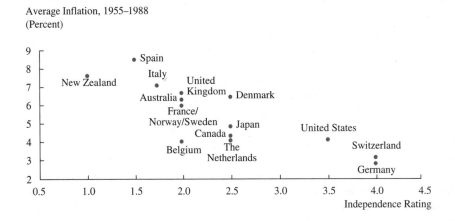

Source: *The Wall Street Journal,* August 26, 1992; data from Alberto Alesina and Lawrence Summers, *Journal of Money, Credit, and Banking,* 1992.

countries. In some countries, such as Germany, the central bank is independent not only of direct political pressure from the electorate but also of direct pressure from other government policy makers, in particular those responsible for fiscal policy. In other countries, such as England, the central bank is much more vulnerable to such pressures, giving it limited independence to decide the stance of its monetary policy. Recently, economists have begun to focus attention on this differential independence as a potential explanation for the very different inflation performances of different countries.

Fiscal policy makers, when their own excessively expansionary policies push up the domestic interest rate or appreciate the currency, often pressure monetary policy makers to offset those effects by engaging in an expansionary (often called an accommodating) monetary policy. If the central bank complies, the long-run result is inflation. Since the 1980s, one broad trend has been for many central bankers to accept price stability or the avoidance of inflation as their primary target. This requires that they "just say no" to fiscal authorities, a step much easier in a system that makes the central bank formally and legally independent.

Early evidence from the pioneering studies suggests that central bank independence may lead to better inflation performance. Figure 20.4 summarizes the results of one study. Before concluding on the basis of inflation performance that all central banks should be independent, we need to ask how independence affects the other major macroeconomic goals. There is no evidence that independence prevents central banks from responding appropriately to achieve real GNP or employment targets. In fact, some evidence indicates that more independent central banks may achieve not only better inflation results, but better output and employment results as well.

In response to poor inflation performance during the 1970s and 1980s, several countries, including Canada and New Zealand, instituted legal changes that make their central banks more independent. New Zealand's law gives the central bank a performance goal of 0–2 percent inflation; failure to meet that goal can lead to dismissal of the bank's policy makers.[48] The Maastricht Treaty requires all EU member countries to establish central bank independence by 1999 in order to qualify for participation in the monetary union. France has altered its laws to meet the requirement, but as of early 1996 the Bank of England remains legally subservient to the Treasury.

Despite the evidence linking independence to lower inflation, central bank independence is likely to remain controversial. During recessions, both elected officials and the electorate may want more expansionary monetary policies—despite evidence that their primary long-run effect is a rise in the price level. The U.S. recession of the early 1990s brought political pressures to limit the Federal Reserve's legal independence from Congress, and the fiscal impact of German unification generates similar concerns about the traditionally fiercely independent Bundesbank.

Some economists and policy makers have argued that a central bank's degree of formal independence may actually matter less than the clarity and narrowness of its mandate. Many central banks, including the U.S. Federal Reserve, are required by law to pursue multiple goals. In the case of the United States the Federal Reserve Bank Act of 1978 assigns the Fed two goals: full employment *and* price stability. Given the mounting evidence that monetary policy cannot affect employment or output in the long run, many economists believe central banks should have a single policy goal: price stability, along with the legal independence to pursue that target free from political pressure and interference.

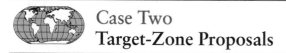

Case Two
Target-Zone Proposals

Since the breakdown of Bretton Woods 25 years ago, skeptics of flexible exchange rates have proposed many reforms of the current system of managed floating. Target-zone proposals are among the most common, especially for the world's key currencies, now the dollar, the mark, and the yen. In fact, we can think of target zones as simply a particular type of managed float. **Target zones** consist of wide trading bands around a set of adjustable pegged exchange rates. Bands of ±10 percent, for example, allow exchange rates to vary by as much as 20 percent before they reach the band's edge and authorities intervene to prevent the exchange rate from moving outside the band.

On the surface, target zones seem an attractive combination of the strengths of fixed and flexible rates. They limit exchange rate volatility but allow policy makers

---

[48]The Waller article in the chapter references discusses the implications of "performance contracts" for central bankers.

some discretion in their monetary policy (so long as the exchange rate remains within the band and requires no intervention). Compared with the current *ad hoc* managed float, target zones provide rules for countries' decisions about when to intervene and, if announced publicly, could anchor foreign exchange market participants' expectations about exchange rate policy.

A closer look at target zones reveals potential weaknesses. First, note the similarities between the European Exchange Rate Mechanism and the target-zone proposal. The ERM's frequent crises, outlined in section 20.8.2, suggest that target zones might fall victim to the same problems. To be effective, target zones must be credible; that is, market participants must believe policy makers will hold exchange rates within their specified bands. But, what would prevent the same expectations of devaluations and revaluations that periodically destabilize the ERM? After all, even ±15 percent bands could not prevent devaluations of the Spanish peseta and Portuguese escudo in 1995. Even with wide target-zone bands, policy makers still must make a credible commitment to defend those bands; otherwise, the system becomes a *de facto* float.

A target-zone system also requires that the central exchange rates, around which the bands lie, be defined. Different proposals differ in exactly how this would be done. One, by John Williamson of Washington's Institute for International Economics, proposes that the central rates be adjusted automatically for inflation differentials and for shocks that alter equilibrium real exchange rates. In other words, Williamson proposes a system of target zones for *real* exchange rates. But existing empirical work provides no clear basis for defining equilibrium real exchange rates over the relatively short time horizons over which policy decisions must be made. Another potential problem arises over allocating the responsibility for intervention when an exchange rate does reach the edge of its target zone. Suppose the dollar, mark, and yen operated under a target-zone system. Which country would be responsible for intervention to maintain the bands? Unless these rules were specified in advance, the system's operation would resemble the current managed float with its *ad hoc* intervention decisions.

Summary

International trade and financial transactions require some means of exchanging one currency for another, known as an *international monetary regime*. The major types of regime include fixed exchange rates, flexible exchange rates, and managed floating. Each arrangement has benefits and costs; so the choice involves trade-offs depending on the individual country's economic situation.

The major strengths attributed to fixed exchange rates include discipline against inflationary policies and reduction in exchange rate uncertainty. Flexible exchange rates, on the other hand, promote adjustment and eliminate the need for foreign exchange market intervention, thereby allowing each country to determine its own monetary policy independently.

Since 1973, the major currencies have operated under a managed float that attempts to capture the benefits of both fixed and flexible exchange rates. Ideally, a managed float would allow the forces of supply and demand to determine the long-run paths of exchange rates while using intervention to smooth out short-term fluctuations. In practice, the lack of information concerning the nature of disturbances when policy decisions must be made makes it difficult to choose the optimal extent of intervention.

Members of the European Union seek to integrate their economies more closely by entering a currency union. However, crises have plagued the early stages of those plans because the transitional period involves the often unstable combination of fixed exchange rates, divergent macroeconomic policies, and capital mobility.

Looking Ahead

We have focused so far on developing general models that provide basic insights into macroeconomic policies, events, and performance for virtually any country. However, some countries face special challenges in designing and implementing sound macroeconomic policies. Two such groups are developing economies and countries in transition from central planning to more market-oriented economic systems. In Chapter Twenty-One, we turn our attention to the problems and prospects facing these countries.

Key Terms

convertible currency
gold standard
mint exchange rate
price discipline
specie-flow mechanism
gold-exchange (gold-dollar) standard
key (reserve) currency
adjustable-peg system
fundamental disequilibrium
tranches
conditionality
liquidity

dollar standard
managed (dirty) float
leaning-against-the-wind policies
Exchange Rate Mechanism (ERM)
European Monetary System (EMS)
European Currency Unit (ECU)
economic and monetary union (EMU)
Euro
convergence indicators
optimal currency area
target zones

Problems and Questions for Review

1. Explain the determination and maintenance of the exchange rate between the German Deutsche mark and the French franc
   (a) Under the gold standard.
   (b) Under the Bretton Woods gold-dollar standard.
   (c) Under the Exchange Rate Mechanism of the European Monetary System.
   (d) Under the economic and monetary union proposal of the Maastricht Treaty.

2. What considerations does the optimal currency area literature suggest a group of countries should take into account in making the decision whether to adopt a common currency? Explain.

3. Comment on the following statement: "A fixed exchange rate regime cannot work as long as policy makers place more importance on internal than on external balance."

4. What is the practical shortcoming of the following rule for policy makers under a managed floating exchange rate system: "Intervene in foreign exchange markets to offset the effects of temporary disturbances, and allow the exchange rate to change in response to permanent disturbances."

5. Some analysts argue that a common European currency cannot work unless all members satisfy the Maastricht convergence indicators *prior* to joining. Others argue that EU member countries should adopt a common currency first and *then* satisfy the convergence indicators. What are some of the pros and cons of each argument?

6. Economists agree that moving from a fixed to a flexible exchange rate regime gives policy makers control of the domestic money stock. Ironically, this fact is used to argue for both fixed and flexible exchange rates. Explain.

7. Explain how proposals for an exchange rate regime based on target zones attempt to capture the benefits of both fixed and flexible exchange rates. In what sense is a target-zone system simply a special type of managed float? What are some of the potential weaknesses of target zones?

8. One possible international monetary regime consists of a world central bank conducting monetary policy and issuing a single currency used throughout the world. What would be the advantages of such a system? The disadvantages?

References and Selected Readings

Bailey, M. J., and G. S. Tavlas. "Trade and Investment Under Floating Exchange Rates: The U.S. Experience." *Cato Journal* 8 (1988): 421–442.
Accessible survey of the literature on exchange rate volatility, trade, and investment.

Bailey, M. J., and G. S. Tavlas. "Exchange Rate Variability and Direct Investment." *Annals of the American Academy of Political and Social Science* 516 (1991): 106–116.
Accessible survey of the literature on exchange rate volatility and foreign investment.

Black, Stanley W. "International Money and International Monetary Arrangements." In *Handbook of International Economics,* Vol. 2, edited by Ronald W. Jones and Peter B. Kenen, 1153–1194. Amsterdam: North-Holland, 1985.
Advanced treatment of alternative international monetary systems.

Bofinger, Peter. "The German Monetary Unification (Gmu): Converting Marks to D-Marks." Federal Reserve Bank of St. Louis *Review* (July–August 1990): 17–36.
Monetary aspects of German unification; for all students.

Bordo, Michael D. "The Gold Standard, Bretton Woods, and Other Monetary Regimes: A Historical Appraisal." Federal Reserve Bank of St. Louis *Review* (March–April 1993): 123–191.
Detailed but accessible examination of modern international macroeconomic experience.

Eichengreen, Barry. "European Monetary Unification." *Journal of Economic Literature* 31 (1993): 1321–1357.
Prospects for a common currency in Europe as of 1993; intermediate.

Eichengreen, Barry. *Golden Fetters: The Gold Standard and the Great Depression, 1919–1939.* New York: Oxford University Press, 1992.

An economic history of the interwar period emphasizing the role of the gold standard in constraining governments' policy responses to the Depression; for all students.

Eichengreen, Barry. *International Monetary Arrangements for the 21st Century.* Washington, D.C.: The Brookings Institution, 1994.
Accessible survey of the history and likely future of the international monetary system.

Eichengreen, Barry, and Jeffrey Frieden. *The Political Economy of European Monetary Unification.* Boulder: Westview Press, 1994.
Collection of papers on political-economy aspects of Maastricht; level of papers varies.

Feldstein, Martin. "The Case Against Trying to Stabilize the Dollar." *American Economic Review Papers and Proceedings* (May 1989): 36–40.
Argues that exchange rate stability represents an additional policy target; see the Williamson article in the same issue for an opposing view. For all students.

Fieleke, Norman S. "The International Monetary Fund 50 Years After Bretton Woods." Federal Reserve Bank of Boston *New England Economic Review* (September–October 1994): 17–30.
The evolution of the IMF's role in the international monetary system; for all students.

Friedman, Milton. "The Case for Flexible Exchange Rates." In *Essays in Positive Economics.* Chicago: University of Chicago Press, 1953.
One of the first serious calls for a change to a flexible exchange rate regime; for all students.

Garber, P., and L. Svensson. "The Operation and Collapse of Fixed Exchange Rate Regimes." In *Handbook of International Economics,* Vol. 3, edited by G. M. Grossman and K. Rogoff, 1865–1912. Amsterdam: North Holland, 1995.
Advanced survey of the theoretical and empirical literatures.

Goldstein, Morris. *The Exchange Rate System and the IMF.* Washington, D.C.: Institute for International Economics, 1995.
Proposal to reform the role of the IMF in the international monetary system; for all students.

Isard, Peter. *Exchange Rate Economics.* Cambridge: Cambridge University Press, 1995.
Intermediate-to-advanced level survey of the literature on exchange rate regimes.

James, Harold. *International Monetary Cooperation Since Bretton Woods.* Oxford: Oxford University Press, 1996.
A comprehensive official history commissioned on the fiftieth anniversary of Bretton Woods.

Kenen, Peter B., et al., eds. *The International Monetary System.* Cambridge: Cambridge University Press, 1994.
Collection of papers on the strengths and weaknesses of the current international monetary system; level of papers varies.

Laurent, Robert D. "Is There a Role for Gold in Monetary Policy?" Federal Reserve Bank of Chicago *Economic Perspectives* (March–April 1994): 2–14.
Another look at one of the enduring questions of international macroeconomics; for all students.

McKinnon, Ronald I. "International Money in Historical Perspective." *Journal of Economic Literature* 31 (1993): 1–44.
A review of international monetary history by an opponent of flexible exchange rates; intermediate.

Mills, Terence C., and Geoffrey Wood. "Does the Exchange Rate Regime Affect the Economy?" Federal Reserve Bank of St. Louis *Review* (July–August 1993): 3–20.
Macroeconomic performance under different exchange rate regimes; for all students.

Neely, Christopher J. "Realignment of Target Zone Exchange Rate Systems: What Do We Know?" Federal Reserve Bank of St. Louis *Review* (September–October 1994): 23–34.
More on target-zone exchange rate systems; intermediate.

Obstfeld, Maurice, and Kenneth Rogoff. "The Mirage of Fixed Exchange Rates." *Journal of Economic Perspectives* 9 (1995): 73–96.
Argues that permanently fixed exchange rates have become infeasible for all but a few countries; accessible to all students.

Persson, T., and G. Tabellini. "Double-Edged Incentives: Institutions and Policy Coordination." In *Handbook of International Economics,* Vol. 3, edited by G. M. Grossman and K. Rogoff, 1973–2030. Amsterdam: North Holland, 1995.
Advanced survey of the literature on governments' interaction in determining macroeconomic policy.

Pollard, Patricia. "Central Bank Independence and Economic Performance." Federal Reserve Bank of St. Louis *Review* (July–August 1993): 103–117.
More on the subject of Case One; for all students.

Pollard, Patricia. "EMU: Will It Fly?" Federal Reserve Bank of St. Louis *Review* (July–August 1995): 3–16.
Prospects for the EMU as of early 1995, focusing on the Maastricht convergence indicators; for all students.

Schlesinger, Helmut. "On the Way to a New Monetary Union: The EMU." Federal Reserve Bank of St. Louis *Review* (May–June 1994): 3–11.
Prospects for a European common currency as of 1994 by the former head of the Bundesbank; for all students.

Session on "Historical Perspectives on International Institutions." *American Economic Review Papers and Proceedings* 85 (May 1995): 317–334.
Evaluations on the 50-year anniversary of the Bretton Woods institutions.

Svensson, Lars E. O. "An Interpretation of Recent Research on Exchange Rate Target Zones." *Journal of Economic Perspectives* (Fall 1992): 119–144.
Accessible survey of one type of managed float, discussed in Case Two.

Tavlas, George. "The Theory of Optimum Currency Areas Revisited." *Finance and Development* 30 (June 1993): 32–35.
Accessible overview of the renewed interest in optimal currency areas.

Tavlas, George. "The 'New' Theory of Optimum Currency Areas." *The World Economy* (1993): 663–685.
Excellent, detailed survey of the current state of the literature on optimum currency areas; for all students.

Waller, Christopher J. "Performance Contracts for Central Bankers." Federal Reserve Bank of St. Louis *Review* 77 (September–October 1995): 3–14.
Evaluates performance contracts as a way of making central bankers accountable for their policy results; for all students.

Williamson, John. "The Case for Roughly Stabilizing the Real Value of the Dollar." *American Economic Review Papers and Proceedings* (May 1989): 41–45.
Accessible article that argues for targeting exchange rate stability (along the lines of the target-zone proposals in Case Two); see the Feldstein article in the same issue for an opposing view.

CHAPTER TWENTY-ONE

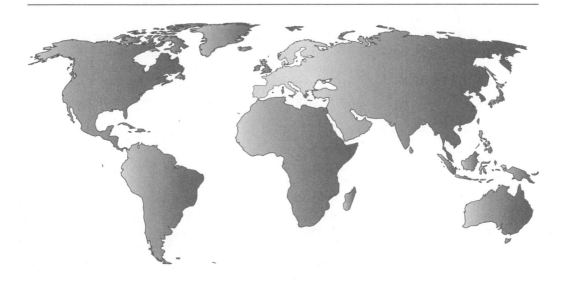

Macroeconomics of Development and Transition

21.1 Introduction

The models developed in Chapters Twelve through Twenty capture the fundamental knowledge economists have acquired about how the international macroeconomy and monetary system work. Those models provide insight into macroeconomic events and policy options for *any* country, and we have used many diverse countries as examples and cases. However, we should remember that not all countries' macroeconomies are alike. The United States and Britain, Kazakhstan, Singapore, and Ethiopia each face different macroeconomic challenges, policy options, and potentials. Important macroeconomic differences arise from countries' unique histories, economic and political systems, legal institutions, economic shocks, size, trading relationships, resource endowments, and many other factors.

Two groups of economies that exhibit distinctive macroeconomic characteristics and encounter special macroeconomic situations as a result are the developing economies and the countries in transition from central planning. Recall that in the *micro*economic portion of the book, we first developed economists' basic trade models in Chapters Two through Ten and then looked in Chapter Eleven at the unique trade-related issues and problems facing developing and transitional economies. Having now mastered the basic *macro*economic models, we are ready to take the analogous step and focus on the unique macroeconomic challenges facing developing and transitional economies.[1]

Macroeconomists have turned more attention to these countries over the last few years for several reasons. The internationalization of output and finance markets, represented by rapidly growing trade in goods, services, and financial assets, creates more numerous and more important linkages between developed and developing economies. These linkages sometimes grow largely unnoticed until a dramatic event—such as the OPEC oil shocks of the 1970s or the debt crisis of the 1980s—thrusts them onto newspapers' front pages. As developing economies grow and integrate themselves further into the world economy, macroeconomic interdependence becomes more pronounced. Events in Mexico following the December 1994 peso devaluation provide just one example in which recent macroeconomic events in a single developing economy exerted dramatic influence on other countries, both developed and developing.[2] Another reason for macroeconomists' increased attention to development-related issues comes from the emergence of a large group of "new" developing economies in the wake of the revolutions that swept the Soviet bloc in 1989–1991. Those economies face the need not only to establish sound day-to-day macroeconomic policies, but also to design economic and political institutions that make such policies sustainable and credible.

We turn first to developing economies in general, and then to the newest group of developing economies—those making the transition to market-oriented economic systems after decades of central planning.

21.2   Development and the Macroeconomy

Recall from Chapter Eleven that the fundamental goal of economic development is an improvement in the well-being of a country's residents. Per capita GDP is the most common, albeit imperfect, measure of development status. Based on 1993 per capita income, the World Bank classifies the 108 countries with annual incomes below $8,626 as developing countries, which the Bank further divides into 22 upper-middle income ($2,786 – $8,625), 41 lower-middle income ($696 – $2,785), and 45 low-income (< $696) countries.[3]

We also noted in Chapter Eleven that important differences exist *among* developing economies.[4] Most of sub-Saharan Africa, where economic development has progressed least, continues to exhibit very low per capita incomes, low or negative growth rates, along with high illiteracy and short life expectancy compared with other countries. Of the 45 countries classified as low income by the World Bank in 1995, 28 were in Africa. In East Asia, many developing countries still have low per capita

---

[1]We should note that division of the problems facing developing and transitional economies into *micro*economic ones and *macro*economic ones is highly artificial, so we hope readers will read or review Chapter Eleven, especially sections 11.5, 11.7, and 11.9, along with this chapter.

[2]Case Three in Chapter Sixteen covers the Mexican crisis.

[3]Table 11.1 ranks countries by per capita income and by the United Nations' Human Development Index. The table also notes countries classified as severely indebted or transitional.

[4]Table 11.2 summarizes some of the relevant differences.

incomes, but recent growth rates have been very high, and life expectancy almost equals that in developed economies. A handful of developing countries, most notably in Latin America, have accumulated such large amounts of external debt that, even after substantial debt rescheduling and forgiveness by creditors, that fact continues to dominate their macroeconomies and development prospects. And, as we shall see later in the chapter, the former centrally planned economies of Eastern Europe and Central Asia enjoy high incomes relative to those in many developing economies, as well as reasonably high life expectancy and literacy rates, but nevertheless saw dramatically negative growth rates during the transitional 1980s and 1990s.

21.2.1 Developing Countries' Prereform Macroeconomic Characteristics

We must keep in mind the important differences among developing economies; still, we can highlight a set of macroeconomic characteristics historically shared by many of these countries prior to their recent reforms. Common characteristics include

1. Pervasive government involvement in the economy, including widespread government ownership of infrastructure, industry, and land, as well as extensive regulation of day-to-day economic activity.
2. Poorly developed financial institutions.
3. Government finance through money creation rather than taxes or domestic borrowing.
4. Fixed exchange rates, accompanied by capital controls or direct government control of foreign exchange transactions.
5. Extensive foreign borrowing to cover current-account deficits.

Much of the reform undertaken by many developing countries during the 1980s and 1990s involves undoing or altering these characteristics, which most economists agree combined to hinder both macroeconomic performance and economic development. We can easily see, based on insights from the macroeconomic models developed in earlier chapters, how the five characteristics listed above would interact to affect economic performance adversely.

Government Ownership and Control
Government directly owns and controls much of the productive capacity in many developing countries. This can create a variety of microeconomic and macroeconomic problems.[5] Because a government typically maintains its ownership and control through its political power rather than by good economic performance that survives the test of the market, many state-owned enterprises exhibit low productivity, technological backwardness, and production patterns that ignore consumer preferences.

---

[5]In addition to the problems discussed here, many economists think that a pervasive state role in the economy creates additional opportunities for corruption; see the Tanzi article in the chapter references.

When governments own large sectors of the economy and engage in detailed management of business enterprises, policy decisions often hinge as much on politics as on economics. Plant managers, realizing that their fate depends more on political connections than on economic performance, have little incentive to enhance the productivity and efficiency of their plants. Wages often are set to reward the politically faithful with high-paying jobs, even if those wages far outstrip labor productivity and result in uncompetitive products. As a result, many state-owned enterprises require constant government subsidies to keep them in operation. In addition, the inefficient enterprises must have protection from foreign competition, so economies with extensive government ownership and control often forgo the gains from international trade. After all, if state-owned domestic producers ignore consumer wants, consumers will try to import goods from abroad (or emigrate) to satisfy those wants. To maintain its control, the government must stifle these attempts to circumvent its rules.

Poorly Developed Capital Markets

In a context of extensive government ownership and control, private capital markets can perform few of the functions they serve in industrial economies where government plays a more limited role. As a result, capital markets and financial services tend not to evolve in developing economies even when they are not restricted legally. The absence of well-developed financial markets then provides a rationale for still *more* government involvement to allocate capital and make investment decisions—tasks performed largely by private capital markets in the major industrial economies. Developing-country governments' poor policy records, bad reputations, and lack of credibility make it difficult for them to borrow by selling long-term bonds. At the same time, widespread government ownership of industry precludes a stock market as a major means of raising private funds to finance investment. This leaves only bank loans as a source of domestic finance; since governments typically control the banking sector, government often determines which enterprises receive financing and which do not. Government also can use credit terms, such as the interest rate charged on loans, to subsidize favored activities and tax unfavored ones.

Money-Financed Fiscal Expenditures

Government's broad role in the typical prereform developing economy dictates high levels of fiscal expenditures. And, as in *all* economies, these expenditures must be paid for. Developing countries often have poorly functioning tax systems for several reasons. Low incomes translate into a small tax base. Any high-income elites in the economy typically enjoy a close political relationship to the government, thereby insulating themselves from pressures to pay high taxes. And tax compliance and enforcement tend to be weak.[6] These characteristics combine to render tax finance of high levels of government expenditure infeasible.

An alternative means of finance is government borrowing from the domestic population. But, as we mentioned, governments with poor policy records and credibility

---

[6]Poorly developed tax systems cause many developing countries to rely heavily on taxes on imports and exports. This imposes an additional cost on the economy by discouraging international trade and forcing the economy to forgo part of the potential gains from trade.

problems find it difficult to borrow by selling long-term bonds to the domestic population. The basic reason is that governments can, after selling bonds, create excessive money growth and inflation, which erodes the real rate of return earned by those who bought the bonds. In fact, if the rate of inflation exceeds the nominal interest rate paid on the bonds, investors actually earn *negative* real rates of return—quite a deterrent to investment. This leaves just one source of domestic financing for government expenditure: money creation. In effect, the central bank prints money that the government then uses to buy goods and services. This combination of expansionary fiscal policy and expansionary monetary policy, of course, produces inflation, along with a bigger "inflation tax," which further reduces governments' ability to borrow.

To keep the required interest payments low on whatever domestic or foreign borrowing the government undertakes, policy makers have an incentive to keep interest rates artificially low. This discourages domestic saving and encourages capital flight, as domestic savers attempt to earn higher and more secure real rates of return by placing their funds in foreign assets.[7] Low interest rates combined with government control over bank lending allows politically favored sectors to receive handsome subsidies in the form of cheap loans. But low interest rates also result in a shortage of capital to finance investment and more opportunity for the government to allocate the scarce capital on political grounds.

Government Control over Foreign Exchange

In an attempt to keep domestic funds in the domestic economy rather than allowing them to escape as capital flight, governments often use capital controls or foreign exchange controls. Regulations may require exporters who earn foreign currencies to sell them immediately to the government in exchange for domestic currency. More generally, exchange controls can render the domestic currency nonconvertible for both current-account and capital-account transactions. These policies give governments even more control over the economy. By choosing to whom to allocate scarce foreign exchange and what exchange rate to charge for it, government can tax or subsidize each transaction.[8] Controls also restrict the domestic population's opportunity to circumvent the government's inflation tax by using a foreign currency instead of the domestic one in everyday domestic transactions.[9] Despite governments' best efforts, large-scale black markets in foreign exchange usually arise and limit official attempts to control access to loans and foreign exchange.

External Debt

Finally, we come to the characteristic that put developing countries on newspaper front pages around the world during the 1980s: external debt. We have discussed the

---

[7]A high rate of private saving is one of the important characteristics that distinguishes the fast-growing East Asian economies from most other developing countries.

[8]Case One contains more detailed discussion of exchange controls.

[9]This phenomenon is called *currency substitution* or, more specifically, *dollarization*. Case Three in Chapter Fifteen noted the recent legalization of dollar transactions in Cuba. Case Six in this chapter notes Russian efforts to restrict dollarization.

widely publicized debt problem of some developing countries at several points in the text. In Chapter Eleven, we analyzed external debt as one element of the general development problems facing developing countries and focused on the microeconomic aspects of their debt. *(We suggest a review of section 11.7.)* Here we note the relationship between the macroeconomic aspects of external debt and the other macroeconomic characteristics of developing countries.

Consider one of the fundamental macroeconomic relationships, the link between domestic investment, saving, the government budget, and the current-account balance. For every economy, it must be true, by definition, that[10]

$$I = S + (T - G) - CAB. \qquad [21.1]$$

Equation 21.1 implies that a country can finance domestic investment (I) in three ways: through domestic private saving (S), through government saving in the form of a budget surplus $(T - G > 0)$, or through a current-account deficit $(CAB < 0)$ and foreign borrowing. We argued above that the typical developing country exhibits a low rate of private saving, high government expenditure, and low tax revenues. Together, these characteristics limit the feasibility of the first two forms of finance.

Developing countries still can take advantage of domestic investment opportunities, but they must run current-account deficits and borrow abroad to finance them. This just represents the intertemporal-gains-from-trade argument again. If developing economies have good domestic investment opportunities but little current income with which to finance them, those countries can borrow from others that have investment funds available but few good domestic investment opportunities. Both parties gain, so long as the borrowing finances investment projects that prove productive enough to bring an economic return sufficient to repay the loan.

Unfortunately, many developing economies in the 1970s borrowed to finance projects that failed this criterion.[11] The projects failed for several reasons. Many of the projects were chosen by governments on a political rather than economic basis. Some funds supported grossly inefficient state-owned enterprises; others paid for military buildups; still others went to unproductive "prestige projects" such as national airlines, steel mills, and new capital cities. Other projects failed because economic conditions changed between the time the projects were undertaken and the time repayment came due. The industrial-country recession of the early 1980s caused primary-product prices to plunge, real interest rates to soar, and the dollar to appreciate dramatically against most developing-country currencies. As a result, borrowers suffered a decline in export earnings from which to make payments, a rise in interest payments, and a rise in the domestic-currency value of their outstanding foreign-currency-denominated loans. This unfortunate combination led many developing countries to the brink of default.

Only years of negotiations, detailed in section 11.7, ended the crisis with no major defaults and minimal long-term damage to the international monetary system.

---

[10]Section 14.7 develops this relationship.
[11]Section 11.7 provides details.

However, as section 11.7.4 makes clear, the debt crisis left a painful legacy and continuing economic problems for many developing countries. It did, however, have some positive effects as well. The debt crisis reminded developed and developing countries once again of their interdependence. The crisis also forced many developing countries to undertake long-needed economic and political reforms.

21.2.2 Reform

In a contest to select the top three events in the international macroeconomy over the past 15 years, policy reform in the developing countries would be a strong candidate for inclusion. One by one, following decades of dismal economic performance, many countries have changed some or all of the five key prereform macroeconomic characteristics listed above.[12] The reforms differ from country to country in their timing and breadth, but the most common changes fall into two groups. **Stabilization reforms** refer to policy changes that aim to achieve macroeconomic *stability*. The most basic elements of this stage of reform include cutting excessive government spending and reducing excessive money growth. Together, these changes help stabilize the value of the domestic currency and reduce inflation. The other major component of reform, **structural reform,** or **structural adjustment,** refers to changes in the basic *structure* of the economy. The most important element involves reducing the extent of government involvement in the economy and increasing the role for markets. Structural reforms attempt to provide stronger incentives for productive economic activities, including production, saving, investment, and international trade based on comparative advantage. Note, however, that stabilization and structural reforms cannot really be separated. After all, the primary forces that cause macroeconomic instability—excessive fiscal spending and money growth—follow directly from government ownership and control of the economy, and reducing government ownership and control requires structural reform.

Although the correspondence is rough and inexact, we can think of stabilization reform as improving control over the aggregate *demand* curve (especially, stopping the continual large rightward shifts that lead to persistent inflation) and structural reform as encouraging rightward shifts of the long-run aggregate *supply* curve, which represents the economy's basic productive capacity. Historically, many developing countries suffered a combination of (1) inefficient government management of the economy, which mired supply far to the left of its potential position based on the countries' resources, and (2) excessively expansionary fiscal and monetary policies, which continually shifted aggregate demand to the right and, given the economies' low productivities, generated persistent inflation and currency devaluations. Panel (a) of Figure 21.1 illustrates these effects. The fundamental policy reforms undertaken by many developing economies during the past 15 years attempt to undo this disastrous combination and move the economies to a situation more similar to that in panel (b) of Figure 21.1. The precise approach to reform and the

---

[12]In some cases, countries instituted reforms at least in part because of pressure from creditors and international organizations such as the International Monetary Fund.

Figure 21.1 ▫ **Macroeconomic Stabilization, Structural Reform, and Aggregrate Demand/Supply**

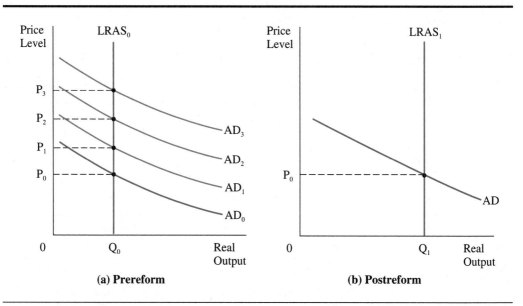

(a) Prereform   **(b) Postreform**

Panel (a) represents the typical macroeconomic situation in developing economies prior to reform. Overly expansionary fiscal and monetary policies shift aggregate demand (AD) continually to the right. Structural inefficiencies hold the long-run aggregate supply curve (LRAS) to the left of its potential position. This combination produces low levels of real output and rising prices. Reform shifts the situation to the one depicted in panel (b). Macroeconomic stabilization stops the continual rightward shift of AD, and structural reform allows LRAS to move to the right. This new policy combination produces higher rates of real output and steady prices.

relative emphasis on the many diverse aspects of reform vary greatly from country to country; however, we can note some common themes.

Privatization and Deregulation

The most basic structural reform involves reducing the role of government in the ownership and day-to-day control of the economy. Many state-owned enterprises have been privatized, or sold to private investors. The goal is to confront the enterprises with a competitive economic environment, forcing them to become more productive, efficient, competitive, and responsive to consumer preferences. Managers and workers in the new environment face stronger incentives to improve production techniques, minimize costs, adopt new technologies, and otherwise improve the enterprises' economic performance.

Privatization, as essential as it is to reform, can be a slow and difficult process. Emerging capital markets and investors find it hard to estimate reasonable prices for the enterprises up for sale, because their earlier performance under government ownership often provides a poor guide to their potential profitability. Foreign purchases of formerly state-owned enterprises can generate resentment of reform among the domestic population. Workers who held subsidized-wage jobs in the enterprises may oppose reforms that ultimately must limit wages to those justified by labor productivity. And, of course, some of the enterprises, established for political reasons, simply have no economic future and eventually must be closed or allowed to go bankrupt.

Financial Integration

Historically, many developing countries deliberately isolated themselves from world capital markets. Authorities prohibited or strictly regulated foreign investment in the domestic economy and tried to prevent any outflow of domestic funds. This isolation gave the domestic government a near monopoly over capital allocation. As a result, economically promising investment projects often went unfunded, while less promising ones received not only initial funding but an endless stream of government-financed subsidies as well.

Financial integration with world capital markets—the macroeconomic counterpart of trade liberalization—plays a vital role in undoing this legacy by replacing government control of the capital-allocation process with more efficiently functioning markets. These markets, by providing capital owners with vehicles to move their funds around the world, allow investors to compare investment projects across countries and to invest in the most economically promising projects. Governments lose their ability to channel funds into politically motivated white-elephant projects. Governments also gain an external check on their macroeconomic policies. If a government strays from the reform path and begins to follow policies not conducive to strong economic performance, investors can shift their funds away from that economy, signaling to the government the riskiness of its path.[13]

The changes associated with financial market integration also encourage domestic saving and create domestic sources of funds to finance investment projects. Even given their low incomes, developing country populations can generate impressive levels of saving—*if* convinced that government will not expropriate those savings, erode them through the inflation tax, or force them into instruments that pay low or even negative real rates of return.

Like privatization, financial market integration can prove politically difficult. Enterprises favored under the government capital-allocation regime may attempt to block reform that would result in their evaluation on economic rather than political criteria. Opening the economy to foreign investment may generate resentment, particularly in economies with colonial histories. And policy makers may not always appreciate the check on their policies provided by investors' ability to shift funds in response to policy changes.

Fiscal Consolidation and Tax Reform

Fundamental reforms of macroeconomic policy include reducing the level of government expenditure and shifting the finance of continuing expenditure away from money

---

[13]Some analysts worry that capital market may *over*react to a government's policy missteps, such as Mexico's 1994 devaluation, thereby worsening macroeconomic performance.

creation and toward taxes or government borrowing. The basic goal is reduction of the rate of growth in aggregate demand in order to reduce the exorbitant rates of inflation common in so many developing economies. Reducing government expenditure requires curtailing the role of government to include only those activities not well suited to markets, such as national defense, law enforcement, and some infrastructure projects. Activities not meeting this criterion can be privatized. Government also must cut subsidies to enterprises that continue under state ownership.

To reduce inflation, government expenditures that continue postreform must be financed more through taxes and government borrowing and less through money creation. Other aspects of reform help accomplish this shift, at least in the long run. For example, as reform improves policy making and economic performance, the government's policy-making reputation may improve to the extent that the domestic population willingly purchases government bonds to finance government expenditures. Integration with world financial markets helps ensure that the rates of return on such bond offerings will be competitive with those available on foreign assets.

As with all other aspects of reform, fiscal consolidation will not be universally popular. The country's elites may have adjusted to inflation and learned to circumvent government controls, so they may actually prefer continued inflation to either paying taxes to finance government expenditures or forgoing government services or subsidies.[14] And, of course, enterprises that lose their government subsidies may oppose reform.

Currency Convertibility

A country cannot enjoy the full gains from trade in goods and services or from intertemporal trade unless its currency is convertible. As long as government maintains control over foreign exchange transactions and sets artificial exchange rates for those transactions, international activity cannot be based on comparative advantage. Potential exporters, for example, have little incentive to produce for export if they know they must sell any foreign currency they earn to the government at artificially low prices. On the other hand, favored elites will import luxury consumption goods from abroad if provided with the requisite foreign exchange at reduced rates.

Currency convertibility implies that the exchange rate, if fixed, cannot be set too far from equilibrium in the foreign exchange market. Convertibility means that international traders and investors can demand that the central bank buy and sell foreign exchange at the pegged rate in amounts sufficient to cover the desired international trade and financial activities. If the pegged exchange rate strays too far from equilibrium, the excess demand or excess supply of foreign exchange will eventually exceed the central bank's ability to intervene and maintain the peg. If the central bank runs short of reserves, market participants may come to expect a devaluation and precipitate a currency crisis similar to Mexico's in December 1994 or to those within the European Monetary System in 1992 and 1993.[15]

---

[14]Brazil's inflation history, discussed in Chapter Nineteen Case Two, provides one example.

[15]On Mexico, see Case Three in Chapter Sixteen. On the EMS, see Case Four in Chapter Twelve, Case One in Chapter Sixteen, Case Three in Chapter Seventeen, and section 20.8.2.

One way to avoid such crises is to operate under a flexible rather than a fixed exchange rate regime. Developing countries undertaking reform often hesitate to make this move for two reasons. For very small developing economies, transactions in the domestic currency may be so infrequent and small that the foreign exchange market would bear little resemblance to the active and competitive markets for U.S. dollars, Japanese yen, and German marks. Forward and futures markets, in particular, may be nonexistent, leaving individuals and firms with little opportunity to hedge foreign exchange risks under floating rates. Perhaps more importantly, a fixed exchange rate, *if* crises can be avoided, can provide a small measure of price discipline as part of the reform process by forcing the central bank to shrink the money stock when the balance of payment shifts to deficit. However, we saw in Chapters Sixteen and Twenty that governments can circumvent such discipline if they are so inclined. Reforming governments may lean too heavily on the exchange rate as an aid to disinflation. If they refuse to devalue even when domestic inflation persistently outpaces foreign inflation, the result is a real currency appreciation (recall that the real exchange rate, or the relative price of domestic goods and services, equals $R \equiv P/eP^*$). This leads to declining exports, rising imports, and a growing current-account deficit. *(Why?)* If foreign-exchange-market participants view this trend as politically unsustainable, a currency crisis erupts.

Another disadvantage of fixed exchange rates comes from interaction between the exchange rate regime and the production structure of the economy. For many developing economies, such as those in Africa, a mere handful of goods—often primary products—account for all export revenues. Figure 11.6 documents this characteristic. World demand for these primary products moves with business-cycle conditions in the major industrial countries, so a recession there can severely reduce demand for a developing country's two or three export products. We learned in section 20.7.3 that a fixed exchange rate can exacerbate the macroeconomic impact of negative shocks to export demand. This happens because the initial decline in demand pushes down the domestic interest rate and leads to a balance-of-payments deficit. To hold the pegged exchange rate, the central bank must place further contractionary pressure on the economy by intervening in the foreign exchange market and shrinking the money stock. Under a flexible exchange rate, on the other hand, the balance-of-payments deficit would cause the domestic currency to depreciate, lower the relative price of domestic goods and services, and improve the competitiveness of the country's products on world markets. *(Illustrate these results in an aggregate demand–aggregate supply diagram.)*

Increased recognition of the limits on the discipline that fixed exchange rates can impose, of the crisis-generating potential of fixed rates with mobile capital, and of the interaction between fixed exchange rates and negative export-demand shocks has led growing numbers of developing economies to adopt more flexible exchange rate regimes as part of their reform packages. Early empirical evidence from these economies suggests that a flexible exchange rate *can* work for developing countries so long as they follow fiscal and monetary policies consistent with macroeconomic stability.[16]

---

[16]The article by Quirk and Cortés-Douglas in the chapter references summarizes some of the empirical studies performed by the IMF on this issue.

Investment Finance and Debt

The debt crisis of the 1980s reminded debtors and creditors alike of the fundamental rules for sound debt management: (1) to avoid insolvency crises, an investment project must produce a rate of return sufficient to cover loan payments; (2) to avoid illiquidity crises, loan maturity and project maturity must match so that returns from the project come in time to make loan payments; and (3) uncertainty regarding future economic events, both domestic and international, constrains the prudent amount of debt accumulation any country can undertake.[17]

Ideally, the aspects of reform already discussed can go a long way toward preventing a repeat of the debt crisis. With government playing more limited roles in the economy of most developing countries, future borrowed funds are less likely to be wasted on unproductive, politically motivated projects. Privatization facilitates the growth of stock markets and equity finance, in which the debtor's obligation to the creditor varies with economic outcomes.[18] This helps avoid the problem that arose in the 1980s when debtors—because their debt took the form of bank loans—owed fixed repayment schedules regardless of their investment projects' outcomes. Active capital markets help potential investors evaluate more accurately the financial return likely from various projects. Removal of capital controls and foreign exchange controls allows investors to express confidence or lack thereof in policy makers' decisions by "voting with their funds." Governments' improved reputations encourage domestic saving and make long-term government bonds a more feasible means of finance. Early evidence indicates that the nature of developing-country borrowing has shifted away from the prereform pattern of predominantly bank loans to developing-country governments and toward debt and equity flows from private lenders to private borrowers.

21.2.3 Lingering Risks

Most analysts' current concerns about developing countries' macroeconomies focus on three issues. First, some countries still have not embarked on meaningful stabilization and structural reform programs. As other developing countries do reform their macroeconomies, those that fail to reform run the risk of becoming even more isolated. International investors, faced with a choice between postreform and prereform countries as hosts for investment, are likely to choose those with the strongest reform programs. Empirical evidence already supports these predictions. During the early 1990s, private capital flows to developing economies grew at a dramatic pace. But most of that capital flowed to a handful of actively reforming recipients: Argentina, Brazil, and Mexico in Latin America, and China, South Korea, and Thailand in Asia.

Second, developing countries remain, as a group, heavily dependent on external sources of finance for investment. These capital inflows will continue only so long as the recipient countries maintain macroeconomic stability and provide attractive

---

[17]Section 11.7.2 develops the economic logic underlying each rule.

[18]Section 11.7.1 treats the distinction between debt and equity finance and its role in the debt crisis.

real rates of return.[19] Fortunately, the same policies conducive to establishing *foreign* investor confidence also promote *domestic* saving and discourage capital flight, so there is some long-term potential for building domestic saving into a viable source of investment finance. In the meantime, the need to maintain foreign investor confidence may constrain policy makers' options. This can help hold countries on the reform path, but it also can make economies prone to expectation-generated crises similar to the one suffered by Mexico in late 1994.

Finally, the lowest income countries remain deeply indebted and largely isolated from participation in world markets. Many have lagged in instituting macroeconomic reforms, and several continue to suffer from wars, both civil and with neighbors. Foreign investors, with the exception of official lenders such as the World Bank, show little interest in investing in these economies.

The largest cluster of such countries lies in sub-Saharan Africa, where real per capita GDP fell by almost 1 percent per year 1980–1985 and by one-half of 1 percent per year 1986–1994.[20] Inflation in the region averaged 24 percent in 1994, excluding Zaire, where hyperinflation reached 23,900 percent. Government involvement in the economies remains high, and many continue to finance large-scale losses incurred by state-owned enterprises. Overall government budget deficits average about 9 percent of GDP per year. Money growth rates are erratic, and real interest rates often are negative as a result of rapid inflation. The countries continue to run large current-account deficits, which implies that they continue to add to already large external debts. By 1994, total debt for the region equaled its total GDP. Between 1991 and 1993, only about 1.5 percent of total foreign investment inflows into developing economies went toward sub-Saharan Africa. Not all these problems result from poor macroeconomic policy. The countries suffered dramatic declines in prices for their highly concentrated primary product exports during the industrial-country recession of the early 1990s. But failure to undertake and maintain strong macroeconomic reforms exacerbated the negative shock's impact on the economies.

21.3   Transition and the Macroeconomy

Prior to the revolutions of 1989–1991, most analysts considered the centrally planned economies of the Soviet bloc to be developed industrialized economies. In one sense, this analysis was correct, because we shall see that industrialization—in fact, *over*industrialization—is a key characteristic of many of these economies. Yet, in other senses the analysis was wrong or misleading, due in part to the lack of reliable economic statistics. The recent revolutions raised the Iron Curtain to reveal economies with low levels of productivity, drastic shortages of consumer goods, outmoded technologies, and severe environmental problems. These characteristics give

---

[19]The Dadush and Brahmbhatt article in the chapter references attempts to identify economic trends that precede foreign investors' decisions to abandon an economy.

[20]Data on sub-Saharan Africa come from International Monetary Fund, *World Economic Outlook*, May 1995, 98-107. For more information on macroeconomic performance among the subset of African countries that use the CFA franc, see Chapter Sixteen, Case Two.

the transitional economies much in common with the developing world, despite the presence of huge industrial plants, sophisticated military capabilities, and relatively high per capita incomes.

21.3.1 Centrally Planned Economies' Prereform Macroeconomic Characteristics

Substantial differences exist *among* the transitional economies, and these differences carry important implications for the countries' prospects. For some countries, such as Poland and Hungary, the histories of central planning are relatively short, and central planning never fully enveloped those countries' highly productive agricultural sectors. For others, such as the former Soviet Union, the history of central planning is much longer, and that planning encompassed and often devastated agriculture.

A few countries, such as China, embarked on market-oriented economic reforms with no explicit political revolution. Another, the former East Germany, actually ceased to exist as an independent state in the reform process.[21] Still others, the 15 republics of the former Soviet Union, became independent states.

For some countries, such as China, dramatic increases in international trade have been a hallmark and important engine of the reform process. For others, such as Bulgaria and some of the former Soviet republics, the events of 1989–1991 brought trade to a virtual halt as the Council for Mutual Economic Assistance (CMEA) dissolved.[22]

The transitional economies also differ substantially in the extent to which they have in place legal and institutional frameworks to support the transition to a market-based economy. Vital elements of these frameworks include many items taken for granted in the major industrial economies: laws to protect private property, laws to enforce contracts, accounting rules and standards, and sound economic policy-making institutions such as central banks.

Despite the important differences among transitional economies, we can make substantial progress toward understanding the macroeconomics of the process by focusing on a few key characteristics of the "typical" prereform centrally planned economy. It will soon become obvious why we treat these economies in the same chapter as more traditional developing ones. Typical macroeconomic features include

1. Extensive government ownership of productive assets; government control over all important aspects of economic activity, prices, and international trade; and government resource and capital allocation according to a centralized economic plan.

2. Overly industrialized economic structure, with underdeveloped financial and services sectors.

---

[21]The article by the authors in the chapter references takes an economic approach to explaining the German choice to unify.

[22]Section 11.9 examines trade-related aspects of transition, including the role of CMEA trade.

3. Government-set prices and capital-allocation procedures that encourage capital-goods production and discourage consumer-goods production, resulting in chronic shortages.

4. Extensive money finance of government expenditure, especially subsidies to large state-owned enterprises.

5. Capital and exchange controls to maintain highly artificial fixed exchange rates.

Government Ownership and Control

Until the mid-1980s, more than 95 percent of production in the Soviet Union was in state hands.[23] This figure puts the Soviet Union at the upper end of the spectrum of state ownership (Hungary, for example, lies at the lower end of the spectrum), but the predominant economic role of the state defines centrally planned economies. Governments own virtually all productive resources. Planners decide what will be produced, in what quantities, by which enterprises, using which inputs, on what schedule, to whom the output will be distributed, and at what prices.

Government planners allocate capital and other resources according to the economy's central plan. State-owned enterprises receive government "credits" that they use to buy nonlabor inputs at state-determined prices. Different enterprises pay different "prices" for inputs according to whether the government wants to tax or subsidize the enterprise's activity. Enterprises that are profitable return the profit to the government as tax revenue; enterprises that earn losses often have their debt forgiven. The fact that losses do not force enterprises into bankruptcy, because the government simply provides more loans and credits regardless of economic performance, means firms face a **soft budget constraint.** In other words, profitability is not a requisite for continued operation under such a system. Workers receive government-set wages, often paid in cash, but the typical shortages of consumer goods imply that much of the cash goes unspent. Officially recorded unemployment hovers close to zero because planners assign workers to jobs.

The government's control also extends to international trade, which is handled through state trading companies rather than directly by individual enterprises. Comparative advantage, which rests on a comparison of relative prices across countries, cannot determine trade patterns when prices are set bureaucratically without regard to market forces. Planners often attempt to keep the economy from relying on imports from market-oriented economies, and state trading companies choose "surplus" goods to export in exchange for the necessary imports.[24]

Overindustrialization

Policy makers in some centrally planned economies use their power over prices and resource allocation to encourage production of capital and military goods and

---

[23]Lipton and Sachs (1992), 219.

[24]In contrast to their disregard of comparative advantage, planners placed heavy emphasis on regional specialization and economies of scale. This produced a set of heavily dependent supplier-customer relationships that the events of 1989-1991 destroyed. This breakdown contributed to dramatic short-term declines in output and continues to constrain prospects for many transitional economies, particularly the former Soviet republics. Section 11.9.2 emphasizes this element of the transition.

Table 21.1 □ **Output Structure of the United States and the Soviet Union**

Sector	Output (Percent of Total Output)	
	United States (1986)	Soviet Union (1988)
Industry	23.5%	48.9%
Construction	6.1	10.7
Agriculture	1.9	9.3
Transportation and communication	5.8	10.1
Trade and distribution	11.2	6.1
Other	1.5	0.8
Services	50.0	13.9

Source: Lipton and Sachs (1992), p. 217.

discourage production of consumer goods and services. Among other tools to accomplish this, governments provide the favored sectors with cheap energy, cheap access to foreign exchange for their imports, and heavy subsidies to cover wages and other costs. Table 21.1, which compares output structures of the United States and the Soviet Union in the late 1980s, reveals the outcome of such policies. Note that industry accounts for twice as large a share of output in the former Soviet Union as in the United States, while the Soviet service-sector output falls short of a third of the U.S. figure. Among the major transitional economies, China appears to have recognized its overemphasis on industry relatively early; it shifted policy in 1979 to create market incentives for agricultural production and build a better balanced productive structure.

In addition to their heavy emphasis on industry, centrally planned economies exhibit a prevalence of very-large-scale state-owned enterprises that hold monopoly positions for their respective products. The sheer size of the firms often surpasses any possible economies of scale, and their monopoly status provides them little incentive to produce high-quality products or adopt new technologies.

Price Controls and Shortages

Government planners set prices administratively for both goods and resources, often ignoring supply and demand. The result, of course, is a situation of chronic shortages of goods that consumers and firms want and surpluses of goods that no one wants. Shortages of consumer goods imply that citizens must stand in line, often daily, to acquire basic goods. Workers often hoard their cash wages because of the lack of availability of goods to purchase with them; these hoarded funds (called **monetary overhang**) give the government a further incentive to levy an inflation tax that erodes the funds' potential purchasing power. Existence of a large monetary overhang means that lifting price controls for any good can lead to a dramatic price increase because of the pent-up money balances.

Price controls also result in shortages of productive inputs for which government planners have set prices too low. This leads to production bottlenecks as downstream firms run short of vital inputs. To avoid these bottlenecks that can cause firms to fall short of their government-assigned output targets, firms often hoard inputs and inventories and attempt to vertically integrate to become as self-sufficient as possible.

Money-Finance of Fiscal Expenditures

Unproductive state-owned enterprises rely on massive government subsidies to keep them in operation. These subsidies, along with other governmental functions, lead to high rates of government expenditure. Tax systems often are poorly developed and overly reliant on the state-owned enterprises for revenues. Governments find it difficult to borrow because of their isolation from world capital markets, their poor credibility, and the domestic population's distrust of government promises to repay debts and avoid inflation that produces negative real rates of return. As a result, governments rely heavily on money finance of government expenditures. In essence, the central bank prints money to keep the state-owned enterprises in operation—an ideal recipe for runaway inflation that price controls attempt to suppress.

Capital and Exchange Controls

Government control over prices in centrally planned economies extends to the price of foreign exchange or the exchange rate. Currencies typically are nonconvertible, and governments maintain monopoly control over foreign exchange transactions. Because international trade is channeled through state-trading companies, the government maintains access to any foreign exchange acquired through exports. Planners then allocate the scarce foreign exchange by selling it at different prices to cover imports that have different priorities under the central plan.

Currency nonconvertibility, along with price controls' distortion of comparative advantage, causes centrally planned economies to forgo most of the potential gains from trade. In particular, nonconvertibility imposes **bilateralism** on trade. Suppose Czechoslovakia exports tractors to the Soviet Union and receives payments in rubles, the Soviet currency. The rubles cannot be sold on the foreign exchange market for dollars, francs, or any other foreign currency. To use the rubles, Czechoslovakia must import a good from a country willing to accept rubles as payment, that is, the Soviet Union. Therefore, each pair of countries ends up importing and exporting approximately equal values of goods from one another, a pattern that eliminates many opportunities for mutually beneficial trade.

Governments also restrict capital inflows and outflows, as well as use of foreign currencies, under central planning. The domestic population may hoard cash because government restrictions prohibit buying foreign assets and because domestic assets may be nonexistent or vulnerable to confiscation, inflation, or other risks. The government represents most enterprises' only potential source of investment funds. Many centrally planned economies report high rates of investment, but the actual productivity of such investment often is low. Government planners, with little knowledge of actual production processes in different sectors of the economy, often provide inappropriate resources and fund inappropriate investments. In the Soviet Union, in particular, newly available evidence suggests that the domestic population was asked to forgo consumption goods in order for the economy to invest in ways that ultimately failed to enhance productivity. In fact, given its usage of labor and capital inputs, the Soviet Union exhibited the lowest growth in the world from 1960 to 1989, due in large part to government control over the capital-allocation process.[25]

21.3.2 Reform

Many economists think that transforming the centrally planned countries into functioning market-oriented economies represents a task of a magnitude unprecedented in modern economic history. One reason for this assessment is that so many types of reform—economic, political, social, and legal—are needed. A high degree of consensus exists on the basic outline of economic reform. Most lingering controversies concern issues of timing. For example, is it better to attempt dramatic and immediate reforms on all margins simultaneously (the **big-bang approach,** often associated with Poland), or to reform more slowly and take the different elements of reform one-by-one (the **gradualism approach,** often associated with China)? One right answer doesn't exist; for example, big bangs may be required in cases of large-scale breakdown of political authority, as in the former Soviet Union, but not in cases of more subtle political transformation, as in China. In the discussion below, we mention several timing dilemmas that confront reformers. Because no historical counterpart exists of so many countries undertaking such a broad array of reforms, economists' ability to answer important questions about the timing of reform is limited. All we can do is apply sound economic theory, watch as different countries take different approaches, and try to learn what works and what does not.

Regardless of approach—big-bang or gradual—successful reforms must include both macroeconomic stabilization and structural reform. Stabilization seeks to halt excessive fiscal spending and money growth in order to prevent continual rightward shifts of the aggregate demand curve that generate chronic inflation. Structural reform seeks to shift the long-run aggregate supply curve to the right in several ways. One is the elimination of gross productive inefficiencies and enhancement of market incentives; these move the economy onto its production possibilities frontier from the interior point associated with central planning. The second and third changes that can shift the supply curve involve improved knowledge and access to more productive technologies along with increased investment; these two processes shift a country's production possibilities frontier outward.

Privatization

Privatization represents the central task of structural reform. Just as government ownership of productive assets defines central planning, private ownership defines a market-oriented or price-based economic system. Privatization includes the sale of state-owned enterprises to private owners, who then run the enterprises on a market basis; that is, buying inputs and selling outputs at market-determined prices,

---

[25]For details, see the Easterly and Fischer article in the chapter references.

deciding what and how much to produce, what production techniques to use, and so on. These changes play several key roles in reform. Together, they harden the soft budget constraint faced by firms; profitability becomes a requisite for continued operation. This contributes to macroeconomic stabilization because it eliminates enterprise losses as a continual drain on the government's budget and reduces the incentive to print money to cover the losses. Privatization can help absorb some of an economy's monetary overhang as individuals spend accumulated cash to buy shares in privatized enterprises, and the revenues raised through privatization also contribute to the all-important reduction of the government budget deficit. By giving investors a clear financial stake in the firm's future, privatization also enhances productivity incentives and avoids the tendency, prevalent in years just prior to reform, for workers to "decapitalize" firms by paying themselves exorbitant wages and counting on government subsidies to cover the shortfall.

In practice, before many of the positive effects of privatization could happen, most transitional economies experienced sudden drops in output as the government's coordination role in the economy—no matter how ineptly performed—disappeared with no short-term replacement. Basic input-supply relationships broke down, because enterprises had no experience interacting directly with one another without the state as an intermediary. Output declined by an average of about 20 percent before the reform process even began; in some cases, such as the Russian oil industry, the declines were even more dramatic.

Overall, privatization has proven to be one of the most politically difficult and slow-moving reforms for most countries, especially in the large-enterprise sector. Part of the reason is easy to see: Before other reforms (especially price liberalization) are in place, how can potential investors evaluate the potential values of the enterprises for sale?

Sectoral Restructuring

Central planning produces an economy in which the supplies of and demands for various goods and resources do not match. This is reflected in many ways, such as overindustrialization, queues for consumer goods, and the existence of large monetary overhangs. Sectoral restructuring occurs when market-determined prices begin to allocate resources so that the economy produces those goods desired by consumers and firms.

Many large state-owned enterprises existed largely on government subsidies and produced poor-quality versions of goods no one wanted. These enterprises must be allowed to adapt or die as part of the reform process, because they represent a huge drain on the economy and a major barrier to stabilizing fiscal expenditures. In other words, the previously soft budget constraint facing state-owned enterprises must become a hard one—an essential step in both long-term macroeconomic stabilization and structural reform.

Many of the transitional economies suffer from poorly developed service and financial sectors, the mirror image of their overindustrialization. A shift toward markets means improvements in retailing and distribution, as well as creation of private financial and banking sectors to replace government control over financial activity in the economy.

A need for sectoral restructuring in *any* economy, centrally planned or otherwise, presents a difficult task. Workers in industries that must shrink have strong incentives to oppose reform, especially when they have been the long-time recipients of heavily subsidized high wages as in many centrally planned countries. Some workers may lack the skills to move to other employment in the growing private sector. The society must devise programs to alleviate the economic hardship imposed on such workers lest they block the necessary reforms and condemn the economy to perpetual stagnation.

Price Liberalization

Privatization and sectoral restructuring cannot occur without large doses of price liberalization. Private investors will be hesitant to purchase enterprises that produce goods whose prices are held down by government price controls, because such enterprises will earn losses rather than profits. And sectoral restructuring, or shifting resources toward the goods wanted by consumers and firms, requires that producers know what consumers and firms want. Prices convey this information by signaling the amount of money the buyer is willing to forgo to obtain the good. From consumers' perspective, price liberalization is the means to eliminate shortages and queues.

All these salutary effects from price liberalization cannot prevent controversy from surrounding this aspect of reform. After all, transition typically means some workers lose their jobs in antiquated, unproductive state-owned enterprises. For those who keep their jobs, the artificially high wages paid under central planning must give way to market-determined wages based on productivity if the products are to compete in world markets. In this context, a rise in consumer-goods prices due to price decontrol is bound to prove unpopular, even if it does fill previously empty store shelves with goods.

Note, however, that price decontrol leads to one-time price adjustments, *not* to ongoing inflation. In the former Soviet Union prices rose by between 350 and 400 percent on decontrol.[26] When—as in Russia—authorities decontrol prices *before* they establish macroeconomic stability and control of inflation, they risk the populace mistakenly attributing the inflation to price decontrol. Such mistaken attribution can lead to a loss of popular support for reform. Does this mean that price liberalization should always wait until *after* authorities can control inflation? Not necessarily. In Russia, policy makers feared that the growing shortages of consumer goods posed a greater threat to support for reform than did further inflation; the only way to fill store shelves was to liberalize prices.

Fiscal Consolidation

Extensive government control of the economy translates into extensive government expenditures. Macroeconomic stabilization, essential as a foundation for longer run structural reforms, requires that these massive expenditures be brought under control. There are two major parts to this task. The first is simply reduction

---

[26]Fischer (1992), 78.

in government expenditure, with much of the reduction coming from curtailed subsidies to unproductive state-owned enterprises. Military spending and unproductive investment expenditures are other candidates for cuts. The second part of fiscal consolidation involves shifting from money finance of expenditure to taxes and government borrowing. This requires both strengthening the tax system (often *ad hoc,* corrupt, and politicized under central planning) by making it simple, transparent, and enforceable, and improving the government's credibility to the point that it becomes able to issue bonds to finance its expenditure.

The whole process of fiscal consolidation involves not only changes in policy makers' day-to-day behavior but changes in the fundamental structure of policy-making institutions. Most notably, the money-supply process must be reoriented toward monetary control as a tool of macroeconomic policy rather than a passive accommodator of fiscal expenditure. We shall see in Cases Five and Six that this presents a particular challenge to the former Soviet republics, where runaway inflation during the early 1990s threatened to drive the economy back to barter.

Financial Integration

A system of central planning with its artificial prices requires isolation from world markets, where demand and supply determine prices. This holds true not only for goods markets, but for capital and foreign exchange markets as well. Uncontrolled contact with world markets makes the central plan's artificial prices unsustainable. Once reform begins, building contacts with world markets serves an important function by helping align prices to their market levels.

Removing capital controls means allowing domestic residents to invest abroad and allowing foreign investors to invest in the domestic economy. Under a market-oriented system, funds to finance investment flow toward projects that offer the most attractive mix of real rate of return and risk, regardless of location. If domestic residents distrust the government's promises, they can place their funds in foreign assets instead. Enterprises attract capital by promising to use it productively, not through their priority in the government's central plan.[27] The banking sector presents significant reform challenges. In the former Soviet Union, for example, the primary assets owned by banks consist of loans to unproductive state-owned industrial enterprises that eventually must go bankrupt. Yet, many analysts believe the banks need to be saved in order to help in the privatization process.

Reform also involves changing the system of state control over foreign-exchange allocation. The domestic currency must be made convertible, particularly for current-account transactions. This openness to international markets allows world market prices to bring artificial domestic prices into line. Governments can choose between fixed and flexible exchange rate regimes, each of which carries advantages and disadvantages, just as is the case for developed and other developing economies. Transitional economies often select some type of pegged exchange rate regime in the

---

[27]Some estimates suggest that half to three-quarters of capital investment in Czechoslovakia, Hungary, and Poland under central planning was wasteful in the sense that it will be useless in a market economy. See Dornbusch and Wolf (1992), 252.

hope that the exchange rate anchor will provide credibility for the government's effort to reduce excessive growth of the money stock.[28] If unaccompanied by fiscal consolidation and monetary restraint, however, a fixed exchange rate loses credibility and becomes prone to balance-of-payments and currency crises. As long as high rates of inflation continue, failure to devalue the domestic currency sufficiently to offset the inflation differential results in real currency appreciation, rising imports, dwindling exports, and a growing current-account deficit that must be financed. Fixed exchange rates during the early stages of transition have an additional advantage for economies with no institutional framework for conducting monetary policy: the simple rules of a fixed rate regime are relatively straightforward, easy to understand, and require a minimum of institutional sophistication to be applied successfully.[29]

21.3.3 Transition Prospects

Prospects for the transitional economies differ substantially depending on the degree of their economic problems, the wisdom and perseverance of their reforms, their political stability to endure the reform process, and their luck in avoiding adverse domestic and international shocks during the transition period. Each country faces unique advantages and disadvantages. Russia, for example, inherited a more complete set of economic institutions than did the other Soviet republics, but it also inherited the Soviet army payroll and the bulk of outstanding Soviet external debt. Generally speaking, most countries' macroeconomic *stabilization* efforts have thus far been more sustained and successful than their *structural* reforms.

By 1994, the early reformers, including Albania, the Baltic countries (Estonia, Latvia, and Lithuania), the Czech Republic, Mongolia, Poland, the Slovak Republic, and Slovenia, began to experience positive real GDP growth, faster growth in some cases than that of the major industrial economies. This contrasts sharply with countries where reforms have lagged, as illustrated in Figure 21.2.[30] Late or timid reformers include Bulgaria and Romania, along with Kazakhstan, Moldova, Kirgizstan, and Ukraine. In Russia, legislative opposition to fiscal consolidation, along with rising military expenditures in 1994, damaged the earlier progress made toward macro stabilization, and the run-up to the June 1996 presidential election stalled reform (see Case Six). Armed conflict has complicated reform efforts in Armenia, Georgia, and the former Yugoslavia. As of 1995, reforms had barely begun in Azerbaijan, Belarus, Tajikistan, Turkmenistan, and Uzbekistan.

By 1995, small private capital flows into the transitional economies had begun, along with repatriation of flight capital. Both trends, however, apply primarily to those countries most advanced in the reform process—particularly the Czech Republic, the Slovak Republic, Hungary, and the Baltic states. And flows have been modest compared with

---

[28]Cases Four, Five, and Six provide examples from China and the former Soviet Union.

[29]Of course, perfectly flexible exchange rates imply simple policy rules as well, but few analysts believe transitional economies could accept the potential for extreme exchange rate volatility during the earliest phases of transition.

[30]Case Four in Chapter Eleven presents more information on the links between growth and the timing and extent of reform.

Figure 21.2 □ **GDP Growth in Transitional Economies, 1994 (Percent)**

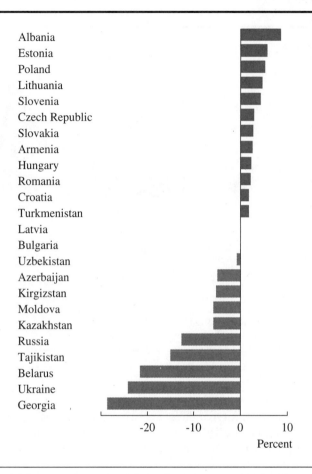

Source: World Bank, *Global Economic Prospects and the Developing Countries, 1995.* Washington, D.C.: World Bank, p. 72.

experts' earlier predictions. The same holds true for foreign direct investment, which potentially can play a vital role in transition by transferring new technology, worker training, and managerial know-how. Opaque legal systems and uncertain governance structures appear as responsible as macroeconomic instability for the dearth of investment inflows.[31]

Figure 21.3 summarizes aggregate net resource flows to Eastern European and Central Asian transitional economies for recent years and breaks those flows down

---

[31]Just one example of the kind of problem that can arise: In 1995, China explained to foreign direct investors that they would not receive contractually promised tax rebates because the government could not afford to pay them!

Figure 21.3 □ **Aggregate Net Resource Flows into East Europe and Central Asia,[a]**
1980–1994 ($ Billions)

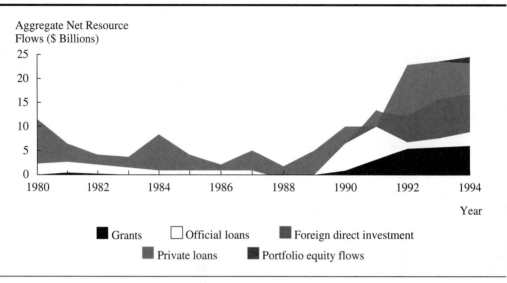

[a]Includes Albania, Armenia, Azerbaijan, Belarus, Bulgaria, Croatia, Czech Republic, Estonia, Georgia, Hungary, Kazakhstan, Kirgizstan, Latvia, Lithuania, Macedonia, Moldova, Poland, Romania, Russia, Slovak Republic, Slovenia, Tajikistan, Turkmenistan, Ukraine, Uzbekistan, and former Yugoslavia.

Source: World Bank, *World Debt Tables,* 1994–95, Vol. 1. Washington, D.C.: World Bank, p. 251.

by type. Aggregate net resource inflows include loans minus principal repayments, plus portfolio investment, foreign direct investment, and grant inflows. After coming to a near halt during the late 1980s, aggregate net resource inflows accelerated dramatically in the 1990s and were relatively evenly divided between private loans, foreign direct investment, and grants.

Continued success in the transition process depends on countries' abilities to maintain the progress made in macroeconomic stabilization and to move forward on the difficult issues of structural reform.

Case One
Exchange Controls and Multiple
Exchange Rates

Exchange controls refer to arrangements by which governments attempt to control purchases and sales of currencies by individuals and firms. These controls were ubiquitous in prereform developing and centrally planned economies; many such

Table 21.2 □ **Official and Black-Market Exchange Rates for Eastern European Currencies, 1989**

	Dollars per Unit of Currency	
	Official Rate	Black-Market Rate
Soviet Union (ruble)	$1.63	$0.10
East Germany (ost mark)	0.54	0.04
Poland (zloty)	0.0003	0.0001
Hungary (forint)	0.17	0.13
Czechoslovakia (koruna)	0.07	0.03

Source: *Business Week*, November 27, 1989, p. 65; data from Bayerische Vereinsbank, Deak International Inc., and *Business Week*.

countries maintain some degree of exchange controls. Under an ordinary fixed exchange rate regime, central banks intervene in the foreign exchange market, but this intervention does not interfere with currency purchases or sales by private agents. By contrast, exchange controls attempt to influence who buys and sells currencies, in what quantities, at what prices, and for what purposes through a variety of rules, regulations, and price manipulations.

Government Monopoly

The simplest and strongest form of exchange control involves a pure government monopoly in foreign exchange. Under such a system, individuals or firms can buy or sell foreign currencies *only* through the national government; no (legal) private foreign exchange market exists. Firms that earn foreign exchange by exporting must turn their earnings over to the government, and they receive domestic currency in exchange, at the official exchange rate. This arrangement gives the government the means to decide which international transactions to permit. Some types of transactions may automatically be disallowed, such as trips abroad or importation of luxury consumer goods.

Government monopolies in foreign exchange tend to fail in dealing with the basic problems of balance-of-payments deficits and chronic shortages of foreign exchange. When foreign currencies are not available through legitimate channels, economic incentives exist for illegal or **black markets** to emerge. Participants in these markets buy and sell foreign currencies at market-determined rates for transactions not sanctioned by the government-run market. In some economies, the volume of transactions flowing through the black markets for currency dwarfs that occurring through legitimate channels, and governments differ considerably in their level of effort to enforce exchange-control rules and eliminate black markets. Table 21.2 reports official and black-market exchange rates for several centrally planned economies, just prior to their reforms. Note the large differentials between the two rates, especially in the Soviet Union and East Germany.

Beginning in 1989, as part of the massive political and economic changes sweeping the Soviet Union and Eastern Europe, governments began to inch toward more realistic values for their currencies and toward an ultimate goal of currency convertibility. In Poland, the government began to devalue the currency substantially to bring the official rate closer to equilibrium. The goal: elimination of the black market in zlotys by making the currency freely convertible in three to five years. The steps for meeting this goal included (1) granting private foreign exchange dealers licenses to handle small trades at market-determined rates and (2) replacing government sales at the artificially low official rate with government auctions of foreign exchange for large transactions. Gradually, the zloty stabilized in foreign exchange markets and by early 1996 traded at about $0.40 per zloty.[32]

In early 1989, the Soviet government also began subtle moves toward its goal of currency convertibility by 2000. Some factories were allowed to auction to other Soviet enterprises foreign exchange earned by exporting; auction rates reportedly were $0.09 to $0.10 per ruble, or less than one-tenth the official rate. In late 1989, Gosbank (the Soviet state bank) announced a 90 percent devaluation for transactions not involving imports or exports. Mikhail Gorbachev made a controversial move late in 1990, ordering all Soviet enterprises to turn 40 percent of their foreign-currency revenue over to the Soviet central government; the currency would go toward payments on the large Soviet foreign debt. Economists, Soviet and otherwise, pointed out that the decree effectively eliminated the incentive for Soviet enterprises to export and earn foreign exchange, since a large percentage of such earnings would be confiscated.

In 1991, the Soviet government raised the ruble price of foreign exchange for Soviet citizens traveling abroad to near the black-market rate, then about $0.04 per ruble. Even more important, a move in April 1991 allowed foreign and Soviet firms to buy rubles for some purposes at rates set by supply and demand in biweekly sessions.[33]

Finally, in July 1992, the Russian ruble began to trade at a single exchange rate, set by the Russian Central Bank and based on biweekly currency auctions. Trading began at 125 rubles per dollar. By early 1996, the ruble traded at 4,700 rubles per dollar (after dropping as low as 5,200 per dollar) and fluctuated widely with the prospects for Russian economic reform. Ruble convertibility remains one of the most controversial aspects of economic reform in the former Soviet Union.[34]

Multiple Exchange Rates

A second means by which the government can affect the types of international transactions undertaken is by selling foreign exchange to be used for various purposes at different prices.[35] This is called a system of **multiple exchange rates.** Developing countries often institute such systems by setting a low price for foreign exchange used in importing items for the public sector and a high price for foreign exchange used in importing items for the private sector. The price differential between the two rates serves as a tax/subsidy scheme.

---

[32]Poland rebased the currency in 1995.

[33]Case Three in Chapter Twelve examines the institutional details of Russia's fledgling foreign exchange market.

[34]See Cases Five and Six.

[35]See the El-Erian article in the chapter references for Arab countries' experiences with multiple exchange rates.

Again, the multiple-rate system creates an incentive for individuals who want to import unfavored goods to buy foreign exchange on the black market. An incentive also exists for individuals to be less than honest in stating the nature of the intended transaction—for example, saying that the foreign exchange will be used for a tractor and then buying a Rolls-Royce. As a result, exchange controls impose not only an efficiency loss by interfering with price signals but high administrative and enforcement costs as well.

Dual Exchange Rates

The most common system of multiple exchange rates is a **dual exchange rate system.** Here, commercial transactions involving trade in goods and services occur at a fixed exchange rate called the **commercial rate.** Capital transactions for short-term capital flows in response to interest rate differentials occur at a floating rate called the **financial rate** (see the listings for the Czech Republic and for Uruguay in Figure 12.1). The goal is to create a stable (that is, fixed) exchange rate to encourage trade in goods and services and to insulate the commercial rate from any volatility caused by short-term capital flows. As with other types of exchange controls, if the commercial and financial rates move very far apart, an incentive emerges to report transactions dishonestly in order to buy or sell foreign exchange at the more favorable rate.

Case Two
Chinese Gradualism

China began its economic reforms in 1979 with a stated goal of increasing the country's productivity and wealth, not of political revolution or creating a "capitalist" economy. The country enjoyed several advantages over the transitional economies of Eastern Europe and the former Soviet Union: no severe political crisis or vacuum of political authority, a relatively stable macroeconomy, little foreign debt, no external trade shocks comparable to those that struck the other transitional economies, and high rates of saving. From the beginning, gradualism characterized the Chinese strategy. Reform began in agriculture, then spread to international trade and industry. The current economic challenges facing the country involve reform of its financial sector and its macroeconomic policy-making institutions.

Structural reform of Chinese agriculture started in 1979 with the decontrol of markets for small household crops. The government allowed agricultural collectives—government-mandated groups of 20 to 30 families that managed Chinese farms during the decades of central planning—to dissolve in favor of family-managed farms. Agricultural production soared. During the 1980s, price liberalization spread to larger agricultural markets, except for grain, which remained under government price controls to keep food prices artificially low.

Prior to reform, a handful of state trading companies held monopolies over international trade. Gradually, the government transferred the right to engage in trade from these national enterprises to regional corporations that competed with one another for business. The Chinese government also created Special Economic Zones, mostly along the southern coast near Hong Kong and Taiwan, where authorities permitted more inward foreign direct investment and other market-oriented economic activities.[36] Exports from the zones grew dramatically, and some of the reforms instituted there spread to other locales.

In a pattern typical of other transitional economies, Chinese macroeconomic policy followed the needs of the state-owned enterprises, which in 1980 produced about 75 percent of the country's industrial output. Loans from the central bank to these enterprises swelled the money stock, and subsidies they received increased the government's fiscal expenditures. China did, however, finance less of its government expenditure with money creation than did most other transitional economies, and this contributed to the country's macroeconomic stability. Chinese citizens traditionally saved a large share of their incomes, and government policy makers kept interest rates high enough to ensure positive real rates of return and to encourage saving.

The main threat to China's macroeconomic stability has come from the link between the banking sector and the state-owned enterprises, half of which earn losses. Current reform efforts center on shifting the financial sector to a more market-oriented basis, but the threat of unemployment if too many state-owned enterprises should fail puts pressure on policy makers to move slowly and often erratically.

Since reforms began, China has experienced real growth rates of near 10 percent, and inflation has emerged as a growing problem. The country's recent macroeconomic performance exhibits a stop-go-stop-go pattern of business cycles that we can understand based on the fundamental dilemma facing policy makers. To maintain support for reform and accomplish their fundamental goal of increasing the nation's wealth, policy makers must maintain expansionary policies and high rates of economic growth. But, given the continued existence of an unreformed sector of large state-owned enterprises, fiscal expenditures and money creation go largely to that sector. Too much expansion leads to inflation, especially in the cities, where rising food prices bring political unrest. Policy makers respond to rising inflation by curtailing fiscal expenditure and, especially, reducing money growth by cutting the state sector's easy access to credit. This restrains inflation, but it threatens the survival of the economically unproductive state-owned enterprises. Eventually, the specter of rising unemployment convinces policy makers to relax their austerity measures, and inflation begins again.

Figure 21.4 illustrates one such cycle. During 1988–1989, inflation rose dramatically and eventually caused policy makers to apply the monetary brakes. Inflation fell, but so did the rate of growth of real output. In 1990, policy makers relented, and the rates of growth of both output and the price level moved up. In mid-1993, inflation pushed policy makers into a new austerity program that lasted until late 1995.

Recent speeches and interviews by high-ranking Chinese policy makers indicate that they understand the stop-go pattern will continue until banking and monetary reform makes bankers, especially those in the provinces, more immune to state-owned enterprises' demands for soft-budget-constraint loans. In early 1996, economic policy makers announced a reform plan aimed at loosening the link between banks, the money stock, and the state-owned sector. The plan involves separating the central

---

[36]Section 9.5.2 contains more information on China's special economic zones.

Figure 21.4 □ **Real GDP and Retail Price Growth in China, 1990–1995 (Percent)**

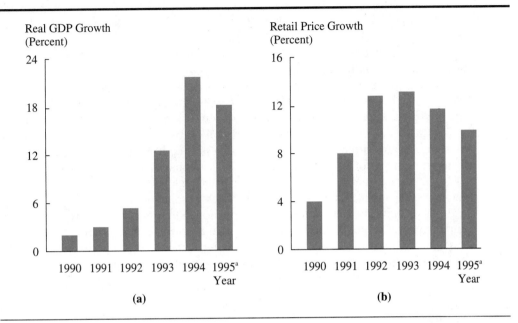

ᵃAnnualized rate, through June.

Source: Craig G. Smith, "As Chinese Inflation Begins to Cool, Attention Turns to Creating More Jobs," *The Wall Street Journal,* July 13, 1995.

bank, which will conduct monetary policy, from commercial banks, which will make loans based on market-oriented criteria. This promises to allow monetary policy makers to determine the rate of growth of the money stock according to macroeconomic goals rather than according to individual enterprises' demands for loans and subsidies. The ultimate goal of the reform includes a system of monetary policy conducted through open market operations, as in most market-oriented industrial economies.

 Case Three
Debt, India, and the Ruble[37]

For years, the Soviet Union provided India large trade credits, denominated in non-convertible rubles, that India used to buy Soviet arms and industrial equipment.

[37]See "Very Present Help in Rouble," *The Economist,* May 16, 1992, 42; and "Russia, India Resolve Dispute," *The Wall Street Journal,* January 29, 1993.

The credits accumulated to a total Indian debt of 10 billion rubles. A 1978 agreement between the two countries linked the definition of the ruble's value to a basket of industrial-country currencies, worth approximately $1.30 in mid-1992. In July 1992, Russia floated the ruble. By early 1993, its value sank to approximately 400 rubles to the dollar, or about *one-fifth of 1 percent* of its 1978 value.[38] Evaluating India's Soviet debt at this new exchange rate would shrink it in dollar terms from around $13 *billion* to approximately $25 *million*.

In 1992, Russia—successor to the Soviet Union—claimed India must repay the debt using the ruble's 1978 value. India claimed otherwise and offered to repay at the 1992 market value for rubles. The two countries needed to negotiate a compromise. Russia desperately needed markets for one of its few salable products, weapons, and India represented a major market. India needed Russian replacement parts for its existing stocks of Soviet weapons and aircraft. India also provided consumer goods (of inadequate quality to sell in Western markets) to Russia. On the other hand, India needed a reduction in its Soviet debt. Such a reduction would shrink India's total external debt by about 15 percent—perhaps enough to restore the country's credit rating to investment grade. In early 1993, the two countries did negotiate a compromise, but they did not disclose the terms of the agreement, which included a Russian promise to construct a factory in India to make military spare parts.

Case Four
The Market(s) for Yuan

During the early years of Chinese economic reform, the government maintained a tight monopoly on foreign exchange. Government monopoly trading companies conducted all foreign trade and turned their foreign exchange earnings over to the People's Bank of China, which also served as the sole legal source of foreign exchange. All legal foreign exchange transactions with the Bank of China occurred at an official fixed exchange rate, which stood at about 1.5 yuan per dollar in 1979. Government priorities determined which requests for foreign exchange purchases were granted and which were denied, because the quantity demanded of foreign exchange always exceeded the quantity supplied at the official exchange rate. *(Illustrate in a foreign exchange market diagram.)* This exchange-control system, along with an active black market in foreign currency, remained more or less intact until 1985, although the government periodically devalued the yuan.

An important part of China's reform program involved encouraging inward foreign direct investment. But foreign firms balked at the exchange-control system, and Chinese policy makers recognized that the government's monopoly over currency trading discouraged foreign investment. Beginning in 1985, when the official

---

[38]This depreciation only hinted at things to come. Within two years, the ruble traded at 5,200 to the dollar! Cases Five and Six provide details.

exchange rate was yuan2.9/$1, authorities began to allow foreign firms and foreign/domestic joint ventures to trade currencies in local "swap centers." The centers started in cities with substantial foreign presences and spread until trading occurred in more than a hundred local markets. Firms still had to turn over a set percentage of any foreign exchange they earned to the People's Bank of China at the official exchange rate, but they could trade the remaining currency in the swap centers at higher yuan per dollar rates. Tourists, new foreign investors, and most Chinese firms remained restricted to the government's official foreign exchange market; but authorities gradually permitted more and more transactions in the swap centers.

By the early 1990s, authorities had raised the official yuan exchange rate to yuan5.8/$1. Exporters still had to sell 20 percent of their foreign-currency earnings to the People's Bank of China at that rate, and government planners determined who could buy dollars at the artificially low rate. All other transactions occurred in the swap centers—still subject to government intervention and restricted access—where rates varied from 8 to 10 yuan per dollar.

One important goal of Chinese trade reforms has been to gain membership in the General Agreement on Tariffs and Trade (GATT), now known as the World Trade Organization (WTO). One step toward such membership requires meeting the organization's demand that China have a unified foreign exchange market with a single exchange rate. The unification process began in 1994 when authorities dissolved the official government foreign exchange market into the network of local swap markets that, in turn, merged into a national market for foreign exchange. The government retained control over which transactions are permitted, and intervention kept the exchange rate within bands determined by the central authorities. Regulations still prohibited Chinese firms from holding bank deposits denominated in foreign currencies, but such restrictions became increasingly difficult to enforce. As of early 1996, the yuan traded in foreign exchange markets at rates between 8 and 10 yuan per dollar, similar to the rates observed in the local swap-center markets prior to the unification of China's foreign exchange markets.

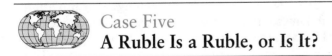

Case Five
A Ruble Is a Ruble, or Is It?

When the Soviet Union dissolved into 15 republics in 1991, each republic faced a decision: continue to use the ruble as its currency or introduce a new national currency. The choice wasn't an easy one. There were several arguments for sticking with the ruble. If Russian economic reforms went well, the ruble would be stable and could provide an important anchor during the difficult transition. If a significant group of republics kept the ruble, interrepublic trade might decline less during transition. Plus, the newly independent republics, with the partial exception of Russia, had no institutions in place and no expertise to manage a currency.

However, there were political and economic arguments on the other side as well. The republics most eager to escape Russian domination, such as the Baltics, saw a national currency as an important element of their long-awaited sovereignty. The republics faced highly divergent economic conditions and reform agendas, and separate currencies would allow them to use the exchange rate as a tool of macroeconomic policy. As long as republics kept the ruble, Russia would determine monetary policy and, indirectly, the pace of many aspects of reform.

Republics that made quick decisions to abandon the ruble—such as Estonia and Latvia—faced many other decisions. Should their new currencies replace rubles currently in circulation in their territories or be issued in addition to existing rubles? How should authorities manage the introduction of new currencies? Should the new currency operate under a fixed or a flexible exchange rate regime? If the exchange rate was to be pegged, to what currency?

Immediately following the breakup of the Soviet Union, each republic's main branch of Gosbank (the former Soviet state bank) started to act as a central bank. The Russian Central Bank issued subsidized ruble credits to each republic's central bank, and those banks in turn used the funds to provide cheap ruble credits to state-owned enterprises. In effect, 15 inexperienced central banks issued rubles.[39] In the struggle between Moscow and the republics for political and economic power, each central bank tried to buy loyalty from the state-owned enterprises by providing ruble credits on demand, ignoring the effects of its decisions on the overall stock of rubles. Given this situation, we should not be surprised that by 1992 inflation had gotten out of control. Russia tried to insulate itself from the inflationary effects of rubles issued in the other republics (especially Ukraine) by declaring that Russian goods could be paid for only with ruble deposits in Russian banks.

As the 15 independent republics continued to issue ruble credits and to reform at different paces, their economic prospects and rates of inflation began to diverge and their ruble credits began to exchange at different rates. In other words, the republics' currencies—while all still called "rubles"—started to trade as distinct currencies. Table 21.3 provides examples of the intraruble exchange rates during the week of September 7, 1992. The republics that issued the largest quantities of ruble credits, such as Ukraine and Kazakhstan, saw their rubles depreciate against those of other more reform-minded republics. In mid-1992, Russia reached an agreement with the International Monetary Fund that, among other provisions, required the Russian Central Bank to stop issuing subsidized ruble credits to other republics' central banks. However, the agreement failed to halt the process (see Case Six).

By 1993, the erratic nature of Russian reforms, the ruble's rapid depreciation, and continuing inability to control the stock of rubles led several republics to abandon the ruble or make plans to do so. Table 21.4 provides information on the republics' currency choices during 1993. In late 1993, Armenia, Belarus, Kazakhstan, Tajikistan, and Uzbekistan reached an agreement with Russia on a "new ruble zone" that gave Russia control over the supply of rubles. The agreement soon broke down as the National Bank of Belarus won from the Russian Central

---

[39]Russia maintained control over the supply of actual paper rubles because all the printing presses were located in Russia; but the ruble money stock included ruble credits in addition to paper rubles.

Table 21.3 □ **Exchange Rates between Republic Rubles and Latvian Rubles, September 1992**

Republic	Republic's Rubles per Latvian Ruble
Ukraine	0.3–0.4
Kazakhstan	0.3
Belarus	0.7–1.0
Moldova	0.7–0.8
Tajikistan	0.8–1.0
Russia	0.95

Source: *The Economist,* September 19, 1992, p. 96; data from Latvian Central Bank.

Bank the right to print rubles and issue subsidized ruble credits to state-owned enterprises. As of late 1995, most members of the Commonwealth of Independent States, a loose confederation of 12 former Soviet republics, still used the ruble as their currency, and many of the problems of monetary control highlighted in this case continued.

Table 21.4 □ **Currencies of the Former Soviet Republics, 1993**

Republic	Currency (April 1993)	Currency (September 1993)
Armenia	Ruble	Ruble
Azerbaijan	Manat and ruble	Manat and ruble
Belarus	Rubel and ruble	Rubel and ruble
Estonia	Kroon	Kroon
Georgia	Ruble and coupon[a]	Coupon
Kazakhstan	Ruble	Ruble
Kirgizstan	Som	Som
Latvia	Latvian ruble	Lats
Lithuania	Talonas	Litas
Moldova	Ruble and coupon[a]	Coupon
Russia	Ruble	Ruble
Tajikistan	Ruble	Ruble
Turkmenistan	Ruble	Ruble
Ukraine	Karbovanets	Karbovanets
Uzbekistan	Ruble and rationing coupon	Ruble

[a]Republics issued "coupons" that circulated as currency in part to overcome the countries' inability to print paper rubles, the printing presses for which remained in Russian hands.

Sources: Grant Spencer and Adrienne Cheasty, "The Ruble Area," *Finance and Development,* June 1993, p. 3; and Hernán Cortés-Douglas and Richard K. Abrams, "Introducing New National Currencies," *Finance and Development,* December 1993, p. 27; data from national central banks.

Only Estonia, Latvia, and Lithuania have completed the transition to relatively stable national currencies. Estonia pegs its kroon to the Deutsche mark. Lithuania pegs the litas to the U.S. dollar. And Latvia operates a managed float for the lats. *(Look up the exchange rate for each Baltic currency in Figure 12.2.)*

Case Six
Central Bank Independence, Moscow Style

During the years of Soviet central planning, Gosbank, the state bank, performed two functions typically undertaken by separate entities in market-oriented economies: monetary policy and business lending. In fact, the Soviet system implied that monetary policy was simply the outcome of lending decisions. Gosbank approved loans and credits to state-owned enterprises, provided cash to the enterprises to cover their wage payments, and printed money to cover much of the government budget deficit. These decisions combined to determine the rate of growth of the Soviet money stock.[40] As David Lipton and Jeffrey Sachs explain the Soviet system circa 1991:

> . . . there was little technical understanding and no tradition of an active monetary policy to limit credit growth. Throughout the period of central planning, credit flows were subordinated to physical commodity flows as assigned in the plan. In other words, enterprises were automatically given the monetary resources to pay for inputs assigned to them in the plan. The idea that bank credit should be limited to restrict the overall growth of the money supply simply did not exist until 1992.[41]

As the Soviet economy collapsed in 1991, Gosbank issued massive amounts of credits to floundering enterprises and printed more money to cover the growing government budget deficit. The money stock expanded rapidly, and inflation grew as the Soviet Union collapsed. As a result, the reform process for the former Soviet republics started in a highly unstable macroeconomic environment.

Almost immediately, disputes arose between the Russian Central Bank (successor to the Gosbank) and other branches of the Russian government over the appropriate conduct of the bank's activities. The Central Bank and the Parliament (to which the bank reported under Russian law) favored continuing credits at negative real interest rates to the state-owned enterprises as a way of keeping those enterprises open—even if they produced goods no one wanted and incurred losses. Proponents of this view argued that keeping the enterprises' budget constraints

---

[40]This is a reversal or "upside-down" version of the process typical in market-oriented economies. There, the central bank determines the rate of growth of the money stock based on macroeconomic considerations of price stability and/or unemployment. The rate of growth of the money stock, in turn, determines the quantity of loans that banks can extend. Commercial banks allocate the available loans by choosing the most credit-worthy borrowers in an effort to maximize the banks' profit.

[41]"Prospects for Russia's Economic Reforms," *Brookings Papers on Economic Activity* 2 (1992), 227.

soft through such policies was the only way to prevent bankruptcies and massive unemployment.

Policy makers in other branches of government, especially the reform-oriented Ministry of Finance, held an opposing view. They argued that reduced rates of money growth were essential to preventing hyperinflation and achieving short-term macroeconomic stabilization. Further, they argued that once prices were liberalized, economically productive enterprises should be able to earn a profit. Enterprises that continued to earn losses were producing noncompetitive products and should be required to adapt or close in order to avoid a continuing drain on the government budget and the economy.

In July 1992, the Russian Parliament appointed Victor Gerashchenko, the former head of Gosbank, head of the Russian Central Bank. Gerashchenko continued his Soviet-style policies despite reform orders from President Boris Yeltsin and the minister of finance. Gerashchenko reportedly stated that the rate of growth of the money stock had no effect on prices and that economic theory did not apply to Russia, and he insisted on strict secrecy in the bank's operations. Continuing rapid money growth led to inflation rates between 2,000 and 2,500 percent in 1992. Gerashchenko's policies caused Jeffrey Sachs, a Harvard University economist and adviser to the Russian government, to conclude in frustration, "I believe on close analysis that Gerashchenko may be the worst central bank governor in history."[42]

In mid-1993, the Russian Central Bank finally signed an agreement with the Ministry of Finance to stop issuing endless cheap credit to the state-owned enterprises. President Yeltsin decreed later in the year that the bank would answer to *him* for its policies, not to Parliament, which contained many antireform members with strong ties to the state-owned sector. But Gerashchenko's erratic policies continued. He issued a plan to confiscate all large-denomination ruble notes, which comprised the bulk of Russian citizens' savings, and he tried to ban use of the dollar in Russia in an attempt to increase demand for the rapidly depreciating ruble.

Russia's new constitution, drafted in 1993, made the Russian Central Bank a bit less dependent on Parliament. Under the new system, the president recommends the bank's chair and Parliament approves (or refuses to approve) the recommendation. Previously, Parliament itself appointed the chair and had to approve bank policies. The constitution also provides the Central Bank with a specific policy mandate: currency stability. [43] The Gerashchenko era hardly satisfied that mandate. In July 1992, when Russia instituted biweekly currency auctions, the ruble traded at 125 per dollar. [44] By late 1994, the ruble's value had fallen to 4,000 rubles per dollar, including a decline of 21.5 percent on October 11 alone.

In late 1994, shortly after the ruble's most dramatic decline, Gerashchenko was replaced as head of the Russian Central Bank by more reform-minded Tatiana Paramonova. Under her leadership, the ruble stabilized and the Russian Central Bank

---

[42]"Rooted in Soviet Past, Russia's Central Bank Lacks Grasp of Basics," *The Wall Street Journal,* September 23, 1993, A1.

[43]On central bank independence in other economies, see Case One in Chapter Twenty.

[44]Case Three in Chapter Twelve covers the mechanics of Russia's first foreign exchange market.

and Ministry of Finance worked together to build confidence in the ruble and in the process of monetary reform. The rate of inflation declined. Russia reached an agreement with the International Monetary Fund under which the Central Bank would stop issuing subsidized credits to the state-owned enterprises. But Paramonova needed Parliamentary approval to remove the "acting" from her title of Central Bank acting chairwoman. Parliament twice refused to approve her appointment. In late 1995, President Yeltsin dismissed her, part of a wave of antireform moves in top policy-making slots as the June 1996 presidential election approached.

Summary

The developing and transitional economies share two major tasks in their pursuit of improved economic performance: macroeconomic stabilization and structural reform. Macroeconomic stabilization includes reformed fiscal and monetary policies that reduce the rate of inflation and stabilize the value of the domestic currency. Structural reform includes reduction of the government's role in the day-to-day management of the economy. Most developing and centrally planned economies have embarked on these tasks. The timing and boldness of reforms differ significantly across countries; early evidence indicates that early, bold, and persistent reform contributes to improved economic performance. Most reforming economies have made greater progress toward macroeconomic stabilization than toward structural reform.

Key Terms

stabilization reforms
structural reform (structural adjustment)
privatization
soft budget constraint
monetary overhang
bilateralism
big-bang approach

gradualism approach
exchange controls
black markets
multiple exchange rates
dual exchange rate system
commercial rate
financial rate

Problems and Questions for Review

1. Describe several macroeconomic characteristics typical of prereform developing economies. Briefly explain each characteristic's likely effect on macroeconomic performance.

2. What are the two key types of economic reform for developing and centrally planned economies? Relate the two to the aggregate demand–aggregate supply model.

3. Describe how reform in developing economies alters the characteristics you listed in problem 1. How is each element of reform likely to affect a country's macroeconomic performance?

4. Describe several macroeconomic characteristics typical of prereform centrally planned economies. Briefly explain each characteristic's likely effect on macroeconomic performance.

5. Describe how reform in transitional economies alters the characteristics you listed in problem 4. How is each element of reform likely to affect a country's macroeconomic performance?

6. Explain why "hardening" enterprises' previously soft budget constraints plays an essential role in economic reform.

7. Distinguish between gradualism and big-bang approaches to economic reform. Name a country that has pursued each approach.

8. Over the last few years, several countries (for example, Hong Kong, Estonia, Singapore, and Lithuania) have established monetary regimes based on currency boards. A currency board works as follows:

   Like a central bank, a currency board issues currency. But unlike a central bank, it does so only according to strict rules: The board prints domestic currency and commits itself to converting it on demand to a specified foreign currency at a fixed rate of exchange. To make this commitment credible, the board holds reserves of foreign currency equal to at least 100 percent of the domestic currency issued at the fixed exchange rate. The board issues currency only when it holds enough foreign-currency denominated assets to back it. And the currency board does little else: no open market operations and no lending to the government.

   (a) Write an equation for the domestic money stock and one for changes in the domestic money stock under a currency board system. *(You may want to review section 15.6.)*

   (b) What are the major implications of such a system in comparison with a more "normal" fixed exchange rate system with a central bank?

   (c) Why might economies in transition, such as Estonia and Lithuania that abandoned the Soviet ruble and established new national currencies, find a currency board system attractive?

References and Selected Readings

Åslund, Anders. *How Russia Became a Market Economy.* Washington, D.C.: The Brookings Institution, 1995.
Accessible, comprehensive account of Russia's transformation.

Bergsman, Joel, and Xiaofang Shen. "Foreign Direct Investment in Developing Countries: Progress and Problems." *Finance and Development* 32 (December 1995): 6–8.
Recent trends in FDI in developing countries, including its relationship to reform; for all students.

Calvo, Guillermo, and Carlos Végh. "Currency Substitution in High-Inflation Countries." *Finance and Development* 30 (March 1993): 34–37.
What happens when inflation causes a country's residents to use an external currency; for all students.

"Challenges of Transition." *Finance and Development* 31 (December 1994): 2–28.
Series of short articles on the major aspects of transition; for all students.

Claessens, Stijn, and Sudarshan Gooptu. "Can Developing Countries Keep Foreign Capital Flowing In?" *Finance and Development* 31 (September 1994): 62–65.
Issues related to reliance on foreign capital to finance investment; for all students.

Cortés-Douglas, Hernán, and Richard Abrams. "Introducing New National Currencies." *Finance and Development* 30 (December 1993): 26–30.
The process of changing currencies; for all students.

Dadush, Uri, and Milan Brahmbhatt. "Anticipating Capital Flow Reversals." *Finance and Development* 32 (December 1995): 3–5.
How developing countries that depend on capital inflows to finance investment can anticipate outflows; for all students.

Dornbusch, Rudiger, et al. "Currency Crises and Collapses." *Brookings Papers on Economic Activity* 2 (1995): 219–293.
Lessons from four currency crises; intermediate.

Dornbusch, Rudiger, and Alejandro Werner. "Mexico: Stabilization, Reform, and No Growth." *Brookings Papers on Economic Activity* 1 (1994): 253–315.
Analysis of Mexico's macroeconomic prospects on the eve of the December 1994 crisis; intermediate.

Dornbusch, Rudiger, and Holger Wolf. "Economic Transition in Eastern Germany." *Brookings Papers on Economic Activity* 1 (1992): 235–272.
The economics of transition in eastern Germany. Intermediate; includes both microeconomic and macroeconomic aspects of transition.

Easterly, William, and Stanley Fischer. "What We Can Learn from the Soviet Collapse." *Finance and Development* 31 (December 1994): 2–5.
Analysis of the Soviet Union's dramatic economic deterioration; for all students.

Easterly, William, and Lant Pritchett. "The Determinants of Economic Success: Luck and Policy." *Finance and Development* 30 (December 1993): 38–41.
Interaction of good policy and "luck" in determining economic performance; for all students.

Edwards, Sebastian. *Crisis and Reform in Latin America.* New York: Oxford University Press for the World Bank, 1995.
Readable account of Latin American developments from 1982 through 1994.

El-Erian, Mohammed A. "Multiple Exchange Rates: The Experience in Arab Countries." *Finance and Development* 30 (June 1993): 2–5.
More on the subject of Case One; for all students.

Fischer, Stanley. "Stabilization and Economic Reform in Russia." *Brookings Papers on Economic Activity* 1 (1992): 77–126.
The economics of transition in the former Soviet Union; intermediate. Includes both microeconomic and macroeconomic considerations.

Haggard, Stephan, et al., eds. *The Politics of Finance in Developing Countries.* Ithaca: Cornell University Press, 1993.
Collection of papers on credit allocation in eight Asian and Latin American developing economies; for all students.

Humpage, Owen F., and Jean M. McIntire. "An Introduction to Currency Boards." Federal Reserve Bank of Cleveland *Economic Review* 31 (1995): 2–11.
A currency system used by some developing countries and economies in transition; for all students.

International Monetary Fund. *World Economic Outlook.* Washington, D.C.: International Monetary Fund, annual.
Overview of economic events and prospects relevant to the developing economies, with data. The May 1995 issue focuses on global saving.

James, Harold. *International Monetary Cooperation since Bretton Woods.* Oxford: Oxford University Press, 1996.
Readable chapters on the relationship between developing and transitional economies and the Bretton Woods institutions, including important precursors to the 1989–1991 reforms.

Lipton, David, and Jeffrey D. Sachs. "Prospects for Russia's Economic Reforms." *Brookings Papers on Economic Activity* 2 (1992): 213–284.
The politics and economics of reform in the former Soviet Union; intermediate.

Little, I. M. D., et al. *Boom, Crisis, and Adjustment: The Macroeconomic Experience of Developing Countries.* New York: The World Bank, 1993.
Comparison of 18 developing countries, 1974–1989.

Meier, Gerald M. *Leading Issues in Economic Development.* New York: Oxford University Press, 1995.
Comprehensive collection of short articles on the many issues that comprise the development process; appropriate for all students.

Obstfeld, Maurice. "International Currency Experience: New Lessons and Lessons Relearned." *Brookings Papers on Economic Activity* 1 (1995): 119–219.
Intermediate-level survey of current knowledge on international monetary regimes, including those of developing economies.

Obstfeld, Maurice, and Kenneth Rogoff. "The Mirage of Fixed Exchange Rates." *Journal of Economic Perspectives* 9 (1995): 73–96.
Argues that permanently fixed exchange rates have become infeasible for all but a few countries; accessible to all students.

Ostry, Jonathan D., and Carmen M. Reinhart. "Saving and the Real Interest Rate in Developing Countries." *Finance and Development* 32 (December 1995): 16–18.
Prospects for raising saving rates in low-income developing economies; for all students.

Quirk, Peter, and Hernán Cortés-Douglas. "The Experience with Floating Rates." *Finance and Development* 30 (June 1993): 28–31.
Recent experience of developing countries with flexible exchange rates; for all students.

Sachs, Jeffrey D., and Andrew Warner. "Economic Reform and the Process of Global Integration." *Brookings Papers on Economic Activity* 1 (1995): 1–118.
The role of openness in economic development and growth; intermediate.

Sahay, Ratna, and Carlos Végh. "Dollarization in Transition Economies." *Finance and Development* 32 (March 1995): 36–39.
Use of external currencies during macroeconomic transitions; for all students.

Spencer, Grant, and Adrienne Cheasty. "The Ruble Area: A Breaking of Old Ties?" *Finance and Development* 30 (June 1993): 2–5.
The pros and cons of former Soviet republics' retaining or abandoning the ruble as their currency; for all students.

Summers, Lawrence H. "The Challenges of Development." *Finance and Development* (March 1992): 6–9.
Summary of the problems and prospects of development; for all students.

Summers, Lawrence. "Research Challenges for Development Economists." *Finance and Development* (September 1991): 2–5.
Survey of unsolved problems; accessible to all students.

Summers, Lawrence H., and Lant H. Pritchett. "The Structural-Adjustment Debate." *American Economic Review Papers and Proceedings* 83 (May 1993): 383–389.
An evaluation of criticisms of the IMF-World Bank structural adjustment loan programs; for all students.

"Symposium on China." *Journal of Economic Perspectives* 8 (1994): 23–92.
Collection of accessible articles on various aspects of China's transition.

Tanzi, Vito. "Corruption, Governmental Activities, and Markets." *Finance and Development* 32 (December 1995): 24–26.
Government involvement in the economy a a possible source of corruption; for all students.

Williamson, John, ed. *Economic Consequences of Soviet Disintegration.* Washington, D.C.: Institute for International Economics, 1993.
The effects of the breakup of the Soviet Union on the former Soviet republics, satellite states, and the rest of the world economy; for all students.

Williamson, John. *International Debt Re-examined.* Washington, D.C.: Institute for International Economics, 1995.
A readable ex post examination of the developing-country debt crisis and responses by the debtors, international capital markets, creditors, developed economies, and international organizations.

Williamson, John, ed. *The Political Economy of Policy Reform*. Washington, D.C.: Institute for International Economics, 1994.
Collection of papers on the different experiences of various developing countries undergoing political and economic reform; for all students.

World Bank. *Bureaucrats in Business: The Economics and Politics of Government Ownership*. New York: Oxford University Press, 1995.
Detailed case studies of state-owned enterprises, privatization, and reform; for all students.

World Bank. *World Debt Tables*, Vol. 1. Washington, D.C.: World Bank, annual.
Comprehensive survey of recent trends in developing-country debt, with data.

World Bank. *World Development Report*. New York: Oxford University Press, annual.
Devoted to examination of various aspects of development; accessible to all students. The 1994 issue examines "Infrastructure for Development," and the 1995 issue focuses on "Workers in an Integrating World." Also contains large collection of data.

Yarbrough, Beth V., and Robert M. Yarbrough. "International Contracting and Territorial Control: The Boundary Question." *Journal of Institutional and Theoretical Economics* 150 (1994): 239–264.
Examines economic aspects of the German decision to unify as a means of East German transition to a market economy; intermediate.

COUNTRY OR ECONOMY INDEX

SUBJECT INDEX